from abba to zoom

FROM abba TO zoom

A Pop Culture Encyclopedia of the Late 20th Century

david mansour

Andrews McMeel Publishing
Kansas City

From
abba
to
zoom

 For information, write Andrews McMeel Publishing, an Andrews McMeel Universal company, 4520 Main Street, Kansas City, Missouri 64111.

05 06 07 08 09 RR4 10 9 8 7 6 5 4 3 2 1

Library of Congress Cataloging-in-Publication Data

Mansour, David.
From Abba to Zoom : a pop culture encyclopedia of the late 20th century / David Mansour.
p. cm.
ISBN-10 0-7407-5118-2
1. Popular culture—United States—History—20th century—Encyclopedias. 2. United States—Civilization—1970—Encyclopedias. I. Title: Pop culture encyclopedia of the late 20th century. II. Title.

E169.12.M327 2005
306'.0973'03—dc22

2004062782

Book design by Holly Camerlinck
Composition by Coleridge Design

Attention: Schools and Businesses
Andrews McMeel books are available at quantity discounts with bulk purchase for educational, business, or sales promotional use. For information, please write to: Special Sales Department, Andrews McMeel Publishing, 4520 Main Street, Kansas City, Missouri 64111.

To my mom and dad,
Jim and Rose Mansour,
with love

acknowledgments

John Bode, Jennifer Breck, Misty Brown, Marcia Cardello, Matt Culley, Patrick Doran, Sherri Elliott, John Escalada, Jimmy Evans, Liz Giffin, Tina Hillhouse, Lendy Kesler, Jeff Lampe, Raymond Lopez, Michelle Maple, Pam Powell, Don Schreiner, Jill Silva, Eden Thorne, Karma, Viva, Cindy, and my salon clients. Thanks for believing!

A respectful thank-you to Tom Thornton, Dorothy O'Brien, Josh Brewster, Nick Kowalczyk, and the staff at Andrews McMeel Publishing for giving an unknown Kansas City writer the chance of a lifetime.

introduction

Hey, gotcha! The title *From ABBA to Zoom* has intrigued you enough to pick up the book (or better yet purchase it) leading you to turn to this page. Now I would like to ask you a series of questions.

WERE YOU BORN IN THE 1950s?

- Did you watch *The Huckleberry Hound Show* while devouring a bowl of roaring Frosted Flakes?
- When asked "Say, kids, what time is it?" did you answer "It's Howdy Doody Time!"?
- Were your favorite toys a Hula-Hoop, Slinky, Mr. Potato Head, and the Easy-Bake Oven?
- Did you go on dream dates with Barbie and Ken?
- Did you wear a coonskin cap while aiming at road signs with a Daisy BB Gun?
- Did you carry a lucky Troll in your pocket on the way to school?
- Did you Swim, Frug, and Twist to The Beach Boys, The Supremes, and The Beatles?
- Did you swoon over Davy Jones or Bobby Sherman?
- Did your raging teenage hormones have you torn between Kansas cutie Mary Ann and Hollywood sexpot Ginger?
- Did you wear go-go boots, miniskirts, love beads, and white lipstick?

- Did you wear your hair in a bouffant flip style, just like TV's *That Girl*'s?
- Did you starve yourself stick-thin to be like British model Twiggy?
- Were you a Gidget or a Robbie Douglas who secretly wished to be a hippie letting-it-all-hang-out at Woodstock?
- Did you utter the words "groovy," "outta-sight," and "far-out"?
- Did *The Sound Of Music* make you think about becoming a nun, or *The Graduate* make you contemplate seducing your girlfriend's mother?
- Are you a Baby Boomer?

WERE YOU BORN IN THE 1960s?

- Did you watch the Saturday-morning adventures of Jonny Quest, H.R. Pufnstuf, and Josie and the Pussycats?
- Did you debate which was the better-tasting cereal, Quisp or Quake?
- Did you consume futuristic Tang with Space Food Sticks while wishing you were in space with Captain Kirk's Starship Enterprise?
- Did you know the address to Boston's Zoom-a-Zoom-a-Zoom; how many Bananas were in the Splits; and the story of a man named Brady?
- Did you play with Creepy Crawlers, G.I. Joe, Hot Wheels, and SSP Racers?
- Did you lovingly hug your Mrs. Beasley and wear a Lucky Locket Kiddle around your neck at the playground?
- Do you know what Super Elastic Bubble Plastic is?
- Were you daring enough to sneak the oft-banned Pop Rocks to school in your Disney School Bus lunch box?
- Did you Hustle, Freak, and Bump to the Bee Gees, Donna Summer, and K.C. and his Sunshine Band?
- Were you crazy over Donny, Michael, Leif, and David and his little brother Shaun?
- Did you lust over a *Charlie's Angels* poster taped to your bedroom wall?
- Were your bell-bottoms wide and your platforms high?
- Did you just *have* to have a pair of Calvin's or Gloria's latest designer jeans?
- Was your hair cut in a shag, a wedge, a wing, a feather, a mushroom, or a bi-level?
- Did you reek of Babe, Stetson, or just plain marijuana?
- Were you the Richie Cunningham type who yearned to shake his groove thang on the Studio 54 dance floor?
- Did *Jaws* scare you out of the sea, *Earthquake* scare you away from L.A., and *The Exorcist* scare you back to church?
- Was The Force with you?
- Or, was it up your nose with a rubber hose?
- Are you confused about whether you're a Baby Boomer or a Generation Xer?

WERE YOU BORN IN THE 1970s?

- Did you ponder Scooby-Doo, where are you? Or "Conjunction junction, what's your function?"
- Did breakfast consist of such toaster favorites as Pop Tarts, Eggos, and Danish-Go-Rounds?
- Did you know how to get to *Sesame Street*?
- Did you think the squeaky Smurfs were just the cutest little blue things in the world?
- Did you collect every single one of the Masters of the Universe action figures?
- Were your high-score initials displayed on Pac-Man, Galaga, and Donkey Kong arcade video games?
- Did you Pogo, Flashdance, and Roger Rabbit to Devo, Michael Jackson, and the New Kids on the Block?
- Did you cry yourself to sleep wishing you could be teen queen Molly Ringwald and hang out with the Brat Pack studs?
- Did you emulate the MTV fashions of Madonna, Boy George, and Duran Duran?
- Was your hair as big as Bon Jovi's, or were your bangs as tall as Tiffany's?
- Were "like, totally," "fer shur," "gnarly," "rad," "tubular," and "to the max" part of your vocabulary?
- Were you a preppie like Blair Warner, a stoner like Jeff Spicoli, or a nerd like "Screech" Powers?
- Did you laugh when Ferris skipped school and cry when E.T. phoned home?
- Are you a Generation Xer?

If you answered "yes" to any of these questions, this book is for you, because it's about you! *From ABBA to Zoom* is an extensive pop culture encyclopedia and reference guide about the late twentieth century. In its pages, you will find entries showcasing the people, places, and things that shaped and influenced Americans born after World War II. With a youth-friendly emphasis, the entries cover toys, dolls, games, books, comics, television shows, movies, celebrities, fictional characters, make-believe lands, fashions, food, drinks, restaurants, songs, dances, slang, fads, events, lists, and much more.

So, sit back, relax, and enjoy this incredible journey of memories past, from ABBA to Zoom, and all pop culture points in between!

note to reader

There are thousands of *outtasight* entries in this book, all of which are brief, easy to read, and contain fascinating facts and personal reflections.

If you'd like to locate an entry for a certain *real-life actor or actress* who catches your fancy, try looking under their last name, such as **Cassidy, David,** or **Fawcett, Farrah**.

If it's the name of a specific *fictional character* from one of your favorite TV shows, movies, books, or comics you're looking for, you can find them listed according to their first name, such as **Alex P. Keaton** or **James Bond**.

Of course, if you're searching to find your favorite *toy, candy, movie, band, TV show, TV character, or anything else that takes you back to the Happy Days,* just flip the pages to the first letter of its name and let the memories fill your mind!

Accompanying many of the entries is an FYI (For Your Information) section that gives a fun tidbit about the subject.

Got it? Groovy!

a

ABBA

Once referred to as the "Swedish Beatles," the superstar music group, formed in Stockholm in 1970, consisted of two highly glamorous and amorous married couples: Agnetha Faltskog and Björn Ulvaeus, and Benny Andersson and Anni-Frid "Frida" Lyngstad. (ABBA is an acronym composed of the first letter of each member's first name.) With foxy Agnetha and Frida harmonizing on lead vocals, the Swedes and their unique Euro-pop sound, employing solemn verses followed by explosive choruses, achieved international stardom in the 1970s with a string of Top Forty hits: "Waterloo" (1974), "SOS" (1975), "Fernando" (1976), "I Do, I Do, I Do, I Do, I Do" (1976), "Mamma Mia" (1976), "Knowing Me, Knowing You" (1977), "Dancing Queen" (1977), "Take a Chance on Me" (1978), and "Does Your Mother Know" (1979). Ultimately, the pressure of success on the couples led to divorce—Agnetha and Björn in 1979, Benny and Frida in 1981—and resulted in the band's breakup.

Despised by the critics but adored by the public, ABBA went greatly underappreciated until the mid-1990s. Now enshrined in kitsch-oriented pop culture, ABBA's music has been revived by other recording artists, such as Erasure, Abbacadabra, Björn Again, and A*Teens, and featured in two film comedies—*The Adventures of Priscilla, Queen of the Desert* (1994) and *Muriel's Wedding* (1995). Their songs also played a lead role in the stage musical *Mamma Mia,* which started its run in 1999.

FYI: ▸ At one time, ABBA was Sweden's biggest import to the world, in front of the Saab automobile.

"ABC"

"Shake it, baby, shake it!" Showcasing twelve-year-old Michael Jackson's intense falsetto, this 1970 chart-topper by The Jackson 5 was about the ABC's of love—which, according to the young Motown heartthrobs, were easy as "A-B-C, 1-2-3, Do-Re-Me. Just you and me, girl!"

ABC AFTERSCHOOL SPECIALS

Hour-long specials, shown occasionally on weekday afternoons from 1972 to 1996, which offered school-age youths something more substantial than the billionth rerun of *Gilligan's Island*. Broadcast on ABC-TV, the Emmy-winning series featured educational documentaries, interviews, cartoons, comedies, and minimovies with cautionary story lines, all covering controversial issues like drug addiction, alcoholism, physical abuse, mental illness, teen pregnancy, homosexuality, and AIDS.

Notable presentations included "Rookie of the Year" (1973), starring Jodie Foster; "Me and Dad's

New Wife" (1976), starring Kristy McNichol; "Schoolboy Father" (1980), starring Rob Lowe; "Stoned" (1980), starring Scott Baio; "The Boy Who Drank Too Much" (1980), also starring Scott Baio; and "Please Don't Hit Me, Mom" (1981), starring Nancy McKeon.

ABC-TV'S FRIDAY NIGHT LINEUP, 1970

Popular with youths of the era, the now-legendary prime-time TV lineup began at 7:30 P.M. (6:30 Central Time) with Mike, Carol, and their blended family on *The Brady Bunch*. Next, at 8:00, was Phoebe Figalilly, the magical Nanny who watched over the Professor's three precocious tots on *Nanny and the Professor*. The groovy *Partridge Family*, featuring teen dreamboat David Cassidy, aired at 8:30, followed by everyone's favorite, *That Girl*'s Ann Marie, at the 9:00 P.M. spot. *Love, American Style* started at 9:30, marking bedtime for many kids because parents felt its racy anthologies were too mature for young minds. Finally, at 10:00, swiveling pop-star Tom Jones made our mothers swoon over his musical variety hour.

ABERCROMBIE & FITCH

Trendy clothing stores, originating out of Ohio, in which young people shop to spend a whole lot of dough on new threads that look worn and tattered. (A pair of used-looking cargo pants can run you more than $60.) A&F recently got flack for allegedly hiring only beautiful, mostly white salesclerks—the kind that look like the semi-naked models appearing in sexy fashion spreads of the retail chain's catalogs.

FYI: ▸ In the newspaper comic strip *Hi and Lois*, Abercrombie and Fitch are a comedic duo of garbage collectors.

ABOMINABLE SNOW MONSTER

"He's mean, he's nasty, and he hates everything to do with Christmas!" Seen in the 1964 Yuletide classic *Rudolph the Red-Nosed Reindeer*, this ferocious roarer of the North Pole gave Rudolph and Hermy a hard time until dental extraction turned him into a gentler, kinder Snow Monster. Nicknamed "Bumbles" by fearless prospector Yukon Cornelius, he was based on the Abominable Snowman, a legendary furry white snow beast from the Himalayas.

ACID-WASHED JEANS

In the early part of the 1980s, denim jeans had to look and feel brand-new. I knew people who would iron every single wrinkle out of a pair after laundering, and God forbid if the deep-blue hue began to fade or a hole was worn in the fabric. By the end of the decade, all that changed when—to the dismay of parents—youngsters purposely purchased jeans, called acid-washed or stone-washed, that looked as if they had been worn in the worst disaster imaginable every day for two years. The colors of these jeans were extremely faded, with white bleach streaks throughout. They tended to acquire rips and holes very easily, making them even more awesome.

Those who weren't allowed to buy jeans in such a state of disrepair would deliberately cut holes in a shiny new pair, then toss them in a washing machine with very hot water and a capful of Clorox for at least five cycles. After drying, the end results: faded color, glaring tears, and total coolness!

ACTION JACKSON

"Do and dare! He's everywhere!" Introduced in 1972, Mego Toys' low-cost, low-quality action figure with a line of vehicles and accessories was nothing but a cheap imitation of G.I. Joe. A.J.'s female counterpart was a tough doll named Dinah-Mite.

ADAM CARTWRIGHT

Ben Cartwright's intelligent but brooding man-in-black eldest son, whose New England–bred mother, Elizabeth, died when he was an infant. Played in the TV western *Bonanza* by actor Pernell Roberts from 1959 until 1965, the year he left for greener pastures and found himself blackballed in Hollywood for quitting a hit series (he felt it was beneath him). His stint in Hollywood purgatory lasted until he was cast as Trapper in *Trapper John, M.D.* in 1979.

ADDAMS FAMILY

Created in the 1930s by Charles Addams as a comic strip for *The New Yorker* magazine, the creepy, kooky, mysterious, spooky, altogether ooky clan, headed by Gomez and Morticia Addams, resided in a ramshackle mansion at 000 Cemetery Lane. The Addamses achieved cult status when they became subjects of a popular prime-time sitcom on ABC-TV

(1964 to 1966), starring John Astin as patriarch Gomez and Carolyn Jones as his wife, Morticia. This was followed by a Saturday-morning cartoon (1973–75) and two theatrical releases, *The Addams Family* (1991) and the sequel *Addams Family Values* (1993). Other members of the Addams family included oddball Uncle Fester, pudgy son Pugsley, weirdo daughter Wednesday, witchy Grandmama, furry Cousin Itt, zombie-like servant Lurch, and Thing (a bodiless hand). Vic Mizzy composed the TV show's contagious finger-snapping title theme.

"ADDICTED TO LOVE"

Robert Palmer's 1986 chart-topper is actually kind of a repetitious song made famous by a music video in which the soulful British rocker fronts a band of slick but vague miniskirted supermodels. Later in the year, he followed the same model-band format with the "I Didn't Mean to Turn You On" video.

ADVENTURES OF GULLIVER

Airing on Saturday mornings from 1968 to 1970, a Hanna-Barbera cartoon chronicling the adventures of Gary Gulliver, who, along with dog Shag, sails to the land of Lilliput in search of his missing father, Lemuel (Jonathan Swift's legendary Gulliver). Once there, he is captured and later befriended by its six-inch-tall citizens. Supporting characters include amiable Bunko, youthful Egger, unlucky Glumm, King Pomp, pretty Flirtacia (Pomp's daughter), and the villainous Captain Leech, who wanted to nab Gulliver's secret treasure map.

ADVENTURES OF PRISCILLA, QUEEN OF THE DESERT

"Being a man one day and a woman the next is not an easy thing."

—BERNADETTE (TERENCE STAMP)

Spirited Australian comedy about three drag queens who drive a pink school bus named Priscilla from Sydney through the Outback to perform their cabaret gig in Alice Springs. The trio, fabulously adorned in Academy Award–winning costumes and gravity-defying wigs, encounter homophobia, engine failure, and past memories while stopping in small desert towns to lip-synch ABBA songs. Directed by Stephan Elliott, the 1993 film starred Terence Stamp as witty Bernadette Bassenger, Hugo Weaving as sad-sack Mitzi Del Bra, and Guy Pearce as the hunky and shallow Felicia Jollygoodfellow.

ADVENTURES OF THE WILDERNESS FAMILY

Family-friendly 1976 film depicting the wholesome Robinson clan, who are fed up with smog, crime, and other hassles of urban Los Angeles and pack it all up to move to a log cabin in the wilderness of Utah. Highlighting the magnificent beauty of the Rocky Mountains region, this was one of the most successful independent features of the 1970s.

AEROSMITH

Formed in 1970, the durable band from Boston, fronted by the Jagger-esque Steven Tyler, is known for a hedonistic spirit and ribald rock tunes. Hit songs include "Dream On" (1973), "Sweet Emotion" (1975), "Last Child" (1976), "Walk This Way" (1976), "Dude (Looks Like a Lady)" (1987), "Angel" (1988), "Rag Doll" (1988), "Love in an Elevator" (1989), and "Janie's Got a Gun" (1989).

FYI: ▸ Beautiful movie actress Liv Tyler (*Stealing Beauty* and *Armageddon*) is Steven's daughter (she inherited his lips).

AFRO

"Black Power!" Fashionable in the late 1960s and 1970s, this kinky, round hairdo symbolized liberation for African-Americans weary of having their hair painstakingly straightened to imitate flat Caucasian styles. (The name came from the wearer's pride in his or her African cultural heritage.) Free at last, blacks allowed their locks to grow naturally full, and the bigger the Afro the better. Those sporting it often carried a large-toothed pick comb sticking right in the Afro, or in a rear pocket of their bell-bottoms, for quick and handy use. So popular was the Afro, by the end of the 1970s, that white celebs like Barbra Streisand, Bette Midler, Ali MacGraw, and Anthony "Luke Spencer" Geary made the mistake of perming their hair into tight, frizzy Afros—a.k.a. Anglo-fros!

FYI: ▸ In old school yearbooks, some students had Afros so huge that they barely fit into the frame of the picture!

AGENT 99

"Oh, Max!" This pretty, brunette secret agent for Washington-based CONTROL partnered with Maxwell Smart (Agent 86) to battle the evil spies of KAOS on the prime-time hit *Get Smart*. Much to Max's dismay, Agent 99 combined her sultriness and mental resources to save the bumbling, stumbling spy from danger. In love with Max, she later became his wife and gave birth to twins, a boy and a girl.

FYI: ▸ The beauty who played Agent 99 was brainy Barbara Feldon, who was once a contestant on TV's *$64,000 Question*. Her knowledge of Shakespeare won her the prize in the show's title!

AIR HOCKEY

During the 1970s, youngsters flocked to pool halls in droves to challenge one another in this hockey-inspired table game. The playing surface had hundreds of tiny holes that jetted enough air to keep the puck airborne. At times the puck would be hammered so fast and hard, back and forth, that it was next to impossible to see it, and if struck at the right angle (watch out!) it became a painful missile!

AIRPORT 1975

"The stewardess is flying the plane!" Actually released in 1974, this cinematic successor to *Airport* (the blockbuster 1970 epic about a passenger airliner crippled by a mad bomber) jets on with more high-flying excitement as a 747 jumbo jet, Columbia Airlines Flight 109, en route to L.A. from D.C., has a disastrous mid-air collision with a small plane. The pilots are wiped out, a gaping hole appears in the cockpit nose, and—omigawd!—stewardess Nancy Pryor (played by cross-eyed Karen Black) must now fly the wounded aircraft. Chuck Heston co-stars as Alan Murdoch, Nancy's lover, a former pilot who courageously enters the cockpit from a helicopter to help land the airplane. Supporting players include *Airport* regular George Kennedy as Joe Patroni, Susan Clark as Mrs. Patroni, Efrem Zimbalist Jr. as Captain Stacy, Sid Caesar as Barney, Linda Blair as Janice Abbott, Nancy Owens as Mrs. Abbott, Dana Andrews as Scott Freeman, Gloria Swanson as herself, Ed Nelson as Major Alexander, Myrna Loy as Mrs. Devaney, Larry Storch as Purcell, Jerry Stiller as Sam, Erik Estrada as Julio, Christopher Norris as stewardess Bette, and pop singer Helen Reddy as Sister Ruth, a nun.

Two more sequels followed: *Airport '77* and the unbelievable *Concorde: Airport 1979*, featuring a supersonic jet with passengers John Davidson, Jimmie "J.J." Walker, Charo, and Martha Raye being chased upside down by Russian missiles.

FYI: ▸ A favorite "so bad, it's good" moment in *Airport 1975* is when guitar-strumming Helen Reddy serenades teen kidney-transplant patient Linda Blair (who comes off much too happy for someone under such extensive care) with an uplifting song.

ALADDIN

Based on the ancient tale from *The Thousand and One Nights*, this Disney adventure-fantasy follows a handsome street urchin named Aladdin who dreams of winning the hand of the beautiful Princess Jasmine, daughter of the Sultan of Agrabah, a mythical Arabian city, while battling the scheming vizier Jafar. He is aided in his quest by faithful monkey friend Abu and an unruly big blue Genie (ad-libbed with lightning-fast glee by comedian Robin Williams). The 1992 film became the highest-grossing animated feature film ever, earning more than $200 million in revenue. It features the Oscar-winning song "A Whole New World," along with "Arabian Nights," "Friend Like Me," and "One Jump Ahead." Followed by two made-for-video sequels: *The Return of Jafar* (1993) and *Aladdin and the King of Thieves* (1996).

ALAN MAYBERRY

Tall, strong, and handsome blond stud from *Josie and the Pussycats* cartoon who was like a roadie or something. He was also Pussycat Josie's main squeeze.

FYI: ▸ Alan M. was initially introduced in the *Josie* comic book number 42 in August 1969 as a folksinger in a band called Alan and the Jesters.

AL BUNDY

"Let's rock!" The balding, middle-aged head of the Bundy family longs for the glory days of 1966, when he was a football hero at Polk High School (he once made four touchdowns in a championship game). Instead he's a low-paid salesman squeezing shoes onto the feet of fat women at Gary's Shoe Emporium at the New Market Mall in suburban Chicago. He comes home hungry at night to his wife, Peg, who's sexually frustrated and doesn't cook or clean, and two dysfunctional kids, trampy Kelly and geeky Bud. At least Al finds relief drinking beer, watching sports on TV, putting his hand into his pants, and joining the fellows at The Jiggly Room, a neighborhood nudie bar. He was played by Ed O'Neill on FOX's *Married . . . with Children* from 1987 to 1997.

ALEXANDER CABOT III

"Hey, they can't get away with that! As manager of the Pussycats, I won't allow it! Uh, one of you girls stop him!" Hippie-ish music promoter and manager of all-female rock group Josie and the Pussycats. The opposite of his conniving sister, Alexandra, he's a quivering scaredy-cat in the vein of Shaggy from *Scooby-Doo*.

FYI: ▸ Radio's Top Forty spokesman Casey Kasem provided both Alexander's and Shaggy's voices in the Hanna-Barbera cartoons *Josie and the Pussycats* and *Scooby-Doo*.

ALEXANDER: THE OTHER SIDE OF DAWN

This 1977 sequel to *Dawn: Portrait of a Teenage Runaway*, starring *Brady Bunch*'s Eve Plumb, was the first TV movie to deal with the down-and-dirty world of male prostitution. It starred Leigh McCloskey as Alexander Duncan, a good-looking fellow who can't land a decent job and ends up hustling his body to both women and men on the streets of Hollywood. He gets involved with a gay pro-football player, Charles Selby (Alan Feinstein), before ex-hooker girlfriend Dawn Wetherby (Plumb) arrives on the scene to help him find legitimate work.

FYI: ▸ Leigh McCloskey went on to star as Mitch Cooper, Lucy Ewing's husband, on the prime-time soap *Dallas* from 1979 to 1982.

ALEXANDRA CABOT

"Ooh, that Josie!" Wealthy music manager Alexander Cabot's scheming, wisecracking, no-talent debutante sis who had a white skunk-stripe in her jet-black hair (just like Disney's Cruella De Vil). Unrelentingly jealous of Josie and the Pussycats (especially Josie, because she dated roadie Alan M., whom Alexandra lusted over), she often got both herself and the all-girl rock band involved in a madcap misadventure. Voiced by Sherry Alberoni, a former Mouseketeer, Alexandra is one of the best-loved bitches of Saturday-morning cartoons. Sebastian is her mischievous cat.

ALEXIS CARRINGTON COLBY

"I'll get you for this! If it's the last thing I do, you'll pay for this, Blake Carrington!" Glamorous and ruthless, the raven-haired bitch—er, I mean Brit—arrived in Denver (after giving Cecil Colby a fatal heart attack during a sexual romp) to vex ex-husband Blake and dig her freshly manicured claws into the padded shoulders of his sweetly devoted second wife, Krystle. Played wonderfully wicked by B-movie sex-symbol Joan Collins on *Dynasty*, Alexis was hands down the most popular TV villainess of the 1980s.

ALEX OWENS

Alexandra Owens, a pretty nineteen-year-old who labors during the day as a welder in a Pittsburgh steel factory but at night works as an exotic dancer at Mawby's Bar, where she douses herself with water amid flashing strobe-lighting. Living in a huge downtown loft the size of a sweatshop, the curly-haired brunette dons leg warmers and torn sweatshirts while dreaming of getting into a prestigious ballet academy (the Pittsburgh Conservatory of Dance). Played by newcomer Jennifer Beals in the 1983 film *Flashdance*.

ALEX P. KEATON

To the bewilderment of his liberal, onetime-hippie parents, this teen from Columbus, Ohio, is an ultraconservative Young Republican who idolizes Richard Nixon, sleeps with a picture of William F. Buckley Jr. over his bed, subscribes to *The National Review*, and regularly wears a suit and tie. After high school, future yuppie Alex attended Leland College, where he studied economics and after graduation joined a Wall Street firm. Played by twenty-one-year-old Michael J. Fox on the TV hit *Family Ties*.

ALF

The cat-hungry, smart-alecky, fur-covered, diminutive 229-year-old space alien from the planet Melmac lived with a suburban Los Angeles family, the Tanners, after crash-landing in their garage. Although his actual name was Gordon Shumway, the Tanners—dad Willie, mom Kate, and kids Lynn and Brian—called him Alf for "Alien Life Form." Voiced by Paul Fusco, Alf was the star of a prime-time sitcom (1986–90) and a Saturday-morning cartoon (1987–90).

ALFRED E. NEUMAN

"What, me worry?" The idiotic, grinning, gap-toothed redhead has been the cover-boy mascot for *Mad* magazine since 1956. Hey, has anybody noticed his resemblance to President George W. Bush?

ALI, MUHAMMAD

"I'm the greatest. I can't be beat." The boxing great was born Cassius Clay on January 17, 1942, in Louisville, Kentucky, before joining the Nation of Islam and changing his name to Muhammad Ali. Celebrated for strength, agility, and the famous "Ali Shuffle," the champ set a career record of fifty-six wins (only five losses), including three heavyweight titles (1964–67, 1974–78, and 1978–79). He was also celebrated for his conceit ("I'm the best-looking, the fastest, the cleverest . . .") and for poetry recitals that mocked opponents like George Foreman and Joe Frazier (". . . float like a butterfly and sting like a bee"). Subject of a reggae-esque Top Forty hit, "Black Superman—Muhammad Ali," by Johnny Wakelin in 1975. He retired in 1981.

FYI: ▸ Muhammad Ali was so famous in the 1970s that even the Pope asked for an autograph.

ALICE NELSON

"Pork chops and applesauce." Most kids who grew up watching *The Brady Bunch* wished they had this nutty live-in housemaid in their home. Played by wisecracking Ann B. Davis, Alice was good-natured and full of funny, practical advice. She wore a blue double-breasted maid's uniform with white apron as she cooked, cleaned, and sewed for the Bradys, who simply adored her. Alice's longtime beau was "unbudgeable bachelor" Sam the Butcher. (He called her his "little lamb chop.")

ALIEN

"In space, no one can hear you scream." In director Ridley Scott's 1979 sci-fi horror film, a futuristic space freighter, the Nostromo, with seven crewmen and a cat, lands on an unexplored planet called LV-426 to investigate a craft that has crash-landed. They unwittingly pick up and become stalked by an alien organism that rapidly develops into an unstoppable and highly carnivorous reptile-like monster with horrific slime-dripping, razor-sharp teeth inside of jaws inside of jaws (designed by Swiss surrealist H. R. Giger). The cast includes Sigourney Weaver as take-charge heroine Lieutenant Ripley, John Hurt as second officer Kane, Tom Skerritt as Captain Dallas, Veronica Cartwright as navigator Lambert, Harry Dean Stanton as Brett, Yaphet Kotto as Parker, Ian Holm as android science officer Ash, and Jonesy, the Nostromo's pet cat. Followed by three sequels: *Aliens* (1986), *Alien 3* (1992), and *Alien Resurrection* (1997).

FYI: ▸ *Alien*'s heart-pounding and gut-wrenching special effects—including the gross-out "rebirth" of the baby alien busting out of John Hurt's stomach—won an Oscar for visual effects.

A-LINE DRESS

Quintessential 1960s dress, first introduced by designer Christian Dior in 1955 and made famous by First Lady Jackie Kennedy in the early 1960s. (She accessorized it with a pillbox hat, little white gloves, and a handbag.) The name of the dress is derived from its A-shaped design, in which the sides angle out slightly from the bustline to form a slightly wider hem.

ALKA-SELTZER

Antacid tablets distinguished by the fizz they make after being dropped into a glass of water, and for being promoted by a trio of now-classic TV commercial catchphrases from the 1970s: "I can't believe I ate the whole thing," "Mamma-mia, thatsa spicy meatball," and "Plop, plop, fizz, fizz / Oh, what a relief it is."

ALLEN, IRWIN

"If I can't blow up the world in the first ten seconds, then the show is a flop." Special-effects master who created and produced many action-packed TV adventures of the 1960s, such as *Voyage to the Bottom of the Sea* (1964–68), *Lost in Space* (1965–68), *Time Tunnel* (1966–67), and *Land of the Giants* (1968–70). His motion picture *The Poseidon Adventure* (1972) single-handedly spawned the popular disaster genre of the 1970s.

ALPHABET BLOCKS

Probably best remembered are the wooden ones by PlaySkool that were embossed with a letter and a picture of an animal that begins with that letter (like a gorilla for G or a zebra for Z) on the side of each.

ALPHA CENTAURI

The intended star-system destination of the Robinson family before Dr. Zachary Smith got them lost in space in the TV sci-fi classic *Lost in Space*.

ALVIN

Mischievous leader of the cartoon's shrilled-voiced Chipmunks, he wore a floor-length red sweater with a big A on the chest, whose grand schemes involving brothers Simon and Theodore usually antagonized peacekeeping manager David Seville ("Aaaalviiin!").

AMANDA BELLOWS

The totally stylish Emmaline Henry on the TV sitcom *I Dream of Jeannie* played Dr. Alfred Bellows's caring but nosy wife, Amanda, from 1966 to 1970.

AMANDA WHURLITZER

The meanest fastballer in Southern California! A foul-mouthed eleven-year-old girl who pitched the hapless "Bad News" Bears to the Little League Championship. Portrayed by Tatum O'Neal in the 1976 movie *The Bad News Bears*.

AMAZING CHAN AND THE CHAN CLAN

Airing on Saturday mornings from 1972 to 1974, this Hanna-Barbera production—noteworthy for being one of the first and only cartoons about Chinese-Americans—featured Charlie Chan, the amazing Oriental sleuth who mixed investigative skills with a healthy dose of ancient Chinese philosophy. The show's catch? Chan was assisted in solving crimes by his eager and somewhat bumbling clan of ten children—Henry, Alan, Stanley, Suzie, Mimi, Anne, Tom, Flip, Nancy, and Scooter and their pet dog Chu Chu. Eldest sons Henry and Stanley fronted the family's rock group and drove a van that could transform into various vehicles.

FYI: ▸ Keye Luke, who played number-one son Lee in the *Chan* movies of the 1930s, provided the voice of Charlie, while juvenile actress Jodie Foster provided the voice of Anne.

AMERICAN BANDSTAND

"It's got a great beat, and you can dance to it." TV's first rock 'n' roll program—hosted by the charismatic and clean-cut Dick Clark, a disc jockey from Philadelphia—captured what was hip and happenin' when it came to the teenage world of dance and music. *American Bandstand* is ABC-TV's longest-running afternoon show, and throughout its thirty-year run the format stayed virtually the same (with the exception of moving the set from Philly to L.A.). There were the bleachers full of beaming teens waiting for their fave pop-star to come onstage, lip-synch his or her latest hit, and then be interviewed by Clark. There were the roving camera shots capturing these trendy-dressed teens dancing to popular tunes. (Many home viewers learned how to dance by imitating the *Bandstand* regulars.) There were the "Rate-a-Record" segments that had four kids grading the "danceability" of a new song on a scale of 35 (bad) to 98 (good). There was the countdown of the week's Top Ten records, the Solo Spotlight couples dance, and the highly touted yearly Dance Contest, in which viewers wrote in to cast ballots for their favorite couple. Why, even Dick Clark stayed the same—perpetually youthful—earning him the label of "America's Oldest Teenager."

American Bandstand has been the inspiration for every teen dance show since its first airing in 1957—*Hullabaloo, Shindig, Soul Train, Dance Party U.S.A.*, and MTV's *Grind*—and found itself spoofed by John Waters's irresistible feature film *Hairspray* (1988). "Bandstand Boogie" was the instrumental theme of the series, performed by Les Elgart and his orchestra and later revamped with words by Barry Manilow.

AMERICAN GIGOLO

Highly visual yet pretentious thriller about Julian Kay (Richard Gere), an Armani-clad (when he's wearing clothes) stud-for-hire who attends to the sexual needs of the rich women of Beverly Hills, including the wife of a California state senator, until the day he is falsely accused of murdering a former client. The 1980 movie is most famous for a full-frontal nudity shot of Gere and for the music score by Giorgio Moroder, including the number-one hit song "Call Me" by Blondie. Paul Schrader directed the film.

AMERICAN GLADIATORS

Syndicated TV spectacle that pitted four athletic contestants (two men, two women) against a lineup of muscle-bound professional jocks known as "Gladiators." Tested on strength, agility, and endurance, the contenders competed in a variety of physical challenges, such as jousting and wall-climbing, while a menacing Gladiator—who bore a name like Gemini, Nitro, or Laser (male), or Blaze, Gold, or Lace (female)—attempted to trounce them along the way. The show ended with the top male and female competitors facing a strenuous obstacle course called "The Eliminator," in which all of the Gladiators were employed to stop the competitors from finishing. Hosts during the program's eight-year run (1989–96) included football greats Joe Theismann and Larry Csonka.

AMERICAN TAIL

Produced by Steven Spielberg and directed by Don Bluth, a 1986 big-screen animated feature about an adorable young Russian mouse named Fievel Mousekewitz who gets separated from his family while immigrating to America in the 1880s. In his new homeland, Fievel has many adventures, while dodging bad cats, and is eventually reunited with his parents and sister. Grossing more than $47 million, *An American Tail* merited the honor of being the highest-grossing animated film of its day. Its platinum-selling song, "Somewhere Out There," performed by Linda Ronstadt and James Ingram, earned an Oscar nomination for Best Song. Followed by a 1991 sequel, *An American Tail: Fievel Goes West.*

AMERICAN WEREWOLF IN LONDON

"Have you ever talked to a corpse?
It's boring."

—JACK GOODMAN (GRIFFIN DUNNE)

Frightful 1981 horror venture about two American college boys, David Kessler (David Naughton) and Jack Goodman (Griffin Dunne), who are viciously attacked by a werewolf while traveling through the British moors. One dies (Jack), and the other is severely mauled and sent to recovery in London (David), where he is nursed back to health by a sweet nurse, Alex Price (Jenny Agutter). David's life becomes even more nightmarish as he begins to turn into a blood-hungry werewolf. Directed by John Landis, this now-classic lycanthropic film is noted for the special-effects scene of Naughton transforming into the hairy beast (the best in cinematic history, rivaled only by *The Howling*) and for Dunne's darkly humorous undead Jack (shown in progressive states of decay), who continuously visits David.

AMITY ISLAND

"Amity Island welcomes you!" The local citizens and tourists at this tranquil Long Island seaside resort were terrorized by an enormous, two-ton thirty-foot man-eating great white shark (*Jaws*) in the summer of 1975. Three years later, the shark attacks reoccurred at Amity (*Jaws 2*).

AMITYVILLE HORROR

In 1977, Jay Anson's supposedly true story of a middle-class family's twenty-eight-day encounter with demons became a runaway best-selling novel, later made into a popular 1979 film. It chronicled the tale of the luckless Lutzes, who moved into the colonial home of their dreams (or, in their case, their nightmares), once the setting of a grisly murder in which young Ronald DeFeo slaughtered his entire family. The new inhabitants are soon terrorized by the house, as toilets ooze black gook, odd noises burst from sights unseen, doors mysteriously slam shut, a rocking chair rocks with no one in it, flies mass by the hundreds, and the attic windows glow like two demon eyes. The movie starred James Brolin as George Lutz, Margot Kidder as his wife, Kathleen, and Rod Steiger overacting as Father Delaney, a priest who tries to exorcise the devilish attitude from the dwelling. Followed by a whole slew of sequels, including a prequel and one done in 3-D.

ANAKIN SKYWALKER

A kindhearted slave boy from the planet Tatooine who grew up to learn the mystical ways of the Jedi

Knight. He later crossed over to the Dark Side to become the terrifyingly evil Darth Vader. Played by nine-year-old Jake Lloyd and later by teen Hayden Christensen in the prequels to George Lucas's *Star Wars* film trilogy: *Episode I: The Phantom Menace* (1999) and *Episode II: Attack of the Clones* (2002).

ANDERSON, LONI

TV sex symbol in the late 1970s who played receptionist Jennifer Marlowe on the sitcom *WKRP in Cincinnati* (1978–82) and screen goddess Jayne Mansfield in the TV film *The Jayne Mansfield Story* (1980). Loni is also famous for her brickhouse body, blonde helmet-hair, and nasty divorce from actor Burt Reynolds.

ANDERSON, PAMELA

The bleached-blonde hair! The augmented breasts! The tanning-salon skin! The "Number-One Sex Goddess" of the 1990s was the Barbie incarnate—all plastic and fake, if ya know what I mean. Some of Pamela's career highlights include being a *Playboy* centerfold (February 1990), playing ever-buoyant lifeguard C. J. Parker on *Baywatch* (1992–97), marrying overtattooed Motley Crue drummer Tommy Lee (1995–98), and voicing a superhero exotic dancer (Erotica Jones) in the adult TV cartoon *Stripperella* (2003). The Canadian actress was born on July 1, 1967, in Ladysmith, British Columbia.

ANDREA THOMAS

Mild-mannered science teacher at Larkspur High School whose alter ego was the beautiful and oh-so-mighty Isis, an ancient Egyptian goddess. At Larkspur, Miss Thomas, a bespectacled brunette, associated with students Renee Carroll and Cindy Lee and fellow school employees Rick Mason and Dr. Barnes. She was played by JoAnna Cameron on the popular mid-1970s Saturday-morning TV series *Isis*.

ANDY GRIFFITH SHOW

Airing from 1960 to 1968, this is one of the best-loved TV sitcoms of all time. Set in Mayberry, North Carolina, it centers on Andy Taylor (played by lanky Andy Griffith), an easygoing and upright sheriff who watched over the daily goings-on of fellow country bumpkins living in the sleepy hamlet. Andy was a widower raising a young son, Opie (Ron Howard), with the help of doting Aunt Bee (Frances Bavier). Other Mayberry townsfolk included Barney Fife (Don Knotts), Andy's deputy sheriff; Ellie Walker (Elinor Donahue), Andy's first girlfriend, a drugstore clerk; Helen Crump (Aneta Corsaut), Andy's later girlfriend, a schoolteacher; Floyd Lawson (Howard McNear), a barber; Howard Sprague (Jack Dodson), the town clerk; Otis Campbell (Hal Smith), the town drunk; Clara Edwards (Hope Summers), the town busybody; Emmett Clark (Paul Hartman), a handyman; Gomer Pyle (Jim Nabors), a gas pump attendant; Goober Pyle (George Lindsey), Gomer's cousin; and Thelma Lou (Betty Lynn), Barney's best gal. Pleasant and likable, the show was the first of CBS-TV's rural-oriented comedies, a lineage that eventually included *The Beverly Hillbillies, Petticoat Junction, Green Acres, Hee Haw,* and two *Andy Griffith* spin-offs, *Gomer Pyle, U.S.M.C.,* and *Mayberry RFD.* "The Fishin' Hole" by Earl Hagen was the cheery theme song whistled over the opening credits.

FYI: ▸ *The Andy Griffith Show* was one of only three series in TV history to end its run at the top of the Nielsen ratings; the others were *I Love Lucy* and *Seinfeld.*

ANGEL FLIGHT PANTS

Fashionable during the disco dance era, a brand of slacks noteworthy for being extremely skintight and having very wide flares. Usually worn with disco jackets, vests, and shiny satin shirts.

ANGELICA PICKLES

"If I wanna be mean, I can be mean. Know why? Cos, I'm the boss." Pigtailed spoiled brat and—at three and a quarter years old—the eldest of the *Rugrats*, who always bullies the younger cousins, whom she calls "babies." Angelica cherishes a Barbie-like doll called Cynthia that often serves as an accomplice in her misdeeds. Cheryl Chase provides Angelica's voice on Nickelodeon's *Rugrats* cartoon show.

ANGEL-SLEEVE BLOUSES

Loose-cut cottony blouses with oversized, billowy "bell-bottom" sleeves. Rock goddess Stevie Nicks sported these as part of the witchy-gypsy look she loved so much.

ANGELYNE

"The image of Angelyne
is said to be as much a part of
Hollywood as the Hollywood sign."
—CNN

Who is she? I'm not really sure. What does she do? I'm not really sure of that, either. Why is she featured in this book? Well, since 1984 this platinum-blonde bimbo has been one of L.A.'s most unique phenomena. Her pouty face and enormous breasts have decorated hundreds of billboards all over town as a means of self-promotion. If you're lucky, you can spot her cruising around the boulevards of Hollywood in a pink Corvette.

FYI: ▸ In a scene from the 2004 global-warming disaster flick *The Day After Tomorrow,* a tornado in Los Angeles rips an ever-present Angelyne billboard off its perch, careens it down a Hollywood street, and kills a news reporter.

ANIMAL REVENGE MOVIES

Killer dogs! Killer birds! Killer frogs! Gasp! What's going on? In the last few decades, ecology concerns have been all the rage, especially during the 1970s (the "give a hoot, don't pollute" era), when a trend in horror films had animals running amok and seeking revenge on two-legged litterbugs and other destroyers of the environment. Renowned animal-revenge movies of the decade include *Day of the Animals* (1977), *Empire of the Ants* (1977), *Food of the Gods* (1976), *Frogs* (1972), *Grizzly* (1976), *Jaws* (1975), *Night of the Lepus* (1972), *Nightwing* (1979), *Orca* (1977), *The Pack* (1977), *Piranha* (1978), *Squirm* (1976), *The Swarm* (1978), *Tentacles* (1971), and *Willard* (1971). So remember, kiddies, be kind to all those furry, feathered, and scaly little critters lurking around your neighborhood, because you wouldn't want any of these alarming tales to become reality.

ANIMANIACS

A trio of black-colored animated characters with long ears who were trapped in the Warner Brothers water tower back in the 1930s for being too screwball for the general public. Sixty years later, talky Yakko Warner, Beatle-accented Wakko Warner, and adorable Dot Warner were finally freed to wreak zany chaos on cartoon lovers everywhere. Presented by Steven Spielberg, the *Animaniacs* TV show was honored with three Emmy Awards for Outstanding Animated Program during its original run in the 1990s.

ANNE WELLES

In the camp film classic *Valley of the Dolls*, Barbara Parkins starred as breathtaking Anne Welles, the small-town New England girl who travels to the bright lights of New York City and becomes the glamorous Gillian Girl, a cosmetics model with the "million-dollar face." "She took the green pills."

ANNIE

"The sun will come out tomorrow." Betcha bottom dollar a lot of little girls wanted to be this frizzy red-headed waif upon seeing the 1982 movie, based on the 1977 Broadway musical, which in turn was inspired by the *Little Orphan Annie* comic strip created by Harold Gray in 1924. The uplifting film starred Aileen Quinn as spunky Annie, Albert Finney as wealthy Daddy Warbucks, Ann Reinking as gracious Grace Farrell, Carol Burnett as dreadful Miss Hannigan (in a scene-stealing performance), Tim Curry as sinister Rooster Hannigan, Bernadette Peters as trampy Lily St. Regis, Geoffrey Holder as mystical Punjab, and Sandy as Annie's faithful mutt. Featured songs included "Tomorrow," "It's a Hard Knock Life," "Dumb Dog," "Easy Street," "I Think I'm Gonna Like It Here," "Little Girls," and "Maybe."

ANN MARIE

"If you find one girl to love / Only one girl to love / Then she'll be That Girl, too!" A wide-eyed (accented by black eyeliner and false eyelashes), squeaky-voiced (she sounded like she had a chronic sore throat), dark-haired (styled in a fab flip) struggling actress, portrayed by Marlo Thomas on prime time's *That Girl*, trying to make it in the Big Apple—New York City. Upbeat and fun-loving, this single gal of the 1960s somehow found time, between looking for acting jobs and flying a kite down Fifth Avenue, to spend with patient boyfriend Don Hollinger and overprotective daddy Lou Marie. Ann's stylish, doll-like fashions—A-line minidresses, colored tights, wide-brimmed bonnets, and go-go boots—were the grooviest around!

ANN ROMANO
Mother of two teen girls, Julie and Barbara, who gets divorced after seventeen years of marriage and moves into a small apartment building in Indianapolis. Adorned with an orange, mushroom-shaped hairdo, Ann was the quintessential single working mother of the 1970s who took it "one day at a time" and rarely lost her sunny disposition even in the worst of times. Played by Bonnie Franklin on CBS-TV's *One Day at a Time*.

ANOREXIA NERVOSA
An eating disorder characterized by deliberate starvation due to excessive dieting or self-induced vomiting (bulimia). The generation of girls who grew up in the shadow of mega-skinny waif model Twiggy and her thin-is-in cover-girl comrades seemed to have been hardest hit by this debilitating illness. In 1983, thirty-two-year-old pop-music star Karen Carpenter's premature death from heart failure, a side effect of anorexia nervosa, put the formerly unknown disease in the headlines and made it a household name.

Ignoring the dangers of anorexia, the fashion world embraced the emaciated waif look in the 1990s, allowing it to make a big comeback among models like Britain's young Kate Moss and shockingly thin TV actresses like Calista Flockhart of *Ally McBeal* and Lara Flynn Boyle of *The Practice*. Outraged feminist groups particularly attacked Moss for projecting an image that's impossible for a woman to achieve. (All over New York City, Kate's Calvin Klein ad photos were defaced with "feed me" spray painted on them.)

ANT, ADAM
Once called "the Prince Charming of new romanticism," the British singer (born Stuart Leslie Goddard on November 3, 1954, in London) fronted a New Wave band in the early 1980s—Adam and the Ants—an act famous for a bizarre array of costumes (swashbuckling pirate, American Indian, and Renaissance dandy), peacock-colored makeup, and avant-garde hairdos. Their hyper, tribal-rhythm "Antmusic," from the 1980s *Kings of the Wild Frontier* LP, was a dance-floor favorite on both sides of the Atlantic. After the Ants disbanded in 1982, the dark-haired cutie with a bad-boy image went solo with songs "Goody Two Shoes" (1982) and "Strip" (1983).

ANT FARMS
After sending off for a supply of live ants in the mail, Baby Boomer kids could watch the busy little insects dig a colony in Uncle Milton's clear-plastic containers with panoramas of a farm. But beware. These caused a big mess in the house, with ants crawling here and there when accidentally dropped or dumped on the floor.

ANTS IN THE PANTS
Kids never knew how much fun having ants in the pants could be until the introduction of this Schaper action game in 1968. Similar to the old-fashioned game of tiddlywinks, players flipped plastic "ants" into the air, shooting toward a big pair of plastic trousers complete with red suspenders. The first player to get all his or her "ants in the pants" won.

APPLE JACKS
I don't really remember kids being that crazy over the apple-cinnamon taste of this breakfast cereal, but its catchy commercial jingle ("A is for Apple! J is for Jacks! Cinnamon-toasted Apple Jacks!"), along with the animated Apple Jacks stick-figure children, excited them enough to force their parents to buy it. Apple Jacks were introduced by Kellogg's in 1965.

AQUAHAMA CITY
Futuristic metropolis, located under a dome in the ocean, that's home to the cartoon shark Jabberjaw and his teenage friends.

AQUALAD
Superhero Aquaman's young son (fondly referred to as "Tadpole" by his pop), who rode a sea pony named Imp and was accompanied by a pet walrus called Tusky. In the *Aquaman* cartoon show airing on Saturday mornings in the late 1960s, Aqualad repeatedly used the expression "Jumpin' Jellyfish!"

AQUAMAN
Created in 1941 by *DC* comics to compete with rival Sub-Mariner of *Marvel* comics, Aquaman is the

golden-haired ruler of the Lost Continent of Atlantis and "King of the Seven Seas," whose mother was an Atlantian and whose dad was an American marine scientist. The aquatic superhero rode into action on a giant seahorse named Storm while battling dastardly villains with his mighty telepathic brain waves. Beautiful wife Mera often accompanied Aquaman on his maritime crime-fighting while riding a pink sea horse.

AQUA NET
This inexpensive aerosol hairspray was used to create big helmet hair with a gluelike hold. No matter which decade, it served its purpose. The fancy bouffant coiffures of the 1960s, the flippy feathered hair of the 1970s, the tall mall bangs of the 1980s—all were held firmly in place with Aqua Net!

ARBY'S
"America's roast beef. Yes sir!" The fast-food chain with restaurants shaped like a big western hat is famous for roast-beef sandwiches and a horseradish condiment known as "Horsey Sauce." Founded by brothers Forrest and Leroy Raffel, the first Arby's opened in Boardman, Ohio, in 1964, serving only roast-beef sandwiches, potato chips, and a beverage. These days, the Arby's menu offers roast beef served in many variations, as well as chicken wraps, ham sandwiches, garden salads, curly fries, potato cakes, apple turnovers, and Jamocha shakes.

ARCADES
Places of childhood abandonment, usually found at shopping malls, where adolescents challenge each other to pinball, foosball, air hockey, and the latest quarter-swallowing electronic games with names like Pac-Man, Donkey Kong, Space Invaders, Asteroids, Galaga, Centipede, Frogger, Dig Dug, Q-Bert, Missile Command, Dragon's Lair, Tron, Tempest, Zaxxon, and more.

ARCHIE ANDREWS
"America's Typical Teenager" is the freckle-faced, redheaded star of the *Archie* comic dynasty. A popular upperclassman at Riverdale High School, Archie is a wholesome lad who drives an old jalopy and fronts a rock 'n' roll band called The Archies. He enjoys hanging out with best bud Jughead Jones and is torn between the affections of good girl Betty Cooper and rich bitch Veronica Lodge.

ARCHIE BUNKER
"Stifle yourself." America's favorite bigot, played by Carroll O'Connor, was seen on Norman Lear's *All in the Family* sitcom on prime-time TV from 1971 to 1983. The blue-collar loudmouth from Queens (704 Houser Street), New York, projected most of his off-the-wall bigotry—about blacks, Hispanics, Italians, Asians, Jews, gays, and every other "un-American" type—toward "dingbat" wife Edith (Jean Stapleton), liberal daughter Gloria (Sally Struthers), and Gloria's hippie husband, Mike Stivic (Rob Reiner), whom Archie referred to as "Meathead." In the early 1970s, a popular bumper sticker found on automobiles read "Archie Bunker for President!"

***ARCHIE* COMICS**
In 1969, the popularity of The Archies, stars of comics, cartoons, and music, hit a phenomenal peak when comic-book sales surged more than a million copies a month (all other leading comics were selling around 300,000 a month). The various titles in the prolific *Archie* comic-book line have included *Archie, Archie and Friends, Archie at Riverdale High, Archie's Girls Betty and Veronica, Archie's Joke Book, Archie's Pal Jughead, Archie's Pals 'n' Gals, Archie's Madhouse, Archie's TV Laugh-Out, Betty, Betty and Me, Betty's Diary, Everything's Archie, Josie and the Pussycats, Jughead's Jokes, Laugh, Life with Archie, Little Archie, Pep, Reggie and Me, Reggie's Wise Guy Jokes, Sabrina the Teenage Witch, Veronica,* and *The World of Archie.*

ARCHIES
Created by Bob Montana, a gang of cartoon teens from Riverdale who have been entertaining generations of kids since 1942, the year Archie Andrews made his debut with the self-titled *Archie* comic. Shortly after, his four best friends—Jughead Jones, Betty Cooper, Veronica Lodge, and Reggie Mantle—appeared in their own comic-book spin-offs: *Archie's Pal Jughead* (1949), *Archie's Girls, Betty and Veronica* (1950), and *Archie's Rival Reggie* (also 1950). Along with these long-lasting comic-book series, The Archies have appeared in a syndicated newspaper strip, in a succession of Saturday-morn-

ing TV cartoons, on records as a bubblegum rock band, and on a variety of merchandising tie-ins, including lunch boxes, cereal premiums, jelly glasses, coloring books, dolls, games, and other toys.

ARCHIE SHOW

On September 14, 1968, *The Archie Show* (produced by Don Kirshner) premiered on Saturday-morning TV and became the top-rated cartoon of the season, garnering an astonishing 75 percent of the Nielsen audience. It had the Riverdale gang appearing in comedy skits, in a dance-of-the-week selection, and as a rock group, The Archies (vocals and music performed by anonymous studio musicians), who actually had four Top Forty songs, including "Jingle Jangle" (1969) and the number-one smash "Sugar, Sugar" (1969). The series aired for more than a decade as a popular Saturday-morning staple in various forms with different titles, such as *The Archie Comedy Hour* (1969–70), Archie's *Fun House* (1970–71), *Archie's TV Funnies* (1971–73), *Everything's Archie* (1973–74), *The U.S. of Archie* (1974–76), and *The Bang-Shang Lalapalooza Show* (1977–78). Three spin-off cartoons were inspired: *Sabrina, the Teenage Witch*, *The Groovie Goolies*, and *Josie and the Pussycats*.

ARE YOU THERE GOD? IT'S ME, MARGARET

First published in 1970, Judy Blume's young adult novel about sixth-grader Margaret Simon—almost twelve and full of questions—who moves with her family from an apartment in New York City to a house in Farbrook, New Jersey. Margaret was growing up and going through the joys and fears that beset a young girl on the brink of womanhood. By talking to God, she examined her thoughts on religion, personal hygiene, wearing a bra, having her first period, and the much-earlier maturity of her two friends, Nancy and Gretchen. It's often considered the most influential book of female adolescents during the 1970s.

ARIEL

Title character of Disney's *Little Mermaid* (voiced by Jodi Benson) is a headstrong sixteen-year-old sea princess (daughter of King Triton) who yearns for a pair of legs in order to go on land to find amore with handsome human Prince Eric. Ariel cuts a deal with sea witch Ursula, trading her beautiful voice for two legs—with a catch: If the now-mute mermaid doesn't find the meaning of true love in three days, she belongs to the evil Ursula forever. Ariel's best friends are crab Sebastian, fish Flounder, and seagull Scuttle.

ARISTOCATS

Everybody wanted to be a cat upon seeing this charming Disney animated feature about a beautiful and privileged Parisian feline, Duchess (voice of Eva Gabor), and her three adorable kittens, Berlioz, Toulouse, and Marie, who are dumped in the French countryside by Edgar the butler. It seems these Aristocats are due to inherit a fortune from doting human mistress Madame Bonfamille, and her scheming butler will collect the money if they're out of the picture. To the rescue comes Thomas O'Malley (voice of Phil Harris), a roguish alley cat, aided by little mouse Roquefort (Sterling Holloway), a pair of gabbling geese known as Abigail and Amelia, and a band of jazz cats led by cool Scat Cat (voice of Scatman Crothers). The 1970 film's catchy tunes included the title theme sung by Maurice Chevalier, "Scales and Arpeggios," "Thomas O'Malley Cat," "She Never Felt Alone," and the bluesy show stopper "Everybody Wants to Be a Cat."

FYI: ▸ Despite being considered by many critics as not up to par with most Disney animations, *The Aristocats* did extremely well at the box office (fifth highest grosser of the year), and especially in Europe, where the French adored it.

ARMOUR HOT DOGS

The dog kids love to bite, particularly "fat kids, skinny kids, kids that climb on rocks, tough kids, sissy kids, even kids with chicken pox." Armour has been serving hot dogs since 1867!

ARMSTRONG, NEIL

The Apollo 11 astronaut was a hero for a generation of boys after he became the first man to set foot on the moon, stating "That's one small step for man, one giant leap for mankind," in 1969.

ARMY JACKETS

Olive-drab outerwear most often worn by stoner guys dragging on cigarettes in high school smoking areas. Usually purchased at Army surplus stores, they were way cool if handed down by your older brother who served in the Vietnam War. Navy peacoats were also popular.

ARMY MEN
Purchased in a bag, bucket, or play set, these inexpensive green-plastic toy soldiers allowed boys to stage multisoldier battles. They returned to prominence in the 1990s as characters in Disney's computer-animated *Toy Story* movies.

ARNOLD HORSHACK
Nasally, geeky, somewhat shy Sweathog who had a strange tic of raising his hand while exclaiming "Oooh! Oooh! Oooh!" and the annoying "Aawwk, aawwk, aawwk" laugh. Played by Ron Palillo on the hit comedy series *Welcome Back, Kotter* from 1975 to 1979.

ARNOLD JACKSON
"What-choo-talkin-about?" On TV's *Diff'rent Strokes*, the role of this wisecracking black orphan from Harlem adopted by a white Park Avenue millionaire was designed as a showcase for pudgy-cheeked, twinkly-eyed Gary Coleman. The precocious juvenile actor had a natural comedic talent and looked younger than his true age of eleven because of a congenital kidney condition that stunted his growth. Coleman would grow up to become a regular in national tabloid headlines because of his dysfunctional lifestyle.

ARNOLD'S DRIVE-IN
Milwaukee malt shop, located near Jefferson High, where Richie Cunningham and pals hung out after school on the popular sitcom *Happy Days*. Arnold's was originally owned by Matsuo "Arnold" Takahashi before being bought by new proprietor Al Delvecchio. Fonzie used the men's restroom as his personal "office."

ARNOLD THE PIG
The intellectual, TV-addicted hog, owned by farmer Fred Ziffel on *Green Acres*, was so popular with TV viewers that he received more fan mail than all the two-legged stars, including Eddie Albert and Eva Gabor.

ASLAN
The lion in the title of C. S. Lewis's book *The Lion, the Witch, and the Wardrobe* (1950)—a majestic, heroic beast aided by four British children in battling the sinister White Witch, who holds the magical and mythical land of Narnia in winter's grip. Aslan is the Turkish word for "lion."

ASTLEY, RICK
Born on February 6, 1966, in Warrington, England, this young pop singer, bestowed with the voice of a middle-aged crooner, achieved the biggest U.K. hit of 1987 with his debut single, "Never Gonna Give You Up." Astley's other hits include "Together Forever" and "It Would Take a Strong, Strong Man" (both 1988).

ASTRO
The enthusiastic Jetson family dog, found as a wandering stray by son Elroy, is walked outside daily by dad George on a futuristic treadmill ("Jane! Stop this crazy thing!"). In *The Jetsons* cartoon show of the 1960s, Astro's "Ruh-Roh!" voice came from Don Messick, who later voiced another cartoon mutt, Scooby-Doo, in the 1970s.

ASTROBOY
"Astroboy, bombs away!" The beloved series about a superpowered robotic youngster was the first Japanese cartoon to be imported onto American TV screens in the mid-1960s (it paved the way for *Speed Racer* and *Kimba*). Astroboy began life as Tetsuan-Atoma (Mighty Atom), a comic-book character introduced by Osamu Tezuka in 1951. The animated show, debuting in 1963, had him created by Dr. Boynton, a scientist whose son, Astor, had been killed in a car wreck. In order to deal with the grief, Boynton created a robot in his son's likeness. Outfitted with a barrage of remarkable powers—including rocket flight, super eyesight and hearing, and machine-gun hips—the black-haired, pint-sized android's mission in life was to do good and fight evil villains.

ASYMMETRICAL HAIRCUT
Popular around the mid-1980s, a trendy, lop-sided hairdo that had one side clipped spiky short and the other side left long (around chin length) and sometimes permed into a kinky clump. (What were we thinking?)

ATHLETES

From the football field to the tennis court, these are fifty great athletes idolized by Baby Boom and Gen-X children. As young fans we supported them faithfully through winning seasons and losing seasons. We waited anxiously outside stadiums hoping to catch a glimpse of our idol and obtain a signature on a trading card or a baseball. Many of us searched endlessly to find certain trading cards, bartering with other sports fanatics for a coveted Reggie Jackson or Roger Staubach. We even pretended to be our adored superjock while playing ball at the neighborhood playing field, ice skating at the local rink, doing tumbles in the backyard, and racing Hot Wheels in our bedroom.

Hank Aaron—Baseball
Andre Agassi—Tennis
Troy Aikman—Football
Muhammad Ali—Boxing
Mario Andretti—Auto racing
Lance Armstrong—Bicycling
David Beckham—Soccer
Johnny Bench—Baseball
Larry Bird—Basketball
Terry Bradshaw—Football
George Brett—Baseball
Wilt Chamberlain—Basketball
Jimmy Connors—Tennis
Larry Csonka—Football
John Elway—Football
Julius "Dr. J." Erving—Basketball
Chris Evert—Tennis
Peggy Fleming—Figure skating
"Mean" Joe Greene—Football
Wayne Gretzky—Hockey
Dorothy Hamill—Figure skating
Bobby Hull—Hockey
Bo Jackson—Baseball/Football
Reggie Jackson—Baseball
"Magic" Johnson—Basketball
Michael Jordan—Basketball
Florence Griffith Joyner—Track
Greg Louganis—Diving
Mickey Mantle—Baseball
Dan Marino—Football
Willie Mays—Baseball
Mark McGwire—Baseball
Joe Montana—Football
Joe Namath—Football
Jack Nicklaus—Golf
Bobby Orr—Hockey
Jim Palmer—Baseball
Pele—Soccer
Richard Petty—Auto racing
Mary Lou Retton—Gymnastics
Cathy Rigby—Gymnastics
Tom Seaver—Baseball
O.J. Simpson—Football
Ken Stabler—Football
Bart Starr—Football
Roger Staubach—Football
Joe Theismann—Football
Mike Tyson—Boxing
Johnny Unitas—Football
Tiger Woods—Golf

ATHLETIC FOOTWEAR

"Just do it!" Popular with jocks and nonjocks alike, some of the best-selling brands since the 1970s have included Adidas, British Knight, Converse, Kaepas, Keds, L.A. Gear, Nike, Puma, and Reebok.

ATOM ANT

"Up and at 'em!" exclaimed Atom Ant, the world's smallest superhero, as he flew from a secret crime laboratory deep, deep under the earth. A pair of atomized eyeglasses gave the muscular, football-helmeted arthropod his mighty strength, and the *Crook Book* gave knowledge for fighting every evildoer on the planet, including karate ant Mr. Mooto, Killer Diller Gorilla, Godzilla Termite, Ferocious Flea, and seductive femme fatale Anastasia Antnik. A Hanna-Barbera favorite, Atom Ant appeared on his own self-titled Saturday-morning cartoon from 1965 to 1967, before joining forces with rodent detective Secret Squirrel as half of *The Atom Ant / Secret Squirrel Show*, from 1967 to 1968.

ATTACK OF THE KILLER TOMATOES!

"I know I'm going to miss her / A tomato ate my sister." Eegawd!!! Run for your life! It's the attack of the purposely culty, low-budget film, an overripe 1978 spoof of bad horror pictures that spawned three sequels and an animated TV cartoon. Directed by John De Bello and featuring a cast of unknowns, this had a rampaging army of giant mutant tomatoes terrorizing the good citizens of sunny San Diego, California. Anybody have some ketchup?

AUGIE DOGGIE AND DOGGIE DADDY
Father-and-son canine team featured as a segment on Hanna-Barbera's *Quick Draw McGraw* cartoon show, airing on Saturday mornings from 1959 to 1966. Their cartoons had Doggie Daddy, a Jimmy Durante soundalike, caught up in some mischievous antics of little offspring Augie Doggie.

AUGUSTUS GLOOP
"I feel sorry for Wonka. It's going to cost him a fortune in fudge." The winner of Willy Wonka's first Golden Ticket and "The Pride of Dusselheim" was this fat German boy who ate everything in sight. The young buffoon's gluttonous greed caused him to drink from a river made of chocolate, into which he fell (or did Wonka kick him in?), and eventually got sucked up a factory pipe.

AUNT BEE TAYLOR
"Oh, fiddle-faddle." Andy Taylor's endearingly fussy aunt (played by character actress Frances Bavier on *The Andy Griffith Show*), a pleasantly plump spinster who tends his house and helps look after son Opie. Rival in Mayberry is town gossip Clara Edwards, with whom Aunt Bee competes in pie-making contests.

AUNT CLARA
Samantha Stephens's delightfully absentminded witch relative (mother Endora's older sister) who would cast spells that went awry. (Clara once blacked out the entire eastern seaboard when trying to turn the lights on at the Stephenses.) However, Clara is Sam's favorite aunt and often acts as babysitter to little Tabitha. Marion Lorne received a 1966 Emmy Award for Best Supporting Actress in a Comedy for her role as Aunt Clara on *Bewitched.*

AURORA MODEL KITS
Highly successful figure and character kits inspired by the monster-movie craze of the 1960s. Monster-loving kids eagerly bought and built these easy-to-assemble kits, beginning with Frankenstein in 1961 and followed by Dracula (1962), The Wolfman (1962), The Mummy (1963), The Phantom of the Opera (1963), Creature from the Black Lagoon (1963), The Hunchback (1964), Dr. Jekyll, Mr. Hyde (1964), King Kong (1964), Godzilla (1964), Bride of Frankenstein (1965), The Witch (1965), Vampirella (1971), Cro-Magnon Man (1971), and—to be at the mercy of all these ghastly ghouls—the beautiful Victim (1971).

Aurora also produced best-selling kits based on popular TV shows, movies, and comic books, including *Land of the Giants, Lost in Space, Star Trek, Man from U.N.C.L.E., Mod Squad, Green Hornet, James Bond, Tarzan, Chitty Chitty Bang Bang, Banana Splits, The Archies, Batman, Superman, Spider-Man,* and *Wonder Woman.*

FYI: ▸ In 1964, Aurora's infamous guillotine model kit, which actually beheaded its unlucky victim, came under fire after concerned parents applied political pressure to have it discontinued.

AUSTIN POWERS
"Yeah, baby, yeah!" Although it was filmed in 1997, thirty years after the spy-crazed 1960s, this funny spoof should be mentioned for being a groovy tribute to James Bond and his fellow secret agents. It starred Mike Myers as dentally challenged Austin Powers, the shagadelic superspy from swingin' Carnaby Street who had been cryogenically frozen since 1967. It's thirty years later, and the "International Man of Mystery" is thawed out by the British Secret Service so he can help stop diabolical archenemy Dr. Evil (also played by Myers) from holding the world hostage for $1 million—excuse me—$100 billion! Co-stars include Elizabeth Hurley as Powers's sexy sidekick Vanessa Kensington, Michael York as Powers's boss Basil Exposition, Robert Wagner as Agent Number Two, Seth Green as Dr. Evil's slacker son Scott Evil, and Internet babe Cindy Margolis as the deadly head Fembot. Mega-popular, the comedy, directed by Jay Roach, inspired two boisterously ribald sequels: 1999's *Austin Powers 2: The Spy Who Shagged Me* and 2002's *Austin Powers in Goldmember.* "Oh, behave!"

AUTOMOBILES
For teenagers of the late 1970s, driving a car meant total liberation—freedom—a great way to escape the hassles of parents and teachers. At high school,

the cars we drove said a lot about our personality and status in life. Cool dude Sean drove a mag-wheeled Trans Am (earned by working late shifts at the local Texaco station); well-to-do drill-teamer Misty had a convertible Corvette (given to her as a Sweet Sixteen gift by her doting parents); and pot-smoking freak Chad could be found toking away in an old VW Bus (a hand-me-down from his old man). For most of us, our first automobiles were never our personal choice—but we were glad just to have wheels, even if it was a turtle-paced Plymouth Volare (way uncool!) instead of a quick-zooming 1960s Ford Mustang (way cool!).

The following is a list of fifty cars that those of us who were in high school in the late 1970s and early 1980s would be familiar with. These were the first we drove and the ones most often seen in our student parking lots.

AMC Gremlin
AMC Javelin
AMC Pacer
Chevrolet Camaro
Chevrolet Chevelle
Chevrolet Corvair
Chevrolet Corvette
Chevrolet Impala
Chevrolet Malibu
Chevrolet Monte Carlo
Chevrolet Nova
Chevrolet Van
Chevrolet Vega
Datsun 240-Z
Dodge Challenger
Dodge Charger
Dodge Dart
Ford Capri
Ford Cobra
Ford "Country Squire" Station Wagon
Ford El Camino
Ford Gran Torino
Ford Maverick
Ford Mustang
Ford Pick-Up Truck
Ford Pinto
Ford Thunderbird
Honda Civic
Jeep CJ-5
Mazda RX-7
Mercury Cougar
MG Midget
Oldsmobile Cutlass
Plymouth Barracuda
Plymouth Duster
Plymouth Road Runner
Plymouth Satellite
Plymouth Volare
Pontiac Bonneville
Pontiac Grand Prix
Pontiac Firebird
Pontiac GTO
Pontiac LeMans
Renault Le Car
Toyota Corolla
Triumph TR-7
Volkswagen Beetle
Volkswagen Bus
Volkswagen Rabbit
Volkswagen Thing

AVENGERS (COMIC)

In 1963, a few of *Marvel* comics' mightiest superheroes—Captain America, Thor, Iron Man, Quicksilver, Ant Man, and the Wasp—united to become an unstoppable crime-fighting team called the Avengers.

AVENGERS (TV SHOW)

British TV import centering on the espionage missions of suave secret agent John Steed (Patrick Macnee) and his female partner, the sexy and cat-suited Emma Peel (Diana Rigg). Aired on American prime-time TV from 1966 to 1969.

AVOCADO

One of the signature colors of the 1970s, popular in kitchenware, appliances, and clothing. Coordinated well with mustard yellow, rusty brown, and tomato-red shades.

AVON

"Ding-dong, Avon calling!" A variety of cosmetic products (lipstick, perfume, soaps, and so on) sold by "Avon ladies" who at one time went door to door in suburban neighborhoods to peddle Avon. These days, Avon ladies host parties, usually in their home, to sell the enduring beauty line. Rival is Mary Kay Cosmetics.

A&W ROOT BEER
Once there was a time when they had drive-up stands with carhops dressed in orange and brown uniforms who served the great-tasting root beer in frosted glass mugs, along with foil-wrapped burgers named after family members (Papaburger, Mamaburger, Teenburger). When the carhop wasn't looking, some diners (including my mom) would steal the mugs—accumulating a superb home collection. Roy Allen and Frank Wright of Lodi, California, created A&W Root Beer and the restaurants in 1919. (The company's moniker comes from the first initial of each last name.)

AYDS
Little squares of chocolate-like appetite suppressors that mothers had to hide from kids who thought it was candy. Disappeared in the early 1980s when the Centers for Disease Control gave a deadly new viral strain a soundalike name, AIDS, for Acquired Immune Deficiency Syndrome.

AZRIEL
Naughty cat, belonging to a naughtier sorcerer, Gargamel, that was always hunting for a smurfalicious blue snack on *The Smurfs* cartoon program.

BABA LOOEY

The short, sombrero-wearing Mexican burro served cautiously as deputy to the blundering Quick Draw McGraw, an equine sheriff of the Southwest, in the classic Hanna-Barbera cartoons.

BABAR

The wise and gentle King of Elephant Land—dressed in a signature gold crown, white spats, and a three-piece green suit—resided in the village of Celesteville with his loving Queen Celeste. His storybook adventures had the two of them journeying around the world accompanied by three offspring—Pam, Flora, and Alexander—along with cousin Arthur and little monkey Zephir. The elephant-enslaving Rhinoceroses, led by evil Retaxes, were the archenemy.

BABA WAWA

"Hewwo. This is Baba Wawa." Comedienne Gilda Radner's humorous spoof of Barbara Walters, the "wegendawy tewevision weportew," was an ongoing feature on NBC's *Saturday Night Live.*

BABE

> "That'll do, pig. That'll do."
>
> —FARMER HOGGETT (JAMES CROMWELL)

Directed by Chris Noonan, this charming fable from Australia became the most talked-about film of 1995 and, as an underdog sleeper, surprised many when it earned an Oscar nomination as Best Picture (it lost to Mel Gibson's *Braveheart*). Combining real animals and animatronics, it told the story of a runt pig, Babe, who had been orphaned as a baby and won as a raffle prize by a kindly farmer, Arthur Hoggett (played by character actor James Cromwell). Raised on Hoggett's farm by a border collie, the little pig defies the odds by learning to be a sheepherder and winning the National Sheepdog Championship. Babe's barnyard buddies include matriarch sheepdog Fly, nervous duck Ferdinand, elderly ewe Maa, pampered house cat Duchess, and a trio of squeaky-voiced singing mice. It was based on the book by Dick King-Smith, *The Sheep-Pig,* and followed by a sequel, *Babe: Pig in the City* (1998).

FYI: ▸ Forty-eight piglets were used for the role of Babe during filming (because baby pigs grow up so fast)!

BABE PERFUME

Produced by Fabergé, this big-selling women's fragrance of the 1970s was notable for being hawked by the model Margaux Hemingway, granddaughter of Nobel Prize–winning author Ernest Hemingway.

BABES IN TOYLAND

This lavishly colorful Walt Disney interpretation of Victor Herbert's operetta was the studio's first live-action musical. It starred Annette Funicello and

Tommy Sands as Mary Quite Contrary and Tom the Piper's Son, two young lovers from Mother Goose Village on the run from the wicked Barnaby (Ray Bolger). Accompanied by several Mother Goose tots—including Boy Blue (Kevin Corcoran) and Bo Peep (juvenile Ann Jillian)—they flee through the dreadful Forest of No Return and end up in wonderful Toyland, overseen by the amusing Toymaker (scene-stealing Ed Wynn) and his assistant, Grumio (Tommy Kirk). Barnaby and his two bumbling henchmen, Gonzorgo (Henry Calvin) and Roderigo (Gene Sheldon), catch up with our nursery-rhyme heroes, and following a miniaturized battle aided by marching toy soldiers, all ends happily for Mary and Tom. The 1961 film, directed by Jack Donohue, was a remake of the far-more-superb 1934 Laurel and Hardy comedy adventure. Songs included "Castle in Spain," "I Can't Do the Sum," "Just a Whisper Away," "Forest of No Return," and Herbert's "Toyland."

BABY ALIVE

"The closest thing to a real baby that any doll could be." Introduced by Kenner Toys, the best-selling doll of 1973 took the "real-life" concept one step further. When little girls fed Baby Alive a spoonful of her specially prepared "food" or a drink from her bottle, her mouth would be activated as if she were really eating. Remove the spoon or bottle, and she continued to chew and swallow for a few more seconds. What made the battery-operated doll even more lifelike were her soft skin and the fact that she actually pooped in her diapers.

FYI: ▸ Sadistic kids enjoyed torturing Baby Alive by feeding her unimaginable stuff like cat doo-doo and Comet cleanser.

BABY BOOMERS

The generation of seventy-eight million Americans born in the post–World War II Baby Boom, between 1943 and 1960. Key words: AIDS, *American Bandstand,* "American Pie," Barbie, Beach Boys, beach movies, Beatles, bell-bottoms, *Big Chill, Dick and Jane* reading books, *Dating Game,* disco, *Easy Rider,* ecology, Elvis, *Father Knows Best,* G.I. Joe, gay lib, go-go boots, *Graduate,* Granola Heads, *Hair,* Hendrix, hippies, *Howdy Doody, Jetsons,* Kennedy assassination, Kent State, *Leave It to Beaver,* LSD, Manson family, marijuana, *Mickey Mouse Club,* miniskirts, Mod invasion, *Mod Squad,* Monkees, moon landing, Motown, Mystery Date, New Age, NOW, peace marches, peace sign, The Pill, punk rock, Rolling Stones, San Francisco, *Saturday Night Fever,* school air-raid drills, sexual revolution, *Soul Train,* Springsteen, streaking, summer of love, thirtysomething, Twiggy, Twister, Vietnam War, Watergate, *Wonder Years,* Woodstock, and yuppies.

FYI: ▸ Over the years, Baby Boomers have been labeled the "Dr. Spock," "Pepsi," "Rock," "Now," "Sixties," "Love," "Protest," "Hippie," "Woodstock," "Vietnam," "Me," "Big Chill," and "Yuppie" Generation.

BABY-DOLL DRESSES

Short, sassy, little-girl-like dresses—printed in pink gingham or frilly flower designs—that were soooo popular with adult women in the swingin' 1960s. Revived in the 1990s with alternative clubbers thanks to Hole's Courtney Love, who paired hers with clunky combat boots and torn fishnet tights. (They were more sexy worn with platform heels and no tights.)

BABY GO BYE-BYE

This blonde, pigtailed doll with the yellow sundress came with a pink car, the Bumpety Buggy, which could be programmed to drive her around in different directions. As the Bumpety Buggy moves, Baby Go Bye-Bye and her pigtails bounce up and down, back and forth, like they're just having the best time ever! Introduced by Mattel Toys in 1969, she remained a popular favorite throughout the 1970s.

BABY HUEY

Born in 1950, *Harvey* comics' five-foot-tall, 250-pound "baby giant" (actually a duck)—dressed in diapers, an undersized T-shirt, and a baby bonnet—whose naiveté and heart of gold is as big as his immense strength. Starred with Casper the Friendly Ghost and Little Audrey on the cartoon series *Matty's Funday Funnies* from 1959 to 1961.

"BABY ONE MORE TIME"

The star-making MTV video to Britney Spears's number-one song featured the teenager as a good Catholic schoolgirl gone wild (every guy's fantasy). In the clip, Britney, with her blonde tresses in pigtails, shimmies around the linoleum-lined hallways of a high school cooing "Baby one more time," while wearing the traditional parochial school plaid skirt (on the short side) with sexy knee-high stockings and a white blouse tied at the midriff (exposing her navel).

FYI: ▸ The Halloween following the video's release in 1998, many girls (and a few men) costumed themselves in Britney's schoolgirl getup.

BABY PUSS

Fred and Wilma Flintstone's pet saber-toothed tiger was the "cat" from the line in the ending theme song of the *Flintstones* cartoon: "Maybe someday Fred will win the fight, then that cat will stay out for the night."

BABY TENDER LOVE

Little Gen-Xers loved playing mommy with this treasured baby doll, released by Mattel in 1969, whose soft rubber body gave her a cuddly, lifelike feel. To add to the realness, she would pee-pee in her panties after drinking water from her bottle. Both a Talking Baby Tender Love and a Living Baby Tender Love were introduced in 1971, followed by a Tearful Baby Tender Love in 1972. In 1976, children could own a Baby Brother Tender Love, complete with a little penis, making him the first anatomically correct doll in toy history.

BACK TO THE FUTURE

"Are you telling me
my mom has the hots for me?"
—MARTY MCFLY (MICHAEL J. FOX)

Nifty blend of comedy and fantasy has 1980s teen Marty McFly (played by Michael J. Fox) accidentally sent back to the 1950s via a time-traveling DeLorean car built by wacky inventor Dr. Emmett Brown (Christopher Lloyd). Once there, he meets the seventeen-year-old versions of his parents, wimpy George McFly (Crispin Glover) and scampy Lorraine Baines (Lea Thompson). To Marty's horror, Lorraine falls for the "new kid" in school (Hill Valley High), and he must ensure his future existence by playing cupid to his mom and dad! Directed by Robert Zemeckis, this was the highest grosser of 1985, and Michael J. Fox's terrific performance turned the quick-witted actor, then best known as conservative Alex Keaton on prime time's *Family Ties*, into a genuine movie star. It inspired two sequels, a Saturday-morning TV cartoon, and an amusement ride at the Universal Studios theme parks in California and Florida.

BAD NEWS BEARS

Funny 1976 film comedy, directed by Michael Ritchie, about a beer-guzzling baseball coach, Morris Buttermaker (Walter Matthau), who turns the Bears, a hopeless Southern California Little League team led by girl pitcher Amanda Whurlitzer (Tatum O'Neal), into contenders. Followed by two sequels, *The Bad News Bears in Breaking Training* (1977) and *The Bad News Bears Go to Japan* (1978), along with a prime-time TV series, *The Bad News Bears* (1979–80), starring Jack Warden as Coach Buttermaker.

FYI: ▸ The team sponsor of the Bears was Chico's Bail Bonds.

BAD RONALD

Adapted from John Holbrook Vance's book, the 1974 made-for-TV shocker starred Scott Jacoby as Ronald Wilby, a misfit teenager slowly slipping into madness. Bad Ronald lived in a secret room built by his mother (Kim Hunter) in the walls of their house to evade the law for accidentally murdering a taunting peer. Years later, Mama has died and a new family moves into the old Victorian, unaware that their three pretty daughters (Cindy Fisher, Cindy Eilbacher, and Lisa Eilbacher) are being watched by this disturbed hidden occupant (bad, bad Ronald).

BAIO, SCOTT

This onetime perpetual favorite of teen rags virtually grew up on TV playing cocky, smooth-talking youths. Born on September 22, 1961, in Brooklyn, the handsome, dark-haired Baio started out as a juvenile model in fashion ads before he began his acting career in 1976 starring opposite Jodie Foster in the all-kiddie musical *Bugsy Malone*. In 1977 and 1978, he was featured in a series of TV sitcoms—*Blansky's Beauties*, *Who's Watching the Kids*, and the show that made him a teen heartthrob, *Happy Days*. On it, the sixteen-year-old played Chachi Arcola, the enterprising young cousin of Fonzie (Henry Winkler) and the boyfriend of Joanie Cunningham (Erin Moran).

In the early 1980s, Baio appeared in several dramatic TV specials with social messages geared toward juveniles, like *The Boy Who Drank Too Much* (1980) and *Stoned* (1980), the latter earning him an Emmy nomination. During and after a long stint as a male nanny in the lame 1980s sitcom *Charles in Charge*, he became a regular in gossip columns for dating—and being dumped by—a succession of lovely blonde TV starlets, including Pamela Anderson, Nicolette Sheridan, Catherine Oxenberg, and the two Heathers, Thomas and Locklear.

BAKKER, JIM, AND TAMMY FAYE

"I take him shopping with me.
I say, 'Okay, Jesus, help me find a bargain.'"
—TAMMY FAYE BAKKER

Prominent televangelist and his spendthrift singing wife. The couple fell from grace after his scandalous fifteen-minute sex affair with dubious church secretary Jessica Hahn in 1987 was followed by charges of skimming more than $52 million from their South Carolina–based PTL (for Praise the Lord) ministry. Jim was convicted and sentenced to forty-five years in prison (the sentence was later reduced to a meager four and a half years). As for teary, mascara-caked Tammy Faye, she divorced Jim, became a regular on the public-appearance circuit, and was the subject of a 1999 big-screen documentary, *The Eyes of Tammy Faye.*

FYI: ▸ A popular Tammy Faye joke making the rounds during the PTL scandal was "What does Tammy Faye Bakker have in common with a ski slope? Answer: Two inches of face topped by three inches of powder."

BALL-ENDED RUBBER BANDS

These elastic bands with attached brightly colored marbles were a happenin' hair accessory for little girls in the 1970s.

BALLOON DROPPING

Juvenile prank in which water-filled balloons are dropped out of windows on unsuspecting people below.

BALOO

A happy-go-lucky bear with Phil Harris's voice whose philosophy in life is "The Bare Necessities"—in other words, sit back and relax. Befriends the little orphan Indian boy named Mowgli in Disney's *Jungle Book* (1967).

BAMM-BAMM RUBBLE

"Bamm! Bamm!" Adopted by Barney and Betty Rubble in the cartoon program *The Flintstones*, Bamm-Bamm is a club-wielding, towheaded baby boy dressed in leopard-spotted fur and gifted with extraordinary strength. Smitten with little Pebbles Flintstone, a next-door neighbor, the irrepressible youth ended up going steady with her as a teenager. His name came from the "Bamm!" sound he made when he struck something with his club.

BANANA CLIP

Banana-shaped plastic hair accessory with teeth that allowed women to pull their hair into a huge horse's mane on the back-top of their head. Greatly popular in the later 1980s, it made those who wore it look like bimbos.

BANANA PAD

The groovy, psychedelic-colored place that the four Banana Splits called their hangout on TV's *Banana Splits Adventure Hour*. They shared the pad with Goofy Gopher, who lives in a flowerpot, and the Cuckoo Clock, which answers questions and occasionally punches someone in the face.

BANANARAMA

Before the Spice Girls, this was the most successful female group in British history and one of many "alternative" girl acts dominating the U.S. charts in the 1980s. Formed in 1981, the cute and rather saucy trio, consisting of Sarah Dallin, Keren Woodward, and Siobhan Fahey, were known for unison vocals and world-beat pop music. They had minor hits with "Shy Boy" (1982) and "Robert DeNiro's Waiting" (1984), before smashing the Top Ten with "Cruel Summer" (1984). In the summer of 1986, their cover of Shocking Blue's "Venus" went straight to number one, becoming an enormous dance hit at clubs around the nation. In 1988, Fahey left the group to marry Dave Stewart of the Eurythmics and was replaced by Jacquie Sullivan.

FYI: ▸ Bananarama's name was a combination of "Banana," from the late 1960s kiddie show *The Banana Splits*, and "Pyjamarama," a 1977 Roxy Music song.

BANANA SEATS
Bicycle seats found on hi-rise bikes, such as the Schwinn Sting-Ray, which were flat and curved into a long banana shape. The cool ones had a wet vinyl look and glittered with far-out colors (for boys) or mod flowers (for girls).

BANANA SPLITS
"One banana, two banana, three banana four / Four bananas make a bunch and so do many more." A far-out foursome who played in a groovy rock band made up of actors dressed in bizarre-looking animal costumes (created by Sid and Marty Krofft) and voiced by veteran voice men of the Hanna-Barbera cartoon studios. There was drummer Bingo (voice of Daws Butler), a hipster gorilla; guitarist Dropper (voice of Allan Melvin), a wise-cracking lion; guitarist Fleegle (voice of Paul Winchell), a lispy beagle; and keyboardist Snorky (voice of Don Messick), a honking baby elephant. The Splits hung out at the Banana Pad, a clubhouse with swirling psychedelic backgrounds, and zoomed about in the Banana Buggy, a six-wheeled, polka-dotted dune buggy.

Their silly nonsense was featured on *The Banana Splits Adventure Hour*, a Saturday-morning TV show, airing from 1968 to 1970, considered groundbreaking in its mix of live action and animation. Throughout the program, the quartet would perform slapstick comedy skits (they basically ran around a lot bumping into each other) and sing bubblegum pop numbers. Their zany interludes were interspersed by three ongoing cartoon series—"The Arabian Knights," "The Three Musketeers," and "The Micro Ventures"—plus a live-action serial, "Danger Island." The theme tune, "The Tra La La Song (One Banana, Two Banana)," landed on *Billboard*'s Hot 100 in 1969. "Hey, Splits, let's split!"

FYI: ▸ *The Banana Splits Adventure Hour* was the priciest Saturday-morning show in its day, costing Hanna-Barbera $135,000 an hour to produce.

BAND-AID
Memorable mid-1970s TV commercials featured a teenaged John Travolta sporting this brand's adhesive bandage over a cut while in a locker room shower singing "I am stuck on Band-Aid / 'Cause Band-Aid's stuck on me."

BANDIT
Feisty little white bulldog with black masklike markings over both eyes (hence his name), belonging to adventuresome cartoon kid Jonny Quest.

BANGLES
America's most successful all-female rock act ever, whose lineup consisted of doe-eyed Susanna Hoffs, sisters Vicki and Debbi Peterson, and ex-runaway Michael Steele. Originated as the Bangs in 1982, but to avoid confusion with another group who had the same moniker changed to The Bangles in 1984. Success came in 1986 with the release of the album *Different Light*, which housed the smash singles "Manic Monday" (penned by Prince), "Walk Like an Egyptian," and "Walking Down Your Street." Other songs: "In Your Room" (1988), "Eternal Flame" (1989)—inspired by the flame that burns by Elvis Presley's grave—and a 1987 cover of Simon and Garfunkel's "Hazy Shade of Winter" from the *Less Than Zero* soundtrack. Disbanded in 1989.

BARBARA COOPER
Pretty and chipper, the fifteen-year-old daughter of single mom Ann Romano was one of the most likable teen characters on prime-time TV in the late 1970s. On CBS-TV's *One Day at a Time*, Barbara was played by Valerie Bertinelli, who later married rocker Eddie Van Halen and starred in a succession of weepy made-for-TV movies in the 1980s.

BARBIE
"We girls can do anything!" The superstar of Toyland has been a playtime favorite for generations of girls and is the biggest-selling doll in the world. (Since her debut in 1959, more than one billion have been sold, at the phenomenal rate of two per second.) The teen fashion queen was created by the

late Ruth Handler (co-founder of Mattel Toys), who named her after her own daughter, Barbara.

At just under a foot tall, Barbie is the girl with most cake—the homecoming queen, the head cheerleader, the bride (never the bridesmaid). She's the blonde (sometimes) All-American beauty with an hourglass frame consisting of long legs, tiny waist, and big boobs. (If she was real, her measurements would be 38-18-28.) The original material girl (Madonna, eat your heart out), glamorous Barbie came with an extensive wardrobe, ranging from groovy mod styles to shiny disco attires and every trend in between. Her limitless accessories include dream homes, ski lodges, country campers, sports cars, speedboats, airplanes, and carrying cases of all shapes and sizes.

As a modern woman, career opportunities are plentiful for Barbie. From nurse to doctor, airline stewardess to astronaut, ballerina to Olympic athlete, supermodel to rock star—she can do it all! Knowing all work and no play makes a dream doll a dull doll, Barbie's recreational activities are abundant. She enjoys dancing at the sock hop, socializing at the malt shop, shopping in the city, relaxing at the beach (preferably Malibu), playing a game of tennis, traveling around the world, and competing in beauty pageants (hey, wasn't she Miss America back in the early 1970s?).

Barbie hangs with a wide circle of girlfriends. There's Midge (her best friend), Francie (her mod cousin), Stacey (her British friend), Christie (her black friend), P.J. (her groovy friend), Truly Scrumptious (her Chitty Chitty Bang Bang friend), Julia (her TV nurse friend), and Twiggy (her supermodel friend). Adoring siblings are preteen Skipper and five-year-old twins Tutti and Todd. Handsome Ken was Barbie's one and only boyfriend, with whom she had been going steady since 1961 (they since broke up). The different types of Barbies have included Twist 'n Turn Barbie, Talking Barbie, Living Barbie, Malibu Barbie, Live Action Barbie, Walk Lively Barbie, Quick Curl Barbie, and SuperStar Barbie.

Barbie's critics accuse her of being a poster child for anorexia as well as for garish body enhancements (boob jobs, cheek implants, lip injections, and so on) and crass materialism. The term "Barbie doll" is used to describe an empty-headed, appearance-obsessed, materialistic woman. Love her or hate her, Barbie is a true pop culture icon.

FYI: ▸ Barbie's full name is Barbara Millicent Roberts, her parents are George and Margaret, she is a Pisces (born March 9), and she is a student at Willow High School (where she met dream date Ken Carson).

BARBIE AND THE ROCKERS

"Hot Rockin' Rockstars!" A neon-hued, big-haired, really rad New Wave band headed by the multitalented Barbie. The multicultural lot included boyfriend Ken, redhead Diva, African-American Dee Dee, Chinese-American Dana, and Mexican-American Derek. Released in 1985, this was Mattel's most popular Barbie line of the 1980s.

BARBIE'S FRIEND SHIP

"Fly the friendly skies!" Introduced in 1973, a carrying case that when opened became a United Airlines jetliner so that everyone's favorite fashion doll could demonstrate her social graces as Stewardess Barbie while her sweetheart did the guy thing as Pilot Ken.

BARETTA

Airing on prime-time ABC-TV from 1975 to 1978, this crime drama starred former child star Robert Blake (of *Our Gang* fame) as Tony Baretta, a tough New York City detective who worked the streets by blending in wearing a variety of undercover disguises. Baretta's friends included Billy Truman (Tom Ewell), an ex-cop who ran the seedy King Edward Hotel where he lived; Rooster (Michael D. Roberts), a street-smart informant; and Fred, his pet cockatoo. Sammy Davis Jr. sang the theme song, "Keep Your Eye on the Sparrow," which became a Top Forty disco hit in 1976 for Rhythm Heritage.

BARNABAS COLLINS

Courtly, dark, and handsome 200-year-old vampire (played by Jonathan Frid on TV's groovy horror soap *Dark Shadows*) who resided at Collinwood in Collinsport, Maine, with blue-blooded cousin Elizabeth and various other relations. Barnabas longed to be rid of vampirism, a "curse" bestowed on him back in 1795 from a kiss by Angelique, a beautiful witch jealous of his love for wife Josette Du Pres. Dr.

Julia Hoffman, a physician in love with Barnabas, helped search for a cure to end his blood-sucking nightmare. Throughout the late 1960s and early 1970s, middle-aged actor Frid became an unlikely sex symbol and teen idol—it was common to find his pix amid those of The Monkees and Bobby Sherman in *16* or *Tiger Beat* magazines—besieged with love letters from fans dying to have him sink his fangs into them.

FYI: ▸ A fangtastic Barnabas Collins joke that made the rounds during the late 1960s: Why does Barnabas use makeup when he goes on TV? Otherwise he'd have *Dark Shadows*.

BARNEY

"I love you, you love me. . . ." With banal cuteness, the purple dinosaur came to life on PBS in 1992 to entertain the very young—and nauseate everyone else.

BARNEY FIFE

"Nip it in the bud!" Don Knotts's Emmy-winning role (five times for Best Supporting Actor in a Comedy Series, *The Andy Griffith Show*) as Andy Taylor's cousin, best friend, and deputy sheriff—a scrawny, nervous, overzealous, often-fumbling fellow—is one of the best comic performances in all of TV history.

BARNEY RUBBLE

Voiced by Mel Blanc on the cartoon show *The Flintstones*, the yellow-haired caveman was Fred Flintstone's cheerful but dense "little buddy," next-door neighbor, and comrade-in-mischief. He is married to pert Betty and has a superstrong adopted son named Bamm-Bamm.

FYI: ▸ In the 1990s, teen girls used the term "Barney" in reference to a second-rate guy who wasn't hot in looks or attitude.

BARNUM'S ANIMAL CRACKERS

> "Animal crackers in my soup / Monkeys and rabbits loop-the-loop / Gosh, oh gee, but I have fun / Swallowin' animals one by one."
>
> —SHIRLEY TEMPLE

Not really crackers, but cookies shaped like wild animals that are packaged in a cardboard carton with an attached string handle designed to look like a circus-wagon cage. These classic treats have been manufactured by Nabisco since 1902!

BARON BOMBURST

The evil, immature toy-loving ruler of Vulgaria resides in a castle with child-despising wife Baroness Bomburst and covets Chitty Chitty Bang Bang, the magical flying car ("I vant dot car!"). The Baron is played by Gert Fröbe in the 1968 movie musical *Chitty Chitty Bang Bang* and by Tony Adams in the smash stage adaptation.

BARON VON REDBERRY AND SIR GRAPEFELLOW

A pair of breakfast cereals, produced by General Mills in 1972. Animated commercials depicted each cereal character as dueling World War I flying aces: Sir Grapefellow from Great Britain ("Tally-ho!") and Baron Von Redberry from Germany ("Achtung! Baron Von Redberry iz der berry goodest!").

BARREL OF MONKEYS

Introduced by Lakeside in 1969, this action game, a distant relative of pick-up sticks, provides a "barrel of laughs" while testing skills at balancing. The game's object is to pick up and link—one by one—twelve brightly colored plastic monkeys by their hook-shaped arms. Impatience and shaky hands cause the chain to break, sending the chimps tumbling to the ground. The monkeys are housed in a small barrel (hence the name).

BARRIS, CHUCK

Called the "King of Bad Taste," the diminutive boyish-looking, curly-haired producer produced a slew of gaudy TV games shows in the 1960s and 1970s, such as *The Dating Game, The Newlywed Game, How's Your Mother-in-Law? The Gong Show* (in which he also served as host), *The $1.98 Beauty Show*, and *Three's a Crowd.*

FYI: ▸ In 2002, actor Sam Rockwell played Chuck Barris in *Confessions of a Dangerous Mind*, a big-screen film in which the game-show impresario claims he worked for the CIA as a hitman!

BARRYMORE, DREW

"I was born ten years old." Beating the odds, this adorable child actress of the 1980s overcame teenage alcoholism and drug addiction to become one of Hollywood's brightest movie stars of the 1990s and the early twenty-first century—and is still just as adorable. Born on February 22, 1975, in Culver City, California, the descendant of the legendary Barrymore acting dynasty (grandfather is matinee idol John Barrymore) made her film debut in the horror film *Altered States* (1980) before charming audiences as kid sister Gertie in Steven Spielberg's *E.T. The Extra-Terrestrial* (1982). She followed the success of *E.T.* by hosting *Saturday Night Live* at age seven, becoming the youngest person ever to do so, and starring in a trio of movies: *Irreconcilable Differences* (1984), *Firestarter* (1984), and *Cat's Eye* (1985).

As a teen in the late 1980s, Barrymore's highly reported bouts with substance abuse sidelined her career (she began drinking and using cocaine at age nine), but she cleaned up her act, wrote *Little Girl Lost* (1989), a book about her experiences with addiction and rehabilitation, and made a successful transition to adult roles. Emphasizing a good-natured personality smoldering with sexuality, her later films have included *Boys on the Side* (1995), *Scream* (1996), *The Wedding Singer* (1998), *Never Been Kissed* (1999), and *Charlie's Angels* (2000). The actress reaped off-screen attention in 1995 when she posed nude for *Playboy* magazine and flashed her boobs to David Letterman on his *Late Night* talk show.

FYI: ▸ Director Steven Spielberg is Drew Barrymore's godfather. Drew is the godmother of Courtney Love's daughter, Frances Bean Cobain.

BART SIMPSON

"I'm Bart Simpson! Who the hell are you?" Potty-mouthed fourth-grade underachiever (and proud of it too) who is preoccupied with skateboarding, Krusty the clown, and driving dad Homer and sister Lisa crazy. Voiced by a woman (yes, a woman, Nancy Cartwright), Bart's sarcastic sayings, such as "Don't have a cow, man!" "Eat my shorts!" "Ay, caramba!" and "Underachiever and proud of it!" became oft-repeated catchphrases with the nation's youth of the 1990s. His bad behavior on *The Simpsons* series caused many concerned parents to announce the program "off-limits" to their children!

BASIL, TONI

Born in September 1950, the onetime high school cheerleading captain from Las Vegas is most famous for her 1982 recording of "Mickey," a cheerleader chant set to an ultrahyper New Wave beat, considered by many to be the best-loved song of the 1980s (or best-hated, depending on your taste in music). Before her singing career, Basil enjoyed success as a choreographer for 1960s rock 'n' roll TV shows (*Hullabaloo* and *Shindig*), a movie actress (1969's *Easy Rider*), and a video director (Talking Heads' "Once in a Lifetime").

BASKIN-ROBBINS

Ice-cream restaurant chain, started in 1948 by Burt Baskin and Irv Robbins, that is distinguished for having thirty-one flavors of ice cream, one for every day of the month. The original thirty-one flavors served at Baskin-Robbins' first shop, located in Glendale, California, were Banana Nut Fudge, Black Walnut, Burgundy Cherry, Butter Pecan, Butterscotch Ribbon, Chocolate, Chocolate Almond, Chocolate Chip, Chocolate Fudge, Chocolate Ribbon, Coffee, Coffee Candy, Date Nut, Egg Nog, French Vanilla, Green Mint, Lemon Crisp, Lemon Custard, Lemon Sherbet, Maple Walnut, Orange Sherbet, Peach, Peppermint Fudge, Peppermint Stick, Pineapple Sherbet, Pistachio Nut, Raspberry Sherbet, Rocky Road, Strawberry, Vanilla, and Vanilla Burnt Almond. Since then, nearly a thousand different ice-cream flavors have been created by Baskin-Robbins and enjoyed by ice-cream lovers at 4,500 stores worldwide.

FYI: ▸ To celebrate the 1969 moon landing, Baskin-Robbins introduced a new flavor called Lunar Cheesecake.

BASS SHOES

Their Weejun penny loafers were *it* when it came to high school footwear, and the moderately expensive line was itself a status symbol throughout the late-1970s and early-1980s preppy era. Kinney's Shoe Stores had a Bass knock-off called GASS (initials for Great American Shoe Store).

BATGIRL
Pretty, scholarly librarian by day, sexy, motorcycling crime-buster by night—young Barbara Gordon, daughter of Gotham City's Police Commissioner Gordon, helped Batman and Robin fight evildoers in Gotham City. Her glittery, skin-tight Batsuit contributed to the wet-dream fantasies of many adolescent boys. Played by Yvonne Craig on the TV series (1967–68) and Alicia Silverstone in the 1997 *Batman and Robin* movie.

BATMAN
"Holy Mackerel!" Created by cartoonist Bob Kane, the Caped Crusader made his debut in *Detective Comics* in May 1939. Mysterious and masked, Batman is the secret identity of handsome Gotham City millionaire Bruce Wayne, who, after seeing his parents gunned down by a holdup man as a child, vows war on all the city's evildoers. Batman battles archfiends like the Joker, the Riddler, the Penguin, and Catwoman by using a collection of climbing ropes, grappling hooks, and boomerangs—all stored on the utility belt worn around his waist. Orphan teen Dick Grayson serves as his sidekick, Robin, the Boy Wonder. The Dynamic Duo live in the Wayne mansion, beneath which is hidden their sophisticated crime lab known as the Batlab, as well as a Batcave for stashing the marvelously equipped Batmobile and futuristic Batplane. They spawned a huge Bat-industry, including comic strips, a TV series, cartoon shows, feature films, and thousands of toys.

***BATMAN* (TV SHOW)**
"Same Bat-time, same Bat-channel. . . ." From 1966 to 1968, Bat-mania took the nation by storm as this prime-time series, starring Adam West as Batman and Burt Ward as Robin, aired on ABC-TV. The wonderfully campy program was like the pages of a comic book come to life. It featured over-the-top acting (except for the wooden West) and silly cliffhanger finales, along with bright psychedelic colors and words like "Pow!" "Bam!" "Thud!" and "Smash!" flashing across the screen during fight scenes. Best of all was the exotic array of celebrity guest stars cast as diabolical archenemies, such as Burgess Meredith as the Penguin, Frank Gorshin as the Riddler, Cesar Romero as the Joker, Julie Newmar as Catwoman (later played by Lee Meriwether and Eartha Kitt), Victor Bruno as King Tut, Vincent Price as Egghead, Milton Berle as Louie the Lilac, Liberace as Chandell, Roddy McDowall as the Bookworm, and Tallulah "Dahl-ling" Bankhead as the Black Widow.

Yvonne Craig joined the cast in 1967, as young librarian Barbara Gordon who moonlighted as Batgirl. Other regulars included Neil Hamilton as Police Commissioner Gordon (Barbara's dad); Alan Napier as Bruce Wayne's butler, Alfred Pennyworth, the only person who knew of Batman's and Robin's secret identities; Madge Blake as Dick Grayson's clueless aunt; and Stafford Repp as Chief O'Hara, who summoned the Dynamic Duo with a searchlight known as the Batsignal. The rousing, surf-oriented "Batman Theme," composed by Neal Hefti, became a smash hit for The Marketts in 1966.

BATMOBILE
Customized, rocket-fast, slick-black supercar driven by the Dynamic Duo, Batman and Robin, to chase and apprehend crooks. Created by George Barris for the 1960s *Batman* TV series.

BATTLE OF THE NETWORK STARS
Televised from the beautiful campus of Pepperdine University in Malibu during the late 1970s and early 1980s, these were a series of specials that featured three teams of prime-time stars—representing each network (ABC, CBS, NBC)—competing in various sports, such as bicycle racing, tennis, swimming, pool canoeing, team tug-of-war, and an obstacle course. *Battle of the Network Stars* was ideal for watching would-be jock actors (including Paul Michael Glaser, Robert Conrad, Parker Stevenson, Richard Hatch, Bill Cosby, and Jamie Farr) show off their athletic prowess at a game of flag football; as well as for seeing TV starlets (for example, Farrah Fawcett-Majors, Lynda Carter, Suzanne Somers, Adrienne Barbeau, Valerie Bertinelli, and Kristy McNichol) jiggle and wiggle in tight T-shirts, little athletic shorts, and calf-high tube socks while running a relay. Sportscaster Howard Cosell served as the play-by-play commentator.

FYI: ▸ ABC, led by captain Gabe Kaplan, captured the very first battle crown on November 13, 1976.

BATTLESHIP

Man your battle stations! Fire when ready! One of America's all-time favorite boxed games and a continual best-seller since Milton Bradley first introduced it in 1967. The two-player naval strategy game's object is to be the first to locate an opponent's fleet of ships ("G-4"), strike a blow ("It's a hit!"), and sink them ("You sank my battleship!"). Battleship contains two plastic game boxes with a Target Grid and Ocean Grid, five ships per player (Carrier, Battleship, Cruiser, Submarine, Destroyer), and colorful red and white firing pegs (red for a hit, white for a miss). In the 1970s, kids could play with an electronic version featuring flashing lights and realistic explosion sounds.

BATTLESTAR GALACTICA

Clearly inspired by the huge success of the motion picture *Star Wars* (1977), this sci-fi saga, showcasing elaborate special effects, was the most costly TV series ever produced (a reported $1 million per hour), not to mention one of the most publicized. It told the story of the battle between good and evil in outer space during the seventh millennium A.D. The battleship Battlestar Galactica and her convoy of 220 smaller spacecraft hurtled through space toward a far-off unfamiliar planet called earth, while avoiding conflict with evil overlord Count Baltar (John Colicos) and his Cylons (half-human, half-robots). The show starred Lorne Greene as wise Commander Adama, Richard Hatch as brave Captain Apollo, Dirk Benedict as dashing Lieutenant Starbuck, Maren Jensen as pretty brunette Athena, Laurette Spang as pretty blonde Cassiopea, and Noah Hathaway as young Boxey. Muffitt was Boxey's pet "daggit," a mechanical dog. It lasted only a single season on ABC (1978–79).

BATTLING TOPS

"Be a champion in the bout of the century!" Introduced in 1968, the goal of this action game by Ideal was to send your top spinning—by using a string attached to a puller—into a plastic arena where it would battle it out with the tops of opponents. The tops came with individual names, like Dizzy Dan, Hurricane Hank, Tricky Nicky, and Twirling Tim. The owner of the last top spinning in the arena won points, and the first to accumulate ten points was the champ.

BAY CITY ROLLERS

During the mid-1970s, the plaid phenomenon known as Rollermania took the adolescent world by storm. Forget Donny Osmond! Forget David Cassidy! Forget Michael Jackson! It was these tartan-clad popsters from Scotland with dodgy haircuts and cheery smiles that had teenybopper gals swooning over their bubblegum tunes and *Tiger Beat* pinups. The five members consisted of Les McKeown (the most scream-inducing), brothers Alan and Derek Longmuir, Eric Faulkner, and Stuart "Woody" Wood. Hits included mega-smash "Saturday Night" (1975), "Money Honey" (1976), and the remake of Dusty Springfield's "I Only Want to Be with You" (1976).

FYI: ▸ Manager Tam Paton picked the group's name after randomly sticking a pin in a map of the United States and finding it stuck on Bay City, Michigan.

BAY CITY ROLLERS SHOW

In 1978, the plaid-attired Bay City Rollers, experiencing waning popularity, became hosts of *The Krofft Superstar Hour*, a Saturday-morning TV musical-variety program retitled *The Bay City Rollers Show*. This revamped series had a short life-span (five months). Soon after, the band, full of animosity toward one another, split.

BAYWATCH

Originally airing on NBC in 1989, when it failed to capture an audience, *Babewatch*—um, *Bodywatch*—er, *Boobwatch*—I mean—*Baywatch* got revived the following year in off-network syndication, where it became the most popular TV show in the entire world with an estimated one billion viewers in 150 countries. It focused on an attractive staff of bare-chested men and silicone-breasted women who worked as red-clad lifeguards patrolling the beaches of greater Los Angeles. Prime-time hunk and German pop-music legend David Hasselhoff starred as earnest Mitch Bucannon, a veteran lifeguard stationed at Malibu Beach who watched over the rescue attempts of these younger lifeguards.

Throughout its eleven-year run, many up-and-coming stars were cast as *Baywatch* lifeguards. Those noteworthy include Erika Eleniak as Shauni McClain, Nicole Eggert as Summer Quinn, David Charvet as

Matt Brody, Pamela Anderson as C.J. Parker, Alexandra Paul as Stephanie Holden, Yasmine Bleeth as Caroline Holden, David Chokachi as Cody Madison, Gena Lee Nolin as Neely Capshaw, Traci Bingham as Jordan Tate, Michael Bergin as J.D. Darius, and Carmen Electra as Lani McKenzie. After looking at this list of actors, it's obvious that to be hired as a *Baywatch* lifeguard you only have to be 100 percent gorgeous—thin and booby for the gals, thin and buff for the guys—look incredible running in slow motion in a tightly stretched swimsuit of skimpy proportions, and act like you know how to rescue a drowning swimmer or stop a shark from attacking an unsuspecting surfer. (Actual acting abilities take second place.)

BAZOOKA BUBBLEGUM

Classic chewing gum manufactured by Topps and distinguished by the tiny Bazooka Joe comic strips found inside every wrapper. Purchase price: one penny.

BB GUNS

If you've ever been shot by a little BB pellet, you'll wonder why any parent would allow a kid to own a BB gun. The most famous BB gun brand: Daisy's Red Ryder, the subject of the delightful 1983 Yuletide film *A Christmas Story*, starring Peter Billingsley as Ralphie Parker.

BEACH BOYS

American rock band whose songs about sun, sand, surfing, and endless summers embodied California's golden days of the 1960s. Brothers Brian, Dennis, and Carl Wilson, cousin Mike Love, and friend Al Jardine formed The Beach Boys while attending high school in the middle-class Hawthorne district of Los Angeles in 1961. Credited for inventing "surfer music," The Beach Boys sang good-natured tunes marked by vibrant vocal harmonies, including "Surfin' Safari" (1962), "Surfin' U.S.A." (1963), "Surfer Girl" (1963), "Little Deuce Coupe" (1963), "Be True to Your School" (1963), "In My Room" (1963), "Fun, Fun, Fun" (1964), "I Get Around" (1964), "Help Me, Rhonda" (1965), "California Girls" (1965), "Barbara Ann" (1966), "Sloop John B" (1966), and the trippy "Good Vibrations" (1966). The Beach Boys' nostalgic appeal made them a popular touring act way into the 1990s.

***BEACH PARTY* MOVIES**

The ultracheap *Beach Party* movies produced by American International Pictures (AIP) were a constant staple of drive-in theaters during the mid-1960s. Brainless and charmingly lowbrow, they all had the same formula: camp comedy, silly plot twists, toe-tapping tunes, nonstop dancing, girls in bikinis, guys in muscles, all-day surfing, all-night partying, and of course, Frankie and Annette. Former teen idol Frankie Avalon and former Mouseketeer Annette Funicello starred five times as cute and cocky beachboy Frankie, a.k.a. the "Big Kahuna," and his sexy but chaste beach bunny Dee Dee.

The films in the series included *Beach Party* (1963), *Bikini Beach* (1964), *Muscle Beach Party* (1964), *Pajama Party* (1964), *Beach Blanket Bingo* (1965), *How to Stuff a Wild Bikini* (1965), and *The Ghost and the Invisible Bikini* (1966). With the exception of the last, William Asher, husband of *Bewitched*'s Elizabeth Montgomery, directed them all.

FYI: ▸ Have you ever wondered why big-breasted Annette's two-piece swimsuits looked rather large and modest compared with the bikinis worn by the other beach girls? It's because the teen queen was still under contract with Disney, and Uncle Walt insisted she keep her navel covered.

BEANBAG CHAIRS

Loungy, bulbous-shaped chairs, overfilled with soft polystyrene beadlike "beans" that conformed to your body, allowing you to sink comfortably while sitting in it. These colorful, cushiony, vinyl-covered chairs were a trendy furnishing during the 1970s, particularly in the bedrooms of adolescents. The downside to a beanbag chair is that if you cause a rip in one, an avalanche of tiny white beads will rush out all over the floor!

BEANIE BABIES

Ty Inc.'s stuffed beanbag animals with creative names like Chocolate the Moose and Wise the Owl sparked a collecting craze of manic proportions in the mid-1990s, bringing out the worst in adult collectors. Greedy grown-ups pushed small kids aside as they clamored for the tiny plush Beanies. They stole from their own children to sell Quackers the Duck and cuddly comrades for top dollar on the

Internet black market. They purchased countless McDonald's Happy Meals, throwing away the food but keeping the Beanie that came inside the box. Thankfully, the craze ended before we had to give these Beanie-obsessed adults an intervention.

BEANY AND CECIL

Created by legendary Warner Brothers animator Bob Clampett, this began as an Emmy-winning puppet show in 1948 before becoming one of the cutest animated TV shows of the 1960s. Airing from 1962 to 1967, the cartoon presented the exciting exploits of yellow-haired Beany Boy, an adventurous lad wearing a cap with a propeller on top who sailed the Seven Seas aboard the Leakin' Lena with his uncle, Captain Horatio K. Huffenpuff. Beany's best pal, the lovable, gullible Cecil the Seasick Sea Serpent, regularly saved him from the dastardly deeds of Dishonest John ("Nya-hah-hah!").

FYI: ▸ Groucho Marx, a fan of *Beany and Cecil,* once said this was the only kids' show adult enough for young daughter Melinda to watch.

"BEANY" CAPS

Throughout the early 1960s, these caps with spinning propellers on top were a national fad for children, fueled by the popularity of the kiddie classic *Beany and Cecil.*

"BEAT IT"

Michael Jackson's follow-up to "Billie Jean," from the mega-successful *Thriller* LP, topped the charts for three weeks in the spring of 1983. The song's accompanying video was an homage to *West Side Story.* It featured Jackson dancing with a gang of balletic badboys and Eddie Van Halen's lead guitar.

"BEATLE" BOOTS

Fashionable male footwear of the 1960s consisting of an ankle-high boot with flat heel and pointed toe, made famous by—you guessed—The Beatles! Also known as Chelsea boots.

BEATLES

Volumes have been written about England's Fab Four, considered the "World's Number-One Rock Group" with a total of forty-nine Top Forty American singles, including twenty number-ones, so I want to give this entry a different slant—a short reflection by someone barely old enough to remember them during their historic arrival in America (me!). I was barely a two-year-old when Paul, John, George, and Ringo invaded the States in January 1964 and caused nationwide hysteria among teenagers, who shook, screamed, and fainted from overwhelming excitement.

My early memories of this time period are fuzzy. I remember my teenage sister Paula groovin' to their "Ya ya ya's" on a 45 rpm that played on a portable phonograph in her heavily guarded bedroom. I remember my older brother Butch trying to grow his hair and sideburns long because the mop-headed foursome wore theirs that way. I remember being a preschooler and go-go dancing spastically to "I Want to Hold Your Hand," "She Loves You," "Twist and Shout," and "A Hard Day's Night." But most of all, I remember watching their Saturday-morning cartoon show, airing from 1965 to 1969, while eating a heaping bowl of Cap'n Crunch and wearing my pajamas. (The Beatles were the first living celebrities adapted as animated characters on network TV.)

BEAUTY AIDS

It's not easy being beautiful. We can be thankful that there are a gazillion beauty products out there to aid in the difficult task of looking good. The following are 100 well-known beauty items and a few health aids (because it's hard to look good if you don't feel good) found in drugstores and supermarkets from the 1960s through the 1990s.

- Aim Toothpaste
- Alberto VO5 Hot Oil Treatment
- Aqua Net Hairspray
- Aquafresh Toothpaste
- Arrid Extra Dry Deodorant
- Bain de Soleil Tanning Lotion
- Ban Deodorant
- Banana Boat Tanning Lotion
- Band-Aid Bandages
- Bic Razor
- Binaca Blast Breath Freshener
- Blistex Lip Balm
- Body On Tap shampoo

Bonne Bell Lip Smackers
Breck Shampoo
Brylcreem Hair Gel
Calgon Bath Oil
Caress Soap
Carmex Lip Balm
Chap Stick Lip Balm
Clearasil Acne Medicine
Coast Soap
Colgate Toothpaste
Coppertone Tanning Lotion
Cover Girl Makeup
Crest Toothpaste
Cutex Nail Polish
Dep Hair Gel
Dial Soap
Dippity-Do Hair Gel
Dove Soap
Dry Look Men's Hairspray
Earth Born Shampoo
Epilady Hair Depilatory
Finesse Shampoo
Gee Your Hair Smells Terrific Shampoo
Gleem Toothpaste
Grecian Formula Men's Hair Color
Hawaiian Tropic Tanning Lotion
Head and Shoulders Dandruff Shampoo
Herbal Essence Shampoo
Ipana Toothpaste
Irish Spring Soap
Ivory Soap
Jergens Body Lotion
Johnson's Baby Oil
Johnson's Baby Shampoo
Kotex Tampons
L.A. Looks Hair Mousse
Lava Soap
Lee Press-on Nails
Lemon-Up Shampoo
Listerine Mouthwash
Long and Lovely Shampoo
Max Factor Makeup
Maybelline Makeup
Milk Plus Six Shampoo
Miss Clairol Hair Color
Mr. Bubble Bubble Bath
Nair Depilatory
Nivea Body Lotion
No More Tears Shampoo
Noxzema Cold Cream
Oil of Olay Facial Moisturizer
Pantene Shampoo
Pearl Drops Teeth Whitener
Pert Plus Shampoo
Pond's Cold Cream
Prell Shampoo
QT (Quick Tan) Self-Tanning Lotion
Q-Tips Cotton Swabs
Rave Hairspray
Revlon Makeup
Right Guard Deodorant
Schick Razor
Scope Mouthwash
Sea & Ski Tanning Lotion
Secret Deodorant
Short n' Sassy Shampoo
Shower to Shower Body Powder
Soft & Dry Deodorant
Speed Stick Deodorant
Stri-Dex Pads Acne Medicine
Suave Shampoo
Sudden Tan Self-Tanning Lotion
Summer's Eve Douche
Sun-In Hair Lightener
Sure Deodorant
Tame Hair Conditioner
Tampax Tampons
Ten-O-Six Acne Medicine
Toni Perm
Ultra Brite Toothpaste
Vaseline Petroleum Jelly
Visine Eye Drops
Vidal Sassoon Shampoo
Wella Balsam Shampoo
White Rain Hairspray
Yucca-Dew Shampoo
Zest Soap

BEAUTY AND THE BEAST
"A tale as old as time." Released for Christmas 1991, Walt Disney's beautiful and exhilarating musical film, featuring the voices of Paige O'Hara (Belle) and Robby Benson (Beast), was based on the classic fairy tale by Madame Leprince de Beaumont. A handsome prince whose heart is too hard to love anyone (besides himself) is turned into a hideous beast by a

witch's spell. Only his learning to love another and be loved in return can break it. Along comes the beautiful and bookish Belle, who is looking for her wayward father, Maurice, a doddering inventor. Belle is made prisoner in the Beast's desolate castle, where the only other signs of life come from servants who had turned into humanized household objects by the spell (for example, clock Cogsworth, candelabra Lumiere, and teapot Mrs. Chips and teacup son Chip). At first, the gutsy Beauty and the ferocious Beast are at odds, but as the film unfolds, Belle sees the poignant soul under his harsh exterior. Just before he is doomed to remain a beast forever, they find true love and the spell is broken.

Beauty and the Beast became the first animated movie in Academy Award history to be nominated for Best Picture. It was also the first animated feature to gross more than $100 million worldwide. Songs include the Oscar-nabbing "Beauty and the Beast," performed by Angela Lansbury in the film and sung by Celine Dion and Peabo Bryson on the radio, plus "Be Our Guest," "Belle," "Gaston," "How Long Must This Go On," "If I Can't Love Her," and "Something There." Two straight-to-video sequels, a Broadway musical, and a TV series followed.

BEAVER CLEAVER

"Ward, I'm a little worried about the Beaver. . . ." Real first name: Theodore. The lovable, round-faced youngest son of Ward and June Cleaver was a seven-year-old attending Grant Avenue Grammar School whose well-meaning curiosity often lands him in a dilemma. Big brother Wally is the Beav's idol, and his best pal is chubby Larry Mondello. Played by Jerry Mathers on the 1950s *Leave It to Beaver* TV show.

FYI: ▸ *Leave It to Beaver*'s creators, Joe Connelly and Bob Mosher, came up with the nickname "Beaver" because they thought it connoted a character that was "all boy."

BEAVIS AND BUTT-HEAD

"Heh-heh, heh-heh. . . ." This MTV cartoon show, created by Mike Judge in 1993, was about two moronic adolescent heavy-metal fans (Metallica for blond Beavis, AC/DC for dark-haired Butt-Head) who amused themselves by reviewing bad music videos on TV and creating chaos in their suburban surroundings. The duo's popularity led to a 1996 big-screen feature, *Beavis and Butt-Head Do America*, and a 1997 spin-off, *Daria*, starring Goth-chick Daria Morgendorffer (Beavis and Butt-Head called her "Diarrhea"). "That sucks."

BEDKNOBS AND BROOMSTICKS

Many of us remember this as the Disney movie with the flying bed. Set in London during the Blitzkrieg of World War II, it starred Angela Lansbury as Miss Eglantine Price, an amateur witch who uses her powers to stop the Nazis from invading England. As for the flying bed, it was a magical brass bedknob that caused it to soar, transporting Miss Price, along with three orphan waifs—Charlie, Paul, and Carrie—to the bottom of the beautiful briny sea and to the Lost Isle of Naboombu, an enchanted island inhabited by soccer-playing animals. Directed by Robert Stevenson, the 1971 musical-fantasy's mix of live action and animation won an Academy Award for Best Visual Effects. The songs, written by Richard and Robert Sherman, included "The Age of Not Believing," "The Old Home Guard," "Portobello Road," "The Beautiful Briny," and "Substitutiary Locomotion." Based on the book by Mary Norton.

BEDROCK

Prehistoric town, population 2,500, located 250 miles below sea level in Cobblestone County and home to the Flintstones and the Rubbles, two modern Stone Age families on TV's *Flintstones*.

BEDROCK ROLLERS

"Nothin' is as groovy as a boom boom boom of the band with the Bedrock beat. . . ." As cartoon teenagers, Pebbles Flintstones and Bamm-Bamm Rubble fronted this groovy music group with cartoon friends Penny, Wiggy, and Moonrock. Pebbles played mallets on dinosaur teeth, Bamm-Bamm pounded on a keyboard of dinosaur bones, Moonrock drummed on two prehistoric turtles, and Penny and Wiggy provided background support.

BEE GEES

Top-selling music act of the 1970s whose name was an acronym from "Brothers Gibb." Born and raised on Great Britain's Isle of Man (home of the tail-less

Manx cat) before relocating to Australia, the group—made up of three brothers, eldest Barry Gibb and twins Maurice and Robin Gibb—was noted for quivering vocals and brotherly harmonies. They had two definitive stages in their recording career. The first was in the late 1960s and early 1970s with a string of lush, tearful ballads: "To Love Somebody" (1967), "Words" (1968), "I've Gotta Get a Message to You" (1968), "I Started a Joke" (1969), and "How Can You Mend a Broken Heart" (1971).

Picking up the pace, the second stage began in the mid-1970s when the trio's supersonic falsettos, particularly showcased on the pulsating, disco-driven Saturday Night Fever soundtrack, defined the "sound" of Top Forty disco. Hits of this era included "Jive Talkin'" (1975), "Nights on Broadway" (1975), "You Should Be Dancing" (1976), "Boogie Child" (1976), "How Deep Is Your Love" (1977), "Stayin' Alive" (1977), "Night Fever" (1978), "Too Much Heaven" (1978), and "Tragedy" (1979). Teen idol Andy "Shadow Dancing" Gibb was their kid brother.

FYI: ▸ "You can tell by the way I use my walk / I'm a woman's man: no time to talk." The way the Bee Gees looked personified manhood of the disco era: blow-dried, feathered hair; skintight, crotch-bulging, flare-legged slacks; polyester shirts, unbuttoned to the navel and exposing a hairy chest adorned with gold medallions; and towering platform shoes.

BEEHIVE

Huge, sky-high coif, shaped like a bee's nest, favored by young "vulgarian" women of the 1960s (think Priscilla Presley, circa 1963, or the actresses in the early films of John Waters) and those gals from the B-52's, Kate and Cindy. Achieving the perfect Beehive took frantic backcombing (a.k.a. teasing or ratting), sometimes a plastic or wire frame to provide support and shape, an extreme amount of Aqua Net hairspray, and a heck of a lot of patience.

BEETLEJUICE

"Beetlejuice! Beetlejuice! Beetlejuice!" If you said his name three times fast, the straggly-haired poltergeist dressed in a garish black-and-white-striped suit would materialize from the Netherworld to wreak comical havoc. Played by Michael Keaton in director Tim Burton's 1988 *Beetlejuice* movie and voiced by Stephen Ouimette in the Saturday-morning cartoon that followed.

BELL-BOTTOMS

A style of pants, mega-fashionable in the late 1960s and throughout the 1970s, that got its name from its unique bell shape (tight from the waist to the thighs, flared from the knees to the bottom). Two general rules for wearing bell-bottoms: the wider the bell, the cooler the wearer; and legs long enough so your shoes won't show (otherwise you look like a geek wearing highwaters). Extras that made them totally awesome: bottom edges frayed from dragging on the ground, metal studs sewn down the seams, and patches with slogans and symbols stitched over well-worn holes (the smiley face or peace sign were faves).

The downside to wearing bell-bottoms: "hearing" the legs of your bells rubbing against each other while walking (this could be really embarrassing in a school corridor, where the smallest noise had a tendency to magnify and echo) and falling off your hi-rise Schwinn bike after the wide cuffs got caught in the spokes. A less radical version of bell-bottoms was the not-as-wide flares.

FYI: ▸ A far-out bell-bottomed look for a groovy guy, circa 1970, would be multicolored striped bells worn with a shirt with wide Tom Jones sleeves accented by a fringed vest, and pointy boots as footwear. For a groovy gal, it would be crushed-velvet hip-hugger bells with an ultrapsychedelic floral-print blouse, accessorized with a funky neon-colored fur vest (fake, of course), a choker necklace, and platform sandals.

BELLE

In Disney's magnificent *Beauty and the Beast* (1991), the lovely auburn-haired heroine, a bookworm daughter of a dotty inventor, finds herself fighting off the unwanted advances of town stallion Gaston and trapped as a prisoner in the castle estate of a heartless prince turned into a lonely beast.

BEMELMANS, LUDWIG

The son of a Belgian painter, this author and illustrator created the enchanting Madeline stories featuring the little French schoolgirl. Beginning with *Madeline* in 1939, these books are highly acclaimed for their cheerful humor, rhythmic text, and, most of all, vivid watercolors of such Paris landmarks as the Eiffel Tower and Notre Dame Cathedral. Others in the series included *Madeline's Rescue* (1953), *Madeline and the Bad Hat* (1958), *Madeline and the Gypsies* (1961), *Madeline in London* (1962), and *Madeline's Christmas* (1962). In 1954, *Madeline's Rescue* won the prestigious Caldecott Medal, and the *New York Times* named it an Outstanding Book of the Year.

FYI: ▸ *Madeline* was inspired by Ludwig Bemelmans's hospital stay in France in which a little girl in the room next to his was having her appendix taken out. The little girl was named after his beloved wife, Madeline.

BEN

"I loved the song and I loved the story. People didn't understand the boy's love for this little creature. He was dying of some disease and his only true friend was Ben, the leader of the rats in the city where they lived. A lot of people thought the movie was a bit odd, but I was not one of them."

—MICHAEL JACKSON

Ben the movie was a horror tale about a boy who loved a misunderstood killer rat; "Ben" the song was Michael Jackson's haunting ode to this varmint. The 1972 film was a follow-up to the previous year's *Willard*, a box-office success about a misfit teen (Bruce Davison) who trained rats as deadly agents of revenge, and based on the book *Ratman's Notebooks* by Stephen Gilbert.

In the sequel, Danny Garrison (Lee H. Montgomery), a sickly boy, befriends an injured rodent named Ben, the super-intelligent leader of Willard's rat pack, and nurses him back to health. The twosome develops a special bond, as Ben is kept hidden and in exile from the boy's family and the authorities. Tragedy strikes when the police catch up with the "King of the Rats" to destroy him and his rodent followers. The title theme, sung by twelve-year-old Jackson, topped the charts in September 1972—a sign of things to come for the biggest-selling recording artist of all time.

BEN AND JERRY'S

Founded in 1978 by childhood pals Ben Cohen and Jerry Greenfield, this Vermont-based ice-cream company employed a hippie image incorporating psychedelic packaging and trippy flavor names like Cherry Garcia, Chunky Monkey, Karamel Sutra, and Wavy Gravy to become one of the world's top-selling ice creams. A percentage of its income goes to charity.

BENATAR, PAT

Don't be fooled by the petite stature and seemingly delicate persona. This rocker could belt out a power ballad like no one else, earning her the honor of being the first major female rock star of the 1980s. Born Patricia Andrzejewski on January 10, 1953, on Long Island, she studied classical singing as a teenager at New York's Juilliard School of Music before signing with Chrysalis Records, where she recorded her debut album, *In the Heat of the Night,* in 1979. Songs: "Heartbreaker" (1979), "We Live for Love" (1980), "Hit Me with Your Best Shot" (1980), "Hell Is for Children" (1980), "Treat Me Right" (1981), "Fire and Ice" (1981), "Promises in the Dark" (1981), "Shadow of the Night" (1982), "Love Is a Battlefield" (1983), "We Belong" (1984), and "Invincible" (1985), the theme from the Helen Slater film *The Legend of Billie Jean.* Teen Pat Benatar wannabes of the early 1980s copied her short, spiky dark hair and trendy rock outfits—headbands, leg warmers, and ankle boots.

BEN CARTWRIGHT

The stern yet kind widower played by silver-haired Lorne Greene on the prime-time hit *Bonanza.* He lived with his three strapping sons (Adam, Hoss, and Little Joe), all born from different mothers, on the prosperous Ponderosa Ranch. Buck was the name of Cartwright's pet horse.

BENITA BIZARRE

"I play a vicious witch, but not really. I live in a jukebox, wear a turkey-feather boa, and want to make a record even though I can't sing. What more could a girl ask?"

—MARTHA RAYE

The aptly named, no-talent, witchy wannabe singer dressed in flamboyant technicolored feather-boa outfits resided in a giant jukebox and terrorized the Bugaloos because she was jealous of their musical abilities. Benita's stooges were Flunky Rat, a Nazi-like rodent chauffeur, and Woofer and Tweeter, a pair of spark-plug-like nincompoops. Played by big-mouthed comedienne Martha Raye.

BENJAMIN BRADDOCK

"Mrs. Robinson, you're trying to seduce me." Idolized Baby Boom character, played by young Dustin Hoffman in the film masterpiece *The Graduate* (1967), who doesn't know what to do with his future after graduation (plastics?) so he gets seduced by Mrs. Robinson, the middle-aged married mother of his girlfriend, Elaine.

BENJI

A blond, shaggy-coated, scrappy little mutt (believed to be a mix of cocker, poodle, and schnauzer)—rescued from a Burbank, California, animal shelter as a puppy in the 1960s—who grew up to become the biggest dog star since the days of Lassie and Rin Tin Tin. The pooch's sweet face, modest personality, and intelligence led him to be greatly adored by viewers, especially children. He was a show-business veteran of TV's *Petticoat Junction* (Uncle Joe's beloved Higgins) when he starred in the *Benji* motion picture in 1974, in which he played a lovable orphan who rescues two children from kidnappers and falls in love with a Pekinese named Tiffany. It became an instant kiddie classic, spawning two sequels: *For the Love of Benji* (1977) and *Benji the Hunted* (1987).

BEN "OBI-WAN" KENOBI

"May The Force be with you." The noble wizard knight and defender of the Old Republic, who instructs young Luke Skywalker in the way of the Jedi, was played by Oscar-nominated Sir Alec Guinness in the revolutionary sci-fi film *Star Wars* (1977).

BENSON, ROBBY

A dark-haired, pale-eyed, soft-voiced actor who enjoyed success in the 1970s as the star of tearjerker, coming-of-age movies. Born on January 21, 1956, in Dallas, Benson's specialty was playing angst-ridden teens: a shy Jewish lad in love for the first time with a gentile girl in *Jeremy* (1973); a youngster dying from a brain tumor in *Death Be Not Proud* (1975); Billy Joe McAllister, who jumped off the Tallahatchie Bridge in *Ode to Billy Joe* (1976); an out-of-control high school drug addict in *The Death of Richie* (1977); a naive college basketball player in *One on One* (1977); a young man whose figure-skating girlfriend is accidentally blinded in *Ice Castles* (1978); and a Chicano gang member in love with a Wasp beauty in *Walk Proud* (1979). In later years, he married New Wave singer Karla DeVito (1981's "Is This a Cool World or What") and voiced Beauty's Beast in Disney's animated *Beauty and the Beast* (1991).

BENTON, BARBI

Nicknamed "Barbi Doll," the astonishingly beautiful brunette from California whose persona was that of a girlish featherbrain experienced enormous popularity in the 1970s for four reasons: (1) *Playboy* centerfold (March 1970); (2) girlfriend of *Playboy*'s Hugh Hefner; (3) "Brass Buckles," a Top Ten country hit in 1975; (4) playing sexpots on TV's *Hee Haw* (1971–76) and *Sugar Time!* (1977–78). So well liked was this curvaceous cutie that she starred in her own TV special, *A Barbi Doll for Christmas.*

BERENSTAIN BEARS

"This way to Bear Country, you'll know when you're there, as soon as you enter, you'll feel like a bear." Tot-oriented picture books, written and illustrated by husband-and-wife team Stan and Jan Berenstain, about the cute Bear family—overbearing Papa Bear, nurturing Mama Bear, eight-year-old Brother Bear, six-year-old Sister Bear, and pet pooch Snuff—who live in a tree in the tiny hamlet of Beartown. Considered one of the top children's book series in the United States, with more than forty-five million copies published. The different titles have included *The Bears' Christmas, Bears in the Night,* and *The Berenstains' B Book.*

BERMUDA SHORTS

Originally worn by the police patrol on Bermuda Island, these knee-length shorts, colored in plain pastels or a bright madras plaid, became an acceptable fashion statement for men in the 1960s and have stayed around ever sense.

BERMUDA TRIANGLE

Scary stuff this Bermuda Triangle, a.k.a. Devil's Triangle or Satan's Triangle—a patch of Atlantic Ocean just off the Florida coast where planes and boats mysteriously vanish, never to be found. In the mid-1970s, the whole country was abuzz about what was causing these disappearances. Was it UFOs? Was it the portal to some kind of time warp? Was it extreme weather conditions? Was it the underwater citizens of long-lost Atlantis? Or, was it—eek!—the devil himself coming up from hell below?

Everybody had an opinion (I tend to think it's the weather), especially author Charles Berlitz, whose book *The Bermuda Triangle*, featuring his theories explaining the disappearances, became a number-one best-seller in 1975. That same year, two TV movies were aired to capitalize on the intriguing craze: *Beyond the Bermuda Triangle*, starring Fred MacMurray, and *Satan's Triangle*, starring Kim Novak. In 1976, Milton Bradley released a cool Bermuda Triangle board game with a moving "Sinister Mystery Cloud" that swallowed unwary ships.

BERT AND ERNIE

Sesame Street roommates dressed in coordinating striped sweaters (vertical on Bert, horizontal on Ernie) who like pigeons and rubber duckies. Playful Ernie often irritated sensible Bert with his endless array of questions. The Christian Right has linked the Muppet roomies to a rumor that they're a gay couple.

FYI: ▸ Voiced by creator Jim Henson, Ernie became a pop-music star when his recording of "Rubber Duckie" landed in the Top Forty in 1970.

BERTIE BOTT'S EVERY FLAVOR BEANS

Jelly beans featured in the Harry Potter book series that come in various flavors, including such yummy ones as banana, marshmallow, and tutti-frutti; such uncertain ones as black pepper, grass, and spinach; and totally disgusting ones, such as boogers, ear wax, and vomit. A funny party prank is making guests randomly pick one and eat it without knowing what flavor they're getting.

BERTINELLI, VALERIE

Born April 23, 1960, in Delaware, the fresh-faced brunette's role as the tomboyish youngest daughter, Barbara, on *One Day at a Time* made her the most likeable teen actress on TV during the 1970s. Girls liked her because she seemed personable and fun, while guys liked her because of her foxy good looks. Bertinelli kept busy in the 1980s and 1990s starring in a steady flow of "women with issues" TV movies (such as *The Seduction of Gina* and *Shattered Vows*) and as the wife of rock-star guitarist Eddie Van Halen (they were married in 1981).

BERT THE CHIMNEY SWEEP

Spindly Dick Van Dyke starred as the soot-covered chimney cleaner and Cockney beau of Mary Poppins in the 1964 Disney classic. He performed the whimsical "Chim Chim Cheree" number, with Mary (Julie Andrews), in the movie.

BEST LITTLE GIRL IN THE WORLD

This compelling "disease-of-the-week" exposé starred Jennifer Jason Leigh as Casey Powell, a perfect teen from a perfect middle-class home who suffers from a secret case of anorexia nervosa. It seems Casey is unable to cope with stress in the family plus social pressure at school, and her gradual starvation is a cry for help. The 1981 TV movie was the first to address the debilitating illness and its effects on the average American family.

BEST OF THE WEST

Inspired by the popularity of Hasbro's G.I. Joe, Marx Toys created this western-oriented action-figure line, starring Johnny West and his cowgirl Jane West, in 1965. The twosome were eleven-inch-tall solid-plastic dolls, fully jointed ("1001 different positions"), that came with a multitude of accessories: horses (Thunderbolt for Johnny, Flame for Jane), camp gear, weapons, equipment, outfits, a covered wagon, and even a frontier homestead called the Circle X Ranch. In 1967, the West clan grew with the addition of son Jamie, daughter Josie, pony Pancho, and dogs Flick and Flack. By the late 1960s, the line developed into a complete series featuring more than a dozen frontier figures (some fictional, some not), including Bart Black, Brave Eagle, Bill Buck, Chief Cherokee, Sam Cobra, Fighting Eagle, General Custer, Sheriff Pat Garrett, Geronimo, Jeb Gibson, Captain Tom Maddox, Princess Wildflower, and Zeb Zachary.

BETSY McCALL
A Baby Boom favorite was this charming brown-haired little girl, who appeared in the pages of *McCall's* magazine from 1951 to 1974 as a monthly paper doll modeling seasonal clothing. She would be re-created successfully in real doll form throughout the 1950s and 1960s for such toy companies as American Character, Ideal, and Uneeda.

BETSY WETSY
This classic doll from Ideal Toys whose moving parts and drinking, wetting, and crying capabilities made her the most realistic baby doll of the Baby Boom era (1950s).

"BETTE DAVIS EYES"
A 1981 pop-music tribute, laden with a heavy synchronized beat, about a femme fatale with enormous eyes. Recorded by blonde-haired, scratchy-voiced Kim Carnes, it topped the charts for nine weeks, falling one week short of tying Olivia Newton-John's "Physical" as the number-one song of the year, and won Grammy Awards as both Record of the Year and Song of the Year.

FYI: ▸ If you're wondering what screen-legend Bette Davis thought about "Bette Davis Eyes," she absolutely adored it!

BETTY BOOP
"Boop-Oop-a-Doop!" Modeled after singer Helen Kane ("I Wanna Be Loved by You"), animator Max Fleischer created this sexy, flirty little jazz baby, with the black pin-curled hair, wide eyes, and squeaky voice, in 1931. Along with faithful dog Bimbo and clown pal Koko, the little flapper vamped and warbled her way through no less than 105 cartoon adventures throughout the 1930s. Her continuing appeal has produced a wide range of licensed merchandise still available today.

BETTY COOPER
Riverdale High's sweetheart, a blonde girl-next-door-type with a ponytail who dreams of being Mrs. Archie Andrews—that is, if best pal / shopping mate / cheerleader comrade Veronica Lodge would keep her well-manicured claws off him.

FYI: ▸ Teens in the 1980s used the comic-book beauty's name to refer to a hot girl: "The babe in the leather miniskirt is a real Betty."

BETTY JO, BILLIE JO, AND BOBBIE JO
Widow Kate Bradley's three beautiful daughters, who are seen skinny-dipping in the Hooterville water tank during the opening title credits of the 1960s *Petticoat Junction* TV show. Blonde Billie Jo Bradley is the smart, talented oldest. Brunette Bobbie Jo Bradley is the optimistic, ditzy middle child. Redhead Betty Jo Bradley is the sweet, tomboyish youngest who marries handsome pilot Steve Elliott and has his baby, Kathy Jo.

BETTY RIZZO
"Listen, fella, if this is a line, I'm not biting." Rizzo is the sassy, trampy leader of the Pink Ladies, a gang of high school girls who hang out with the hoodlum T-Birds. Many fans of the movie *Grease* (1978) often say this bad girl with a heart of gold is their favorite character, especially because of Stockard Channing's awesome performance.

BETTY RUBBLE
Spirited and sensible brunette, married to Barney Rubble, who is Wilma's best girlfriend and shopping-spree partner ("Charge it!") in the children's series *The Flintstones*. TV actress Bea Benaderet, best known as Cousin Pearl on *The Beverly Hillbillies* and as Kate Bradley on *Petticoat Junction*, provided Betty Rubble's voice from 1960 to 1964.

FYI: ▸ Betty Rubble's maiden name was Betty Jean McBricker.

BEVERLY HILLBILLIES
"Come 'n listen to my story 'bout a man named Jed . . ." Airing on CBS-TV from 1962 to 1971, this much-loved sitcom was the top-rated prime-time show of the 1960s. (During its first two years, it attracted up to sixty million viewers a week.) It told the story of the Clampetts, a clan of poor country bumpkins who became millionaires after striking oil ("black gold, Texas tea") on their property in the hills of the Ozarks (near Bug Tussle). After loading up their decrepit truck, they moved to "Californy" to live in a posh mansion in Beverly

Hills (518 Crestview Drive), complete with a "cement pond" out back, much to the dismay of their snobbish neighbors. The major players include Buddy Ebsen as sensible widower Jed Clampett, Irene Ryan as his testy mother-in-law Granny, Donna Douglas as Jed's beautiful daughter Elly May, Max Baer Jr. as thick-headed nephew Jethro Bodine, Raymond Bailey as scheming bank president Milburn Drysdale, Harriet MacGibbon as his snooty socialite wife Margaret, Nancy Kulp as Drysdale's prudish assistant Miss Jane Hathaway, and Bea Benaderet as crazy Cousin Pearl, Jethro's mother.

The Beverly Hillbillies spawned two country-cousin spin-offs: *Petticoat Junction* (1963–70) and *Green Acres* (1965–71). The bluegrass team of Lester Flatt and Earl Scruggs performed the well-known theme song, "The Ballad of Jed Clampett." "Y'all come back now, y'hear!"

BEVERLY HILLS 90210

The TV series with the most famous zip code in the world was a *Peyton Place* for the teen set. First airing in 1990, the FOX prime-time soap focused on a set of sixteen-year-old twins, Brandon and Brenda Walsh (Jason Priestley and Shannen Doherty), whose family moved from Minneapolis to Beverly Hills 90210. The twins enrolled at West Beverly Hills High, where they managed to fit in with a student body of pampered children of the rich and famous. Their new crowd consisted of beautiful but vain Kelly Taylor (Jennie Garth), moody surfer Dylan McKay (Luke Perry), insecure Donna Martin (Tori Spelling, daughter of TV producer Aaron Spelling), jaded Steve Sanders (Ian Ziering), brainy Andrea Zuckerman (Gabrielle Carteris), and naive David Silver (Brian Austin Green).

What set *Beverly Hills 90210* apart from the other high school fare of the day was its realistic spin on modern teenage issues, such as alcoholism, drug abuse, suicide, eating disorders, date rape, safe sex, and teen pregnancy. Its devoted audience of young and mostly female viewers made pinup idols of handsome male leads Jason Priestley and Luke Perry and spawned a spin-off aimed at the twentysomething demographic: *Melrose Place*, starring Heather Locklear as vixen Amanda Woodward.

BEWITCHED

> "*Bewitched* is not about cleaning the house with a magic wave or zapping up the toast or flying around the living room. It's about a very difficult relationship. And I think people pick up on this. They know there's something else going on besides the magic."
>
> —ELIZABETH MONTGOMERY

The bewitching fantasy sitcom stars Elizabeth Montgomery as a pretty witch named Samantha who, to the utter disbelief of her supernatural family, forsakes witchcraft to marry Darrin Stephens, a mere mortal, and settle down as a suburban housewife in Westport, Connecticut (1164 Morning Glory Circle). The honeymoon is over when Sam finds herself compelled to use witchy powers to rescue her beleaguered hubby from all types of spells cast by his troublesome in-laws. Regular cast members include Dick York and, later, look-alike Dick Sargent as Darrin; twins Erin and Diane Murphy as daughter Tabitha; twins David and Greg Lawrence as son Adam; Agnes Moorehead as Samantha's mother, Endora; Maurice Evans as Samantha's father, Maurice; Paul Lynde as Uncle Arthur; Marion Lorne as Aunt Clara; Alice Ghostley as housekeeper Esmeralda; Bernard Fox as Dr. Bombay; David White as Darrin's boss, Larry Tate; Alice Pearce and, later, Sandra Gould as neighbor Gladys Kravitz, and George Tobias as her husband Arthur; and "Pandora Sparks" (Liz Montgomery) as Samantha's dark-haired, naughty "twin" cousin Serena. Hanna-Barbera Productions created the show's now-famous animated opening credits.

Airing from 1964 to 1972, *Bewitched* was one of the best-loved TV shows of the 1960s and, on into 1977, ABC-TV's highest-rated sitcom ever.

FYI: ▸ A debatable question over the years has been "Who has the greater powers, *Bewitched*'s Samantha or *I Dream of Jeannie*'s Jeannie? In 1994, Nick at Nite asked TV viewers that question, with some 1.4 million call-in votes registered. The winner: Samantha with 58 percent of the vote!

B-52'S

Formed in Athens, Georgia, in 1977, a wacky New Wave group consisting of drummer Keith Strickland; vocalists Fred Schneider, Kate Pierson, and

Cindy Wilson; and guitarist Ricky Wilson (Cindy's brother, who died of complications from AIDS in 1985). The B-52's were notable for their highly visual stage show—showcasing retro-1960s fashions (miniskirts, go-go boots, capri pants, and Nehru jackets), jerky dance steps, and quirky party music—featuring Fred's distinctive singing-shouting and the girls' singing-yodeling. They developed a cult following during the late 1970s and early 1980s, especially in university towns, where they received the most airplay because of cutting-edge college radio programming. Their kitsch-oriented, postpunk, prealternative dance tunes included "Rock Lobster" (1979), "Planet Claire" (1979), "Dance This Mess Around" (1979), "Private Idaho" (1980), "Quiche Lorraine" (1980), "Future Generations" (1983), and "Legal Tender" (1983).

Superstardom eluded The B-52's until the very end of the 1980s, when they scored their biggest smash with "Love Shack" (1989), a million-seller, followed by "Deadbeat Club" (1990) and "Roam" (1990). *Rolling Stone* magazine bestowed them the "Comeback of the Year" honor in 1989.

FYI: ▸ The B-52's name is Southern slang for the sky-high beehive hairdo worn by Cindy and Kate. (The hairstyle's nickname came from its resemblance to the vast B-52 bomber.)

BICENTENNIAL

July 4, 1976, America's 200th birthday. On that historic summer day, Americans reveled in fervent patriotism—a Spirit of '76—unseen since the valiant G.I.'s arrived home from World War II. Cities and towns from coast to coast celebrated this "mother" of all Fourth of Julys with parades, fluttering flags, sizzling hot dogs, sailing ships, and blazing fireworks.

Memorable Bicentennial festivities included a sixty-square-foot cherry pie baked by residents of the town of George, Washington; 1,776 Frisbees whirled through the air in Sheboygan, Wisconsin; a reenactment of a Revolutionary War battle in Western Springs, Illinois; the biggest parade of the day, covering eleven miles of palm-lined streets in Los Angeles; the largest fireworks celebration, with a price tag of $200,000, in Washington, D.C. (the crowd of one million went crazy when laser guns shot the message "1776–1976, Happy Birthday, U.S.A."); "Operation Sail" in the New York Harbor, which had sixteen of the world's tallest windjammers and thousands of other ships sail past the Statue of Liberty; and the Freedom Train, traveling more than 17,000 miles to eighty cities, with eleven cars of Americana exhibitions.

Glorious red-white-and-blue was everywhere. Thanks to innumerable Bicentennial promotions, practically everything and everyone was wearing these patriotic shades. From head to toe, we wore red, white, and blue on tennis shoes, socks, bell-bottoms, shirts, and baseball caps. In every suburb and small town, kids painted fire hydrants in various Stars-and-Stripes patterns. We rode special-edition Bicentennial bicycles and carried Bicentennial lunch boxes called Yankee Doodles to school. Our school yearbooks were red, white, and blue inside and out (the yearbook staff worked hard to reflect the spirit of the Bicentennial). A common essay topic in classrooms was "What the Bicentennial means to me."

Barbie and Ken dolls took part in the celebration as well: she in a quaint Betsy Ross-esque gown and he in a patriotic jacket. The U.S. Treasury introduced the Bicentennial coin set: a quarter, a half-dollar, and the ill-fated Susan B. Anthony dollar coin—a coin that was doomed because it was easily mistaken for the quarter, which was around the same size. And finally, a popular bumper sticker found on automobiles summed it all up: "America, Love It or Leave It."

BIG

"Have you ever had a really big secret?" Director Penny Marshall's age-swapping film (1988) is a delightful comedy fable about a young boy, Josh Baskin (David Moscow), who asks a genie in a carnival wish machine to make him "big." The next morning he awakens to find his wish has turned him into a thirty-year-old Tom Hanks. Remaining a boy inside a man's body, he is thrown out of the house by his confused mother (Mercedes Ruehl), who thinks the adult Josh is a nutty intruder and that her son is missing. Aided by best-pal Billy (Jared Rushton), he moves to New York City and tries to adapt to the strange world of grown-ups with hopes of returning to his twelve-year-old form. Josh's childlike outlook lands him a job in the competitive world of product testing for a toy company headed by Mr.

MacMillan (Robert Loggia), which leads to his very own high-rise apartment and a first romantic involvement with a yuppie colleague named Susan (Elizabeth Perkins). *Big* highlights: Josh and boss Loggia tap-dancing on a giant keyboard in an FAO Schwarz toy store, and uptight Susan rediscovering the child inside as she jumps with little-girl delight on the trampoline in Josh's apartment.

FYI: ▸ Tom Hanks's movingly sweet performance as the man-boy Josh in *Big* earned the gifted actor his first Academy Award nomination.

BIG BIRD

The warm, lovable, huggable, eight-foot-tall yellow canary with the innocence of a six-year-old is the Muppet most associated with the children's educational series *Sesame Street*. Muppets creator Jim Henson's associate Frank Oz once played this life-sized guy.

BIG BLUE MARBLE

Emmy-winning children's educational TV series, airing on PBS in the mid-1970s and marked by filmed snippets showcasing kids from other areas of the world. Because "Big Blue Marble" refers to what the earth looks like when seen from space, that became the title.

BIG BOY

The smiling, well-fed advertising kid dressed in the trademark red-and-white checkerboard jumper and named after the double-decker cheeseburger first sold at Bob Wian's restaurant in Glendale, California (Bob's Big Boy).

BIG BUDDY

Popular in the 1970s, this chewing gum from Bazooka was unique because of its twelve-inch-long, one-inch-wide ruler shape. It came in the usual sickeningly sweet flavors (Bubblegum, Grape, Cherry, and so on), and those of us who chewed it usually carried it in the back pocket of our pants (like the big comb, it always stuck out).

BIG COMB

Okay, you really had to have been a youth of the 1970s to understand the importance of this. An essential fashion accessory was a big plastic comb, usually manufactured by Goodie, which we stuck in the rear pocket of our pants. Why did we do such a silly thing, you ask? Remember, this was the era of feathered hair worn to perfection, and every so often we had to touch up the feathers because they would start to flounder (unless you glued them in place with Aqua Net Extra Super Hold hairspray, which wasn't the carefree and natural look desired). So, by wearing a handy big comb, all you had to do was reach in the back of your Angel Flights, pull it out, and feather away. Why was the comb so big? It had to be big enough to feather a whole side of hair in a single swipe, and the small black barber's combs just didn't do the job. The big drawback was when the school bully came up from behind and flicked you in the rear end with your own big comb. Black kids with Afros kept a big plastic pick in their back pockets.

BIG ETHEL MUGGS

This gangly, goofball of a bucktoothed gal from *Archie* comic books had a colossal crush on "Burger Boy" Jughead Jones, whose interest in girls, especially her, was zilch.

BIG EYES

"People either love them or hate them.
There's no middle ground."
—MARGARET KEANE

Believe it or not, these kitschy paintings of doleful waifs with extraordinary oversized eyes—which eerily followed a viewer around the room—were the best-selling art of the 1960s. San Francisco husband-and-wife artists Walter and Margaret Keane came up with the idea for the "Big Eyes" style after seeing the homeless postwar orphans of Europe while studying art in Paris during the 1940s. Their paintings depicted an emaciated child standing in a gloomy alleyway or dreary tenement hall, sometimes with a single teardrop streaming out of an eye or an equally undervalued kitten or puppy grasped in their hands. You couldn't help but feel sorry for them. The hoity-toity art world considered Keane paintings the epitome of bad taste, but the public loved them. (One sold for a $100,000, and another, titled "Tomorrow Forever," was chosen for the Hall of Education at the 1964 New York World's Fair.)

By the end of the 1960s, mass-produced prints of Keane Big Eyes, along with knockoffs by other artists—like Bruno Di Maio's harlequin-clad ballerinas, Lee's mod go-go kids, and Gig's puppies and kitties—were snatched up at dime stores and hung in homes across the nation. The wide-eye fad also inspired an array of dolls for little girls to nurture, such as Fun World's Suzy Sad Eyes and Hasbro's Little Miss No Name.

FYI: ▸ It's true! It's true! Keane was commissioned by film actress Joan Crawford to paint a portrait of her in the Big Eyes style (she placed it proudly in the living room of her Hollywood mansion), and comedian Jerry Lewis had one painted of him and his family, including their household pets.

BIGFOOT

Mythical North American apelike beast, allegedly seen in the forests of the Pacific Northwest and the swamps of the Deep South, also known as a Sasquatch.

BIGFOOT AND WILDBOY

Airing in 1979, a Saturday-morning adventure series originally seen as a segment of *The Krofft Supershow* from 1977 to 1978. Set in the wilderness of the Pacific Northwest, it centered on the adventures of a blond teen called Wildboy (Joe Butcher) who had been raised and cared for by benign Bigfoot (Ray Young), the hairy beast of American folklore.

BIG GULP

"The Big Gulp was the most profound invention of my generation."
—WINONA RYDER

The gigantic thirty-two-ounce 7-Eleven fountain drink that you served yourself was the first of its kind. Scary enough, but today the Big Gulp is a rather small drink compared to 7-Eleven's pee-inducing forty-four-ounce and sixty-four-ounce fountain drinks.

BIG HAIR

This was the trendy look in hair for the last half of the 1980s—a style so big, so wild, that it looked as if a woman had spent hours inside a dishwasher! Its early roots (no pun intended) were seen in the 1978 movie *Grease* when Olivia Newton-John's virginal Sandy metamorphosed into the "Tell me about it, Stud" spandex-wearing slut for the "You're the One That I Want" musical number. Olivia's smooth, blonde hair had been teased into an arousing and pretty messy 'do, unlike the "good girl" bob she had sported in earlier scenes. However, it wasn't until the mid-1980s that big hair, reminiscent of a bird's nest, caught on with younger women who were influenced by trendsetting Madonna (she adorned her disarrayed locks with lace and scarves).

To achieve this big, big look, after shampooing you had to blow-dry your hair—scrunch-styling as it dried (holding your head upside during this process helped a lot), then afterward tease it up and out while using a multitude of products, such as gels, hair sprays, and that great 1980s invention—mousse. If your hair wasn't blessed with any natural body, perms, particularly the spiral kind, and crimping irons helped. This all led the way to the horrifying sky-high mall-bang worn by female mall rats in the late 1980s and early 1990s.

BIG JIM

Introduced for boys in 1973, Mattel's answer to Hasbro's popular G.I. Joe was this dark-haired, seven-inch-tall action figure notable for biceps that actually bulged when his arms were flexed. But unlike warmonger Joe, a "fighting man from head to toe," Jim was a big jock, excelling in such sports-oriented activities as football, basketball, baseball, soccer, karate, camping, scuba diving, arctic exploration, and being a cowboy. He came with a variety of accessories, including a Corvette, a sports camper, a dune buggy, a speedboat, a safari jeep, a karate studio, and an Olympic ski run. Big Jim had three loyal buddies who joined him on outdoor adventures: bearded Big Josh, blond Big Jeff, and black Big Jack.

BIG MAC

Added to the McDonald's menu in 1968, this is the most famous of all fast-food hamburgers, thanks partly to a popular commercial jingle released during the Christmas 1974 season: "Two-all-beef-patties-special-sauce-lettuce-cheese-pickles-onions-on-a-sesame-seed-bun!" It listed all the hearty burger's ingredients, including the secret special sauce, which tasted a lot like Thousand Island salad dressing.

BIG WHEEL

Throughout the 1970s, it seemed as if every neighborhood in America echoed with the sound of this durable riding toy's big wheels zooming down sidewalks and driveways. Introduced by Marx Toys in 1969, the revolutionary Big Wheel was similar to a tricycle but more kick-ass! The low-slung, ground-hugging plastic rider had a trio of wheels: two wide ones in the back below the adjustable seat, and a big one (hence the name) in the front where the pedal was. Kids loved it because it was easy to ride, could go very fast, rarely tipped over during tight turns, and had a hand brake that created awesome spinouts. Some even came equipped with a rear "saddlebag" to store important stuff like candy, baseball cards, and rock collections.

FYI: ▸ Although geared toward children ages three to ten, the Big Wheel became popular with teenagers of the 1970s, who would steal them from neighborhood yards and use them for rowdy high jinks.

BIKER SHORTS

A late-1980s fashion statement, originating as apparel of sporting bicyclists. Made of stretchy and skin-tight Lycra material, these looked great worn by hot MTV dancers (especially peekabooing underneath a short skirt), but not so great on fat-ass women and men shopping at the local Wal-Mart.

BI-LEVEL

The most popular—and most overdone—hairdo of the 1980s was cut short on the sides, left longer in the back, spiked on the top, and looked great with headbands. Singer Olivia Newton-John is often credited with introducing it to the masses during her "Let's Get Physical" phase back in the early 1980s. Variations of the cut were seen on rock divas Pat Benatar, Chrissie Hynde, Joan Jett, and Sheena Easton. More recently, the outdated bi-level, a.k.a. Mullet, can often be found on male soccer players, trailer park trash, and lesbians.

BILL AND TED

"Excellent!" Whoa! In 1989, Bill S. Preston and Ted "Theodore" Logan, two airhead teens from San Dimas, California, took an "excellent adventure" through history via a time-traveling telephone booth. Two years later, they had a "bogus journey" to the afterlife, where they challenged the Grim Reaper in hell and met the almighty God. Played by dark-haired Keanu Reeves (Ted) and blond Alex Winter (Bill) in the movies *Bill and Ted's Excellent Adventure* and *Bill and Ted's Bogus Journey*. "Party on, dudes!"

FYI: ▸ The garage band Bill and Ted perform in is called Wyld Stallyns (both youngsters play the guitar).

BILL DAVIS

Surly but soft-spoken bachelor, living in a swank Manhattan penthouse with an English butler, who becomes a surrogate dad to his brother's three children: teenage Cissy and precious twin tots Buffy and Jody. Bill, played by Brian Keith on TV's *Family Affair*, worked as a highly paid consulting engineer.

"BILLIE JEAN"

Landing on the top of the charts for an incredible seven weeks in early 1983, Michael Jackson's song had him denying being the father of Billie Jean's illegitimate baby. It boasted a superstar-making music video in which Jackson displayed his now-legendary dance moves. The video also made history for being the first by a black artist to receive wide airplay on MTV.

BILLY BLASTOFF

"America's first boy in space!" Young lads of the late 1960s had hours of imaginary playtime with the plastic action-figure whose battery-operated jet pack powered his many space-age vehicles. Joined by robot friend Robbie, Billy could travel through rugged alien terrain in the Exploration Tractor, chart the moon's surface in the Lunar Crawler, or zip across wide-open intergalactic plains in his Space Car. The adventurous space scout came with a handy ray gun to give those dastardly Martians a zap or two.

"BILLY, DON'T BE A HERO"

This antiwar ditty, awash in a rousing drum roll, was one of the many tragic-story songs crowding the radio airwaves in the 1970s. It told the tale of Billy, an overenthusiastic fellow who enlists as a "Soldier

Blue" in spite of the wishes of his young fiancée. After being sent off to war, her desperate pleas of "Billy, don't be a hero / Don't be a fool with your life / Billy, don't be a hero / Come back and make me your wife" go unheard as he volunteers to aid his fellow soldiers in action. Subsequently, his bride-to-be receives the letter telling her that Billy had died a hero (she threw it away). The 1974 pop tune was first recorded by the British band Paper Lace ("The Night Chicago Died"), whose rendition hit number one in the United Kingdom, and later by Yankees Bo Donaldson and The Heywoods, who landed at the top of the American charts for two weeks.

BILLY JACK

"Once in a generation, a hero becomes a legend." Surprise 1971 box-office sensation, made popular by kids who loved its pseudo-hippie philosophy, thrilled over the kung fu action scenes, and sang along with the Top Forty theme song "One Tin Soldier" by pop group Coven ("Go ahead and hate your neighbor / Go ahead and cheat a friend . . ."). Peace-loving flower children at an interracial freedom school in rural Arizona are terrorized by rednecks from a nearby town. After the schoolteacher is raped and an Indian boy is killed, Billy Jack comes to the rescue. Half-Indian, half-white, this Vietnam vet (a Green Beret) and master of karate (hapkido, to be exact) believes in "an eye for an eye" and takes the law into his own hands to obtain justice.

The irony of this "champion of the helpless" (played by stone-faced Tom Laughlin) is that for being such a peace-preaching pacifist he uses a ton of violence to get the point across! Laughlin also directed, and real-life wife Delores Taylor played his girlfriend Jean, the raped teacher. Two sequels followed the cult film: *The Trial of Billy Jack* (1974) and *Billy Jack Goes to Washington* (1977).

BILLY JOE McALLISTER

Troubled Mississippi teen who jumped off the Tallahatchie Bridge in Bobbie Gentry's legendary 1967 country ballad "Ode to Billy Joe."

BINGO

The orange gorilla with the crazy grin who played the bongos for The Banana Splits rock group on their *Banana Splits* Saturday-morning TV program.

BIONIC WOMAN

A successful 1976 spin-off from the hit action series *The Six Million Dollar Man*, starring Lindsay Wagner as Jaime Sommers, onetime fiancée of astronaut Steve Austin (Lee Majors). After a skydiving accident left Jaime near dead, the same doctors who worked on Steve's operation reconstructed her body. The operation left her with superhuman capabilities—two bionic legs for great speed, a bionic right arm for powerful strength, and a bionic ear for incredible long-distance hearing. The Bionic Woman began her new life employed as an undercover agent on secret missions for the Office of Scientific Information (OSI), supervised by Oscar Goldman (Richard Anderson), working overtime as Steve's boss on the other Bionic series. The TV show ran until 1978.

BIRCHWOOD ELEMENTARY

The grade school attended by Charlie Brown and pals in Charles Schulz's beloved comic strip *Peanuts*.

BIRD

Side-stepping dance, involving hip movements and arms flapping like bird wings, that originated in Prince's 1984 film *Purple Rain* with the song "The Bird," performed by Morris Day and The Time. In 1987, another tune was added to the silly dance: Pee-Wee Herman's beach-oriented "Surfin' Bird" from *Back to the Beach*, starring Frankie Avalon and Annette Funicello.

BIRDS

> "It could be the most terrifying motion picture I have ever made!"
> —ALFRED HITCHCOCK

Still startling today, this horror masterpiece directed by Alfred Hitchcock was based on the ominous short story by Daphne du Maurier. The 1963 movie focuses on a small seaside town, Bodega Bay, in northern California, which came under a vicious attack by thousands of our usually benign feathered friends. Its cast is headed by icy blonde (a standard in Hitchcock movies) Tippi Hedren as Melanie Daniels, a spoiled socialite from San Francisco who comes to Bodega Bay bearing a gift of lovebirds for attractive, idealistic lawyer Mitch Brenner (Rod Taylor). Supporting actors include Jessica Tandy as Mitch's mother, Lydia, Veronica Cartwright as Mitch's little sister, Cathy, and Suzanne Pleshette as schoolteacher Annie Hayworth. Favorite scene: Melanie witnessing the steady arrival of hundreds of blackbirds outside the Bodega Bay school as the children inside sing a melancholy roundelay-type song ("She combed her hair but once a year / Ristle-te, rostle-te, now, now, now . . .") and the subsequent attack on the students as they flee from the school.

FYI: ▸ Alfred Hitchcock makes his customary cameo appearance at the start of the film, walking a pair of dogs (his own terriers) past the pet shop where Melanie purchases the lovebirds.

BIRKENSTOCKS

The ugly-looking but orthopedic-friendly soft-soled sandals with moldable footbed came to the United States from Germany in 1966. Most often seen on the feet of hippies, granola heads, and lesbians.

BIZZY BUZZ BUZZ

First manufactured in the 1960s, this buzzing electric pen in the shape of a busy bee wrote in squiggly, wiggly lines by way of its stinger.

B.J. AND THE BEAR

Capitalizing on the trucking and CB craze, this NBC-TV adventure (1979–81) starred handsome Greg Evigan as Billie Joe "B.J." McCay, a Vietnam vet from Milwaukee who traveled American highways as a trucker driving a big red-and-white eight-wheeler with a chimpanzee named Bear riding shotgun. The series had independent trucker B.J. hounded by a succession of corrupt law officers, most notable being Sheriff Elroy P. Lobo (Claude Akins). A no-brainer (ideal for those who thought the sophomoric plots of *The Dukes of Hazzard* were hard to follow), the fast-moving show played it for laughs and dished up plenty of scantily clad women, along with wild car- and truck-chase scenes.

In 1981, B.J. and his Bear settled down to run a trucking company in Southern California, Bear Enterprises, aided by a crew of seven foxy female truckers, including ditzy blonde Stacks (played by ditzy blonde Judy Landers) and twins Teri and Geri (played by real-life twins Candi and Randi Brough, a.k.a. the Wrigley's Doublemint Twins). Multitalented Evigan sang the theme song.

FYI: ▸ B.J.'s CB handle was "Milwaukee Kid."

BLACK BEAUTY

The nickname of superhero Green Hornet's slick, supercharged jet-black 1966 Chrysler Imperial sedan, which was driven by his chauffeur-sidekick Kato.

BLACK BELT JONES

Popular 1974 blaxploitation flick starring Jim Kelly in the title role as a relentless kung-fu fighter battling the sinister Syndicate to save his school of martial arts, located in the Watts area of Los Angeles.

BLACK CAULDRON

"Whosoever uses the Black Cauldron for evil will be all-powerful, for my blood will flow with his, and together we will either rule the world or destroy it." Released in 1985, Disney's twenty-fifth full-length animated film is notable for not having a single song or musical number in it. Centuries ago, in the land of Prydain, a young pig-keeper named Taran is given the task of protecting Hen Wen, a magical pig who knows the whereabouts of the mystical Black Cauldron, a device of immeasurable power. With pig in tow, the heroic lad is sent on a quest to find the cursed Black Cauldron and destroy it. This is not an easy task, for an evil despot—the deep-voiced, skull-faced Horned King—and his undead army will stop at nothing to get the Cauldron. Carrying a magic sword, Taran is helped along the way by mischievous Gurgi, an indescribable creature; spunky Eilonway, a princess held captive by Horned King; and cowardly Fflewddur Fflam, a wandering minstrel.

The Black Cauldron was based on Lloyd Alexander's *Chronicles of Prydain*, a five-volume fantasy based on Welsh mythology, first published in 1965. Costing $25 million, one of Disney's most expensive films, it is rumored to have been in production for up to ten years, plagued with delays throughout by animator retirements, strikes, and management changes. However, its uniqueness in story and beautiful watercolor animation make it a must-see not only for Disney fans but also for those who enjoy a good sword-and-sorcery yarn.

BLACK STALLION

Outstanding screen version of Walter Farley's 1941 story about a young American boy and a wild Arabian stallion stranded on a deserted island after surviving a shipwreck. Distant strangers at first, Alec Ramsey (Kelly Reno) and the majestic black thoroughbred eventually warm up to each other and develop a strong friendship. When rescued, they are brought to Alec's hometown, where "the Black" is considered uncontrollable until he's trained for a championship race. Directed by Carroll Ballard, the 1979 movie's forty-five-minute island sequence, sans dialogue, has to have some of the most stunning imagery ever filmed. *The Black Stallion* costarred Teri Garr as Alec's mother and Mickey Rooney (giving an Oscar-nominated performance) as Henry Dailey, a retired horse trainer. A sequel, *The Black Stallion Returns*, followed it in 1983.

FYI: ▸ Galloping alongside Black as well-loved equines of children's lit are Anna Sewell's *Black Beauty*, Marguerite Henry's *Misty of Chincoteague* and *Sea Star*, and Mary O'Hara's *Flicka* and *Thunderhead* (son of Flicka).

BLACULA

Entertaining black-oriented horror movie about eighteenth-century African Prince Mamuwalde (William Marshall), who is turned into a vampire after being bitten by the original Count Dracula. Mamuwalde wakes up a century later in modern-day Los Angeles, circa 1972, where he roams the city streets to drink the blood of homosexuals, whores, and—potentially—sexpot Pam Grier. Followed by a sequel, *Scream Blacula Scream* (1973), and a score of soul-brother fright films, including *Blackenstein* (1973), *Black Werewolf* (1974), and *Dr. Black, Mr. Hyde* (1976).

FYI: ▸ In the 1980s, William Marshall played the King of Cartoons, a crown-adorned royal who regularly introduced a cartoon short on Saturday morning's *Pee-Wee's Playhouse*.

BLAIR, LINDA

Born on January 22, 1959, the chubby-cheeked, baby-voiced actress made a spectacular film debut as the head-spinning, vomit-spitting, devil-possessed Regan in the 1973 horror classic *The Exorcist*. The performance earned the fourteen-year-old an Oscar nomination for Best Supporting Actress (she lost to even younger Tatum O'Neal) and stereotyped her as America's favorite put-upon teen. Big-screen roles to follow were pretty uneventful, as she was cast in mediocre movies: *Airport 1975* (1974), *Exorcist II: The Heretic* (1977), and *Roller Boogie* (1979).

A trio of controversial TV movies in the 1970s is what Blair became better known for. In these, she played youths who suffer from a number of indignities, including a fourteen-year-old runaway sent to a tough detention home where she is raped with a broom handle (*Born Innocent*); a fifteen-year-old AA candidate (*Sarah T.: Portrait of a Teenage Alcoholic*); and a sixteen-year-old kidnapped by an escaped mental patient and whisked away to his "Xanadu" (*Sweet Hostage*). She made headlines in 1979 when she was put on probation for three years after being found guilty on drug charges. As a mature actress, she maintained her baby face and childlike quality and once again became typecast, this time as a put-upon adult suffering numerous indignities in violent R-rated exploitation horror and prison flicks, most notably *Hell Night* (1981), *Chained Heat* (1983), and *Red Heat* (1985).

BLAIR WARNER

"I just had one of my brilliant ideas." Rich, beautiful, and snobbish, the blonde debutante thought the world revolved around her. She attended the distinguished Eastland School for Young Women, and later Langley College, on the TV sitcom *The Facts of Life*. Played by juvenile actress Lisa Whelchel, formerly of *The New Mickey Mouse Club*.

FYI: ▸ In 1999, a spoof of indie horror sensation *The Blair Witch Project* was titled *The Blair Warner Project*.

BLAIR WITCH

In Burkittsville, a small town nestled among the thick trees of the Black Hills Forest in North Central Maryland, the townfolk whisper an age-old legend about an evil being called "The Blair Witch." Back in 1785, a woman named Elly Kedward in the township of Blair (where Burkittsville now stands) was accused of witchcraft by a group of children. After being found guilty, Elly was banished from Blair during a particularly hard winter and cast out into the surrounding woods, where she died. Or did she? Ever since, the region has been stricken with supernatural disappearances and murders, including a series of child killings in the 1940s.

The last known incident occurred in October 1994, when three Montgomery College filmmakers—Heather Donahue, Joshua Leonard, and Michael Williams—disappeared in the woods near Burkittsville while shooting a documentary about the Blair Witch. So, if you happen to be in the woods and come across creepy stick figures, stop what you are doing. Leave right away! It could be a warning sign that Elly Kedward, the Blair Witch, is nearby.

In 1999, *The Blair Witch Project*, a mock documentary filmed by young directors Daniel Myrick and Eduardo Sanchez on a budget of only $40,000, grossed a whopping $130 million at the box office! Its shaky camerawork made many moviegoers motion sick.

BLAKE CARRINGTON

Veteran TV actor John Forsythe starred as the debonair, silver-haired family patriarch and millionaire oil tycoon (Denver-Carrington Oil Company) on prime time's *Dynasty* from 1981 to 1989.

BLANC, MEL

Bugs Bunny. Daffy Duck. Porky Pig. Speedy Gonzalez. Elmer Fudd. Tweety Pie. Sylvester the Cat. Yosemite Sam. The Road Runner. As often as not, the voices of the legendary Warner Brothers cartoon characters, known as Looney Tunes, were contributed by comic genius Mel Blanc (1908–89), "The Man of 1,000 Voices." Blanc also provided the voice of many Hanna-Barbera characters, such as Barney Rubble, Dino the Dinosaur, Secret Squirrel, Speed Buggy, and Captain Caveman.

FYI: ▸ Mel Blanc's tombstone reads "That's All, Folks."

BLAXPLOITATION

"Black is Beautiful!" A genre of filmmaking whose name was derived from Hollywood's exploitation of the hip and happenin' black culture of the early 1970s. These quick-paced, low-budget, ultraviolent, action-packed films were generally set in an urban black community and centered on a sexy cool dude or a foxy chick who battled white racists, drug kingpins, pimps, and other lowlife street criminals. The archetypal blaxploitation flick was often named after the story's central hero (for example, *Shaft*, *Coffy*, *Cleopatra Jones*, *Black Belt Jones*, *Black Caesar*, *Slaughter*, *Superfly*, and *Sweet Sweetback's Baad Asssss Song*) and featured a predominantly black cast.

BLESS THE BEASTS AND CHILDREN

The 1971 movie about six young misfits at the Box Canyon Boys Camp in Arizona who rebel against their counselors to liberate a herd of buffalo from slaughter at a nearby reserve. Based on the 1971 novel by Glendon Swarthout, the pro-ecological drama was directed by Stanley Kramer and starred Billy "Will Robinson" Mumy as Teft, along with Barry Robins as Cotton, Miles Chapin as Shecker, Darel Glaser as Goodenow, Bob Kramer as Lally 1, and Marc Vahanian as Lally 2. Its soundtrack featured the Oscar-nominated title song by The Carpenters and the haunting instrumental "Cotton's Dream" by Barry DeVorzon and Perry Potkin Jr.

BLOB

"Whatever it is, it's getting bigger!" A red blob of goo from outer space that grows larger and larger as it gulps up every living thing it comes in contact with. The Blob dislikes cold temperatures. Featured in the 1958 movie *The Blob*, starring Steve McQueen and followed by a 1972 sequel *Beware! The Blob* and by a 1988 remake, *The Blob*. Also the subject of a Top Forty song, "The Blob" (1958), by The Five Blobs.

BLONDIE **(COMIC STRIP)**

Cartoonist Chic Young's beloved newspaper comic strip about quintessential middle-class husband and father Dagwood Bumstead and his dingy but somehow sensible blonde wife, Blondie, in which Dagwood's domestic misadventures took center stage. Since 1930, the durable strip has had hapless Dagwood dealing with the shenanigans of offspring, son Alexander (formerly "Baby Dumpling") and teen daughter Cookie, clashing with know-it-all neighbor Herb Woodley and irascible boss Mr. Dithers, colliding with postman Mr. Beasley, and attempting ill-fated afternoon naps. All this while lovable spouse Blondie—competent as always—watches, ready to help him out of a jam. The Bumstead's pet dog, Daisy, seemed to be always having puppies. The popularity of *Blondie* inspired a movie series with more than two dozen films (from 1938 to 1950), starring Penny Singleton as Blondie and Arthur Lake as Dagwood, a 1940s radio program, and two prime-time TV shows (one airing on NBC in 1957 and the other on CBS in 1968).

FYI: ▸ Dagwood had an affection for oversized, multilayered sandwiches, which became known as "Dagwoods" in pop culture lingo.

BLONDIE (ROCK BAND)

The band from New York City that got its name from the bleached-blonde locks of charismatic lead singer Deborah Harry, once labeled the "sex symbol of punk rock" because of her Marilyn Monroe-esque demeanor. Other members included Harry's guitarist boyfriend Chris Stein, guitarist Frank Infante, bassist Gary Valentine, keyboardist Jimmy Destri, and drummer Clem Burke. Blondie's innovative Top Forty hits included the disco-flavored "Heart of Glass" (1979), the reggae-inspired "The Tide Is High" (1980), the surreal rap "Rapture," (1981), "One Way or Another" (1979), "Dreaming" (1979), and "Call Me" (1980), from the Richard Gere movie *American Gigolo*.

FYI: ▸ Blondie's original band name was Angel and The Snakes.

BLOODY MARY

Bloody Mary (Yikes!). Bloody Mary (Eek!). Bloody Mary (Oh my gawwwwwd!). The famous urban legend has it that if you say Bloody Mary's name three times while standing in front of a mirror, her ghostly spirit will emerge to murder you. This was the basis for the 1992 horror film *Candyman*, starring Virginia Madsen and Tony Todd.

BLOSSOM

NBC-TV sitcom, airing from 1991 to 1994, starring Mayim Bialik as Blossom Russo, a feisty thirteen-year-old who used a "video diary" to record her daily feelings and thoughts. She lived with her divorced musician father, Nick Russo (Ted Wass), and two older brothers: substance-abusing Anthony (Michael Stoyanov) and dim-witted cutie-pie Joey (Joey Lawrence). Jenna Von Oy co-starred as Blossom's quirky pal Six, so-named for being the sixth child in her family. The program's young female audience made Joey the hot teen heartthrob of the early 1990s. His popularity led to minor success as a recording artist with the 1993 hit "Nothin' My Love Can't Fix."

BLUE FALCON

Alias of millionaire Bradley Crown, a blue-caped superhero with a modulated voice who teamed up with a clumsy robot canine in Hanna-Barbera's Saturday-morning cartoon show *Dynomutt, Dog Wonder*. The duo resided at Crown's mansion, called Falcon's Lair, and sped about in the awesome Falcon Car to fight criminals in Big City.

BLUE LAGOON

Released in the summer of 1980, this was nothing more than a soft-core porn flick aimed at teenagers. It starred dark-haired teen sex symbol / Calvin Klein model Brooke Shields as Emmeline, and curly-haired blond stud muffin Christopher Atkins as Richard, two nineteenth-century teenagers shipwrecked since childhood on a South Seas island. Directed by Randal Kleiser, the movie focused on their growing love and sexual feelings for each other while offering gorgeous tropical scenery mixed with teasing peekaboo shots of the sexy leads (including a view of Atkins's penis during a swim scene).

FYI: ▸ While shooting *The Blue Lagoon*, Brooke had to have her long locks glued to her budding breasts so nothing would show.

BLUES BROTHERS

Dan Aykroyd and John Belushi's sketch as Jake and Elwood Blues, black-suited, sunglass-wearing leaders of a blues musical revue on NBC's *Saturday Night Live*, led to a blockbuster 1980 movie, *The Blues Brothers*, and a string of Top Forty hits, "Soul Man" (1979), "Rubber Biscuit" (1979), and "Gimme Some Lovin'" (1980). Revived in the 1990s with *Roseanne*'s John Goodman replacing the deceased Belushi, who had died from a drug overdose on March 5, 1982.

BLUME, JUDY
Controversial best-selling author of teenage fiction (born February 12, 1938, in New Jersey), whose novels and their frank and sometimes explicit treatment of touchy subjects—such as sexual development, menstruation, masturbation, and losing one's virginity—were coveted by a generation of female puberty victims. Works include the legendary *Are You There God? It's Me, Margaret* (1970), *Freckle Juice* (1971), *Tales of a Fourth Grade Nothing* (1972), *Otherwise Known as Sheila the Great* (1972), *Deenie* (1973), *Blubber* (1974), *Forever* (1975), *Starring Sally J. Freedman as Herself* (1977), *Superfudge* (1980), and *Tiger Eyes* (1981). She is frequently the target of so-called "family values" advocates who are fond of censoring books.

BLUTH, DON
A former animator for Disney who set up his own film company in the 1980s and made high-quality features like *The Secret of NIMH* (1982), *An American Tail* (1986), *The Land Before Time* (1988), *All Dogs Go to Heaven* (1989), *Rock-a-Doodle* (1991), *Thumbelina* (1994), *The Pebble and the Penguin* (1995), and *Anastasia* (1997). Bluth also created the video games Dragon's Lair (1983) and Space Ace (1984).

BLUTO
Popeye's archrival, a big, brutish lug of a man also known as Brutus, who was out to steal the good-hearted sailor's spindly rosebud, Olive Oyl, in the *Popeye* cartoons. Bluto got his just desserts when Popeye ate spinach, which gave him superhuman powers.

BLYTHE
Introduced by Kenner Toys in 1972, Blythe was one of the weirdest fashion dolls around. She had a gigantic oversized head and enormous round eyes, which made her look as if she'd stepped out of a Keane Big Eyes picture. But the really odd thing about her was that by pulling a ring attached to a string on the back of her head, her eyes would close and reopen with a different color and expression. Imagine: orange eyes looking downward, blue eyes looking upward, green eyes looking right, and pink eyes looking left. Pretty eerie.

BOARD GAMES
Board games, with their colorful packaging, enticing game boards, and iconic playing pieces, are popular with just about everyone. No matter what your taste, there's a game out there for you. Besides testing your knowledge (Go to the Head of the Class) or skill (Operation) or luck (Trouble), they are fun to play and a great way to interact socially with others. Milton Bradley has been by far the leading producer of board games, followed by Parker Brothers. Ideal Toys was the main producer of action games during the 1960s and 1970s.

The following is a list of fifty classic board and action games that have been favorites of ours from early childhood (Candy Land) to adult years (Trivial Pursuit). Some are associated strictly with the Baby Boom generation (Rock 'Em Sock 'Em Robots), while others are playtime mainstays that have been around for decades (Monopoly). Hopefully this will bring back happy memories of the games you played, in which you chanced it all at the spin of a wheel or the toss of dice. After each game's name are the manufacturer and debut year.

Aggravation—Co-5 Company, 1962
Ants in the Pants—Schaper, 1968
Barrel of Monkeys— Lakeside, 1969
Battleship—Milton Bradley, 1967
Battling Tops— Ideal, 1968
Booby-Trap—Parker Brothers, 1965
Candy Land—Milton Bradley, 1955
Chutes and Ladders—Milton Bradley, 1943
Clue—Parker Brothers, 1949
Connect Four—Milton Bradley, 1979
Cootie—Schaper, 1948
Don't Break the Ice—Schaper, 1967
Don't Spill the Beans—Schaper, 1967
The Game of Life—Milton Bradley, 1960
Gnip Gnop—Parker Brothers, 1971
Go to the Head of the Class—Milton Bradley, 1938
Green Ghost—Transogram, 1965
Hands Down—Ideal, 1964
Headache—Kohner, 1968
Hi-Ho Cherry-O—Whitman, 1960
Hungry Hungry Hippos—Milton Bradley, 1980
Kaboom—Ideal, 1966
KerPlunk—Ideal, 1967

The Last Straw—Schaper, 1966
Mastermind—Invicta, 1972
Miss Popularity—Transogram, 1961
Monopoly—Parker Brothers, 1935
Mouse Trap—Ideal, 1963
Mystery Date—Milton Bradley, 1965
Operation—Milton Bradley, 1965
Ouija—Parker Brothers, 1967
Pass Out: The Drinking Game—Pass Out, 1962
Perfection—Lakeside, 1973
Pictionary—Western Publishing, 1985
Rebound—Ideal, 1971
Risk!—Parker Brothers,1959
Rock 'Em Sock 'Em Robots—Marx, 1966
Scrabble—Selchow & Righter, 1953
Skittle-Bowl—Aurora, 1969
Sorry—Parker Brothers, 1950
Stay Alive—Milton Bradley, 1971
Stratego—Milton Bradley, 1961
Time Bomb—Milton Bradley, 1964
Tip-It—Ideal, 1965
Toss Across—Ideal, 1969
Trivial Pursuit—Selchow & Righter, 1981
Trouble—Kohner, 1965
Twister—Milton Bradley, 1966
Which Witch?—Milton Bradley, 1970
Yahtzee—E. S. Lowe, 1956

BOBA FETT
Mean and menacing, the helmet-wearing *Star Wars* character is the best bounty hunter in the whole Galaxy.

BOBBY BRADY
The imaginative youngest son of the Brady clan who tags alongside his older brothers, Greg and Peter, and idolizes western outlaw Jesse James and football great Joe Namath. Bobby was ultrasensitive about his small size (it didn't help matters that Sam the Butcher referred to him as "Shrimpo"). Played by Mike Lookinland (born December 19, 1960, in Utah) on the TV sitcom *The Brady Bunch*.

BOBBY EWING
Unlike his evil brother J.R., the youngest Ewing son (played by Patrick Duffy on the hit prime-time soap opera *Dallas*) was blessed with good morals. Bobby married sexy Pamela Barnes, daughter of the Ewing family's rival Digger Barnes, and one year he died—but it was only a dream.

BODEGA BAY
A freaky thing happened to this tranquil California coastal town, located south of San Francisco, in 1963. Hundreds of birds of every variety swarmed the fictional Bodega Bay and in turn attacked the unsuspecting citizens, including schoolchildren and diners at a local restaurant. Seen in director Alfred Hitchcock's silver-screen thriller *The Birds*.

BO DONALDSON AND THE HEYWOODS
The Cincinnati-based group—Bo Donaldson, Rick Joswick, Mike Gibbons, Nicky Brunetti, Gary Coveyou, Dave Krock, and Scott Baker—was a favorite of the *Tiger Beat* crowd because every single member was cute and hunky. Their version of Paper Lace's "Billy, Don't Be a Hero" sold a million copies and landed at the top of the American charts in 1974.

BO DUKE
John Schneider's Southern charm and country-blond good looks made this TV character from *The Dukes of Hazzard* one of TV's hottest hunks of the early 1980s.

BODY ON TAP
Shampoo enriched with beer (yes, beer), because in the 1970s it was believed that the nutrients in beer gave extra body and shine to lifeless hair. However, for those looking to get drunk, this shampoo wasn't recommended for drinking.

BODY PIERCING
Do you remember when it was considered taboo for a man to wear an earring? And that if he did, it had to be in the left ear because an earring in the right meant he was gay? The late 1980s saw a change in attitude as men started piercing the left ear, the right ear, or even both ears (those too chicken to pierce clipped ear cuffs on their lobes). During this era, daring women multipierced their earlobes. In the 1990s, having holes in the ear wasn't cool enough, so youths pierced their nose, eyebrows, lips, tongue, navel, nipples, and genitalia (a ring in the penis is known as a "Prince Albert"). Many did it to look hip

or for shock value, but by today's standards body piercings are common and go unnoticed.

FYI: ▸ Alicia Silverstone's belly-button ring in the 1993 Aerosmith "Cryin'" video is credited as inspiring young women to partake in body piercing.

BODY SNATCHERS

"You're next!" Invading space pods that duplicate humans while they sleep, turning them into emotionless humanoids. Seen in the 1956 sci-fi classic *Invasion of the Body Snatchers* and the 1978 and 1994 remakes.

BOLO TIES

Introduced to the mainstream fashion world following the Urban Cowboy craze of the 1980s, these country neckties were skinny cords of leather worn around the neck and held together in the center with some sort of ornate clip. (You got extra fashion points if the clip had a turquoise design.)

BOMBER JACKETS

Brown leather aviation jackets made fashionably popular by Tom Cruise in his hit 1986 movie *Top Gun*.

BONANZA

Airing Sunday nights on NBC from 1959 to 1973, this was the second longest-running western in the history of TV (*Gunsmoke* was first) and one of the highest-rated programs throughout the 1960s. Set in Virginia City, Nevada, in the 1860s, it told the story of the Cartwrights, prosperous owners of a ranch called the Ponderosa. The patriarch of the homestead was widower Ben Cartwright (Lorne Greene), who had raised three sons alone: eldest Adam (Pernell Roberts), middle son Hoss (Dan Blocker), and youngest Little Joe (Michael Landon). Chinaman Hop Sing (Victor Sen Yung) was the household's loyal cook. Family friendly, the show focused more on the relationships between the Cartwrights and the cowpokes they encountered each week (played by different guest stars), and when a disagreement arose—put away the six-shooters—they settled it with peaceful words or, if that failed, a good old-fashioned fistfight.

FYI: ▸ *Bonanza* was the first western to be televised in color.

BONGO

A red-jacketed little circus bear riding a unicycle who leaves the big top, where he had been mistreated, and falls in love with a sweet girl bear named Lulubelle. But before he can win her heart, he has to confront a villainous rival bear, Lumpjaw. Based on a story by Sinclair Lewis and featured in Walt Disney's big-screen compilation *Fun and Fancy Free* (1947).

BON JOVI

New Jersey hard-rock band, fronted by photogenic, big-tressed Jon Bon Jovi (born John Francis Bongiovi on March 2, 1962), the son of a former Playboy Bunny mother and hairdresser father. With such hits as "You Give Love a Bad Name" (1986), "Livin' on a Prayer" (1987), "Wanted Dead or Alive" (1987), and "Bad Medicine" (1988), Bon Jovi opened the Top Forty door for other "hair metal" bands of the era, such as Poison and Motley Crue. Other members included guitarist Richie Sambora, keyboardist Dave Bryan, bassist Alec Such, and drummer Tico Torres. Cutie-pies Jon and Richie gave teen girls—who wore their hair as huge as Bon Jovi's record sales—an alternative to then-current New Wave heartthrobs, like Duran Duran, George Michael, and Corey Hart.

FYI: ▸ Call it smooth, savvy, or just plain lucky, Bon Jovi's producers had selected teens rate thirty of the tunes being considered for the *Slippery When Wet* (1986) LP. The highest-rated one made it onto the album, which topped the American charts for eight weeks and sold fourteen million copies worldwide.

BONNE BELL LIP SMACKERS

"I'm crackers over Lip Smackers!" For most teeny-bopper girls, a tube of this classic lip gloss, which came in a gazillion yummy flavors, was the first cosmetic their parents allowed them to wear. Introduced in 1973, Bonne Bell Lip Smackers are commonly found at drugstores and five-and-dimes. They come in two sizes: "the small one," often carried in the back pocket of a girl's jeans alongside her plastic comb, and the "big one," worn on a rope around her neck. For Christmas, Lip Smackers are packaged in a clear candy-cane-shaped container that makes a swell stocking stuffer.

The extraordinary Lip Smackers flavors over the years have included Cola, Dr. Pepper (the most popular flavor), 7-Up, Root Beer, Orange, Grape, Cherry, Strawberry, Raspberry, Watermelon, Lemon, Lime, Banana, Coconut, Peppermint, Wintergreen, Bubble Gum, Tootsie Roll, Good & Plenty, Chocolate, Cherry Chocolate, and Chocolate Mint.

FYI: ▸ It used to be that when a teen girl had a hot date the Lip Smacker she chose was important because it would be her date's first taste when his lips touched hers. (We hope he liked Dr. Pepper.)

BOO
Feline specter from the year 1776 who wore a feathered Revolutionary War cap and belonged to cowardly Jonathan Muddlemore, a specter as well, on the 1970s cartoon show *The Funky Phantom*. Boo loathed the unghostly bulldog Elmo.

BOO BERRY
Introduced in 1972, an amiable blue ghost with Peter Lorre's voice who advertises the same-named cereal featuring blueberry flavor marshmallow bits. Boo Berry is part of General Mills' popular monster cereal line, which includes Frankenberry, Count Chocula, and both the late great Fruit Brute and Yummy Mummy.

BOO BOO BEAR
"I don't think the ranger's gonna like this, Yogi." Yogi Bear's little cub companion at Jellystone Park who—although loyally abetting—continually points out the evil of Yogi's freeloading, basket-nabbing ways. Boo Boo is featured in Hanna-Barbera's classic *Yogi Bear* cartoons.

BOO BOO KITTY
This black stuffed toy cat was Shirley Feeney's beloved good-luck charm on ABC-TV's *Laverne and Shirley*. I think Shirley's brawny boyfriend Carmine Ragusa won it for her at a carnival, or something like that.

BOOGEYMAN

> "I check under my bed every night for the boogeyman."
> —TORI SPELLING, ACTRESS

No one actually knows who he is or what he looks like, we just know he's real scary and hides under the bed, in closets, upstairs in the attic, or down in the basement!

BOONE'S FARM STRAWBERRY HILL
A rite of passage for many teens in the 1970s was getting drunk for the first time. Not just drunk, but stinking drunk from a bottle of this inexpensive (okay, cheap), sweet-tasting pink wine. After chugging the bottle empty (back then, there was no such thing as pacing), you weren't prepared for how stumbling wasted you got: falling everywhere, making a fool out of yourself until eventually retching pink chunks all over the place (hopefully not in your best friend's car), passing out, and waking up the next morning feeling like death warmed over.

Of course, if mom found out about your hangover, she wouldn't have any sympathy. First came the guilt trip about how disappointed she is and something about higher expectations. Next came the booming noises as she vacuumed in close proximity, moved furniture around, and banged pots and pans in the kitchen. (Even though you were on the other side of the house, a hangover made it seem like you were right beside her.) Then she would make you get out of bed at nine o'clock on Saturday morning to do some unnecessary chore that could wait until next week, if not next month. You swear under your breath that you will never touch a drop of alcohol again. The next weekend you chug a bottle of Mad Dog 20-20. . . .

FYI: ▸ The legal drinking age back in the 1970s was eighteen.

BOP BAGS
Made out of inflatable vinyl, these standing punching bags had weighted bottoms that allowed them to bounce back up after being karate chopped. They came as colorful characters, including Bamm-Bamm Rubble, Magilla Gorilla, Bullwinkle, Popeye, and Bozo the Clown.

BOP IT
"Twist it! Pull it! Bop it! Pass it!" Lively electronic party game that has players twisting, pulling, and bopping a button, knob, or ratchet on a thingamajig, making all kinds of beat rhythms before passing

it on to the next person. First manufactured by Parker Brothers in 1997, the game's object—besides annoying those not playing—is for challengers to follow a sound-effects pattern without messing up (it's similar to Milton Bradley's Simon).

"BORDERLINE"

This early tune, released in the spring of 1984, was Madonna's very first gold single (more than twenty more gold singles would follow) and her first to land in *Billboard* magazine's Top Ten. Its video clip had everyone's favorite "boy-toy" angst-in-love over a James Dean-esque guy at a pool hall.

BORN FREE

> "She was born free,
> she has the right to stay free."
> —JOY ADAMSON, NATURALIST

Classic best-selling book (number one for thirteen weeks in 1960) about the adventures of Kenyan game warden George Adamson and his wife, Joy (the author), who raised an orphaned lion cub named Elsa in captivity. When the lioness reaches maturity, she is threatened with confinement in a zoo, but George and Joy set her free"as free as the wind blows, as free as the grass grows"—by teaching her how to survive in the African wilderness. The heartwarming tale inspired two sequels, *Living Free* and *Forever Free*, and an enormously popular 1966 motion picture, *Born Free*, starring Bill Travers and Virginia McKenna (married in real life) as George and Joy. Its uplifting title theme, by John Barry and Don Black, won an Academy Award for Best Song and became a Top Forty hit for Roger Williams (Matt Munro sang it in the movie).

FYI: ▸ *Born Free* was the grandmother of the "save the animals" film genre, whose litter included *Charlie, the Lonesome Cougar* (1967), *Gentle Giant* (1967), *Bless the Beasts and Children* (1971), *Napoleon and Samantha* (1972), *All Creatures Great and Small* (1974), *The Bears and I* (1974), *Free Willy* (1993), *Andre* (1994), and *Fly Away Home* (1996).

BORN INNOCENT

The once-controversial tele-pic contained the shocking shower scene of Linda Blair being raped with a broomstick in a girl's juvenile detention home by her fellow inmates. (The infamous footage is now cut from the film due to complaints from parental watch groups.) Blair starred as Chris Parker, a fourteen-year-old delinquent and habitual runaway who has the misfortune of being sent to the California Home for Girls, where she is forced to adapt to its terrifying environment. Airing in 1974, this marked Blair's TV movie debut as everyone's favorite put-upon teen. It was also a precursor of her future motion-picture roles. Throughout the 1980s, she starred in a series of R-rated, low-budget women's prison dramas, including *Chained Heat* (1983), *Savage Island* (1985), *Red Heat* (1985), and *Bail Out* (1989).

BOSOM BUDDIES

Before Tom Hanks became a big movie star, hailed as "the Jimmy Stewart of the 1990s," he acted in this silly but charming TV sitcom airing on ABC from 1980 to 1982. Paying homage to the guys-in-drag story line of the Tony Curtis–Jack Lemmon–Marilyn Monroe classic *Some Like It Hot* (1959), it starred Hanks and Peter Scolari as Kip Wilson and Henry Desmond. Fresh out of college and working at a Manhattan ad agency, these two ordinary guys disguise themselves as sisters, Buffy (Hanks) and Hildegarde (Scolari), so they could live at a low-rent, all-girl residence, the Susan B. Anthony Hotel. Buffy and Hildy weren't pretty girls—they were rather masculine—but the female hallmates at the hotel never really caught on to the charade; they just thought they were two homely gals with good personalities.

Supporting cast included former Miss Virginia Donna Dixon as hallmate Sonny Lumet, a naive blonde bombshell (in the Monroe mold) who worked as a nurse and would later become Kip's girlfriend (she thought Kip was Buffy's brother); Wendie Jo Sperber as hallmate Amy Cassidy, a plump jokester with a whopping crush on Henry, who was a receptionist where the boys worked and co-conspirer of their masquerade; and Telma Hopkins (of Tony Orlando and Dawn fame) as hallmate Isabel Hammond, a sassy aspiring actress.

BOSSA NOVA

Sexy, sophisticated music and dance movement combining samba and jazz. Originating from the beaches of Rio de Janeiro, particularly the beach of Ipanema, it became a household word of Middle America in the 1960s. The best of bossa nova would include the jaunty "Blame It on the Bossa Nova" (1963), performed by Eydie Gormé, and Antonio Carlos Jobim's Grammy-winning "The Girl from Ipanema" (1964), recorded by saxophonist Stan Getz and vocalist-guitarist João Gilberto and featuring the wistful vocals of Astrud Gilberto (João's wife), the Brazilian spokeswoman of bossa nova.

FYI: ▸ The term "bossa nova" is Portuguese for "new wave."

BOWIE, DAVID

Known as the "Thin White Duke" because of his fair skin and slender appearance, the British superstar was an androgynous-looking, bizarrely decorated theatrical-based singer whose ever-changing career influenced future generations of musicians from various rock-music genres—psychedelic, glam, glitter, punk, New Wave, modern, techno, and Goth. He was born David Jones on January 8, 1947, and his musical breakthrough occurred with the release of the futuristic conceptual album *The Rise and Fall of Ziggy Stardust and the Spiders from Mars*. Hit songs: "The Man Who Sold the World" (1972), "Space Oddity" (1973), "Young Americans" (1975), "Fame" (1975), "Golden Years" (1976), "Ashes to Ashes" (1980), "Let's Dance" (1983), "China Girl" (1983), "Modern Love" (1983), and two duets: "Under Pressure" (1981) with Queen, and a remake of Martha Reeves's hit "Dancing in the Street" (1983) with Mick Jagger.

Beginning in 1976, Bowie added movie star to his roster, playing an extra-terrestrial in the cult sci-fi film, *The Man Who Fell to Earth*. Other movies included *Just a Gigolo* (1979), *The Hunger* (1983), *Merry Christmas, Mr. Lawrence* (1983), *Absolute Beginners* (1986), and *Labyrinth* (1986). Although an open bisexual (he allegedly had a sexual affair with Jagger), his sexual preference seems to be strictly the female sex, most notable being first wife Angie Barnett (they named their son Zowie Bowie) and second wife Iman, the supermodel from Ethiopia.

FYI: ▸ David Bowie possesses two-different colored eyes: one blue, the other brown.

BOY BANDS, 1990S

Backstreet Boys. 'N Sync. 98 Degrees. You had to have been a teenage girl in the late 1990s to tell these bands apart. Characterized by pretty-boy members singing danceable bubblegum pop and whiny ballads, the three bands seemed slickly manufactured. Their every move—from singing to dancing to personal habits—appeared calculated.

Well, since I wasn't a teen in the 1990s, and definitely not of the female gender, I'll keep this simple. The Backstreet Boys from Orlando, Florida, consisted of five boys: Nick Carter, Howie Dorough, Brian Littrell, A. J. McLean, and Kevin Richardson. Their big hit: "Quit Playing Games (With My Heart)" (1997). 'N Sync, also from Orlando, counted Lance Bass, Josh Chasez, Joey Fatone, Chris Kirkpatrick, and Justin Timberlake as members. Their hit: "Bye, Bye, Bye" (1999). Not from Orlando, but from Cincinnati, 98 Degrees was brothers Nick and Drew Lachey with Justin Jeffre and Jeff Timmons. Hit: "Because of You" (1998). Nick Carter, Justin Timberlake, and Nick Lachey were the most crush-worthy hotties of each group. Love them (screaming girls) or hate them (screaming guys), the boy bands dominated the pop-music charts through to the new millennium.

BOY IN THE PLASTIC BUBBLE

In the 1976 TV movie, young John Travolta plays Tod Lubitch, a teenager born without immunities and forced to live inside an isolation bubble. When he falls in love with the girl next door, Gina Biggs (Glynnis O'Connor), he must make a life-or-death decision about continuing his existence in the bubble or living outside like a normal teen. Robert Reed and Diana Hyland (in an Emmy-winning performance) co-star as Tod's parents, Johnny and Mickey Lubitch. The theme song "What Would They Say?" was written by Paul Williams and sung by Travolta.

FYI: ▸ Off the set, Diana Hyland was John Travolta's much-older girlfriend (he was twenty-two, she forty). She died of cancer in 1977.

BOY TEN FEET TALL

Long-forgotten little gem, also known as *Sammy Going South*, that most of us probably saw during our grade-school years while viewing a late-night movie or Saturday matinee on TV. Young Fergus McClelland starred as Sammy, an engaging ten-year-old British lad living in Port Said whose parents are killed by an air strike during the 1956 Suez crisis. He travels alone, and on foot, 4,500 miles through Africa to reach his only surviving relative, an aunt living in Durban. Directed by Alexander Mackendrick, the 1963 children's film, noted for gorgeous cinematography, co-starred veteran actor Edward G. Robinson as Cocky Wainwright, a wily soldier of fortune. Two other children-off-on-their-own features from the era worth viewing are *Lord of the Flies* (1963) and *A High Wind in Jamaica* (1965).

BOZO THE CLOWN

"You're Kazowee!" Before Ronald made the scene in McDonaldland, it was hard to imagine any other clown more famous than Bozo, the host of TV's longest-running kiddie show. The likeable circus clown—with the white face, red nose, tufts of red hair, blue uniform, and oversized red shoes—was originally the star of comic books and children's records in the late 1940s. In 1956, Larry Harmon purchased the rights to use the character on a daily half-hour TV series. His concept was to have local TV stations use their own live Bozo the Clown (trained by Harmon himself), who would entertain the studio audience of children and introduce Bozo cartoon shorts. (Willard Scott, weatherman for NBC's *Today Show*, served as a local Bozo in Washington, D.C., during the 1960s.) By 1966, the character could be seen on more than 240 stations in more than forty countries. In the cartoons, Bozo resided at a circus with sidekick Butch the Circus Boy and his dog, Elvis. "That's a real rootin' tootin' trick!"

FYI: ▸ Bozo has entered the pop culture lexicon as a word used to describe someone who does something stupid: "You're such a bozo!"

BRADY BUNCH

The TV show most often associated with those born on the generational cusp of the Baby Boom and Generation X. Debuting on September 26, 1969, it told the story of a lovely lady (widow Carol Martin) with three golden-haired daughters (Marcia, Jan, and Cindy) who marries a man named Brady (widower Mike Brady) with three brown-haired sons of his own (Greg, Peter, and Bobby). Together they form a cheery combined family, including housemaid Alice, residing at 4222 Clinton Avenue in a contemporary split-level home (dig those hues of burnt orange, harvest gold, and avocado green) in suburban Los Angeles.

The typical *Brady Bunch* story line centers around the somewhat trivial issues of the kids—for example, Greg having to choose between Marcia or his girlfriend for Westdale High's head cheerleader; Marcia breaking a date because "something suddenly came up"; Peter's voice changing while recording a rock tune; Jan having to wear "positively goofy" glasses; Bobby's hang-up about his short stature; and Cindy's missing Kitty Karry-All doll. Attentive parents Mike and Carol are on hand to give helpful talks with simple advice, such as "Find out what you do best and then do your best with it" or "You're great just the way you are."

The Bradys' prime-time stint on ABC ended in 1974, but thanks to after-school reruns they have lived on to become America's favorite TV family. Their legacy includes a Saturday-morning cartoon (*The Brady Kids* [1972–74]), dozens of merchandising items, several record albums, a live nationwide music tour (billed as The Brady Kids), a 1977 variety prime-time show (*The Brady Bunch Hour*), TV movies (*The Brady Girls Get Married* [1981] and *A Very Brady Christmas* [1988]), an early-1990s stage show (*The Real Live Brady Bunch*), and two successful big-screen spoofs (*The Brady Bunch Movie* [1995] and *A Very Brady Sequel* [1996]).

The reason behind our generation's love of *The Brady Bunch* is actually very simple: They represent the ideal household we wanted to be part of. We were born and raised in an era of war, riots, violence, and a skyrocketing divorce rate. There was conflict in Vietnam, the Manson family created Helter Skelter, President Nixon was snooping in Watergate, drugs ran rampant in schools, and we were becoming the first of the "latchkey" children. In the land of the Bradys, every day was a superduper "Sunshine Day" where none of these real-life issues existed.

FYI: ▸ *The Brady Bunch* was inspired by the 1968 Lucille Ball–Henry Fonda comedy movie *Yours, Mine, and Ours.*

BRADY BUNCH VARIETY HOUR

"I did it because I didn't have anything better to do. I was going to school and I really wanted to work. It was fun. But it was also really embarrassing."

—SUSAN "CINDY BRADY" OLSEN

Oh no. America's favorite polyester-clad family made a return to prime-time via this stink-o-rama variety hour, premiering in November 1976 and airing sporadically throughout 1977. Produced by Saturday-morning puppeteers Sid and Marty Krofft, the TV program was inspired by a highly rated episode of *The Donny and Marie Show* (also produced by the Kroffts) in which Flo Henderson and the Brady Kids guest starred. This new Brady show had the original cast—minus Eve Plumb (she was off being Dawn the Teenage Runaway), replaced by Geri Reischal (a.k.a. "Fake Jan")—trading in their suburban home for a beach pad after Mike (Robert Reed) quit his architect job to manage the family's variety act.

They sang (you haven't heard anything until you hear housemaid Alice's rendition of "Thank God I'm a Country Girl"). They danced (and you haven't seen anything until you see the whole clan shake their booty to a disco beat). They did comedy skits on a stage adjacent to a swimming pool (into which one of the Bradys would inevitably fall) accompanied by the Water Follies Swimmers and the Krofftette Dancers. And it was all just so dang awful.

But wait. To make matters worse, the show featured the Bradys wearing horrible 1970s fashion, including platform heels, elephant bells, and wide lapels, plus Afro perms on the guys, and feathered bangs on the gals. Its guest-star roster was a sight to behold as well: Lee and Farrah Fawcett-Majors (at the time, America's golden couple), Kaptain Kool and The Kongs, Rick Dees (quacking "Disco Duck"), the *What's Happening!* gang, Mayor H. R. Pufnstuf, and Donny and Marie Osmond (on roller skates)!

BRADY KIDS

Airing from 1972 to 1974, this Saturday-morning cartoon focused on the adventures of the Brady kids, living unsupervised without parents Mike and Carol or housemaid Alice. The far-out family now resided in a tree house, where they formed a rock band—Greg on guitar, Marcia on tambourine, Peter on bass, Jan on the organ, Bobby on drums, and Cindy on junior guitar—singing tunes like "Time to Change" and "It's a Sunshine Day." Joining them was a menagerie of pets: talking canine Mop Top, magical mynah bird Marlon, and Chinese-speaking twin panda bears named Ping and Pong. (Apparently Mike and Carol took family dog Tiger when they abandoned the kids at the tree.)

FYI: ▸ The Brady Kids is also what the real-life actors—Barry, Maureen, Chris, Eve, Mike, and Susan—called themselves when they toured America performing live musical shows. One amazing stint at the Hollywood Bowl in 1973 had them sharing a bill with Krofft Brothers faves H. R. Pufnstuf, Jack Wild, Johnny Whitaker, and The Bugaloos.

BRAIN FREEZE

A momentary, rather painful sensation that occurs inside your head when you slurp an ice-cold Slurpee, popsicle, or other frozen treat too fast. Also called "Coldeye," because a brain freeze makes your eyes feel like they're an Arctic Circle blizzard!

BRANDON AND BRENDA WALSH

Sixteen-year-old fraternal twins who move with their parents from the Midwest (Minneapolis) to the posh California zip code of 90210. Brandon's a goody-goody, Brenda's a bitch, but both are pretty and popular, so they quickly fit in with the cool crowd at West Beverly Hills High. Best friends include Donna Martin, Kelly Taylor, and Dylan McKay. Played by Jason Priestley (Brandon) and Shannen Doherty (Brenda) in FOX-TV's *Beverly Hills 90210*.

"BRANDY (YOU'RE A FINE GIRL)"

This Top Forty chart-topper told of a love that could never be. Brandy was a barmaid living in a harbor town on a western bay who served whiskey and wine to lonely soldiers passing the time away. They all thought she was a fine girl, someone who would make a good wife, but her heart belongs to a sailor (she wore his name on a locket) whom she couldn't have because he loved only the sea. The 1972 song was recorded by Looking Glass, a rock quartet fronted by Elliot Lurie.

BRAT PACK

"It's kind of magical, like being a part of a fraternity of freaks."
—ANDREW MCCARTHY, ACTOR

A clique of attractive twentysomething actors with seemingly self-absorbed personalities who were ultrapopular around the mid-1980s. The term "Brat Pack" was coined by writer David Blum for a June 1985 *New York Magazine* cover story after witnessing high-living hunks Emilio Estevez, Rob Lowe, and Judd Nelson mobbed by a crowd of star-gazing groupies at L.A.'s Hard Rock Café. Other members of the prestigious Brat Pack were Anthony Michael Hall, Andrew McCarthy, Demi Moore, Molly Ringwald, and Ally Sheedy. Those on the fringe included Tom Cruise, Jon Cryer, Matt Dillon, Robert Downey Jr., C. Thomas Howell, Mary Stuart Masterson, Lou Diamond Phillips, Charlie Sheen, James Spader, Kiefer Sutherland, Lea Thompson, and Mare Winningham.

Posturing and spoiled, the Brat Pack ruled young Hollywood during the yuppie decade, dominating movie screens in ensemble films like *The Outsiders* (1983), *The Breakfast Club* (1985), *St. Elmo's Fire* (1985), *Pretty in Pink* (1986), and *Young Guns* (1988). They also dominated the gossip columns with excessively bad behavior, including Demi's and Ally's battles with substance abuse, and Rob's nude hotel-room romp with a minor that was caught on video. Beyond the ensemble cast, the Brat Pack's solo roles were mediocre stuff (did anyone actually see *Oxford Blues, From the Hip, Maid to Order, Mannequin,* or *She's Having a Baby?*), which today is probably the main reason most of them have experienced floundering movie careers, often showing up in straight-to-video films and starring in prime-time TV shows.

BRATZ DOLLS

"The girls with a passion for fashion!" Characterized by big eyes, full lips, and funky fashions, these teen fashion dolls are Barbie's number-one challenger of the millennium. (After forty years of dominating the market, Barbie is finding herself outsold by these beautiful hipsters.) Well-dressed and ultra-accessorized, blonde Cloe ("Angel"), brunette Dana ("Sugar Shoes"), Asian Jade ("Kool Kat"), redhead Meygan ("Funky Fashion Monkey"), African-American Sasha ("Bunny Boo"), and Latin Yasmine ("Pretty Princess") are the main Bratz girls. Their equally well-dressed boyfriends, known as Bratz Boyz, are Cade, Cameron, Dylan, Eitan, and Koby. Introduced by MGA Entertainment in the late 1990s, the T.O.T.Y. (Toy of the Year)–winning dolls are acclaimed for themed doll sets with extensive wardrobes, such as "Formal Funk," "Girls' Nite Out," "Sun-Kissed Summer," and "Wintertime Collection," and highly detailed play sets, like a "Late Night F.M. Limo," "Stylin' Salon 'n' Spa," and "Super-Stylin' Runway Disco." There is also a miniature Lil' Bratz doll line.

BREAK DANCING

The 1980s urban-oriented dancing in which the participants (mostly male) looked like they were having an epileptic seizure as they spun on the ground with a body part. Best break-dancing songs included "Breakin' . . . There's No Stopping Us" (1984) by Ollie and Jerry and "Breakdance" (1984) by Irene Cara.

BREAKFAST CLUB

Written and directed by John Hughes, this is considered by most to be the quintessential 1980s teen flick. Set at Shermer High School in suburban Chicago, it told the story of five students from different social backgrounds who serve a nine-hour Saturday detention period sitting in the school library ("The Breakfast Club"). To pass the time , the diverse set of youngsters bare their innermost secrets, smoke a doobie, dance, and become friends. Perceptive and sensitive, the 1985 movie starred a Brat Pack ensemble cast: Molly Ringwald as popular princess Claire Standish, punished for cutting class to go shopping; Emilio Estevez as buff athlete Andrew Clark, punished for taping a guy's hairy butt cheeks together during P.E.; Anthony Michael Hall as nerdy brain Brian Johnson, punished for bringing a flare gun to school; Judd Nelson as burned-out criminal John Bender ("Demented and sad, but social"), punished for delinquency; and Ally Sheedy as weird basket-case Allison Reynolds, punished for, er, well, she just didn't have anything better to do (she's so weird she eats Cap'n Crunch and Pixy Stix sandwiches). Paul Gleason co-starred as Richard Vernon, the hard-ass dean of students. The soundtrack featured the chart-topper "Don't You (Forget About Me)" by Simple Minds.

BRECK
Shampoo brand best known for its Miss Breck advertisements that feature spokes-models marked by long, luscious locks—the kind of hair everyone envies. The Miss Breck alumnae included future starlets Cybill Shepherd, Jaclyn Smith, Kim Basinger, and Brooke Shields.

BREYER HORSES
These realistically detailed and very beautiful model horses with an average height of nine inches have been popular collectibles of children, mainly the female segment, since 1950. Commonly showcased with love on a girl's bedroom shelves, favorite Breyer equine breeds have included the American Quarter Horse, the Arabian, the Clydesdale, the Palomino, the Thoroughbred, the Mustang, and the Chincoteague pony, as well as such famous horses as Black Beauty, Seabiscuit, and Roy Rogers's Trigger.

BRIAN'S SONG
Telecast in 1970, the tearjerker (one of the highest viewed TV movies of all time) was about the interracial friendship between Chicago Bears football players Gale Sayers (Billy Dee Williams) and Brian Piccolo (James Caan), who bravely battled cancer that ended his life at the age of twenty-six. Based on Sayers's book *I Am Third.* The haunting title theme was composed by Michel Legrand, who later would win an Oscar for Best Original Score with *Summer of '42* (1971).

BRIDE OF FRANKENSTEIN
Frankie's reluctant future wife who has the most outtasight hairdo of all the ghouls—aw, I mean girls. Originally played by character actress Elsa Lanchester in the 1933 classic *The Bride of Frankenstein.*

BRINKLEY, CHRISTIE
"Modeling is a nine-to-five business with me. I don't take it seriously." Blonde supermodel of the 1980s who maintained a remarkable career way after most models peaked in their early twenties. Born February 2, 1954, the Malibu-born and -raised All-American daughter of a TV producer was discovered while studying art in Paris. A statuesque beauty (around six feet tall), her lithe body graced the coveted cover of three *Sports Illustrated* swimsuit issues (1979, 1980, and 1981), fueling her status as the world's top cover girl. (By 1984, she had appeared on more than 200 different magazine covers.) In 1983, Brinkley met husband-to-be singer Billy Joel while starring opposite him in his "Uptown Girl" music video. The tall, fair-haired Californian and the dark-haired, squat Long Islander made an unusual pair but proved that a guy didn't have to be handsome to win the heart of a beautiful girl (he just needed to be a successful rock star). They were married from 1985 until 1994 and had one child, daughter Alexa Ray. Brinkley played Chevy Chase's Ferrari-driving fantasy babe in *National Lampoon's Vacation* (1983).

BROTHERS, DR. JOYCE
Petite blonde shrink best known for her constant guest appearances and cameos on televised game shows, beauty pageants, sitcoms, and so on.

BROWN, JULIE
Kooky comedienne who specializes in spoofing pop culture figures, especially featherbrained starlets and supermodels. She first drew attention in 1984 when critics praised her comedy album *Goddess in Progress,* which housed the ditties "I Like 'Em Big and Stupid," "'Cause I'm a Blonde," "Earth Girls Are Easy," and the classic "The Homecoming Queen's Got a Gun." The comic hosted her own MTV variety series titled *Just Say Julie* (1986–92) before starring in the big-screen venture *Earth Girls Are Easy* (1989), a comedy based on her song and co-starring Geena Davis. She can also be seen in *The Spirit of '76* (1991), a spoof of the 1970s, sporting former teen idols David Cassidy and Leif Garrett; *Medusa: Dare to Be Truthful* (1992), a made-for-cable spoof of Madonna's infamous documentary; and *Clueless* (1995), playing Alicia Silverstone's butch P.E. teacher, Ms. Stoeger.

FYI: ▸ She is known as "West Coast" Julie Brown, not to be confused with MTV's V.J. "Downtown" Julie Brown.

BROWN HORNET
Dashing but totally inept superhero who is idolized by Fat Albert in Bill Cosby's Saturday-morning cartoon *Fat Albert and the Cosby Kids.*

BRUCE WAYNE
Handsome Gotham City millionaire whose secret identity is that of Batman, the Caped Crusader.

BRYLCREEM
"A little dab'll do ya!" Nondrying hair gel for men, used to achieve the 1950s greased-back Fonzie look.

BUBBLEGUM MUSIC
Bubblegum music is defined by one dictionary as "simplistic music for young listeners." Popular with teenyboppers of the late 1960s and early 1970s, this genre of music was named after the sugary-sweet rock tunes associated with it. These ear-candy ditties featured cute juvenile lyrics along with danceable and contagious finger-snapping cords of the electric organ, bass guitar, drums, and essential tambourine. You only have to listen to TV music acts like The Archies, Josie and the Pussycats, The Banana Splits, and The Partridge Family to hear the sound.

The best of bubblegum would include these twenty-five chart-smashing, sugarcoated songs and the artists who recorded them:

- "ABC" (1970) by The Jackson 5
- "Apple, Peaches, Pumpkin Pie" (1967) by Jay and the Techniques
- "Brand New Key" (1971) by Melanie
- "Build Me Up Buttercup" (1969) by The Foundations
- "The Candy Man" (1972) by Sammy Davis Jr.
- "Daydream Believer" (1967) by The Monkees
- "Dizzy" (1969) by Tommy Roe
- "Green Tambourine" (1968) by The Lemon Pipers
- "Happy Together" (1967) by The Turtles
- "Heartbeat—It's a Lovebeat" (1973) by The DeFranco Family
- "I Think I Love You" (1970) by The Partridge Family
- "I Think We're Alone Now" (1967) by Tommy James and the Shondells
- "Indian Lake" (1968) by The Cowsills
- "It's a Sunshine Day" (1971) by The Brady Bunch Kids
- "Julie, Do Ya Love Me" (1970) by Bobby Sherman
- "Little Willy" (1973) by The Sweet
- "Nice to Be with You" (1972) by Gallery
- "One Bad Apple" (1971) by The Osmonds
- "Playground in My Mind" (1973) by Clint Holmes
- "Simon Says" (1968) by 1910 Fruitgum Company
- "Sugar, Sugar" (1969) by The Archies
- "The Tra La La Song (One Banana, Two Banana)" (1969) by The Banana Splits
- "Tracy" (1969) by The Cuff Links
- "Windy" (1967) by The Association
- "Yummy Yummy Yummy" (1968) by The Ohio Express

FYI: ▸ Actual bubblegum was invented by Walter E. Diemer, an accountant for the Fleer chewing gum company, in 1928.

BUBBLE SKIRTS
Created by designer Christian LaCroix in the mid-1980s, these fancy skirts distinguished by a bubble-like poof gave fashion-conscious women who wore them a bubble butt. Also known as the poof skirt.

BUBBLE YUM
Giving their jaws a workout, kids often have big wads of this soft and juicy, sugary-sweet, cavity-inducing chewing gum in their mouths, because it's great for blowing big bubbles and the flavor lasts "a long, long, loooong time!" Introduced by Life Savers Inc. in 1974, Bubble Yum originally came in two flavors, Bubble Gum and Grape, before being offered in Spearmint, Tropical Punch, Pink Lemonade, Wild Cherry, Strawberry, Banana Split, Chocolate, and other funky flavors. Rumored to be the gum of choice for egg-laying spiders.

BUCK
The large shaggy mutt belonging to the Bundys on *Married . . . with Children* was the only family member with a lick of common sense. Every once in a while, TV audiences would hear the long-suffering Buck's scornful musings about his dysfunctional household.

BUCKWHEAT
"O-Tay!" The pint-sized, nappy-haired lad from the *Little Rascals* became superpopular in the early

1980s when comedian Eddie Murphy spoofed him as an adult pop-music star on NBC's *Saturday Night Live*.

BUCKY BEAVER

Buck-toothed cartoon mascot of Ipana toothpaste, popular back in the late 1950s and early 1960s. During the classic "Slumber Party" scene in *Grease* (1978), Jan (Jamie Donnelly) imitates Bucky and sings his Ipana commercial jingle ("Brusha, brusha, brusha . . ."). Bucky's worst enemy was D. K. Germ.

BUD BUNDY

Nerdy yet egotistical, the youngest of the Bundy household on the trashy TV sitcom *Married . . . with Children* (played by David Faustino) is a teenage schemer who takes constant ribbing from trashy older sister Kelly about his short stature and inability to score with the girls.

BUDDY L

Toy company from Moline, Illinois, originating in the 1920s, known for making large, heavy-duty pressed-steel trucks and cars that were tough enough to be played outside. Two memorable Buddy L vehicles of the 1960s were the Kennel Truck, which came with twelve plastic dogs (introduced in 1964), and the Traveling Zoo, which housed six plastic jungle animals (introduced in 1966). Buddy L was an alternative to the widely popular Tonka Truck toy line.

BUDDY LAWRENCE

Doug and Kate Lawrence's youngest daughter (real name: Letitia) was a spunky, sometimes troubled tomboy who enjoyed skateboarding on the streets of Pasadena, California. Fifteen-year-old Kristy McNichol's performance as Buddy on TV's *Family* brought her great acclaim and two Emmy Awards in 1977 and 1979.

BUFFALO SANDALS

Fashionable in the 1970s, these wedge-heeled leather sandals were characterized by four straps: two across the toes and two across the ankles. Girls would wear toe socks with them in the wintertime.

BUFFY DAVIS

Half of a set of nauseatingly cute five-year-old twins (the other was brother Jody), a freckle-faced, curly-pigtailed lass who carried and conversed with a bespectacled rag doll named Mrs. Beasley. Played by the late Anissa Jones on the sitcom *Family Affair*, little Buffy was one of the most popular child characters on TV during the 1960s.

BUFFY SUMMERS

"Don't you get it?
I don't want to be the Chosen One!
I don't want to spend the rest of my life
chasing after vampires.
All I want to do is graduate
from high school, go to Europe, marry
Christian Slater, and die!"

—BUFFY, THE VAMPIRE SLAYER

Blonde cheerleading babe at Sunnydale High in Los Angeles who reluctantly discovers that she is a descendant of a long line of vampire slayers that goes back to the Dark Ages. The sixteen-year-old's destiny is to hunt down and kick butt of bloodsuckers and other ghouls stalking Southern California at night. Played first by Kristy Swanson in the *Buffy the Vampire Slayer* movie (1992) and then by Sarah Michelle Gellar on the cult-inducing *Buffy the Vampire Slayer* TV series (1997–2003).

BUGALOOS

"The Bugaloos, the Bugaloos, we're in the air and everywhere. . . ." Sid and Marty Krofft produced this live-action Saturday-morning TV show about a mod rock group whose teenage members were part human, part insect. Equipped with guitars, wings and antennae, and British accents, the singing and flying quartet consisted of butterfly Joy (Caroline Ellis), bumblebee Harmony (Wayne Laryea), grasshopper I.Q. (John McIndoe), and male ladybug Courage (John Philpott). They lived in a psychedelic-hued place called Tranquility Forest with a firefly friend named Sparky (Billy Barty). Airing from 1970 to 1972, the fantasy program revolved around the band's continuous clash with archenemy Benita Bizarre (Martha Raye), a tone-deaf wannabe singer who lived in a giant jukebox and was envious of the Bugaloos' talent.

BUGS BUNNY
The long-eared gray rabbit who chomped on carrots and spoke in a Brooklyn accent (voiced by Mel Blanc) is not only the quintessential Looney Tunes star but also one of the most famous cartoon characters in the whole world. The "screwy" smart-alecky hare made his debut in the Warner Brothers cartoon "*Porky's Hare Hunt*" in 1938 opposite stuttering Porky Pig, and has since been the star of more than 150 animated shorts, including the Academy Award–winning "*Knightly Knight Bugs*" (1958). Along with Porky, Bugs Bunny has had long-running feuds with befuddled hunter Elmer Fudd, hot-tempered cowpoke Yosemite Sam, and wise-quacking Daffy Duck. In 1960, Bugs hopped into prime time for two seasons, headlining *The Bugs Bunny Show*, and two years later became an ongoing fixture of Saturday-morning TV. The "wascally wabbit" is known for the inquisitive greeting "Eh . . . What's up, Doc?"

FYI: ▸ One of Bug Bunny's creators claimed that the sight of Clark Gable eating a carrot in the 1934 classic *It Happened One Night* inspired the character.

BUGSY MALONE
Directed by Alan Parker in 1976, a musical spoof of gangster flicks featuring an all-kiddie cast headlined by fourteen-year-old Scott Baio as mobster Bugsy Malone and thirteen-year-old Jodie Foster as nightclub singer Tallulah. What's fun about this unusual movie is that, instead of employing real bullets, the gangsters use "splat guns" that cover the victim in whipped cream.

BUG TUSSLE
Nestled somewhere among the hills of the Ozarks, this fictional backwoods community was where the Clampett hillbilly clan lived in a tiny cabin before striking it rich and moving to a mansion in Beverly Hills, Californy.

BULLWINKLE MOOSE
"Watch me pull a rabbit out of my hat!" Simple-minded but lovable, bristle-haired, big-antlered moose from Jay Ward's *Rocky and Bullwinkle Show*. On the cartoon program, he hosted "Bullwinkle's Corner," a poetry segment, and "Mr. Know-It-All," featuring his foolish answers to viewers' questions. In the 1960s, Bullwinkle bobbed overhead as a favorite float in the Macy's Thanksgiving Day Parade and peddled cereals for General Mills ("I'm just a moose with Cheerios to sell!").

FYI: ▸ Jay Ward got the name Bullwinkle from Bullwinkle Ford, a car dealership near his home in Berkeley, California.

BUMP
The hottest dance craze of the mid-1970s, involving a movement of bumping your butt and various other body parts (hips, sides, arms, legs, and so on) simultaneously with a dance partner while rising up and squatting down to the rhythm of the music. Its dancers often wore towering platform shoes, which made squatting while bumping a most challenging feat (it wasn't uncommon to see dancers fall on their fannies). Great songs to bump your rump are "Rock Your Baby" (1974) by George McCrae; "Rockin' Chair" (1974) by Gwen McCrae (George's wife); "Rock Your Boat" (1974) by The Hues Corporation; "Bump Me Baby" (1975) by Dooley Silverspoon; "Shake Your Booty" (1976) by K.C. and the Sunshine Band; and "Ain't Gonna Bump No More (With No Big Fat Woman)" (1977) by Joe Tex.

BUNGEE JUMPING
Extreme sport of flinging yourself off a very high bridge or tower with only an elastic bungee cord attached to your ankles to break the fall. Believed to have originated as a rite of passage for boys using vines, called "land diving," on the South Pacific island of Pentecost. The first modern bungee jump occurred in 1977 when four Oxford University students jumped off a bridge in England.

BUNNY HOP
A chain dance, similar to the conga but mixed with forward hops and backward hops (like a bunny), which is popular with tipsy revelers at weddings and bar mitzvahs.

BUNSON BERNIE
Liddle Kiddle Land's intrepid fire chief, dressed in a yellow vinyl slicker, who zooms around in a miniature fire engine. The blue-eyed, redheaded firefighter is a favorite among today's collectors of Liddle Kiddle dolls.

BURGER CHEF
Closing its last door in 1996, this now-defunct fast-food chain once was a major competitor of McDonald's and Burger King. Its advertisements featured a teen employee named Jeff ("Burger Chef and Jeff!").

BURGER KING
"Hold the pickles, hold the lettuce / Special orders don't upset us / All we ask is that you let us / Serve it your way / Have it your way at Burger King!" The fast-food home of flame-broiled hamburgers and the enormous Whopper is the second-largest burger joint in the world—after McDonald's. Founded in Miami, Florida, in 1954 by James McLamore and David Edgerton.

BURGERMEISTER MEISTERBURGER
"There will be no more toys!" The tyrannical ruler of Sombertown who once broke his funny bone after tripping on a toy, an act that caused him to declare all toys unlawful! Burgermeister is featured in the 1970 Yuletide special *Santa Claus Is Comin' to Town.*

BUS STOP
Popular disco line dance from the late 1970s and early 1980s found recently in different variations, such as the Electric Slide, the Tootsie Roll, the Train, and the Macarena.

BUSTER BROWN
"I'm Buster Brown, and I live in a shoe. That's my dog, Tige, and he lives there too!" This line of classic footwear for juveniles employs a little blond-haired boy and his pet pooch as its advertising icons. Buster Brown was actually an early comic-strip star who first appeared in 1905 in the *New York Herald Tribune.*

BUSTIERS
Worn to enhance a woman's breasts by pushing them up with underwiring, boning, and padding, these strapless undergarments became fashionable outerwear in the mid-1980s when pop-star Madonna paired them with crinoline skirts and capri pants.

FYI: ▸ Bustier is French for "boost."

BUTCH CASSIDY AND THE SUNDANCE KIDS
Produced by Hanna-Barbera from 1973 to 1974, this was another in a long line of cartoons revolving around a teenage rock group. Fronted by dreamy Butch Cassidy, a David Cassidy-esque lead singer, the Kids moonlighted as undercover spies for the World Wide Travel Agency—led by a computer called Mr. Socrates—while traveling the world to perform at concert gigs. Other members included sensible blonde tambourine-player Merilee, brunette guitarist Steffy, foolhardy redheaded drummer Harvey (voiced by ex-Monkee Mickey Dolenz), and mischievous dog Elvis. Like numerous animated bands of the era, Butch and the gang always took a break from their TV adventures to deliver a groovy, finger-snapping, toe-tapping bubblegum song.

BUTCH EVERETT
The blond middle son on *Nanny and the Professor* was a mischievous eight-year-old who always got into everything. Real first name: Bentley. Young actor Trent Lehman (born July 23, 1961), who played Butch for two TV seasons (1970–71), committed suicide on January 18, 1982, after typecasting as a cutie-pie moppet led to years of rejection by Hollywood.

BUZZ LIGHTYEAR
"To infinity and beyond!" The cocky Space Ranger action figure, complete with flashy laser action and pop-out wings—who doesn't realize he's a toy—is one of the leading characters in the *Toy Story* movies. Buzz rivaled pull-string cowboy Woody as little Andy's new favorite toy after being received as a birthday present. Voiced with much enthusiasm by comedian Tim Allen, the courageous spaceman starred in a TV cartoon titled *Buzz Lightyear of the Star Command* in 2000.

zabc

CABBAGE PATCH KIDS
Created by artist Xavier Roberts, these pudgy, blubber-faced rag dolls caused the biggest toy-buying frenzy of the 1980s (or any other decade, for that matter). Originating out of a cabbage patch located in Georgia's BabyLand General Hospital, the yarn-haired moppets, all one-of-a-kind with individual names and birthdays, were "adopted" by little girls (each came with an adoption certificate). When Coleco Toys released the dolls in June 1983, the public's interest in them was lukewarm, and many of the dolls landed on store clearance tables by summer's end. But as the Christmas season neared, the ugly-looking dolls grew on people and ended up number one on every girl's Santa Claus wish list. Unable to keep up with the Cabbage Patch demand, stores became terribly understocked. Our parents, temporarily insane as usual, camped outside malls and toy stores overnight, waiting to be the first to grab a doll once the doors opened. When they did go through the doors—watch out—all hell broke loose, as suburban moms and dads scrambled and beat one another up for one of the "must have" Cabbage Patch Kids. By Christmas Day, two and a half million had been sold.

CADBURY
Resourceful butler employed as Richie Rich's personal valet who often came to the aid of the "Poor Little Rich Boy" in his comic-book adventures.

CAESAR CUT
Forward-combed and close-cropped, this male haircut, with roots all the way back in the days of Augustus Caesar of ancient Rome, was a trendy style in the 1960s worn by mod studs like James Coburn and Steve McQueen. Thanks to pop-singer George Michael and *E.R.* actor George Clooney, it made a comeback in the early 1990s, first among gay men (always on the fashion forefront), then crossing over to the straight population.

CALAMITY JIDDLE
The rootin' tootin' little blonde cowgirl who rode a black-spotted palomino rockin' pony in the land of Liddle Kiddle is another sought-after favorite from Mattel Toys' diminutive doll line of the 1960s.

CALGONITE
Ancient Chinese secret, huh? No, a modern-day American laundry detergent that's memorable for its 1970s TV commercial spots set in a Chinese laundry.

"CALIFORNIA DREAMIN'"
A Top Ten smash in 1966, this was The Mamas and the Papas' harmonious hymn to the West Coast—particularly San Francisco's hippie haven Haight-Ashbury. Dig the flute solo at the end.

CALIFORNIA RAISINS
A hipster bunch of overdried grapes (actually animated Claymation) seen in a slew of popular com-

mercials created by Will Vinton in 1986 for the California Raisin Advisory Board. Their signature song: the Motown classic "I Heard It Through the Grapevine" by Marvin Gaye.

CALVIN AND HOBBES

Delightful comic strip about an overactive kid—six-year-old Calvin—who spends most of his time raising hell with his stuffed tiger doll, Hobbes. Wise and philosophical, Hobbes comes to life only in Calvin's daydreams. Created by former political cartoonist Bill Watterson and distributed by Universal Press Syndicate, it first appeared in newspapers in 1985.

CALVIN KLEIN JEANS

During the designer-jeans craze of the early 1980s, these were the most prestigious to wear. Success is credited to a series of controversial TV commercials in 1980 featuring beguiling teen model Brooke Shields and her seductive tease: "Know what comes between me and my Calvins? Nothing." These ads increased the fashion designer's jeans sales by 300 percent in ninety days, reflecting the mood of status-seeking Americans who would let "nothing" come between them and their Calvins.

CAMEL TOE

Terminology used to describe what happens when a chick wears her pants tighter than tight. Her crotch area becomes outlined with the seam riding up the crack, making it resemble the toe of a camel. I should add that only slutty girls would be caught with camel toe.

CAMERON, KIRK

Born October 12, 1970, in California, the squeaky-clean cutie with the dimply crooked smile and gangly body was the major teen dreamboat of the late 1980s, receiving more than 10,000 letters a month. He played oldest son Mike Seaver on the prime-time sitcom *Growing Pains* (1985–92). An avowed Christian, he can be seen miscast as newshound Buck Williams in *Left Behind* (2000), co-starring wife Chelsea Noble as a flight attendant, a big-screen film based on the best-selling book series about the allegedly approaching biblical Apocalypse, written by Tim LaHaye and Jerry Jenkins.

CAMOUFLAGE

Once associated with uniforms for G.I.'s, who wore it to blend in with the jungle habitat during combat, camouflage became quite popular as a fashion statement for Rambo wannabes in the early 1980s.

CAMPBELL, GLEN

The boyish-appearing singer-guitarist with the easy-going but somewhat cornball disposition dominated the country-and-western charts in the late 1960s, crooning ballads like "Gentle on My Mind" (1967), "By the Time I Get to Phoenix" (1967), "Wichita Lineman" (1968), and "Galveston" (1969). In the 1970s, Campbell's hit songs, all crossovers on the pop charts, included "Rhinestone Cowboy" (1975), "Country Boy (You Got Your Feet in L.A.)" (1975), and "Southern Nights" (1977). Other ventures: hosting a well-received variety show on prime-time TV, *The Glen Campbell Goodtime Hour* (1968–72), and starring opposite John Wayne and Kim Darby in the big-screen western *True Grit* (1969).

In the early 1980s, he had a much-publicized on-again, off-again affair (fueled by alcohol, cocaine, and abuse) with younger singer Tanya Tucker. Once claiming he'd been physically and spiritually cleansed after finding God, Campbell was arrested in November 2003 in Phoenix on DUI and hit-and-run charges (he allegedly drunkenly plowed his BMW into another vehicle at an intersection and left the scene) and aggravated assault on a cop (he kneed a police sergeant during arrest). His pitiful mug shot glared from the front page of tabloids nationwide.

FYI: ▸ Born on April 22, 1936, in Delight, Arkansas, Glen Campbell was the seventh son of a seventh son.

CAMPBELL KIDS

"Mmm! Mmm! Good!" Created by Philadelphia artist Grace Dayton, these chubby, rosy-cheeked urchins have helped promote the company's canned soup since 1904.

CAMP CRYSTAL LAKE

This dangerous summer camp locale should be avoided at all costs, especially if you are a promiscuous teen counselor, if it's Friday the thirteenth, and if you are in a *Friday the 13th* movie. You see, this is the home of boogeyman Jason, who wears a hockey goalie mask, wields every sharp object imaginable, and hacks, chops, and even drills his victims to death.

CAMP INCH
Summer camp where identical-looking Sharon McKendrick and Susan Evers (played by the identical-looking Hayley Mills) meet and discover they are twin sisters, separated by divorce, in Disney's *Parent Trap* (1961).

CAMP LITTLE WOLF
The summer-camp setting where Ferris Whitney and Angel Bright place a bet on who could lose their virginity first in the *Little Darlings* movie (1980).

CAMP NORTH STAR
Summer camp where the misfit kids go (the snotty rich kids go to rival Camp Mohawk) in the 1979 film comedy *Meatballs*. Overseen by lead counselor Tripper Harrison (Bill Murray), whose philosophy is to have a good time all the time ("It just doesn't matter!").

CANDID CAMERA
"Smile, you're on Candid Camera." Classic Baby Boom–era TV show, hosted by Allen Funt, that featured a series of pranks and stunts performed on unsuspecting members of the public. Spawned a few copycats over the years, such as *People Do the Craziest Things*, *Totally Hidden Video*, and MTV's *Punk'd*, starring Ashton Kutcher.

CANDIES
The gotta-have-it footwear, thanks to a kicky 1979 ad campaign by director Adrian Lyne (*Flashdance*) and the sight of sassy Olivia Newton-John wearing a pair in the blockbuster movie *Grease*. More than fourteen million pairs were sold during the late 1970s and early 1980s, with one out of three women ages fifteen to twenty-five owning them. These sexy, inexpensive shoes were desired because they looked casual enough to be worn with designer jeans for a hot disco date yet were dressy enough to be worn with a sophisticated evening gown for prom night. The task of staying upright in a pair of these high-heeled mules, a.k.a. slides (because you just slide them on), was a challenge of towering proportions, because they were three to four inches high, plus strapless and backless. It became a common sight at the disco to see a spandex-clad dancing queen take an embarrassing fall while doing the Rock Freak in her Candies.

"CANDLE IN THE WIND"
Elton John's poignant tribute to screen goddess Marilyn Monroe was first recorded for his *Goodbye Yellow Brick Road* LP in 1973. Fourteen years later, a version of the ballad recorded live in Australia with the Melbourne Symphony Orchestra landed in the American Top Ten. Sadly, in 1997 it was used as a eulogy to Princess Diana, a good friend of Elton's. He rewrote the lyrics ("Goodbye, Norma Jean" became "Goodbye, England's Rose") and performed it mournfully at her funeral. Known as "Candle in the Wind 1997," it became the best-selling single of all time, and all profits from sales were donated to the Diana, Princess of Wales Memorial Fund.

CANDY
The following list is special. It does not need an explanation. There is no reason for commentary. As people who were once kids, we know what it is all about. C-A-N-D-Y! It's a delightful list of 100 delicious, gooey, sweet-tasting candy we just could not—and still cannot—do without. So enjoy.

Almond Joy
Atomic Fire Balls
Baby Ruth
Bit-O-Honey
Black Cow
Boston Baked Beans
Bottle caps
Butterfinger
Cadbury Creme Egg
Candy cigarettes
Candy corn
Candy necklaces
Caramel Creams
Charleston Chew
Chewels
Cherry Mash
Chic-O-Stix
Chunky

Circus Peanuts
Clark Bar
Conversation hearts
Dots
Dum Dum suckers
Dweebs
Everlasting Gobstoppers
Fun Dip
Goo Goo Cluster
Goobers
Good & Plenty
Gummi Bears
Heath Bar
Hershey's Chocolate Bar
Hershey's Kisses
Hot Tamales
Jawbreaker
Jelly Belly
Jolly Ranchers
Jujyfruit
Junior Mints
Kit Kat
Krackel Bar
Laffy Taffy
Lemonheads
Life Savers
M&M's
Mallo Cup
Marathon Bar
Mars Bar
Mary Janes
Mentos
Mike and Ike
Milk Duds
Milk Shake
Milky Way
Mounds
Mr. Goodbar
Nerds
Nestlé Crunch
Nestlé $100,000 Bar
Now and Later
Oh Henry!
PayDay
Peeps
Pixy Stix
Pom Poms
Raisinets
Razzles
Red Hots
Reese's Peanut Butter Cups
Reese's Pieces
Rolo
Runts
7th Avenue
Sixlets
Skittles
Smarties
Snickers
Sno-Caps
Sprees
Starburst
Sugar Babies
Sugar Daddy
Sugar Mama
Sweetarts
Three Musketeers
Tootsie Pop
Tootsie Roll
Twix
Twizzler
Wacky Wafers
Wax cola bottles
Whatchamacallit Bar
Whoppers
Willy Wonka's Oompas
Willy Wonka's Scrunch Bar
York Peppermint Patty
Zagnut
Zero Bar
Whistle Pops
Zotz

FYI: ▸ The average American consumes more than twenty pounds of candy each year.

CANDY CIGARETTES

Chalky-tasting candy cigarettes once sold to children in little cigarette boxes back in the days when it was cool to smoke. Of course, now that we believe they probably influenced kids to puff on real cigarettes ("cancer sticks"), they, along with cohorts chocolate cigarettes and bubblegum cigars, have been banned. Many candy cigarettes came with a pink tip, to make them look as if they were lit.

CANDY LAND

"A sweet little game, for sweet little people." An all-time childhood classic created by Eleanor Abbott, a San Diego woman recovering from polio, as a game for youngsters who suffered from the crippling disease. Aimed at those too young to read or count, Candy Land's rules are simple: move a gingerbread-man playing piece to the game-board space that matches the color on the game card—red, purple, yellow, blue, orange, or green. Players pass through oh-so-tasty places along the colorful board—Candy Hearts, Peppermint Stick Forest, Gingerbread Plum Tree, Gumdrop Mountains, Crooked Old Peanut Brittle House, Lollipop Woods, and Ice Cream Floats—while avoiding the sticky Molasses Swamp, until they reached yummy Candy Castle. "The Legend of the Lost Candy Castle," a fairy tale about all the Candy Land characters, is printed on the inside of the box. Manufacturer Milton Bradley estimates that more than 100 million children have played with the thirty million sets sold since debuting in 1949.

"CANDY MAN"

The happiest (and sappiest) song of the summer of 1972 was recorded by Sammy Davis Jr. and performed in his distinctively hip style (he even added a "groovy" to describe a lemon pie). Containing bubblegum lyrics, such as "chocolate-covered sunrises sprinkled with dew" and "sun-soaked rainbows wrapped in sighs," the record was number one for three weeks, earning the Rat Packer a Grammy nod for Best Male Pop Vocal. Leslie Bricusse and Anthony Newley wrote the sweet tune for the 1971 kiddie movie *Willy Wonka and the Chocolate Factory*. It was used in the scene where Bill (Aubrey Woods) sings to the candy-greedy schoolchildren inside his candy shop upon hearing Wonka had a new one called the Scrumdidilyumptious Bar.

CANNONBALL

"Come and ride the little train that is rolling down the tracks to the Junction, Petticoat Junction. . . ." Archaic steam-driven train (an 1890s locomotive) controlled by engineers Charley Pratt and Floyd Smoot that took passengers (and TV viewers) to Kate Bradley's Shady Rest Hotel on the sitcom *Petticoat Junction*. Homer Bedloe, vice-president of the more modern CF&W Railroad, was constantly trying to put it out of business.

CAN'T STOP THE MUSIC

"This is the eighties!
You're going to see a lot of things
you've never seen before."

—SAMANTHA SIMPSON (VALERIE PERRINE)

Can't stand the music is more like it, when it comes to this awful 1980 disco musical notable for being the Village People's first and only big-screen venture. Loosely based on the Village People's true life story, it starred boyishly cute Steve Guttenberg as aspiring composer Jack Morell (loosely based on Village People creator Jacques Morali), who forms an act with six men decked out in "Macho Man" outfits—cop, cowboy, construction worker, soldier, biker, and American Indian—to perform his disco tunes. Aided by supermodel roomie Samantha Simpson (the ample Valerie Perrine) and tax lawyer Ron White (the stiff Bruce Jenner), Jack takes his costumed boys from the boogie streets of Greenwich Village to disco glory in San Francisco. Best number: the gay musical sequence for "Y.M.C.A.," which had the Village People performing in an actual Y.M.C.A. among a bevy of half-naked studs. Directed by TV actress Nancy Walker and produced by the elaborate Allan Carr, this jive turkey is considered one of the worst films ever made and probably helped contribute to the death of disco.

CAPES

Not the kind found around the necks of superheroes in comic books, but a stylish winter cloak with slits in each side to stick your arms out of, worn by girls during the early 1970s. This fashionable outerwear is believed to have been inspired by the blue cape Phoebe Figalilly wore on the TV sitcom *Nanny and the Professor*.

CAPEZIO

Flat-soled, soft-leather dance shoes that became stylish streetwear for modern girls of the 1980s. Of course, they would accessorize these with leg warmers bunched around the ankles.

CAP GUNS

Realistic but harmless pistols that made loud popping sounds—Pow! Pow!—from little spots of gunpowder. It was also fun to lay the strips of gunpowder down on a sidewalk and pound a rock on them.

CAP'N CRUNCH

"It's got corn for crunch, oats for punch, and it stays crunchy even in milk!" If a cereal was picked to represent a favorite from late twentieth-century childhoods, it's a sure bet that this would be the choice. Introduced in 1963 by Quaker Oats, the popular breakfast treat had kid appeal written all over it. For one thing, it's advertised with amusing animated TV spots created by Jay Ward (*Rocky and Bullwinkle*) and starring Cap'n Horatio Crunch—the fun-loving, blue-uniformed sea captain of the S.S. *Guppy*. They show him, along with canine first mate Seadog and a crew of children (Brunhilde, Alfie, Dave, and little Carlyle), on all sorts of seafaring adventures, where he encounters zany foes—pirate Jean LaFoote, Smedley the Elephant, and evil sea creatures called Soggies—who tried to plunder the ship's precious cargo of Cap'n Crunch cereal. The sugary-sweet taste of the barrel-shaped nuggets isn't bad either, and for variety there are different Cap'n Crunch flavors to chose from: Crunch Berries, Peanut Butter Crunch, Punch Crunch, Cinnamon Crunch, Choco Crunch, and Vanilly Crunch. Cap'n Crunch never seems to get soggy, staying crunchy down to the last spoonful (many of us can recall how it sandpapered the roof of our mouths and left our gums sore). Finally, there are all those great premium offers and giveaways, such as comic books, coloring books, cloth dolls, banks, whistles, rings, a story scope with disks, and a Seadog Spy Kit.

FYI: ▸ Country singer Garth Brooks once claimed his only addiction was a bedtime snack of Cap'n Crunch cereal.

CAPRI PANTS

Shapely Italian gals on the resort island of Capri originally wore these slim calf-length pants before they were introduced to the United States by American tourists who adopted the look while vacationing there. However, we'll have to give leggy Mary Tyler Moore credit as the celeb who brought them into vogue after sporting them on *The Dick Van Dyke Show* in the early 1960s. In the late 1990s, capris returned as a hot retro fashion item, spurred on by capricious Gap and Old Navy ads.

CAPTAIN ACTION

Introduced by Ideal Toys in 1966, a versatile action figure that came with an assortment of interchangeable costumes and accessories, allowing transformation into various superheroes. One minute he could be the Green Hornet or the Phantom, a few minutes later (after changing his uniform and face mask), he could be the Lone Ranger, Captain America, or Spider-Man. He had a young sidekick named Action Boy, and together they became companion crime fighters—Superman and Superboy, Batman and Robin, Aquaman and Aqualad—driving a supercar called the Silver Streak. Because every hero needs an archenemy, the deformed-looking Dr. Evil was created in 1967 and came with alter-ego villain outfits, such as the Joker (Batman) and the Red Skull (Captain America).

CAPTAIN AMERICA

Adorned in patriotic red, white, and blue (including his round shield), this World War II superhero and defender of democracy against Nazi foes was created by the legendary *Marvel* comics team of Jack Kirby and Joe Simon in 1941. He gained his superpowers by drinking a secret potion. Alias: Steve Rogers.

CAPTAIN AND TENNILLE

Toni Tennille and Daryl Dragon met in 1971, married in 1974, and as The Captain and Tennille became one of the most popular music duos of the 1970s. Vocalist Tennille was tall (around six feet), had a toothsome smile, and wore her hair in a bouncy style reminiscent of a mushroom cap. Keyboardist Dragon's trademark was the nautical headgear he always wore on stage, which got him nicknamed "the Captain" by Mike Love when he played for The Beach Boys in the early 1970s. In the summer of 1975, their happy love song "Love Will Keep Us Together" skyrocketed the couple to fame as it landed at the top of the charts, sold a million copies, and became the number-one single of the year. Other smash tunes included "The Way I Want to Touch You" (1975), "Lonely Night (Angel Face)" (1976), "Shop Around" (1976), "Muskrat Love" (1976), and "Do That to Me One More Time" (1979).

In 1976, they were given a much-hyped musical-variety TV series, *The Captain and Tennille* show, but the reserved Captain (who never said much) and the perky Tennille seemed uncomfortable with the comedy routines and it never lived up to expectations of becoming another *Sonny and Cher Comedy Hour.*

CAPTAIN CAVEMAN AND THE TEEN ANGELS

Saturday-morning cartoon produced by Hanna-Barbera from 1977 to 1980 and featuring a pint-sized Stone Age superhero who wore a leopard-skin cape and carried a club that allowed him magical powers. After thawing out from a prehistoric chunk of glacier ice, he teamed up with the Teen Angels, an investigative trio (inspired by prime-time's *Charlie's Angels*) consisting of brainy African-American Brenda Chance, scaredy-cat brunette Taffy Dare, and easygoing blonde Dee Dee Sykes. Nicknamed "Cavey," the woolly hero used the blustery cry of "Captain Caveman-n-n-n-n!" as he came to the rescue and helped the Angels solve a variety of mysteries. Logical-minded Cave Bird was his purple-feathered friend. "Go get 'em, Cavey!"

FYI: ▸ "No redeeming values." A 1980 *TV Guide* survey placed *Captain Caveman* at the very bottom of twenty-seven children's shows studied by a board of experts.

CAPTAIN DANIEL GREGG

The "ghost" in the TV sitcom *The Ghost and Mrs. Muir* (played by Irish actor Edward Mulhare). A handsome nineteenth-century sea captain whose afterlife spirit haunts his former home, Gull Cottage, scaring off all potential renters—that is, until the day gutsy Mrs. Carolyn Muir moves in . . .

CAPTAIN JAMES T. KIRK

Hammy thespian William Shatner starred as the heroic commander of the starship Enterprise in the *Star Trek* TV series and motion pictures. Bold and handsome, with chiseled chin and broad shoulders, Captain Kirk frequently was the object of female affection, both human and alien.

CAPTAIN KANGAROO

One of the longest-running children's programs in TV history, airing from 1955 to 1984. Geared for kids of preschool age, the easy-paced show starred Bob Keeshan as the gray-haired, amply mustached Captain Kangaroo, so called because of the large pockets on his trademark jacket that were always stuffed with fun surprises. Unlike most kiddie-show hosts, Captain Kangaroo was a gentle, kindhearted man with a nonpatronizing manner who seemed to talk one-on-one with young viewers. Regular visitors at his Treasure House residence included farmer Mr. Green Jeans (Hugh Brannum) and an array of puppets: shy Bunny Rabbit, mischievous Mr. Moose, curious Miss Frog, soft-spoken Mr. Whispers, scholarly Word Bird, Dancing Bear, and rhyme-speaking Grandfather Clock.

CAPTAIN MERRILL STUBING

Serious-minded with a slightly sunny disposition, Captain Stubing served as the bald-headed skipper of ABC-TV's *Love Boat* from 1977 to 1986. Played by Gavin MacLeod, who was familiar to TV viewers for his earlier role as sarcastic newswriter Murray Slaughter on *The Mary Tyler Moore Show* (1970–77).

CAPTAIN PLANET

"The power is yours!" Blue-skinned environmental superhero who, along with a team of international teens, The Planeteers—African Kwame (Earth), Soviet Linka (Wind), American Wheeler (Fire), Asian Gi (Water), and South American Ma-Ti (Heart)—used mighty powers to combat polluting eco-villains on planet earth (for example, Hoggish Greedly, Looten Plunder, Duke Nukem, Sly Sludge, Verminous Skumm, and Dr. Blight). Captain Planet and the Planeteers were the stars of a long-running TBS cartoon series (1990–95) based on an original idea by media czar Ted Turner.

CARACTACUS POTTS

Enthusiastic and rather eccentric inventor of the flying Chitty Chitty Bang Bang automobile—every kid's "fine four-fendered friend." Lives in an old windmill in the English countryside along with his twin children Jemima and Jeremy, senile Grandpa Potts, and an English sheepdog called Edison. Fond of beautiful Truly Scrumptious, the daughter of the local candymaker. Portrayed by Dick Van Dyke in the 1968 big-screen musical *Chitty Chitty Bang Bang.*

CARANGI, GIA

Iconoclastic supermodel (born January 19, 1960, in Philadelphia) of the late 1970s and early 1980s whose smoldering Italian-American looks and streetwise persona redefined the industry's standard of beauty. Sadly, her $10,000-a-day high-fashion shoots were overshadowed by her brash, often-selfish behavior, volatile lesbian affairs, and drug abuse. Heroin addiction led to Gia's death from AIDS in 1986 at age twenty-six. (She was one of the first women in America to succumb to the deadly disease.) The 1998 HBO bio-flick *Gia*, starring Angelina Jolie, told her life story.

FYI: ▸ Supermodel Cindy Crawford was nicknamed "Baby Gia" when she entered the modeling industry in the 1980s, because of her resemblance to Gia Carangi. Some fashion insiders cruelly suggest that if it wasn't for Gia's untimely demise look-alike Crawford would not have received the modeling jobs that led to cover-girl success.

CARE BEARS

"Caring is what counts!" Cuddly teddy bears in pastel colors featured in a TV cartoon and based on a line of characters created by American Greeting Cards in 1981. Aimed at the preschool set, the Care Bears' feelings are expressed by symbols on their tummies that match their names: Funshine Bear, Love-a-Lot Bear, Grumpy Bear, Bedtime Bear, Friend Bear, Cheer Bear, Share Bear, Tenderheart Bear, Wish Bear, Good Luck Bear, and Birthday Bear. Riding in cloudmobiles from a star-speckled, rainbow-trimmed cloud world called Care-a-Lot, the Care Bears arrive on earth to make it a happier place with a motto of caring and sharing. When trouble menaces, they get together to send a rainbow beam of goodwill from their bellies ("Care Bear . . . Stare!"), which softens the toughest of hearts, like that of nemesis Professor Coldheart. Accompanying the cartoon and greeting cards in the 1980s were a toy line by Kenner and a host of big-screen movies and TV specials.

CARGO PANTS

Trousers characterized by multiple pockets first popular in 1930s England for military men to stash weapons and other ammunition. Sixty years later, high-profile retail chains like The Gap and Old Navy reintroduced cargo pants so young people could use the many pockets to store cell phones, Game Boys, and other electronic gadgets.

CARLISLE, BELINDA

The former high school cheerleader from Hollywood (born August 17, 1958) was a member of the legendary all-girl New Wave quintet The Go-Go's. Known for a quivering singing style (some critics liken her voice to that of a sheep's baa), the cute and pudgy Carlisle with the changing hair color (pink, blue, red, white—you name it)—shared lead vocals with elfish Jane Wiedlin in memorable hits like "Our Lips Are Sealed" (1981) and "We Got the Beat" (1982). After The Go-Go's disbanded in the mid-1980s, Carlisle sobered up, slimmed down, grew her hair long, highlighted it blonde, and transformed into one of pop music's hottest nymphets. Solo hits included "Mad About You" (1986), "Heaven Is a Place on Earth" (1987), "I Get Weak" (1988), and "Circle in the Sand" (1988).

CARLOS RAMIREZ

Good-looking, suave, and wealthy, the playboy owner of a swingin' discotheque in San Juan, Puerto Rico, was smitten with a flying American nun named Sister Bertrille. Portrayed by Alejandro Rey on the 1960s TV sitcom *The Flying Nun*, co-starring Sally Field as Sister Bertrille.

CARL'S JR.

Home of the famous Super Star Hamburger, this West Coast burger chain was at one time acclaimed for having the best french fries around. Its eastern affiliate is Hardee's.

CARMEN SANDIEGO

World-class female thief who is hunted around the world by the Acme Crime Detective Agency assisted by a trio of teen contestants on PBS-TV's educational geography game show, *Where in the World Is Carmen Sandiego?* Originally a popular computer game that many schools used to educate children on world geography in the 1980s.

CARMINE RAGUSA
Amorous and masculine, "The Big Ragu" was Shirley Feeney's on-again, off-again boyfriend. Played by Eddie Mekka, a former opera singer, on *Laverne and Shirley* from 1976 to 1983.

CARNABY STREET
Not far from Oxford Circus tube station, this London locale was the heart of the Swinging 1960s and renowned for boutique shops stocked with the latest mod threads and groovy go-go clubs packed with frugging dancers. If lucky, you could spot miniskirt designer Mary Quant, model Twiggy, or one of the Beatles hanging about.

CAROL ANN FREELING
"They're heeere!" Angelic, wide-eyed, tow-headed five-year-old who stares at a static screen talking to the "people in the TV" and gets stuck somewhere unseen in her suburban California home by evil spirits. Rescued by clairvoyant Tangina, who beckons her to "come to the light." Portrayed by the late Heather O'Rourke in the *Poltergeist* film series.

CAROL BRADY
"Sometimes when we lose, we win." In the TV sitcom *The Brady Bunch,* Florence Henderson starred as the polyester-pantsuited housewife and mom of three girls and stepmom of three boys. She had the most outtasight shag haircut around. Hubby Mike Brady's term of endearment for Carol was "Twinkles."

FYI: ▸ Mrs. Brady once won a Twist contest as a teenager.

CAROL BURNETT SHOW
"I'm so glad we had this time together." Beloved variety TV hour hosted by redhead Carol Burnett, a daffy comedienne whose awesome versatility allowed her to sing, dance, and deliver a deafening Tarzan yell. Co-starring with Carol was a troupe of supporting regulars: comics Harvey Korman and Tim Conway, hunk Lyle Waggoner, and look-alike newcomer Vicki Lawrence. Along with a celebrity guest star, each week they would perform skits that spoofed popular movies and TV, and ongoing sketches featuring recurring characters: "Mr. Tudball and Mrs. Wiggins," an incompetent, blonde secretary (Burnett) and her long-suffering employer (Conway); "Ed and Eunice," a squabbling couple (Korman and Burnett) constantly at odds with her mother (Lawrence); "As the Stomach Turns," a soap-opera parody; "Went with the Wind," a *Gone with the Wind* takeoff; and Burnett's poignant Cleaning Lady. Every broadcast opened with friendly Burnett answering questions from the audience and ended with her singing the theme song, "It's Time to Say Goodbye," and doing her trademark earlobe tug (a gesture of saying "hello" to her grandmother). As prime time's last great variety series, *The Carol Burnett Show* aired for eleven years on CBS-TV (1967–78), winning an astounding twenty-five Emmy awards and spawning a 1980s sitcom, *Mama's Family,* starring Vicki Lawrence as Thelma Harper (Burnett occasionally guest-starred).

FYI: ▸ Carol Burnett's lucky charm was good friend Jim Nabors, who by tradition always appeared as the guest star on the opening telecast of each season.

CAROLYN MUIR
Attractive, take-charge writer who after the death of her husband moved with her two young children to a cottage in Schooner Bay, a coastal community in New England, that was haunted by the ghost of a sea captain. Oscar-winning actress Hope Lange starred as Carolyn on prime time's *The Ghost and Mrs. Muir* (1968–70).

CARPENTERS
Referred to by President Richard Nixon as "young America at its very best," the brother-and-sister duo sold nearly 100 million records, won three Grammy Awards, and became one of the most successful music acts of the 1970s. Their vocals were one of a kind: Karen's expressive crystalline voice, intermittently happy and sad, was blended with older brother Richard's mellow pop tones, creating a densely layered sound. Blond Richard was the brain of the act, but brunette Karen was its heart, de-

scribed best by *Rolling Stone* magazine writer Tom Nolan: "Fascinating contrasts: youth with wisdom, chilling perfection with warmth."

Born in Connecticut, The Carpenters moved with their parents to Downey, California, in the 1960s, where Richard, a talented pianist, formed a jazz trio with Karen as drummer and school friend Wes Jacobs as bassist. Performing "The Girl from Ipanema," they took top honors at the Battle of the Bands competition at the Hollywood Bowl in 1965. Jacobs left the trio in 1968 to study music, and with a shy Karen reluctantly at vocals, the duo cut a series of demos that eventually reached Herb Alpert, who signed them on his A&M label.

Under Alpert's guidance, The Carpenters released the gushy single "(They Long to Be) Close to You," penned by Burt Bacharach, in 1970. It topped the charts for four weeks, sold one million copies, and was the first of sixteen consecutive Top Twenty hits, including the perpetual wedding song "We've Only Just Begun" (1970), plus "For All We Know" (1971), "Rainy Days and Mondays" (1971), "Superstar" (1971), "Sing" (1973), "Yesterday Once More" (1973), "Top of the World" (1973), and "Please Mr. Postman" (1974). The group headlined its own NBC-TV variety show, *Make Your Own Kind of Music*, during the summer of 1971.

The Carpenters seemed to be on top of the world, but in reality the pressures of stardom caused agonizing personal problems: Richard's addiction to prescription narcotics (quaaludes) and Karen's battle with anorexia nervosa, a mental illness characterized by obsessive dieting. In 1975, The Carpenters were forced to call off a global concert tour because Karen, at five foot four and weighing a painful ninety pounds, was too weak too perform. On February 4, 1983, she lost her long fight against the eating disorder and died of cardiac arrest at the age of thirty-two. Today, a rebirth of interest in the oft-derided group has occurred, particularly with Karen becoming more revered now than ever in her short lifetime.

CARRIE

"They're all gonna laugh at you!" A huge hit with high school teens of the late 1970s, this horror classic made them think twice about picking on outcast, nerdy classmates. Directed by Brain De Palma, the 1976 film was a stylish adaptation of Stephen King's 1975 million-selling novel.

Set in the Maine township of Chamberlain, it starred newcomer Sissy Spacek as mousy Carrie White, a senior at Bates High School, gifted (or cursed) with telekinetic powers. Lonely and painfully shy, Carrie is abused by a man-hating, Jesus Freak mother (Piper Laurie) and persecuted by the school's "in crowd." Her life takes a shocking turn on discovering for the first time menstrual blood while in the gym shower at school, causing her to freak out, fearing she was bleeding to death. The other girls in the locker room, led by bitch Chris Hargensen (Nancy Allen), pelt her with tampons, chanting "Plug it up! Plug it up!" which leads to their punishment of grueling calisthenics. Infuriated, Chris and hoodlum boyfriend Billy Nolan (John Travolta) devise a malicious prank by having Carrie nominated for prom queen and being escorted by unsuspecting Tommy Ross (William Katt), the most handsome and popular boy in the class.

On the big night, Carrie and Tommy are elected king and queen (due to rigged votes), and as she stands on stage beaming—for once, feeling accepted by the student body—she is doused by a bucket of pig's blood. The cruel joke unleashes Carrie's pent-up rage and she turns her awesome telekinetic powers on her classmates. After destroying the school, she goes home to throw every knife in the kitchen at her crazed mom. It concludes with one of the greatest surprise endings of all time: a dream sequence in which Carrie's bloody hand reaches out from the grave to grab Sue Snell (Amy Irving), a remorseful classmate who had encouraged boyfriend Tommy to take Carrie to the prom and whose attempts to stop the bloody joke went unheeded.

The frightfest put both De Palma and King on the map and advanced the careers of its young cast, especially Spacek, who earned a Best Actress Oscar nomination for her role as Carrie White. It inspired other telekinetic revengers, such as *Jennifer* (1978), *The Fury* (1978), and *Scanners* (1981), as well as a sequel twenty years later, *The Rage: Carrie 2*, starring Emily Bergl as Rachael Lang, Carrie's half-sister.

FYI: ▸ Stephen King got the concept for *Carrie* when he was a high school English teacher observing the social pecking-order among his students.

CARRIE NATIONS

Big-boobed and groovy, this all-girl rock band from Texas, originally called The Kelly Affair, went to Hollywood to make it big but found only sex, drugs, and psychedelic deceit. The trio includes cute and curvy Kelly MacNamara, the lead singer; voluptuous Casey Anderson, the guitarist; and hip soul-sister Pet (short for Petronella) Danforth, the drummer. Hit songs: "Look on Up from the Bottom," "In the Long Run," and "Find It." Featured in breast-loving Russ Meyer's deliciously bad *Beyond the Valley of the Dolls* (1970).

CARS

Rock group, formed in Boston in 1976, that makes one recall old-fashioned memories of skinny ties, straight-leg jeans, high-top sneakers, and spiky hair. Driven by lanky, towering lead singer Ric Ocasek, The Cars mixed New Wave and power pop and rode the music charts during the late 1970s and the 1980s. Hit songs include "Just What I Needed" (1978), "My Best Friend's Girl" (1978), "Let's Go" (1979), "Touch and Go" (1980), "Shake It Up" (1981), "You Might Think" (1984), "Magic" (1984), and "Drive" (1984). Voted Best New Band of the Year by *Rolling Stone* magazine in 1979. Disbanded in 1988.

CARTER, AMY

Born on October 19, 1967, the only daughter and youngest child of President Jimmy Carter, the peanut farmer from Plains, Georgia, she had the fortune (and misfortune) of being thrust into the limelight at the age of nine. She was fortunate in that it's almost every kid's wish to be the child of the President of the United States. Just think how cool it would be to live in the White House, have Secret Service Agents follow you to school, and meet famous people from all over the world.

On the other hand, the whole world got to witness little Amy go through puberty. Imagine your preteen years, nine through twelve, on public display (not a pretty sight). And physically speaking, poor Amy had it rough. She was the prototypical nerd, and also adorned with the Carter family toothy grin, long, stringy reddish-blonde hair, and thick black eyeglasses that overwhelmed her pale, freckled face. She seemed to be an odd girl who marched to the beat of a different drummer. In fact, the only memories I have of Amy are of her being gawky in the background while newsmen were interviewing her dad. In college, Amy was involved in various forms of political activism.

CASPER THE FRIENDLY GHOST

The friendliest ghost we know! A childlike white specter who prefers helping people instead of scaring them. Casper yearns only to make a friend, which could be difficult because his see-through appearance usually scares everyone off ("It's a g-g-ghost!"). Created by Joe Oriolo and Sy Reit, the cute apparition first materialized in 1945 as a star of theatrical cartoon shorts produced by Paramount Pictures Famous Studios. He started his best-selling comic-book career for *Harvey* comics in 1958, eventually headlining thirteen different titles, including *The Friendly Ghost Casper, Casper's Ghostland, Casper and the Ghostly Trio, Casper and Wendy, Casper's Space Ship, TV Casper and Company*, and *Casper and Richie Rich*.

Casper's TV career began in 1959 as a regular cartoon segment, along with Little Audrey and Baby Huey, on *Matty's Funday Funnies* (1959–61), a series sponsored by Mattel Toys. In 1963, he was given his own half-hour series, *Casper the Friendly Ghost*, which haunted ABC's Saturday-morning schedule for the rest of the decade. Other friends who appeared with Casper were good little witch Wendy, tuff little ghost Spooky, galloping ghost horse Nightmare, and the mischievous Ghostly Trio. Casper and pals resided in the Enchanted Forest. In 1995, the "World's Most Famous Ghost" was the star of a high-tech Hollywood movie starring Christina Ricci and Bill Pullman.

FYI: ▸ On April 16, 1972, Casper's name was used for the command ship on the Apollo 16 space mission.

CASSIDY, DAVID

Teenland's grooviest heartthrob played bell-bottomed, pukka-shelled Keith Partridge, eldest son and lead singer of the TV rock group The Partridge Family (1970–74). Born April 12, 1950, in New York City, he was no stranger to show business. His father was comic actor Jack Cassidy, his mother was actress-singer Evelyn Ward, and his stepmother (Jack's second wife) was Oscar winner Shirley Jones, who also portrayed his mom on *The Partridge Family*. Along with starring on the smash sitcom, Cassidy simultaneously had several Top Forty hits with The Partridge Family: "I Think I Love You" (1970) and "I Woke Up in Love This Morning" (1971), and, as a solo artist, "Cherish" (1971).

His irresistibly cute face, sparkling green eyes, outtasight shag cut, slender bod, cool yet slightly silly personality, and sweet singing voice sent young girls into chaotic rages of hormonal overload. *Life* magazine reported in 1971: "Attendance at a David Cassidy concert is an exercise in incredulity. Hordes of girls, average age eleven and a half, with hearts seemingly placed inside their vocal cords, shout themselves into a frenzy. They also wave at him, snap his picture and send him presents backstage. Afterward, being unable to rip off a piece of David's clothing or a hunk of his hair or a limb of his body, they rush out to buy David Cassidy records or posters or send away for mysterious items like the David Cassidy Lover's Kit."

At times the attention turned menacing, as fans mobbed Cassidy almost everywhere no matter how private the situation (his hospital room was invaded after he had his gall bladder removed). At a London concert in 1974, ambulance workers treated more than 1,000 overexcited fans, six were hospitalized, and a fourteen-year-old suffered a fatal heart attack. Feeling partly responsible for the incident, a remorseful Cassidy decided to shed his teen idol image by quitting *The Partridge Family* and escaped from the spotlight to a peaceful estate in Hawaii. He has since hosted a retro video show on VH-1, acted in the Broadway play *Blood Brothers* (co-starring younger half-brother Shaun Cassidy), and written a 1994 autobiography, *C'mon, Get Happy.*

FYI: ▸ The David Cassidy Lover's Kit, purchased exclusively from *16 Magazine* for a mere two bucks, contained "a life-sized, full-length portrait, an autographed maxiposter three times life-size, a complete biography and childhood photo album, forty wallet-sized photos, a secret love message from David, and a lovers' card with his name and yours." Wow!

CASSIDY, SHAUN

With the success of a hit TV series and a concurrent singing career, along with intense good looks, he followed in the footsteps of older brother David to become the second teenybopper sensation to strike the Cassidy family in a decade. Born on September 27, 1958, to actress Shirley Jones and actor Jack Cassidy, Shaun became famous playing Joe Hardy on TV's *Hardy Boys Mysteries* in 1977. The same year, he had a fabtastic singing career with three Top Ten hits: "Da Doo Ron Ron," "That's Rock 'n' Roll," and "Hey, Deanie." Hazards of being a teen idol are that your adolescent fans will grow up or move on to the next heartthrob. This sure enough happened to Cassidy, and by the end of the 1970s his meteoric career took a nosedive into obscurity.

CASTLE GRAYSKULL

Sword-and-sorcery fortress on the war-torn planet Eternia housing the wise Council of Elders, in which burly-chested He-Man and his Masters of the Universe are guarded from supreme bad guy Skeletor. Based on the *He-Man* cartoon series, Castle Grayskull came as an awesomely cool multilevel play set, complete with drawbridge, elevator, and hidden trapdoor, in the Masters of the Universe action-figure toy line of the 1980s.

CATES, PHOEBE

Born July 16, 1963, dark-haired, bright-eyed teen model turned actress (frequently seen in *Seventeen* magazine during the late 1970s), best known for the teen-oriented classic *Fast Times at Ridgemont High* (1982). In it she played fifteen-year-old Linda Barrett, the embodiment of teen experience, who instructs best pal Stacey Hamilton on fellatio by giving head to a carrot and is also the bare-breasted wet dream for masturbating Brad, Stacey's older brother. Also seen as the female lead in *Paradise* (1982), *Private School* (1983), *Gremlins* (1984), *Bright Lights, Big City* (1988), and *Shag* (1989). In 1984, Cates played Lili, the heroine of the highly rated TV miniseries *Lace.* Contemporaries included Brooke Shields, Kim Delaney, Lori Loughlin, and Nia Peeples. She married actor Kevin Kline in 1990.

CAT-EYE GLASSES

Boys don't make passes at girls who wear glasses. That's a bunch of cat poop! They'll think a gal is the cat's meow after catching a glimpse of her sporting these cat-eye-style glasses, fashionable in the late

1950s and '60s and characterized by slightly oblong frames with ends pointed upward (reminiscent of the eyes of a Siamese kitty). Extra points for those who wear a pair decorated with sparkly jewels or fanciful etchings, like leopard print or a whirly pattern.

CATHY

"Ack!" Full name: Cathy Andrews. Created by Cathy Guisewite, this wide-eyed, perpetually single heroine of a long-lasting newspaper comic strip made her debut in 1976. *Cathy* chronicles the personal and professional life of a young career woman as she struggles with an unappreciative corporate boss (Mr. Pinkley), a noncommital boyfriend (Irving), an oh-so-perfect friend (Andrea), an over-doting set of parents (Anne and Bill Andrews), and dieting from never-ending weight gain. At least pet dog Electra (and millions of readers) loves Cathy unconditionally. *Cathy* is distributed by Universal Press Syndicate. In 1993, Cathy Guisewite won the National Cartoonists Society's Reuben Award.

FYI: ▸ Did hell freeze over? After twenty-eight years of on-again, off-again dating, Cathy and Irving finally tied the knot on February 5, 2005. Now, if only the Little Red-Haired Girl will have lunch with Charlie Brown . . .

CAT IN THE HAT

"Ten years ago, Dr. Seuss took 220 words, rhymed them, and turned out *The Cat in the Hat*, a little volume of absurdity that worked like a karate chop on the weary world of Dick, Jane, and Spot."

—ELLEN GOODMAN, DETROIT FREE PRESS

"It is fun to have fun, but you have to know how. . . ." First published in 1957, this beloved children's book written by Dr. Seuss was loaded with easy and fun rhyming words, to encourage youngsters to read "all by themselves." It starred his most famous creation—the Cat in the Hat, a six-foot-tall feline wearing a large red-and-white striped stovepipe cap and red bow-tie. It's a "cold, cold wet day," and a brother and sister (along with a worrisome pet fish) are left alone indoors with nothing to do. After hearing a surprise bump at the door, they find the fast-moving, fast-talking Cat in the Hat, who's full of games, tricks, and mischievous fun. The madcap visitor, with the aid of Thing One and Thing Two (who came in a box), makes a mess of the house, but before Mother returns he proves to be a kid's best friend by magically cleaning up the chaos with a giant Sweep-Up Machine. In 1971, the whimsical tale was made into an animated TV special complete with such off-the-wall songs as "Cat's Hat," "Nuthig, Nuthig to Do," and "Calulatus Eliminatus."

FYI: ▸ The Cat in the Hat's hat was a popular fashion accessory for X-tripping revelers at techno-driven rave parties throughout the 1990s.

CATS

Inspired by the poetry of T. S. Eliot's *Old Possum's Book of Practical Cats*, this elaborate production by Andrew Lloyd Webber became Broadway's longest-running musical after opening in 1982. It features spectacular feline makeup, costumes, and dance scenes, as well as memorable tunes, including the heartfelt "Memory," sung by Grizabella the Glamour Cat. Other Broadway shows created by Andrew Lloyd Webber include *Joseph and the Amazing Technicolor Dreamcoat* (1968), *Jesus Christ, Superstar* (1971), *Evita* (1978), *Starlight Express* (1984), *Phantom of the Opera* (1987), and *Sunset Boulevard* (1993).

CATWOMAN

The purr-fectly wicked and sexy cat-suited Batman villainess played in succession by Amazonian starlet Julie Newmar, former Miss America Lee Meriwether, and sultry singer Eartha Kitt in the 1960s TV series, ultracool Michelle Pfeiffer in the film *Batman Returns* (1992), and most recently Halle Berry in 2004's *Catwoman*. (Male filmgoers loved Berry's torn and tattered skin-hugging Catwoman garb, even though the film was a big-screen bomb.) The Feline Felon's real name: Selina Kyle. Meow!

CAULIFLOWER BANGS

A frumpy hairstyle that involved a woman cutting a wide section of short bangs atop her head (all the way back to the crown, which is just wrong), then curling them up and back with a curling iron and overdosing it stiff with spray lacquer. This round bang look reminds me of something you would find on a vegetable party-tray, so I refer to it as "cauliflower bangs."

CAVEMOBILE

This is the name of cartoon caveman Fred Flintstone's foot-powered, thatched-top convertible with stone wheels. Also called the Flintmobile.

CB RADIOS

"Breaker, Breaker!" During the Bicentennial summer, "First Mama," also known as First Lady Betty Ford, was a CB enthusiast who called out "breakers" from the White House. Before Betty and other "cotton pickers" (nontruckers) became obsessed with CB radios in the mid-1970s, they were chiefly operated by "good buddies" (truck drivers) as a way of communicating with other truckers on the nation's highways. Adopting anonymous "handles" (names) and speaking in a creative, folksy lingo, these "racket jawers" (CB operators) used the two-way, twenty-three-channel electronic transmitters to warn one another not to go over "double nickel" (the national speed limit of fifty-five miles an hour) because a "Smokey" (patrolman) with a "Kodak" (radar) was lurking ahead, or to alert them to the whereabouts of a foxy "beaver" (woman) in a "four-wheeler" (car). CBs were also used to warn of bad weather conditions; to aid motorists who were lost, stranded, or involved in accidents; and just to have a friendly chat while driving alone on long trips. The CB boom spawned songs, "Convoy" (1975) by C. W. McCall and "White Knight" (1976) by Cledus Maggard; a prime-time TV show, *Movin' On* (1974–76), starring Claude Akins and Frank Converse; and three motion pictures: *Citizen's Band* (a.k.a. *Handle with Care*) (1977), *Smokey and the Bandit* (1977), and *Convoy* (1978). "That's a big ten-four, good buddy."

"CENTERFOLD"

The J. Geils Band's chart-topping 1981 tribute to the fantasy babes of dirty magazines was joined by a video featuring the red-blooded rock group from Boston playing in a classroom full of nightie-clad schoolgirls.

CENTRAL PERK

The cozy coffeehouse in Greenwich Village is where the *Friends* gang gathers or works (Rachel, ineptly), lounging on oversized sofas and catching up on things while uttering witty quips over a latte or cup of cappuccino.

CEREAL

"We were about to enter that precarious palace of the puff, that fare-thee-well fortress of flakes, that sanctuary of sweetness, sugar, and trisodium mononitrate: the cereal aisle!"

—COMEDIAN JERRY SEINFELD

As kids, part of the ritual of accompanying our moms on weekly visits to the grocery store was to help choose a favorite brand of boxed cereal. If you weren't there to help her pick out the "most important meal of the day," she would bring home nutritional, boring brands like Corn Flakes, Special K, or Grape-Nuts. Since we were bombarded and influenced by a week's worth of TV ads from the three big cereal magnates (Kellogg's, General Mills, and Post), our hearts thumped fast with anticipation as we reached the cereal aisle—for now it was time to choose a brightly colored box of sugary delight. This momentous decision was always difficult to make, so we were stuck in the cereal aisle for a long time.

Breakfast cereals were fun! They feature zany characters (for example, Cap'n Crunch, Quisp Martian, Trix Rabbit, and Lucky Leprechaun). You can play with them while eating (like Alpha-Bits, Crispy Critters, and Lucky Charms). And, they're yummy-tasting (Cocoa Krispies, Froot Loops, and Sugar Frosted Flakes, for instance). Another great thing about cereals was the cool toy premium found inside the boxes or obtainable by mail.

The following is a list of fifty best-loved cereals:

Alpha-Bits
Apple Jacks
Boo Berry
Cap'n Crunch
Cheerios
Chex
Cinnamon Toast Crunch
Cocoa Krispies
Cocoa Pebbles
Cocoa Puffs
Cookie Crisp
Corn Flakes
Corn Pops
Count Chocula
Crispy Critters
Crunch Berries
Frankenberry

Freakies
Froot Loops
Frosted Flakes
Frosty O's
Fruit Brute
Fruity Pebbles
Golden Grahams
Honey Nut Cheerios
Honeycomb
Jets
Kaboom
King Vitamin
Kix
Life
Lucky Charms
Maypo
Mini-Wheats
Nut & Honey Crunch
Peanut Butter Crunch
Puffa Puffa Rice
Quake
Quisp
Raisin Bran
Rice Krispies
Sir Grapefellow
S'mores
Smurf-Berry Crunch
Spoon-sized Shredded Wheat
Sugar Crisp
Sugar Smacks
Trix
Twinkles
Wheaties

FYI: ▸ The average child consumes fifteen pounds of cereal a year.

CHACHI ARCOLA
Teen favorite Scott Baio played the adorable younger cousin of Arthur Fonzarelli (the Fonz was Chachi's idol) and sweetheart of Joanie Cunningham on the 1970s TV sitcom *Happy Days* and its 1980s spin-off, *Joanie Loves Chachi*. Chachi's first name? Charles.

CHAIRRY
Sweet-talking, fluttery-eyed, aqua-blue chair found inside *Pee-Wee's Playhouse*. Found the marvelous Miss Yvonne to "smell pretty" whenever she sat on him.

CHA-KA
The littlest member of the monkey-like Pakuni tribe who was the Marshall family's friendly but prankish companion (they saved his life during a T-Rex attack). Daughter Holly spent extra time teaching Cha-Ka to speak English. He was played by eleven-year-old child actor Philip Paley on Saturday morning's *Land of the Lost*.

CHAP STICK
"There's a Chap Stick for every pair of lips." Perky blonde ski bunny Suzy Chaffee, a.k.a. Suzy Chap Stick, hawked this lip balm on TV ads in the 1970s.

CHARIOTS OF THE GODS
A best-selling book, and later movie, that raised the speculative question "What if visitors from outer space helped advance mankind's knowledge centuries ago?" The 1968 book featured author Erich Von Daniken's theories about the extra-terrestrial origins of man's great feats. According to his philosophy, these space travelers helped build great ancient civilizations (Incan and Mayan) and landmarks (Egyptian pyramids). They also upgraded our ancestors' intelligence levels by teaching them arithmetic. In 1974, a German-produced big-screen documentary based on the book was released in America. Although the film's theories have never been proved, it made a great travelogue of exotic locales.

CHARLES, SUZETTE
First Runner-Up to Vanessa Williams, this Miss New Jersey succeeded the scandal-stricken Miss America after she resigned from the throne, and for a mere eight weeks in 1984 she reigned as the second African-American in history to hold the pageant's title.

CHARLIE AND THE CHOCOLATE FACTORY
First published in 1963, Roald Dahl's legendary masterpiece about a virtuous but poor lad, Charlie Bucket, who visits Willy Wonka's magical candy kingdom in the company of four decidedly obnoxious children: Augustus Gloop, Veruca Salt, Violet Beauregarde, and Mike Teevee. The book was followed by a sequel, *Charlie and the Great Glass Elevator* (1972), and two movies, *Willy Wonka and the Chocolate Factory* (1971), starring Gene Wilder as Willy Wonka, and *Charlie and the Chocolate Factory* (2005), starring Johnny Depp as Willy Wonka.

CHARLIE BROWN

"Good grief!" Dressed in a trademark yellow sweater with a zigzag black stripe across the middle, he's the good ol' star of the Peanuts cartoons, called "Blockhead" by friends and "that round-headed kid" by pooch Snoopy. A wishy-washy lad, Charlie Brown's unending optimism leads him to believe that for just once the innocent-appearing tree will not eat his kite (it does), that antagonist Lucy will not pull the football away before he can kick it (she does), that he'll pitch his winless baseball team to a victory (he doesn't), and that his school crush, the Little Red-Haired Girl, will one day share his lunch at Birchwood Elementary (she doesn't). "Rats!"

CHARLIE BROWN CHRISTMAS

"It's Christmas time again.
And every year the same thing happens.
Everyone is full of cheer—everyone but me."
—CHARLIE BROWN

First airing in 1965, a heartwarming TV special that taught Charles Schulz's Peanuts characters (making their animation debut) the "true" meaning of the Yuletide holiday. The story has Charlie Brown lacking the Christmas spirit because its message is lost amid all the seasonal glitz. He finds beagle Snoopy trying to win a cash prize by decorating his doghouse for the Super-Colossal Neighborhood Lights and Display Contest, while little sister Sally is writing a letter to Santa asking him to bring her money, "preferably tens and twenties." To make matters worse, he hasn't received one Christmas card or been invited to a Christmas party or even asked to go Christmas caroling. During a visit to Lucy's psychiatric-advice booth, she suggests he get involved with the holiday festivities by directing their Christmas play. To decorate the stage, our hapless hero sets out to find the "perfect" Christmas tree.

Searching through aluminum and plastic monstrosities at a Christmas-tree lot, he rescues a tiny, scrawny real tree nobody would ever want. The gang is shocked to see the pathetic tree Charlie Brown brings back, and after his placement of the first ornament causes it to droop, he declares, "Augh! I've killed it." Linus later finds the tree abandoned in the snow and, realizing it just needs a little love, tenderly drapes his security blanket around it. One by one, the rest of the Peanuts come to hang decorations on it. The spirit of the season comes shining through, causing the little tree to grow beautifully fuller.

Directed by Bill Melendez, *A Charlie Brown Christmas* is the longest-running animated special in TV history, winning Emmy and Peabody awards for program excellence. It is highlighted by Vince Guaraldi's delightfully boppish jazz score, including "Christmas Time Is Here" and "Linus and Lucy" (the tune associated with the Peanuts).

"CHARLIE BROWN" CHRISTMAS TREE

Many people who grew up watching *A Charlie Brown Christmas* every Yuletide purposely choose a scraggly inexpensive tree over a much fuller, costlier one—as a declaration of love for the timeless holiday story and, of course, as a statement against the hype and commercialism of the modern holiday season.

CHARLIE BROWNS

A man's wingtip shoe similar in appearance to a saddle shoe; usually beige but with the middle (or saddle) section brown, navy, or burgundy.

CHARLIE BUCKET

The central hero of *Charlie and the Chocolate Factory* is a poor boy who lives in a small one-room house with his family, including four bedridden grandparents. Honest and good-hearted, young Charlie helps his parents out by working a paper route after school. He spends all the money he earns to buy a loaf of bread to go with the family's daily dinner of cabbage water. Charlie has dreams of winning a Golden Ticket so that he can visit Willy Wonka's fantastic chocolate factory.

FYI: ▸ Twelve-year-old Peter Ostrum played Charlie Bucket in the 1971 *Willy Wonka* film. It was Ostrum's only acting credit, for he grew up to become a veterinarian.

CHARLIE COLOGNE

"There's a new fragrance that's coming to town and they call it Charlie. . . ." For many women of the 1970s, Charlie was "the" smell. Sold in drugstores, the inexpensive fragrance, created by Revlon in

1973, was "kinda here, kinda now, kinda here, kinda wow!" and gave its wearer a feeling of self-confidence, glamour, and high class. The rest of us were left with the nauseating aroma of her strong, oversprayed cologne that lingered in the room (phewww!). Charlie's popularity was spurred by spirited TV ads featuring blonde model Shelley Hack strutting with high self-regard around an array of glamorous hot spots in the big city. Hack would later become associated with a different Charlie, as in *Charlie's Angels*, when she replaced Kate Jackson on the detective series in 1979.

CHARLIE'S ANGELS

"Once upon a time there were three little girls who went to the police academy. . . ." The ABC series that launched a thousand jiggles was the most popular new program of the 1976–77 TV season, and its principal attraction seemed to be the braless sex appeal of its leading ladies. It starred Kate Jackson as cool intellectual Sabrina Duncan, Jaclyn Smith as Southern beauty Kelly Garrett, and Farrah Fawcett-Majors as sporty blonde Jill Munroe. The foxy trio, all recent police-academy graduates, were taken from mundane day-jobs of writing parking tickets to work undercover at Charles Townsend Associates, a private detective agency. Their boss was the never-seen Charlie (voiced by John Forsythe), who communicated with them by speakerphone. Known as "Angels," the gals were aided by Charlie's contact man, Bosley (David Doyle), on daring assignments that had them going undercover at health spas, women's prisons, casinos, roller-derby rinks, and other places where they could wear skimpy clothing, such as bikinis, hot pants, bath towels, and so on.

In 1977, Farrah (hands down the most popular Angel) and her frosted hair became an overnight sensation. So feeling a bit heady (sorry, I couldn't help myself), Fawcett-Majors quit the crime drama to embark on a career in motion pictures. She was replaced by Cheryl Ladd, who held her own playing Jill's blonder kid sister, Kris Munroe. Subsequently, the replacement of an Angel became a yearly event: Jackson was replaced by Charlie cologne model Shelley Hack as Tiffany Welles in 1979, and a miscast Hack was replaced by Tanya Roberts as Julie Rogers in 1980.

As producer Aaron Spelling's first mega-hit (he later gave us *Dynasty*, *Beverly Hills 90210*, and *Melrose Place*), *Charlie's Angels* ended its remarkable run in 1981, but not before inspiring a few jiggle-prone imitators: *The American Girls* (1978), *Flying High* (1978–79), *Roller Girls* (1978), *Sugar Time!* (1977–78), and *Hee Haw Honeys* (1978–79). It also inspired an incredible amount of mass merchandise, featuring the Angels' gorgeous faces on such items as dolls, toys, T-shirts, notebooks, stickers, pinups, and even a beanbag chair. Farrah summed up the show's popularity when she told *TV Guide* in 1977: "When the show was number three, I figured it was our acting. When we got to be number one, I decided it could only be because none of us wears a bra."

In the 2000s, *Charlie's Angels* was remade into a set of action-packed blockbuster films starring Cameron Diaz as Natalie Cook, Drew Barrymore as Dylan Sanders, and Lucy Liu as Alex Munday—the new generation of Angels (2000's *Charlie's Angels* and 2003's *Charlie's Angels: Full Throttle*).

FYI: ▸ Which Angel were you? From talking with women of today's thirtysomething age-group, I've found that many pretended to play *Charlie's Angels* as young girls. More often than not, they say they fought with their girlfriends over who got to be Jill (Farrah) or Kelly (Jaclyn), but hardly anyone ever wanted to be Sabrina (Kate). "Freeze, turkey!"

CHARLIE THE OWL

"Very wise and very smart is Charlie the Owl . . ." Inventing, intellectual owl who wore a graduation cap and lived in a tree house, equipped with an elevator for easy access, on the kiddie program *New Zoo Revue*.

CHARLIE THE TUNA

Ambitious but luckless, the blue-finned fish, dressed in a red cap and black eyeglasses, tries to acquire "good taste" so that Star-Kist would consider him worthy of being packed into a can of tuna. Created in the mid-1960s, animated TV commercials featured Charlie demonstrating refined activities—reading poetry, painting a masterpiece, listening to classical music—only to be rejected by a sign on a fishhook that reads "Sorry, Charlie," followed by a voiceover saying "Sorry, Charlie. Star-Kist doesn't want tuna with good taste. Star-Kist wants tuna that tastes good." Herschel Bernardi provided the voice of Charlie the Tuna.

CHARLIE TOWNSEND

Mysterious, unseen proprietor of Charles Townsend Associates, a private detective agency in Los Angeles, who gave his female agents (known as "Angels") assignments via a speakerphone. Voiced by John Forsythe on the 1970s TV series *Charlie's Angels*.

CHARLOTTE'S WEB

Acclaimed by the Children's Literature Association as the "Best American Children's Book of the Past 200 Years," this spun the story of a spunky little girl named Fern Arable, a runt pig named Wilbur, a gluttonous rat named Templeton, and an enchanting spider named Charlotte. The story is set on a farm in New England. Wilbur and Charlotte lived together in a barn where one day the naive pig learns he is slated to become ham and bacon. The wise Charlotte (a true friend and a good writer) enlists the aid of Templeton and comes up with a plan to save Wilbur's life by weaving the words "SOME PIG" in her web. This extraordinary act causes Wilbur to become a local celebrity, drawing crowds who are eager to see the miraculous hog, and convincing superstitious Farmer Zuckerman not to slaughter him. Written by E. B. White in 1952, the beloved classic was later made into an animated big-screen musical in 1973, featuring the voices of Debbie Reynolds (Charlotte), Henry Gibson (Wilbur), Pamelyn Ferdin (Fern), Paul Lynde (Templeton), Agnes Moorehead (Goose), and Charles Nelson Reilly (Ram).

CHARMIN' CHATTY

Tall, gangly, eyeglass-wearing pal of doll Chatty Cathy, who was introduced in 1962, came with sixteen interchangeable records and could say an amazing 120 different phrases.

CHARO

In the 1970s, the vivacious blonde from Seville, Spain, was omnipresent on American TV as the hip-wiggling, guitar-strumming "cuchi-cuchi" girl who spoke in broken English. Kids of the era will remember her as Aunt Charo on *Chico and the Man* and as April Lopez on *The Love Boat*.

FYI: ▸ Charo was the winner of *Guitar Player* magazine's Readers Poll as Best Flamenco Guitarist two years in a row.

CHATTY CATHY

"Will you play with me?" The adorable, freckle-faced playmate for a generation of girls was the second most popular doll ever (Barbie is number one). Her success can be credited to the fact that she talked. By pulling a ring attached to a string on her back, you could make her say eleven different phrases, such as "I love you," "Please brush my hair," "May I have a cookie?" and "Give me a kiss." How did she work, you ask? Very simple: A miniature record player was concealed inside her. When the pull-string, called a "Chatty Ring," was yanked, the record randomly played one of her many sayings.

Debuting in 1960, Mattel's Chatty Cathy was modeled after the typical little girl next door. Realistic-appearing, she could be bought as a blonde or a brunette with either blue or brown eyes that opened and closed. Mattel expanded the "Chatty" line with a Chatty Baby (1962), twins Tiny Chatty Baby and Tony Chatty Brother (1963), nerdy-looking Charmin' Chatty (1963), and Singin' Chatty (1965). Her sales dwindled around 1970 after she received a redesigned face with painted eyes, a shorter stature, and spoke only nine phrases (the one good thing was a new voice provided by Maureen McCormick of *The Brady Bunch*). Kids weren't interested in that new Chatty Cathy, though, and she was soon discontinued. In spite of that unhappy ending, Chatty Cathy left her mark in toy history and will always be known for leading the way for hundreds of other "Chatty-Ring" talkers.

FYI: ▸ Today, Chatty Cathy's name is used to describe a talkative person—for example, someone who babbles on and on at a card game might be called a "Chatty Cathy" by another player.

CHEECH AND CHONG

A comedy duo whose humor about scoring dope, sexy chicks, and private parts made them popular among the drug counterculture of the 1970s. Originating from Vancouver, the hippie twosome consisted of Richard "Cheech" Marin, a dopey-eyed, heavy-mustached Mexican-American, and Tommy Chong, a bespectacled, bushy-bearded Chinese-French-Irish Canadian. In the early 1970s, they experienced success on *Billboard*'s record charts with a series of comedy LPs titled *Cheech and Chong* (1972), *Big Bambu* (1972), *Los Cochinos* (1973), and *Cheech and Chong's Wedding Album* (1974), along with the album cuts "Earache, My Eye," "Basketball Jones," and "Sister Mary Elephant." In 1978, Cheech and Chong ventured onto the silver screen with *Up in Smoke*, a hilarious no-brainer about their journey to find the best pot available. It became one of the highest-grossing movies of the year and was followd by *Cheech and Chong's Next Movie* (1980), *Cheech and Chong's Nice Dreams* (1981), and *Cheech and Chong's Still Smokin'* (1983). The pair became victims of Nancy Reagan's antidrug era and broke up the act in 1985. Chong is the father of actress Rae Dawn Chong, seen in the films *Quest for Fire* (1981), *The Color Purple* (1985), and *Commando* (1985).

CHEE-CHEE
Pet chimp of Doctor Dolittle, the world-famous veterinarian who could converse with animals. Featured in a series of children's novels by Hugh Lofting and in the 1967 *Dolittle* movie.

CHEERFUL TEARFUL
Introduced in 1966, the realistic baby doll from Mattel could actually change her expression to reflect her mood. When her arm was lifted and lowered, she smiled or pouted and cried real tears as well.

CHEERIOS
"Goodness in toasted oat cereal." The wholesome grain cereal in the shape of little O's has been a family favorite for almost sixty years. Variations of Cheerios include Apple Cinnamon, Frosted, Multi-Grain, and Honey Nut ("It's a Honey of an O"). From 1959 to 1970, Rocky and Bullwinkle served as its on-again, off-again advertising mascots.

CHEETAH
Not the speedy African prairie cat, but the mischievous chimpanzee tagalong of ape-man Tarzan in the *Tarzan* film series.

CHEF
School chef (velvet-voiced soul singer Isaac Hayes) who croons sexually explicit songs as a way of teaching Comedy Central's *South Park* elementary boys various life lessons. Chef scored a smash hit with the song "Chocolate Salted Balls" in 1999. Real name: Jerome McElroy.

CHEF BOYARDEE
Does anyone remember this canned pasta's late 1960s TV ads that had a little lad running through the back streets of an Italian city gleefully shouting, "We're having Beefaroni!"? For me, it's an endearing memory. In 1959, Chef Boyardee also introduced a pizza-making kit that brought pizza into American households before the days of frozen and home-delivery pizzas.

FYI: ▸ Chef Boyardee is named after founder Chef Hector Boiardi, who once catered President Woodrow Wilson's wedding.

CHEMISTRY SETS
Along with microscopes, these were ideal for budding scientists to do secret experiments in the privacy of their own bedrooms (as long as they didn't blow up the house).

CHER
Born Cherilyn Sarkisian LaPierre on May 20, 1946, in California, the enduring superstar of music, TV, and film who—just when you think she's in outsville—reinvents herself to revitalize her career. Tall and slim, with black hair, a husky voice, and a daring wardrobe, Cher has experienced a spectacular career in showbiz, marked with a variety of phases and expanding over five decades. When she was a teenager in the 1960s, she worked as a backup singer for producer Phil Spector, where she met sweetheart Sonny Bono at a recording session. In 1964, Cher married the much-older, much-shorter Sonny and they formed a recording duo, Sonny and Cher, marked by groovy threads and folksy ballads ("The Beat Goes On").

In the 1970s, Cher, wearing extremely long, straight hair, was a household name whose life took many directions: a TV star with impeccable comedy timing opposite hubby Bono on *The Sonny and Cher Comedy Hour* (1971–75); a pop chanteuse who had three number-one hits: "Gypsies, Tramps, and Thieves" (1971), "Half-Breed" (1973), and "Dark Lady" (1974); a divorcée after ending her eleven-year marriage to Sonny in 1974; a mother to daughter Chastity Bono and son Elijah Blue Allman, from her short-lived marriage to rocker Gregg Allman, 1975–77; and a glamorous clothes-horse whose revealing Bob Mackie–designed fashions brought much-publicized controversy as Cher fought the network censors to bare her belly button (she won). She ended the Me Decade as a disco diva—and with a disco smash, "Take Me Home" (1979)—performing campy cabaret-style shows in Vegas.

Cher began the 1980s sporting a spiky punk hairdo and singing in the short-lived heavy-metal rock group Black Rose. In 1982, Broadway actress was added to her repertoire when she made her debut in Robert Altman's *Come Back to the Five and Dime, Jimmy Dean, Jimmy Dean.* The play's success led to an acclaimed motion-picture career, which included the 1982 film version of *Jimmy Dean,* along with *Silkwood* (1983), *Mask* (1985), *Moonstruck* (1987)—earning her the coveted Best Actress Oscar—*Suspect* (1987), *The Witches of Eastwick* (1987), and *Mermaids* (1990). During her movie-star days, Cher moonlighted as a hard-rocker, scoring eight Top Forty singles, including "I Found Someone" (1988) and "If I Could Turn Back Time" (1989). Throughout this period, the outspoken star shown a penchant for tattoos and plastic surgery, an even more exhibitionist fashion sense, and a thing for much younger men (actor Eric Stoltz and Bon Jovi's Richie Sambora). More recently, her main focus has been a string of exercise videos and infomercials.

CHER HOROWITZ

"As if." This modern-day *Emma* is a Beverly Hills brat whose mission in life is to play matchmaker and give total makeovers to those more clueless. The blonde teen who made wearing kilts to school (with knee-high stockings no less) seem so sexy was portrayed by the charmingly petulant Alicia Silverstone in the movie *Clueless* (1995)—and was named after the subject of the preceding entry.

"CHEVY VAN"

Sammy John's Top Ten hit song about being seduced in his van after picking up a girl hitchhiker. Fueled by the custom-van craze, it sold more than a million copies in the spring of 1975.

CHEWBACCA

The 200-year-old, eight-foot-tall woolly Wookie was the strong and fearless co-pilot of smuggler Han Solo's Millennium Falcon in the *Star Wars* saga.

CHEWING GUM

> "I chew gum all the time,
> except when I eat dinner.
> Then, I take it out of my mouth and
> stick it behind my ear."
>
> —VIOLET BEAUREGARDE,
> IN *WILLY WONKA AND THE CHOCOLATE FACTORY*

Hey, all you Violet Beauregardes out there! Here's a list of twenty-five favorite brands of chewing gum.

Bazooka
Big Buddy
Big League Chew
Big Red
Black Jack
Blow Pops
Bubblicious
Chiclets
Cinn-a-Burst
Dentyne
Double Bubble
Doublemint
Freshen-Up
Fruit Stripe
Garbage Pail Kids
Gold Rush
Gum balls
Hubba Bubba
Joe Blo
Juicy Fruit
Rain-Blo
Super Bubble
Topps Baseball Cards
Trident
Wacky Packages

CHIC
Pronounced "Chick," these rivaled Gloria Vanderbilts as one of the world's top-selling jeans for women of the 1980s. The reason? They were more affordable (they could be found at Kmart) and were the first to offer the waist-inseam method of male-sizing for females. Characterized by the orange cursive "Chic" scrawled across the back pocket.

CHICKEN OF THE SEA
According to its jingle, "If you ask any mermaid you happen to see, What's the best tuna? she'll respond 'Chicken of the Sea!'" The canned tuna is advertised by a pretty, blonde mermaid who first appeared on the Chicken of the Sea label in 1952.

FYI: ▸ Chicken of the Sea tuna was thought to be actual chicken by ditzy blonde Jessica Simpson on the pop singer's MTV *Newlyweds* show in 2003.

CHICO AND THE MAN
Airing from 1974 to 1978, this sitcom is notable for being the first series with a Hispanic lead character and for being the first set in a Mexican-American neighborhood. It told the story of Ed Brown (Jack Albertson), the testy owner of a run-down garage located in the barrio of East Los Angeles, and Francisco "Chico" Rodriguez (Freddie Prinze), his quick-talking employee. Although different as night and day—Ed: old, cynical, and Caucasian; Chico: young, optimistic, and Chicano—the two worked well together turning the floundering business around. Supporting regulars included garbage man Louie (Scatman Crothers), mailwoman Mabel (Bonnie Boland), Chico's friend Mando (Isaac Ruiz), and Ed's landlady Della Rogers (Della Reese). In January 1977, troubled and drug-addled Prinze committed suicide at the height of his success. The show continued without its main star by adding a new "Chico" in the form of twelve-year-old Raul Garcia (Gabriel Melgar), a runaway from Tijuana who gets adopted by Ed. Also joining the NBC program was Charo as Raul's sexy Aunt Charo. Latin pop-star José Feliciano composed and performed the theme song.

CHIEF
"Sorry about that, Chief." Maxwell Smart's white-haired superior at CONTROL, an intelligence agency in Washington, D.C., was played by Edward Platt in the 1960s spy spoof *Get Smart*. The Chief used the Cone of Silence, which enveloped his entire desk, so conversations regarding evil KAOS would be kept top secret. TV viewers knew only his first name, Thaddeus.

CHIEF BIG MAC
Advertising character for McDonald's who is the leader of the police force in McDonaldland and has a head shaped like a Big Mac hamburger.

CHIFFON MARGARINE
This brand of margarine is well known for a set of slogans—current retro favorites—from its TV commercials: "It's not nice to fool Mother Nature!" and "If you think it's butter but it's not—it's Chiffon!"

CHILD CATCHER
Featured in 1968's *Chitty Chitty Bang Bang*, the dark and creepy fiend who snatches children to be imprisoned in Baron Bomburst's castle had to be the most frightful villain in any kid-oriented film of the era.

CHILDREN OF THE CORN
The 1984 horror movie based on a Stephen King novella about sinister juvenile devil-cultists who live in the cornfields of Nebraska. It starred Peter Horton and Linda Hamilton as Burt and Vicky Robeson, and Courtney Gains as the spooky Malachai. At least half a dozen sequels were spawned.

CHILLY WILLY
The cute mute penguin, who wore a snowball cap and walked stiff-legged like silent-screen great Charlie Chaplin, was created in 1953 by animator Walter Lantz (Woody Woodpecker). Chilly Willy's sophomore cartoon short "I'm Cold" earned an Academy Award nod for Best Short Subject in 1954.

CHIM CHIM
The name of the mischievous monkey belonging to Speed's kid brother, Spridal, on the cartoon program *Speed Racer*. Chim Chim is not to be confused with soundalike Chee-Chee, Doctor Dolittle's chimp.

CHINA FLATS
Imported from China, the mid-1980s alternative crowd shuffled around in these simple yet fashionable

black cloth shoes with thin cotton insoles. Also known as China Dolls (females) and Kung Fu shoes (males).

CHINESE FIRE DRILLS

Okay, we all did this silly act at least once. It involved stopping your car at a red light (usually at a busy intersection). Everyone on the driver's side would get out, race around the car, and get in on the passenger's side. Those on the passenger's side would dart around and get in on the driver's side. It was finished before the light turned green.

CHIP DOUGLAS

The third son of Steve Douglas and brother of Mike, Robbie, and youngest Ernie on the classic TV sitcom *My Three Sons*. Chip's best pal was Sudsy Pfeiffer, and best gal was college sweetie Polly Williams, with whom he would later elope. Actual first name: Richard.

FYI: ▸ Juvenile actor Stanley Livingston, who played Chip from 1960 to 1972, often threw away fan mail unread and married a go-go dancer at the age of eighteen (to the disdain of TV dad Fred MacMurray). These actions got him labeled the "black sheep" of the *My Three Sons* family.

CHIPMUNKS

The most enduring novelty pop group of all time, whose squeaky-voiced recordings—played unceasingly on childhood phonographs—drove parents out of their minds. It is said that singer-songwriter Ross Bagdasarian conceived the idea of the little cartoon rodents after nearly running over a squirrel on a country road. Under the stage name of David Seville, he had previous success in 1958 with the oddity song "Witch Doctor" ("Oo-ee, oo-ah-ah, ting-tang, walla-walla, bing-bang"), in which his voice was recorded at twice the speed of the musical accompaniment. Applying the same concept in 1959, he recorded the chart-busting "Chipmunk Song" using a trio of voices under the group name The Chipmunks.

Three years and five million records later, the three mischievous Chipmunks—Alvin, Simon, and Theodore—along with harried manager David Seville, starred in an animated TV series, *The Alvin Show* (1961–65). After Bagdasarian's death in 1972, the high-voiced group's career was put on hiatus until the early 1980s, when his son, Ross Jr., resurrected them with new recordings and a Saturday-morning cartoon titled *Alvin and the Chipmunks*, co-starring the Chippettes. Over the years, their records have sold more than thirty-five million copies, including the LPs *Let's Sing with the Chipmunks* (1959), *Sing Along with the Chipmunks* (1960), *Christmas with the Chipmunks* (1962), *The Chipmunks Sing The Beatles* (1964), *The Chipmunks See Doctor Dolittle* (1968), *Chipmunk Punk* (1980), *Urban Chipmunk* (1981), and *Chipmunk Rock* (1982).

"CHIPMUNK SONG"

"Christmas, Christmas time is here. . . ." The definitive Yuletide novelty song, featuring the sped-up voices of Ross Bagdasarian's Chipmunks, was 1958's fastest-selling single, landing at the top of the charts for four weeks and capturing three Grammy Awards: Best Comedy Performance, Best Recording for Children, and Best Engineered Record.

CHIP 'N' DALE

Two squeaky-voiced, fast-talking chipmunks, featured in Walt Disney cartoons since 1943, who—when not squabbling with each other—are usually pestering the cranky Donald Duck or the lovable pooch Pluto. Headlined a cartoon series on the Disney Channel, *Chip 'n' Dale Rescue Rangers* (1988–89), that had them starring in cliff-hanger adventure tales, à la Indiana Jones. If you are wondering how to tell the look-alike critters apart—scatterbrained Dale has a large, red nose, while the slightly more logical Chip has a smaller, black nose.

CHIPPENDALES

An all-male exotic dance troupe (fancy words for strippers) who by bumping and grinding their manhood turned normal, everyday housewives, college coeds, and brides-to-be into whooping, lust-crazed, dollar-waving maniacs. The are named after Chippendales, a Hollywood nightspot with a ladies-only door policy, where they have been performing since 1979. The average Chippendale looked like he'd stepped out of the centerfold of *Playgirl* magazine. One hundred percent beefcake, complete with handsome mug, muscles, and six-pack abs, he teasingly stripped down to a smaller-than-small G-string with a bulging "package," which was never exposed. These dancers projected studly stereotypes—cowboy, fireman, policeman, lifeguard, construction worker, and Latin lover—and could whip the most demure gal into a horny she-devil. When not dancing on stage, the Chippendales wore a working uniform consisting of little more than a tuxedo collar, a bow tie, cuffs, and black, skintight Lycra pants.

By the end of the early 1980s, a male stripper fad was in full swing. There were Chippendales calendars, posters, greeting cards, playing cards, videotapes, and underwear to be purchased at Spencer Gifts. Gregory Harrison played a stripper in the 1981 TV movie *For Ladies Only,* as did Christopher Atkins in the 1983 motion picture *A Night in Heaven.* New Waver Adam Ant sang about stripping on a 1983 record appropriately titled "Strip." Across the nation, other nightclubs began showcasing their own brand of male stripper troupes. Most of these dancers were not on a par with the Chippendales—they were cheesy (think of a Fabio type pushing his G-string-covered crotch toward your face) and added a slimy element to the whole business.

CHIPPETTES

All-girl singing group—Brittany, Eleanor, and Jeannette—who often competed against their male counterparts, The Chipmunks, in talent contests. Made their debut in 1983 on the *Alvin and the Chipmunks* cartoon show.

CHIPS

An action-packed hour of car chases and crashes, embraced by younger viewers who made it one of TV's most-watched police dramas throughout the late 1970s and early 1980s. Airing from 1977 to 1983, it dealt with the adventures of two motorcycle patrolmen—blond cutie Jonathan Baker (Larry Wilcox) and Hispanic hottie Francis "Ponch" Poncherello (Erik Estrada)—who are oh-so-sexy in their snug-fitting CHiPs uniforms. The twosome cruised the busy freeways of L.A., aiding motorists and apprehending criminals. Featured regulars included Sergeant Joe Getraer (Robert Pine), Officer Baricza (Brodie Greer), and Officer Bonnie Clark (Randi Oakes).

Dedicated friends on screen, Larry and Erik were not friends off. Their stormy relationship and personal differences caused Wilcox to quit the NBC show in 1982. He was replaced by Tom Reilly as Officer Bobby "Hot Dog" Nelson. Bruce Penhall, a pro motorcycle racer, played his half-brother Bruce Nelson, an officer-in-training. CHiPs is an acronym for California Highway Patrol.

CHIQUITA BANANA

"I'm Chiquita Banana and I've come to say / Bananas have to ripen in a certain way. . . ." If popular Brazilian film singer-dancer Carmen Miranda were reincarnated as a fruit, she would be this saucy spokes-banana for the United Fruit Company. The familiar Chiquita Banana jingle, penned by Garth Montgomery and sung by Patti Clayton, first aired on radio in 1944.

CHITTY CHITTY BANG BANG

"Oh, you pretty Chitty Chitty Bang Bang, Chitty Chitty Bang Bang, we love you. . . ." A delightful 1968 children's film about the spectacular car that could fly in the air and float on the sea, based on the 1964 book by Ian Fleming (*James Bond*) and loosely adapted for the screen by director Ken Hughes and author Roald Dahl (*Charlie and the Chocolate Factory*). Gangly Dick Van Dyke starred as Caractacus Potts, an eccentric inventor who spruces up a derelict racing car and gives it unique qualities, like fins for floating, and wings and propellers for flying. Named after the wonderfully strange sound its engine makes ("Bang bang chitty chitty bang bang"), the auto takes Potts, his twin children Jemima (Heather Ripley) and Jeremy (Adrian Hall), and truly scrumptious lady friend Truly Scrumptious (Sally Ann Howes) on an incredible adventure. They land in the kingdom of Vulgaria, a faraway place where children are forbidden. There they meet a host of nonsensical characters, including the toy-loving ruler Baron Bomburst (Gert Fröbe), his child-hating wife, Baroness Bomburst (Anna Quayle), the kindly Toymaker (Benny Hill), and the feared Child Catcher (Robert Helpmann). Songs, written by the Sherman Brothers of Disney fame, include the Oscar-nominated title tune along with "Truly Scrumptious," "Hushabye Mountain," "Toot Sweets," "You Two," "Doll on a Music Box," and "Chu-Chi Face."

Dearly loved by kids of the 1960s (including

this author), the musical fantasy spawned a variety of toy tie-ins, such as Corgi's six-inch replica of the winged auto ("the most fantasmagorical Corgi in the history of everything!"), Chitty Chitty Bang Bang Liddle Kiddles, a talking Mr. Potts doll, a talking Truly Scrumptious Barbie Doll, and an actual Toot Sweet candy maker ("Tweet 'em 'n Eat 'em"), which made real candy whistles out of Tootsie Rolls!

FYI: ▸ Chitty Chitty Bang Bang's license plate read GEN II (meaning "gentle"), and its automobile make was a Paragon Panther.

CHOCKLIT SHOPPE

In the *Archie* cartoons, this after-school hangout in Riverdale, owned by kindly Pop Tate, is where you can find lovable teenagers Archie and Betty and Reggie and Veronica frugging to a groovy tune playing on the jukebox (probably the latest from Josie and the Pussycats), while Jughead sits in a booth nearby consuming a mound of burgers and avoiding Big Ethel.

CHOKER

A tight-fitting, Victorian-style necklace consisting of a wide black-velvet ribbon, ornamented with an oversized cameo (like the kind Laurie Partridge wore). In vogue first in the early 1970s before undergoing a revival—influenced by dance-club divas Madonna and Lady Miss Kier of Deee-Lite—twenty years later in the 1990s. Teen boys favored leather cord variations decorated with pukka shells, shark teeth, gems, or beads (like the kind Bobby Sherman wore).

CHOO-CHOO CHARLIE

"Charlie says. . . ." Cute animated TV commercials airing throughout the 1960s featured little Charlie, a train engineer wannabe, shaking a full box of Good & Plenty (black licorice–flavored candy in the shape of pill capsules colored pink and white) to create the sound of a choo-choo train chugging along the tracks, and blowing on an empty box to produce a train whistle. Inspired us kids to save our empty Good & Plenty boxes to use as whistles. "Love my Good & Plenty."

CHRIS HARGENSEN

Catty high school bitch (played by Nancy Allen in the 1976 movie *Carrie*) who has it out for telekinetic-possessed geek Carrie White. As punishment for taunting Carrie during gym class, Chris is given a grueling set of exercises by Miss Collins. She refuses to do them and ends up suspended from school. She dates motorhead Billy Nolan, and together they plot to ruin Carrie on the night of the senior prom (Chris is the one who pulls the cord that gives Carrie a bloody shower). Chris and Billy die in a car accident caused by the power of Carrie.

CHRIS PARTRIDGE

The Partridge Family's youngest son, the archetypal seven-year-old suburban boy, who plays the drums in the rock band. Portrayed by dark-haired Jeremy Gelbwaks (1970–71) and later by blond Brian Forster (1971–74).

CHRISSY SNOW

Real name: Christmas. Suzanne Somers's jiggly dum-dum, who wears her blonde hair in a variety of ponytails remindful of a pampered puppy dog and who snorts when she laughs at her own lame jokes, on the late-1970s sitcom *Three's Company*. During the day, Chrissy works as a typist. In the evening, she shares an apartment in Santa Monica with another girl, Janet Wood, and a guy, Jack Tripper. Chrissy's country and western, just-as-airheaded cousin Cindy Snow took her place as a roommate when Chrissy moved back home to Fresno to take care of her ailing mother.

CHRISTIE

Toy history was made in 1968 when Mattel introduced Christie as Barbie's first African-American friend. It should be mentioned, however, that she wasn't the first black Barbie doll; that distinction goes to a "colored" version of cousin Francie in 1967, which sold poorly because most white households of the times couldn't accept Barbie's having an African-American relative! Christie wore her hair in a far-out Afro and shared Barbie's passion for wild psychedelic mod fashions. Handsome boyfriend Brad was added to the collection in 1970, so that Christie could double-date with Barbie and Ken. Other notable African-American Barbie friends have included nurse Julia, based on the Diahann Carroll late-1960s sitcom, and 1974's Cara and Curtis. In 1985, Mattel started producing black versions of Barbie, along with Christie, who still remains a best pal.

CHRISTINE

"It's furious!" The name of the demon-powered automobile, a bright-red 1958 Plymouth Fury, that literally takes over the life of high school outcast Arnie Cunningham. Featured in Stephen King's same-titled best-selling 1982 novel and in John Carpenter's 1983 film adaptation.

CHRISTMAS SONGS

Ho, ho, ho! It's Christmas time. Deck the halls and hang the mistletoe. Here's my list of the twenty-five best Yuletide tunes from the Baby Boom and Generation X childhood years (1950s through to the 1980s). These favorites of the holiday season should stir up youthful memories of snowmen, reindeer, elves, candy canes, sugar cookies, glittering lights, greeting cards, wrapped gifts, Christmas trees, and of course the jolly ol' fellow himself: Santa Claus. So snuggle up in front of a cozy fireplace (with chestnuts roasting and stockings hanging), grab yourself a glass of creamy eggnog and a slice of succulent fruitcake, and let these joyful recordings take you back to the merry Christmases of yesterday.

- "Blue Christmas" (1957) by Elvis Presley
- "Chipmunk Song" (1958) by The Chipmunks
- "Christmas Time Is Here" (1965) by Vince Guaraldi Trio
- "Christmas Wrapping" (1982) by The Waitresses
- "Do They Know It's Christmas?" (1984) by Band Aid
- "Feliz Navidad" (1970) by José Feliciano
- "Frosty the Snowman" (1950) by Jimmy Durante
- "Grandma Got Run Over by a Reindeer" (1979) by Elmo and Patsy
- "Happy Xmas (War Is Over)" (1971) by John Lennon and Yoko Ono
- "Holly Jolly Christmas" (1964) by Burl Ives
- "Heat Miser / Snow Miser" (1974) by George S. Irving and Dick Shawn
- "I Saw Mommy Kissing Santa Claus" (1952) by Jimmy Boyd
- "Jingle Bell Rock" (1957) by Bobby Helms
- "Last Christmas" (1984) by Wham!
- "Little Drummer Boy" (1958) by The Harry Simeone Chorale
- "Little Saint Nick" (1963) by The Beach Boys
- "Mary's Boy Child" (1956) by Harry Belafonte
- "Merry Christmas, Darling" (1970) by The Carpenters
- "Peace on Earth / Little Drummer Boy" (1977) by David Bowie and Bing Crosby
- "Rockin' Around the Christmas Tree" (1958) by Brenda Lee
- "Rudolph the Red-Nosed Reindeer" (1949) by Gene Autry
- "Santa Baby" (1953) by Eartha Kitt
- "Welcome Christmas" (1966) by Boris Karloff
- "We're a Couple of Misfits" (1964) by Billie Richards and Paul Soles
- "Wonderful Christmas Time" (1979) by Paul McCartney

CHRISTMAS STORY

"A tribute to the original, traditional, 100 percent red-blooded, two-fisted, all-American Christmas." An endearing holiday comedy centering on a nine-year-old Indiana lad named Ralphie Parker who wants nothing more than a genuine Red Ryder BB gun for Christmas. Unfortunately for our young hero, his parents and teacher don't think it's a good idea ("You'll shoot your eye out!"). Released in 1983, this nostalgic look at the Christmas holiday in the 1940s was based on an autobiographical story by humorist Jean Shepherd from his book *In God We Trust, All Others Pay Cash.* Cast includes Peter Billingsley as determined Ralphie, Darren McGavin as his gruff father, Melinda Dillon as his long-suffering mother, Ian Petrella as his wimpy brother Randy, Tedde Moore as his teacher Miss Shields, and Scott Schwartz as his pal Flick, who gets his tongue stuck on a frozen flag pole. Film highlights include Mr. Parker's obsession with a gaudy fishnet-hosed leg lamp, Ralphie uttering the "F-word" in front of his dad, and a visit to a monstrous department-store Santa. The film classic was directed by Bob Clark, the man who gave us *Porky's*.

CHRISTMASTOWN

According to the Rankin/Bass 1970 TV special *Santa Claus Is Comin' to Town*, the first castle on the left is where you'll find its number-one citizen—Santa Claus! It's better known as the North Pole.

CHRISTOPHER ROBIN

British author A. A. Milne based the imaginative young lad, whose stuffed animals came magically to life in the *Winnie the Pooh* tales, on his own son, Christopher Robin.

CHRONICLES OF NARNIA

These were seven separate children's books written by C. S. Lewis from 1950 to 1956 in Great Britain. In the 1960s, Macmillan Publishing Company introduced the classic tales to American children. The most popular book of the Chronicles was the first one, *The Lion, the Witch, and the Wardrobe* (1950). It told the story of four children—Edmund, Lucy, Peter, and Susan—who discovered the wonderful land of Narnia by stepping over a magic line in the back of a large wardrobe closet. Narnia was under a spell cast by the wicked White Witch, who made it "always winter and never Christmas." The children befriended the heroic lion Aslan and helped him challenge the witch's evil rule. In 1979, this tale was made into an animated TV special that won an Emmy Award for Outstanding Animation Program. The other books in the series were *Prince Caspian* (1951), *The Voyage of the Dawn Treader* (1952), *The Silver Chair* (1953), *The Horse and His Boy* (1954), *The Magician's Nephew* (1955), and *The Last Battle* (1956).

CHUCK E. CHEESE

"Where a kid can be a kid." Noisy pizza and game emporium for little rug rats, featuring token-devouring arcades, inane indoor rides, and cardboard pizza crust. First opened in 1977, the restaurant chain is named after the eatery's mouse mascot.

CHUCKY

Deadly "Good Guy" doll from the *Child's Play* film series who is possessed by the evil spirit of Charles Lee Ray, a.k.a. the Lake Shore Strangler, a serial killer who terrorized Chicago in the 1980s. Right before dying after being gunned down by the police, the psychopathic Ray used black magic to transport his soul into the freckle-faced Chucky doll with red hair. Chucky will be "your friend to the end."

CHURCH LADY

"Well, isn't that special." Enid Strict, the judgmental hostess of *Church Chat,* a religious talk show, smugly accused every celebrity guest of being a friend of Satan, and she did a swell Superior Dance as well. Created by comic Dana Carvey on NBC's *Saturday Night Live.*

CINDY BEAR

Yogi Bear's love interest in the Hanna-Barbera cartoons is this sweet Southern Belle bear dressed in a skirt and known for the dainty exclamation of "Ah do declare!"

CINDY BRADY

"Baby talk, baby talk, it's a wonder you can walk!" The *Brady Bunch*'s "baby-talking" youngest one in (blonde, pigtailed) curls was known for whining, snooping, tattling, and of course lisping. Played by actress Susan Olsen (born August 14, 1961, in Santa Monica, California).

CINDY LOU WHO

Little Who from Dr. Seuss's Whoville who caught the loathsome Grinch dressed as Santa Claus and stealing her family's Christmas tree. When she asked him why he was taking it, he replied: "I'm taking it home to fix it, dear."

CISSY DAVIS

Pert and pretty fifteen-year-old who wore her auburn hair in a perky flip hairdo. Portrayed by actress Kathy Garver, Cissy was the overprotective big sister of darling twins Buffy and Jody on the TV sitcom *Family Affair.*

CLACKERS

The insufferable noise of clack, clack, clack was heard everywhere when Clackers (a.k.a. Klackers or Click-Clacks) made the scene back in the early 1970s. Clackers were two ping-pong-ball-sized heavy marbles, each attached to the end of two cords with a ring in the middle, that you would swing back and forth so the balls would bounce off each other. Enthusiastic owners got them clicking and clacking so hard that at times all you could see was a blur, and if they were really talented they could do neat-o tricks with them. Clackers were discontinued in 1971 after the government issued a warning because they allegedly could shatter, sending shrapnel-like glass flying in the air, plus kids often used these toys as a weapon (ouch).

CLAMDIGGERS
Cool style of pants—straight-legged, mid-calf length—popular with both guys and gals during the beach-surfing craze of the mid-1960s. Name is derived from rolling up your pant legs to the middle of the calves while digging for clams just off the shore.

CLAM-HEAD
Redheaded best buddy of a cartoon shark, Jabberjaw, who played bass for The Neptunes, an underwater rock band, and exclaimed "Wowee, wow, wow, wow, wow!" when excited.

FYI: ▸ Actor Barry Gordon, who voiced Clam-Head on the *Jabberjaw* cartoon show, performed the 1950s Christmas novelty tune "I'm Getting Nuttin' for Christmas."

CLARABELL THE CLOWN
Horn-squeaking, seltzer-spraying, nontalking clown from *The Howdy Doody Show* who spoke his first and only words ("Goodbye, kids") when the kiddie program aired its final show in 1960. Played by Bob Keeshan, the future Captain Kangaroo.

FYI: ▸ Clarabell's last name was Hornblow.

CLARENCE THE CROSS-EYED LION
Beloved cockeyed jungle feline of the same-titled 1965 film—the basis for the hit TV show *Daktari* (1966–69). Along with Lassie and Flipper, this gentle sweetie was one of the more popular animal stars of the 1960s.

CLARICE
Bow-headed, long-lashed, pretty doe who accepts her sweetie, Rudolph the Red-Nosed Reindeer, for all of his differences, especially the young buck's "handsome" nose. Janet Orenstein voiced Clarice in the animated TV special *Rudolph the Red-Nosed Reindeer* (1964).

CLARK KENT
Reporter for the *Daily Planet* in Metropolis who uses a mild manner, a bumbling demeanor, and eyeglasses to mask his secret identity of superhero Superman, the Man of Steel.

CLEARASIL
This medicated zit cream for teens came skin-colored to conceal pimply breakouts but only made the condition more obvious because it dried "cakey."

CLEOPATRA JONES
Groovy Tamara Dobson starred as the title character, a slick and sexy secret agent out to stop a notorious drug ring led by the menacing mommy (Shelley Winters), in this quick-paced 1974 blaxploitation favorite. Sequel *Cleopatra Jones and the Casino of Gold* followed it the next year.

CLIFF BARNES
Played by actor Ken Kercheval, Barnes is the key adversary of the powerful Ewing clan on *Dallas*, a district attorney out to avenge his father's downfall by the Ewings. (Jock Ewing had tricked ex-partner Digger Barnes out of his share of an oil strike, as well as stealing his sweetheart Miss Ellie.) To his dismay, younger sister Pam married Bobby Ewing.

CLIFFORD THE BIG RED DOG
Little Emily Elizabeth's pet is the biggest, reddest dog on her street and one of the most popular book characters ever aimed at preschool readers. Originally published in 1963 as a black-and-red paperback, the playfully illustrated story by Norman Bridwell has spawned a book series with such titles as *Clifford and the Big Storm, Clifford and the Grouchy Neighbor, Clifford Goes to Hollywood, and Clifford's Thanksgiving Visit.*

CLING AND CLANG
Driving the bell-ringing Rescue Racer, these tiny, mute, birdlike, twin cops assisted Mayor Pufnstuf in combating kooky Witchiepoo on the Saturday-morning classic *H. R. Pufnstuf*. How to tell Cling and Clang apart? Cling wears the red uniform, Clang wears the blue!

CLOGS
I don't know about you, but I can still hear the echoing sound—clomp, clop, clomp, clop, clomp,

clop—produced by feathered-haired gals wearing a pair of the "must have" footwear of the 1970s. Originating out of Europe, cloddish clogs were wooden platform-style shoes characterized by a leather or vinyl open or closed toe area and a strapless heel. Trendy chicks matched them with miniskirts, maxiskirts, bell-bottoms, and gauchos. They looked especially groovy with rainbow-striped toe socks with each toe a different color. The hazards of wearing clogs were twisting an ankle while walking, or kicking one off while doing the latest disco move on the dance floor. Pity the poor disco dancer who ended up with a flying clog in the face.

CLOSE 'N' PLAY

For youngsters, there was no better way to play your Jackson 5 or Osmonds 45 rpm records than on this automatic phonograph from Kenner. Introduced in 1966, the battery-operated record player was simple to use: put a record on the turntable, switch on, close lid (needle was attached to lid), and it played automatically (hence the name). And, because it was conveniently portable you could carry it to a friend's house for an outtasight slumber party!

CLOWNS

Some people find clowns cute and amusing. They like to go to the circus and wave gleefully at these costumed funnymen. Their day would be made if a clown came over to greet them and perform a hilarious mime. The good clowns are Bozo, Ronald McDonald, and Emmett Kelly, a.k.a. Weary Willie, of the Ringling Brothers Barnum and Bailey Circus. Others find clowns simply frightening. It had to be torture for them to sit through magic tricks performed by a rented clown at a childhood birthday party. Did they wonder what evil lurked behind the grease-paint smile and honking red nose? The bad clowns are Stephen King's It (Pennywise), serial killer John Wayne Gacy, and the Killer Klowns from Outer Space.

FYI: ▸ Coulrophobia is the fear of clowns.

"CLUB TROPICANA"

A little-known Wham! tune from the 1983 *Fantastic* album, best remembered for its breezy music video of the cute pop duo George Michael and Andrew Ridgely as flight attendants joined by a pair of gorgeous female flight attendants, frolicking at a resort swimming pool in the Caribbean. Ahhhhh! Bring me another piña colada!

CLUE CLUB

Two cowardly bloodhounds, Woofer and Wimper, and a quartet of precocious teenage detectives—Dotty, D.D., Larry, and Pepper—were the stars of this cartoon show, a *Scooby-Doo* imitation produced by Hanna-Barbera and seen on Saturday mornings from 1976 to 1979.

CLUELESS

"Sex. Clothes. Popularity. Is there a problem here?" Amy Heckerling, director of the 1980s teen classic *Fast Times at Ridgemont High,* gave moviegoers an update with this sassy spin on 1990s high school culture. Described as "Jane Austen's *Emma* meets *Beverly Hills 90210,*" the 1995 comical satire focuses on pampered but well-meaning Beverly Hills brat Cher Horowitz (Alicia Silverstone), a popular high-schooler whose task in life is to make things better for those she knows. Accompanied by best friend and shopping buddy Dionne Davenport (Stacey Dash), Cher plays matchmaker to two lonely teachers, Miss Geist and Mr. Hall (Twink Caplan and Wallace Shawn), gives clueless transfer student Tai Frasier (Brittany Murphy) a makeover, tries to make cute new guy Christian Stovitz (Justin Walker) fall for her only to learn he is gay, and finally finds love with her idealistic ex-stepbrother, Josh (Paul Rudd). Other prominent characters include Cher's father Mel Horowitz (Dan Hedaya), Dionne's boyfriend Murray Duvall (Donald Faison), pot-smoking surfer Travis Birkenstock (Breckin Meyer), cocky jock Elton Tiscia (Jeremy Sisto), the deliciously bitchy Amber Mariens (Elisa Donovan), and butch P.E. instructor Coach Miss Deemer (Julie Brown). Like Heckerling's earlier *Fast Times, Clueless* showcases the teen fads and slang ("As if" and "Whatever") of an era. It spawned a TV show (1996–99) starring Rachel Blanchard as Cher. "Whatever. . . ."

FYI: ▸ Cher and Dionne were both named after famous singers of the past who now do infomercials.

CLYDE CRASHCUP
Zany, self-deluded scientist-inventor featured in a separate cartoon segment of *The Alvin Show* (1962–65). Leonardo, his bald assistant, accompanied Crashcup in his misadventures.

COBAIN, KURT
"It's better to burn out than fade away." Blond, lanky, long-haired singer-guitarist from Seattle (born February 20, 1967) who fronted the grunge band Nirvana and was labeled the "voice" of a generation. The band was universally credited with introducing alternative rock to the mainstream in the early 1990s. Nirvana's hit songs, like "Smells Like Teen Spirit" (1991) and "Come as You Are" (1992), spoke to an audience of disenchanted twentysomethings. Cobain's troubled lifestyle, fueled by heroin addiction, disdain for stardom, and a tumultuous marriage to Courtney Love (lead singer of Hole), led to his death by a self-inflicted shotgun blast on April 5, 1994.

FYI: ▸ Kurt Cobain joined the ranks of Janis Joplin, Jimi Hendrix, and Jim Morrison—all rock legends who died at the age of twenty-seven during the height of their careers.

COCA-COLA
Ahh, where do you even begin to describe Coke—the most popular soft drink in the world—in a few short paragraphs? How about a list of fun trivia points?

- Atlanta pharmacist John S. Pemberton originally concocted Coca-Cola in 1886 as a headache and indigestion tonic, a syrupy mixture containing kola nuts, coca leaves (the source of cocaine), caffeine, and mysterious other ingredients.
- Pemberton's bookkeeper, Frank Robinson, penned Coca-Cola's trademark cursive lettering in 1887.
- In 1887, Pemberton sold the Coca-Cola recipe to another pharmacist, Asa G. Candler, for a mere $284.24. Candler marketed it as a refreshing drink and made millions. Pemberton died penniless.
- Coca-Cola's curvaceous, green-tinted glass bottle debuted in 1916.
- The image of Santa Claus changed from a tall, thin, elfish man to a pleasantly plump, jolly fellow when he appeared in a series of Coca-Cola Christmas print ads, illustrated by Haddon Sundblom, beginning in 1931.
- Catchy Coca-Cola advertisement slogans over the years: "Coke adds life," "Coke is it," "Have a Coke and a smile," "It's the real thing," "The pause that refreshes," "Things go better with Coke," and "Zing! What a refreshing new feeling!"
- One of Coca-Cola's best remembered TV commercials is the 1971 spot in which young people gathered on a hilltop to sing "I'd like to buy the world a Coke," a peaceful counterpoint to a turbulent era. A Top Forty pop hit was adapted from the jingle—"I'd Like to Teach the World to Sing (in Perfect Harmony)" by The Hillside Singers.
- Almost a million Americans drink Coca-Cola for breakfast.
- All the Coca-Cola consumed in the world each year would fill more than 3.5 million bathtubs.
- The Chinese translation for Coca-Cola is "Bite the Wax Tadpole."
- The stringently noncommercial BBC wouldn't play The Kinks' "Lola" (1970) until they changed a Coca-Cola reference to "cherry cola."
- In 1985, Coca-Cola became the first soft drink consumed in space.
- Also in 1985, Coca-Cola executives changed the formula and called it "New Coke." The public simply didn't like it (the new taste sucked), and when sales quickly plummeted, the old Coke was brought back as Coca-Cola Classic.
- The many other beverages produced by the Coca-Cola Company include Diet Coke, Fresca, Mello Yello, Mr. Pibb, and Sprite.
- Coca-Cola's number-one rival is Pepsi-Cola, or just plain Pepsi.

COCAINE
"If coke's a joke I can't wait for the next line." The magical powder from South America was the drug of choice for the glamorous jet set, disco queens, and rock gods of the late 1970s and early 1980s. For these fancy folks, there was something seductively alluring about seeing a mound of white powder, freshly separated into lines on a mirror by a razor blade, waiting to be snorted up the nose with a rolled-up dollar bill. Coke became unglam after leaving addicted users in rehab or, worse, rock-bottom broke and on the inner-city streets trying to

score, alongside thugs and whores, its cheaper and more addictive relative—crack cocaine. Slang names for cocaine are Big C, blow, devil's dandruff, flake, nose candy, snow, and white horse.

FYI: ▸ So prevalent was cocaine at Manhattan's Studio 54 that above the bustling dance floor a huge moon-face was displayed with a coke spoon that would actually move up toward the nostrils.

COFFEE, TEA, OR ME?

Best-selling 1967 book disclosing the "uninhibited memoirs" of two swingin' stewardesses—authors Trudy Baker and Rachel Jones—that did nothing for women of the high-flying profession but make them out to be objects of sexual desire for male passengers. The sexy stereotype changed by the 1980s as a result of unions, fueled by the women's lib movement, which helped fight sexist weight and age restrictions (before that time, almost all airlines required a stewardess to quit before the age of thirty—if marriage didn't come first—and to go through the embarrassing "weigh in" each workday). Eventually the working title "flight attendant" replaced "stewardess," to accommodate the many males now employed in the once strictly female industry. The book was followed by a sequel, *Round-the-World Diary* (1971), and a made-for-TV movie, *Coffee, Tea, or Me?* (1973), starring bubbly Karen Valentine and John Davidson.

COFFY

"They call her Coffy and she'll cream you!" In her biggest hit, beautiful Pam Grier, "the queen of blaxploitation," plays a tough nurse who uses her street wits, sexy body, and loaded shotgun to seek vengeance against the junkies who hooked her kid sister on smack. A groovy Ray Ayers soundtrack accompanies the 1973 movie.

COLORFORMS

"No scissors, no paste, never a mess!" Created by husband-and-wife art students Harry and Patricia Kislevitz in 1951, Colorforms are brightly colored, precut, self-adhesive vinyl pieces that you apply and remove from a laminated scene board in endless recombinations. Housed in a flat box, Colorforms sets are inspired by the popular licensed characters, movies, and TV programs of the day (Barbie, Batman, Mickey Mouse, Popeye, Snoopy, Sesame Street, and so on). The advertising slogan said it all: "Colorforms plastic stick like magic!"

COMIC STRIPS

Drawn in black-and-white every day except on Sundays, when they can be found in glorious color, comic strips are a kid's favorite part of the newspaper. Forget about the headline news! Forget about the sports section! Forget about Dear Abby! Children want to see what their beloved comic characters with the word-filled balloons above their heads are up to. And if a kid is lucky, mom or dad will read the strip to him (talk about family bonding).

The following is a list of fifty best-loved newspaper comic strips we enjoyed growing up with. Some of them have been around since our grandparents were young (*Blondie*, *Dick Tracy*, *Little Orphan Annie*); others were short-lived (*Miss Peach*, *Tumbleweeds*, *Wee Pals*); while others are becoming faves of our own children (*Calvin and Hobbes*, *Garfield*, *Marvin*). Below, each comic-strip's title is accompanied by the name of the cartoonist who made it famous and the year it debuted in newspapers.

Alley Oop—Vincent T. Hamlin, 1933
Andy Capp—Reginald Smythe, 1963
Archie—Bob Montana, 1947
B.C.—Johnny Hart, 1958
Batman—Bob Kane, 1943
Beetle Bailey—Mort Walker, 1950
Blondie—Chic Young, 1930
Brenda Starr—Dale Messick, 1940
Broom Hilda—Russell Myers, 1970
Calvin and Hobbes—Bill Watterson, 1985
Cathy—Cathy Guisewite, 1976
Dennis the Menace—Hank Ketcham, 1951
Dick Tracy—Chester Gould, 1931
Dilbert—Scott Adams, 1989
Dondi—Irwin Hasen, 1955
Doonesbury—Gary Trudeau, 1970
The Family Circus—Bil Keane, 1960
The Far Side—Gary Larson, 1979
Flash Gordon—Alex Raymond, 1934
For Better or For Worse—Lynn Johnston, 1979
Funky Winkerbean—Tom Batiuk, 1972
Garfield—Jim Davis, 1978

Hagar the Horrible—Dik Browne, 1973
Heathcliff—George Gately, 1973
Henry—Carl Anderson, 1932
Hi and Lois—Dik Browne, 1954
Li'l Abner—Al Capp, 1934
Little Orphan Annie—Harold Gray, 1924
The Lockhorns—Bill Hoest, 1968
Love Is . . . —Kim Casali, 1970
Mandrake the Magician—Phil Davis, 1934
Mark Trail—Ed Dodd and Jack Elrod, 1946
Marmaduke—Brad Anderson, 1954
Marvin—Tom Armstrong, 1982
Mary Worth—Martha Orr, 1934
Miss Peach—Mell Lazarus, 1957
Momma—Mell Lazarus, 1970
Nancy—Ernie Bushmiller, 1938
Peanuts—Charles Schulz, 1950
The Phantom—Ray Moore, 1936
Pogo—Walt Kelly, 1948
Prince Valiant—Harold Foster, 1937
Steve Canyon—Milton Caniff, 1947
Superman—Joe Shuster, 1939
Tank McNamara—Bill Hinds, 1974
Tarzan—Harold Foster, 1929
Tumbleweeds—T. K. Ryan, 1965
Wee Pals—Morrie Turner, 1965
The Wizard of Id—Johnny Hart and Brant Parker, 1964
Ziggy—Tom Wilson, 1971

COMMANDER ADAMA

Silver-haired Lorne Greene starred as the stoic leader of the intergalactic starship of freedom fighters on *Battlestar Galactica*, during the seventh millennium A.D.

COMMANDER K-9

Marvin the Martian's green-skinned canine companion who accompanies the cartoon space alien on his missions to blow up planet earth in the Looney Tunes cartoon shows.

COMPACT PUSSYCAT

Seemingly a cross between a feline and a cosmetics compact, this fluttery-lashed pink convertible came with a parasol top to keep the harsh sun away from the delicate features of its driver, the sumptuous Penelope Pitstop. As car number five, Miss Pitstop raced the Compact Pussycat in an ongoing transcontinental competition in the Hanna-Barbera Saturday-morning classic *The Wacky Races*.

CONAN THE BARBARIAN

Created by pulp writer Robert E. Howard, the muscle-bound, sword-wielding warrior made his *Marvel* comics debut in October 1970. Set in the land of Cimmeria 20,000 years ago during the Hyborian Age—a time of mysticism, sorcery, and savagery—Conan's quest had him seeking vengeance against the evil warlock Thulsa Doom, who enslaved him as a child after brutally murdering his parents. His allies were Subotai the Mongol and Valeria, Queen of Thieves. In 1982, Conan's adventures were made into an epic motion picture starring the magnificently muscled Arnold Schwarzenegger. Its success spawned a 1984 sequel, *Conan the Destroyer*, not to mention hordes of low-budget sword and sorcery imitators, including *Beastmaster* (1982), *Ator the Fighting Eagle* (1983), *Deathstalker* (1983), *Hercules* (1983), *Krull* (1983), *Yor the Hunter from the Future* (1983), *Barbarian Queen* (1985), *Red Sonja* (1985), *Masters of the Universe* (1987), and *Gor* (1988).

CONCENTRATION

NBC-TV's longest-running game show, airing from 1958 to 1979, had contestants matching numbered tiles in order to obtain clues to a giant rebus. The first to solve the puzzle won all prizes accumulated. The program's hosts have included Hugh Downs, Jack Barry, Art James, Bill Mazer, Ed McMahon, Bob Clayton, and Jack Narz.

CONEHEADS

Featured as a comedy skit on NBC's *Saturday Night Live*, this alien family from the planet Remulak included leader-husband Beldar, a.k.a. Fred Conehead (Dan Aykroyd); wife Prymaat, a.k.a. Joyce Conehead (Jane Curtin); and teenage daughter Connie (Laraine Newman). Though they had bald, cone-shaped heads, they disguised themselves as middle-class suburbanites residing in a colonial-style home in Parkwood, New Jersey, and claimed they were originally from "France," if anyone asked. In 1993, Aykroyd and Curtin reprised their roles of Beldar and Prymaat for a poorly received big-screen comedy based on the 1970s skits.

"CONJUNCTION JUNCTION"
"Conjunction Junction, what's your function?" By far the most recognized *Schoolhouse Rock* tune, performed by jazz singer Jack Sheldon. First airing in 1973, its animated episode featured the distinctive train conductor dressed in blue overalls and puffy hat at a railroad track (Conjunction Junction) where boxcars are hooked together by words, phrases, and clauses.

CONKY 2000
The robot who talked in an echoing synthesized voice was responsible for the day's secret word on *Pee-Wee's Playhouse*, which made everyone scream real loud ("Ahhhhhhhhhhhh!!!") whenever the secret word was spoken.

CONNECT FOUR
A hybrid of checkers and tic-tac-toe played upright, this two-player game is best remembered for a TV commercial in which a brother gets beaten by his sister and exclaims, "Pretty sneaky, Sis!" Connect Four was introduced by game genius Milton Bradley in 1974.

"CONVOY"
In 1975, country singer C. W. McCall mined the CB radio fad with this number-one song on both the pop and country charts—a saga about a good ol' boy trucker with the handle "Rubber Duck." In 1978, it provided the basis for the movie of the same title starring Kris Kristofferson and Ali MacGraw.

FYI: ▸ Chip Davis, co-writer of "Convoy" (the other was Bill Fries), later formed an instrumental New Age act called Mannheim Steamroller.

COOKIE MONSTER
"C is for cookie, that's good enough for me / Oh, cookie, cookie, cookie, starts with a C!" A blue furry beast found on *Sesame Street* with an addiction for sweet, yummy cookies. "Me want cookie!"

COOKIES
Here's a list 'specially for you, Cookie Monster, so go ahead and salivate over these twenty-five cookie favorites:

- Animal crackers
- Butter cookies
- Chocolate chip cookies
- Deluxe graham striped cookies
- Fig Newtons
- Fortune cookies
- Ginger snaps
- Girl Scouts Thin Mints
- Lemon Coolers
- Macaroons
- Mallomars
- Milanos
- Nutter Butters
- Oatmeal raisin cookies
- Oreo cookies
- Peanut butter cookies
- Pecan Sandies
- Pinwheels
- Pirouettes
- Shortbread cookies
- Snickerdoodles
- Sugar cookies
- Sugar wafers
- Vanilla wafers
- Vienna Fingers

COONSKIN CAPS
"Davy, Davy Crockett, king of the wild frontier. . . ." First worn by early frontiersmen in the 1800s, these raccoon-skin caps with tail became the biggest fashion fad for young boys of the 1950s, made popular by Disney's *Davy Crockett* TV show.

COOPER, ALICE
Today's kids have Marilyn Manson to shock parents and religious leaders, but back in the early 1970s we had this other guy with a girl's name, labeled by the press as the "Devil of Depravity" from whom the youth of America must be rescued. Born Vincent Furnier, a preacher's son, on February 4, 1948, in Detroit, the rock star changed his name to Alice Cooper in 1968 (allegedly the name came from a spirit via a Ouija session). Wearing long, shaggy dark hair and heavy kohl eye makeup, he was known for violent-themed songs and bizarre, often gory stage performances. His props consisted of snakes, electric chairs, gallows, mutilated dolls, chickens, and bucketfuls of raw meat. (Contrary to

popular rumor, Cooper never bit off the head of a chicken during a concert.) Before the public lost interest in Cooper's outrageous antics, he was able to score a few hits, most notably the youth-oriented anthems "Eighteen" (1972) and "School's Out" (1972).

COOTIE CATCHER

These handmade fortune-tellers were all the rage in grade school, and it seemed that everywhere you went there would be some kid with one stuck on fast-moving fingers. As a minor form of origami, a Cootie Catcher was easy to make and fun to create. There were four common steps:

- Fold all four corners of notebook paper inward so that the points meet in the center.
- Turn over and fold all four corners toward center once more.
- Pick four different colors (typically red, blue, green, and yellow) for the outside leaves, number the eight inside leaves (one to eight), and under the flap of each number write a lucky (or unlucky) fortune.
- Fold in half, color side out, and slip fingertips underneath flaps. You're ready to go.

After placing the Cootie Catcher on your fingers, you would ask a friend to pick a color. If she chose, for example, "green," you opened and closed the Cootie Catcher five times for each letter in the word *green,* stopping on the inner leaves that revealed four of the eight numbers. Then your friend picked a number and you opened and closed accordingly; for example, if she picked three you opened and closed three times. From there, she would pick one final number and you'd lift up its flap to reveal the mysterious fortune. The fortunes were pretty basic stuff, ranging from nice—"You are smart!" "You are cute!" or "(*name of hunk or fox*) loves you!"—to naughty: "You smell like a swamp rat!" "You are ugly!" or "(*name of nerd or nerdette*) loves you!"

COOTIE GAME

"C'mon dice, roll me a head!" For wee folks, a cootie was more than an imaginary disease caught by touching a member of the opposite sex, it was a multicolored plastic bug assembled piece by piece by the roll of a dice. Cootie was created around World War I and originally played as a paper-and-pencil game. In 1949, Minnesota woodworker Herb Schaper designed the "exciting, educational construction game" featuring the plastic Cootie bug after his hobby of crafting fishing lures gave him the idea. By the following year, more than 1.2 million sets had been sold. Playing Cootie was simple (its target age-group is three to seven): Each number on a rolled dice represented a body part (1) body, (2) head, (3) antenna, (4) eye, (5) mouth, (6) leg, and the first player to put together a complete bug won the game.

COOTIES

Something—bugs? germs?—you could catch from members of the opposite sex, especially if you played with them during recess in elementary school.

FYI: ▸ Cooties is the slang term used for lice, coined by World War I Doughboys who shared trenches with the pesky insects.

"COPACABANA (AT THE COPA)"

The Copacabana was the hottest spot north of Havana, at least according to Barry Manilow's 1978 single featuring a cast of characters, like showgirl Lola, who did the cha-cha, and Rico, the suave proprietor of the Cuban nightclub. This perky disco ballad tended to throw its listeners into a tropical climate—a world of rumbas and sambas in a room full of smoke and laughter and cocktails sporting umbrellas. It was a popular choice for many high school girls who sashayed and cha-cha-ed in a Latin outfit at the annual talent show or beauty pageant. Manilow adapted the Grammy-winning song into a hit stage musical in 1994.

COPPERTONE GIRL

"Don't be a paleface!" The pigtailed blonde kid with the cocker spaniel tugging on her swimsuit has been associated with Coppertone suntan products since 1953. It's rumored that Jodie Foster as a toddler was a model for the Coppertone Girl in the 1960s, but actually the two-time Oscar-winning actress only starred in a Coppertone TV commercial (making her acting debut at age three).

CORAL KEY PARK
Watched over by benevolent TV ranger Porter Ricks, this actual marine preserve and wildlife refuge located in the Florida Keys was the home of Flipper, the well-loved dolphin star.

CORDUROY
Once called the "poor man's velvet," cords enjoyed huge popularity in the 1970s as a fabric for men's clothing. Consisting of a ridged velveteen made of a dense cotton weave, it was used in suits, blazers, shirts, and—my one-time favorite—jeans (Levi's bootleg style, colored baby blue or tan, were cool).

COREY BAKER
Little six-year-old black boy (played by Marc Copage on TV's *Julia*) who was raised by his widowed mother, Julia Baker, after his Air Force pilot father was shot down over Vietnam. Corey's best bud is Earl J. Waggedorn, a dorky redheaded white kid.

COREYS
As in Feldman (born July 16, 1971) and Haim (born December 23, 1971). Two promising child actors of the 1980s (*The Goonies, Stand by Me, The Lost Boys,* and *License to Drive*) who simultaneously grew up, did awful films, had drug problems, became has-beens, and now do straight-to-video movies.

CORGI
Toy company, hailing from Wales in the United Kingdom, advertised by the Welsh Corgi—you know, the intelligent dog breed Queen Elizabeth so adores. Notable for small, well-crafted, die-cast cars ("The first with windows"), especially those of famous movie and TV vehicles, like the Batmobile, the Monkeemobile, Chitty Chitty Bang Bang (with actual wings that fold out), and James Bond's Aston Martin. First manufactured in 1956, Corgi's chief competitors are Matchbox and Hot Wheels.

CORNROWS
In 1980, following the success of the comedy *10*, silly white women across America imitated the film's sexy lead actress, Bo Derek, by wearing their hair in beaded dangly cornrows—a traditional African hairstyle that looks best on black women (or Bo Derek).

CORVETTE
First manufactured by Chevrolet in 1953, this automobile is considered the first American sports car (MGs, Jaguars, and Porsches are from Europe). Most of us recall the Corvette of the 1970s, characterized by a long, lean fiberglass body with powerful bulges and curves (maybe colored lipstick-red) and a raspy, aggressive V-8 engine sound—the vehicle driven by studly Burt Reynolds or sexy Farrah Fawcett (Miss Fawcett's car got christened "Farrah's Foxy Vette"). Famed pop culture Corvettes would be the one George Maharis and Martin Milner drove around the country in the 1960s TV series *Route 66*, and the one Prince sang about in the 1983 hit "Little Red Corvette."

COSBY SHOW

> "The most positive portrayal of black family life that has ever been broadcast."
> —CORETTA SCOTT KING

As the most popular TV series of the 1980s, *The Cosby Show* gave America a much needed view of a happy upper-middle-class African-American family with traditional parents. Before its 1984 premiere, most shows depicted black families as living (struggling) in urban ghettos and in single-parent households (*Sanford and Son, Good Times, What's Happening!*). *The Cosby Show* centered around the everyday lives of a loving but firm obstetrician, Heathcliff Huxtable (comedian Bill Cosby), and his charming attorney wife, Clair (Phylicia Rashad, sister of Debbie Allen), who resided in a well-furnished townhouse in Brooklyn with their five precocious offspring. The Huxtable children were oldest daughter Sondra (Sabrina Le Beauf), the sweet-natured Princeton University grad; Denise (Lisa Bonet), the feisty free spirit; middle-child Theo (Malcolm-Jamal Warner), the lovable underachiever and the Huxtables' only son; Vanessa (Tempestt Bledsoe), the moody fourth child; and little Rudy (Keshia Knight Pulliam), the adorable baby of the family. The Emmy-winning NBC show had a successful spin-off, *A Different World*, when Denise Huxtable left to attend Hillman College in 1987.

COSMO G. SPACELY
George Jetson's bossy boss at Spacely Space Sprockets, who communicates with his much-harried em-

ployee via a TV phone on *The Jetsons* cartoon show. A loudmouthed, short-statured chap, Mr. Spacely is married to the snobbish Stella.

"COTTON'S DREAM"

Instrumental piece by Barry DeVorzon and Perry Botkin Jr. originally featured in the movie *Bless the Beasts and Children* (1971). Later used as the theme song for the TV soap *The Young and the Restless* and finally as performance music for Romanian gymnast Nadia Comaneci during the 1976 Summer Olympics—which caused it to hit the pop charts as "Nadia's Theme."

COUNT CHOCULA

"I vant to eat your cereal!" One-fanged, chocolate-loving vampire named after the sugary-sweet cereal featuring bits of chocolate-flavor marshmallows, which he has hawked for General Mills since 1971. In a long-running series of animated TV commercials, the Count quarreled with monster pals Boo Berry and Frankenberry over who had the best cereal.

COUNT DRACULA

"I vant to suck your blood." Bram Stoker's plasma-thirsty Transylvanian is the legendary leader of all vampires. If you ever have the misfortune of encountering the Count or a member of his type in the dark of the night, just remember that vampires fear stakes through the heart, garlic, sun rays, and the almighty crucifix (unless they're Jewish). Although he has been played by many actors in countless movies, my pick for the best cinematic Dracula is a toss-up between Bela Lugosi (1931) and Christopher Lee (1958).

COUNTRY CAMPER

"The swinginest camper on wheels!" Back in the 1970s, whenever Barbie Doll felt outdoorsy and had a hankering to explore the countryside, this was the orange recreational vehicle, equipped with a fold-out tent and pull-down picnic table, that she traveled around in.

COUNTRY SONGS

For those of you who are country-and-western inclined, here are fifty best-loved tunes—chock-full of Southern lovers, cheatin' hearts, divorcin' spouses, honky-tonk women, urban cowboys, CB truckers, and good ol' country sunshine—from the 1960s to the early 1990s.

- "All My Ex's Live in Texas" (1987) by George Strait
- "All the Gold in California" (1979) by Larry Gatlin
- "Before the Next Teardrop Falls" (1975) by Freddy Fender
- "Behind Closed Doors" (1973) by Charlie Rich
- "The Closer You Get" (1983) by Alabama
- "Coal Miner's Daughter" (1970) by Loretta Lynn
- "Could I Have This Dance" (1980) by Anne Murray
- "Country Bumpkin" (1974) by Cal Smith
- "Country Sunshine" (1973) by Dottie West
- "Crazy" (1961) by Patsy Cline
- "Delta Dawn" (1972) by Tanya Tucker
- "The Devil Went Down to Georgia" (1979) by Charlie Daniels Band
- "D-I-V-O-R-C-E" (1968) by Tammy Wynette
- "Don't It Make My Brown Eyes Blue" (1977) by Crystal Gayle
- "Drivin' My Life Away" (1980) by Eddie Rabbitt
- "Elvira" (1981) by Oak Ridge Boys
- "Flowers on the Wall" (1965) by Statler Brothers
- "Forever and Ever, Amen" (1987) by Randy Travis
- "Friends in Low Places" (1990) by Garth Brooks
- "The Happiest Girl in the Whole U.S.A." (1972) by Donna Fargo
- "Harper Valley P.T.A." (1968) by Jeannie C. Riley
- "He Stopped Loving Her Today" (1980) by George Jones
- "Hello Darlin'" (1970) by Conway Twitty
- "Help Me Make It Through the Night" (1971) by Sammi Smith
- "I Love" (1973) by Tom T. Hall
- "Jolene" (1973) by Dolly Parton
- "Killin' Time" (1989) by Clint Black
- "King of the Road" (1965) by Roger Miller
- "Kiss an Angel Good Mornin'" (1971) by Charley Pride
- "Lookin' for Love" (1980) by Johnny Lee

- "Lucille" (1977) by Kenny Rogers
- "Luckenbach, Texas (1977) by Waylon Jennings
- "Mama He's Crazy" (1984) by The Judds
- "Mammas Don't Let Your Babies Grow Up to Be Cowboys" (1978) by Waylon Jennings and Willie Nelson
- "Nobody" (1982) by Sylvia
- "Ode to Billy Joe" (1967) by Bobbie Gentry
- "Okie from Muskogee" (1969) by Merle Haggard
- "On the Road Again" (1980) by Willie Nelson
- "Rhinestone Cowboy" (1975) by Glen Campbell
- "Ring of Fire" (1963) by Johnny Cash
- "Rose Garden" (1970) by Lynn Anderson
- "Rub It In" (1974) by Billy "Crash" Craddock
- "Satin Sheets" (1973) by Jeanne Pruett
- "Sleeping Single in a Double Bed" (1978) by Barbara Mandrell
- "Smoky Mountain Rain" (1980) by Ronnie Milsap
- "Somebody Should Leave" (1985) by Reba McEntire
- "Stand by Your Man" (1968) by Tammy Wynette
- "Take This Job and Shove It" (1977) by Johnny Paycheck
- "Tulsa Time" (1978) by Don Williams
- "You're the Reason God Made Oklahoma" (1981) by David Frizzell and Shelley West

COUNT VON COUNT

"Greetings! I am the Count. They call me the Count, because I love to count things!" *Sesame Street*'s resident vampire who taught young viewers how to count. He had a pet bat named Creepy.

COURTSHIP OF EDDIE'S FATHER

"People, let me tell ya' 'bout my best friend. . . ." Bill Bixby starred as widower Tom Corbett, a California magazine publisher responsible for raising his seven-year-old son and "best friend," Eddie, played by Brandon Cruz. The precocious youngster had a matchmaking habit that regularly put his father into awkward situations, consequently leading to the sitcom's story lines. Japanese actress Miyoshi Umeki played their housekeeper, Mrs. Livingston, and from time to time juvenile Jodie Foster appeared as Eddie's school friend Joey Kelly. Airing on prime time from 1969 to 1972, it was based on the novel by Mark Toby and the 1963 movie starring Glenn Ford and Ron Howard. The theme, "Best Friend," was sung by pop singer Harry Nilsson, whose other songs included "Everybody's Talkin'" (1969), "Me and My Arrow" 1971), "Without You" (1972), and "Coconut" (1972).

COUSIN ITT

The diminutive, hairy (from head to toe), gibberish-talking (only Gomez Addams can understand his strange babble) relative of *The Addams Family* is supposedly a playboy irresistible to those of the opposite sex!

COUSIN OLIVER

"This is your cousin Oliver." Robbie Rist, a miniature John Denver look-alike, starred as the annoying relative who jinxed the Brady Bunch when he came to stay with them during their last TV season. Many fans believe cousin Oliver contributed to the cancellation of the popular prime-time show.

COVER GIRL CLEAN MAKEUP

Natural-appearing liquid makeup notable for ads peddled by fresh-faced "Cover Girl" models, such as Cheryl Tiegs, Christie Brinkley, and Kim Alexis.

COWBOY BOOTS

The traditional country-and-western footwear was really, really trendy among urban cowboys and cowgirls throughout the 1980s. A pair of Tony Lama boots, often made from the skin of an exotic animal, was considered the best to own.

COWBOY CURTIS

Soon-to-be movie star Laurence Fishburne played the rootin' tootin' chaps-wearing African-American cowboy on *Pee-Wee's Playhouse*, from 1986 to 1991. Fishburne would be nominated for a Best Actor Oscar for his role as bad-boy musician Ike Turner in *What's Love Got to Do with It* (1993).

COWSILLS

Billed as "America's First Family of Music," they were the real-life inspiration for TV's *Partridge Family* and the precursor to such pop dynasties as The

Osmonds, The Jacksons, The De Francos, and The Sylvers. Originating from Newport, Rhode Island, the group consisted of five fresh-faced brothers—Bill, Bob, Paul, Barry, and John—a cute-as-a-button little sister, Susan; and a groovy mother, Barbara. They were known for harmony-laced rock ballads, including the million-selling singles "The Rain, the Park, and Other Things" (1967), "Indian Lake" (1968), and "Hair" (1969), the title song from the Broadway musical. Disbanded in 1972 after various members left for college and careers outside the music industry.

CRACKED MAGAZINE

First published in May 1958 by John Severin, this is a copycat of *Mad* magazine complete with similar movie parodies and an imbecilic coverboy-mascot (the yellow-haired Sylvester P. Smythe).

CRACKER JACK

"Buy me some peanuts and Cracker Jack, I don't care if I never get back. . . ." The delicious blend of caramel-covered popcorn and salty peanuts, packaged in a small box with a tiny toy surprise inside, has been a best-selling snack food for more than 100 years. Jack is the name of the young lad wearing the sailor suit on the Cracker Jack box.

CRAWFORD, CINDY

Born on February 20, 1966, the gorgeous brunette, known in the modeling industry as "The Face," defined the term "supermodel" in the early 1990s. Since shooting her first *Vogue* cover (August 1986), Crawford (and her trademark mole above her lip) has graced more magazine covers than any other model in the world, boasting more than 600 so far. Other Crawford career highlights include competing as a finalist in Elite Model Management's Look of the Year contest (1983), being the first modern supermodel to pose nude for *Playboy* (1988), signing a multi-million-dollar contract with Revlon cosmetics (1989), hosting MTV's fashion program *House of Style* (1989), becoming the first supermodel to advertise Pepsi (1991), starring in a series of best-selling exercise videos (1992), and authoring a book titled *Cindy Crawford's Basic Face: A Makeup Workbook* (1996). She experienced an ill-fated marriage to actor Richard Gere from 1991 to 1994.

FYI: ▸ Cindy Crawford was the valedictorian of her senior class at DeKalb High School in suburban Chicago. She received a scholarship to study chemical engineering at Northwestern University.

CRAYOLA CRAYONS

"Crayola. Childhood isn't childhood without it." For children, a great joy in life is receiving a brand-smacking new box of Crayola crayons with each colorful waxy stick standing perfectly straight, ready to be felt, smelled, and even licked. In fact, their scent is so wonderful some kids try to eat them (I remember one little girl in my second-grade class throwing up the purple Crayon), and according to a recent Yale University study they are among the twenty fragrances most recognizable to American adults.

Cousins Edwin Binney and C. Harold Smith, who had already created a successful line of retail products—shoe polish, printing ink, and slate pencils—invented Crayola crayons. Packaged in the famous yellow carton with the green serpentine stripes, the first box of eight colors, introduced in 1903, contained the same blue, red, green, yellow, violet, orange, brown, and black crayons found today. In 1958, Binney & Smith debuted the popular 64-box, which came with a built-in sharpener and a wide range of exotic shades, such as carnation pink, aquamarine, magenta, silver, burnt sienna, and periwinkle. Crayola manufactures two billion crayons a year.

FYI: ▸ Binney's wife, Alice, is credited with coming up with the Crayola name after she combined the French word "craie" (for chalk) with "olea" (from oleaginous, referring to the oily paraffin wax used in the crayons).

CRAZY FOAM

"The toy that cleans." This festive 1960s bath-time product for kids came in colorful canisters with lids shaped as wacky characters that spewed foam soap out of their mouths. Competitor was Silly Soap ("Makes bathing fun").

CREATURE FEATURE

Scaring the crap out of pajama-clad children, these movie programs, airing on local UHF stations on weekend afternoons or late at night, showed a standard fare of classic 1930s and 1940s horror, 1950s atomic-age monsters, and 1960s and 1970s low-budget schlock. Not all were called "Creature Feature." Depending on what part of the country you lived in, the titles could have been *Chiller Cinema, Graveyard Theater, Nightmare Theater, Shock Theater, Fright Night, Jeepers Creepers,* or *Elvira's Movie Macabre.* The programs were hosted by a local actor, usually dressed as a costumed fiend, who would introduce the featured film and give tidbits about it before and after commercial breaks. Favorite *Creature Feature* hosts seen on TV throughout the 1970s and 1980s included Bob Wilkins (San Francisco), Chuck Acri (Peoria), Dick "Count Gore De Vol" Dyszel (Washington, D.C.), Carl "The Creature" Grayson (Chicago), Lew "The Creep" Steele (New York City), Roberta "Crematia Mortem" Solomon (Kansas City), Dale Dorman (Boston), Dick "Dr. Paul Bearer" Bennick (Winston-Salem), John "Dr. San Guinary" Jones (Omaha), and Russ "Sir Cecil Creape" McCown (Nashville).

CREATURE FROM THE BLACK LAGOON

Unofficially known as a "Gill Man," the Creature from the Black Lagoon, located deep in the jungles of the Amazon, is discovered on an expedition and gets horny for pert brunette Julie Adams. The rubber-suited monster was first seen in the horror classic *Creature from the Black Lagoon* (1954) and its sequel, *Revenge of the Creature* (1955), both directed by Jack Arnold.

CREEPY CRAWLERS

Kids have always been fascinated by monsters, and they enjoy making a gooey mess, so it seemed only fitting in 1964 that Mattel would advance its line of Vac-U-Form machines with the introduction of Creepy Crawlers. This casting set featured a sludgy, liquid plastic called Plastigoop, which you poured into prestamped molds of insects and other scary critters. The metal molds were then inserted into a small electric heating contraption called the Thingmaker (a.k.a. Vac-U-Form). After baking for a few minutes (remember that peculiar smell of melting plastic?), the molds were removed and cooled off, resulting in a squirmy plastic rendition of a scary bug. (Real cool.)

The enormous success of Creepy Crawlers—in their debut year they were second only to Hasbro's G.I. Joe as the best-selling toy—inspired Mattel to manufacture a slew of other Thingmaker sets: Creeple People (wacky troll-like creatures), Fright Factory (ghoulish monster makeup), Fighting Men (soldiers with combat and field equipment), Batman Bat-Maker (different kinds of bats), Fun Flower (assorted flowers), Picadoos (matrix dot patterns), Eeeeks (icky bugs with mix-and-match heads), Zoofie Goofies (zoo animals with interchangeable body parts), and Incredible Edibles (digestible Creepy Crawlers, made with sugarless Gobbledegook).

CRICKET IN TIMES SQUARE

George Selden's heartwarming tale about Chester, a liverwurst-loving cricket from Connecticut who is accidentally brought to the Big Apple by the way of a picnic basket. Stranded in Times Square, he is befriended by Tucker Mouse, Harry Cat, and Mario Bellini, a young lad whose parents own a failing newspaper stand near the subway station. To help the struggling Bellinis, the courteous Chester uses his talent of rubbing his wings together to perform beautiful violin arias at rush hour as a way of attracting business to the newsstand. First published in 1960, the book's success led to a series of sequels—*Tucker's Countryside, Chester Cricket's New Home,* and *Harry Cat's Pet Puppy*—and a 1973 animated TV special. The well-crafted special was awarded the Parents' Choice Award for excellence in TV programming.

CRINOLINE SKIRTS

Traditionally used as underwear beneath skirts to make them more full and frilly, these became fashionable outerwear in the mid-1980s, thanks to the influence of pop starlets like Madonna, Cyndi Lauper, Stacey Q, and Jody Watley. Crop tops, bolero jackets, footless stretch leggings, ankle boots, and armfuls of bangles completed the look.

CRISPY CRITTERS

"The one and only cereal that comes in the shape of animals!" Animal-shaped, sugar-frosted oat cereal manufactured by Post throughout the 1960s. Besides appearing on the cereal box and in televised commercials, its spokes-lion, Linus the Lionhearted, ruler of Africa's animal kingdom, headlined his own

Saturday-morning cartoon show from 1964 to 1966. Post reissued the name Crispy Critters in 1987 for a cereal now advertised by a furry hybrid of a teddy bear and an alien.

FYI: ▸ In 1967, Crispy Critters cereal featured a nifty Pushmi-Pullyu shape as a tie-in with the just-released *Doctor Dolittle* movie starring Rex Harrison.

CRISSY

"With hair that grows and grows and grows!" Most women who played with dolls back in the late 1960s and early 1970s have fond memories of beautiful Crissy, whose luxurious auburn hair could go from short to long and back to short again. Debuting in 1969, the eighteen-inch-tall fashion teen with expressive, lifelike eyes was one of Ideal Toys' "grow hair" dolls. Wound on a spool inside her belly, Crissy's hair "grew" by pressing a button on her tummy and yanking her long ponytail up and out from the top of the head. To make it short again, you turned a knob on her back. Just think, one minute she could have a sassy, short bob, then next a swingin' shoulder-length flip, and finally a flowing knee-length sweep. The concept for Crissy came from Tressy, a "grow hair" fashion doll produced by American Character from 1963 to 1967. (Ideal acquired the patent rights after American Character went bankrupt.)

Crissy's popularity led to a family of "grow hair" dolls, including smaller (fifteen-inch-tall) cousin Velvet and Velvet's even smaller (twelve-inch-tall) sister Cinnamon, along with friends Tressy, Kerry, Brandi, Mia, Cricket, Dina, and Tara. There was also a twenty-five-inch-tall Baby Crissy and African-American versions of Crissy and Velvet. Cool threads for Crissy and the whole gang included miniskirts, bell-bottoms, hot pants, granny gowns, jumpers, ponchos, capes, pom-pom hats, and knee-high go-go boots.

FYI: ▸ Lionel Weintraub, president of Ideal Toys from 1963 to 1983, claims Crissy was his favorite doll.

CROCE, JIM

The record "Bad, Bad Leroy Brown" (1973) was Jim Croce's fourth Top Forty hit and first chart-topper before his death in a plane crash at age thirty on September 20, 1973, in Natchitoches, Louisiana. This tragedy robbed the music world of a remarkable singer and songwriter at the dawn of stardom. Other Croce hits included "You Don't Mess Around with Jim" (1972), "Operator (That's Not the Way It Feels)" (1972), and the posthumous "I Got a Name" (1973) and "I'll Have to Say I Love You in a Song" (1974). As if to seal his own fate, Croce sang these words in the number-one song "Time in a Bottle" (1973): "There never seems to be enough time to do the things you want to do once you find them."

CROCHETED BEER CAN HATS

Labels of beer cans were cut into square or oval shapes and crocheted together to form a hat. Tacky, I know, but the Budweiser caps were kinda cool.

CROCODILE DUNDEE

"G'day mate!" The 1986 film starring Paul Hogan as the likeable, easygoing Aussie who saves a pretty American reporter, Sue Charlton (Linda Kozlowski), from a crocodile attack in the Outback and follows her to the strange jungle of New York City. As the year's surprise blockbuster comedy, it made the blonde Hogan, previously known for a series of TV ads promoting Australian tourism ("We'll put another shrimp on the barbie"), an international star and was followed by two sequels.

CROCODILE HUNTER

"Holy smokes! That was close!" First airing in 1996, this Animal Planet documentary series stars blond Australian Steve Irwin, a charismatic herpetologist who runs a wildlife refuge in Queensland with wife Terri. Fearless and sometimes foolish, Irwin likes to get up close and personal with crocodiles and other dangerous reptiles. The TV show regularly has him wrangling a big ol' croc that has nestled too close to civilization so he can return it back to the wild, or digging his arm into a muddy hole in an attempt to grab a poisonous snake.

CROP TOPS

Belly-baring shirts for gals first made popular by Madonna in the mid-1980s before youngsters Britney Spears and Christina Aguilera adopted 'em as their own sometime around the millennium. Also known as midriffs and belly shirts.

CRUELLA De VIL

"Poison them, drown them, bash them in the head!" Deliciously bad, Cruella is possibly the meanest villainess ever created by the Disney Studios. Seen in 1961's *101 Dalmatians*, the eccentric chain-smoker with the gravelly voice and two-tone hair (black and white) wants to make coats from the fur of adorable Dalmatian puppies. Glenn Close played Cruella brilliantly over-the-top in the 1996 live-action remake and its sequel, *102 Dalmatians* (2000).

CRUISE, TOM

> "If you're going to pay anybody too much to star in the movie you're spending too much to make, pay Tom Cruise. He's the only bona fide movie star of his generation."
>
> —*MOVIELINE* MAGAZINE

Determined actor who broke away from the Brat Pack to become one of the top movie stars of the 1980s and 1990s (he was the number-one box office draw in 1986 and 1987). Born Thomas Cruise Mapother IV on July 3, 1962, in Syracuse, New York, the boyishly handsome dark-haired actor—with the great smile—first drew attention as the headstrong military cadet, opposite Timothy Hutton, in *Taps* (1981). Next came the Brat Pack association, when he was cast as one of the Greasers in the 1983 big-screen adaptation of S. E. Hinton's *The Outsiders*. But the role establishing Cruise as a star was that of high school senior Joel Goodsen in the comedy *Risky Business* (1983), which featured the memorable scene of him dancing around the living room playing an air guitar to Bob Seger's "Old Time Rock 'n' Roll" while wearing nothing but white socks, shirt tails, and underwear briefs.

At five foot nine (rumored to be a diminutive five foot six), he is best at playing hotshot characters, such as the hotshot fighter pilot in *Top Gun* (1986), the hotshot pool shark in *The Color of Money* (1986), the hotshot barman in *Cocktail* (1988), the hotshot L.A. hustler in *Rain Man* (1988), the hotshot race car driver in *Days of Thunder* (1990), the hotshot Irish farmhand in *Far and Away* (1992), the hotshot Navy lawyer in *A Few Good Men* (1992), the hotshot law student in *The Firm* (1993), and the hotshot secret agent in *Mission: Impossible* (1996). He played against type as the Keeper of Unicorns in the sword-and-sorcery opus *Legend* (1986), as well as Vietnam vet Ron Kovic in Oliver Stone's *Born on the Fourth of July* (1989) and angst-ridden bloodsucker Lestat in Anne Rice's *Interview with the Vampire* (1994). In 1990, Cruise married Australian actress Nicole Kidman, and for ten years the extraordinarily perfect twosome reigned as Hollywood's leading couple.

C-3PO

Prissy and verbose, this golden protocol droid, whose primary functions are etiquette and translation, aided freedom-fighting Princess Leia and Luke Skywalker in the *Star Wars* movies. Threepio is often paired with lively R2-D2, a smaller maintenance droid, and the furry Ewoks hail him as a god.

CUJO

A slobbering, rabid Saint Bernard that terrorizes its owners—a mother and her young son—trapped in a stalled car in the middle of nowhere during the heat of the summer. Featured in the best-selling 1981 thriller *Cujo*, by Stephen King, and in the 1983 movie adaptation.

CULOTTES

Hmmm? Shorts that look like a skirt—or was it a skirt that looked like shorts? This 1970s style was a relative of gaucho slacks.

CULTURE CLUB

"America knows a good drag queen when it sees one!" exclaimed gender-bending Boy George as he accepted the 1983 Best New Artist Grammy for his band Culture Club. How right he was—Americans do know a good drag queen when they see one and made Boy George and his bandmates the pop-music phenomenon of the 1980s. Formed in London in 1981, the group starred Boy George (born George O'Dowd on June 14, 1961), the soft-spoken lead singer whose striking trademark appearance consisted of androgynous clothing, long hair customarily styled in dreadlocks wrapped in colorful rags or scarves, and glamorous full-face makeup (he enjoyed giving beauty tips to adolescent girls—and boys!). Boy George was joined by keyboardist Roy Hay, bassist Michael Craig, and drummer Jon Moss.

Made famous by MTV, Culture Club was the darling of the music network. Its campy videos showcased Boy George bobbing and dancing to a New Wave easygoing sound, which included six Top Ten singles in one year (1983): "Do You Really Want to Hurt Me," "Time (Clock of the Heart)," "I'll Tumble 4 Ya," "Church of the Poison Mind," "Karma Chameleon," and "Miss Me Blind."

In July 1986, Boy George made media headlines when his heroin addiction was revealed after an arrest for drug possession. The group never recovered from this and other negative publicity, and it disbanded the following year. In the 1990s, solo and drug-free Boy George reinvolved himself with the club music scene, scored a hit with "The Crying Game" (1992), and hung out with the Hare Krishna sect.

CURIOSITY SHOP

An educational TV series, put together by famed Warner Brothers cartoonist Chuck Jones and designed to help kids (ages six to eleven) examine and explore everyday subjects and objects with the aid of puppets, cartoons, filmed segments, and interviews. Each show focused on a singular theme, such as Flight, Rules, Laughter, Tools, Memory, or The Senses. The setting was a magical place called the Curiosity Shop, owned by Mr. Jones and featuring a puppet-populated calliope wall and an elevator "to anywhere." Fanciful puppets inhabiting the program included Flippo the Hippo, Darwin the Chimpanzee, Eunice the Seal, Hermione the Giraffe, Nostalgia the Elephant, Woodrow the Groundhog, Hudson the Talking Rock, Eeek A Mouse, Oogle, Onomatopoeia, Monsieur Cou Cou, Professor S. I. Trivia, Gittle the Bumbling Witch, and Baron Balthazar (who could talk to animals, just like Dr. Dolittle). Airing Saturday mornings on ABC from 1971 to 1973, the hour-long show unfortunately suffered low ratings because it ran opposite CBS's more popular and less educational *Sabrina, the Teenage Witch* and *Josie and the Pussycats.*

CURIOUS GEORGE

"He was a good little monkey and always very curious. . . ." An inquisitive chimp wearing a red cap and red shirt who starred in a series of picture books written and illustrated by the wife-and-husband team of Margret and H. A. Rey. The series began in 1941 with *Curious George* and was followed by *Curious George Takes a Job* (1947), *Curious George Rides a Bike* (1952), *Curious George Gets a Medal* (1957), *Curious George Flies a Kite* (1958), *Curious George Goes to the Moon* (1963), and *Curious George Learns the Alphabet* (1963). To the delight of toddlers worldwide, these lively tales had the irrepressible monkey getting into numerous misadventures as a result of his abundant curiosity. Lucky for Curious George, the Man with the Yellow Hat who drove a blue car always managed to rescue him from trouble. Known as Zozo in Great Britain.

CURLY-Q RIBBONS

These brightly colored, spiral-shaped hair ribbons (like the ones Eve Plumb wore on *The Brady Bunch*) were another happenin' hair accessory for little girls in the 1970s.

CURTIS, JAMIE LEE

The daughter of Janet Leigh and Tony Curtis made her motion-picture debut at age nineteen in John Carpenter's horror classic *Halloween*, playing teen babysitter Laurie being stalked by psycho-killer Michael Meyers on Halloween night in 1978. Curtis made several more horror films—*Prom Night* (1980), *Terror Train* (1980), *The Fog* (1980), and *Halloween 2* (1981)—earning the nickname "Hollywood Scream Queen." Moved on to more respectable work, such as *Trading Places* (1983) and *A Fish Called Wanda* (1988). In 1981, she starred as doomed *Playboy* centerfold Dorothy Stratten in the TV movie *Death of a Centerfold: The Dorothy Stratten Story* (1981).

CUSTOM VANS

In the post-Nixon years of the 1970s, these were make-out pads on wheels for horny single dudes. A guy who drove a van was smooth, hip, sexy, sleazy—a with-it stud whose wheels reflected his taste from the inside and out. And that taste included murals involving unicorns, comic superheroes, jungle animals, galaxy fantasies, and well-built foxy chicks airbrushed on the exterior of the van. The decor inside came customized with fuzzy shag carpet stapled onto the floor, ceiling, and walls—or, if carpeting wasn't used—fake fur, crushed velvet, or spongelike Naugahyde did the job. Because custom vans were roomy inside, they were typically equipped with numerous luxuries to guarantee nights of seductive pleasure. A gal's chastity didn't stand a chance against items like a wet bar to serve Tequila Sunrises or Strawberry Daiquiris, a hot tub for relaxing while toking on a good Colombian doobie, a satin-sheet-strewn bed (usually a couch that could convert into a bed), mirrored ceilings, black lights and black velvet posters, and sensual mood music—The Moody Blues, Eagles, or Barry White—coming from an eight-track player. You could make love in a busy parking lot or on a secluded stretch of road and nobody outside would ever know, because the vans provided complete privacy. A bumper sticker of the day featured the slogan "If This Van's a Rockin', Don't Bother Knockin'!" Popular makes of vans: the Dodge Econoline and the Chevy Van.

CYCLOPS

A legendary one-eyed, carnivorous giant who can be seen tormenting the Robinson family trapped in their Space Chariot vehicle on an October 1965 episode of TV's *Lost in Space*.

CYLONS

Diabolical half-human, half-robot beings led by Count Baltar, whose mission was to annihilate the human race, particularly those aboard TV's *Battlestar Galactica.*

"DADDY, DON'T YOU WALK SO FAST"
The heartfelt song about the impact of divorce on a father and his young child struck a chord with youngsters of the 1970s because it came out at a time (summer of 1972) when the divorce rate reached an all-time high and many experienced the trauma of having their parents split up. The song is about a dispirited dad leaving home for good, and as he gets halfway down the highway his little girl runs behind pleading for him not to "walk so fast." This experience so moves the father that he decides to go back and give his marriage a second shot. Penned by Peter Callander and Geoff Stephens, the million-seller was pop singer Wayne Newton's first and only Top Ten hit. He began his singing career with 1963's "Danke Schoen" and more recently was the top-drawing entertainer in Las Vegas and Branson, Missouri (where he is thought of as "Mr. Excitement").

DAFFY DUCK
This lisping, web-footed black Looney is Warner Brothers' continuous second banana to the more popular Bugs Bunny. A quick-talking schemer, he's able to play a few tricks on dim-witted hunters Porky Pig and Elmer Fudd but meets his match with antagonist Bugs Bunny, who always leaves an outsmarted Daffy sputtering, "You're dethpicable!" Daffy first appeared in the cartoon short "Porky's Duck Hunt" in 1937. From 1978 to 1982, he gained his own Saturday-morning cartoon, *The Daffy Duck Show*.

FYI: ▸ Warner Brothers' Daffy Duck and Disney's Donald Duck dueled each other on pianos in a scene from *Who Framed Roger Rabbit* (1988). A put-off Daffy couldn't believe he had to work with a duck that had a speech impediment!

DAHL, ROALD
British writer (1916–90) famous for dark-humored children's stories like *James and the Giant Peach* (1961), *Charlie and the Chocolate Factory* (1964), *The Magic Finger* (1966), *Fantastic Mr. Fox* (1970), *Charlie and the Great Glass Elevator* (1972), *The Witches* (1983), and *Matilda* (1988). In 1968, wrote the screenplay for the movie *Chitty Chitty Bang Bang*. He was married to American actress Patricia Neal from 1953 to 1983.

DAILY BUGLE
Fictional New York City newspaper where young Peter Parker, alias Spider-Man (of comic-book fame), works as a photographer along with reporter Betty Brandt and editor-in-chief J. Jonah Jameson.

DAILY PLANET
"Always first with the news." Fictional Metropolis newspaper where Clark Kent, alias Superman (of comic-book fame), works as a reporter along with fellow newshound Lois Lane, photographer Jimmy Olsen, and editor-in-chief Perry White.

DAIRY QUEEN

Founded in 1940 by Alex and J. F. McCullough in Joliet, Illinois, the nation's leading ice-cream chain seems to have at least one restaurant in nearly every small town in America. Known for such "scrumpdillyishus" yummies as soft-serve ice cream, chocolate-dipped cones, Blizzards, Mister Mistys, and Peanut Buster Parfaits, along with Brazier foods (hamburgers, fries, and other fried foods). Comic-strip icon Dennis the Menace has been its advertising kid since the 1970s. Main rivals: Tastee-Freez, Mister Softee, Carvel, and Baskin-Robbins.

DAISY DUCK

Donald Duck's attractive and rather flirtatious girlfriend made her debut in his 1937 cartoon short "Don Donald" playing fiery Mexican Donna Duck. In the love-struck eyes of the irascible Donald, this long-lashed sweetie can do no wrong. But look out! If she doesn't get her way she's just as irascible, if not more, than Donald.

DAISY DUKE

The Dukes of Hazzard's Southern sexpot was a brown-haired beauty (actress Catherine Bach) who adorned her curves in skimpy outfits and waited on tables at the Boar's Nest Restaurant. Daisy aided cousins Bo and Luke Duke by employing both her body and her brains to halt the bad guys.

DAISY DUKES

Mega-short, butt-cleaving denim cut-offs, a countrified version of hot pants inspired by and named after Catherine Bach's Daisy Duke on *The Dukes of Hazzard* (Bach made them herself). This sexy fashion trend was reignited in the 1990s by the rap song "Dazzey Duks" by Duice, and they remain today a mainstay in short fashions.

DAISY "GRANNY" MOSES

Jed Clampett's ornery, pipe-smoking mother-in-law who spends her time brewing homemade potions, cooking vittles made out of such critters as possum and muskrat, and trying to find tomboy granddaughter Elly May a suitable husband. (Granny thinks the blonde bombshell is an old maid because she's past the age of fourteen.) Played by Irene Ryan on CBS-TV's *Beverly Hillbillies* from 1962 to 1971.

DAKTARI

"Daktari" in Swahili means "doctor," but to Americans it's a late-1960s African-adventure TV show. Airing on CBS from 1966 to 1969, it starred Marshall Thompson as Dr. Marsh Tracy, an American veterinarian at the Wameru Game Preserve and Research Center in Africa. Called the "Great White Vet" by the locals, Dr. Tracy was assisted by his pretty seventeen-year-old daughter, Paula (Cheryl Miller), and native African conservationist Mike (Hari Rhodes). They had two distinctive pets: mischievous chimp Judy and cross-eyed lion Clarence, who ended up becoming more popular with viewers than the show's human actors. Baby hippo Ethel, elephant Margie, and water buffalo Foghorn were other notable *Daktari* animals. During its final season, young Erin Moran joined the cast as seven-year-old Jenny Jones, an orphan adopted by the Tracy household. (Hey, did little Jenny Jones grow up to become a 1990s talk-show hostess?) Moran would later play teen Joanie Cunningham on the 1970s TV sitcom *Happy Days*. Based on producer Ivan Tors's 1965 movie *Clarence the Cross-Eyed Lion*.

DALLAS

The most successful prime-time soap opera since the days of *Peyton Place* (1964–69), its popularity paralleled the nation's Reagan-era fascination with big money and big business. Airing on CBS-TV from 1978 to 1991, the show focused on the wealthy Ewing clan of Southfork, a sprawling ranch on the outskirts of Dallas, Texas, and their struggles with power, wealth, revenge, and sex. At the center of the family's oil and cattle empire was eldest son J.R. Ewing, referred to by TV critics as "the man viewers loved to hate." Played by Larry Hagman, J.R. was scheming, manipulative, greedy, and out to ruin his opponents, deceive his friends, outfox his brothers, institutionalize his wife, and mislead his mistresses—all this while wearing a smile on his handsome face and a twinkle in his baby-blue eyes.

Joining Hagman in the central cast were Jim Davis as silver-haired patriarch Jock Ewing, Barbara Bel Geddes as Jock's wife, Miss Ellie, Patrick Duffy as "good" youngest son Bobby Ewing, Ted Shackelford as black-sheep middle son Gary Ewing, Linda Gray as J.R.'s beautiful but troubled wife, Sue Ellen, Victoria Principal as Bobby's sexy wife, Pamela, Charlene

Tilton as Gary's daughter and family slut Lucy Ewing, Steve Kanaly as ranch foreman and Jock's illegitimate son Ray Krebbs, and Ken Kercheval as Pam's brother and Ewing nemesis Cliff Barnes. *Dallas* spawned a spin-off, *Knots Landing* (1979–92), and a legion of imitators: *Dynasty* (1981–89), *Falcon Crest* (1981–90), *Flamingo Road* (1981–82), *King's Crossing* (1982), and *The Secrets of Midland Heights* (1980–81).

DALLAS COWBOYS CHEERLEADERS

Like most NFL teams, the Dallas Cowboys originally used local high school and college girls who did old-fashioned "two-bits, four-bits, six-bits, a dollar" cheers. All that changed in the mid-1970s when the Texas football franchise introduced a new "professional" cheerleading squad, made up of beautiful buxom women clad in scanty uniforms, known as the Dallas Cowboys Cheerleaders.

Shaking pom-poms and wearing a uniform consisting of a white fringed vest, a royal-blue blouse (knotted bare-midriff style), white hot pants, and white knee-high boots, the feathered-hair foxes wiggled and jiggled their "T & A" (tits and ass) to flashy jazz-disco dance routines loaded with synchronized high kicks (yee-hah!). They brought added excitement and showmanship to the football games—along with much publicity and attention from lingering TV cameramen. They also brought controversy, because some people felt they took away from the wholesome image of cheerleading and set the women's movement back years. But the fans of Dallas—and apparently everywhere else—loved the dazzling Cowgirls, and by 1977 virtually every NFL team hired its own squad of sexy professional cheerleaders, such as the Oakland Raiderettes, the Los Angeles Embraceable Ewes, the Denver Pony Express, the Chicago Honey Bears, the Washington Redskinettes, the Miami Dolphin Starbrites, and the Seattle Sea Gals.

The popularity of the Dallas Cowboys Cheerleaders led to colorful, top-selling posters, calendars, and playing cards. There were also two highly rated Dallas Cowboys Cheerleaders TV movies, a prime-time special appropriately titled "The 36 Most Beautiful Girls in Texas," and a couple of cruises aboard *The Love Boat*. They inspired a notorious 1978 porno film, *Debbie Does Dallas*, starring real-life Cowgirl reject Bambi Woods.

DAMIEN THORN

The son of an American ambassador, he's the Antichrist in juvenile form, according to *The Omen* movies. (If you don't believe me, I dare you to look for the satanic number 666 on his scalp.)

DANCERINA

"Because girls dream about being a ballerina, Mattel makes Dancerina." Fueled by popular TV commercials, this was one of the "must have" dolls of the late 1960s. Unlike hair-growing Crissy or diminutive Liddle Kiddles, Dancerina has not yet found her niche in today's nostalgia market. Introduced in 1968, the twenty-four-inch-tall, angelic-looking blonde ballerina—whose toes were permanently on point—came wearing a shocking pink tutu, leotards, ballet slippers, and a "magic" tiara. By grasping a knob in the center of the tiara and flipping on a switch, little girls could control the battery-operated Dancerina, making her twirl, turn her head, stop, twirl again, turn head again, and so on. She could pirouette, toe-dance, strike classic poses, and bow gracefully—just like a real ballerina! Dancerella was her ten-inch-tall brunette little sister.

DANCE FEVER

In 1979, disco was hot, and so was this weekly dance program that capitalized on the burning mania by featuring four competing couples hustling, swinging, spinning, and bumping to pulsating music and flashing lights. Considered the nation's best disco dancers, these competitors were rated on originality, style, and talent—as judged by a panel of guest celebrities. The winning couple went on to the Grand Prix finale at season's end, when they could win as much as $50,000. The syndicated TV show was hosted by dark-haired choreographer Deney Terrio, noteworthy for teaching John Travolta his dance moves for *Saturday Night Fever* (1977). Two female dancers called Motion assisted Terrio, and the three of them would perform a spectacular disco routine each week. In 1985, Terrio's cocaine habit caused him to be replaced by *T. J. Hooker*'s Adrian Zmed, who had once been a guest judge on the show.

FYI: ▸ Deney Terrio made tabloid headlines in the late 1980s when he accused Merv Griffin of sexual harassment.

DANCING FLOWERS
This amusing yet short-lived fad of the early 1990s featured a shades-wearing daisy that bobbed in time to whatever music was being played. An electronic sound chip in its plastic flowerpot base made it dance.

"DANCING IN THE DARK"
The hook-driven song from the highly successful *Born in the U.S.A.* album was accompanied by a music video directed by Brian De Palma that had singer Bruce Springsteen giving an exciting live concert performance. The video ended with Springsteen yanking prestardom Courteney Cox (*Friends*) out of the audience to dance on stage.

"DANCING QUEEN"
Considered to be ABBA's biggest single ever, this topped the charts not only in America (their only U.S. chart-topper) but in numerous other countries as well, including Austria, Australia, Belgium, Germany, Great Britain, New Zealand, Norway, Sweden, and Switzerland. The Swedish hit machine originally performed the zingy 1977 disco hit at the wedding reception of the King of Sweden and his bride Silvia Sommerlath. The song captured the attitude of young and free Dancing Queens, who universally flocked to discos on weekend nights.

FYI: ▸ The archetypal look of a real-life Dancing Queen consisted of hair feathered, winged, or tied into a knot atop her head; and trendy clothing, such as a skin-tight pair of spandex pants or a slinky wraparound skirt worn with a shimmering halter top or Lycra bodysuit—accessorized by a netted fashion scarf and platform-soled espadrilles or Candies slides with three-inch-high spiked heels for footwear. Her cosmetics included Robin's Egg Blue frosted eye shadow, Maybelline's gooey Kissing Sticks on the lips, a dusting of body glitter for bare shoulders, and a spritz or two of sweet-smelling Charlie or Enjoli perfume. Dig it!

DANGER ISLAND
Live-action adventure serial seen as a regular segment on *The Banana Splits Adventure Hour* (1968–70), centering around five people stranded on a remote jungle island who do battle with deadly natives and pirates. It featured a mute jungle boy named Chongo and starred a really young Jan-Michael Vincent.

DANNY "DANNO" WILLIAMS
"Book 'em, Danno!" Detective Steve McGarrett's number-one assistant, played by James MacArthur, son of actress Helen Hayes and playwright Charles MacArthur, on *Hawaii Five-O* from 1968 to 1969.

DANNY PARTRIDGE
Redheaded, freckle-faced middle son and guitarist of The Partridge Family. Danny's sharp tongue and quick wit made him seem older and wiser than his ten years of age.

FYI: ▸ Do they take a class for this or what? Let me see . . . Dysfunctional Child Actor 101, or is it more like Advanced Tabloid Scandals? Danny Bonaduce, who played Danny Partridge from 1970 to 1974, followed the ill-fated burn-out path of other Hollywood tots (including Carl "Alfalfa" Switzer, Tommy Rettig, Anissa Jones, Adam Rich, Leif Garrett, and the *Diff'rent Strokes* kids) by experiencing his own share of controversial headlines, including being arrested for cocaine possession and assaulting a cross-dressing prostitute.

DANNY ZUKO
"You see, Sandy, I got this image. . . ." The coolest of the T-Birds at Rydell High, a greaser hood—tough on the outside, soft on the inside—who fell for goody-two-shoes Sandy, his "summer love." Played by slick-haired cutie John Travolta in the smash motion picture *Grease* (1978).

DAPHNE BLAKE
Trouble-prone, miniskirted redhead in the *Scooby-Doo* cartoons, considered one of the hottest babes of Saturday-morning cartoons. (Other beauties include Wonder Woman, Judy Jetson, Penelope Pitstop, Archie's Betty and Veronica, and Josie and the Pussycats.)

DARIA MORGENDORFFER
"My hormones don't rage. Oh, sure, they get mad sometimes, but then they just stop speaking to each other." Title character of the late-1990s MTV car-

toon series *Daria* (1997–2001), a spin-off from *Beavis and Butt-Head.* Loosely based on comedienne Janeane Garofalo, Daria (voiced by Tracy Grandstaff, not Garofalo as some believe) is an intelligent and quite cynical seventeen-year-old living in suburban Lawndale with yuppie parents Helen and Jake and a prettier younger sister, Quinn. As a junior at Lawndale High School, Daria isn't popular (unlike the shallow Quinn, whom others adore), but she actually prefers not to be popular. She has high disdain for the faculty, especially the principal, Ms. Li, and shoots sharp sarcasm toward her fellow students, particularly Quinn's snooty Fashion Club comrades (Sandi, Stacey, and Tiffany), ditzy head cheerleader Brittany Taylor, dumb football QB Kevin Thompson, and a trio of clueless Quinn admirers called the Three Js (for Joey, Jeffy, and Jamie). Thankfully, there's Jane Lane, Daria's equally intelligent and cynical best pal (plus she has an edgy older brother, Trent Lane, who plays in an alternative rock band, Mystik Spiral).

DARK SHADOWS

"My name is Victoria Winters . . ." began the afternoon serial that had us kids racing home from school so we wouldn't miss a single eerie minute of it! Airing on ABC from 1966 to 1971, this TV drama added a radical twist to the soap genre by combining otherworldly individuals (vampires, ghosts, werewolves, witches, and zombies) and their supernatural practices (black magic, exorcisms, and reincarnations) with the traditional daytime tales of greed, deceit, lust, romance, and heartbreak. Unique to this "horror soap" were the story lines that often switched between the contemporary characters and their nineteenth-century ancestors (played by the same actors).

Set at solemn Collinwood, a gloomy Gothic mansion resting on the edge of a wave-battered cliff in the Maine seaside town of Collinsport, it centered on the dark secrets of the Collins family. Key players included reclusive matriarch Elizabeth Collins Stoddard (played by veteran movie actress Joan Bennett), 200-year-old vampire cousin Barnabas Collins (Jonathan Frid), Elizabeth's teenage daughter, Carolyn Stoddard (Nancy Barrett), family governess Victoria Winters (Alexandra Moltke), Elizabeth's brooding drunken brother, Roger Collins (Louis Edmonds), Roger's troublemaking teenage son, David Collins (David Henesy), physician Julia Hoffman (Grayson Hall), beautiful witch Angelique (Lara Parker), werewolf Quentin Collins (David Selby), and ghost Daphne Harridge (Kate Jackson, in her first TV role).

Awash with machine-made fog, creaking doors, spooky theme music, hambone acting, on-camera bloopers, cheap special effects, hypnotic pacing, and far-out plot turns, *Dark Shadows* became a daytime phenom, developing a huge cult following among housewives and youngsters alike. It inspired two big-screen movies (1970's *House of Dark Shadows* and 1971's *Night of Dark Shadows*), a 1969 record album, a 1969 Top Twenty single ("Quentin's Theme" by Charles Randolph Grean Sounde), twenty or so paperbacks, and a heap of toy tie-ins.

DARK SIDE OF THE MOON

The supersensory 1973 album by the English progressive rock band Pink Floyd set the all-time record for longevity by charting for an astounding fourteen years (no other in the history of any chart has charted longer). Housed among the lush, multilayered tracks is the Top Forty single "Money." A must for all pot-smoking philosophy students.

DARRIN STEPHENS

On the TV series *Bewitched*, dark-haired Dick York, later replaced by look-alike Dick Sargent, starred as Samantha's mortal husband, a conservative, hard-working advertising account executive at McMann & Tate. Worried about what people would think of his wife's being a witch, Darrin insists that Sam suppress her nose-twitching powers, to no avail. He is detested by mother-in-law Endora, who always mispronounces his name (Darwin, Darwood, Durwood, Dagwood, Dobbin, Dumbo, and Dum-Dum, to list a few) and is referred to as "tall, dark, and nothing" by Samantha's naughty cousin Serena.

FYI: ▸ Darrin Stephens attended the University of Missouri, Class of 1950. "Go Tigers!"

DARTH VADER

"If you only knew the power of the Dark Side. . . ." Black-masked, black-robed, respiratory-impaired former Jedi Knight who went over to the Dark Side and transformed into the fear-inspiring military leader of the evil Galactic Empire in the *Star Wars* film franchise. Darth Vader is the father of freedom-fighting Luke Skywalker of the Rebel Alliance.

DASTARDLY AND MUTTLEY IN THEIR FLYING MACHINES

"We're on Muttley's side.
And I guess we're on Dastardly's side.
Anyway, how do you know
they're the bad guys? Maybe they're good.
In wars, everybody thinks they're on
the good side, so how can you say
who's bad or good?
It depends on which side you're on."

—ANONYMOUS EIGHT-YEAR-OLD TV VIEWER, 1969

Spinning off from Saturday morning's enormously popular *Wacky Races*, despicable bad guy Dick Dastardly and his snicker-prone canine accomplice, Muttley, headlined their own TV cartoon, which aired from 1969 to 1971. A cross between the 1965 film *Those Magnificent Men in Their Flying Machines* and Snoopy's Red Baron, the show featured the dirty duo as World War I flying aces and leaders of a villainous and incompetent aerial squadron. Each week they were given orders from the general to capture heroic Yankee Doodle Pigeon, an American courier pigeon carrying secret messages. Their comical Rube Goldberg–esque attempts to catch the bird always ended in vain, resulting in a furious Dastardly ("Drat. And double drat!") and a snickering Muttley. Weirdos Klunk and Zilly were the squadron's good-for-nothing mechanics.

DATING

I was a teen in the late 1970s, attending high school from the fall of 1976 to the summer of 1980. When I think of dating back in that era of Jimmy Carter, disco music, and *Charlie's Angels*, I think of—

- **School dances.** We actually used the term "boogie," as in "Let's go boogie," and slow songs like Styx's "Babe" often led to kissing and groping on the dance floor (until an adult supervisor broke it up).
- **Movie theaters.** If the movie was real boring, you'd end up making out. Actually, for that matter, if it was really good you'd end up making out too.
- **Drive-in movies.** Major make-out places; if you went to one on a date, you knew you were probably going to get to third base.
- **Make-out parties.** Hickeys ruled, as these gatherings usually involved four to six couples all making out in someone's parents' rec room.
- **Rock concerts.** The guy would buy the girl a T-shirt with the band's logo (Styx, KISS, Journey, Foreigner) as a memento.
- **Roller rinks.** A big one for the under-sixteen crowd, especially the couples skate.
- **Pizza Hut.** A great place to get to know each other before a movie, or after. Tacky, I know, but hey—at least it wasn't McDonald's, which would be known as a cheap date.
- **Prom.** The ultimate date, for which what you wore (a frilly baby-blue gown or a glitzy disco number?), who your date was (the captain of the football team or the mysterious college student?), where you ate dinner (Ponderosa or Steak & Ale?), and where you ended up after prom (home or at a keg party in room 161 at the local Holiday Inn?) sealed your high school reputation.

However, I think for most teens of the era it was more fun to travel in packs and go to beer parties in the woods or at an absent parents' house; go cruisin' down the main drag in a jacked-up car (high points for Trans Ams, Firebirds, and Boss Mustangs); go to the beach; or go to the mall—all great places to meet and hang out with someone of the opposite sex.

DATING GAME

Classic game show featuring a lovely bachelorette seated in front of a mod flower backdrop asking vaguely sexy questions of three hopeful male contestants (bachelors) hidden from her view. After the round of questions (and the commercial break), the bachelorette would pick the one whom she'd like to go out with. The other half of the show was then played with one dreamy bachelor choosing from among three bachelorettes. Winners received an all-expense-paid date—with a chaperone—to some fun vacation spot. The show ended with the winning two couples and host Jim Lange blowing a big kiss to the home audience. Lange presided as host of *The Dating Game* from 1965 to 1974. "Spanish Flea," by Herb Alpert and the Tijuana Brass, was the boppy instrumental theme.

DAVE STARSKY

The cute, dark-haired half of the *Starsky and Hutch* TV detective duo, played by Paul Michael Glaser, was the more rugged one, dressed in a "street" uniform of sneakers, jeans, and trademark cardigan sweater. Starsky drove a cool souped-up 1974 Ford Torino.

DAVEY AND GOLIATH

"But Daaavey." A long-running (produced from 1960 to 1965), fifteen-minute, God-friendly kids' series, conceived by Art Clokey (creator of *Gumby*) and funded by the Lutheran Council of Churches. Employing Clokey's stop-motion photography process (pixillation), it featured morality lessons for children involving the adventuresome ten-year-old Davey Hanson from Anywhere U.S.A., and a cautionary Goliath, his talking dog. Many Christian-based TV stations are still airing it today.

DAVID SEVILLE

Dark-haired cartoon character and harried manager of the capricious Chipmunks who was loosely based on singer-songwriter Ross Bagdasarian, creator of the famed singin' rodents.

DAVIS, MAC

Country-and-western singer who experienced crossover pop success in the mid-1970s. Born on January 21, 1942, the Texan—known for his curly-haired good looks and friendly, laid-back manner—began his career as a songwriter, penning "In the Ghetto" (1969) and "Don't Cry Daddy" (1969) for Elvis Presley, and "Watching Scotty Grow" (1971) for Bobby Goldsboro. As a solo artist, Davis scored a number-one song with "Baby, Don't Get Hooked on Me" in 1972. Other hits included "I Believe in Music" (1972), "One Hell of a Woman" (1974), and "Stop and Smell the Roses" (1974). From 1974 to 1976, he hosted his very own musical-variety TV series, *The Mac Davis Show*, notable for his improvising of songs from suggestions submitted by the studio audience and for introducing us to the mime duo Shields and Yarnell. Davis starred as an NFL jock in the 1979 film *North Dallas Forty*, co-starring Nick Nolte, and appeared as Will Rogers in the Broadway musical *Will Rogers Follies* during the 1990s.

DAWN DAVENPORT

"My parents will be really sorry if I don't get them cha-cha heels!" Obese teenage schoolgirl whose being denied cha-cha heels for Christmas leads to her running away, getting raped, and becoming a single mother (the "retarded" Taffy), a criminal (along with sleazy cohorts Concetta and Chicklette), the wife of a hippie (Aunt Ida's Gator), a glam model (for beauticians Donald and Donna Dasher), a mass murderer, and finally rendezvousing with the electric chair. Played by the divine Divine in John Waters's 1975 camp classic *Female Trouble*.

DAWN DOLL

At only six inches tall, this groovy fashion doll reminds you of a Barbie doll but has a diminutive style all her own. Manufactured by Topper Toys from 1970 to 1972, Dawn had long, middle-parted blonde hair and real eyelashes and came wearing a blue-and-white halter-top minidress. She was the beautiful model-proprietor of the Dawn Model Agency who employed an assortment of cover-girl chums: Angie (a lovely brunette), Jessica (a blonde stewardess with a daring short cut), Dale (an African-American with an outtasight Afro), Glori (a radiant redhead), Longlocks (who had extremely long, dark hair, hence her name), and Gary, Ron, and Van (the handsome boyfriends). What set these dolls apart from others of the era was that their bodies could move: When their arms were moved up and down, they mechanically swung their legs and swiveled their hips, as if they were dancing or walking.

The world of Dawn included a wide range of fab accessories. There was the Dawn Fashion Show, complete with a revolving stage so the dolls could walk and model dazzling mod fashions with far-out names like "Gala Go-Go," "Peek-a-Boo Poncho," "Skinny Mini," "Groovy, Baby, Groovy," "Pink Pussycat," and "Socko Swirls." Then there was the Dawn Beauty Pageant, in which the doll contestants actually walk down the runway, swivel, and return to the stage to compete for the golden crown.

The Dawn's Disco, with the psychedelic revolving dance floor, let Fancy Feet Dawn and boyfriend Kevin go-go the night away. There was also a Dawn's Beauty Parlor with an actual working sink; Dawn's Dress Shop, complete with a three-way mirror so the dolls could see how they looked in their glam frocks; Dawn's Action Car, a fast-driving blue convertible; and a collection of colorful carrying cases to take Dawn on the go.

FYI: ▸ One Dawn doll (Dawn Head-to-Toe), introduced in 1971, came with three removable wiglets: a glamorous long-flowing fall that swept to the floor, an elegant braided up-do, and a bouncy *I Dream of Jeannie* ponytail.

DAWN OF THE DEAD

"When there's no more room in hell, the dead will walk the earth."
—PETER (KEN FOREE)

In 1979, director George A. Romero returned to the zombie film genre with the apocalyptic sequel to his cult masterpiece *Night of the Living Dead* (1968). Society is on the verge of collapse, and a band of survivors—two SWAT team members, Peter and Roger (Foree and Scott Reiniger); and a chopper pilot, Stephen (David Emge), and his beautiful TV anchor girlfriend, Francine (Gaylen Ross)—flee from zombie-infested Pittsburgh, Pennsylvania, in a stolen traffic-news helicopter. Running low on fuel, the quartet land on the roof of a huge suburban shopping mall (Monroeville Mall), where they take refuge within. After killing the living dead shuffling inside and barricading all the doors, the shopping complex seems like a safe haven. (And who wouldn't want a whole mall all to themselves?) However, there is an ever-expanding army of cannibalistic zombies trying to break through the barricades, and when a renegade gang of human bikers opens the mall doors, allowing hundreds of walking corpses to enter, the survivors—including a now-pregnant Fran—flee for safety.

Filmed in glorious bloody color, the gore-loaded, stomach-churning movie is acclaimed as a scathing commentary on American consumerism (the dead return to the mall on some sort of residual instinct). It is followed by a 1985 sequel (the third and final installment in Romero's *Dead* trilogy) and a 2004 remake (in which the zombies run like marathon racers).

DAWN: PORTRAIT OF A TEENAGE RUNAWAY

This 1976 made-for-TV movie had the distinction of starring angst-ridden Brady Bunch gal Eve Plumb as a young streetwalker on seedy Hollywood Boulevard. Popular with teenage viewers—who enjoyed seeing the usually clean-cut Plumb play a scruffy hooker—it became one of the biggest hits of the TV year. In it, fifteen-year-old Dawn Wetherby (Eve Plumb), the unhappy daughter of a cocktail waitress, runs away to sunny Hollywood, where she becomes a prostitute when she is unable to land a legitimate job to pay her rent. While on the streets, she befriends a good-looking male hustler named Alexander (Leigh McCloskey), who helps her get off the Boulevard. But can she help him too? Watch the sequel, *Alexander: The Other Side of Dawn* (1977), and you will find out. Inspired a few other TV movies about youthful whores, including *Little Ladies of the Night* (1977) and *Off the Minnesota Strip* (1980). Soundtrack featured "Comin' Home Again," performed by Shaun Cassidy, and "Cherry Bomb," performed by The Runaways.

DAWN WIENER

"Why do you hate me?" "Because you're ugly." Unattractive, dorkily dressed with awful horn-rimmed glasses, and painfully geeky, this seventh-grader is the heroine of director Todd Solondz's indie film *Welcome to the Dollhouse* (1995). Anyone with hurtful memories of middle school can relate to Dawn, the archetypal picked-on adolescent. At the junior high she attends in suburban New Jersey, life is hellish at best. Dawn has no friends (not even the other nerds like her). The whole student body calls her "Wiener Dog" and "Dog Face." Her school locker is splattered with awful, derogatory phrases. She has no one to sit with at lunch in the cafeteria. And the cheerleading squad taunts her for being a lesbian (she's not). Thirteen-year-old actress Heather Matarazzo won the Independent Spirit Award for Best Debut Performance for her role as Dawn.

DAY AFTER

It seems as if every generation of the latter part of the twentieth century had fears of some sort of foreign attack or invasion. During the 1940s, our grandparents worried about submarine-roving Nazis from Hitler's Germany and high-flying Japanese kamikazes attacking U.S. coastlines from under and over the seas. Our parents feared the Communist Party would secretly take over their suburban neighborhoods in the 1950s. Young Baby Boomers of the 1960s cold war feared the atomic bomb and were instructed on how to "duck and cover." Gen-Xers came of age in the 1980s under the threat of nuclear war.

This 1983 TV movie portrayed a grim picture of why all generations should avoid nuclear war, by depicting the catastrophic consequences of a Soviet blast on Lawrence, Kansas (home of the University of Kansas), located on the outskirts of Kansas City. One chilling scene (out of many): The sight of missiles flying out of their silos suddenly disrupts an ordinary, peaceful day in the midwestern countryside. Terrifying and highly rated, *The Day After* was the most controversial made-for-TV film of its time because of its topical subject. Critics accused ABC-TV of airing Soviet propaganda, and that provoked a firestorm of debate among politicians, the media, antinuclear groups, and peace activists.

DAY OF THE ANIMALS

"For centuries they were hunted for bounty, fun, and food. Now it's their turn." The 1977 animal-revenge flick has woodland critters in the High Sierras going nuts after being exposed to the sun's radiation when earth's ozone is depleted. You just have to pity the two-legged humans, such as Lynda Day George, hubby Christopher George, and Leslie Nielsen, who happen to be hiking in the woods that day. William Girdler, who filmed another killer animal tale the previous year, *Grizzly*, directed the low-budget thriller.

DAY OF THE WEEK PANTIES

Monday, Tuesday, Wednesday . . . no confusion here, folks, these feminine undergarments made it clear which one to wear each day of the week.

DAYDREAMER

An entertaining, kid-oriented motion picture mixing live actors with the stop-motion animated puppets of Arthur Rankin Jr. and Jules Bass. This was the first big-screen venture from the duo responsible for giving us wonderful holiday TV specials like *Rudolph the Red-Nosed Reindeer* and *A Year Without a Santa Claus*. It told the story of thirteen-year-old Hans Christian Andersen (Paul O'Keefe), whose daydreams take him to the famous fairy-tale adventures he would later grow up to write about: "The Emperor's New Clothes," "Thumbelina," "The Little Mermaid," and "The Garden of Paradise."— Featured were Jack Gilford as Papa Andersen, Ray Bolger as the Pieman, and the voices of Tallulah Bankhead as the Sea Witch, Victor Borge as the Second Tailor, Patty Duke as Thumbelina, Margaret Hamilton as Mrs. Klopplebobbler, Sessue Hayakawa as the Mole, Burl Ives as Father Neptune, Boris Karloff as the Rat, Hayley Mills as the Little Mermaid, Terry-Thomas as the First Tailor, and Ed Wynn as the Emperor. Robert Goulet sang the 1966 film's title song.

DAZED AND CONFUSED

"It was the last day of school in 1976. A time they'd never forget—if only they could remember!" Forget TV's *That '70s Show* if you really want to see what teens of the 1970s were like. Director Richard Linklater's *Dazed and Confused* (1993) captures it superbly (trust me, I lived it). This hilarious piece of nostalgia follows a varied group of suburban Texas teens (freaks, jocks, and geeks) on the last day of school in late May 1976. The upperclassmen of Robert E. Lee High School are hazing the incoming freshmen ("All right, you freshmen bitches!"), while everyone else is looking to get stoned, drunk, laid, or score Aerosmith concert tickets. The talented ensemble cast (all then unknown) includes Jason London as football quarterback Randall "Pink" Floyd, Joey Lauren Adams as foxy sophomore Simone Kerr, Milla Jovovich as freaky Michelle Burroughs, Rory Cochrane as stoner Ron Slater, Adam Goldberg as rebellious nerd Mike Newhouse, Ben Affleck as bully Fred O'Bannion, Parker Posey as bitchy cheerleader Darla Marks, Matthew McConaughey as long-since-graduated motorhead David Wooderson, and Wiley Wiggins as freshman-to-be Mitch Kramer. The soundtrack contains carefully selected period music, such as "Slow Ride" by Foghat, "Low Rider" by War, "School's Out" by Alice Cooper, "Jim Dandy" by Black Oak Arkansas, "Love Hurts" by Nazareth, "Fox on the Run" by Sweet, "Tuesday's Gone" by Lynyrd

Skynyrd, and "Rock 'n' Roll All Nite" by KISS. "Finally, a movie for everyone who *did* inhale!"

D.C.

Initials stood for "Darn Cat." A seal-point Siamese belonging to teenage owner Patti Randall, who helped solve the mystery of a woman bank teller kidnapped by bank robbers. Feline star Syn, who starred as the scene-stealing tomcat in the 1965 Disney comedy *That Darn Cat*, also played Tao in the 1963 adventure *The Incredible Journey*.

DEADHEADS

Tie-dye-wearing, acid-dropping hippie loyalists of Jerry Garcia's Grateful Dead who faithfully roam the country in old VW buses to attend the ceaseless tour band's performances. In the late 1980s, the Dead developed an even larger following, particularly among well-to-do college students who weren't even born when the psychedelic rockers first formed in San Francisco back in 1966. This strange phenomenon nabbed the aging group their first Top Ten hit with "Touch of Grey" (1987). Garcia died of a heart attack on August 9, 1995.

DEAD MAN'S POINT

In the Saturday-morning TV series *Sigmund and the Sea Monsters*, this is the forbidden cove off Southern California's Cypress Beach, where the Ooz family, a clan of evil sea monsters headed by Big Daddy and Sweet Mama, reside in a cave.

DEATH OF RICHIE

In the tradition of the youth classic *Go Ask Alice*, this sobering 1977 TV movie was derived from a nonfiction book about the tragic effects of drug abuse on a teenager. Based on the 1973 novel *Richie* by Thomas Thompson, it starred heartthrob Robby Benson as Richie Werner, a confused teen whose drug addiction leads to erratic outbursts at school and clashes with his family, particularly his straight-as-an-arrow father. In a moment of self-defense, the youngster, in a violent, drug-influenced rage, is shot to death by his dad, who is consequently put on trial for murder. The film co-starred Ben Gazzara as father George Werner, Eileen Brennan as mother Carol Werner, and Lance "James at 15" Kerwin as Russell Werner, Richie's little brother.

DEBBIE DOES DALLAS

Notoriously successful 1978 porno film inspired by the popularity of pro football's Dallas Cowboys Cheerleaders. It starred Cowboys Cheerleader reject Bambi Woods, an energetic blonde who in real life tried out for the squad but didn't make the cut. In the movie, young Debbie Benton and her high school cheerleading pals travel to Dallas for cheerleader tryouts and end up screwing every man in sight for a spot on the pom-pom-shaking team. Spawned two *Debbie Does Dallas* sequels in 1981 and 1985.

DEBBIE THE BLOOP

Strange space-chimp adopted as a pet by young Penny Robinson on TV's *Lost in Space*. In real life, Debbie was actually a monkey made to look like an alien Bloop by using chenille bump ears.

De BRUNHOFF, JEAN

French author and postimpressionist painter (1899–1937) who wrote and illustrated the beloved children's book series about Babar, the Little Elephant, based on bedtime stories invented by his mother, Cecile. After his death, son Laurent de Brunhoff took over as Babar's author. Titles in the series included *The Story of Babar the Little Elephant, Babar the King, Babar's Travels, Babar in America, Babar and Father Christmas*, and *Babar Visits Another Planet*.

DEE DEE

Annette Funicello's sexy but chaste Southern California beach bunny who likes dancing, singing, parties, and Frankie (when he's not taking her for granted), from the 1960s *Beach Party* films.

DEELY BOBBERS

Also known as deely boppers. A crazy 1980s fad that had people wearing an antennae-like contraption secured atop the noggin by a headband and made out of colorful Styrofoam balls or other wacky objects attached to always-jiggling slinky springs.

DeFRANCO FAMILY, FEATURING TONY DeFRANCO

The pop-music family act from Toronto, Canada, featured the youngest sibling, thirteen-year-old Tony, as lead singer (official name: Tony DeFranco and The DeFranco Family). Tony's selling point (besides being a cutie-pie) was a Donny Osmond resemblance and an oh-so-dreamy singing voice. He was joined by brothers Nino and Benny and sisters Merlina and Marisa. Pop hits included the million-selling "Heartbeat—It's a Lovebeat" (1973), "Abra-Ca-Dabra" (1974), and a remake of The Drifters' "Save the Last Dance for Me" (1974). Like most teen idol bands of the era, Tony and Family were immortalized in the pages of teenybop rags like *Tiger Beat*, *16*, *Fave*, and *Teen Beat*.

Del RUBIO TRIPLETS

Seeing and hearing is believing when it came to these go-go-booted, miniskirted, guitar-strumming, identical blonde sisters—Milly, Elena, and Eadie—who made their splash in kitsch culture at the age of sixty-five with tone-deaf covers of rock hits, like "Walk Like an Egyptian," "Neutron Dance," "Y.M.C.A.," "Whip It," and "These Boots Are Made for Walkin'." In 1988, they starred on FOX's *Married . . . with Children* as Peg Bundy's singing and dancing aunts, The Wanker Triplets. Originally performed as the singing group 3 Gals, 3 Guitars.

"DELTA DAWN"

At one time, "Delta Dawn" was the prettiest woman you ever laid eyes on, but by the 1970s folks around Brownsville thought she was crazy. You see, she walked around town wearing a faded rose, carried a suitcase while looking for a mysterious dark-haired man, and at age forty-one was still called "baby" by her daddy. This poor soul was the subject of a 1973 song that simultaneously became a colossal hit both for Australian songbird Helen Reddy and for thirteen-year-old country superstar Tanya Tucker. A number-one pop single for Reddy, it marked the first of a trio of songs about some rather dysfunctional women, including "Leave Me Alone," with big ol' Ruby Red Dress, and "Angie Baby," a special lady who lived in a world of make-believe.

DENNIS THE MENACE

Dennis Mitchell, the late Hank Ketcham's five-year-old towheaded enfant terrible, first appeared in a daily single-panel newspaper cartoon on March 12, 1951, and became immensely popular. Americans enjoyed reading about the little hero's well-meaning but mischievous antics in his suburban town of Hillsdale, especially toward long-suffering next-door neighbor George Wilson. Other characters in the *Dennis* comics included harried parents Henry and Alice Mitchell, best pal Joey MacDonald, know-it-all nemesis Margaret Wade, Italian-American tomboy Gina, and shaggy dog Ruff. In 1959, *Dennis the Menace* began a four-year-run as a prime-time sitcom starring Jay North. The tiny troublemaker also appeared in a cartoon segment on Saturday morning's *Curiosity Shop* (1971–73) and was the spokeskid for the Sears Christmas Wish Book and for Dairy Queen restaurants. In 1993, a well-made film, scripted by John Hughes of 1980s Brat Pack fame, played at theaters.

FYI: ▸ Cartoonist Ketcham's real-life son was named Dennis. The inspiration for the comic strip came one day when his wife remarked, "Our son Dennis is a menace."

DENNY'S

This low-priced restaurant chain, known for serving breakfast night and day, is where most of us ended up for a cup of stimulating coffee and much-needed nourishment to soak up the booze after a heavy night of partying. After three in the morning (known as the "graveyard" hours), its patrons are a sight to behold: drunken club kids mixing with those who've just finished working late-night shifts (for example, cops and strippers), alongside local riffraff—all being served by hardened, cigarette-voice waitresses. Originally named Danny's Donuts, Denny's was founded by Harold Butler in Lakewood, California, in 1953. Today, it is America's leading family restaurant, with more than 1,500 restaurants. Look for its famous yellow-and-red sign and try its best-known meal, the Grand Slam Breakfast, consisting of two buttermilk hotcakes with two eggs, two strips of bacon, and two sausage links.

DENVER, JOHN

The singer-songwriter with the blond mop-top, granny glasses, perky personality, and folksy voice epitomized the 1970s middle-of-the-road music scene. Born Henry Deutschendorf on December 31, 1943, in Roswell, New Mexico, he adopted the showbiz surname after his favorite city in Colorado and began singing and playing guitar at folk-music joints in L.A. during the mid-1960s. In 1969, his composition of "Leaving on a Jet Plane" became a number-one hit for Peter, Paul, and Mary, establishing a strong basis for impending success. Denver's career took flight with a string of million-selling singles: "Take Me Home, Country Roads" (1971), "Rocky Mountain High" (1973), "Sunshine on My Shoulders" (1974), "Annie's Song," written for his wife Ann Martell (1974), "Back Home Again" (1974), "Sweet Surrender" (1975), "Thank God I'm a Country Boy" (1975), "I'm Sorry" (1975), "Calypso," dedicated to famed marine biologist Jacques Cousteau, whose ship was called *Calypso* (1975), and "Fly Away," with Olivia Newton-John on backing vocals (1975). He made his acting debut in the 1977 comedy movie *Oh, God!* co-starring cigar-smoking George Burns, as God.

On October 12, 1997, Denver died when the private plane he was flying crashed into California's Monterey Bay. He had spent his entire life active in environmental issues and the world hunger movement. Denver's favorite environment: the Colorado mountains. ("Rocky Mountain High" was written in honor of those majestic peaks.)

DEPP, JOHNNY

"I don't pretend to be Captain Weird. I just do what I do." Hollywood star with not-so-clean pretty-boy looks (often looking like he needs a good shave and a shower, he self-dubbed himself "Mr. Stench") who is renowned for picking eccentric movie roles over more commercial ones. Born June 9, 1963, in Kentucky, and raised in Florida, the dark-haired Depp moved to Los Angeles in the early 1980s to play guitar in a rock band called The Kids. He turned to acting after ex-wife Lori Allison, a makeup artist, introduced him to actor Nicolas Cage, who in return introduced him to his agent. His big-screen debut came in the first *Nightmare on Elm Street* movie in 1984.

It was starring as Officer Tommy Hanson on TV's *21 Jump Street* that gained him popularity as a teen heartthrob in the late 1980s. Fortunately for Depp, he was able to shake off the teen-dream image by choosing unusual film roles. The best of these characters include Wade "Cry-Baby" Walker in *Cry-Baby* (1989), Edward Scissorhands in *Edward Scissorhands* (1990), Sam in *Benny and Joon* (1993), Gilbert Grape in *What's Eating Gilbert Grape?* (1993), Edward Wood Jr. in *Ed Wood* (1994), Ichabod Crane in *Sleepy Hollow* (1999), George Jung in *Blow* (2001), and Jack Sparrow in *Pirates of the Caribbean* (2003). Depp was a co-ower of the sizzling L.A. club dubbed The Viper Room, located on Sunset Boulevard in West Hollywood.

FYI: ▸ Johnny Depp had "Winona Forever" tattooed on his arm when dating actress Winona Ryder. After they broke up, he had the final "n" and the "a" surgically removed to say "Wino Forever."

DEPUTY DAWG

Created in 1960 by Terrytoons, this dim-witted Southern lawman muttered in slurred speech and fumbled his way to upholding law and order in the small hamlet of Creek Mud, Mississippi. Lawbreaking pranksters in Deputy Dawg's cartoon life include Vince Van Gopher, Ty Coon the Raccoon, Muskie the Muskrat, and Pig Newton.

DEREK, BO

Throughout the early 1980s, the sex symbol with pale-blue eyes, blonde hair, high cheekbones, and a well-endowed figure was considered the definition of beauty. Born Mary Cathleen Collins on November 20, 1956, she grew up the archetypal California beach girl in Long Beach. In 1979, director Blake Edwards introduced the world to Bo when he cast her in the raunchy comedy *10*, co-starring Dudley Moore and Julie Andrews. (The title refers to her perfect rating on the beauty scale of 1 through 10.) She played newlywed Jenny and the focus of middle-aged Moore's obsession—a young, free-spirited Southern Californian who wears her hair in cornrows, smokes marijuana, and screws to Ravel's "Bolero." At the age of sixteen, Bo married Svengali actor-director John Derek, thirty years her senior. He photographed her in the nude for several *Playboy* magazine layouts and directed her in awful career-stunting flicks, such as *Tarzan the Ape Man* (1981) and *Bolero* (1984).

FYI: ▸ Bo Derek's questionable acting abilities once led late-night TV host David Letterman to introduce a plank of cedarwood as her acting coach.

DEREK FLINT
"Introducing America's Playboy Hero!" *Our Man Flint*, the best of the countless James Bond parodies of the 1960s, centered around zesty Derek Flint (played tongue-in-cheek by James Coburn), the "world's greatest secret agent" (and lover), who worked for Z.O.W.I.E. (Zonal Organization World Intelligence Espionage). Flint spends his time in the 1966 film stopping mad scientists from destroying the world with their earthquake machine and seducing Russian femme fatale Gila (Gila Golan). Followed by *In Like Flint* (1967), spy spoofery at its best as an evil society of beautiful women in the Virgin Islands schemes to take over the world by using subliminal brainwashing hair dryers!

DERRY DARING
Called the "Queen of the Stuntwomen," she was the female counterpart to Evel Knievel. However, unlike the motorcycle stunt king, she wasn't a real person—she was a doll. Introduced for girls in 1975 by Ideal Toys—which had experienced success the previous year with the Evel Knievel action figure—the seven-inch-high Derry Daring had a poseable body and long blonde hair and wore a pink-and-silver jumpsuit equipped with matching helmet. She came riding the Trick Cycle, which could be revved up by the Gyro-Power Winder for thrilling wheelies and stunt jumps. Derry's other exciting accessories included the three-in-one Pop-Top Camper, which converted into a camper or a pickup or a smart-looking utility vehicle, and the Wheelie Car, an amazing action car capable of long-distance vertical wheelies and high-flying ramp jumps.

DESERT BOOTS
These ankle-high, sand-colored suede shoes by Clarks were the first-choice casual footwear among youths (males and females) of the 1970s.

DeSHANNON, JACKIE
Singer-songwriter who had a couple of Top Ten hits during the late 1960s—"What the World Needs Now Is Love" (1965) and "Put a Little Love in Your Heart" (1969)—and co-wrote, along with Donna Weiss, "Bette Davis Eyes" (1981) for Kim Carnes.

DESIGNER JEANS
Expensive, form-fitting jeans, popular in the late 1970s and early 1980s, that featured the name of someone famously chic on the ass pocket. According to pop culture authors Jane and Michael Stern in their *Encyclopedia of Bad Taste*, the famous moniker on the designer jeans "gives them status and therefore makes the person who wears them feel more important than someone who wears ordinary Levi's." No matter if a person was socially insecure or cursed with lower-class status—once they wiggled their fanny into a pair of these elitist pants, they had an instant sense of elegance and sex appeal. Designer jeans started to become oh-so-trendy around 1978, when the Nakash brothers introduced their french-cut, elegant-appearing Jordache jeans, featuring the pants' logo—a pony—on the back pocket. Then in 1979, socialite Gloria Vanderbilt's signature appeared stitched on the right rear pocket of her jeans line, along with a swan embroidered on the front coin pocket, giving women the "million-dollar look"! In 1980, designer denim was at its fashion high after Calvin Klein's suggestive ads appeared, showcasing a seductive Brooke Shields squiggling into hers or an assortment of hunky shirtless male models posing in theirs.

Other notable names to grace the butts of label-conscious Americans were Sergio Valente, Bonjour, Chic, Angel Flights, Cotler, Diane von Furstenberg, Cheryl Tiegs, Ralph Lauren, Yves St. Laurent, Chemin de Fer, Chams de Baron, Brittannia, and "Ooh, La! La!" Sassoon.

DESPERATELY SEEKING SUSAN
In this funky comedy by director Susan Seidelman, Rosanna Arquette stars as Roberta, a bored suburban New York housewife who spices up her life by reading the personals in the daily newspaper. Roberta is intrigued by one particular love-column adventure, between a mysterious New Wave temptress and her lover, under the recurring headline entry "Desperately Seeking Susan." On a whim, she journeys to Manhattan to catch a peek at the lovebirds and finds herself buying Susan's just-sold leather jacket from a secondhand clothing store. Wearing the jacket, Roberta is accidentally conked on the head and assumes Susan's identity after experiencing amnesia. Unfortunately (but fortunately

for laughs), there are unpleasant people seeking Susan, including a hit man contracted to kill her, and Roberta finds herself caught in the middle. Costars included pop-star Madonna as Susan, the wildly dressed, free-spirited kook, and blue-eyed dreamboat Aidan Quinn as Dez, the brooding movie projectionist who befriends Roberta. Released during the summer of 1985, the film's surprise success is credited with the popularity of Madonna, whose songs were all over the airwaves—including "Into the Groove," featured on the soundtrack.

DEVIL'S TOWER
Located in northeastern Wyoming, this steep-sided national monument was made globally famous in 1977 when it became the alien landing pad in Steven Spielberg's blockbuster movie *Close Encounters of the Third Kind.*

DEVO
They were not men, they were Devo, a futuristic rock act performed by nerds (or, in their words, "spuds") from Akron, Ohio—brothers Jerry and Bob Casale, brothers Mark and Bob Mothersbaugh, and nonbrother Alan Myers, who met while studying at Kent State in the mid-1970s. It was there that they formed an experimental group, originally called the De-Evolution Band, based on a self-invented theory of the regression of mankind. Shortened to Devo, the band was known for a nonconformist robotic style, industrial uniforms, and quirky, mechanical-sounding music. Tunes included a fractured rendering of The Rolling Stones' "(I Can't Get No) Satisfaction" (1977), "Jocko Homo" (1977), "Whip It" (1980), "Working in the Coal Mine" (1981), "That's Good" (1982), and "Peek-a-Boo" (1982). "Whip It" was their best-selling single and only Top Forty hit. Devo is noteworthy for being one of the forerunners of the New Wave synthesized sound, inspiring such songs as "Pop Muzik" (1979) by M and "Cars" (1980) by Gary Numan.

DEXTER SHOES
Indistinctive 1980s footwear known for a thick rubber sole and its brown color (indistinctive like this descriptive!).

DIAMOND, NEIL
Some find him cheesy, others think he's God, but there's no denying that this entertainer, marked by overdramatic, middle-of-the-road ballads, has made an impact on American Top Forty radio. Born on January 24, 1941, in Brooklyn, Diamond first found success as a songwriter for other artists (he penned "I'm a Believer" for The Monkees). As a recording artist, he cranked out hit after hit with such songs as "Girl, You'll Be a Woman Soon" (1967), "Sweet Caroline" (1969), "Solitary Man" (1970), "Cracklin' Rose" (1970), "I Am . . . I Said" (1971), "Song Sung Blue" (1972), "Play Me" (1972), "Longfellow Serenade" (1974), "Forever in Blue Jeans" (1979), and "September Morn'" (1980). His duet "You Don't Bring Me Flowers" with fellow Brooklynite Barbra Streisand topped the charts for two weeks and sold more than a million copies in 1978. Diamond made his acting (if you can call it acting) debut in 1980 with an updated version of Al Jolson's *The Jazz Singer*. Although a flop, it earned him three more hits: "Love on the Rocks," "Hello Again," and "America." He wrote the score for the 1973 film *Jonathan Livingston Seagull.*

FYI: ▸ Neil Diamond became somewhat cool in the mid-1990s when two of his songs were prominently featured in movies: "Girl, You'll Be a Woman Soon" from *Pulp Fiction* (1994) and "Sweet Caroline" from *Beautiful Girls* (1996).

DIANA, PRINCESS
"I would like to be a queen in people's hearts. Someone's got to go there and love people." Born on July 1, 1961, pretty Lady Diana Spencer was a shy nineteen-year-old kindergarten teacher who married thirty-three-year-old Prince Charles, heir to the throne of England. Their fairy-tale wedding on July 29, 1981, was one of the most anticipated and reveled ceremonies of the twentieth century (more than 750 million people watched worldwide). Affectionately nicknamed Di, she was referred to as "the People's Princess" because of the friendly and caring rapport she had with "everyday people." She brought a breath of fresh air to stuffy ol' Buckingham Palace, but that freshness also made her seem out of place next to the dowdy royal family. (I'll al-

ways remember a photograph of Di receiving a disapproving glance from husband Chuck because she dared to groove to the music at a rock concert in London.) The Prince and Princess of Wales procreated two sons, William and Harry, before their marriage came to a turbulent end in 1992 because of obvious generational differences, alleged infidelities by both parties, and his apparent jealousy of her massive popularity.

Throughout the 1980s and 1990s, Diana was a fashion trendsetter. Women all over the world copied her short, blonde hairstyles, as well as her designer threads (Di's favorites: Versace, Valentino, and Dior). More famous than a movie star, the princess used her celebrity to focus attention on international issues: AIDS, breast cancer, domestic violence, homelessness, world hunger, war orphans, and the carnage wrought by land mines. In 1995, in recognition of her charity work, she received the International Humanitarian of the Year Award. The downside to her enormous fame was the curse of living life as if in a fishbowl, with the world's media and tabloid photographers stalking Diana's every move.

Tragically, on August 31, 1997, Princess Diana was killed, along with millionaire companion Dodi Fayed, when the Mercedes they were traveling in crashed inside a Paris traffic tunnel after being pursued by a gang of motorcycle-riding paparazzi. Her death stunned the world, leaving millions mourning and throwing Great Britain into a state of shock and sadness. On the day of her funeral, September 9, 1997, more than one and a half million people said farewell.

For those of us born in the same decade as Diana, her sudden death is comparable to the shock our parents must have felt after President Kennedy's assassination in 1963. To our generation, she was more than just the most famous woman in the world. Diana was a role model, an inspiration, someone whose life seemed destined for greater things, and, most important, a peer whom we probably could have known, palled around with, and, yes, grooved with at a rock concert, if given the chance.

DIANA PRINCE

Alter ego of comic-book star Wonder Woman, who works for the armed forces in Washington, D.C., as a secretary for pilot Steve Trevor. In between typing and filing, the crown princess of Paradise Island fights for American rights as a star-spangled superheroine with bullet-deflecting bracelets and a magic lasso.

DIARY OF A TEENAGE HITCHHIKER

The 1979 TV flick made youngsters think twice about thumbing a ride from strangers. Both sleazy and corny, the moralistic tale starred blonde dumpling Charlene Tilton—taking a break from *Dallas*—as Julie Thurston, a defiant Southern California chick with a penchant for skimpy clothing and a knack for ignoring her parents' advice. (Sounds like a typical teen to me.) Like her other friends, seventeen-year-old Julie is a member of the local hitchhiking scene (it's a free ride to the beach)—that is, until the day a drooling maniac picks her up and she learns a lesson. It co-starred Dick Van Patten and Katherine Helmond as parents Herb and Elaine Thurston, and *Brady Bunch*'s Christopher Knight as boyfriend Nick.

DICK AND JANE

"Look, Jane, look. See Spot run." A series of children's readers, *Fun with Dick and Jane*, widely used in American grammar schools from the 1930s to the 1970s. In a simple style—centering around the playful antics of Dick, younger sister Jane, baby sister Sally, family dog Spot, and family cat Fluff—these primers taught youngsters one new vocabulary word per page. Eleanor Campbell illustrated them.

DICK DASTARDLY

Dirty, despicable, diabolical, and devious—this dark-haired, mustachioed cartoon character is one of Saturday morning's all-time favorite villains. Along with snickering canine sidekick Muttley, Dastardly first appeared driving the Mean Machine (car number 00) on Hanna-Barbera's *Wacky Races* (1968–70). In every episode, he set out to sabotage the other drivers competing for the title of "World's Wackiest Racer." The popularity of Dastardly and Muttley led to a spin-off, *Dastardly and Muttley in Their Flying Machines*, which had the terrible twosome as World War I flying aces trying to "Stop That Pigeon."

DICK TRACY
Jut-jawed comic-strip police detective, created by Chester Gould in 1931, who employs cunning street smarts to fight colorful Prohibition-style criminals such as ghastly Mrs. Pruneface, faceless Blank, and the insect-infested Flyface. Came to the big screen in 1990 starring Warren Beatty as Tracy, Glenne Headly as his girlfriend, Tess Trueheart, and Madonna as gangster moll Breathless Mahoney.

DIFF'RENT STROKES
Airing from 1978 to 1986, the premise of this TV sitcom was two black orphans from Harlem becoming residents of Park Avenue, where they are introduced to the cushy, upper-class lifestyle after being adopted by a white millionaire (their deceased mother had been his maid). It starred juvenile-star-of-the-moment Gary Coleman as wisecracking Arnold Jackson, Todd Bridges as his reserved older brother, Willis, Conrad Bain as wealthy widower Philip Drummond, Dana Plato as Drummond's blonde teenage daughter, Kimberly, and Charlotte Rae as dizzy housekeeper Mrs. Edna Garrett, who would leave in 1980 to become a housemother at the prestigious Eastland School for Girls (the spin-off *Facts of Life*). The popular NBC show addressed many sensitive topics, including child molestation, hitchhiking, and drug abuse. (First Lady Nancy "Just Say No" Reagan appeared on a 1983 episode that dealt with the dangers of illegal substances.)

FYI: ▸ The original working title of *Diff'rent Strokes* was "45 Minutes from Harlem."

***DIFF'RENT STROKES* KIDS**
After *Diff'rent Strokes* ended its eight-year run, all three of its child stars became regulars in tabloid headlines. Dana Plato posed nude for *Playboy*, then in 1991 was charged with armed robbery of a Las Vegas video store and given five years probation for forging pill prescriptions. Gary Coleman filed suit against his parents and a former manager, claiming they had mishandled his earnings, and later he was sued for punching an autograph-seeking fan. Todd Bridges found himself charged in a drug-related murder (he was acquitted) and had numerous arrests for drug possession. (Where's Nancy Reagan when you need her?) Before Plato's fatal overdose in May 1999, all three were regulars on the talk-show circuit, discussing the plight of kid actors who are worshiped as adorable tots but too often discarded by Hollywood when they grow up.

DIG 'EM FROG
"Dig 'em!" Cool green frog in a baseball cap who has been the mascot for Kellogg's Sugar Smacks cereal—renamed Honey Smacks—since 1972.

DIGGER THE DOG
Adorned with a red detective hat, this yellow canine pull toy leaned over as though sniffing tracks for an undercover clue. So, what was Digger searching for? Clues to a crime? A hidden stash of bones? The Hot Wheel you lost in the backyard last week? The only person who could answer these questions was the imaginative little tot who owned a Digger. The toy was introduced by Hasbro Toys in 1974.

DILLON, MATT
The dark-haired, thick-browed, fair-skinned movie actor epitomized the streetwise urban youth of the late 1970s and early 1980s. Born on February 18, 1964, in New Rochelle, New York, Dillon was discovered in the hallway of his junior high school by a talent scout. At age fifteen, he was cast by director Jonathan Kaplan as the ill-fated ruffian Richie White in *Over the Edge* (1979), a film about rebellious suburban youths. Teen heartthrob appeal came after Dillon played Randy, the stud who deflowered Kristy McNichol at summer camp in *Little Darlings* (1980), and Melvin Moody, the thug who bullied Chris Makepeace in *My Bodyguard* (1980). Both these roles portrayed him as a brooding James Dean–type, complete with blue jeans, white T-shirt, and cigarette dangling from his mouth. Next came a trilogy of movies based on S. E. Hinton's novels about disenchanted youths: *Tex* (1982), *The Outsiders* (1983), and *Rumble Fish* (1983). Despite the teen idol status (which he detested) and a brief association with Hollywood's Brat Pack, Dillon went on to demonstrate an acting range in both comedy and drama films, such as *The Flamingo Kid* (1984), *Drugstore Cowboy* (1989), *Singles* (1992), *To Die For* (1995), *There's Something About Mary* (1998), and *Wild Things* (1998).

FYI: ▸ Matt Dillon is the great-nephew of cartoonist Alex Raymond, who created the comic strips *Flash Gordon* and *Jungle Jim*.

DILTON DOILY

Scrawny, bespectacled brainiac in the *Archie* comic books who is the smartest boy at Riverdale High School. Dilton hangs out with The Archies when not busy working on a chemistry lab project or writing for a science magazine titled *Dilton's Strange Science*.

DINO

This prehistoric "dog" was a small purple dinosaur owned by the cartoon Flintstone family of Bedrock. He regularly pounced on Fred, showering him with slobbery licks. Dino's favorite dog-food brand was called Shlump.

DINO BOY

This Hanna-Barbera adventure was a companion cartoon to the interplanetary crime-fighter *Space Ghost* on Saturday mornings from 1966 to 1968. It featured the adventures of Tod, a young boy who accidentally parachuted into a strange prehistoric world, the Lost Valley, and rode around on a brown-spotted brontosaurus called Bronty. Ugh, a cave-dwelling Neanderthal, was Tod's rescuer and friend.

DINOSAURS

Brontosaurus! Stegosaurus! Triceratops! Pterodactyl! Woolly mammoths! Saber-tooth tigers! Tyrannosaurus Rex! In the 1960s and 1970s, dinosaurs were the rage—children loved these prehistoric creatures! Along with viewing them on TV (*The Flintstones* and *Land of the Lost*) and at the movies (*One Million Years B.C.* and *The Land That Time Forgot*), kids played with plastic dinosaur herds packaged in blister-carded bags purchased from the dime store. In the early 1960s, Marx Toys produced a best-selling play set, Prehistoric Times, complete with a realistic terrain base (rock formations, caves, palm trees, and lagoon), cavemen, and a variety of colorful dinosaurs.

DIPPITY-DO

Popular in the 1960s, this goopy pink gel packaged in a jar was used by moms and big sisters to roller-set their hair for that nifty bouffant flip. These days, Dippity-do is marketed to intensely active youths of both genders who need stiff gel to hold their radical cuts in place.

DIRTY DANCING

> "Nobody puts Baby in a corner."
> —JOHNNY CASTLE (PATRICK SWAYZE)

Directed by Emile Ardolino, this little musical was the surprise box-office hit of 1987. Set in 1963, it's a coming-of-age tale about a sheltered teen girl named Frances "Baby" Houseman (Jennifer Grey) vacationing for the summer with her upper-class family at Kellerman's, a hotel resort in New York's Catskill Mountains. Bored with the hotel's recreational programs, Baby discovers fun with the working-class dance staff, who dirty-dance (sexy, crotch-grinding moves) off hours. She also develops a heavy crush on the hot dance instructor from the "wrong side of the tracks," Johnny Castle (Patrick Swayze). When Johnny's regular dance partner, Penny Johnson (Cynthia Rhodes), becomes incapacitated following a botched abortion, Baby volunteers to be his partner. Johnny teaches Baby how to dance, and despite the difference between upper class and lower class—ahhhhhhhhh—they end up in love. *Dirty Dancing* boasts appealing performances, hot dance sequences, and a great soundtrack, including the Oscar-winning song "(I've Had) The Time of My Life" by Bill Medley and Jennifer Warnes.

DIRTY DOG

Nasty dance that looks the way it sounds: The guy stands behind the gal and dances as if he's humping from behind, just like two dogs mating. It's freaky!

DIRTY HARRY

"Go ahead, make my day." Harry Callahan—Clint Eastwood's rule-breaking San Francisco cop who totes a .44 Magnum and an everlasting sneer on his stoic face. First seen in the riveting action film *Dirty Harry* (1971), followed by *Magnum Force* (1973), *The Enforcer* (1976), *Sudden Impact* (1983), and *The Dead Pool* (1988). Set the mold for revenge-seeking, violence-laden films of the era, most notably *Billy Jack* (1971), *Walking Tall* (1973), and *Death Wish* (1974). "Feeling lucky, punk?"

DISASTER MOVIES

Inspired by the disaster-movie genre of the 1970s, my kid sister and I used to make up catastrophe scenarios with her Barbies. We would put the Barbie Townhouse over the crack of two twin beds pushed together, then we would shake the beds until the crack widened and the house collapsed through. Afterward, we'd crash the Barbie Airplane into the Barbie Camper. It was such an incredible calamity in Toyland, with only favorite Barbie dolls surviving (stewardess P.J. parachutes out of a burning 747 to safety) and the least desirable "killed" off (bye-bye Skipper). Macho man G.I. Joe was always on hand to save the day!

Popular throughout the 1970s and early 1980s, disaster movies were spectacular events, featuring the latest special effects and huge all-star casts. Set in familiar places, such as airplanes (*Airport 1975*), cruise ships (*The Poseidon Adventure*), office buildings (*The Towering Inferno*), and the city of Los Angeles (*Earthquake*), they had basically the same formula: a handful of people from every walk of life thrown in the midst of a cataclysm (for example, a plane crash, a tidal wave, a blazing skyscraper, an earthquake, an avalanche, a volcanic eruption, or a falling meteor), where half will perish in some form or another before the others can make it to safety. The sick pleasure of watching was to see who would die and in what way. In the late 1990s, the genre experienced a reemergence with such computer-generated disasters as *Armageddon* (1998), *Dante's Peak* (1997), *Deep Impact* (1998), *Titanic* (1997), *Twister* (1996), and *Volcano* (1997).

DISCO

Spinning mirror balls. Flashing strobe lights. Thumping music beat. Friday nights. Studio 54. Xenon. 2001. The Bump. The Hustle. The Bus Stop. "Le Freak." "Boogie Oogie Oogie." "Stayin' Alive." "Hot Stuff." "I Love the Nightlife." "Y.M.C.A." "Shake Your Groove Thing." "Dancing Queen." John Travolta. Bee Gees. Donna Summer. Village People. K.C. and the Sunshine Band. Deney Terrio. *Saturday Night Fever. Xanadu. Roller Boogie.* Hot pants. Platform heels. Designer jeans. Sequins. Spandex. Lycra. Gold lamé. White polyester. Poppers. Quaaludes. Cocaine. 'Nuf said.

"DISCO DUCK"

The silliest and most despised song to come out of the disco era, recorded by Memphis D.J. Rick Dees in 1976. The novelty ditty was about a man who went to a party and changed into a clucking duck while disco-dancing. During the chorus, listeners were subjected to the foul fowl (doing a Donald Duck impersonation) sputtering out disco slang like "Get down mama!" "Dy-no-mite!" "Shake your tail feather," and "Try your luck, don't be a cluck!" Dees's success with this chart-topper led to a long-running and profitable career as one of America's top radio D.J.'s. He hosted TV's *Solid Gold* from 1984 to 1985 and the short-lived late-night talk show *Into the Night*.

DISCO HITS

Hey, all you lovers of the night life! Put on your dancin' shoes, get down, and shake your booty to these fifty disco hits, circa 1975 to 1980. These are essential if you want your funky dance party to be the jam of the year.

- "Bad Girls" (1979) by Donna Summer
- "Best of My Love" (1977) by The Emotions
- "Boogie Fever" (1976) by The Sylvers
- "Boogie Nights" (1977) by Heatwave
- "Boogie Oogie Oogie" (1978) by A Taste of Honey
- "Boogie Wonderland" (1979) by Earth, Wind, and Fire and The Emotions
- "Born to Be Alive" (1979) by Patrick Hernandez
- "Brick House" (1977) by The Commodores
- "Car Wash" (1976) by Rose Royce
- "Dance (Disco Heat)" (1978) by Sylvester
- "Dancing Queen" (1977) by ABBA
- "Disco Inferno" (1978) by The Trammps.
- "Disco Lady" (1976) by Johnnie Taylor
- "Don't Leave Me This Way" (1977) by Thelma Houston
- "Fly, Robin, Fly" (1975) by Silver Convention
- "Funkytown" (1980) by Lipps Inc.
- "Get Dancin'" (1975) by Disco Tex and The Sex-o-Lettes
- "Get Down Tonight" (1975) by K.C. and the Sunshine Band
- "Get Off" (1978) by Foxy
- "Get Up and Boogie" (1979) by Silver Convention

- "Got to Be Real" (1979) by Cheryl Lynn
- "The Groove Line" (1978) by Heatwave
- "Heaven Must Have Sent You" (1979) by Bonnie Pointer
- "The Hustle" (1975) by Van McCoy
- "I Feel Love" (1977) by Donna Summer
- "I Love the Nightlife" (1978) by Alicia Bridges
- "I Will Survive" (1979) by Gloria Gaynor
- "In the Bush" (1978) by Musique
- "Instant Replay" (1978) by Dan Hartman
- "Knock on Wood" (1979) by Amii Stewart
- "Lady Marmalade" (1975) by Patti LaBelle
- "Last Dance" (1978) by Donna Summer
- "Le Freak" (1978) by Chic
- "Love Hangover" (1976) by Diana Ross
- "Love Rollercoaster" (1975) by Ohio Players
- "Macho Man" (1978) by Village People
- "More, More, More" (1976) by Andrea True Connection
- "Night Fever" (1978) by Bee Gees
- "Play That Funky Music" (1976) by Wild Cherry
- "Ring My Bell" (1979) by Anita Ward
- "Shake Your Booty" (1976) by K.C. and the Sunshine Band
- "Shake Your Groove Thing" (1979) by Peaches and Herb
- "Shame" (1978) by Evelyn "Champagne" King
- "That's the Way (I Like It)" (1975) by K.C. and the Sunshine Band
- "Turn the Beat Around" (1976) by Vickie Sue Robinson
- "Upside Down" (1980) by Diana Ross
- "We Are Family" (1979) by Sister Sledge
- "Y.M.C.A." (1978) by Village People
- "You Sexy Thing" (1975) by Hot Chocolate
- "You Should Be Dancing" (1976) by Bee Gees

DISNEYLAND

"To all who come to this happy place—welcome!"

—WALT DISNEY, 1955

The first and foremost of the Magic Kingdom theme parks is the place children of the Baby Boom generation dreamed of visiting the most. And who could blame them? Created by and named after Walt Disney, Disneyland opened on July 17, 1955, in sunny Anaheim, near Los Angeles, on 160 acres of land once covered with orange groves. A spectacular and pristine wonderland (it set the standard for future amusement parks), Disneyland is divided into seven interconnecting sections—Fantasyland, Adventureland, Frontierland, Tomorrowland, New Orleans Square, Toontown, and Critter Country—as well as an entrance area, Main Street U.S.A., modeled after a turn-of-the-century small town. Each "land" features thrilling rides and other attractions based on the classic Disney movies. All-time favorites among these are the Mad Tea Party, King Arthur Carousel, Dumbo the Flying Elephant, It's a Small World, Matterhorn Bobsleds, Jungle Cruise, Autopia, Space Mountain, Astro Orbiter, Mark Twain Steamboat, Tom Sawyer Island, Pirates of the Caribbean, Haunted Mansion, Splash Mountain, and the Disneyland Monorail, which provides transportation from Tomorrowland to the Disneyland resort hotels. Lucky kids get to greet a life-sized Mickey Mouse or Donald Duck, who wander all over the park, and give them a great big hug.

The success of Disneyland, which has entertained more than 420 million guests from every corner of the world, inspired the enormous Walt Disney World complex located in Orlando, Florida, which opened on October 1, 1971, and was followed by the adjoining Epcot Center on October 1, 1982; Tokyo Disneyland on April 15, 1983; Disneyland Paris on April 12, 1992; and California Adventure (next to Disneyland) on February 7, 2001.

DITTOS

In the pre–designer jean era of the late 1970s, these "must-have" denim slacks were the ultimate in foxy feminine hipness. Dittos were distinguished by the trademark saddleback—a horseshoe shape design around the butt—and infamous for giving embarrassing "camel toe."

DIVINE

"Of course, the last thing my parents wanted was a son who wears a cocktail dress that glitters, but they've come around to it." The delightful 300-pound drag queen (real name Harris Glenn Milstead, born October 19, 1945) made a name for himself as director John Waters's favorite leading lady (they were childhood friends in their native Baltimore). Called the ultimate cult star, Divine played some of the most off-kilter females in film history: Babs

Johnson, "the world's filthiest person," who actually ate doggie poo-poo in *Pink Flamingos* (1972); Dawn Davenport, whose disappointment at not getting cha-cha shoes for Christmas led to a life of crime, in *Female Trouble* (1974); Francine Fishpaw, a lonely alcoholic housewife with a strong sense of smell, in *Polyester* (1981); and Edna Turnblad, Ricki Lake's iron-toting mom, in *Hairspray* (1988). Divine died of a heart attack, a result of obesity, in 1988 while in Los Angeles to film a segment of *Married . . . with Children*, in which he was to play Peg Bundy's uncle.

DIXIE RIDDLE CUPS

Introduced in the 1970s, these little paper bathroom cups had illustrations and silly riddles printed on them, making the tedious routine of brushing and rinsing your teeth more exciting, Youngsters would take a cup from the Dixie cup dispenser and ask each other a kid-oriented riddle, such as "What do you call a sleeping bull?" (A bulldozer!), "What did The Beatles say during the avalanche?" (Watch out for The Rolling Stones!), "What do you get when a cow is caught in an earthquake?" (A milkshake!), and "What do skeletons say before dining?" (Bone appetit!).

"DIZZY"

As soon as the opening chick-a-boom and shimmy drum track started—along with the beginning line "I'm so dizzy my head is spinning"—kids would dance and spin around until they dropped from dizziness. Recorded by Tommy Roe in 1969, this bubblegum classic was number one on the pop charts for four weeks.

DOC MARTENS

What go-go boots were to the swingers of the 1960s, and platforms were to the disco kids of the 1970s, these clunky combat-boot-like shoes with thick rubber soles—designed primarily for orthopedic comfort in 1945—were to alternative Gen-Xers of the 1990s. "Docs" were originally worn by skinheads and punk-rockers before becoming a footwear staple of nonconformist young people from all over the world.

DOCTOR DOLITTLE

"Imagine talking with a tiger, chatting with a cheetah. . . ." Released in 1967, this musical movie was based on the classic Hugh Lofting adventure tales about John Dolittle, a nineteenth-century veterinarian who could talk to animals. Directed by Richard Fleischer, it starred Rex Harrison as the top-hatted Dr. Dolittle; Samantha Eggar as his pretty fiancée, Emma Fairfax; Anthony Newley as jaunty Matthew Mugg; William Dix as little Tommy Stubbins; and Geoffrey Holder as Willie Shakespeare the Tenth, tribal chief of the floating Sea Star Island. The doctor and friends sing and dance and sail off to the South Seas in search of the elusive Great Pink Sea Snail and the Giant Lunar Moth. Dolittle's menagerie of animals included loyal parrot companion Polynesia, Labrador retriever Jip, pig Gub-Gub, white duck Dab-Dab, shortsighted horse Toggle, chimp Chee-Chee, lovesick seal Sophie, and bizarre, two-headed llama Pushmi-Pullyu.

An expensive and colossal production, *Doctor Dolittle* was four years in the planning, plus a year in preproduction and nine months for filming. More than 1,500 animals had to be precisely trained for their appearances. The popular children's movie spawned a mass assortment of *Dolittle* toys and earned a 1967 Academy Award nomination for Best Picture and an Oscar for Best Song: "Talk to the Animals," written by Leslie Bricusse. But despite all, *Doctor Dolittle* was a critical and financial dud, infamous for being the film that nearly bankrupted the 20th Century Fox Studios.

In 1998, African-American comedian Eddie Murphy filmed a spin on the *Doctor Dolittle* tale. This *Doctor Dolittle* had no relation to Lofting's stories, except that Murphy's Dolittle, a modern-day vet, could gab (and share crude jokes) with the animals. Unlike Harrison's *Dolittle* film, it was a huge box-office hit and was followed by a sequel, *Dr. Dolittle 2*, in 2001.

DOCTOR KITS AND NURSE KITS

Complete with candy pills and plastic instruments, these toy kits helped body-curious Baby Boom youngsters play "doctor."

DODGEBALL

Action game that kids used to play during grade-school phys ed. Participants were divided into two teams, with one team forming a circle around the other team. The outer team would then throw a rubber ball at members of the team in the middle, who made attempts to dodge it. Ow, watch the head! When a player was hit (which could be painful) her or she was banished from the inner circle. The last player standing in the middle was the winner. These days, dodgeball is banned at most schools because of the likelihood of injury and because bullies would take direct aim at classmates they enjoyed tormenting. Today, adults play in professional dodgeball tournaments, which is the premise of the 2004 Ben Stiller comedy *Dodgeball: A True Underdog Story*.

DODIE HARPER DOUGLAS
Precocious little girl who became the stepdaughter of Steve Douglas after he married her schoolteacher mom, Barbara Harper. In the vein of Buffy Davis from *Family Affair*, Dodie carried a funny-looking doll named Myrtle. Played by Leif Garrett's younger sister Dawn Lyn on *My Three Sons* from 1969 to 1972.

DOHERTY, SHANNEN
Bitchy TV actress (born April 12, 1971) who habitually made tabloid headlines in the 1990s for a lifestyle of drunken brawls on Hollywood's Sunset Strip. Doherty got herself canned from the hit prime-time soap *Beverly Hills 90210* by producer Aaron Spelling in 1994 because of her constant conflicts with fellow cast members. Her bitch trend continued in 2001, when she was dismissed from the sitcom *Charmed* for fighting with co-star Alyssa Milano and accused of being rude to next-door neighbor Molly Ringwald in their Hollywood neighborhood.

DOLLAR
The loyal Dalmatian dog with black dollar signs in place of the traditional round spots was owned by wealthy cartoon kid Richie Rich. First appeared in *Richie Rich* comic book number 65 in 1967.

$1.98 BEAUTY CONTEST
Tacky parody of beauty pageants featuring "everyday" contestants competing in swimsuit and talent routines to win a mere $1.98 in coins, plus a bouquet of vegetables. The most memorable competitor was the 200-pound lady plumber who did the "Dance of the Sugar Plum Fairy." The most famous winner was gap-toothed, frizzy-haired Sandra Bernhard, using the pseudonym of Malvena Ray, who warbled Dolly Parton's "Here You Come Again." Airing for only one year (1978), the brainless TV show was produced by Chuck Barris and hosted by oddball, walrus-mustached Rip Taylor.

DOLL BUGGIES AND STROLLERS
These doll accessories are made to help little girls play "mommy" and show off their precious "babies" by pushing them around the neighborhood.

DOLLHOUSES
The ones from the 1950s and 1960s were modeled after modern suburban homes (split-levels, colonials, and ranch houses) and made with easy-to-assemble lithographed steel. They came accessorized with little doll families and plastic furniture to fill the individual rooms. Marx Toys was the leading producer of the era's dollhouses.

DOLLS
Hello, dolly! For most girls (and some boys) their favorite childhood playmate was a beloved doll. Dolls provided hours of imaginary playtime. Girls could pretend to be mommy while playing house, to be a teacher overseeing a class of dolls, to put on a fashion show, or even to host a beauty pageant. The best thing about a doll was that a girl could love her, cuddle her, and tell her secrets, because she knew the doll would love her back and never, ever tell a soul. During the 1960s and 1970s, such toy companies as Mattel, Ideal, Kenner, Hasbro, Remco, Topper, and Uneeda were at mass-manufacturing peaks and offering children an abundance of dolls. I randomly asked 100 women born between 1959 and 1971 to vote for their favorite childhood doll. This Top Ten list is the result:

Barbie
Raggedy Ann
Mrs. Beasley
Crissy
Chatty Cathy
Liddle Kiddles
Baby Alive
Dawn
Holly Hobbie
Baby Tenderlove

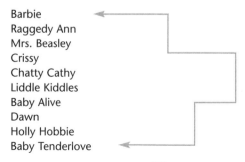

DOLLS, ACTION

Girls born after the 1950s were a generation totally under the influence of TV. Purportedly, they had short attention-spans caused by too much rapid-paced TV and needed the kind of dolls that did more than just cry "mommy," wet panties, or just stand around looking pretty. Besides having a great wardrobe, a doll needed to actively do things—like walk, dance, tumble, giggle, eat, poop, bathe, blink, grow hair, or drive a car. Following are twenty-five dolls capable of doing things besides crying, peeing, and—sorry Chatty Cathy—talking.

- **Baby Alive.** She eats, drinks, and poops (Kenner, 1973).
- **Baby Crawl-Along.** She crawls along the floor (Remco, 1967).
- **Baby First Step.** She walks and roller-skates (Mattel, 1965).
- **Baby Fun.** She blows a horn, a balloon, and bubbles (Mattel, 1968).
- **Baby Go Bye-Bye.** She drives a buggy car (Mattel, 1970).
- **Baby Say 'n See.** She talks, moving her mouth while her eyes glance around (Mattel, 1967).
- **Bizzie Lizzie.** She does housework: ironing, sweeping, and dusting (Ideal, 1971).
- **Cheerful Tearful.** She cries real tears with a smile that turns into a pout (Mattel, 1966).
- **Crumpet.** She pours tea and serves cookies (Kenner, 1971).
- **Dancerina.** She does pirouettes and other ballet moves (Mattel, 1968).
- **Gabbigale.** She repeats everything you say (Kenner, 1972).
- **Giggles.** She giggles and rolls her eyes (Ideal, 1967).
- **Hi Dottie.** She has a conversation with you on the phone (Mattel, 1971).
- **Jumpsy.** She jumps rope (Remco, 1970).
- **Kissy.** She puckers her lips and kisses (Ideal, 1961).
- **Lazy Dazy.** She closes her eyes and slowly falls asleep (Ideal, 1972).
- **Lucky Lisa.** She plays a variety of board games (Wards, 1971).
- **Peggy Pen Pal.** She writes and draws pictures (Horsman, 1970).
- **Saucy.** She makes eight different facial expressions (Mattel, 1972).
- **Shoppin' Sheryl.** She shops at a toy grocery store (Mattel, 1971).
- **Sketchy.** She draws pictures on a playboard (Mattel, 1970).
- **Tearful Baby Tender Love.** She changes her mood from happy to sad (Mattel, 1972).
- **Timey Tell.** She tells time from her wristwatch (Mattel, 1971).
- **Tippee Toes.** She rides a tricycle, a horse, and a baby walker (Mattel, 1967).
- **Tippy Tumbles.** She does somersaults and headstands (Remco, 1969).

DOLLY DARLINGS

These cute four-inch-high dolls with coy facial expressions came in hatbox cases, each with themed accessories, like "Beth at the Supermarket," "Cathy Goes to a Party," "John and His Pets," "Shari Takes a Vacation," "Susie Goes to School." The popularity of Dolly Darlings, manufactured by Hasbro Toys from 1965 to 1968, influenced similar doll lines of the same period, such as Uneeda's Tiny Teens, Deluxe Reading's Go-Go's, and Ideal's Flatsy.

DOLLY MADISON

Snack-cake competitor of Hostess whose best-selling products are creme-filled Zingers and the powdered donuts Gems. In the late 1950s, Dolly Madison hired Charles Schulz's Peanuts as spokeskids to appeal to youngsters of postwar America. (The company's commercials aired during the *Charlie Brown* holiday specials on TV.)

DOLLYWOOD

Amusement theme park opened by and named after country-music superstar Dolly Parton in 1986. Located in her home state of Tennessee, at Pigeon Forge, on the edge of the Smoky Mountains.

DOLPHIN SHORTS

Onetime popular brand of satinlike, elastic-waist, short shorts—marked by slit sides, rounded corners, contrasting-color trim, and a dolphin appliqué. Generally worn with white tube socks for a night out at the disco roller rink.

DOMINO'S PIZZA
"One call does it all!" Restaurant chain, founded in 1960, notorious for car-crashing-fast pizza deliveries. In the 1980s, advertised by the Noid, a devilish character out to ruin pizza by making it cold or soggy.

DONALD DUCK
Walt Disney's best-recognized character, after Mickey Mouse. The often cranky, scratchy-voiced fowl (distinctively squawked by Clarence "Ducky" Nash) dressed in blue sailor garb made his debut in the Silly Symphony cartoon "The Wise Little Hen" in 1934. With an inclination toward greed and revenge, Donald is a not-as-sweet but still-lovable fellow, jealous of any attention given to others, especially goody-goody pal Mickey. Supporting regulars in his cartoons and comic books include flirtatious girlfriend Daisy Duck, hellion triplet nephews Huey, Dewey, and Louie (their mother is Donald's sister, Dumbella), miserly millionaire uncle Scrooge McDuck, German-accented uncle Professor Ludwig Von Drake, and pesky chipmunks Chip 'n' Dale. Duckburg, located in the heart of Calisota, was Donald Fauntleroy Duck's original hometown. In 2004, Donald received a Walk of Fame Star in Hollywood (in front of Disney's El Capitan Theatre at 6840 Hollywood Boulevard) to honor his seventy years in show business.

FYI: ▸ Mickey Mouse might be the most popular Disney star, but feisty Donald Duck is the hardest worker, appearing in far more cartoon shorts than the rodent (last count: 150).

DONALD HOLLINGER
"Ohhh, Dawwwwnald!" The handsome redhead was Ann Marie's ever-patient, long-suffering boyfriend, who worked as a junior executive for *Newsview* magazine. Played by Ted Bessell on *That Girl* (1968–71).

DON DIEGO De La VEGA
"My sword is a flame / To right every wrong / So heed my name." Foppish alter ego of Zorro, the swashbuckling masked swordsman who sought vengeance against military tyrants of Spanish California circa 1820. Zorro's trademark was the sign of the "Z," which he slashed with his sword. Created by author Johnston McCulley, he has been the subject of several movies and a popular Walt Disney TV series starring Guy Williams.

DONKEY KONG
The one that started it all for Nintendo, a former playing-card company, was this early arcade game introduced in 1981 starring Donkey Kong, the skyscraper-climbing ape, and his archnemesis, Jumpman, an early incarnation of Super Mario. It was one of the decade's top-playing games, spawning two sequels, Donkey Kong Jr. and Donkey Kong 3, and a Saturday-morning cartoon (1983–85) co-starring Q-Bert and Frogger, two other game characters of the era. In 1994, after taking a break from the limelight, the oversized monkey found himself discovered by a new generation in Donkey Kong Country, a game for the Super Nintendo home system.

DONNY AND MARIE
She was a little bit country. He was a little bit rock 'n' roll. Together as Donny and Marie, they were one of the best-loved brother-and-sister pop acts of the 1970s. In 1974, seventeen-year-old teen idol Donny Osmond teamed up with his pretty fifteen-year-old sister, Marie (born October 13, 1959), who experienced moderate success in country music with the remake of Anita Bryant's "Paper Roses" (1973). As a duo, they had several hit records, including the million-selling "I'm Leaving It All Up to You" (1974), along with "Morning Side of the Mountain" (1974), "Deep Purple" (1976), "Ain't Nothing Like the Real Thing" (1977), and "On the Shelf" (1978).

Capitalizing on Donny and Marie's huge popularity, ABC-TV gave the toothy, look-alike siblings their own family-friendly show (1976–79). The variety program blended comedy skits (peachy-sweet Marie poking fun at squeaky-clean Donny) and musical numbers—the perky twosome performing their teenybopper songs. The other Osmond Brothers were featured, including the annoying youngest Jimmy, and so were a flashy ice-skating troupe called the Ice Angels. Sid and Marty Krofft of Saturday-morning fame produced the series, and Bob Mackie (Cher's outfitter) designed the elaborate costumes.

DON'T BE AFRAID OF THE DARK

A young couple, Sally and Alex Farnham (Kim Darby and Jim Hutton), inherit a creepy Victorian mansion inhabited by light-fearing, troll-like demons. Sally's redecoration of the old place unleashes these evil creatures, who begin to terrorize her. When Sally tells hubby and friends of her frightening experiences, such as an ugly imp's head popping out of the floral centerpiece at the dinner table, she is dismissed as being neurotic and maybe a little wacko. The story ends when the diminutive demons take Sally away to make her one of their own. Seen originally in 1973 as an ABC Movie of the Week, this is one of those scary TV movies (like Karen Black's *Trilogy of Terror*) that is remembered vividly today for really freaking viewers out. In fact, the morning after the movie aired, it was obvious to me that my fellow classmates who viewed it were still white-faced from having the shit scared out of them, and sleepy-eyed from staying awake worrying about troll-like demons in their basement.

DON'T BREAK THE ICE

"The game begins, the ice is thin. Be careful or you may go in!" An action game geared toward little children, introduced by Schaper Toys in 1967. Kids take turns using a mallet to knock out plastic "ice blocks" on a raised grid with a fisherman standing in the middle. The first to hit the wrong block causing the "frozen lake" to cave in, dumping the fisherman in the icy water (Brrrrr!), was the loser.

"DON'T GO BREAKING MY HEART"

The snappy duet between Elton John and Kiki Dee topped the U.S. pop charts for four weeks in the summer of 1976. "Don't Go Breaking My Heart" TV highlights: On *The Muppet Show*, Elton performed it with Miss Piggy, and on *One Day at a Time*, Barbara (Valerie Bertinelli), impersonating Elton, and Julie (Mackenzie Phillips), impersonating Kiki, did an early form of karaoke with their rendition.

"DON'T YOU WANT ME"

Referred to as the "granddaddy of New Wave pop" because it was the first British New Wave single to land at the number-one spot on the American Top Forty in 1982. Recorded by the Human League.

DON WEST

Dark-haired, handsome young pilot enlisted to assist the Robinson family on their journey through outer space. This major had eyes only for blonde beauty Judy, the oldest Robinson daughter, and an intense rage toward traitorous Dr. Smith. Portrayed by Mark Goddard on the TV sci-fi series *Lost in Space*.

DOOGIE HOWSER

Before he could grow facial hair, this boy genius with the dorky nickname (his real first name was Douglas) whizzed through high school, college, and med school to become a sixteen-year-old doctor at Eastman Medical Center in Los Angeles. Played by Neil Patrick Harris on the *Doogie Howser, M.D.* TV show, from 1989 to 1993.

DOPEY

Gentle Dopey was the pet baby brontosaurus that Holly Marshall rode periodically on Saturday morning's *Land of the Lost*. He was hatched on September 21, 1974, in an episode titled simply "Dopey."

"DO THEY KNOW IT'S CHRISTMAS?"

"And there won't be snow in Africa this Christmas time." Bob Geldof's haunting Yuletide song created to raise money for the famine-stricken in Ethiopia. Released in November 1984, it quickly debuted at number one in Great Britain, becoming the fastest- and biggest-selling single (more than three million copies) in that country's history, until Elton John's "Candle in the Wind 1997" took the honor. It featured a collection of British artists performing under the name of Band Aid, including Bananarama, Culture Club, David Bowie, Duran Duran, Eurythmics, Frankie Goes to Hollywood, Heaven 17, Human League, Kool and The Gang, Paul McCartney, Paul Young, Phil Collins, Spandau Ballet, Sting, Style Council, and U2. It was the first benefit record from which neither artists, manufacturers, nor retailers took any profit, and it inspired other musical benefit songs and concerts: U.S.A. for Africa (Band Aid's American equivalent), Live Aid, Farm Aid, and Northern Lights.

DOVE

Many a young person's fantasy was stirred by this 1974 movie, based on sixteen-year-old Robin Lee

Graham's real-life adventures around the world. The teen (played by Joseph Bottoms) sets off alone in a twenty-three-foot sloop to sail to every imaginable port of call. Graham's seafaring journey takes five years to complete, and along the way he falls in love with a girl (played by model Deborah Raffin) who ends up accompanying him. Directed by Charles Jarrott, the film is memorable for magnificent photography of exotic scenery.

DOWN-FILLED VESTS
Once a staple of the ski set, the sleeveless outer garment characterized by puffy quilts and flashy zigzag colors became a chic fashion item during the late 1970s and early 1980s even away from the ski slopes.

DR. ADAM BRICKER
"Doc," the Love Boat's chief physician, was a divorced swinger who seemed preoccupied with bedding the beautiful women traveling as passengers. Otherwise, he did take his job pretty seriously. Played by Bernie Kopell on *The Love Boat* from 1977 to 1986.

DR. ALFRED BELLOWS
"Fine. I'll accept that. It's no more ridiculous than any of your other explanations." Self-important NASA shrink who thought Major Tony Nelson suffered from delusions because the astronaut claimed to own a wish-granting entity named Jeannie. Dr. Bellows was portrayed by Hayden Rorke on the sitcom *I Dream of Jeannie* from 1965 to 1970.

DR. BENTON QUEST
Jonny Quest's bearded dad from the hit Hanna-Barbera cartoon is the superscientist and brave leader of a research intelligence team that travels the world to investigate strange goings-on.

DR. BOMBAY
"Calling Dr. Bombay! Calling Dr. Bombay! Emergency! Emergency! Come right away!" Eccentric, globe-trotting witch doctor (played by character actor Bernard Fox) who is called for when spells go wrong on *Bewitched*.

DR. DAVID BRUCE BANNER
"Don't make me angry. You wouldn't like me when I'm angry." When angered, this mild-mannered scientist transforms into the green-skinned, superstrong, simpleminded Incredible Hulk. When he reverts to normal, he has no recollection of events that took place while he was the Hulk. Dr. Banner was played by Bill Bixby on *The Incredible Hulk* prime-time series (1978–81) and by Eric Bana in *The Hulk* movie (2003).

DR. DEMENTO
Novelty-record D.J. (real name: Barret Sherman) who for more than thirty years has hosted a national radio show, airing every Sunday night from Los Angeles, showcasing a mad mix of music and comedy by the likes of Spike Jones, Tom Lehrer, Allen Sherman, Monty Python, Weird Al, and Tiny Tim.

DR. DOOM
Victor Von Doom, the fiendish ruler of Latveria and number-one foe of the Fantastic Four, wears an iron mask to hide severe scars from an experiment that exploded in his face. First appeared in *Marvel* comics' *Fantastic Four*, issue number 5, in July 1962.

DREAM PETS
A menagerie of little critters—made out of colorful feltlike material on the outside and tightly stuffed sawdust on the inside—such as Penny Poodle, Lucy Lamb, Pancho Donkey, Firehouse Fritz Dalmatian, and Hawaiian Hound, a lei-adorned pink pooch reclining on a plastic surfboard. Manufactured by Dakin in the 1950s and 1960s, these charming collectibles were sort of the predecessors to Ty's Beanie Babies, but cooler.

DRESSY BESSY AND DAPPER DAN
Introduced in 1970, Playskool's pigtailed Dressy Bessy and brother Dapper Dan were cuddly cloth dolls that came with layers of sewn-on clothing and shoes that could be buttoned, zipped, snapped, buckled, laced, and tied. The purpose of these twenty-inch-tall playmates was to teach tots ages three to six how to dress themselves—and according to many of my friends who owned one, they did the job.

DR. EVIL (*AUSTIN POWERS*)
"I have one simple request. And that is to have sharks with frickin' laser beams attached to their

heads!" A totally different evil arrived in the late 1990s: Dr. Evil, groovy secret agent Austin Powers's archenemy, a bald, scar-faced baddie who wanted to take over the world for "one meeeellion dollars." Former *Saturday Night Live* comedian Mike Myers worked overtime playing both Evil and Powers in the *Austin Powers* film trilogy.

DR. EVIL (CAPTAIN ACTION)

"The Sinister Invader of Earth!" The deformed-appearing, green-skinned alien was the nemesis of 1960s action figure Captain Action. Dr. Evil transposed into such villains as the Joker and the Red Skull.

DR. FRANK N. FURTER

"Come up to the lab and see what's on the slab!" Tim Curry's classic gender-bending performance, in *The Rocky Horror Picture Show* (1975), as the "Sweet Transvestite" from the planet Transsexual in the galaxy Transylvania. The mad scientist traveled to earth in a space castle to create Rocky Horror, the ultimate sexual man. Dr. Frank N. Furter's wardrobe consisted of high-heeled platform shoes, a high-collared black-satin cape, a bodice, panties, a garter belt, thigh-high fishnet stockings, and heavy makeup.

DRILL TEAMS

Thoughts of high school football half-times bring back memories of a smile-struck squad of thirty to fifty girls dressed in sparkly uniforms—typically white boots, double-faced gloves, and scandalously short skirts—who performed on the gridiron with precision high-steps, dance routines, and amazing straight-kicks above their heads. A drill team's purpose is to entertain at pep rallies, sporting events, band competitions, parades, and other community events. Almost every large high school and college and university around the nation has its own version of a drill team or dance team commonly known for energetic routines fusing military marching, dancing, high-kicking, and sometimes colorful props, such as pom-poms, flags, streamers, and stepladders. These teams often get their monikers by combining the school's mascot name with the "ette" suffix (for example, Indianettes, Eaglettes, Raiderettes, Cardettes). The typical drill team member is a pretty girl (usually slender and long-legged) with good grades whose popularity in school could rival a cheerleader. The first and most famous drill team: the legendary high-kicking Rangerettes from Kilgore College in Texas, formed in 1940 by feisty Gussie Nell Davis.

FYI: ▸ When you think of a classic drill-team movement, synchronized high kicks usually come to mind (most guys can recall the remarkable line of "crotch shots" when forty or so different legs were simultaneously kicked straight up in the air), but another well-known move would be the Contagion, where split-second movements ripple down the line of girls and back again. As for those high kicks, a drill-teamer should be able to kick her toe to the brim of an imaginary hat with ease and proper form (known as the "Hat Test").

DRIVE-IN THEATERS

"Hurry up! Show's about to start. . . ." These outdoor theaters on the outskirts of town, with enormous screens that hovered above patrons watching movies from their automobiles, seem to have become a thing of the past. As a tribute to the drive-in, I offer twelve recollections:

- Idling in your car first in line at the entry gate to get the best parking spot (front center, about the eighth row back from the large screen)
- Sneaking in by lying on the backseat floorboards with blankets and pillows on top to conceal you, or lying about your age to take advantage of the "children under twelve get in free" deal
- Mom parking the station wagon backward so we could recline in the wagon section with sleeping bags while she sat out in a folding lawn-chair
- Viewing a triple feature with low-budget movies of the same theme, like "youths on the run" (*Dirty Mary Crazy Larry*, *Macon County Line*, and *Moonshine County Express*) or "gross-out horror" (*Last House on the Left*, *Mark of the Devil*, and *Texas Chainsaw Massacre*) or "Bruce Lee martial arts" (*Chinese Connection*, *Enter the Dragon*, and *Fists of Fury*)
- Listening to the film with a crackling echo coming from a speaker hooked up inside the car window. ("Please remember to replace the speaker on the post when you leave the theater.")

- Couples on dates who ignored the movie because they were busy making out. (The steamed-up windows from hot breath wouldn't let them view it anyway.)
- Adolescent voyeurs scoping out the horny couple making out in the car next door
- Parties of teens—drunk and disorderly—being told to "quiet down" by nearby families
- Going to the snack stand (positioned in the middle of the drive-in) during intermission to pick up hot dogs, sliced pizza, popcorn, and soda. (Why did drive-in food taste so much better than the food you packed from home?)
- The previews of upcoming releases, plus the animated intermission advertisement starring dancing and singing concession food
- Restless, bored children playing on the playground equipment during the movie, often unaccompanied by an adult. (It seemed much safer in the 1970s to leave your kid alone.)
- Fighting drowsiness during the second feature but losing to sleep, only to wake up snug in bed after dad carried you from the car to the house

---

FYI: ▸ The first drive-in theater opened in June 1933 in Camden, New Jersey.

DR. JEKYLL
Classic author Robert Louis Stevenson's tormented scientist from *Dr. Jekyll and Mr. Hyde,* who transforms into evil alternative personality Mr. Hyde when he drinks a potent elixir he concocts in his laboratory. Jekyll's first name: Henry.

DR. JOHN DOLITTLE
Commonly referred to as Dr. Dolittle, a top-hatted veterinarian, or "animalitarian," from Puddleby-on-the-Marsh, England, who could converse with animals. A self-taught linguist, the eccentric doctor had an animal-language repertoire that included 498 different tongues, ranging from "Alligatorese" to "Zebran." Played by Rex Harrison in the 1967 movie musical *Doctor Dolittle.*

DR. LEONARD McCOY
"It's dead, Jim." Nicknamed "Bones," the dry-humored head physician of the starship Enterprise enjoyed poking fun at nonlogical first officer Mr. Spock. Played by DeForest Kelly in the *Star Trek* TV series and in big-screen films.

DR. MARSH TRACY
Handsome and compassionate, the American veterinarian-conservationist at the Wameru Study Center for Animal Behavior in Africa courageously battled lawless men who killed animals for the sake of killing or who traded in hide, ivory, or captive wildlife. Called the "Great White Vet" or "Daktari" (for "doctor") by the natives. Played by Marshall Thompson in the 1960s TV series *Daktari.*

DROOPER
Wiseacre, bass-playing lion of Saturday morning's Banana Splits who ran an advice column called "Dear Drooper" and moonlighted as Super Drooper, a caped crusader out to do battle with such unscrupulous foes as the Infamous Inner Tube Inflater or the Fiendish Fluffy Feather Filcher.

DROWSY
Introduced in 1965, Mattel Toys' blonde moppet was so-o-o, so-o-o sleepy—her eyes were always half shut (she could barely stay awake)—and when you pulled her talk-ring she said things in a drowsy voice like "I wanna stay up," "Mommy, kiss me good night," and "Mommy, I want another glass of water." The sleepyhead's soft cloth body—adorned in pink flannel pajamas with white polka dots—made her the perfect pal for little girls to cuddle and snuggle with at bedtime. Unquestionably a classic childhood doll for those women born on the Baby Boom and Gen-X cusp (1959–70).

DR. PEPPER
"I'm a Pepper, he's a Pepper, she's a Pepper, we're a Pepper, wouldn't you like to be a Pepper too?" First airing in 1978, Dr. Pepper's elaborate TV commercials, featuring peppy actor David Naughton singing and dancing about being a Pepper, were some of the best of the era. The dark-colored soft drink is renowned for an original taste, a mix of twenty-three different fruit flavors (the ingredients are a corporate secret), and for having so much caffeine that anyone consuming it would feel like a peppy Pepper. Mr. Pibb is Dr. Pepper's main competitor.

DR. PHIBES

"Love means never having to say you're ugly." Vincent Price made famous the horribly deformed and disturbed doctor out for revenge on those he blamed for the death of his beloved wife, in *The Abominable Dr. Phibes* (1971) and its sequel, *Dr. Phibes Rises Again!* (1972). Besides murdering in creative ways, Phibes's other pet project was creating a life-sized windup band called the Clockwork Wizards.

DR. RUTH

"America's First Lady of Love," Ruth Westheimer, the pint-sized (four foot seven) sex therapist with the garbling German accent, experienced major fame hosting TV talk shows (*Good Sex! with Dr. Ruth* and *Ask Dr. Ruth*) in the 1980s. On the programs, she talked openly about sexual issues (masturbation, premature ejaculation, delayed orgasm, and so on), instructing us not to be ashamed of our bodies, and taking phoned-in questions from viewers.

DR. SCHOLL'S

In 1961, Dr. William Scholl, an orthopedic specialist, created this contoured wooden sandal as a means of exercising the foot and leg muscles while casually walking around all day. Who would've guessed these understated (okay, ugly) shoes would become a trendy fashion for young women during the 1960s and 1970s? Dr. Scholl's was the forerunner of today's ortho footwear, including such shoe lines as Clinic, Drew, Tela, Worishofer, Zeeta, and the popular Birkenstock.

DR. SEUSS

The premier writer-illustrator of children's literature of the late twentieth century. His stories, commingling inventive wordplay with colorful illustrations, featured the most outtasight places imaginable, populated by such far-out creatures as the mischief-making Cat in the Hat, the Christmas-hating Grinch, the tree-saving Lorax, and the ever-persuasive Sam I Am. Born Theodor Seuss Geisel on March 2, 1904, in Springfield, Massachusetts, he created his pen name by adding "Dr.," believing it would sound more important, and dropping his first and last names. In 1954, Dr. Seuss launched the "beginner book" industry, starting with the good-hearted elephant of *Horton Hears a Who!* Making learning to read easy and fun, his other books included such classics as *The Cat in the Hat* (1957), *How the Grinch Stole Christmas* (1957), *Dr. Seuss's ABC* (1960), *Green Eggs and Ham* (1960), *One Fish, Two Fish, Red Fish, Blue Fish* (1960), *Hop on Pop* (1963), *Fox in Socks* (1966), and *There's a Wocket in My Pocket* (1974). Dr. Seuss died in 1991, but even after death he was still able to deliver one more fanciful tale, *Daisy Head Maizie*, a twenty-year-old unpublished manuscript found among his office papers.

DRUGS

Acid, angel dust, bennies, cocaine, crack, crank, crystal, dope, downers, ecstasy, grass, hash, heroin, LSD, MDA, marijuana, meth, mushrooms, opium, PCP, peyote, poppers, pot, quaaludes, reefers, sleeping pills, smack, special K, speed, uppers, Valium, and weed—these are the many types of recreational drugs that a generation of young people has experimented with since coming of age in the shadow of the 1960s drug culture. For better or worse, drugs have been glorified in our popular culture via books (*Bright Lights, Big City*, *Go Ask Alice*, *Less Than Zero*, and *Valley of the Dolls*), films (*Easy Rider*, *Woodstock*, every Cheech and Chong comedy, and virtually all teen flicks released since the late 1960s), and songs ("Bennie and the Jets," "Lucy in the Sky with Diamonds," "One Toke over the Line," "Purple Haze," "Cocaine," and "White Rabbit").

Over the years, youngsters have been warned that along with drug use comes the danger of addiction, overdosing, and "frying one's brain like an egg." Throughout the 1980s, First Lady Nancy Reagan fronted a zealous antidrug campaign aimed at kids with the slogan "Just Say No." Mrs. President's oversimplified attempt at teaching America's youth not to use drugs was futile at best, particularly when it was revealed that Nancy—allegedly, according to rumor—liked her doctor-prescribed pills chased with alcohol. (Hypocritically, our parents' generation believed that if a drug is prescribed by a physician, then it's okay, although their drug of choice was usually liquor.)

It's been said that druggies use drugs because of peer pressure or to escape from personal demons. But let's face the facts: Druggies do drugs because they're fun. Drugs make them feel good (sometimes). It's exciting getting recklessly high with friends at a party (unless you make a fool out of yourself by saying or doing something stupid during a blackout). And part of being young and high is the feeling of carefree invincibility. (Yeah, just ask the late Anissa Jones, Freddie Prinze, Gia Carangi, Kurt Cobain, River Phoenix, and Dana Plato. I wonder if they would wish they'd "just said no.")

DR. ZACHARY SMITH

A foreign spy who sabotages the Robinson family's maiden voyage to the Alpha Centauri star system and accidentally becomes a stowaway on their Jupiter 2 spacecraft as it veers irreparably off course into the recesses of an uncharted solar system. Pompous yet cowardly, his scheming ways usually put the family—particularly young Will Robinson—in danger. Jonathan Harris played Dr. Smith in the sci-fi series *Lost in Space* (1965–68).

DUCHESS

Pampered and beautiful, the furry white feline with the voice of Eva Gabor finds herself and her three kittens dumped in the dreadful outskirts of Paris, and later helped by rascally alley cat Thomas O'Malley, in Walt Disney's animated film *The Aristocats* (1970).

DUCK SHOES

Quack! Quack! Advertised in preppy-oriented Lands' End catalogs, the Top-Sider-esque footwear made of waterproof rubber was a hot fashion item in the early 1980s. To avoid having soggy socks, prepsters wore these in the rain, snow, and other events involving water.

DUDLEY DO-RIGHT

Square-jawed and with a modulated voice, the blond Royal Canadian Mountie was originally featured in a segment of *The Bullwinkle Show* before headlining his own spin-off cartoon show from 1969 to 1970. A noble but highly inept do-gooder, Dudley spent his day constantly rescuing the apple of his eye, Nell—the pretty daughter of his boss, Inspector Fenwick—from the sinister clutches of Snidely Whiplash. The lovely Nell never returned his love, for she had a thing for Horse, Dudley's faithful white steed.

DUKE

A real-life dog named Stretch starred as Jed Clampett's lazy hound dog on the sitcom *The Beverly Hillbillies*. To the disgust of uppity next-door neighbor Mrs. Drysdale, old Duke once fathered the pups born to her pampered French poodle.

DUKES OF HAZZARD

Comedy-adventure series about two fast-driving, hot-looking good ol' boys who lived in rural Hazzard County, somewhere in the southern United States. Blond Bo Duke (John Schneider) and brunet Luke Duke (Tom Wopat) were more than just relatives (cousins, to be exact); they were buddies playing countrified Robin Hoods by bending the law and outwitting corrupt local officials, headed by Jefferson Davis "Boss" Hogg (Sorrell Booke) and his buffoonish henchmen, Sheriff Roscoe P. Coltrane (James Best) and Deputy Enos Strate (Sonny Shroyer). Bo and Luke's specialty was speeding around in the souped-up General Lee, an orange 1969 Dodge Charger. Their accomplices were wise Uncle Jesse (Denver Pyle) and beautiful Daisy Duke (Catherine Bach), their curvaceous cousin, who dressed in scanty clothing. Country-music star Waylon Jennings was the off-screen narrator and sang the show's fitting theme, "Good Ol' Boys."

Airing on Friday evenings from 1979 to 1985, *The Dukes of Hazzard* was a lead-in to the soap *Dallas* on CBS-TV. In 1982, following the path of big-headed TV stars (*Bonanza*'s Pernell Roberts, *Charlie's Angels*' Farrah Fawcett, *Three's Company*'s Suzanne Somers, and *CHiPs*' Erik Estrada, for example), Schneider and Wopat quit the show over a salary dispute and were replaced by look-alikes Byron Cherry and Christopher Mayer as Coy Duke and Vance Duke (more Duke cousins). The ratings were sluggish without Bo and Luke, so a settlement was reached allowing the original country studs to return to Hazzard County in late February 1983.

With an emphasis on high-flying car chases combined with slapstick, the series was an instant hit with youths and led to the licensing and manufacturing of countless *Dukes*-related merchandise (toys, games, T-shirts, and so on). It inspired a host of Southern imitations, including *B.J. and the Bear* (1979–81), *Lobo* (1979–81), *Harper Valley P.T.A.* (1981–82), and *Enos* (1980–81), a *Dukes* spin-off.

DUNE BUGGY

The friendly-looking recreational vehicle symbolized the carefree beach crowd of the late 1960s and early 1970s. Dune buggies were commonly found careening over sand dunes of North America's beaches and deserts, especially around the shores of Florida and Southern California and in the desert regions of California's Mojave Desert and Mexico's Baja California. Made of lightweight fiberglass, the custom-made, topless car had a squat, round appearance without flat lines (often they were modified VW Beetle bodies with rear VW engines), and fat wheels with thick treads for traction while driving in loose sand (on most models, the rear tires were much larger than the front ones). A safety rollbar kept occupants from being crushed if flipped over while flying across the dunes. They came in bright shades—cherry red, lime green, orange, yellow, purple, and turquoise—coated with a dazzling silver flake finish, and some owners decorated them with colorful Rickie Tickie Stickie flower decals, befitting the personality of these happy-go-lucky little cars.

Famous dune buggies of pop culture include the Funky Phantom's Looney Dooney, The Banana Splits' Banana Buggy, teenage Bamm-Bamm's Cave Buggy, Wonderbug from *The Krofft Supershow*, Speed Buggy, Hot Wheels' Dune Daddy, Matchbox's Beach Hopper, Big Jim's Dune Devil, and Malibu Barbie's Sun 'n Fun Buggy.

FYI: ▸ The image of the dune buggy took a diabolical turn when it became known as the favorite method of transportation for the Manson Family on their infamous trips through the rugged terrain of California's Death Valley. Charlie had his own command buggy, equipped with a scabbard next to the steering wheel to hold the sword he used to slice victims.

DUNGEONS & DRAGONS

Fantasy role-playing game popular with socially inept nerds of the late 1970s and early 1980s. Created by Gary Gygax for the company Tactical Studies Rules in 1974, the game was set against a medieval background and involved a complex theoretical war strategy. It allowed players to assume alter egos—a human fighter, a dwarf thief, a magic elf, a wizard, and so on—while acting out various adventures (they pretended to cast spells and fight dragons, ogres, and a huge eyeball known as the Beholder). Participants were educated about the wonders of Mythos, Satanism, medieval weaponry, and the Renaissance Faire. Throughout its popularity, geek kids would have D&D sleepovers, playing the game all night long and taking the role-playing so seriously that it would continue for days afterward. It also inspired a TV movie, *Mazes and Monsters* (1982), starring a pre–movie star Tom Hanks, and a Saturday-morning cartoon, *Dungeons & Dragons* (1983–87).

DUNKIN' DONUTS

"Time to make the donuts." Founded in 1950 by William Rosenberg, this is America's number-one donut chain. Dunkin' Donuts sells almost 6.4 million donuts every day (a yearly total that could circle earth twice), its glazed donut being the best seller. Rival donut chains include Krispy Kreme and Winchell's.

DURAN DURAN

British New Wave supergroup, formed in 1980, whose name came from a villain played by Milo O'Shea in the Jane Fonda sci-fi film *Barbarella*. The quintet of pretty boys was known for techno-ish power pop ballads accompanied by imaginative music videos. (An old saying went "If video killed the radio star, it made Duran Duran.") They were also known for a glamorous androgynous look consisting of full makeup and moussed hair (Duran Duran wore more eyeliner and lip gloss than the teenybopper girls squealing over them) and for marrying fashion models like Yasmin Parvanah and Julie Anne. Sultry and brooding, Duran Duran's fab five members consisted of lead vocalist Simon Lebon, keyboardist Nick Rhodes, guitarist Andy Taylor, bassist John Taylor, and drummer Roger Taylor (none of the Taylors were related). Top Forty songs included "Hungry Like the Wolf" (1983), "Rio" (1983), "Union of the Snake" (1983), "New Moon on Monday" (1984), "The Reflex" (1984), "The Wild Boys" (1984), "Save a Prayer" (1985), and "A View to a Kill" (1985), from the James Bond movie of the same title.

In 1985, the band split into two groups: Andy and John formed The Power Station, joined by

Robert Palmer, and scored two hits with "Some Like It Hot" and a revival of T-Rex's "Get It On (Bang a Gong)," while Simon, Nick, and Roger formed Arcadia and had a smash with "Election Day," featuring narration by Grace Jones. Duran Duran re-formed in the 1990s.

FYI: ▸ A question I've always had about Duran Duran: Does anyone actually know what they're singing about in their songs? What's the Union of the Snake? The New Moon on Monday? The Reflex?

DUSTER JACKETS

Long, knee-length leather jackets—sort of a western version of a trench coat—that made guys look really cool in the late 1980s. Not so cool today, they are often associated with weird computer types.

DUSTY

A doll for robust tomboy types who liked sports and other outdoorsy activities. (Did these girls even play with dolls?) Issued by Kenner in 1974, the "fashion-action" doll—with freckles, a platinum-hued shag cut, and a terrific suntan—could actually swing her arm, allowing her to play an assortment of sports. Dusty could hit a tennis ball, swing a golf club, serve a volleyball, and whack a baseball. She enjoyed going on fun-filled vacations, such as fishing trips, skiing on snowy mountain slopes, wild African safaris, and trail rides astride her beautiful Palomino horse called Nugget. Dusty's friends were Cliff, her pacesetting boyfriend, and Skye, an exciting black girl. When the threesome weren't on the go, they enjoyed hanging out at Dusty's Swingin' Cabana, a round, inflatable vacation home.

DWAYNE SCHNEIDER

Actor Pat Harrington's apartment building superintendent, seen on TV's *One Day at a Time*, who was simply called "Schneider" by his tenants. Regarding himself as "the Rudolph Valentino of Indianapolis," this mustachioed macho man was a member of a fraternal lodge called the Secret Order of Beavers.

DYLAN McKAY

The brooding California surfer was a character played by sideburned hunk Luke Perry on the teen TV hit *Beverly Hills 90210*.

DYNASTY

Inspired by the success of supersoap *Dallas*, this was another popular prime-time serial of the 1980s, and like its Texas competitor it focused on a lavishly wealthy clan (the Carringtons) living west of the Mississippi (Denver) whose fortune came from the oil business. Airing on ABC from 1981 to 1989, *Dynasty* epitomized the Reagan-era obsession with big business and big money. The Carringtons of Denver were glamorous sophisticates—forever bedecked in tuxedos, evening gowns, and elaborate coiffures (the show boasted a weekly wardrobe budget of more than $10,000, thanks to Nolan Miller's glitzy, eye-popping frocks and Cartier's dazzling jewels)—who sipped champagne and exchanged clever, straight-to-the-point insults.

The principal players included John Forsythe as oil tycoon Blake Carrington; Linda Evans as his devoted second wife, Krystle; Joan Collins as vengeful ex-wife Alexis; Pamela Sue Martin, and later Emma Samms, as spoiled daughter Fallon; Al Corley, and later Jack Coleman, as sexually confused son Steven; John James as Fallon's do-gooder husband, Jeff Colby; Heather Locklear as Krystle's trampy niece Sammy Jo; Gordon Thomson as long-lost son Adam; and Catherine Oxenberg as long-lost daughter Amanda. Supporting regulars included Lloyd Bochner as Cecil Colby; Pamela Bellwood as Claudia Blaisdel; Kathleen Beller as Kirby Anders; Geoffrey Scott as Mark Jennings; Deborah Adair as Tracy Kendall; Michael Nader as Dex Dexter; Diahann Carroll as Dominique Deveraux; and Rock Hudson as Daniel Reece. (It was while Hudson starred on *Dynasty* that the world learned of his homosexuality and affliction with AIDS.)

Dynasty took a campy approach to its cast of characters, dialogue, and plot twists. It featured over-the-top story lines, such as Alexis and Krystle's hair-pulling catfight in the lily pond, or the "Moldavian Massacre" season finale, in which virtually every character was gunned down by machine-gun-toting terrorists. Every episode seemed to be filled with outrageous backstabbing and a bitchy word or two between its dueling shoulder-padded divas. Fans couldn't get enough, and by the 1984–85 TV season *Dynasty* was the number-one show on the air.

DYNOMUTT

Created by Hanna-Barbera, Dynomutt, the Dog Wonder, was a perpetually malfunctioning bionic pooch partnered with a muscular superhero called the Blue Falcon. Although voiced by Frank Welker, Dynomutt sounded a lot like Art Carney's Ed Norton from *The Honeymooners*. Introduced as half of *The Scooby-Doo/Dynomutt Hour* in 1976 before Dynomutt headlined his own Saturday-morning cartoon show in 1978.

EARTHQUAKE

"This used to be a helluva town." Released at the peak of the 1970s disaster craze, this action-packed movie depicts what happens when the long-predicted "Big One" hits Los Angeles. What occurs is devastation never before seen on the big screen: A superquake—a 9.9 on the Richter Scale—shudders and shakes the City of Angels. Chasms open, freeways buckle, buildings quiver then collapse, jam-packed high-rise elevators plummet, the world-famous Hollywood sign tumbles, homes somersault down the Hollywood Hills, the enormous Hollywood Reservoir Dam crumbles, flooding the Southern California metropolis—and all this right before your very eyes!

Directed by Mark Robson, the 1974 film, boasting Oscar-winning special effects, was filmed in startling, earsplitting Sensurround, a sound technique using low-frequency vibrations to allow theater audiences to feel "tremors" during the earthquake scenes. The all-star cast included Charlton Heston as rugged construction engineer Stewart Graff; Ava Gardner as his spoiled wife, Remy; Geneviève Bujold as his mistress, Denise Marshall, a single mother whose son, Corry, winds up unconscious on the paved bottom of a river runoff; Lorne Greene as Remy's father and Stewart's boss, Sam Royce; George Kennedy as police officer Lew Slade; Richard "Shaft" Roundtree as daredevil cyclist Miles Quade; Afroed Victoria Principal as beautiful Rosa; Marjoe Gortner as wig-wearing psychotic Jody; and Walter Matthau as a drunk at a neighborhood bar. *Earthquake* is infamous for the mismatched casting of Gardner as Greene's daughter (Greene was only seven years older than Gardner!).

FYI: ▸ Before viewing *Earthquake*, audiences were given a disclaimer warning them about Sensurround: "Please be aware that you will feel as well as see and hear realistic effects such as might be experienced in an actual earthquake. The management assumes no responsibility for the physical or emotional reactions of the individual viewer." Some were shaken with fear by Sensurround's low-frequency hum and actually had to leave the movie theater!

EARTH SHOES

Dowdy-looking, funny-shaped, dirt-colored, orthopedic-pleasing shoe designed by Anne Kalso, a yoga instructor from Denmark. Kalso's Earth Shoe was characterized by a corrugated rubber wedgie sole, wide and high at the toe and narrow and low at the heel. This design relieved the toes of forward pressure and promoted better posture, allowing the wearer to "walk the way nature intended." (I always thought they seemed to waddle like ducks.) It supposedly did wonders for people with bunions, corns, calluses, hammer toes, and bad backs. Earth Shoes were introduced in the United States on Earth Day, April 22, 1970. They became one of the biggest shoe fads of the 1970s—selling over two million pairs and spawning more than eighty-five copycats. (You could purchase the Kalso brand only at one of the 135 Earth Shoe stores in the United States.) Ironically, the shoe's main footwear competitor—the elevated platform—was an orthopedic nightmare.

EASTLAND SCHOOL FOR YOUNG WOMEN

The fictional prep school for well-to-do girls located in upstate New York, near Peekskill, is where you would find students Blair Warner, Natalie Green, Tootie Ramsey, and Jo Polniaczek—supervised by housemother Mrs. Edna Garrett—learning about the facts of life on TV's *Facts of Life* (1979–88).

EASTON, SHEENA

The beautiful, dark-haired Scottish lass—with the coolest bi-level cut around—was one of pop music's favorite female singers of the 1980s. Born in Glasgow as Sheena Orr, she began her career singing frothy female anthems, including her only American number one, "Morning Train (Nine to Five)" (1981), as well as "Modern Girl" (1981), "For Your Eyes Only" (1981), "You Could Have Been with Me" (1982), "Telefone (Long Distance Love Affair)" (1983), and "Almost over You" (1984). She won the Best New Artist Grammy in 1981. Halfway through the decade, Easton adopted a bawdier image with tunes like "Strut" (1984), "Sugar Walls" (1985), and "U Got the Look" (1987), a duet with Prince.

FYI: ▸ Because of the erotic lyrics, such as "Blood races to your private spots" and "Come spend the night inside my sugar walls," Easton and her "Sugar Walls" (allegedly slang for "vagina") found themselves—among other naughty recording artists (Prince, Madonna, Cyndi Lauper, Frank Zappa, and Twisted Sister's Dee Snider)—under attack in the mid-1980s by Senator Al Gore's blonde, helmet-haired wife, Tipper, for the use of profanity in rock music.

EASY-BAKE OVEN

"Bake your cake and eat it too!" Play kitchens have always been a favorite pastime of juvenile June Cleavers, but when Kenner introduced the Easy-Bake Oven in 1964, girls could go beyond make-believe and actually bake yummy cakes, pies, cookies, candy, brownies, fudge, biscuits, pretzels, and pizza—just like mom! The turquoise plastic mini-oven (sixteen by eighteen inches) baked exclusively by heat generated from two ordinary 100-watt light bulbs. Girls mixed the gooey batter (the real fun) and poured it into tiny slide-through baking pans. Each pan was then placed on grooved rails and slid through an enclosed oven, where it would bake for what seemed like an eternity. After that, it was on to the cooling chamber—then out a slot where eager little fingers couldn't wait to frost and then devour the freshly baked goodie. In 1971, a contemporary-looking, forest-green Super Easy-Bake Oven was manufactured, equipped with two ovens, double-sized slide-through pans, and a viewing window. The shape of the Easy-Bake Oven has been modernized today to resemble a microwave oven. For more than three decades, the Easy-Bake Oven has remained the best-selling non-doll toy among girls.

EB DAWSON

Dressed in his trademark plaid jacket and green cap, this lanky country bumpkin (played by Tom Lester) was Oliver Douglas's klutzy, birdbrained farmhand on the TV sitcom *Green Acres*.

ECSTASY

"I can feel my hair growing!" First surfacing on the nightclub scene in the mid-1980s, X is today's illegal drug of choice for young people caught up in the world of raves and circuit parties. This synthetic drug (MDMA) with amphetamine-like and hallucinogenic qualities is used to keep you dancing and for mood enhancement. At dance-oriented clubs nationwide, you can spot those tripping on ecstasy (known as X-ing) by their senseless jabbering, ceaseless dancing, bottled-water gulping, and glow-stick chewing (to keep from grinding the teeth).

FYI: ▸ Invented in Germany in 1917 as an appetite suppressant, ecstasy was legal in the United States as recently as 1986.

ECTO-1A

Souped-up white hearse that the Ghostbusters team drove on gigs to rid Manhattan of troublesome spooks, in the *Ghostbusters* film comedies and Saturday-morning cartoon.

EDDIE CORBETT

Cute seven-year-old who had a habit of trying to find his widowed father, Tom Corbett, a prospective wife. Eddie lived with his dad and an Asian housekeeper, Mrs. Livingston, in a high-rise apartment in San Francisco, California. Portrayed by freckle-faced Brandon Cruz (born May 28, 1962) in the TV comedy *The Courtship of Eddie's Father* from 1969 to 1972.

EDDIE HASKELL

The cheating, two-faced friend of Beaver Cleaver's older brother, Wally, is regarded as the first nasty youngster featured as a regular in a TV series. This no-good weasel bullied the younger kids and tried to score points with Mr. and Mrs. Cleaver by being phony polite. ("My, Mrs. Cleaver, you look especially lovely today!")

FYI: ▸ Ken Osmond, who played Eddie Haskell on *Leave It to Beaver*, grew up to be a cop for the LAPD. He was awarded a medal for valor.

EDDIE MUNSTER

Full name: Edward Wolfgang Munster. Herman and Lily's young son on *The Munsters* TV sitcom was a wolf-boy with pointed ears and a major widow's peak who dressed in a velvet Lord Fauntleroy suit and attended fifth grade at Mockingbird Heights Elementary School. He always carried with him a stuffed werewolf doll named Woof-Woof. Eddie was played by eleven-year-old Butch Patrick, who later, as a teen, starred in the Saturday-morning kids' series *Lidsville*.

ED GRIMLEY

"I'm going mental!" Played by Martin Short on *Saturday Night Live*, a nerdy character (as in wearing pants pulled up too high, shirt buttoned up all the way, and hair gelled into a point on top of his head) whose passions were playing the triangle and watching Pat Sajak's *Wheel of Fortune*.

EDITH ANN

Lily Tomlin's bratty, raspy-voiced little girl, who sat on an oversized rocking chair while sharing opinions about her juvenile world. Originally introduced as a regular character on *Rowan & Martin's Laugh-In* TV show. "And that's the truth!"

EDWARD SCISSORHANDS

"His story will touch you, even though he can't." Director Tim Burton's dark fairy tale about a man-made boy with scissors for hands (Johnny Depp) created by a benevolent inventor (Vincent Price). Living completely alone in a Gothic castle after his creator dies, sweet-natured Edward is befriended by a cheery Avon Lady, Peg Boggs (Dianne Wiest). Feeling compassion for the strange orphan, Peg takes him to live in a surreal suburb, where he makes friends with her teenage daughter, Kim Boggs (Winona Ryder). Despite Edward's talent for using his finger blades to create works of art with hair and lawn hedges, the suburban community is close-minded and can't accept someone who is different. Released for Christmas of 1990, this visually colorful film is highlighted by a magical Danny Elfman score.

EEYORE

Oh-so-doleful ("sigh") purple donkey stuffed with sawdust whose tail constantly drops off despite being pinned on ("Most likely lose it again"). A friend of Winnie the Pooh, Eeyore lives at his "Gloomy Place" in the 100 Acre Woods, where he likes to eat thistles.

EGGHEAD JR.

The son of hen-house matriarch Miss Prissy, this eyeglass-wearing lad is the brainiest chick in the Looney Tunes barnyard. Loud-mouth rooster Foghorn Leghorn regularly spends time instructing Egghead Jr. on something ("Pay attention, boy. Now listen here"), only to have the quiet youngster devise his own extraordinary solution.

EGGO

Frozen breakfast waffle from Kellogg's, distinguished by its round shape and famous for TV ads featuring an early-morning twosome hovering over a toaster while bickering "Leggo of my Eggo." "No, *you* leggo of *my* Eggo." Eggo flavors have included Buttermilk, Blueberry, Strawberry, Apple Cinnamon, Banana Bread, Nut & Honey, and Chocolate Chip.

EIGHT IS ENOUGH

Once acclaimed as "America's Favorite Family Program," this hour-long comedy-drama, centering on a family with eight very different children, aired on prime time from 1977 to 1981. Set in California, it starred bald, pudgy Dick Van Patten as Tom Bradford, the regularly flustered father who worked as a newspaper columnist for the *Sacramento Register*, and pretty, blonde Diana Hyland as Joan, the more-patient mother and Tom's wife of twenty-five years. Best known for being teen idol John Travolta's much-older girlfriend, Hyland died of cancer after five episodes were filmed. She was replaced by Betty Buckley as Abby Abbott, a widow and teacher at Memorial High (the alma mater of the Bradford teens), who became Tom's new wife. The Bradford brood were played by Grant Goodeve as twenty-three-year-old David, Lani O'Grady as twenty-one-year-old Mary, Laurie Walters as twenty-year-old Joannie, Susan Richardson as nineteen-year-old Susan, Dianne Kay as eighteen-year-old Nancy, Connie Needham as fifteen-year-old Elizabeth, Willie Aames as fourteen-year-old Tommy, and Adam Rich as eight-year-old Nicholas. Later cast additions included Joan Prather as Janet McArthur, David's attorney wife; and Brian Patrick Clarke as Merle "The Pearl" Stockwell, Susan's baseball-pitcher husband. (David and Susan were married in a double wedding in 1979.) In 1980, future Brat Packer Ralph Macchio joined the ABC show as Jeremy, Abby's troubled teenage nephew. *Eight Is Enough* was based on the autobiography of Washington columnist Tom Braden.

ELECTRAWOMAN AND DYNAGIRL

"ElectraWow!" Seen on Saturday mornings from 1976 to 1977, this ElectraSuper program is the best remembered of the adventure serials showcased on *The Krofft Supershow*. Airing at a time when TV viewers were captivated with female superheroes (The Bionic Woman, Wonder Woman, Isis), this cliff-hanger show appealed to girls who now loved to play crime-fighters—the same way boys have always played Batman and Robin. It starred feathered-haired blonde Deidre Hall as Lori, a brave and determined reporter for *Newsmaker* magazine, and pigtailed brunette Judy Strangis as Judy, Lori's perky and younger protégé.

When trouble arose, the twosome turned into ElectraFantastic superheroines—via the Electra-Change—clad in spandex costumes and wearing ElectraComps, a wrist mechanism that sent out forceful ElectraBeams. The amazing ElectraCar, a triangular-shaped, three-wheeled, superpowered dune buggy, drove them in battles against ElectraEvil villains, such as the Sorcerer, Miss Dazzle, the Empress of Evil, and the Pharaoh. Electronics wizard Frank Heflin (Norman Alden) assisted them from a secret headquarters at ElectraBase. Deidre Hall later played Dr. Marlena Evans on the afternoon soap *Days of Our Lives*.

ELECTRIC BOOGIE

The 1980s dance movements associated with break-dancing, consisting of hand waves, robot-like actions, and Michael Jackson's moonwalking.

ELECTRIC COMPANY

"Heeeyyy, yooouu guuuyyys!" An entertaining yet educational TV program from the producers of *Sesame Street*, airing on PBS from 1971 to 1981. It was aimed at older youngsters, ages seven to ten, who had graduated from *Sesame Street*'s simple lessons of letters and numbers. Emphasizing the development of reading skills, it used the phonics method to teach letters, combinations of letters, complete words, and sentences employing those words. It also taught simple arithmetic. Lessons were interwoven with short sketches, songs, dances, cartoons, and mini-documentaries. Comedian Bill Cosby and actress Rita Moreno headed the repertory cast, which included a teenage rock band called Short Circus.

ELECTRIC FOOTBALL

The Dallas Cowboys, Washington Redskins, Pittsburgh Steelers, Green Bay Packers, Miami Dolphins, Los Angeles Rams—just imagine being able to coach one of these superstar NFL teams. Electric football games allowed this fantasy to come true as kids placed their team of tiny plastic players—ends, tackles, guards, and offensive and defensive backs—in different formations at the line of scrimmage on a highly detailed football field complete with goal posts, yard markers, grandstand, bleachers, and little NFL pennants. The quarterback passes the magnetic ball, and with the press of a button—buzzzzzz—the teams vibrated around the metal gridiron. You could control the degree of vibration, moving the players at a pace from slow motion to fast speed. If the power was turned up too high, they gyrated spastically in every direction or fell down.

ELEPHANT BELLS

Wildly oversized bell-bottoms with legs that resembled an elephant's. Instead of purchasing jeans in this style, some kids preferred to cut their bells at the seam, then sew a big piece of material into the slit, making the legs astonishingly huge. Real cool.

ELLIOT

Disney's enchanted cartoon dragon from Fantasy World who spans thirty feet and has bright-green skin, tiny pink wings, a potbelly, and a jolly but somewhat bumbling disposition. He befriends and protects a troubled orphan boy named Pete—the only person who can see him—and becomes "Pete's dragon." Charlie Callas provided Elliot's voice in the 1977 Disney film *Pete's Dragon*.

ELLIOTT

Young California boy who befriends E.T. and helps the stranded alien get back home. Elliott's special bond with the extra-terrestrial is so great that when E.T. gets seriously sick, Elliott suffers as well. Elliott's big brother is Michael, and Gertie is his baby sister. Played by child actor Henry Thomas (born September 9, 1971) in Steven Spielberg's *E.T.* movie.

ELLIOTT, MAMA CASS

"I feel hip bones are overrated." A persistent rumor says that this rotund singer choked to death on a ham sandwich. The truth is that her early demise was only partly due to eating—she died of a heart attack brought about by chronic obesity. (The rumor exists because she was eating a ham sandwich at the time of her death in London on July 29, 1974.) Born Ellen Naomi Cohen on September 19, 1941, in Baltimore, Mama Cass is best remembered for having a vocal talent as large as her bountiful girth—on her five-foot-five-inch frame she carried more than 200 pounds. She was also known for her self-mocking sense of humor and for wearing psychedelic-printed muumuus. An original member of The Mamas and the Papas, a 1960s hippie folk band, she experienced solo success as a ballad singer when the group disbanded in 1968, with songs "Dream a Little Dream of Me" (1968), "It's Getting Better" (1969), and "Make Your Own Kind of Music" (1969). Mama Cass was deliciously evil as flamboyant Witch Hazel in the movie version of the TV classic *H. R. Pufnstuf* (1970) and fantastically animated on the Saturday-morning *Scooby-Doo* special "The Haunted Candy Factory" (1971).

ELLIS, BRET EASTON

Literary wunderkind who at age twenty-one penned *Less Than Zero* (1985), the nihilistic bestseller that captured the shallow "die young, stay pretty" mentality of young Americans during the "have it all" 1980s. Later universally panned for writing the graphically violent *American Psycho* (1991), a stomach-turning novel about a yuppie serial killer named Patrick Bateman. Ellis was a member of literature's "Brat Pack," a group of youthful novelists whose alumni included Jay McInerney (*Bright Lights, Big City*), Tama Janowitz (*Slaves of New York*), and Douglas Coupland (*Generation X*).

ELLY MAY CLAMPETT

Jed Clampett's tomboy daughter, a curvaceous bombshell who is prettier than a 'possum and stronger than an ol' wildcat. Elly May loved critters more than fellas and preferred pigtails, denim, and gingham over fancy coiffures and elegant dresses. Played by gorgeous blonde Donna Douglas, a former Miss Louisiana, on TV's *Beverly Hillbillies*.

FYI: ▸ More than 500 animals appeared as Elly May's adored "varmints" on *The Beverly Hillbillies*, including Bobbie the bobcat, Sidney the kangaroo, Gertrude the duck, Eleanor the chicken, Earl the rooster, Clyde the raccoon, Smelly the skunk, Florabelle the pigeon, Skipper the chimp, and Rusty the cat.

ELMER FUDD

"Sssshhh! Be vew-wy, vew-wy quiet. I'm hunting wabbits. Heh-heh-heh-heh-heh!" Dim-witted, bald-headed hunter whose cartoon adventures often had him in pursuit of screwy Bugs Bunny or sputtering Daffy Duck. First featured in the 1939 cartoon short "Dangerous Dan McFoo."

ELMO

"Oh, no! That tickles!" Lanky little red-hued *Sesame Street* Muppet who—during the Christmas of 1996—became the biggest toy fad since the Cabbage Patch Kid craze of the mid-1980s with the wildly sought-after Tickle Me Elmo doll.

ELOISE

Along with contemporaries Madeline and Pippi Longstocking, this irrepressible six-year-old is one of the classic storybook girls of Baby Boom childhood. Living in Manhattan's Plaza Hotel with a British nanny, pug Weenie, and turtle Skipperdee, adorable Eloise plays in the elevators, roller-skates down the corridors, and "cawn't" help herself when she terrorizes the hotel staff. And just like Madeline and Pippi, the success of her first story in 1955 spawned a book series with such titles as *Eloise in Paris*, *Eloise in Moscow*, and *Eloise at Christmastime*. The Eloise books were written by actress Kay Thompson (*Funny Face*) and illustrated by Hilary Knight.

ELROY

George and Jane Jetson's young son was an inquisitive, gadget-obsessed lad who wore a futuristic beanie on his head and studied at the Little Dipper School in Orbit City. Best pal was Astro, the family pooch. Cartoon legend Daws Butler provided Elroy's voice on *The Jetsons*.

ELSA

Orphaned lion cub rescued and raised by Joy and George Adamson in Kenya; subject of the beloved book and movie *Born Free*.

ELSIE THE COW

Since 1939, the demure Jersey heifer with the fresh daisy necklace and cooking apron has been the spokes-cow for Borden dairy products. She is married to Elmer (from Borden Elmer's Glue), and they have two children, Beulah and Beauregard.

ELVIRA

Sassy and witty, the black-haired and big-boobed Mistress of the Dark hosted B-movie horror flicks on TV (*Elvira's Movie Macabre*) during the 1980s and 1990s. Her true identity is that of Cassandra Peterson, a former Las Vegas showgirl, born September 17, 1949, in Manhattan, Kansas.

ELVIS, MARILYN, AND JAMES DEAN

> "Live fast, die young, and leave a good-looking corpse."
> —JAMES DEAN

Even though this trio of Hollywood legends actually belongs to our parents' generation, they have had just as much influence over our pop culture as such contemporary idols as Michael Jackson, Tom Cruise, and Madonna. For those of you who have been living on Planet Mars and don't know who they are, here's a short summary: Elvis Presley was the dark-haired, lip-sneering, handsome "King of Rock 'n' Roll" whose blues-inspired music and hip-swiveling stage performances made our mothers overheat from excitement. Gentlemen did prefer blondes when it came to Marilyn Monroe, the breathy-voiced sex goddess with limp-lidded eyes, a quivering half-smile, and a left-cheek beauty mark, gifted with a wiggly hourglass figure and a vulnerable childlike personality full of humorous not-so-dumbness. Good-looking, blond James Dean embodied all that was cool, an original "rebel without a cause" who played by his own rules and who, because of a tragic auto accident, had a short career consisting of only three major films.

Since we were mere infants, these one-of-a-kind icons, chiefly popular during the 1950s, have been a part of our lives. We watched their movies—Dean's *East of Eden*, Monroe's *Seven Year Itch*, and Presley's *Viva Las Vegas*—on the TV late show and on videotape. We read the many tell-all biographies written about them. Their images have been mass-produced on virtually every type of object imaginable, particularly T-shirts, posters, and dolls. Our favorite fashions are a reflection of their impact: Dean's white T-shirts and blue denim jeans, Presley's black leather jackets, Monroe's red lipstick and peroxide-blonde hair. A high percentage of us were raised in dysfunctional homes, so we relate to beautiful Marilyn's sad life and even understand her dependency on drugs, alcohol, and men to escape from reality. We identify with the recklessness of the angst-ridden James Dean, which led to his untimely death in a car crash. We mourned along with our parents the sorrowful bathroom death of the reclusive Elvis in Graceland.

Their pop culture legacy has left us with many mysterious and unanswered questions. Does James

Dean's ghost really haunt the highways of Southern California in his sporty Porsche Spyder? Was Marilyn Monroe's fatal overdose an accident, a suicide, or a murder arranged and covered up by the Kennedys? Is Elvis alive and eating a burger at a fast-food joint somewhere in the Midwest?

EMERGENCY!

"Squad 51, 10-4!" Airing on NBC-TV from 1972 to 1977, this prime-time adventure series showcased the rescue efforts of Squad 51, a team of paramedics for the Los Angeles County Fire Department. It starred Randolph Mantooth and Kevin Tighe as John Gage and Roy DeSoto, a pair of handsome paramedics who spent each episode doing daring rescues that were either comical or heartrending. Gage and DeSoto, along with canine mascot Boots, were associated with the emergency staff at nearby Rampart General Hospital: Dr. Kelly Brackett (Robert Fuller), Dr. Joe Early (Bobby Troup), and nurse Dixie McCall (onetime torch singer Julie London). For those who couldn't get enough emergencies, including kids who loved the fast-moving show, a cartoon spin-off, *Emergency + Four*, was shown on Saturday mornings from 1973 to 1976.

EMILY LITELLA

"Never mind." Lovable Gilda Radner's Weekend Update editorial correspondent on *Saturday Night Live* was a spinster with poor hearing who misinterpreted the headlines. ("What's all this fuss I hear about the 1976 presidential erections?")

EMPIRE OF THE ANTS

Bell-bottomed, pant-suited Joan Collins and fellow vacationers in Florida are terrorized by ants that have mutated into giant-sized monsters after feeding on radioactive waste. Loosely based on the intriguing sci-fi story by H. G. Wells, the 1977 movie is absurd and outdated, but fun to watch if you're in the mood for a bitchy Collins performance. Directed by low-budget master Bert I. Gordon (*Earth vs. the Spider, Attack of the Puppet People, Village of the Giants, Picture Mommy Dead*, and *Food of the Gods*).

ENCHANTED FOREST

Casper the Friendly Ghost lived in this bewitching comic-book land, which was filled not only with ghosts but also with witches, fairies, elves, giants, trolls, little devils, and every other magical creature imaginable.

ENDLESS LOVE

"It's not over! It's not over!" Even though based on an acclaimed novel by Scott Spencer, the 1981 youth melodrama was panned by critics nationwide, who considered it one of the worst of its time. It focused on the overheated love affair of David (overemoting Martin Hewitt) and Jade (underemoting Brooke Shields). Jade's parents think the precocious teens are too serious and demand that they spend time apart from each other. David's agony over the breakup turns into obsession, and finally madness, as he burns down Jade's family home. This endless film is noteworthy for the endless title song by Lionel Richie and Diana Ross and for marking the debut of superstar Tom Cruise (he played Billy, a bit part). Directed by Franco Zeffirelli, who in 1968 gave moviegoers a more superior and better-received film about young romance: Shakespeare's *Romeo and Juliet*, starring Leonard Whiting and Olivia Hussey.

ENDLESS SUMMER

Legendary documentary written, directed, and shot by Bruce Brown that is credited with introducing the world to the awesome sport of surfing. Released in 1966, it starred two young California surfers, Robert August and Mike Hynson, on an "Endless Summer" quest, traveling around the world to exotic locales—Africa, Australia, New Zealand, Tahiti, Hawaii, and South America—in search of the perfect wave. Along with the breathtaking surfing and locale photography, Brown's amusing tongue-in-cheek narrative (just like an old travelogue) and The Sandals' gentle guitar theme mark the film. In 1994, Brown filmed a just-as-superior sequel, with Patrick O'Connell and Robert "Wingnut" Weaver as the next generation of globe-trotting surfers.

FYI: ▸ If you're wondering where to find the perfect wave, according to *Endless Summer* it's the break off Cape Saint Francis in South America.

ENDORA

Samantha's colorfully Pucci-clad, heavily eye-shadowed meddlesome mother is a batty witch who utterly detested mortal son-in-law Darrin "Darwood" Stephens. Marvelously played by character actress Agnes Moorehead on the *Bewitched* TV sitcom.

ENERGIZER BUNNY

Since 1980, this sunglass-wearing, drum-thumping pink rabbit "keeps going and going and going" as the advertising icon for Energizer batteries.

ENGLISH LEATHER

Cheap-smelling men's cologne that was advertised by 1970s TV spots featuring a gorgeous model exclaiming, "My man wears English Leather or he wears nothing at all!"

ERASURE

Late 1980s electro-pop group featuring the multitalented Vince Clarke (formerly of Depeche Mode and Yazoo) and Andy Bell, whose dance-floor hits included "Oh L'Amour" (1986), "Chains of Love" (1988), and "A Little Respect" (1989). In 1989, recognized as the Best British Group at the eighth annual Brits Awards in London.

ERECTOR SETS

> "Erector is far more than a toy—it trained several generations of engineers, giving them the feel of metal. I'm terrified that today's computer-trained engineers will lack this vital skill—with disastrous results!"
>
> —ARTHUR C. CLARKE, AUTHOR OF *2001: A SPACE ODYSSEY*

"Build yourself a great kid." Since 1913, the longtime favorite metal construction sets by A. C. Gilbert allowed future engineers to build skyscrapers, robots, planes, and motorized carnival rides, such as ferris wheels and merry-go-rounds.

ERICA KANE

"I warn you, I've got claws." Everyone's favorite love-to-hate soap-opera character is this gorgeous and glamorous brunette vixen from Pine Valley, seen on ABC-TV's *All My Children*. Those legions of fans who have been faithful to the show since its debut year (1970) have seen Erica grow from a scheming, self-centered teenager into a scheming, self-centered adult. Her quest in life is to become a supercelebrity. She has been a high-fashion model, a movie actress, a cosmetics executive, a TV hostess, and an author (her biography is *Raising Kane*). She'll do anything to get ahead, and she is capable of seducing Pine Valley's most rich and powerful men. Her constantly expanding moniker—Erica Kane (Jeff) Martin (Phil) Brent (Tom) Cudahy (Mike) Roy (Adam) Chandler (Travis) Montgomery (Travis) Montgomery (Dimitri) Marick (Dimitri) Marick—is proof of that seduction.

FYI: ▸ Actress Susan Lucci, who plays Erica Kane, experienced an astonishing eighteen-year losing streak as a Best Actress in a Daytime Series nominee. She finally won the Emmy on her nineteenth try in 1999.

ERIC CARTMAN

The chubby antihero of the *South Park* gang is a loud-mouthed, know-it-all, self-centered, greedy pain-in-the-butt who eats a lot of Cheesy Poofs, which probably contributes to his being overweight. Cartman once had his anus probed by space aliens and didn't know who his father was because his slutty mom slept with every man in town. In 2003, he was picked as one of VH1's 200 Greatest Pop Culture Icons (at number 198).

ERIC VON ZIPPER

"I come here to tell you that these beach bums is bums." Comedian Harvey Lembeck's moronic leader of the Rat Pack—a motley gang of leather-jacketed cyclists who detest surf "bums," particularly Frankie and Annette—was a funny regular in the *Beach Party* movies of the 1960s. Von Zipper threatened the surfers with a disabling technique called the Himalayan Suspension (you find a certain pressure point on the skull, and it paralyzes the victim) but accidentally zapped himself every time.

ERNESTINE

"One ringy-dingy, two ringy-dingies. . . . Is this the party to whom I am speaking?" One of the best-loved characters on *Rowan & Martin's Laugh-In* was this sarcastic, nasal-voiced telephone switchboard operator played by comic Lily Tomlin.

ERNEST P. WORRELL

"Knowhutimean?" The bungling, know-it-all Kentucky bumpkin was the alter ego of the rubber-faced comic Jim Varney. He became famous in the 1980s as a TV advertising spokesman pitching various consumer products to an unseen pal named Vern ("Hey, Vern"). In 1987, he hit the big screen with *Ernest Goes to Camp* followed by *Ernest Saves Christmas* (1988), *Ernest Goes to Jail* (1990), *Ernest Scared Stupid* (1991), and *Ernest Rides Again* (1993).

ERNIE DOUGLAS
Goofy but sweet orphan adopted by Steve Douglas, the father of best-buddy Chip, on the TV classic *My Three Sons*. Ernie was played by Barry Livingston, younger brother of Stanley Livingston, who co-starred as Chip.

ERNIE KEEBLER
The pudgy-faced sprite cheerfully promotes Keebler cookies and crackers while overlooking the Keebler elves, who are busy at baking inside a hollow tree.

ESCAPE TO WITCH MOUNTAIN
Live-action Disney fantasy, based on Alexander Key's 1968 sci-fi book, about two orphan siblings with supernatural powers—thirteen-year-old Tony Malone (Ike Eisenmann) and eleven-year-old Tia Malone (Kim Richards)—being pursued by evil millionaire Aristotle Bolt (Ray Milland), who wants to use them for corrupt deeds. The unusual children have a secret: They are extra-terrestrials and must meet up with their spaceship at Witch Mountain. Eddie Albert co-starred as Jason O'Day, a gruff bachelor who helps the kids. Directed by John Hough, the 1975 movie featured great special effects, including the memorable scene in which O'Day's Winnebago flies through the air while being chased by a helicopter. A box-office smash, it was followed by a 1978 sequel, *Return from Witch Mountain*.

ESKIMO PIE
The first chocolate-coated ice-cream bar, invented by Christian K. Nelson in 1921. Legend has it that a little boy went into Nelson's ice-cream shop in Onawa, Iowa, and had a difficult time deciding between a chocolate candy bar and an ice-cream bar, because he wanted both but had enough money for only one. The boy's dilemma got Nelson thinking about covering a vanilla ice-cream bar with chocolate candy coating, and the classic Eskimo Pie was born. Its advertising mascot is a happy Eskimo lad dressed in a fur parka.

ESMERELDA
The shy, ditzy witch who had lost most of her powers served as a maid for Darrin and Samantha Stephens on TV's *Bewitched*. Esmerelda suffered from allergy sneezing and bouts of hiccups that would inadvertently activate supernatural catastrophes!

ESPADRILLES
A gal's favorite footwear during the 1970s, these were platform-type shoes involving cork-wedgie soles and canvas tops.

ESTRADA, ERIK
The Hispanic actor (born March 16, 1949, in New York's Spanish Harlem) came into prominence in the late 1970s playing motorcycle-cop Frank Poncherello on the police series *CHiPs* (1977–83). Estrada's toothy white grin, thick jet-black locks, muscular build, and macho demeanor made Ponch a hot TV sex symbol and pinup. Although he doesn't speak Spanish, he starred in a Mexican soap opera, *Dos Mujeres, un Camino*, in the 1990s. (During shooting, his lines were fed to him over a hidden earphone.)

ETCH-A-SKETCH
One of the classic toys of our times, actually invented in France by Arthur Granjean, who originally called it L'Ecran Magique (The Magic Screen). The Ohio Art Company purchased the rights to the toy in 1959, changed the name to Etch-a-Sketch, and introduced it to the public on July 12, 1960. An instant success, it has sold more than sixty million since its original release. Kids spend challenging hours drawing masterpieces by turning two white control knobs—one vertical, the other horizontal—on a red-framed, silver-screened TV-like contraption, only to erase the image with a shake. (Some lost their work of art prematurely after it was accidentally dropped or shaken.)

How does an Etch-a-Sketch work? The reverse side of the glass screen is a compartment filled with a mixture of powdered aluminum and plastic beads. The knob controls on the front are connected to a hidden metal stylus that causes straight perpendicular lines to appear in the gray particles. Curved or diagonal lines are possible, but it takes coordinated, simultaneous movements of the two knobs. Shake the Etch-a-Sketch, and the lines disappear as the powder becomes redistributed again.

E.T. THE EXTRA-TERRESTRIAL

"E.T. phone home." Directed by Steven Spielberg, this was once the number-one box-office champ of all time—until Spielberg's own *Jurassic Park* topped it in 1995. An enchanting sci-fi fantasy starring Henry Thomas as Elliott, a lonely ten-year-old in suburban California who finds a cute, limp-eyed alien in the backyard and—with the aid of Reese's Pieces—entices it into his home. Called E.T. (for Extra-Terrestrial), the little space visitor had been accidentally left behind on earth during an interplanetary scouting expedition. The youngster befriends the stranded creature by giving it secret refuge in his bedroom. When devious government types come searching, protective Elliott must save his new friend by getting him home to the mother ship. The 1982 film co-starred Dee Wallace as Elliott's single mother, Mary, Robert MacNaughton as older brother Michael, and an adorable seven-year-old Drew Barrymore as Gertie, the kid sister who dresses E.T. in drag.

A testament to Spielberg's incontestable strength as "one of cinema's most skillful craftsmen," according to film critic James Pallot, are scenes showcasing "E.T.'s too-cute encounters with suburban living" and "the undeniable exhilaration felt when Thomas's bicycle magically soars into the air." Fueled by an explosion of merchandise tie-ins, such as trading cards, toys, and T-shirts, *E.T.* was quickly embraced by audiences worldwide, and the alien waif became a pop culture icon. In 1983, Michael Jackson did a story album, accompanied by a booklet featuring photos of him cuddling E.T.

FYI: ▸ Actress Debra Winger contributed to the voice of E.T.

EURYTHMICS

In the summer of 1983, the haunting "Sweet Dreams (Are Made of This)" climbed to the top of the charts, introducing America to one of the most compelling female singers of modern rock, Annie Lennox. Born in Scotland on Christmas Day 1954, Lennox sings like a diva and has a personal appearance consisting of anything from bleached-blonde or fiery-red crew cuts, to an assortment of wigs, including an Elvis one, and an odd array of costumes and androgynous clothing. Deriving their name from a dance form in which children were taught music through movement, the Eurythmics were formed by Lennox and her musician-producer boyfriend Dave Stewart, after the 1980 breakup of their previous group, The Tourists.

In the 1980s, the duo's songs were accompanied by artistic and imaginative videos, making them favorites of the MTV Generation: "Love Is a Stranger" (1983), "Here Comes the Rain Again" (1984), "Who's That Girl?" (1984), "Would I Lie to You" (1985), "There Must Be an Angel (Playing with My Heart)" (1985), "Sisters Are Doin' It for Themselves" (1984)—a feminist anthem with Aretha Franklin—"Missionary Man" (1986), and "I Need a Man" (1988). The Eurythmics separated in the early 1990s, Stewart married Bananarama's Siobhan Fahey, and Lennox went on to have a highly acclaimed solo career.

EVANGELISTA, LINDA

"It was God who made me beautiful. If I weren't, then I'd be a teacher." Born on May 10, 1965, the chameleon-like Canadian beauty joined forces with cover-girl cohorts Christy Turlington and Naomi Campbell to form The Trinity, an elite trio of supermodels who reigned over all other models in fame, fortune, and attitude in the early 1990s. Evangelista modeled for several years, picking up considerably mediocre work (earning about $600 per photo shoot), and then her long hair was chopped into the now-famous boyish cut (colored regularly in various shades of brunette, blonde, and red), making her the hottest model around (earning fees of more than $10,000 a day). She had a lengthy engagement to *Twin Peaks* actor Kyle MacLachlan from 1996 to 1998.

"EVERGREEN"

The love theme from *A Star Is Born* (1976), composed and sung by the movie's Afro-permed diva Barbra

Streisand (diminutive Paul Williams was the other composer). In early 1977 it went to the top of the pop charts for three weeks and won the Academy Award for Best Song. The easy-listening ballad became a homecoming and prom standard at schools and was often used as the event's title theme (for example, "Evergreen Memories: Prom 1977" or "Evergreen Homecoming 1977"). Imagine, if you will, teen guys dressed in baby-blue bell-bottomed polyester tuxes slow-dancing with gals in frilly, floral-printed maxigowns and baby's breath stuck in their feathered hair, while La Streisand warbled sappy lyrics like "Love, soft as an easy chair, love, fresh as the morning air." It was just a matter of time before the overplayed song made someone go insane. So it seemed only appropriate that it played in the background when comedienne Julie Brown's homecoming queen (Debby Dickey) got a gun and went on a mad shooting rampage, knocking off her high school peers during the halftime ceremony (an event sung about in Brown's 1984 novelty tune "The Homecoming Queen's Got a Gun").

EVERLASTING GOBSTOPPERS

"Did you say Everlasting Gobstoppers?" Yes, these jawbreaker candies from the *Willy Wonka and the Chocolate Factory* movie never dissolve, so they are "everlasting." Became an actual candy, part of Nestlé's Wonka line, manufactured as small jawbreakers that change colors and flavors.

EVIL DEAD

"There's something out there." Director Sam Raimi's low-budget 1983 gorefest about five college students camping out in a remote cabin in the woods of Tennessee who uncover the ancient Sumerian Book of the Dead and a tape recording of an archaeologist translating it. When the tape is played, it awakens an evil demonic force in the woods that viciously stalks and murders the campers (including a horrendous tree rape scene). Raimi's landmark film, starring Bruce Campbell as Ash Williams, is noted for blood-splattering, limb-ripping violence so over the top that it's comical. It has become a powerful cult favorite over the years, influencing a whole new breed of horror filmmakers. Followed by two superior sequels: *Evil Dead 2: Dead by Dawn* (1987) and *Army of Darkness* (1993).

EVINRUDE

The brave little dragonfly from Disney's *The Rescuers* (1977) who serves as an air carrier for sleuthing mice, Bernard and Bianca, to save a small orphan girl named Penny from the evil clutches of swamp-dwelling Madame Medusa.

EVOLUTION REVOLUTION

Lance Link, the secret agent chimp, fronted this groovy all-monkey rock combo. They performed one of their psychedelic tunes, such as "Sha-La Love You" or "Rollin' in the Clover," at the end of each episode of the *Lancelot Link, Secret Chimp* TV show.

EWOKS

Cute, furry, diminutive denizens of the forest moon of Endor who aided the Rebel Alliance led by Luke Skywalker in defeating the evil Imperial Force (Battle of Endor). First introduced in *Return of the Jedi* (1983), the peace-loving tribe, headed by Chief Chirpa, later starred in two made-for-TV movies, *The Ewok Adventure* (1984) and *Ewoks: The Battle for Endor* (1985), and in a Saturday-morning cartoon show, *The Ewoks* (1985–86). Best known Ewok: Wicket, the young scout who discovered the wounded Princess Leia in *Return of the Jedi.*

EXORCIST

The most terrifying movie of its day—so terrifying that it scared the hell out of audiences, creating mass hysteria. People literally fainted and threw up. After watching the frightfest, many worried that Satan would invade their bodies and possess their souls. Some even blamed their own bad conduct on manipulation by Lucifer, giving new meaning to the phrase "The devil made me do it!"

As Mike Oldfield's haunting "Tubular Bells" tinkles on the soundtrack, the chilling 1973 tale unfolds in Washington, D.C., at the Georgetown townhouse of Mrs. MacNeil (Ellen Burstyn), a famous movie actress alarmed about her young daughter's repulsive behavior. It appears that the wholesome Regan (Linda Blair) has been peeing on the living-room carpet in front of shocked party guests, as well as levitating over her bed, doing an amazing 360-degree head spin, spewing pea-green vomit all over the place, growling and spurting cuss words like a drunken sailor (vocalized by veteran actress Mercedes Mc-

Cambridge), and masturbating with a crucifix. On top of all that, her physical appearance has been transformed into a pustule-covered, yellow-eyed demon. Realizing Regan is possessed, the distraught mother enlists the aid of Father Karras (Jason Miller), a troubled young priest with self-doubts, and Father Merrin (Max von Sydow), a staunch elder who specializes in exorcisms, and together they proceed to cast the devil out of the young girl.

Directed by William Friedkin, *The Exorcist* was adapted from William Peter Blatty's best-selling 1971 novel, loosely based on a factual incident involving a possessed fourteen-year-old Maryland boy. Packed with state-of-the-art special effects and makeup, the R-rated movie was extremely controversial because of its vulgar language, flagrant sexual overtones, and a fixation with the darker side of religion. Moviegoers everywhere lined up around the block and made it the highest-grossing horror film of all time (until 1996's *Scream* took away the honor). It earned ten Oscar nominations, including Best Picture, Best Director (Friedkin), Best Actress (Burstyn), Best Supporting Actress (Blair), and Best Supporting Actor (Miller), and won for Sound and for Blatty's screenplay. The sequels—*Exorcist II: The Heretic* (1977) and *The Exorcist III* (1990)—and countless imitations were spawned.

FYI: ▸ Two F/X secrets from *The Exorcist*: Regan's projectile vomit was created by a mixture of oatmeal and pea soup pumped through a tube hidden in an apparatus on her lower lip, and the spinning head was created by using a mechanical double of Linda Blair complete with radio-controlled blinking eyes.

EXTENDABLE TUNNELS

Indoors or out, tots could crawl through nine feet of steel hoops covered with colorful vinyl for all kinds of fun make-believe play.

EXXON TIGER

Since 1959, the animated tiger's famous roar, "Put a Tiger in your tank," has been the advertising slogan for the Oklahoma-based gasoline company.

FACIAL STUBBLE

Not shaving your mug in order to sport a permanent five o'clock shadow was a scratchy fashion trend in the late 1980s. Inspiration came from British recording artist George Michael and *Miami Vice* actor Don Johnson.

FACTS OF LIFE

The NBC-TV spin-off from *Diff'rent Strokes* began in 1979, when housekeeper Mrs. Edna Garrett left the Drummonds to be a housemother at the Eastland School for Young Women, a boarding academy in upstate New York. Played by Charlotte Rae, Mrs. Garrett was wise and sympathetic—both friend and substitute parent to those in her care. The first season featured a large regular cast of students (including future Brat Packer Molly Ringwald), but in the fall of 1980 it was trimmed down to include only four girls: Lisa Whelchel as spoiled deb Blair Warner, Mindy Cohn as chubby wiseacre Natalie Green, Kim Fields as naive Tootie Ramsey, and Nancy McKeon as streetwise Jo Polniaczek.

One of the longest-running sitcoms of the 1980s, it went through numerous changes as the girls matured into young women. The most significant change occurred in 1983, when an underpaid, unappreciated Mrs. Garrett switched careers by opening Edna's Edibles, a gourmet-food shop in nearby Peekskill. Blair and Jo (now attending school at Langley College) and Tootie and Natalie (still at Eastland) moved in, and *The Facts of Life* continued until 1988. Another noticeable change was the young actresses' embarrassing weight gain, which became the butt of jokes, especially after comedienne Joan Rivers referred to them as "The Fats of Life" (maybe they devoured too many of Edna's edibles).

FAITH

When singer George Michael broke up his bubbly pop act Wham! with Andrew Ridgeley in 1986, he experienced continued success as a solo artist with this album. Released in November 1987, it sold more than nine million copies, topped the U.S. charts for twelve weeks, won the coveted Album of the Year category at the Grammy Awards, and became one of the ten best sellers of the decade. It housed the horny and controversial "I Want Your Sex" (in the era of AIDS, one out of three U.S. radio stations banned this song about carnal pleasure), along with "Father Figure," "One More Try," "Monkey," "Kissing a Fool," and the butt-wiggling title track. *Faith* also marked a new look for pretty-boy Michael: facial stubble, shades, leather jackets, blue jeans, and boots.

FALL GUY

Action-adventure TV series starring Lee Majors as Colt Seavers, a studly movie stuntman who moonlights as a bounty hunter tracking down crooks who skipped out on bail. Assisting Colt on his assignments were zealous younger cousin Howie Munson (Douglas Barr) and stunning stunt gal Jody Banks (Heather Thomas). Airing on ABC from 1981 to 1986, each episode of *The Fall Guy* featured spectacular stunt work and the country-tinged opening theme "The Unknown Stuntman," sung by Lee Majors.

FALLON CARRINGTON

Pretty brunette Pamela Sue Martin and, later, British-accented Emma Samms played the spoiled and devious daughter of Blake and Alexis Carrington on TV's *Dynasty*. Fallon was married to handsome do-gooder Jeff Colby (John James), son of Carrington rival Cecil Colby.

FAME

> "You got dreams? You want fame? Well, fame costs. And right here is where you start paying. In sweat."
>
> —LYDIA GRANT (DEBBIE ALLEN)

Fame found fame as a successful big-screen movie, a hit song, and a popular TV series. Directed by Alan Parker, the 1980 musical-drama focused on a diverse group of students at New York's High School of the Performing Arts, the renowned educational institution for aspiring actors, dancers, and musicians. Filmed vignette-style, it followed the dreams, ambitions, and struggles of the talented teens from their freshman year through graduation. The energetic cast included Irene Cara as determined singer-dancer Coco, Paul McCrane as sensitive gay actor Montgomery, Maureen Teefy as timid actress Doris, Gene Anthony Ray as streetwise dancer Leroy, Lee Curreri as headstrong keyboardist Bruno, Barry Miller as Puerto-Rican comic Ralph, Laura Dean as underachieving dancer Lisa, and Antonia Franceschi as promiscuous prima ballerina Hilary. Playing faculty members were Anne Meara as English teacher Elizabeth Sherwood, Albert Hague as music instructor Benjamin Shorofsky, and Debbie Allen as dance teacher Lydia Grant. Songs included the Oscar-winning "Fame," along with "Out Here on My Own," "I Sing the Body Electric," "Red Light," and "Hot Lunch Jam." Irene Cara scored a Top Ten single with "Fame" during the summer of 1980.

Fame the highly praised prime-time TV show aired on NBC from 1982 to 1983 and, later, in first-run syndication from 1983 to 1987. Debbie Allen, Albert Hague, Gene Anthony Ray, and Lee Curreri repeated their roles from the film (Allen also choreographed the elaborate dance sequences). Joining them was a cast of newcomers, most notable being Erica Gimpel as Coco Hernandez, Carlo Imperato as Danny Amatullo, Valerie Landsburg as Doris Schwartz, Lori Singer as Julie Miller, P. R. Paul as Montgomery, Cynthia Gibb as Holly Laird, Billy Hufsey as Christopher Donlon, Nia Peeples as Nicole Chapman, and pop-star Janet Jackson as Cleo Hewitt.

FAMILY AFFAIR

Wholesome ABC-TV sitcom—featuring the dazzling psychedelic-kaleidoscope opening credits (Da-da-da-DAH! da-da-da-da-da . . .)—about a swingin' Manhattan bachelor who finds himself guardian of his deceased brother's three young children from Indiana. Its story lines had the gruff yet soft-spoken Bill Davis (Brian Keith) and his very proper British manservant, Mr. French (Sebastian Cabot), adapting to having to share their chic Fifth Avenue penthouse apartment with the supercute orphans while helping them with a variety of personal dilemmas and acting as substitute parents. The kids were played by Cathy Garver as pretty teenager Cissy, Johnny Whitaker as five-year-old Jody, and Anissa Jones as his twin sister, Buffy. Airing from 1966 to 1971, *Family Affair* was a huge hit with youngsters of the era, who made Buffy and Jody, along with Buffy's beloved rag doll, Mrs. Beasley, household names. Their adorable faces were marketed on a multitude of merchandise, such as board games, coloring books, lunch boxes, and dolls. (How many of you ladies out there had a talking Mrs. Beasley doll?)

Following the cancellation of *Family Affair*, Johnny Whitaker experienced further success starring in a number of Disney films and on the Saturday-morning kiddie program *Sigmund and the Sea Monsters* (1973–74). On the flip side, Anissa Jones's luck ran out: typecast as Buffy, she rarely found work in Hollywood and died of a drug overdose at the age of eighteen in 1976.

FAMILY CIRCUS

Bil Keane's heartwarming cartoon revolving around the humorous everyday events in an average American family. Premiering on February 19, 1960, the newspaper cartoon—drawn within a single circle to symbolize a circus ring—is modeled on Keane's real-life wife and children. There's doting cartoonist Daddy, loving housewife Mommy, and four children: eldest brother Billy, ponytailed sister Dolly, middle brother Jeffy, and baby brother P.J. (added in 1962). Rounding out the principal characters are pet dogs Barfy and Sam, feline Kittycat, and widowed Grandma. *The Family Circus* is the most widely syndicated comic panel, appearing in more than 1,500 newspapers worldwide. Its popularity led to more than sixty *Family Circus* paperbacks and three animated TV specials: *A Special Valentine with the Family Circus* (1978), *A Family Circus Christmas* (1979), and *A Family Circus Easter* (1982). Keane has the distinction of receiving the Reuben Award for Best Cartoonist.

FYI: ▸ Bil Keane's son Glen, who served as the inspiration for the *Family Circus* Billy, grew up to be a prominent animator for the Walt Disney Studios. He designed and animated the Beast for Disney's *Beauty and the Beast* (1991) and more recently did the animation on *Tarzan* (1999).

FAMILY FEUD

"Survey says . . ." ABC-TV's longest-running daytime game show (1976–93) had two teams of five family members competing against each other by answering responses to previously asked questions. Smoochy Brit Richard Dawson is the best-known host (1977–85) of this popular, fast-paced show. It was later rekindled in the 1990s (hosted by Ray Combs) and again in the twenty-first century, with separate stints hosted by Louie Anderson and Richard Karn.

FAMILY TIES

One of the more popular sitcoms of the 1980s, airing on NBC prime time from 1982 to 1989. Set in Columbus, Ohio, the show focused on and drew laughs from the generation gap between a onetime hippie couple who still maintained their liberal 1960s ideas, and their three rather conservative and materialistic Reagan-era offspring. It starred Michael Gross and Meredith Baxter-Birney as parents Steven Keaton, a manager at WKS-TV, the local public TV station, and Elyse Keaton, an architect and community activist. Playing the children were Michael J. Fox as yuppie-in-training Alex, Justine Bateman as underachieving mall-rat Mallory, and Tina Yothers as youngest daughter Jennifer, the only Keaton kid with an inkling of liberalism. A fourth child, Andrew (Brian Bonsall), joined the show in 1986 (he went from being a baby one season to about four years old the next!). Memorable supporting regulars on *Family Ties* included Marc Price as nerdy neighbor Erwin "Skippy" Handleman, Scott Valentine as Mallory's handsome boyfriend Nick Moore, Tracy Pollan (Fox's future wife) as Alex's first girlfriend, Ellen Reed (1985–86), and Courteney Cox as Alex's second girlfriend, Lauren Miller (1987–89). The theme song, "Without Us," was sung by Johnny Mathis and Deniece Williams.

FYI: ▸ Ronald Reagan named *Family Ties* as his favorite TV show during his presidency.

FAMOLARE

"Footloose and Famolare!" Wedgy platform-esque shoe created by Joe Famolare Jr. in the 1970s and noted for having a foot-friendly, four-wave shock-absorbent sole. Famolare's big-selling shoe (the "Get There") was not only comfy but also foxy with a pair of Jordache jeans while doing the boogie-oogie on the disco dance floor!

FANNY PACK

Introduced sometime in the late 1980s, a zippered pouch strapped beltlike around the waist and worn mainly by tourists to store money and other things while sightseeing. They're now considered tacky and a fashion faux pas.

FANTASTIC FOUR

Created in 1961 by Jack Kirby and Stan Lee, this fantastic foursome marked the beginning of the "*Marvel* revolution," an exciting new wave of comic books featuring such superheroes as the Amazing Spider-Man, the Incredible Hulk, Iron Man, Silver Surfer, Sub-Mariner, Thor, and The X-Men. The Fantastic Four were a quartet of scientists who were blasted by strange cosmic rays while flying their rocket ship through space. The radiation exposure transformed Dr. Reed Richards into elastic Mr. Fantastic; his wife, Susan, into vanishing Invisible Girl; her brother, Johnny Storm, into blazing Human Torch; and Ben Grimm into the beastly, granite-like Thing. They donned blue tights, had the number "4" emblazoned on their chests, and zoomed about in the elaborately implemented Fantasticar to battle evildoers, such as the iron-masked Dr. Doom, Mole Man, and Diablo. From 1967 to 1970, a *Fantastic Four* Saturday-morning cartoon was produced by Hanna-Barbera.

FANTASTIC VOYAGE

Based on the novel by Isaac Asimov, this 1966 sci-fi movie told the futuristic tale of a medical team in a hi-tech submarine who are miniaturized to microscopic size, then injected into the body of a wounded defector scientist from the Soviet bloc to perform a delicate brain surgery. Trouble arises when it is discovered that one of the crew is a double agent sent to botch the voyage. Things get even dicer when the doctors are threatened by the body's natural defense system and race against time to complete the journey before their bodies revert to normal size. Directed by Richard Fleischer, the fantastic film starred Stephen Boyd as Grant, Raquel Welch as Cora Peterson, Donald Pleasence as Dr. Michaels, Arthur Kennedy as Dr. Duvall, and William Redfield as Captain Bill Owens. An unforgettable scene shows sexy Raquel, wearing a clingy rubber bodysuit, being menaced by giant antibodies. The amazing special effects and eye-dazzling production designs won Academy Awards. Inspired a cartoon show that aired on Saturday mornings from 1968 to 1970.

FANTASY ISLAND

Welcome to Fantasy Island, a tropical resort where guests come to live out their dreams. Airing on ABC-TV from 1978 to 1984, this adventure series was similar to *The Love Boat*, which it followed on Saturday evenings. Each episode had two interwoven tales and starred such has-been celebs as Sonny Bono, Georgia Engel, Roddy McDowall, Barbi Benton, and Marcia Wallace. Greeting each visitor as they arrived by plane was handsome and suave Mr. Roarke (Ricardo Montalban), the mysterious proprietor of the glamorous island paradise. He was assisted by Tattoo (Hervé Villechaize), a dwarf with a heavy accent. Most of the stories were morality lessons, as each guest came to realize that their everyday life back home wasn't so bad after all.

FARM PLAY SETS

Like dollhouses of the Baby Boom era, the barns and silos were made of easy-to-assemble lithographed metal. Typical sets consisted of plastic animals, fences, and farm equipment, such as tractors and plows.

FARRAH FAWCETT FEATHERED HAIR

The biggest hair trend of the 1970s, thanks to the luscious frosted locks of Farrah Fawcett-Majors, Wella Balsam shampoo spokes-model and star of TV's *Charlie's Angels*. Farrah wore her blonde hair long and in layers, with each layer feathered back—using a blow-dryer or curling iron—to form airy, bouncy waves. She had the look of a carefree California fox, and teen girls nationwide coveted that look. The most outtasight chicks in high school were the ones who could wear their hair most like Farrah's. These girls were often both envied and despised by those whose fine, wimpy hair would never feather, or, when it did, usually became flat or made limp wienie rolls before the day was over. In fact, in 1978 one Farrah look-alike at a Texas high school had acid thrown in her face by a jealous rival. By the end of the decade, virtually every girl in America had a variation of Farrah's feathered hair!

FYI: ▸ "I'm sure you'll find something beautiful happens to your hair," purred Farrah about her Farrah Fawcett Shampoo, made especially for her and for those who wanted to be her. Fabergé manufactured the Farrah Fawcett line of hair products and beauty soaps in 1978.

FARRAH FAWCETT POSTER

Selling more than eight million copies, this was the most sensational pinup since the days of World War II when movie bombshells Betty Grable and Rita Hayworth looked out on the barracks of lonely G.I.'s. This poster featured a kittenish Farrah wearing an undersized, one-piece red swimsuit standing in front of a multicolored striped Indian blanket, displaying major nipple erection while flashing a radiant Ultra Brite smile with her frothy blonde mane flowing freely around her shoulders. Almost all the boys in America had Farrah pinned up on their bedroom walls or wore her as an iron-on transfer on T-shirts. Released by Pro Art in the fall of 1976, the poster generated a pinup renaissance, with sexpots like Lynda Carter, Suzanne Somers, Susan Anton, Cheryl Ladd, Cheryl Tiegs, and the Dallas Cowboys Cheerleaders hopping on the cheesecake bandwagon.

FAR SIDE

Created by cartoonist Gary Larson, the single-panel comic full of bizarre cows, clowns, cavemen, and fat ladies was considered by some newspaper readers as too weird (they didn't get it), while many others simply worshiped it. Following its 1980 debut in the *San Francisco Chronicle*, the strip soared to great popularity, leading to a number of paperback anthologies and other merchandising items, such as day-to-day desk calendars and greeting cards. Unexpectedly, Larson terminated *The Far Side* in 1995.

FASHION PLATES

Introduced by Tomy Toys in the early 1970s, this creative toy allowed little fashion designers to create an endless array of ensembles by mixing and matching different types of clothing combinations. First you arranged the plastic Fashion Plates, which had indented shapes of various skirts, pants, and tops in the cradle base. Then you placed drawing paper on top and ran a black crayon over the shape. The next step was to flip the plates over to choose from different raised-up patterns and prints (for example, houndstooth, paisley, polka dots, or zig-zag stripes), and likewise run a crayon over that. Finally, you colored in your couture creation.

FAST FOOD

Not only did fast food give our parents a break from time-consuming cooking, it also gave us kids a break from our parents' cooking. As children we loved fast-food restaurants. We were charmed by their advertising icons (Ronald McDonald, Burger King, Big Boy, Chuck E. Cheese, Colonel Sanders, and so on), who enticed us with delicious-tasting, grease-laden foods that came in boxes called Happy Meals (McDonald's) or Fun Meals (Burger Chef). Fast-food joints were also significant spots for juvenile social happenings, like birthday parties, Little League game banquets, or teen after-school hangouts (where the social-pecking order would be established). And with their low, minimum-wage pay, they became the first place of employment for most teenagers—and often the only jobs they could get. The following are fifty of America's best-known fast-food chains from the 1960s through to the twenty-first century.

A&W Root Beer stands
Arby's
Arthur Treacher's
Back Yard Burgers
Big Boy
Blimpie
Burger Chef
Burger King
Captain D's
Carl's Jr.
Chick-Fil-A
Chuck E. Cheese
Church's Chicken
Dairy Queen
Del Taco
Der Wienerschnitzel
Domino's Pizza
Dunkin' Donuts
Godfather's Pizza
Hardee's
In-n-Out Burgers
Jack in the Box
Kentucky Fried Chicken
Koo Koo Roo
Long John Silver's
McDonald's
Mr. Goodcents
Pizza Hut
Pizza Inn
Ponderosa
Popeye's
Pup 'n' Taco
Rax
Red Barn
Roy Rogers
Sambo's
Shakey's Pizza

Show Biz Pizza
Sonic
Steak 'n' Shake
Straw Hat Pizza
Subway
Taco Bell
Taco Bueno
Taco John's
Taco Via
Texas Tom's
Wendy's
Whataburger
White Castle

FYI: ▸ A fast-food joke making the rounds during the 1980s, Q: What did Wendy say when Ronald McDonald pulled down his pants? A: Where's the beef?

FAST TIMES AT RIDGEMONT HIGH

"At Ridgemont High, only the rules get busted." In the fall of 1979, *Rolling Stone* magazine writer Cameron Crowe, baby-faced at age twenty-two, went undercover as a student for a year at an unnamed American high school (rumored to be Clairemont High in San Diego) to chronicle the life of suburban teenagers. Observing their language, fashions, and lifestyle, he turned the exposé into a book, *Fast Times at Ridgemont High*. In 1982, the story was made into a funny, cool, and extremely influential movie about a year in the life of several students who attended Ridgemont High in Southern California and worked at the Sherman Oaks Galleria in the San Fernando Valley.

Written by Crowe and directed by Amy Heckerling, the film was a launching pad for an assembly of young talent, most notably Jennifer Jason Leigh as Stacey Hamilton, a shy, naive fifteen-year-old whose yearning for love and sex leads to an abortion. Others included Judge Reinhold as Stacey's fast-food-employed older brother, Brad Hamilton; Phoebe Cates as Stacey's more experienced best friend, Linda Barrett; Sean Penn as stoned surfer Jeff Spicoli; Robert Romanus as weaselly ticket scalper Mike Damone; and Ray Walston as resolute teacher Mr. Hand. Featured in small bits were Eric Stoltz, Anthony Edwards, Nicolas Cage, and Forest Whitaker. The soundtrack contained a legion of early-1980s pop tunes, including Jackson Browne's Top Ten single "Somebody's Baby," plus others by Oingo Boingo, Quarterflash, Billy Squier, Stevie Nicks, Sammy Hagar, and The Go-Go's.

Fast Times has become a cult favorite, showcasing many pop culture icons of the 1980s, such as Pac-Man, designer jeans, and Pat Benatar look-alikes. Its fast-moving pace and clever dialogue set the standard for dozens of teen comedies to follow, like *Valley Girl* (1983), *Sixteen Candles* (1984), *Better Off Dead* (1985), *Ferris Bueller* (1986), *Pretty in Pink* (1986), *Can't Buy Me Love* (1987), *Some Kind of Wonderful* (1987), and *Say Anything* (1988). In 1995, director Heckerling filmed another high school comedy for a new generation of teens: the brilliant *Clueless*, starring Alicia Silverstone as popular matchmaker Cher Horowitz.

FAT ALBERT AND THE COSBY KIDS

Hey, hey, hey! It's Faaaaaaaaat Albert—and you're gonna have a good time with Bill Cosby's highly praised Saturday-morning cartoon show, airing on CBS-TV from 1972 to 1980. Hosted by the Cos himself, it was based on his stand-up comedy routines about the gang of boyhood friends he grew up with in North Philadelphia. The leader was bighearted, oversized Fat Albert, lover of food and fun, who used the signature rumbling of "Hey, hey, hey." Fat Albert was heavy and strong—so heavy that he caused the ground to shake when he fell down, so strong that the pavement cracked when he dribbled a basketball. The other Cosby Kids included athletic funster Bill (based on Bill Cosby himself), Bill's little brother Russell, gangly Weird Harold, scheming Rudy, buck-toothed Bucky, oafish Dumb Donald, and oddball Mushmouth. They lived in brownstones in the older section of the city and hung out at a landfill by the railroad tracks, where they formed a boppy musical band with instruments made out of an assortment of junk.

A landmark cartoon, *Fat Albert* was the first geared toward African-American children who lived in ghettos, a segment of the population ignored by Saturday-morning programming. However, its thought-provoking messages about feelings, ethics, and values became popular with kids of all races and social backgrounds.

FATHER GUIDO SARDUCCI

Comedian Don Novello's chain-smoking gossip columnist for the Vatican newspaper *L'Osservatore Romano*, seen on NBC's *Saturday Night Live* in the 1970s.

FAUX TUXEDO SHIRTS

Long-sleeved T-shirts imprinted with the front of a black-tie tuxedo that were often worn by class-clown types to important events like the high school prom.

FAWCETT, FARRAH

> "I saw in Farrah the possibility of a real legend—baseball, apple pie, and Chevrolets."
> —JAY BERNSTEIN, FARRAH'S MANAGER

Remember the hair? The smile? The body? The jiggle? The poster? If you were alive in the 1970s, you had to be brain-dead not to remember the phenomenal popularity of this All-American golden girl, the number-one sex symbol of the decade.

Born February 2, 1947, in Corpus Christi, Texas, the blonde beauty with the dazzling smile attended the University of Texas, where at age eighteen she was voted one of the school's Ten Most Beautiful Women. In 1969, she left Texas for Hollywood to become an actress. Farrah started her career as a model in commercials, best known for hawking Noxzema shaving cream, Ultra Brite toothpaste, Wella Balsam shampoo, and Mercury Cougars. Coinciding with this period, she played bit parts in movies (1970's *Myra Breckinridge* and 1976's *Logan's Run*) and appeared in guest roles on network shows (*Marcus Welby* and *Harry-O*). In 1973, she married actor Lee Majors, and as his "six million dollar wife" used the hyphenated name of Farrah Fawcett-Majors.

Farrah became an overnight sensation in the fall of 1976 when she was cast as one of a trio of girl detectives on the TV series *Charlie's Angels*. Starring as sporty Jill Munroe, she teased, bounced, and jiggled her way through nonsensical plots (remember the skateboard escape or the roller-derby scene?). Her frosted, tousled tresses launched a hairstyle fad, inspiring legions of women to bombard beauty salons for feathered "Farrah" cuts. And then there was the poster featuring Farrah in a red bathing suit. It became the most spectacular seller since World War II and led to a revival in cheesecake pinups. Her face and image also graced scores of merchandising items, including dolls, toys, T-shirts, notebooks, beanbag chairs, hundreds of magazine covers, and a line of Farrah Fawcett hair and beauty products by Fabergé.

Growing tired of the weekly grind, Farrah quit the enormously popular series after only a single season. She wanted to prove herself as a movie actress, but only made a string of mediocre films: *Somebody Killed Her Husband* (1978), referred to by one critic as "Somebody Killed Her Career"; *Sunburn* (1979); and *Saturn 3* (1980). By the end of the 1970s, she split from Lee, dropped the hyphen, moved in with boyfriend Ryan O'Neal, and sheared her trademark locks. Farrah strived for legitimacy as an actress, earning the respect of her critics with both the 1983 off-Broadway production of *Extremities*, playing a battered rape victim who turns the tables on her rapist, and the 1984 TV movie *The Burning Bed*, starring as an abused wife who kills her sadistic husband (one of the highest-rated made-for-TV movies ever).

In later years, Farrah experienced controversy due to an infamous June 6, 1997, appearance on David Letterman's *Late Show*. Promoting her Playboy Channel TV special, the blonde bombshell came off disoriented while rambling and straining to finish sentences, prompting speculations of drug addiction and mental illness. She denied the accusations, claiming she was only being playful and that her behavior was intentional. Comedienne Janeane Garofalo drew laughs on a later Letterman episode when she lost her train of thought and exclaimed, "I'm so Farrah right now!" Despite having her private life scrutinized by the tabloids, Farrah perseveres, and she seems to be heading toward a new career as a character actress in such films as Robert Duvall's *The Apostle* (1998).

FEBRUARY 3, 1959

The day the music died. Rock 'n' roll legends Buddy Holly, Ritchie Valens, and the Big Bopper were tragically killed when their tiny aircraft crashed in a field near Mason City, Iowa, during a snowstorm. Inspired Don McLean to write and record the million-selling single "American Pie" in 1971.

"FEELINGS"
Whoa. Whoa. Whoa. "Feelings," written and sung in such a heartfelt way by Brazilian Morris Albert, was a Top Ten hit in the summer of 1975. It became one of the "cliché" songs of the 1970s, rivaling "Evergreen" and "You Light Up My Life" as an overplayed staple at weddings, proms, and lounge piano bars. The million-seller earned two Grammy nominations: Song of the Year and Best Male Pop Vocal Performance.

FELIX THE CAT
Created by cartoonist Otto Messmer in 1919, the "wonderful, wonderful" cat was once the best-known animated figure in the world (in the years before Walt Disney's Mickey Mouse). Spunky and clever, the wide-eyed black feline who could turn his expressive tail into anything first appeared in a series of silent cartoon shorts, before debuting as a newspaper comic strip (1920s) and a comic book (1930s). Felix's appearance was revamped by animator Joe Oriolo in 1960 to appeal to young Baby Boomers and given a new gimmick: his bag of magic tricks.

FERDIN, PAMELYN
Prolific nasal-voiced, redheaded child TV actress, circa 1965–75 (born February 4, 1959, in Los Angeles), better known for providing the voices of Lucy Van Pelt in the *Peanuts* cartoons and Fern Arable in the animated *Charlotte's Web* movie (1973). On TV, Ferdin starred as a regular cast member on the educational series *Curiosity Shop*; as a friend of Johnny and Scott Stuart on *Sigmund and the Sea Monsters*; and as Felix Unger's daughter on *The Odd Couple*. Today she is an avid animal-rights activist.

FERNANDO
"You look marvelous!" In the mid-1980s, Spanish-accented movie star Fernando Lamas, the papa of cheesy action-star Lorenzo, was spoofed hilariously by Billy Crystal on NBC's *Saturday Night Live*. Crystal played him as a silver-haired, starry-eyed host of a TV talk show, *Fernando's Hideaway*, whose philosophy was "It is better to look good than to feel good."

FERN ARABLE
From the well-loved book *Charlotte's Web* comes this imaginative farm girl who befriends Wilbur the pig, Charlotte the spider, and a barnyard of other animals on her uncle Homer Zuckerman's farm.

FERNWOOD
Small fictional hamlet, seen in the mock TV soap *Mary Hartman, Mary Hartman*, is the Ohio home of neurotic housewife Mary Hartman, aspiring country singer Loretta Haggers, the penis-exposing Fernwood Flasher (Mary's grandfather Raymond Larkin), and the cheesy talk show *Fernwood Tonight* on local station WZAZ-TV, Channel 6, hosted by Barth Gimble.

FERRIGNO, LOU
The famous bodybuilder, a former Mr. America (1973) and Mr. Universe (1973 and 1974), who was 60 percent deaf and had a halting speech defect. Played Bill Bixby's monstrous alter ego in *The Incredible Hulk* from 1978 to 1982. The muscleman's dimensions: six foot five, 275 pounds, fifty-nine-inch chest, nineteen-inch neck, and twenty-two-inch biceps.

FERRIS BUELLER'S DAY OFF

"Life moves pretty fast.
If you don't stop and look around
once in a while, you could miss it."
—FERRIS BUELLER (MATTHEW BRODERICK)

The 1986 comedy movie was a hit among teenagers who enjoyed beating the system made up of parents and teachers. Directed by John Hughes, it starred Matthew Broderick as seventeen-year-old Ferris Bueller, a self-confident, smooth-talking, well-liked whiz kid in dire need of a day off. Ferris fakes sick and skips school (Glenbrook North High in suburban Chicago), accompanied by pretty British girlfriend Sloane Peterson (Mia Sara) and reluctant best pal Cameron Frye (Alan Ruck). The crazy threesome borrow Cameron's father's prized 1961 Ferrari convertible without permission and head for downtown Chicago. Once there, they cut loose at the top of the Sears Tower, catch a Cubs game at Wrigley Field, and "twist and shout" at the German-American Appreciation Day Parade. However, our hero's nemeses—suspicious Principal Ed Rooney (Jeffrey Jones) and jealous sister Jeannie Bueller (Jennifer Grey)—are hot on his tracks, hell-bent on catching him in the act of ditching school. Plucky Edie McClurg gives a humorous spin as Grace, Rooney's nosy secretary.

The *Ferris* soundtrack features an eclectic mix of music, including Yello's "Oh Yeah," Wayne Newton's "Danke Schoen," and The Beatles' "Twist and Shout. In 1990, the film inspired a short-lived TV sitcom, *Ferris Bueller*, starring Charlie Schlatter as Ferris and, before she was a *Friend*, Jennifer Aniston as sister Jeannie. "Save Ferris!"

FESTRUNK BROTHERS

Extremely funny *Saturday Night Live* skit of the late 1970s, starring Dan Aykroyd as Georg and frequent guest Steve Martin as Yortuk, two "wild and crazy" political refugees from Czechoslovakia who, wearing loud, unbuttoned polyester shirts and tight slacks, cruise New York City bars looking for "foxes!" and their big American breasts.

FIELD, SALLY

Sunny TV actress turned film star whose prime-time role as *The Flying Nun* (1967–70), as well as the earlier surf bunny *Gidget* (1965–66) and, later, ESP-endowed *Girl with Something Extra* (1973–74), was difficult for her to live down. In the late 1970s and 1980s, she broke stereotype by proving herself a serious actress, winning an Emmy Award in 1976 for *Sybil*, followed by not one but two prestigious Oscar statuettes as Best Actress for *Norma Rae* in 1979 and *Places in the Heart* in 1984. (The latter led to her infamous and often mocked acceptance speech: "The first time I didn't feel it, but this time I feel it and I can't deny the fact you like me. Right now, you like me!") Had a greatly publicized romance with male sex symbol Burt Reynolds in the mid-1970s.

FIEVEL MOUSEKEWITZ

An American Tail's sweet Jewish mouse emigrating from Russia who gets separated from his family as they're about to arrive at their new homeland, America, at the turn of the century. Fievel believes that this New Land has no cats and that the streets are paved with cheese.

5th DIMENSION

Imagine, if you will: It's a beautiful day at the park—the sky is blue, the sun is shining, the birds are singing, the butterflies are flittering, and you and your best pal are lazily lounging on a blanket in the grass. A picnic basket full of tasty morsels lies nearby, as well as a chilled bottle of white Zinfandel. In the background, a radio plays a groovin' 5th Dimension song. Life doesn't get any better than this. Popular during the late 1960s and early 1970s, the L.A.-based vocal quintet—known for easy California soul—consisted of Marilyn McCoo, Florence LaRue, Billy Davis Jr., LaMont McLemore, and Ron Townson. Their string of hits includes "Up, Up and Away" (1967), "Stoned Soul Picnic" (1968), "Aquarius/Let the Sunshine In" (1969), "Wedding Bell Blues" (1969), and "One Less Bell to Answer" (1970). Sweethearts McCoo and Davis were married in 1969 and left the band in 1975 to perform as a duo. In 1976, they had a million-selling chart-topper, "You Don't Have to Be a Star (To Be in My Show)."

FYI: ▸ In 1962, at the age of nineteen, Marilyn McCoo was crowned Miss Bronze California, and won the pageant's Grand Talent Award and Miss Congeniality. The following year, she returned to give her crown to the new Miss Bronze California—Florence LaRue!

FILMATION STUDIOS

Animation production studio whose Saturday-morning cartoon shows rivaled Hanna-Barbera throughout the late 1960s and 1970s. Gave us *The Archies* (1968–78), *Aquaman* (1968–69), *Batman* (1969–70), *Superman* (1969–70), *The Hardy Boys* (1969–71), *Sabrina, the Teenage Witch* (1970–74), *The Groovie Goolies* (1970–72), *The Brady Kids* (1972–74), *Fat Albert and the Cosby Kids* (1972–79), *Lassie's Rescue Rangers* (1973–74), *Star Trek* (1973–75), *The New Adventures of Gilligan* (1974–77), and *Tarzan* (1976–79). Later produced the syndicated *He-Man and Masters of the Universe* (1983) and sister show *She-Ra: Princess of Power* (1985).

FINGER

An action given when one was really pissed off: extending the middle finger upward as an obscene gesture. Also known as "flipping someone off" or "the bird."

FINGER DINGS

Finger-powered "puppet" dolls in which you placed two fingers inside the legs to make them walk, run, dance, skate, kick, and jump. Introduced by Remco

Toys during the Swingin' '60s (1969, to be exact), there were three Finger Dings: mincing and leaping Betty Ballerina, go-go dancing Millie Mod, and figure-eight-skating Sally Ice Skater. In an attempt to appeal to boys, Remco issued Adventure Boy with three different actions sets, consisting of a snowmobile, a spacecraft, or a skymobile.

FINGERLESS GLOVES

Some kids would simply cut the fingers off their winter gloves, but the height of 1980s cool were the lacy black ones worn by pop stars Prince and Madonna. They were reminiscent of the fingerless gloves that pickpocketing vagabonds (like characters from a Charles Dickens book) would've warn in the late 1800s.

FIREBALL XL-5

Captivating British TV import noted for employing "supermarionation," a seemingly "live" puppet effect using wires and plastic models, invented by Gerry and Sylvia Anderson. Airing from 1963 to 1965, the futuristic kids' show centered around Colonel Steve Zodiac from Space City, who piloted the 300-foot-long Fireball XL-5 spacecraft on adventures throughout the galaxy. Accompanying him were the beautiful blonde doctor Venus, eccentric scientist Professor Matic, automaton autopilot Robert the Robot, and pet Zoonie, a lazoon who mimicked his human masters. Other puppet shows created by the Andersons were *Thunderbirds*, *Stingray*, *Supercar*, and *Captain Scarlet*.

FISHER-PRICE CHATTER PHONE

Introduced in 1962 by Fisher-Price, this is an all-time favorite pull toy for youngsters of preschool age. When pulled, the telephone makes a unique "chatter-chatter" sound and its eyes roll up and down giving a friendly expression. When you dial, a bell makes a happy ring-a-ling noise ("ring, ring"). Another well-loved Fisher-Price telephone is the Pop Up Chime Phone, introduced in 1965: You press the numbers to play musical chimes and a blonde doll pops up and out when you press "O" for Operator.

FISHER-PRICE CORN POPPER

"Poppety-pop-pop. . . ." A classic childhood toy from Fisher-Price. Preschoolers pushed this plaything across floors and other flat surfaces to make the multicolored balls pop, pop, pop inside its clear popper dome. The Corn Popper was launched in 1968.

FISHER-PRICE PLAY FAMILY SETS

For those born after the 1950s, it was almost impossible to have grown up without one or more of these play sets. It all started around 1959, when Fisher-Price Toys introduced the happy Safety School Bus, which came with six removable wooden students known as Fisher-Price Little People. (Do you remember the blonde with pigtails, or the scowling bully with the side-cap?) Shortly afterward, a whole village of Play Family sets were created, keeping energetic tots busy in their playrooms. There was the Play Family Fire Station, Schoolhouse, Hospital, Airport, Auto Garage, Farm, Zoo, Family House, Houseboat, Camper, Western Town, Castle, Circus Train, Ferris Wheel, and even a Sesame Street Play Family complete with Big Bird, Cookie Monster, and Bert and Ernie. Like the school bus, all these came with the cute peg-type people and animals designed to fit securely into play furniture and moving play vehicles. Parents liked the Play Family sets because they were durable and could be handed down from sibling to sibling.

FISHER-PRICE PULL TOYS

Since 1930, the toy company has been the leader in pull toys aimed at preschool children. These enduring playthings featured cheerful lithographed wooden and plastic characters set on polyethylene wheels that wobbled, twirled, and chimed their way into a youngster's heart. Which of these engaging favorites did you drag around as a toddler: The Snoopy Sniffer? Queen Buzzy Bee? Cackling Hen? Tuggy Turtle? Big Bill Pelican? Suzie Seal? Wobbles the Dog? Prancing Pony? Jolly Jalopy? Toot-Toot Engine? Safety School Bus? Eight-Key Pull-a-Tune Xylophone? The Chatter Telephone?

FISHER-PRICE TV-RADIOS

Wind up wooden music boxes in the shape of portable radios, equipped with carrying handles and spring aerial, which played nursery-rhyme melodies (like "Farmer in the Dell," "Jack and Jill," and "Ten Little Indians") while a dial turned to illustrate the tune.

FISHNET STOCKINGS
Resembling the open-weave material used by fishermen to net fish, these sultry mesh stockings were fashionable among pinup girls of the 1950s, mod females of the 1960s, punk chicks of the 1970s, New Wave women of the 1980s, and Goth gals of the 1990s.

FIZZIES
Manufactured by the Warner-Lambert Pharmaceutical Company from 1962 to 1970, these "mystic" tablets dissolved and fizzled when dropped in a glass of water (sort of like Alka-Seltzer), becoming an instant soft drink once ice was added. The different Fizzies flavors included Orange, Grape, Cherry, Cola, Root Beer, Strawberry, and Lemon-Lime.

FYI: ▸ Fizzies only had four calories per drink, making them ideal for chubby kids between and during meals!

FLANNEL SHIRTS
Once associated with brawny lumberjacks and western wranglers, the colorfully plaid flannel became a fashion staple of male slacker-types during the grunge movement of the 1990s. Their typical uniform consisted of a flannel shirt over an old concert T-shirt (preferably Pearl Jam or Nirvana), along with worn-out jeans and combat boots.

FLASHDANCE
"Something happens when she hears the music. It's her freedom. It's her fire. It's her life." During the mid-1980s, Americans were stricken with a strange fever that caused them to wear torn, oversized, shoulder-baring sweatshirts, wrap their foreheads in decorative headbands, take leg warmers outside the ballet studio as a fashion statement, and dance like a maniac. The origin of this intense frenzy was *Flashdance*, a little film that became the monster sensation of 1983, grossing more than $50 million. Showcasing glitzy choreography, high-energy music, great clothing ideas, and a fairy-tale ending, it starred dark-haired, doe-eyed Jennifer Beals—a then unknown nineteen-year-old college student—as Alex Owens, steel welder by day, sexy flashdancer by night. Living in Pittsburgh, Pennsylvania, Alex is adored by her grumpy pop, Frank (Phil Burns), and ice-skater sis, Jeanie (Sunny Johnson). She aspires to get into a professional ballet school and is mentored by a saintly old woman, Hanna Long (Lilia Skala), who was once a legendary prima ballerina. Along the way, she falls in love with her handsome steel-mill boss, Nick Hurley (Michael Nouri). The Giorgio Moroder soundtrack became as big a hit as the movie, spawning two number-one hits: the bouncy "Flashdance . . . What a Feeling" by Irene Cara, and the ultrahyper "Maniac" by Michael Sembello. Adrian Lyne directed.

FYI: ▸ Jennifer Beals didn't do her own flashdancing; dancer Marine Jahan doubled for her, wearing a curly wig.

FLATSY
"They're flat—and that's that!" From 1968 to 1970, Ideal Toys produced this line of five-inch-high fashion dolls whose name came from their flat shape, measuring a mere half an inch thick. A Flatsy had long hair that came in wild psychedelic colors, such as blue, green, pink, orange, and yellow. A wire ran through the body (just like Gumby), allowing her to be bendable and poseable. Like Mattel's Liddle Kiddles, produced earlier in the decade, each Flatsy came packaged in a play set (a picture frame) with accessories to match her personality: sailor Bonnie, birthday girl Candy, weather girl Dewie, chef Cookie, cowgirl Filly, nurse Nancy, car racer Rally, beach girl Sandy, and train engineer Casey (the only male). As the dolls gained popularity, Ideal introduced others in various sizes, like the eight-and-a-half-inch Fashion Flatsies, the two-and-a-half-inch Mini Flatsies, and a Spinderella Flatsy who pirouetted on a stage.

FLAT-TOP
All the cool guys in the 1960s and 1970s had long hair, so it was understandable that boys hated getting their hair cut: It meant dad took them to the barber, where they would end up with a short cut seen only on dorks and squares. The flat-top, circa 1987, was the first time in decades that guys actually wanted an extreme clipper cut, one that resembled the style worn in the military. Fellows flocked to barbershops and salons to have the top of their hair snipped short to the scalp (about half an inch

long) and shaped perfectly flat on top, while the sides were clipped so close you could see right through to the skin. Wicked dudes, like white rapper Vanilla Ice, had head-lines (a.k.a. fades) shaved into the sides and back (the hair was shaved off to form lines, patterns, logos, and initials).

FLEEGLE
Fleegle was the Banana Splits' guitar-strumming beagle and "top banana" who had the lispy voice and the pink tongue always hanging out of his mouth. On *The Banana Splits Adventure Hour*, he moonlighted as The Great Fleegali, a magician whose tricks usually bombed.

FLEMING, PEGGY
The pretty brunette from California was the top female figure-skater of the 1960s. She was the U.S. champion from 1964 to 1968, the world champion from 1966 to 1968, and received the Olympic gold medal in 1968.

FLEX
Remember this shampoo's wild TV commercial from the 1980s? It featured model Patti Hansen in a blue-satin cowgirl outfit equipped with white cowboy hat and cowboy boots and holding and shooting her blow-dryer like a pistol. The ads claimed to provide hair with maximum Flex-ability!

FLEXIBLE FLYER SLEDS
Created by Samuel Leeds Allen in 1889, this original brand of wooden snow sleds had steel runners that were steered by movable crossbar handgrips. Sloshes up childhood memories of awakening on Christmas morning to find that Santa had left one near the Christmas tree, and of spending frosty afternoons sledding on daring hills overlooking low-lying areas, or creating sled chains on snow-stricken neighborhood side streets. The Flexible Flyer spawned hundreds of imitations.

FLINTSTONES
Created by William Hanna and Joseph Barbera in 1960, this now-legendary TV show was prime time's first cartoon before becoming a Saturday-morning fixture from 1967 through the late 1980s. *The Flintstones* centers on a boisterous caveman named Fred Flintstone who, along with dim-witted little buddy and next-door neighbor Barney Rubble, causes all sorts of chaos in the prehistoric town of Bedrock. Fred's wife is levelheaded Wilma, whose best friend is pixyish Betty, Barney's wife. Each couple has one infant child: ponytailed Pebbles Flintstone and superstrong Bamm-Bamm Rubble. Dino, a doglike runtasaurus, is Fred's loyal pet.

Loosely inspired by Jackie Gleason's *Honeymooners* (1955–56), *The Flintstones* is a parody of modern-day suburban life set in prehistoric days—Fred and Wilma lived in a split-level cave house on 345 Stonecave Road. Among the cool Stone Age renderings of twentieth-century gadgetry are a baby mastodon as a vacuum cleaner, a hungry pigasaurus under the kitchen sink as a garbage disposal, a grass-eating dinosaur on wheels as a lawn mower, a bird with a long beak for a needle as a record player, and a pterodactyl as an airliner. In 1994, a live-action *Flintstones* film was produced, starring John Goodman as Fred, Elizabeth Perkins as Wilma, Rick Moranis as Barney, and Rosie O'Donnell as Betty; followed by a sequel, *Flintstones in Viva Rock Vegas* (2000).

Besides appearing on lunch boxes and gazillions of other kiddie merchandise, the Bedrock characters are featured as chewable vitamins for One A Day. On Saturday mornings, youngsters can choose between two sugary-sweet breakfast cereals, Fruity Pebbles or Cocoa Pebbles, while watching reruns of *The Flintstones* and several spin-off series, including *The Pebbles and Bamm-Bamm Show* (1971–76), *The Flintstones Comedy Hour* (1972–73), *Fred and Barney Meet the Shmoo* (1979–80), and *The Flintstone Kids* (1986–88).

FLINTSTONES VITAMINS
"Yabba-dabba-doo!" Finally, moms could get kids to take daily vitamins hassle-free with these chewable, fruity-flavored favorites shaped like the beloved Bedrock characters—Fred, Wilma, Pebbles, Dino, Barney, Bamm-Bamm, Cavemobile—minus Betty. (It wasn't until the 1990s that Betty became a vitamin.) Introduced in 1969 by One A Day.

FLIP
The official hairdo of the 1960s, generally worn somewhere above the collarbone, ends flipped up and out neatly and evenly all around the circumference, with

the crown area teased and a whole lot of Aqua Net sprayed to hold it all in place. Brings back memories of fun-loving young gals adorned in mod A-line dresses and white knee-high boots who held "status" careers of the 1960s, such as airline stewardess, go-go dancer, and Playboy Bunny. This was the style of choice for perky actresses—like Doris Day, Patty Duke, Sally Field, Annette Funicello, Mary Tyler Moore, Elizabeth Montgomery, and the queen of the flip, "That Girl" Marlo Thomas (she had the best around).

FLIP-FLOPS

These humble foam-rubber sandals are perfect for a day at the pool. The name came from the "flip-flop, flip-flop, flip-flop" sound created when walking around in a pair.

FYI: ▸ In the Australian dragfest *The Adventures of Priscilla, Queen of the Desert* (1994), one of the outlandish outfits created by Oscar-winning costume designer Lizzy Gardiner included a dress completely made out of pink flip-flops!

FLIPPER

"Faster than lightning" dolphin star, called TV's "King of the Sea," whose weekly adventures aired on prime time from 1964 to 1968. As the aquatic equivalent of Lassie, Flipper was a smart, kind, and gentle creature who befriended two boys, fifteen-year-old Sandy (Luke Halpin) and ten-year-old Bud (Tommy Norden). The youngsters lived with their widower dad, Porter Ricks (Brian Kelly), a marine preserve ranger, in a cottage near the Florida shore community of Coral Key Park. "Clickety click! Clickety click!" chirped Flipper as he guided and aided the family in protecting the marine refuge from wrongdoers. Popular with kids, the wholesome NBC series was based on the 1963 motion picture, starring Chuck Connors.

FYI: ▸ Although Flipper was a male dolphin, he was played by a female named Susie. He was not the first or last gender-bending animal star. The many collies who portrayed Lassie over the years were all male, a female simian named Vicky starred as Cheetah on the *Tarzan* TV series, and, more recently, the macho Taco Bell Chihuahua was played by a lovely muchacha named Gidget.

FLIP WILSON SHOW

"The devil made me do it!" The hippest show on prime-time TV during the 1970s, and the first variety hour to star a black performer. Airing from 1970 to 1974, it was hosted by stand-up comic Flip Wilson, who played a collection of humorous characters based on outrageous Harlem stereotypes. There was the not-so-honest, gospel-preaching Reverend Leroy of the Church of What's Happening Now; private-eye Danny Danger; Good-Time Ice-Cream man Herbie; Wilson's everyman, Freddie Johnson; and everyone's favorite: sassy hussy Geraldine Jones. Different guest stars joined Flip in various sketches or to sing a song or two. In 1970, Shindana Toys released a talking, two-sided Flip Wilson doll featuring Flip on one side ("Don't touch me. You don't know me that well!") and the blonde Geraldine on the other ("The devil made me buy this dress!").

FYI: ▸ Born Clerow Wilson in New Jersey, Flip was later nicknamed for his naughty, "flip" humor.

FLOCK OF SEAGULLS

New Wave band whose lead singer, Mike Score, had the distinction of having the weirdest hairdo around (and, believe me, there was a lot of competition). He styled the sides of his bleached-blond hair up to the center, flattened it on top, and pointed it toward the front. It looked like the bow of an old windjammer ready for sailing. Other members of the group included Frank Maudsley, Paul Reynolds, and Score's brother, Ali. Besides the odd hair, they were known for three Top Forty hits: "I Ran (So Far Away)" (1982), "Space Age Love Song" (1983), and "Missing (If I Had a Photograph of You)" (1983).

FLORIDA EVANS

Esther Rolle's housemaid on *Maude*, who would later have her own hit TV spin-off, *Good Times*. Diligent and devoted, Florida worked hard providing for her three children (J.J., Thelma, and Michael) and protecting them from the hardships of ghetto life in Chicago's South Side. Became a widow after husband James was killed in a car wreck.

FLORIDA ORANGE BIRD

Created by the Walt Disney Studios in the early 1970s, a cheery bird with an orange for its head, used by Florida's Department of Citrus to promote the sale of citrus fruit. Orange Bird's TV ads had him fluttering around the head of homophobe Anita Bryant as she sang about the joys of Florida O.J.

FLOUNDER (DOCTOR DOLITTLE)
The windjammer in which Doctor Dolittle and friends sailed off to the South Seas in search of the Giant Pink Sea Snail and Great Lunar Moth.

FLOUNDER (*LITTLE MERMAID*)
Ariel's rotund flounder fish friend that tags along with the mermaid princess in the 1989 Disney animated classic.

FLOWER CHILD

> "If you're going to San Francisco,
> be sure to wear some flowers in your hair."
> —SCOTT MCKENZIE, SINGER

A hippie person from the days of Haight-Ashbury in San Francisco, circa Summer of Love 1967, who was peace-loving and garnished his or her hair with flowers (usually daisies). Poet Allen Ginsberg coined the hippie phrase "flower power" during a rally against the Vietnam War.

FLUFFERNUTTER
Classic childhood sandwich containing gooey Marshmallow Fluff and peanut butter, preferably eaten on white Wonder Bread while watching *Bewitched* or *I Dream of Jeannie*.

FLUFFY
Carol's cat, who, along with Mike's dog, Tiger, caused the ruckus at the Brady wedding. The orange-colored feline (real name: Rhubarb) was seen only during the first season of *The Brady Bunch* (1969–70).

FLYING NUN
A classic TV fantasy about an American nun at Convent San Tanco—located atop the highest hill in San Juan, Puerto Rico—who had the ability to fly. It starred Sally Field in the title role as bubbly, high-spirited Elsie Ethrington, who took vows as Sister Bertrille and whose petite size (five foot two and ninety pounds) and wide, wing-shaped white cornet sent her soaring when the tropical trade winds blew. She used this unusual gift in her efforts to do good for the community, but awkward landings often left her in wacky sitcom predicaments. Costarring were Alejandro Rey as rich and handsome playboy Carlos Ramirez, Madeleine Sherwood as the strict Mother Superior, Marge Redmond as funny Sister Jacqueline, and Shelley Morrison as Sister Sixto—a Puerto Rican nun whose English wasn't very good. Airing on ABC from 1967 to 1969, the entertaining show was based on the 1965 book *The Fifteenth Pelican* by Tere Rios.

FYI: ▸ The Flying Nun explained her ability to fly: "When lift plus thrust is greater than load plus drag."

FOGHORN LEGHORN
The loudmouth Southern rooster, I say the loudmouth Southern rooster, had a habit of repeating himself, a fondness for the song "Camptown Races," and a strong dislike for spunky Henery Hawk, the little chicken hawk who was always trying to catch him. Foghorn Leghorn made his debut in the Warner Brothers cartoon short "Walky Talky Hawky" in 1946.

FONDUE
Back in the 1970s, eating fondue was a social event. At parties around the nation (or for that matter around the world, because this social dish originated in Zurich, Switzerland), guests would gather around a fondue pot containing bubbling hot melted cheese and dunked chunks of fruit, bread, or meat speared on long forks. These feasts popped up everywhere, from intimate dinners of four to large buffets for twenty-four, from festive birthday parties and proud bar mitzvahs to elegant Yuletide celebrations. Creative hosts would come up with a variety of fondue recipes to serve to happy guests, including Teriyaki Beef Fondue, Seafood Fondue, Mexican Fondue Monterey, and Pigs-in-the-Blanket Fondue. And for those with a sweet tooth, there was a gooey Milk Chocolate Fondue in which you dipped whole strawberries, chunks of pineapple, and angel-food-cake cubes.

FONZIE
One of the most popular icons of the 1970s was Arthur Fonzarelli (a.k.a. the Fonz or Fonzie), a TV

character played by Henry Winkler in the hit series *Happy Days* from 1974 to 1984. Fonzie was a streetwise, motorcycle-riding greaser who wore his dark hair slicked back and a uniform consisting of a black leather jacket, a white T-shirt, Levi's denim jeans, and black cycle boots. He was a high school dropout who worked hard as an auto mechanic and lived in an apartment above Howard and Marion Cunningham's garage (he called them Mr. and Mrs. C; Marion called him Arthur). A ladies' man, the Fonz had magical powers over chicks and could make any girl in Milwaukee swoon (except motorcycle queen Pinky Tuscadero). People did what he said at the snap of his fingers, and when it was time for a serious meeting, everyone gathered in his "office"—the men's restroom at Arnold's Drive-In.

The epitome of 1950s cool, Fonzie started out as a supporting character on *Happy Days*, sharply contrasting with Richie Cunningham's goody-goody image. After catching the fancy of younger viewers, he became an overnight star with many of the show's antics centering on him—and Henry Winkler's salary jumped from $750 an episode to $80,000. Fonzisms such as "Aaaayyh!" "Sit on it!" "Correctamundo!" and a thumbs-up gesture became trademarks that kids loved to mimic. Today, his leather jacket is enshrined at the Smithsonian Institution in Washington, D.C.

FOOSBALL

Exciting table action game popular at arcades, bars, fraternities, and bachelor apartments—like Joey and Chandler's pad on *Friends*—that let players control an entire soccer team. Each opposing side of the foosball table has four handles attached to rods with eleven traditionally outfitted, three-dimensional soccer players attached to them. Players manipulate the rods to control the team, allowing them to hit the soccer ball, score points, and make the winning goal. The kids who play foosball are often very good; those who aren't, don't bother playing.

FOOTLOOSE

Inspired by the box-office success of the previous year's *Flashdance*, this energetic 1984 youth musical starred Kevin Bacon as Ren McCormack, a teenager from a big city (Chicago) who finds himself uprooted to a small conservative town in the middle of the Bible Belt (Bomont, Iowa) where rock music and dancing have been made illegal. Unable to control his dancing feet, the free-spirited city slicker confronts the town's small-minded preacher, the Reverend Shaw Moore (John Lithgow), to make it legal again. It won't be easy, because the crusading Reverend Moore blames sinful rock 'n' roll for the accidental death of his son. Directed by Herbert Ross, the film's supporting cast includes Lori Singer as Ariel, Reverend Moore's rebellious daughter and Ren's love interest, and Chris Penn (Sean's brother) as Willard, the oafish country hick whom Ren teaches how to dance. The soundtrack spawned a number of Top Ten hits, including the inspiring title tune by Kenny Loggins, "Let's Hear It for the Boy" by Deniece Williams, "Dancing in the Sheets" by Shalamar, "Holding Out for a Hero" by Bonnie Tyler, and "Almost Paradise . . . Love Theme from *Footloose*" by Heart's Ann Wilson and Loverboy's Mike Reno.

FORD TORINO

Here I'm talking about the 1974 jacked-up version, colored bright red with a white stripe down the side, known as the "Starsky" car, from the one driven by Paul Michael Glaser on the 1970s TV show *Starsky and Hutch*. Youngsters (like my kid sister) used to squeal with delight when a look-alike came zooming down the neighborhood street.

FOSTER, JODIE

Born on November 19, 1962, in Los Angeles, the movie actress began her long career in show business at the age of three, doing commercial work—she was a model for the little Coppertone girl. Blonde and tomboyish, she was a precocious child star who first came to attention in 1970 playing Joey Kelly, a friend of Eddie Corbett's on the primetime series *The Courtship of Eddie's Father*. Her early film work consisted of Disney fare: *Napoleon and Samantha* (1972), *Tom Sawyer* (1973), *Freaky Friday* (1976), and *Candleshoe* (1977). In 1976, she shocked filmgoers with her Oscar-nominated portrayal of Iris Steensman, a fourteen-year-old prostitute in Martin Scorsese's *Taxi Driver*. Never one for mainstream roles, her teen-movie roster included the offbeat *Bugsy Malone* (1976), *The Little Girl Who Lives Down the Lane* (1976), *Carny* (1980), and *Foxes* (1980).

As a Yale freshman in the fall of 1980, Foster was painfully thrown in worldwide headlines after John Hinckley's attempted assassination of President Ronald Reagan. A crazed fan, Hinckley had been stalking Foster and thought killing the President would impress her. (His inspiration came from the story line of *Taxi Driver.*) The unplanned notoriety following the tragic shooting made Foster a target of the deranged, resulting in her temporary retreat from the Hollywood limelight.

Today, she is an accomplished adult actress and director, the recipient of two Best Actress Oscars (1988's *The Accused* and 1991's *Silence of the Lambs*), and star of acclaimed films, such as *Stealing Home* (1988), *Little Man Tate* (1991), *Sommersby* (1993), *Maverick* (1994), *Nell* (1994), and *Contact* (1997).

FOX, MICHAEL J.

On prime time's *Family Ties* (1982–89), the squeaky-clean, young-looking, diminutive actor (born June 9, 1961, in Edmonton, Canada) stole the show as archconservative teenager Alex Keaton. He would later become a huge star in films, such as *Back to the Future* (1985) and its two sequels, along with *Teen Wolf* (1985), *The Secret of My Success* (1987), *Bright Lights, Big City* (1988), *Casualties of War* (1989), and *Doc Hollywood* (1991). In 1996, he starred in another prime-time series, *Spin City.* Stricken with Parkinson's disease since 1991, he quit the popular sitcom in the spring of 2000 to spend time combating the debilitating illness. Married to actress Tracy Pollan, who played his girlfriend Ellen on *Family Ties.*

FYI: ▸ A rock 'n' roll fanatic, Michael J. Fox once purchased a pair of guitars owned by Eric Clapton at an auction for $79,000.

FOX AND THE HOUND

A touching 1981 movie about the unlikely friendship between Tod, an orphaned fox cub, and Copper, a bloodhound puppy. Although natural enemies, the adorable twosome become the best of friends one summer, under the watchful eye of plump owl Big Mama and kindly human Widow Tweed. Mean-spirited hunter Amos Slade, believing it is against the law of nature for a fox and a hound to get along, takes Copper away for the winter to train him as a hunting dog. Widow Tweed takes Tod to the safety of a game preserve, where he falls in love with Vixey, a beautiful vixen. The story turns bittersweet the next spring when the grown-up dog and fox become hunter and hunted. Friendship conquers all when Copper steps in the line of Slade's gunfire to save Tod's life. Based on the book by Daniel P. Mannix, this was one of the better Disney animated features of the early 1980s. Providing voices were Keith Coogan as young Tod, Mickey Rooney as adult Tod, Corey Feldman as young Copper, Kurt Russell as adult Copper, Sandy Duncan as Vixey, Jack Albertson as Amos Slade, Pearl Bailey as Big Mama, and Jeanette Nolan as Widow Tweed. The soundtrack includes Bailey's heartfelt "Best of Friends."

FOXES

"Teenage dopers. What a waste."
—DEIRDRE (KANDICE STROH)

A 1980 teen exposé about four suburban girls coping with social and emotional problems (drugs, sex, broken homes, and abusive parents) brought on by growing up in L.A.'s sprawling San Fernando Valley. Jodie Foster heads the cast as Jeanie, a sensible sixteen-year-old trying to understand her life while besieged with the problems of her three best friends: Annie, Madge, and Deirdre. Starring as the other Foxes were feathered-haired, bleached-blonde Cherie Currie (former lead singer of The Runaways) as drug-addicted runaway Annie; Marilyn Kagan as overweight, big-hearted Madge; and Kandice Stroh as flirtatious Deirdre. The film's most sobering moment occured when Annie, a totally wasted hitchhiker, accepts a lift from a pair of married perverts whose attempt to molest her led to her premature death. Co-stars included *Tiger Beat* hunk Scott Baio as the Foxes' skateboarding ally, Brad; Randy Quaid as Madge's much-older boyfriend, Jay, whose pad gets wrecked when a party gets out of control; and Sally Kellerman as Jeanie's embittered mom. The soundtrack contains a driven Giorgio Moroder music score and the melancholy disco ballad "On the Radio" by Donna Summer. Adrian Lyne, a former TV commercial director, made his big-screen directorial debut with *Foxes.* (Renowned as a visual stylist, he would go on to film *Flashdance, 9 1/2 Weeks, Fatal Attraction,* and *Indecent Proposal.*)

FOXY BROWN

Radically violent blaxploitation film, released in 1974, starring sexy Pam Grier as an angry nurse who infiltrates a Mafia drug ring disguised as a hooker to avenge the slaying of her undercover federal-agent boyfriend.

FYI: ▸ Foxy Brown, a popular 1990s female rapper from Brooklyn, took her stage name from Pam Grier's action character. Foxy's real name: Inga Marchand.

FOZZIE BEAR

"The comedian's a bear." The fuzzy yellow bear—a Jim Henson Muppet named after puppeteer Frank Oz, who also voices the character—is a stand-up comic who continuously tells unfunny jokes and gets pelted by rotten tomatoes. "Wocka! Wocka!"

FRACTURED FAIRY TALES

A regular supporting segment on the *Bullwinkle and Rocky* cartoon program, featuring twisted send-ups of classic childhood fairy tales. Narrated by character actor Edward Everett Horton.

FRAGRANCES

> "What do I wear to bed?
> Why, Chanel No. 5, of course."
> —MARILYN MONROE

What was your smell? Was it spicy, like Yves Saint Laurent's Opium? Floral, like Gloria Vanderbilt? Musky, like Jovan's unisex Musk? Preppy, like both Ralph Lauren's Polos? Or sweet, like Love's Baby Soft? Did you smell like your mom (White Shoulders)? Your dad (Old Spice)? Kid sister (Tinkerbell)? Big brother (Hai Karate)? Or worse, your grandma (Chantilly)?

Following is a list of fifty colognes and perfumes that we grew up with (twenty-five women's, twenty-five men's). Some, such as Chanel No. 5, are classics found only at fine department stores like Macy's or Saks Fifth Avenue. Others, like Macho or Aphrodisia, were trendy five-and-dime types and went the way of polyester leisure suits and metallic jumpsuits. So, what was your first fragrance? And what's your all-time favorite?

Women's:

Avon's Sweet Honesty
Babe
Chanel No. 5
Chantilly
Charlie
Chloe
Ciara
Coty's Wild Musk
Emeraude
Enjoli
Giorgio
Halston
Jean Naté
Jontue
Lauren
Liz Claiborne
Love's Baby Soft
Maxi
Obsession
Opium
Shalimar
Tabu
Vanderbilt
White Shoulders
Windsong

Men's:

Aqua Velva
British Sterling
Brut
Calvin Klein
Canoe
Chaps
Chaz
Drakkar
English Leather
Grey Flannel
Hai Karate
Jade East
Kouros
Lagerfield
Macho
Mennen Millionaire
Old Spice
Oleg Cassini
Paco Rabonne
Paul Sebastian

Pierre Cardin
Polo
Royal Copenhagen
Sex Appeal
Stetson

FRAMPTON, PETER
With his cute dimpled smile and long, curly locks, this singer-guitarist was the foxy alternative for girls in the 1970s who didn't find those other blond pop idols—Shaun Cassidy, Leif Garrett, or Andy Gibb—their cup of teenybopper tea. Born on April 22, 1950, in England, Frampton started his music career forming a succession of rock bands, including The Herd (1966), Humble Pie (1969), and Frampton's Camel (1971). As a solo artist, he experienced commercial breakthrough in 1976 with the release of the chart-busting *Frampton Comes Alive!* the top-selling live album of all time. Frampton's follow-up album, *I'm in You* (1977), although favorably received by critics and fans, couldn't duplicate the success of *Alive!* and his career took a nosedive. It didn't help that he was in a near-fatal car crash in the Bahamas, starred in the movie stinker *Sgt. Pepper's Lonely Hearts Club Band*, co-starring the Bee Gees, and had bouts with depression and alcoholism. In recent years, Frampton has performed as a session artist or "guest" guitarist for singers like David Bowie and Karla Bonoff.

FRAMPTON COMES ALIVE!
Peter Frampton's tour de force was the biggest-selling live LP in rock history (more than fifteen million copies) and stayed on the charts for two years, including ten weeks at number one. Recorded on stage at Winterland in San Francisco, this double album featured his trademark sound, called the Voicebox, a guitar trick of making words by channeling the music through a mouthpiece. Hit singles included "Baby, I Love Your Way," "Do You Feel Like We Do," and "Show Me the Way."

FRANCES "BABY" HOUSEMAN
A nice Jewish seventeen-year-old who goes on summer holiday with her parents to a resort in the Catskills and discovers love, sex, and "dirty dancing" with the resort's hunky dance teacher, Johnny Castle.

FYI: ▸ The curly spiral-perm bob worn by Jennifer Grey as Baby Houseman in the *Dirty Dancing* film became one of the hot hair trends of the late 1980s.

FRANCIE
"The kookiest, kickiest, most MODern cousin a girl could ever have!" Introduced during the height of the British Invasion, mod cousin Francie became the grooviest new member of Barbie Doll's family in 1966. At just a little over eleven inches tall, Francie Fairchild was shorter than older Barbie and lacked her curves, but it didn't matter, for she was the just the right size to wear all the hip, happenin' fashions then in vogue (go-go boots, miniskirts, and so on). Francie looked like a teenage Sally Field Gidget with British model Jean Shrimpton's trademark long straight hair. Her best chum was an ultramod English lass named Casey, who arrived on the scene from London's Carnaby Street in 1967 and who wore her hair in a just-so-fab geometric bob. The twosome adored The Beatles, Twiggy, Frug dancing, and watching TV's *Hullaballoo* and *Shindig*. Happy-go-lucky and very spur-of-the-moment, Francie and Casey were always off being groovy together.

FRANCIS PONCHERELLO
"Ponch" for short. Hunky Hispanic Erik Estrada starred as the daring and fun-loving California Highway Patrol (*CHiPs*) motorcycle cop who worked the freeways of L.A. with by-the-book partner Jon Baker.

FRANKENBERRY
Since 1971, the effeminate pink Frankenstein monster with pink nail polish has been the spokes-creature for a same-name General Mills cereal enhanced by strawberry-flavored marshmallow bits. Rivals are chocolate-craving Count Chocula and friendly ghost Boo Berry.

FYI: ▸ Is this true or just another urban legend? In an accident in the 1970s, Frankenberry cereal caused a bunch of kids to shit pink.

FRANKENSTEIN JR.
A giant robot (about ten yards tall) invented by courageous boy genius Buzz Conroy, son of distinguished scientist Professor Conroy. Buzz used a radar ring to control the masked and caped Junior,

who somewhat resembled the Frankenstein monster, and with the bellow of "Allakazoom!" the two of them would blast off from their laboratory—hidden in the mountains—to battle bad guys. This Hanna-Barbera cartoon shared air time with The Impossibles, a trio of crime-fighting agents, on Saturday mornings from 1966 to 1968.

FRANKENSTEIN'S MONSTER

Author Mary Shelley's man-made monster, created by and named after Dr. Henry Frankenstein in her *Frankenstein* novel, was a towering, seven-foot-tall patchwork of formerly dead body parts with a flat head and electric bolts sticking out of his neck. Gentle-voiced Boris Karloff is the actor most associated with playing Frankenstein's monster. Karloff starred as the lumbering creature in director James Whale's *Frankenstein* (1931) and *The Bride of Frankenstein* (1935).

FRANKIE

Cute and cocky beachboy who was fond of surfing, singing, parties, and Dee Dee (when some other shapely bikini-adorned honey wasn't catching his eye). Played by dark-haired teen heartthrob Frankie Avalon in a series of beach-party movies released throughout the mid-1960s, including *Beach Party* (1963), *Bikini Beach* (1964), *Muscle Beach Party* (1964), and *Beach Blanket Bingo* (1965).

FRANKLIN

Introduced in 1968 when Charlie Brown met him at the beach, he is the Peanuts' African-American pal who attends a different elementary school across town with good friends Peppermint Patty and Marcie. Franklin's so religious he can quote verbatim the Bible's Old Testament.

FREAK

"Freak out—C'est Chic—Le Freak!" This disco dance was made up of a light shimmy and snapping fingers while partners lurched the top half of their bodies back and forth over each other. Best tunes to freak out: "Le Freak" (1978) by Chic and "Disco Nights (Rock Freak)" (1979) by GQ.

FREAKIES

Unless you were a child of the 1970s, you won't remember this breakfast cereal of the colorful animated TV commercials featuring the legendary Freakies song: "We are the Freakies / We are the Freakies / And this is our Freakies Tree / We never miss a meal / Because we love our cereal." Introduced by Ralston in 1973, it was advertised by a group of mutated creatures known as Freakies who resided around a magical tree from which the cereal sprouted abundantly. The Freakies consisted of Boss Moss, handsome Snorkledorf, weird-nosed Hamhose, grumpy Grumble, sweet Cowmumble, smart Gargle, and righteous Goody-Goody. As an advertising promo during the summer of 1973, one of seven different plastic Freakies figures was packaged inside each cereal box ("Free Freakies Inside!"). Kids got so desperate to own all the figures that they would purchase a box, dig right away for the Freakies premium, and not even eat the sweetened cereal, which tasted a lot like Quisp or Cap'n Crunch.

FREAKS AND GEEKS

"Everything you remember from high school—that you choose to forget." Wistful TV show about two group of teens, the freaks (cool) and the geeks (uncool), dealing with life at McKinley High School in suburban Michigan around 1981. Linda Cardellini and John Francis Daley starred as the show's central characters, siblings Lindsay Weir (freak) and Sam Weir (geek). Although short-lived on NBC-TV in the late 1990s, *Freaks and Geeks* developed a loyal following.

FYI: ▸ In May 2004, *Freaks and Geeks* ranked twenty-fifth in *TV Guide*'s "25 Top Cult Shows Ever!"

FREAKY FRIDAY

"When I woke up this morning, I found I'd turned into my mother. . . ." Based on the 1972 best-selling book by Mary Rodgers, this funny Disney fantasy starred Jodie Foster as Annabel Andrews, a thirteen-year-old tomboy, and Barbara Harris as Ellen Andrews, her overburdened mother. The two of them never saw eye to eye—until one freaky Friday, when they magically changed personalities and had to live each other's lives. Released in 1976, the film was directed by Gary Nelson and co-starred John Astin as Bill Andrews, the bewildered husband and father. It inspired several late-1980s big-screen comedies about generational identity-switching, including *Like Father, Like Son* (1987), starring Dudley Moore and Kirk Cameron; *Vice Versa* (1988), starring Judge Reinhold and Fred Savage; *18 Again* (1988), starring George Burns and Charlie Schlatter; and *Big* (1988), starring Tom Hanks and David Moscow. In 2003, Disney remade *Freaky Friday*, starring Lindsay Lohan and Jamie Lee Curtis.

FRECKLES FRIENDLY
Lower-class, freckle-faced best buddy of Richie Rich, the "Richest Kid in the World." Freckle's tagalong little brother was named Pee-Wee.

FREDDIE WASHINGTON
"Hi, there." Played by Lawrence Hilton-Jacobs, the suave black basketball dude with the million-dollar smile was one of Mr. Kotter's Sweathogs on the sitcom *Welcome Back, Kotter*. Nickname: Boom Boom.

FREDDY JONES
This brawny All-American blond hunk with the orange ascot was the leader of the *Scooby-Doo* gang who drove the Mystery Machine and had a thing for babe Daphne Blake.

FREDDY KRUEGER
"One, two, Freddy's comin' for you / Three, four, better lock your door / Five, six, grab a crucifix / Seven, eight, gonna stay up late / Nine, ten, never sleep again." The "bastard son of a hundred maniacs" is a barbecue-faced, finger-knifed, wisecracking ghoul, adorned in a dirty striped sweater and a slouchy fedora hat, who lethally haunts the dreams of sleeping teenagers. Freddy's the star of the now-classic horror film series *A Nightmare on Elm Street*.

FYI: ▸ In 1988, the talking Freddy Krueger doll got pulled from toy shelves because it was too scary for little kids!

FREDDY THE FLUTE
Talking magic golden flute that evil Witchiepoo constantly tried to snitch from teenager Jimmy on the kiddie classic *H. R. Pufnstuf*. In 1995, the original Freddy was stolen from the Krofft Brothers storage warehouse in Los Angeles. Two months after the Kroffts posted a $10,000 reward, Freddy was returned anonymously to a Los Angeles TV station.

FREDDY THE FROG
"Lots of spark with lots of parties, Freddy the Frog . . ." Seen on the *New Zoo Revue*, he was a human-sized, childlike, happy-go-lucky frog who wore a beige turtleneck sweater with the initial "F" on the front. Freddy's sister was named Freeda.

FRED FLINTSTONE
"Yabba-Dabba-Doo!" Voiced by Alan Reed, this husky, loudmouthed caveman who wore leopard skins and had a permanent five o'clock shadow is one of the best-known characters from late twentieth-century animation. When Fred wasn't working hard as an operator of a dinosaur-powered crane at Mr. Slate's rock quarry, he enjoyed bowling and attending lodge meetings as a member of the Royal Order of Water Buffaloes. Dim-witted Barney was his best pal, Wilma was his ever-patient wife, and Pebbles was his adorable daughter.

FYI: ▸ Blessed with a hearty prehistoric appetite, Fred Flintstone loved to eat. Some of his favorites included brontosaurus burgers, deviled dodo eggs, steakasaurus ribs, sweet-and-sour pterodactyl, mastodon chow mein, gravelberry pie, rockshore pudding, and, to wash it all down, Cactus Cola.

"FREE BIRD"
"If I leave here tomorrow, would you still remember me?" The 1975 Lynyrd Skynyrd anthem and perennial favorite on FM classic rock stations was a slow-dance favorite in the 1970s. The only complaint: The song's hard-rocking guitar finale would cause amorous couples on the dance floor to separate from a passionate clench, leaving them dancing in a fast frenzy, as if they'd taken a hit of speed. ". . . 'Cause I'm as free as a bird now."

FYI: ▸ Lynyrd Skynyrd, renowned Southern rockers, named themselves after their Jacksonville, Florida, high school gym teacher, Leonard Skinner.

"FREEDOM '90"
The music video to George Michael's 1990 song didn't star the former Wham! singer, who obsti-

nately refused to appear. Instead, it starred an assemblage of supermodels who lip-synched the words: Christy Turlington, Linda Evangelista, Naomi Campbell, Cindy Crawford, and Tatiana Patiz. It also featured the burning of Michael's biker jacket and the blowing up of the jukebox from the "Faith" video (supposedly these images symbolized the end to his pretty-boy, ass-shaking heartthrob image).

FREE TO BE YOU AND ME

Much-lauded liberal-inclined children's TV special based on the book of the same title and produced and hosted by Marlo Thomas. Airing on the ABC network in 1974, the variety extravaganza used stories, songs, and dance to teach youngsters that it was okay to be yourself and that they should accept others who are different. It won the Emmy Award for Outstanding Children's Special. The songs—featuring the singing voice of Thomas, along with "friends" Alan Alda, Mel Brooks, Jack Cassidy, Shirley Jones, Diana Ross, Michael Jackson, Harry Belafonte, Dustin Hoffman, Rosey Grier, and Carol Channing—were released on vinyl. In 1988, Thomas followed all this up with a sequel titled *Free to Be . . . a Family* (which also won an Emmy for Outstanding Children's Special).

FREE WILLY

A 1993 family film about a troubled twelve-year-old boy named Jesse (played by Jason James Richter) who befriends a three-ton killer whale called Willy held captive at an aquatic amusement park. As a young pup, Willy had been separated from his parents by fishermen and eventually ended up in a cramped tank at the park and being exploited by the seedy owner. Jesse will risk everything to set Willy free. Directed by Simon Wincer, the hit movie was followed by two sequels, *Free Willy 2: The Adventure Home* (1995) and *Free Willy 3: The Rescue* (1997), and a cartoon TV series (1994). Michael Jackson performs its closing theme, "Will You Be There?"

FRENCHY

Squeaky-voiced actress Didi Conn's cosmetology-school dropout who was a member of the girl gang Pink Ladies in the movie musical *Grease*. Frenchy once had a dream fantasy in which Frankie Avalon appeared as the Teen Angel crooning "Beauty School Drop Out" after she mistakenly dyed her hair bright pink.

FRESHEN UP

Manufactured by Warner Lambert, the square-shaped, breath-freshening chewing gum is nicknamed "Cum Gum" because it has a liquid center that bursts in your mouth as you chew it.

FRESH PRINCE OF BEL-AIR

Playing like a cartoon show, this TV sitcom's emphasis was on the clash of cultures as streetwise rapper Will Smith is sent to stay with rich relations in posh Bel-Air, California (805 Saint Cloud Road), after things get too rough in his West Philly hood. Will's new crib is a lavishly furnished mansion, which he shares with his lawyer-uncle Philip Banks (James Avery), Philip's wife, Vivian Banks (Janet Hubert-Whitten), narcissistic teen cousin Hilary (Karyn Parsons), aspiring preppy cousin Carlton (Alfonso Ribeiro), unpretentious youngest cousin Ashley (Tatyana Ali), and an impertinent butler named Geoffrey (Joseph Marcell). He attends the exclusively snooty Bel-Air Academy with his three cousins. Airing on NBC from 1990 to 1996, the series' executive producer was the legendary Quincy Jones.

FYI: ▸ A rap star in real life (as D.J. Jazzy Jeff and the Fresh Prince, he and partner Jeff Townes won a Grammy for the 1988 hit "Parents Just Don't Understand"), Will Smith would become one of cinema's hottest black actors—demanding $15 million a picture for such blockbusters as *Independence Day* (1996) and *Men in Black* (1997).

FRIDAY THE 13th

In the summer of 1980, director Sean S. Cunningham's splatterfest became a surprise box-office hit, fostering numerous imitations and ten equally gory sequels (including one in 3-D). Despite the warnings from local townspeople of a "death curse," seven teenage counselors arrive on Friday the thirteenth to reopen Camp Crystal Lake, a woodsy summer camp that had been closed for more than twenty years after a series of unsolved murders. As the movie unfolds, the unsuspecting teens are stalked one by one and then violently murdered by an unseen psycho. The killer turns out to be a seemingly harmless mother, Mrs. Voorhees (Betsy Palmer), avenging the 1957 death of her young son Jason, a drowning camper whose calls for help went unnoticed because his counselors were too busy getting it on. (The underlying moral message of the *Friday the 13th* series is that if you have sex you will meet a bloody demise.) Perky Adrienne King played Alice, the lone survivor, and prestardom Kevin Bacon starred as Jack, the stud who is the recipient of the film's most shocking slaying. (He and his girlfriend get speared together, like a shish kebab, right after—you guessed it—having sex.) Horror master Tom Savini did the gruesome special effects, and the scary "ssh-ssh-ssh-aah-aah-aah" music score was the work of Harry Manfredini.

The first sequel, *Friday the 13th, Part 2*, introduced moviegoers to unstoppable hockey-masked Jason Voorhees and his penchant for knocking off victims in horrifying and creative ways. (At last count, he's axed, hacked, chopped, stabbed, drilled, crushed, electrocuted, and decapitated more than 124 people.)

FRIEDA

The girl with the naturally curly hair who hangs out with snooty school friends Lucy and Violet in Charles Schulz's beloved *Peanuts* cartoons.

FRIENDS

> "*Friends* works because it's a fantasy family at a time when the family is so dysfunctional for this generation."
>
> —DAVID "ROSS" SCHWIMMER

"Everyone needs friends." The highly successful NBC sitcom, premiering in 1994, is important for being the first to focus on Generation X as young adults striking out on their own in the big city. In this case, the city is New York and the "friends" are six fabulously hip, funny, and gorgeous twentysomethings. There was Monica Geller (Courteney Cox), the obsessive-compulsive neat-freak and trained chef; Rachel Green (Jennifer Aniston), the pampered rich girl who shared an apartment with Monica after leaving her fiancé at the altar; Phoebe Buffay (Lisa Kudrow), the flaky masseuse with a heart of gold; Ross Geller (David Schwimmer), Monica's nerdy paleontologist brother whose wife dumped him for another woman; Joey Tribbiani (Matthew LeBlanc), the cute but dim-witted aspiring actor ("How you doin'?"); and Chandler Bing (Matthew Perry), the corporate jokester. Despite having seemingly low-paying jobs at which they apparently never worked because they were always hanging out at the Central Perk coffeehouse, the sextet lived in fantastic pads in Greenwich Village and wore the latest haircuts and designer threads. Each episode followed the intertwined life experiences of the quirky-natured "Friends," as they tried to build careers, find romance, and become responsible "adults." The series instantly found a niche with an audience of twentysomething viewers who wanted to be like the characters and, most important, have friends like "Friends."

FRIENDSHIP BRACELETS

Teens of the late 1980s gave each other one of these bracelets woven from colorful embroidery string to be worn tied permanently on your wrist. I think the story behind them was that you wore it until the string disintegrated and fell off, which then symbolized a true friendship with the person who gave it to you.

FRIGHT FACTORY

Mattel Thingmaker set introduced in 1965, featuring molds to make frightfully fun monster makeup items to wear on your own face and body, such as bloodshot eyes, claws, fangs, and scars.

FRINGED SUEDE JACKETS

Suede jackets with swingy long fringe around the middle and/or bottom and/or sleeves have been a hot on-again, off-again fashion statement since western hero Davy Crockett ruled the TV screen back in the 1950s. The style led to the 1960s fringed suede vest, which was groovy for a night of go-go dancing.

FRISBEE

"When a ball dreams, it dreams it's a Frisbee!" A plastic disc you throw in the air—where it will then whiz, whirl, then gently land in a waiting partner's hand. (Its flight is controlled by a sharp backhand flick of the wrist.) Manufactured by the Wham-O toy company since 1957, more than 100 million Frisbees in a variety of sizes and colors, including a glow-in-the-dark model, have been produced. An estimated nine out of ten Americans have played with one at least once in their lives. As a recreational sport, Frisbee was particularly popular in the late 1960s and early 1970s among free-spirited men of high school and college age who viewed it as a noncompetitive alternative to contact sports, such as football, basketball, and baseball. In 1975, Wham-O started an annual World Frisbee Disc Championship, which included everything from distance throwing and catching to a dog-catch competition.

FYI: ▸ The Frisbee was named in honor of the Frisbie Baking Company of Bridgeport, Connecticut, whose metal pie-tins had been tossed in fun by college youths at nearby Yale University since the 1920s.

FRITO BANDITO

"Ayiee, yie-yie-yieeee. . . ." He was the Frito Bandito, an animated pistol-packin', sombrero-wearing, mustachioed Mexican bandit out to nab Fritos Corn Chips in a series of TV ads airing during the late 1960s and early 1970s. Although greatly popular with youngsters, the Bandito was often criticized by the Latin American community for being a racist stereotype, which led to its discontinuation in the mid-1970s. A cool school-age memory was owning the Frito Bandito pencil topper, a premium found in Frito-Lay snack packs. First manufactured in 1968, these two-inch-tall erasers were hot items coveted by just about every kid in school. Frito-Lay later released pencil toppers of two other advertising icons: W. C. Fritos and the Muncha Bunch.

FROGGER

Popular arcade game, introduced in 1981, which had players trying to guide a daredevil frog (Frogger) across a busy stretch of highway without getting squashed, and through a crowded swamp without becoming lunch for hungry snakes and alligators. (He just wanted to get home to the safety of his lily pad.)

FROGS

"Today the pond! Tomorrow the world!" Produced by Roger Corman and directed by George McCowan, a 1972 low-budget shocker about malevolent swamp critters taking revenge on an ecologically incorrect family. It starred Sam Elliott as Pickett Smith, an environmental research photographer who has the misfortune of winding up at the island estate of a wheelchair-bound tyrant, Jason Crockett (Ray Milland), in the Florida Everglades. It is patriarch Crockett's July Fourth birthday, and his self-centered kin have gathered to celebrate. But before the fireworks can go off, the frogs have organized masses of bugs, spiders, snakes, lizards, alligators, snapping turtles, and other creepy crawlers (including Spanish moss) to annihilate the humans. The horror film co-starred Joan Van Ark as decent daughter Karen Crockett; Adam Roarke as former football-hero son Clint Crockett; Lynn Borden as Clint's spoiled, beautiful wife, Jenny; Nicholas Cortland as fashion photographer cousin Kenneth; and Judy Pace as Bella Garrington, the black fashion model. Following the end credits, don't miss the campy closing scene of the cartoon frog gulping down a human hand.

FROSTBITE FALLS

A cartoon town in middle Minnesota that Bullwinkle Moose and his friend Rocky J. Squirrel call home.

FROSTED FLAKES

Tony the Tiger's sugar-coated cornflakes cereal used to be called Sugar Frosted Flakes. Then the health-conscious 1970s hit, and the nasty word "sugar" was nixed from the title. This inspired other sugar-loaded cereals of the era to follow suit: Sugar Pops became Corn Pops, Sugar Smacks became Honey Smacks, and Super Sugar Crisp became Super Golden Crisp.

FROSTY PALACE

Burger and shake joint in the movie *Grease* where Sandy, Danny, and other students from Rydell High hang out after school. Items on the menu included the Polar Burger and the Dog-Sled Delight (a hot dog).

FROSTY SNO-MAN SNO-CONE MACHINE

Introduced by Hasbro in 1963, this classic toy was a white-plastic ice-shaving machine in the shape of a snowman. When kids wanted "a real tasty treat," they put ordinary ice cubes in Frosty's top, turned the manual crank on the back—which shaved the cubes—and caught the ice in a pointy snow-cone cup. After adding syrup (ten different flavors to choose from) and topping with candy sprinkles, they had an icy cup of delicious goodness. Replaced by the Snoopy Sno-Cone Machine in the early 1980s.

FROSTY THE SNOWMAN

"Haaappy Birthday!"
—FROSTY THE SNOWMAN'S FIRST WORDS

Following in the footsteps of *Rudolph the Red-Nosed Reindeer* and *The Little Drummer Boy*, Arthur Rankin Jr. and Jules Bass brought another classic Christmas carol to life in 1969 with this perennial favorite. Based on the 1950 record by singing cowboy Gene Autry and narrated by Jimmy Durante, the animated TV special told the story of the lovable snowman who came to life "one magic Christmas Eve" after a little girl named Karen and her school chums placed a magic hat belonging to a sinister magician, Professor Hinkle, on top of his head. Threatened by rising temperatures and pursued by Hinkle, who wants his hat back, Frosty and Karen set off for the cooler North Pole. Once there, Karen is unable to endure the freezing climate, so Frosty puts her in a toasty greenhouse full of holiday evergreens. He gets trapped there himself by Hinkle and melts down to a puddle. All is well when Santa Claus saves the day by restoring Frosty to his old self, allowing him to return every Yuletide, because he was made of "Christmas Snow." As for Hinkle, Santa threatens to never bring him another present if he doesn't change his evil ways. (As punishment the hapless magician has to write "I am very sorry for what I did to Frosty" 100 zillion times.) Voiced by comedian Jackie Vernon, Frosty—with his corncob pipe, button nose, and two eyes made of coal—later starred in three other Rankin/Bass specials: *Frosty's Winter Wonderland* (1976), *Rudolph and Frosty's Christmas in July* (1979), and *Frosty Returns* (1992).

FRUG

Quintessential 1960s dance, popular with go-go dancers and everyone else, that combined a slow Jerk and Pony feet with arms and wrists rhythmically thrust up and over head.

FRUIT BRUTE

Least popular of the General Mills monster cereals. Introduced in 1972, it was advertised by a crafty werewolf who wore multicolored striped overalls and howled over the multicolored fruit-flavored marshmallow bits found in the cereal. In 1977, poor Fruit Brute disappeared from the cereal aisle, leaving him all but forgotten.

FRYE BOOTS

Fashionable in the 1970s, this tan-colored masculine footwear, featuring a bulky toe and chunky heel, went hand in hand with Levi's boot-cut jeans and flannel shirts. Dingo boots, advertised by O.J. Simpson, was its competitor.

FYI: ▸ Frye boots have a long history dating back to America's Civil War, when soldiers for both sides wore them.

FULL HOUSE

Taking the *Brady Bunch* postnuclear family concept one step further, this much-loved TV sitcom, airing on ABC from 1987 to 1995, showcased three men and three kids living together as one big, happy family. Set in San Francisco, it dealt with Danny Tanner (played by Bob Saget), a morning talk-show host whose wife died, leaving him with the task of raising a trio of young daughters: ten-year-old Donna Jo "D.J." (Candace Cameron), five-year-old Stephanie (Jodie Sweetin), and baby Michelle (twins Mary-Kate and Ashley Olsen). Needing extra help to raise the ultraprecocious girls, Danny enlisted his brother-in-law Jesse Katsopolis (John Stamos), a rock musician, and friend Joey (Dave Coulier), a stand-up comic, to move in. In 1991, Jesse married Rebecca Donaldson (Lori Loughlin), co-host of Danny's *Wake Up, San Francisco* TV show. Rebecca moved in, gave birth to twins, and the *Full House* became even fuller.

FUNICELLO, ANNETTE

Practically growing up in the public eye, this pert, pretty brunette has been America's sweetheart since the late 1950s. Her lengthy career took her from child Mouseketeer on TV's *Mickey Mouse Club* to teenage leading lady of Disney films (*Babes in Toyland*, *The Shaggy Dog*, and *The Monkey's Uncle*) and star of pop music ("Tall Paul"), then on to Dee Dee in the *Beach Party* movie series, and finally to commercial spokes-mom for Skippy peanut butter. She has been suffering from multiple sclerosis since 1987.

FUNKY CHICKEN

Silly dance in which you flap your arms like a hen on a speed trip. (Why am I conjuring up an image of how Jan Brady would dance?) Willie Henderson's hit song "The Funky Chicken" fueled this dance craze in 1970.

FUNKY PHANTOM

A Saturday-morning cartoon show about a 200-year-old New England specter named Jonathan Muddlemore who lived during the American Revolutionary War. Muddlemore, a well-to-do coward, and his pet cat, Boo, became trapped in a grandfather clock after hiding from pursuing Redcoats in 1776. One stormy night in 1976, a trio of teenagers—Skip, Augie, and April—and their gruff bulldog, Elmo, take refuge in Muddlemore's abandoned mansion. After resetting the clock's hands to twelve, they free the now-ghostly Spirit of '76 and his kitty. Nicknamed "Muddsey," the elated but still skittish phantom joins the teens, riding their Looney Dooney dune buggy around the country in a series of scary adventures derived from American folklore and colonial history. Airing from 1971 to 1973, the Hanna-Barbera TV favorite featured the voices of Daws Butler as Jonathan Muddlemore and former Monkee Micky Dolenz as Skip.

FUNKY WINKERBEAN

A representative of the average American teenager, Funky was the title character of a long-running newspaper comic strip created by twenty-three-year-old schoolteacher Tom Batiuk in 1972. The strip focused on the offbeat (and sometimes topical) antics of Funky and various classmates and faculty at Westview High School, located in suburban Akron, Ohio. At Westview High, Harry L. Dinkle, "the world's greatest band director," leads the marching band, and the Scapegoats were always the losing football team. Tony Montoni's pizza parlor was where Funky worked after school (after graduating, he became its co-owner).

FUNNY FACE

"There's a laugh in every glass!" Like Kool-Aid, these powdered soft-drink mixes came in little packages, but unlike its rival you didn't have to add sugar because the mix was already presweetened. Introduced by Pillsbury in 1965, the ultracool thing about Funny Face was that each of the ten flavors came with a wacky character to match: Goofy Grape (the leader), Freckle Face Strawberry, Lefty Lemon, Choo Choo Cherry, Jolly Olly Orange, Loudmouth Punch, With-It Watermelon, Frooty Tooty Fruity, Rootin' Tootin' Raspberry, and Chug-a-Lug Chocolate. In 1969, the company offered a cool "send away" premium featuring each Funny Face on a plastic drinking mug.

FYI: ▸ Does anyone remember Funny Face characters called Chinese Cherry and Injun Orange? Probably not, because they were deemed racist and replaced by Choo Choo Cherry and Jolly Olly Orange.

FURBY

Resembling Gizmo, the furry Mogwai from the movie *Gremlins*, this cute interactive plush pet with eye, ear, and mouth movements was the hot sold-out toy of Christmas 1998. Furby could speak its very own language (called Furbish), and when placed next to other Furbys he would chatter with them. In the first year of production, more than twelve million were sold.

FYI: ▸ In Furbish, "ah-may koh koh" means "pet me more," "noo-loo" means "happy," "mee mee a-tay" means "very hungry," and "dah doo-ay wah" means "big fun!"

FURY

"The story of a horse and the boy who loved him." Children's TV adventure about a troublesome twelve-year-old orphan, Joey (Bobby Diamond), who is adopted by a bachelor, Jim Newton (Peter Graves), and sent to live on his spacious Broken Wheel Ranch near Capitol City in the Southwest, where he befriends a beautiful black stallion named Fury (played by Gypsy). Friendly Pete (William Fawcett) is the old-timer employed as the ranch's handyman. The popular series ran for eleven years (1955–66) on Saturday mornings (the last six years were repeats).

GABE KOTTER
Wisecracking teacher of a class made up of academically challenged students called the Sweathogs. Mr. Kotter was once a Sweathog himself at James Buchanan High in Brooklyn, and has compassion for the "misfits" in his remedial classroom. Gabe is married to the patient Julie, who endures her hubby's stories about his wacky relatives. ("Did I ever tell you the one about my uncle?") Played by Gabe Kaplan on the 1970s TV sitcom *Welcome Back, Kotter.*

GALAXIANS
Four ghost monsters—shadow Blinky (red color), speedy Pinky (pink color), bashful Inky (blue color), and pokey Clyde (orange color)—whom Pac-Man tried to avoid (unless he was flashing blue) while scoring points in the varying mazes of his electronic video game.

GAMEBOY
Introduced in 1989—the smaller, easier to hold, colorful version commonly seen today was released in 1996—Nintendo's portable video-game player keeps little ones occupied while waiting for parents to do those darn parent things that take forever. For grown-ups without children, owning a Gameboy is great for passing the time while waiting at airports and other places that take forever. My kid niece's favorite Gameboy game is Pokemon.

GAMES
These fifty games were not found in fancy cardboard boxes manufactured by Milton Bradley or Parker Brothers. They are classic childhood games in which all you need to do is follow the rules, have a little skill, and possess a kid's worth of imagination.

Baseball
Basketball
Charades
Chicken fights
Chinese fire drills
Cops and robbers
Cowboys and Indians
Crab soccer
Croquet
Doctor
Dodgeball
Duck Duck Goose
Football

Freeze
Heads Up Seven Up
Hide-and-seek
Hockey
Hopscotch
Jump rope
Kick the can
Kickball
King of the hill
London Bridge
Marco Polo
Miss Susie
Monster
Mother, may I?
Musical chairs
One, two, three, red light
Pin the tail on the donkey
Post office
Red light, green light
Red Rover
Relay races
Ring around the rosy
Rock, paper, scissors
Simon says
Smear the queer
Snowball fights
Soccer
Softball
Speedball
Spin the bottle
Swing the statue
Table football
Tag
Tic-tac-toe
Truth or dare
Tug-of-war
Whip it

GAP

Named after "generation gap," The Gap started life in San Francisco in 1969 as a single shop specializing in Levi's blue jeans for hippies of both sexes. In just under three decades, it grew into the world's largest retailer (more than 3,000 stores globally), specializing in low-end clothing for yuppies of both sexes. Critics claim that The Gap dresses everyone in a uniform of conformity ("Gapification"): generic khakis, blue jeans (they replaced Levi's with their own Gap brand), black pocket T's, polo shirts, and more. The Gap Girls on NBC's *Saturday Night Live* spoofed the store's employees as vapid, low-intelligence sales clerks who fold jeans ("Didja cinch that?"). Current Gap competitors include Abercrombie & Fitch, The Buckle, American Eagle, Banana Republic, and Old Navy (the last two stores are both owned by The Gap).

GARANIMALS

"Garanimals and kids. Wow, what a match!" Introduced in 1972, mix-and-match clothing separates for young children age five and under that you put together by matching the jungle animal ("Garanimal") on the hangtag. The hangtag system made it easy for kids to select their own clothes and dress themselves.

GARBAGE PAIL KIDS

What Wacky Packages were to the kids of the 1970s, these trading cards were to the kids of the 1980s. Manufactured by Topps from 1985 to 1988, the Garbage Pail Kids, selling at twenty-five cents for a pack of five cards, crudely spoofed the Cabbage Patch Kids phenomenon. A GPK card featured a sticker on the front with a graphic of a disfigured kid, resembling a Cabbage Patch Doll, whose name matched his or her dysfunctional scenario. Some of the Kids in the first series (there were fifteen series in all) included vomiting Up Chuck, electric-chaired Fryin' Brain, lightning-struck April Showers, zombie Dead Ted, street drunk Boozin' Bruce, Itchy Ritchie, straitjacketed Wacky Jackie, pimply Crater Cris, obese Slobby Robbie, hirsute Hairy Mary, sickly Virus Iris, and skeletal Bony Joanie. Blasted Billy, the lad with a mushroom cloud exploding from the top of his head, is the "poster child" for GPK (he's the most familiar one). Positively disturbing, yes, but young boys, who despised the girly cuteness of Cabbage Patch Dolls, loved the Garbage Pail Kids and made them big sellers. On the other hand, the gross-out antics angered parents, teachers, and the makers of Cabbage Patch Kids. Topps stopped producing them after being sued by the CPK people over copyright infringement. Inspired a big-screen motion picture in 1997 starring Valerie Vomit, Windy Winston, Foul Phil, Nat Nerd, Ali Gator, Greaser Greg, and Messy Tessie.

GARFIELD

"Show me a good mouser and I'll show you a cat with bad breath." Rotund, gluttonous, lazy, finicky, grouchy, cynical, stubborn, mischievous, lovable—these are just a few of the words that describe this feline superstar of the comic world. The furry, orange tabby was created by cartoonist Jim Davis, who modeled and named him after his cantankerous grandfather Garfield. In 1981, four years after debuting for United Feature Syndicate, Garfield headlined the most popular comic strip in the nation, and by the end of the 1980s more than 1,900 worldwide newspapers carried his strip. In 1982, he became a TV star with a series of animated specials—*Here Comes Garfield* (1982), *Garfield on the Town* (1983), *Garfield in the Rough* (1984), *Garfield's Halloween Adventure* (1985), *Garfield in Paradise* (1986), and *Garfield Goes Hollywood* (1987)—and a Saturday-morning cartoon, *Garfield and Friends* (1988–95). Lorenzo Music, most famous for playing Carlton the Doorman on prime time's *Rhoda*, provided Garfield's sarcastic voice on these programs. Garfield's passions in life were consuming ample amounts of food (especially lasagna), catnapping lazily, tormenting both his owner, Jon Arbuckle, and the simpleminded dog Odie, and flirting with pink Persian Arlene.

GARGAMEL

Baneful wizard who tried but never succeeded in capturing the blue Smurfs via his Great Book of Spells. ("So many uncast spells! So many uncaught Smurfs!") Azriel was Gargamel's wicked kitty accomplice.

GARRETT, LEIF

Hot stuff during the late 1970s, Leif Garrett was a poor man's (in his case a poor girl's) Peter Frampton, Shaun Cassidy, and Andy Gibb. True, he was a cute teen heartthrob with long, curly blond hair, but his hair wasn't as long or as curly as Frampton's golden locks. Like Cassidy, he had a prime-time TV show, *Three for the Road*, but it lasted only a scant two months in 1975. Like all three, he made records, but only one made it as high as number ten on the *Billboard* Top Forty ("I Was Made for Dancin'" in 1978). He even starred in a so-so successful movie capitalizing on the then current skateboard fad, titled—what else?—*Skateboard* (1978). What he did have was the ability to turn millions of adolescent girls into raving maniacs, and in doing so he became the spandex-clad pinup prince of teenybopper rags whose concerts at amusement parks around the nation were sold-out events.

Leif (pronounced "Layf," rhymes with "safe") was born November 8, 1961, in Hollywood, California. He is the older brother of Dawn Lyn, better known as little Dodie Douglas on TV's *My Three Sons*. Throughout the 1990s, a very grown up and handsome Leif (with a lot less hair) appeared frequently as a guest V.J. on TV's VH-1, hosting 1970s revival programs. Unfortunately, he has also been the subject of a much-publicized battle with heroin addiction.

GARY EWING

Black sheep, recovered alcoholic, middle brother of the Ewing clan who was seldom seen in Dallas, Texas, because he lived in suburban Knots Landing, California. Daughter is slutty blonde Lucy Ewing. Gary was married to long-suffering Valene before scheming Abby got her claws in him. Played by the blond Ted Shackelford in the prime-time serial *Dallas* and its spin-off, *Knots Landing*.

GASTON

Egotistical and chauvinistic, the handsome (and hairy-chested) lout and supporting antagonist of the Disney fairy-tale *Beauty and the Beast* found it difficult to believe that bookish heroine Belle didn't love him when everyone else in town seemed to adore him. Good-looking on the outside, vile on the inside, Gaston was the opposite of the Beast, who was outwardly repulsive but beautiful within.

GAUCHOS

Girls' culotte-type pants, trendy in the mid-1970s, that went just below the knees, flared out, and were often paired with knee-high leather boots that laced up. They had a Spanish chicness to them.

GAY PURR-EE

Sophisticated big-screen musical cartoon about the story of three French country kitties who travel to "ze beeg seety of Purr-ee." It features the legendary voice of Judy Garland as the naive Mewsette, a lovely white kitty who journeys to the City of Lights in search of new adventures. Once in Paris, she encounters Madame Rubens-Chatte (Hermione Gingold), the fat pink proprietor of a feline beauty parlor, and the villainous Meowrice (Paul Frees), a smooth-talking city slicker who kidnaps Mewsette in order to sell her off to a rich old cat in America. To the rescue comes Mewsette's ever-devoted boyfriend Juane-Tom (Robert Goulet), a hardy tomcat and self-proclaimed "greatest mouse-catcher in the world," and his tiny companion, Robespierre (Red Buttons). This 1962 movie includes the tunes "Mewsette," "The Money Cat," "Take My Hand, Paree," "Paris Is a Lonely Town," "Bubbles," and "Roses Red, Violets Blue."

GEE, YOUR HAIR SMELLS TERRIFIC

"Gee, your hair smells terrific!" That's what handsome strangers would whisper to you when they caught a whiff of your terrific-smelling hair—according to the ads for the shampoo with the same name.

GENE GENE THE DANCING MACHINE

An overweight black stagehand for TV's *Gong Show* who would periodically appear on stage dancing crazily (he had no rhythm), which resulted in the rowdy celebrity judges' throwing various objects at him.

GENERAL

The loyal horse of storybook moppet Pippi Longstocking. Lives on her front porch at Villa Villekulla in Sweden.

GENERAL HOSPITAL

In 1981, Chuck and Di's royal "wedding of the century" wasn't the only matrimonial event making headlines. Across the Atlantic, Americans had turned the nuptials of a soap-opera twosome, *General Hospital*'s Luke and Laura, into a nationwide phenomenon. Premiering as a medical drama in 1963, the ABC-TV serial—airing weekday afternoons—developed a large teen following during the late 1970s and early 1980s because its story lines were rich in romance and adventure. The most famous of these tales was the tumultuous love affair of bad-boy Luke Spencer (Anthony Geary) and teen sweetheart Laura Vining (Genie Francis).

Luke and Laura's relationship began with controversy. On October 5, 1979, Luke raped Laura in his deserted disco. After dealing with the attack by attending group counseling for rape victims, Laura found herself enthralled with the charismatic rogue—a development that sent shivers down the spines of feminists everywhere—and eventually split from her husband, Scotty Baldwin (Kin Shriner), and ran off with Luke, who at the time was hiding from the mob. As their romance grew, so did the ratings, and on November 11, 1981, the day Luke and Laura said "I do," more than fourteen million viewers tuned in—the largest audience ever to watch a daytime dramatic series!

Soon after the wedding, a boating mishap left Laura missing and presumed drowned (this plotline gave actress Francis a break from the series). Searching for her to no avail, Luke united with secret agent Robert Scorpio (Tristan Rogers) to save Port Charles (hometown of *General Hospital*) from the villainous Cassadine family's attempt to put everything into a cryogenic deep-freeze. This sci-fi plotline, referred to as the "Ice Princess," drove the show's ratings so high that even legendary film actress Elizabeth Taylor—an immense fan—asked to make a guest appearance (she played the Widow Cassadine).

Under producer Gloria Monty's leadership, *General Hospital* was TV's top-rated soap from 1979 to 1988. Along with Luke, Laura, Scotty, and Scorpio, other favorite characters during this golden era included Dr. Lesley Webber (Denise Alexander), Rick Webber (Chris Robinson), Tracy Quartermaine (Jane Elliot), Monica Quartermaine (Leslie Charleson), Alan Quartermaine (Stuart Damon), Ruby Anderson (Norma Connolly), Bobbi Spencer (Jackie Zeman), Joe Kelly (Douglas Sheehan), Susan Moore (Gail Rae Carlson), Heather Grant (Robin Mattson), Amy Vining (Shell Kepler), Tiffany Hill (Sharon Wyatt), Jackie Templeton (Demi Moore), Laura Templeton (Janine Turner), Noah Drake (Rick Springfield), Jimmy Lee Holt (Steve Bond), Victor Cassadine (Thaao Penghlis), Holly Sutton (Emma Samms), Blackie Parrish (John Stamos), Felicia Cummings (Kristina Malandro), and Frisco Jones (Jack Wagner).

FYI: ▸ In 1981, a female quartet called the Afternoon Delights had a Top Forty hit with "General Hospi-Tale," a musical parody of the hit soap.

GENERAL LEE

Some say the real star of TV's *Dukes of Hazzard* was Bo and Luke's jacked-up orange 1969 Dodge Charger with a decal of the Rebel flag on top and the number "01" on both doors. Because wear and tear from the jump stunts was so high on the car the show went through 300 look-alikes during its seven seasons of production.

GENERATION X

"I didn't come up with
the name for a generation.
I came up with a title for a novel."
—DOUGLAS COUPLAND, AUTHOR OF *GENERATION X*

The seventy-nine million or so Americans born from 1961 to 1981, the years following the great mid-century Baby Boom. Name was tagged after Douglas Coupland's 1990 cult book about a group of disenchanted twentysomethings. Technically known as the "13th Generation" because it refers to the thirteenth generation of Americans born since colonial days. Key words: *Archies*, *Beverly Hills 90210*, body piercing, *Brady Bunch*, Brat Pack, *Bright Lights, Big City*, Brooke Shields, *Charlie's Angels*, Doc Martens, Duran Duran, Ecstasy, Bret Easton Ellis, extreme sports, *Friends*, *Generation X*, grunge, *H. R. Pufnstuf*, *Heathers*, John Kennedy Jr., latchkey kids, *Less Than Zero*, Lollapalooza, Madonna, McJobs, *Melrose Place*, Moby, Molly Ringwald, MTV, New Wave, Nirvana, Osmonds, *Partridge Family*, Pearl Jam, Persian Gulf War, personal computers, Princess Diana, *Prozac Nation*, Quentin Tarantino, R.E.M., rap music, raves, *Real World*, *Reality Bites*, *Schoolhouse Rock*, *Scooby-Doo*, Seattle, *Sesame Street*, *Simpsons*, *Sixteen Candles*, *Slacker*, slasher films, tattoos, Tom Cruise, twentysomething, Valley Girls, video games, *Willy Wonka*, and *Zoom*.

FYI: ▸ Over the years, Gen-Xers have been labeled the Baby Buster Generation, the Blank Generation, the Boomlet Generation, the Brady Bunch Generation, the Computer Generation, the Grunge Generation, the Hip-Hop Generation, the Latchkey Generation, the MTV Generation, the New Lost Generation, the Nintendo Generation, the Post-Yuppie Generation, the Repair Generation, the Slacker Generation, the Thirteenth Generation, the Tweener Generation, the Twentysomething Generation, and the Whatever Generation.

GENTLE BEN

Airing on CBS prime time from 1967 to 1969, an adventure show about a 650-pound American black bear adopted as a pet by a family in the Florida Everglades. It starred Clint Howard as Mark Wedloe, the eight-year-old son of a game warden, whose best pal was a friendly and gentle creature called Ben (played by Bruno the Bear). Dennis Weaver played Mark's father, Tom, and Beth Brickell was his mother, Ellen. Based on the 1967 theatrical release *Gentle Giant*, also starring Weaver and Howard, the fondly remembered series was produced by Ivan Tors, creator of two other animal-oriented hits: *Flipper* (1964–68) and *Daktari* (1966–69). Howard is the younger brother of actor-director Ron Howard.

GEOFFREY THE GIRAFFE

Animated giraffe mascot of the nationwide Toys "R" Us toy supermarkets. Geoffrey's female mate is bow-headed GiGi, and their child is Baby Gee.

GEORGE JETSON

Meet George Jetson, the good-natured, hardworking head of a futuristic household in Orbit City who commutes on the intergalactic skyways in an atomic-powered, glass-bubble car to his job as a computer operator for Spacely Space Sprockets. (With a three-hour day and a three-day-a-week schedule, the poor fellow is considered overworked.) His family consists of attractive and supportive wife Jane, complex teenage daughter Judy, boy-genius son Elroy, and pet dog Astro. Voiced by George O'Hanlon for the 1960s *Jetsons* cartoon show.

GEORGE OF THE JUNGLE

"George, George, George of the Jungle. . . ." The coolest if not the klutziest swinger in Africa, with brawn bigger than brain, was this black-haired, loin-clothed, vine-swinging, cartoon jungle hunk. George lived a happy existence in Imgwee Gwee Valley near a native village called Umbwebwe. He was joined by confidant Ape, an Oxford-educated talking gorilla, and pet elephant Shep, whom he thought was a large puppy. Buxom redhead Ursula served as his "Jane." Before you could say "Watch out for that tree!" the clumsy tree-smacker would find himself in all kinds of kooky misadventures, usually involving the local natives or nasty animal poachers. Created by animator Jay Ward, *George of the Jungle* aired from 1967 to 1970 on Saturday mornings. Two other cartoon segments accompanied it: *Super Chicken* and *Tom Slick*. In 1997, the beloved show was made into a live-action Disney pic starring Brendan Fraser as George.

GEORGE WILSON

"Heeey, Mr. Wilson!" Dennis the Menace's elderly next-door neighbor was a crabby sort who, when trying to avoid the devilish tot, enjoyed working in his prized flower gardens and walking pooch Fremont. This cartoon character was married to the more patient Martha Wilson.

GERALDINE JONES

"What you see is what you get, honey!" Comedian Flip Wilson's female alter ego was a brassy, bigmouthed, liberated black woman from Harlem, fond of wearing a blonde flip wig and mod psychedelic-print minidresses. On *The Flip Wilson Show*, Geraldine flirted with other fellows even though she had a severely jealous boyfriend named Killer (or so she said).

GERE, RICHARD

Born August 31, 1949, in Philadelphia, this spiritually inclined actor's brooding good looks and perfectly muscled body made him one of the top male sex symbols of the 1980s. Films included *Days of Heaven* (1978), *Yanks* (1979), *American Gigolo* (1980), *An Officer and a Gentleman* (1982), *Breathless* (1983), *The Cotton Club* (1984), *Internal Affairs* (1990), *Pretty Woman* (1990), *Sommersby* (1993), and *Primal Fear* (1996). Had a highly publicized marriage to supermodel Cindy Crawford from 1991 to 1994. (The couple took out an ad in the *Times* of London in May 1994 to deny rumors they were each homosexual and were maintaining the union for appearances only.)

FYI: ▸ Richard Gere is plagued by a rather nasty urban legend that has something to do with gerbils and his butt.

GET ALONG GANG

Saturday-morning cartoon starring six lovable, childlike critters—moose Montgomery, dog Dotty, cat Zipper, lamb Woolma, porcupine Portia, and beaver Bingo—who lived together in the Clubhouse Caboose in the village of Greenmeadow. Airing from 1984 to 1986, the show was based on a line of greeting cards from American Greetings.

GET SMART

A prime-time spy spoof created by Mel Brooks and Buck Henry and inspired by the 1960s secret-agent movie genre. Airing on NBC-TV from 1965 to 1970, the sitcom starred Don Adams as Maxwell Smart, a.k.a. Agent 86, a well-meaning but inept secret agent who worked for CONTROL, a Washington-based counterintelligence agency. Smart accepted his orders from a boss known simply as Chief (Edward Platt) and his partner was the beautiful Agent 99 (Barbara Feldon), who used her intelligence and ingenuity to bail the bumbling spy out of trouble. Their assignments took them on missions to thwart the sinister agents of KAOS, an organization dedicated to evil and world dominance. CONTROL colleagues included master of disguise Agent 13 (Dave Ketchum), dim-witted Agent Larrabee (Robert Karvelas), and literal robot Hymie (Dick Gautier). Max and Agent 99 became enamored of one another, and in 1968 the mismatched lovebirds became husband and wife. Years later, the series would be followed by a big-screen film, *The Nude Bomb (The Return of Maxwell Smart)* (1980) and by a reunion TV movie, *Get Smart Again* (1989), which reunited Don Adams and Barbara Feldon.

FYI: ▸ The cool thing about *Get Smart* was all the spy gadgets, such as Maxwell Smart's shoe phone and an anti-eavesdropping device called the Cone of Silence, used for secret conversations by CONTROL. Also cool were his pet expressions, such as "Would you believe?" "Missed it—by that much," and "Sorry about that, Chief," which became catchphrases of the era.

GHIDORAH

In the 1965 sci-fi film *Ghidorah, the Three-Headed Monster*, this flying triple-headed space dragon from outer space rampaged Tokyo before the fire-breathing protector Godzilla, assisted by supermonsters Mothra and Rodan, could stop him.

GHOST AND MRS. MUIR

Airing on TV from 1968 to 1970, this fantasy sitcom starred Hope Lange as pretty Carolyn Muir, a recently widowed author who relocated with her two young children to the quaint New England coastal town of Schooner Bay. They settled into Gull Cottage, a little rented house overlooking the sea, that seemed perfect for these new occupants until the discovery of one thing—it was haunted by the spirit of a former owner, Captain Daniel Gregg (Edward Mulhare), a nineteenth-century ship captain. At first, the salty spook resented the Muir family, but he later began to look out for their best interests (especially the pretty Mrs. Muir). Supporting cast members were Harlen Carraher as son Jonathan Muir, Kellie Flanagan as daughter Candy Muir, Reta Shaw as housekeeper Martha Grant, Scruffy as the family pooch, and Charles Nelson Reilly as Claymore Gregg, the Muir's landlord and fussy mortal nephew of the ghostly captain. Based on the 1947 film that starred Rex Harrison and Gene Tierney.

GHOSTBUSTERS

"Who ya gonna call? Ghostbusters!" A 1984 big-screen adventure about a team of poltergeist hunters called on to rid New York's Big Apple of an array of off-the-wall spooks, including the slime-spewing Green Blob and the titanic Stay-Puff Marshmallow Man. "Afraid of no ghosts," the proton-powered Ghostbusters consisted of paranormal scientists—sarcastic Peter Venkman (Bill Murray), buffoon Raymond Stantz (Dan Aykroyd), brainiac Egon Spengler (Harold Ramis), and friend Winston Zeddemore (Ernie Hudson)—who worked out of an old firehouse and drove a souped-up hearse called the Ecto-1. Sigourney Weaver co-starred as a beautiful concert cellist, Dana Barrett, who hires the Ghostbusters to rid her upscale Manhattan pad of a demon God housed in her refrigerator. Written by Aykroyd and Ramis and directed by Ivan Reitman, the film's slapstick special effects led it to become the highest-grossing comedy of all time. It spawned a 1989 sequel, two Saturday-morning cartoons, and a line of action figures. Ray Parker Jr., former lead singer of Raydio, scored a number-one hit with the theme song.

GHOSTLY TRIO

Three people-spooking older ghost uncles named Stretch, Stinkie, and Fatso, with whom Casper the Friendly Ghost shares a haunted house in the Enchanted Forest.

GHOSTS

The invisible beings that go bump in the night. Some specters are friendly, like Casper; others are not friendly, like those in *The Amityville Horror* and *The Shining.*

GIBB, ANDY

Kid brother (born March 5, 1958, in England) of the superstar group Bee Gees who became a top-selling singer on his own merits. One of these merits included good looks—wavy golden locks, a gleaming white smile, a sexy hairy chest, and a nice bulge showcased by spandex pants—which put him among the ranks of the teen idol elite of the late 1970s. If you looked in the school locker of the archetypal teen girl, you would find his pinups among those of then-current heartthrobs Shaun Cassidy, Leif Garrett, and John Travolta. Gibb's recording hits included the chart-toppers "I Just Want to Be Your Everything (1977), "(Love Is) Thicker Than Water" (1977), and "Shadow Dancing" (1978). In 1980, he dueted with gal-pal Olivia Newton-John on "I Can't Help It."

Around 1982, the pop star's professional and personal life hit rock bottom. All-night binges on booze and cocaine got him fired as host of TV's *Solid Gold* for no-showing on several tapings, and canned from the Broadway production of *Joseph and the Amazing Technicolor Dreamcoat* for missing twelve performances in one month. Gibb's careless lifestyle caused his fiancée, *Dallas* star Victoria Principal, to call off their engagement, leaving him outwardly brokenhearted. After a long fight with substance abuse, he died of a heart ailment on March 10, 1988, at the age of thirty.

GIBBONS, EUELL

Harvest-praising naturalist from Pennsylvania who became famous in the mid-1970s for advertising crunchy Post Grape-Nuts cereal in a series of TV commercials.

GIBSON, DEBBIE

Sweet teen queen of pop music, born August 31, 1970, in Long Island, who scored big in the late

1980s with a string of Top Forty hits: "Only in My Dreams" (1987), "Shake Your Love" (1987), "Out of the Blue" (1988), "Foolish Beat" (1988), and "Lost in Your Eyes" (1989). She was the subject of the oft-asked question among electric youths: "Who do you like better, Tiffany (her rival) or Debbie Gibson?" My answer? Gibson, of course. Unlike redhead Tiffany, who held concerts in shopping malls (tacky, tacky), the blonde girl-next-door had the better singing voice, wrote all her songs, and is still around today performing in Broadway musicals like *Les Misérables* and Disney's *Beauty and the Beast*.

GIBSON, MEL

Dark-haired, blue-eyed, boyishly handsome Australian hunk who became an international star and sex symbol—chosen as *People* magazine's "Sexiest Man Alive of 1985"—after playing the futuristic desert wanderer in a trio of *Mad Max* movies. Other prominent films include both the Australia-produced *Tim* (1979) and *Gallipoli* (1981), along with *The Year of Living Dangerously* (1982), *The Bounty* (1984), *Tequila Sunrise* (1988), *Hamlet* (1990), *Forever Young* (1992), *Maverick* (1994), *Braveheart* (1995), which won him an Oscar for Best Director, *Ransom* (1996), *The Patriot* (2000), and *Signs* (2002). In 1987, the actor bared his cute derriere in the cop thriller *Lethal Weapon* (1987). A devout Catholic, Gibson filmed his take on the final hours and crucifixion of Jesus Christ with the extremely violent moneymaker *The Passion of the Christ*, one of 2004's most controversial movies. Currently, he tops the list as a Hollywood power player, demanding paychecks as high as $25 million a picture (*The Patriot*), and is ranked number one in *Forbes* as the highest-paid celebrity of 2004 (he reportedly earned $210 million from *The Passion of the Christ*).

FYI: ▸ Mel Gibson was actually born in America—Peekskill, New York, to be exact. When Gibson was twelve, his father (a native of Australia) moved Gibson and his eleven siblings to his home country so the boys could avoid being drafted into the Vietnam War. Whatever his nationality, Gibson is proof that they grow them better Down Under, paving the way for Hollywood's current crop of Aussie hunks, such as Russell Crowe, Guy Pearce, Heath Ledger, and Hugh Jackman.

GIDGET

"Toodles!" Airing on ABC-TV from 1965 to 1966, a sitcom starring young Sally Field as Frances "Gidget" Lawrence, a plucky fifteen-year-old Southern California girl who yearns for good times in the Malibu sun with her surfer pals. Co-stars included Don Porter as Gidget's widowed dad, Professor Russell Lawrence, Betty Conner as older sister Anne, and Lynette Winter as best friend Larue, who claimed to be allergic to the sun. The "Gidg" and Larue attended school at Westside High. The show was based on the book by Frederick Kohner and the *Gidget* film series, the first of which starred Sandra Dee in the title role (1959).

FYI: ▸ The nickname "Gidget" stands for "girl midget."

GIDNEY AND CLOYD

Gidney was mustached, Cloyd was barefaced, and the pair of trigger-happy but friendly moonmen was featured in the first animated *Rocky and Bullwinkle* story, "Jet Fuel Formula," in 1959.

GIGANTOR

Flying space-age robot star of a Japanese-produced cartoon who, according to the theme song, "was bigger than big, taller than tall, quicker than quick, stronger than strong, and ready to fight for right against wrong." Controlled by twelve-year-old Jimmy Sparks, son of creator Dr. Sparks, Gigantor was built as a jet-propelled weapon of war but later reprogrammed to act as protector of peace against interplanetary evil. Based on the Japanese series *Tetsujin 28 Go*, the show first aired on American syndicated TV in 1965. It was produced by the same folks who gave us *Astro Boy* and *Speed Racer*.

GIGGLES

"When Giggles giggles, everybody giggles!" The happiest doll in the world was introduced by Ideal Toys in 1967. Eighteen inches tall, she had big blue eyes and blonde, rooted hair, and, as her arms were moved apart, she would cock her head, look right and then left, and giggle, giggle, giggle. When her hands were put back together, she would giggle some more.

G.I. JOE

G.I. Joe, "America's Movable Fighting Man," is the most famous action figure of all time. His main mission has always been to help little boys have fun. Introduced by Hasbro in 1964, Joe was created by freelance toy designer Stan Weston from a composite of twenty Congressional Medal of Honor recipients. Buyers, retailers, and some parents at first sneered at the twelve-inch-tall war hero, claiming that a doll for boys would never sell, but the skeptics were proven wrong when first-year sales topped more than $17 million. By 1965, it was the best-selling toy among children under the age of twelve.

Initially G.I. Joe came in four different sets, based on the branches of the U.S. military: Action Soldier, Action Sailor, Action Marine, and Action Pilot—all with trademark fuzzy crew-cut, battle-scarred cheek, and multiple-jointed body. Commonly we think of Joe wearing clunky combat boots, fatigues, and a dog tag and carrying an arsenal of weapons, including pistols, rifles, machine guns, hand grenades, and bazookas. In 1966, he was joined by three foreign allies (British Commando, Australian Jungle Fighter, and French Resistance Fighter), who helped him combat a trio of enemies (German Storm Trooper, Japanese Imperial Soldier, and Russian Infantry Man). The following year we saw the introduction of a Talking G.I. Joe, who barked battlefield commands like "We must get there before dark. Follow me!" and "Medic, get that stretcher!" There were also many exciting accessories, including pup tents, jeeps, rafts, helicopters, jet fighter planes, a sea sled, a space capsule, a headquarters, and a footlocker to store all Joe's equipment.

In 1970, because of antiwar sentiment over the conflict in Vietnam, his fighting image was softened with the Adventure Team Joe line. He could now be bought as an Air Adventurer, Sea Adventurer, Land Adventurer, and so on. This new nonmilitary image had Joe trekking off on global explorations in a series of action sets with exciting titles like "Capture of the Pygmy Gorilla," "Fangs of the Cobra," "White Tiger Hunt," "Search for the Abominable Snowman," "Mystery of the Boiling Lagoon," and "Perils of the Raging Inferno."

Little boys during the Reagan-powered 1980s are more familiar with the G.I. Joe that was a four-inch-tall plastic action figure with a slew of comrades: Scarlett, Snake Eyes, Stalker, Breaker, Short-Fuze, Grunt, Flash, Zap, and Rock 'n' Roll. Introduced in 1983, these action figures battled a ruthless terrorist organization known as Cobra. It helped launch a *G.I. Joe* comic-book series and a Saturday TV cartoon, *G.I. Joe: A Real American Hero.*

A likeable TV ad airing in the mid-1990s featured a G.I. Joe–type doll driving a miniature Nissan over to a toy townhouse and sweeping a Barbie-type doll away from her Ken-type boyfriend. In reality, most girls never wanted their Barbies to date the "World's Greatest Action Figure," because he was too rugged (and too ugly) for the "Queen of Fashion Dolls." They preferred that compliant Ken escort Malibu Barbie on her dream dates. "Now you know, and knowing is half the battle."

FYI: ▸ "G.I.," a popular slang term for American foot soldiers during World War II, stood for "Government Issue."

GILBERT, MELISSA

Winsome child star, born May 8, 1964, in Los Angeles, known best for playing freckle-faced, pigtailed tomboy Laura Ingalls on prime time's *Little House on the Prairie*. Gilbert grew up on TV, first in commercials (more than thirty by age seven), then in guest appearances on such shows as *Gunsmoke* and *Emergency!* and finally on the highly rated *Little House.* For nine seasons (1974–83), faithful viewers watched Laura mature from a nine-year-old to a young woman, becoming a teacher, a wife (Mrs. Almanzo Wilder), and a mother (to daughter Rose). Gilbert's impressive work in TV movies has included remakes of classic big-screen films: *The Miracle Worker* (1979), *The Diary of Anne Frank* (1980), and *Splendor in the Grass* (1981). During the 1980s, she had a lengthy love affair with the Brat Pack's Rob Lowe. Younger sister is Sara Gilbert, who played free-spirited Darlene Conner on TV's *Roseanne.*

GILLEY'S

This country-and-western nightclub in Pasadena, Texas, owned by singer Mickey Gilley ("Stand by Me"), was the epicenter of the Urban Cowboy craze of the 1980s. At Gilley's you would find country superstars crooning their latest hits on stage, and patrons two-stepping, line-dancing, sipping long-neck beers, playing pool, bar-brawling, and riding the bucking mechanical bull. After eighteen years of operation, the club announced its final last call in 1989.

GILLIGAN

"Oh, Gilligan, not again!" Dressed in a perennial wardrobe of red shirt, white pants, and sailor's cap, actor Bob Denver's Gilligan was the lovable first mate of the shipwrecked S.S. *Minnow* on prime time's *Gilligan's Island.*

FYI: ▸ According to Bob Denver and the show's creator-producer Sherwood Schwartz, Gilligan's first name was Willie, even though it was never revealed.

GILLIGAN'S ISLAND

Considered by many to be the silliest TV sitcom of all time, this is the tale about a wildly diverse group of seven who set sail on a three-hour boating tour in the South Pacific only to run into a tropical storm that wrecks their tiny ship, the S.S. *Minnow,* on an uncharted isle. Hapless and marooned, these castaways include the *Minnow*'s skipper, Jonas Grumby (Alan Hale Jr.), first mate Gilligan (Bob Denver), millionaire Thurston Howell III (Jim Backus) and his socialite wife, Lovey Howell (Natalie Schafer), movie star Ginger Grant (Tina Louise), science professor Roy Hinkley (Russell Johnson), and Kansas farm girl Mary Ann Summers (Dawn Wells). A typical episode had the castaways concocting a somewhat far-fetched plan to get off the island with half-wit Gilligan usually screwing it up, or they're visited by some cartoonish character who never seems to be able to help them get back home.

The show was extremely loved by kids and hated by grown-ups. ("It's difficult to believe *Gilligan's Island* was written, directed, and filmed by adults," wrote the *San Francisco Chronicle.*) After its three-year prime-time run on CBS (1964–67), it went into rerun syndication and has been a cult hit ever since. A cartoon version, *The New Adventures of Gilligan,* aired on Saturday mornings from 1974 to 1977. Later, the cast (minus Tina Louise, replaced by Judith Baldwin) was reassembled for three made-for-TV films: *Rescue from Gilligan's Island* (1978), *The Castaways on Gilligan's Island* (1979), and *The Harlem Globetrotters on Gilligan's Island* (1981). A frequently asked pop culture question among Gen-Xers is "Who do you think is sexier, Ginger or Mary Ann?"

FYI: ▸ Something I've always pondered: If the castaways were just going on a three-hour cruise, why did they have enough clothing and other belongings to last three years: Ginger's array of cocktail gowns, the professor's laboratory equipment, and the Howells' trunks of furs, diamonds, money, and booze?

GILLIGAN'S ISLAND THEME

"Just sit right back and you'll hear a tale, a tale of a fateful trip. . . ." An obscure vocal group, The Wellingtons, performed the theme song to the adored TV sitcom. Officially titled "The Ballad of Gilligan's Island," it was written by George Wyle and Sherwood Schwartz, creator of *Gilligan's Island.*

GINGER GRANT

Glamorous, redheaded Hollywood star (in the slinky Marilyn Monroe mode with beauty mark) who was once voted Miss Hourglass—because her sand was in all the right places! Ginger's film credits include *Housewives from Mars, The Hula Girl and the Fullback,* and *Sing a Song of Sing-Sing.* Actress Tina Louise supposedly despised playing sex-goddess Ginger on *Gilligan's Island,* believing that the role typecast her and ruined her chances of becoming a serious movie actress. She doesn't take part in any *Gilligan* reunion shows and loathes interview questions about the beloved sitcom.

FYI: ▸ Rumor has it that the buxom Jayne Mansfield, not Marilyn Monroe, was the original model for sexy Ginger Grant. Mansfield allegedly turned down the part.

GIRL FROM U.N.C.L.E.

Airing on prime time from 1966 to 1967, this female-oriented spin-off from NBC-TV's popular *Man from U.N.C.L.E.* starred newcomer Stefanie Powers as April Dancer, a pretty American spy—"108 pounds of dynamite"—who was teamed with a dashing agent from London, Mark Slate (Noel Harrison).

GIRL GROUPS

In the mid-1960s, the girl-group sound rivaled that of the British, Motown, Surf, and Psychedelic music genres. Consisting purely of high school glee-club-type vocalists (Chiffons, Dixie Cups, and Supremes, for example) or vulgarian cycle chicks (Ronettes, Shangri-Las, and the like), these all-female acts melted the hearts of Americans with simple yet catchy songs about boyfriend angst. Throughout most of the 1970s, the popularity of girl groups had waned, but periodically a female act, such as LaBelle or Sister Sledge, would strike heat with some disco anthem. The 1980s saw a strong reemergence of the girl group led by a force known as The Go-Go's and other total-girlie New Wavers (for example, Bananarama and The Bangles). The 1990s ended with "Girl Power" at full throttle, as a British quartet, The Spice Girls, racked up a string of chart-toppers.

"GIRLS JUST WANT TO HAVE FUN"

In 1984, Cyndi Lauper's bouncy signature song set the mood for what it was like to be young, female, and in the middle of the Go-Go decade (the 1980s). You see, thanks to the previous generation of feminists, it was okay, if not encouraged, for gals coming of age to be independent, free-thinking, strong, and sexually assertive. After working hard all day, they wanted to play even harder. They dressed in sexy New Wave fashions from stores such as Merry-Go-Round or in kooky vintage clothing from thrift stores. Makeup was worn wild, vivid, and colorful—forget natural—and they often dyed their hair any color of the rainbow. Best of all, a girl could stay out all night long, dancing and gallivanting till the sun came up.

GIVE-A-SHOW PROJECTOR

Popular in the 1960s and early 1970s, this Kenner toy allowed kids to put on a show anytime, anywhere (usually on a sheet hanging on the bedroom wall). The battery-operated plastic projector displayed big (eight-by-eight-foot) shows from 35 mm color slides (each slide had seven scenes) involving favorite cartoon characters, from familiar superheroes like Mighty Mouse, Spider-Man, and Batman to revered TV stars including Casper, Scooby-Doo, and Fred Flintstone.

GIZMO

Cuddly, furry, big-eyed Mogwai given to Billy Peltzer as a Christmas present. He spawned a gang of rambunctious, reptile-like gremlins after rules about the care and feeding were broken. (Don't expose him to bright light, don't get him wet, and don't feed him after midnight.) In the movie *Gremlins* (1984), comedian Howie Mandel provided Gizmo's voice.

GLADYS KRAVITZ

This busybody snoop lived across the street from Samantha and Darrin Stephens on *Bewitched*. Gladys has a long-suffering husband who plainly ignored her screams of "Abner!" after she'd just witnessed something unusual over at the Stephens house.

GLADYS ORMPHBY

A character on TV's *Laugh-In* played by comedienne Ruth Buzzi. Gladys was a crotchety spinster who continually used her purse or umbrella as a weapon on dirty old man Tyrone (Arte Johnson), who snuggled up to her on a park bench.

GLAMOUR GALS

Standing a mere four inches, these Lilliputian fashion dolls with vinyl bodies and rooted big hair were manufactured by Kenner Toys in the early 1980s (1981–82). Jessie, Danni, Loni, Shara, and Jana came with beautiful clothes, handsome boyfriends, and great accessories, such as the Fancy Firebird sports car, the Party Place hangout, and the Ocean Queen cruise ship. Mattel Toys followed suit by introducing their small-sized Dazzle doll line in 1982.

GLAMOUR HEAD STYLING CENTERS

Little hairdressers could apply makeup and style the hair on large doll-head replicas of favorite celebs like Farrah Fawcett, Marie Osmond, Brooke Shields, Barbie, and the Bionic Woman.

GLASS, MARVIN

Acclaimed designer wiz for board-game manufacturers, such as Ideal, Milton Bradley, Parker Brothers, and Schaper, noted for inventing many of the classic action-games played by children of the 1960s and 1970s. Best-known games: Mouse Trap

(1963), Time Bomb (1964), Hands Down (1965), Operation (1965), Tip It (1965), Rock 'Em Sock 'Em Robots (1966), Tiger Island (1966), Feeley Meeley (1967), Ants in the Pants (1968), Kooky Carnival (1969), Toss Across (1969), Which Witch? (1970), and Gnip Gnop (1971).

GLOBEY

Wise and worldly globe who talked in a French accent on Saturday-morning TV's *Pee-Wee's Playhouse*. His duty in the Playhouse was to introduce Pee-Wee Herman and home viewers to faraway foreign places by using vintage travelogues.

GLORIA GLAD

Rich kid Richie Rich's pretty, middle-class, redheaded girlfriend in his comic books was fond of saying "Neat-o!" I think Richie Rich liked Gloria because, unlike everyone else, she wasn't overly impressed with his vast wealth.

GLORIA VANDERBILT JEANS

While Calvin was king of designer jeans, the Manhattan socialite, once dubbed America's "poor little rich girl," was the queen. Vanderbilt's best-selling, high-dollar jeans were fabulously supertight (many wearers had to slowly squeeze into a pair by lying horizontal on a bed, or even the floor) and colored a perfect deep indigo (you didn't dare machine-dry them for fear of unfashionable fading). Each pair had Vanderbilt's moniker scrawled across the back right pocket and a trademark swan stitched over the front coin pocket. Gloria also experienced tremendous success with floral-scented Vanderbilt perfume, one of the top fragrance lines of the 1980s.

GLO WORM

Introduced in 1982, Hasbro's stuffed worm with the cheery face helped keep those scary "things that go bump in the night" away from toddlers by providing a comforting glow when its snuggly body was squeezed.

GNIP GNOP

"You're trying to out-Gnip him, while he's trying to out-Gnop you!" Introduced in 1971, this variation of ping-pong was one of the most successful action-games for Parker Brothers. Players whacked keys simultaneously, shooting six colorful balls through holes in the center panel of a see-through plastic dome. The balls would collide furiously in mid-air or bounce up against the sides as they tried to pass through the holes. The player to empty his side first was the winner. If you are wondering what the odd name Gnip Gnop means, it's ping-pong spelled backward.

GNOME-MOBILE

"Take off your brakes and laugh!" Released in 1967, a marvelous Disney fantasy directed by Robert Stevenson and based on a children's book by Upton Sinclair. Character actor Walter Brennan stars in a dual grandfather role as D. J. Mulrooney, a curmudgeonly lumber tycoon, and Knobby, a friendly 943-year-old gnome. While on a day trip in California's Redwood Forest, Mulrooney and his young grandchildren, Elizabeth and Rodney Winthrop (played by "the *Mary Poppins* kids," Karen Dotrice and Matthew Garber), discover a pair of gnomes, Knobby and his grandson Jasper, trying to find their lost colony. They set off in Mulrooney's fancy 1930s Rolls-Royce (the Gnome-Mobile of title) in search of the other gnomes and to protect them from being exploited in a carnival freak show. The title song was written by Richard and Robert Sherman.

GO ASK ALICE

"Sugar and spice and everything nice. Acid and smack and no way back." The must-read book for teenagers back in the 1970s was at one time considered shocking because it was the actual diary of an anonymous fifteen-year-old drug user. Alice was an average middle-class teen whose journals chronicled a nightmarish struggle with drugs—particularly acid, pot, and speed—and the desperate attempt to fight her way back to the real world. She died of a mysterious drug overdose after making the decision to stay clean and stop writing in a diary. Since first being published in 1971, *Go Ask Alice* has sold more than three million copies. In 1973, the story was adapted into an excellent TV movie of the same title, starring Jamie Smith-Jackson as Alice.

FYI: ▸ The title, *Go Ask Alice*, was taken from the 1967 drug-trippy song "White Rabbit" by Jefferson Airplane: "One pill makes you larger / And one pill makes you small / And the ones that mother gives you don't do anything at all / Go ask Alice, when she's ten feet tall. . . ."

GOATEE

The pointy billy-goat beard once brought to mind the era of bongo-playing, "Daddy-O" Beats (or Satan) before becoming part of the essential uniform of Gen-X males in the 1990s. A variation of the goatee is the soul patch, a patch of fuzz between the chin and bottom lip. Guys who wear these often think they're real cool.

GOBBLEDEGOOK

Kids squeezed various flavors—cinnamon, licorice, cherry, raspberry, root beer, butterscotch, mint, and tutti frutti—of this sugarless goo into a silly-faced oven, the Sooper Gooper, to make wiggly, squiggly, and truly digestible Incredible Edibles. Don't worry, mothers. The fun-to-say Gobbledegook had the Good Housekeeping Seal of Approval.

GOD'S EYE

Grade-school art project for which you wrapped cheerfully colored yarn around two popsicle sticks until you created a work of art supposedly resembling the eye of God.

GODZILLA

Godzilla. Just the mere mention of the name brings back memories of being a kid sitting mesmerized in front of the TV set on weekend afternoons, watching badly edited black-and-white movies of the rubber-suited monster destroying the megalopolis of Tokyo while Japanese actors—whose mouths moved out of synch to poorly dubbed English—sought ways of combating the rampaging beast. Godzilla originated as a simple prehistoric reptile, a Godzillasaurus, exposed to radiation after his South Pacific island habitat was used for atomic testing in the mid-1950s. This exposure turned him into a towering, greenish-gray monster capable of mass destruction and delivering devastating atomic blasts with his breath. When not menacing Tokyo, Godzilla was off fighting a parade of seemingly unbeatable enemies, such as humongous moth Mothra, big mutant pterodactyl Rodan, three-headed flying space dragon Ghidorah, mammoth cockroach Megalon, sea monster Ebirah, smog monster Hedora, mechanical replica Mecha Godzilla, and giant ape King Kong.

The "king of the monsters" made his cinematic debut in the 1954 Japanese film *Gojira* (pronounced "Godzilla," it's a translation of a word combo: "gorilla" and "whale"), directed by Ishiro Honda. Created as a symbol of the devastation wreaked on Japan by the American atom bomb, *Gojira* was taken very seriously by the Japanese people, making it one of their all-time most popular and critically acclaimed hits. In 1956, a poorly cropped and dubbed version was released in America: *Godzilla, King of the Monsters* (containing unnecessary footage of Raymond "Perry Mason" Burr as a reporter and commentator). Of course, Americans loved the movie, and its 250-foot-tall, 400-ton, fire-breathing, radioactive star became a household name and cultural icon, inspiring more than fifteen sequels, countless imitations, and a 1998 update starring Matthew Broderick and a New York–trashing Godzilla that looks nothing like the original.

GO-GO BOOTS

"Are you ready, boots? Start walkin'. . . ."
—NANCY SINATRA

When I think of 1960s footwear, the first thing that comes to mind are these low-heeled, mid-calf-high white boots. Introduced in 1965 by French designer André Courrèges during the peak of mod fashion, they were named after the miniskirted go-go girls who wore them while dancing at discotheques around the nation. During their heyday, groovy go-go boots were seen on the most trendsetting celebs, like Dusty Springfield, Petula Clark, Jeannie C. Riley, The Shangri-Las, Twiggy, Ann-Margret, and Raquel Welch—who wore a fur version in the 1966 dinosaur epic *One Million Years B.C.* But the Queen of Boots was Nancy Sinatra, whose boots threatened to "walk all over you," or at least according to her 1966 homage to footwear, "These Boots Are Made for Walkin'." (While on tour to promote the song, Sinatra carried 250 pairs of go-go boots of every style, shape, and color.) By decade's end, the boot fad was still kicking, and the age of wearers was even younger: grade-school girls adored boots endorsed by little Buffy from TV's *Family Affair* in 1969. Boots of the 1970s came in a variety of colors and heights, including the standard knee-high ones sported by pro football cheerleading squads, such as the Dallas Cowboys Cheerleaders and the Oakland Raiderettes.

GO-GO GIRLS

Sexy women, often dressed in bikinis or fringed minidresses and go-go boots, who demonstrated the latest dance crazes—the Twist, Swim, Jerk, and Frug—inside elevated cages at the famed Whiskey A-Go-Go in Hollywood and other American nightclubs in the 1960s. Later became associated with sleazy strippers.

FYI: ▸ In 1970, a sixteen-year-old British girl named Jane Berins set a world record by go-go dancing for eighteen hours!

GO-GO'S

In the early 1980s, this enthusiastic all-female quintet—noted for quirky, straightforward songs about having fun, heartbreak, and other matters important to the young—took the country by storm, becoming the most influential girl group of the decade. During the band's reign, it was a common sight to see dance floors filled to capacity with club kids "go-go"-ing to the peppy beat of their retro surf-meets-Valley-Girl sound. Along with the music, their thrift-store finery and New Wave hairdos easily inspired other 1980s girl acts, including The Waitresses, The Bangles, Bananarama, Toni Basil, and even Madonna.

Formed originally as a punk band in Los Angeles in 1978, The Go-Go's were two twenty-year-old lead singers: cute and chubby fair-haired Belinda Carlisle and cute and impish dark-haired Jane Wiedlin. Rounding out the group were guitarist Charlotte Caffey, bassist Kathy Valentine, and drummer Gina Schock. Their maiden album, *Beauty and the Beat*, went multiplatinum in 1981, topping the charts for six weeks and spinning off two smash singles: "Our Lips Are Sealed" and "We Got the Beat." The next year, they followed suit with the summer-oriented ditty "Vacation," accompanied by a cool music video featuring the girls doing synchronized waterskiing. As a result of personal conflicts, like the customary rock 'n' roll ego trips and drug problems, The Go-Go's disbanded in 1985. Carlisle and Wiedlin both went on to have solo careers marked with hits: Belinda's "Mad About You" (1986) and Jane's "Blue Kiss" (1985).

GOLDDIGGERS

A group of gorgeous young women assembled as singers and dancers for *The Dean Martin Show* in the late 1960s. The sexy troupe also performed as a Vegas act and on the Bob Hope Christmas Show in Vietnam.

FYI: ▸ The term "gold digger" is used to describe a woman, often attractive, who hooks a much older man and marries him for his wealth. Famous gold diggers: Marilyn Monroe's Lorelei (from *Gentlemen Prefer Blondes*), Zsa Zsa Gabor, Anna Nicole Smith, and any gal who dates Donald Trump.

GOMER PYLE

"Gaa-aw-leeh!" The goofy, likable yokel was first seen in *The Andy Griffith Show* (played by Jim Nabors) working as a filling-station attendant at Wally's, before becoming a marine stationed at California's Camp Henderson and headlining his own *Gomer Pyle* TV show on CBS from 1964 to 1969. "Shazam!"

FYI: ▸ In spite of his rural twang, Nabors has a booming singing voice, well suited for show tunes and hymns, and he enjoyed a second career as a recording artist.

GOMEZ ADDAMS

Cigar-smoking, mustachioed, wild-eyed Latino lawyer who was the family patriarch on *The Addams Family*. Gomez liked to follow his estate's fortune on a stock ticker-tape machine, wreck model train sets violently, and have wife Morticia speak French (it drove him mad with passion). Portrayed by John Astin (TV) and Raul Julia (film).

GONG SHOW

The epitome of bad TV was this talent show for people with no talent. Premiering in 1976, the bizarre and often tasteless daytime program featured a panel of three B-grade celebrities who judged a sequence of unusual amateur acts performing questionable talents. Equipped with handy mallets, the celebrity panel had a large gong nearby, and when an act was awful (and about one-third were) it got gonged off the stage. But if an act had enough talent to get by the mercy of the raucous judges, it was rated on a scale of one through ten, with the show's winner receiving a cash award of $516.32 plus a Golden Gong.

Typical of *The Gong Show* talents were a musician who played a trumpet with his belly button; an elderly fellow who pirouetted in a tutu; a man who meowed the song "Alley Cat"; and a fat lady dressed as an oversized Shirley Temple warbling "On the Good Ship Lollipop." *The Gong Show* was produced and created by Chuck Barris (nicknamed "Chucky Baby"), who moonlighted as host. Among the celebs who frequented the outrageous program were Jaye P. Morgan, Jamie Farr, Rex Reed, Arte Johnson, Michele Lee, Phyllis Diller, Rip Taylor, Steve Garvey, and Dr. Joyce Brothers. Regular performers featured during interludes included the paper-sacked Unknown Comic and the rhythmless Gene Gene the Dancing Machine. Barris also produced two classic game shows: *The Dating Game* and *The Newlywed Game*.

FYI: ▸ Disco diva Cheryl Lynn (1979's "Got to Be Real") was discovered on *The Gong Show*!

GONZO THE GREAT

A blue hook-nosed "whatever-he-is" creature whose job on *The Muppet Show* was to open each program with a trumpet fanfare (which he always botched).

GOOBER AND THE GHOST-CHASERS

Hanna-Barbera cartoon show, another *Scooby-Doo* knockoff airing from 1973 to 1975, about a stick-thin dog named Goober teamed up with a trio of young reporters—Gilly, Ted, and Tina—who hunted apparitions for *Ghost Chasers* magazine. When frightened, Goober would become invisible (except for the stocking cap atop his head). From time to time, various members of TV's *Partridge Family*, including Laurie, Danny, Chris, and Tracy, would tag along with the gang on their ghost-chasing antics.

GOOD HUMOR ICE CREAM

Every summer afternoon, like clockwork, kids would hear the "ring-a-ding-a-ling, ring-a-ding-a-ling" coming from down the street. It was the white Good Humor ice-cream truck. And hurry! If mom didn't dish out money quickly enough, you could miss it (or so it seemed to an excited child). Offering favorites like Strawberry Shortcake and Chocolate Eclair Bars, Sundae Twists, Neapolitan Sandwiches, and King Cones, Good Humor's frozen delights were the perfect remedy for beating the heat on a sweat-oozing summer day. Good Humor ice cream was founded by Harry Burt in Youngstown, Ohio, in 1920. Today, it is a leading ice-cream brand and can be found in most grocery stores.

GOOD TIMES

Black-oriented TV sitcom notable for being the first spin-off of a spin-off (it was descended from *Maude*, which in turn was descended from *All in the Family*). Airing on CBS from 1974 to 1979, it concerned the "scratching and surviving" of Maude Findlay's former maid, Florida Evans, as she struggled to raise her lower-class brood in a high-rise housing project on Chicago's South Side. Florida (played by hefty, gap-toothed Esther Rolle) was a loving mother who struggled to make ends meet and guard her children from the negative influences of ghetto life. Other family members included Florida's frequently unemployed husband, James Evans (John Amos), who died in a car accident in 1976 (Amos wanted out of his contract), jive-talking eldest son J.J. (for James Jr.) Evans (Jimmie Walker), pretty daughter Thelma Evans (BernNadette Stanis), and youngest son Michael Evans (Ralph Carter). Sexy Willona Woods (Janet Dubois) was Florida's best friend and next-door neighbor. In 1977, pre–pop star Janet Jackson joined the cast as Penny, an abused little girl adopted by Willona.

GOODY BARRETTES

These plastic baby barrettes were a significant fashion staple for preschoolers who needed help keeping strands of baby-fine hair from falling out of place. They came in cheerful colors—blue, pink, purple, and yellow—and were found in way-too-cute shapes, including butterflies, bunnies, daisies, and duckies. Became a silly retro fad when adult women sported them in their coifs in the 1990s (movie princess Drew Barrymore, grunge queen Courtney Love, Beverly Hills brat Tori Spelling, and material girl Madonna).

GOOFY

Appearing rather dilapidated, the half-witted black dog is one of Walt Disney's "Classic Five" cartoon characters (the others included Mickey Mouse, Minnie Mouse, Donald Duck, and Pluto). Known for a gutteral laugh that goes something like "Uh-hyulk, uh-hyulk . . . yep . . . uh-hyulk," the lovable goof first appeared in a Mickey Mouse short called

"Mickey's Revue" in 1932. From 1992 to 1996, he starred opposite bratty son Max in *Goof Troop*, an afternoon TV series on the Disney Channel that inspired a full-length animated feature, *A Goofy Movie*, in 1995.

GOOFY GRAPE

This zany purple vineyard fruit with the Napoleon cap was the spokes-grape and the best known of Pillsbury's Funny Face drink mix characters.

GOONIES

"Truffle Shuffle." Hellishly noisy 1985 Steven Spielberg production about a band of outcast kids, called "The Goonies," on an adventurous search for an old pirate treasure hidden in a spooky underground cavern that is peppered with secret passageways and booby traps. The Goonies must find the loot in order to save their small seaside community from the hands of greedy property developers who want to turn it into a golf course. Unfortunately for our young heroes, a pursuing family of criminals, led by mean Mama Fratelli (Anne Ramsey) and hulking, Baby Ruth–loving son Sloth (John Matuszak), is closing in. The Goonies consisted of heroic brothers Michael "Mikey" Walsh (Sean Astin) and Brandon "Brand" Walsh (Josh Brolin), along with wiseacre Clark "Mouth" Devereaux (Corey Feldman), chubby Lawrence "Chunk" Cohen (Jeff Cohen), spunky Andrea "Andy" Carmichael (Kerri Green), computer geek Richard "Data" Wong (Jonathan Ke Quan), and smart-mouth Stefanie "Stef" Steinbrenner (Martha Plimpton). It was directed by Richard Donner (*Superman*). Cyndi Lauper had a hit single with its theme, "The Goonies 'R' Good Enough."

GOOSEBUMPS

> "I've never turned into a bee.
> I've never been chased by a mummy
> or met a ghost. But many of the ideas in my
> books are suggested by real life.
> For example, one Halloween my son, Matt,
> put a mask on and then
> had trouble pulling it off. That gave me
> the idea for *The Haunted Mask*."
>
> —R. L. STINE

Highly successful horror-book series aimed at gradeschoolers age eight to eleven, created in 1992 by author R. L. Stine, a former editor of *Bananas* magazine. Stine's stories were scary tales revolving around ghastly and just plain weird predicaments that enthralled kids, who couldn't stop reading no matter how many chilling goosebumps they got. Best known of these titles include *Stay Out of the Basement, Say Cheese and Die! Monster Blood, Swamp Fever, Welcome to Camp Nightmare, The Curse of the Mummy's Tomb, Night of the Living Dummy*, and *Revenge of the Lawn Gnomes*. In October 1995, just in time for Halloween, the live-action *Goosebumps* series premiered on the FOX-TV network.

FYI: ▸ R. L. Stine was named best-selling author by *USA Today* for three straight years, from 1994 to 1996. The *Goosebumps* books have sold more than 220 million copies.

GOPHER SMITH

First name: Burl. He's the always-optimistic yeoman-purser on *The Love Boat*. Following the hit TV show's cancellation, actor Fred Grandy—who played Gopher—returned to his home state of Iowa and got himself elected to the U.S. House of Representatives in 1986.

GORE, LESLEY

The golden-blonde teenager from New Jersey was one of America's top pop-female singers of the mid-1960s, known best for the explosive "It's My Party" ("and I'll cry if I want to") and sequel tune "Judy's Turn to Cry" (both produced by Quincy Jones in 1963). Another notable hit for Miss Gore is the chilling "You Don't Own Me" (1964), a prefeminist anthem performed years later by Goldie Hawn, Diane Keaton, and Bette Midler at the closing of the 1996 film *The First Wives Club*.

GOTHAM CITY

Fictional crime-riddled metropolis where you would find its most famous denizen, Batman, a.k.a. Bruce Wayne, raging battle against such evildoers as The Joker, The Penguin, and Catwoman.

GRANDMAMA ADDAMS

Veteran comic actress Blossom Rock (sister of Jeanette MacDonald) played Gomez Addams's brew-stirring, haggish witch mother on *The Addams Family* TV show.

GRANDPA DRACULA

On TV's *The Munsters*, character actor Al Lewis starred as Lily's very old (somewhere between the ages of 62 and 479) vampire father who, on a whim, would turn into a bat and was always concocting a scheme in his basement laboratory.

GRANNY (SYLVESTER AND TWEETY)

Gingerly matron who owned Tweety Pie and Sylvester the Cat. This Warner Brothers cartoon character had no qualms about giving bird-hungry Sylvester a whack with her broom, but, as we all know, the big-eyed, baby-voiced yellow canary could do no wrong (at least in the eyes of sweet Granny).

GRANNY DRESSES

Prudish, country-style dresses characterized by long sleeves, high necks, floor-length ruffled hems, and floral prints. Although they were embraced by hippie chicks who seemed to dig the old-fashioned romantic allure of the style, I can recall only flat-chested, preteen girls wearing granny dresses.

GREASE

"Ramalamadingdong!" *Grease* was "the word" in 1978, when the big-screen version of the long-running Broadway sensation—about the days of Hula-Hoops, poodle skirts, and slick duck-tails—became the year's number-one box-office moneymaker and the highest-grossing movie musical ever. Set at Rydell High in Southern California during the fab 1950s, it starred recording artist Olivia Newton-John as blonde Sandy Olsson, a wholesome transfer student from Australia pining for her tender summer love, who, unknown to her, is a leather-jacketed rebel at the new school. Snake-hipped hunk John Travolta (fresh from *Saturday Night Fever*) played dark-haired Danny Zuko, leader of the greaser T-Bird gang, who—for the sake of his "image"—pretends to be too cool for his sweet seaside flame ("You see, Sandy, I got this image . . ."). Danny's T-Bird buddies were best pal Kenickie (Jeff Conaway), Sonny (Michael Tucci), Putzie (Kelly Ward), and Doody (Barry Pearl). The female equivalents to the T-Birds were the scandalous Pink Ladies, consisting of sassy leader Betty Rizzo (Stockard Channing), Frenchy (Didi Conn), Jan (Jamie Donnelly), and Marty Maraschino (Dinah Manoff).

Other teenage characters included chirpy cheerleader Patty Simcox (Susan Buckner), nerdy Eugene Felsnick (Eddie Deezen), football jock Tom Chisum (Lorenzo Lamas, with dyed-blond hair), dirty-dancer Cha Cha DiGregorio (Annette Charles), and crater-faced T-Bird rival Leo (Dennis C. Stewart). A who's who of 1950s actors were cast in supporting adult roles: Eve Arden as staunch Principal McGee ("If you can't be an athlete, be an athletic supporter"); Dody Goodman as McGee's scatter-brained assistant, Blanche; Sid Caesar as Coach Calhoun; Alice Ghostley as auto-mechanic instructor Murdock; Fannie Flagg as the school nurse Wilkins; Joan Blondell as warmhearted waitress Vi; Edd "Kookie" Byrnes as *National Bandstand* emcee Vince Fontaine; Frankie Avalon as the Teen Angel; and Sha Na Na as Johnny Casino and the Gamblers.

Directed by Randal Kleiser, *Grease* was an electrifying showcase of energetic dancing (choreographed by Patricia Birch) and lively tunes. Its million-selling soundtrack album featured four Top Ten singles: the duos "You're the One That I Want" and "Summer Nights" by Newton-John and Travolta, "Hopelessly Devoted to You" by Newton-John, and title track "Grease" by Frankie Valli. Other songs included "Born to Hand Jive," "Greased Lightning," "Look at Me, I'm Sandra Dee," "Sandy," "There Are Worse Things I Could Do," and "We Go Together." Despite stars who were actually too old to portray teens (Newton-John was thirty, Channing was thirty-four) and the message that you'll get your man if you act like a cigarette-smoking tramp ("How's it hangin', stud?"), the movie was enormously popular with youths of the 1970s, who just couldn't get enough of 1950s nostalgia. Like shades of *Rocky Horror*, many fans saw *Grease* repeatedly at the theater, memorizing the complete dialogue and copying the dance movements. In 1982, a weak sequel—*Grease 2*—was released, starring Michelle Pfeiffer and Maxwell Caulfield.

GREATEST

Released in 1977, the autobiographical big-screen flick in which conceited boxing great Muhammad

Ali, the "Louisville Slugger," played himself. A so-so movie, it's most notable for introducing singer George Benson's wondrous "The Greatest Love of All," later recorded by Top Forty diva Whitney Houston in 1985.

GREAT GAZOO

Appearing in later *Flintstones* episodes, this recurring cartoon character was a miniature green space visitor (voiced in a pseudo-English accent by Harvey Korman) from the planet Zetox whose sole purpose on earth was to grant Fred's every wish (he appeared only to Fred). Gazoo answered to boss Gazaam.

GREAT GRAPE APE

"Grape Ape don't know his own strength." Hanna-Barbera's thirty-foot purple cartoon gorilla who palled around with a quick-speaking dog named Beegle while inadvertently wreaking havoc in the city of Anytown U.S.A.

GREAT LASH MASCARA

Created in 1971, Maybelline's famous mascara in the familiar pink-and-green tube is the world's number-one cosmetic product, selling at the rate of one every 1.9 seconds!

GREAT PUMPKIN

According to Linus Van Pelt on the animated TV special *It's the Great Pumpkin, Charlie Brown* (1966), every Halloween night this supernatural entity arrives at the Peanuts' neighborhood pumpkin patch "with his bag of toys for all the good children." (Obviously the blanket-toting tot had his holidays mixed up.)

GREAT SPACE COASTER

Syndicated TV show, airing from 1981 to 1986, featuring educational songs, jokes, and skits for kids presented by three teens—Francine, Danny, and Ray—and a variety of puppets. Life-sized and small, the puppets included Goriddle Gorilla, Knock Knock the Woodpecker, Edison the Elephant, and the program's biggest star, newscaster Gary Gnu ("No g-news is good g-news, with Gary Gnu"). In 1983, the series won a Peabody Award for an episode filmed at a riding camp for disabled children.

GREEN ACRES

Airing on CBS prime time from 1965 to 1971, this reversal of *The Beverly Hillbillies* featured a wealthy couple leaving behind a luxurious city life to live on a farm in the countryside. Successful Manhattan lawyer Oliver Wendell Douglas (Eddie Albert) longed to live in the country as a farmer. His ditzy blonde wife, Lisa (Eva Gabor), an always glamorous Hungarian-accented socialite, had no desire to leave penthouse life on Park Avenue. With Lisa reluctantly in tow, Oliver purchased a 160-acre farmstead (sight unseen), complete with a ramshackle house, on the outskirts of rural Hooterville.

Once on greener acres, they find farming is not quite what Oliver thought it would be, especially after encountering the kooky denizens of Hooterville. There was fast-talking con-artist/salesman Mr. Haney (Pat Buttram), befuddled agricultural agent Hank Kimball (Alvy Moore), naive and gangly handyman Eb Dawson (Tom Lester), feisty storekeeper Sam Drucker (Frank Cady), inept brother-and-sister carpenter team Alf and Ralph Monroe (Sid Melton and Mary Grace Canfield), pig farmer Fred Ziffel (Hank Patterson), his plump wife Doris Ziffel (Barbara Pepper), and the Ziffels' scene-stealing pet pig, Arnold. The well-known *Green Acres* theme song ("The chores! The stores! Fresh air! Times Square!"), sung by Albert and Gabor, was composed by Vic Mizzy, who also did the theme for *The Addams Family*.

GREEN EGGS AND HAM

"I do not like them, Sam-I-Am. I do not like green eggs and ham." Written and illustrated by Dr. Seuss in 1960, this best-selling rhyming tale starred Sam-I-Am, a pushy and persuasive fellow who liked green eggs and ham. He liked them so much that he spent the entire story convincing the book's other character, a cantankerous chap with no name, that he should like them too (" . . . in a box . . . with a fox . . . in a house . . . with a mouse . . ."). *Green Eggs and Ham* personified the genius of Dr. Seuss's work. Kids found it so fun to read and look at that they never noticed it was teaching something. The lesson? How do you know you don't like something until you try it?

GREEN GOBLIN

Greatest of all Spider-Man foes is this comic-book villain—real name: Norman Osborn II—with the green skin and pointed ears. His pumpkin bombs can be a big pain in the butt for the amazing web-slinger.

GREEN HORNET

Although *The Green Hornet* has been around since the late 1930s, as a radio show and later a comic book created by George Trendle, most of us are familiar with the dedicated superhero because of the mid-1960s TV series. Airing from 1966 to 1967 on ABC, it starred hunky Van Williams as millionaire playboy Britt Reid—grandnephew of John Reid, better known as The Lone Ranger—a crusading newspaper publisher by day (*Daily Sentinel*) and half-masked crime-fighter by night (The Green Hornet). He battled not exotic villains like Batman's Joker or Spider-Man's Green Goblin but mobsters, bootleggers, and an assortment of other gangster types. Martial-arts legend Bruce Lee co-starred as karate-chopping Kato, Reid's loyal houseboy and chauffeur of his supercharged Black Beauty. Also aiding him were the Hornet Gas Gun, which fired a green knockout gas, and the Hornet Sting, which fired a laser beam capable of penetrating steel. Kato and District Attorney F. P. Scanlon (played by Walter Brooke) were the only people who knew Reid's secret identity.

GREEN MACHINE

"For guys eight to ten years old who really know how to ride." Introduced by Marx Toys in 1975, the green-hued, high-tech, boy-friendly rival of the low-slung Big Wheel (also manufactured by Marx) was longer, sleeker, and could achieve tighter turns without tipping over.

GREG AND JENNY

The star-crossed love affair of Greg Nelson and Jenny Gardner (played by Laurence Lau and Kim Delaney) on *All My Children* was the younger, sweeter alternative to the hot-and-heavy romance of Luke and Laura on sister show *General Hospital* in the early 1980s. The two Pine Valley teens came from different sides of the track: clean-cut Greg was the son of prim, affluent Enid Nelson, while good-hearted Jenny was the daughter of tacky, white-trash Opal Gardner. They faced constant meddling from others, who tried to break them up: Tad "the Cad" Martin, Jenny's natural brother whose blackmailing ways usually affected the reputation of his sister; Mrs. Nelson, Greg's mother, who thought her son was too good for Jenny; and Liza Colby, their wicked classmate, who seized every opportunity to make Jenny feel unworthy of Greg (Liza wanted him all to herself). Streetwise African-American Jesse Hubbard and his girlfriend Angie Baxter were supporting friends. Despite the intrusions, Greg and Jenny found romance, and their popular story lines became the core of *All My Children* from 1981 to 1984.

GREG BRADY

The groovy and good-looking eldest *Brady Bunch* son was an aspiring rock star (Johnny Bravo), surfing buff, and teenage "Casanova of Clinton Avenue" (according to housemaid Alice). Barry Williams played Greg Brady.

GREMLINS

It's Christmas in the picture-perfect town of Kingstown Falls, and a teenager named Billy (Zach Galligan) receives a present from his gadget-inventing dad, Rand Peltzer (Hoyt Axton). The gift turns out to be an exotic Asian critter known as a Mogwai. Named Gizmo, the cute, furry, wide-eyed, cooing creature comes with three warnings: "Keep him out of the light. Don't get him wet. And never, never feed him after midnight." When Billy breaks the rules, little Gizmo spawns an army of nasty and ugly gremlins who turn the quaint hamlet into a battle zone. These malicious monsters gleefully foul up traffic, tear up a movie theater, trash the town, get drunk, and kill off the town grinch, Mrs. Deagle (Polly Holliday). The film co-starred fresh-faced Phoebe Cates as Kate, Billy's sweetheart, and Frances Lee McCain as Lynn Peltzer, Billy's mom, who uses her kitchen microwave to nuke a marauding gremlin.

A "Steven Spielberg Presentation" directed by horror master Joe Dante (*Piranha* and *The Howling*), *Gremlins* came under fire for violence far too extreme for its target audience: children. Despite the scares and gore, moviegoers took to the 1984 comedy-fantasy, making it a top moneymaker of the year. In 1990, an excellent sequel, *Gremlins II: The New Batch*, was hatched.

GREY POUPON

The horseradish-mustard spread became famous in the 1980s with a series of TV advertisements featuring a haughty rich fellow in the back of a chauffeured limousine pulling up alongside average people, rolling down his window, and asking: "Pardon me, do you have any Grey Poupon?"

GRIER, PAM

Born May 26, 1949, the North Carolina–bred actress, once called "the black Raquel Welch" because of similar attributes (gorgeous face and big breasts), was known as "the queen of blaxploitation films." Started her career in the early 1970s in a series of low-budget women-in-prison flicks: *The Big Doll House* (1971), *The Big Bird Cage* (1972), and *Women in Cages* (1972). But it was four films in which she played the title character that made Grier a cult figure and the sex symbol for men of all races and ages: *Coffy* (1973), *Foxy Brown* (1974), *Sheba Baby* (1975), and *Friday Foster* (1975). In these, her Afroed heroines were independent, strong, cool chicks out for revenge against drug lords, pimps, and other evildoers of the inner city.

When the blaxploitation genre dimmed, so did Grier's career. She resorted to playing character roles, like a drug-crazed hooker in 1981's *Fort Apache, The Bronx* and a witch in 1983's *Something Wicked This Way Comes.* A major comeback occurred in 1997 when director Quentin Tarantino—a fan of the fast-paced, low-budget, violence-oriented blaxploitation films—cast her as the lead character in *Jackie Brown.* Footballer-turned-actor Rosie Grier is her cousin.

GRIMACE

Introduced in 1971, this big, purple, bloblike creature with stumpy arms was so absolutely crazy about McDonald's milkshakes that he would steal them from young children. Happy-go-lucky and inquisitive, but a little slow and clumsy, Grimace used simple expressions such as "Uh" and "Duh." More recently, Ronald McDonald's best pal has reformed from milkshake-nabbing and is doing TV ad spots with billionaire Donald Trump.

GRIZZLY ADAMS

Airing from 1977 to 1978, a family-oriented prime-time adventure starring burly, bearded Dan Haggerty as James "Grizzly" Adams, a frontier fugitive accused of a crime who flees to the rugged Northwest during the late 1800s and finds harmony with nature. His best friend and companion was Ben, a 500-pound grizzly bear he saved from a mountain ledge as a cub. Serving as narrator of the show was Denver Pyle, who also co-starred as Mad Jack, Adams's pal, along with Don Shanks as Nakuma, Adams's Indian blood brother. The NBC-TV series was based on the 1976 film *The Life and Times of Grizzly Adams*, also starring Haggerty.

GROCERY FOOD

For most American families, the weekly (or monthly) expedition to the grocery store was a household ritual. Moms had a big job ahead upon entering the grocer's automatic doors, for they had to get enough food to feed a hungry horde, often on a single-income budget heavily dependent on redeeming coupons cut from magazines and newspapers. Kids lucky enough to be "dragged" along knew they would have a big say in which trendy food items would go into the family grocery cart, and thus into their mouths.

Here's a list of 100 brand-name food items commonly found in grocery carts at such supermarkets as Safeway, A&P, Piggly Wiggly, Winn-Dixie, Milgram's, Kroger, Vons, Ralph's, Food Lion, and Giant—circa, let's say, 1973.

A-1 steak sauce
Armour hot dogs
Aunt Jemima pancake mix
Betty Crocker cake mix
Bird's Eye Frozen Vegetables
Bisquick
Blue Bonnet margarine
Bottled soft drinks
Boxed cereal
Bumble Bee canned tuna
C&H sugar
Campbell's soups
Carnation instant breakfast
Chef Boyardee canned ravioli
Chicken-of-the-Sea tuna
Chiffon margarine
Chiquita bananas
Cool Whip
Danish-Go-Rounds
Dannon yogurt

- Dinty Moore stew
- Dole canned pineapple
- Eggo waffles
- French's mustard
- Fritos corn chips
- Funny Face packets
- Gerber baby food
- Goober Grape
- Green Giant canned vegetables
- Grey Poupon
- Hamburger Helper
- Hawaiian Punch
- Heinz 57 Sauce
- Heinz ketchup
- Hellmann's mayonnaise
- Hershey's chocolate syrup
- Hi-C canned juice
- Hostess snack cakes
- Hungry Jack pancake mix
- Hunt's Snack Pack canned puddings
- Jell-O
- Jeno's frozen pizza
- Jiffy Pop popcorn
- Keebler cookies
- Koogle Spread
- Kool-Aid packets
- Kraft macaroni and cheese
- Kraft sliced cheese
- LaChoy chicken chow mein
- Land O Lakes butter
- Lay's potato chips
- Libby's canned vegetables
- Lipton Cup-a-Soup
- Lipton tea bags
- Little Debbie snack cakes
- Log Cabin syrup
- Manwich sloppy joe mix
- Marshmallow Fluff
- Maxwell House instant coffee
- Miracle Whip
- Morton pot pies
- Morton salt
- Mrs. Butterworth's syrup
- Mrs. Paul's fish sticks
- Nestea iced-tea mix
- Nestlé Quik
- Oscar Mayer bologna
- Ovaltine
- Pepperidge Farm cookies
- Peter Pan peanut butter
- Pillsbury cookie dough
- Pop-Tarts
- Popsicles
- Pringle's potato chips
- Quaker Oats oatmeal
- Ragu spaghetti sauce
- Rice-a-Roni
- Ritz crackers
- Sara Lee frozen cakes
- Shake 'n Bake
- Smucker's jams
- Spaghetti-Os
- Spam
- Starkist tuna
- Steak-Ums
- Stove Top stuffing
- Sunkist oranges
- Swanson TV dinners
- Swiss Miss hot-chocolate mix
- Tang
- Tropicana orange juice
- Uncle Ben's rice
- Underwood deviled ham
- V8 vegetable juice
- Van Camp's pork and beans
- Velveeta pasteurized processed cheese
- Vlasic pickles
- Welch's jelly
- Wishbone salad dressing
- Wonder Bread

GROCERY FOOD II

Fifty favorite dinner (or supper) entrées of the average suburban American family, circa 1973:

- Barbecued spare ribs
- Beef stew
- Beef stroganoff
- BLT sandwiches
- Chicken and dumplings
- Chicken cacciatore
- Chicken-noodle soup
- Chicken-fried steak
- Chicken teriyaki
- Chili
- Clam chowder

Corned beef and hash
Creamed chipped beef
Fish sticks
Fried chicken
Fried-egg sandwiches
Glazed baked ham
Grilled-cheese sandwiches
Hamburgers
Hot dogs
Hungarian goulash
Lamb chops
Lasagna
Liver and onions
Meat loaf
Monte Cristo sandwiches
Pizza
Pork chops
Pot roast
Quiche lorraine
Ravioli
Roast turkey
Salisbury steak
Salmon cakes
Sauerkraut and pork
Shepherd's pie
Shish kebabs
Sloppy joes
Spaghetti and meatballs
Steak
Stuffed cabbage
Stuffed green peppers
Submarine sandwiches
Swedish meatballs
Swiss steak
Tacos
Tamale pie
Tuna casserole
Tuna-fish sandwiches
Veal parmigiana

Twenty-five perfect side dishes to accompany these meals:

Applesauce
Baked beans
Black-eyed peas
Coleslaw
Corn bread
Corn on the cob
Cottage cheese
Creamed corn
Deviled eggs
French fries
Fried okra
Garlic bread
Green beans
Hash browns
Macaroni and cheese
Macaroni salad
Mashed potatoes
Potato salad
Scalloped potatoes
Spanish rice
Succotash
Sweet potatoes
Tater tots
Three-bean salad
Wild rice

Saving the best for last—twenty-five yummy-for-our-tummy desserts:

Ambrosia
Apple dumplings
Apple pie with vanilla ice cream
Banana cream pie
Banana split
Boston cream pie
Bread pudding
Carrot cake
Cheesecake
Chocolate cake
Chocolate cream pie
Coconut cream pie
Crêpes suzette
Hot-fudge sundae
Jell-O
Key lime pie
Lemon meringue pie
Marble cake
Neapolitan ice cream
Peach cobbler
Pecan pie
Pineapple upside-down cake
Rice pudding
Pumpkin pie with Cool Whip
Strawberry shortcake

"GROOVE IS IN THE HEART"

The 1990 dance club hit marked by a funky music video showcasing Deee-Lite, the dance band from New York City fronted by groovy redhead Lady Miss Kier among colorful psychedelic acid-tripping graphics.

FYI: ▸ Deee-Lite's name was inspired by the tune "It's De-lovely," from the 1936 Cole Porter musical *Red, Hot, and Blue.*

GROOVIE GOOLIES

You're probably pondering what the heck is a Groovie Goolie? Well, in case you weren't watching Saturday-morning TV back in the early 1970s, this was a *Laugh-In*–inspired cartoon, airing from 1970 to 1972, about a group of cool monsters residing in a spooky castle called Horrible Hall.

Count Dracula ("Drak" to his friends), the owner of Horrible Hall, lived there with his plump wife, Hagatha, a green-skinned witch with a mischievous broom named Broom Hilda, and his lovable son Frankie, a Frankenstein monster. Other inhabitants included Bella La Ghostly, the morbidly glamorous switchboard operator who read the daily Horror-scope via the Tel-Bone; Wolfie, the skateboarding and surfboarding werewolf; Bonapart, the accident-prone skeleton who always fell apart; Mummy, the TV commentator who always became unwound; Dr. Jekyll-Hyde, the schizophrenic two-headed doctor; Hauntleroy, the jokester ghost; Ghoulihand, the disembodied hand; Tiny Tomb and Miss Icky (Tiny Tim and Miss Vicky—get it?), the hippie ukulele player and his girlfriend; Ratso and Batso, two vampire kids; Rover, Frankie's pet dinosaur; and Lovesick Loveseat, a sofa with the hots for Drak. On each episode, the ghoulish gang would gather to form a rock band, The Groovie Goolies, and perform a surf-ish bubblegum tune, including such originals as "C'mon, C'mon to the Goolie Picnic," "The Goolie Garden," and "The Goolie Get-Together."

The Goolies were created to support Sabrina the Teenage Witch when the young sorceress was separated from the *Archies* and given her own cartoon program in 1970 (titled *Sabrina and the Groovie Goolies*). The following year, Sabrina and the Goolies went their own way when they received individual self-titled shows.

GROVER

"Hello every-bod-eeeee!" Playful blue monster Muppet on *Sesame Street* who doesn't use contractions when he speaks and who pretends to be a superhero called SuperGrover.

GROWING PAINS

Durable if nondescript family sitcom of the 1980s that starred Alan Thicke as Jason Seaver, a New York psychiatrist who began practicing from his suburban home in order to watch over his spunky brood after his wife, Maggie (Joanna Kerns), returned to work as a newspaper reporter for the *Long Island Herald.* The Seaver children were Mike (teen idol Kirk Cameron), the troublesome wisecracking eldest; Carol (anorexic-to-be Tracey Gold), the shy and intellectual middle child; and sweet-natured Ben (cute Jeremy Miller). Premiering in the fall of 1985, the ABC show aired for eight seasons, which allowed home viewers to see the kids evolve from students at Thomas E. Dewey High (home of the Hooters) to young adults in college. In 1988, Maggie had another child, a baby girl named Chrissy, who matured amazingly fast (in a span of two years she was a six-year-old). The milquetoast theme, "As Long as We Got Each Other," was sung by B. J. Thomas and Jennifer Warnes.

GROWING UP SKIPPER

"She's two dolls in one, for twice as much fun!" Back in 1974, Barbie Doll's kid sister could really be two dolls in one: She was a doll of elementary-school age, but she could become the "other" doll by a turn of the left arm, which caused her to grow taller (three-quarters of an inch), develop a curvy bustline, and emerge into a slimmer teenager. This unusual Skipper is considered to be one of the most controversial dolls of its era, because mothers thought it would give little girls the wrong idea. Of what? I bet there were many flat-chested prepubescents who wished they could turn an arm around and evolve into a taller, bustier teen. In 1975, Mattel introduced redhead Growing Up Ginger as fair-haired Skipper's best friend.

GRUESOMES

Spooky neighbors of the Flintstones, modeled after the Addams Family and consisting of father Weirdly, mother Creepella, and son Goblin, who owned a menagerie of odd pets. Residing at Tombstone Manor, the ghastly Gruesomes thought everyone in Bedrock was a bit peculiar and they were the "normal" ones.

GRUMPY

This is what the Marshall family nicknamed the menacing Tyrannosaurus Rex on Sid and Marty Krofft's *Land of the Lost*.

GRUNGE

Gen-X youth movement of the early 1990s, founded on flannel shirts, drug use (heroin was the trip of choice), and a cluster of alternative rock bands from the rainy metropolis of Seattle (Nirvana, Pearl Jam, Hole, Alice in Chains, Soundgarden, and Stone Temple Pilots) whose songs contain lyrics churning with apathy and desolation.

GUMBY

Idealistic green clayboy with tilted bumped head, bulging eyes, and bell-bottom legs who was created by artist Art Clokey and introduced on the kiddie classic *The Howdy Doody Show* in 1956. Made out of Plasticine, Gumby was filmed with stop-motion animation: shoot a few frames, move the figure a little, and so on (a technique later used in holiday TV specials, such as *Rudolph the Red Nosed Reindeer*). In 1957, he received his own Saturday-morning series, *The Gumby Show*, which became syndicated in 1966. Beginning with the opening of a book, each episode had Gumby experiencing the typical boy's fantasy adventure, with such titles as "Moon Trip," "The Fantastic Farmer," "Robot Rumpus," and "Gumby Crosses the Delaware." Gumby's best pal was orange-hued Pokey, a spunky yet skeptical pony. Other Gumby characters included dad Gumbo, mom Gumba, little sister Minga, pet dog Nopey, dinosaur friend Prickle, blue mermaid Goo (Gumby's best girl), and the Blockheads, twin foes who had "G" and "J" alphabet blocks for heads.

In 1964, Gumby and Pokey were being manufactured by Prema Toy Company as bendable toy figures. An immediate success with children of the Baby Boomers, they can still be found at most toy stores, delighting a whole new generation of youngsters. Comedian Eddie Murphy hilariously spoofed the clayboy on *Saturday Night Live* in the mid-1980s, portraying him as a bitter, over-the-hill Jewish entertainer ("I'm Gumby, dammit!").

GUMMI BEARS

Candymaker Heide's clear, chewy, fruity, bear-shaped confection spawned a myriad of imitations in the 1980s, including the wiggly Gummi Worms, and a Disney cartoon show, *The Gummi Bears* (1985–91).

HACKY SACK

Created in 1972 by Mike Marshall and John Stalberger of Oregon, a modern recreational sport in which players keep a small bean-filled bag, known as a Hacky Sack or "footbag," from hitting the ground using anything except their hands. After Marshall died of a heart attack in 1975, Stalberger sold the rights for the Hacky Sack to Wham-O, a toy company famous for manufacturing the famed Frisbee flying disc. Over the years, different varieties of the sport have evolved, including "Footbag Net," a form of volleyball, and "Freestyle Footbag," where participants stand in a circle and do tricks while passing it around the circle.

HADJI SINGH

Hadji is cartoon kid Jonny Quest's turbaned East Indian buddy who has the mysterious power of levitation and hypnotism. He once saved Dr. Benton Quest (Jonny's dad) from an assassination attempt during a lecture in India.

HAI KARATE

"Be careful how you use it." Once superpopular, now a defunct men's aftershave and cologne advertised in the late 1960s as the aroma (a cheap lemony-lime scent) that drove girls so wild you would have to fight them off with karate chops. Hai Karate's competitors included Brut, Old Spice, and Jade East.

HAIR METAL BANDS

Big-haired (we're talking bleached, moussed, teased, scrunched, mountain-high, ocean-wide hair here) heavy-metal boy bands of the last half of the 1980s who took the trashy "sex, drugs, and rock 'n' roll" mantra literally as a lifestyle. Major players included Bon Jovi, Cinderella, Europe, Guns n' Roses, Motley Crue, Poison, Quiet Riot, Ratt, Scorpions, Warrant, Wasp, and Whitesnake. These fellows had outrageous sex orgies with multitudes of groupies, drank and drugged like there was no tomorrow, and played hard-rock music that remarkably all sounded the same. They usually dated and married supermodels, porn stars, or blonde *Baywatch* babes.

HAL EVERETT

The oldest son on the TV sitcom *Nanny and the Professor* was a twelve-year-old science wiz obsessed with experiments, played by David Doremus.

HALEY, JACKIE EARLE

Born July 14, 1961, juvenile movie actor of the 1970s whose most memorable role was that of

Kelly Leak, Tatum O'Neal's Little League teammate, in *The Bad News Bears* (1976). Other films included *Damnation Alley* (1977) and *Breaking Away* (1979).

"HALF-BREED"

I still recall an old *Cher Show* episode in which Cher appeared amid a fog wearing a Bob Mackie–designed Indian feather headdress and skimpy Indian costume and riding tall on a white horse—to wail "Half-Breed." In 1973, Cher recorded this song dealing with a racial issue (Native Americans), and it landed at the top of the pop charts for two weeks. It was her second number-one without Sonny Bono (her first: 1971's "Gypsies, Tramps, and Thieves"), and it confirmed her career as a solo artist. The song's subject matter related the experience of a woman who was not accepted by either side of her roots: Cherokee or Caucasian. Somehow, because of Cher's physical appearance (long, straight raven hair, prominent nose, and eternal golden tan) people instantly assumed that she was an American Indian, and surmised that she was speaking from personal angst of her own experience. However, her ancestry was actually a Heinz 57 of Armenian, French, German, Greek, and just a small amount of American Indian.

HALLOWEEN

"The night he came home!" Poor Laurie Strode. It's Halloween in Haddonfield, Illinois, and it seems like the pretty seventeen-year-old is the only teen without a date. Unlike her girlfriends, Annie and Lynda, who are out for a night of hot action, she settles in for a quiet evening of babysitting and watching old horror flicks on TV. Unknown to Laurie, it's not going to be just another Halloween in Haddonfield. You see, a psychopath named Michael Meyers has escaped from the mental hospital after serving fifteen years for fatally butchering his big sister with a knife when he was a child—and he has returned to his hometown with only one thing on his mind: to relive the crime! The creeping maniac has his eye on Laurie (who turns out to be his younger sister), and before evening's end her high school chums will be slaughtered and she will be terrorized over and over again.

Considered the ABC of slasher films, director John Carpenter's *Halloween* (1978) has become a modern horror classic, inspiring endless sequels and numerous clones (for example, *Friday the 13th* and *Nightmare on Elm Street*). It's a very scary movie, saturated with atmospheric, heart-pounding suspense and accompanied by a bone-chilling music score (written by Carpenter himself) and prowling camera angles showing the white-masked boogeyman lurking behind windows and doors (way creepy). The cast includes Jamie Lee Curtis as Laurie, Nancy Loomis as wisecrack Annie, P. J. Soles as boy-crazy Lynda, Donald Pleasence as psychiatrist-in-pursuit Dr. Loomis, and Tony Moran as butcher-knife-wielding Michael Meyers.

HALLOWEEN SONGS

Booooooo! Forget those goody-goody Yuletide and Easter holidays. For many boys and ghouls, the evening of October 31, Halloween, is the ghastly holiday of choice. To honor this witchy day of masked trick-or-treaters, grimacing jack-o'-lanterns, and apple-bobbing contests at the local haunted house, I've picked the twenty-five best Halloween songs of pop culture—essential ditties for a spooky night of scaring the neighborhood kids and doing the Monster Mash at a costumed bash.

- "Bad Moon Rising" (1969) by Creedence Clearwater Revival
- "Black Magic Woman" (1970) by Santana
- "The Blob" (1958) by The Five Blobs
- "Clap for the Wolfman" (1974) by The Guess Who
- "Devil Woman" (1976) by Cliff Richard
- "Dinner with Drac" (1958) by John "The Cool Ghoul" Zacherle
- "(Don't Fear) The Reaper" (1976) by Blue Oyster Cult
- "Frankenstein" (1973) by The Edgar Winter Group
- "Ghostbusters" (1984) by Ray Parker Jr.
- "Godzilla" (1977) by Blue Oyster Cult
- "Monster" (1985) by Fred Schneider
- "Monster Mash" (1962) by Bobby "Boris" Pickett
- "Nightmare on My Street" (1988) by D.J. Jazzy Jeff and the Fresh Prince
- "People Are Strange" (1967) by The Doors
- "Planet Claire" (1979) by The B-52's
- "The Purple People Eater" (1958) by Sheb Wooley
- "Season of the Witch" (1966) by Donovan
- "Spooky" (1968) by Classics IV

- "Thriller" (1983) by Michael Jackson
- "Tubular Bells" (1973) by Mike Oldfield
- "Weird Science" (1985) by Oingo Boingo
- "Welcome to My Nightmare" (1975) by Alice Cooper
- "Werewolves of London" (1978) by Warren Zevon
- "Witch Doctor" (1958) by David Seville
- "Witchy Woman" (1972) by The Eagles

HALTER TOPS

Fashionable in the 1970s, these skimpy, shoulder-baring, triangle-shaped tops for young women are held together by a string tied around the neck. Had a fashion comeback early in the twenty-first century when teen singing nymphet Britney Spears sported them in her pop-music videos.

HAMBURGER HELPER

"Hamburger Helper . . . when you need a helping hand!" Introduced in 1970 by General Mills, this meal in a box provided a helping hand for busy mothers at dinnertime. After a long day of work, including toting kids back and forth to various activities (school, ball games, ballet, scouts, and more), moms didn't have a lot of time to cook a meal, so a box of Hamburger Helper came in handy. Each box contained uncooked pasta and a package of seasoning mix that when combined with ground beef in a skillet created an instant casserole. A family could have a different meal each night of the week because there were so many types to choose from: Potatoes Au Gratin, Beef Noodle, Cheeseburger Macaroni, Chili Macaroni, Pizza Pasta, Zesty Mexican, Zesty Italian, Rice Oriental, Lasagna, and this author's personal childhood favorite, Potato Stroganoff. The popularity of this inexpensive "real good, feel good" meal spawned two other Helpers in 1972: Chicken Helper and Tuna Helper.

In the annals of pop culture, Hamburger Helper rates right up there with such other "bad taste" food items as Spam, Easy Cheese, Slim Jims, Twinkies, and TV dinners—because if you really think about it, how much help does a pound of hamburger really need?

HAMBURGLAR

Promo character who is a masked crook, dressed in black-and-white prison garb, who loves McDonald's hamburgers and will do anything to get one—including steal them. He spends most of his time being chased around McDonaldland by police officer Chief Big Mac.

HAMMER, M. C.

"It's Hammer time!" Stanley Kirk Burrell (born March 30, 1962), known simply as Hammer, a singer whose catchy bubblegum rap (1990's megasmash "U Can't Touch This"), flamboyant fashion sense (voluminous genie-like trousers), and flashy dance moves made him the top hip-hop artist of the early 1990s. The success of his landmark album, *Please Hammer Don't Hurt 'Em*, which went to number one on the pop charts (the first time ever for a rap recording), netted him millions. Overexposure from hawking countless products, such as Pepsi, Taco Bell, KFC, Mattel dolls, and a Saturday-morning cartoon, *Hammerman*, earned the egomaniac rapper backlash from anyone over preteen age. Overspending his fortune (he purchased seventeen luxury cars and blew dough on an entourage of 250), Hammer ran out of money around the time his career fizzled. He filed for Chapter 11 bankruptcy and today is a rapping reverend of a Christian church in his hometown of Oakland, California.

FYI: ▸ Hammer is nicknamed for childhood hero Hammerin' Hank Aaron of the Oakland A's. (In the 1970s he was a batboy for the baseball team at the Oakland Coliseum.)

HAND JIVE

This hand dance—accompanied by feet alternating pigeon-toed then bow-legged—was featured in the 1978 movie musical *Grease* (Sha Na Na's "Born to Hand Jive") during the *National Bandstand* dance contest at Rydell High.

HANDS DOWN

"The slaphappiest game ever!" In 1965, Ideal Toys had a hit on their hands, as kids got slaphappy with this fast-moving action-game based on the child's card game Snap. The object of Hands Down was for four players to draw cards and try to be the first to slap the hand-shaped plastic molds on the "colorful exciting Slam-O-Matic." The last player holding cards was the winner.

HANG TEN SHIRTS

The hoop-neck T-shirts with the famous embroidered footprint logo and multicolored stripes were favorites of surf dudes back in the 1960s and 1970s. Created by a San Diego surfer named Duke Boyd in 1962. The term "hang ten" is surf-speak for the act of hanging all ten toes over the front of the surfboard.

HANKS, TOM

The most successful movie actor of the recent turn of the century, often likened to a young James Stewart or Jack Lemmon, whose early acting roots included the low-budget slasher-thriller *He Knows You're Alone* (1981) and cross-dressing in the prime-time sitcom *Bosom Buddies* (1980–82). After the *Buddies* ended its run, the tall, dark-haired leading man (born July 9, 1956, in California)—versatile in both comedy and drama—went on to become a huge star in such films as *Bachelor Party* (1984), *Splash* (1984), *Big* (1988), and *Philadelphia* (1993), for which he won his first Best Actor Oscar playing a lawyer dying of AIDS, followed by *Sleepless in Seattle* (1993), *Forrest Gump* (1994), for which he earned his second Best Actor Oscar, and then *Apollo 13* (1995), *That Thing You Do* (1996), *Saving Private Ryan* (1998), and *You've Got Mail* (1998). Married to actress Rita Wilson.

HANNA-BARBERA

Once called the "General Motors of Animation" by *60 Minutes*, animators William Hanna and Joseph Barbera were first teamed together in 1938 at the MGM Studios, where they created the popular Tom and Jerry theatrical cartoon series. Their TV legacy began in 1957 with Ruff and Reddy, followed by the much-loved Huckleberry Hound and Quick Draw McGraw. Today, Hanna-Barbera's cartoon empire of more than 350 different shows and thousands of colorful cartoon characters extends to the far corners of the world. Their wacky heroes—Yogi Bear, Top Cat, the Flintstones, the Jetsons, Atom Ant, Secret Squirrel, Magilla Gorilla, Jonny Quest, Space Ghost, Banana Splits, Dastardly and Muttley, Penelope Pitstop, Josie and the Pussycats, Scooby-Doo, Speed Buggy, Hair Bear Bunch, Funky Phantom, Hong Kong Phooey, Jabberjaw, Dynomutt, Captain Caveman, Smurfs, the Powerpuff Girls, and more—have delighted generations and will forever be a part of twentieth-century childhood folklore.

HANS AND FRANZ

"We just vant to pump . . . you up!" *Saturday Night Live*'s Dana Carvey (Hans) and Kevin Nealon's (Franz) funny send-up (*Pumping Up with Hans and Franz*) of pumped-up Austrian "veight" lifters as cousins of Arnold Schwarzenegger who came to America to follow in their famous relative's footsteps.

HAN SOLO

Daredevil Corellian smuggler and pilot of the Millennium Falcon who, along with Wookie sidekick Chewbacca, aids the Rebel Alliance in battling the Galactic Empire. Harrison Ford's performance as roguish Han Solo in the three *Star Wars* movies made the evasive actor a big Hollywood star (he was the top box-office draw in 1997). His other best-known films include the *Indiana Jones* series—beginning with *Raiders of the Lost Ark* (1981), as well as *Blade Runner* (1982), *Witness* (1985), *Frantic* (1988), *Presumed Innocent* (1990), *Patriot Games* (1992), and *The Fugitive* (1993).

HANSON

Folksy teen idol group of three blond brothers—oldest Isaac Hanson, middle Taylor Hanson, and youngest Zac Hanson—from Tulsa, Oklahoma, who had one major hit, the catchy "MMMBop" (1997), before getting walloped by the thundering bubblegum pop of those flashy boy-bands Backstreet Boys and 'N Sync.

HAPPINESS IS A WARM PUPPY

This childhood classic featuring Lucy hugging Snoopy on the cover was a best-selling book that showcased Charles Schulz's *Peanuts* characters in a compilation of adorable aphorisms. Reading it brought comfort and whimsy and reminded us that it's the little things in life that bring the most happiness. Among the sayings and accompanying illustrations were "Happiness is a thumb and blanket" (thumb-sucking Linus with his security blanket); "Happiness is a smooth sidewalk" (bun-headed Violet roller-skating); "Happiness is a pile of leaves" (Charlie Brown jumping in a pile of raked leaves); and "Happiness is finding someone you like at the door" (pianist Schroder at Lucy's front door). As the number-one nonfiction book of 1963 (more than a million copies were sold), it spawned a whole series featuring the spunky Peanuts gang and their pithy philosophies, including *Security Is a Thumb and a Blanket* (1963), *Christmas Is Together Time* (1964), *I Need All the Friends I Can Get* (1964), *Home Is on Top of a Doghouse* (1966), and *Happiness Is a Sad Song* (1967). It also inspired two spoofs by *Tonight Show* host Johnny Carson: *Happiness Is a Dry Martini* (1965) and *Misery Is . . . a Blind Date* (1967).

HAPPY DAYS

Throughout the 1970s, nostalgia for the 1950s was big stuff. We viewed *American Graffiti* (1973), *The Buddy Holly Story* (1978), and *Grease* (1978) at movie theaters; listened to "At the Hop," "Johnny B. Goode," and "Rock Around the Clock" on oldies-but-goodies radio stations; wore poodle skirts, bobby sox, and duck-tails for Fifties Day at school; and most of all, tuned in Tuesday evenings to this TV series. Originating as a skit titled "Love and the Happy Days" on a *Love, American Style* episode, the long-running ABC sitcom, airing from 1974 to 1984, was created by Garry Marshall (brother of Penny).

Set in Milwaukee, Wisconsin, in the late 1950s, *Happy Days* centered on the middle-class Cunningham family—particularly teenage son Richie, the archetypal "boy next door," and his pals at Jefferson High. The main cast of characters included former child actor Ron Howard as nice-guy Richie Cunningham, Henry Winkler as hoodlum dropout Arthur "Fonzie" Fonzarelli, Anson Williams as cute but geeky Warren "Potsie" Weber, Donny Most as loudmouth prankster Ralph Malph, Tom Bosley as caring dad Howard Cunningham, Marion Ross as doting mom Marion Cunningham, Erin Moran as kid sister Joanie Cunningham, and Pat Morita as Matsuo "Arnold" Takahashi, proprietor of Arnold's Drive-In, a malt shop where much of the action took place.

Two years after premiering, *Happy Days* became TV's number-one hit and one of the biggest shows of the 1970s, with more than fifty million viewers watching every week during peak years. A major part of its success is credited to Henry Winkler's skillful performance as the Fonz. Starting out as a supporting character, Winkler's "rebel without a cause" caught the fancy of young audiences, who turned him into the star of the sitcom by the second season. His cool Fonzisms, such as "Aaaayyh!" accompanied by a thumbs-up gesture, were copied by kids everywhere.

As *Happy Days* evolved over the years, so did the characters. The fall of 1977 saw Richie, Potsie, and Ralph enrolling at the University of Wisconsin at Milwaukee; little Joanie becoming a flirtatious teen; and Fonzie getting his high school diploma and beginning a career as the auto mechanics teacher at Jefferson High. Notable cast additions included Al Molinaro as Arnold's new owner, Al Delvecchio; Scott Baio as Fonzie's cute younger cousin Charles "Chachi" Arcola; Lynda Goodfriend as Richie's girlfriend, Lori Beth Allen; Cathy Silver as Joanie's boy-crazy friend, Jenny Piccolo; Ted McGinley as Marion's Yale-educated nephew, Roger Phillips; Crystal Bernard as Howard's Southern-bred niece K. C. Cunningham; Linda Purl as Fonzie's divorcée girlfriend, Ashley Pfister; and Heather O'Rourke as Ashley's little daughter, Heather Pfister.

Happy Days had three prime-time spin-offs: *Laverne and Shirley* (1976–83), *Mork and Mindy* (1978–82), and the unsuccessful *Joanie Loves Chachi* (1982–83). At first, the show used Bill Haley's "Rock Around the Clock" as its opening theme, but later it was replaced by the original composition "Happy Days" by Pratt and McClain, which became a Top Ten hit in 1976.

FYI: ▸ Another pop culture question I've wondered about: Whatever happened to jock older brother Chuck Cunningham (Gavan O'Herlihy), seen on *Happy Days*' first season only to disappear, never to be referred to again?

HAPPY MEALS

McDonald's inexpensive meal for children, packaged in a colorful activity fun box and consisting of a small beverage, small fries, a hamburger or Chicken McNuggets, and, best of all, a surprise toy premium—usually some kind of tie-in for the latest Disney movie. Other fast-food joints followed suit with their own versions, such as Burger Chef's Fun Meals and Wendy's Kid Meals.

HARD-ROCK GROUPS

If you want to be cool among the freaks in school, you can't go wrong by picking one of the following fifty hard-rock / heavy-metal groups circa 1971 to

1990. To make sure you know what you're talking about, a signature song is listed with each. And remember, if you are ever asked who your favorite group is, never, ever mention The Captain and Tennille or The Carpenters—or, for that matter, ABBA, the Bay City Rollers, Donny and Marie, Dawn, the Bee Gees, or Air Supply.

AC/DC—"You Shook Me All Night Long" (1980)
Aerosmith—"Walk This Way" (1976)
Bachman-Turner Overdrive—"Takin' Care of Business" (1974)
Bad Company—"Feel Like Makin' Love" (1975)
Black Oak Arkansas—"Jim Dandy" (1974)
Black Sabbath—"Iron Man" (1972)
Blue Oyster Cult—"(Don't Fear) The Reaper" (1976)
Bon Jovi—"You Give Love a Bad Name" (1986)
Boston—"More Than a Feeling" (1976)
Cheap Trick—"I Want You to Want Me" (1979)
Deep Purple—"Smoke on the Water" (1973)
Def Leppard—"Pour Some Sugar on Me" (1988)
Eagles—"Hotel California" (1977)
Fleetwood Mac—"Dreams" (1977)
Foghat—"Slow Ride" (1976)
Foreigner—"Hot Blooded" (1978)
Grand Funk Railroad—"We're an American Band" (1973)
Guns n' Roses—"Sweet Child O' Mine" (1988)
Heart—"Magic Man" (1976)
Jefferson Starship—"Miracles" (1975)
Joan Jett and The Blackhearts—"I Love Rock 'n' Roll" (1982)
Journey—"Open Arms" (1982)
Judas Priest—"You've Got Another Thing Comin'" (1982)
Kansas—"Carry on Wayward Son" (1977)
KISS—"Rock and Roll All Nite" (1975)
Led Zeppelin—"Stairway to Heaven" (1971)
Loverboy—"Working for the Weekend" (1982)
Lynyrd Skynyrd—"Free Bird" (1975)
Steve Miller Band—"Fly Like an Eagle" (1977)
Moody Blues—"Nights in White Satin" (1972)
Motley Crue—"Girls, Girls, Girls" (1987)
Nazareth—"Love Hurts" (1976)
Tom Petty and The Heartbreakers—"Refugee" (1980)
Pink Floyd—"Another Brick in the Wall" (1980)
Poison—"Every Rose Has Its Thorn" (1988)
Queen—"Bohemian Rhapsody" (1976)
Quiet Riot—"Cum on Feel the Noize" (1983)
REO Speedwagon—"Keep on Loving You" (1981)
Rolling Stones—"Brown Sugar" (1971)
Rush—"Tom Sawyer" (1981)
Scorpions—"Rock You Like a Hurricane" (1984)
Steely Dan—"Hey Nineteen" (1980)
Styx—"Come Sail Away" (1977)
Supertramp—"The Logical Song" (1979)
Three Dog Night—"Joy to the World" (1971)
Van Halen—"Jump" (1984)
Whitesnake—"Here I Go Again" (1987)
Who—"Squeeze Box" (1976)
Wings—"Band on the Run" (1974)
ZZ Top—"Legs" (1984)

HARDY BOYS

Mystery book series created in 1927 by Edward Stratemeyer under the pseudonym Franklin W. Dixon, and continued after his death by his daughter Harriet Stratemeyer Adams, who kept her father's pen name. The father-daughter team was also responsible for mass-producing several other juvenile mystery book series, including *Nancy Drew*, *Tom Swift*, *The Rover Boys*, and *The Bobbsey Twins*. The *Hardy Boys* books told about the sleuthing adventures of teen brother detectives, sixteen-year-old Joe Hardy and eighteen-year-old Frank Hardy, sons of world-renowned crime investigator Fenton Hardy. Brunet Frank and blond Joe lived with their mother and Aunt Gertrude in the small coastal town of Bayport. Working out of a makeshift crime lab in the family barn, and assisted by devoted high school pal Chet Morton, they were able to solve every case.

From 1969 to 1971, the youthful sleuths were

featured in a self-titled Saturday-morning cartoon, doubling as musicians in a groovy rock band called The Hardy Boys Plus Three (and joined by pals Pete, Chubby, and Wanda). In 1977, The Hardy Boys Mysteries, a prime-time series, alternated every other Sunday night on ABC-TV with Nancy Drew (starring Pamela Sue Martin). With a contemporary feel that appealed to teenagers of the late 1970s, the program featured heartthrobs Shaun Cassidy and Parker Stevenson as Joe and Frank. Cassidy found time to sing a song, and his version of "Da Do Ron Ron" from an April 1977 telecast became a number-one smash.

HARLEM GLOBETROTTERS

The most famous basketball squad in the world was organized by Abe Saperstein not in New York City's famous uptown neighborhood but in Chicago, Illinois, in 1926. Playing to the infectious theme of "Sweet Georgia Brown," the all-black team—dressed in red-white-and-blue uniforms—is known for exhibition games in which the players combine world-class ball-playing with tricks, such as passing the ball between the legs and behind the back then back between the legs. The most familiar Globetrotters during their popularity peak of the 1960s and 1970s were George "Meadowlark" Lemon, Freddie "Curly" Neal (the bald one), Hubert "Geese" Ausbie, Bobby Joe "B.J." Mason, J. C. "Gip" Gipson, Nate Brown, Charles "Tex" Harrison, Marquis Haynes, John Smith, and Theodis Lee. From 1970 to 1973, the fun-loving pranksters came to Saturday-morning TV as a Hanna-Barbera cartoon, *The Harlem Globetrotters*, with Scatman Crothers providing the voice of Meadowlark Lemon. The show had them trotting around the globe playing various opponents, assisted by elderly Granny, the white driver of the squad's Stars and Stripes bus, and long-legged dog Dribbles, the team mascot.

FYI: ▸ NBA superstar Wilt Chamberlain played with the Harlem Globetrotters from 1958 to 1959.

HARLEM GLOBETROTTERS ON GILLIGAN'S ISLAND

This lower-than-low 1981 TV movie featured the world-famous basketball team crash-landing on the atoll inhabited by Gilligan and fellow castaways and playing basketball against a squad of robots (yes, robots).

HAROLD AND THE PURPLE CRAYON

"One night, after thinking it over for some time, Harold decided to go for a walk in the moonlight. . . ." Simple yet wonderful picture book for very young readers about a little boy who can't sleep taking an oversized purple crayon and drawing a path, a moon, and an assortment of adventures. Written and illustrated in 1955 by Crockett Johnson, it was followed by *Harold's ABC, Harold's Circus*, and *Harold's Trip to the Sky*.

"HARPER VALLEY P.T.A."

"Well, this is just a little Peyton Place, and you're all Harper Valley hypocrites." Country singer Jeannie C. Riley's sassy ballad about miniskirted mom Mrs. Johnson, who socked it to the Harper Valley P.T.A. board members after her teenage daughter brought home a note questioning her parenting abilities. The note complained that Mrs. Johnson, a widow, wore her dresses way too high and was drinking, running around with men, and going wild. Aware of the board members' own extracurricular activities—and we're not talking bowling here—Mrs. Johnson marched into the afternoon meeting to point out to those hypocrites that they were all drunks, adulterers, or both. Written by Tom T. Hall, "Harper Valley P.T.A." was a mega-smash in the spring of 1968. It sold 1.6 million copies in its first ten days of release and simultaneously topped both *Billboard*'s country chart and the Hot 100 pop chart. The record inspired a theatrical comedy movie that in turn inspired a prime-time TV series on NBC, both starring Barbara Eden as the sexy and outspoken widow Stella Johnson.

HARRY POTTER

"We are pleased to inform you that you have been accepted at the Hogwarts School of Witchcraft and Wizardry." The eleven-year-old British orphan destined for great wizardry is the hero of a massively popular book and movie series created by rags-to-riches author J. K. Rowling. Her stories follow bespectacled Harry, with a lightning-bolt shaped scar on his forehead, who is rescued from a dreary life with nonmagic (Muggles) relatives when it comes to light that he's the son of two legendary wizards who were murdered by an evil comrade. Young Potter is sent away to his parents' alma mater, the

Hogwarts School of Witchcraft and Wizardry, secretly hidden somewhere in northern England. Assigned to Gryffindor House, Harry befriends best pals Hermione Granger, a smart know-it-all, and Ron Weasley, a redheaded chess expert. At Hogwarts, the three classmates encounter wondrous things, such as gentle giant Hagrid, snowy-owl Hedwig, wicked Lord Voldemort, troublemaking poltergeist Peeves, bank-teller goblin Griphook, three-headed canine monster Fluffy, a baby Norwegian Ridgeback dragon, chocolate frogs, jellybeans that come in every flavor, including awful ones, Phoenix-feathered wands, wizard sport Quidditch, mirrors that reflect your heart's desire, invisibility cloaks, the Leaky Cauldron Pub, the conjurer shopping district Diagon Alley, and Hogwarts Express at Platform 9 3/4.

First published in 1998, the best-selling Harry Potter books, starting with *Harry Potter and the Sorcerer's Stone*, cast a spell over the world. Brilliantly written in an enchanting and humorous style reminiscent of Roald Dahl of earlier days, it had children (and many adults) overtly excited about reading and eagerly awaiting the next title. Subsequent titles are *Harry Potter and the Chamber of Secrets*, *Harry Potter and the Prisoner of Azkaban*, *Harry Potter and the Goblet of Fire*, *Harry Potter and the Order of the Phoenix*, and *Harry Potter and the Half-Blood Prince*. Unique to each book, Harry and schoolmates, including archrival Draco Malfoy of Slytherin House, age one more year and advance to the next school grade at Hogwarts. Daniel Radcliffe stars as Harry Potter in the film series.

HART, COREY

Ear-ringed and moussed, the dark-haired cutie from Canada (born May 31, 1962, in Montreal) was a fave heartthrob of pop music during the mid-1980s. He's most famous for a keyboard-driven ditty, the overserious "Sunglasses at Night" (1984), and the touching love song "Never Surrender" (1985).

***HARVEY* COMICS**

Harvey, one of the leading comic-book publishers in the United States, was founded in 1939 by brothers Alfred, Leon, and Robert Harvey. In the early 1950s, the brothers acquired the rights to publish comic books based on popular Paramount Pictures cartoon characters Casper the Friendly Ghost, Little Audrey, Baby Huey, and Herman and Katnip. Other *Harvey* comic stars include Wendy the Good Little Witch, Richie Rich, Little Dot, Little Lotta, Spooky, and Hot Stuff. Mascot symbol is a jack-in-the-box.

HARVEY KINKLE

High school boy-next-door-type from Riverdale who dates Sabrina the Teenage Witch. (Even though he is often tangled up in some kind of witchy weirdness, Harvey never figures out that she has magical powers.)

HASBRO

Founded by brothers Henry and Helal Hassenfeld in Providence, Rhode Island, in 1923, this persevering toy company is a worldwide champ with annual sales of more than $3 billion. Hasbro's toy line has included such big sellers as Mr. Potato Head, Frosty Sno-Man Sno-Cone Machine, G.I. Joe, Lite-Brite, Weebles, Transformers, Jem, My Little Pony, My Buddy, and Glo Worm. One reason Hasbro has remained a leader in the toy industry: its aggressive acquisitions of other toy manufacturers, such as Ideal, Kenner, PlaySkool, Milton Bradley, Parker Brothers, Tonka, Romper Room, and Knickerbocker.

HASSELHOFF, DAVID

Tall (six-foot-four), good-natured actor known more for his hunky good looks—handsome face, twinkling blue eyes, dark, wavy hair, hirsute chest, tight jeans—than for his acting talents. Nevertheless, he's had major success starring in a trio of TV programs: daytime's *The Young and the Restless* (1975–82), as Snapper Foster; prime time's *Knight Rider* (1982–86), as crime-fighting loner Michael Knight; and syndication's *Baywatch* (1989–99), as aging Malibu lifeguard Mitch Buchannon.

FYI: ▸ David Hasselhoff is a recording superstar in Europe. His concert tours have taken him to Austria and Germany, where he once performed for 500,000 people in front of the Berlin Wall!

HAUNTED MANSION

"Welcome, foolish mortals, to the Haunted Mansion." The Disneyland attraction, located in New Orleans Square, is the home of 999 ghosts—including "room for one more." Styled after a stately antebellum manorhouse and enclosed by ornate wrought-iron gates, the Haunted Mansion was under construction for more than a decade until its opening on August 9, 1969. (The exterior of the building was actually finished in 1963, tantalizing park visitors for the next six years.) Upon entering the mansion through creaky doors, guests embark in black Doom Buggies that carry them past spooky scenes brought to life by state-of-the-art computer-controlled special effects. Some of the resident haunts "just dying to meet you" include fortune-telling Madame Leota and a trio of hitchhiking ghosts. "Grim Grinning Ghosts," composed by Buddy Baker with lyrics by Xavier Atencio, is the rollicking theme song played throughout the attraction. *The Haunted Mansion*, a big-screen adaptation loosely based on the theme ride, starred comedian Eddie Murphy in 2003.

FYI: ▸ The organ located in the Haunted Mansion's ballroom is the same instrument used by Captain Nemo in Walt Disney's classic film *20,000 Leagues Under the Sea* (1954).

HAWAIIAN PUNCH

Since 1963, the canned fruit drink's mascot, Punchy, a cartoon bully wearing a red crown and blue-striped shirt, has been asking unsuspecting folks, "How about a nice Hawaiian Punch?" and when they said "Sure!" he promptly punched them. The various flavors of the Texas-based fruit-juice company have included Fruit Juicy Red (its best-known flavor), Apple Red, Great Grape, Sunshine Orange, Lemon Pink, Pineapple, Very Berry, and its original flavor.

HAWAIIAN SHIRTS

Retro fun! In the early 1980s, these short-sleeved shirts—printed with loud, colorful tropical flowers, native villages, hula dancers, and surfing scenes—went beyond being just a vacation souvenir from Hawaii, or the uniform of choice for a lounge lizard at the local tiki-tiki hut, when young men adopted them as a favorite summer clothing item. Also known as aloha shirts, they were first created in 1931 by a Hawaiian clothing merchant named Ellery Chun.

HAWAII FIVE-O

Airing on CBS-TV from 1968 to 1980, this prime-time cop drama had the absolute coolest opening-credit sequence of any show from its era. Beginning with a massive ocean wave, it showcased a rapid-moving montage of exciting Hawaiian beach scenes, like hula dancers, surfers, and bikinied babes, pulsating to a rousing guitar-based instrumental theme ("da-da-da-da-da-daa, da-da-da-da-dah . . . "), performed by The Ventures. Set in Honolulu (and filmed entirely on location), the hit series starred Jack Lord as Detective Steve McGarrett, the no-nonsense head of Five-O, the Hawaii State Police elite investigative unit that reported straight to Governor Philip Grey (Richard Denning). Detectives Danny "Danno" Williams (James MacArthur), Chin Ho Kelly (Kam Fong), and Kono Kalakaua (Zulu) assisted McGarrett in thwarting all sorts of crooks in paradise, particularly the mysterious and ruthless criminal Wo Fat (Khigh Dhiegh). *Hawaii Five-O* sets the record for the longest continuously running police series in the history of TV.

HAWN, GOLDIE

"I have a light personality and a deep-thinking brain." Born in Washington, D.C., on November 21, 1945, this adorable blonde with the huge eyes and "tee-hee-hee" giggle was first seen as the go-go dancing ding-a-ling on the 1960s TV comedy *Laugh-In* before becoming one of the best-loved movie comediennes of the 1970s and 1980s. Most memorable of Hawn's free-spirited scatterbrains of film include her Oscar-winning Toni from *Cactus Flower* (1969), Marion from *There's a Girl in My Soup* (1970), Jill from *Butterflies Are Free* (1972), Jill from *Shampoo* (1975), Gloria from *Foul Play* (1978), Judy from *Private Benjamin* (1980), Paula from *Best Friends* (1982), Sunny from *Protocol* (1984), Molly from *Wildcats* (1986), and Joanna/Annie from *Overboard* (1987). Actress Kate Hudson is Hawn's daughter from her marriage to Bill Hudson (1976–79).

FYI: ▸ Before she was almost famous, Goldie Hawn worked on a can-can line at the 1965 World's Fair, followed by an actual stint as a go-go dancer in Jersey and as a chorus girl at the Desert Inn in Vegas.

HAZEL

"Oh, Mr. B!" Based on Ted Kay's *Saturday Evening Post* cartoon character, the sitcom starred Shirley Booth as cheery know-it-all Hazel Burke, a housekeeper wearing a maid's uniform who ran the entire Baxter family residence more efficiently than they did. Airing on NBC-TV from 1961 to 1966, it costarred Don DeFore as corporate lawyer George Baxter, Whitney Blake as his wife, Dorothy, and Bobby Buntrock as their young son, Harold. An accomplished actress with both a Tony and an Oscar for *Come Back, Little Sheba*, Booth won two Emmy Awards for her role as Hazel in 1962 and 1963 (making her one of the few to receive all three prestigious acting honors).

HEADBANDS AND LEG WARMERS

Often associated with each other, these two fashion accessories from the 1980s were made popular by the aerobics craze, and by one person in particular—Olivia Newton-John. Olivia's 1981 music video "Physical" featured the trendsetting Aussie, with a new bi-level haircut, aerobicizing around a fitness center wearing the essential Lycra bodysuit accompanied by a matching headband tied around her forehead and a pair of leg warmers bunched around her ankles. In no time, women and—I'm afraid to say—many men copied Olivia's headband and leg-warmer ensemble. They wore them not only while working out at health clubs and dance studios but also as everyday wear at school, at the office, and for a night out on the town.

Women preferred headbands that were thin, corded, and colored in a multitude of shades to match various items of clothing, while men favored bandannas and wide headbands for a butcher look. As for leg warmers, they were great for jazzing up the ankles of a pair of skintight designer jeans worn with either high-heel pumps or boots and for dressing up a black-leather miniskirt (like the headband, leg warmers always color-coordinated with the top or blouse). Along with Olivia, other celebs known for sporting this ultratrendy look were rocker Pat Benatar, flashdancer Jennifer Beals, *Dynasty*'s Linda Evans, movie-actress-turned-aerobics-queen Jane Fonda, Loverboy's Mike Reno, and John Travolta in *Staying Alive* (the *Saturday Night Fever* sequel).

HEAD & SHOULDERS

Classic dandruff shampoo manufactured by Procter & Gamble for those unlucky enough to be afflicted with noticeable white flakes and an itchy scalp.

HEARST, PATTY

In 1974, the pretty nineteen-year-old newspaper heiress was kidnapped from her Berkeley, California, apartment by the Symbionese Liberation Army (SLA), a radical terrorist organization, and brainwashed into becoming the bank-robbing "Citizen Tania." Captured by the FBI in 1975, Patty served twenty-two months of a seven-year prison term (she was released after President Jimmy Carter commuted her sentence). She is now a favorite of cult director John Waters, appearing in his movies *Cry-Baby* (1990), *Serial Mom* (1994), *Pecker* (1998), and *Cecil B. DeMented* (2000).

FYI: ▸ The punk band The Misfits wrote a song about Patty Hearst titled "She."

HEART

Led by sisters Ann and Nancy Wilson, this hard-rockin' band was one of the few in the 1970s fronted by females (others included Jefferson Airplane's Grace Slick, Big Brother and The Holding Company's Janis Joplin, Stone Poneys' Linda Ronstadt, and Fleetwood Mac's Stevie Nicks and Christine McVie). Formed in Seattle in 1973, the group was originally known as The Army, then White Heart, and finally just Heart in 1974. Heavily influenced by Led Zeppelin, their hits included the singles "Crazy for You" (1976), "Magic Man" (1976), "Barracuda" (1977), "Heartless" (1978), and "Straight On" (1978) and the albums *Dreamboat Annie* (1976), *Little Queen* (1977), and *Dog and Butterfly* (1979). In the mid-1980s, Heart pulled an Aerosmith with renewed popularity after a five-year slump with the songs "What About Love?" (1985), "These Dreams" (1986), "Alone" (1987), and "All I Wanna Do Is Make Love to You" (1990). In 1984, Ann dueted with Loverboy's Mike Reno on "Almost Paradise," the love theme from the movie *Footloose*. Nancy is married to movie writer-director Cameron Crowe (*Almost Famous*).

"HEARTLIGHT"

In 1982, Neil Diamond wrote and sang this tribute to E.T. the Extra-Terrestrial ("Turn on your heartlight . . ."). It was a reference to the way the little space alien's heart glowed through his skin when feeling love and affection.

HEATHCLIFF
George Gately created the clever, orange-striped fat tomcat of comic-strip fame in 1973. Although a highly independent feline, Heathcliff claims the Nutmegs—Grandpa, Grandma, and youths Iggy and Marcy—as his nominal family. His sweetheart is a Persian named Sonja.

HEATHERS (ACTRESSES)
A duo of sexy TV actresses—Heather Locklear and Heather Thomas—whose California-blonde looks turned red-blooded guys on during the 1980s. (Both the Heathers were actually California natives, raised in the Los Angeles area.) Locklear played mischievous Sammy Jo on *Dynasty* and later naughty Amanda Woodward on *Melrose Place*. Thomas was more sugar than spice as stuntwoman Jody Banks on *The Fall Guy*.

***HEATHERS* (MOVIE)**
A smart dark comedy directed by Michael Lehmann and starring wry Winona Ryder as Veronica Sawyer and devilish Christian Slater as Jason "J.D." Dean. Veronica is the fourth wheel of a powerful Westerburg High School clique composed of three bitch-queens, all named Heather: wicked leader Heather Chandler (Kim Walker), green-with-envy Heather Duke (Shannen Doherty), and spineless cheerleader Heather McNamara (Lisanne Falk). Well-coiffed and coutured, the Heathers rule Westerburg's hallways and lunchrooms, striking fear in the unpopular girls—especially one poor fat lass nicknamed Martha Dumptruck—with as much as a clever put-down or a simple roll of the eyes. Fed up with the Heathers—in fact, fed up with the entire school caste system—Veronica joins cute but nutty J.D., a newcomer at Westerburg. Together they hatch a plan to murder the Heathers and their bullying jock boyfriends by disguising the crimes as suicides. Kudos to scenarist Daniel Waters for penning this cleverly worded tale, cited by Winona Ryder as "one of the greatest pieces of literature I have ever read."

FYI: ▸ Following the release of the movie in 1989, "Heathers" became a slang term used in high school to describe guilelessly bitchy girls who hang around in popular social cliques.

HECKLE AND JECKLE
Inseparable pair of conniving look-alike black magpies with two distinct personality traits: one talked in a Brooklyn accent (Heckle), the other in a more refined British tone (Jeckle). Created in 1956 by animator Paul Terry, Heckle and Jeckle were among the most popular Terrytoons characters, second only to the extraordinary Mighty Mouse. What set them apart from other cartoon icons of the era is that they favored outwitting their opponents by employing fast-talking pestering over physical slapstick.

HEE HAW
Best described as the country cousin of *Laugh-In*, this variety TV program enjoyed brief popularity with high ratings from 1969 to 1971, before it was canceled after the CBS network decided to rid itself of rural-oriented shows. It then went into syndication with all-new shows, where it remained a hit into the early 1990s (in 1977, it was the nation's top non-network series). Filmed in Nashville, the fast-paced, cornball *Hee Haw* consisted of a hodgepodge of songs, skits, one-liners, running gags, and guest appearances by the biggest names in country music, such as Loretta Lynn, Conway Twitty, Tammy Wynette, George Jones, Merle Haggard, and Johnny Cash. It was co-hosted by singers Roy Clark and Buck Owens, who were joined by a large stable of overall- and gingham-clad bumpkins, including Cathy Baker, Archie Campbell, Grandpa Jones, George Lindsey, Minnie Pearl, Lulu Roman, Junior Samples, Stringbean, twins Jim and Jon Hager, and a bevy of buxom *Hee Haw* Honeys. Every once in a while, a cartoon donkey appeared, providing a "hee haw" as a reaction to the corny humor.

Favorite *Hee Haw* segments: the "Gloom and Despair" song ("Where, oh where, are you tonight? Why have you left me here all alone? I've searched the world over and thought I'd found true love, but you met another, and . . . Phhfftt! . . . you were gone"), rotund Junior Samples's used-car commercials ("Call BR549 . . . "), blonde-bobbed Cathy Baker getting a swat on the butt by a loose fence-board after telling a lame joke, and the *Hee Haw* salute to an American small town and its population, featuring the whole cast in a cornfield ("Hog's Breath, Tennessee. Population 99. Saaaalute!"). Sleepy-eyed Beauregard Jr. was the show's bloodhound mascot. "That's all!"

HEE HAW HONEYS

What the curvaceous country-cuties on the variety show *Hee Haw* were known as. Regular Honeys included Barbi Benton, Marianne Gordon, Gunilla Hutton, Kathie Lee Johnson (yes, the future Mrs. Frank Gifford and co-host of *Live with Regis and Kathie Lee*), Jeannine Riley, Misty Rowe, Linda Thompson, and Lisa Todd. Two of them—sexy Misty and cute Kathie Lee—starred in a short-lived, stink-o-rama spin-off called *Hee Haw Honeys* in 1978.

HEIDI

In 1968, with the New York Jets leading the Oakland Raiders and fifty seconds left, NBC cuts from the game broadcast to this made-for-TV movie, totally missing Oakland's win after they score two touchdowns in the last nine seconds. This network decision caused protest from football-loving males everywhere. Despite the controversy, the film is a fine adaptation of the classic children's tale by Johanna Spyri. It was scripted by Earl Hamner Jr. of *The Waltons* fame and starred Jennifer Edwards, daughter of director Blake Edwards, as the little Swiss girl Heidi.

HEIDI POCKETBOOK DOLL

Introduced in 1966, the really cute, diminutive blonde, housed in a plastic pocketbook case, was the best-seller of Remco's 1960s doll line. Heidi had a Japanese friend named Jan, and each had a secret button on their stomach that allowed them to wave "hi" when pressed. Later additions to Heidi's Pocketbook line were little sister Hildy, little brother Herbie, little friend Pip, and tomboy friend Spunky. However, it's Heidi and Jan in the Pocketbook family that most women remember from childhood.

HELEN LAWSON

"The only hit that comes out of a Helen Lawson show is Helen Lawson, and that's *me*, baby, remember?" In the camp film-classic *Valley of the Dolls*, Susan Hayward portrayed steely-eyed Helen Lawson, the ballsy, brassy diva of Broadway who didn't like Neely O'Hara or Capricorns. "She took the yellow pills."

HELLO KITTY

"After all, you can never make too many friends," or apparently too many products featuring Hello Kitty, the most popular cartoon character to come out of Japan since the days of Speed Racer. Beginning with a simple coin purse in 1974, Sanrio's bow-headed white feline has appeared on innumerable licensed products (some estimate there have been more than 15,000 items), including school supplies, clothing, jewelry, toys, and furniture. Important stats on Hello Kitty: She lives in London with her parents and twin sister, Mimmy; she is in the third grade; her birthday is November 1; her boyfriend is Tippy; and her best friends are bunny Cathy, mole Morey, and monkey twins Tim and Tammy.

HELP! IT'S THE HAIR BEAR BUNCH

Airing from 1971 to 1974, Hanna-Barbera's Saturday-morning cartoon was reminiscent of the earlier favorite, *Top Cat* (1961–69), but instead of a gang of hip cats residing in an alley, it starred a bunch of cool bears living at the zoo. A trio of cousins, the Hair Bears consisted of frizzy-haired leader Hair Bear, logical Bubi Bear, and dopey Square Bear. They lived in Cave Block 9 at the Wonderland Zoo, where they spent their time seeking better living conditions and outwitting ill-tempered zookeeper Mr. Peevely and his silly assistant Botch.

HELTER SKELTER

Originally the title of a Beatles song, Helter Skelter took on a gruesome new meaning on August 9, 1969, when homicidal members of Charles Manson's "Family" entered the secluded Hollywood Hills estate of actress Sharon Tate, the beautiful wife of film director Roman Polanski. On that sweltering summer night, Tate and three jet-set friends—coffee heiress Abigail Folger, celebrity hairstylist Jay Sebring, and Polish writer-producer Voyteck Frykowski (Polanski's childhood chum)—were brutally shot, stabbed, and clubbed to death. Also murdered was Steven Parent, an eighteen-year-old visiting the property caretaker at the guesthouse, who didn't even know the other victims (talk about being in the wrong place at the wrong time). What made the crime even more incomprehensible was that when Sharon Tate, nearly nine months pregnant, begged for the life of her unborn baby, one of her killers replied, "Look, bitch, I have no mercy for you."

Two nights later, the bloodletting continued with the murder of wealthy Los Angeles supermarket chain owner Leno LaBianca and his wife, Rosemary. Similar to the Tate slayings, the victims' blood was used to write crazed sayings on the walls and doors, such as "Pig," "Rise," "War," and the misspelled "Healter Skelter." The gruesome murders, seemingly random, fueled rumors of retribution by satanic cults or of a drug deal gone wrong. It threw Southern California into a panic, causing citizens to arm themselves with guns, guard dogs, and bodyguards. Officially called the Tate-LaBianca murders, these crimes went unsolved for five months until linked with Charles Manson, the thirty-four-year-old leader of a communal cult of young hippie drifters whom he had brainwashed into spaced-out maniacs.

Consisting of twenty-five members or more, the Manson Family practiced free love, dropped LSD, believed in half-baked religiosity, and worshiped Charlie like a divine prophet (they believed he was Jesus Christ). Influenced by the 1968 Beatles song "Helter Skelter," Manson preached that an apocalyptic race war would take place in the near future. The black race would rise up and wipe out the entire white race, with the exception of the Manson Family, who would be hiding out in the Mojave Desert. Manson also believed blacks would be inept at running things—and that's when the Manson Family would come out from their desert hideaway as the new world leaders. Because this war wasn't happening anytime soon, Manson decided to give it a jump start by sending a handful of followers to commit helter skelter at the Tate and LaBianca residences. (Manson theorized that the crimes would be blamed on blacks, that whites would retaliate, and that the race war would then begin.)

On July 24, 1970, the Tate-LaBianca trial began with no-nonsense Vincent Bugliosi as the prosecutor. During the trial, Manson and his gang showed no remorse for the crimes—they even laughed and smirked when grisly details of the murders were described. It became one of the longest (July 24, 1970, to January 26, 1971) and most sensational trials in American history, ending with the guilty convictions and death-penalty verdicts against Manson, Susan Atkins, Patricia Krenwinkel, Leslie Van Houten, and Charles "Tex" Watson. (After California's death penalty was abolished, the sentences were commuted to life imprisonment.)

In 1974, Bugliosi's story of the murders and trial became a best-seller, *Helter Skelter: The True Story of the Manson Murders*. It was made into an explosive highly rated TV movie, *Helter Skelter*, in 1976, starring George DiCenzo as Vincent Bugliosi and Steve Railsback as Charles Manson, and remade in 2004. Once called "the most dangerous man alive" by *Rolling Stone* magazine, Manson is currently in solitary confinement at the State Prison in Corcoran, California, where he psycho-babbles to news cameras every chance he gets. And if that isn't bizarre enough, anti-establishment types around the world have come to worship him as a martyr of sorts, and his cult still survives.

FYI: ▸ After the bloody massacre at 10050 Cielo Drive in Bel Air, it became the "in thing" to claim at Hollywood parties: "I was supposed to have been at Sharon's that ghastly night."

HE-MAN

Alter ego of Prince Adam, handsome blond son of King Randor and Queen Marlena, who ruled over Castle Grayskull in the land of Eternia. When trouble emerged, usually initiated by wicked Skeletor from Snake Mountain, Prince Adam would shout "By the power of Grayskull! I have the power!" and transform into mighty-chested, sword-wielding He-Man, Master of the Universe. His virtuous cohorts included Stratos, Teela, Man-at-Arms, funny sidekick Orko, and sister Adora, a.k.a. She-Ra, the Princess of Power. Fierce Battle Cat was He-Man's trusty mount.

HE-MAN WOMAN HATERS CLUB

After suffering through a dismal Valentine's Day, the *Our Gang* boys made a pact to hate all women and formed this antifemale fraternity led by juvenile male chauvinists Alfalfa Switzer and Spanky McFarland. The sanctity of the club is ruined when love-struck Alfalfa goes gaa-gaa over crush-worthy Darla Hood, the club's secretary (!).

HENERY HAWK

Since 1942, the spunky young chicken-hawk's sole purpose has been to catch a chicken to eat. However, he doesn't really know what a chicken looks like, so he settles for boisterous rooster Foghorn Leghorn, in the Warner Brothers cartoon shorts.

HENRIETTA HIPPO

"Delicate and feminine is Henrietta Hippo. . . ." Extravagant hippopotamus star of the 1970s juvenile classic *New Zoo Revue* who had a diva personality similar to that of Miss Piggy. Henrietta had a dainty Southern accent of sorts, gigantic nostrils, and carried a handkerchief and parasol. Her constant yakking about her dazzling beauty annoyed everyone on the TV show (and viewers at home, too.)

HENRY

Mute, bald-headed comic-strip kid created by Carl Anderson in 1932. Henry's escapades centered on his street antics, in which girlfriend Henrietta and bully Butch often join.

HENRY, MIKE

The Tarzan that children of the 1960s viewed at movie theaters was played by this former L.A. Rams linebacker in three films, *Tarzan and the Valley of Gold* (1966), *Tarzan and the Great River* (1967), and *Tarzan and the Jungle Boy* (1968). Henry—whose studly six-foot-three-inch frame was distinguished by hairy, muscular pecs and legs—played loinclothed Tarzan as well-spoken, educated, and kind of groovy, a cross between a modern superhero and a secret agent. The dark-haired actor's run as the jungle lord lasted only a brief time because of the harsh working environment while shooting on location in Mexico and Brazil. Enduring food poisoning, animal bites, infections, and extensive hours of filming, Henry later sued *Tarzan* producer Sy Weintraub for "maltreatment, abuse, and working conditions detrimental to my health and welfare."

HERBAL ESSENCES

The green-colored organic shampoo from Clairol was distinguished in the 1970s for its advertisements and bottle label that featured a pretty earth-goddess, with long, flowing golden locks garnished with flowers, birds, and butterflies, emerging from a pond. In the first decade of the twenty-first century, contemporary TV commercials for Herbal Essences products have been very popular. These fun ads feature young women, including Julia Louis-Dreyfuss of *Seinfeld* fame, getting orgasmic while shampooing their hair with Herbal Essences in public spots like a courtroom or a city bus.

HERBIE

Lovable white Volkswagen Beetle, amazing race car 53, that actually had a mind of its own. It was the star of the live-action Disney hit *The Love Bug* (1969) and sequels, *Herbie Rides Again* (1974), *Herbie Goes to Monte Carlo* (1977), and *Herbie Goes Bananas* (1980).

HERE COMES PETER COTTONTAIL

Stop-motion animator Rankin/Bass takes a break from Christmas and gives the Easter holiday a shot with this fanciful, pastel-colored yarn. Hosted by magician Seymour S. Sassafrass (voice of Danny Kaye), it recounts the story of hippety-hopping Peter Cottontail (voice of Casey Kasem), who wants to be the Chief Easter Bunny of April Valley (home of all Easter bunnies). Problem is, Peter ignores the cautionary song "In Spring the Easter Bunny Never Sleeps" and oversleeps on the day of the egg-delivery contest, losing out to his sinister rival, Irontail (voice of Vincent Price), who becomes Chief Easter Bunny. Sassafrass then allows Peter to use his magical Yestermorrow Mobile, piloted by caterpillar Antoine, to travel back through time—making unplanned stops at other holidays before reaching Easter—to fix the mistake of oversleeping. The 1971 musical was inspired in part by the famous song by Gene Autry and by a book, *The Easter Bunny That Overslept*, by Priscilla and Otto Friedrich.

FYI: ▸ When Peter Cottontail tells a lie, his left ear bends.

HERE COME THE DOUBLE DECKERS

"Ring the bell, toot the horn. . . ." A live-action kiddie TV show imported from Great Britain and airing on weekend mornings from 1970 to 1972. It was about the Double Deckers, a gang of seven rambunctious youngsters (ages nine to sixteen) living in London who hung out and played together in an old double-decker bus, their clubhouse. The program starred Michael Audreson as Brains, Gillian Bailey as Billie, Bruce Clark as Sticks (the only American member of the group), Peter Firth as Scooper, Brinsley Forde as Spring, Debbie Russ as Tiger, Douglas Simmonds as Doughnut, and Melvyn Hayes as street cleaner Albert, their adult chum. Their mascot was a stuffed tiger belonging to Tiger (of course).

HERMAN MUNSTER

Actor Fred Gwynne's seven-foot-three-inch green-skinned Frankenstein monster, who had a lightning-shaped scar on his forehead and electric bolts protruding from his the neck, was the goofy patriarch on TV's *The Munsters.* Though 150 years old, Herman is prone to childish, earthshaking tantrums when life and his vampire-like wife, Lily, don't give him his way. A devoted family man, he works hard as a funeral director at Gateman, Goodbury, and Graves in Mockingbird Heights.

HERMAN, PEE-WEE

"I know you are, but what am I?" Who was childlike, smart-alecky, cute, silly, wise, retro, funky, and punk all at the same time? If you said Michael Jackson, you're wrong. It's Pee-Wee Herman—the man-child comic superstar of the 1980s. The alter ego of comedian Paul Reubens (born August 27, 1952, in Peekskill, New York), Pee-Wee was a petulant twelve-year-old trapped in a grown man's body who talked in an excitable high-pitched voice, wore a trademark outfit consisting of a too-small gray suit, red bow-tie, white-buck shoes, and cropped hair gelled back. He started on the nightclub and talk-show circuit, before starring in a 1982 cable TV special for HBO, *The Pee-Wee Herman Show,* an off-the-wall adult-oriented takeoff of 1950s kiddie shows, which brought him national exposure.

In 1985, Pee-Wee headlined his first big-screen vehicle, *Pee-Wee's Big Adventure,* directed by Tim Burton, featuring him on a cross-country trek in search of a stolen bicycle. The film's success spawned a sequel, *Big Top Pee-Wee* (1988), and a Saturday-morning TV series, *Pee-Wee's Playhouse* (1986–91). Combining childish whimsy and double-entendre humor, the TV program quickly caught on with both kids and young adults, making it a cult favorite of the late 1980s. In July 1991, Paul Reubens made tabloid history after his arrest for openly masturbating in a Florida porno theater. This bad publicity led CBS to pull *Pee-Wee's Playhouse* off the air and caused Reubens to shelve the Pee-Wee Herman character altogether. "Yeah, right."

FYI: ▸ The name of the XXX-rated movie comedian Paul Reubens was viewing when he got caught playing with his peewee was titled *Naughty Nurses.*

HERMAN'S HERMITS

A product of the British Invasion, this pop group from Manchester experienced Top Forty American success in the mid-1960s with the songs "I'm into Something Good" (1964), "Mrs. Brown, You've Got a Lovely Daughter" (1965), "I'm Henry the Eighth, I Am" (1965), and "There's a Kind of Hush" (1967). Led by the adorable Peter "Herman" Noone—a teen magazine coverboy who was a mere teen himself (born November 5, 1947)—the Hermits consisted of guitarists Derek Leckenby and Keith Hopwood, bassist Karl Green, and drummer Barry Whitwam. They were distinguished by their cheeky antics, showcased in such films as *Hold On!* (1966) and *Mrs. Brown, You've Got a Lovely Daughter* (1968).

FYI: ▸ The Herman's Hermits name derived from the cartoon character Sherman of TV's *Bullwinkle Show.*

HERMEY

"Hermey doesn't like to make toys!" Blond-haired elf from the TV special *Rudolph the Red-Nosed Reindeer* who doesn't want to work the assembly line at Santa's toyshop. He wants to be a dentist! Who ever heard of an elf as a dentist? So he runs away with fellow misfit red-nosed reindeer Rudolph to find fame and fortune.

HERSHEY'S

Candy-maker Milton S. Hershey founded the world's largest chocolate factory in 1905 in the rural township of Derry Church, now known as Hershey, Pennsylvania. The company's foundation is the classic Hershey's milk-chocolate bar, developed in the 1890s, called the "Great American Chocolate Bar."

Other principal Hershey candy brands include Almond Joy, Kisses, Kit Kat, Milk Duds, Mounds, Mr. Goodbar, PayDay, Reese's Peanut Butter Cups, Twizzlers, Whoppers, and York Peppermint Patties. Hershey Park—an amusement park geared around Hershey's chocolate—is the home of sixty rides and attractions.

HEXUM, JON-ERIK

A handsome young actor whose promising career was ended by an accidental self-inflicted gunshot on the set of the prime-time show *Cover Up*. Born on November 5, 1957, in Tenafly, New Jersey, Hexum began his showbiz career by putting his genetically superior good looks—sapphire-blue eyes, wavy hair, chiseled face, and muscles (we're talking *Gattaca* here)—to work as a model for beefcake calendars. Soon after moving to Los Angeles in 1982, he won the lead role of time-traveler Phineas Bogg in the short-lived sci-fi TV series *Voyagers* (1982–83). With a growing reputation as Hollywood's new hunk, Hexum starred in his most famous role—down-to-earth coverboy—Burnett, opposite vixen Joan Collins, in the 1983 tele-film *The Making of a Male Model*. In September 1984, Hexum was cast as Mac Harper, a secret agent disguised as a male model, in *Cover Up*, co-starring supermodel-turned-actress Jennifer O'Neill. It was on the ill-fated day of October 18, 1984, on the set of *Cover Up* that Hexum, in an act of showing off, shot himself in the forehead with a pistol loaded with blanks. The incident put him in a short coma and he died shortly afterward at age twenty-six.

FYI: ▸ Jon-Erik Hexum carried a California organ donor's card. When he died, at least five people received transplants of his viable organs, including his heart.

HI AND LOIS

Newspaper comic strip about a contemporary nuclear-age family that was a result of a collaboration of two cartoonists—Mort (*Beetle Bailey*) Walker and Dik (*Hagar the Horrible*) Browne. It centers around hardworking district sales manager Hiram "Hi" Flagston, his attractive wife, Lois, and their four fair-haired offspring: procrastinating fifteen-year-old Chip, mischievous eight-year-old twins Ditto and Dot, and precocious baby Trixie. Trixie's best friend is the Sunbeam that shines down on her face. Additional characters include lazy next-door neighbor Thirsty, his frustrated spouse, Irma, Hi's callous boss, Mr. Foofram, and neighborhood garbagemen Abercrombie and Fitch. Debuting in 1954, the strip has enjoyed long-lasting popularity because of its warmhearted and honest approach to the average middle-class American family.

"HI, BOB!"

This frequently spoken greeting on the TV sitcom *The Bob Newhart Show* inspired a beer-drinking game in the 1970s. The game was easy to play: When somebody on the show said "Hi, Bob!" boozing participants shouted "Hi, Bob!" back and took a swig of beer. Because the show's characters said "Hi, Bob!" many times throughout its half-hour airing, it was guaranteed that those playing the game were gonna cop a beer buzz.

***HIGHLIGHTS* MAGAZINE**

"Fun with a purpose!" Most of us first became acquainted with this "monthly book for children" while waiting in the reception rooms of medical offices. First published in 1946, *Highlights* is known for kid-friendly features including stories, games, puzzles, activities, readers' artwork and poems, jokes and riddles, hidden pictures, and the Goofus and Gallant, Timbertoes, and Berenstain Bears comic-strip segments. Inspired other elementary-school mags, like *Boy's Life*, *Ranger Rick*, *Humpty Dumpty*, *Children's Digest*, and *Jack and Jill*.

HIGH SCHOOL REUNION

The class reunion is approaching. For some, it's time to lose weight, dye the gray, get a facial, switch to contact lenses, shop for a flattering outfit, call long-lost buds to see if they'll be attending, and take stock of their life. No matter if it's your tenth or twentieth, a high school reunion is a momentous event that forces people to think about everything they've accomplished, or didn't accomplish, since graduation. What if you didn't do anything exciting with your life? Should you fabricate an elaborate story about acquiring enormous wealth from inventing something like Post-it Notes? No, that didn't work for Romy and Michele, and it probably won't work for you either. It's easier just to be up-front about your accomplishments or lack of accomplishments—unless you starred in porno movies or spent some time locked away in prison. The following is a fictional account of a class reunion:

The minute of the hour of the night of the reunion arrives. The function is taking place at a ritzy hotel in the large city hovering over the suburbs where I grew up. I enter alone through the doors of a grand ballroom that is dimly lit by huge chandeliers twinkling above and filled with tables set formally with floral arrangements and tea-light candles. I'm nervous as hell. Maybe I should've brought a date for moral support. I go straight to the cash bar and buy an alcoholic beverage to calm the nerves. It's probably not a good idea, because I already had two glasses of wine in my hotel room, which gave me confidence to head down to the ballroom. I missed the last reunion, and it's been so many years . . . wait . . . who are all these mature faces, strange yet somehow familiar? They don't recognize me either—yet. Thank God for the name tags with yearbook photos on 'em.

Right away I start mingling with my aged schoolmates. There's Susan, once a member of the school's drill team and a class beauty. Still beautiful, she reminds me of the time we skipped school to go to the beach and got caught by Miss Frost, the English teacher. Nearby are Jimmy and Jimmy, two chums who go way, way back to the early days of grade school. Now married with children, the Jimmys have done well with their lives as successful business owners. Tammy confesses that she always had a crush on me; I confess to Laura that I've always had a crush on her. She's married; I am not available anyway. Onetime freak Sandy, now a police officer, wants me to go outside and sneak a smoke, just like the good ole days. The night is actually turning out to be fun.

Smile, everybody! Gather together, it's time for the class portrait (I totally missed it because I was out smoking with Sandy). Former classmates are everywhere. Some line up in the food line for the buffet-style dinner (remindful of the school lunchroom), while others catch up with one another waiting in the bar line. (Watch those drinks, guys. You don't want to end up a wobbling drunk like Debbie over there, who's telling everyone in earshot about her sexual escapades with various football players behind the bleachers after game night.) A rented disc jockey on stage plays old Top Forty favorites, packing the ballroom dance floor with quasi-toasted revelers attempting to boogie like they once did. (Tammy wants me to dance to a Bob Seger tune. I tell her no but eventually give in, for old times' sake.)

Hardworking Connie, former class president and current reunion-committee president, takes over the stage to announce a handful of awards. Donna receives the Least Changed award (doesn't she realize the Farrah hairdo went out of style in 1980?); David, dressed in high-fashion Armani, wins the Most Changed award (I wonder when he ditched the long locks, the pukka-shell necklaces, and the surfer threads); Eric gets the honor of Most Miles Traveled to Attend award (he flew in all the way from the Persian Gulf, where he's based as a Navy pilot); and drunk Debbie wobbles on stage to pick up the Most Surprising Profession award (once the captain of the varsity cheerleaders, she's now a proud Vegas stripper). Some of us weren't surprised about Debbie's surprising profession.

All this made me wonder about the girl once voted Most Likely to Succeed. Everyone thought Becky would become CEO of some large corporation, but I hear she's a stay-at-home wife and mother of three happily living in the suburbs. What happened to Kelli, the homecoming queen? No way, that can't be her happily shuffling on the dance floor with an extra 100 pounds on her once-petite frame. The varsity-football star Kenny? Well, he flunked out of State U and now sells used Oldsmobiles at a local car lot. Wow, can you believe what became of the geek from chemistry lab? Ricky invented a magical hair-growth substance and made millions selling it to a shampoo conglomerate.

The reunion has turned out to be quite an interesting surprise and, believe it or not, I actually had a good time. So, take it from someone who's been there. If you are planning on attending your next high school reunion—relax! The truth is, you turned out just fine. Life happens the way it's supposed to, and no one did better than you (unless you are the geek from chemistry lab). Remember to say "Hey" to the old gang, and give Bob Seger a dance.

FYI: ▸ A couple of wonderful films worth renting before heading off to your high school reunion are *Grosse Pointe Blank* (1997), starring John Cusack, and *Romy and Michele's High School Reunion* (1997), starring Lisa Kudrow and Mira Sorvino.

HIGH SCHOOL SOCIAL CLIQUES

"There're freaks, heads, jocks, fags, and frocks.
The fags are the people you call brains.
A head I consider a really hard freak,
the type that is always stoned.
Freaks are like weekend partiers.
The jocks get superdrunk off one beer.
Some people are really in between.
One guy I know is kind of a jock and
kind of a freak. I guess he's a frock.
It's very confusing, really."

—ANONYMOUS HIGH SCHOOL FRESHMAN, *LIFE* MAGAZINE'S SPECIAL REPORT ON THE NEW YOUTH, FALL 1977

In the 1986 youth comedy *Ferris Bueller's Day Off*, school secretary Grace describes to Principal Rooney how important Ferris is among his peers: "He's very popular. The sportos, motorheads, geeks, sluts, dweebies, wastoids, they all adore him." The line is a hilarious (and often cruel) reminder of how we were labeled (often unfairly and unfortunately) and divided into various social groups during our school years. The following is a list of the numerous cliques found in American high schools, from the 1970s through to the 1990s. As we all know, it was hard not to be associated with at least one of these crowds, and some of us could easily intermingle with many different ones. So, get ready to relive everyone's so-called favorite time of his or her life. (Doesn't the thought send shivers up your spine and put butterflies in your stomach?) Which group did you belong to?

- **Alkies.** Remember *Sarah T: Portrait of a Teenage Alcoholic*? These kids often carried thermoses spiked with hard liquor to school. In the middle of the school year, they would mysteriously disappear for at least a semester due to stints in rehab.
- **Artsy-fartsies; band geeks; drama freaks; thespians.** Talented kids who were wrapped up in the arts (band, choir, drama, art, and journalism). Band geeks weren't all nerds, though quite a few were, and drama freaks were *Fame* wannabes who would break out in song in a crowded lunchroom.
- **Babes; foxes.** These school beauties were very desirable and very off-limits (think teenage Farrah Fawcett or Christie Brinkley). Often left dateless on weekend nights because guys assumed they were already taken or would turn them down.
- **Big men on campus (or BMOCs); hunks; studs.** Good-looking dudes with hot bods and even hotter cars who could have any girl they preferred.
- **Bitches; Heathers; prom queens.** A mystery is how these mean queens of the social pecking order could be cruelly snooty to everyone except their own kind—the popular kids—but still always sweep school-wide voting competitions (for things like homecoming queen and class elections) and merit yearbook superlatives.
- **Brains; dorks; dweebs; geeks; nerds; trekkies; urkels; weirdos.** Highwater pants, pens and pencils in the front shirt-pocket, eyeglasses, violin cases, oily hair, and a peculiar sense of humor—today's CEOs of computer-software companies.
- **Burnouts; druggies; freaks; headbangers; heshers; hoods; potheads (or 'heads); stoners.** Long-haired antisocials who were into heavy-metal music, rebellion, and drugs.
- **Cowboys; kickers; ropers.** "Yee-ha!" Tobacco-chewing fellas who wore cowboy hats, cowboy boots, and Wranglers and drove American-made pickup trucks while Willie or Waylon crooned on the radio. Blue-jacketed members of FFA (Future Farmers of America).
- **Flower children; granola heads; hippies; tree huggers.** "Peace, man!" Long-haired followers of Jerry Garcia's Grateful Dead and Creedence Clearwater Revival; into bare feet, love beads, karma, incense, Greenpeace, and LSD. Somehow felt cheated because they missed out on the 1967 Summer of Love because they weren't even born.
- **Frocks; in-betweeners.** Combo of freak and jock; boy- or girl-next-door types who could

hang out with the hoods during lunch or be seen among cheerleaders after school. Average students who were often nominated for class vice-president and usually didn't win. Molly Ringwald as Samantha Baker in *Sixteen Candles* (1984) would be the ideal prototype.

- **Ghetto kids; trailer trash; white trash.** Poor in both finances and in grades, these often disobedient classmates lived in trailer parks or low-income housing projects and were the types you'd see as guests on *The Jerry Springer Show.*
- **God Squad; holy rollers; Jesus freaks.** Ultrareligious students who couldn't understand why prayer wasn't allowed in public schools. Fond of witnessing and hayrides.
- **Goody-two-shoes; squares; straight asses; teacher's pets.** In the words of rocker Adam Ant, "Don't drink, don't smoke . . . What *do* you do?" Uptight kids and goody-goody tattletales—actually, trying to get an education—disturbed by unruly students and by kids trying to copy off their tests.
- **Goths; mods; New-Wavers; progressives; punk rockers.** Students fond of black clothing, Doc Martens, odd hairstyles, body-piercing, tattoos, and alternative music.
- **Greasers; motorheads.** Hollering, beer-guzzling guys who hung out in the school parking lot admiring one another's "boss" muscle cars (Trans Ams, Mustangs, GTOs, and the like). Commonly found in industrial-arts classes.
- **"In" crowd; jocks; rah-rahs; socials (or socs); sportos.** Popular athletes, cheerleaders, drill-teamers, pom-pom girls, and their hangers-on who ruled the school and rarely socialized outside their celebrated circle. Actually got excited about pep rallies or class-officer and homecoming elections.
- **Loners; losers; slackers; wastoids.** Who? These are the faces and names you can't recall as you reminisce through your old yearbook—because they didn't do anything in high school.
- **Outcasts.** Simply scorned by every single social clique (even the nerds and the wastoids), these misfits didn't have any friends and were easy prey for bullies. Think of the taunted Carrie White from Stephen King's *Carrie* (1976) or today's ultimate high school nightmare: the oft-taunted kid who comes to class one day shooting a semi-automatic rifle.
- **Party animals.** The kids who threw cop-busting house parties when their parents were out of town. Aspired to be members of the toga-clad, party-loving Delta fraternity seen in the 1978 film comedy *National Lampoon's Animal House.*
- **Pizza gang.** Geeky, pimple-faced kids who thought they were cooler than you and hung out at pizza restaurants on weekend nights ordering continuous pitchers of Coca-Cola.
- **Preppies; preps; snobs; Young Republicans.** The wealthy students (and wealthy wannabes)—named Biff, Skip, Muffy, or Buffy—adorned in madras plaid, khaki, Izod, Top-Siders, and sweaters draped over shoulders (they look like they stepped out of a Lands' End or L. L. Bean clothing catalog). Today's yuppie or Martha Stewart clone.
- **Rednecks.** Troublemaking types named Billy Bob, Kenny Boy, Bobbi Sue, or Bubba, who didn't like blacks, Mexicans, Asians, Indians, Italians, Jews, long-haired hippies, liberals, feminists, gays, or any other "non-American" types.
- **Retards; short bus crowd.** The special-education students (I know this is mean, but high school can be ruthless) who often arrived at school in squatty school buses for the handicapped.
- **Skaters.** Pesty, immature guys found skateboarding in packs in parking lots and on sidewalks of commercial business areas.
- **Sluts.** Lots of girls were unfairly called this, but a few sporting camel toes, braless halter tops, baby-blue eye shadow, and hickeys actually deserved it. A girl's reputation was shot when her name appeared on the boy's bathroom wall in the form of "For a good time call —— ."
- **Surfers.** "Hey, dude, surf's up!" Fond of pukka shells, Hang Ten, and the Pacific Coast Highway, these kids headed for the beach more often than to school. Sean Penn as Jeff Spicoli in *Fast Times at Ridgemont High* (1982) and Bo Derek as Jenny in *10* (1979) were the perfect role models.
- **Valley Girls.** "Oh my gawd! It's s-o-o-o-o tubular . . . fer shur!" Materialistic, bubbleheaded, spoiled girls associated with L.A.'s San Fernando Valley. Variations can be found at every mall in every suburb of every American city.

HIGH SCHOOL YEARBOOKS

"To a very sweet guy. It's been really fun knowing you this year. Good luck in the future and stay cool always. Love, Jennifer"
—ARCHETYPAL YEARBOOK AUTOGRAPH

Some people love their high school yearbook, because they're in so many of the photos and there are so many autograph scribbles from friends—all demonstrating how popular and active they were in the past school year. Others cringe, because their yearbook has few, if any, pictures of them, because they weren't in any clubs or sports or at any dances, so there might be only a terrible class photo forever capturing a bad haircut, a gawky grimace, or even worse, closed eyes (we won't even mention the mere handful, or less, of autographs).

Part of a rite of passage each spring, yearbooks were thick, handsome, photo-glutted hardcover annuals that documented a year's worth of school events. Commonly, these chapters sectioned yearbooks off:

- **Student Life.** Candid shots of students hanging out in halls and the schoolyard, plus photographs of traditional ceremonies: pep rallies, dances, homecoming pageants, stage musicals, car washes, awards, and graduation
- **Sports.** Team photos, including cheerleaders, and action shots
- **Organizations.** Group photos of organized clubs, such as the drill team, marching band, choir, orchestra, thespians, student government, debate, chess, newspaper, and yours truly the yearbook staff
- **Faculty.** Photos of teachers, principals, office workers, and other school employees
- **Senior Class.** A picture of the class officers (president, vice-president, secretary, treasurer) preceded the formal head shots of graduating seniors, each accompanied by a summary list of his or her activities from all years of high school
- **Senior Class Superlatives.** Well-liked seniors were awarded distinct honors by ballot voting from fellow students, such as "Most Popular," "Most Likely to Succeed," "Class Clown," "Best Dressed," "Best Looking," "Most Athletic," "School Spirited," and so on
- **Underclassmen.** Separated by class (juniors, sophomores, freshmen), this part featured tiny head shots of students in alphabetical order
- **Advertisements.** Showcasing students posing in front of locally owned businesses that gave money to sponsor the yearbook

Unique to high school yearbooks is trying to get everyone you know (and then some) to sign your yearbook. Some would even have yearbook parties for that purpose.

HIGHWATERS

"Hey, where's the flood?" Pants with legs that are unintentionally too short, associated with nerds. A childhood taunt to those who wore highwaters went: "The flood is over / The mud is dry / Why are you wearing your pants so high?"

HIGH WIND IN JAMAICA

Once-popular 1960s family film based on the Richard Hughes adventure novel about a group of aristocratic children unwittingly taken hostage by pirates. Believed to be "uncivilized" by their parents after growing up in Jamaica, the Thornton brood are put on a ship to England to be placed in boarding schools to learn proper Victorian manners. Their ship is seized by pirates on the Caribbean Sea, and during the attack the kids do what you would expect kids to do: They venture onto the pirate vessel to explore it. Not realizing that the youngsters are trapped aboard, the pirate ship sails off. Months go by before the children are released back to civilization, and in the meantime they develop unruly pirate-like behavior while clashing with the pirates, led by Captain Chavez (Anthony Quinn), who come to view them as bad-luck symbols. Alexander Mackendrick, who previously filmed another youth classic in 1963, *A Boy Ten Feet Tall*, directed this 1965 movie. Two standouts: young actress Deborah Baxter's performance as feisty ten-year-old Emily Thornton, and harmonica virtuoso Larry Adler's mood-provoking score.

HILLBILLY BEARS

An idiotic backwoods bear clan composed of Paw Rugg, Maw Rugg, Floral Rugg, and Shag Rugg—get it?—whose cartoon adventures were a supporting segment of *The Atom Ant Show*.

HILLBILLY MOBILE
The actual name of the Clampetts' decrepit flatbed truck, a 1921 Oldsmobile, on *The Beverly Hillbillies.* Jethro does most of the driving, while Granny sits in a rocking chair in the back of the vehicle.

HINTON, S. E.
Best-selling author from Tulsa, Oklahoma, whose novels for teenagers, such as *The Outsiders* (1967), *Tex* (1979), and *Rumble Fish* (1983), were best-sellers in the 1980s, especially after being made into big-screen movies starring Matt Dillon. Hinton's initials stood for Susan Eloise.

HIP-HUGGERS
Sexy and daring, these navel-baring slacks were cut low and tight at the hips and had a bell-bottom look. First worn by mod chicks in the swingin' sixties and later by teen tarts in the early twenty-first century.

HIPPETY HOPPER
In the Warner Brothers cartoon short "Hop, Look, and Listen" (1948), Sylvester the Cat finds himself entangled with this silent baby kangaroo—freshly escaped from a city zoo—whom he mistakes for an overgrown mouse.

HI-RISE BIKES
During their heyday (the late 1960s and early 1970s), "flashy" and "racy" were the words to describe the eye-stopping beauty of a kid's hi-rise bicycle, commonly known as the Schwinn Sting-Ray, or one of its competitors: the Sears Spyder, the Wards Mustang, the Huffy Slingshot, the AMF Fast One, and the Ross Apollo. The hi-rise originated around the mid-1960s, when the design of bicycles for juveniles took on a radical new look inspired by cool chopper cycles. These bikes had tires that were much smaller than regular bikes, with the front wheel smaller than the rear wheel, giving it the distinctive hi-rise appearance. Their handlebars were extended with the handle grips pulled down into U-shapes (called suicide bars) and equipped with brake grips for sudden stops. Along with the hand brakes, there were foot-pedal brakes (a.k.a. coaster brakes) for totally cool skids. The seats were flattened out and curved into a banana-shaped "banana seat" affixed to a chrome backrest. Some hi-risers had "wet vinyl" banana seats that glittered with far-out colors or psychedelic daisies, and a forty-two-inch backrest known as a sissy bar, equipped with a back pad, to protect kids from falling off while doing all those wicked wheelies and stunt jumps. These speedy-looking vehicles also had three-speed or five-speed stick shifts on the console and safety reflectors on the rear.

Hi-rise bikes came in groovy glossy shades, like lunar blue, kelly green, cherry red, lemon-lime, burnt-orange, gold, silver, magenta, and peppermint pink. A girl could make her hi-rise ultragirly by decorating each handle grip with multicolored vinyl streamers that blew crazily in the wind, and by placing between the handlebars a woven basket trimmed with gaily-colored mod flowers to match the floral banana seat. Kids also had a penchant for clothes-pinning playing cards on the tire spokes to produce a flap-flap-flapping sound as they rode through the neighborhood.

HITCHHIKE
Dance from the early 1970s in which participants grooved with their thumbs up, as if they were hitching a ride. I believe the Brady Kids used the Hitchhike in their dance routine while performing the groovy rocker "Keep on Moving" on *The Brady Bunch.* (If they didn't, they should've.)

"HIT ME WITH YOUR BEST SHOT"
Pat Benatar's first million-seller single, from the rock-driven *Crimes of Passion* LP (1980), which earned her a Grammy Award for Best Rock Vocal Performance.

HOCUS POCUS
The cute white rabbit resided in the magic hat of evil Professor Hinkle in the Rankin/Bass animated holiday classic *Frosty the Snowman* (1969). Friendly and resourceful, the bouncy hare aided jolly Frosty and little Karen on their journey to the North Pole.

HOGAN, HULK
Wild and outrageous, the platinum-blond "Hulkster," born Terry Bollea in Augusta, Georgia, was the superstar wrestler of the 1980s. He paved the way for today's showy WCW and WWF body slam-

min' professionals, like "Macho Man" Randy Savage, Stone Cold Steve Austin, Goldberg, and the Rock. Hogan's popularity made him the star of cartoon (1985's *Hulk Hogan's Rock 'n' Wrestling*), film (1993's *Mr. Nanny*), and TV commercials (Honey Nut Cheerios).

FYI: ▸ Hulk Hogan is the number-one most requested celebrity for the "Make-a-Wish" children's foundation.

HOGAN'S HEROES

Great 1960s sitcom about a ragtag band of international soldiers imprisoned in a German Nazi camp during World War II. *Hogan's Heroes* made light of a serious subject by having the Allied prisoners, cool and in complete control, outfoxing the Germans at Stalag 13, who were both comical and incompetent. The POWs had access to a hidden tunnel system, which they used to assist the Allied forces and thereby sabotage the enemy's war effort. They could also sneak off the prison grounds (the barbed-wire fence was rigged like an electrical garage door), and they had such creature comforts as a steam room, a barbershop, a lounge with a vintage wine cellar, and a French chef. Airing on CBS from 1965 to 1971, the TV show starred dark and handsome Bob Crane as Colonel Robert Hogan, a U.S. Air Force officer who served as the inmates' ringleader. His cohorts included African-American Sergeant James Kinchloe (Ivan Dixon), British Corporal Peter Newkirk (Richard Dawson), French Corporal Louis LeBeau (Robert Clary), and country-bumpkin American Sergeant Andrew Carter (Larry Hovis). Monocled bumbler Colonel Wilhelm Klink (Werner Klemperer) and his idiotic assistant Sergeant Hans Schultz (John Banner) were the camp commandants. Cynthia Lynn and Sigrid Valdis played Colonel Klink's blonde and buxom secretaries Helga and Hilda.

FYI: ▸ On June 29, 1978, Bob Crane was found bludgeoned to death and strangled with an electrical cord in a hotel room in Scottsdale, Arizona. It was later revealed that he had been involved in kinky pornography in which he filmed himself and others having sex. His killer is still a mystery.

HOGWARTS

For more than a thousand years, the world's largest school of magic has instructed youths ages eleven to seventeen on how to be great witches and wizards. Hogwarts is a castle secretly located somewhere in remote northern England and divided into four school houses named after the four founding wizards: brave Gryffindor, loyal Hufflepuff, wise Ravenclaw, and cunning Slytherin. Broom-riding Quidditch is the official sport.

HO HOS

Hostess snack-cake favorites that are creme-filled chocolate rolls covered with chocolate candy. Remember when they came individually wrapped in aluminum foil?

HOLLY HOBBIE

Based on the greeting-card character introduced by American Greetings in 1967, the rag doll—with the caramel-colored braids and patchwork frocks—appealed to girly-girl types who liked Gunne Sax dresses and watched TV's *Little House on the Prairie*. Extremely adored, Holly and her bonnet-headed petticoat friends—Amy, Carrie, and brother Robby Hobbie—were mass-produced on various merchandise items, such as bed sheets, clothing, watches, stationery, posters, toys, games, and lunch boxes. She was the predecessor of Betsy Clark, Strawberry Shortcake, Rainbow Brite, and the Precious Moments moppets—all of which experienced similar success in the 1980s.

HOLLY MARSHALL

"Run, Holly, run!" Young daughter in the 1970s version of *Land of the Lost*, played by Kathy Coleman on the TV show, whose curiosity frequently got her family in some kind of dangerous predicament. Holly's trademark was blonde hair worn in braided pigtails, and a plaid shirt.

HOLLYROCK

Entertainment capital near Bedrock where you would find prehistoric stars, such as Ann-Margrock, Gina Lollobrickada, Cary Granite, Rock Hudstone, Stony Curtis, along with music conductor Leonard Bernstone, songwriter Stony Carmichael, dance instructor Arthur Quarry, "really big" TV host Ed Sullystone, lawyer Perry Masonry, and canine star Sassie.

HOLLYWOOD SQUARES

This legendary TV game show featured two contestants playing a giant tic-tac-toe game made up of a panel of nine celebrities, with wiseacre Paul Lynde regularly occupying the center square. Hosted by Peter Marshall from 1966 to 1982. Revived in 1998 with host Tom Bergeron and film comedienne Whoopi Goldberg in the center square.

HOLMES, JOHN C.

Porn king whose amazing endowment (estimated at more than thirteen inches long when erect) and insatiable sexual appetite made him a legend in the California adult-film industry of the 1970s and 1980s. A former Bible student from Ohio, he appeared in more than 2,275 X-rated flicks, including one in 3-D, and claimed to have had sex with 14,000 women. His most famous role was that of Johnny Wadd, a horny private investigator seen in several movies, including *Liquid Lips* (1976), *Jade Pussycat* (1977), and *Blonde Fire* (1979). In later years, he fell victim to cocaine abuse and was acquitted of participating in the grisly drug-related murder of two men and two women on Wonderland Avenue in L.A.'s Laurel Canyon (July 1981). He died of AIDS in 1988. The movie *Boogie Nights* (1997), starring Mark Wahlberg as Dirk Diggler, is loosely based on the life of John C. Holmes.

"HOMECOMING QUEEN'S GOT A GUN"

"Everybody run! The homecoming queen's got a gun!" Comedienne Julie Brown's wicked satire on America's fascination with pageantry and violence. Featured on her 1984 comedy album *Goddess in Progress*, the song told the tragic but funny story of Debby Dickey, the homecoming queen at John Wayne High School in Van Nuys, California, who went on a mad shooting rampage during the halftime ceremonies. As the band played "Evergreen," the blonde and blue-eyed Debby, wearing pink chiffon and her tiara, was atop the float when suddenly she whipped out a .38 caliber automatic from her brassiere and began firing wildly into the "stoked" crowd. Before the police could get there, the trigger-happy queen had picked off half her class, including the entire Glee Club ("No big loss") and the cheerleaders ("Buffy's pom-pom just blew to bits, Mitzi's head just did the splits"). After being blown out of her float by a SWAT-team helicopter, Debby lay dying in the arms of her best friend and Brooke Shields look-alike Julie Brown, who thought the dreadful event was "just like *Carrie* or something." Embarrassed by her friend's shooting spree, Julie asked the queen why she freaked out. Debby replied, "I did it for Johnny."

HOMER SIMPSON

"D'oh!" Lazy, selfish, bald-headed slob of a dim-witted dad from *The Simpsons* cartoon, who works at the Springfield nuclear power plant and enjoys his time off by guzzling Duff beer (his drink of choice) at Moe's Tavern and bowling strikes at Barney's New Bowlerama. Married his high school sweetheart, Marge Bouvier, and settled down with three kids—Bart, Lisa, and Maggie—in Evergreen Terrace, the "nicest upper-lower-middle-class section of Springfield."

FYI: ▸ In 2003, *People* magazine picked Homer Simpson as one of their "Fifty Favorite TV Stars," a list that includes such luminaries as Lucille Ball, Walter Cronkite, and Lassie.

HONEY BEES

"Bzzzzzz. . . ." What Ginger, Mary Ann, and Mrs. Howell called themselves after forming a go-go-booted girl group with honey-bee-striped sweaters on *Gilligan's Island*. Their song: "You Need Us."

HONEYCOMB CEREAL

"Honeycomb's big / Yeah, yeah, yeah! / It's not small / No, no, no! / Honeycomb's got a big, big taste! / Big, big taste for a big, big bite!" Hey, grab your Post Honeycomb cereal, and let's meet at the Honeycomb Hideout. Oh, and don't forget to bring all those great premiums found inside the cereal box, like the Honeycomb Kid Ring, the *Chitty Chitty Bang Bang* model car, and the Josie and the Pussycats pencil toppers! The "sweet crisp corn cereal" was introduced in 1966 and originally advertised by the Honeycomb Kid, a rope-twirling rodeo cowboy.

HONEYCOMB HIDEOUT

The clubhouse where all those cool kids hung out in the Honeycomb cereal TV commercials of the early

1970s. (If I remember correctly, I think it was some kind of tree house.)

HONEY HILL BUNCH

Gang of five-inch-tall rag dolls with vinyl heads and rooted hair and a wide range of childhood personality types. There was Batter, a redheaded tomboy; Darlin', a blonde beauty; I.Q., an Asian scholar; Solo, a dark-skinned musician; Spunky, a "tuff" lad; Sweetlee, a momma's helper; and Li'l Kid, the youngest, who follows the older children around. The Honey Hill Bunch rode around in a vehicle called the Rickety Rig and hung out at their "special place," the Honey Hill Bunch Clubhouse. Produced by Mattel Toys from 1976 to 1978.

HONEY, I SHRUNK THE KIDS

A 1989 Disney fantasy about a hapless suburban inventor, Wayne Szalinski (Rick Moranis), whose electromagnetic shrinking machine accidentally shrinks his and the neighbors' kids to the size of ants. When they are mistakenly tossed out with the garbage, the microscopic youths trek through a treacherous jungle that was once the backyard to get back home. Followed by a sequel, *Honey, I Blew Up the Kid*, in 1992.

HONEY WEST

TV series about an arousing female private eye, played by blonde, beauty-marked Anne Francis, who had a pet ocelot named Bruce and used a customized tube of lipstick that housed a radio transmitter. It aired on ABC-TV from 1965 to 1966.

HONG KONG PHOOEY

This Hanna-Barbera cartoon (airing from 1974 to 1981) featured a bumbling superpooch whose secret identity was that of Penrod "Penry" Pooch, a mild-mannered janitor employed at a police station. Penry worked alongside rigid boss Sergeant Flint and sweet telephone operator Rosemary. Whenever trouble menaced the city, Penry would leap into a file cabinet, clang a gong, and emerge as the kung-fu–fighting "Mutt of Steel" dressed in a karate robe and black mask. The hopelessly clumsy crime-fighter's chops and kicks were often ineffective, but with the help of a loyal feline assistant named Spot, along with the *Hong Kong Kung Fu Book of Tricks* and the occasionally unreliable Phooeymobile, evildoers didn't stand a chance. Veteran actor Scatman Crothers provided the voice of Hong Kong Phooey and sang the show's theme song, considered by many to be an all-time great of Saturday-morning TV.

HOOTENANNY

Popular on college campuses in the 1960s, an informal gathering of young people who got together to sing folk music, such as "Kumbaya," "He's Got the Whole World in His Hands," and other tunes made famous by beloved folk acts of the era, like The Kingston Trio, Joan Baez, Bob Dylan, the New Christy Minstrels, and Peter, Paul, and Mary.

HOOTERVILLE

Small farming community, somewhere in rural America, where the TV classics *Petticoat Junction* and *Green Acres* are set. Prominent citizens include Sam Drucker, the general store owner, and Kate Bradley, proprietor of the Shady Rest Hotel. It's unofficially the Rutabaga Capital of the World.

HOPPITY HOP

Jump on, kiddies, grab the handle, give a big leap, and hop and hop and hop to your heart's content! Introduced by the Sun Rubber Company in 1969, this was an eighteen-to-twenty-inch-diameter riding toy ("The ball with hops of fun") made of inflatable ultra-thick rubber with a ring handle molded into the top. It came in blue or red, and when it was fully inflated you could squat on it and travel all over the neighborhood with spastic jumps of joy. Other Hoppity toys included a western-style Hoppity Horse (which had a horse's head instead of a ring handle and came equipped with bridle, saddle, and fenders), a Hoppity Donald Duck, and a Hoppity Spider-Man.

HOPPY

A honking prehistoric kangaroo, known as a hopperoo, owned as a pet by Barney and Betty Rubble on *The Flintstones* cartoon show.

HORATIO J. HOO DOO

Villainous green-skinned magician who terrorized the happy Hat People of the land of Lidsville. Hoo Doo blasted bombs from his fingers and flew about in a top-hat hovercraft called the Hatamaran. He commanded a dumb-bunny sidekick (Raunchy Rabbit), four evil hats (executioner, gangster, pirate, and vampire), and a deck of oversized playing cards to do his dirty work. Played disturbingly over-the-top by comic actor Charles Nelson Reilly on the Saturday-morning series *Lidsville* (1971–73).

HORRIBLE HALL
Cobwebbed castle where the groovy, if not gruesome, Goolies, overseen by Count Dracula, reside on their Saturday-morning *Groovie Goolies* TV cartoon.

HORSE
This loyal white steed, dressed in a Canadian Mountie hat and suit, belonged to Dudley Do-Right on animator Jay Ward's *Dudley Do-Right Show*. On the cartoon program, Dudley's sweetheart, Nell Fenwick, was more in love with Horse than with Dudley.

HORTON HEARS A WHO!
"A person's a person, no matter how small!" This 1954 children's fable is notable for being the book that launched Dr. Seuss's legendary storytelling career. Written in whimsical rhyme, it's the tale of a gentle, good-hearted elephant named Horton who came to the rescue of Whoville, a microscopic community. Horton resided in the Jungle of Nool, when one day (the fifteenth of May) he heard the faint sound of a Who (Dr. Whoovy) coming from a speck of dust the size of a pin. Generous to all creatures great and small, Horton set out to protect his tiny new friends and to prove to the other jungle animals (who thought he was a fool) that other worlds actually existed. In 1970, the story was made into an animated TV special.

HOSS CARTWRIGHT
Real name: Eric. The middle son of Ben Cartwright on *Bonanza* was a gentle giant whose Swedish mother, Inga, was killed during an Indian attack. Hoss rode a horse called Chuck. Dan Blocker played Hoss from 1959 until his unexpected death just before beginning production on the TV western's thirteenth season. His demise contributed to an enormous drop in the ratings, leading to cancellation of the show in January 1973.

FYI: ▸ Hoss means "big, friendly man" in Swedish.

HOSTESS SNACK CAKES
"You get a big delight in every bite!" Since the 1930s, Hostess has delighted the taste buds of sugar-craving food junkies with an assortment of snack-cake confections. These treats have included the chocolaty goodness of Cup Cakes, Ding Dongs, Ho-Hos, Hostess O's, and Suzy Q's, as well as the sweet bliss of Big Wheels, Fruit Pies, Pudding Pies, Sno Balls, and Twinkies. The Continental Baking Company, which also produces the best-selling white bread, Wonder Bread, is the owner of the Hostess label. Competitors include Dolly Madison, Little Debbie, and Lance.

HOT COMB
The men's styling apparatus from the late-1970s disco era was an electrical hybrid of the blow dryer and comb. Its purpose: to give a man full feathered locks while drying his hair at the same time!

HOT DOG
The big and white shaggy sheepdog was the mascot for the singing Archies rock group of comic and cartoon fame. Hot Dog had an appetite just as ravenous as his two-legged master, Jughead Jones.

HOT PANTS
When The Royal Teens sang the provocative question "Who wears short shorts?" back in 1958, they probably had no idea that a decade later, during the winter of 1971, this trendy fashion would have almost every female claiming, "I do! I do!" Riding high alongside the miniskirt craze, hot pants were a shorter, tighter, and flashier version of the 1950s short shorts. Designed in every color and fabric combination imaginable (red satin, black leather, purple velvet, yellow suede, white silk, green broadcloth, brown wool, or blue denim), hot pants were so sizzling that clothing stores couldn't keep up with the demand (Alexander's in New York City sold 1,500 a week). And despite the cold temperatures outside, women everywhere were sporting skimpy hot pants, generally underneath a stylish overcoat or a thigh-high slit midiskirt, with knee-high boots. Hot pants were seen on jet-set celebs like Jackie O, Ursula Andress, Raquel Welch, Jane Fonda, Marlo Thomas, and Susan Dey. They became acceptable attire for just about all events, from afternoon shopping

expeditions to glitzy black-tie affairs to late nights at the discotheque. They even looked stunning in a sea-cruise disaster—check out Carol Lynley and Pamela Sue Martin in *The Poseidon Adventure* (1972) and you'll see hot pants at their fashionable best. (Pamela wore hers under a revealing thigh-high midi that was conveniently removed once the going got rough.) The popularity of hot pants faded sometime around the mid-1970s as more conservative mid-length skirts became the rage. By the end of the decade—with the exception of the Dallas Cowboys Cheerleaders—they were seen only on trampy rock-groupies and sleazy streetwalkers, who wore them with halter tops, fish-net stockings, and platform heels.

FYI: ▸ Hot pants were variously known as cool pants, happy legs, les shorts, shortcuts, and shortootsies.

HOT-ROLLER HAIR

Adored by preppy sorority girls and suburban Valley Girls during the 1980s, this style involved long hair that was often blow-dried upside down (for height at the roots) and then rolled with hot rollers (a.k.a. electrically heated curlers). After ten minutes or so, the rollers were removed and the hair would be styled big and fluffy, with the ends falling in a cascade of curls. If a girl had bangs, she would curl them with a curling iron into a puff shaped something like a cauliflower (bangs were often too short to wrap around a hot roller). Finally, the style was glued in place by heavy-duty hairsprays, such as Aqua Net, Final Net, or Rave. The downside to the look was that many girls were left with the ends of their hair split and frizzy from daily use of the hot appliance. Teen model Brooke Shields, teen actress Lisa Whelchel (*The Facts of Life*), and teen soap queen Genie Francis (*General Hospital*) hot-rolled their hair to the max!

HOT STUFF

"Blazing fun for everyone!" Like his contemporaries Casper, Wendy, and Spooky, the Little Devil was another *Harvey* comics character created in a supernatural manner. Hot-tempered and decidedly more devilish than the friendly Casper, the cute red fellow started his sizzling comic-book career in October 1957. Hot Stuff had stereotypical devil traits, such as horns, pointed ears, a tail, a pitchfork (which he used to give some pesky soul a poke in the hind quarters), but he wore a not-so-stereotypical white diaper. He lived in a cave in the Enchanted Forest with his doting Aunt Clinker and was charmed by a sweet fairy named Princess Charma.

HOT WHEELS

Introduced by Mattel Toys in 1968, these miniature (around three inches long) die-cast metal vehicles appeal to kids who are mesmerized by mag-wheeled, souped-up, colorful hot rods. The first generation of Hot Wheels were typically "California custom-styled" renditions of classic cars, generally sporty numbers like the Camaro, Charger, Corvette, Cougar, Mustang, T-Bird, or VW bug, colored in a "dazzling Spectraflame paint job" of magenta, aqua, orange, or olive. There were also many futuristic concept cars with such outtasight names as "Beatnik Bandit," "Deora," "King Kuda," "Mutt Mobile," "Red Baron," "Silhouette," "Splittin' Image," and "Turbofire." Gravity-powered and superfast, Hot Wheels raced on "miles" of bright-orange tracks that could be bent or looped at an incredible 360-degree angle, allowing the cars to travel straight, sideways, and upside-down and to jump ramps without falling off. There was even a Super Charger that made the already fast Hot Wheels go even faster. When the racing action ended, kids housed them in a wheel-shaped Super Rally case. Currently, the "fastest cars in the world" are treasured collectibles, as many men today grew up playing with them as boys. (The original sixteen custom classics presented the first year are especially coveted.)

FYI: ▸ Ouch! Some irate parents used the plastic Hot Wheels tracks as an alternative to a belt or stick when punishing bad kids.

HOUSEHOLD ITEMS

The year: 1977. The place: suburban America. The setting: an eight-room split-level house in a quiet cul-de-sac. The family: fortysomething parents, sixteen-year-old son, and ten-year-old daughter. The following is a room-by-room description of various household items found in the typical middle-class home.

- **Kitchen.** This hub of the household has wallpaper printed with mushrooms on it and a floor done in fake-brick linoleum. The appliances are avocado green, including the dishwasher and trash compactor (how modern!). On the kitchen counter you can find a Mr. Coffee, a coffee mug tree, an electric percolator wrapped snugly in a quilted cozie, a McCoy smiley-face cookie jar full of Oreo cookies, a toaster oven, and an Amana Radar Range microwave. Inside the Frigidaire—with the automatic icemaker—are leftover goodies, like last night's Hungarian goulash, stored in plastic Tupperware containers. Dad likes to cook and has a whopping fetish for gadgets, so hidden away in the lower kitchen cabinets are a Crock-Pot, an electric skillet, a Fry Baby, Ginsu knives, a hot-air popcorn popper, a La Machine food processor, Presto's Hotdiggity, Presto's Presto Burger, Ronco's Veg-O-Matic food slicer, the Salad Shooter, and a Seal-a-Meal. Above the kitchen sink window is a fern that hangs in a macramé plant-sling, while a Chia Pet and a glass containing an avocado seed sprouting a twig are happily sitting on the sill. Over in the corner, underneath a black Kit-Kat clock with swaying tail and moving eyes, sits a yellow Formica dinette set where the family eats breakfast off Franciscan Dinnerware—the kind with the nifty starburst pattern—each morning.

- **Dining Room.** The wallpaper is chocolate brown with royal-blue stripes, and a freshly raked, harvest-gold shag carpet speckled with orange and olive flecks covers the floor. A large Spanish-style oak table, accompanied by six red-velvet-cushioned chairs, dominates the center of the room. On the tabletop rests a wooden bowl full of real-looking plastic fruit. Lying on the matching oak hutch are decoupaged wine bottles (cleverly crafted by mom), a fondue set, a Lazy Susan serving dish, and a pair of rather large pepper mills. Hanging on the walls is a set of giant wooden fork and spoon plaques and a painting of a Spanish matador in action.
- **Living Room.** The walls are painted slate blue, and the harvest-gold shag with the orange and olive flecks, so prominent in the dining room, continues in this cozy room. Dad, king of this modern-day castle, enjoys reclining in his throne, a La-Z-Boy rocker with a magazine pouch attached to the side (the current issues of *TV Guide* and *Sports Illustrated* are housed there), while mom prefers to snuggle nearby on the poppy-red crushed-velvet love seat, partly covered with a crocheted wrap, for chilly nights. The focus of this large room is an Eames-style couch placed between two octagonal end tables garnished with matching lamps (the kind you magically switch on, off, and dim by lightly tapping the side of the lamp). On the boomerang-shaped coffee table in front of the couch roosts a big and gaudy ashtray made by mom in her ceramics class (that mom, she's a crafty gal). On top of the twenty-five-inch RCA console color TV set is a Sony Betamax VCR, a sign of things to come. A TV-tray set is not too far away, so the family can watch favorite prime-time shows—*All in the Family*, *Happy Days*, *Hawaii Five-O*, and *60 Minutes*—during supper. On the shelves lining the main wall, you can find framed school pictures of the children, candle art (which you don't dare light unless you want to face the wrath of your mother), some more decoupage, a few of mom's favorite knick-knacks, including Hummel figurines, and a complete set of *Funk and Wagnall's Encyclopedia*. A swingin' swag lamp hangs in the corner, and nearby on a wall is a dandy windjammer done in string art and a big macramé owl wall-hanging. Catnapping lazily in the bay window is Callie, the family's calico.
- **Parents' Bedroom.** The beige shag carpeting in this large bedroom offsets the olive-green walls. A queen-sized waterbed, with tiger-striped bed sheets and matching faux-fur comforter, dominates the room. On the nightstand next to the bed is a digital alarm clock (easier to tell time with during those groggy early mornings), and tucked not-so-secretly inside a drawer are racy issues of *Penthouse*, *Qui*, and *Viva*. Lying on mom's vanity is a lighted three-way mirror (for day, office, or evening lighting), a steam roller set, a Vidal Sassoon hot-styling comb, and a little statue of a wide-eyed, goofy guy with his arms spread out that reads "I Love You This Much," a romantic gift from dad on their last anniversary. Alongside the bedroom furniture are a wicker chair and sofa set and a pair of potted palm trees (artificial, for low maintenance). Brass butterfly plaques suspended on the wall appear to flutter about.

- **Daughter's Bedroom.** A very girly room with hot-pink walls and white shag carpeting. The ten-year-old shares her white-framed canopy bed with a menagerie of stuffed animals and dolls (Mrs. Beasley grins gleefully). On the walls are a series of Keane knock-off prints featuring those big-eyed waifs whose doleful stares follow you around the room, and a poster of a cat hanging from a branch with the slogan "Hang in there, baby!" Coexisting with the bedroom furniture are an inflatable chair and a child-sized desk, on which you'll find a plastic mushroom-shaped lamp, a pink Princess phone, a Miss America jewelry box with a tiny dancing ballerina inside, a stack of paperbacks recently ordered from Scholastic Book Services through the school, and Kenner's Close 'n' Play phonograph to listen to 45s of dreamy Shaun Cassidy. Overhead lingers a constantly turning and twirling butterfly mobile. Barbie's towering Townhouse, occupied by Malibu Barbie and gang, is proudly on display next to a toy chest full of juvenile treasures.
- **Son's Bedroom.** This sixteen-year-old's private domain is colored in robin's-egg blue (Sherwin-Williams on the walls) and brown (more of that popular shag carpeting). He still sleeps in his childhood bunk bed, but now the top bunk has become an excellent place to toss an assortment of discarded junk—dirty laundry, half-eaten sandwiches, sports equipment, comics, and unopened schoolbooks—and to conceal dad's missing copies of *Playboy*. A red-white-blue beanbag chair purchased the previous year's Bicentennial summer is plopped nearby. The walls are decorated with sports pennants (Redskins are number one), rock-star pinups (KISS is number one), and a Farrah Fawcett-Majors poster (Farrah's number one too). Perched on stackable yellow-plastic shelves are Little League and high school sports trophies, a Lava Lite with swirling electric blue lava, an eight-track tape player, and a portable twelve-inch TV, ideal for an exciting round of Atari's Pong. Love beads hanging in the window hide a budding marijuana plant (clueless mom thinks it's exotic flora).
- **Bathroom.** This is a happy room, thanks to the sunshine-yellow walls—where a school of ceramic fish and a fanciful ceramic mermaid swim about—and the purple shag rug. The top of the bathroom sink is home to a Dixie Cup dispenser, a Water Pik (helps Sis get food particles out of her braces), a Mr. Dentist automatic toothbrush, and dad's Schick Hot Lather dispenser. For comfort, there is a soft toilet seat. Earlier in the decade, mom got creative with the tile walls in the shower and stuck mod Rickie Tickie Stickie flower decals all over—which still remain today.
- **Rec Room** (short for recreation room, a.k.a. the family room or rumpus room). This huge room with faux-wood paneling and zebra-striped carpeting (nonshag) can be found in the lower half of the split-level. Placed in the room's center is a comfortable leopard-spotted conversation-pit sofa that dwarfs a nearby contemporary-looking cone fireplace. The brand-new console stereo is state-of-the-art with a variety of options, including an AM-FM radio, a turntable, an eight-track tape player, and a reel-to-reel player. A record cabinet holds mom and dad's favorite LPs: easy-listening jazz favorites such as Bobby Darin, Nancy Wilson, Stan Getz, Tom Jones, Sergio Mendes, and Dionne Warwick. Sitting on dad's wet bar—which he keeps fully stocked—is a mélange of wine and whiskey decanters, a cocktail shaker (dad's rule: "A swell martini is shaken, not stirred"), a groovy Go-Go Girl Drink Mixer, and a revolving multicolored fountain light. A futuristic-looking white pod-shaped chair with a built-in radio is nearby. The room's wall art includes a few paint-by-number items and a black-velvet portrait of Elvis (mom's favorite). For recreational fun, there is a Ping-Pong table and a game wall (shelves stocked with popular board games, including Monopoly, The Game of Life, Scrabble, Clue, Stratego, Twister, and Yahtzee). In a big storage closet near the Whirlpool washer and dryer is a home-movie projector, a slide projector, Panasonic's Toot-a-Loop transistor radio, Polaroid's Instamatic camera, the aluminum Christmas tree and its multicolored revolving light, a sunlamp for winter tanning, and an unused Popeil's Pocket Fisherman (given to dad one Father's Day). Outside the glass sliding doors near the backyard patio is the hot tub, strictly off limits to the kids and used only by the parents and their swinging adult friends.

HOUSTON, WHITNEY
Fashion model (appeared on the covers of *Seventeen* and *Glamour* in the early 1980s) turned rhythm-and-blues superstar whose glorious roaring voice, which effortlessly spans five octaves, led her to become one of the most successful female singers of all time. Born on August 9, 1963, in East Orange, New Jersey, the beautiful daughter of gospel star Cissy Houston and cousin of Dionne Warwick made an impressive recording debut when her first album, *Whitney Houston*, sold twelve million copies in 1985. Following her debut single, "You Give Good Love" (1985), she scored seven consecutive number-one songs on *Billboard* magazine's Top Forty: "Saving All My Love for You" (1985), "How Will I Know?" (1985), "The Greatest Love of All" (1986), "I Wanna Dance with Somebody (Who Loves Me)" (1987), "Didn't We Almost Have It All?" (1987), "So Emotional" (1987), and "Where Do Broken Hearts Go?" (1988). Houston also scored on the big screen, starring in *The Bodyguard* (1992), *Waiting to Exhale* (1995), and *The Preacher's Wife* (1996). Her smash version of Dolly Parton's melancholy ballad "I Will Always Love You," from *The Bodyguard* soundtrack, held the number-one spot for fourteen weeks and became the top-selling single of the year. Early in this twenty-first century, she endured intense media scrutiny for a turbulent marriage to bad-boy singer Bobby Brown, for her backstage diva tantrums, and for her emaciated, haggard appearance, which fueled persistent rumors of drug addiction (backed up by her two—at this writing—stints in rehab).

HOWARD, RON
Born March 1, 1954, in Oklahoma, a precocious, redheaded, freckle-faced child actor of TV who played Opie on *The Andy Griffith Show* (1960–68) and grew up to star as milk-fed teen Richie Cunningham on the long-running *Happy Days* during the 1970s. He matured into an acclaimed film director, considered one of the best in Hollywood, whose roster includes *Splash* (1984), *Cocoon* (1985), *Willow* (1988), *Parenthood* (1989), *Backdraft* (1991), *Far and Away* (1992), *Apollo 13* (1995), and *A Beautiful Mind* (2001). Older brother of Clint Howard, who appeared as Mark Wedloe on the prime-time series *Gentle Ben*.

HOWARD CUNNINGHAM
Richie and Joanie's gruff but caring father and Marion's devoted husband, who owned a hardware store in Milwaukee (Cunningham Hardware), was portrayed by character actor Tom Bosley on the nostalgic sitcom *Happy Days*.

HOWARD EVERETT
On prime time's *Nanny and the Professor*, Richard Long starred as the widower whose busy and often chaotic life as single dad to three young children—Hal, Butch, and Prudence—and mathematics professor at Clinton College in Los Angeles leads him to hire a magical nanny named Phoebe Figalilly.

HOWDY DOODY
"Say, kids, what time is it?" "It's How-w-w-w-dy Doody time!" The greatest icon of the Baby Boomer childhood during the 1950s was this freckle-faced, redheaded, plaid-shirted cowboy marionette—the star of TV's first and most popular kiddie show, broadcast from 1947 to 1960. Designed by former Disney animator Milt Neil, Howdy Doody resided in colorful Doodyville, a circus town populated by a daffy assortment of puppets and humans. His madcap Doodyville pals included buckskin-clad host Buffalo Bob Smith, horn-honking silent Clarabell the Clown, storekeeper Cornelius Cobb, Chef Pierre, Indian Chief Thunderthud ("Kowabunga!"), Indian Princess Summer-Fall-Winter-Spring, wrestler Ugly Sam, miserly Mayor Phineas T. Buster, lame-brained carpenter Dilly Dally, salty seaman Captain Scuttlebutt, private eye John J. Fadoozle, half-dog, half-duck Flubberdub, sister Heidi Doody, and Howdy's twin, Double Doody.

FYI: ▸ Howdy Doody's favorite word was—you guessed it—"Thingamajigs!"

HOW THE GRINCH STOLE CHRISTMAS
"Christmas Day is in our grasp, as long as we have hands to clasp!" Dr. Seuss's deliciously delightful Yuletide tale became popular first as a 1957 book and later as a 1966 animated TV special. Captivating generations of kids, it tells the story of the mean-spirited, Christmas-hating Grinch who has green skin and a heart "two sizes too small" and lives north of Whoville at the top of snowy Mount

Crumpit. The Grinch loathed the cheerful, tiny Whos who inhabited Whoville, and he despised their love of Christmas even more. One Christmas Eve, he disguised himself as Santa and, with reluctant dog Max dressed as a reindeer to pull his sleigh, set off to steal the holiday from the Whos. While the Whos were tucked snugly in their beds, the sinister Grinch crept into their homes and looted every bit of Yuletide joy—presents, stockings, decorations, Christmas trees, and even the "roast beast" for the holiday feast. Upon returning to Mount Crumpit with the stolen loot, his wicked satisfaction soon turned to confusion when he heard the heartwarming chorus of "Fah who for-aze! Dah who dor-aze!" rising from Whoville. Witnessing the giftless Whos rejoicing in the spirit of the season, the Grinch learned the true meaning of Christmas, and his heart grew three sizes larger.

Broadcast annually on TV since debuting, *How the Grinch Stole Christmas* is just about everyone's favorite Christmas special. It was narrated in tongue-twisting rhyme by inimitable horror actor Boris Karloff, and it features wonderful songs—"You're a Mean One, Mr. Grinch" and "Welcome Christmas"—performed by ultrabasso Thurl Ravenscoft. The grouchy Grinch later starred in two more specials, *Halloween Is Grinch Night* (1977) and *The Grinch Grinches the Cat in the Hat* (1982). The manic Jim Carrey played him in a live-action big-screen adaptation of the tale in 2000.

H. R. PUFNSTUF

"Once upon a summertime / Just a dream from yesterday / A boy and his magic golden flute / Heard a boat from off the bay. . . ." Who's your friend when things get rough? Why, it's H. R. Pufnstuf, the delightful denizen of our wonderfully whacked-out Saturday-morning memories. Airing from 1969 to 1971, this was the first of Sid and Marty Krofft's psychedelic fantasy TV shows, mixing live actors with life-sized puppets (others include *The Bugaloos*, *Lidsville*, and *Sigmund and the Sea Monsters*).

After setting sail one day, a boy named Jimmy (played by British teen heartthrob Jack Wild) and his talking flute, Freddy, find themselves shipwrecked on Living Island, an enchanted land populated with kooky characters. It seems Jimmy was lured to the isle by a spell cast by wicked Witchiepoo (character actress Billie Hayes), an ugly old witch obsessed with owning magical Freddy the Flute. To the rescue comes H. R. Pufnstuf ("Can't do a little, 'cuz he can't do enough"), a yellow dragon with a Texas drawl who wears go-go boots and serves as mayor of Living Island. When Witchiepoo, flying on her Vroom Broom, makes things rough for Jimmy, helpful Pufnstuf arrives in the nick of time to protect him from her sinister clutches.

Other Living Island inhabitants include twin midget cops Cling and Clang (driving the Rescue Racer vehicle), wise owl Dr. Blinky, con artist Ludicrous Lion, goofy vulture Orson, hapless spider Seymour, aptly named Stupid Bat, the Four Winds (East, West, North, and South), the fearsome looking Evil Trees, Judy the Frog (a Judy Garland soundalike), and Miss Shirley Pufnstuf, Puf's movie-star sister (a Shirley Temple look-alike). The Boyds, a bird rock band, sang the show's closing theme. Successful in the Saturday-morning ratings, the series spawned a 1970 feature film titled *Pufnstuf*, which had additional cast members: Martha Raye as Boss Witch, and Mama Cass Elliott as Witch Hazel.

FYI: ▸ Rumor has it that the trippy show's title *Pufnstuf* is slang for smoking marijuana and that the initials *H. R.* stand for "hand rolled." (Truth be told, they actually stood for "Royal Highness" turned around.)

HUARACHE SANDALS

Two-strap woven-leather sandals with wooden soles, popular in the 1970s, that made a squeaky noise when you walked.

HUCKLEBERRY HOUND

Introduced to older children of the Baby Boom in the self-titled cartoon show, the lovable blue dog is TV's first animated superstar. Huckleberry Hound speaks in a slow Southern drawl, sings an off-key rendition of the song "Clementine," and is too easygoing to be bothered by the comical mishaps that plague him. From 1958 to 1962, he headlined *The Huckleberry Hound Show,* Hanna-Barbera's first major TV hit and the first cartoon series to win an Emmy Award. It housed three other animated segments, "Pixie and Dixie," "Hokey Wolf," and "Yogi

Bear." (Debuting on the show, Yogi went on to star in his own top-rated series in 1961.)

FYI: ▸ The friendly canine was so adored that an island in the Antarctic was actually named Huckleberry Hound by the U.S. Coast Guard.

HUDSON BROTHERS

A mid-1970s musical-comedy act consisting of three zany yet charming brothers from Oregon: Bill, Mark, and Brett. The dark-haired, polyester-clad trio were notable for hosting a short-lived TV variety show during the summer of 1974, *The Hudson Brothers Show*, followed by a live Saturday-morning series, *The Hudson Brothers Razzle Dazzle Comedy Show* (1974–75), and a syndicated half-hour comedy program, *Bonkers* (1979). Hyped as a "cross between the Marx Brothers and The Beatles," the Hudsons didn't actually become household names, but they were popular enough among the under-twenty-one crowd to dominate their share of space in the pages of teen magazines (hunky Brett was the hands-down favorite). As musical artists, they almost had a Top Twenty hit with "So You Are a Star" (1974). From 1976 to 1979, eldest brother Bill was married to actress Goldie Hawn, with whom he sired two offspring, actors Kate Hudson and Oliver Hudson.

HUEY, DEWEY, AND LOUIE

These angelic-looking triplet ducklings with devilish demeanors have been wreaking havoc in the life of their uncle, cantankerous Donald Duck, since debuting in the appropriately titled cartoon short "Donald's Nephews" in 1937 (they were the sons of Donald's sister, Dumbella). Fifty years later, the impish threesome starred with great-uncle Scrooge McDuck, a miserly millionaire, on the Disney Channel cartoon series *DuckTales* (1987). Huey, Dewey, and Louie were members of a scouting organization called Junior Woodchucks.

HUGGY BEAR

Starsky and Hutch's pimp-daddy informant, who dressed in the traditional pimp regalia: flashy polyester suits, fedoras, gold jewelry, and platform shoes. Huggy owned The Pits, a Los Angeles bar whose patrons were hookers and hustlers. Played by black actor Antonio Fargas on ABC-TV's *Starsky and Hutch*.

HUGHES, JOHN

Born February 18, 1950, in Chicago, this filmmaker had his finger on the pulse of what a 1980s generation of suburban teenagers were actually thinking and feeling with his flicks *Sixteen Candles* (1984), *The Breakfast Club* (1985), *Weird Science* (1985), *Ferris Bueller's Day Off* (1986), *Pretty in Pink* (1986), and *Some Kind of Wonderful* (1987). Lost his touch when he started making tot-oriented movies, beginning with the commercially successful *Home Alone* (1990), starring Macaulay Culkin, followed by sequel *Home Alone 2: Lost in New York* (1992), *Curly Sue* (1991), *Dennis the Menace* (1993), and *Baby's Day Out* (1994).

HULA-HOOPS

One of the biggest fads in toy history was the Hula-Hoop, an oversized plastic hoop named after the Hawaiian hula hip gyrations needed to keep it spinning. Introduced by Wham-O in 1958, more than twenty-five million were sold within four months of its debut. Skilled Hula-Hoopers can spin the rings not only around the waist but also on legs and feet, arms and wrists, and even the neck and head. In the late 1960s, they came loaded with metal beads inside that made a peculiar whirring sound. In 1987, Roxanne Rose at Washington State University spun a Hula-Hoop for ninety hours, and in 1990, some 2,000 people in New Brunswick, Canada, set the world record for the most people simultaneously Hula-Hooping.

FYI: ▸ Believing it to be an example of the "emptiness of American culture," Russian Communist leaders didn't think the Hula-Hoop was such a great idea.

HUMAN LEAGUE

Distinguished by a synthesized postmodern pop sound, this music act was one of the first British New Wave groups to be played on American Top Forty radio stations. The group—lead singer Philip Oakey, Joanne Catherall, and Susanne Sulley—struck gold in 1982 with the catchy "Don't You Want Me." Other hits included "(Keep Feeling) Fascination" (1983), "The Lebanon" (1984), and "Human" (1986). Oakey's androgynous appearance and asymmetrical hairdo (short on one side, long on the other) inspired men in other New Wave bands (Culture Club and Duran Duran, for example) to follow suit, sporting full-face makeup (including tweezed eyebrows) and unisex haircuts.

HUMANOIDS FROM THE DEEP
Mutated half-salmon, half-human scaly monsters that attacked Pacific Northwest fishing villages to mate with big-breasted women. Featured in the 1980 low-budget horror movie of the same name.

HUMAN TORCH
"Flame on!" The superhero identity of young scientist Johnny Storm, who could burst into a streak of flame at will. When not headlining his comic book, this hot number (he's a blond cutie) joined sister Susan, a.k.a. The Invisible Girl, as a member of *Marvel*'s crime-fighting Fantastic Four.

HUNDRED ACRE WOODS
Enchanting woodland, based on England's Ashdown Forest, where you will find the homes of A. A. Milne's Winnie the Pooh and storybook friends, such as Pooh Corner, Eeyore's Gloomy Place, and Tigger's Bouncing Place.

HUNGRY HUNGRY HIPPOS
"The Frantic Marble Munching Game!" Introduced in 1978 by Milton Bradley, an insane action game in which four participants each control a pastel-colored hippopotamus by a lever and greedily gobble up marbles with its mouth. Once all the marbles are gulped down, the hungry, hungry hippo that eats the most wins!

HUSH PUPPIES
Since 1958, a cute, mopey-looking basset hound has advertised this classic, casual soft-suede footwear touted as "The World's Best-Loved Shoes!"

HUSTLE
"Do the Hustle!" The original Hustle (a.k.a. the New York Hustle), done most commonly with Van McCoy's 1975 hit single "The Hustle," was a couples dance with hands connected at the waist. The feet movement consisted of sideways toe point on each side for the first two beats, and then three short steps, alternating forward and back taking up counts three and four. Many stunts took place amid these simple steps, such as turns, multiple eight-count turns, and even a pretzel or two. The next Hustle to make the disco scene was the West Coast Hustle, whose steps were similar to New York Hustle steps, except hands were not joined. The late-1970s line dances were all variations of the Hustle, including the L.A. Hustle, the Bus Stop, and the mega-popular Saturday Night Fever Hustle (for example, the Bee Gees' "Night Fever," an underlit and blinking dance floor with spinning disco ball, twenty or so dancers, and John Travolta doing right-handed pointing to the sky in fours, and other disco moves simultaneously, at a Brooklyn discotheque). Many instructional "how to" record albums and eight-track tapes were available so that novice dancers could learn to Hustle in the privacy of home before boogying at the disco.

HYPERCOLOR SHIRTS
Faddish tops, popular around 1991, that changed color as the wearer's body-temperature changed, creating amazing tie-dye patterns.

efghij

"I AM WOMAN"
She was woman, hear her roar! A 1973 song by Australian singer Helen Reddy, later adopted as an anthem for the feminist movement ("I am strong. I am invincible"). After she won the Best Female Pop Vocalist award for the recording, Reddy's acceptance speech at the 1973 Grammy Awards, in which she thanked God "because she makes everything possible," caused controversy. It was the first time someone had publicly acknowledged the possibility that God could be of the "weaker" sex.

ICE CASTLES
Three-Kleenex weeper about a pretty farm girl from Iowa named Alexis Winston (Lynn-Holly Johnson), a figure skater on the way to the top who becomes blinded in a freak accident (first Kleenex—Boo-hoooo!). Encouraged by love and support from her hockey-player boyfriend, Nick Peterson (Robby Benson), and widowed father, Marcus Winston (Tom Skerritt), Lexie beats the odds and skates again (second Kleenex—Boo-hoooo!). Directed by Donald Wrye, the 1979 movie is most remembered for Melissa Manchester's emotional love song, "Through the Eyes of Love" (third Kleenex—Boo-hoooo!).

ICEE
"Icee . . . Cool, delicious, and full of fun!" Slushy beverage competitor of 7-Eleven's Slurpee, advertised by a fanciful polar bear wearing a red turtleneck sweater. Found at a variety of convenience stores—except for 7-Eleven, of course.

IDEAL TOYS
One of the more prominent toy manufacturers of the twentieth century—founded by Morris and Rose Michtom in 1903 in Brooklyn, New York. The company's Baby Boomer favorites included action toys, dolls, and games like Captain Action, Evel Knievel, Mr. Machine, King Zor, Battling Tops, Hands Down, Kaboom, KerPlunk, Mouse Trap, Rebound, Tip-It, Toss Across, Tammy, Crissy, Flatsy, Kissy, Lazy Dazy, Betsy Wetsy, Thumbelina, Tiffany Taylor, and the Shaker Maker.

"I'D LIKE TO TEACH THE WORLD TO SING"
Of all the Coca-Cola TV advertisements, the most memorable has to be the early-1970s spot featuring an international group of young people on a hilltop in Italy singing "I'd like to buy the world a Coke, in perfect harmony. . . ." In 1971, the Hillside Singers adapted the jingle into a pop-music recording that became one of the year's hottest singles.

IDOL, BILLY

The sneering rock rebel, distinguished by bleached-blond spikes and black rubber threads, was born Willem Broad on November 30, 1955, in London. From 1977 to 1981, the newly christened Billy Idol fronted Generation X, a punk band notable for the album *Valley of the Dolls* and the masturbation-theme song "Dancing with Myself." He went solo in the mid-1980s, and his hits included both the rousing "Hot in the City" (1982) and "White Wedding" (1983), the melodic "Eyes Without a Face" (1984), and a revival of Tommy James and The Shondells' "Mony Mony" (1987). Throughout the 1990s, music's bad boy faced his share of infamy: A 1990 motorcycle accident severely injured his right leg (he ran a stop sign and smashed into a car); assault and battery charges in 1991 after punching a female companion in the face outside a West Hollywood restaurant; and two apparent drug overdoses in 1994.

I DREAM OF JEANNIE

Fondly remembered 1960s prime-time sitcom starring handsome Larry Hagman as Major Tony Nelson, a NASA astronaut whose space capsule crash-lands on a deserted island in the Pacific, where he discovers an elaborately jeweled bottle that has washed ashore. After he uncorks the bottle, out pops beautiful blonde Barbara Eden—amid a spray of pink smoke—as a harem-outfitted genie named Jeannie who promptly accepts Major Nelson as her one and only master ("Thou may ask anything of thy slave, Master!"). Tony, a confirmed bachelor, reluctantly transports Jeannie, hidden inside the bottle, to his home in Cocoa Beach, Florida, where she causes all sorts of magical mischief. Adding to the humor, Tony's friends and co-workers at NASA do not believe Jeannie exists, because she refuses to appear for anyone but her master (they think he's a little nutty from too much space travel). At first, Tony and Jeannie officially had a master-slave relationship, but the oft-jealous genie was very much in love with her astronaut and, after three years on TV succeeded in convincing him that he loved her enough to marry her.

Airing on NBC from 1965 to 1970, *I Dream of Jeannie* co-starred Bill Daily as Tony's best pal, Major Roger Healey, the only other person who knew about genie Jeannie; Hayden Rorke as Dr. Alfred Bellows, a NASA psychiatrist who questioned Tony's sanity; and Emmaline Henry as Amanda Bellows, Alfred's busybody wife. A highlight of the show is the groovy animated opening title credits with a bouncy Hugo Montenegro musical theme ("Duuuh-dah! Dah, dah, dah-dah, dah!"). From 1973 to 1975, a cartoon adaptation of this series, *Jeannie*, aired on Saturday mornings.

FYI: ▸ Along with dreamy Jeannie, other genies of recent pop culture include Shazzan! Weenie the Geenie, Sheldon the Sea Genie, Pee-Wee's Jambi, and the blue genie from Disney's *Aladdin.*

IF I WERE A CARPENTER

The Carpenters' tribute album, released in 1994, featured their pop songs covered by ultrahip alternative rock acts, such as "Top of the World" by Shonen Knife, "Superstar" by Sonic Youth, "Close to You" by Cranberries, "It's Going to Take Some Time" by Dishwalla, "Solitaire" by Sheryl Crow, "Let Me Be the One" by Matthew Sweet, and "Bless the Beasts and Children" by 4 Non Blondes. The album's cover had an illustration of the superstar duo done in the Big Eyes style of Margaret and Walter Keane.

"I GOT YOU, BABE"

The pounding love song by Sonny and Cher had the real-life husband and wife pop duo vowing mutual devotion, in spite of people saying that Sonny's hair was too long and they didn't have the money to pay the rent. A smash hit in 1965, it topped the charts for three weeks, selling more than three million copies and making pint-sized, nasal-voiced Sonny Bono and slinky, husky-voiced Cher overnight stars.

I KNOW WHAT YOU DID LAST SUMMER

Screenwriter Kevin Williamson, the man who made *Scream* (and made you scream), followed his 1996 horror smash with this slasher yarn starring four of the hottest teen actors of the day: Jennifer Love Hewitt, Sarah Michelle Gellar, Ryan Phillippe, and Freddie Prinze Jr. After celebrating graduation in Southport (North Carolina), high school friends—brainy heroine Julie James (Love Hewitt), beauty queen Helen Shivers (Gellar), football jock Barry Cox (Phillippe), and regular guy Ray Bronson

(Prinze)—accidentally hit a fisherman while driving on an oceanside roadway. Panicked that the accident will destroy their future, the foursome swear secrecy and dumps the body into the sea. A year later, they receive strange messages from an unknown source stating, "I know what you did last summer." Soon each is viciously stalked by a vengeful maniac whose costume is a fisherman's slicker and a fatal ice hook. Based on Lois Duncan's novel and directed by Jim Gillespie, the 1997 movie was followed by a sequel, *I Still Know What You Did Last Summer*.

IMGWEE GWEE VALLEY

Isolated African locale where you would find the native village of Umbwebwe, as well as the tree home of ape-man George, on the cartoon series *George of the Jungle*.

IMPERIAL BUTTER

Those who taste this butter would instantly feel like a king and even have a crown magically appear on top of their head—at least according to the TV commercials.

IMPOSSIBLES

The Impossibles, the "World's Greatest Fighters for Justice," were a trio of government agents disguised as a Beatles-type rock group. When Chief Big D summoned them on a teeny television stashed on the flip-side of a guitar, they would shout "Tally-Ho!" and transform into marvelous superheroes. There's Coil Man, who becomes a human spring; Multi Man, who becomes multiple bodies of himself; and Fluid Man, who converts into liquid. The Impossibles traveled in the stupendous Impossicar on crime-fighting assignments, leaving battled villains everywhere protesting, "Those Impossibles are impossible!" Premiering alongside *Frankenstein Jr.* on CBS-TV in 1966, the Hanna-Barbera cartoon series ended abruptly two years later after parents protested the violence in this and other cartoons.

"I'M TOO SEXY"

Right Said Fred's "I'm Too Sexy" novelty song about models on the catwalk who are too sexy for love, for their shirt, their hat, their car, Milan, New York, Japan, your party, and a pussy cat. The tongue-in-cheek dance ditty by the British Baldies was an American number-one for a trio of weeks in early 1992.

INCHWORM

Introduced by Romper Room Toys in the early 1970s, the juvenile riding toy, shaped like a bright-green smiley-face worm on two wheels at either end, inched forward when you bounced up and down on the saddle in the middle.

INCREDIBLE EDIBLES

"Cook up some fun! Frightfully delicious! Sugarless!" Introduced in 1966, these wiggly worms and other critters were featured as a digestible version of Mattel's enormously popular and successful Creepy Crawlers. Incredible Edibles allowed kids to gross out unsuspecting grown-ups (and one another) by swallowing a worm (ugh!), munching on a frog (yuck!), or gobbling down a caterpillar (eeek!). The Incredible Edibles toy sets came with an electric oven in the shape of a head with a goofy face called a Sooper Gooper. Kids poured different flavors of a sugarless goo—Gobbledegook—into aluminum baking molds containing a wild variety of scary shapes. Inserting the molds into the Sooper Gooper, they could whip up a batch of butterscotch turtles or cinnamon lizards, cherry spiders or a root-beer octopus, licorice crabs or mint beetles. For those who were faint of heart, there were molds featuring not-so-scary shapes, like butterflies, flowers, leaves, berries, stars, and gingerbread men.

INCREDIBLE HULK

One of *Marvel* comics' best-known characters, the "half-man, half-monster" superhero created by cartoonist Stan Lee in 1962. While researching the effects of stress on physical strength, mild-mannered scientist Dr. David Bruce Banner was accidentally exposed to a massive dose of radiation. Then Banner found that when he became enraged he transformed into a green-complexioned beast with savage outbursts and tremendous strength. These transformations took a toll not only on his wardrobe but on his social life as well, so the scientist took off around the country searching for a cure. A prime-time adaptation aired on CBS from 1978 to 1982, starring Bill Bixby as Dr. Banner and champion bodybuilder Lou Ferrigno as The Incredible Hulk. In 2003, the *Hulk* came to the big screen, with Eric Bana as Dr. Banner and a CGI (computer-generated imagery) Hulk.

INCREDIBLE JOURNEY

In this 1963 live-action Disney adventure, a trio of household pets—elderly bull terrier Badger, simple-minded Labrador retriever Luath, and wise Siamese cat Tao—mistake their owners' intentions when they leave for a summer vacation. Believing that their masters will never return, the animals set out on a 250-mile "incredible journey" through rugged Canadian terrain to find them. Along the way, they find themselves up against fast-flowing rivers, porcupines, a mountain lion, and a grizzly bear. Directed by Fletcher Markle, the movie—taken from Sheila Burnford's well-loved 1960 book—is noted for beautiful scenery and amazing animal stunts. Disney remade it in 1993 as *Homeward Bound: The Incredible Journey*.

INCREDIBLE TWO-HEADED TRANSPLANT

The head of an insane murderer and the head of a mental retard share the same body—if you don't believe me, check out the campy 1971 movie of the same title to see for yourself.

INDIANA JONES

University professor Dr. Henry Jones Jr., or just plain Indy, was a globe-trotting archaeologist, adventurer, and daredevil (except when it came to snakes), around the 1930s. Played by Harrison Ford in director Steven Spielberg's blockbusters *Raiders of the Lost Ark* (1981), *Indiana Jones and the Temple of Doom* (1984), and *Indiana Jones and the Last Crusade* (1989).

FYI: ▸ Henry Jones got the nickname "Indiana" from his boyhood pet dog of the same name.

INDIAN EARTH

This powder blush by Revlon, housed in a small terra-cotta jar with a cork lid, gave women who brushed it heavily over the cheeks, shoulders, and upper chest a shadowy yet glisteny appearance—perfect for nights at the disco during the early 1980s.

INITIATION OF SARAH

Cheesy but fun 1978 TV movie with a *Revenge of the Nerds* meets *Carrie* plot line. A mousy, withdrawn college freshman gifted with strange telekinetic powers, Sarah Goodwin (Kay Lenz) joins a sorority of nerdy misfits whose housemother is the batty Mrs. Erica Hunter (Shelley Winters). Meanwhile, Sarah's black-haired, blue-eyed beautiful and ingenuous sister, Patty Goodwin (Morgan Brittany), joins a popular sorority overseen by snobbish blonde Jennifer Lawrence (Morgan Fairchild). Queen Jennifer and her Barbie doll horde viciously torment Sarah's lowly sorority and eventually force Patty to cast her sister away. Encouraged by Mrs. Hunter during a histrionic sorority ritual with demonic overtones, Sarah uses her psychic powers to exact revenge on the bitches.

INSPECTOR GADGET

"Go, Gadget, go!" On the long-running cartoon series (1983–92), Don Adams (*Get Smart*) voiced the bumbling detective employed by Interpol who was endowed with an arsenal of gadgets affixed to his body for nabbing crooks. Part-human/part-bionic, the trenchcoated crime-buster had the ability to fly (because of a propeller attached to the top of his hat), bounce (because of springs at the bottom of his feet), and stretch his arms to great lengths (because of extendable limbs). Young niece Penny and trusty dog Brain aided him. In 1999, Matthew Broderick starred as Inspector Gadget in a live-action film for the Disney studio.

INSPECTOR JACQUES CLOUSEAU

Bungling, mustachioed Parisian police officer played by British comic actor Peter Sellers in *The Pink Panther* film series: *The Pink Panther* (1963), *The Return of the Pink Panther* (1975), *The Pink Panther Strikes Again* (1976), and *Revenge of the Pink Panther* (1978).

IN THE NEWS

In 1970, CBS-TV created a series of minute-long informational featurettes, geared for children ages six to twelve, that appeared on the Saturday-morning lineup between cartoons. Originally, they were called *In the Know* and featured different CBS cartoon characters—Sabrina the Teenage Witch, The Groovie Goolies, and Josie and the

Pussycats—introducing facts and trivia about the world (the Pussycats sang the theme song). A year later, these vignettes were revamped with a new title: *In the News*. They now featured various guest celebrities speaking on current topics, and the show ran this way until CBS discontinued the programming in 1992. Unique to *In the News* was its swirling globe logo and weird Moog-like background music.

"INTO THE GROOVE"

Believe it or not, pop goddess Madonna's sizzling dance hit from the summer of 1985 never charted on *Billboard*'s Hot 100 because it appeared only on the B-side of the twelve-inch "Angel." It was featured in the big-screen comedy *Desperately Seeking Susan* (1985), starring Rosanna Arquette, Aidan Quinn, and Madonna.

INVISIBLE GIRL

Pretty, blonde Susan Richards, a scientist, was endowed with the power to vanish after being exposed to cosmic rays while traveling through outer space. Joined by husband Reed Richards (Mr. Fantastic), brother Johnny Storm (Human Torch), and family friend Ben Grimm (The Thing) as a member of a superhero crime-fighting team, The Fantastic Four, for *Marvel* comics.

INVISIBLE MAN

Now you see him, now you don't. He's the inspiration of many a kid's make-believe fantasy! Just imagine having the ability to be invisible—you could create all sorts of mischief on unsuspecting people, like these ten possibilities:

- Play "ghost" tricks on your bratty sister at home, like floating an object across the room to spook her
- Sneak into your best friend's house at night, to see if the rumor that he sleeps in footed bunny pajamas is true
- Trip the class bully in the hallway at school
- Look in your teacher's desk drawer for the answers to tomorrow's quiz
- Sneak a peek at the half-dressed pom-pom squad in the girl's locker room
- Eat "free" candy right there in the aisle at the store
- Place unwanted items in carts of shoppers (they will be perplexed about how they got there), such as feminine hygiene products in a bachelor's basket, or a box of condoms in an uppity society matron's cart
- Walk right past the cinema's ticket booth to see an R-rated movie that's usually off-limits
- Stand directly behind someone, say their name, lightly tap them, and try not to giggle when they turn around in fright
- When you think someone is catching on to your invisibility—be still, they can't see you, so they'll never be able to find you!

IRISH SPRING SOAP

Manly, yes, but women like it too! According to the TV commercials, this deodorant soap made both men and women feel "fresh as an Irish spring morning."

IRON MAN

The "invincible" alter ego of billionaire industrialist Tony Stark was a red-and-gold armor-suited superhero once wounded in Vietnam who often battles a longtime foe, the Mandarin, and teams with other mighty heroes as a crime-fighting Avenger. Created by Stan Lee for *Marvel* comics in 1963.

ISAAC WASHINGTON

Your bartender on *The Love Boat* was a compassionate, ear-lending, African-American hipster played by actor Ted Lange on the long-running TV program (1977–86).

ISIS

"O zephyr winds that blow on high, lift me now so I can fly!" Created in 1975 for Saturday-morning TV, this live-action children's series starred brunette beauty JoAnna Cameron as Andrea Thomas, a complacent science teacher who could metamorphose into mighty Isis, an Egyptian superheroine endowed with the powers of nature. Andrea's amazing might came from a mystical amulet she discovered while on an archaeological dig in Egypt. The possessor of the golden amulet could run with the speed of gazelles, soar as high as a falcon, and command the elements of earth, sky, and water. Andrea's secret identity was unknown to everyone—from close friends to the students and fellow teachers at Larkspur, the high school where she taught. When confronted with wrongdoers, Andrea would clutch the amulet worn around her neck, recite a magic incantation ("O mighty Isis!"), and—in a flash of lightning—change into the ancient Egyptian goddess wearing a short-skirted white tunic, an ornate necklace, and a gold headband and grasping a cobra-headed staff. Isis employed rhyming couplets (for example, "I came from afar, to freeze this car" or "Electric forces spinning round, return safely to the ground") in her crime-fighting efforts. Magical Tut was her devoted pet crow.

The program was half *The Shazam!/Isis Hour*, and following cancellation of *Shazam!* in 1977 it stayed on the air for another year as *The Secrets of Isis*. Noted for being a TV product of the women's lib movement, the success of the show prompted the *Isis* comic-book series.

ISLAND OF MISFIT TOYS

Seen on the classic Christmas special *Rudolph the Red-Nosed Reindeer*, an Arctic isle inhabited by outcast toys that are unwanted by children because of imperfections. On the Island of Misfit Toys, you'll find a choo-choo with square wheels, a water pistol that shoots jelly, a spotted elephant, a swimming bird, an ostrich-riding cowboy, a sinking boat, an unloved doll, and a Charlie-in-the-Box (!). They are ruled over by King Moonraiser, a flying lion who searches the entire the world for misfit toys to bring back to the island.

I SPY

Airing on prime time from 1965 to 1968, this NBC-TV show took a lighthearted approach to the then-popular espionage theme. It starred Bill Cosby as Alexander Scott and Robert Culp as Kelly Robinson—a team of scholarly secret agents who used the disguise of a professional tennis player (Kelly) and his trainer (Alexander) on globe-trotting assignments. Most significant is its distinction of being the first drama series to feature an African-American (Cosby) in a regular lead role.

"I THINK I LOVE YOU"

"I'm afraid that I'm not sure of, a love there is no cure for. . . ." TV's popular singing clan The Partridge Family scored their first and only number-one hit with this dynamic and innovative tune (in a bubblegum sorta way) in the fall of 1970. Written by Tony Romeo, the song—featuring groovy vocals by David Cassidy and Shirley Jones, and a fab harpsichord interlude—crested at the top of the charts for three weeks, sold more than five million copies, and became the group's most familiar anthem. In 1996, Levi Strauss played on our nostalgia by using "I Think I Love You" in a smart TV ad showing two 501-wearing strangers on an elevator who eye each other, then simultaneously have the same daydream of love, marriage, and children (gasp!); after the ride ends, they falter, then go their own way.

FYI: ▸ On their TV series, The Partridge Family performed "I Think I Love You" on episode 8, "But the Memory Lingers On." It was the episode in which a skunk invades the family's bus and Mr. Kincaid makes everyone bathe in tomato juice to get rid of the stinky smell.

IT'S ABOUT TIME

Silly, short-lived TV sitcom (1966–67), often overlooked today, about a pair of astronauts, Mac and Hector (Frank Aletter and Jack Mullaney), who accidentally zoom through a time barrier and crash-land in earth's Stone Age. There they are befriended by a prehistoric cave family: a cordial couple, Shadd and Gronk (Imogene Coca and Joe E. Ross), and their two children, Breer and Mlor (Pat Cardi and Mary Grace). During the show's mid-season, the astronauts repair their damaged space capsule and return to modern-day Los Angeles with the Stone Agers in tow. Many laughs unfold as the cave clan adjusts to life in the twentieth century.

IT'S ALIVE!

"There's something wrong with the Davis baby!" And there's something wrong with this dreadful 1977 horror flick about killer mutant babies and the many sequels it inspired.

IT'S A SMALL WORLD

"Join the happiest cruise that ever sailed 'round the world!" Walt Disney's salute to the children of the world first appeared at the 1964–65 New York World's Fair, before moving to Disneyland in 1966 (opening on May 28). The Fantasyland theme-park attraction, lined by a topiary garden of animal shapes, features a unique pastel-colored structure with playful spires and finials, representing various world landmarks, including France's Eiffel Tower, Italy's Leaning Tower of Pisa, and India's Taj Mahal. Designed by artist Mary Blair, this beautiful structure's centerpiece is a huge ticking clock that features a parade of dolls marching around every fifteen minutes. As guests voyage aboard boats through the Tower of the Four Winds entry, they are greeted inside by the most amazing sight: hundreds of doll-like Audio-Animatronic characters (297 children and 256 toys set in 100 different regions of the world) dressed in native costumes and gleefully singing and dancing to the simple tune of "It's a Small World," written by Richard and Robert Sherman. The cuteness of the ride and its repetitive song, played in various languages, can be a pleasure for some but torture for others.

FYI: ▸ During the Christmas season, the attraction is transformed into the spectacular "It's a Small World" Holiday. The outside is all lit up and glowing from Christmas lights, and on the inside the holiday traditions of numerous nations are displayed with the theme song interwoven with "Jingle Bells."

IT'S THE GREAT PUMPKIN, CHARLIE BROWN

"That stupid blockhead brother of mine
is out in the pumpkin patch
making his yearly fool of himself!"
—LUCY VAN PELT

This was the Peanuts gang's third animated outing and one of the first TV specials to honor Halloween. Premiering in 1966, it centered around security-blanking-clutching Linus Van Pelt's anticipation of the Great Pumpkin, the Halloween equivalent of Santa Claus, and Charlie Brown's delight at being invited to his first trick-or-treat party. According to Linus, on every Halloween night the Great Pumpkin rises from the pumpkin patch to reward good children with gifts. Nobody supports his faith in this spooky entity except for trusting Sally Brown, who has a crush on Linus. Sally waits with him in the local pumpkin patch but later becomes furious after forfeiting a night of candy-grabbing for a Jack-o'-Lantern that never came. Meanwhile, an elated Charlie Brown, dressed as a ghost in a multiholed white sheet, joins Lucy Van Pelt and the rest of the gang for a night of trick-or-treating. His elation turns to disappointment after he always receives rocks in his bag, instead of candy. The special is notable for introducing viewers to Snoopy's fantasy sequence: Flying the Sopwith Camel (his doghouse), the brave beagle engages German rival the Red Baron in bloodthirsty aerobatics battles.

ITTY BITTY TITTY COMMITTEE

This was an unofficial club for females cursed or blessed (depending on how you see it) with a flat chest.

IZOD SHIRTS

"Save an alligator, kill a preppy." These short-sleeved tennis/polo shirts that came in a variety of pastel hues and are marked by the little green alligator symbol on the chest were the epitome of preppydom. Prepsters thought they were extra-cool when worn with the collars turned up. Tennis pro René Lacoste was the founder of the Izod label. Main rival during the early-1980s preppy craze was the more expensive Ralph Lauren polo (with the polo player symbol), while its poorer imitations included Le Tigre (leaping tiger symbol), Hunter's Run (horse symbol), and J. C. Penney's (fox symbol).

fghij

JABBA THE HUTT
This 600-year-old, grotesquely obese, sluglike creature was the Galaxy's top criminal underlord. He resided in a palace on the planet Tatooine, where he once kept lovely Princess Leia captive as a harem girl. First seen in director George Lucas's *Return of the Jedi* (1983).

JABBERJAW
"I don't get no respect!" *Jabberjaw*, the "latest, greatest shark you ever saw," was created by Hanna-Barbera for a Saturday-morning cartoon show that aired from 1976 to 1978. Lovable but goofy (and sounding a lot like Curly Howard from the Three Stooges), the great white shark resided in Aquahama City, a domed oceanic metropolis in the year 2076, where he played drums in a teenage rock band called The Neptunes. His fellow musicians (and friends) consisted of gallant lead singer Biff, ditzy keyboardist Bubbles, prima-donna tambourine player Shelly, and excitable bassist Clamhead, Jabberjaw's best buddy. Touring in the Aquacar on their underwater gigs, the group encountered a collection of villains—Sourpuss Octopuss, Phantom Kelp, El Eeel, and the Piranha—who predictably involved them in a slapstick chase while a Neptune bubblegum tune played in the background. The cartoon was loosely inspired by the shark craze of the mid-1970s, fueled by Steven Spielberg's phenomenal motion picture *Jaws* (1975).

JACK AND JILL
Magazine for youngsters ages seven to ten, loaded with short stories, biographies, fun facts, comics, puzzles, activities, crafts, and poetry.

JACKIE JOKERS
Young, dark-haired comedian, called the "Clown Prince of Show Biz," whose popularity as a supporting character in the *Richie Rich* comics during the mid-1970s led to his own spin-off comic book.

JACK IN THE BOX
Founded in San Diego by Robert O. Peterson in 1951, a fast-food hamburger joint associated with a creepy-looking Jack in the Box clown mechanism, whose head you spoke into when ordering at the drive-thru. In 1980, the company literally dynamited their icon (officially known as Jack the Clown) on network TV, signaling a move away from a focus on kids and toward more adult-oriented tastes. Jack

was reintroduced in 1995. Signature burger: The Jumbo Jack.

FYI: ▸ Jack in the Box was the first restaurant to have a drive-thru, plus the first to introduce a breakfast sandwich and a prepackaged portable salad.

JACK-IN-THE-BOXES

The tin lithographed musical boxes produced by Mattel during the 1960s featured Bugs Bunny, Casper, The Cat in the Hat, Dr. Dolittle, Flipper, Mother Goose, Snoopy, and a slew of other kid-friendly characters who abruptly popped out from under the lid after the hand crank was turned.

JACK SKELLINGTON

In Tim Burton's *Nightmare Before Christmas* movie, spindly limbed Jack Skellington, the pumpkin king, gets tired of doing the same old Halloween every year. By accident, he discovers a fascinating universe called Christmastown. Jack then kidnaps Santa Claus (whom he calls "Sandy Claws") so that he and the other spooky denizens of Halloweentown can have their macabre version of Christmas. Sally, a sewn-together rag doll, admires him.

JACKSON, JANET

The youngest member of the Jacksons (born May 16, 1966), a recording star herself since the mid-1980s. Her long string of energetic dance-oriented hits has included "What Have You Done for Me Lately?" (1986), "Nasty" (1986), "When I Think of You" (1986), "Miss You Much" (1989), "Rhythm Nation" (1989), "Escapade" (1990), "Black Cat" (1990), "That's the Way Love Goes" (1993), and "Together Again" (1997). Miss Jackson also acts, having appeared at age ten in the TV sitcom *Good Times* (1977–79) and then in *Diff'rent Strokes* (1981–82), *Fame* (1984–85), and the movie *Poetic Justice* (1993).

At 2004's Super Bowl, Jackson had a "wardrobe malfunction" while performing live with singer Justin Timberlake during the glitzy halftime ceremony. After singing their duet, Timberlake ripped at Jackson's bralike top, causing her nipple-pierced breast to tumble out in front of millions. This act outraged TV viewers and the Federal Communications Commission, which in response fined CBS-TV $550,000. As a punishment, that year's Grammy Awards banned Jackson, a former Grammy-winner, from appearing (though Timberlake, who apologetically claimed innocence in the boob display, was able to perform at the show).

FYI: ▸ Janet appeared publicly for the first time on stage with The Jackson 5 in 1973 doing impressions of Cher and Mae West!

JACKSON, MICHAEL

Born on August 29, 1958, Michael Jackson was the seventh child of Katherine and Joe Jackson. At age five, he became the lead singer in his older brothers' group, The Jackson 5, with his intense falsetto—which could later be heard in such Top Forty hits as "ABC" (1970) and "Never Can Say Goodbye" (1971). Displaying major teen-dream appeal (he was to black youths what Donny Osmond was to white youths), the sweet, soft-spoken, cherub-faced youngster set out on a solo career with the songs "Got to Be There" (1971), "Rockin' Robin" (1972), and "Ben" (1972). In 1978, he played the Scarecrow opposite friend Diana Ross's Dorothy in the film version of Broadway's *The Wiz*. Jackson's success as an adult singer came with the LP *Off the Wall*. Released in late 1979, it bridged the gap between 1970s disco and early-1980s dance and contained the electrifying chartbusters "Don't Stop 'Til You Get Enough" and "Rock with You."

In the 1980s, Jackson was the most internationally recognized star of the times, the most famous man in the world, the self-proclaimed "King of Pop." On December 1, 1982, his landmark album *Thriller* was released—and the music world would never be the same. It sold a record-setting forty million copies worldwide, hit number one in every western country, spent a record thirty-seven weeks at the top of the charts in America, became the best-selling LP in history, and received a record twelve Grammy nominations—winning eight, including Album of the Year. An unprecedented seven Top Ten singles came off that album: "Billie Jean," "Beat It," "Wanna Be Startin' Somethin'," "Human Nature," "P.Y.T. (Pretty Young Thing)," "Thriller," and "The Girl Is Mine," a duet with Paul McCartney. Jackson's innovative music videos, showcasing his high-pitched cry of "Woo-hoo," crotch-grabbing, and self-choreographed dance moves like the Moonwalk, were monumental in breaking the color barrier on MTV, a network previously reluctant to air "black" videos.

Youths everywhere copied and mocked Jackson's boyishly handsome appearance and trendsetting fashion. There was the Jheri-Curled hair with a spit curl falling on the forehead, the dark sunglasses, the brocade leather jackets, the tight flood pants exposing white socks, the preppy loafers, and—most significant—the single sequined glove worn on the right hand (the press nicknamed him "The Gloved One"). By the end of the decade, Jackson had sold more than 110 million records and had become the first entertainer to earn more than $100 million in a year.

However, somewhere along the way something went wrong. The once seemingly normal mega-star of records, radio, and rock video had developed into a Howard Hughes–like recluse or a pixie-ish Peter Pan isolated far away in his never-never land—a fantastic castle outside Santa Barbara complete with an exotic animal zoo and amusement park, appropriately named Neverland Valley.

Labeled "Wacko Jacko" by tabloids, Jackson's weird behavior lived up to that cruel title. For starters, he went from looking like an African-American to looking like a phantom, because of an overabundance of plastic surgery (what's up with the nose?) and his increasingly paler skin. He tried to buy the remains of John Merrick, otherwise known as the Elephant Man. His hair went up in flames during the making of a Pepsi-Cola commercial. He sleeps in a hyperbaric oxygen chamber to forestall aging, bathes in pure Evian water, and walks around in surgical masks (I think to protect himself from germs or to hide the latest nose job).

Then there are his odd friendships with child stars Brooke Shields, Emmanuel Lewis, and Macaulay Culkin, along with movie veteran Liz Taylor, a chimp named Bubbles, and E.T. the Extra-Terrestrial. And let's not forget about his quickie marriage to Lisa Marie Presley, his on-and-off-again estrangement from sisters Janet and LaToya, his addiction to painkillers, his fathering offspring with a woman he's not involved with, his sleepovers with young boys, and, most serious of all, the allegations of child molestation. It's really sad for the fans who grew up with Michael to witness what he has become.

JACKSON, REGGIE
Baseball star, an outfielder for the New York Yankees, whose popularity in the 1970s led to a chocolate candy bar being named after him: the Reggie Bar. He was nicknamed "Mr. October" because he blasted three home runs in one game during the World Series on October 18, 1977.

JACKSON 5
The five siblings from the blue-collar town of Gary, Indiana, were the first black music group to become national teen idols. From Savannah to St. Louis, San Diego to Seattle, their Afroed images crossed the boundaries of skin color, decorating the bedroom walls not only of urban black girls but also of suburban white girls who often had no day-to-day contact with a person of "color." All through the first half of the 1970s, they were the only African-American act to compete with Caucasian acts—The Osmonds, The Partridge Family, and The Brady Bunch—that were gracing the covers and pages of such teenybop mags as *Flip*, *16*, *Teen Beat*, and *Tiger Beat*.

The Jackson 5 was composed of precocious, charismatic, good-looking, and extremely talented brothers: Jackie, the oldest and wisest; Tito, the most musically inclined; Jermaine, the sexiest; Marlon, the shyest; and Michael, the gentle-spoken, prodigious star. They were formed, groomed, and rigorously coached by their father, Joe Jackson, in the mid-1960s. After winning several talent shows and playing nightclub gigs throughout the Midwest, the quintet came to the attention of Berry Gordy, who signed them to his famed Motown Records in 1969. (They would become the last major act to rise from the once-mighty label.)

Overnight, The Jackson 5 (or simply "J5" to die-hard fans) showcasing young Michael's standout vocals, exploded on the record charts with bubblegum soul tunes. Their first four singles—"I Want You Back" (1969), "ABC" (1970), "The Love You Save" (1970), and "I'll Be There" (1970)—were consecutive number-one hits. Other notable songs include "Never Can Say Goodbye" (1971), "Dancing Machine" (1974), and "Enjoy Yourself" (1976). The Jackson 5's high-energy stage performances, featuring dazzling dance moves, inspired a self-titled Saturday-morning cartoon TV show, from 1971 to 1973.

In 1976, the group changed its name to The Jacksons, after switching labels (Epic Records) and replacing Jermaine with youngest brother Randy. (Married to Berry Gordy's daughter, Hazel, Jermaine stayed with Motown for a solo career.) Sisters Rebbie, LaToya, and Janet did backing vocals for the band and later starred with them in a short-lived TV variety series, *The Jacksons* (1976–77). Sweet and outgoing Michael, the superidol of the family, experienced success as a soloist with a string of hits. After leaving The Jacksons in the 1980s, he emerged as a mega-superstar, the most talked about artist in pop music since the days of Elvis and The Beatles. Kid sister Janet didn't do so badly either. A superstar in her own right, she signed a $32 million contract with Virgin Records in 1991.

FYI: ▸ Contrary to popular belief, Diana Ross didn't discover The Jackson 5. It was Bobby Taylor, leader of the Motown group The Vancouvers, who convinced Berry Gordy to give them an audition. The Ross rumor—fabricated for publicity—remains alive because she was the one who formally introduced the quintet to the press before their debut performance at the Daisy Club in Beverly Hills in 1969, and, because their first album was titled *Diana Ross Presents The Jackson 5* and they were once the opening act for The Supremes.

JACK TRIPPER

John Ritter's good-time, skirt-chasing chef who faked homosexuality in order to share an apartment with two gorgeous girls, Janet and Chrissy, on the TV sitcom *Three's Company*. Like his surname, the fun-loving bumbler was always tripping over an object, such as a sofa, doorstep, or potted houseplant. True to his dreams, in 1982, he opened his own restaurant, Jack's Bistro, specializing in French cuisine, and dated a stewardess named Vicky Bradford.

JACOBY, SCOTT

Dark-haired, curly-headed juvenile actor of the 1970s best known for his work in made-for-TV movies, such as *That Certain Summer* (1972), earning him a Best Supporting Actor Emmy Award for his role of Nick Salter, the young son of a homosexual father; *Bad Ronald* (1974); and *The Diary of Anne Frank* (1980).

JAFAR

> "Jafar, Jafar, he's our man,
> if he can't do it—great!"
> —GENIE (ROBIN WILLIAMS)

In Disney's *Aladdin* (1992), Jafar (voiced by Jonathan Freeman) is the cruel adviser to the Sultan of Agrabah who has a thirst for ruling the Sultan's desert kingdom and the hand of his beautiful daughter, Princess Jasmine. His talking parrot, Iago, provides comic relief in the midst of his master's evil doings.

JAI

Orphaned jungle boy, befriended by Tarzan, who appeared in the Ape Man's prime-time TV adventure, from 1966 to 1968. Manuel Padilla Jr., who played the scrawny Jai, also starred as an orphaned jungle-boy befriended by Tarzan in two big-screen releases: Ramel in *Tarzan and the Valley of Gold* (1966) and Pepe in *Tarzan and the Great River* (1967).

JAIME SOMMERS

Tennis-pro-turned-superwoman after her human body-parts—legs, arm, and ear—injured from a skydiving accident, were replaced with bionic body parts (bionic ex-boyfriend Steve Austin referred Jaime for this top-secret operation). When Jaime wasn't working for OSI fighting evildoers, she doubled as a schoolteacher at the Ventura Air Force Base near her hometown of Ojai, California. Her loyal pet dog was Max, a bionic German shepherd. Played by the lovely blonde Lindsay Wagner on the sci-fi adventure series *The Bionic Woman*.

JAKE RYAN

Hunk deluxe! The most popular boy in school, a handsome senior, who ends up with Samantha Baker, a sophomore "everygirl," in *Sixteen Candles* (1984). Fueled the hopes of average-looking high school girls in the 1980s that they too could have a dreamy "Jake Ryan."

JAMBI THE GENIE

Jambi was a blue-tinted disembodied magic head, belonging to writer John Paragon, who lived in a box on *Pee-Wee's Playhouse*. The turban-wearing genie with dishy gay mannerisms would grant master Pee-Wee a wish by chanting the magical phrase: "Mekka-lekka-hi, mekka-heiny-ho!"

JAMES AND THE GIANT PEACH

Written in 1961 by acclaimed author Roald Dahl, this is the extraordinary story of a wildly imaginative young boy who is sent to live with two cruel aunts, Aunt Spiker and Aunt Sponge, at the English seaside after his parents are eaten by a rhinoceros. One day a strange old man appears and gives orphan James a bag of magic crocodile tongues, which he accidentally spills near a peach tree and produces a house-sized peach. After the giant peach crushes his nasty aunts, James crawls into it through a worm hole, making friends with its human-sized insect occupants: a centipede, a silkworm, a ladybug, a cricket, and a spider. With the aid of a flock of seagulls (not the New Wave band from the 1980s), the peach is lifted into the air and flies across the Atlantic Ocean to New York City. The fantastic tale inaugurated Dahl's career as a writer of children's literature, whose books later included *Charlie and the Chocolate Factory* (1964) and *Matilda* (1988). In 1996, *James and the Giant Peach* was made into a motion picture, produced by Tim Burton (*The Nightmare Before Christmas*), using stop-motion animation.

JAMES AT 15

This family drama was one of TV's more realistic attempts at depicting what growing up was like in the latter half of the 1970s. It starred blond Lance Kerwin as James Hunter, a bright, sensitive fifteen-year-old with a love for photography and an inclination for daydreaming. James moves with his family from Oregon to suburban Boston after his college-professor father accepts a new teaching position. Adjusting to a different city and attending a new school (Bunker Hill High) was difficult for James at first (he tried running away). Over time, he learns to fit in, making friends with a black hipster, Ludwig "Sly" Hazeltine (David Hubbard), and an intellectual female, Marlene Mahoney (Susan Myers).

Airing from 1977 to 1978, the NBC series covered serious and somewhat risqué subject matter, such as teen alcoholism, drug use, premarital sex, and sexually transmitted diseases. However, on February 9, 1978, it aired its most controversial episode, in which James on his sixteenth birthday loses his virginity to a Swedish exchange student, Christina Kollberg (Kirsten Baker). Starting with that episode, the title changed to *James at 16*. If it had not been canceled in July 1978, presumably the name would have changed annually—*James at 17*, *James at 18*, *James at 19*, and if it continued to air today, it would be known as *James at 43*!

JAMES BOND

The most famous secret agent in pop culture history was Bond, James Bond—author Ian Fleming's daring and dashing Agent 007 of Her Majesty's Secret Service. Who knew the cold war could be so much fun, as the British superspy sped about in his fabulously equipped Aston Martin DB5, rigged with tire-slashers, an oil-slick squirter, a smoke-screen device, a bulletproof windshield, and an ejector seat. With a license to kill, our unflappable hero traveled to exotic locales (Jamaica, Istanbul, Moscow, Japan, Las Vegas) risking life and limb saving the world from fiendish foes—Dr. No, Goldfinger, Oddjob, Blofield, Jaws—while seducing a bevy of luscious babes with double-entendre names: Honey Rider, Pussy Galore, Holly Goodhead, Plenty O'Toole, Kissy Suzuki. His first cinematic venture, *Dr. No* (played by sexy Sean Connery, the best Bond by far), was a 1962 box-office smash that spawned a long series of sequels, including *From Russia with Love* (1963), *Goldfinger* (1964), *Thunderball* (1965), *You Only Live Twice* (1967), and *Diamonds Are Forever* (1971).

Actors following Connery as 007 included Roger Moore in the films *Live and Let Die* (1973), *The Man with the Golden Gun* (1974), *The Spy Who Loved Me* (1977), *Moonraker* (1979), *For Your Eyes Only* (1981), and *Octopussy* (1983); Timothy Dalton in *The Living Daylights* (1987) and *Licence to Kill* (1989); and more recently, Pierce Brosnan in *Tomorrow Never Dies* (1997), *The World Is Not Enough* (1999), and *Die Another Day* (2002). Bond's popularity inspired a legion of secret-agent imitators, most notably Dean Martin's boozy Matt Helm, James Coburn's zesty Derek Flint, and Don Adams's bumbling Maxwell Smart.

FYI: ▸ James Bond was a connoisseur of the martini ("large and very strong and very well made"), a cocktail traditionally made with gin and dry vermouth. In *Casino Royale* (Ian Fleming's 1953 book and a 1967 movie), Agent 007 introduced millions to the Vesper martini—a.k.a. vodka martini.

JAMES BUCHANAN HIGH

Inner-city public school in Brooklyn, New York, where the Sweathogs—Vinnie Barbarino, Juan Epstein, Arnold Horshack, and Freddie Washington—attended classes on the sitcom *Welcome Back, Kotter.*

JAMS

Colorfully printed knee-length shorts with an elastic waist that were originally sported by male surfers in the 1960s and had a fashion renaissance in the mid-1980s.

JAN AND JAYCE

Masked and caped teenage duo who tagged along with crime-fighter Space Ghost on his interstellar Saturday-morning *Space Ghost* cartoon adventures. They had a tiny pet space-monkey named Blip.

JAN BRADY

Jan Brady was the epitome of angst-ridden adolescence of the 1970s. Played by teen actress Eve Plumb on *The Brady Bunch*, she was the continual middle child whose wish was to be the lone child ("I wish I were an only child!")—especially because she was always in the shadow of older, prettier, more popular Marcia ("Why does Marcia always get everything? Marcia! Marcia! Marcia!"). Actually, she was just as pretty as Marcia, more levelheaded, and had blonder hair, which she wore with sideburn banana curls similar to those of a Hasidic Jew. Jan repeatedly put herself down ("What a dumbhead I am!"), and because of her insecurities, she thought the other Brady kids were always poking fun at her.

As Jan fans, we understood when she wore a silly black Afro wig to try to find her own identity. We felt for her when she bombed trying to make the pom-pom squad, unlike Marcia who made head captain. We watched freckle-faced Jan as she experienced the trauma of wearing a mouthful of braces and dreadful glasses ("Glasses! I'll look positively goofy!"), and we related to her because we were all going through the same identity-crushing times. Jan got her reward for persevering—by the end of the sitcom's final season she was voted the "Most Popular Girl" in school.

JANE HATHAWAY

This "Plain Jane" beanpole was bank president Milburn Drysdale's highly efficient assistant ("Yes, Chief!") and Clampett confidant. Played by Nancy Kulp on *The Beverly Hillbillies.*

JANE JETSON

George Jetson's charming spouse, a busy futuristic housewife who, when not doting on her family, spends time shopping (by pushing a button on a computerized machine), cooking (by pushing another button), and having her hair done (by pushing still another button). Resourceful robot Rosie took care of Jane's housework. Actress Penny Singleton, best known for playing Blondie Bumstead in the *Blondie* film series, provided Jane's voice for the popular *Jetsons* cartoon show of the 1960s.

JANE PORTER

"Me Tarzan, you Jane." Attractive lass rescued by vine-swinging Tarzan while on a treacherous African expedition. She falls in love with the mighty Ape Man and chooses to stay in the jungle as his mate, where they build a cozy home high in a tree. The twosome were joined by chimpanzee pal Cheetah and later an adopted son, whom they call "Boy." Throughout the 1930s, Maureen O'Sullivan, mother of Mia Farrow, starred as Jane in the *Tarzan* movie series, produced by MGM Studios.

JANET WOOD

This intelligent, curly-haired brunette (played by Joyce DeWitt) who worked at a florist shop is the sensible one of the roommate trio on *Three's Company*. She's overprotective of ditzy roomie Chrissy, a well-built blonde who's too dim to realize she's being hit on by all the wolves, er . . . men. Janet takes naps in her favorite sky-blue, sport-style jersey T-shirt.

JASON VOORHEES

A skulking monster in a hockey mask with an inclination for murdering teenagers at Camp Crystal Lake on any given Friday the thirteenth. Out for revenge after drowning many years ago, Jason is a powerful force that nothing can stop. And just when you think he's down for the count—he pops back up for more bloodletting (and for one more *Friday the 13th* movie). He did battle with dream demon Freddy Krueger from Elm Street in 2003's *Freddy vs. Jason*.

JAWAS

Band of diminutive scavengers with hooded cloaks and glowing eyes who seized robots C-3PO and R2-D2 on the desert planet Tatooine in the first *Star Wars* film (1977).

JAWS

The movie that scared us away from the sea and into the safety of swimming pools during the summer of 1975, leading to shark hysteria up and down America's shorelines and all points between. From the opening scene of a skinny-dipping woman being fatally attacked by the unseen shark, to the battle climax aboard seaman Quint's boat, viewers experienced one nerve-racking, eye-covering, edge-of-your-seat thriller. Based on author Peter Benchley's best-seller, *Jaws* is the spine-tingling tale of a peaceful Massachusetts beach resort, Amity Island (actually filmed at Martha's Vineyard), that is terrorized by a ravenous, two-ton, thirty-foot great white. Concerned police chief Martin Brody (Roy Scheider) must stop this oversized shark from munching on swimmers and ruining Amity's tourist business. He enlists the aid of young marine biologist Matt Hooper (Richard Dreyfuss) and salty shark-hunter Quint (Robert Shaw), and the trio succeed at stopping the lethal fish—or at least until the next sequel, 1978's *Jaws 2*.

Directed by Steven Spielberg, *Jaws* was a box-office phenomenon that became the year's top moneymaker and the highest grosser ever (until Spielberg's own *E.T.* in 1982). It spawned a school of less-equal sequels and imitators, and, along with composer John Williams's menacing score ("dunn-dunn-dunn-dunn-*dunn-dunn-dunn-dunn*"), has a strong place in pop culture history.

FYI: ▸ The hydraulically operated mechanical shark created for *Jaws* was named "Bruce" by the film crew.

JEAN LaFOOTE

This barefoot French pirate is Cap'n Crunch's most notorious nemesis, an insidious scoundrel out to steal the seafaring S.S. *Guppy*'s precious cargo—golden Cap'n Crunch cereal.

JEAN NATÉ

Created in 1935 by Charles of the Ritz, a lemon-scented body splash packaged in bright-yellow containers that bring back memories of somebody's grandmother. Also came in talcum powder, soap, and deodorant.

JEANNIE

"Yes, master!" Played by Barbara Eden on prime time's *I Dream of Jeannie*, this beautiful 2,000-year-old magical genie (born in 64 B.C. in Baghdad), resides in a bejeweled bottle owned by her master, astronaut Tony Nelson. Wearing blonde hair piled high in an elaborate ponytail and a harem outfit, playful Jeannie is ready to grant Major Nelson his every wish (even when he doesn't wish it), with crossed arms, a nod of the head, and a blink of her twinkling eyes. She also has a sultry and devious dark-haired look-alike sister also named Jeannie.

FYI: ▸ Sexy Barbara Eden attracted male attention with the breezy midriff-revealing pink and magenta Arabian Nights costume, but TV censors forced her to cover her belly button with high-waisted harem pants.

JED CLAMPETT

Poor mountaineer, played by onetime movie hoofer Buddy Ebsen on the CBS-TV sitcom *The Beverly Hillbillies*, who moves his scatterbrained clan from the hills of the Ozarks to the hills of Beverly after striking oil on his property.

JEFF COLBY

On the prime-time serial *Dynasty*, cutie John James played the devoted husband of Fallon and the virtuous son-in-law of Blake Carrington. His father was Cecil Colby, deceased rival of Blake's and late husband of evil Alexis, Fallon's mother and Blake's first wife. (Are you following me?)

JEFFERSON DAVIS HOGG

Known as "Boss" Hogg, a white-suited, potbellied politico who corruptly runs Hazzard County U.S.A.

with the assistance of dim-witted brother-in-law Sheriff Roscoe P. Coltrane, bumbling Deputy Enos Strate, and a lazy basset hound called Flash. "Those Duke boys," cousins Bo and Luke Duke, were the thorns in his tubby side and the pain in his redneck. Played by Sorrell Booke on *The Dukes of Hazzard*, a comedy adventure TV show.

JEFFERSON HIGH

Located in suburban Milwaukee, this is the school that Richie Cunningham, his younger sister, Joanie, Potsie Webber, and Ralph Malph attend on TV's *Happy Days*. School colors: blue and white.

JEFF SPICOLI

> "All I need are some tasty waves,
> a cool buzz, and I'm fine."
> —JEFF SPICOLI (SEAN PENN)

"Hey, bud, let's party!" Sean Penn's hilarious star-making spin as the bong-toking, spaced-out teen in *Fast Times at Ridgemont High* was the prototype of all Valley surfer-stoner dudes of the 1980s. Wearing his sun-bleached hair at shoulder length and sporting a totally awesome pair of checkered Vans, Spicoli dreams of national fame by surfing the ultimate wave. But first he has to make it through Mr. Hand's history class, during which he makes the famous mistake of ordering a pizza. Bill and Ted, Wayne and Garth, and Pauly Shore were all created in his mold. "Whoa!"

JELLIES

Inexpensive clear-plastic shoes for girls found in a variety of bright colors. They had a particular smell to 'em (especially after sweating in 'em all day).

JELL-O

> "Gelatin, no matter what it's in,
> always gives a gay, party air to things."
> —EDITH BUNKER (JEAN STAPLETON)

With its shimmering bright colors and tasty fruit flavors, General Foods' brand of gelatin packaged in a powdered mix was one of the traditional "fun" foods of the twentieth century. The wiggly-jiggly treat is also the largest-selling prepared dessert in the world, preferred by many as a cool, low-cal alternative to cakes and pies. Creative homemakers mold aspic with Jell-O or add fruit cocktail to it, then top it with a glob of whipped cream. Creative college students use Jell-O as a party favor called "Jell-O Shooters." (The Jell-O is mixed with grain alcohol instead of water and then lovingly chilled.)

JELLY BELLY

The tiny jelly bean skyrocketed to popularity in the early 1980s after President Ronald Reagan proclaimed them to be his favorite snack (he served them in the Oval Office and on Air Force One). Manufactured by the Herman Goelitz Company of Fairfield, California, since 1976, the candy is famous for its endless variety of gourmet flavors. The more unusual of these flavors include Buttered Popcorn, Cantaloupe, Cappuccino, Champagne Punch, Jalapeno, Margarita, Piña Colada, Sizzling Cinnamon, Strawberry Cheesecake, Tangerine, Toasted Marshmallow, and Top Banana. Jelly Belly became the first jelly bean in space when served on the Challenger space shuttle in June 1983—the same mission that boasted America's first female astronaut Sally Ride as a crew member.

JELLYSTONE NATIONAL PARK

Overseen by hardworking Ranger John Smith, this is the government-protected habitat that picnic-basket-stealing Yogi Bear calls home in the *Yogi Bear* cartoon series. Its name is a take on picturesque Yellowstone National Park, located in Wyoming, Montana, and Idaho, famous for geysers and hot springs.

JEM

Truly outrageous rock 'n' roll heroine of an MTV-influenced doll line (1985) and cartoon (1986–87) produced by Hasbro Toys. Virtuous do-gooder Jerrica Benton, Jem's alter ego, was a beautiful blonde business executive (Starlight Music) and supervisor at a home for young orphan girls (Starlight Foundation), who transformed into a flashy and pink-haired rock star via Synergy, a hologram-projecting computer. Jem fronted the all-girl Holograms: red-haired sister Kimber, blue-haired Aja, lavender-haired Shana, pink-haired Raya, and rainbow-haired choreographer Danse. Taking a fashion nod from Madonna and Cyndi Lauper, the girls dressed in rad threads and Day-Glo makeup while battling rival girl band The Misfits, led by mean Pizzazz. Handsome Rio—serving as both Jerrica's boyfriend and Jem's road manager—never realized that the two were the same person.

JENGA

Milton Bradley's "edge-of-your-seat" game has players removing one wooden block at a time from a tower and stacking it higher on top. The last person to stack a block without making the tower topple wins the game. Jenga was invented in the 1970s by Leslie Scott of Great Britain. Alder is the tree used to make the wooden Jenga blocks.

JENNIFER KEATON

On *Family Ties*, nine-year-old Tina Yothers starred as this somewhat boring but cute and very blonde youngest daughter of the Keaton family. Compared with yuppie brother Alex and materialistic sister Mallory, she was the one most likely to take after her liberal parents, Steven and Elyse.

JENNIFER NORTH

"All I know how to do is take off my clothes." In the camp film classic *Valley of the Dolls*, Sharon Tate played gorgeous Jennifer North, an international sex symbol whose dependency on her magnificent body—long legs and big tits—led to suicide when faced with a mastectomy. "She took the red pills."

JENNY PICCALO

Joanie Cunningham's free-spirited, slutty girlfriend on *Happy Days*. Since the sitcom's premiere in 1974, viewers only got to hear about Jenny's bad-girl exploits—through Joanie—before finally seeing her in the person of Cathy Silvers (daughter of comedian Phil Silvers), who played her from 1980 to 1983.

JERK

This mid-1960s dance involved jerking the upper body to the rhythm of the music (a double-time Frug) while keeping the lower body somewhat still. Not recommended for those suffering back problems! Jerk songs included "The Jerk" (1965) by The Larks and "Cool Jerk" (1966) by The Capitols.

JESSICA RABBIT

"I'm not bad. I'm just drawn that way." Voluptuous (you can just hear the wolf whistles), slinky, red-headed human wife of frantic Roger Rabbit. In her feature film Disney's *Who Framed Roger Rabbit* Kathleen Turner provided Jessica's sultry speaking voice while Amy Irving did her singing.

FYI: ▸ Jessica Rabbit once owned a lingerie shop at Pleasure Island, located in Florida's Walt Disney World resort.

JETHRO BODINE

Jed Clampett's nephew (played by Max Baer Jr. on *The Beverly Hillbillies*), a good-looking, well-built, girl-chasing dimwit with a third-grade education. Has a hulking twin sister named Jethrene (also played by Baer), who lives with their yodeling ma, Pearl, back yonder in Bug Tussle.

JET SCREAMER

Slick singer who had a pop hit with the far-out "Eep Op Ork Ah-Ah (Means I Love You)." In the 1962 *Jetsons* episode "A Date with a Jet Screamer," teenager Judy Jetson wins a contest in which first prize is a date with her idol, Jet Screamer.

JETSONS

Created by Hanna-Barbera, this space-age counterpart to the Stone Age *Flintstones* first aired on prime-time TV in 1962 before moving to Saturday mornings the following year, where it remained a classic fixture for the next two decades. The show revolves around the Jetsons, a "typical" twenty-first-century family who live in suburban Orbit City, located in outer space, in an ultramodern apartment building called the Skypad. The household consists of nice-guy George Jetson, lovely wife Jane, teenage daughter Judy, young son Elroy, and faithful dog Astro. Other characters in the cartoon include Rosie the robot maid, George's boss, Cosmo S. Spacely, his spouse, Stella, and a little alien pet called Orbity. In 1990, a feature-length theatrical version of *The Jetsons* was released, featuring teen pop-star Tiffany as Judy Jetson's voice.

JEWELL, GERI

Comedienne with cerebral palsy who occasionally played Blair Warner's cousin Jeri on *The Facts of Life* from 1981 to 1984. Known for her humor making light of her handicap, she has been one of the few disabled persons ever to have a recurring role on a TV series.

JHERI CURL
A messy hair substance used by African-Americans in the 1980s to make their hair look glossy and curly (like Michael Jackson's "Thriller" look). It's extremely out of fashion today. In fact, calling someone a "Jheri Curl" can be a big insult.

JIFFY POP
"Fun to make! Fun to eat!" This brings back pleasant childhood memories (before microwaves) of watching the flat foil pan of popcorn kernels on the stovetop grow and grow and grow—pop, pop, pop, pop—into an expanded dome on the verge of exploding. Some never got it right; they always burned it over the range, leaving a smoke odor that lasted for hours.

FYI: ▸ Here's a fun pop culture tidbit: Drew Barrymore was making Jiffy Pop before she got slashed to death in the movie *Scream* (1996).

JILL MUNROE
Sporty, sexy California-blonde undercover agent working for Charlie Townsend, who was dyn-ooo-mite at skateboarding, roller derby, tennis, and flipping back her feathered locks. She retired from crime-fighting to become a Grand Prix race driver in Europe. Played by former Wella Balsam pitch-babe Farrah Fawcett-Majors on *Charlie's Angels* from 1976 to 1977.

JIMMY
"Come and play with me, Jimmy!" Young lad who gets shipwrecked, along with his magic golden flute, Freddy, on the mysterious Living Island, where he is befriended by its mayor, H. R. Pufnstuf, a cowboy dragon. Spent his entire time (or at least an hour of our Saturday mornings) on the isle trying to find the Magic Path to get home, while avoiding trickery caused by Witchiepoo, "a kooky old witch" who coveted Freddy. English teen idol Jack Wild (*Oliver*'s Artful Dodger) starred as Jimmy in the enormously popular *H. R. Pufnstuf* TV show.

JIMMY OLSEN
Young reporter/photographer for the *Daily Planet* in Metropolis who was buddies with Clark Kent, a.k.a. Superman. (Jimmy didn't know the older Kent was the idolized flying superhero.)

J. J. EVANS
"Dyn-o-mite!" Florida Evans's eldest kid on TV's *Good Times*, played by comic Jimmie Walker, was a seventeen-year-old jive-talking aspiring artist, who let his desire to get out of the ghetto involve him in a multitude of get-rich schemes that always backfired. Initials stood for James Jr.

JOANIE CUNNINGHAM
Richie Cunningham's cute but pesky thirteen-year-old sister who grew up to be a well-liked teenager attending Jefferson High in Milwaukee, Wisconsin. A good girl, Joanie fantasized about being naughty, especially considering that her best gal was bad-girl Jenny Piccalo and her best guy was bad-boy Chachi Arcola. The Fonz called her "Shortcake." Portrayed by child-actress Erin Moran in the TV sitcom *Happy Days* and its spin-off, *Joanie Loves Chachi.*

FYI: ▸ In the early 1980s, snooty Valley Girls referred to a plain-looking, boring female as "a Joanie," a reference to Joanie Cunningham's average looks and unhip personality.

JOANIE LOVES CHACHI
The short-lived 1982 spin-off from *Happy Days* had the two teenage lovebirds, played by Erin Moran and Scott Baio, leaving Milwaukee for Chicago to warble in a rock 'n' roll band. Moran and Baio performed the sitcom's theme song, "You Look at Me."

JOCK EWING
Actor Jim Davis's manipulative silver-haired patriarch of the *Dallas* clan and head of Ewing Oil, who cheated his partner Digger Barnes out of both his half of a prosperous oil strike and his true love, Eleanor "Miss Ellie" Southworth. Sons are corrupt J.R., rebel Gary, virtuous Bobby, and illegitimate Ray Krebbs.

JODY DAVIS
Scratchy-voiced, freckle-faced, curly-haired five-year-old orphaned redhead sent to live with his Uncle Bill in Manhattan, along with twin Buffy and teen sis Cissy, after his parents died in an accident.

Played by Johnny Whitaker on the classic 1960s sitcom *Family Affair.*

JOEY MACDONALD
The dark-haired little pip-squeak was the best pal of Dennis Mitchell in the *Dennis the Menace* comic strip.

JOHN, ELTON
Music superstar noted for dynamic stage performances in the 1970s, dressed in outrageous platform shoes, bizarre spectacles, funky feather boas, and garish costumes (including a gorilla suit and a sequined L.A. Dodgers uniform). Born Reginald Kenneth Dwight on March 25, 1947, in Middlesex, England, the balding and pudgy singer-pianist came up with his stage moniker by combining the first names of two members of his first band, Bluesology: Elton Dean and John Baldry. In 1969, Elton partnered with lyricist Bernie Taupin, forming a union responsible for some of the best-loved songs of the rock era: "Your Song" (1970), "Rocket Man" (1972), "Crocodile Rock" (1973), "Daniel" (1973), "Bennie and the Jets" (1974), "Philadelphia Freedom" (1975), and "Someone Saved My Life Tonight" (1975). An unstoppable hit-maker by 1976, Elton sold more than eighteen million singles and forty-two million albums, which included *Honky Chateau* (1972), *Don't Shoot Me I'm Only the Piano Player* (1973), *Goodbye Yellow Brick Road* (1973), *Caribou* (1974), and the autobiographical *Captain Fantastic and the Brown Dirt Cowboy* (1975).

Elton John's career took a decline in the late 1970s following an admittance of bisexuality and bouts with depression and chemical dependency. However, he came back in style in the 1980s with a string of hits—more easy listening than rock—like "Little Jeannie" (1980), "I Guess That's Why They Call It the Blues" (1983), "Sad Songs (Say So Much)" (1984), "Nikita" (1986), and "Candle in the Wind" (1987). He played the Pinball Wizard in the 1975 film version of The Who's *Tommy.*

FYI: ▸ Elton John is godfather to John and Yoko Lennon's son Sean.

JOHN BOSLEY
Round-faced David Doyle starred as this chipper yet somewhat fretting go-between for the unseen Charlie Townsend and his crime-fighting Angels. In 2000, Bosley was played by comedian Bill Murray in the big-screen remake of *Charlie's Angels* (2000) and by Bernie Mac (yes, an African-American) in its 2003 sequel, *Charlie's Angels: Full Throttle.*

FYI: ▸ John Bosley's surname was an in-joke reference to the fact that David Doyle was often mistaken for look-alike actor Tom Bosley (*Happy Days*).

JOHN-BOY WALTON
Supersincere eldest son of John and Olivia Walton who is simply adored by his six younger siblings—Jason, Mary Ellen, Ben, Erin, Jim-Bob, and Elizabeth. Portrayed by Richard Thomas, a boyish-appearing actor with trademark mole on his cheek, on *The Waltons* TV drama, John-Boy aspires to be a writer and keeps a journal about the events surrounding his large family's upbringing on Walton's Mountain in rural Virginia during the Great Depression. "Goodnight, John-Boy."

"JOHNNY, ARE YOU QUEER?"
Perky popster Josie Cotton's West Coast hit caused quite a stir in 1982 when Los Angeles radio station KROQ-FM began airing it. Her landmark song—one of the first to deal openly with the subject of homosexuality—angered born-again zealots, who picketed the trendsetting music station, claiming that it would turn teen listeners gay. The gay community defended the song as being funny and nonderogatory, an innocent ode from a girl to a boyfriend whom she suspected was gay ("I saw you today, boy, walking with them gay boys . . . "). Originally sung by The Go-Go's as part of a club set, "Johnny, Are You Queer" was offered to Cotton after they failed to record it. Cotton warbled it on stage during the high school prom scene in the 1983 cult movie *Valley Girl.*

JOHNNY BRAVO
Groovy rock-star alter ego of teen heartthrob Greg Brady (Barry Williams) seen in a 1973 episode titled "Adios, Johnny Bravo" on *The Brady Bunch.* Also the title name of the blond, buff-chested animated character who appeared on *Johnny Bravo,* a Cartoon Network TV series, in the late 1990s.

JOHNNY CASTLE
Hunky dance instructor employed at Kellerman's, a resort in New York's Catskills, who dirty-danced after hours with his fellow dance troupers but fell in love with hotel guest "Baby" Houseman. Played by classically trained ballet dancer Patrick Swayze in the 1987 musical film *Dirty Dancing*.

JOHNNY LIGHTNING
"Race with the winners!" The other competitor of Hot Wheels and Matchbox that—despite having some rather kick-ass cars—experienced a short life span during the late 1960s and early 1970s. It's been said that these die-cast vehicles equipped with "lightning motion" were faster than superfast Hot Wheels and made Matchbox cars seem like something granny would drive. Introduced by Topper in 1969, Johnny Lightning cars came with trademark friction-free mag wheels and sleek designs with names like "Fabulous Fin," "Mako Shark," "Manta Ray," "Screamer," and "Twin Blaster." Their track sets included the torturous Cyclone 500, a vertical ninety-degree climb leading to a double loop-the-loop at the top, and the El Dorado, containing four death-defying curves and banks. While playing with these, boys could wear the Johnny Lightning helmet, complete with goggles—just like the ones pro race-car drivers wore!

FYI: ▸ In 1970, racing champ Al Unser drove a real-life Johnny Lightning Special in the Indianapolis 500. He won.

JOHNNY WEST
Twelve-inch-tall cowboy action-figure from the Best of the West toy line, manufactured by Marx Toys from 1965 to 1970. When not hanging out at the Circle X Ranch with kinfolk (including wife Jane and children Jamie and Josie), Johnny spends his days range-riding on ardent steed Thunderbolt and fending off Indian attacks (except for friend Chief Cherokee).

JOKER
Garish and giggling, this deranged "Clown Prince of Crime" is considered Batman's number-one foe in the *Batman* comics. The Joker's calling card is a poison that makes his victims laugh themselves to death. Real name: Jack Napier. Played by onetime Hollywood Latin lover Cesar Romero on the 1960s *Batman* TV show, and by Jack Nicholson in the 1989 *Batman* motion picture.

JOLLY GREEN GIANT
"Ho, ho, ho!" Buff, green-hued spokes-giant for Green Giant's canned and frozen vegetables, who dressed in a green tunic, lived in a valley, and palled around with wee Little Green Sprout.

JON ARBUCKLE
Comic feline Garfield's eternally geeky, girl-loser owner who worked as cartoonist. His other pets included dim-witted dog Odie and the world's cutest kitten, Nermal.

JONATHAN BAKER
Jon for short. Blue-eyed blond Larry Wilcox starred as the straitlaced California Highway Patrol motorcycle cop who worked the busy freeways of L.A. with vivacious partner Ponch (Erik Estrada) on TV's hit crime drama *ChiPs* (1977–83).

JONATHAN LIVINGSTON SEAGULL
Publishers Weekly called 1972 the "Year of the Bird," a reference to Richard Bach's tale about a seagull named Jonathan Livingston. The book soared to the top of the best-seller lists, became the year's number-one seller, and broke the hardcover record set back in 1936 by Margaret Mitchell's *Gone with the Wind*. A nonconformist, Jonathan Livingston found himself alone after being banished from his flock of fellow seagulls. Upon hearing "behind and to the right" coming from a mysterious voice, he meets an elite group of gulls who instruct him on how to achieve perfect flight, and is then lifted to a higher world for feathered friends. Heavy in allegories and metaphors, the uplifting tale envisioned a world of love, understanding, individuality, achievement, and hope. It was somewhat of an inspirational bible for older Baby Boomers who were coming out of the drug culture and doing some very heavy soul-searching. By the mid-1970s, *Jonathan Livingston Seagull* swelled into a full-blown phenomenon—spawning pendants, posters, and a 1973 movie shot from a bird's-eye perspective and featuring a Neil Diamond soundtrack.

JONATHAN MUDDLEMORE

An American patriot during the Revolutionary War who became trapped inside a grandfather clock at Muddlemore Mansion while fleeing the Redcoats. Two centuries later, his spirit, freed by a group of teenagers, became the subject of a TV cartoon titled *The Funky Phantom*. A cowardly spook, "Muddsey" turns invisible whenever he gets frightened.

JONES, ANISSA

Those who were kids in the 1960s will fondly remember this enormously popular juvenile actress as the oh-so-adorable Buffy Davis, twin sister of Jody, from TV's *Family Affair* (1966–71). On the show, the freckled moppet had blonde, curly pigtails, talked in a childish lisp, and carried a beloved doll named Mrs. Beasley. Anissa's sweet face endorsed a multitude of merchandising items, including dolls (Mattel's Talking Buffy and Mrs. Beasley), toys (Buffy's Make-Up and Hairstyling Set), and books (*Buffy Finds a Star* and *Buffy's Cookbook*), as well as children's clothing, go-go boots, wig cases, and even a Buffy Halloween costume. Anissa was a ministar, the envy of almost every little girl who ever dreamed of living in a big Fifth Avenue penthouse with a doting Uncle Bill and Mr. French.

In reality, life for Anissa (born March 11, 1958) wasn't as wonderful as we were led to believe. Unhappy with being an actress on a hit series, she wanted to be a normal kid with a normal life—a kid who went to school during the day and played with friends afterward, instead of spending long days on the set, where a visiting tutor came to instruct her and Johnny "Jody" Whitaker in daily lessons and where playtime was a rare occasion. She despised the cutesy doll-like clothes she was forced to wear, but *Family Affair*'s producers insisted that the frilly outfits were necessary for Buffy's cuddly appeal. Furthermore, her aggressive stage-mother had signed a lucrative contract with a children's clothing company, requiring Anissa to wear them on the show and for public appearances. During the last season, thirteen-year-old Anissa's budding breasts were strapped down underneath Buffy's puffy crinoline dresses.

After cancellation of *Family Affair*, Anissa found herself typecast as Buffy and unable to find work as an actress. With TV stardom over and childhood lost, it was difficult adapting to life as a normal teenager attending public school (her classmates treated her as a weirdo for playing Buffy, now considered uncool). To cope, she turned to the Southern California drug scene. On August 29, 1976, at age eighteen, Anissa died from a lethal mixture of quaaludes and alcohol at a friend's party in San Diego. The San Diego coroner said that the amount of drugs found in her body was the largest he had ever seen.

FYI: ▸ Actress Susan Olsen (curly-pigtailed Cindy Brady) is often confused with Anissa Jones (curly-pigtailed Buffy Davis). People comment: "I thought you were dead."

JONES, DAVY

Born December 30, 1945, this cute and short (five foot three) Cockney Brit was the Monkee with the most teenybopper appeal. One of his biggest supporters was Marcia Brady, president of the Fillmore Junior High chapter of the Davy Jones fan club, who persuaded her idol to perform at the school prom (he sang his solo hit "Girl"). Before Jones was a Monkee, he did a two-year run on Broadway as the Artful Dodger in the musical *Oliver!* The role earned him a Tony nomination.

JONES, DEAN

Easygoing and handsome lead actor for Walt Disney Studios who starred in a string of lightweight theatrical comedies: *That Darn Cat* (1965), *The Ugly Dachshund* (1966), *Monkeys, Go Home!* (1967), *Blackbeard's Ghost* (1968), *The Horse in the Gray Flannel Suit* (1968), *The Love Bug* (1968), *The Million Dollar Duck* (1971), *Snowball Express* (1972), and *The Shaggy D.A.* (1976).

JONES, TOM

In 1969, Sunday nights at my house were intensely exciting. As a first-grader, it was fun (and rather peculiar) to watch my mother get turned on over this ultragroovy, ultracool Welsh singer named after Henry Fielding's bawdy eighteenth-century hero. You see, Jones had a musical-variety TV show titled *This Is Tom Jones*, and from the moment he sang the opening theme, "It's Not Unusual," his energetic and sexy style turned my normally calm mom and thousands of her contemporaries across the nation into lustful, drooling maniacs. (It was a sight to behold. Average housewives acted as if possessed by the love devil.) But, really, you couldn't blame them. Like his fictional counterpart, this Tom Jones of the 1960s was sexually provocative.

The handsome entertainer with the wavy hair and twinkling eyes wore his pants crotch-bulging tight and his shirts open to the navel, exposing a hirsute chest. His booming baritone voice had a seductive growl, and the passion of his hip-swiveling performance produced perspiration for which he always had a scarf handy to wipe his face, then toss to the audience of anxious and squealing women. (In return, those fans were busy tossing their underpanties at him on stage.) His hit songs include "It's Not Unusual" (1965), "What's New Pussycat?" (1965), "Green, Green Grass of Home" (1967), "Delilah" (1968), "I'll Never Fall in Love Again" (1969), and "She's a Lady" (1971).

In the 1990s, a new generation of adults rediscovered Tom Jones, finding him extremely hip and, yes, still sexy (mom was right). His 1989 remake of Prince's "Kiss," produced by the electronic pop group Art of Noise, confirmed this hipness, as well as the 1994 Top Forty album *The Lead and How to Swing It*, including the dance-club hit "If I Only Knew" and a rousing cover of Yaz's "Situation."

FYI: ▸ At one time, "It's Not Unusual" was banned by BBC radio for being too "overtly sexual," and American soul stations thought Tom Jones was African-American.

JONNY QUEST

After years of being known for such funny cartoons as Huckleberry Hound and Yogi Bear, Hanna-Barbera made a radical change with *Jonny Quest*, TV's first animated action-adventure show. Originally premiering on prime time in 1964 before moving to Saturday mornings in 1967 (where it aired until the mid-1970s), the program followed the sci-fi exploits of spunky, yellow-haired Jonny Quest (voiced by young Tim Matheson), the eleven-year-old son of Dr. Benton Quest, famous scientist and head of a globe-trotting research intelligence team. Assisting them were bodyguard-pilot Roger "Race" Bannon, East Indian orphan Hadji, and Jonny's bulldog, Bandit. With the aid of a futuristic computer called the Unitized Neutronic Information Center, the team left their home base, Palm Key, an island in the Caribbean, to travel to exotic parts of the world, where they fought a variety of enemy spies, terrorists, thugs, and monsters. Regular villains included the Fu Manchu-esque Dr. Zin and femme fatale Jezebel Jade. One of the most nostalgically popular cartoons of the 1960s, *Jonny Quest* was a great show then—and it's a classic now.

JO POLNIACZEK

On prime time's *Facts of Life*, she was the streetwise sixteen-year-old from the Bronx—a combo of Henry Winkler's Fonz (*Happy Days*) and Kristy McNichol's Angel (*Little Darlings*)—who attended the prestigious Eastland School for Young Women on a scholarship. Although bestowed with a heart of gold, Jo maintained a tough exterior to mask her insecurities and self-doubts. She was constantly clashing with snooty rich bitch Blair Warner.

FYI: ▸ Although not gay, Jo and teen actress Nancy McKeon (who played her) are often credited with being the first childhood crush of many lesbians. Other lesbian icons of pop culture: Velma (*Scooby-Doo*), Sabrina Duncan (*Charlie's Angels*), Jane Hathaway (*Beverly Hillbillies*), Buddy Lawrence (*Family*), Zelda Gilroy (*Dobie Gillis*), George Fayne (*Nancy Drew*), Peppermint Patty (*Peanuts*), Chris Cagney (*Cagney and Lacey*), and every character played by actress Jodie Foster.

JORDACHE

Did you have the Jordache look? According to the whopping sales of these tight-fitting, European-cut designer jeans, most of you did—back when they were oh so popular back in the 1970s. Introduced in 1978 by the Nakash Brothers of Israel, Jordache's contemporaries included Sergio Valente and—ooh-la-la—Sassoon. A wild-maned horse on the rear pocket was the trademark.

JORDAN, MICHAEL

I don't know what amazes me more about this basketball superstar (born February 17, 1963), considered to be the greatest player in the history of the NBA. Maybe it's his superhuman ability to "catch air" by jumping higher than what seems possible. Maybe it's the astounding career stats as guard (number 23) with the Chicago Bulls (1984–98): 1,072 games; 41,011 minutes; 5,633 assists; 6,672 rebounds; six NBA championships; five MVP awards; and thirteen All-Star games. Maybe it's Jordan's whopping basketball salary of $35 million a year. It could be this money-machine's gazillion endorsements, particularly with Nike (Air Jordan footwear), earning him $80 million a year (in 1987, he was earning an estimated $178,100 a day). Could it be his amazing good looks (the shaved-head six-foot-six hunk was chosen as one of the fifty Most Beautiful People in the World by *People* magazine in 1991)? Wait, I know what it is! I'm amazed that Jordan had the honor of slam-dunking with legendary cartoon star Bugs Bunny in the 1996 film *Space Jam*. Whew!

FYI: ▸ Michael Jordan has a tattoo of the Greek letter "Omega" over his heart, representing Omega Psi Phi fraternity, of which he was a member at the University of North Carolina.

JOSEPHINE THE PLUMBER

Cordially helpful plumber (played by Jane Withers) who gave a thumbs-up for Comet household cleanser in a series of TV commercials that ran throughout the 1970s. One of Hollywood's great child actresses of the 1930s, Withers was best known as Shirley Temple's bratty rival, Joy Smythe, in the movie *Bright Eyes* (1934).

JOSIE AND THE PUSSYCATS

"We are the swingin' Pussycats, and we are here to make the scene, so tune us in on CBS, and see just what we mean!" At one time the flagship of CBS-TV's early-1970s Saturday-morning lineup, this outtasight cartoon was about an all-girl rock band whose concert tours took them to exotic locales, where they encountered all types of adventures. Dressed in leopard-print outfits with "long tails, and ears for hats," the purr-fectly marvelous trio consisted of Josie McCoy, the earnest lead singer and guitarist; Valerie Brown, the sensible African-American tambourine player; and Melody Valentine, the dumb-blonde drummer. Also on hand were cute stagehand Alan Mayberry, nervous manager Alexander Cabot III, his scheming sister Alexandra Cabot (Josie's pain in the neck), and Alexandra's mischievous cat Sebastian. Each show had a mixture of slapstick, mystery, music, and a dynamic "let's get out of here" chase scene showcasing the band running from nasty bad guys while a groovy Pussycat song played in the background. In the fall of 1972, the Hanna-Barbera program became known as *Josie and the Pussycats in Outer Space*, after the gang accidentally got blasted off into space.

As the all-female counterpart of The Archies, the Pussycats were also friends of the Riverdale gang, and the two groups frequently appeared in each other's comic books. Intensely popular with kids of the 1970s, they could be found as a variety of toy premiums, including stickers and patches inside loaves of Wonder Bread, or pencil topper erasers (Melody was the coveted one) and plastic cereal spoons shipped inside Honeycomb cereal boxes. Decades later, *Josie and the Pussycats* was filmed as a live-action, big-screen movie starring Rachael Leigh Cook as Josie, Rosario Dawson as Valerie, and Tara Reid as Melody and targeted to a teen audience that wasn't around during their initial appeal and that couldn't care less about them today.

FYI: ▸ Providing the singing voices of Josie and the Pussycats were Cathy Dougher (Josie), Patrice Holloway (Valerie), and future Charlie's Angel Cheryl Ladd (Melody).

JOSIE McCOY

The central character of the *Josie and the Pussycats* comic books and cartoon show was created in 1963 by animator Dan DeCarlo, who named her after his own wife, Josie. Competent and strong-willed, the redhead performed as the lead singer-guitarist for The Pussycats, an all-female rock band. Blond roadie Alan Mayberry was Josie's object of affection.

"JOY TO THE WORLD"

"Jeremiah was a bullfrog (da da dant). . . ." The biggest-selling single of 1971, performed by Three Dog Night and written by Hoyt Axton, spent a joyous six weeks at number one. It gave unsuspecting teenyboppers a pseudo-inspirational lesson on the Old Testament prophet Jeremiah. Some Christians in school choruses refused to sing the song because they felt it was "sacrilegious."

J.R. EWING

Called "that human oil slick" by *Time* magazine, the Texan from *Dallas* was the man TV viewers loved to hate throughout the 1980s. As mentioned before (see the *Dallas* entry), J.R. was scheming, manipulative, greedy, and out to ruin his opponents, deceive his friends, outfox his brothers, institutionalize his wife, and mislead his mistresses—all this while wearing a smile on his handsome face and a twinkle in his baby-blue eyes. Full name: John Ross Ewing Jr. Played wonderfully wicked by Larry Hagman, formerly of *I Dream of Jeannie* fame.

JUAN EPSTEIN

"My mother, the saint." Afro-puffed Puerto Rican Jewish kid (played by actor Robert Hegyes) seen as one of Gabe Kotter's delinquent Sweathogs on the TV sitcom *Welcome Back, Kotter*. He was known for daily taking to school excuse notes for his tardiness and unfinished homework—always signed "Epstein's Mother." Full name: Juan Luis Pedro Phillipo de Huevos Epstein.

JUDGE JUDY

"Justice with an attitude." Hard-as-nails Judy Sheindlin, a former family-court judge from New York, doesn't take any bull crap dealing with real-life small-claims cases on her syndicated courtroom TV show (1996–).

JUDY

Playful and prankish chimpanzee owned by teenage Paula Tracy on the hit family TV drama *Daktari* (1966–69). Judy also starred with Annette Funicello and Tommy Kirk in Walt Disney's *Monkey's Uncle* (1965). In the film's opening scene, she plays tambourine alongside The Beach Boys!

JUDY JETSON

Pretty and popular, the blonde, ponytailed pink-outfitted teenybopper from Hanna-Barbera's *Jetsons* cartoon attended Orbit High, where she danced the Solar Swivel and mooned over rock idol Jet Screamer.

JUDY MILLER

Gilda Radner's precocious, Brownie-outfitted youngster who hosted a variety show from her suburban family's living room on NBC's *Saturday Night Live*: "Oh, it's the show of the day / It's the show of the way / I am in it, oh, yes, I am, oh / It's the show of your life / It's the Ju-dy Mil-ler Show!"

JUDY ROBINSON

Norwegian blonde beauty queen Marta Kristen played the eldest teenage daughter on TV's sci-fi classic *Lost in Space* from 1965 to 1968. Pubescent lads of the era went ga-ga over this shapely knockout—dressed in a formfitting silver spacesuit—wishing they could get lost in space with her.

JUGHEAD JONES

This crown-wearing beanpole, from the *Archies* comics, was a bumbling, food-loving, lazy slacker-type who preferred hanging out with faithful mutt Hot Dog and buddy Archie Andrews to dating—ugh—girls! Jughead's real name: Forsythe P. Jones III.

JULIA

This pioneering TV sitcom was the first to depict a black female as an educated and independent professional (previous shows, such as *Beulah*, had featured them as domestics). Airing on NBC from 1968 to 1971, it starred singer Diahann Carroll as Julia Baker, a beautiful nurse working in the medical office of Astrospace Industries, a Los Angeles–based aerospace firm, for testy Dr. Morton Chegley (Lloyd Nolan). Living in a modern, integrated apartment building, Julia was the widowed mother of little Corey, played by Marc Copage (her husband, an Air Force pilot, had been killed in Vietnam). Other characters included Corey's best friend and white neighbor Earl J. Waggedorn (Michael Link), Earl's mother Marie Waggedorn (Betty Beaird), chief nurse Hannah Yarby (Lurene Tuttle), and Dr. Chegley's wife, Melba (Mary Wickes). In 1970, hunky Fred Williamson joined the cast as Steve Bruce, Julia's new boyfriend. A talking Julia doll, introduced as a friend of Barbie's by Mattel Toys in 1969, has become a highly sought-after collectible of recent years.

JULIE COOPER

The rebellious, headstrong seventeen-year-old daughter of Ann Romano on *One Day at a Time* was portrayed by Mackenzie Phillips, daughter of The

Mamas and the Papas' John Phillips. Julie later married Max Horvath, an airline flight attendant, and moved from Indianapolis to Houston.

JULIE McCOY

From 1977 to 1984, perky Lauren Tewes played *The Love Boat*'s perky cruise director with a perky Dorothy Hamill wedge haircut (and a perky cocaine addiction). Replaced in 1984 by sister Judy McCoy (Pat Klous).

JUMANJI

"In the jungle you must wait, 'til the dice roll five eight 8." Jumanji is a magical old board game with an African-safari theme that can trap players inside the game as well as unleash wild jungle animals loose in the neighborhood. Featured in the same-titled 1981 children's book by Chris Van Allsburg and in the 1995 movie starring Robin Williams as Alan Parrish, a twelve-year-old who gets trapped while playing Jumanji in 1969 and doesn't get released until twenty-six years later.

JUMPSUITS

We're not talking fat Elvis jumpsuits here; these are the shiny, metallic-looking, one-piece ones that zipped up the front and belted at the waist. In the early 1980s, they looked cool and sexy on rocker chicks like Joan Jett and Cherie Currie.

JUMP THE SHARK

On September 20, 1977, an episode of *Happy Days* had Fonzie overcoming his fear of sharks by water-skiing over a caged one—while wearing his leather jacket, no less. This totally absurd plotline left viewers with the feeling that the once-hot show had reached a peak and it would be all downhill from then on. Due to the Fonz's infamous stunt, the term "jump the shark" is used as a reference for the defining moment (like Cousin Oliver's arrival on *The Brady Bunch* and Laverne and Shirley's move from Milwaukee to Los Angeles) when a good TV show turns bad.

JUNE CLEAVER

Archetypal suburban mother and wife of 1950s TV, from the sitcom *Leave It to Beaver*, who cooked and cleaned house in heels and pearls. Her name today is used to describe a too-perfect mom and wife: "You're a regular June Cleaver."

FYI: ▸ Reportedly, Barbara Billingsley, who played June Cleaver, always wore a string of pearls as a self-conscious attempt to cover up a deep neck wrinkle.

JUNGLE BOOK

Brimming with cheerful animation and jazzy tunes, Disney Studio's nineteenth animated feature was loosely based on the classic tales of Rudyard Kipling. It told the story of ten-year-old Mowgli, the Man-Cub, who is abandoned at birth and raised by wolves in the jungle of India. A brave and wise panther, Bagheera, befriends and attempts to return the lad to the "man village." Reluctant to leave the jungle, Mowgli runs away and meets Baloo, a happy-go-lucky bear who teaches him the "bare necessities of life." After Mowgli is kidnapped by the devious ape leader King Louie and terrorized by both the evil tiger Shere Khan and the slithering snake Kaa, Bagheera and Baloo team together to rescue the boy. At the end, Mowgli falls in love with a beautiful Indian girl on the edge of the forest and is lured to civilization.

Directed by Wolfgang Reitherman, the 1967 film featured a talented cast of actors providing voices: Phil Harris as Baloo, Sebastian Cabot as Bagheera, Bruce Reitherman (the director's son) as Mowgli, Louis Prima as King Louie, George Sanders as Shere Khan, Sterling Holloway as Kaa, and J. Pat O'Malley as Colonel Hathi, leader of the "dawn patrol" of elephants. Its extremely catchy songs include "I Wanna Be Like You," "Trust in Me," "My Own Home," "Colonel Hathi's March," and the Oscar-nominated "The Bare Necessities." This was the last film personally supervised by Walt Disney.

JUNGLE OF NOOL

The forest home of Horton, the beloved storybook elephant in the Dr. Seuss books *Horton Hears a Who* and *Horton Hatches the Egg*.

JUNK FOOD

All right, let's pretend it's 1978 and you are hosting a happenin' shindig for twenty of your closest friends. Partying is a lot of work, so the gang will inevitably work up a serious case of the munchies. So, here is my recommended list of favorite snacks to have readily available for all those teenage junk-food junkies.

- **Chips.** Bugles; Cheetos; cheese puffs; Cheez Doodles; Chex Party Mix; Doo Dads; Doritos; Fritos Corn Chips; Funyuns; Guys Potato Chips; Lay's Potato Chips; Mr. Salty Pretzels; Munchos Potato Chips; O'Boise's Potato Chips; Potato Sticks; Pringles Potato Chips; Ruffles Potato Chips; and Wise Potato Chips
- **Crackers.** Cheez-Its; Chicken in a Biskit; Goldfish; Hi Ho Crackers; Keebler Townhouse Crackers; and Ritz Crackers
- **Dips.** Bean dip; Cheez Whiz; Easy Cheese; fondue; guacamole; Hidden Valley Ranch dip; onion dip; Ro-Tel and Velveeta cheese dip; and salsa
- **Sweets.** Brach's Bridge Mix; brownies; Chips Ahoy Chocolate Chip Cookies; Cracker Jack; Crunch 'n Munch; Fiddle Faddle; Fig Newtons; graham crackers; Hostess Snack Cakes; Krispy Kreme Donuts; Lemon Coolers; M&M's; Mallomars; marshmallows; Moon Pies; Nutter Butters; Oreo Cookies; Rice Krispies Treats; Scooter Pies; Screaming Yellow Zonkers; and S'mores
- **Miscellaneous.** Beef Jerky; Corn Nuts; deviled eggs; Jeno's Pizza Rolls; Jiffy Pop popcorn; Pigs-in-a-Blanket; Planters Peanuts; relish tray consisting of olives, pickles, and raw vegetables (carrots, cauliflower, broccoli, and celery) for dipping; Slim Jims; Spam slices; sunflower seeds; Sunmaid raisins; and Vienna Sausages

JUPITER 2

In *Lost in Space*, the Robinson family rockets through space—hopelessly lost—in this spacecraft-home. Shaped like a silver-tinted, upside-down pie pan, the Jupiter had all the luxuries of futuristic life, circa 1997, including cryo-hibernation tubes to put each family member in a deep sleep for sound-breaking space travel.

JURASSIC PARK

Fantastic amusement park located on Isla Nubar, a remote island off the Costa Rican coast, where a zoo houses live dinosaurs cloned from DNA extracted from prehistoric fossils. Unfortunately, the theme park's concept is too good to be true, as employee sabotage causes the security system to break down, permitting the creatures to escape from their pens and hunt the visitors. The island's predicament is the premise of Michael Crichton's 1990 best-selling novel and director Steven Spielberg's 1993 thrill-adventure film, starring Sam Neill as Alan Grant, Laura Dern as Ellie Sattler, and Jeff Goldblum as Ian Malcolm. A triumph of technology, the movie leaves you awestruck upon viewing footage of live action blended with computer-generated imagery, allowing dinosaurs, such as a brachiosaurus or a triceratops, to look more realistic than ever. The most frightening scenes are the earth-thundering T-Rex attack on two stalled theme-park vehicles, and the marauding raptors chasing two little kids through a restaurant's abandoned kitchen. Spielberg's *Jurassic Park* knocked his own *E.T.* (1982) out of first place as the highest-grossing film of all time ($900 million worldwide). Like all good moneymakers, it spawned three sequels and an action-figure toy line.

JUSTICE LEAGUE OF AMERICA

A collection of superhero crime-fighters based on the *DC* comic books. Included Aquaman, Batman and Robin, the Flash, the Green Lantern, Superman, and Wonder Woman. The dishonorable Legion of Doom, led by Superman's archenemy Lex Luthor, were the JLA's evil emissaries.

ghijkl

KABOOM

The classic balloon-busting game was introduced by Ideal in 1966. The idea was to put a balloon on the plastic Kaboom machine (shaped like an old factory) and to take turns pushing on a pump that would cause it to inflate. The player who pumped the most times without causing the balloon to go "kaboom" won the game. Parents didn't really like Kaboom; the noise of bursting balloons made them nervous, and they worried that exploding balloon bits might put an eye out.

KANGA AND ROO

Marsupial twosome—kindly mother (Kanga) and playful baby (Roo)—featured in the *Winnie the Pooh* stories. Young Clint Howard (Ron's brother) voiced little Roo in the very first Disney cartoon featurette, *Winnie the Pooh and the Honey Tree* (1966).

KAOS

Featured on the prime-time spy spoof *Get Smart*, the diabolical underground agency with plans to rule the world was the nemesis of CONTROL, an American government agency. Two of KAOS' most sinister agents were Conrad Siegfried, a menacing German who was related to the infamous Red Baron, and the Groovy Guru, a hippie baddie who wanted to take over the minds of America's teenagers.

KAPTAIN KOOL AND THE KONGS

Made-to-order rock band assembled as hosts of *The Krofft Supershow*, airing on Saturday mornings from 1976 to 1978 and consisting of Kaptain Kool (Michael Lembeck), Superchick (Debra Clinger), Turkey (Mickey McMeel), and Nashville (Louise DuArt). Besides singing crappy bubblegum tunes, the KK&K's job was to introduce the different serial installments that appeared on the variety program, like ElectraWoman and DynaGirl, Wonderbug, and Dr. Shrinker.

FYI: ▸ Michael Lembeck is the son of Harvey Lembeck, remembered best for playing biker Erich Von Zipper in the *Beach Party* films of the 1960s. He would later co-star as Max Horvath (Julie Cooper's hubby) on prime time's *One Day at a Time* and become an Emmy-winning sitcom director (*Friends, Mad About You,* and *NewsRadio*). His sister Helaine Lembeck played goody-two-shoes Judy Borden on *Welcome Back, Kotter.*

KARAOKE
A barroom pastime that translates in Japanese as "really bad singing," particularly after suffering through liquored-up would-be singers belting out tone-deaf renditions of "I Will Survive," "Love Shack," or "Friends in Low Places." All kidding aside, the actual Japanese translation of karaoke is "empty orchestra."

KARATE KID
In the 1984 movie, a lonely New Jersey teen, Daniel LaRusso (Ralph Macchio), moves to a new high school in Southern California after his single mother is transferred with her job. Because of his dark Italian looks and East Coast accent, Daniel is bullied by the school's blond-maned surfer crowd, led by karate champ Johnny Lawrence (William Zabka). Daniel's only friend is a pretty classmate, Ali Mills (Elisabeth Shue), who happens to be the ex-girlfriend of the jealous Johnny. Upon receiving a bloody beating by Johnny and his karate-chopping buds, Daniel is rescued by an elderly Okinawan handyman, Mr. Miyagi (Oscar-nominated Noriyuki "Pat" Morita), who teaches him the secrets of martial arts. Following months of training, "Daniel-San" gets revenge against his tormentors in the All Valley Karate Championship. Directed by John G. Avildsen, this feel-good film in the *Rocky* vein gave birth to three sequels and a Saturday-morning cartoon.

KAREN
In the perennial Christmas favorite *Frosty the Snowman*, this little grammar-school girl with the blonde ponytail and red winter coat befriends Frosty and travels with him to the wintry North Pole.

KAREN CARPENTER STORY
The highly rated 1989 made-for-TV bio-pic, starring Cynthia Gibb as Karen Carpenter and Mitchell Anderson as big brother Richard Carpenter, showcased the dark side of the sunny pop star's rise to fame and her death from anorexia nervosa. Louise Fletcher co-starred as Karen's controlling, overbearing mother, Agnes Carpenter.

KATE BRADLEY
Bea Benaderet's good-natured widow who ran Hooterville's Shady Rest Hotel with her three gorgeous daughters—Billie Jo, Bobbie Jo, and Betty Jo—on TV's *Petticoat Junction*. Kate was always at odds with the fancy-suited executives at the CF&W Railroad, because they were trying to shut down the train tracks to the Shady Rest and put out of business the Cannonball, an old-fashioned steam-driven train (the only transit to her hotel).

KATIE MILLER
Impertinent Tina Cole played the pretty, blonde sweetheart of Robbie Douglas, whom she met at college in Los Angeles, on *My Three Sons*. After getting married, the newlyweds moved in with Robbie's family and later gave birth to triplets: Steve Jr., Charley, and Robbie II.

KATO
"Faster, Kato!" Kato was the karate-chopping, kick-boxing manservant and sidekick of the Green Hornet, who also chauffeured the superhero's slick Black Beauty automobile. Legendary martial-arts star Bruce Lee played him on the classic *Green Hornet* TV series from 1966 to 1967.

K.C. AND THE SUNSHINE BAND
Rhythm-and-blues group at the forefront of the 1970s disco dance revolution, known for horn-driven party music. Formed in Florida by singer-keyboardist Harry "K.C." Casey and bass guitarist Richard Finch, the largely interracial Sunshine Band consisted of seven to eleven members, including the original lineup of guitarist Jerome Smith, drummer Robert Johnson, and conga player Fermin Goytisolo. In the summer of 1975, they scored their first number-one smash with the distinctive-sounding "Get Down Tonight" ("Do a little dance / Make a little love / Get down tonight . . . "). It was followed by the risqué—"uh-huh, uh-huh"—"That's the Way (I Like It)" (1975), along with "Shake Your Booty" (1976), "I'm Your Boogie Man" (1977), "Keep It Comin' Love" (1977), "Boogie Shoes" (1978), and the ballad "Please Don't Go" (1979). In January 1982, the group's career was put on hiatus following K.C.'s life-threatening auto accident in his hometown of Hialeah, Florida. The accident left K.C. with a nerve injury that caused him to lose all feeling on the right side of his body and to be unable to walk for almost a year. Today, he is fully re-

habilitated, and the Sunshine Band can be seen playing their funky horns at disco revival shows.

KEANE, WALTER AND MARGARET
Husband-and-wife artist team who created the Big Eyes paintings of the 1960s—you know, the rather creepy, undernourished-looking waifs (my friend Jennifer refers to them as the heroin-addicted children) whose oversized eyes follow you around the room no matter where you stand. It's now known that Margaret painted all the Keane paintings and that her abusive husband took all the credit (allegedly he threatened to kill her if she told the truth). They divorced.

KEDS
Canvas sneakers, popular with youngsters, especially girls. The name was a contraction of "kid" and "ped."

KEEBLER ELVES
According to the TV ads, the delicious Keebler cookies and crackers were baked in a "magic oven" by little elves who lived in a hollow tree. Created in 1966, these sprites were named after Godfrey Keebler, a baker who founded the United Biscuit Company, which later evolved into Keebler. Over the years, there have been three head advertising elves. First was an uptight fellow named J. J. Keebler, who was followed briefly by a lackluster boss, Ollie Keebler, and finally by Ernie Keebler, who's been playfully promoting the company's "uncommonly good" products ever since. Best known of the Keebler goodies: Chips Deluxe, E. L. Fudge, Fudge Shoppe, Pecan Sandies, Town House Crackers, Wheatables, and Zesta Saltines.

"KEEP AMERICA BEAUTIFUL"
The disheartening antipollution public-service announcement featuring the tearful Native American (Iron Eyes Cody) standing on a hillside overlooking a littered landscape. Originally aired on the first Earth Day, in 1971.

"KEEP ON TRUCKIN'"
Expression used in the 1970s as an alternative to good-bye. It was commonly spotted on T-shirts and posters paired with a comic character depicting a long-haired Grateful Dead–type wearing archetypal hippie gear: Birkenstocks, bell-bottoms, tie-dye, peace-sign pendant, headband, and granny sunglasses.

KEITH PARTRIDGE
Teen dream king David Cassidy played the sixteen-year-old lead singer of The Partridge Family from 1970 to 1974. Keith's cute high school looks, with dreamy green eyes and kissable smile, made him an irresistible pinup boy for teenage gals. His pukka-shell choker necklaces, rib-tight shirts, and blow-dried, shoulder-length shag made him a fashion role-model for young men.

KELLY, EMMETT
America's most famous circus clown, known best for his portrayal of "Weary Willie," the hobo character who performed the "Sweeping the Spotlight" routine, which now has become a pantomime classic. Kelly was a star attraction of the Ringling Brothers Barnum and Bailey Circus for more than fifteen years, and was Eastman Kodak's Ambassador of Goodwill at the 1964 New York World's Fair.

KELLY BUNDY
On *Married . . . with Children*, Christina Applegate's hot blonde bimbo was full of ignorant malapropisms, playfully called Kellyisms ("I'm an Aquarium," "It's so hot you could lay an egg on the sidewalk," or "E before O except before E-I-E-I-O"). As a teenager, Kelly attended James K. Polk High School in suburban Chicago, where she dated hoodlums and aspired to be a floozy.

KELLY GARRETT
The brown-haired Texas beauty, an ex-stewardess and former Vegas showgirl with a past, was one of three supersleuths on prime time's *Charlie's Angels.* Played by former Breck Shampoo girl Jaclyn Smith.

KEN

"I never bothered with romance, or gave any boy a second glance, and then I met Ken."
—BARBIE DOLL

"Ken. He's a doll!" In 1961, this cute twelve-inch-tall boy-next-door was introduced as Barbie Doll's one and only love interest and named after the son of Elliot and Ruth Handler, owners of Mattel Toys and creators of Barbie. (Barbie was named after their daughter Barbara.) Although slightly on the skinny side, Ken made the perfect dream date for Barbie. He was the football player to her cheerleader. The prom king to her prom queen. The Romeo to her Juliet. And yes—the groom to her bride. Ken mysteriously disappeared in 1968—and in spite of coming back a year later as a Talking Ken sporting a groovy new look, he couldn't shake the rumors about running off to Canada to avoid the Vietnam War draft. Completely redesigned, he was now more handsome—resembling TV's Major Tony Nelson—with a mod haircut, long sideburns, and a thicker, hunkier body (including well-defined calves). Through the years there have been many different styles of Ken Dolls, most notably Malibu Ken (1970), Busy Ken (1971), Mod Hair Ken (1972), Sun Valley Ken (1973), Now Look Ken (1975), SuperStar Ken (1977), Sport & Shave Ken (1979), All Star Ken (1981), Dream Date Ken (1982), and Great Shapes Ken (1983). One thing that hasn't changed is Ken's lack of male genitalia, but despite criticism for being sexless and dull, he still excites our dear Barbie—or he did up until Valentine's Day 2004. On the eve of Cupid's romantic holiday, dolldom's perfect pair announced they have called it splits. (A spokesperson for Mattel said Barbie and Ken "will remain friends.")

FYI: ▸ Ken wasn't the only guy in Barbieland. Other fellows included Allan, Ken's best friend and Midge's boyfriend; Brad, Christie's black boyfriend; Curtis, Cara's black boyfriend; Derek, Ken's Hispanic "Rocker" friend; Ricky, Skipper's preteen boyfriend; and Todd, Barbie's little brother and twin of Tutti.

KEN "HUTCH" HUTCHINSON

The handsome, fair-haired half of the crime-battling "buddy" team *Starsky and Hutch* was also the better-dressed, more educated, and more gentle half. Surly David Soul, who portrayed Hutch from 1975 to 1979, previously co-starred as Joshua Bolt on prime time's *Here Come the Brides* (1968–70) and scored a chart-topping Top Forty single, "Don't Give Up on Us" (1977).

KENICKIE

"A hickey from Kenickie is like a Hallmark card." Danny Zuko's tough-talking best pal and fellow T-Bird was played by Jeff Conaway in the movie musical *Grease* (1978).

KEN-L RATION

The dog food brand's TV ads had kids singing: "My dog's better than your dog / My dog's better than yours / My dog's better 'cause he eats Ken-L Ration / My dog's better than yours!"

KENNEDY, JOHN, JR.

The son of John and Jacqueline Kennedy was born on November 25, 1960, sixteen days after his father was elected as the youngest President in U.S. history. As an infant in the land of Camelot (the Kennedy White House), he was America's prince—affectionately called John-John by the press—who played under his doting dad's desk in the Oval Office. On the day of his third birthday, the world wept as the littlest Kennedy bravely saluted the coffin of his assassinated father when it passed before him. He would grow up in the public eye, having inherited his father's relaxed attitude and his mother's genius for being teasingly aloof—two traits that allowed him to appear comfortable around the ever-lurking paparazzi cameras.

In the 1980s, Kennedy had matured into a tall, handsome man with a head of thick, wavy brown hair, a lean, muscular body, and a broad chest. Athletic and outgoing, he was occasionally seen rollerblading, jogging, cycling, or playing Frisbee in New York's Central Park. He attended Brown University to study law and experienced the highly publicized (and highly human) misfortune of failing the New York bar exam not once but twice ("Hunk Flunks" screamed tabloid headlines). It didn't matter that John Jr. came off as slacker material, because he was America's most eligible bachelor, whom *People* magazine dubbed "The Sexiest Man Alive!"

On September 21, 1996, millions of women were left brokenhearted when prince charming married his princess—statuesque blonde Carolyn Bessette—in a supersecret wedding ceremony, outfoxing the always-prying media. Kennedy set out to prove that he was not just another rich kid getting by on a famous name. He showed evidence of inheriting his dad's flair for politics and journalism by becoming the founder and editor of the offbeat political magazine *George*. Among other things, he donated $50,000 to a Harlem school program and established Reaching Up, a charity to help the poor and disabled. It seemed fitting that some day he might be President.

On the night of July 16, 1999, the dreadful Kennedy family curse struck again. Kennedy, his wife, Carolyn, and her sister Lauren Bessette set off on his single-engine Piper Saratoga to attend cousin Rory Kennedy's wedding in Hyannisport. Apparently confused by the thick haze on a hot summer night, they plunged into the Atlantic Ocean off the coast of Martha's Vineyard. After a five-day search, the bodies were found amid the wreckage of the plane strewn on the ocean floor.

Like the sudden death of Princess Diana, John's tragic demise stunned the world—especially those of us too young to remember his father as President. We grew up with him even though we did not know him personally. He came off like a regular guy—okay, a good-looking, glamorous, rich one, but a regular guy nevertheless—whom we could hang out with, chat with, share a cappuccino with, and rollerblade with. Unlike a lot of people born into famous families (Princess Stephanie, Lisa Marie Presley, Paris Hilton, and some of the Kennedy cousins), he never came across as a spoiled brat, only friendly and well mannered. JFK Jr. tried to make a difference in this world and will be missed for all the great things he would have accomplished.

KENNER TOYS

"It's Kenner—it's fun!" The Cincinnati-based toy manufacturer enjoyed success in the Baby Boomer years with the Easy-Bake Oven, Give-a-Show Projector, Spirograph, Smash-Up Derby, SSP Racers, Baby Alive, Close 'n' Play phonograph, and Girder and Panel building set. Kenner's Gen-X favorites included Care Bears, Strawberry Shortcake, Darci, Stretch Armstrong, Sit 'n' Spin, and the best-selling *Star Wars* action-figure line. Formed in 1947 by the Steiner brothers—Albert, Philip, and Joseph—the company is named after its original office location on Kenner Street.

KENNINGTON

If you were to wear a plushy velour or terrycloth V-neck pullover shirt back in the late 1970s and early 1980s, this would have been the cool brand to sport.

KENNY McCORMICK

"Oh my god, they killed Kenny! You bastards!" Every week, millions of TV viewers tune in to the *South Park* cartoon show on Comedy Central to find out what horrible way this ill-fated little boy wearing the orange hooded coat will die. Extremely poor, muffled-voice Kenny lives in a run-down shack with his violently drunk family.

KENTUCKY FRIED CHICKEN

Founded by Colonel Harlan Sanders in Kentucky in 1939, a fast-food restaurant chain famous for pressure-cooked deep-fried chicken that's "finger lickin' good" and served in family-sized buckets. Renamed KFC in order to eliminate the word "fried" for the health-conscious 1990s.

FYI: ▸ In one year, KFC sells 541 million chickens worldwide.

KERMIT THE FROG

The personable, wisecracking green amphibian was the reporter for *Sesame Street* news before becoming master of ceremonies on TV's *Muppet Show* and later a big-screen star (*The Muppet Movie*) and recording artist ("Rainbow Connection"). Continually avoids the amorous advances (and karate chops) of prima donna Miss Piggy, his lovesick sidekick, in most *Muppet* ventures. Muppet creator the late Jim Henson originally voiced Kermie.

KERPLUNK

"To win it all, don't let the marbles fall!" Introduced in 1967 by Ideal Toys, this classic was described as "a tantalizing game of nerve and skill." To play Kerplunk, you stuck thirty plastic toothpicks into the midsection of a clear-plastic cylinder, then poured forty marbles in through the top. Each player took turns removing the toothpicks one at a time without triggering a marble avalanche ("kerplunk!"). Other great action games by Ideal included Battling Tops, Crazy Clock, Hands Down, Kaboom, Mouse Trap, Poppin' Hoppies, Rebound, Snake's Alive, Tip-It, and Toss Across.

KEVIN ARNOLD

"In seventh grade, who you are
is what other seventh-graders say you are."
—KEVIN ARNOLD (FRED SAVAGE)

Inquisitive and very observant teenager whose growing-up experiences in suburban America in the late 1960s were captured superbly in the TV sitcom *The Wonder Years*. Portrayed by juvenile actor Fred Savage.

KEVIN McCALLISTER

Child star Macaulay Culkin played this resourceful eight-year-old who battles inept burglars after his parents accidentally leave him "home alone" in suburban Chicago when they fly to Paris for the Christmas holiday. Following the box-office success of *Home Alone* (1990), sweet-faced Culkin became cinema's top juvenile actor of the 1990s, starring in *My Girl* (1991), *Home Alone 2* (1992), *The Pagemaster* (1994), and *Richie Rich* (1994)—before puberty ended his sizzling career.

KEWPIE

Most people today associate Kewpie, whose name means "small cupid," with a prize won at a carnival, but almost a century ago the round-faced, big-eyed doll with the curly topknot was the rage of the toy world. In all shapes and sizes, every little girl had to have a Kewpie (just like their future granddaughters had to have a Cabbage Patch Kid in the 1980s). The happy elfin was modeled on illustrations created in 1909 by Rose O'Neill for *Ladies' Home Journal* before being manufactured as a doll in 1913. As a treasured collectible today, fervent Kewpie collectors gather in the Ozark town of Branson, Missouri, for the yearly Kewpiesta.

KICKBALL

If you were a kid during the 1970s, it was nearly impossible not to have participated in a rousing game of kickball, a popular elementary-school team sport played with mixed teams of boys and girls. Its rules were similar to baseball, including game layout: a diamond-shaped field with bases (first, second, third, and home) and pitcher's mound. But instead of baseballs, gloves, and bats, the only equipment necessary was a soft rubber dodgeball.

To play kickball, players were divided into two teams, and then the refereeing teacher tossed a quarter to see who kicked first. The pitcher rolled the ball to the kicker-up, who attempted to kick it. The secret was to kick it low and hard so it careened far to the outfield. If you kicked it too high, the opposing team could catch it, putting you out. After kicking, you ran to first base while trying to dodge the ball, which was picked up from the ground and thrown at you (many kids ended up with the air knocked out of them from being hit too hard). Then you waited for the next player to kick the ball before you made a mad dash to second base. The object was to make it to home base without getting tagged. Usually, after three or four innings, the teams with the most points won.

Unfortunately, with kickball the teams were chosen by captains (always the best jocks in class) who would take turns picking players one by one, giving many of us the humiliating experience of being the last one picked. Teachers with compassion for the athletically challenged would do the "even-odd" thing!

KIDDIE CHANTS

Here are fifty well-known jingles, jump-rope rhymes, and singsong parodies that we kids chanted while we playing in schoolyards, playgrounds, and on backyard swing sets, teeter-totters, and jungle gyms:

- "Beans, beans, good for your heart / The more you eat the more you fart."
- "Bubblegum, bubblegum in a dish / How many pieces do you wish?"
- "Chinese, Japanese, dirty knees / Look at these." (Point to your tits.)
- "Cinderella, dressed in yellow, went upstairs to kiss her fellow / Made a mistake and kissed a snake / How many doctors did it take? / One, two, three, four. . . ."
- "Coca-Cola went to town / Pepsi-Cola knocked him down / Dr. Pepper fixed him up / Then they all drank Seven-Up."
- "Cross my heart, and hope to die / Stick a needle in my eye."
- "Don't say ain't, your mother will faint / Your father will fall in a bucket of paint / Your sister

will cry / Your brother will die / Your cat and dog will call the F.B.I."

- "Eeny, meeny, miny, mo / Catch a tiger by his toe / If he hollers let him go / My mother said to pick the very best one, and you are not it."
- "Fatty and Skinny, lying in bed / Fatty rolled over, and Skinny was dead / Fatty called the doctor, and the doctor said: 'One more roll and we'll all be dead.'"
- "Fatty, Fatty, two by four / Can't fit through the kitchen door."
- "Find a penny, pick it up, and you will always have good luck."
- "Firecracker! Firecracker! / Boom, boom, boom! / Firecracker! Firecracker! / Boom, boom, boom! / The boys got the muscles / The teachers got the brains / The girls got the pretty looks, and we won the game!" (As a cheerleader chant, participants would shake their hips vigorously during the "Boom, boom, boom" part.)
- "Fuzzy Wuzzy was a bear / Fuzzy Wuzzy had no hair / Fuzzy Wuzzy wasn't fuzzy was he?"
- "Glory, glory, hallelujah / Teacher hit me with a ruler / Hid behind the door with a loaded forty-four / And my teacher ain't teachin' no more."
- "Happy Birthday to you / Happy Birthday to you / You look like a monkey, and you smell like one too."
- "Here comes the bride, all fat and wide / Here comes the groom, thin as a broom."
- "Here I sit, all brokenhearted / Came to shit, but only farted."
- "I love myself, I think I'm grand / I sit and hold my pretty hand / When I grow up, I'll marry me / And try to raise a family."
- "I scream, you scream, we all scream for ice cream."
- "I see London / I see France / I see (*insert name*)'s underpants."
- "I'm Popeye the sailor man / I live in a garbage can / I eat all the worms, and suck all the germs / I'm Popeye the sailor man."
- "I'm like rubber, you're like glue / What you say bounces off me, and sticks to you."
- "(*Insert boy's name*) and (*insert girl's name*) sitting in a tree / K-I-S-S-I-N-G / First comes love, then comes marriage / Then comes [same girl's name] with a baby carriage."
- "Ip dip, dog shit / You are not it!"
- "It's about time / It's about space / It's about time to wash your face."
- "It's raining, it's pouring / The old man is snoring / Jumped in bed and bumped his head / And didn't get up in the morning."
- "Jingle bells, Batman smells, Robin laid an egg / Batmobile lost its wheel, and the Joker got away."
- "King Kong played ping-pong with his ding-dong."
- "Liar, liar / Pants on fire / Nose as long as a telephone wire."
- "Lizzie Borden took an axe and gave her mother forty whacks / When she realized what she'd done, she gave her father forty-one."
- "Mama Mia, Papa Pia, Baby's got the diarrhea."
- "Marijuana, marijuana / LSD, LSD / College kids make it / High school kids take it / Why can't we, why can't we?"
- "McDonald's is our kind of place / Hamburgers in your face / French fries up your nose / Apple pies between your toes / And don't forget those chocolate shakes / They taste like polluted lakes / McDonald's is our kinda place!"
- "Me Chinese / Me play joke / Me put pee pee in your Coke."
- "Milk, milk / Lemonade / 'Round the corner fudge is made."
- "Miss Susie had a steamboat / The steamboat had a bell / Miss Susie went to heaven / The steamboat went to hell."
- "Missed me, missed me / Now ya gotta kiss me."
- "My brother lies over the ocean / My sister lies over the sea / My daddy lies over my mommy / And that's how they created me."
- "No more pencils / No more books / No more teacher's dirty looks / When the teacher rings the bell / We'll drop our books and run like hell."
- "On top of spaghetti, all covered with cheese / I lost my poor meatball, when somebody sneezed / It rolled off the table, and onto the floor / And then my poor meatball rolled out of the door."
- "One potato, two potato, three potato, four / Five potato, six potato, seven potato, more."
- "One, two, buckle my shoe / Three, four, shut the door / Five, six, pick up sticks / Seven, eight, lay them straight / Nine, ten, do it again."

- "Pease porridge hot / Pease porridge cold / Pease porridge in the pot four days old."
- "Rain, rain, go away / Come again some other day."
- "Sticks and stones may break my bones, but words will never hurt me."
- "There's a place in France / Where the naked ladies dance / There's a hole in the wall / Where the men can see it all."
- "Trick or treat, smell my feet / Give me something good to eat / If you don't, I don't care / I'll pull down your underwear."
- "We need a pitcher, not a belly-itcher / We need a catcher, not a belly-scratcher."
- "When you're sliding into first, and you feel something burst / Diarrhea, cha-cha-cha! Diarrhea! / When you're sliding into third, and you lay a juicy turd / Diarrhea, cha-cha-cha! Diarrhea! / When you're sliding into home, and you feel something foam / Diarrhea, cha-cha-cha! Diarrhea!"
- "The worms crawl in / The worms crawl out / In your stomach, and out your mouth."

KIDDLE KOLOGNES

"Really smells sweet, just like her name!" Introduced in 1968, two-inch-tall Liddle Kiddles that came housed inside plastic perfume bottles. Each doll was scented with the floral-sweet fragrance of its name: Rosebud, Violet, Honeysuckle, Sweet Pea, Apple Blossom, Orange Blossom, Bluebell, Gardenia, and Lily of the Valley. Along with Lucky Locket Kiddles, these are probably the best remembered of Mattel's enormously popular Kiddles doll line, and those who played with them can still recall their unique smell to this day.

KID GLOVES

Pristine-white wrist-length gloves, nicknamed "kid gloves" because they were commonly worn by little girls for dress-up occasions (church, weddings, holidays, the theater, and so on) throughout the 1950s and '60s. Although not little girls, adult sexpots in the Ginger Grant mode would wear longer, elbow-length gloves (if a guy was lucky, she'd strip-tease them off) with sexy evening gowns (and if he was even luckier, she'd strip that off too).

KID 'N PLAY

Hip-hop music duo of the 1990s who became stars of a hit feature film, *House Party* (1990), plus two sequels. Also, cartoon characters of a short-lived Saturday-morning series, *Kid 'n Play* (1990). To tell the likeable rappers apart, Kid (Christopher Reid) was the one with the sky-high flat-top and Play (Christopher Martin) was the one without the sky-high flat-top.

KID POWER

"White, yellow, black, or red, it's up to Kid Power!" From 1972 to 1974, cartoonist Morrie Turner's *Wee Pals*, a multicultural gang of schoolchildren seen in newspapers as a comic strip, starred in their own Saturday-morning cartoon series, produced by Rankin/Bass. "Kid Power is beautiful, baby!"

"KIDS IN AMERICA"

"New York to East California, there's a new wave comin', I warn ya. . . ." When Kim Wilde sang these words in her 1982 hit single, who would have guessed that this Brit was accurately predicting the coming New Wave music invasion that saturated U.S. airwaves throughout the 1980s? Ironically, she left out the kids living in L.A. and the rest of western California, where most of the American music scene was happening. For a lot of post-Boomer kids, the song was an anthem of sorts. After many years of being bombarded with easy-listening soul (for example, Kool and the Gang and Lionel Richie), easy-listening soft rock (Air Supply and Hall and Oates, for instance), and easy-listening pseudo-punk rock (including Loverboy and Quarterflash), they wanted something new, something different, and "Kids in America," with its spunky blend of synthesized rhythms mixed with bubblegum pop, was it. The daughter of 1960s singer Marty Wilde, Kim (born November 18, 1960) would later top the U.S. charts with the 1986 remake of The Supremes' "You Keep Me Hangin' On."

KIMBA THE WHITE LION

An animated gem from the 1960s about the adventures of kindhearted Kimba, a rare white lion cub who ruled an inherited animal kingdom in Africa 4,000 years ago. A friend of all, the little lion-prince bravely followed in the pawprints of his father, patrolling the jungle in order to maintain the peace. Kimba's father, King Caesar, was killed by hunters, and his mother, Queen Snoweene, was trapped by hunters and taken to a zoo. Kimba was joined on his adventures by sweet feline female companion Kitty and an assortment of other animal pals, including Bucky Deer, Dodie Deer, Dan'l Baboon, Pauley Cracker, King Speckle Rex, and mysterious Cassius the Panther. Archnemesis Claw, a wicked lion, along with a pair of evil hyena henchmen, Tab and Tom, wanted to take over Kimba's harmonious kingdom. Based on Japan's 1950s animated series *Jungle Taitei* (translation: Jungle Emperor), this Japanese-produced cartoon aired on American syndicated TV from 1966 to 1967. Its animation team went on to create the legendary *Speed Racer* in 1967.

FYI: ▸ Disney's popular *Lion King* (1994) seems to parallel *Kimba the White Lion*. For example, both have cub heroes who inherit an African kingdom (Kimba / Simba); cub girlfriends (Kimba's Kitty / Simba's Nala); jungle pals (Simba had Pumbaa and Timon); wise advisers (Kimba's Cassius / Simba's Rifiki); and lion bad-guys with hyena henchmen (Kimba's Claw / Simba's Scar).

KIMBERLY DRUMMOND

The ill-fated Dana Plato appeared as millionaire Philip Drummond's fair-haired teenage daughter on the TV sitcom *Diff'rent Strokes* from 1978 to 1984. She becomes the big "sister" of two black youths from Harlem, Arnold and Willis.

KING, BILLIE JEAN

American tennis champion who beat male chauvinist Bobby Riggs in the heavily promoted "Battle of the Sexes" match on September 20, 1973, at the Houston Astrodome.

FYI: ▸ Billie Jean King became the first female athlete in history to earn more than a million dollars in a single year.

KING, STEPHEN

The greatest horror-fiction writer of modern times. Born on September 21, 1947, in Portland, Maine, the blockbuster novelist has been referred to as the undisputed master of psychological terror and the contemporary equivalent of Edgar Allan Poe. King's spine-chilling, supernatural stories, set in the everyday world among ordinary middle-class citizens (often in the fictional hamlet of Castle Rock, Maine), are famous for displaying the evil lurking in the dark side of the human soul. His best-sellers include the novels *Carrie* (1974), *Salem's Lot* (1975), *The Shining* (1977), *The Stand* (1978), *The Dead Zone* (1979), *Firestarter* (1980), *Cujo* (1981), *Christine* (1983), *Pet Sematary* (1982), *It* (1986), *Misery* (1987), *The Tommyknockers* (1987), and *The Dark Half* (1989), plus the short stories *The Body* (a.k.a. *Stand by Me*), *Cycle of the Werewolf* (a.k.a. *Silver Bullet*), *Trucks* (a.k.a. *Maximum Overdrive*), *Children of the Corn*, and *Rita Hayworth and the Shawshank Redemption* (a.k.a. *The Shawshank Redemption*). Almost all King's works have been adapted to both the big screen and the small screen, with different degrees of success, the most notable being *Carrie* (1976), starring Sissy Spacek; *The Shining* (1980), starring Jack Nicholson and Shelley Duvall; *Misery* (1990), starring James Caan and Kathy Bates; and *The Shawshank Redemption* (1994), starring Tim Robbins and Morgan Freeman.

FYI: ▸ Stephen King says his favorite holiday is—you guessed it—Halloween!

KING BOWSER KOOPA

Sinister, fire-breathing dragon-dinosaur creature that kidnaps Princess Toadstool, heir to the throne of Mushroom Kingdom, in Nintendo's original *Super Mario Brothers* video game. Bowser's black magic turns the princess' once-loyal citizens into his evil-doing cronies, such as the mushroom-like Goombas, turtle-esque Koopa Troopas, and Piranha Plants. Where's courageous Super Mario when you need him?

KING KONG

Giant ape "beast" from Skull Island, a jungle habitat, who ventures to the Big Apple, where he snatches his blonde "beauty" (actress Fay Wray) and makes a fateful ascent to the top of the Empire State Building. Kong was featured in several movies, including the 1933 *King Kong* classic and the 1976 remake, starring Jessica Lange and Jeff Bridges. From 1966 to 1969, he appeared in animated form as the pet of little Bobby Bond in the Saturday-morning TV cartoon *King Kong*.

FYI: ▸ King Kong once duked it out with Japanese monster Godzilla atop Mount Fuji (1963's *King Kong vs. Godzilla*)!

KINGS ISLAND

Marked by a scaled-down replica of the Eiffel Tower, this amusement park located near Cincinnati, Ohio, made pop culture history when visited by The Brady Bunch in 1973. There the TV family filmed the episode in which Jan Brady buys a Yogi Bear poster and accidentally substitutes it for Mike Brady's architecture blueprints of a new addition to the theme park. The mix-up causes the whole Brady family to go on a frantic search throughout the park until the blueprints are found. You just gotta love the shot of the Bradys screaming on The Racer roller coaster!

"KING TUT"

Nightclub comic Steve Martin's goofy tribute to King Tutankhamen, a teenage Egyptian pharaoh whose unearthed golden relics were being exhibited at museums across the nation during 1978. Martin first performed the novelty ditty on NBC's *Saturday Night Live* before recording it with backup singers called the Toot Uncommons.

KIRA

An ethereal roller-skating muse—the mythological goddess of dance—dressed in a sundress and leg warmers and looking like beautiful Olivia Newton-John, circa 1980, who comes down to earth every forty years or so to help inspire down-on-their-luck musicians and artists. Kira's story is told in the movie musical *Xanadu*.

KIRK, TOMMY

Likeable leading man who made a string of films in the late 1950s and early 1960s for the Walt Disney Studios, playing bungling but well-meaning teenagers. The best of his roles includes Travis Coates in *Old Yeller* (1957), Wilby Daniels in *The Shaggy Dog* (1959), Ernst Robinson in *Swiss Family Robinson* (1960), Biff Hawk in *The Absent-Minded Professor* (1960) and *Son of Flubber* (1963), and Merlin Jones in *The Misadventures of Merlin Jones* (1964) and *The Monkey's Uncle* (1965).

KISS

These cartoonish heavy-metalers disturbed parents, critics, and religious leaders alike, because they were idolized by a legion of mostly male teen fans—known as the KISS Army—whose adoration rewarded them with a multitude of platinum and gold records. What set them apart from other acts of the era were the sinister-looking makeup (they never went out in public without it), black and silver S&M-like costumes, satanic imagery (KISS is rumored to be the initials for Knights In Satan's Service), and over-the-top pyrotechnic stage shows. Formed in New York City, KISS consists of blood-spitting bassist-leader Gene Simmons (the Demon) and his astonishing long tongue, along with hairy-chested guitarist Paul Stanley (the Star Child), guitarist Ace Frehley (the Space Ace), and drummer Peter Criss (the Catman). Best-selling albums included *Dressed to Kill* (1975), *Alive!* (1975), *Destroyer* (1976), and *Love Gun* (1977). Hit singles: "Rock and Roll All Nite" (1975), "Shout It Out Loud" (1976), "Beth" (1976), "Hard Luck Woman" (1977), "Christine Sixteen" (1977), "Calling Dr. Love" (1977), and "I Was Made for Loving You" (1979). The quartet was so huge that you could see their devilish images on lunch boxes, board games, dolls, comic books, and in a 1978 TV movie, *KISS Meets the Phantom of the Park*, portraying them as superheroes. They're still around today.

KITT

Short for "Knight Industries Two Thousand," the computerized superauto—driven by crime-fighter Michael Knight (a.k.a. Knight Rider, played by David Hasselhoff)—was a black Pontiac Trans-Am capable of powerful speeds (up to 300 miles an hour), air leaps (up to fifty feet), and an ability to survive assaults unscathed. It also came loaded with an arsenal of weapons, including flame-throwers, smoke bombs, and an infrared sensory mechanism. KITT had an actual personality (a little on the snooty side), allowing it to think, talk, and be friends with the good-natured Knight Rider.

FYI: ▸ George Barris, creator of Batman's Batmobile, the Green Hornet's Black Beauty, the Munsters' Koach, and the Monkees' Monkeemobile, customized KITT for the *Knight Rider* TV series.

KITTY CUSTARD

This pink feline belonged to Strawberry Shortcake, the sweet-smelling heroine of greeting cards, toys, and cartoons.

KITTY KARRY-ALL

Just as Buffy Davis had her Mrs. Beasley, and Dodie Douglas had her Myrtle, this doll, with blonde pigtails and a red jumper dress with multiple pockets holding accessories, was owned by little Cindy Brady of *The Brady Bunch*. In Episode 3, "Kitty Karry-All Is Missing," airing November 7, 1969, Cindy's favorite doll is missing and the family thinks brother Bobby has hidden it from her. Earlier, Bobby had angrily told Cindy that he hoped her favorite doll got lost. When the doll disappears, Cindy points the finger of blame at Bobby. Eventually Kitty Karry-All, along with Bobby's kazoo and other lost Brady items, turns up inside the doghouse of kleptomaniac pooch Tiger.

KITTY KAT

Furry, black domestic feline owned by TV's Munster family that didn't meow like a typical cat—it roared like a ferocious African lion. The Addams family, rivals of the Munsters on another channel, also had a pet named Kitty, but this one was a real lion that had the temperament of a regular housecat.

KIX CEREAL

"We like Kix for what Kix have got / Moms like Kix for what Kix have not." We didn't like Kix, but our moms would make us choose this healthful cereal, characterized by round puffs, over the sugary-sweet good stuff like Sugar Crisp or Froot Loops. Kix has been manufactured by General Mills since 1937.

KLINGONS

This alien species, made up of hostile warriors from the planet Kronos, continually clashes with the valiant crew of the starship Enterprise in the *Star Trek* television and film series.

KNIEVEL, EVEL

The risk-taking pioneer of ramp-launched motorcycle jumping, called the "World's Wildest Daredevil" and "King of the Stuntmen," whose jumps involved rows of cars, trucks, bonfires, people, and even a canyon. Some of Knievel's most heart-stopping stunts included jumping over a water tank full of man-eating sharks; springing over the fountain at Caesar's Palace in Las Vegas (unfortunately he crash-landed himself into a month-long coma); clearing fourteen Greyhound buses at Ohio's Kings Island; and an unsuccessful one-mile leap over Idaho's Snake River Canyon, some 2,500 feet above ground, in the rocket-powered X-2 Sky Cycle (his parachute opened too soon). In 1972, George Hamilton portrayed the daredeviling cyclist in the bio-flick *Evel Knievel*, and in 1977 Knievel played himself in the action-adventure *Viva Knievel!* Taking advantage of Knievel's popularity among children, Ideal Toys came out with a bendable Evel Knievel action figure in 1974. It came with a variety of cycles and stunts, plus a female counterpart named Derry Daring. Gutsy son Robbie Knievel (born 1962) replaced Knievel when he retired in 1975.

FYI: ▸ Evel Knievel is listed in *The Guinness Book of World Records* for having broken more bones than anyone in recorded history.

KNIGHT RIDER

TV action series starring "Hunk of the Hour" David Hasselhoff as Michael Young, an undercover cop who, after being severely wounded and disfigured by a shot in the face, was saved by a mysterious millionaire (Wilton Knight). Brought back to life from the brink of death, Michael was given a new appearance through plastic surgery and a new identity—Michael Knight. He was also given a new plan for fighting crime: stopping lawbreakers with the aid of a supercar called KITT, a slick, computerized Trans-Am capable of fast speed, weaponry, thinking, and talking (voiced by Williams Daniels). Airing from 1982 to 1986, *Knight Rider* was the hit of its first season. Its large viewing audience included many youngsters, who loved the special F/X-laden KITT, and many women, who loved the handsome Hasselhoff in his post–*Young and the Restless*, pre-*Baywatch* days.

KNOTTS, DON

Following his success as Barney Fife on prime time's *Andy Griffith Show*, the scrawny, bug-eyed, squawky-voiced comedian (born July 21, 1924, in West Virginia) was popular with younger movie audiences as the star of a series of low-budget comedies in the 1960s: *The Incredible Mr. Limpet* (1964), *The Ghost and Mr. Chicken* (1966), *The Reluctant Astronaut* (1967), and *The Shakiest Gun in the West*

(1968), and as comic relief in Disney films in the 1970s: *The Apple Dumpling Gang* (1975), *No Deposit, No Return* (1976), *Gus* (1976), and *Herbie Goes to Monte Carlo* (1977). He later appeared on *Three's Company*, from 1979 to 1984, as irascible landlord Ralph Furley.

KOLCHAK: THE NIGHT STALKER

Cool prime-time show about Carl Kolchak (played by Darren McGavin), a wiseass reporter for Chicago's Independent News Service who stumbles on macabre creatures from the supernatural world during his investigations. His skeptical editor, Tony Vincenzo (Simon Oakland), had problems believing Kolchak's reports of aliens, mummies, vampires, werewolves, zombies, and Satan worshipers. Chris Carter supposedly credits this as his inspiration for creating *The X-Files*.

FYI: ▸ *Kolchak* made its TV premiere on Friday the thirteenth (September 1974). It ran for a single season.

KOOGLE

"Peanut Butter Koogle with the goo goo googly eyes!" A Baby Boomer lunchtime favorite in the 1970s was this peanut butter spread in a jar with swirls of chocolate, banana, cinnamon, or strawberry jelly mixed in.

KOOL-AID

Inexpensive instant soft-drink packaged in little envelopes that comes in a wide variety of powdered flavors, like Grape, Orange, Cherry, Black Cherry, Raspberry, Strawberry, Lemon-Lime, Lemonade, Pink Lemonade, and Fruit Punch. For most youngsters, it's the next best thing to soda pop and often the only sugary drink parents give permission to drink. Kool-Aid is so easy to make that any child can do it. Pour powder contents into pitcher, add one cup of sugar, add two quarts of water, add some ice, stir to your heart's desire, and—presto!—you have a pitcher of refreshing delight. Edwin Perkins, a chemist from Nebraska who also specialized in mail-order spices and other flavors, developed Kool-Aid in 1927. By 1931, the drink mix had become so successful that Perkins discontinued everything else, dedicating all his time and energy to the manufacturing of the little packets. In 1953, Kool-Aid became part of General Foods, which gave it a smiling-pitcher advertising character called the Kool-Aid Kid. Today, more than seventeen gallons of Kool-Aid are gulped, guzzled, and sipped every second across America!

FYI: ▸ Kool-Aid at summer camp is called "Bug Juice"!

KOOL-AID MAN

Remindful of the smiley-face symbol, the pitcher character beaming at us from packages of Kool-Aid was created in 1953 by Marvin Potts, an advertising-agency artist whose inspiration came from the designs his son had traced on a frosty windowpane. For thirsty children of the 1970s, the Kool-Aid Man is best known as the star of TV ads who breaks through walls after being summoned ("Hey, Kool-Aid!").

KOOSH BALLS

Soft, rubbery porcupine-like balls in psychedelic colors, created by an engineer named Scott Stillinger in 1987. Named "Koosh" because of the sound the balls make when they land in your hand.

KRAZY IKES

"Make hundreds of interesting toys!" These construction sets by Whitman, consisting of colorful hard-plastic pieces with interlocking ball-and-socket joints, kept youngsters busy making all sorts of funny people and animals. These were popular in the 1960s.

KRIS MUNROE

When blonde Jill Munroe (Farrah Fawcett) retired as one of Charlie Townsend's crime-walloping Angels, she was replaced by her spunkier and blonder kid sister, Kris Munroe (Cheryl Ladd).

FYI: ▸ On her first day on the set of *Charlie's Angels*, Cheryl Ladd wore a T-shirt with the inscription "Farrah Fawcett Minor" as a way of breaking the ice with her new costars and crew.

KRISTIN SHEPARD

She did it! She did it! The little vamp shot J.R.! Kristin was played by Mary Crosby (born September 14, 1959), daughter of crooner Bing Crosby and actress Kathryn Grant, on the prime-time soap *Dallas* from 1979 to 1981.

KROFFT, SID AND MARTY
H. R. Pufnstuf. Witchiepoo. Benita Bizarre. Weenie the Genie. Sigmund Ooze. The Sleestaks. Kaptain Kool and the Kongs. ElectraWoman and DynaGirl. Wonderbug. Wow (and whew)! If it weren't for the way-out minds of the Krofft brothers, today's adults wouldn't have the psychedelic-hued memories of these wild and wacky Saturday-morning individuals. The offspring of many generations of circus puppeteers, Sid and Marty Krofft got their start in 1960 with an adults-only puppet review, *Les Poupées de Paris*, that appeared in nightclubs and at the New York World's Fair. They later went on to create and produce all those fantastic kiddie TV shows of the 1970s, featuring live actors starring opposite giant-sized puppet-people, like *H .R. Pufnstuf* (1969–71), *The Bugaloos* (1970–72), and *Lidsville* (1971–74). The Kroffts were also responsible for designing the groovy animal costumes worn by Hanna-Barbera's Banana Splits and for producing several "legendary bad" prime-time variety shows, particularly *The Brady Bunch Hour* (1976–77), *Donny and Marie* (1976–79), and *Pink Lady and Jeff* (1980). In 1976, they gave name to the world's first indoor high-rise amusement park, The World of Sid and Marty Krofft, inside Atlanta's Omni International structure.

KROFFT SUPERSHOW
Airing on Saturday mornings from 1976 to 1978, this Sid and Marty Krofft production showcased a collection of kid-friendly, cheaply made, serialized adventures. It was hosted by Kaptain Kool and the Kongs, a rock band put together just for the program, consisting of Michael Lembeck (Kaptain Kool), Debra Clinger (Superchick), Mickey McMeel (Turkey), and Louise DuArt (Nashville). In addition to singing, the Kongs introduced each of the various filmed serials, which included *ElectraWoman and DynaGirl, Wonderbug, Dr. Shrinker, The Lost Saucer, Magic Mongo*, and *Bigfoot and Wildboy*. In the fall of 1978, *The Krofft Supershow* changed formats after it became *The Krofft Superstar Hour*. The nontalented Kaptain Kool and the Kongs were given the hook and replaced by the Bay City Rollers, a plaid-covered pop group from Scotland who were the big deal among preteens. This revamped show, an hour-long variety musical, was dreadful (in other words, it sucked) and lasted five months too long.

KRUSTY THE KLOWN
On *The Simpsons* cartoon series, Bart Simpson's most beloved idol is Krusty, a clown who hosts a kids' show seen on a local Springfield TV station. Krusty's real name: Herschel Krustofsky.

KRYPTO
"The Dog of Steel!" Furry white pet dog belonging to Superman that had superstrength, like his master, and wore a flowing red-and-yellow cape attached to his yellow collar.

KRYPTON
Home planet of comic superhero Superman (Kal-El) and his cousin Supergirl (Zor-El) that exploded into smithereens. Green fragments from the long-dead planet, known as Kryptonite, can leave these two mighty superheroes hapless.

KRYSTLE CARRINGTON
On *Dynasty*, honey-voiced, blue-eyed blonde Linda Evans starred as Blake Carrington's angelic yet tough-as-nails (manicured, of course) shoulder-padded second wife who was constantly battling it out with his wicked first wife, Alexis. Her popularity inspired a sweet-smelling fragrance line called simply Krystle.

K-TEL RECORDS
"As seen on TV!" A record label famous for explosive 1970s and early-1980s TV spots advertising compilation albums and eight-track tapes showcasing "20 original hits, 20 original stars." What set K-Tel Records aside were the eclectic collections found on each. (Only on K-Tel could you hear a disco song followed by a New Wave hit followed by a country-rock tune followed by a heavy-metal ditty followed by a sappy love ballad.) Check out this lineup on 1976's *Power House*: "Get Up and Boogie" by Silver Convention, "Country Boy" by Glen Campbell, "Sara Smile" by Hall and Oates, "Feelings" by Morris Albert, "Crazy on You" by Heart, "Love Is the

Drug" by Roxy Music, "You're No Good" by Linda Ronstadt, "More, More, More" by The Andrea True Connection, "Junk Food Junkie" by Larry Groce, "I'm Easy" by Keith Carradine, "You Sexy Thing" by Hot Chocolate, and "Lorelei" by Styx. To store the albums, K-Tel offered the Record Selector, a modern method of storing and selecting your favorite music. You placed the LPs in the Record Selector, and by moving the first one forward the others followed automatically. When the Selector reached the album you wanted to play, you simply stopped it and removed the record.

KUKLA, FRAN, AND OLLIE

A beloved TV staple for Baby Boom children featuring singer-actress Fran Allison, who fraternized in front of a puppet stage with a pair of hand puppets—worrywart Kukla (Russian for "doll") and lovable one-toothed dragon Ollie (short for Oliver J. Dragon). The classic program first aired in 1947 as a local Chicago show, before going national from 1949 to 1962. In 1967, Kukla, Fran, and Ollie hosted the *CBS Children's Film Festival* on Saturday afternoons. On this long-running program, the trio introduced and commented on children's films from around the world. Burr Tillstrom created the puppets and provided their voices.

KUNG FU

"Hi-yaaa!" Airing from 1972 to 1975, a philosophy-oriented TV western starring David Carradine as drifter Kwai Chang Caine, a soft-spoken, barefoot, shaven-headed Buddhist priest who traveled the American frontier in the 1880s. Half-Chinese and half-American, Caine was raised in a Shaolin temple in China, where he studied to become a monk and learned the martial art of kung fu. He fled to the American West after accidentally killing a member of China's royal family. Once there, he searched for a missing brother, while eluding capture by Chinese agents and American bounty-hunters. The ABC show was noteworthy for its surrealistic slow-motion fight scenes and flashbacks showing juvenile Caine being disciplined in the mystical philosophies ("the oneness of all things") and the use of kung fu for self-protection. Co-starring in the flashback sequences were Keye Luke as Master Po, Philip Ahn as Master Kan, and Radames Pera as the juvenile Caine, affectionately known as "Grasshopper."

FYI: ▸ David Carradine is the son of character actor John Carradine and oldest brother of actors Keith and Robert Carradine.

KYLE BROSLOFSKI

The intelligent one of the *South Park* gang, whom everyone, particularly the obnoxious Cartman, tends to make fun of because of his Jewish heritage. Kyle has an adopted younger brother, Ike, from Canada that he plays kick-the-baby with, and at Christmas he gets visited by "imaginary" friend Mr. Hanky, the Christmas Poo. Underneath his cap, which he never removes, he has a severe red Afro.

FYI: ▸ Creator Matt Stone named Kyle's parents after his own parents, Gerald and Sheila (he also provides the voice of Kyle).

LAKER GIRLS

The NBA's most popular cheerleading squad was the focus of a lame 1990 TV movie about three candidates (one being plain-looking Tina Yothers) aspiring to cheer for the legendary L.A. Lakers basketball team. Pop singer and *American Idol* judge Paula Abdul became a member and head choreographer in 1982. She helped turn the Laker Girls from routine cheerleaders to the dazzling dance team adorned in scanty yellow-and-purple outfits that fans think of today.

LAMBADA

The Forbidden Dance. A saucy, sexy Brazilian dirty dance featuring lots of bumping and grinding. Should be called the Forgotten Dance because it never really caught on in North America.

LAMBCHOP

This baby-talking white lamb was a famous hand puppet belonging to ventriloquist Shari Lewis. From 1960 to 1963, the too-cute duo starred on a children's TV series, *The Shari Lewis Show*, in which they sang and told stories along with puppet pals—Louisiana-accented Hush Puppy and goofy Charlie Horse.

LAMBDA LAMBDA LAMBDA

Seen in the film comedy *Revenge of the Nerds* (1984), a lovable fraternity whose members are outcasts and misfits. Located on the campus of Adams College, the Tri-Lambs are frequently taunted by the cocky jocks of the Alpha Beta fraternity and their beauty-queen girlfriends. Sister sorority is the Omega Mu (Moooooo!).

LANCELOT LINK, SECRET CHIMP

"He stands for justice, he has no fear. . . ." Really strange Saturday-morning TV show about chimpanzee secret agents that's sort of a mixture of TV's *Get Smart,* cinema's *Planet of the Apes*, and music's The Monkees. It starred a bunch of clothed apes with voices dubbed by humans, and according to ABC-TV's PR department was a "Swiftian satire in which a world like ours is peopled entirely by chimpanzees." The principal Monkey 007 was Lancelot Link, a secret agent who liked his banana daiquiris shaken not stirred. He worked for A.P.E. (Agency to Prevent Evil) under Commander Darwin and moonlighted in a groovy rock combo called The Evolution Revolution. Assisted by blonde-bewigged Mata Hairi, the simian spy battled the evil C.H.U.M.P. (Criminal Headquarters for the Underground

Master Plan), intent on ruling the world. Dastardly primate Tonga, whose cronies included Baron von Butcher and lackey Creto, Dr. Strangemind, Dragon Woman, Wang Fu, and Ali AssaSeen, headed C.H.U.M.P. Airing in 1970, this "have to be seen, to be believed" spy spoof ran for only one season on ABC before rerunning on syndicated TV, where it developed a huge cult following. "Oh, Lance Link, what'cha gonna do?"

LAND BEFORE TIME

Don Bluth's endearing animated feature about five orphaned baby dinosaurs—brontosaurus Lightfoot, triceratops Cera, stegosaurus Spike, anatosaurus Ducky, and pterodactyl Petrie—in search of the Great Valley, a legendary land of lush vegetation where all creatures reside in peace. On their journey, the youngsters encounter life-threatening obstacles, including a menacing Tyrannosaurus Rex called Sharp Tooth, while learning lessons about life. Followed by five straight-to-video sequels.

LANDO CALRISSIAN

The suave soldier-of-fortune once owned the Millennium Falcon spacecraft before losing it to Han Solo in a game of sabacc. Resides in Cloud City, where he is the Baron Administrator. First introduced to moviegoers in *The Empire Strikes Back* (1980), Lando was played by African-American sex symbol Billy Dee Williams.

LAND OF THE GIANTS

A sci-fi series about seven earthlings (and a dog) stranded in a strange world inhabited by a race of giants. Airing from 1968 to 1970, it takes place in the mid-1980s (June 12, 1983, to be exact), with the crew and passengers flying aboard the Spindrift, a commercial rocket ship traveling from Los Angeles to London. The Spindrift is drawn into a space warp's magnetic force and crash lands on an earthlike planet that had occupants and objects a dozen times larger. Struggling to repair the wounded craft, the castaways find themselves threatened by giant "everyday" creatures (cats, snakes, spiders, and children) and hunted by scientists interested in examining them. *Land of the Giants* starred Gary Conway as Captain Steve Burton, Don Marshall as co-pilot Dan Erickson, Heather Young as stewardess Betty Hamilton, Deanna Lund as jet-set heiress Valerie Scott, Don Matheson as tycoon Mark Wilson, Kurt Kasznar as villainous Alexander Fitzhugh, Stefan Arngrim as twelve-year-old Barry Lockridge, Chipper as Barry's pet dog, and Kevin Hagen as Inspector Kobrick, a giant-sized security agent working for a totalitarian government and responsible for apprehending the "little people." F/X master Irwin Allen was creator and executive producer of this fondly remembered ABC series.

LAND OF THE LOST

Airing on Saturday-morning TV from 1974 to 1978, this Sid and Marty Krofft production told the story of forest ranger Rick Marshall (Spencer Milligan) and his two children, Will and Holly (Wesley Eure and Kathy Coleman), who plunge into a time warp following an earthquake while rafting on the Colorado River. The Marshalls find themselves transported back to the days of the dinosaurs in a lost land of three moons. They encounter all kinds of adventures while searching for a way back to the twentieth century and are befriended by a gentle, monkey-like tribe called the Pakunis, particularly by one member, Cha-Ka. They are also terrorized by the hostile Sleestacks, half-human, half-lizard cave-dwelling creatures. Dopey was Holly's pet baby brontosaurus.

Land of the Lost was a lot more serious than the Kroffts' earlier live-action programs—pure sci-fi, while the others were silly fantasies. There were no cute dancing puppets, no friendly sea monsters, no singing insect bands, only strange prehistoric beings who more often than not were stupendously life-threatening (for example, Grumpy the T-Rex, Torchy the fire-breathing dinosaur, and the Abominable Snowman). Those of us weaned on *Pufnstuf* and *Lidsville* during the early 1970s were becoming too old (or too cool) for most of the cartoons seen on Saturday morning, but we actually enjoyed watching this (even if the special effects seemed fake), and to this day many of our younger siblings can recall how the Sleestacks scared the shit out of them.

LAND SHARK

One of *Saturday Night Live*'s earlier ongoing comedy skits in which the once-popular *Jaws* craze of 1975 was spoofed. It had Chevy Chase inside a flimsy shark costume trying to get through the front doors of unsuspecting victims by offering a candygram, a telegram, plumbing, flowers, and so on.

LANE, DIANE
Beautiful teenager (born January 22, 1965) whose performance at age sixteen in *A Little Romance*, as love-struck runaway Lauren, put her on the cover of *Time* magazine in 1979. Along with Jodie Foster, Tatum O'Neal, Kristy McNichol, and Brooke Shields, she was heralded as one of the new generation of adolescent film actresses. It wasn't until recent years that Lane made the often-difficult transition from child star to adult star, with critically applauded roles in *A Walk on the Moon* (1999), *The Perfect Storm* (2000), and *Unfaithful* (2002). Other notable movies include *The Outsiders* (1983), *Rumble Fish* (1983), *The Cotton Club* (1984), *Streets of Fire* (1984), and *The Big Town* (1987).

FYI: ▸ Diane Lane dated rocker Jon Bon Jovi in the mid-1980s before marrying Christopher "Highlander" Lambert in 1988 (they were divorced in 1994).

LARRY DALLAS
Jack Tripper's best friend, a hopeless swinger who lived in a neighboring upstairs apartment. Played by Richard Kline on the sitcom *Three's Company* from 1978 to 1984.

LARRY TATE
"Darrin, you son of a gun!" David White starred as Darrin Stephens's self-serving boss at McMann & Tate, an advertising firm in New York City, on the *Bewitched* TV series. Larry's wife is the socially inclined Louise.

LASSIE
The greatest animal star of all is this heroic, loyal, and intelligent collie with a talent for rescuing her human owners from harmful predicaments. Lassie originated in Eric Knight's best-selling 1940 novel *Lassie Come Home*. In 1943, the book was made into a successful MGM movie of the same title, starring child actors Roddy McDowall and Elizabeth Taylor. It spawned more than a half-dozen sequels, including *Son of Lassie* (1945), *Courage of Lassie* (1946), *Challenge to Lassie* (1949), and, most recent, *Magic of Lassie* (1978) co-starring James Stewart. Most Baby Boomers remember Lassie best as the star of a long-running, family-friendly adventure series—a Sunday night fixture on CBS-TV from 1954 to 1971—which experienced many changes in format and cast. Lassie's most notable masters on the program were young Jeff Miller (Tommy Rettig, 1954–57), young Timmy (Jon Provost, 1958–64), and forest ranger Corey Stuart (Robert Bray, 1964–68). Rudd Weatherwax owned and trained Lassie. (By the way, Lassie was actually a laddie, named Pal.)

LASSIE'S RESCUE RANGERS
An ecology-oriented cartoon show starring famed TV collie Lassie. On the program, she and other forest animals help the Turner family organize a Forest Force rescue team in the Rocky Mountains. Aired on Saturday mornings from 1973 to 1975.

LAST STRAW
"Who will place the straw that breaks the camel's back? The loser—that's who!" Introduced in 1966 by Schaper (the folks who gave us Cootie and Ants in the Pants), this was often referred to as the "don't break the camel's back" game. It featured a plastic camel consisting of two halves connected by a tension band. The camel was set on four wheels and had a two-sided cargo basket between its two humps. Each player took turns putting wooden straws in the basket, hoping his or her straw would not be the one that overloads it and causes the camel to "break his back." One by one, players were eliminated, the winner being the last player remaining.

LATCHKEY KIDS
Children who are left home alone and unsupervised while their parents are at work. The term originated in the early 1970s after mothers began to work outside the home, either because of economic hardship or as a result of the feminist movement. Generation X is sometimes referred to as the Latchkey Generation.

LAUGH-IN
Innovative TV variety show marked by its psychedelic look and a fast pace, and teeming with jokes, sight

gags, double entendres, and political statements. Officially known as *Rowan & Martin's Laugh-In*, this madcap groovefest was hosted by the nightclub comedy duo of Dan Rowan (the straight man) and Dick Martin (the funny man). It featured a repertory cast of talented young comics, including Ruth Buzzi, Judy Carne, Richard Dawson, Patti Deutsch, Henry Gibson, Teresa Graves, Goldie Hawn, Arte Johnson, Alan Sues, Lily Tomlin, Jo Anne Worley, and Gary Owens, the program's overmodulated announcer. Regular highlights: Johnson's German soldier Wolfgang; both Tomlin's sarcastic telephone operator Ernestine and her precocious juvenile Edith Ann; Buzzi's dowdy little old Gladys Ormphby; Gibson's broadminded Parson; big-mouth Worley's raucous laugh; Carne's "Sock it to me!" girl, who constantly got splashed with a bucket of water; and giggly Hawn's shimmying go-go in a bikini with funny sayings painted all over her body.

Other prominent highlights were the Swingin' Cocktail Party; the Flying Fickle Finger of Fate; Letters to Laugh-In; Laugh-In Looks at the News; and the mod-colored Joke Wall at the end of the program, where cast members took turns popping out of windows to deliver a quick one-liner. The series also featured cameos by famous showbiz celebs and politicians (nowhere else could you find conservative President Richard Nixon stating "Sock it to me," or tough-guy John Wayne dressed as the Easter Bunny). The zany sayings heard on *Laugh-In* provided the late 1960s and early 1970s with a lexicon of pop culture catchphrases: "You bet your Bippy!" "Beautiful downtown Burbank!" "Look that up in your Funk & Wagnalls!" "Verrrry interesting!" "Here come de Judge!" and of course, "Sock it to me!"

Premiering on NBC in 1968, *Laugh-In* was the number-one show on prime time during its first two seasons, but because of high cast turnover, the ratings dropped, and cancellation followed in 1973.

FYI: ▸ The title *Laugh-In* is a reference to the late-1960s hippie "love-in."

LAUPER, CYNDI

When Cyndi Lauper appeared on the music scene in 1983, it seemed as if she had stepped out from a comic-strip panel. Her hair was cut into an odd asymmetrical style (one side longer than the other) and colored in a variety of primary hues (blue, pink, yellow, and more). She wore clashing ragtag clothing found at secondhand stores (Manhattan's Screaming Mimi's was her favorite). And she talked and sang in a squeaky, high-pitched Betty Boop-ish voice.

Born on June 20, 1953, in Queens, New York, Lauper performed in dive bars in and around the Big Apple and fronted a band, Blue Angel, before hitting the big time with her 1984 debut album, *She's So Unusual.* The LP went platinum, generating four Top Ten singles, including the fun-loving anthem for a girls' night out, "Girls Just Want to Have Fun," "She Bop" (a witty tribute to masturbation), and two heartfelt ballads, "Time After Time" and "All Through the Night." With repeated exposure on MTV, Lauper was one of the first stars created by the music-video revolution. For a short while, she was involved with the pro-wrestling circuit, palling around with wrestler Captain Lou Albano, and even finding time to manage Wendy Richter, the female world wrestling champion. Considered the most promising female singer of the mid-1980s (she won the 1984 Best New Artist Grammy Award), the talented Lauper's quirky cartoon image stereotyped her, so that the music-buying public never really took her seriously.

LAURA INGALLS

Based on the real-life author of the *Little House* books, the pigtailed, tomboy middle child of Charles and Caroline Ingalls was played by Melissa Gilbert on the prime-time series *Little House on the Prairie.* Laura's recollections of growing up on the American frontier in the 1870s became the basis for the books and subsequent 1970s TV show. Affectionately nicknamed "Half-Pint" by her father, she would grow up to become a teacher and marry Almanzo Wilder.

LAURA PALMER

"She's dead. Wrapped in plastic." Who killed Laura Palmer? Not since the days of "Who shot J.R.?" has a question so mesmerized American TV audiences. The discovery of the popular prom queen's plastic-wrapped and serenely beautiful dead body in a local lake, and the ensuing murder investigation by coffee-swigging FBI agent Dale Cooper, was the main plotline of *Twin Peaks* (1990–91), a dreamlike nighttime soap created by cult-film director David Lynch. So who did kill the seventeen-year-old whose blonde wholesomeness masked her true identity: a drug-addicted tramp? The answer: Laura's father, Leland Palmer, an upstanding citizen of Twin Peaks (a small logging town in the Pacific Northwest) who was secretly possessed by Killer Bob.

LAURA VINNING SPENCER

In 1976, fair-haired Genie Francis (born May 26, 1962) was cast to star as Dr. Lesley Webber's illegitimate daughter on the mega-popular daytime serial *General Hospital*. Her teenage love affair with dashing scoundrel Luke Spencer made her one of the most popular romantic leads in soap-opera history.

LAURIE PARTRIDGE

Stick-thin teen model Susan Dey starred as the pretty eldest daughter and keyboard player on TV's *Partridge Family*. As the dark-haired alternative to blonde Marcia Brady from rival sitcom *The Brady Bunch*, Laurie was a sensible fifteen-year-old liberal activist/feminist who enjoyed ribbing cute but cocky brother Keith. She once experienced the humiliation of picking up radio broadcasts via the metal braces in her mouth.

LAURIE STRODE

The scholarly and virginal seventeen-year-old from Haddonfield, Illinois, was stalked and terrorized by homicidal maniac Michael Meyers while babysitting one Halloween night. Laurie's best pals, Annie and Lynda, didn't survive the unholy night of terror. (True to slasher-film tradition, they were killed off because they were naughty girls.) Portrayed by Jamie Lee Curtis, daughter of actors Tony Curtis and Janet Leigh, in the *Halloween* film series.

LAVA LITES

"A motion for every emotion." Once again, for the pop culture illiterate out there (come out from underneath your rocks): Lava Lites, an oozing symbol of the 1960s Age of Aquarius, are lighted glass urns containing a clear liquid and a ball of colored wax (lava). When turned on, a forty-watt lightbulb located at the bottom heats a metal coil, causing the lava to melt, rise, and then fall, forming all kinds of slow-swirling, ever-changing shapes and sizes. They were commonly found in black-lighted rooms with hippies stoned on drugs who would watch the pulsating, glowing globs of goo rise up and down in a hypnotic slow-motion dance of psychedelia—or in a swingin' bachelor's love pad, where they were sensual mood-lighting to help seduce lovely chicks into getting horizontal on a waterbed.

Originally called the Astrolight, the Lava Lite was invented by an Englishman named Craven Walker in 1964. Lava-mania began the following year, after Chicago businessman Adolph Wertheimer purchased the rights to manufacture the Astrolight in the United States and renamed it. By the end of the decade, he'd sold two million of them, and during the 1970s more than five million of these trippy lights were purchased—before they joined the other icons of the day (the peace sign, love beads, tie dyes, mod flowers, and the smiley face) as out-of-style relics. In the 1990s, a demand for hippie kitsch ignited a new lava-wave, and almost everyone under the age of forty had at least one of the colorful lamps at home or in the workplace. Groovy.

LAVERNE AND SHIRLEY

A rare example of a spin-off proving just as popular as the founding TV series. The gals from Milwaukee were seen briefly on *Happy Days* as girlfriends of the Fonz, before headlining their own show in 1976. An instant hit, it starred Penny Marshall as wisecracking, man-hungry Laverne DeFazio, and Cindy Williams as perky, naive Shirley Feeney. Laverne and Shirley were best friends who shared a basement apartment at 730 Hampton Street and worked together as bottle cappers at the Shotz Brewery. The sitcom centered around the twosome's trying to find romance as well as a way out of their blue-collar world of the 1950s. Supporting regulars included David L. Lander and Michael McKean as the girls' ding-a-ling neighbors, Lenny and Squiggy, Eddie Mekka as Shirley's Romeo boyfriend, Carmine Ragusa, Phil Foster as Laverne's dad, Frank DeFazio, and Betty Garrett as the girls' landlord, Mrs. Edna Babish (she later married Frank).

Laverne and Shirley experienced high Nielsen ratings, surpassing *Happy Days* as the number-one show of the 1977–78 and 1978–79 TV seasons. In 1982, however, after a long rivalry between Marshall and Williams, trouble erupted when Cindy—tired of working long hours and feeling that Penny was shown favoritism because her brother, Garry Marshall, was the executive producer—walked off. The ABC show ended its run shortly thereafter. In recent years, Penny Marshall has directed critically acclaimed motion pictures, including *Big* (1988), *Awakenings* (1990), and *A League of Their Own* (1992)—and has been a TV commercial spokesperson for Kmart, along with pal Rosie O'Donnell. As for Cindy Williams, well, she hasn't been heard from much since leaving *Laverne and Shirley*.

FYI: ▸ "Schimiel" and "Schlimauzel"—chanted by Laverne and Shirley right before the show's opening theme song, "Making Our Dreams Come True," sung by Cyndi Greco—mean "fool" and "loser" in Hebrew.

LAVERNE DeFAZIO

The blonde half of *Laverne and Shirley* (played by Penny Marshall), a tough-talking, boy-crazy jokester whose daily uniform consisted of a tight sweater with the initial "L" monogrammed on it. Laverne's father, Frank DeFazio, owned the Pizza Bowl, a combination pizza parlor / bowling alley in Milwaukee that was the local hangout for Laverne and her best friend, Shirley Feeney. Laverne's favorite drink: a Pepsi-and-milk mixture.

LAWRENCE, JOEY

Sweet-looking, shaggy-haired teen idol for the early-1990s *Sassy* crowd who is most famous for playing Joey Russo on the TV series *Blossom* (1991–95). Born April 20, 1976, in Pennsylvania, hardworking Lawrence was already an acting veteran by the time he appeared as Blossom's dum-dum but adorable brother. He debuted on Nell Carter's *Gimme a Break* (1983–87), at age five, playing little Joey Donovan, and voiced the title character in Disney's *Oliver and Company* (1988). He even managed to have a minor singing career with the LP *Joey Lawrence*, which carried the Top Twenty hit "Nothin' My Love Can't Fix." After shedding his Tiger Beat looks, he matured into a handsome leading man (still hunky but with far less hair), starring in big-screen fare, such as *Urban Legends: Final Cut* (2000). Two younger siblings—Matthew and Andrew—followed his career from child actor to adult actor. The three brothers starred together on the TV sitcom *Brotherly Love* (1995–97) and in the Disney tele-flick *Jumping Ship* (2001).

FYI: ▸ Toddler Joey Lawrence once dazzled Johnny Carson on *The Tonight Show*, singing "Give My Regards to Broadway"!

LAY'S POTATO CHIPS

"Betcha can't eat just one" of these best-selling potato chips, introduced in 1938 by Frito-Lay. Other snack chips manufactured by the Texas-based company include Cheetos, Doritos, Fritos, Funyuns, Munchos, Ruffles, and Tostitos.

LEAKIN' LENA

Seafaring vessel commanded by Captain Horatio K. Huffenpuff, uncle of propeller-capped Beany Boy, in the *Beany and Cecil* cartoons.

LEATHERFACE

Squealing inbred fiend, wearing a mask stitched out of human skin (yuck!), who torments his victims with sledgehammers, meat hooks, and of course the chainsaw. Responsible for a chainsaw massacre in Texas during the summer of 1974, in which he and his ghoulish family butchered five unlucky teenagers. Leatherface's blood relations sometimes call him "Bubba" or "Junior." Gunnar Hansen played him in the cult horror film *The Texas Chainsaw Massacre*.

LEATHER PANTS

Sometimes they're cool, like Billy Idol; sometimes they're cheesy, like a Village People. These nightclubbing pants' fashionableness in the early 1980s led to the hot, hot, hot leather miniskirt look for women. An inexpensive plastic version of leather, known as pleather, has been somewhat popular in recent years.

LEAVE IT TO BEAVER

Much-celebrated series that reaps cult status today among older Baby Boomers, perhaps because of its nostalgic, "picture perfect" depiction of the American family of the 1950s. Set in the mythical suburban land of Mayfield U.S.A.—where homes are kept immaculate and nothing really bad happens—the sitcom focused on the nice middle-class Cleaver family, residing at 211 Pine Street. The breadwinner of the household was Ward Cleaver (Hugh Beaumont), the levelheaded dad who worked as an accountant for Mr. Rutherford. Devoted June Cleaver (Barbara Billingsley) was the ideal wife and mother who regularly dressed in heels, pearls, and shirtwaist dresses even when vacuuming the floors and baking cookies. Their adorable offspring were Wally (Tony Dow), the popular All-American oldest son, and Theodore, better known as the Beaver (Jerry Mathers), the puckish youngest son.

Airing from 1957 to 1963, each episode of *Leave It to Beaver* usually centered on the good intentions of the Beav, which often backfired, landing him—and dopily protective Wally—in some "kinda sorta" trouble. Supporting characters included Wally's pals, Eddie Haskell (Ken Osmond) and Clarence "Lumpy" Rutherford (Frank Bank), and Beav's friends, Larry Mondello (Rusty Stevens), Whitey Whitney (Stanley Fafara), and Gilbert Bates (Stephen Talbot). Prime-time contemporaries of the show were *The Adventures of Ozzie and Harriet* (1952–66), *Make Room for Daddy* (1953–65), *Father Knows Best* (1954–63), and *The Donna Reed Show* (1958–66).

LEE, BRUCE

The king of martial-arts films, dubbed the "Fastest Fist in the East," was born Lee Yuen Kam on November 27, 1940, in San Francisco. Of Chinese and European descent (his name means "protector of San Francisco"), he was called Bruce Lee by a nurse who thought he should have an American name. Lee began his martial-arts training while studying philosophy at the University of Washington. He first achieved national recognition as Kato, the loyal manservant on TV's *Green Hornet* (1966–67). In 1972 and 1973, Lee starred in a string of low-budget kung-fu fighting films made in Hong Kong: *Fists of Fury* (1972), *The Chinese Connection* (1973), *Enter the Dragon* (1973), and sequel *Return of the Dragon* (1973). These violent movies featured him as the underdog fighting authoritarian villains (and their armies) while displaying explosive athletic abilities, superhuman street-fighting skills, a charismatic personality, and sexy good looks. All this made him popular with youths—especially the male segment—and brought him worldwide movie stardom.

On July 20, 1973, Lee died under mysterious circumstances during production of the movie *Game of Death*. Some believe his death was from a brain hemorrhage after hitting his head during a movie stunt, while others say a fatal reaction to the prescription painkiller Equagesic did him in. Then there are those who theorize that he was a victim of a deadly three-generation curse, or fatally punished for revealing too many ancient kung-fu secrets, or a victim of a "delayed death strike." His early demise at age thirty-two only enhanced Lee's reputation as an international cult figure who had defined the martial-arts movie genre, leading the way for other chop-socky heroes, such as Jackie Chan, Sonny Chiba, Chuck Norris, and Don "the Dragon" Wilson.

Son Brandon Lee began a film career in the 1990s but died in a freak accident during filming of *The Crow* in 1993 at the age of twenty-eight. (Now, what about that three-generation curse?) Unrelated actor Jason Scott Lee starred in the 1993 bio-pic *Dragon: The Bruce Lee Story*.

LEGEND OF ZELDA

In the mystical world of Hyrule, a young warrior named Link is asked by Princess Zelda to find the eight fragments of the Triforce, a golden triangle with magical powers, before the evil wizard Gannon does. Along the way, Link encounters many pitfalls—and so do this video game's players. In the short history of video gaming, Nintendo's Legend of Zelda is one of the most innovative, influential, and enduring. Introduced in 1986, it was followed by Zelda II: The Adventure of Link (1989), The Legend of Zelda: A Link to the Past (1991), The Legend of Zelda: Link's Awakening (1993), The Legend of Zelda: Ocarina of Time (1998), The Legend of Zelda: Majora's Mask (2000), The Legend of Zelda: Oracle of Ages (2001), and The Legend of Zelda: The Wind Walker (2002).

L'EGGS

"Our L'eggs fit your legs / They hug you / They hold you / They never let you go!" Inexpensive and durable pantyhose cleverly packaged in a plastic egg-shaped container (hence the name). Extremely popular throughout the 1970s, L'eggs is best remembered for a commercial starring leggy dancer Juliet Prowse performing high kicks in a pair.

FYI: ▸ Kids often took the discarded white L'eggs cylinder and made swell art projects, like Christmas and Easter ornaments, or stored loose change in them.

LEGION OF DOOM

A bad boys' club headed by Lex Luthor and made up of troublemakers: the Riddler, Scarecrow, Toyman, Sinestro, Bizarro, Giganta, Cheetah, Brainiac, Black Manta, Grod, and Captain Cold. The Legion of Doom was the foe of the superheroic Justice League of America and seen on their 1970s *Super-Friends* Saturday-morning cartoon.

LEGO

"A new toy every day!" This favorite construction toy of juvenile architects permitted children to build endless combinations of houses, skyscrapers, cars, trucks, planes, ships, and whatever else their young imaginations could think of. For those of you who are unfamiliar with Legos, they are interlocking plastic bricks in bright primary colors (red, blue, green, yellow, and white) with studs on top and corresponding holes on the bottom that allow them to be easily stacked together with structural stability. They are nearly indestructible and can be found in mixed play sets, accompanied by an assortment of accessories (including wheels, windows, doors, people, garden plants, and more) to make all kinds of movable toys and buildings.

A Danish carpenter named Ole Kirk Christiansen, whose earlier toy creations were made out of wood before the switch to plastic after World War II, founded the Lego Company in 1932. Lego is an abbreviation of the Danish words *leg godt*, meaning "play well." (Lego also means "assemble" in Latin.) Christiansen's company began selling the "Automatic Building Blocks" in 1949; they were a prototype of what would become the well-known Lego building bricks in 1955. By the end of the 1950s, Lego sets were one of Europe's best-selling toys; and in 1961 they became available for purchase in the United States. Today, Lego blocks can be found in half of all American households.

Duplo is the name for the Legos aimed at younger kids, between the ages of eighteen months and five years. They are eight times the size and less complicated than the basic Lego set.

FYI: ▸ In Ole Kirk Christiansen's hometown of Billund, Denmark, there is a twenty-five-acre theme park called Legoland. It was built in 1968 and is home to an astonishing collection of Lego structures, including the U.S. Capitol, the Statue of Liberty, Mount Rushmore, the Parthenon, and life-sized Lego replicas of animals and famous people.

LEIGH, JENNIFER JASON

Young film actress of the 1980s and 1990s (born February 5, 1962) fondly remembered for her early movie role as fifteen-year-old Stacy Hamilton, a naive high-schooler who ends up getting an abortion in Amy Heckerling's *Fast Times at Ridgemont High* (1982). Other films include *The Best Little Girl in the World* (1981), *Heart of Midnight* (1988), *Last Exit to Brooklyn* (1989), *Miami Blues* (1990), *Rush* (1991), *Single White Female* (1992), *The Hudsucker Proxy* (1994), and *Georgia* (1995). She is the daughter of the late Vic Morrow, who died in a freak accident in 1983 while filming *The Twilight Zone* movie (he was decapitated by a helicopter blade following a misguided explosion).

LEMON-UP

Now-defunct shampoo that smelled lemony fresh and had a plastic yellow lemon for its screw-on cap. I believe Lemon-Up's coordinating conditioner, Lime-Up, had a lime fragrance and a plastic lime-shaped bottle cap.

LENNY AND SQUIGGY

Lenny Kosnowski and Andrew "Squiggy" Squiggman were the nutty neighbors of Laverne and Shirley who also worked with them at the Shotz Brewery, employed as truck drivers. After the girls would mention something disgusting, the pesty twosome would usually walk in the room ("Hell-o-o-o-o"). Michael McKean and David L. Lander played Lenny and Squiggy on ABC-TV's hit sitcom *Laverne and Shirley* (1976–83).

LESS THAN ZERO

Brett Easton Ellis's 1985 cult novel about a group of spoiled, wealthy, directionless young people (postcollege age) hooked on an aimless round of drugs, parties, and sex. Vermont college student Clay Easton returns home to Los Angeles for the Christmas holidays to find his old friends burned out by all-night partying fueled by an excessive abundance of cocaine. He reunites with ex-girlfriend Blair Kennedy, a coke-snorting model who requests his help in rescuing pal Julian Wells, a coke-addicted lost soul disowned by his rich parents and forced to have sex with men to pay off a $50,000 debt owed to Rip, a coke-dealing yuppie. In 1987, *Less Than Zero* was made into a motion picture, directed by Marek Kanievska and starring Andrew McCarthy as Clay, Jami Gertz as Blair, Robert Downey Jr. as Julian, and James Spader as creepy Rip.

Although having an ultracool visual style, the movie was considered by many to be a box-office turkey (viewers either loved it or hated it) with an antidrug message that actually came off glamorizing the reckless and decadent world the dispirited characters lived in. Two saving graces were Downey's standout performance (sadly foretelling his real-life addiction with narcotics in the 1990s) and the collection of tunes housed on the soundtrack, including L. L. Cool J's hip-hop "Going Back to Cali" and The Bangles' thrashy remake of Simon and Garfunkel's "Hazy Shade of Winter."

LET'S MAKE A DEAL

Airing from 1963 to 1976, a fun TV game show featuring excitable audience members ("Pick me, pick me!") dressed in wacky outfits who were selected by wheeling-and-dealing host Monty Hall to choose between "Door Number One, Door Number Two, or Door Number Three," hoping for the "Big Deal of the Day" and not a worthless "Zonk." In the last few minutes of the show, Hall would pay cash to audience members for various items on their person. Lovely Carol Merrill served as the display model, while Jay Stewart served as announcer.

LEVI'S 501 BUTTON-FLY

"Button your fly." The cool and comfortable 501-style jeans, marked by the button-fly front and red tag attached to the right back pocket, has been the flagship of the Levi Strauss denim-jean empire since 1890. It's important to note that guys with great bodies look best in them.

LEWIS, EMMANUEL

Born March 9, 1971, in New York, the cute pipsqueak friend of Michael Jackson was in reality a young teenager playing half his age as the star of TV's *Webster* (1983–87).

LEWIS, JERRY

"Laaa-dy!" Dark-haired, nasal-voiced comic who is simply revered by the French for his geeky, spastic humor in such 1960s films as *The Bellboy* (1960), *Cinderfella* (1960), *The Nutty Professor* (1963), *Who's Minding the Store?* (1963), *The Disorderly Orderly* (1964), *The Family Jewels* (1965), *Way, Way Out* (1966), and *Hook, Line and Sinker* (1969). The citizens of France made Jerry Lewis a member of the French Legion of Honor in 1984. Lewis's mass appeal in America seems to be with children, particularly those of the 1960s, who identified with his childlike, often sweet-natured characters. For most adult Americans, his comedy style is an acquired taste—they either love it ("Brilliant!") or hate it ("Annoying!"). But there's no question that people of all nationalities and all ages like him best for his fund-raising for fighting muscular dystrophy for fifty-plus years with his annual Jerry Lewis Telethon every Labor Day weekend. (In 1977, his charity work earned him a nomination for the Nobel Peace Prize.) From 1950 to 1956, he teamed with the suave Dean Martin, creating a comic duo that was the world's number-one movie draw. By himself, Lewis was the top box-office earner in 1957 and 1959 and from 1961 to 1964.

FYI: ▸ Jerry's oldest son, Gary Lewis, and his pop-rock group, The Playboys, had several pop hits in the mid-1960s, including "This Diamond Ring" (1965), "Count Me In" (1965), and "Everybody Loves a Clown" (1965).

LEX LUTHOR

Superman's archnemesis, the "World's Greatest Criminal Mind," who threatened the world with one mad invention after another and knew that the potent Man of Steel was vulnerable to power-diminishing Kryptonite.

LIBBY'S

All there is to say about this brand of canned vegetables is: "When it says Libby's, Libby's, Libby's on the label, label, label / You will like it, like it, like it on the table, table, table!"

LIBERACE

The flamboyant pianist whose trademarks were sequined tuxedos, fur capes, garish jewelry, a bouffant black hairdo, and a gleaming white smile and who playfully grinned and winked while tinkling enthusiastic versions of classics by Chopin and Rachmaninoff on a custom-made Steinway with lighted candelabras atop. First popular in the 1950s (his album sales actually rivaled Elvis's). Most of us recall the campy "Lee" as a Las Vegas performer and as the villainous Chandell on the *Batman* TV show. Although blatantly gay, Liberace denied his homosexuality even after ex-boyfriend Scott Thorson filed a palimony lawsuit (they settled out of court in 1986). Liberace died from AIDS the following year.

LIDDLE KIDDLES

"Meet the teeniest, tiniest Little Persons." Introduced by Mattel Toys in 1966, these diminutive imps enchanted the hearts and caught the imagination of children born at the tail-end of the Baby Boom and at the beginning of Generation X. Derived from the words "little kids," Liddle Kiddles were cute, doe-eyed miniature dolls (ranging in heights from one inch to four inches) with oversized heads on itty-bitty bodies. Reflecting what a child might want to be when she grew up, each Kiddle came with a plastic play set and accessories, along with a catchy name that matched his or her personality: fire chief Bunson Bernie, cowgirl Calamity Jiddle, nurse Florence Niddle, sailor Lola Liddle, auto driver Babe Biddle, tea-party hostess Greta Griddle, barbeque expert Sizzly Friddle, rock star Beat a Diddle, surfer Surfy Skiddle, snow-sledder Freezy Sliddle, pilot Windy Fliddle, and fishing tomboy Kampy Kiddle.

As the popularity of Liddle Kiddles grew, so did the variety. There were walking Skediddle Kiddles, wearable Lucky Locket Kiddles, and floral-scented Kiddle Kolognes. There were Kola Kiddles, Kiddle Lollipops, Kiddle Kones, Kozmic Kiddles, Storybook Kiddles, Holiday Kiddles, Animiddle Kiddles, and even Chitty Chitty Bang Bang Kiddles! By the late 1960s, more than 200 different Kiddle items could be purchased, including coloring books, paper dolls, games, puzzles, vinyl playhouses, carry cases (or karry kases), and a lunch box. Kiddles kicked off the miniature-doll craze of the 1960s, inspiring toy lines like Hasbro's Dolly Darling, Ideal's Flatsy, Remco's Heidi, Topper's Dawn, Uneeda's PeeWee, and Whitman's PeePul Pals. Liddle Kiddles skediddled out of toy stores when they were discontinued in 1971.

FYI: ▸ Liddle Kiddles made ideal babies for Barbie and her friends.

LIDSVILLE

Weird, odd, bizarre—those are the best ways to describe this Sid and Marty Krofft production. Airing on Saturday mornings from 1971 to 1973, the live-action TV show told the tale of a shag-haired boy named Mark (teenage Butch Patrick, formerly of *The Munsters*) from Jackson City who fell into an enlarged magician's cap at an amusement park (Six Flags Texas) and landed in kooky, kicky, groovy Lidsville. In this world populated by singing and dancing Hat People, these strange Lidsville citizens had human bodies with oversized hat-heads based on stereotypical occupations and personalities: a pointed birthday-party hat, a British colonel's pith helmet, a chef's cap, a beany cap (complete with spinner), a country bumpkin's straw hat, a cowboy hat, a fireman's helmet, a football helmet, a French beret, a feathered Indian hat, a motorcycle helmet, a nurse's cap, and an operatic hat.

Horatio J. Hoo Doo (Charles Nelson Reilly), a sinister, green-skinned magician, tried to imprison Mark because he thought the lad was a spy for the "good" hats. Hoo Doo was aided by Raunchy Rabbit, a simpleton white hare, and four "bad" hats: an executioner, a gangster, a pirate, and a vampire. Bumbling Weenie the Genie (Billie Hayes), housed in a magic ring once owned by Hoo Doo, befriended Mark and helped him out of many zany predicaments.

LIEUTENANT RIPLEY

Statuesque Sigourney Weaver's noble and courageous officer, blasting slimy space monsters to bits in four *Alien* movies, set the standard for tough, take-charge heroines in sci-fi films.

LIEUTENANT UHURA

Striking African-American, dressed in a velveteen minidress and black ankle boots, who was the communications officer of the starship Enterprise. She hailed from the United States of Africa, where in Swahili the name "Uhura" translates to "freedom." Nichelle Nichols, who played the lovely Uhura on the sci-fi classic *Star Trek*, was one of a handful of African-American women seen in leading roles on TV during the 1960s. Her contemporaries included Diahann Carroll's Julia Baker (*Julia*), Gail Fisher's Peggy Fair (*Mannix*), and Eartha Kitt's Catwoman (*Batman*).

"LIKE A PRAYER"

Madonna at her controversial best—stigmata, cross-burning, crucifixion, and kissing a black Jesus Christ—all seen in the promo video for this gospel-tinged song from the parent album *Like a Prayer* (1989). The clip was banned by the Vatican for "blasphemous" religious imagery, and Pepsi quickly dropped Madonna as its current pitch-girl. It did, however, win the Best Viewers Choice Video at the MTV Awards.

LI'L JINX

Cartoonist Joe Edwards's precocious, pigtailed blonde girl whose one-page comic-strip adventures have been featured as a regular segment in the *Archie* comic books since July 1947.

LILY MUNSTER

Maiden name: Lily Dracula. Age: 137. Herman Munster's graciously charming wife is a vampire-ish homemaker whose hauntingly beautiful appearance includes ghastly pale makeup and a skunk stripe running through her long black hair. (She resembles Vampira, a horror-movie hostess on TV during the 1950s.) Lily's perfume of choice is Chanel No. 13. Portrayed by Yvonne De Carlo on *The Munsters* sitcom from 1964 to 1966.

LIMBO

"How low can you go?" Classic dance, introduced by dance-master Chubby Checker (1962's "Limbo Rock"), involving a limbo stick that gets lower and lower and lower. It's popular at luaus, frat parties, and roller rinks.

LINCOLN LOGS

Since 1916, generations of kids have experienced the rugged and exciting days of America's untamed frontier with these beloved construction sets. Lincoln Logs were created by John Lloyd Wright (son of America's most distinguished architect, Frank Lloyd Wright), whose inspiration came from a Japanese technique for constructing earthquake-proof buildings (crisscross beaming). A typical Lincoln Log set—consisting of tiny interlocking logs made of real wood from the forests of Oregon, and flat green pieces used for the roofs, gables, and a chimney—allowed youngsters to make realistic-looking cabins, forts, corrals, and bridges. In the 1940s, Playskool Toys acquired Lincoln Logs, and the following decade they became a massive hit because of America's fascination with Davy Crockett and the Wild West. By the mid '70s, one million sets of Lincoln Logs were sold a year!

FYI: ▸ Typifying "the spirit of America," Lincoln Logs were named after our sixteenth President and his log-cabin birthplace.

LINUS VAN PELT

This *Peanuts* cartoon character is Charlie Brown's deep-thinking, subtly intelligent, and oversensitive best pal, who can't cope without his powder-blue security blanket and has unsupported faith in the elusive Great Pumpkin. He is the younger brother of the crabby, bossy, and opinionated Lucy Van Pelt.

LIONEL TRAIN SETS

Invented in 1900 by Joshua Lionel Cowen, who gave the Michigan-based company his middle name, these realistically detailed HO-scale sets were simply the best when it came to model railroading. Traditionally in the Baby Boomers' childhood years, many boys would wake up Christmas morning to find a Lionel electric train set—complete with engines, cabooses, and other railroad cars—circling the Christmas tree.

LION KING

The popularity of Walt Disney big-screen animation continued in 1994 with the record-breaking success of *The Lion King*. (It earned more than $312 million worldwide, to become the highest-grossing animated movie in history.) Set amid the stunning beauty of Africa's Serengeti, this coming-of-age adventure centers on willful lion cub Simba, son of proud ruler

King Mufasa and destined to be the leader of the animals. Treacherous uncle Scar—second in line to the throne—plots with a trio of wicked hyenas to kill Mufasa, and in doing so tricks nephew Simba into believing that his actions had caused his father's death. Guilt-ridden, the young cub escapes into exile and sheds his identity as the future king. He is befriended by carefree meerkat Timon and his warthog pal Pumbaa (two of the film's best-loved characters), who instruct Simba on "hakuna matata," a Swahili phrase meaning "no worries." Meanwhile, Scar takes over the grassy savanna, where his incompetence turns it into a parched wasteland. After maturing into an adult lion during exile, Simba is persuaded by lioness Nala, his childhood girlfriend, to return home to overthrow Scar, reclaim his kingdom, and complete nature's "Circle of Life." Other noteworthy *Lion King* characters include hornbill Zazu and shaman baboon Rafiki.

The soundtrack features Elton John's "Can You Feel the Love Tonight," which won a Best Song Oscar, and "The Circle of Life," plus "Hakuna Matata," sung by Timon and Pumbaa. A musical stage show based on *The Lion King* opened on Broadway in 1997.

LISA DOUGLAS

"Dahling, I love you, but give me Park Avenue!" On *Green Acres*, this glamorous socialite (played by Zsa Zsa's sister Eva Gabor) finds herself yanked from a cushy Manhattan lifestyle to live on a dilapidated farmstead in Hooterville by much-adored hubby Oliver Wendell Douglas. Once there, she befriends all the farm animals, including a cow she names Eleanor, and learns to cook some rather indigestible forms of "hotscakes." Because of her thick Hungarian accent, the Hooterville locals usually misunderstand everything she says, and she in return usually misunderstands everything they say.

LISA FRANK

Since 1979, this artist's colorful graphics of big-eyed teens, kittens, dolphins, and unicorns, splattered on all sorts of trendy merchandise items, particularly school supplies, has been the "stuff girls love."

LISA SIMPSON

Voiced by Yeardley Smith, Lisa Marie Simpson is the extremely brainy (159 I.Q.), socially conscious (budding feminist, vegetarian, and Buddhist) saxophone prodigy (Bleeding Gums Murphy is her jazz-blues mentor) who is highly misunderstood and undervalued by her daft cartoon family on TV's *The Simpsons*. She attends second grade at Springfield Elementary School.

LITE-BRITE

"Lite-Brite, makin' things with light / What a sight, making things with Lite-Brite!" A fondly remembered toy, infamous for annoying moms because of the oodles of small, colorful pegs that were swallowed up in shag carpeting only to reemerge as an enemy of bare feet when stepped on. Introduced in the 1960s, Hasbro's Lite-Brite, with the illuminated electric pegboard, was easy to use. You placed a precut black paper pattern over the pegboard, inserted colored glow-pegs into the holes of the pattern, peeled away the paper, and were left with a colorfully lit clown, horse, parrot, windmill, sailboat, or whatever else your imagination could come up with. Moms enrolled in ceramics classes would create miniature Christmas trees with holes in them for Lite-Brite pegs, so that when a lightbulb in the base of the ceramic tree was lit, the pegs glowed in glorious living color!

LITTLE ANNIE FANNY

Created by Harvey Kurtzman (the founder of *Mad* magazine) in 1962, the buxom blonde appeared for twenty-six years in an adult-oriented comic strip featured in the back pages of *Playboy* magazine. Lampooning the social changes of America (the space race, civil rights, women's lib, Miss America, The Beatles, and so on), the colorful strip usually depicted clueless Annie's involvement in some escapade in which her clothes are taken off. It was loosely based on Harold Gray's *Little Orphan Annie*. (Orphan Annie had a benefactor named Daddy Warbucks, while Annie Fanny had a benefactor named Sugardaddy Bigbucks.)

LITTLE AUDREY

The wide-eyed little girl who wore a trademark red dress and brown hair styled in ponytails on both the top and the lower back of her head was *Harvey* comics' biggest female character. Sweet, playful, and gifted with a huge imagination, Little Audrey was first seen as the star of theatrical cartoon shorts for Paramount Pictures, beginning with "Santa's Surprise" in 1947 (Mae Questel provided her voice). She headlined her comic-book series, published by St. John from 1948 until 1952, the year she moved to *Harvey*. She was greatly adored throughout the 1950s and 1960s. Little Audrey's popularity led to spin-off comic books, including *Little Audrey Clubhouse* and *Little Audrey TV Funtime*, a newspaper comic strip, and a multitude of toy products. From 1959 to 1960, her theatrical cartoons were played on TV's *Matty's Funday Funnies*, along with other *Harvey World* favorites, such as Casper and Baby Huey. Audrey's best pals were prankster Melvin and buck-toothed Lucretia. In 1976, the publication of *Little Audrey* comics and those of the other *Harvey* gals (*Little Dot*, *Little Lotta*, and *Wendy the Good Little Witch*) were halted to make more room for Richie Rich's then-growing comic-book line.

LITTLE BLACK DRESS

In the 1990s, the short miniskirt style returned once more, only this time it was more respectable than ever. Now known as the little black dress, it became a modern woman's fashion staple, worn to various events ranging from power lunches to cocktail parties to wedding receptions.

LITTLE DARLINGS

"Don't let the title fool you." Once-controversial movie about two rival fifteen-year-old girls at a summer camp, Camp Little Wolf, who settle their differences through a loss-of-virginity contest. Teen queens Tatum O'Neal and Kristy McNichol star as rich, well-bred Ferris Whitney and poor, street-smart Angel Bright. To win their bets, Ferris tries to make it with the much-older camp counselor Gary Callahan (played by handsome French actor Armand Assante), while Angel falls for Randy (played by young heartthrob Matt Dillon), a stud across the lake at the boy's camp. Fourteen-year-old Cynthia Nixon (of today's *Sex and the City* fame), starred as Sunshine, Ferris and Angel's hippie roomie. Ronald F. Maxwell directed the 1980 comedy.

FYI: ▸ Who wins? Ferris lies and says she lost her virginity first to Gary, while Angel actually loses hers to Randy.

LITTLE DEBBIE

Packaged in family-friendly cartons, these snack cakes were created in 1960 by O. D. McKee, who named them after his four-year-old granddaughter, Debbie (she's the advertising mascot in the straw hat and blue gingham dress). Best known of the Little Debbie goodies are the Banana Twins, Fudge Brownies, Honey Buns, Nutty Bars, Oatmeal Creme Pies, Pecan Spinwheels, Star Crunch, Swiss Cake Rolls, and Zebra Cakes.

LITTLE DOT

Cute little lass from the comic pages of *Harvey* who was just plain dotty over dots. Premiering in 1953, Little Dot wore only dotted clothing (her trademark dress was red covered with black polka dots) and always kept her black hair tied in a ponytail with a polka-dotted bow. Her bedroom was full of every polka-dotted object imaginable, and to the bewilderment of her folks, she constantly brought home anything and everything circular or dot-shaped. Little Dot had an endless supply of eccentric uncles and aunts who enjoyed sending their favorite niece peculiar dotted items that involved her in zany comic-book adventures. Friends included tubby Little Lotta and poor little rich boy Richie Rich.

FYI: ▸ Little Dot's last name was Polka. (Get it? Polka, Dot!)

LITTLE DRUMMER BOY

"Blessed are the pure at heart, for they shall see God." The most solemn of the holiday TV specials to come out of the 1960s featured the stop-motion animation of Rankin/Bass and narration by legendary screen actress Greer Garson. It told the story of little Aaron, an orphaned drummer boy full of hate toward all people after bandits destroyed his family's farm with fire and killed his parents. Aaron wanders the desert with a surrogate family of surviving farm animals that dance to his drumbeat: Sampson the donkey, Joshua the camel, and Bim Baa Baa the lamb. One day, Aaron and the animals are taken prisoner by two desert rats, greedy Haramed and his second-banana, Ali, who force them to serve as an entertainment troupe. After Joshua is sold to one of the Three Kings journeying to Bethlehem led by the Star of David, the Little

Drummer Boy, with the help of Sampson and Bim Baa Baa, escape from the thieves and set off to reclaim the beloved camel.

Once in the city of Bethlehem, Bim Baa Baa is struck and gravely injured by a speeding chariot (a heart-wrenching moment). Cradling the wounded creature, Aaron sorrowfully arrives at the manger just as the Three Kings are giving their gifts to the baby Jesus. Having no gift, Aaron gives the only thing he has—a song on his drum ("parum-pa-pum-pum"), which brings joy to the Christ Child. Miraculously, Bim Baa Baa is healed by the Savior's powers and Aaron feels love in his heart again. Premiering for Christmas 1968, this touching special was based on the classic Yuletide song made famous by the Harry Simeone Chorale in 1958.

LITTLE GOLDEN BOOKS

Since 1942, these books with the famous gold-foil bindings not only sparked the imagination of children but also introduced them to the wonderful world of reading. Many happy hours were spent reading the wide variety of stories and staring at the colorful, inviting illustrations. The Little Golden Book series was up-to-date in featuring popular character and cartoon icons, as well as classic fairy tales and books on educational subjects. Best of all were all the charming tales associated only with the Golden Book line, such as *The Little Engine That Could, The Poky Little Puppy, The Saggy Baggy Elephant, Scruffy the Tugboat, The Shy Little Kitten,* and *The Tawny Scrawny Lion.* Inspired many other book series aimed at small children, including Rand McNally's Elf Books, Wonder Books, Tell-a-Tales, Big Little Books, Golden Shape Books, Disney's Wonderful World of Reading, and Beginner Books by Dr. Seuss.

FYI: ▸ More than one billion Little Golden Books have reached the hands of children!

LITTLE HOUSE ON THE PRAIRIE

Family-friendly prime-time drama based on the stories of Laura Ingalls Wilder, notable for introducing a new generation to her *Little House* book series. Set in Walnut Grove, Minnesota, in the 1870s, the books centered on Laura Ingalls's farm family and their experience with homesteading on the American frontier. Airing on NBC from 1974 to 1983, the hour-long TV show advocated good old-fashioned values and traditions (you know, like family, home, and hard work) rarely seen on prime time anymore. Starring as the Ingalls family were Michael Landon as Charles the hardworking father; Karen Grassle as Caroline the loving mother; Melissa Sue Anderson as Mary the golden-haired eldest daughter; Melissa Gilbert as Laura the pigtailed middle daughter and narrator of the show; alternating twins Lindsay and Sidney Greenbush as Carrie the youngest daughter; and Barney as Jack the family dog. Regulars included Richard Bull as general-store proprietor Nels Oleson, Katherine MacGregor as his haughty wife, Harriet Oleson, Alison Arngrim as their bratty daughter, Nellie Oleson, Jonathan Gilbert (Melissa's brother) as their nasty son, Willie Oleson, Charlotte Stewart as schoolteacher Miss Beadle, Karl Swenson as mill owner Lars Hansen, Victor French as farmer Isaiah Edwards, and Bonnie Bartlett as his wife, Grace. In addition to his starring role, Landon served as the executive producer and regularly wrote and directed.

LITTLE JOE CARTWRIGHT

Rancher Ben Cartwright's baby-faced youngest son (played by handsome Michael Landon on TV's *Bonanza*) was the romantic hothead who rode a horse called Cochise. Little Joe's Southern-belle mother, Marie, died after falling from a horse.

LITTLE LOTTA

Called the "World's Champion Eater" and the "Strongest Young Lady on the Planet," Lotta Plump was one of *Harvey* comics' leading female stars of the 1960s and 1970s (others: Little Audrey, Little Dot, and Wendy the Good Little Witch). Born in 1955, Little Lotta had an enormous appetite for lots and lots of food, which made her a lot of a gal. Along with the hefty size, she was fun-loving, hot-tempered, and very strong (Lotta didn't realize the power of her own strength). The freckled lass wore every day a uniform consisting of a green sweater, a white pleated skirt, and a red bow in her bobbed blonde hair. She aspired to join her hometown police department when she got older. Comic-book pals include dotty Little Dot, rich Richie Rich, and diminutive brainhead Gerald.

LITTLE LULU

First appearing in the *Saturday Evening Post* in 1935, Marjorie Henderson Buell's popular comic-strip and cartoon character—a little moppet full of childish wit and corkscrew curls—was the forerunner of such mischief-making lasses as Little Audrey and Nancy. Lulu's on-again, off-again fellow was next-door neighbor Tubby Tompkins.

LITTLE MERMAID

After a decade or so of insipid animated motion pictures, the delightful 1989 spin on the Hans Christian Andersen story about the young mermaid who yearns to be a two-legged human ushered in a renaissance for the Disney studio. Redheaded mermaid Princess Ariel, daughter of King Triton, ruler of the seas, saves the life of a shipwrecked human. He turns out to be a handsome prince named Eric, with whom she falls hopelessly in love. Against her father's wishes, she longs to join Prince Eric as a land-dwelling person. Evil Ursula, an octopus-legged sea witch, comes into play by granting Ariel two legs in exchange for her beautiful voice. The rest of the yarn goes: Newly mute Ariel, sans fish tail, finds Eric on land; he falls in love with her; Ursula plots to overtake King Triton's undersea kingdom; Ariel and Eric, with the help of faithful ocean pals—Sebastian the Jamaican crab, Flounder the fish, and Scuttle the albatross—foil Ursula's attempts, and everyone lives happily ever after.

The overwhelming success of *The Little Mermaid* (grossing a record $84.4 million at the box office), including two Academy Awards for Best Score and Best Song ("Under the Sea"), led to a whole new run of Disney animated films in the 1990s. These well-crafted, computer-enhanced features, loosely adapted from classic folk and fairy tales, included *Beauty and the Beast* (1991), *Aladdin* (1992), *The Lion King* (1994), *Pocahontas* (1995), *The Hunchback of Notre Dame* (1996), *Hercules* (1997), *Mulan* (1998), and *Tarzan* (1999). Enchanting brand-new heroes and heroines were showcased (all soon to be classic Disney characters), along with lovable supporting characters, wonderfully wicked villains, and unforgettable, toe-tapping musical numbers. The downside to this new wave in Disney animation is the thousands and thousands of toys and merchandise tie-ins cluttering the current pop culture landscape.

LITTLE PRINCE

Written by Antoine de Saint-Exupéry in 1943, a fable about the adventures of a young boy from the faraway asteroid of B-612 who travels through the galaxy on a series of comets. When he reaches earth, the little space traveler encounters a pilot who had crash-landed in the barren Sahara who teaches the lad about life and love. In 1974, this children's classic was made into a musical motion picture directed by Stanley Donen and starring Steven Warner as the Little Prince and Richard Kiley as the pilot. Gene Wilder and choreographer Bob Fosse co-starred as a fox and a snake.

LITTLE RED-HAIRED GIRL

Maybe someday our beloved Charlie Brown will get up the nerve to ask the Little Red-Haired Girl to share his school lunch at Birchwood Elementary in the *Peanuts* comic strip.

LITTLE ROMANCE

Director George Roy Hill's enchanting romance about teenage puppy love. Based on the novel by Patrick Cauvin, the 1979 film told the tale of an intelligent and lonely American girl named Lauren (Diane Lane) living in Paris with her five-times-married actress mother, Kay King (Sally Kellerman), and understanding stepfather, Richard King (Arthur Hill). Lauren falls in love with Daniel (Thelonious Bernard), a charming (and just as intelligent) lower-class French lad, and together they become each other's "Bogie" and "Bacall." After their "little romance" comes under fire from both sets of parents, the youngsters—chaperoned by a dapper old con man named Julius (Laurence Olivier)—run away to Venice. In that Italian city, a romantic myth says that if two lovers kiss under the Bridge of Sighs at sunset when the bells of Campanile toll, their love will last for eternity. The heart-tugging ending is guaranteed to make you feel all warm and fuzzy on the inside, and weepy and smiley on the outside.

LITTLES

Meet the Little family: Mr. Little, Mrs. Little, their kids, Tom and Lucy, Granny, and Uncle Pete, a group of six-inch-tall humans with long tails and pointy ears who live in a house owned by Mr. and Mrs. Biggs. The Littles use big-people-sized objects for their furnishings, like sardine cans for beds and thread spools for tables, and avoid life-threatening hazards, such as household cats own by the giant people. Featured in the best-selling children's book series by John Peterson, which began in 1967, the Littles also starred in a much-watched Saturday-morning cartoon, airing from 1983 to 1986.

LIVING ISLAND

Magical isle found in the make-believe Land of Krofft, where animals sing, trees dance, Witchiepoo rules the sky, and the mayor is a talking cowboy dragon named H. R. Pufnstuf.

LIZA COLBY

"I'll make Jenny Gardner pay!" Scheming teen bitch from the daytime soap *All My Children* who seized every opportunity to ruin the romance of school classmates Greg Nelson and Jenny Gardner. Liza cheated her way into the 1982 Miss Junior Pine Valley Contest in order to beat the real winner, Jenny, out of the crown.

LOCH NESS MONSTER

Alleged sea creature believed to live in Loch Ness, the largest freshwater lake in the British Isles, located in the Highlands of Scotland. Few have seen "Nessie," but those who have say she has the appearance of a Plesiosaurus, an aquatic dinosaur marked by a long, tapering neck with a serpentine-like head, a huge humped back, and fins for legs. Along with Bigfoot and the Abominable Snowman, the Loch Ness Monster is one of the great mythical monsters of contemporary times.

FYI: ▸ That famous picture of the Loch Ness Monster—you know, the blurry one with Nessie swimming in the lake—taken by Colonel Robert Wilson in the 1930s, was acknowledged as a fake by Wilson's accomplice, Christian Spurling, on his deathbed in 1993. Spurling stated that he had helped build the model of the monster used in the photograph.

LOCK, SHOCK, AND BARREL

Ill-behaved trio of tots wearing trick-or-treat costumes who reside in Halloweentown and have a hand in the kidnapping of "Mr. Sandy Claws" in *The Nightmare Before Christmas*.

LOCO-MOTION

The 1960s dance inspired by Little Eva's "The Loco-Motion" (1962) is best described by the song's lyrics: "a chug-a-chug motion like a railroad train."

LOGAN'S RUN

"The only thing you can't have in this perfect world of total pleasure is your thirtieth birthday. Logan is twenty-nine." In the sci-fi flick, it's the year 2274 and a hedonistic society resides in an underground domed city where the citizens are only allowed to live to the ripe old age of thirty. Every person has a red crystal planted in the palm of his or her hand, and when it starts to flash on the eve of their thirtieth birthday, they are required to attend "renewal" at the Carousel, a ritual ceremony that executes these unsuspecting citizens. There are "Runners," who decide to reject this rite of passage by escaping to a mysterious utopia on the outside world called "Sanctuary." It is then up to the Sandmen, an elite government police force, to chase, apprehend, and slay these rebellious resisters.

Good-looking British actor Michael York stars as Logan 5, a Sandman with a blinking palm who decides to run, with the help of love-interest Jessica (Jenny Agutter). The fleeing twosome are hunted by Francis (Richard Jordan), a colleague of Logan's who is determined to stop his friend from running. On their journey, Logan and Jessica encounter the wild orphan children of the Cathedral; evade facial mutilation from a laser machine belonging to insane cosmetic surgeon Doc (Michael Anderson Jr.); and almost become frozen dinner for an Ice-Cyborg named Box (Roscoe Lee Browne). Once they reach the safety of Sanctuary, the couple stumble on the ruins of Washington, D.C., where they meet the cat-loving wise Old Man (Peter Ustinov), the first and only elderly person they have ever seen. Feathered-haired Farrah Fawcett-Majors makes an early career performance as Holly, the beautiful assistant of Doc, who sacrifices her life to save Logan and Jessica.

Directed by Michael Anderson and based on the novel by William F. Nolan and George Clayton Johnson, the fast-paced 1976 thriller features spectacular futuristic sets and vivid special effects. It inspired a brief prime-time series, *Logan's Run* (1977–78), starring Gregory Harrison as Logan and Heather Menzies as Jessica.

LOIS LANE

No-nonsense newshound whose longing to get the ultimate story puts her in life-threatening situations in which mighty Superman has to come to the rescue. Lois had the hots for Superman, but she doesn't know that Clark Kent, her bumbling co-reporter at the *Daily Planet* (who had the hots for Lois), is her hero's alter ego.

LOLLAPALOOZA

Established by former Jane's Addiction frontman Perry Farrell in the summer of 1991, a nomadic music festival made up of alternative rock bands (like the Butthole Surfers, Red Hot Chili Peppers, and Nine Inch Nails), body modification sideshows (like piercings and tattoos), and T-shirt vendors. The name Lollapalooza came from a 1960s slang term for an extraordinary thing, person, or event.

LONE RANGER

Who was that masked man? Why, it's the mysterious Lone Ranger (a.k.a. John Reid), astride horse Silver and joined by faithful Indian sidekick Tonto, who battled dastardly outlaws of the Old West. The white-hatted hero with the black half-mask was played by Clayton Moore on the hit ABC-TV western *The Lone Ranger* from 1949 to 1957.

FYI: ▸ The Lone Ranger's familiar instrumental TV theme was Rossini's bouncy "William Tell Overture."

LONG DUK DONG

"Whatsa happenin', hot stuff?" Asian-American actor Gedde Watanabe's looney party animal, named after a "duck's dork," is cited by many as the most unforgettable character in John Hughes's teen classic *Sixteen Candles* (1984). A foreign-exchange student from China, Long stays with Howard and Dorothy, the clueless grandparents of put-out Samantha Baker.

LONGET, CLAUDINE

Pretty brunette singer from Paris known for soft renditions of others' hits (examples: "The Look of Love" and "Love Is Blue"), which she sang in a wispy voice with a strong French accent. Discovered by crooner Andy Williams in Las Vegas while performing as the lead dancer in the *Folies-Bergère* show, she married him in 1961 and had three children. Although divorced from Williams in 1967, Longet and her children—daughter Noelle and sons Andrew and Christian—continued appearing for many years on his annual TV Christmas specials as one big happy family. In 1976, Longet's ethereal image turned nightmare heavy when she accidentally shot and killed her lover, professional skier Spider Sabich, in Aspen, Colorado. Following a highly publicized murder trial (there are those who believe she killed Sabich in cold blood over a souring romance), Longet was convicted of criminal negligence and sentenced to thirty days in jail. These days, she remains in quiet retirement in Aspen with husband Ron Austin, her defense attorney in the Sabich case.

LONG, STRAIGHT, CENTER-PARTED HAIR

After the flip bouffant and before Farrah Fawcett feathers, long, straight hair with a severe middle part was the most common hairstyle for girls during most of the 1970s. The style's roots originated in the late 1960s among hippie chicks who wanted a natural look and didn't like fussing with contemporary cuts, styling, and hair products. Forget painstaking roller sets and back-combing—those were for squares and moms. Young gals were now laying their long tresses on an ironing board while a friend used a clothes iron to flatten out all the kinks, giving it that groovy extrastraight look so coveted in the halls of school.

Two trendsetting prime-time teens spurred this popular look: blonde Maureen McCormick, who played Marcia on *The Brady Bunch*, and brunette Susan Dey, who played Laurie on *The Partridge Family*. Peggy Lipton as hipster Julie on TV's *Mod Squad*, and Ali MacGraw as the dying Jenny in the 1970 flick *Love Story*, wore their hair this way. The long, flat tresses of earthy pop singers Cher, Melanie, and Carly Simon also helped make it the look of the decade.

FYI: ▸ Looking back at my 1975 junior high yearbook, I saw the impact of this hairstyle—all eighteen girls on my school's two cheerleading squads were sporting the zipper-headed straight style!

LOONEY DOONEY
The name of the dune buggy driven by the teen gang and ghostly Jonathan Muddlemore on the Saturday-morning cartoon *The Funky Phantom*. It had a large American flag decal on the hood.

LOONEY TUNES
A wacky array of cartoon characters who appeared in hundreds of short films for the Warner Brothers studios. Created by such legendary animators as Tex Avery, Friz Freleng, Chuck Jones, Bob Clampett, and Robert McKimson, these witty and funny cartoons were once shown before the feature movie at theaters. Looney Tune favorites included Porky Pig, Daffy Duck, Bugs Bunny, Elmer Fudd, Tweety Pie, Sylvester J. Pussycat, Yosemite Sam, Foghorn Leghorn, Pepe Le Pew, Marvin Martian, Road Runner, Wylie E. Coyote, Speedy Gonzalez, and Tasmanian Devil. In the 1960s and 1970s, as the popularity of Saturday-morning cartoons boomed, the Looney Tunes became staples of TV, often headlining their own shows: *The Bugs Bunny Show* (1960–62), *The Porky Pig Show* (1964–67), *The Road Runner Show* (1966–72), *Sylvester and Tweety* (1976–77), *The Daffy Duck Show* (1978–82), and, more recent, *Taz-Mania* (1991–93).

LORELEI
A mysterious and beautiful blonde mermaid (played by Marta "Judy Robinson" Kristen) who rescues and falls in love with surfing nitwit Bonehead (Jody McCrea) in *Beach Blanket Bingo* (1965). Also, the name of Marilyn Monroe's luscious gold digger in *Gentlemen Prefer Blondes*.

LOST BOYS
"Sleep all day. Party all night. Never grow old. Never die. It's fun to be a vampire." Directed by Joel Schumacher, a 1987 youth-oriented horror flick about two brothers, Mike and Sam Emerson (played by Jason Patric and Corey Haim), who move with their single mother, Lucy (Dianne Wiest), to live with their Grandpa (Barnard Hughes) in Santa Clara, California, a beachfront burgh renowned for its large amusement park and a plague of murders. A gang of Gothic teen vampire bikers led by wicked David (Kiefer Sutherland), who live in an oceanside cavern, is the reason for all the murders. Mike falls for beautiful bloodsucker Star (Jami Gertz), and, worried that his older brother is turning into a vampire, Sam enlists comic-book-crazed friend Edgar Frog (Corey Feldman) to help destroy the Lost Boys. (Where's Buffy the Vampire Slayer when you need her?) Billy Wirth and Alex Winter co-star as vampires Dwayne and Marko.

LOST IN SPACE
An exciting sci-fi TV classic loosely based on Gold Key's *Space Family Robinson* comic books and created by "Master of Disaster" Irwin Allen (*Voyage to the Bottom of the Sea* and *Land of the Giants*). Airing on prime time from 1965 to 1968, the CBS-TV series told the story of the Robinsons, a wide-eyed family sent by the U.S. government in 1997 to start a colony on a planet in the Alpha Centauri star system. Unfortunately for them, an enemy-agent stowaway, Dr. Zachary Smith, sabotages the mission, and their Jupiter 2 spaceship is thrown radically off course. Now lost in space, the Robinson family roam from planet to planet, trying desperately to find a way home, only to encounter dangerous space monsters and other bizarre life-forms. Each episode ended with a "how are we going to get out of this?" cliffhanger, usually instigated by devious Dr. Smith. ("To be continued next week, same time, same channel!")

Lost in Space starred Guy Williams as astrophysicist Professor John Robinson, the head of the space-age household, and June Lockhart as Maureen Robinson, the devoted wife and mother. Other cast members included Marta Kristen as eldest daughter Judy Robinson, Angela Cartwright as youngest daughter Penny Robinson, Billy Mumy as son Will Robinson, Mark Goddard as young pilot Don West, Jonathan Harris as cowardly adversary Dr. Smith, and Bob May as the Robot B-9.

Popular with children—who enjoyed the special effects (even if they were on the cheesy side) and the odd alien creatures—*Lost in Space* spawned dozens of toys, including a board game by Milton Bradley, a Switch 'n Go play set by Mattel, View-Master reels, model kits by Aurora, a domed lunch box by Aladdin, and a battery-operated twelve-inch-tall robot by Remco. In 1998, a big-screen remake was released, starring William Hurt as John, Mimi Rogers as Maureen, Matt LeBlanc as Don, Heather Graham as Judy, and Gary Oldman as Dr. Smith.

FYI: ▸ The *Lost in Space* theme was composed by John Williams. (Remember the opening credits with the animated Robinsons dangling in space?) The prolific Williams later scored the sci-fi movies *Jaws* (1975), *Star Wars* (1977), *Close Encounters of the Third Kind* (1977), *Superman* (1978), *Raiders of the Lost Ark* (1981), and *E.T.* (1982).

LOST SAUCER

Airing from 1975 to 1976, this silly Saturday-morning TV program starred Ruth Buzzi and Jim Nabors as Fi and Fum, a pair of alien androids from the year 2369 who sail their flying saucer through a time warp and land in modern-day Chicago. They befriend nine-year-old Jerry (Jarrod Johnson) and his teenage babysitter Alice (Alice Playten). Upon inviting the youngsters aboard to check out the craft, things go awry. The police arrive, and Fum panics and accidentally hits the launch button, sending the spaceship, now with Jerry and Alice as passengers, back through the time warp, where they get hopelessly lost. Dorse, a creature with a dog's torso and horse's head, was Fi and Fum's resident pet. After cancellation, *The Lost Saucer* reappeared as a segment of *The Krofft Supershow.*

LOU GRANT

Edward Asner played the gruff producer of the Six O'Clock News on WJM-TV in Minneapolis, and later the city editor of the *Los Angeles Tribune* on CBS-TV's *Mary Tyler Moore Show* (1970–77) and its spin-off *Lou Grant* (1977–82). Mr. Grant's bark is worse than his bite. He's a pussycat underneath the bulldog exterior.

LOUNGE MUSIC

After almost three decades of being oh-so-dreaded by the hip and young, easy-listening music (a.k.a. martini or elevator music) from the 1950s and 1960s—yes, our parents' tunes—came to be appreciated by a new audience in the 1990s, thanks to cocktail revivalist groups, like Combustible Edison, Love Jones, and Big Bad Voodoo Daddy, and to compilation CD series, such as *Space Age Bachelor Pad* and *Ultra-Lounge*. Favorite lounge recording acts include Herb Alpert, Burt Bacharach, Tony Bennett, Nat "King" Cole, Bobby Darin, Sammy Davis Jr., Martin Denny, Juan Garcia Esquivel, Ella Fitzgerald, Tom Jones, Peggy Lee, Henry Mancini, Dean Martin, Frank Sinatra, Mel Torme, and Nancy Wilson.

LOVE BEADS

Representing brotherly love, these dangly necklaces in various lengths made out of tiny, multicolored beads were essential to the hippie look back in the 1960s.

LOVE BOAT

Where did stars go when fame had faded? Where could you see has-been celebs like Marcia Wallace, Tom Bosley, Nanette Fabray, Don Adams, Pearl Bailey, and Jerry Stiller find first-rate romance on the high seas? Why, on prime time's Love Boat, a.k.a *Pacific Princess*, the luxurious cruise ship that sailed weekly on romantic and funny voyages across tropical waters to Mexico's exotic Puerto Vallarta.

Patterned after the comedy vignettes of *Love, American Style* (1969–74) and loosely based on Jacqueline Saunders's book, *The Love Boats* (drawn from her adventures as an actual cruise-ship hostess), this hit series became a Saturday-night fixture, airing from 1977 to 1986 on ABC-TV. Every episode featured different interwoven tales of amour involving famous guest stars of yesterday and today. *The Love Boat*'s sunny crew included earnest Captain Merrill Stubing (Gavin MacLeod), perky social director Julie McCoy (Lauren Tewes), swingin' physician Dr. Adam Bricker, a.k.a. Doc (Bernie Kopell), goofball assistant purser Burl "Gopher" Smith (Fred Grandy), and sympathetic bartender Isaac Washington (Ted Lange). Later, regular add-ons included Vicki (Jill Whelan), Captain Stubing's twelve-year-old daughter; Judy McCoy (Pat Klous), Julie's sister and social director replacement (Klous substituted for Tewes after drug abuse led to Lauren's departure in 1984); Ashley "Ace" Evans (Ted McGinley), the ship's photographer; April Lopez ("cuchi-cuchi" Charo in a recurring role), a singer-guitarist; and the Love Boat Mermaids, a team of lovely singer-dancers. *The Love Boat* theme was sung by Jack

Jones ("Love, exciting and new / Come aboard, we're expecting you . . .").

LOVE BUG

Based on the story *Car-Boy-Girl* by Gordon Buford, an engaging Walt Disney romp about a Volkswagen Beetle with a mind of its own, named Herbie, that follows a down-on-his-luck race-car driver, Jim Douglas (Dean Jones), home. After being adopted by Jim, the amazing Herbie—car number 53—wins race after race. He also performs outrageous stunts while being chased through the streets of San Francisco by villainous former owner Peter Thorndyke (David Tomlinson), who wants to sabotage "the little car." Other human characters in the film include Jim's pretty girlfriend Carole Bennett (Michele Lee) and silly mechanic Tennessee Steinmetz (Buddy Hackett). Directed by Robert Stevenson, *The Love Bug* was the highest-grossing American film of 1969 (it earned a staggering $23 million), and at the time the second-biggest film in Disney history, behind *Mary Poppins* (1964). It inspired three sequels: *Herbie Rides Again* (1974), *Herbie Goes to Monte Carlo* (1977), and *Herbie Goes Bananas* (1980).

LOVE CONNECTION

The Dating Game, 1980s style! Potential dates are selected through videotaped interviews. After the initial date, the couple return to the game show to report the outcome—good or bad—of their rendezvous. Hosted by Chuck Woolery.

LOVE IS . . .

Adorable syndicated newspaper cartoon created by New Zealander Kim Casali in 1970 as a way of expressing her love for husband Roberto. It hit a 10 on the "Aaahhh, ain't that cute" scale. The single-panel comic strip featured a totally naked (minus genitalia), childlike, lovesick couple accompanied by different sayings, like "Love is . . . to be proud of your partner wherever you go," "Love is . . . paying her a compliment," "Love is . . . rubbing her feet after a hard day at work," and "Love is . . . making desserts for him when you're on a diet." Popular throughout the 1970s and 1980s, the *Love Is . . .* twosome and their warm aphorisms were often cut out of the newspaper and placed on a refrigerator door or tucked inside the pages of a scrapbook. They were also found on numerous merchandise items, such as music boxes, statuettes, drinking glasses, puzzles, and even in a series of paperback books.

"LOVE IS A BATTLEFIELD"

The storytelling video to Pat Benatar's 1983 million-selling single starred the rock star as a hooker who leads fellow prostitutes in forming a now-clichéd dance cavalcade (for example, Donna Summer's "She Works Hard for the Money" and Michael Jackson's "Thriller") against an abusive pimp.

"LOVE ROLLER COASTER"

This funky soul song by The Ohio Players is infamous for being part of an urban legend. According to popular myth, during the second chorus you can hear a woman screaming—which is true—supposedly because she was being raped or murdered or both while the song was being recorded in the studio. In my research, I've found no evidence of this being true (maybe she was screaming because she was riding the "roller coaster of love, oooh oooh oooh"). Despite the notoriety—or maybe because of it—the single became a million-selling chart-topper in 1975.

LOVE'S BABY SOFT

Introduced in 1974 by the Mem Company, a young woman's fragrance unique in that it was the first cologne for those coming of age in the late 1970s and early 1980s. Love's Baby Soft had an intoxicating baby-powder scent and came packaged in a small spray bottle convenient for storing in purses and large pockets. Other fragrances popular with teen gals of the era were Babe, Charlie, Enjoli, Wild Musk, and Avon's Sweet Honesty.

"LOVE SHACK"

The biggest hit and first million-seller of the B-52's, inspired by a fun-time dance club in rural Georgia, was accompanied by the best video of the day. The clip featured the B-52's and a gang of pals, including Afro-puffed drag queen RuPaul, shimmying the night away at the "Love Shack." Won an MTV Music Video Award for Best Group Video and voted Best Single of 1989 in *Rolling Stone* magazine's Music Awards.

LOVEY HOWELL
Mr. Howell's dingy socialite wife on TV's *Gilligan's Island* was played by film character actress Natalie Schafer from 1964 to 1967. Lovey loved furs, jewels, and Gold Dust No. 5—her favorite perfume.

LSD
"Blow your mind!" The hallucinogenic of choice for peace-loving, long-haired hippies of the 1960s and 1970s. Remember viewing film footage of the Woodstock rock festival showing hippies dancing as if they were wildly insane? Well, most likely they were on an LSD trip. This potent mood-changing drug is also known as "acid" because it's manufactured from lysergic acid diethylamide (LSD), which is found in ergot, a fungus that grows on grains.

LUCKY CHARMS

> "Do you know the joy of getting a scoop of Lucky Charms and having four mini-marshmallows in one scoop?"
> —COMEDIAN ROSIE O'DONNELL

Introduced in 1964 by General Mills, this "magically delicious" cereal is a favorite of kids because of its brightly colored and sugary-sweet mini-marshmallow charms: green clovers, orange stars, pink hearts, and yellow moons (in 1975, blue diamonds were added). The breakfast cereal is also famous for its spokes-elf, Lucky the Leprechaun, featured on the box front and in a long-airing series of animated TV ads.

LUCKY LOCKET KIDDLES
"Wear me and be lucky!" Manufactured from 1967 to 1970, a line of ticklishly small (two inches tall) Liddle Kiddles, packaged inside plastic lockets encrusted with colorful jewels, that could be taken out for play. Little girls dangled these highly versatile good-luck lockets on a gold chain around the neck or wrist or wore them clipped on a belt, headband, or purse.

LUCKY THE LEPRECHAUN
Advertising mascot for Lucky Charms cereal whose real name was L. C. Leprechaun. In animated TV commercials, this possessive sprite was regularly thwarted by a group of rambunctious children who tried to take away his precious pot of Lucky Charms.

LUCY EWING
Charlene Tilton and her blonde sexiness starred as the spoiled, trampy teenage daughter of seldom-seen Gary Ewing who resided at Southfork with her relatives on prime time's *Dallas*.

LUCY VAN PELT
Three things the beloved *Peanuts* character and crabby older sister of Linus Van Pelt takes delight in:

- Tormenting "blockhead" Charlie Brown
- Giving out five-cent advice from her neighborhood therapy booth
- Lounging seductively on musical genius Schroeder's piano (he's her crush)

LUDICROUS LION
"Buttons, buttons, who's got the buttons?" The quick-talking, con-artist feline was featured as one of the regular characters on Sid and Marty Krofft's Saturday classic *H. R. Pufnstuf*.

LUKE DUKE
Singer-actor Tom Wopat played the dark-haired half of the two hot-looking guys on prime time's *Dukes of Hazzard* from 1979 to 1985.

LUKE SKYWALKER
Fair-haired young farmer who lives with his aunt and uncle on the planet Tatooine. He aspires to be a light-saber-wielding Jedi Knight and bravely commits himself to helping the Rebel Alliance fight the Imperial Force's Dark Side. Played by Mark Hamill in the *Star Wars* movie trilogy.

LUKE SPENCER
Perm-head Anthony Geary starred as the popular antihero of TV's daytime soap *General Hospital*. Cynical in a charming sort of way, this rogue's tempestuous love affair with teen queen Laura Vinning made them the hot couple of daytime soaps in the early 1980s.

LUNCH BOXES
It used to be a ritual for children all across the nation to get a new lunch box every September at the beginning of the school year. These square pails with the squeaky hinges and coordinating ther-

moses were more than just containers for carrying food from home to school; they actually signaled the personality of an elementary-school kid. For example: Little beauty queens carried Barbie or Miss America; boy-next-door types had G.I. Joe or Hot Wheels; class clowns lugged Bullwinkle or The Banana Splits; future rock stars brought The Monkees or KISS; and bookworms usually clutched the boring standard plaid.

Originating in 1950 (Hopalong Cassidy was the first) and made of vinyl or lithographed metal, lunch boxes colorfully showcased the stars, shows, and interests of the times. Just imagine how totally cool it was to have your bologna sandwiches and Hostess Sno Balls transported via a Flipper, Scooby-Doo, or Dukes of Hazzard lunch box. By the early 1970s, more than 100 million lunch boxes had been sold. In the mid-1980s, these wonderful steel boxes—works of art in their own right—were banned because crusading moms claimed they could be used as deadly weapons (God forbid if little Tiffany got banged on the head by her Strawberry Shortcake lunch pail). Aladdin and King Seeley Thermos were the leading manufacturers of lunch boxes.

FYI: ▸ The all-time best-selling lunch box was the domed Walt Disney School Bus, with more than nine million sold from 1961 to 1973. Shaped like a yellow school bus, it featured Goofy as the driver, and other Disney characters (Mickey, Donald, Bambi, Dumbo, Pinocchio, Alice in Wonderland, and more) as passengers.

LURCH

The Addams Family's seven-foot-tall, 250-pound, zombie-like butler who plays the harpsichord and answers his eerie employers' loud gong with a ghoulish, deep-voiced "Youuuu raaang?"

LYDIA GRANT

"Show time, gentle people!" Attractive, hard-driving dance instructor at New York's High School of the Performing Arts. Played by actress-choreographer Debbie Allen in both the *Fame* movie and the TV series. Allen's snazzy choreography for the show won her two Emmy Awards.

LYN, DAWN

Born in 1963, the dark-haired, freckle-faced younger sister of teen hottie Leif Garrett played Steve Douglas's stepdaughter Dodie on *My Three Sons* from 1969 to 1972. Also starred in the big-screen films *Shootout* (1971), opposite Gregory Peck, and *Walking Tall* (1973), along with her brother.

jklm

MACARENA

"Hey Macarena!" A Spanish novelty song about a prostitute, performed by Los Del Rio (Bayside Boys Mix), that launched the number-one biggest dance craze of the 1990s. Most people either really loved this line dance (former Vice-Prez Al Gore, for one) or totally loathed it (this author). To do the Macarena (according to the box instructions of 1996's Hey Macarena Doll by Fun Source Toys):

- Put your right hand out, palm down. Then put your left hand out, palm down.
- Put your right hand out, palm up. Then your left hand out, palm up.
- Cross your right hand to your left elbow. Next, your left hand to your right elbow.
- Touch your right hand to your right ear. Then your left hand to your left ear.
- Cross right hand to your left hip. Next, left hand to your right hip.
- Put your right hand on your right hip. Then left hand on your left hip.
- Finally, sway your hips back and forth three times. Make a quarter turn to your right and repeat everything from the beginning.

MACARONI MOSAIC

Tacky craft project from the 1970s for which one glued together, then painted, uncooked pasta noodles—macaroni, shells, rigatoni—to create wondrous works of art featuring owls, mushrooms, windjammers, and even Jesus Christ.

MACH V

The Formula One Mach V, driven by brave teenager Speed Racer in his *Speed Racer* cartoon series, is the fastest, coolest, most high-tech race car in the world. Aerodynamically designed with trademark pointed fenders, the white convertible came equipped with a variety of functions, all of which could be activated by these eight alphabetical buttons located on the steering wheel:

A. Powerful automatic jacks for jumping over obstacles
B. Extragrip tires for slick roadways
C. Saw blades to cut through road-blocking trees
D. Releases bullet-proof canopy to keep water and deadly gases out of the cockpit
E. Extra headlight illumination
F. Seals off the cockpit for thirty minutes of oxygen to travel underwater
G. Activates a remote-control bird to carry important messages
H. Sends the remote-control, message-carrying bird directly to Speed's loyal pit crew

MACRAMÉ

A versatile craft—based on making two easy knots, the clove hitch and the square knot. Associated with hippies and other earthy types of the 1960s and 1970s. (Macramé expressed their back-to-nature attitudes and gave them something easy to do with their hands during all those acid trips.) Macramé's versatility allowed its products to be used as home decorations, such as hanging plant holders, place mats, lamp shades, toilet paper cozies, and wall hangings resembling something like a large hoot owl—or, worn as a fashion accessory, like a purse, belt, headband, tunic, vest, and even a far-out poncho. For kids of the 1970s, art class was the place to show off macramé skills by creating pot holders for mom or a tool belt for dad. Today at flea markets these crafts can be found side by side with pop-top hats, macaroni mosaics, string art, and candle art.

FYI: ▸ In 1981, moviegoers were shocked when teenage Lu-Lu Fishpaw used macramé to kill in John Waters's "odorama" comedy, *Polyester.*

MADAME MEDUSA
Evil pawnshop owner in Disney's *The Rescuers* (voiced by Geraldine Page) who kidnaps an orphan girl, Penny, to aid in retrieving the sought-after Devil's Eye diamond hidden away in a swamp. Brutus and Nero were two brutish alligators assisting Medusa.

MADELINE
"In an old house in Paris / That was covered with vines / Lived twelve little girls / In two straight lines. . . ." Since 1939, generation after generation has adored Madeline, the little redheaded schoolgirl and spunky heroine of a series of splendid picture books. Created by Belgian author-illustrator Ludwig Bemelmans, Madeline was the smallest and smartest of twelve schoolgirls attending an old boarding school overseen by headmistress Miss Clavel near the Eiffel Tower in Paris.

MADGE THE MANICURIST
Enlightening nail technician at the Salon East Beauty Parlor who soaked her clients' nails in Palmolive dishwashing liquid ("You mean I'm soaking in it?") in a series of long-running TV commercials.

MADISON
Beautiful mermaid from offshore Cape Cod who arrived completely naked at New York's Statue of Liberty in search of human beau Allen Bauer, whom she twice saved from drowning (once as a child and once as an adult). Named after the avenue, Madison loves to gnaw on lobsters at restaurants, and her screeching fish notes can shatter TV screens. When totally dry, her mermaid tail will turn into legs, but she can't survive out of water longer than six days. Blonde Daryl Hannah's performance as Madison in the comedy film *Splash* (1987) made her one of the hottest young actresses of the decade.

MAD LIBS
A wacky party game where one player would read a page-long short story littered with blank spots throughout, and the other players would take turns inserting random words based on different parts of speech in the blanks. The game taught unsuspecting kids the difference between nouns, verbs, adjectives, and adverbs. The fun thing about playing Mad Libs was players' topping one another by coming up with really gross or naughty words, like "dingleberry," "toe jam," "pus-filled," "vomit breath," and "butt-muncher."

***MAD* MAGAZINE**
For many adolescents, this monthly magazine, with its radical slant on the world, gave them their first taste of rebellion, not to mention a sense of satire and parody. Referred to as the twelve-year-old boy's bible, *Mad* was full of all kinds of cool and gross humor, as well as elaborate spoofs of popular TV shows, movies, sheet music, celebrities, advertisements, and everyday American family life. *Mad* began in August 1952 as a comic book poking fun at other comic books. In 1955, publisher Bill Gaines changed its comic-book format to a magazine format—starting with issue number 25—and in that form it grew to become one of the nation's leading humor periodicals. Its ever-present coverboy-mascot is a grinning, gap-toothed nitwit named Alfred E. Neuman, famous for the expression "What, me worry?" Other regular features and characters include madcap cartoonist Don Martin's thick-jawed goons, Dave Berg's everyday folks in "The Lighter Side," "Spy vs. Spy," "A Mad Look at . . . ," and the "Mad Fold-In." *Mad* magazine inspired a few clones, the most notable being *Cracked* magazine and *Crazy* magazine (now defunct).

MAD MAX
Australian superstar Mel Gibson played Max Rockatansky, a.k.a. Mad Max, the ex-cop drifter who—after seeking revenge for the brutal murder of his wife and child—roams the desolate, barbaric,

postapocalypse world of the not-too-distant future. The wandering loner was first seen in director George Miller's kinetically paced sci-fi thriller *Mad Max*. This 1979 grade-B movie was a surprise runaway hit, becoming Australia's most successful film of all time ($100 million in worldwide rentals alone). It inspired two sequels: *The Road Warrior* (1982), featuring cynical Max speeding around in a souped-up auto while reluctantly helping a peaceful community of fuel-manufacturing pacifists fight off a pillaging biker gang sporting punk haircuts and medieval-like weaponry; and *Mad Max Beyond Thunderdome* (1985), with the brooding hero preparing for combat as a gladiator in a futuristic arena known as "Thunderdome" ruled over by the evil Aunty Entity, played by rock star Tina Turner. The *Mad Max* saga invented a new genre—post-apocalypse movies—that gave us such forgettable low-budget offerings as *Survival Zone* (1984), *Def-Con 4* (1985), *Hell Comes to Frogtown* (1987), *Aftershock* (1988), *Warlords* (1988), and *World Gone Wild* (1988).

MAD MONSTER PARTY

"Crawl, fly, slither, and slink to the underground party of the year!" Released in 1967, this big-screen musical comedy featured Animagic puppets from Rankin/Bass lampooning the horror-film genre. It stars Baron Von Frankenstein (voice of Boris Karloff), the "King of the Monsters," who throws a bash on the Isle of Evil to announce his retirement. The baron invites a horde of classic creepies to this big blowout in which one will be chosen to take his place as the leader of the Worldwide Organization of Monsters. Topping the ghoulie guest list are Frankenstein's Monster and his Phyllis Diller look-alike wife, the Monster's Mate (voiced by Ms. Diller herself), who henpecks her hubby (she calls him Fang) to death—except that he's already dead. Other partygoers include the Peter Lorre-esque Yetch, Dracula, the Werewolf, the Mummy, Dr. Jekyll and Mr. Hyde, the Creature from the Black Lagoon, the Hunchback of Notre Dame, the Invisible Man, "It" (a.k.a. King Kong), and Little Tibia and The Phibbeans, a rock band made up of skeletons. Also on hand is the baron's nerdy hypochondriac nephew, Felix Flankin, who falls in love with his uncle's assistant, the vampy and well-endowed redhead Francesca.

Over the years, *Mad Monster Party* has become a perennial Halloween favorite, enjoyed by film buffs because of all the references made about the classic movie monsters. "At long last a motion picture with absolutely no cultural value!"

MADONNA

"I'm tough, ambitious, and I know exactly what I want. If that makes me a bitch, okay!" Do you love to love her? Do you love to hate her? Regardless of how you feel, there is no dismissing Madonna—the self-confident, overdetermined, independent, reinventing, controversial sex goddess of the video generation. Since the 1980s, she has been pop music's most influential woman, rivaling Elvis and The Beatles as the most successful chart artist ever (with 100 million albums sold worldwide). Despite pushing the limits of decency and good taste, Madonna is a postfeminist role model who ushered in the age of female independence, teaching us to "express" ourselves. (She made it okay for a gal to be sexually provocative without the old-time stigma of being labeled a "slut.")

Born Madonna Louise Ciccone on August 16, 1958, the former high school cheerleader left her hometown of Bay City, Michigan, in 1979 in search of fame in New York City. As a struggling performer, she worked in various dance troupes, got a scholarship to the Alvin Ailey dance school, and joined disco artist Patrick Hernandez ("Born to Be Alive") as a backup singer. In the early 1980s, she became part of New York's club scene, where she wrote songs, made demo tapes, and went to clubs like Danceteria in hopes of getting noticed by the "right people."

The ambitious singer—whose voice was once likened to "Minnie Mouse on helium"—gained early attention with two dance-club successes, "Everybody" and "Physical Attraction," which preceded her first chart hit, "Holiday," from her debut album, *Madonna* (1983). Beginning with "Lucky Star" in 1984, she began an unprecedented run of sixteen U.S. Top Five singles, including "Like a Virgin" (1984), "Material Girl" (1985), "Crazy for You" (1985), "Live to Tell" (1986), "Papa Don't Preach" (1986), "Open Your Heart" (1986), "Like a Prayer" (1989), "Express Yourself" (1989), "Cherish" (1989), and "Vogue" (1990).

Many credit her phenomenal rise to fame to the merchandising of songs via music videos (a Madonna video premiere on MTV is an "event").

Young fans, known as Madonna Wannabes, emulated her sexy ragtag clothing and ratty hairstyles. From 1985 to 1989, Madonna experienced a stormy marriage with Hollywood bad boy Sean Penn ("the coolest guy in the universe"), whose violent brawls with photographers got the couple labeled the "Poison Penns" by gossip rags. She launched a movie career with 1985's *Desperately Seeking Susan*. Although a debatable movie actress, she had further success with *Dick Tracy* (1990), *Madonna: Truth or Dare* (a 1991 documentary of her "Blonde Ambition Tour"), *A League of Their Own* (1992), and the opera *Evita* (1996).

Madonna has always stirred up controversy. At the live telecast of the MTV Music Video Awards in 1984, she strutted across and humped the stage—dressed in a wedding gown—while performing "Like a Virgin." She outraged Catholics with her "Like a Prayer" video by incorporating religious imagery, burning crosses, and an interracial kiss—causing Pepsi to drop her ad campaign. Her video "Justify My Love" was so naughty that even often-naughty MTV banned it. In 1992, a steel-covered, pseudo-pornographic book, *Sex*, featured Madonna hitchhiking nude, tied-up in bondage, and having lesbian sex. And in 1994, on *The Late Show with David Letterman*, she swore incessantly, including uttering the F-word thirteen times, and gave host Letterman a pair of her panties to smell (he didn't).

We never thought it would happen, but the Madonna of later years has mellowed into a gentler, kinder Madonna. Less controversial, the newly middle-aged singer is a mother of two (daughter Lourdes and son Rocco), a wife (British film director Guy Ritchie), and a children's book author (*The English Roses*). She practices mystical Kabbalah, an ancient Jewish religion, and many of her last hits, such as "Frozen" and "Ray of Light," have a metaphysical air.

FYI: ▸ When Madonna made her national TV debut on *American Bandstand* in 1984, host Dick Clark asked her what her ambition was. Her answer: "To rule the world." That she has.

MADONNA WANNABES
The throng of young and mostly teenage female fans who copied Madonna's tough, sexy "boy-toy" appearance back in the mid-1980s. To look like Madonna, you wore underwear as outerwear, net tops over black midriff T-shirts to display the belly button, crinoline skirts, armfuls of black rubber bracelets and clunky bangles, crucifixes dangling from ears and neck, fingerless gloves, ankle-high boots, and rags tied in heavily frosted, ratted hair.

MAGAZINES
Fifty weekly and monthly periodicals read by us over the years:

Bananas
Boys' Life
Circus
Cosmopolitan
Cracked
Creem
Dynomite
Easy Riders
Ebony
Family Circle
Glamour
GQ
Heavy Metal
Highlights
High Times
Hit Parader
Hot Rod
Hustler
Interview
Jet
Life
Mad
Mademoiselle
McCall's
National Enquirer
National Geographic
National Lampoon
Newsweek
Penthouse
People
Playboy
Playgirl
Popular Mechanics
Popular Science
Reader's Digest
Right On
Rolling Stone

Rona Barrett's Gossip
Seventeen
Sassy
16
Spin
Sports Illustrated
Teen
Teen Beat
Tiger Beat
Time
TV Guide
Us
Vogue

MAGGIE SIMPSON
Pacifier-sucking Simpson baby from *The Simpsons* prime-time cartoon show who couldn't walk or talk but could spell her own name with an Etch-a-Sketch.

MAGIC BUS
In 1964, hippie author Ken Kesey painted an old school bus with psychedelic swirls of color. Its front destination sign read "Further," and with Neal (*On the Road*) Cassidy at the wheel, Kesey and his band of Merry Pranksters rode the bus across the United States to spread a message of love and the wonders of mind-altering drugs (there were jugs of LSD punch on board). Tom Wolfe chronicled the trippy journey in his book *The Electric Kool-Aid Acid Test* (1967).

FYI: ▸ In many American cities today, you can take a ride back to the 1960s with a local version of the Magic Bus. For a nightly rental fee, these brightly painted vehicles, equipped with love beads, Lava Lites, a well-stocked liquor bar, and a groovy sound system, will transport your drunken party from bar to bar and club to club across the city. It's more fun than riding around in a stuffy limousine, plus it's a safe alternative to drinking and driving.

MAGIC 8-BALL
Hi, Magic 8-Ball! This is Kellie Marie. I'm eleven years old and have a totally important question to ask you. Does Donny Osmond love me? (Shake, shake, turn over) "My sources say no." Bananas! Okay, then, like, does David Cassidy? (Shake, shake, turn over) "Reply hazy, try again." Oh c'mon, I'm Keith Partridge's number-one fan, so does he love me, or what? (Shake, shake, turn over) "Outlook not so good." That's not what I want to see. Okay, how about Barry Williams? (Shake, shake, turn over). . . .

Sound familiar? It should if you were typical of a kid who had a Magic 8-Ball. Holding the hard, black-plastic, grapefruit-sized ball with a billiard-style "8" on top, you'd ask it questions about life's most perplexing issues ("Will Gramma visit?" "Will I get the candy-apple-red Spyder bike with banana seat and sissy bar for my birthday?" "Am I popular?" "Is Whit Lewis a two-faced know-it-all?" . . .). Then, you'd turn the ball upside down and gaze into the little window that showed the polyhedron-shaped piece floating in murky blue-colored liquid and imprinted with twenty different fortunes that would reveal the answer (for instance, "Without a doubt," "Don't count on it," "Better not tell you now," or "Yes, definitely"). This continually best-selling toy was introduced by the Alabe Crafts Company in 1946 before being purchased and marketed by Ideal Toys in the early 1950s.

MAGIC EYE BOOKS
A series of novelty books that involved readers' staring for a long time at an image on a page to eventually see a hidden 3-D illusion. Some people could figure out the picture right away, while others—like me—could never quite get it.

MAGIC MOUNTAIN
Southern California Six Flags amusement park, located in Valencia and famed for having the largest collection of roller coasters on the planet. In fact, it currently holds the Guinness Book world record for most coasters—sixteen at last count, including these nerve-rattling rides: Batman the Ride, Canyon Blaster, Colossus, Flashback, Goldrusher (the park's first coaster), Goliath, Ninja, Psyclone, Revolution (the first looping coaster ever built), Scream, Superman the Revenge, Viper, and X.

MAGIC SCREEN
On *Pee-Wee's Playhouse*, this Etch-a-Sketch-like TV allowed Pee-Wee Herman to play "connect the dots" on its screen and to ride whatever vehicle the dots made for him.

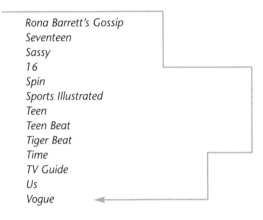

MAGIC SLATES
Write a secret message to a friend, then lift the oversheet, and—voila!—everything magically disappears. Like coloring and sticker books, Magic Slates are a staple of childhood playtime and feature licensed characters on them (for example, Donald Duck, Batman, and Flipper).

MAGILLA GORILLA
In 1964, Hanna-Barbera introduced this friendly, good-natured ape to their ever-growing cartoon zoo (joining the ranks of Huckleberry Hound, Quick Draw McGraw, and Yogi Bear). Wearing a derby hat, a bow tie, and shorts with suspenders, Magilla lived in the display window of a pet shop owned by ever-weary Mr. Peebles, whose work goal was to sell the banana-eating, mischief-making primate. The enormous gorilla could never find a master to take him home permanently, but when he did ("Somebody wants little old me?") he either created so much trouble that no one kept him for long, or he was used for various criminal schemes. Magilla's best friend was a little neighborhood girl named Ogee who wanted to be his owner.

Airing from 1964 to 1967, *The Magilla Gorilla Show* featured three additional cartoon segments: "Ricochet Rabbit," starring a sheriff hare with the ability to move lightning quick and whose deputy was the slow-poke Droop-a-Long Coyote; "Mushmouse and Punkin' Puss," a hillbilly saga of a rat and a cat feuding like the Hatfields and McCoys; and "Breezly and Sneezly," featuring a polar bear and an Arctic seal who hung out at Camp Frostbite, an Alaskan army base.

FYI: ▸ Character actor Allan Melvin, better known as Sam the Butcher, Alice's boyfriend on *The Brady Bunch*, voiced Magilla Gorilla.

MAGNA DOODLE
"Draw like magic, erase like magic!" Etch-a-Sketch-like creative toy complete with magnetic dust behind a screen, but instead of a knob to turn you use a magnet-tipped pen to doodle and scribble. To erase, simply slide the magnet bar attached at the bottom across the screen. Introduced in 1980, the Magna Doodle has sold more than forty million sets and is currently distributed by Fisher-Price.

MAJOR MATT MASON
From 1966 to 1969, boys could explore the far reaches of the galaxy with Mattel's "Man in Space," a poseable six-inch-tall action-figure astronaut (an inner wire made him bendable). Wearing a white space suit and detachable helmet, the adventure-seeking Mason lived, worked, and completed exploratory assignments in the two-tiered Moon Station with a courageous crew of buddies: red-suited Sergeant Storm, yellow-suited radiologist Doug Davis, and blue-suited rocketry specialist Jeff Long. The interplanetary team was assisted by an assortment of aliens, including Captain Laser from Planet Mars, a thirteen-inch-tall superstrong spaceman with flashing eyes; Callisto from Planet Jupiter, who had green skin and a transparent brain that gave him advanced mental powers; and Scorpio from the planet Scorpio, the red-coated, bug-eyed villain. The Major Matt Mason toy line came with separate accessories, vehicles, and equipment, such as the motorized Space Crawler, the Space Sled, the Space Cannon, the Jet Propulsion Pak, the Cat Track Space Tractor, and the Uni-Tred.

MALEFICENT
Evil fairy featured in Disney's animated classic *Sleeping Beauty* (1959) whose gift to the baby Princess Aurora is a curse: on her sixteenth birthday she will sleep forever after pricking her finger on the spindle of a spinning wheel (Aurora can be awakened, but only by a true-love kiss). Maleficent has the ability to transform herself into an enormous fire-breathing dragon (as if her dark, witchy robe and horned headdress weren't ominous enough).

MALIBU BARBIE
Mattel founder and Barbie creator Ruth Handler came up with the idea of the fabulous Malibu series in 1971 after falling in love with the famed California beach community, north of L.A., that had become her new home. Known as "The Sun Set," Malibu Barbie and her friends—Ken, Francie, Skipper, P.J., and Christie—reflected the easygoing, laid-back, sun-loving West Coast attitude. They came with golden tans and sun-streaked hair—worn long and straight with deep side parts and no bangs (very Malibu)—brightly colored bathing suits, terrycloth beach towels, and groovy sunglasses. Their accessories included an assortment of cool beach paraphernalia, like surf-

boards, a speedboat, a Beach Bus camper, and a Sun-n-Fun dune buggy covered with groovy daisy decals.

Wildly successful, the Malibu Barbie line was intended to be an inexpensive line with no frills and relatively plain packaging. Understated in appearance, these dolls lacked the "lifelike" eyelashes and elaborate hairdos of earlier Barbies and marked the start of a new era for the "Queen of Fashion Dolls." The original Malibu series stayed around for several years before Mattel's annual introduction of a new collection of low-budget bathing-suit dolls, such as 1979's Sun Lovin' Malibu Barbie (with real tan lines), 1982's Sunsational Malibu Barbie, 1986's Tropical Barbie, and 1989's Beach Blast Barbie.

FYI: ▸ To achieve the perfect 1970s Malibu look (it's the same for both guys and gals—the only difference is that girls often had the longer hair), you need these:

- A Hang Ten, Ocean Pacific (OP), or Pacific Coast Highway (PCH) shirt
- A pair of Levi's light-blue or tan-colored boot-cut cords
- A pair of Van sneakers or camel-hued desert boots
- A pukka-shell or shark's-tooth choker necklace
- Long, straight, sun-bleached hair with a deep side-part (no bangs)
- A deep, dark suntan (sunburns don't count)

MALL

Shop till you drop! At one time, the typical shopping plaza was a strip of stores—grocery store, shoe store, pet store, five and dime, and so on—but in the 1970s the face of shopping changed. Gigantic concrete, multilevel compounds known as malls or gallerias began popping up in suburbs across the United States. These hubs were typically made up of national and regional retail shops, restaurants, movie theaters, and recreational facilities.

Those of us who were born after 1960 were the first generation(s) to spend the formative years shopping in malls. Whether you lived in New York, Nebraska, or New Mexico, all of us had a similar experience, because each mall was basically the same as the next one. We were the original mall rats whose parents dropped us off on Saturday afternoons, trusting us to behave (yeah, right), and came back to retrieve us later in the day (the mall served as a kind of babysitter). We would spend our weekly allowance, and the lucky few would use dad's credit card, on all types of important stuff: faddish clothing (gotta have those leg warmers and headbands), records (gotta have Blondie's and Journey's latest), odd bric-a-brac (gotta have the Scott Baio poster and the unicorn candle), arcade games (gotta play Asteroids or Frogger), and junk food (gotta eat the cheese-smothered pretzel and drink a strawberry slushie). We shopped, hung out, visited with friends, flirted with each other, fell in love, and got our first jobs at the mall.

If we died and went to the great shopping mall in the sky, these would be the fifty mall-friendly stores waiting for us there:

Aladdin's Castle
Abercrombie & Fitch
B. Dalton Bookstore
Banana Republic
Benetton
Bloomingdale's
Camelot Music
Casual Corner
Charlotte Russe
Chess King
Claire's Boutique
County Seat
Deb
Fashion Bug
Fashion Gal
Foot Locker
Foxmoor
Function Junction
Gap
Gift Horse
Glamour Shots
Hallmark Cards
J. C. Penny
Hickory Farms
Kay-Bee Toys
Kinney's Shoes
Lane Bryant
Limited
Macy's
Merry Go Round
Montgomery Ward
Mr. Bulky's
Musicland

National Shirt Shop
Orange Julius
Petland
Pier 1
Sam Goody's
Sears
Spencer's Gifts
Taco Via
Topsy's Popcorn
Tower Records
Up Against the Wall
Ups-n-Down
Victoria's Secret
Waldenbooks
Wicks 'n' Sticks
Wild Pair
World Bazaar

FYI: ▸ America's first shopping mall opened in Appleton, Wisconsin, in 1955.

MALL BANGS
Another one of those "what were we thinking" fashion trends? These were astonishingly sky-high bangs, hair-sprayed stiffly in place as if saluting the heavens, worn by young female mall rats in the late 1980s and early 1990s. Also known as rooster bangs.

MALLORY KEATON
Fifteen-year-old underachieving mall rat whose main concerns are her looks, popularity, boys, clothes, and junk food (in no particular order). Dated handsome Nick Moore, a high school dropout and aspiring sculptor. Pretty brunette Justine Bateman, sister of *The Hogan Family*'s Jason Bateman, starred as Mallory on *Family Ties* from 1982 to 1989.

MAMAS AND THE PAPAS
Hippie rock group whose sweet four-part harmonies were the "in" thing among flower children during the Summer of Love. Formed in 1963, the group consisted of two guys, the Papas (Denis Doherty and John Phillips), and two gals, the Mamas (Cass Elliott and Michelle Phillips, John's wife). Hits included "California Dreamin'" (1966), "Monday, Monday" (1966), "Creeque Alley" (1967), and a remake of The Shirelles' "Dedicated to the One I Love" (1967). Disbanded in 1968.

FYI: ▸ John Phillips is the father of TV actress Mackenzie Phillips and pop singer Chynna Phillips (the gals are half-sisters).

MAN FROM ATLANTIS
Short-lived sci-fi TV series (1977–78) starring Patrick Duffy—donning eerie green contact lenses—as amphibious humanoid Mark Harris, the last surviving denizen of the fabled lost continent. Equipped with superhuman powers, the aquatic hero had the capacity to breathe underwater (his lungs were gills) and swim fast like a fish (his hands and feet were webbed). One day, while researching along a beach, a pretty marine biologist named Dr. Elizabeth Merrill (Belinda J. Montgomery) stumbled upon an injured and unconscious Man from Atlantis washed ashore. She took him back to the Foundation for Oceanic Research to help him regain his health. Once healthy, Mark decided to stay and work with Dr. Merrill, and their adventures had them trekking under the sea in the Cetacean, a submarine-like vehicle, to combat an array of mad scientists and odd alien beings. In 1978, the cute, dark-haired Duffy signed on for his most famous role: J.R. Ewing's "good" brother, Bobby Ewing, in the prime-time soap *Dallas*.

FYI: ▸ *Man from Atlantis* was the first American TV show to be aired in the People's Republic of China.

MAN FROM GLAD
Derived from the James Bond genre, this classic TV commercial starred an espionage agent who saved our moms from giving us stale bologna sandwiches, with the help of Glad's "fold-lock top" sandwich bags.

MAN FROM U.N.C.L.E.
Ultracool prime-time favorite, airing from 1964 to 1968, about a team of secret agents who worked undercover for the United Network Command for Law and Enforcement (U.N.C.L.E.). It featured Robert Vaughn as supersuave American Napoleon Solo, and David McCallum as his handsome, blond Russian counterpart, Illya Kuryakin. Their mission: to protect the civilized world from the spread of evil. In 1966, it launched a female-friendly spin-off, *The Girl from U.N.C.L.E.*, starring Stefanie Powers as April Dancer.

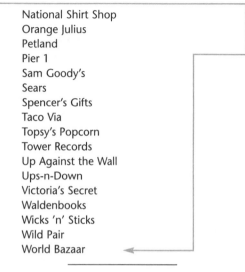

FYI: ▸ The last word of all the *Man from U.N.C.L.E.* episode titles ended with "Affair"—for example, "The Doomsday Affair," "The Mad Scientist Affair," and "The Mind-Twister Affair."

MANILOW, BARRY

He wrote the songs that made the whole world sing, and by doing so became the darling of the easy-listening circuit. Born on June 17, 1946, in Brooklyn, Manilow studied at the prestigious Juilliard School of Music in New York. In the early 1970s, he wrote and sang jingles for commercials (Dr. Pepper, Pepsi, McDonald's) and penned the world-famous slogan "You Deserve a Break Today." As a pianist at a gay cabaret in the Big Apple, Manilow met a young, unknown singer named Bette Midler. Their friendship led him to produce Midler's first two albums and tour as her piano player and music director.

In 1974, Manilow's big break came with the number-one song "Mandy." Other Top Ten hits included "It's a Miracle" (1974), "Could It Be Magic" (1975), "I Write the Songs" (1975), "Tryin' to Get the Feeling Again" (1976), "Looks Like We Made It" (1977), "Can't Smile Without You" (1978), and the disco ballad "Copacabana (At the Copa)" (1978). By pop-music standards, Manilow isn't the most exciting performer in the business—in fact, he's rather bland—but his capacity to sell millions of records and fill stadiums in superstar proportions is extraordinary!

MARBLES

Even though they've been around since ancient times, collecting these smooth, colorful glass balls was a huge fad throughout the 1950s and 1960s. Different types of marbles include Aggies, Cat's Eyes, Marine Puries, Moonies, Rainbows, and Jumbo Shooters.

MARCIA BRADY

"Marcia! Marcia! Marcia!" Teen babe Maureen McCormick played the pretty and popular, overachieving, self-absorbed older sister on *The Brady Bunch.* Some of Marcia's accomplishments included senior-class president, student-body president, cheerleader captain, school-banquet hostess, editor of the *Fillmore Flyer*, the school newspaper, and president of the Davy Jones Fan Club (she persuaded the teen idol to perform at her junior high prom). Marcia frequently competes with older brother Greg but often takes his advice on dating boys ("Tell someone something suddenly came up"). Younger middle-sister Jan is totally jealous of her.

MARCIE JOHNSON

Book-smart and full of common sense, this bespectacled introvert was Peppermint Patty's dutiful ally in the *Peanuts* cartoon strip, constantly referring to her as "sir." Patty and Marcie both have a crush on Charlie Brown, but there are those who speculate that Marcie could also have a crush on Peppermint Patty.

MARCY D'ARCY

Formerly Marcy Rhoades, a yuppie feminist once married to banker Steve Rhoades (he left her to become a park ranger) and currently married to gigolo house-husband Jefferson D'Arcy (he gives her good sex). Marcy (played by actress Amanda Bearse) detests living next door to the Bundy family on the FOX sitcom *Married . . . with Children.* Maybe Marcy would like her neighbors better if Al Bundy stopped his ongoing insults about her chicken figure and flat chest.

FYI: ▸ Amanda Bearse directed many episodes of *Married . . . with Children*, becoming the first woman in TV history ever to direct a show.

MARGARET WADE

> "You're lucky, mom. If you were Margaret's mother, you'd hafta kiss her goodnight!"
>
> —DENNIS THE MENACE

Margaret is the redheaded, curly-haired, freckle-faced, eyeglass-wearing know-it-all foe of Dennis Mitchell in the *Dennis the Menace* cartoons. She has a crush on the tousled-haired Menace, but her affections are returned only with rejections (and sometimes an aptly targeted snowball or a slimy frog in the face).

MARGE SIMPSON

Devoted wife to the boorish Homer, a practical peacemaker and caring mother who has the biggest hairdo—a towering blue beehive—of any cartoon character from pop culture history. Julie Kavner of *Rhoda* fame (she played Brenda Morgenstern, Rhoda's sister) gives voice to Marge on cartoonist Matt Groening's *Simpsons* TV show.

MARILYN MUNSTER
The unfortunate niece of the Munsters spends her life bemoaning the curse of being blonde, blue-eyed, and beautiful. Oblivious to the rest of the clan's ghastly appearance, the college coed blames her "ugly" looks for scaring off potential male suitors. Poor Marilyn. Played by two actresses: Beverly Owen, from September 1964 to December 1964 (she left *The Munsters* TV series to get married), and Pat Priest, from December 1964 to September 1966.

MARION CUNNINGHAM
"Are you feeling frisky, Howard?" Actress Marion Ross's doting housewife (Mrs. Howard Cunningham) and loving mother (of Richie and Joanie), who joins the likes of June Cleaver, Margaret Anderson, Donna Stone, Carol Brady, and Shirley Partridge as one of the great moms of TV land. Referred to as "Mrs. C" by Richie's friends.

MARK WEDLOE
On the family-friendly prime-time hit *Gentle Ben*, Ron Howard's little brother, Clint, starred as the young son of a Florida Everglades wildlife officer who befriends a gentle black bear named Ben.

MARMADUKE
Lovable Great Dane owned by Phil and Dottie Winslow whose prankish hijinks have been entertaining comic-strip fans since 1954. Marmaduke's favorite food is peanut butter sandwiches, and he likes to roller-skate around the Winslows' suburban home. Created by Brad Anderson.

MARRIED . . . WITH CHILDREN
"Bundys are losers, not quitters." This gloriously raunchy sitcom rescued us from the cutesy family fare that dominated TV airwaves in the 1980s (*Family Ties, Growing Pains, Full House, The Cosby Show,* and so on). Teeming with lowbrow toilet humor, it focuses on the twisted Bundys, a dysfunctional white-trash family living in suburban Chicago. The head of the household is chauvinistic Al Bundy (played by Ed O'Neill), an underpaid shoe salesman at a shopping mall—with balding hair, bad breath, and stinky feet—whose wife and kids don't give him any respect. Although once a heralded high school football star, the closest Al gets to the gridiron these days is the living-room TV set, which he watches as a loaf on the couch—hands resting inside the waist of his pants—drinking a six-pack beer. Al's spouse of fifteen years is high school sweetheart Peg Bundy (Katey Sagal), a spandex-clad, teased-hair, undersexed, and overbored housewife who loathes cleaning and cooking but loves devouring bonbons and spending Al's meager paychecks. Their troublesome brood consists of fifteen-year-old Kelly Bundy (Christina Applegate), a bleached-blonde vixen with a low I.Q.; eleven-year-old Bud Bundy (David Faustino), an up-and-coming con artist obsessed with losing his virginity; and put-upon family mutt Buck (played by a dog named Michael). Steve and Marcy Rhoades (David Garrison and Amanda Bearse), a yuppie banker and his staunch feminist wife, serve as the Bundys' wholesome next-door neighbors.

Premiering in 1987, *Married . . . with Children* became the most popular series on the fledgling FOX network. It aired for more than a decade and at one point was the longest-running sitcom on TV. The Bundys repeatedly came up against protest boycotts from conservatives, like Michigan housewife Terry Rakolta, who failed to get the "offensive" show pulled. The theme song was "Love and Marriage," sung by Frank Sinatra.

MARTIANS
Space invaders from Mars whose mission is to take over and/or destroy earth and its puny human inhabitants. Famous pop culture Martians: Marvin the Martian and *My Favorite Martian*'s Uncle Martin.

MARTIN, STEVE
Born August 14, 1945, in Waco, Texas, the prematurely gray stand-up comedian tickled the funny bone of young America during the late 1970s. His trademark shtick was that of a "wild and crazy guy," a nincompoop with "happy feet," a goofball sarcastically exclaiming "Well, excuuuuuuse me!" to those who seemed put off by his outrageous silliness. Thanks to guest stints on TV's *Saturday Night Live* and Johnny Carson's *Tonight Show,* Martin became one of the hottest names in show business, with sold-out concerts and hit records, including the novelty single "King Tut." In 1978, he made his movie debut, enacting The Beatles' "Maxwell's Silver Hammer" in the flop musical *Sgt. Pepper's Lonely Hearts*

Club Band, co-starring Peter Frampton and the Bee Gees. Martin's first star vehicle was 1979's *The Jerk*, in which he played the poor white stepchild of black sharecroppers (loosely based on some of his comic routines). In the 1980s and 1990s, after changing his whacked-out, cornball humor to a kinder and gentler style, he became one of Hollywood's biggest stars with films that grossed multimillions at the box office. These have included *Pennies from Heaven* (1981), *Dead Men Don't Wear Plaid* (1982), *All of Me* (1984), *Little Shop of Horrors* (1986), *Planes, Trains, and Automobiles* (1987), *Roxanne* (1987), *Dirty Rotten Scoundrel* (1988), *Parenthood* (1989), *Father of the Bride* (1991), and *L.A. Story* (1991).

MARTY MARASCHINO

"Maraschino. Like the cherry." Marty is the star-struck sex kitten and member of the rebel Pink Ladies, a girl gang in the musical *Grease*.

MARTY McFLY

The 1980s California teenager who goes "back to the future" to play Cupid to his teenage mom and dad at Hill Valley High School, circa 1950s. Seventeen-year-old Marty rides a totally rad skateboard and plays a mean "Johnny B. Goode" on the guitar. Played by Michael J. Fox in a trio of blockbuster *Back to the Future* films.

MARVEL THE MUSTANG

Hey, little cowpokes, put on your spurs, jump in the saddle, press foot bars on front legs, hop up and down, and the frisky pony is off galloping across the playroom (coil springs made hinged legs move on hidden wheels). Marx Toys introduced this classic riding toy in 1967.

MARVIN THE MARTIAN

Diminutive, highly intelligent, ray-gun-zapping, green-skinned extra-terrestrial from Mars whose mission is to blow up planet earth because it blocks his view of Venus. Co-piloting Marvin's zooming Saucer X-2 spacecraft is sidekick Commander K-9, a space canine. Although he made an earth-shattering debut in the 1948 Bugs Bunny cartoon short "Haredevil Hare," his most famous appearance was opposite Daffy Duck and Porky Pig in 1953's "Duck Dodgers in the 24½ Century."

MARX PLAY SETS

Throughout the 1950s and 1960s, Marx Toys produced hundreds of play sets consisting of plastic figures, buildings, vehicles, landscapes, and other accessories. Combined with the abundant imagination of a kid, these sets produced endless make-believe adventures in lands filled with dueling medieval knights, battling cowboys and Indians, roaring prehistoric beasts, buzzing war planes, and zooming rocket ships. The best remembered of the Marx play sets included The Alamo; Battle of Iwo Jima; Ben-Hur; Blue and Gray Battle; Cape Canaveral Missile Center; Fort Apache; Jungle Jim; Medieval Castle Fort; Noah's Ark; Operation Moon Base; Prehistoric Times; and Robin Hood Castle. Numerous play sets were based on popular TV shows of the era, such as *The Rifleman*, *Wagon Train*, *The Untouchables*, *Zorro*, *Daktari*, *The Flintstones*, and *Yogi Bear*. Marx play sets were sold primarily through large department stores like Sears and Montgomery Ward.

MARX TOYS

Louis Marx, a genius when it came to designing, marketing, and manufacturing the modern toy, founded the world's largest toy company of the 1950s in 1921. Called the "King of Toys," Marx not only popularized the play sets (mentioned in previous entry) but also created tin windups, yo-yos, trains, guns, dolls, and other well-loved Baby Boomer toys, such as the Johnny West action-figure line, the Rock 'Em Sock 'Em Robots, Marvel the Mustang, and the Big Wheel.

MARY ANN SUMMERS

On the sitcom *Gilligan's Island*, this sweet and naive farm girl from Horner's Corner, Kansas, was a sharp contrast to glamorous Hollywood sexpot Ginger Grant. Mary Ann liked pigtails, gingham, and coconut cream pies.

FYI: ▸ Raquel Welch auditioned for the role of Mary Ann but lost it to Dawn Wells, a former Miss Nevada who participated in the 1960 Miss America Pageant.

MARY INGALLS

In 1974, crystal-eyed, golden-haired twelve-year-old Melissa Sue Anderson was cast as the oldest daughter in the long-running *Little House on the Prairie* TV series. As a teenager, Mary lost her sight and was sent to a school for the blind, where she met Braille instructor Adam Kendall, her future husband.

MARY JANES

Usually colored black, these shiny, patent-leather, flat-soled shoes for little girls were generally worn for dress-up occasions, like Sunday church services, birthday parties, and holidays (Christmas and Easter).

MARY POPPINS

Based on the books by P. L. Travers, *Mary Poppins* starred Julie Andrews—in her screen debut—as the sweet-singing British nanny who flew in one day on the East Wind to transform the lives of the Bates children at 17 Cherry Tree Lane in London circa 1910. "Practically perfect in every way," Mary Poppins was no ordinary nanny: She could fly with the aid of her umbrella, use magical powers to take youngsters in her care on marvelous adventures, and believed that "a spoonful of sugar makes the medicine go down." Other cast members included gangly Dick Van Dyke as chimney sweep Bert, Matthew Garber and Karen Dotrice as young charges Matthew and Jane Banks, David Tomlinson and Glynis Johns as proper parents Mr. and Mrs. Banks, Hermione Baddeley as the Bankses' housekeeper, Ellen, Ed Wynn as Mary's eccentric Uncle Albert, and Jane Darwell as the Bird Woman.

A 1964 Walt Disney production of *Mary Poppins* is frequently acclaimed as the greatest children's film of its day. Employing a revolutionary blend of live action and animation, it was the forerunner of such Disney gems as *Bedknobs and Broomsticks* (1971), *Pete's Dragon* (1977), and *Who Framed Roger Rabbit* (1988). It earned a remarkable thirteen Academy Award nominations—including Best Picture—with Andrews winning for Best Actress. Brothers Richard and Robert Sherman penned the unforgettable hum-worthy tunes, including "Chim Chim Cheree," "A Spoonful of Sugar," "Let's Go Fly A Kite," "Supercalifragilisticexpialidocious," and "Jolly Holiday."

MARY TYLER MOORE SHOW

After playing housewife Laura Petrie on *The Dick Van Dyke Show* (1961–66), Mary Tyler Moore "turned the world on with her smile" as Mary Richards, the ideal independent woman of the 1970s. Airing on CBS from 1970 to 1977, this was one of the highest rated sitcoms of the day, earning more Emmy Awards than any other in TV history (twenty-nine statuettes) and spawning three spin-offs: *Rhoda* (1974–78), *Phyllis* (1975–77), and *Lou Grant* (1977–82).

Mary Richards was a warm, levelheaded, spunky, somewhat vulnerable, attractive, thirtysomething career gal who wore her brunette hair in a swingin' pageboy flip and dressed in tasteful maxiskirted and pantsuited fashions. After breaking up with her boyfriend, she moved to Minneapolis to make it on her own—throwing her hat high in the air as a sign of independence. She rented a small apartment, where she hosted notoriously bad parties and preferred to stay home on Saturday nights rather than go on dates that usually ended up disastrous. She strived to be an equal in a "man's world" doing a "man's job," which happened to be associate producer of the low-rated WJM-TV News program on Channel 12.

The Mary Tyler Moore Show's talented supporting cast included Edward Asner as Lou Grant, Mary's tough producer boss; Ted Knight as Ted Baxter, WJM's incompetent, preening anchorman; Gavin MacLeod as Murray Slaughter, a sarcastic news writer; Betty White as Sue Ann Nivens, a manipulative TV hostess; Valerie Harper as Rhoda Morgenstern, Mary's best friend and neighbor; Cloris Leachman as Phyllis Lindstrom, Mary's busybody landlord; and Georgia Engel as Georgette Franklin, Ted's sweet airhead spouse.

In 1977, Mary Tyler Moore and husband Grant Tinker, producer of the series, decided it was time to cease production after seven years and 168 episodes, regardless of being on top of the ratings. On September 3, 1977, *The Mary Tyler Moore Show* aired its last episode. It ended with the selling of the WJM-TV station, and the entire staff, except for Ted Baxter, being canned by the new management. After tearful hugs and farewells, a wistful Mary is the last one to leave WJM. She takes a final glance across the newsroom, then turns out the light. "Meow."

FYI: ▸ The theme song for *The Mary Tyler Moore Show* is "Love Is All Around," written and sung by Sonny Curtis, an original member of Buddy Holly's Crickets.

MASHED POTATO

Hard-to-do 1960s dance (only those who were coordinated could do it) was a variation of the Twist with feet and legs moving as if mashing potatoes. Inspired by the song "Mashed Potato Time" (1962) by Dee Dee Sharp and inspired the song "Monster Mash" (1962) by Bobby "Boris" Pickett and a sequel dance called the Gravy.

MASTERS OF THE UNIVERSE

Mattel toy line and cartoon adventure starring brawny, sword-wielding He-Man (Prince Adam) from Castle Greyskull on the war-ravaged Planet Eternia, who, along with robust sister She-Ra (Princess Adora), clashed with the evil Skeletor. The extensive He-Man action-figure line, introduced in 1981, was one of the biggest-selling toys of the 1980s. The syndicated TV show, premiering in 1983, was one of the most watched, though most critics cited it as nothing but a half-hour-long commercial. In 1986, *Masters of the Universe* was made into a live-action sword-and-sorcery movie starring Swedish android Dolph Lundgren as blond He-Man and *Dracula* veteran Frank Langella as skull-faced Skeletor.

MATA HAIRI

"Oh, Lance Link, whatcha gonna do?" Sexy (for an ape), blonde secret agent who assisted spy chimp Lancelot Link on crime-combating missions for A.P.E. on Saturday morning's *Lancelot Link, Secret Chimp* TV show.

MATCHBOX CARS

Miniature die-cast automobiles, trucks, tractors, buses, and emergency vehicles, originally packaged in little yellow cardboard boxes that resembled a matchbox (hence the signature name). At roughly three inches in length, these palm-sized cars were known for meticulous and detailed scale reproductions. First introduced in Great Britain in 1953 by the Lesney Corporation, the Matchbox vehicles didn't zoom into U.S. toy stores until 1956. Their affordable price and diverse assortment made them an instant smash with American kids, who collected them by the dozen, storing them in vinyl Matchbox carrying cases (one late-1960s case could hold seventy-two cars) and foldout Matchbox cities complete with roads, bridges, and skyscrapers.

In 1968, Lesney was caught off guard when Mattel introduced the gravity-driven, ultrafast Hot Wheel line. This hot new rival caused the U.S. sales of Matchbox to drop from $28 million to $6 million in less than two years. To compete, Matchbox transformed its cars into a line called SuperFast, sporting faster wheels that could be raced on plastic track layouts with loop-the-loops just like Hot Wheels. By the 1970s, Lesney eventually lost the head-to-head battle with the more aggressive Mattel and went into receivership. In a twist of fate, Matchbox was eventually bought out by the American toy company Tyco, which was later bought out by Mattel. (The toy conglomerate still keeps a separate Matchbox line.)

MATCH GAME

The much-watched TV game show of the 1970s had two contestants filling in a missing word to the "blank" in a sentence and winning points if their answers matched those of the six-celebrity panel. The sentences were generally suggestive rhymes prompting naughty double entendre answers from the panelists, including regulars Brett Somers, Richard Dawson, and Charles Nelson Reilly. Hosted by Gene Rayburn from 1973 to 1979.

"MATERIAL GIRL"

Epitomizing the wealth-obsessed 1980s, this postfeminist pop song had everyone's favorite "boy-toy" singing about the virtues of being a modern-day gold digger. Madonna had no qualms and made no apologies about living in her "material world," coquettishly chirping lines like "'Cause the boy with the cold hard cash is always Mister Right" and "Only boys that save their pennies make my rainy day." Written by Peter Brown and Robert Rans, it was the second single off her million-selling LP *Like a Virgin*, peaking at the number-two spot for two weeks in February 1985.

"Material Girl" was accompanied by one of the decade's most memorable videos—a delightful retooling of Marilyn Monroe's "Diamonds Are a Girl's Best Friend" scene from the classic 1953 film *Gentlemen Prefer Blondes*. As a tribute to her idol, it featured Madonna wearing an imitation of Marilyn's hot-pink satin dress and dancing on an identically designed set surrounded by a group of enamored, gift-bearing suitors. The song and video appropriately earned Madonna the nickname "Material Girl" and the title "Marilyn Monroe of the 1980s."

MATTEL TOYS

The greatest toy company of the twentieth century, founded by Elliot Handler, wife Ruth, and friend Harold "Matt" Matson in 1944. Mattel gave children such classics as Barbie, Hot Wheels, Chatty Cathy, Liddle Kiddles, Baby Tender Love, Drowsy, Dancerina, Swingy, Mrs. Beasley, The Sunshine Family, Major Matt Mason, Big Jim, Creepy Crawlers, Incredible Edibles, Masters of the Universe, and the See 'n Say. Crown-wearing Matty Mattel serves as its advertising mascot.

FYI: ▸ The company's name came from a union of the first names of Matt Matson and Elliot Handler: Matt + El = Mattel.

MATT HELM

Crooner Dean Martin's boozy spin as a James Bond–era secret agent who worked for I.C.E. (Intelligence Coordination and Exploitation) in *The Silencers* (1966) and three sequels: *Murderers' Row* (1966), *The Ambushers* (1967), and *The Wrecking Crew* (1969).

MATTY MATTEL AND SISTER BELLE

"You can tell it's Mattel. It's swell!" Those of the Baby Boom generation should remember orange-haired Matty Mattel, the crowned "King of Kid-dom," and his yellow-haired sibling, Sister Belle. Matty was the official advertising mascot of Mattel Toys during the late 1950s and early 1960s. When he wasn't serving as a spokes-kid, he and Sister Belle moonlighted as animated hosts of a Mattel-sponsored children's TV show titled *Matty's Funday Funnies* (1959–61), featuring the *Beany and Cecil* cartoon program, as well as classics from Harvey Films, such as *Casper the Friendly Ghost*, *Little Audrey*, and *Baby Huey*. In 1961, Mattel manufactured Matty and Belle as seventeen-inch-high pull-string talking rag dolls that were among the very first of the kind. These lovable playmates were programmed with a variety of phrases, like playful Matty's "Let's play cowboy" and "Let's have a picnic," and sweet-talking Sister Belle's "Sing me a song" and "I'm glad we're friends."

MAUREEN ROBINSON

Another great mom of the TV era (played pleasantly by June Lockhart on *Lost in Space*) whose devotion to her family—plus dedication to space-age housework while drifting aimlessly through space and encountering bizarre alien beings—was the archetype of what the 1960s thought a housewife of the future should be.

MAX

Benevolent, ultra-expressive pooch who is reluctantly dressed as a one-antler reindeer to pull the Christmas-nabbing Grinch's sleigh in Dr. Seuss's beloved classic *How the Grinch Stole Christmas*.

MAX HEADROOM

Computer-generated TV character (Canadian actor Matt Frewer) whose fifteen minutes of fame in the mid-1980s had him starring in a sci-fi series, doing an interview talk show for the Cinemax cable network, and pitching Coca-Cola. His niche was popping onto TV screens at odd times to mock his human creators.

MAXIE

Hasbro's teenage fashion-doll line rivaled Mattel's Barbie for a short while in the late 1980s. Introduced in 1988, blonde Maxie attended Surfside High School in Malibu and typified teen girls of the era by wearing her hair with big fluffed-out bangs and dressing in bebop clothing: stretch jersey material, faded denim, lace, slouched socks, and high-top sneakers or white ankle boots. To be totally honest with you, Maxie was a rather boring doll who did the standard things boring teens do—cheerleading, going to the prom, shopping, hanging out at the beach—accompanied by a boring set of friends (Ashley, Carly, Simone) and a boring jock boyfriend, Rob. She starred in an animated TV series, *Maxie's World*, which was paired with the not-boring *Jem*, another doll line and cartoon show from Hasbro Toys, on the USA Network.

MAXISKIRTS

First fashionable in the early 1970s, these seemingly floor-sweeping skirts (about ankle length) were the alternative to the thigh-high mini; variations included granny dresses and peasant skirts. Frankly, I always thought that many of these skirts, particularly those made out of frilly lace or quilt-like fabrics with floral or gingham patterns, made women appear as if they were wearing their bedtime nightgowns out in public.

MAXWELL SMART

"Would you believe . . . ?" Enthusiastic yet inept secret agent working for Washington's CONTROL as Agent 86. Lovely and cool-headed partner Agent 99 helped him combat the evil spies of KAOS. Played by Don Adams on TV's *Get Smart* from 1965 to 1970. "Missed it by that much!"

MAYA

TV adventure show based on the 1966 film of the same title, starring Jay "Dennis the Menace" North as Terry Bowen, an American teen traveling in the jungles of India on the back of an elephant named Maya, searching for his missing father. Accompanying Terry was Raji (Sajid Khan), an orphaned Indian lad to whom faithful Maya belonged. Although short-lived (1967–68), the NBC series is notable for making young Hindu actor Sajid Khan a rather huge teen idol in the latter half of the 1960s, competing with the likes of Desi Arnaz Jr., Davy Jones, and Bobby Sherman for page space in *Tiger Beat* magazine.

MAYBELLINE KISSING POTION

Slimy, glossy goo in a glass tube with a plastic ball on top that you rolled all over your lips. Flavors included Strawberry, Mighty Mint, Krazy Kola, Cherry Smash, and Cinnamon Stick.

MAYBELLINE KISSING SLICKS

Gooey lip gloss in a glass tube with a sponge-tip applicator that you gobbed all over your lips. Flavors included Sinnamon Sin and Wild Strawberry.

MAYBERRY

Small, peaceful hamlet in rural North Carolina where folksy Sheriff Andy Taylor and fellow country bumpkins reside on TV's *Andy Griffith Show*.

MAYDA MUNNY

Made of money. Spoiled, scheming rich girl, with long, straight dark hair who had a colossal crush on Richie Rich in his comic books.

MAYFIELD

The picture-perfect setting of the sitcom *Leave It to Beaver* was the model for suburban hometowns for family-oriented TV shows of the 1950s and 1960s.

MAYOR McCHEESE

Politico of McDonaldland with the quivering voice who had an enormous cheeseburger for a head and whom Chief Big Mac—a policeman who had an enormous Big Mac hamburger for a head—helped promote McDonald's hamburgers.

MAYTAG REPAIRMAN

Nicknamed "Ol' Lonely" in the classic TV commercials because Maytag appliances supposedly never broke down, leaving him with nothing to repair and no house calls. Played by actor Jesse White from 1967 to 1989.

McDONALDLAND

Freaky place where you can find shaggy Fry Guy creatures grazing in fields of salty french fries, schools of Filet-O-Fish in the pond, apple-pie trees, and burger-snatching crooks. Its most famous inhabitant is a friendly, fun-loving clown named Ronald McDonald.

McDONALD's

"Over 99 billion sold!" For many of us, our first job experience was as a pimply-faced teenager dressed in a silly polyester uniform apathetically saying "Have a nice day" to customers while working for minimum wage at the local McDonald's. All the while, we hoped that the cute girl on the pep squad or the hunky guy in sixth-period biology wouldn't come into the fluorescent-lit restaurant and spot us working behind the counter.

The first McDonald's—a simple, no-frills hamburger stand—was opened in Pasadena, California, in 1937 by two brothers, Maurice and Richard McDonald. The restaurant's success encouraged them to open a second joint two years later in San Bernardino. In the new restaurant, the brothers fine-tuned their fast-food philosophy with a small, standardized menu, low prices, quick service, and streamlined efficiency—all housed in a building with two neon-lit yellow arches poking through the roof. In 1954, Ray Kroc, a milkshake-mixer salesman, approached the McDonald brothers with an offer to sell the restaurant as a franchise, with the first store opening in Des Plaines, Illinois. By 1961, Kroc had licensed more than 200 McDonald's, and later in the year he bought the entire operation. At last count, there are more than 18,000 McDonald's fast-food restaurants in some eighty-nine countries, and—for better or worse—the Golden Arches have become an internationally recognized symbol of American enterprise and capitalism.

McDonald's has contributed much to pop culture over the years. In 1963, the company created a benevolent advertising clown, Ronald McDonald, who lived in a trippy world called McDonaldland with pals Chief Big Mac, Grimace, Mayor McCheese, Hamburglar, Captain Crook, Birdie, the Gobblins, and the Fry Guys. The food items on McDonald's menu are also well known—just the mere mention of a Big Mac, a Quarter Pounder, a Filet-O-Fish, an Egg McMuffin, Chicken McNuggets, a McDLT, a McRib, a Happy Meal with its toy premium, and french fries (the best of any fast-food place) can conjure up mouthwatering memories. Then there are all those memorable commercial jingles and slogans, such as "Your kind of place," "You deserve a break today," "You, you're the one," "Nobody can do it like McDonald's can," and "It's a good time for the great taste of McDonald's."

FYI: ▸ Slang for McDonald's is "Mickey D's."

McGRUFF

"Take a bite out of crime!" Trench-coated dog detective created in 1980 by the National Crime Prevention Council as the star of TV commercials promoting crime prevention for children.

McNICHOL, JIMMY

Born July 2, 1961, in Los Angeles, the brother of Kristy McNichol enjoyed a minor stint as a teen heartthrob in the late 1970s, starring in two short-lived TV dramas, *The Fitzpatricks* (1977–78) and *California Fever* (1979). In 1978, he teamed with Kristy as half of a satin-jacketed recording duo that had a pseudo-hit, a cover of "He's So Fine" by The Chiffons, but failed to give the other sibling act, Donny and Marie Osmond, a run for the money.

McNICHOL, KRISTY

Kristy McNichol was one of the top teen actresses of the late 1970s and early 1980s; her contemporaries included Tatum O'Neal, Jodie Foster, and Brooke Shields. Unlike brat Tatum or eccentric Jodie or pretty-baby Brooke, Kristy was the girl-next-door (someone you could hang with and dish the dirt) and the best-loved young star of her day. Born September 11, 1962, in Los Angeles, the talented youngster first gained notice as Patricia Apple, one of the daughters in the TV drama *Apple's Way* (1974–75). A year later, she hit the big time playing tomboy Buddy Lawrence in the acclaimed *Family* (1976–80), a role that earned her two Emmy Awards for Supporting Actress (1977 and 1979). Praised as the girl to become the "next Jane Fonda," McNichol gave earnest performances in TV movies—*Summer of My German Soldier* (1978) and *My Old Man* (1979)—and in big-screen films: *The End* (1978), *Little Darlings* (1980), and *Only When I Laugh* (1981). A series of flops—*The Night the Lights Went Out in Georgia* (1981) and *The Pirate Movie* (1982)—along with emotional problems caused by manic depression, led to a lengthy break from acting. In 1988, she returned to prime-time TV as cop Barbara Weston on the sitcom *Empty Nest*.

FYI: ▸ While filming the teen flick *Little Darlings*, dreamy co-star Matt Dillon taught Kristy McNichol "the cool way" to smoke cigarettes.

MELODY VALENTINE

Ditzy, giggly drummer for Josie and the Pussycats whose ears wiggled whenever she sensed danger. As a gorgeous blonde knockout, Melody is simply clueless that she drives all the boys berserk. Cherie Moore, now better known as Cheryl Ladd of *Charlie's Angels* fame, provided this lovable heroine's singing voice on the Saturday-morning cartoon show.

MELROSE AVENUE

Called a "funky stretch of street," Melrose Avenue (between Highland Avenue and La Cienega Boulevard) in West Hollywood was once known for underground rock and artist hangouts before morphing into the epicenter of everything young and hip in L.A. in the 1990s. The street dotted with trendy shopping boutiques (Notorious, Red Balls, Retail Slut, Wasteland, and so on), casual sidewalk cafés, and fine restaurants (for instance, Ago, Chianti, Emilio's, and Tommy Tang) was the place to be seen. Inspired Aaron Spelling's popular prime-time soap opera *Melrose Place* (1992–99), starring Heather Locklear, Andrew Shue, and Courtney Thorne-Smith.

MEMBERS ONLY JACKETS

I had one. You had one. We all had one. These were the trendy must-have fashion outerwear of the early 1980s. Purchased at shopping malls everywhere, the expensive windbreaker-like jacket was characterized by shiny parachute-like material that came colored in gawdawful shades of black, blue, burgundy, gray, and tan. Its trademark, however, was the useless straps-with-snaps on each shoulder and around the neck, plus the Members Only label on the left-hand chest pocket. Aimed at the active young man, the jacket became uncool when it came to be associated with aging older men trying to hold on to their youth and with slimy drug dealers who wore the sleeves hiked up to the elbows. Wearing one of the countless imitation brands was even uncooler.

FYI: ▸ Anthony "Luke Spencer" Geary was the Members Only celebrity spokesman.

MEN IN BLACK

Mystery government agents clad in nondescript black suits who keep the earth safe from the universe's predatory aliens. I don't know whether they really exist, but they're the premise for the Will Smith and Tommy Lee Jones *Men in Black* films.

MEN'S BLOW-DRIED, FEATHERED HAIR

The common style worn by most guys in the 1970s was longish hair (about mid-ear length) with long bangs feathered down the middle, parted on the side, or swooshed straight over the forehead, giving it a somewhat poofy appearance. Men achieved this look by using a blow dryer or a styling apparatus known as The Hot Comb, an electrical cross between the blow dryer and the comb. It inspired a men's hair spray called The Dry Look ("The Wet Head Is Dead"), which kept masculine locks perfectly in place. It is interesting that teenage men in 2004 started wearing their hair similar to this (but less blow-dried and feathered)!

MENTOS

"The freshmaker!" A series of cheesy but memorable TV spots, featuring a catchy jingle ("Fresh goes better") that made this chewy mint candy from Europe, packaged in rolls of assorted flavors, all the rage in the 1990s.

MENUDO

Irresistibly cute, spunky, and young—this Latino pop quintet sent Spanish-speaking girls into fits of puppy-love frenzy. Formed in 1983, the group had a unique trait—besides being totally Hispanic—a rule that said members had to retire at the old age of sixteen and be replaced by younger and fresher blood. The first of the all-boy teen idol groups of the 1980s, Menudo never really caught on with non-Spanish-speaking American teens, but in Latin America they were mega-superstars. Their legacy includes DeBarge, New Edition, and the five babes from Boston—New Kids on the Block. Menudo's original six members were Miguel Cancel, Rene Farriat, Johnny Lozada, Charlie Masso, Ricky Melendez, and Ray Reyes. Its most famous member: Ricky "Shake Your Bon-Bon" Martin, the pop-singing sensation of the late 1990s, was a member from 1983 to 1987.

FYI: ▸ In the 1990s, when twentysomething Generation X was all the media talked about, there were cynics who likened it to the Menudo age rule: When you turn thirty you get booted out of the generation. (The media usually referred to only those in their twenties as Generation X, ignoring older members after they had turned thirty.)

MEOW MIX CAT FOOD

Meow . . . Meow . . .

FYI: ▸ At a college dorm party in the mid-1980s, someone secretly poured half a box of Meow Mix into the bowl of Chex Mix sitting on the food table. Those in on the joke laughed among themselves while watching one particularly overweight chap, who had been grazing the food all night long, chow down on the Chex Mix. He never knew the difference.

MESH HAIR TIES

In the 1980s, girls copied their idol Madonna by tying pieces of black or white mesh fabric throughout their ratted-out tresses.

MESH SHIRTS

Nylon fishnet-like tops worn over tank tops, bras, or a bare chest. This was another of the many hot looks pop singer Madonna "owned."

MESSY MARVIN
Seen in televised commercials airing in the mid-1980s, the accident-prone lad (played by Peter Billingsley) would spill everything he touched except for Hershey's Chocolate Syrup. In 1983, the towheaded, bespectacled Billingsley starred as Ralphie in the funny Yuletide yarn *A Christmas Story*.

METRIC SYSTEM
"If you don't learn this, you'll have a lot of problems," cautioned sixth-grade math teacher Mr. George. "In the future, measurements in America will be converted into metrics, just like in Europe." During the mid-1970s, Mr. George's concerns were echoed by teachers everywhere. They scared students into thinking that if they didn't learn the exciting world of metrics—a decimal measuring system that transformed ounces, pounds, gallons, inches, feet, yards, and miles into grams, kilograms, liters, meters, decameters, centimeters, millimeters, kilometers, kilowatts, and megawatts—they would not be universally consistent with the rest of the world. Well, guess what, Mr. George? With the exception of lightbulbs (watts), soda pop (liters), and drugs (grams), it didn't happen. Los Angeles is still 3,000 miles from New York City, the Washington Monument is still 555 feet tall, gas is still pumped by the gallon, hamburger is still bought by the pound—and we're still not universally consistent with the rest of the world.

METROPOLIS
Fictional American city with towering skyscrapers and a bustling population (similar in size to New York or Chicago)—and an abundance of crooks that reporter Clark Kent, alias Superman, calls home in the *Superman* comics.

MEWSETTE
Inexperienced furry white feline with a beauty mark on her face who wants more out of life than just being a pretty kitty in the French countryside, so she ventures off to find fame and fortune in the big city of Paris. Voiced by the legendary Judy Garland in the animated classic *Gay Purr-ee* (1962).

MIAMI VICE
Airing from 1984 to 1989 on NBC, this was the coolest cop show on TV. Set in Florida's glamorous Gold Coast, it dealt with the seedy underworld (corruption, drug trafficking, and prostitution) of Miami, a world that was a stark contrast to a city known for colorful art deco buildings, palm-tree-lined streets, beautiful beach resorts, and breathtaking sunsets. Don Johnson and Philip Michael Thomas starred as detectives Sonny Crockett and Ricardo Tubbs, a duo of hip, sexy, and extremely well-clothed cops who worked undercover to bust Miami's criminal kingpins. Edward James Olmos co-starred as their moody boss, Lieutenant Martin Castillo, head of the Organized Crime Bureau. In 1987, singer Sheena Easton joined the cast as rocker Caitlin Davies, who married Crockett—only to be killed off later in the season.

Influenced by MTV, the action series was known for having more style than substance—containing quick-cut editing effects, lavish imagery showcasing the bright pastel hues associated with Miami, and an aggressive rock-music soundtrack featuring artists such as Glenn Frey, Don Henley, Phil Collins, Lionel Richie, and The Rolling Stones. Jan Hammer's pulsating synthesized electronic theme went to number one on the pop charts in 1985. Reflecting the 1980s—a decade known for excess and indulgence—*Miami Vice* captured America's obsession with fancy cars, big boats, designer clothing, large-breasted women, free-spending, and cocaine. For men's fashion, it spawned three hot trends: pastel-colored suit jackets worn over T-shirts, Italian-style loafers sans socks, and two-day facial stubble.

FYI: ▸ A noteworthy guest star on *Miami Vice* was Melanie Griffith, Don Johnson's ex-wife, who played a hooker in a 1987 episode. This onscreen reunion reignited their off-screen relationship.

***MIAMI VICE* JACKETS**
Fashion trend for trendy men, inspired by the NBC prime-time action series. Popular during the summer of 1985, these lightweight jackets came colored in cheesy pastel hues—peach, lemon-yellow, baby blue, and lavender—and guys wore them with white or colored T-shirts and casual slacks.

MIA/POW BRACELETS
Made from various metals (silver, gold, brass, aluminum, or stainless steel), these bracelets were engraved with the names of military heroes serving in

Vietnam, plus the date they were captured (POW for "prisoner of war") or disappeared (MIA for "missing in action"). They were worn by everyday Americans at home in the States to keep the plight of the missing in the public eye so they would not be forgotten.

MICHAEL EVANS

On TV's inner-city sitcom *Good Times*, Ralph Carter starred as Florida's serious—to the point of being militant—eleven-year-old youngest.

MICHAEL MEYERS

At age six, Michael Meyers knifed his teenage sister, Judith, to death after watching her make love to her boyfriend on Halloween night. As an adult, the knife-wielding, white-masked killing machine, an escapee from an institution for the criminally insane referred to as "pure evil" by his psychiatrist, is said to haunt the streets of Haddonfield (his hometown) each Halloween looking for sexually active young people to butcher. He was played by Tony Moran in the first two *Halloween* movies (1978 and 1981).

"MICKEY"

Toni Basil scored a chart-topping hit in 1982 with this perky tune composed of an infectious pep-squad refrain ("Hey, Mickey! Hey, Mickey!") and foot-stomping cheerleader-on-speed beat. It was accompanied by one of the most memorable music videos of the early 1980s: pop-eyed, mannequin-like Basil mechanically leading a group of strapping cheerleaders (an actual squad from Dorsey High in L.A.) in cheerleading routines to the hyper rhythm of "Mickey."

MICKEY MOUSE

Mickey Mouse is the most famous cartoon character in the world—hands down! Created by Walt Disney in 1928 (who originally supplied his squeaky voice), America's sunny little hero has been the star of more than 100 animated shorts ("Steamboat Willie"), films (*Fantasia*), TV shows (*The Mickey Mouse Club*), records ("Mickey Mouse Disco"), and comics. Dressed in a trademark uniform of red shorts, yellow shoes, and white gloves, he is the keystone of Disney's kingdom whose button-eyed face has appeared on hundreds of thousands of merchandise items, including cookie jars, lunch boxes, telephones, and the classic Mickey Mouse wristwatch with arms that point to the time. In fact, Mickey's image is the number-one most reproduced around the world, surpassing even Jesus Christ (second place) and Elvis Presley (third). When not starring in something or being mass-produced, Mickey happily welcomes guests of all ages at his hometowns of Disneyland in Anaheim, Walt Disney World in Orlando, Disneyland Paris, and Tokyo Disneyland. His best pals are gangly Goofy, irascible Donald Duck, playful pup Pluto, and loyal sweetheart Minnie Mouse, who has been at his side since the beginning.

FYI: ▸ On June 6, 1944, D-Day—when Allied forces began the invasion of Hitler's Europe at Normandy—General Dwight D. Eisenhower's password was "Mickey Mouse."

MICKEY MOUSE CLUB

"Who's the leader of the club, that's made for you and me?" "M-I-C-K-E-Y M-O-U-S-E!" A classic children's TV series of the 1950s, airing weekday afternoons from 1955 to 1959, that employed two dozen adolescent performers, all wearing Mickey Mouse–ear caps. They were called the Mouseketeers (the standout being young Annette Funicello). Led by adult leader Jimmie Dodd, the youngsters sang, danced, introduced Walt Disney cartoons (Mousecartoon Time), and starred in such filmed adventure serials as *The Hardy Boys*, *Annette*, and *Spin and Marty*. Each day of the week, the show had a special themed event: Mondays, "Fun with Music Day"; Tuesdays, "Guest Star Day"; Wednesdays, "Anything Can Happen Day"; Thursdays, "Circus Day"; and Fridays, "Talent Round-up Day." For subsequent generations it was revived twice: in the contemporary-looking but lackluster *New Mickey Mouse Club* (1977) and in the Disney Channel's teen-oriented *All-New Mickey Mouse Club* (1989–94).

MICRO MACHINES

You thought Hot Wheels were small—well, wait till you get a look at the really, really, really tiny Micro Machine vehicles—barely an inch or two long. Introduced by Galoob in 1988, this big-selling toy line consisted of multivehicle sets of die-cast cars, cycles, trains, planes, military machines, and construction equipment with such themes as "Corvettes," "Cops 'n Robbers," "Fire Rescue," "Heavy Haulers,"

"Railway Engines," "Airliners," "Apollo 13," "Indiana Jones," and "Star Wars."

MIDGE

Barbie Doll's first and best girlfriend—her confidante and sidekick, like Lucy's Ethel Mertz, Wilma's Betty Rubble, Mary's Rhoda Morgenstern, and Laverne's Shirley Feeney. Introduced by Mattel in 1963, Midge was less glamorous than fashion queen Barbie. She was the bridesmaid not the bride, the homecoming attendant but never the queen, the pep-squad alternate and not the cheerleader. Perky and freckle-faced, Midge had big blue eyes and wore her reddish hair in a fashionable flip style. She swooned over Allan, and the two of them double-dated alongside Barbie and Ken (Allan and Ken were best buds as well). Sadly, on the eve of the psychedelic 1960s, Midge found herself discontinued. Considered old-fashioned and square, Mattel replaced her with a trio of hipper chicks: mod British model Stacey, Afro-puffed black Christie, and groovy blonde P.J. Twenty years later, she renewed her friendship with Barbie as a contemporary-looking Midge—still wearing those familiar freckles—and became part of the California Dream Barbie in 1988.

MIDISKIRTS

Skirts, ranging from knee length down to mid-calf, for those too conservative to wear short minis but too liberal to wear the longer maxis.

MIGHTY DUMP TRUCK

Introduced in 1964, this big and clunky construction vehicle marked by huge wheels and a tipping truck bed is the all-time best-selling Tonka toy. These days, the Mighty Dump Truck is made mostly out of plastic instead of steel, but it still has the familiar yellow hue.

MIGHTY HEROES

Saturday-morning cartoon series featuring an unusual team of superheroes—each with a big "H" imprinted on his costume—led by a deep-voiced baby named Diaper Man. Joining the powerful infant in the weekly battle against evil were Cuckoo Man, Rope Man, Strong Man, and Tornado Man. Airing in 1966 and 1967, this superhero spoof was directed by Ralph Bakshi, who would later direct innovative and controversial adult-oriented animated films, such as *Fritz the Cat* (1972), *Heavy Traffic* (1973), *The Lord of the Rings* (1978), and *Cool World* (1992). *The Mighty Heroes* was produced by Terrytoons, creators of crime-fighting rodent Mighty Mouse and fast-talking magpies Heckle and Jeckle.

MIGHTY MORPHIN' POWER RANGERS

"It's morphin' time!" The hottest kids' TV show of the 1990s was a live-action sci-fi adventure about a gang of teens from Angel Grove High who morphed into helmeted, colorfully attired karate choppers in order to fight earth-attacking space aliens. Summoned by someone named Zordon, the superhero quintet comprised Jason (Red Ranger), Zack (Black Ranger), Kimberly (Pink Ranger), Trini (Yellow Ranger), and Billy (Blue Ranger). Typical of youth-oriented programs of the era, the Power Rangers littered the land with seemingly thousands of merchandise tie-ins, including an action-figure line that became the best-selling toy of 1993.

MIGHTY MOUSE

"Here I come to save the day!" Rodent equivalent of Superman who arrives just in the nick of time to rescue beloved Pearl Pureheart and other citizens of Mouseville from a battalion of villainous cats, such as Powerful Puss, Sour Puss, and Oil Can Harry. Created by Paul Terry for Terrytoons in 1942, the brawny, caped supermouse first appeared in a series of animated short films for the big screen before starring in a long-running, highly rated Saturday-morning cartoon show on TV, *Mighty Mouse Playhouse*, from 1955 to 1966.

In 1987, Mighty Mouse returned to TV with all-new cartoons on a show titled *Mighty Mouse: The New Adventures*, produced by animator Ralph (*Fritz the Cat*) Bakshi, who had directed *The Mighty Heroes* for Terrytoons back in the 1960s. This new show attracted controversy because of an infamous episode showing the pint-sized superhero regaining his powers by sniffing a handful of crushed flowers up his nose. Media watchdog the Reverend Donald Wildmon, of the conservative American Family Association, claimed Mighty Mouse had actually snorted cocaine, so the scene was edited out of reruns!

FYI: ▸ Mighty Mouse was originally billed as Super Mouse, "The Mouse of Tomorrow."

MIKE BRADY
"You can't take a step forward with two feet on the ground." The firm but loving dad and husband on TV's *Brady Bunch* always dished out fatherly advice and worked as an architect designing far-out suburban split-levels. Mr. Brady likes his coffee "black and with a smile." Actor Robert Reed played this dad of all dads from 1969 until 1974, and in various *Brady Bunch* reunion shows afterward. He died of AIDS in 1993.

MIKE TEEVEE
The TV-obsessed (he likes westerns the best), mischief-making youngster from *Willy Wonka and the Chocolate Factory* (played by twelve-year-old Paris Themmen) who is shrunk down to a few inches when transmitted in the Wonkavision (the contraption's purpose is to downsize large chocolate bars). Afterward, Mike is carried in his distraught mother's purse to Wonka's taffy-pulling machine so he can be stretched back to regular size.

MIKEY
Young character of a 1972 Life cereal TV commercial, one of the most popular in advertising history, who won't eat anything. Mikey's two older brothers at the breakfast table persuade him to try Life cereal ("He won't eat it. He hates everything"), and to their surprise he likes it. Its star, Michael Gilchrist, was the subject of an urban legend that had him dying from swallowing a lethal mixture of Pop Rocks and Coca-Cola (it caused his stomach to explode).

MILBURN DRYSDALE
Money-hungry president of Commerce Bank of Beverly Hills, guardian of the Clampett funds (more than $95 million) and the Clampetts' next-door neighbor. His snobbish wife, Margaret, owner of a pampered French poodle called Claude, couldn't stand living next to the backwoods yokels and tried to find ways to make them move back to the hills of the Ozarks. Played by Raymond Bailey on TV sitcom *The Beverly Hillbillies* from 1962 to 1971.

MILLENNIUM FALCON
Twenty-seven-meter-long Corellian stock freighter flown by a daring pilot, Han Solo, and his Wookie co-pilot and engineer, Chewbacca, in the *Star Wars* movies.

MILLION DOLLAR DUCK
In the 1971 Walt Disney film, struggling scientist Albert Dooley (Dean Jones) brings a radiation-zapped white duck named Charley (Webfoot Waddle) home from his laboratory as a pet for his young son, Jimmy (Lee Montgomery). When Charley hears the barking of a dog, he miraculously starts laying golden eggs. Dooley and his pert wife, Katie (Sandy Duncan), use the newfound riches to pay off debts until the Treasury Department finds out and tries to put an end to the caper. Directed by Vincent McEveety, the movie is typical of the mediocre live-action comedies produced by the Disney Studios in the 1970s.

MILLI VANILLI
Rasta-headed Euro-pop duo—Rob Pilatus and Fabrice Morvan—who fooled the Top Forty, the Grammys, and everyone else by lip-synching to other singers' voices on four hit singles in 1989: "Girl You Know It's True," "Baby Don't Forget My Number," "Girl I'm Gonna Miss You," and "Blame It on the Rain." The act was stripped of its 1989 Best New Artist Grammy Award for the deceit.

MILLS, HAYLEY
Fair-haired, blue-eyed, wistful juvenile actress who was the world's top child-star of the 1960s. Born on April 18, 1946, in London, Mills is famous for a series of highly popular family films for Walt Disney: *Pollyanna* (1960), *The Parent Trap* (1961), *In Search of the Castaways* (1962), *Summer Magic* (1963), *The Moon-Spinners* (1964), and *That Darn Cat!* (1965). Her best non-Disney movie was *The Trouble with Angels* (1966), in which she played Mary Clancy, a juvenile prankster at the St. Francis Academy for Girls, opposite Rosalind Russell's Mother Superior.

MILLS, JULIET
The daughter of legendary British actor Sir John Mills and older sister of Disney star Hayley Mills, remembered best for her role as Phoebe Figalilly on the hit TV sitcom *Nanny and the Professor* (1970–71). In recent years, Mills could be seen playing a witch, Tabitha Lenox, on the campy daytime soap *Passions*. She is married to handsome actor Maxwell Caulfield (1982's *Grease 2*), who is eighteen years her junior (she was born in 1941, he in 1959).

MILTON BRADLEY

"Another Milton Bradley key to fun and learning." The greatest board game manufacturer of the twentieth century was actually founded by namesake Milton Bradley in the nineteenth century (Springfield, Massachusetts, in 1861). The company is known for games that have been passed on from generation to generation: Battleship, Candy Land, The Game of Life, Go to the Head of the Class, Operation, Stratego, Twister, Connect Four, and the electronic noisemaker Simon.

MINDY MCCONNELL

Model-turned-actress Pam Dawber's kindhearted earthling on the TV sitcom *Mork and Mindy* who befriends a strange alien named Mork, from the planet Ork, after his eggshell-shaped spaceship lands in her town of Boulder, home of the University of Colorado. The pretty All-American brunette worked as a clerk at her father's music store before becoming a local newscaster for KTNS-TV.

MINISKIRTS

"It's a bad joke that won't last.
Not with winter coming."
—DESIGNER COCO CHANEL, 1966

Even though English designer Mary Quant is credited with inventing the miniskirt, a 1960s fashion legend has it that during a publicity tour of Australia for a fabric company, supermodel Jean Shrimpton found there wasn't enough material for the dress she was planning to wear. She told the dressmaker, "Make the outfit a bit shorter. No one's going to notice." Enchanted, the fashion world did take notice of the dress—which ended four inches above the knee—and the mini was born.

A thigh-high favorite, the mini is a slim little skirt worn four inches to a wolf-whistling ten inches above the knee. First associated with mod London girls on Carnaby Street, the miniskirt became fashionable in the United States following the British Invasion of the mid-1960s. In 1968, the fun and sexy skirt came to symbolize female liberation after Jeannie C. Riley's free-spirited Mrs. Johnson socked it to the hypocritical P.T.A. of Harper Valley because they found her "dresses way too high." In the early 1970s, younger gals adorned miniskirts with bright-colored leotards or knee-high knit stockings, accompanied by trendy footwear like knee-length go-go boots and platform heels (think TV's *Brady Bunch* girls, and you'll get the picture). Miniskirts went out of vogue in the late 1970s, but short skirts made a brief comeback during the "New Wave meets Valley Girl meets Physical" fashion period of the early 1980s. The minis of this era were made out of leather (patent or faux) or a sweatsuit-like material (fleece) and resembled pleated cheerleading skirts. Gals paired them with Candies pumps, anklets or leg warmers, striped Danskin leotards, and headbands. In the 1990s, an updated form of the mini known as the little black dress became a fashion staple for modern career women.

MINISKIRT TEST

Back in grade school, there were two common tests teachers used to determine whether a gal's skirt was too short: the Kneel Test and the Thumb Test. The Kneel Test required the hem of the skirt to touch the floor when she knelt; the Thumb test required the skirt to be longer than the thumbs when her arms were extended down to the sides. If a girl flunked, either mom was called to bring different clothing, or the student was sent home to change threads.

MINNIE MOUSE

Forever loyal, she is the sweetheart of Mickey Mouse. Together they made their debut in the animated short "Steamboat Willie" in 1928. Minnie's pet dog is Fifi.

MISER BROTHERS

"I'm Mr. Green Christmas, I'm Mr. Sun, I'm Mr. Heat Blister, I'm Mr. One Hundred and One. . . ." "I'm Mr. White Christmas, I'm Mr. Snow, I'm Mr. Icicle, I'm Mr. Ten Below. . . ." These two mean-spirited, weather-controlling brothers, teeming with sibling rivalry, consisted of fire-haired Heat Miser, who liked it hot, and ice-haired Snow Miser, who liked it cold. For many of us, the outrageous Miser brothers, seen in the Rankin/Bass Yuletide special *Year Without a Santa Claus* (1974), have become unforgettable pop culture icons of Christmas. They're too much!

MISFITS

All-girl rock band, from the 1980s *Jem* cartoon and doll line, composed of punk chicks—leader Pizzazz, Roxy, Stormer, Clash, and Jetta—with wicked streaks, and we're not talking hair here. The Misfits are the bitchy rivals of "truly outrageous" Jem and the Holograms.

MISS AMERICA

"The Pageant has endured
because it survived scandal, depressions,
wars, and scathing criticism.
All survivors are winners, and the
Miss America Pageant is one fabulous winner!"

—PHYLLIS GEORGE, MISS AMERICA 1971

"There she is, Miss America. There she is, your ideal. . . ." Once upon a time—before the day of Gloria Steinem's feminist movement and Hillary Clinton's political correctness—a little girl could actually dream of growing up to become a sexist stereotype: an airline stewardess, a Playboy Bunny, a Dallas Cowboys Cheerleader, or the ultimate girly-girl symbol—Miss America! She could dream of being one of the fifty most beautiful women in America parading proudly down the boardwalk of Atlantic City. She could dream of wearing lovely evening gowns and provocative swimsuits in front of millions of TV viewers. She could dream of twirling a baton to "Yankee Doodle Dandy" or tinkling Beethoven's Fifth Symphony on the piano. And she could dream of answering those tough interview questions, like "Why is my beauty important to the world's environment?"

The Miss America Pageant began in 1921 when Margaret Gorman from Washington, D.C., was crowned winner as a publicity stunt to draw tourist business to Atlantic City. By its first TV broadcast in 1955, Miss America had become one of the nation's most sacred annual ceremonies. Her popularity peaked in the 1970s, when girls played with a Miss America Barbie, carried a Miss America lunch box to school, and even won at Parker Brothers' Miss America board game. Oh to be Miss America—wearing a sparkling diamond crown and red-velvet cape trimmed with white fur, and carrying a glittering crystal scepter, walking the runway, waving to the adoring crowd—elbow-elbow-wrist-wrist-wrist!

FYI: ▸ Miss America was the only TV program President Nixon let daughters Julie and Tricia watch.

MISS CLAIROL HAIRCOLOR

Hmmmm . . . "Does she or doesn't she? Only her hairdresser knows for sure." These days, it's somewhat of a status symbol for a woman to get her hair colored—also known as dyed, bleached, tinted, highlighted, frosted, tipped, or streaked—so not only does her hairdresser know, but you do and I do as well.

MISS EGLANTINE PRICE

A novice witch from the small village of Pepperinge Eye who has a magical bedknob that makes beds soar and stops Nazi troops from invading England during the Blitzkrieg. Like all good witches, Miss Price has a token pet cat she calls Cosmic Creepers. Played by Angela Lansbury in Disney's *Bedknobs and Broomsticks* (1971).

MISS ELLIE

Formerly Eleanor Southworth, she married Jock Ewing and years later became the kind, stolid matriarch who kept the peace among the conniving residents of Southfork in *Dallas*. Played by Emmy-winning Barbara Bel Geddes.

MISSION: IMPOSSIBLE

"Your mission, should you decide to accept it . . ." Long-running TV hit, seen on CBS-TV from 1966 to 1973, about an elite crew of top-secret government agents working for IMF (Impossible Missions Force) who use high-tech gadgetry on intricate global assignments. Jim Phelps (Peter Graves) led the group of courageous risk takers consisting of master-of-disguise Rollin Hand (Martin Landau), seductress Cinnamon Carter (Barbara Bain), electronics whiz Barney Collier (Greg Morris), and muscleman Willy Armitage (Peter Lupus). New additions to the team in later years included Leonard Nimoy as Paris, Sam Elliott as Doug, Lesley Ann Warren as Dana, Lynda Day George as Lisa, and Barbara Anderson as Mimi. Lalo Schifrin composed the show's urgent, pulsating jazz theme. Movie superstar Tom Cruise brought *Mission: Impossible* to the big screen not once (1996) but twice (2000 sequel), as slick yet overstylized spectacles that lack the charm of the vintage TV series (even if they did make a gazillion bucks at the box office). "This tape will self-destruct in five seconds."

MISS JESSICA
Sweet and pretty, the redheaded schoolteacher (voiced by Robie Lester) helped Kris Kringle on his mission to bring toys to the deprived children of Sombertown in the TV special *Santa Claus Is Comin' to Town* (1970). Jessica later wed Kris and became Mrs. Santa Claus.

MISS PIGGY
"Moi?" The enchanting blonde sow is the incomparable prima donna of stage and screen, and if you disagree she will give you a karate chop—"Hi-Yah!" She's hopelessly in love with Kermit the Frog, whom she calls "Kermie."

FYI: ▸ Ballet great Rudolf Nureyev once danced a pas de deux from "Swine Lake" with Miss Piggy on her TV series *The Muppet Show.*

MISS YVONNE

> "Pardon me, m'am, excuse my stare, but you have got the biggest hair!"
> —PUPPETBAND'S DIRTY DOG

The "most beautiful woman in Puppetland," whose perfectly groomed hair was as big as her perfectly fabulous ego. Played by Lynne Stewart on *Pee-Wee's Playhouse* from 1986 to 1991.

MISTER ROGERS' NEIGHBORHOOD
"Hello, television neighbor!" Amiable real-life Presbyterian minister Fred Rogers was the host of PBS's longest-running children's TV program, from 1967 to 2001. From the moment Mr. Rogers entered the studio set representing his home and slipped on his trademark cardigan sweater and comfortable sneakers, all the while singing the show's opening theme song, "Won't You Be My Neighbor," youngsters knew it was going to be "a beautiful day in the neighborhood." Using simple conversation (he chatted to the camera as if conversing with viewers), songs, puppets, and human guest stars, Mr. Rogers gently educated kids about values, feelings, and fears, such as jealousy, anger, failure, rejection, impatience, and death. In the early 1980s, black comic Eddie Murphy did a ghetto-ridden lampoon of Mr. Rogers on *Saturday Night Live,* titled *Mr. Robinson's Neighborhood* ("It's one hell of a day in my neighborhood / A hell of a day for a neighbor . . . ").

M&M'S
Tiny, round chocolate candies covered with a hard candy shell, making them resistant to heat so they "melt in your mouth, not in your hand." Introduced in 1941, the M&M's name came from the initials of the last names of its two developers, Forrest Mars and Bruce Murries. There are two common types: the smaller, plain ones with a milk-chocolate center—advertised by Mr. Plain—and the larger, peanut ones with a chocolate-covered peanut in the center, advertised by Mr. Peanut. The candy-coated colors in the typical M&M's batch are brown, red, yellow, orange, green, tan, and the more recent blue (added in a 1995 election held by the Mars Candy Company).

According to popular urban folklore, the colors are pretty significant: the green ones make you horny, the yellow ones make you gay, the orange ones make you lucky, the brown ones make you unlucky, the tan ones give you diarrhea, and the red ones give you cancer. (In 1976, red M&M's were discontinued because of a scare about the "red dye no. 2" used in food being linked to cancerous tumors in laboratory rats; after years of "bring 'em back" fan mail, they reappeared in 1987.) Today, more than 100 million M&M's are consumed daily in the United States.

FYI: ▸ Superstar rock band Van Halen's concert contracts used to require bowls of M&M's backstage with all the brown ones removed!

MOCCASINS
Soft suede frontier-style footwear with fringe across the top loved by kids who want to be Pocahontas or Daniel Boone.

MOCKINGBIRD HEIGHTS
Normal suburban community that found itself home to the lovable but not normal Munster family on prime time's *Munsters* series. Unlike the rest of the neighborhood, the Munsters' property had a continuous thunderstorm overhead. (They would think it was another beautiful day outside!)

MOD
This euphemism for "modern" was bold, daring, groovy, and anything British, circa 1960s. Particularly The Beatles, The Who, Herman's Hermits,

James Bond, swingin' Carnaby Street and Kings Road in London, youthquake fashion designer Mary Quant, short miniskirts, vinyl go-go boots, Nehru jackets, Vespa scooters, Twiggy, Jean Shrimpton, *Blow-Up*, and the geometric Vidal Sassoon haircut. It's all so fab and smashin'—tally-ho, darlings!

MODEL KITS

Popularized by such companies as AMT, Aurora, Hawk, Lindberg, Monogram, and Revell, these plastic building kits contained miniature replicas of automobiles, aircraft, ships, and figures that you either glued or snapped together.

MOD HAIR KEN

Best-selling Ken doll of 1973 that had real rooted dark hair (collar-length and side-parted) and came with reusable facial hairpieces (beard, mustache, and sideburns).

MOD SQUAD

"Danger is their bag!" The coolest, grooviest, most hip-hot-happenin' prime-time TV show of the late 1960s and early 1970s focused on a trio of young people, each a rebellious dropout from society (a.k.a. the Establishment), who were on probation for various run-ins with the law. There were Pete Cochran (Michael Cole), the shaggy rich kid nabbed for stealing a car after his parents kicked him out of their Beverly Hills home; Lincoln "Linc" Hayes (Clarence Williams III), the African-American from the ghetto arrested during the Watts riots; and Julie Barnes (Peggy Lipton), the blonde daughter of a San Francisco hooker who ran away from home and was busted for vagrancy in Hollywood. The threesome found themselves recruited by Captain Adam Greer (Tige Andrews) to be members of a special investigative task force—the Mod Squad—for the L.A.P.D. Their mission: to go undercover and infiltrate the hippie counterculture and bag dangerous criminals preying on drop-out youths. The ABC series aired from 1968 to 1973.

FYI: ▸ In 1999, *The Mod Squad* was made into a lame big-screen feature starring Giovanni Ribisi (Pete), Omar Epps (Linc), and Claire Danes (Julie). When will Hollywood realize that the TV classics from our childhood (for example, *The Avengers, The Beverly Hillbillies, McHale's Navy, My Favorite Martian, Wild Wild West,* and *Josie and the Pussycats*) rarely make good movies?

MOGWAI

A cute, wide-eyed, cooing, furry little creature (about one foot tall), from the Himalayan region of Asia, that you never want to expose to light, get wet, or feed after midnight (see the 1984 *Gremlins* movie). If you break these rules, a Mogwai will spawn an army of marauding gremlins.

MOHAWK

Originating among the Mohican Indian tribe, this hairdo found itself fashionable with both male and female punk rockers of the 1980s. It involved a completely shaved head with the exception of a streak of hair that ran vertically from the forehead to the nape of the neck. Punkers used strong household glues to spike it straight up and would dye it a variety of bright colors. Those who sported this hairstyle thought they were menacing but usually came off looking rather silly. Famous Mohawk wearers include Robert DeNiro as deranged Travis Bickle in the Martin Scorsese film *Taxi Driver*, Annabella Lwin of the fun New Wave band Bow Wow Wow, and professional bad-ass Mr. T.

***MOMMIE DEAREST* (BOOK)**

Written in 1978, the notorious best-seller was Christina Crawford's posthumous attack on her adoptive mother, legendary movie star Joan Crawford. In the book, she reveals how nightmarish it was to grow up with her tyrannical and abusive, both verbally and physically, mother. According to Christina, unmarried Joan adopted her, then son Christopher, and eventually "twin" daughters Cathy and Cindy, for publicity purposes only. On the outside, she came off as a loving and generous mother, but behind the walls of her twenty-two-room Beverly Hills mansion the treatment of the children was harsh and punitive. Life was sheer terror as "Mommie Dearest" went on mad rampages (allegedly fueled by her alcoholism). The children's birthday and Christmas presents were given away to orphanages, they were forced by obsessive neat-freak Joan to scrub bathrooms past the point of perfection, Christina's blonde hair was chopped off for mimicking her mother in front of a mirror, and her bedroom was trashed for hanging her dresses on wire hangers instead of wooden ones.

MOMMIE DEAREST (MOVIE)

In 1981, Christina Crawford's tell-all story became a feature film starring Faye Dunaway as shoulder-padded, movie bitch-goddess Joan Crawford. Because of Dunaway's over-the-top performance and way-out-there dialogue—"I'm not mad at you. I'm mad at the dirt!" and "No more wire hangers!"—it has become a cult classic, establishing wide-eyed Faye as the "Queen of Camp."

MONCHICHIS

"Monchichi, Monchichi / Oh so soft and cuddly. . . ." These cute, monkey-like creatures were the thumb-sucking subjects of a popular toy line, originating from Japan, and a Hanna-Barbera cartoon series (1983–84). Under the guidance of kindly wizard Wizzar, the Monchichis—Moncho, Kyla, Tootoo, Patchitt, and little Thumkii—lived high up in trees in a forest world called Monchia and battled the wicked Grumplins, led by the nasty Horgg.

"MONEY FOR NOTHING"

Dire Straits' innovative, award-winning video clip, directed by Steve Barron, was one of the first to employ computer-engineered 3-D animation. It won 1985's Best Video and Best Group Video categories at the MTV Video Awards. The repeated lead-in refrain, "I want my MTV," performed by Sting (who co-wrote the song with frontman Mark Knopfler), became the cable station's catchphrase.

MONKEEMOBILE

Famed car customizer George Barris created The Monkees' customized zingy red GTO-ish station wagon with the white convertible ragtop that they drove on their hit TV series. From 1968 to 1970, Corgi Toys produced a downsized version of the Monkeemobile, complete with plastic figures of the four-member pop band.

MONKEES

Hey, hey, they're The Monkees—Michael, Peter, Micky, and Davy—the sensationally phenomenal teen idol group of the late 1960s. In the fall of 1965, a now-famous ad appeared in the Hollywood trade papers, searching for "four insane boys, age 17–21," to be assembled for a TV musical-sitcom loosely based on The Beatles and their films *A Hard Day's Night* (1964) and *Help!* (1965). Nearly 500 hopefuls auditioned to be a Monkee, including Danny Hutton (of Three Dog Night), Harry Nilsson, Stephen Stills, Paul Williams, and (gasp!) Charles Manson. The lucky four selected were diminutive Brit Davy Jones, the cute one; former child actor Micky Dolenz, the kooky one; lanky Texan Michael Nesmith, the cool one; and fresh-faced Peter Tork, the not-so-bright one.

Premiering on NBC in 1966, the fast-paced comedy featured The Monkees on various madcap adventures while lip-synching along to their bubblegum tunes and driving the customized Monkeemobile. It was an instant smash, particularly with preteens, and won an Emmy Award as 1966's Best Comedy Series. When The Monkees' prime-time stint ended in 1968, they were seen in reruns on Saturday mornings (following *The Archie Comedy Hour*) until 1973.

Outside the TV show, The Monkees were adored rock stars whose records sold millions, including the Top Forty singles "Last Train to Clarksville" (1966), "I'm a Believer" (1966), "(I'm Not Your) Steppin' Stone" (1966), "A Little Bit Me, a Little Bit You" (1967), "Pleasant Valley Sunday" (1967), and "Daydream Believer" (1968). The success of their recording career angered many rock critics, who felt they were blatantly "manufactured." They said their music was prerecorded and that the boys did voice-overs altered by high-tech recording equipment, which gave them a more polished sound. Monkeemania went on a decline in 1968 when a disgruntled Nesmith announced to the press that they did not play their own music ("We're being passed off as something we aren't"). Tork quit in December 1968, and the band disbanded in 1969.

Today, The Monkees are embraced by younger musicians, such as R.E.M.'s Michael Stipe, who believes they should be inducted into the Rock and Roll Hall of Fame because they were the first taste of rock music for millions of adolescents.

FYI: ▸ Michael Nesmith's mother was the inventor of Liquid Paper correction fluid.

MONSTER CEREALS

Introduced in 1971, a line of General Mills cereals named after and advertised by animated monster characters—Boo Berry, Count Chocula, Frankenberry, and Fruit Brute—and that came with flavored marshmallow bits (à la Lucky Charms). In commercials, these lovable kooks took a nod from Quisp and Quake by arguing about who was the scariest (none) and who had the better-tasting cereal (all). Actually, the sweet-tasting cereals seemed to be more than 50 percent sugar, and the marshmallow bits were rather chalky and would turn slimy in your mouth.

MONSTER MAGNET

This large and powerful red magnet shaped like a scary genie with two outstretched arms was manufactured by Wham-O in 1964.

"MONSTER MASH"

"The dumbest thing I ever heard."
—ELVIS PRESLEY

Spoofing the dance craze fad of the early 1960s, this novelty song in which Frankenstein's monster does a dance called the Mash ("a graveyard smash") is the rock 'n' roll anthem of Halloween. Performed by Bobby Pickett (doing an eerie Boris Karloff imitation), it reached number one in October 1962. A decade later, it reentered the charts twice (1970 and 1972) and sold more than four million copies. Pickett's backup band was called The Crypt-Kickers.

MONTGOMERY, LEE H.

Child movie actor of the 1970s (born November 3, 1961) who played Jimmy Dooley in Disney's *Million Dollar Duck* (1971), Danny Garrison in *Ben* (1972), and David Rolfe in *Burnt Offerings* (1976).

MONTGOMERY "SCOTTY" SCOTT

"Beam me up, Scotty!" *Star Trek*'s puckish chief engineer, who spoke in a Scottish brogue. Actor James Doohan, starring as Captain Kirk's trusted comrade, wasn't native to Scotland; he was born and raised in Vancouver, British Columbia, Canada.

"MONY MONY"

Reaching as high as number three on the charts in 1968, the song, first recorded by Tommy James and the Shondells, hit the number-one spot in 1987 when it was rerecorded "live" by bad-boy rocker Billy Idol. It was Idol's only American chart-topper, and dancers at dance clubs universally accompanied it with a chant that went something like "Hey? Hey what? Get laid, get screwed!"

MOOD LIPSTICK

As a fashion fad of the mid-1980s, this amazing lipstick mysteriously changed after touching the warmth of your lips, from the color of green in the tube to various shades of pink and red.

MOOD RINGS

Novelty jewelry that had a brief reign of faddish popularity in the 1970s by letting its wearers know what kind of mood they were experiencing. The mood ring's oval-shaped stone consisted of a heat-sensitive liquid crystal encased in clear quartz that detected a person's feelings by body temperature and turned an appropriate color in response. Blue meant happy, green was okay, yellow meant bored, brown was cranky, reddish-brown meant insecure, and—worst of all—black was gloom and doom. Created by Joshua Reynolds, heir to the R. J. Reynolds tobacco fortune, the chameleon-like ring sold more than twenty million during the summer and fall of 1975. It inspired many incarnations, such as mood necklaces, mood bracelets, mood pendants, mood belt-buckles, mood watches, mood nail-polish, mood shoes, mood T-shirts, and even mood underwear. The craze ended after a year or so because the liquid crystals tended to lose their mood-changing zest, causing the rings to turn an everlasting shade of black.

FYI: ▸ Italian movie star Sophia Loren made tabloid front-page news in 1975 when her mood ring turned "bad karma" black and sent her into a panic at a press conference.

MOON BOOTS

One—two—three . . . Blast off! Cushy, futuristic platform-esque boots fashionable during winter months of the early 1980s. Also called space boots, they were so named because they looked like the footwear planet-hopping spacemen would wear. Trendy modern-day Uggs, the comfy boot made out of sheepskin and first worn by male Australian surfers before experiencing worldwide popularity, is a throwback to the moon boot.

MOON LANDING

"One small step for man,
one giant leap for mankind."
—NEIL ARMSTRONG

July 20, 1969. The day millions of people crowded around TV sets to see the astounding sight of Apollo 11 touching down on the moon and astronaut Neil Armstrong taking mankind's first walk on it. This is one of those history-making events that people remember for a lifetime (like the assassinations of President Kennedy and Martin Luther King Jr.). They remember where they were, what they were doing, and who they were with. Conspiracy theorists claim that the whole thing was a fake and that Armstrong took those famous steps on a stage of a TV studio.

MOONROCK

Bespectacled young inventor who was a member of the teenage Pebbles and Bamm-Bamm gang on the popular 1970s Saturday-morning cartoon show. Pebbles, a well-meaning schemer, often involved Moonrock in inventing some prehistoric doohickey that more often than not ended up backfiring. He played drums in the groovy Bedrock Rollers rock band, along with Pebbles, Bamm-Bamm, Penny, and Wiggy.

MOOSE MASON

This hulking jock from the *Archie* comic books is Riverdale High's most brainless student (Moose believes the consistent F's he scores on tests at school stand for "fantastic"). He also has a short fuse, especially when it comes to clobbering Reggie Mantle, who has a fatal attraction to Midge Klump, Moose's intellectual and pretty girlfriend.

MOP-TOP CUT

Influenced by the unshorn tresses of The Beatles, this shaggy hairstyle for men stirred up a lot of controversy in the mid-1960s. The name came from its similarity to a cleaning mop. Tame by today's standards, it was once despised by the older generation, who believed young men should have short cuts with hair snipped above the ears. Hair touching a man's ears was just too rebellious, and many guys found themselves expelled from school or fired from jobs for wearing it this way.

MORAN, ERIN

Born October 18, 1961, in California, the freckled, curly-haired brunette with the engaging personality virtually grew up in front of the TV cameras. She first played Jenny Jones, the little orphan girl on *Daktari* (1966–69), and, later, Richie Cunningham's kid sister, Joanie, on the prime-time smash *Happy Days* (1974–84).

MORK AND MINDY

The most popular new show of the 1978–79 TV season was this spin-off from an episode of *Happy Days* in which a nutty alien tried to kidnap Richie Cunningham. It featured improvisational comic Robin Williams as Mork, a free-spirited misfit from the planet Ork, a world void of emotion and humor. Mork was sent to earth by his Orkan leader, Orson, to study the emotional behavior of its citizens. After landing his egg-shaped spaceship in the middle of Boulder, Colorado, he befriended a kind and pretty earthling named Mindy McConnell (played by former cover-girl Pam Dawber). Mindy sheltered him in her attic and taught him about the world of humans. By the fall of 1981, the two mismatched roomies fell in love, married, and (Mork!) gave birth to Jonathan Winters. Riding on the crest of the sitcom's popularity, Mork's nutty lingo, "Nanu, Nanu" (good-bye) and "Shazbat" (drats) became common catchphrases of the era.

MORK FROM ORK

Red-suited alien from the planet Ork, an outcast for having emotions and a sense of humor, who flew a giant egg to earth on a mission to study the "crazy" conduct of its inhabitants. Some of his strange habits included conversing with plants, sleeping upside down in a closet, and drinking soda pop from his finger. Married a humanoid named Mindy McConnell.

"MORK" SUSPENDERS

Please tell me we didn't mimic zany space alien Mork from Ork by wearing these rainbow-striped suspenders. Those of us who were guilty of it would stick various pin-backed buttons with topical sayings and slogans up and down them.

MOROCCO MOLE

Secret agent Secret Squirrel's fez-wearing, vision-impaired rodent sidekick who sounded a lot like character actor Peter Lorre on the mid-1960s Hanna-Barbera cartoons.

MORRIS THE CAT

Called the "Robert Redford of Catdom" by the *New York Daily News*, the hairy orange superstar with the round head was rescued from being put to sleep in a Chicago animal shelter by trainer Bob Martwick. Originally called Lucky, the fortuitous fellow would become Morris, the revered spokes-tabby for 9-Lives cat food, in 1969. These TV commercials showcased him as a fussy and finicky feline who just couldn't resist the taste of 9-Lives. The American public loved Morris, and he became an overnight star who rode around in limousines, flew first class, and received truckloads of fan mail. In 1973, he won a Patsy Award, the animal kingdom's equivalent of the Oscar. (Other nominees that year included the rat from *Ben*, the lion from *Napoleon and Samantha*, a stallion from *Bonanza*, and five Doberman pinschers from *The Doberman Gang*.)

FYI: ▸ In 1987, Morris ran for president of the United States, with Walter Mondale's daughter, Eleanor, serving as his campaign manager.

MORTICIA ADDAMS

The beautiful but somber *Addams Family* wife and mother who enjoyed horticulture (she was always snipping those pesky rose blooms off her beloved thorny stems) and speaking French (which drove hubby Gomez so mad with desire that he'd kiss her from fingers to elbow). Cleopatra, a man-eating African Strangler plant, is her much-pampered pet. Morticia was played by 1950s movie starlet Carolyn Jones on *The Addams Family* TV series, and later by Anjelica Huston in two big-screen versions.

MOSQUITOES

Beatles-esque rock band from America consisting of Bingo, Bango, Bongo, and Irving, who once made a visit to *Gilligan's Island*. Their refusal to help the castaways off the isle led the girls to form the singing Honey Bees, hoping it would change their mind. The Honey Bees' talent only intimated The Mosquitoes, causing them to flee on a helicopter. See the 1965 *Gilligan's Island* episode titled "Don't Bug the Mosquitoes."

MOTHER NATURE

Matriarch of all things natural on earth who doesn't like to be fooled by Chiffon margarine (thunderclap roar, earthquake rumble). Believe it or not, she's the mother of those nasty Miser brothers, Heat and Snow, featured in the animated TV special *The Year Without a Santa Claus* (1974).

MOTHRA

Colorful, fast-moving, giant moth—controlled by the Alilenas, a pair of six-inch-tall twin princesses—who could fire ultrasonic wave beams from its antennae and produce devastating winds with its humongous wings. Mothra is the archenemy of Godzilla (1964's *Godzilla vs. Mothra*).

FYI: ▸ Emi and Yumi Ito, who had an actual singing career in Japan as the Peanuts, played The Alilenas.

MOTOWN

"The sound of young America." Rhythm-and-blues record company founded in Detroit, a.k.a. "Motor City," in 1959 by Berry Gordy Jr. The soulful Motown Sound, featuring throbbing bass lines, luscious harmonies, and danceable beats, crossed the barriers of race in the 1960s by appealing to American teenagers both black and white. The company's legion of stars included Marvin Gaye, Diana Ross and The Supremes, The Temptations, Jackie Wilson, Mary Wells, The Marvelettes, Martha Reeves and The Vandellas, Smokey Robinson and The Miracles, The Four Tops, Stevie Wonder, Gladys Knight and The Pips, and The Jackson 5. A Baby Boomer's greatest-hits LP would not be complete without a Motown ditty or two, like "Shop Around" (1960), "Please Mr. Postman" (1961), "Dancing in the Street" (1964), "My Guy" (1964), "Baby Love" (1964), "My Girl" (1965), "I Can't Help Myself (Sugar Pie, Honey Bunch)" (1965), "Uptight (Everything's Alright)" (1966), and "I Heard It Through the Grapevine" (1968).

FYI: ▸ The nickname of Motown Records is "Hitsville U.S.A."

MOUNT CRUMPIT

Wintry peak north of Whoville, where the Christmas-loathing, green-skinned Grinch dwells in Dr. Seuss's *How the Grinch Stole Christmas*.

MOUSEKETEERS
Mouseketeer roll call: Sherry, Sharon, Bobby, Lonnie, Tommy, Johnny, Dennis, Annette (the most popular), Darlene, Cheryl, Cubby, Karen, Paul, Doreen . . . A group of child actors dressed in trademark uniforms—white T-shirts, with their first name embroidered on the chest, and black mouse-ear caps—who sang, danced, and performed other talents on Walt Disney's *Mickey Mouse Club* (1955–59). In 1977, the Mouseketeers were revived for the next generation of TV fans on *The New Mickey Mouse Club*. This disco-dancing Disney bunch of twelve, including Lisa Whelchel (the future Blair Warner of *The Facts of Life*), wore modern Day-Glo uniforms and colored mouse-ears. They were revived once more, from 1989 to 1994, on the Disney Channel's *All-New Mickey Mouse Club*, which nixed the distinctive mouse-ear hats but featured big hair and the soon-to-be fabulously famous teen stars Britney Spears, Christina Aguilera, Keri "Felicity" Russell, and 'N Sync's Justin Timberlake.

MOUSE TRAP
"It's fun to build this comical wonder, but woe to the mouse who gets caught under!" A classic game of our youth designed by Marvin Glass and released by Ideal Toys in 1963. The gadget-laden action game has players taking turns building an elaborate three-dimensional, Rube Goldberg-esque contraption on a playing board. When the zany mechanical wonder is complete, players take turns, through a chain reaction of events, trying to trap the opponent's playing piece (a plastic mouse). It works like this: A player turns a crank that rotates a gear causing a lever to move and push a stop sign against a shoe; the shoe tips a bucket that holds a metal ball; the ball rolls down a rickety staircase and into a drainpipe, allowing it to hit a helping-hand rod; this causes a bowling ball to fall from the top of the helping-hand rod, through the thingamajig and a bathtub, and land on a diving board; the weight of the bowling ball then catapults a diver through the air and right into a washtub, causing a cage to fall from the top of a post and trap an unsuspecting mouse. Mouse Trap was a huge success, becoming the best-selling game of 1963 and 1964 after selling more than two million copies. It is still in production today.

MOUSSE
Foamy hair product invented in the 1980s that fizzed out of a bottle and when applied would give hair lots of volume (making thin hair thick and flat hair full). Two mousse classics: Paul Mitchell's Sculpting Foam and Sebastian's Fizz.

MOWGLI
The young lad, abandoned at birth and raised as a wolf cub in the jungles of India, was seen in Disney's 1967 animated movie *The Jungle Book*, based on Rudyard Kipling's tales.

MR. BILL
Forget Gumby and the Pillsbury Doughboy, everyone's favorite Play-Doh man of the late 1970s was the repeatedly abused Mr. Bill. The animated hero with the cheery disposition and high-pitched whine made his debut in 1976 on "The Mr. Bill Show," an ongoing segment of NBC's *Saturday Night Live*. He and loyal dog Spot were at the mercy of Mr. Hands, a sadistic pair of hands that pretended to be Mr. Bill's friend but always set him up for horrendous pratfalls. "Oh, noooooooo!" cried Mr. Bill as he found himself flattened, smashed, crushed, chopped, conked, diced, amputated, decapitated, knifed, boiled, baked, blended, and squished. Thuggish bully Sluggo, also made out of clay, was Mr. Bill's nemesis.

MR. BUBBLE
"Mr. Bubble in your tubble makes you nice and clean!" Advertised by a pink soap-bubble called Mr. Bubble, this brand of bubble bath made getting clean as much fun as getting dirty.

MR. CLEAN
The bald-headed, muscular genie would emerge from a white tornado to hawk Mr. Clean All-Purpose Cleaner to inept housewives on now-legendary TV commercial spots.

MR. DOO BEE
Were you a Do Bee or a Don't Bee? Yellowjacket mascot from TV's *Romper Room* who helped preschoolers learn good manners, like "Do Bees comb their hair and are happy and good." His naughty brother, Mr. Don't Bee, taught ill manners,

such as "Don't Bees never comb their hair and are grouchy and bad."

MR. ED

"Gee, Wilbur." This was one of the first of the nonsensical fantasy sitcoms airing on prime time throughout the 1960s (for example, *Bewitched, The Flying Nun, I Dream of Jeannie, My Favorite Martian, My Mother the Car*, and *The Munsters*). Broadcast on CBS from 1961 to 1966, it was the story of a friendly architect, Wilbur Post (Alan Young), who moves to the quiet countryside with his pretty wife, Carol (Connie Hines), to escape the hustle and bustle of the big city. The spacious ranch house they'd bought came with a barn that housed a handsome palomino. The horse looked like any other horse, but it wasn't just any horse ("of course, of course"). It happened to be the famous Mr. Ed, the talking horse (voiced by Allan "Rocky" Lane). Wilbur was the first and only two-legged person Mr. Ed spoke to (nobody before him was worthy of the effort), and the show's plots, centered on the confusion caused by a horse, teemed with one-liners and dry, witty comments.

FYI: ▸ *Mr. Ed* was awarded the 1963 Golden Globe for Best Television Program.

MR. FANTASTIC

The leader of *Marvel* comics' Fantastic Four superhero team was a scientist named Dr. Reed Richards, whose body could be pulled and stretched infinitely. He's married to Sue Storm, a.k.a. the Invisible Girl.

MR. FRENCH

On prime time's *Family Affair*, Sebastian Cabot starred as the impeccable English Gentleman's Gentleman to swingin' Manhattan playboy Bill Davis, who finds himself serving as a surrogate parent to Davis's orphaned nieces, Cissy and Buffy, and nephew Jody. First name: Giles.

MR. GREEN JEANS

Captain Kangaroo's farmer friend (played by Hugh Brannum), an amateur inventor and nature expert who was always introducing live animals on the beloved kiddie show. Mr. Green Jeans's name came from the color of the jeans he wore regularly on the *Captain Kangaroo* kid show.

MR. HAND

"C. D. F. F.—What are you people on? Dope?" In the 1982 teen movie *Fast Times at Ridgemont High*, Ray Walston starred as the punctilious history teacher who faces off with Sean Penn's stoned surfer dude, Jeff Spicoli. Previously, Walston played Uncle Martin on the TV sitcom *My Favorite Martian* (1963–66).

MR. HANKEY

"Howdy Ho!" Mr. Hankey, the Christmas Poo, is a talking piece of poop from the sewer that visits the children of the *South Park* cartoon—actually, only the *South Park* kids who have fiber in their diet—to sing holly jolly Yuletide tunes.

MR. MAGOO

"Oh, Magoo, you've done it again!" Since 1949, crotchety old Quincy Magoo has been the nearsighted star of hundreds of theatrical and TV cartoon shorts. The typical Mr. Magoo story was about how his infamous bad eyesight got him involved in an unintentional funny situation—for example, he couldn't tell the difference between a bear and his nephew in a fur coat. In 1962, *Mr. Magoo's Christmas Carol*, a feature-length version of Charles Dickens's classic tale starring Magoo as Ebenezer Scrooge, aired on prime time for the holidays. It was TV's first animated cartoon special and inspired a prime-time series, *The Famous Adventures of Mr. Magoo* (1964–65), in which he portrayed legendary figures from both history and literature, such as Long John Silver, William Tell, Rip Van Winkle, and Don Quixote. Over the years, he has been the advertising spokesman for various products, including General Electric, Timex, Ideal Toys, Colgate-Palmolive, Rheingold Beer, and the National Heart Association. Jim Backus, of *Gilligan's Island* fame (Thurston Howell III), supplied Magoo's crinkly voice.

MR. MICROPHONE

The Ronco product was known best for an early-1980s TV commercial featuring a carload of fun-loving guys wooing a pedestrian cutie with the bellowing "Hey, good-looking! We'll be back to pick you up later!" The company's other gimmicky products included the Veg-O-Matic Food Slicer ("It slices! It dices! It chops! It juliennes!"), plus the Pocket Fisherman and the Inside the Shell Electric Egg Scrambler.

MR. MONOPOLY
The top-hatted, mustached millionaire carrying a bag of money has been the mascot of Monopoly, the classic board game marketed by Parker Brothers, since 1935. His official name is Rich Uncle Pennybags.

MR. PEABODY
Wealthy, eyeglass-wearing dog-genius who, along with pet boy Sherman, travels back through time by means of his Wayback Machine in a supporting segment of the *Rocky and Bullwinkle* cartoon show titled "Peabody's Improbable History."

MR. PEEBLES
"We've got a gorilla for sale." Weary owner of Peebles Pet Shop who tries desperately to sell mischievous Magilla Gorilla to no avail on Hanna-Barbera's *Magilla Gorilla* cartoon show.

MR. POTATO HEAD
"Meet Mr. Potato Head, the most wonderful friend a boy or girl could have!" When Hasbro introduced this classic toy created by model-maker George Lerner in 1952, kids were allowed to do what they did best—play with their food. And boy did they play, turning ordinary everyday potatoes into Picasso-like fellows with plastic eyes, noses, ears, lips, torsos, hats, eyeglasses, and smoking pipes sticking out of everywhere. Mr. Potato Head's popularity among children of the Baby Boom led to wife Mrs. Potato Head, son Spud, daughter Yam, and pets called the Spud-ettes—Bushy Bear, Kitten Head, Dinkey Donkey, and Piggly Wiggly. In 1964, real potatoes were no longer required when plastic ones were included in each kit. By the mid-1960s, Hasbro added a whole smorgasbord of lovable fruit and veggie friends. There were the Tooty Frooty Friends—Cooky the Cucumber, Katie the Carrot, Oscar the Orange, and Pete the Pepper—as well as 1966's Picnic Pals, consisting of Frankie Frank, Frenchy Fry, Willy Burger, Mr. Ketchup Head, Mr. Mustard Head, and Mr. Soda Pop Head (those guys came with onion- and pickle-shaped mouths and ears). There was also Dunkie Donut-Head, a 1967 exclusive for Dunkin' Donuts restaurants.

Still around today, Mr. Potato Head has a slick new look (his head and body are now one piece) and has starred in two computer-animated Disney films, *Toy Story* (1995) and sequel *Toy Story 2* (1999), while moonlighting as a spokes-potato for Burger King.

FYI: ▸ Mr. Potato Head was the first toy ever advertised on TV.

MR. ROARKE
"Welcome to Fantasy Island!" The elegant, white-suited man with a Spanish accent owned the island resort where visitors could have their wildest dreams come true. Played by Ricardo Montalban, a onetime Hollywood Latin lover, on the *Fantasy Island* TV series. "Smiles, everyone, smiles!"

MRS. BEASLEY
In the late 1960s, kids who regularly watched *Family Affair* simply adored the freckled, pigtailed Buffy and her inseparable Mrs. Beasley doll. As TV's favorite doll, Mrs. Beasley resembled a comforting nanny dressed in a polka-dotted blue ensemble with matching apron and cape, granny glasses, and a sweet smile on an elderly face. The twosome were so popular that little girls wanted to be just like Buffy and have their own Mrs. Beasley. In 1967, their wish came true when Mattel Toys released a twenty-two-inch-tall talking Mrs. Beasley doll (just as big, soft, and lovable as the one featured on the series). On *Family Affair*, Mrs. Beasley talked only to Buffy, but now girls across America could hear what she had to say—and to their delight it was happy phrases in a friendly granny voice, like "Speak a little louder, dear, so Mrs. Beasley can hear you" and "Gracious me, you're getting to be a big girl." Today, Mrs. Beasley brings back fond memories and has become a sought-after collectible.

MRS. BUTTERWORTH
"The original butter syrup." This talking syrup bottle resembling a domestic who looks a lot like an Aunt Bee Taylor wannabe, has been the star of a long-lasting series of TV commercials for Mrs. Butterworth syrup and pancake mix.

MRS. EDNA GARRETT
Somewhat ditzy housekeeper who worked for the Drummonds of Park Avenue before leaving to take a position as housemother at the Eastland School for Young Women, a prestigious girls' boarding academy in upstate New York. Wise and understanding, Mrs. Garrett acted as a surrogate mother to those in her charge, particularly Blair Warner, Natalie Green, Jo Polniaczek, and Tootie Ramsey. Later changed careers and opened Edna's Edibles, a gourmet food shop in nearby Peekskill. Played by comedienne Charlotte Rae on NBC-TV's *Diff'rent Strokes* and its spin-off, *The Facts of Life.*

MR. SLATE
Fred Flintstone's demanding boss at the Rock Head & Quarry Cave Company in Bedrock. When it comes to appearance, the cartoon Mr. Slate looks something like producer Melvin Cooley (Richard Deacon) from *The Dick Van Dyke Show.*

MRS. LIVINGSTON
Oscar-winning actress Miyoshi Umeki played the philosophical housekeeper to a widower and his young son (Tom and Eddie Corbett) whose Japanese upbringing left her occasionally befuddled by American culture on TV's *Courtship of Eddie's Father.*

MR. SPOCK
"It is highly illogical." On *Star Trek*, black-haired, exotic-featured Leonard Nimoy played the completely logical and emotionless first science officer and closest chum to Captain Kirk absolutely perfectly, and became one of the most beloved characters in TV history. Half-Vulcan, half-earthling (his father was a Vulcan and his mother an earthling), Mr. Spock had pointy ears, sharp eyebrows, and a green complexion. He was capable of a handy nerve pinch, which disabled a combatant, and greeted with a V-fingered salute. "Live long and prosper."

MRS. POTATO HEAD
This demure spud has been Mr. Potato Head's spouse since 1953. In Disney's computer-animated *Toy Story* movies of the 1990s, her voice was provided by Estelle Harris, known previously for playing George Costanza's mother on the TV comedy *Seinfeld.*

MRS. POTTS AND CHIP
Mother and young son who were once human household servants but turned into animated objects, a teapot (Mrs. Potts) and a teacup (Chip), by a witch's spell. They befriend Belle when she is made prisoner in the Beast's gloomy mansion in Walt Disney's *Beauty and the Beast* (1991). Actress Angela Lansbury voiced Mrs. Potts.

MR. T
"I pity the fool." Professional bad-ass and star of the hit TV series *The A-Team* (1983–87). Born Lawrence Tero in Chicago, he started out as a bodyguard for celebs like Michael Jackson before he got a big acting break in 1982 with *Rocky III*, in which he played scowling Clubber Lang, adversary to Sylvester Stallone. Sporting a Mohawk coif, a ton of gold chains, bulging biceps, and attitude for miles, Mr. T was greatly worshiped by small kids, who made him a multimedia cult hero with a Saturday-morning cartoon (*Mr. T and the Force*), a comic book, an action figure, and even his own cereal. "You better watch out, sucker!"

FYI: ▸ In 1980, Mr. T won a nationwide "Toughest Bar Bouncer" contest.

MR. WEATHERBEE
When cartoon hero Archie Andrews and teen cohorts—Jughead, Betty, Veronica, and Reggie—cause scholastic havoc in the classrooms of Riverdale High School, this bald, plump principal becomes easily irked. His first name: Waldo.

MR. WHIPPLE
"Ladies, please don't squeeze the Charmin!" Frustrated grocer who has to keep pleading with his customers to stop copping a feel off rolls of Charmin bathroom tissue. Portrayed by actor Dick Wilson in TV advertisements for Charmin since 1964.

MS. PAC-MAN
In 1982, this bow-headed heroine, gifted with an appetite as equally strong as her immensely popular boyfriend, Pac-Man, was given her own arcade video game geared toward girls. The same year, in September, the "wakka-wakka-wakka" sweethearts became stars of a Saturday-morning cartoon TV se-

ries, *The Pac-Man Show* (1982–85). It had them residing in Pac-Land (the Power Forest, to be exact), married, and with an energetic offspring named Pac-Baby, plus two pets, Chomp Chomp the Dog and Sour Puss the Cat.

MTV

Not since the invention of the phonograph has music undergone a more profound change than with the union of video and rock 'n' roll. At midnight on August 1, 1981, Warner-Amex Satellite Entertainment broadcast the prophetic "Video Killed the Radio Star" by The Buggles, and launched MTV (Music Television). For twenty-four hours a day, every day, cable's all-music channel aired short video clips of rock artists performing interpretations of their latest singles. Originally five video jockeys (V.J.'s, for short) introduced the music videos: Martha Quinn, J. J. Jackson, Alan Hunter, Mark Goodman, and Nina Blackwood.

MTV was an absolute must for those coming of age in the 1980s (the MTV Generation), who sat glued in front of TV sets waiting for favorite videos to air. The channel quickly became synonymous with youth culture and instrumental in registering teenage taste. It was its play lists, rather than those of radio stations, that set the trend in music and gave birth to new pop superstars. In the MTV era, a band's look was as important as its sound (if not more so). First-timers could become overnight sensations with the right concoction of cuteness, sexiness, cockiness, and outlandish costumes and makeup, assembled into a highly stylized, eye-catching video. Acts such as Madonna, Cyndi Lauper, Eurythmics, Culture Club, Duran Duran, George Michael, and Prince were awarded instant attention that they might not have received from the radio.

Reaching more than fifty-five million homes across America, MTV established the music video as an art form. Its production style and technique—rapid-fire editing, jumpy camera angles, lavish imagery, and aggressive music soundtrack—influenced other forms of media, from films (*Flashdance* and *Less Than Zero*) to TV shows (*Miami Vice* and *21 Jump Street*), and virtually every TV commercial. MTV is considered to be the cutting edge of pop music and the champion of multiculturalism. Where else could you see a roster like Whitney Houston, Public Enemy, Nirvana, New Kids on the Block, and Aerosmith performing within the same half-hour? While music videos are the staple of MTV's programming, the network also hosts regular programs: cartoons, comedies, game shows, and interviews (for example, *Remote Control, Singled Out, The Real World, Road Rules, Beavis and Butt-Head, Daria, The Grind, House of Style, Yo! MTV Raps, Alternative Nation, Unplugged*, and *The Week in Rock*). In 1984, the annual MTV Video Music Awards began, and in 1985 sister channel VH-1 was launched.

Critics of MTV claim that videos have placed greater emphasis on the appearance of the artist than on the substance of the music. Some blame the "MTV-style editing"—cutting from image to image within seconds—for shortening the attention span of young Americans. Others say that the network has become too self-important, rarely plays videos anymore, and has all but abandoned the original MTV Generation, who supported them during the infant years, because they are too busy wooing tomorrow's teens.

FYI: ▸ As a revolutionary statement, MTV's logo is a jazzed-up version of the 1968 moon landing.

MUFFY TEPPERMAN

"It behooves me to say. . . ." Dark-haired Jami Gertz's funny performance as the preppy cheerleading captain on the short-lived sitcom *Square Pegs* (1982–83), brilliantly captures the quintessential self-centered teen bitch.

MULLET

Now this is what we call "business in the front, party in the back"! A male haircut derived from the 1980s female-oriented bi-level—short on the top and sides, extralong and bushy in the back. The typical guy sporting this Supercuts specialty would have been a working-class youth or a white-trash hick who wore acid-washed jeans, drove a Camaro, and jammed to Springsteen. Two celebrity mulletheads: Patrick Swayze and Billy Ray Cyrus.

MUMMY

Also known as Im-Ho-Tep. A malicious and very dusty cloth-wrapped high priest, in the form of actor Boris Karloff (1932's *The Mummy*), brought back to life after centuries of burial to destroy those who desecrated his Egyptian tomb. Most recently, Im-Ho-Tep was given a new incarnation in a set of rousing adventure films, starring handsome Brendan Frasier (1999's *The Mummy* and 2001's *The Mummy Returns*).

MUMY, BILLY

Born in 1954, the redheaded youngster is considered a top juvenile actor of the 1960s. Best remembered for playing the inquisitive Will Robinson on the TV series *Lost in Space* from 1965 to 1968, as well as for a particularly chilling *Twilight Zone* episode, "It's a Good Life," airing in 1962. It's the one where he plays Anthony Fremont, the little boy who makes people disappear when they upset him.

MUNSTERS

"*The Munsters* are
one of the best damn shows ever!"
—HOWARD STERN

One of two sitcoms about creepy clans to premiere on prime time in the fall of 1964 (the kooky and spooky *Addams Family* was the other). Airing for two seasons on CBS-TV, this funny fantasy features a lovable family of monsters hailing from Transylvania and residing in a musty, cobweb-strewn Victorian mansion at 1313 Mockingbird Lane in Mockingbird Heights U.S.A. Living everyday domestic lives, the Munsters consider themselves ordinary citizens, but to those they encounter they are anything but. The head of the family, Herman Munster (Fred Gwynne), is a seven-foot-tall Frankenstein creature, and his homemaking wife, Lily (Yvonne De Carlo), looks like a vampire. The other members include Eddie (Butch Patrick), their werewolf-like young son; Grandpa (Al Lewis), Lily's ancient Dracula-type father; and Marilyn (Beverley Owen, for the first half-season, and, later, Pat Priest), the unfortunate niece cursed with being normal and beautiful. Beloved pets included fire-breathing dragon Spot, lion-roaring feline Kitty Kat, Eddie's pet snake Elmer, family bat Igor, and wisecracking cuckoo clock bird Raven. After relegation to syndication heaven for fifteen years, the Munsters reunited for a TV movie, *The Munsters' Revenge*, in 1981.

***MUNSTERS* KOACH**

When you're a strange family, you need a strange car, so that's why Herman Munster chauffeured his supernatural clan (Lily, Eddie, Marilyn, and Grandpa) around Mockingbird Heights in this ghastly-looking hot rod. Designed by George Barris, the same man who invented the Batmobile.

MUPPET MOVIE

The first movie starring Jim Henson's lovable Muppets was a musical-comedy that had Kermit the Frog and Miss Piggy heading to Hollywood in search of fame and fortune. It earned Kermit a Top Forty hit single, "Rainbow Connection." Followed by *The Great Muppet Caper* (1981), *The Muppets Take Manhattan* (1984), *The Muppet Christmas Carol* (1992), *Muppet Treasure Island* (1996), and *Muppets from Space* (1999).

MUPPETS

Muppets are lovable puppets featuring a wide range of shaggy animals, monsters, and humanoids, whose name came from a combination of "marionette" and "puppet." Created by Jim Henson, Muppets were first seen throughout the 1950s on TV commercials and network series like *The Ed Sullivan Show* and *The Tonight Show*. They achieved great fame as regular players—Ernie, Bert, Grover, Oscar the Grouch, Cookie Monster, and Big Bird—on the kiddie classic *Sesame Street* in 1969.

In 1976, the Muppets acquired their own prime-time TV series, *The Muppet Show*, which was the most popular first-run syndicated series in history, reaching hundreds of millions of viewers in more than 100 countries. It starred personable Kermit the Frog as the host of a madcap theatrical troupe made up of Muppets and guest celebrities who seemed to make chaos out of every production number. The cast included glamorous prima donna Miss Piggy, along with Fozzie Bear, Rowlf, Zoot, Animal, Gonzo the Great, and a showcase of more than 400 other Muppets. Two ongoing segments were "Pigs in Space," a takeoff of *Star Trek*, and "The Swedish Chef," a spoof of cooking shows. Among the many famous luminaries to join the weekly mayhem were Lily Tomlin, Elton John, Raquel Welch, Steve Martin, Gilda Radner, Debbie Harry, Brooke Shields, Dom DeLuise, Liberace, and Rudolf Nureyev. The success of *The Muppet Show* led to a series of big-screen ventures, beginning with 1979's *The Muppet Movie* and all forms of

Muppet merchandise, such as toys, dolls, posters, and other tie-ins—making them the best-marketed characters since Disney's Mickey Mouse, Warner's Bugs Bunny, and Hanna-Barbera's Flintstones.

MURRAY SLAUGHTER

Bald and lovable, Gavin MacLeod's Murray Slaughter was the quick-witted news writer for WJM's Six O'Clock News in Minneapolis. Perky Marie was Murray's wife and mother of his three daughters, Bonnie, Ellen, and Laurie.

FYI: ▸ As a teenager, Oscar-winner Helen Hunt appeared as Laurie Slaughter on *The Mary Tyler Moore Show* in 1977.

MUSHMOUTH

Peculiar character from the *Fat Albert* cartoon who wore a stocking cap covering most of his face and always mumbled in a low voice something unintelligible, like "Boomba mummba dubba gummba." Although Saturday-morning viewers never knew what he was saying, Fat Albert always did. Mushmouth later became slang for "drunken blather."

MUSHROOM HAIRDO

This 1970s hairdo, a derivation of the Dorothy Hamill wedge, gave its wearer's hair the look of a toadstool. If you can't visualize it (and I don't blame you), imagine a bouncy bowl-cut with the ends curled under by a curling iron (frightful image, huh?). Credit for sporting this one goes out to Toni Tennille, Bonnie Franklin, both members of the Shields and Yarnell mime duo, and goody-goody girls from grammar school.

MUSIC VIDEOS

It's odd to think that at one time we had to use our imaginations to visualize what the words in a song were telling us. (I always thought 1976's "Afternoon Delight" was about fireworks, because of the line "Sky rockets in flight, afternoon delight.") Well, that was before 1981, the year MTV made its broadcast debut, and ever since it only seems fitting for a song to be linked to a video.

"MUSKRAT LOVE"

"Muskrat, muskrat candlelight / Do the town and doin' it right. . . ." An annoying juvenile song from the Captain and Tennille about Muskrat Susie and Muskrat Sam—muskrats in love at Muskrat Land. I don't know about you, but I really didn't need to hear a tune about two aquatic rodents in love. Nevertheless, it reached number four on *Billboard*'s Top Forty and sold a million copies in 1976.

MUSTANG

> "Heads turned, drivers of other cars gaped, and a busload of schoolchildren began chanting, 'Mustang! Mustang! Mustang!'"
>
> —*TIME* MAGAZINE, DESCRIBING THE APPEAL OF THE MUSTANG

Introduced in the spring of 1964 (as a 1964-and-a-half, because new models of cars traditionally debut in the fall), Ford Motor Company's now-legendary pony car was like no other in its day. Named for the free-spirited southwestern horse, the Mustang was small, sporty-looking (in a cute, pert sort of way), and irresistibly affordable (around $2,400). It came with more than thirty-five standard items, fifty different extracost options, and a zippy engine. Carefree and youthful, Ford's Mustang quickly captured the nation's imagination, selling more than a million in less than two years and becoming the only automobile ever to receive the prestigious Tiffany Award for Excellence in American Design. In 1966, soul singer Wilson Pickett honored it with the song "Mustang Sally." Hollywood's most famous Mustang is the dusty-green fastback that actor Steve McQueen drove in the San Francisco chase scene of 1968's *Bullitt*. In the early 1970s, Ford turned the sprightly Mustang into a macho muscle car, featuring a longer and wider frame, heavier body, and a 375-horsepower engine called "The Boss."

MUTTLEY

Fumbling dog sidekick of evildoer Dick Dastardly, known best for his signature wheezy snicker ("Shackle-razzle-futzal-craz"). Seen in the Saturday-morning cartoons *Wacky Races* (1968–70) and *Dastardly and Muttley in Their Flying Machines* (1969–71).

MY BODYGUARD

For those who were the unfortunate target of a school bully, this 1980 movie answered the oft-thought question: "What if I could hire my own personal bodyguard to protect me?" After nine years of private education, scrawny fifteen-year-old Clifford Peache (Chris Makepeace) is the new kid at Lake View, a big public high school in central Chicago. He finds himself harassed by a group of punks led by nasty Melvin Moody (Matt Dillon), a young thug who extorts money from the other students—that is, until Clifford hires a king-sized loner named Ricky Linderman (Adam Baldwin) as a bodyguard to protect him. Directed by Tony Bill, the sensitive comedy co-starred Martin Mull as Clifford's hotel-manager dad and Ruth Gordon as Clifford's feisty gramma. Look for sixteen-year-old Joan Cusack (in her film debut) as nerdy, frizzy-haired Shelley, one of Clifford's friends.

MY BUDDY

"My buddy, my buddy / Wherever I go, he goes. . . ." Alas, a doll for little boys (hey, G.I. Joe was an action figure), introduced by Hasbro Toys in 1985. The success of the freckle-faced, baseball-capped Buddy led to a sequel doll for girls known as Kid Sister and inspired the *Child's Play* horror-film franchise, featuring the demonic Chucky.

MY LITTLE PONY

In an enchanted countryside known as Dream Valley (where the rainbow ends) is where you'll find Hasbro's stable of sweet ponies with long, luxurious, pastel-colored manes that little girls could comb and style. The original My Little Pony toy line of 1982 consisted of six horsies: Blossom, Blue Belle, Butterscotch, Cotton Candy, Minty, and Snuzzle. In 1986, a Saturday-morning cartoon—*My Little Pony and Friends*—was one of the many shows based on existing toy lines of the 1980s (others were, for example, *G.I. Joe*, *He-Man*, *Transformers*, *Care Bears*, *Pound Puppies*, and *Rainbow Brite*).

"MY SHARONA"

In the late summer of 1979, this song by The Knack power-popped onto Top Forty radio, topping the charts for six weeks and selling four million copies in just over a month. By the end of 1979, it had sold five million worldwide and became the number-one song of the year. Suggestively leering, it was about a guy trying to get a girl (Sharona) to go out with him ("Oh, my little pretty one, pretty one / When you gonna give me some time, Sharona?"). Formed in Los Angeles in 1978, The Knack consisted of lead singer Doug Fieger, guitarist Berton Averre, bassist Prescott Niles, and drummer Bruce Gary. The group was one of the most celebrated and talked-about acts on the budding New Wave scene. Unfortunately, they were constantly compared with The Beatles, causing a critical backlash that eventually affected record sales. By the spring of 1980, The Knack's once-sizzling career seemed over, and they disbanded in 1982. In 1994, "My Sharona" recharted on the *Billboard* Top 100 after being featured in the Winona Ryder Gen-X comedy *Reality Bites*.

FYI: ▸ If you are wondering who Sharona was, she's Sharona Alperin, Doug Fieger's teenage girlfriend. Today, Sharona is a high-powered Hollywood real-estate agent whose celebrity clientele includes Leonardo DiCaprio, Claire Danes, Julianne Moore, and *Melrose Place* creator Darren Star.

MY SO-CALLED LIFE

"This life has been a test.
If this had been an actual life,
you would have received instructions on
where to go and what to do."
—ANGELA CHASE (CLAIRE DANES)

This ABC-TV teen drama didn't air long enough (six months in 1994), but it didn't stop teens who embraced the realistic subject matter from giving it a cult following and a reprise with MTV. The series starred Claire Danes as ultramoody fifteen-year-old Angela Chase, a sophomore at Liberty High in suburban Pittsburgh, Pennsylvania. It centered on Angela's relationships with fellow classmates: androgynous Rickie Vasquez (Wilson Cruz, TV's first gay teen regular), wild druggie Rayanne Graff (A. J. Langer), and dreamy Jordan Catalano (Jared Leto). Like all teens, Angela had problems relating to adults, particularly parents Graham and Patty Chase (Tom Irwin and Bess Armstrong). After *My So-Called Life*'s short run, Danes went on to become one of her generation's finest film actresses and was featured in *Little Women* (1994), *William Shakespeare's Romeo + Juliet* (1996), *U Turn* (1997), *The Mod Squad* (1999), *The Hours* (2002), and *Terminator 3: Rise of the Machines* (2003).

MYSTERY DATE

"Open the door . . . to your . . . Mystery Date!" Introduced in 1965, a Milton Bradley fantasy boardgame directed at adolescent gals who dreamed of romance with a little mystery. The object was for each girl to assemble date-time attire for either a beach party, a ski trip, a formal dance, or a night of bowling. Then she would open the plastic "Mystery Door" in the center of the game board, which would reveal the right dream date or the wrong dream date or—God forbid—the "Dud." Opening the door to find the "Dud" waiting was the worst thing that could happen in Mystery Date. He had messy hair, was unshaven, and wore raggedy, sloppy clothes—plus you lost valuable time trying to get rid of him (he sounds a lot like today's slacker grunge guy). The dream dates were cute, clean-cut collegiate types ready to take you on a fun date. "Is your date behind the door?"

MYSTERY IN DRACULA'S CASTLE

Made-for-TV Disney movie notable for pairing juvenile actors Johnny Whitaker and Scott Kolden, who later starred as Johnny and Scott Stuart on the Saturday-morning classic *Sigmund and the Sea Monsters* (1973–75). In this 1973 tale, two boys, Alfie (Whitaker) and Leonard (Kolden), restless and living in a resort town, are filming their own vampire horror movie in an abandoned lighthouse. One afternoon, Alfie and Leonard befriend a stray dog that brings them a stolen necklace. The youngsters decide to use the necklace in their film and are soon chased by the jewel thieves who had stolen it. After a series of misadventures, the crooks are apprehended. Whitaker and Kolden were best buds in real life.

MYSTERY MACHINE

This turquoise-colored Mystery Machine with eye-popping psychedelic graphics was the van that the teenage *Scooby-Doo* gang tooled around in on their mystery-busting travels to creepy places menaced by phantoms and other haunts. The teens' official sleuthing title was Mysteries Inc. (Daphne's rich father provided the funds.)

MY THREE SONS

One of TV's longest-running (1960–72) and most successful sitcoms, which was also one of the first in a long line depicting single-parent households (others were, for example, *The Andy Griffith Show, The Ghost and Mrs. Muir, Julia, The Courtship of Eddie's Father, The Partridge Family*, and *Nanny and the Professor*). It starred film actor Fred MacMurray as even-tempered Steve Douglas, a widower residing at 837 Mill Street in the suburbs of Bryant Park, a city in the Midwest, with three rambunctious sons: eighteen-year-old Mike (Disney star Tim Considine), fourteen-year-old Robbie (ex-Mouseketeer Don Grady), and seven-year-old Chip (Stanley Livingston). Rounding out the family was Steve's father-in-law Bub O'Casey (William Frawley, a.k.a. Fred Mertz of *I Love Lucy*), a delightful "old coot" who helped with cooking and cleaning, and Tramp, the pet dog.

In 1965, the show and cast changed as the sons grew up, started college and careers, and eventually married. That year, Uncle Charley (William Demarest), a crusty ex-sailor with a soft interior, joined the clan, replacing brother Bub, who had taken a trip to Ireland (Frawley had passed away). Mike married girlfriend Sally Morrison (Meredith MacRae) and moved to the East Coast to teach psychology at a college (Considine had tired of his role and was written off). Steve subsequently adopted little orphan Ernie (played by Stanley Livingston's brother Barry), maintaining the show's "Three Sons" concept.

In 1967, more changes and cast add-ons occurred when the family moved to Los Angeles. College student Robbie met perky blonde Katie Miller (Tina Cole), and they were married in 1968. Soon afterward, he had his own "Three Sons" when Katie gave birth to triplets: Steve Jr., Robbie II, and Charley. Steve remarried in 1969 after falling in love with pretty widow Barbara Harper (Beverly Garland), one of Ernie's teachers, and became stepfather to a small daughter named Dodie (Dawn Lyn). And in 1970, Chip eloped with college girlfriend Polly Williams (Ronne Troup). Whew!

NABOOMBU

Legendary lost island in Disney's *Bedknobs and Broomsticks*, inhabited by animated talking animals who play soccer and by a lion ruler, King Leonidas. Here witch Eglantine Price finds the magic spell that helps the British defeat the German Nazis.

NAGEL WOMAN

The late artist Patrick Nagel (1945–84) was the person behind the most recognizable artwork of the 1980s. His simple yet distinctive two-dimensional style, reminiscent of Japanese woodblock prints and art deco, featured sexy, self-assured contemporary gals known as the "Nagel Woman," posed at unusual angles and painted with bold, black lines, and flat, cool hues on white backdrops. Nagel's work first came into view as graphic art in the monthly *Playboy* magazine before appearing as poster prints on the walls of nearly every yuppie's bachelor pad in America. In 1983, he painted the cover of Duran Duran's number-one album *Rio*.

NAMATH, JOE

In 1969, the quarterback from Beaver Falls, Pennsylvania, led the underdog New York Jets to an astonishing Super Bowl victory against the much-ballyhooed Baltimore Colts, marking him as pro football's first bona fide superstar and a sports hero for a generation. After playing at the University of Alabama under Paul "Bear" Bryant's guidance, the nation's number-one draft pick was signed by the Jets in 1965 for a then-record $400,000. Namath's record-breaking performance on the playing field (he was the first quarterback in history to pass for more than 4,000 yards, for example) single-handedly helped give the fledging AFL affiliation credibility against the already-established NFL.

Nicknamed "Broadway Joe" and wearing jersey number 12, Namath was a huge media sensation. His dark, handsome features, easy grin, and charismatic personality made him a welcome guest on virtually every TV talk show, as well as a spokesman for products in numerous commercials. Best-known of these include the Hanes pantyhose spot in which he proved too macho to care by donning a pair ("If these can make my legs look good, imagine what they could do for you") and the Noxzema shave cream ad in which he gets "creamed" by golden girl Farrah Fawcett-Majors. Namath wasn't as lucky on the Hollywood screen as he was on the playing field. His film debut *C.C. and Company* (1970), a motorcycle drama co-starring sexy Ann-Margret, found no company at the box office, and *The Waverly Wonders*, a prime-time sitcom, couldn't do any wonders (it aired only three episodes in the fall of 1978). In 1973, Namath did a memorable guest stint playing himself on a *Brady Bunch* episode, "Mail Order Hero," as little Bobby

Brady's idol. The Jets traded him to the Los Angeles Rams in 1977, and he retired at season's end due to ailing knees.

FYI: ▸ Namath was nicknamed "Broadway Joe" because of his fast lifestyle. ("I like my girls blonde and my Johnny Walker Red.")

NAME THAT TUNE

"I can name that tune in three notes. . . ." Airing on TV from 1974 to 1980, this song-guessing game show was hosted by Dennis James, later Tom Kennedy, and featured the vocal talents of pretty Kathie Lee Johnson (soon-to-be TV hostess).

NANCY

The spunky, chunky lass with the black, bristled hairdo and round cheeks has been the star of cartoonist Ernie Bushmiller's comic strip since 1933. Marked by simple artwork and flat humor, the strip centers around Nancy's inquisitive, somewhat self-centered mischief-making with tough boyfriend Sluggo Smith. She is one of the classic girls of twentieth-century animation; contemporaries were Little Lulu, Little Audrey, and Little Orphan Annie.

NANCY DREW

In juvenile mysteries created by Edward Stratemeyer under the feminine pseudonym Carolyn Keene, this teen supersleuth was the female counterpart to his *Hardy Boys*. Clever, spunky, and determined, the titian-haired eighteen-year-old resides in River Heights, a suburb of New York, with widowed father Carson Drew, a famous attorney, and housekeeper Hannah Gruen. Her crime-solving cohorts include collegian boyfriend Ned Nickerson and tomboy pal George Fayne. The Nancy Drew series began in 1930 with *The Secret of the Old Clock*. Nancy has since starred in more than fifty books, four movies, and a popular 1970s TV series.

From 1977 to 1978, the prime-time *Nancy Drew* alternated every other Sunday night with *The Hardy Boys*, starring Shaun Cassidy and Parker Stevenson. Pamela Sue Martin (pre-*Dynasty*'s Fallon Colby) played Nancy until being replaced by teen cover-girl Janet Louise Johnson because of a contract dispute in January 1978.

NANNY

Pretty Fran Drescher of the whiny, nasal voice (comparable to fingernails being scratched on a chalkboard) and loud fashions starred as Fran Fine, a Jewish-American Princess (JAP) from middle-class Queens, in CBS-TV's popular sitcom airing from 1993 to 1999. One day, while going door-to-door as a cosmetics saleswoman, Fran knocks at the mansion home of widower Maxwell Sheffield (played by Charles Shaughnessy), a British Broadway producer, and gets mistaken for a new nanny applicant. She forges her nanny experience and is hired.

Full of working-class common sense spiked with a little kookiness, outspoken Fran quickly befriends the Sheffield children—Maggie (Nicholle Tom), Brighton (Benjamin Salisbury), and Gracie (Madeline Zima)—as well as Niles (Daniel Davis), the household's eavesdropping butler. Just as quickly, Fran offends stuffy C. C. Babcock (Lauren Lane), Maxwell's business associate, who is totally jealous because she has romantic feelings for him. Following years of sexual tension with her boss, the Nanny finally becomes Mrs. Maxwell Sheffield during the show's ending season. Sylvia Fine (Renée Taylor) is Fran's smothering, mother whose costumed fashions are more outrageous than her daughter's. Ann Hampton Calloway performs "The Nanny Named Fran" theme song that plays over the cartoon-drawn opening credits of the sitcom.

NANNY AND THE PROFESSOR

A cute sitcom, not particularly successful but popular among kids of the early 1970s because it was part of the infamous ABC-TV Friday night lineup, sandwiched between *The Brady Bunch* and *The Partridge Family*. Airing from 1970 to 1971, it starred Juliet Mills as Phoebe Figalilly, better known as Nanny, a "wise and wonderful" housekeeper-governess from England gifted with the power of ESP. Driving an antique car named Arabella, Nanny arrived unannounced one day to bring order and love to the Los Angeles home of widowed college professor Harold Everett (Richard Long) and his three young children: Hal (David Doremus), Butch (Trent Lehman), and Prudence (Kim Richards). A menagerie of pets rounded out the household, including sheepdog Waldo, rooster Sebastian, and guinea pigs Mike and Myrtle.

NAPOLEON AND SAMANTHA

Directed by Bernard McEveety, a first-rate 1972 Disney adventure about two kids and their love for an elderly lion. Following the death of his grandfather, newly orphaned Napoleon (Johnny Whitaker) is afraid of losing beloved pet Major, a gentle retired circus lion. Napoleon hooks up with pal Samantha (Jodie Foster, in her movie debut), and with Major in tow they trek off through the rugged Oregon terrain in search of Danny (Michael Douglas), the only person who can help.

FYI: ▸ At sixteen years of age and weighing more than 500 pounds, Major was a Hollywood veteran featured in 1960s *Tarzan* movies and TV show opposite Mike Henry and Ron Ely.

NATALIE GREEN

Natalie Green was teen actress Mindy Cohn's chubby class clown, who attended the Eastland School for Young Women on the well-loved 1980s sitcom *The Facts of Life*. What Natalie lacked in looks she made up in good-humored personality.

FYI: ▸ Being the least attractive didn't stop Natalie from being the first of the girls to lose her virginity. She lost it to a boyfriend named "Snake" in 1988.

NATASHA AND BORIS

Natasha Fatale, a slender femme fatale with a husky Slavic accent ("You have plan, dahlink?"), and Boris Badenov, a pint-sized master of disguise with beady eyes, were the devilish duo from faraway Pottsylvania who battled our Saturday-morning cartoon heroes Rocky J. Squirrel and Bullwinkle Moose. Highly scheming yet highly hapless, these no-good international agents of evil worked for Mr. Big, a midget underworld gangster whose fearless orders were quite simple: "Must kill Moose and Squirrel!"

NATIONAL LAMPOON'S ANIMAL HOUSE

> "Fat, drunk, and stupid is no way to go through life, son."
>
> —DEAN WORMER (JOHN VERNON)

"It was the Deltas against the rules. The rules lost!" Runaway hit 1978 comedy about the disreputable party animals of the Delta Tau Chi fraternity at fictional Faber College. Set in 1962, these beer-swilling, underachieving degenerates occupy a rundown residence (the Delta House) and spend their time at college indulging in wild toga parties, pranks, and disputes with Dean Vernon Wormer, who tries to get them kicked off campus. Assisting Wormer are the stuffy rich boys of neighboring Omega House and their stuck-up cheerleader girlfriends. Bloated John Belushi leads the cast as John "Bluto" Blutarsky, the biggest slob of them all. Others include Tim Matheson as Eric "Otter" Stratton, Tom Hulce as Larry "Pinto" Kroger, Peter Riegert as Donald "Boon" Schoenstein, and Stephen Furst as Kent "Flounder" Dorfman.

Best scenes: the food fight where Bluto mimics a zit with a hard-boiled egg, and the homecoming parade from hell. Lewd, crude, and rude, the gross-out shenanigans of *Animal House* set the trend for a whole new style of movie comedy aimed at young audiences. It sired a number of low-budget imitations, a short-lived TV series titled *Delta House* (1979), and a thousand toga parties.

NATIONAL LAMPOON'S VACATION

Directed by comedian Harold Ramis, this 1983 film comedy told the madcap tale of a suburban Chicago middle-class family's cross-country journey to a Disney-like amusement park called Wally World. *Saturday Night Live* alum Chevy Chase starred as bumbling Clark Griswold, the square and sappy dad bound and determined that his family—mild-mannered wife Ellen (Beverly D'Angelo) and bored kids Rusty and Audrey (Anthony Michael Hall and Dana Barron)—were going to have the vacation of a lifetime. Along the way, the Griswolds became involved in one hysterical disaster after another: a St. Louis ghetto detour gone awry; an overnight stay in Kansas with demented white-trash relatives (headed by Randy Quaid as Eddie); cantankerous Aunt Edna's sudden death and destination of her body (played by legendary comedienne Imogene Coco); the totaling of the car after Clark falls asleep at the wheel; and Clark's highway and motel poolside encounters with gorgeous supermodel-of-the-moment Christie Brinkley. Three sequels followed: *National Lampoon's European Vacation* (1985), *National Lampoon's Christmas Vacation* (1989), and *National Lampoon's Vegas Vacation* (1997).

NAUGHTON, DAVID

Boyishly good-looking brunet actor best remembered for the late-1970s Dr. Pepper ads on TV in which he sang and danced about the joys of being a Pepper ("I'm a Pepper . . . "). A well-rounded talent, Naughton also starred in the short-lived, disco-themed TV sitcom *Makin' It* (1979) and had a Top Ten hit with its title song. In 1981, he played David Kessler in John Landis's *American Werewolf in London*, a frightful film about an American student who is bitten by a werewolf in the foggy British moors.

"NEED YOU TONIGHT / MEDITATE"

Great music video to a great song has Australia's INXS, headed by the late Michael Hutchence (he committed suicide in 1997), imitating Bob Dylan as each member holds up signs to the different words of "Meditate." "Need You Tonight," from parent album *Kick* (1987), was the group's first U.S. number-one single. Their other hits included "Devil Inside" (1988), "New Sensation" (1988), and "Suicide Blonde" (1990).

NEELY O'HARA

"I have to get up at five o'clock in the morning and Sparkle, Neely, Sparkle!" In the camp film classic *Valley of the Dolls*, eighteen-year-old Patty Duke starred as the determined Neely O'Hara, a nice kid singer who turns into a doll-popping, booze-swilling, foul-mouthed, self-destructive egomaniac after becoming a big star. "She took the red pills."

NEHRU JACKETS

Slim-fitting, hip-length jackets characterized by high-standing banded collars and large buttons, brought to the 1960s mod fashion forefront by The Beatles. Named after East Indian prime minister Jawaharlal Nehru.

NELL FENWICK

In the *Dudley Do-Right* cartoon show, Nell frequently found herself tied to the rails of a train track or some other perilous setup by menacing Snidely Whiplash. To the rescue came patriotic Canadian Mountie Dudley Do-Right, serving loyally under her father, Inspector Fenwick, who at the very last second always saved this lovely pigtailed redheaded lass.

NELLIE OLESON

Everyone's favorite TV brat of the 1970s was the only daughter of Nels and Harriet Oleson, the well-to-do proprietors of Walnut Grove's general store. She was also Laura Ingalls's number-one adversary on NBC's *Little House on the Prairie*.

FYI: ▸ Teen actress Alison Arngrim (born January 18, 1962), who played curly-haired, know-it-all Nellie Oleson from 1974 to 1981, was the younger sister of Stefan Arngrim, seen in the 1960s sci-fi TV adventure *Land of the Giants*.

NEPTUNES

Popular in the year 2076, a bubblegum rock band from Aquahama City, located undersea, whose members consisted of Biff (lead singer), Shelly (tambourine player), Bubbles (keyboardist), Clam-Head (bassist), and a great white shark named Jabberjaw (drummer). The Neptunes could be seen (and heard) on Hanna-Barbera's Saturday-morning cartoon *Jabberjaw*.

NERD

Were you a nerd? Did you wear black, thick-rimmed glasses? Were your pants highwater floods belted really tight high above the waist or held up by suspenders? Did you wear a short-sleeve button-up shirt with a pocket protector full of pens and pencils? Was your hair oily because you washed it only once a week? Have you ever been on the receiving end of a "snuggie" or a "wedgie"? In high school, did you play an instrument in the orchestra or marching band? Were you a member of the flag corps instead of a cheerleader or drill-teamer? Did you ace math, science, or computer skills? In fact, did you belong to your school's science or calculus club?

Along with being a nerd, were you frequently taunted as a doofus, a dork, a dweeb, a geek, or a spaz? On weekend nights, did you spend your time mastering arcade games at Malibu Grand Prix, or role-playing with Dungeons & Dragons, or hanging out at the local library? Did you prefer Richie Cunningham over Fonzie, Arnold Horshack over Vinnie Barbarino, or Natalie Green over Blair Warner? When watching the movie *Revenge of the Nerds*, did you relate to the members of the Lambda Lambda Lambda fraternity? Was Microsoft's Bill Gates one of your idols? If you answer yes to any of these questions, you probably were a nerd.

FYI: ▸ Dr. Seuss coined the word "nerd." He first used it in his children's book *If I Ran the Zoo* (1950).

NERF BALL

"The world's first indoor ball!" Created by Parker Brothers in 1972, the Nerf Ball was an instant hit with kids because you could play with it inside the house. Parents liked it as well, because the ball's nearly weightless, spongelike material made it more-or-less harmless to lamps, vases, and other treasured household objects that got in the way. Its popularity spawned many Nerf accessories, including Nerf basketball hoops (which attached to the back of doors), Nerf baseball equipment (featuring a flyweight bat), and other Nerf products, like a football, a dart gun, and a sponge disc resembling a Frisbee.

NESTLÉ QUIK

"Nestlé Quik + Milk = Chocolaty Fun!" Introduced to early Baby Boomers in 1948, this chocolate powder that you mixed with milk came packaged in a square metal container with a hole on the top just big enough to dip a spoon in. Its TV commercials were an endearing part of Baby Boom childhood. Who could forget the cute Nestlé Quik Bunny drinking a delicious glassful of ice-cold chocolate milk, trying not to sip it too fast through a straw, only to give in and slurp it all up at once? In 1999, Nestlé changed the powdered drink's name to the contemporary Nesquik, a combination of Nestlé and Quik. For variety, Nestlé offers pink strawberry-flavor Quik. "You can't drink it slow if it's Quik!"

NEVERENDING STORY

In this 1984 fantasy film directed by Wolfgang Petersen, sensitive ten-year-old Bastian (Barret Oliver) takes refuge in a bookshop after being bullied by older youths. He finds a magical storybook that sweeps him off to Fantasia, a land of marvelously strange creatures. There he shares the adventures of a heroic boy warrior, Atreyu (Noah Hathaway), on a quest to save Fantasia from destruction by Nothingness, a stormlike entity that makes people forget their hopes and dreams. Limahl, former lead singer of Kajagoogoo, sang the theme song, "The Neverending Story."

NEW ADVENTURES OF HUCKLEBERRY FINN

Airing Sunday evenings from 1968 to 1969, this Hanna-Barbera production offered a different twist on Mark Twain's classic. Combining live actors with animation, it had Huck Finn (Michael Shea), Tom Sawyer (Kevin Schultz), and Becky Thatcher (Lu Ann Haslam) caught in a swirling time warp after being chased by villainous Injun Joe (Ted Cassidy). Each episode had the youngsters transported to a different animated setting, varying from historical to modern, while trying to find their way back to Missouri.

NEW KIDS ON THE BLOCK

The hottest teen idol phenomenon of the 1980s were five youths from working-class Boston: Joey McIntyre, Donnie Wahlberg, Danny Wood, and brothers Jon and Jordan Knight. Slickly manufactured by musical entrepreneur Maurice Starr, the group formed in 1985 as the white answer to the already successful New Edition group ("Cool It Now"), which featured the voice of Bobby Brown (Mr. Whitney Houston). Trying to pull off the image of tough urban dudes, the NKOTB and their music was bubblegum at best, a sterilized mix of pop, rap, and dance at worst. Impressionable as always, teenybopper girls fell for the act and awarded them nine Top Ten hits, including "You Got It (The Right Stuff)" (1988), "I'll Be Loving You (Forever)" (1989), "Hangin' Tough" (1989), "Cover Girl" (1989), and "Step by Step" (1990). The NKOTB are noted for being the precursors to today's pretty-boy dance bands, like Backstreet Boys, 'N Sync, and 98 Degrees. Wahlberg is the older brother of rapper-actor Marky Mark / Mark Wahlberg (*Boogie Nights*, *Three Kings*, and *Perfect Storm*).

FYI: ▸ In 1990, *Rolling Stone* magazine readers picked the New Kids on the Block as the Worst Band and—whoa-oh-oh-oh-oh—"Hangin' Tough" as the Worst Single.

NEWLYWED GAME

Host Bob Eubanks's long-running TV game show (1966–97) featured four newly married couples competing for prizes by predicting how their off-stage spouses will respond to tasteless questions like "What animal would you compare your mother-in-law to?" or "What is the oddest place you've ever had sex?" Created by Chuck Barris, this was the perfect companion piece to *The Dating Game*, with which it was often paired on ABC-TV.

NEWTON-JOHN, OLIVIA

When it came to sugar and spice (and everything nice), nobody was sweeter than this fresh-faced pop star from the Land Down Under. The blonde Aussie with the honey voice was actually born in England on September 26, 1948, but she immigrated to Melbourne, Australia, with her family at the age of five. Her music career began in the mid-1960s after winning a talent contest—which brought her back to England, where she sang at pubs and cabarets. Music mogul Don Kirshner recruited Olivia in the early 1970s as a member of his ill-fated bubblegum band, Toomorrow, and to tour as a guest singer with Cliff Richard.

In 1971, her cover of Bob Dylan's "If Not for You" became the first of twenty-seven U.S. Top Forty hits, five of those topping the charts: "I Honestly Love You" (1974), "Have You Never Been Mellow" (1975), "You're the One That I Want" (1978), "Magic" (1980), and "Physical" (1981). Throughout the 1970s, Olivia projected a wholesome image. Her fondness for country music influenced early soft-rock ballads that crossed over to the country-and-western radio stations. Hits during this country-rock phase include a cover of John Denver's "Take Me Home, Country Roads" (1973), "Let Me Be There" (1973), "If You Love Me (Let Me Know)" (1974), and "Please Mr. Please" (1975). Because she wasn't an American, many in the country-music industry were angry after she won the 1974 Country Music Association's Female Vocalist of the Year Award. (That caused prominent CMA members to split and form the Association of Country Entertainers.) By the late 1970s and early 1980s, Olivia reigned as the most successful female vocalist in America, complemented by numerous gold records and Grammy Awards.

In 1978, she was cast opposite John Travolta in the film version of the smash Broadway musical *Grease* as Sandy, the virginal cheerleader transformed into a spandex-clad dominatrix. Olivia's own personal style would reflect Sandy's sexy makeover, as did her songs during this "naughty but nice" career phase, such as "Hopelessly Devoted to You" (1978), "A Little More Love" (1978), and "Totally Hot" (1979). In 1981, she released the mega-hit "Physical." It became the biggest-selling single of the decade, giving her another image change: the sexually aggressive woman-of-the-eighties. Later hits include "Make a Move on Me" (1982) and "Twist of Fate" (1983).

When Olivia's music career declined, she stayed busy by exploring other avenues. She married actor-dancer Matt Lattanzi in 1984; gave birth to daughter Chloe Rose in 1986; became a business proprietor with a chain of Australian-oriented clothing boutiques (Koala Blue); courageously survived a battle with breast cancer; and fights for the environment, animal rights, and AIDS awareness. Kudos to her for being a major influence in pop culture fashion by introducing sundresses, wing bangs, Candies slides, spandex pants, big teased hair, headbands, leg warmers, multicolored aerobic outfits, and the bi-level haircut. (Okay, maybe these all looked better on Livvy, but you have to give yourself credit for trying.)

FYI: ▸ In the 1960s, Olivia Newton-John won a contest as the girl who looked most like teen film star Hayley Mills.

NEW WAVE ACTS

According to the dictionary, the definition of New Wave is "post-punk rock, involving bizarre clothing, popular in United States, during 1980s." Here's a list of fifty favorite New Wave acts from 1979, when groups like Blondie and The Cars first appeared on Top Forty radio with heavily synthesized songs (the trademark sound of New Wave), to 1986, which is, in my opinion, the last year of the music genre. (In the late 1980s, New Wave evolved into alternative or modern rock.) Each group's signature song is also noted .

ABC—"The Look of Love" (1982)
Adam and the Ants—"Antmusic" (1981)
B-52's—"Rock Lobster" (1979)
Berlin—"No More Words" (1984)
Blondie—"Heart of Glass" (1979)
Boomtown Rats—"I Don't Like Mondays" (1979)
Bow Wow Wow—"I Want Candy" (1982)
Bronski Beat—"Smalltown Boy" (1985)
Cars—"Shake It Up" (1981)
Clash—"Train in Vain" (1980)

Culture Club—"Do You Really Want to Hurt Me" (1983)
Cure—"In Between Days (Without You)" (1985)
Depeche Mode—"People Are People" (1985)
Devo—"Whip It" (1980)
Duran Duran—"Hungry Like the Wolf" (1983)
Echo and the Bunnymen—"Bring on the Dancing Horses" (1986)
English Beat—"Save It for Later" (1982)
Eurythmics—"Sweet Dreams (Are Made of This)" (1983)
Fine Young Cannibals—"Johnny Come Home" (1985)
Flock of Seagulls—"I Ran (So Far Away)" (1982)
Frankie Goes to Hollywood—"Relax" (1984)
General Public—"Tenderness" (1984)
Go-Go's—"We Got the Beat" (1982)
Haircut One Hundred—"Love Plus One" (1982)
Human League—"Don't You Want Me" (1982)
INXS—"One Thing" (1983)
Kid Creole and the Coconuts—"Endicott" (1986)
Knack—"My Sharona" (1979)
Madness—"Our House" (1983)
Men at Work—"Who Can It Be Now" (1982)
Men Without Hats—"The Safety Dance" (1983)
Missing Persons—"Walking in L.A." (1982)
New Order—"Bizarre Love Triangle" (1986)
Oingo Boingo—"Weird Science" (1985)
Orchestral Maneuvers in the Dark (or OMD)—"If You Leave" (1986)
Pet Shop Boys—"West End Girls" (1986)
Police—"Every Breath You Take" (1983)
Pretenders—"Brass in Pocket" (1980)
Psychedelic Furs—"Pretty in Pink" (1981)
Romantics—"What I Like About You" (1980)
Soft Cell—"Tainted Love" (1982)
Squeeze—"Tempted" (1982)
Style Council—"My Ever Changing Moods" (1984)
Talking Heads—"Once in a Lifetime" (1980)
Tears for Fears—"Shout" (1985)
Thompson Twins—"Hold Me Now" (1984)
U2—"Pride (In the Name of Love)" (1984)
Waitresses—"I Know What Boys Like" (1982)
Wang Chung—"Dance Hall Days" (1984)
Yazoo (or Yaz)—"Only You" (1982)

NEW ZOO REVUE

This kiddie program could be called the forerunner of today's juvenile favorite *Barney*, starring the sickeningly sweet purple dinosaur ("I love you, you love me. . . ." Yecch!). Coming right at you on syndicated TV from 1972 to 1981, the show featured actors dressed in foam-rubber animal costumes who sang sappy musical numbers to educate young viewers. The main animal stars were childish Freddy the Frog, flamboyant Henrietta the Hippo, and wise Charlie the Owl. Guitar-strumming Doug (Douglas Momary) and his helper Emmy Jo (Emily Peden) were their human friends. The show's action centered around a gazebo.

NICHOLAS BRADFORD

On ABC-TV's *Eight Is Enough*, precociously cute Adam Rich (born October 12, 1968), with a Toni Tennille hairdo, appeared as this youngest member of the Bradfords from 1977 to 1981.

FYI: ▸ In the years following *Eight Is Enough*, Adam Rich has had several bouts with the law, including getting arrested for shoplifting, drunk driving, and breaking and entering. (TV dad Dick Van Patten bailed him out of jail after he smashed a pharmacy window in an attempt to steal drugs.)

NICK THE LOUNGE SINGER

Bill Murray's cheesy vocalist and self-described "kinda fun guy" who performed cheesy renditions of songs like "Star Wars Theme" or "A Horse with No Name" at cheesy lounges, like the Zephyr Room at Lake Minnehonka's Breezy Point Lodge, the Powder Room at Meatloaf Mountain, or the Honeymoon Room at the Pocomount. Seen on NBC's *Saturday Night Live* throughout the late 1970s.

NIGHTMARE

Casper the Friendly Ghost's galloping ghostly horse, who headlined his own comic-book series in the 1960s and 1970s.

NIGHTMARE BEFORE CHRISTMAS

Director Tim Burton dreamed up this twisted holiday fantasy, featuring stunning stop-motion animation, when he worked as an animator for the Disney Studios back in the 1980s. Spindle-limbed Jack Skellington, the Pumpkin King of Halloweentown—a land of monsters and creepy weirdos—is bored with doing the same thing every year for Halloween. Upon discovering the snowy cheer of neighboring Christmastown, he decides with great zeal to take over a new holiday. Jack kidnaps Santa Claus and replaces him by setting off in a coffin sleigh with skeleton reindeer to deliver creepy-crawly presents (toys that shriek, bite, and give chase) to unsuspecting kids on Christmas Eve. However, his well-meaning plan inadvertently puts Santa in the hands of dangerous Oogie Boogie Man and creates a nightmare for all good little girls and boys worldwide.

Jack is joined in this wonderfully warped tale by pet Zero, his ghost dog; true love Sally, a lonely stitched-together rag doll; her creator, Dr. Finkelstein, a wheelchair-bound mad scientist; the two-faced Mayor of Halloweentown; and Lock, Shock, and Barrel, a trio of diabolical trick-or-treaters. Frequent Burton collaborator Danny Elfman provides the 1993 film's lively music score (he also provides Jack's singing voice) and the tunes "This Is Halloween," "What's This," "Making Christmas," and "Oogie Boogie's Song."

NIGHTMARE ON ELM STREET

It has always been said that if you die in your dreams you'll never wake up. In 1984, director Wes Craven took that dream myth and tweaked it into this modern horror tale. A group of suburban teenagers living on Elm Street in Springwood, Ohio, are fatally stalked in their dreams by razor-fingered boogeyman Freddy Krueger (Robert Englund). A decade ago, neighborhood vigilantes had torched Freddy alive for being a child murderer, so now he has come back from the depths of hell to invade the dreams and bodies of the children whose parents once murdered him. One by one, the teens try to stay awake, but eventually they give in to sleep and get knocked off in a creatively gory manner (young Johnny Depp, in his film debut, is eaten alive by a bed)—all except for resilient Nancy Thompson (Heather Langenkamp), who undertakes a battle to bring the fiendish Freddy out of her dreams to destroy him. Following in the tradition of *Halloween* (1978) and *Friday the 13th* (1980), *A Nightmare on Elm Street* inspired a handful of sequels, and like Michael Myers and Jason Voorhees, Freddy Krueger became a favorite horror villain of the 1980s. Other scary delights from Wes Craven included *The Hills Have Eyes* (1977), *Deadly Blessing* (1981), *The People Under the Stairs* (1991), and *Scream* (1996).

NIGHT OF THE COMET

In this 1984 low-budget sci-fi movie, it's Christmastime in Los Angeles and a comet is approaching earth. People all over California, and the rest of the world, are merrily celebrating its arrival. That is, except for two Val-Gal teen sisters, Regina and Samantha Belmont, who for different reasons are spending the night in steel-lined rooms. The passing of the comet—the same one that visited earth sixty-five million years ago, when the dinosaurs vanished—wipes out onlookers worldwide, turning them either into piles of red dust or into crazed zombies.

Awakening as sole survivors to a "freaked-out world," Regina and Samantha reunite and head to a radio station that's still broadcasting, in hopes of finding another human (it's only an automated tape). Then they head for the mall and delightedly rampage through a deserted department store, trying on clothes while dancing to "Girls Just Want to Have Fun." It's there that the sisters happily discover another survivor, handsome Hector Gomez, and unhappily discover zombie store clerks and a team of evil government agents.

Written and directed by Thom Eberhardt, the film starred Catherine Mary Stewart as older sis Regina (Reggie), a video arcade devotee who survived the comet's fallout after sleeping over with her projectionist boyfriend in a steel-lined booth at the theater; and Kelli Maroney as younger sis Samantha (Sam), a petulant cheerleader who survived the night in a toolshed after running away from her bitchy stepmother. Co-starring were Robert Beltran as Hector the hunky truck driver, and Mary Woronov and Geoffrey Lewis as Audrey and Carter, a pair of mad scientists living in an underground lab. If you haven't seen this end-of-the-world gem, check it out. It's awesome!

NIGHT OF THE LIVING DEAD

"They won't stay dead!" Director George A. Romero took the terrifying concept "What if people who have recently died came back to life as flesh-eating zombies?" and filmed this 1968 horror classic.

Produced with a budget of only $114,000 and shot in grainy 35 mm black and white (giving it a nightmarishly authentic feel), *Night of the Living Dead* was originally panned by critics for its ghoulish and gory effects—considered extremely violent for its day. Rejected by all the major studios, the frightfest was commonly shown as the third feature on a triple bill at drive-in theatres before finding its niche as a midnight movie favorite. Today, it is one of the most talked about, influential, and successful cult flicks of all time, referred to as "the first truly modern horror film."

A rocket launch returning to earth introduces a mysterious contagion into the atmosphere, causing corpses to rise as shambling zombies with a single purpose: to eat the flesh of the living. A random group of people, barricaded inside a rural Pennsylvania farmhouse near a graveyard, tries to survive a night of terror from an ever-increasing throng of zombies who lay siege to the building. The horror and suspense magnifies as the seven survivors make one mistake after another and discover that their enemy is not only the Living Dead but also one another.

The cast of nonprofessional actors included Judith O'Dea as Barbara, the near-catatonic blonde ("What's happening?"); Russell Streiner as Johnny, Barbara's teasing brother; Duane Jones as Ben, the survivalistic black hero; Keith Wayne as Tom, a brave teenager; Judith Ridley as Judy, Tom's pretty girlfriend; Karl Hardman as Harry Cooper, the bigoted white coward; Marilyn Eastman as Helen Cooper, Harry's fed-up wife; and Kyra Schon as Karen, the Coopers' injured and dying young daughter (she was bit by a zombie: "I hurt").

Shocking scenes: the killing of Johnny in the Evans City cemetery by a ghoul after he taunts Barbara ("They're coming to get you, Barbara. Look, there's one now!"); Tom and Judith's inability to leave a burning truck, resulting in the young sweethearts' becoming a hot meal for the ravenous dead; newly deceased Karen feeding on her daddy and mommy with the aid of a gardening spade; a mass of zombies really getting Barbara—led by her Living Dead brother, Johnny; and the somber ending, when Ben, the only survivor, is mistaken for a zombie and shot to death by a posse of redneck hunters.

Romero went on to complete his *Living Dead* trilogy with 1978's superior *Dawn of the Dead* and 1985's tepid *Day of the Dead*. In 1990, *Night of the Living Dead* was remade and updated in glorious color. It basically followed the original's story line, but this time heroine Barbara (Patricia Tallman) was much more active and assertive.

In 2005, Romero released the long-awaited *Land of the Dead,* depicting a world where the last-surviving humans subsist in a walled-in city while the walking Dead, who outnumber the living by 500,000 to 1, wait hungrily on the outside for a chance to break in.

FYI: ▸ An original print of *Night of the Living Dead* is held in the New York Museum of Modern Art archives.

"NIGHT THE LIGHTS WENT OUT IN GEORGIA"
Moonlighting from *The Carol Burnett Show,* comedienne Vicki Lawrence went to the top of the pop charts in 1973 with this moody tune (her only hit record) that warned listeners about Southern backwoods lawmen. Written by Bobby Russell, Lawrence's husband, it told the tale of an innocent man framed for the murder of his best friend, who had been sleeping with his wife (the narrator of the song, the innocent man's little sister, actually committed the crime). Originally offered to Cher, no stranger to woeful story songs herself, then-husband Sonny Bono rejected the ballad because he thought listeners in the South would be offended. A 1981 movie with the same title, starring Kristy McNichol, Mark Hamill, and Dennis Quaid, was loosely based on it.

"99 LUFTBALLONS"
Recorded in both German and English by Nena, a songstress born Gabriele Kerner in Hagen, Germany, the peppy song was about a child's red balloon that accidentally started World War III. It landed at the number-two spot on the American Top Forty in 1984.

NODDERS
Also known as bobbleheads and wobblers, these are plastic or ceramic figurines whose noggins, attached by springs, violently nod and nod and nod to the slightest motion. Once commonly spotted as hip-swiveling hula girls or nodding canines on the

dashboards of automobiles. In recent years the nodder fad has been revived because of the popularity of Funko Inc.'s wobbling pop culture characters found at novelty stores, featuring devils, surfers, tiki gods, beatniks, and a staple of well-known cartoon heroes.

NOID

"Avoid the Noid!" In the 1980s, this skinny, red-suited advertising character's mission was to delay delivery of your fresh, hot Domino's pizza.

NO MORE TEARS

Moms used this classic Johnson & Johnson juvenile shampoo because it didn't irritate little eyes when the suds got in them. The company also made a detangler called No More Tangles to help comb out those tangled rats.

NOOGIE

This juvenile act of torture involved holding someone by the neck with an arm and rubbing knuckles over their head. Todd DiLaMuca subjected Lisa Loopner to lots and lots of noogies on the *Saturday Night Live* skit "The Nerds."

NORELCO ELECTRIC RAZOR

Throughout the mid-1960s, it was promoted at Christmastime by whimsical TV advertisements featuring an animated Santa Claus sledding over snowy hills on a razor. (Wheeeee!) I remember spotting the ads during commercial breaks of *Rudolph the Red-Nosed Reindeer* when it originally aired on NBC-TV.

NORMAN BATES

"We all go a little mad sometimes." The ultimate mama's boy! You can bet that Marian Crane, an embezzling bank teller on the run, wished she'd never taken that fateful shower during her stay at the Bates Motel. Anthony Perkins played this schizophrenic murderer in the Alfred Hitchcock classic *Psycho* (1960).

NORTH, JAY

Born August 3, 1951, a juvenile actor best known for playing Dennis Mitchell on prime time's *Dennis the Menace*, from 1959 to 1963. Throughout the first half of the 1960s, he was one of TV's most recognizable kids. Big-screen ventures included Disney's *Zebra in the Kitchen* (1965) and the jungle adventure *Maya* (1966). Later provided the voice for teenage Bamm-Bamm Rubble on Saturday morning's *Pebbles and Bamm-Bamm Show* (1971–76).

NOVA

In the 1968 sci-fi classic *Planet of the Apes*, the loin-clothed mute primitive is captured, along with American astronaut George Taylor, by highly evolved simians and taken to the ape city to become caged experiments. Befriended by Taylor, the dark-haired beauty escapes with him to find freedom in the Forbidden Zone. Nova returns in the sequel, *Beneath the Planet of the Apes* (1970), to aid newly crashed astronaut John Brent in his search for the missing Taylor. Played by luscious Linda Harrison, a former Miss Maryland and Miss America runner-up (1965) who was once married to Hollywood movie producer Richard Zanuck (1968–78).

NOVELTY SONGS

Silly little ditties that either charmed you or drove you nuts with their nonsensical tales about foolish characters and their predicaments (often fueled by current fads, like CB radios, disco, streaking, and arcade games). Here's a list of thirty classic novelty tunes played on Top Forty radio from the 1960s throughout the 1980s.

- "Ahab the Arab" (1962) by Ray Stevens
- "Alley-Oop" (1960) by Hollywood Argyles
- "The Bertha Butt Boogie" (1975) by The Jimmy Castor Bunch
- "Convoy" (1975) by C. W. McCall
- "Disco Duck" (1976) by Rick Dees
- "Does Your Chewing Gum Lose Its Flavor (On the Bedpost over Night)" (1961) by Lonnie Donegan
- "Eat It" (1984) by Weird Al Yankovic
- "Gitarzan" (1969) by Ray Stevens
- "The Homecoming Queen's Got a Gun" (1984) by Julie Brown
- "Junk Food Junkie" (1976) by Larry Groce
- "King Tut" (1978) by Steve Martin
- "May the Bird of Paradise Fly Up Your Nose" (1965) by Little Jimmy Dickens
- "Monster Mash" (1962) by Bobby "Boris" Pickett
- "Mr. Jaws" (1975) by Dickie Goodman

- "Muskrat Love" (1976) by Captain and Tennille
- "My Ding-a-Ling" (1972) by Chuck Berry
- "On Top of Spaghetti" (1963) by Tom Glazer
- "Pac-Man Fever" (1982) by Buckner and Garcia
- "Puff the Magic Dragon" (1963) by Peter, Paul, and Mary
- "Rubber Duckie" (1970) by Ernie (Jim Henson)
- "Short People" (1978) by Randy Newman
- "Snoopy vs. The Red Baron" (1966) by The Royal Guardsmen
- "The Streak" (1974) by Ray Stevens
- "Take Off" (1982) by Bob and Doug McKenzie
- "Telephone Man" (1977) by Meri Wilson
- "They're Coming to Take Me Away, Ha-Haaa!" (1966) by Napoleon XIV
- "Tie Me Kangaroo Down, Sport" (1963) by Rolf Harris
- "Tip Toe Thru the Tulips with Me" (1968) by Tiny Tim
- "Valley Girl" (1982) by Frank and Moon Unit Zappa
- "Wooly Bully" (1965) by Sam the Sham and the Pharaohs

NOW LOOK KEN

Wow! Introduced in 1975, this Ken doll got with the times by having groovy long hair cascading down past his shoulders. He came wearing an out-tasight leisure suit (in the swingin' beige color) with a scarf tied around his neck. Far-out, man!

NOXZEMA COLD CREAM

Packaged in the famous royal-blue jar, this distinctive-smelling cold cream is smeared all over women's faces and worn as a mask for a short while (giving many husbands a fright!). Its major competitor is Pond's.

NOXZEMA SHAVE CREAM

"I'm gonna get creamed." This men's shaving product was once highlighted by an arousing early-1970s TV commercial that had then-unknown Farrah Fawcett applying foamy shaving cream on the mug of beefy football great Joe Namath in a shower room while seductively whispering, "Take it off, take it all off."

mnop

OCEAN PACIFIC
Casual surfing clothing line launched by San Diego surfer Jim Jenks in the early 1970s. The corduroy board shorts emblazoned with an embroidered "OP" on the left leg are classics. Other well-known manufacturers of surf-oriented fashions include Body Glove, Hang Ten, Hobie, O'Neill, PCH (for Pacific Coast Highway), and Quicksilver.

ODE TO BILLY JOE
"It was the third of June, another sleepy, dusty delta day. . . ." Bobbie Gentry's haunting ballad and subsequent big-screen film about Billy Joe McAllister, who jumped off the Tallahatchie Bridge. Sung in the narrative style of a Southern farm girl, it told her tale of hearing the dinnertime news of her boyfriend's fatal leap, for unknown reasons, into the muddy waters of Mississippi's Tallahatchie River. The country song swept the nation in 1967, crossing over to the pop charts, where it crested at number one for four weeks.

But what was the secret that drove Billy Joe to jump off the bridge up at Choctaw Ridge on that dusty summer day? The mystery wasn't revealed until nine years later, when *Ode to Billy Joe*, a 1976 movie directed by Max Baer Jr. (Jethro Bodine), gave up the answer. It seems that seventeen-year-old Billy Joe (played goofy but cute by blue-eyed Robby Benson) was madly in love with fifteen-year-old Bobbie Lee Hartley (Glynnis O'Connor), heroine of the Ode, but devastated after he'd had a homosexual encounter. ("I ain't all right! I have been with a man, which is a sin against nature, a sin against God!") The guilt drove him to commit suicide.

ODIE
Gushy, dim-witted dog whom Garfield enjoys tormenting. (The comic-strip feline calls him "Bonebreath.")

OFFICER DIBBLE
Do-gooder Manhattan policeman who had an extreme dislike for crafty feline Top Cat and his street gang and continually tried to nab them in their never-ending schemes, in Hanna-Barbera's *Top Cat* cartoon series.

OGEE
"How much is that gorilla in the window?" Oh, gee, she's the little girl who wanted to buy fun-loving Gorilla Magilla as a pet from the Peebles Pet Shop in *Magilla Gorilla* cartoons of the 1960s.

OLIVE OYL

Popeye the Sailorman's flirty sweetie from Sweethaven, physically a pitiful example of womanhood (skinny like a toothpick, flat-chested, with big feet), who often had to be rescued from the brutal clutches of he-man Bluto. Her brother was the harebrained Castor Oyl.

FYI: ▸ Olive Oyl's shoe size was a whopping 14AAAAAA!

OLIVER!

"Please, sir, I want some more." Directed by Carol Reed, this rollicking big-budget movie musical of Dickens's *Oliver Twist* was the Oscar-winning Best Picture of 1968 (Reed also won an Oscar for Best Director). It stars angelic Mark Lester as the luckless urchin who runs away from an orphanage and joins a band of boy pickpockets in London who are trained by the scurrilous Fagin (played by scene-stealing Ron Moody). Co-stars are Jack Wild as the spunky Artful Dodger, Oliver Reed (Carol Reed's nephew) as street thug Bill Sikes, and Shani Wallis as caring barmaid Nancy. Lionel Bart's captivating songs (which all became standards of youthful choirs in the 1970s) include "Food, Glorious Food," "Where Is Love?" "Consider Yourself," "Pick a Pocket or Two," "I'd Do Anything," and "As Long as He Needs Me."

OLIVER WENDELL DOUGLAS

"Keep Manhattan, just give me that countryside!" Eddie Albert's big-time city lawyer who, longing for the farming life, moves himself and his pretty Hungarian socialite wife, Lisa (Eva Gabor), to prime time's *Green Acres*—a farm outside the country town of Hooterville.

OLSEN TWINS

Who would ever have thought that Mary-Kate and Ashley Olsen, the funny-looking twins (okay, they're adorable) who took turns playing little Michelle on TV's *Full House* (1987–95), would grow up to be a billion-dollar industry? Their commercial empire—four TV shows, thirteen movies, twenty straight-to-video films (including *The Adventures of Mary-Kate and Ashley* crime-solving series), 169 books, video-game cartridges, a cartoon (*Mary-Kate and Ashley in Action!*), a record (*Brother for Sale*), a magazine, Mattel fashion dolls, and a clothing line for Wal-Mart—earns a phenomenal billion dollars annually. I'm way past the Mary-Kate and Ashley age-group (Generation Y), so I don't really get the appeal, but I'd guess the secret to their success has to do with their likeable, inquisitive nature, plus the whole twin mystique.

On June 13, 2004, the countdown ended for eager overage males everywhere when the girls, now hot babes, turned eighteen.

FYI: ▸ How to tell the look-alike twins apart? Mary-Kate is shorter by an inch and has darker hair than Ashley. Ashley, who is older than Mary-Kate by three minutes, has a freckle beneath her nose. Also of interest, Ashley is right-handed and Mary-Kate is left-handed.

OMEN

In this spooky supernatural thriller, the Antichrist arrives in the form of an angelic-looking five-year-old named Damien (Harvey Stephens), the surrogate son of a prominent U.S. Ambassador to England, Robert Thorn (Gregory Peck), and his beautiful wife, Katherine (Lee Remick). A series of bizarre and gory deaths occurs, accompanied by the menacing strains of "Ave Satani": A nanny commits suicide by hanging herself at Damien's birthday party; a grisly decapitation by flying plate-glass; an impalement by a lightning rod; and Mrs. Thorn's fatal fall over the second-floor railing after being struck by Damien manically pedaling his tricycle. The ambassador soon suspects that Damien might be the son of Satan, and his discovery of the number 666 on the tot's scalp confirms this suspicion. Directed by Richard Donner, the 1976 horror film co-stars David Warner as Jennings, a priest out to warn Thorn of his son's identity, and Billie Whitelaw as Mrs. Baylock, Damien's evil replacement nanny. A box-office hit, *The Omen* spawned three mediocre sequels that traced the satanic lad's rise to power from childhood through adulthood: *Damien—Omen II* (1978), *The Final Conflict* (1981), and *Omen IV: The Awakening* (1991).

ONE DAY AT A TIME

Popular CBS-TV sitcom about the trials and tribulation of being a single working mother in the 1970s. Bonnie Franklin starred as Ann Romano, a divorced "everywoman" living with two teenagers in a small apartment building in Indianapolis. Ann's daughters were Julie (Mackenzie Phillips), a headstrong seventeen-year-old rebel, and Barbara (Valerie Bertinelli), the prettier and better behaved fifteen-year-old. Pat Harrington Jr. co-starred as Dwayne Schneider, the macho superintendent of the apartment building. Premiering in 1975, *One Day at a Time* lasted for nine seasons with viewers witnessing Ann and the girls growing up and going through many life changes, including Mackenzie's being written off the show during the 1979–80 season because she had to go into rehab for a serious cocaine problem.

100 LITTLE DOLLS

"What an incredible deal!" That's what kids must have thought after coming across the ad in the *Archie* comic books for "100 Little Dolls" for only one dollar. Just think, baby dolls, nurse dolls, dancing dolls, foreign dolls, clown dolls, cowboy dolls, Indian dolls, bride dolls, and so many more—100 different types for a penny a doll! After sending their hard-earned allowance dollar, plus fifty cents for postage and handling, they waited for more than six weeks for the dolls to arrive, only to be disappointed once they opened the package. You see, the ad was misleading—it didn't mention the dolls' size or color. They were only two inches high and made of pink-colored styrene plastic and hard synthetic rubber, and you got only thirty different types—the rest were duplicates. In 1993, the alternative rock group Belly showcased these dolls on their *Star* album cover.

101 DALMATIANS

Adapted from Dodie Smith's book, this charming animated Disney film was told from the doggies' point of view. Flamboyant villainess Cruella De Vil kidnaps adorable and cuddly Dalmatian puppies to make a coat out of their fur (gasp!). Can Dalmatian parents Pongo and Perdita, with the aid of the "Twilight Bark," a canine communications network, rescue their fifteen pups plus eighty-four others from extermination? Of course they can—this is a Disney movie! Released in 1961, *101 Dalmatians* was the number-one box-office hit of the year. One of the Disney Studio's most popular theatrical reissues, it spawned so many Dalmatian toys and merchandising tie-ins that the whole world has been left seeing black spots. A live-action version starring Glenn Close as Cruella and 101 real-life Dalmatians was released in 1996.

FYI: ▸ Handsome Australian-born actor Rod Taylor provided the voice of Dalmatian papa Pongo. He is known best for the lead roles in *The Time Machine* (1960) and *The Birds* (1963).

ONE MILLION YEARS B.C.

"Raquel Welch wears mankind's first bikini!" Hammer Studios' dino-epic was no *Jurassic Park*, but in 1966 it gave kids what they wanted: scary and ferocious dinosaurs, warring caveman tribes, and alpine-breasted Raquel Welch. The movie told the prehistoric saga of handsome Tumak (John Richardson) of the Rock People, a dark, hairy, hostile tribe, who is exiled from his cave in the mountains. After wandering a distance, Tumak finds himself among the Shell People, a fair-haired, gentle, beach-dwelling tribe, and falls in love with their most beautiful member, Loana (Raquel Welch, looking soooo 1960s with skimpy fur bikini, fur go-go boots, white lipstick, liquid eyeliner, false eyelashes, and teased blonde hair). Together, the Stone Age sweethearts, cut off from tribal support, decide to face the harsh world outside, where they encounter a host of primeval creatures and brutal cavemen.

This sci-fi classic was a remake of 1940's *One Million B.C.*, starring Victor Mature and Carole Landis. Favorite scenes include the one in which Loana is carried off by a pterodactyl to be din-din for its babies; Loana and Tumak's frightful venture into a cave occupied by a more primitive species; and the earth-shattering volcanic eruption at the film's finale. Other highlights were the unique "grunt" dialogue invented especially for the movie (no English was spoken); Ray Harryhausen's groundbreaking stop-motion special effects (archaic by today's computer-graphics standards); and the haunting percussive score by Mario Nascimbene. *One Million Years B.C.* helped establish Raquel Welch as a household name and—to her disdain—as a world-famous sex symbol, thanks to the quasi-posed "cavegirl bikini" publicity photo showcasing her physical charms and later to become a best-selling pinup.

FYI: ▸ Other boffo dinosaur flicks of the era were *The Valley of Gwangi* (1969), *When Dinosaurs Ruled* *the Earth* (1970), *The Land That Time Forgot* (1975), *At the Earth's Core* (1976), and a TV movie, *The Last Dinosaur* (1977).

O'NEAL, TATUM

"I couldn't be more spoilder than I am now!" In 1973, at nine years of age, O'Neal became the youngest actor ever to win an Academy Award. She won for her performance as the orphan Addie Loggins (her film debut), a rough-talking, cigarette-smoking, bible-hawking con artist, in the comedy *Paper Moon*, starring opposite real-life dad Ryan O'Neal as Moses Pray. Tatum was born to Ryan and actress Joanna Moore on November 5, 1963, and raised by her father when they divorced in 1967. By 1976, she was the hottest juvenile star in Hollywood and being offered hand-tailored roles. She was receiving the highest fee of any child performer for her role as ace pitcher Amanda Whurlitzer in the Little League Baseball comedy *The Bad News Bears*. Other prominent movies included *Nickelodeon* (1976), *International Velvet* (1978), and *Little Darlings* (1980). Known for having a spoiled-brat temperament, she was nicknamed "Tantrum" by co-workers and members of the world press. Tatum retired from acting when she married tennis star John McEnroe, another notable brat, in 1986 (the union has since ended), and she recently penned a tell-all book about her Hollywood upbringing.

ON YOUR OWN

> "Of all the things I've done, what I love the most is the freedom, the fun, the challenge of growing up and taking charge.
> I've filled these pages with everything I've learned to help you make the most of starting out on your own."
>
> —BROOKE XX

Movie star, supermodel, college coed—in 1985, the world's most famous teen, Brooke Shields, added another notch to her multitalented career—author, with the self-help book *On Your Own*. Drawn from the Pretty Baby's own lifetime experiences ("both happy and sad"), the publication was geared toward young women headed to college. It was full of all kinds of personal advice and beauty tips, such as how to avoid a nervous breakdown before exams, how to survive dormitory food without gaining weight (known as "the freshman fifteen," as in pounds), how to deal with a yucky roommate, how to assemble the perfect weekend wardrobe that'll fit into a backpack, why smoking spoils your looks, and why virginity is important.

OOGIE BOOGIE MAN

"If you ain't shakin', then there's something very wrong." Thoroughly ghastly sack of evil, and enemy of Pumpkin King Jack Skellington, Oogie held Santa Claus captive in Tim Burton's *Nightmare Before Christmas*. Oogie's bumpy body is filled with worms, spiders, and other nightmarish creepy-crawlers.

OOMPA LOOMPAS

Orange-skinned, green-haired dwarfs who were seen as loyal employees inside Willy Wonka's Chocolate Factory. Following the demise of each of the film's brats—Augustus, Violet, Veruca, and Mike—the Oompa Loompas would come out from places unseen and sing a rhyming riddle about the child's bad habit ("Oompa Loompa Doo-pa-Dee-do / I've got another riddle for you . . ."). In the *Charlie and the Chocolate Factory* book by Roald Dahl, the Oompa Loompas were members of a pygmy tribe imported directly from Africa (they were altered for the 1971 movie to avoid racial undertones).

OPERATION

"It takes a very steady hand." Introduced by Milton Bradley in 1965, this is another classic game from our childhood. It features a cardboard patient lying on an operating table who suffers from various plastic ailments, such as a Broken Heart, Funny Bone, Writer's Cramp, Butterflies in Stomach, Charlie Horse, or Water on the Knee. The participants take turns playing "doctor" by eliminating one of these problems with the Electro Probe, a pair of electric tweezers connected to a buzzer. Those with shaky hands lose a turn if they touch the metal edge and cause a startling "buzz-buzz-buzzing" noise, which makes the patient's nose light up. Operation is actually a fun game to play at parties when you and your friends are totally shit-faced.

OPIE TAYLOR

"Golly, Pa, you know just about everything, don't you?" Sheriff Andy Taylor's rambunctious, freckle-faced, redheaded six-year-old son who idolizes his widowed dad and respects his spinster aunt, Bee, the next best thing to a mother. Little Ron Howard—future Academy Award–winning director (2001's *A Beautiful Mind*)—played this All-American lad on *The Andy Griffith Show*.

ORBIT CITY

Located way, way out in outer space, this twenty-first-century metropolis is home to the space-age Jetsons of Hanna-Barbera cartoon fame.

ORBITY

A tiny alien creature with springy legs and suction-cup feet acquired as a pet by the futuristic Jetson family on their mid-1980s cartoon series.

OREO

> "Health food may be good for the conscience, but Oreos taste a hell of a lot better."
> —ROBERT REDFORD

Since debuting in 1912, Nabisco's Oreo chocolate sandwich cookies have ruled as the number-one cookie in America. Everyone has his or her own way of eating an Oreo—I like to twist the cookies apart and lick off all the white creme icing from the center before consuming the rest. Various types of Oreos have included Double Stuf Oreo (a double dollop of creme filling), Mini Oreo (bite-sized cookies), and Fudge Covered Oreo. According to Nabisco: "If every Oreo cookie ever made were stacked on top of each other (over 362 billion), the pile would reach to the moon and back more than five times."

FYI: ▸ The slang term "Oreo" is used as a put-down aimed at a black person with so-called white mannerisms ("White on the inside, black on the outside").

ORLANDO, TONY, AND DAWN

A 1970s pop trio consisting of Tony Orlando, the lead singer with Greek and Puerto Rican heritage, and Telma Hopkins and Joyce Vincent, two African-American backup vocalists known simply as Dawn. Orlando experienced a so-so recording career in the 1960s before uniting with Hopkins and Vincent in 1970. Called Tony Orlando and Dawn (and sometimes just "Dawn"), they experienced initial success with the singles "Candida" and "Knock Three Times" in 1970. Major stardom came in 1973 with the blockbuster "Tie a Yellow Ribbon 'Round the Ole Oak Tree," a song that topped the charts for four weeks, sold more than six million copies internationally, and became the year's best-selling single. Other hits include "Say, Has Anybody Seen My Sweet Gypsy Rose" (1973), "Who's in the Strawberry Patch with Sally" (1973), and "He Don't Love You (Like I Love You)" (1975).

Tony Orlando and Dawn starred in a self-titled musical-variety TV show in 1974. The program showcased a smooth rapport between the charismatic and handsome Orlando and the sassy Dawn, which viewers loved enough to keep the show on the air for two years. In 1977, the threesome disbanded when a weary Orlando temporarily withdrew from show business following the devastating suicide of a best pal, comedian Freddie Prinze. Telma Hopkins later had success as a comedic TV actress, playing Isabelle Hammond on *Bosom Buddies* (1980–82) and Addy Wilson on *Gimme a Break* (1984–87).

OSCAR GOLDMAN

Government boss with the OSI (Office of Scientific Information), based in Washington, D.C., who worked double-time supervising bionic agents Steve Austin and Jaime Sommers. Played by busy Richard Anderson on the TV adventure programs *The Six Million Dollar Man* and *The Bionic Woman*.

OSCAR MAYER

The leading producer of meat goods notable for giving pop culture two highly unforgettable TV commercial jingles: "I wish I were an Oscar Mayer wiener / That is what I'd truly like to be / 'Cause if I were an Oscar Mayer wiener / Everyone would be in love with me" and "My bologna has a first name, it's O-S-C-A-R / My bologna has a second name, it's M-A-Y-E-R / I love to eat it every day and if you ask me why I'll say / 'Cause Oscar Mayer has a way with B-O-L-O-G-N-A." To help promote their hot dog, the Wisconsin-based company created the peculiar-looking Wienermobile and offered a Wienermobile whistle premium you could use to accompany the Oscar Mayer wiener song.

FYI: ▸ To keep up with America's taste for hot dogs, Oscar Mayer rolls 36,000 wieners an hour off its "hot dog highway."

OSCAR THE GROUCH

"Go away!" Continually pissed-off furry green fellow whose home is a garbage can on the PBS children's TV series *Sesame Street*. He's never seen outside of his trash can.

OSMOND, DONNY

As Osmondmania swept the nation in the early 1970s, this young heartthrob stood out from his brothers to become the number-one teen idol of the decade. Born December 9, 1957, Donny joined his older siblings as a member of The Osmond Brothers in 1963 at the age of six. In 1971, following the group's Top Forty success with "One Bad Apple" and "Yo-Yo," recording studio MGM—aware of Donny's youthful good looks and growing admiration among adolescent females—wisely recorded him as a solo artist with the LP *The Donny Osmond Album*. Girls bought his music in droves, bestowing the dark-haired cutie with gold record after gold record, including "Go Away Little Girl" (1971), "Sweet and Innocent" (1971), "Hey Girl" (1971), "Puppy Love" (1972), and "The Twelfth of Never" (1973).

By mid-decade, Donny Osmond was everywhere. His popularity rivaled that of Elvis or The Beatles, and his concerts and public appearances drew record numbers of screaming, frenzied fans. He was the hands-down winner of the most coverage in teen rags, with such headline grabbers as "Donny's Love Affair!" "Donny Can't Marry You!" "Donny's Awful Secret!" or "Donny to Be a Priest!" All over America, Donny's posters and magazine pinups were plastered on the bedroom walls of almost every preteen gal.

In September 1974, a new chapter in his career began when he and younger sister Marie embarked as a toothsome recording duo with the songs "I'm Leaving It All Up to You" and "Morning Side of the Mountain." The squeaky-clean brother and sister co-hosted their own *Donny and Marie* variety TV program from 1976 until 1979. In recent years, Donny has been a favorite guest star on comedienne Rosie O'Donnell's TV talk show (she admits to being one of his prepubescent fans back in the 1970s) and has toured as Joseph in the musical *Joseph and the Amazing Technicolor Dreamcoat*.

FYI: ▸ Donny's trademark was purple socks (purple's his favorite color).

OSMOND, MARIE

In the 1970s, she was the envy of practically every adolescent girl in America, if not the whole world, because of four simple words: Sister of The Osmonds.

OSMONDS

Born to a large Mormon family headed by George and Olive, The Osmond Brothers formed in 1959 as a juvenile barbershop quartet singing at church social functions in their hometown of Ogden, Utah. While performing at Disneyland in 1962, the four boys—Alan, Wayne, Merrill, and Jay—were discovered by singer Andy Williams, who signed them as regulars on his weekly TV variety series. The following year, six-year-old Donny joined his brothers on *The Andy Williams Show*, a stint lasting until 1971 that allowed the family-friendly group to build a strong fan base composed mainly of youngsters.

In 1971, their name was shortened to The Osmonds, after Mike Curb, president of MGM Records, signed the siblings to a recording contract to compete with Motown's well-received brother act, The Jackson 5. The Osmonds' first single, "One Bad Apple" (1971), exploded onto the charts, where it stayed for four months and reached number one for five weeks, selling more than a million copies. Other hits included "Yo-Yo" (1971), "Down by the Lazy River" (1972), and "Crazy Horses" (1972). Referred to as the "Os Bros" by teenybop magazines, the handsome brown-haired brothers, led by fave rave Donny, wore white-fringed Elvis-like jumpsuits while performing electrifying sold-out concerts.

For most of the first half of the 1970s, Osmondmania sent young girls all over the world into scream-inducing hysteria not seen since the days of The Beatles. From 1972 to 1974, the group was caricatured, along with the chubby little brother, Jimmy, on a Saturday-morning cartoon series titled *The Osmonds*. Born in 1963 and billed as Little

Jimmy Osmond, the youngest Osmond at age nine had a minor solo career (his 1972 debut "Long Haired Lover from Liverpool" was the biggest-selling song of the year in the United Kingdom, topping the charts for five weeks) before signing up as a member of his brothers' band. Their saga was told in a 1982 TV movie, *Side by Side: The True Story of the Osmond Family*, starring sister Marie as mother Olive. Currently, the "Os Bros," minus Donny, can be found performing country music in Branson, Missouri, down in the Ozarks.

OTTER POPS

"There's an otterly fantastic place. . . ." Refreshing sugary, fruit-flavored frozen treats packaged in foot-long, plastic-wrapped cylinders that you cut the top off and slurped away. Otter Pops were advertised by cute otter characters whose names and personalities matched their individual flavor: Alexander the Grape, a Roman emperor; Louis Bloo Raspberry, a beret-wearing French otter; Sir Isaac Lime, an explorer; Puncho Punch, a sombrero-adorned, poncho-clad Mexican; Strawberry Short Kook, an actress; Little Orphan Orange, an otter girl with a pet pooch (à la Little Orphan Annie).

OUIJA BOARD

"Yes." "No." "Good-bye." Since 1967, Ouija by Parker Brothers has allowed players to allegedly contact and communicate with spirits from the otherworld. Its game board has "yes" written in the upper left corner, "no" in the upper right corner, "good-bye" at center bottom, and the letters of the alphabet and numbers 0 through 9 in the middle. To play Ouija, participants lightly placed their fingertips on the message indicator called the "Mystifying Oracle" and then asked the contacted spirit a question. Magically the indicator would effortlessly glide across the board to point out "yes" or "no" or to spell out a more detailed answer. Skeptics say that it's the players who are pushing the indicator to the answers, but those of us who have ever played know better.

Beware! Playing Ouija can be a mighty spooky experience, especially if you summon an evil spirit like the one Tawny Kitaen contacted in the 1984 horror film *Witchboard*. Disguising itself as the ghost of a small boy, this demon used the board as a portal to the real world to haunt and slaughter Tawny's friends. During the late 1960s and early 1970s, Ouija's popularity inspired a host of supernatural games, including The Green Ghost Game, Jeane Dixon's Game of Destiny, Ka-Bala, Kreskin's ESP, The Mystery Zodiac Game, Mystic Skull, Voodoo, and Which Witch?

FYI: ▸ The name Ouija is a combination of the French ("Oui") and German ("Ja") words for yes.

OUR GANG

Produced by Hal Roach from 1926 to 1938, *Our Gang* has entertained generations of viewers with more than 220 short film comedies about a ragtag group of tykes involved in various hijinks, such as playing hooky from grammar school, go-cart racing, putting on talent shows, and forming a He-Man Woman Haters Club. Although it starred a large ensemble of child actors, most fans recall five major players from the later years: freckled Alfalfa Switzer, with the straight-up cowlick, who serenaded his beloved Darla with off-key crooning and regularly clashed with neighborhood bully Butch; chubby Spanky McFarland, the gang's leader, who used the catchphrase "Okeydokey!" and did open-mouthed double-takes while smacking his forehead when something went wrong; dark-haired cutie Darla Hood, the target of Alfalfa's unrequited love and the only member with any common sense; token "Negro" Buckwheat Thomas, who had a bushy hairdo, large, animated eyes, spoke mangled English (for instance, "Here I is"), and palled around with a little white kid named Porky Lee; and Pete the Pup, a mutt with a black ring circling his right eye. One *Our Gang* film, "Bored of Education," won an Oscar in 1936. Renamed *The Little Rascals* when it aired on syndicated TV from 1954 to 1965.

OUTSIDERS

Acclaimed director Francis Ford Coppola's 1983 big-screen adaptation of the best-selling youth novel by S. E. Hinton. Set in Tulsa, Oklahoma, in 1966, this semi-classic told the story of a teenage gang from the wrong side of the tracks ("greasers") and their conflicts with their more affluent high school peers ("socs," short for "socialites"). Reading like a who's who of young lead actors of the 1980s, the list of cast members included Matt Dillon as Dallas Winston, Ralph Macchio as Johnny Cade, C. Thomas Howell as Ponyboy Curtis, Patrick Swayze as Darrel Curtis, Rob Lowe as Sodapop Curtis, Emilio Estevez as Two-Bit Matthews, and Tom Cruise as Steve Randle. Also featured were Diane Lane as rich girl Sherri Vallance, and former teen-idol Leif Garrett as soc Bob Sheldon. Author Hinton made a cameo appearance as a nurse.

OVER THE EDGE

Director Jonathan Kaplan's realistic tale about alienated youths on the rampage in America's suburban wasteland (in this case it was New Granada, a planned community near New York City). Although filmed in 1979, it was shelved due to heavy violence and finally released after star Matt Dillon—making his debut as doomed rebel Richie White—struck it big two years later. The soundtrack featured music by The Cars, The Ramones, and Cheap Trick.

OVERALLS

At one time associated with country bumpkins, overalls became fashionable in the mid-1970s among teenage studs, who would wear them without a shirt. In the late 1990s, the trend was to wear overalls with one shoulder strap buttoned and the other unbuttoned and dangling down.

OWL

The wise old owl (aren't they all) full of pseudo-advice was seen as a character in the *Winnie the Pooh* films and books.

PACER

Introduced by the American Motors Corporation (AMC) in 1975, the bulbous automobile is considered one of the great "lemons" of the decade. The Pacer, heralded for its unique and imaginative design far advanced in its concept of driver and passenger comfort and convenience, seemed destined for success. A small car, it offered as much interior room as a larger one, and featured an extralong curbside door for easy entry and exit, plus a convenient rear hatch.

Why did the Pacer become such a notorious bomb? Well, for one thing, it was supposed to be economically friendly, but it had terrible gas mileage. Electrical and carburetor glitches caused it to stall frequently. The steering seized. The brakes suffered from defects. The interior and exterior were riddled with blotches, including a poor finish, doorframes prone to rust, and bad body-panel fittings. And, just when you think it couldn't get any worse, the tortoise-shaped vehicle's vibrations and rattles made driving as much fun as being in a 6.5 California earthquake. In 1980, the Pacer's poor history caused AMC to discontinue production of the ill-fated auto.

FYI: ▸ Throughout the 1970s and early 1980s, the smell of lemon was in the air, and the Pacer wasn't alone. Other stinkaroo cars of the era included the Ford Pinto, the Chevrolet Vega, the Dodge Aspen, the Plymouth Volare, the Volkswagen Dasher, the AMC Gremlin, the Pontiac Fiero, the Suzuki Samurai, and the Yugo.

PAC-MAN

Pac-Man was the first great superstar of the video game era and called the "Mickey Mouse of the 1980s." His popularity landed him *Time* magazine's coveted Man of the Year cover story in 1982. The round yellow fellow remindful of a souped-up smiley face was created in Japan by Namco Limited, a computer and robotics company. Namco based him on a character from Japanese folklore known for a legendary appetite and named him after *paku*, meaning "to eat" in Japanese. In 1980, Bally obtained the rights to manufacture the Pac-Man game in the U.S. and introduced it to arcades the following year.

With mouth wide open, Pac-Man went "Wakka-wakka-wakka" as he scored points by swallowing up dots and fruits while racing through a colorful electronic maze. The more he ate, the more points a player—controlling his progress with a joystick—collected. He also tried to avoid being eaten by the Galaxians, four goblins who resided in the maze.

After arriving in America, the great gobbler instantly outdid the current video-game leader, Space Invaders, as the most played video game in the nation. In his first eighteen months, he gulped up an estimated one billion dollars in quarters!

Pac is noted for being the first game to attract girls into the boy-dominated arcades. During the late 1970s, these places had a reputation for being all-male hangouts ruled by video games with guy-friendly themes, such as auto racing, sporting events, military encounters, and space battles. Pac-Man changed all that, and even introduced a sequel aimed at the fairer sex, Ms. Pac-Man. Setting off a tidal wave of merchandising, the omnivorous heroes turned up on more than 200 consumer products, including cereal, lunch boxes, watches, clothing items, bed sheets, mugs, and dozens of toys. Musicians Jerry Buckner and Gary Garcia released "Pac-Man Fever," a song that cracked *Billboard* magazine's Top Ten in January 1982. In September 1982, Pac-Man and Ms. Pac-Man came to Saturday-morning TV as the married stars of a cartoon series, *The Pac-Man Show.*

FYI: ▸ An original Pac-Man game now resides in the Smithsonian Institution.

PADDINGTON BEAR

A lost little bear dressed in trademark blue overcoat and oversized red hat, found at London's Paddington Station by Mr. and Mrs. Brown, who raise him as their own child. The lovable bear's success in the 1960 storybook *A Bear Called Paddington,* written by Michael Bond and illustrated by Peggy Fortnum, led to a children's book series of more than ten titles, plus all sorts of licensed merchandise items to be found everywhere.

PAINTER'S PANTS

These straight-legged white pants worn by painters and carpenters and distinguished by several pockets and one tab on the side for holding tools became a huge fashion item among teens of the late 1970s. Worn by both gals and guys, they looked great with just about any kind of shirt or sweater, plus the gazillion pockets were excellent for holding pens, pencils, and plastic combs and for tucking away secret notes. In their heyday, painter pants could be found in a multitude of colors, such as blue, green, orange, purple, red, and yellow. Dickies were the better-known brand.

PAKUNIS

A tribe of naive and gentle monkey-like people, led by Paku, who befriended the Marshalls on *Land of the Lost.*

FYI: ▸ Sid and Marty Krofft, creators and producers of *Land of the Lost,* based the Pakuni language on the Akan languages of present-day Ghana.

PAMELA BARNES EWING

On the blockbuster TV soap *Dallas,* the soft-spoken, Jhirmack shampoo redhead model Victoria Principal starred as Bobby's sexy young wife and sister of Ewing rival Cliff Barnes.

"PAPA DON'T PREACH"

This recording and accompanying music video by Madonna is noteworthy for two things: introducing the first of her many "new looks" and featuring the controversial subject of unmarried teen pregnancy. Madonna—an ever-changing pop chameleon who reinvents herself every year or so—now sported a sleek, slimmer body (good-bye, baby fat), cropped platinum blonde hair (farewell, overhighlighted bird's nest), and figure-revealing clothing, consisting of 1960s-style capri pants and bustier top (bye-bye, thrift-store duds and excessive bangles).

In the video, Madonna portrays a teenager who tells her working-class dad (played by actor Danny Aiello) that she's pregnant, in love with her boyfriend, and wants to keep the baby. She also appears as the singing narrator who sings and dances energetically to the teen's monologue ("Papa don't preach, I'm in trouble deep . . ."). The song came under fire because some believed that it glorified teen pregnancy, even though Madonna donated a percentage of its profits to programs advocating sexual responsibility. "Papa Don't Preach" went to the top of the charts in August 1986, and the video earned Madonna an MTV Music Video Award for Best Female Video.

PAPA SMURF

In the Hanna-Barbera cartoon series of the 1980s, the insightful village leader of the blue-hued Smurfs often rescues the younger Smurfs from the clutches of evil wizard Gargamel. Although he was 543 years old, many thought white-bearded Papa Smurf "didn't look a day over 530!"

PAPER DOLLS

Booklets with colorful paper dolls based on popular characters. The paper dolls' clothing was cut out and attached to their flat bodies with little tabs. Popularity declined drastically after the 1960s when three-dimensional fashion dolls—particularly Barbie and Dawn—made the scene. Other popular activity books of the era included coloring books, sticker books, and press-out books.

PARACHUTE PANTS

As a fashion sensation in the early 1980s, these were the "must have" articles of clothing for boogaloo break-dancers and cool New Wave dudes. Getting their name from the shiny parachute-like material they were made out of, parachute pants were traditionally baggy with elastic at the waist, zippers or snaps at the ankles, and zippered pockets all over. They went well with tight-fitting shirts that were striped or printed with Japanese symbols, as well as Members Only jackets, Van sneakers, and headbands.

PARADISE

Released in 1982, this poor imitation of *The Blue Lagoon* starred blond, curly-haired Willie Aames (doing a poor imitation of blond, curly-haired Christopher Atkins) and dark-haired teen model Phoebe Cates (doing a poor imitation of dark-haired teen model Brooke Shields), as sexually active teenagers marooned in a desert oasis instead of a tropical island.

"PARADISE BY THE DASHBOARD LIGHT"

The rock operetta by hefty rocker Meat Loaf was the ultimate "make-out" song. In it, a bitter couple reminisce about once being seventeen-year-olds making out in a car by the lake. As sportscaster Phil Rizzuto does a play-by-play account of a baseball game on the car radio, the teen lovers' act of passion ends temporarily because the girl (vocals by Ellen Foley) won't go any further unless she knows for sure that the boy loves her enough to marry. Caught up in the heat of the moment, he swears to love her to the end of time. Now it's the present, and the beleaguered fellow is praying for the end of time to hurry up and arrive. Written by madcap composer Jim Steinman, this classic was a release from Meat Loaf's 1978 concept album, *Bat Out of Hell*. In recent years it has been a favorite among the karaoke crowd.

FYI: ▸ In 1975, Meat Loaf (born Marvin Lee Aday on September 27, 1951, in Dallas, Texas) played the deceased greaser boyfriend of Little Nell in the cult classic *The Rocky Horror Picture Show* (in both the Broadway and the movie musicals).

PARADISE ISLAND

The home isle of superheroine Wonder Woman, ruled over by her mother, Queen Hippolyte, is an all-girl utopia populated by voluptuous Amazonian beauties whose strength comes from a mineral called Feminum. Wonder Woman is known as Princess Diana in this fictional kingdom (or in the case of Paradise Island, queendom).

PARENT TRAP

"Let's get together, yeah, yeah, yeah. . . ." Well-loved cinematic tale of two thirteen-year-old look-alike girls, Sharon McKendrick from California and Susan Evers from Boston, who go to summer camp (Camp Inch) and discover they are actually twin sisters separated as infants when their parents divorced. The twins scheme to bring their folks back together by switching places—and the fun begins. Trick photography employing double-exposure and split-screen shots made it possible for child star Hayley Mills to play the dual role of both Sharon and Susan. Co-starring were Brian Keith and Maureen O'Hara as the estranged parents, Mitch Evers and Maggie McKendrick, and Joanna Barnes as Vicky Robinson, Mitch's gold-digging girlfriend. Directed by David Swift, the 1961 Walt Disney movie was based on the book *Das Doppelte Lottchen* (*Lottie and Lisa*) by Erich Kastner. Annette Funicello and Tommy Sands, who the same year starred together in Disney's *Babes in Toyland*, sang the title theme.

PARKER BROTHERS

Founded in Salem, Massachusetts, in 1883 by George S. Parker, this board-game manufacturer is known for producing tried-and-true games that stand the test of time—Clue, Sorry, Risk, and the continuously popular Monopoly.

PARKER LEWIS CAN'T LOSE

Airing on FOX from 1990 to 1993, this youth-oriented TV comedy—a *Ferris Bueller* clone—chronicled the exploits of Parker "Not a Problem" Lewis (Corin Nemec), a hip junior at suburban Santa Domingo High who, along with best buds Mikey Randall (Billy Jayne) and Jerry Steiner (Troy Slaten), cleverly managed to evade all the school's rules. Comedienne Melanie Chartoff co-starred as Parker's archnemesis, Ms. Grace Mussa, Santa Domingo's repressive, coldhearted principal.

PARTNERSHIP FOR A DRUG-FREE AMERICA

Out of the "Just Say No" 1980s came this TV commercial featuring a close-up of an egg frying as a voiceover lectures, "This is your brain on drugs."

PARTON, DOLLY

Busty and blonde are words that best describe this much-loved female country singer of the 1970s and 1980s. Born in poverty on January 19, 1946, Parton, the fourth of twelve children, was raised in a two-room shack in the Smoky Mountains of Tennessee. As a five-year-old, she started writing songs, and she received her first guitar at the age of eight. The day after high school graduation in 1964, Parton headed for Nashville. Early success came as Porter Wagoner's singing partner on his syndicated country-music TV show in the late 1960s.

Gifted with a twangy soprano singing voice as ample as her cartoonish curves and mountainous curlicue wigs, Parton evoked tender memories of a humble beginning with her self-penned songs. The self-confident "Dumb Blonde" was her first country smash in 1967. Others hits included "Joshua" (1970), "Coat of Many Colors" (1971), "Jolene" (1973), "I Will Always Love You" (1974), "Love Is Like a Butterfly" (1974), "Here You Come Again" (1977), and a duet with Kenny Rogers, "Islands in the Stream" (1983). "I Will Always Love You" later became a mega-hit for soul artist Whitney Houston in 1992.

In 1980, Parton began a well-received acting career by playing office secretary Doralee Rhodes opposite Jane Fonda's Judy Bernly and Lily Tomlin's Violet Newstead, in the film comedy *Nine to Five* (the catchy title theme was her first number-one song on the pop charts). More movies followed, showcasing Parton as an adept comedienne—sort of a tamer version of Mae West—including *The Best Little Whorehouse in Texas* (1982), *Rhinestone* (1984), *Steel Magnolias* (1989), and *Straight Talk* (1992). In 1986, the multifaceted superstar opened a theme park, Dollywood, in the Smoky Mountains.

FYI: ▸ Dolly Parton cites "Coats of Many Colors" as her favorite self-penned song.

PARTRIDGE FAMILY

"Hello, world, here's a song that we're singing . . ." Airing on ABC-TV from 1970 to 1974, "America's First Family of Prime-Time Pop" was inspired by the success of The Cowsills, a family music act ("Indian Lake" and "Hair") popular during the late 1960s. Embraced by young viewers, the series focused on a widowed suburban mother and her five offspring, who hit the big time as a rock group after their garage tape-recording of "I Think I Love You" went to the top of the charts. Residing in the fictitious community of San Pueblo in California, The Partridge Family consisted of beautiful mother Shirley Partridge (Shirley Jones), dreamy eldest son Keith (David Cassidy, Jones's actual stepson), pretty eldest daughter Laurie (Susan Dey), precocious middle son Danny (Danny Bonaduce), kid brother Chris (Jeremy Gelbwaks, and later Brian Forster), youngest Tracy (Suzanne Crough), and family dog Simone. Reuben Kincaid (Dave Madden) served as the band's fast-talking manager.

As the coolest family around, the Partridges wore maroon crushed-velvet, bell-bottom pantsuits as stage costumes, had groovy long hair, and drove a school bus painted in far-out colors. In real life, The Partridge Family became recording superstars with several smash singles. Led by Cassidy's singing vocals, their signature "I Think I Love You" sold four million copies and topped the pop charts for three weeks in the fall of 1970. Other chartbusters included "Doesn't Somebody Want to Be Wanted" (1971), "I'll Meet You Halfway" (1971), and "I Woke Up in Love This Morning" (1971). Spurred on by the show's success, Cassidy was the hottest teen idol of the early 1970s and experienced a solo hit with a cover of The Association's "Cherish" in 1971. From 1974 to 1975, a Saturday-morning cartoon sequel, *The Partridge Family: 2200 A.D.*, featured the family rockin' and rollin' in outer space.

FYI: ▸ Only the singing voices of Shirley Jones and David Cassidy were used on The Partridge Family recordings. Professional studio musicians provided the rest of the vocals. And no, Susan Dey didn't actually play the keyboard, and neither did Danny Bonaduce play the guitar, or Brian Forster play the drums, or Suzanne Crough play the tambourine (but she looked awfully convincing shaking it).

PARTRIDGE FAMILY BUS

Retired school bus—used by the Partridges on their rock gigs (Shirley and Keith shared the driving)—custom-painted in the colorful geometric style of Dutch abstract painter Piet Mondrian. Had the motto "Caution: Nervous Mother Driving" painted on the back.

PASSWORD

The TV game show, hosted by Allen Ludden from 1961 to 1975, had two-member teams (one celebrity, one noncelebrity) trying to guess the "password" by providing each other with clues. The winners went on to a "lightning round."

PATTY DUKE SHOW

Airing from 1963 to 1966, the popular ABC sitcom starred seventeen-year-old Patty Duke—at the time the youngest person in TV history to headline a series—in a dual role as blonde look-alike cousins, Patty and Cathy Lane. These two laughed alike, walked alike, sometimes even talked alike, but they were as different as night and day. Outgoing Patty, the classic American teen, loved rock 'n' roll and hot dogs (which made her lose control), and more reserved Cathy, a British lass, adored minuets, the ballet route, and crêpes suzette. A world traveler who had lived almost everywhere ("from Zanzibar to Berkeley Square"), cousin Cathy stayed with Patty's family in the middle-class neighborhood of Brooklyn Heights, New York, while her father was working overseas. Both girls attended Brooklyn Heights High School, where they often fooled everyone by mischievously switching identities. Also featured were Patty's parents, Martin and Natalie Lane (William Schallert and Jean Byron); Patty's pesty younger brother, Ross (Paul O'Keefe); and Patty's boyfriend, Richard Harrison (Eddie Applegate).

FYI: ▸ Rita McLaughlin played the back of Patty/Cathy's head (she doubled as one girl when Patty Duke faced the camera as the other).

PATTY SIMCOX

"It's Patty Simcox,
the bad seed of Rydell High."
—BETTY RIZZO (STOCKARD CHANNING)

Rydell High's ultraperky, extrachirpy cheerleader with a swinging ponytail whose ingratiating personality made her the girl you love to hate in the movie *Grease* (1978). While schmoozing votes for student council vice-president, Patty (played by Susan Buckner) persuaded Sandy Olsson, the new student from Australia, to become a member of the cheerleading squad and garnered disdain from tough-talking Betty Rizzo, the leader of the Pink Ladies gang.

PAVEL CHEKOV

Hotheaded young navigator from Russia who assisted Mr. Sulu, chief helmsman of the starship Enterprise. Portrayed by American actor Walter Koenig on the classic *Star Trek* TV series from 1967 to 1969.

PEACE SIGN

How did the peace sign originate? A good question, probably never given much thought. Called "the ubiquitous icon from the Aquarian age" in the pop culture dictionary *Retro Hell*, the peace sign was designed by Britain's Controlled Nuclear Development antiwar lobby in 1964. By 1967's Summer of Love, hippies and nonhippies alike had adopted this circle utilizing the semaphore letters "N" and "D" (for nuclear disarmament), as an emblem of peace during the turbulent Vietnam War. It was common to see it silk-screened on T-shirts, dangled as medallions on chains, spray-painted on walls, and doodled on notebooks. Another symbol for peace is the one you give by holding up your middle and index finger on one hand. "Peace, man!"

FYI: ▸ Those dang right-wingers. A notorious early-1970s bumper sticker likened the peace sign to the foot of a bird, exclaiming "Footprint of the great American chicken."

PEACH PIT
The trendy L.A. restaurant where high-schooler Brandon Walsh worked part time to earn extra cash was also the hangout of his *Beverly Hills 90210* pals.

PEANUT GALLERY
What the live studio audience made up of a dozen or so children sitting on bleachers was called on the children's TV program *The Howdy Doody Show.*

PEANUTS
For more than fifty years, millions of fans have laughed with and loved Charles Schulz's sentimentally perceptive tykes with the oversized heads, making *Peanuts* the most successful comic strip in history. Created in 1950, the Peanuts tykes have appeared in more than 2,000 newspapers in twenty-six different languages in more than seventy countries around the world. They have starred in numerous books (more than 200 million sold thus far, including the classic *Happiness Is a Warm Puppy*); TV specials (most notably, the award-winning *A Charlie Brown Christmas*); motion pictures (*Snoopy Come Home*); a Broadway musical (*You're a Good Man, Charlie Brown*); and a hit record ("Snoopy vs. The Red Baron" by The Royal Guardsmen). They have been spokes-kids in ad campaigns (Metropolitan Life insurance, Dolly Madison snack cakes, and Weber's bread), have appeared on greeting cards (particularly for Hallmark), and are the subject of an annual billion-dollar merchandise industry (remember the Snoopy Sno-Cone Machine?).

The main Peanuts characters were the ever-hopeful Charlie Brown (the strip's hero), his little sister Sally, crabby Lucy Van Pelt, her sensitive brother Linus, pianist Schroeder, tomboy Peppermint Patty, her assistant Marcie, dirty Pig Pen, curly-haired Frieda, snooty Violet, black Franklin, yellow bird Woodstock, and Charlie Brown's beloved dog, Snoopy. These ageless youngsters seem to live in an adult-free world where they lightheartedly ponder the fears, anxieties, confusions, and frustrations common to childhood.

Rats! All good things must come to an end. In 1999, Schulz announced the retirement of Charlie Brown and friends due to his failing health. He died the following year. "Sigh."

FYI: ▸ Charles Schulz originally called his strip *Li'l Folks*, which was changed against his wishes to *Peanuts* by United Feature Syndicate, which had bought the rights in 1950. The title came from the youngsters who sat in the "Peanut Gallery" of the *Howdy Doody* TV show's studio audience.

PEARL, MINNIE
Country-music comedienne (real name: Sarah Colley) from Grinders Switch, Tennessee, who was a regular on the TV variety show *Hee Haw*. Minnie's trademarks are a straw hat with a $1.89 price tag still attached and a "Howdeee!" shout when she walks out on stage.

PEARL BODINE
Jethro and Jethrene Bodine's daft mother (played by Bea Benaderet), who when not visiting her relations in Californy resides back home among the hillbillies in the Ozarks. Cousin Pearl's crazy high-pitched yodeling tends to attract an array of animal critters and policemen to the Clampett estate in Beverly Hills.

PEARL PUREHEART
What Lois Lane was to Superman, and Sweet Polly Purebred was to Underdog, this blonde sweet patootie was the damsel-in-distress to Mighty Mouse. She met the rodent superhero in a cartoon titled "Fight to the Finish" in 1947.

PEASANT SKIRTS
Earthy hippie chicks really dug these ankle-length skirts made out of light gauzy cotton with exotic prints reminiscent of the kind poor working women from Eastern Europe wear.

PEBBLES AND BAMM-BAMM SHOW
In 1971, Hanna-Barbera gave the Flintstone and Rubble offspring their own spin-off Saturday-morning cartoon show. On this program, the two infants were now prehistoric sweethearts who attended Bedrock High School. Redheaded Pebbles Flintstone matured into a gorgeous and vivacious young

woman, with her trademark ponytail still wrapped around a bone. Towheaded Bamm-Bamm Rubble had grown up to be a handsome and muscular young man sporting a turtle-shell cap and driving the Cave Buggy, a dune buggy. The twosome hung out with a gang of friends: inventor Moonrock, sensible and short-statured Penny, astrology buff Wiggy ("Starrific!"), and depressed Schleprock. A stuck-up duo of rich brats, Cindy and Fabian, were the antagonists.

The gang's adventures centered on a Stone Age twist of modern teenage life (dating, finding work, earning money, and eating brontoburgers), and, like many cartoon teens of the era—the Archies, the Pussycats, the Hardy Boys, the Sundance Kids, and the Brady Kids—they performed in a groovy rock band, The Bedrock Rollers. In later episodes, they had to deal with the Bronto Bunch, a disruptive cycle gang who challenged Bamm-Bamm in drag-race competitions. Actors providing voices included Sally Struthers as Pebbles, Jay North (of *Dennis the Menace* fame) as Bamm-Bamm, and comedienne Mitzi McCall as Penny.

PEBBLES CEREALS

Introduced in 1969, two different Post cereals advertised by Fred Flintstone and Barney Rubble of *The Flintstones* cartoon. Fred, who liked chocolate, boasted about the chocolaty Cocoa Pebbles, while Barney, who liked fruit, bragged about the colorful Fruity Pebbles. They were always wrangling over which cereal was the best. Cocoa Pebbles was similar in taste and appearance to Kellogg's Cocoa Krispies but a little crunchier (it didn't get as soggy swimming in a bowl of milk).

PEBBLES FLINTSTONE

"Yabba-dabba-goo!" In February 1963, Wilma and Fred Flintstone gave birth to this superadorable, goo-gooing, ponytailed baby girl at the Rockapedia Hospital in Bedrock. Pebbles grew up to be a pretty and popular teenager, headlining her own Saturday-morning cartoon show with sweetheart Bamm-Bamm Rubble. "Yabba-dabba-doozy!"

PEDAL CARS

Sleek and stylish kiddie riding vehicles made out of sturdy steel and driven by pedal-power. Two favorites of the Baby Boom era were the Mustang convertible and the firefighting hook and ladder complete with flashing red lights and a siren. Popularity declined when the more durable and faster Big Wheel arrived in the late 1960s.

PEDAL PUSHERS

Shorter version of the fashionable capri pants, cut just below the knee. Great for gals riding bicycles, because the length didn't get caught in the chain—that's why they're called pedal pushers!

PEEPS

The yellow marshmallow confection shaped like little chicks is the candy most associated with the Easter holiday. A kid's Easter basket just wouldn't be the same without a few of these tossed in. Manufactured since 1953 by Just Born Inc., which claims that one billion Peeps are produced each year. They're probably right, because these days Peeps can be found year-round for many holidays, such as Halloween (ghost-shaped Peeps), Christmas (Christmas tree-shaped Peeps), Valentine's Day (heart-shaped Peeps), and Fourth of July (star-shaped Peeps).

PEE-WEE'S PLAYHOUSE

"C'mon in, and pull yourself up a chair. . . ." This was the coolest children's program to air on TV in the 1980s. Seen on Saturday mornings from 1986 to 1991, *Pee-Wee's Playhouse* combined live action, animation, Claymation, and computer graphics, along with a surreal mix of childish whimsy and double-entendre humor. It was popular not only with kids but also with young adults, who turned it into a cult favorite. (Not wanting to get up early on a weekend morning, we would videotape it and watch it later.) The show's star and host was Pee-Wee Herman, alter ego of Paul Reubens, a smart-alecky boy trapped in a grown man's body. Pee-Wee lived in the whacked-out, retro-design Playhouse located in the heart of Puppetland.

An array of talking furniture, animals, and puppets resided in the Playhouse with Pee-Wee, including Pterri, Pee-Wee's pet pterodactyl; Conky 2000, a robot; Magic Screen, an Etch-a-Sketch-esque TV; Clocky, a talking U.S.A.-shaped clock; Chairry, a talking chair; Globey, a talking globe; Billy Baloney, Pee-

Wee's ventriloquist puppet; Randy, a bully puppet; Cowntess, a tiara-wearing cow; the Puppetband, a jazz combo; Mr. Window, a cheerful window; the tiny Dinosaur Family, whose home was a mouse hole in the wall; the Three Flowers, who occupied a window box; the Ants, who inhabited an ant farm; Penny, a storytelling Claymation girl with pennies for eyes; and Jambi, a disembodied genie head.

Throughout the show, Pee-Wee and his Playhouse would play host to a regular cast of human pals, including the fabulous Miss Yvonne (Lynne Stewart), vigorous Latin-American Ricardo (Vic Trevino), frisky African-American Cowboy Curtis (Laurence Fishburne), busybody Jewish neighbor Mrs. Rene (Suzanne Kent), efficient mail lady Reba (S. Epatha Merkerson), wayward sailor Captain Carl (Phil Hartman), and the jovial King of Cartoons (William Marshall).

FYI: ▸ Cyndi Lauper warbled the *Pee-Wee's Playhouse* theme song.

PEE-WEE'S PLAYHOUSE CHRISTMAS SPECIAL

In December 1988, this hour-long holiday treat aired on prime-time TV, featuring sweet-natured imp Pee-Wee Herman and his off-the-wall Playhouse gang having a swell Yuletide party decked with fruitcakes, dreidels, piñatas, and an assortment of celebrity guests, including Frankie Avalon, Annette Funicello, Charo, Grace Jones, k.d. lang, Little Richard, Magic Johnson, Whoopi Goldberg, Joan Rivers, Dinah Shore, Oprah Winfrey, Zsa Zsa Gabor, the Del Rubio Triplets, and, of course, Santa Claus.

PEG BUNDY

Al Bundy's ditzy spouse, who teases her auburn hair big and wears tacky, cleavage-bulging leopard-skin outfits with stiletto heels. Slothful and horny, Peg wastes her time watching daytime TV talk shows (Oprah is a favorite), eating chocolate bon-bons, forcing sex on disinterested Al, and spending his measly income at the beauty salon and the shopping mall. Played by Katey Sagal on the FOX-TV sitcom *Married . . . with Children.*

FYI: ▸ Peg Bundy's maiden name is Wanker. Her family is from fictional Wanker County, Wisconsin, and she once held the title of Miss Teenage Wanker.

PENELOPE

Harried American black feline mistaken for a fellow skunk by persistent French loverboy Pepe Le Pew after a white stripe is accidentally painted down her back, in 1949's classic Warner Brothers cartoon short "For Scent-Imental Reasons."

PENELOPE PITSTOP

If prepubescent boys of the late 1960s through the early 1970s were asked to choose their favorite cartoon sex symbol, most likely they would have picked this wide-eyed blonde, heralded as "the glamour gal of the gas pedal." Dressed in a pink driving suit, a helmet, and white boots, the beautiful Penelope premiered in 1968 as one of eleven racers—driving the Compact Pussycat, car number 5—on Hanna-Barbera's *Wacky Races.* Proven popular with young TV viewers, she garnered her own spin-off the following year, *The Perils of Penelope Pitstop.* This new program had Penelope, a wealthy heiress, driving the parasol-topped Pussycat in international racing competitions. Along the way, Penelope clashes with her lawyer Sylvester Sneekly (disguised as the sneering Hooded Claw) and his Bully Brothers henchmen who would inherit her vast fortune if she were out of the picture. Aided by protective gangsters, the dwarfish Ant Hill Mob (also from *The Wacky Races*), and her own handy resources (nail files work great for cutting rope), our fair-haired bombshell regularly escapes the near-fatal dilemmas ingeniously created by Sneekly.

FYI: ▸ Janet Waldo provided Penelope Pitstop's dainty Southern belle accent. She also gave voice to space-age teen Judy Jetson and Josie of the Pussycats.

PENGUIN

Real name: Oswald Cobblepot. Bizarre, pointy-nosed Batman villain who wore a top hat, tails, and a monocle. Played by Burgess Meredith on the cult TV show and by Danny DeVito in the 1992 movie *Batman Returns.*

PENNY LOAFERS

Classic flat-soled brown footwear, particularly the Bass Weejun, worn by prepsters. Name came from the penny placed in the slit on the shoe's top.

PENNY ROBINSON
Dark-haired Angela Cartwright, a top child actress of the 1960s once called "America's little darling," played the sincerely charming and inquisitive youngest Robinson daughter on *Lost in Space* from 1965 to 1968.

FYI: ▸ Angela is the younger sister of Veronica Cartwright—herself a juvenile star of the 1960s (TV's *Daniel Boone* and film's *The Birds*). Veronica grew up to be an acclaimed character actress in such movies as *Invasion of the Body Snatchers* (1978), *Alien* (1979), and *The Witches of Eastwick* (1987).

PEPE Le PEW
Based on French matinee idol Charles Boyer, the suave, amour-struck cartoon skunk's first feature was 1947's "Scent-Imental over You." The helpless romantic from Paris won an Academy Award for his starring role in "For Scent-Imental Reasons" in 1949.

PEPPER ANDERSON
Fortysomething movie actress Angie Dickinson gave those younger female crime-fighters on TV—*Wonder Woman*'s Lynda Carter, *Bionic Woman*'s Lindsay Wagner, and *Charlie's Angels*' Kate, Jaclyn, and Farrah—a run for the money as this sexy cop who worked undercover for the L.A.P.D. on *Police Woman*.

PEPPERMINT PATTY
Redheaded, freckle-faced, sandal-wearing, extroverted tomboy (real name: Patricia Reichardt) from the *Peanuts* cartoons obviously nicknamed after York's chocolate-mint candy. Although a friend of Charlie Brown's (whom she calls "Chuck"), she and close pals Marcie and Franklin don't attend Birchwood Elementary; they go to a different school on the other side of town. What Patty lacks in brains at school (she has a D+ average) she makes up for on the baseball field. She thinks Charlie Brown's dog, Snoopy, is "the funny-looking kid with the big nose."

PERFECTION
"When you're into Perfection, stay on your toes, you gotta be quick, 'cause here's how it goes. . . ." A fun family game created by Lakeside in 1973. Players have to fit twenty-six different plastic geometric shapes into the correct holes of a yellow base unit before the sixty-second timer runs out and suddenly pops everything into the air. "Practice makes Perfection."

PERRY WHITE
"Great Caesar's ghost!" Gruff, blustering editor-in-chief of the *Daily Planet* in Metropolis, seen in the *Superman* comic-book adventures.

PERT PLUS
Procter & Gamble's wonder of modern technology—a shampoo and conditioner in one—gives you "lighter and livelier" hair!

PETE DIONASOPOLIS
"Cheeseboogie, cheeseboogie, cheeseboogie, cheeseboogie! Pepsi! Pepsi!" Rotund John Belushi's Greek proprietor of the Olympia, a diner famous for always being out of food items, on NBC's *Saturday Night Live*. "No Cheeseboogie!"

PETE MITCHELL
"I feel the need . . . the need for speed." Cocky young lieutenant, nicknamed Maverick and also known as Top Gun, who strives to be the Best of the Best at the Navy's elite Fighter Weapons School. His breath is taken away by sexy civilian instructor Charlotte "Charlie" Blackwood. Maverick was played by film idol Tom Cruise in 1986's *Top Gun*.

PETER BRADY
"When it's time to change, you have to rearrange." Cutie Christopher Knight (born November 7, 1957) played Mike's even-tempered middle son on *The Brady Bunch*. Peter liked pork chops and applesauce, and his investigative skills for the school newspaper got him nicknamed "Scoop Brady." He had the misfortune of going through squeaky-voiced puberty change in front of millions of TV viewers.

"PETER PAN" BOOTS
Purchased at trendy shoe stores like Wild Pair, these impish throwbacks to go-go boots were a hot fashion item during the New Wave era of the 1980s. Made out of thin leather or suede, the tops of these inexpensive ankle-high boots could be cuffed (looked ultracool when worn with pinstripe jeans tucked into) or uncuffed (a spicy statement when

matched with a leather miniskirt). Urban country girls preferred their boots lined with dangly fringe at the top. Also known as elf boots.

PETER PARKER

Young college student and part-time photographer for New York's *Daily Bugle* who moonlights undercover as the web-throwing, villain-nabbing Amazing Spider-Man. Parker's sweethearts include the late Gwen Stacy (she was killed by his nemesis, the Green Goblin) and Mary Jane Watson (whom he later married).

PETER PAUL

"Sometimes you feel like a nut, sometimes you don't." Connecticut-based manufacturer of the "indescribably delicious" Almond Joy (nut) and Mounds (no nuts) chocolate bars. Hershey Foods Corporation purchased Peter Paul in 1988.

PETE'S DRAGON

Directed by Don Chaffey, this 1977 Disney musical fantasy followed the tradition of *Mary Poppins* (1964) and *Bedknobs and Broomsticks* (1971) by mixing animation with live action. Set in Passamaquoddy, a Maine fishing village, circa 1910, it told the story of a lonely nine-year-old orphan boy named Pete (Sean Marshall) who runs away from his wicked backwoods foster parents, Lena and Merle Gogan (Shelley Winters and Charles Tyner), with the help of Elliot, a magical cartoon dragon that only he can see. Voiced by comedian Charlie Callas, the jolly and mischievous Elliot spans thirty feet, has bright-green skin, pint-sized pink wings, and a potbelly and is Pete's friend and protector. The boy and his unusual pet find sanctuary at a lighthouse run by friendly Lampie (Mickey Rooney) and fair daughter Nora (Helen Reddy), to avoid capture by the Gogans and greedy Dr. Terminus (Jim Dale), who is out to exploit Elliot. The movie featured the Oscar-nominated song "Candle on the Water," sung by Reddy.

PET ROCK

Of all the silly fads to come out of the 1970s, this had to be the silliest by far. Released in the fall of 1975 by entrepreneur Gary Dahl, the Pet Rock was nothing but a sedentary clump of stone housed in a cardboard box with air holes and wacky instructions on care and training. Forget frisky Lassie, finicky Morris, and flighty Tweety—you didn't have to bother with feeding, grooming, and walking this pet. It didn't bite. It didn't scratch. And it never, ever soiled the carpet or destroyed the furniture. More than 1.2 million Americans parted with their money, at four bucks apiece, to own one!

PET SHOP BOYS

Formed in 1981, British two-man synthesizer and vocalist outfit consisting of singer Neil Tennant and keyboardist Chris Lowe, known for wordy, intellectual, danceable pop music. Characterized by Tennant's wry lyrics and lush synthesized melodies, their parade of hits included "West End Girls" (1986), "Opportunities (Let's Make Lots of Money)" (1986), "It's a Sin" (1987), "Always on My Mind" (1988), "Domino Dancing" (1988), "Left to My Own Devices" (1988), and the collaboration with the legendary Dusty Springfield, "What Have I Done to Deserve This?" (1988). They won the Brit Award for Best British Group in 1988.

FYI: ▸ The pop duo named themselves the Pet Shop Boys after pals who worked in an Ealing pet shop.

PETTICOAT JUNCTION

The second of a trilogy of well-loved rural sitcoms, produced by Paul Henning, that ran on CBS-TV during the 1960s (the other two were *The Beverly Hillbillies* and *Green Acres*). Airing from 1963 until 1970, the show took place at the Shady Rest Hotel, located down the tracks at Petticoat Junction on the outskirts of the small farming town of Hooterville. The Shady Rest was owned and operated by kindly widow Kate Bradley (Bea Benaderet). Helping her run the hotel were three gorgeous daughters—blonde eldest Billie Jo (first played by Jeannine Riley, then Gunilla Hutton, and finally Meredith MacRae), brunette middle daughter Bobbie Jo (Pat Woodell and later Lori Saunders), and redhead youngest Betty Jo (Linda Kay Henning, daughter of producer Henning)—all eligible and fond of swimming in the town's water tank. The girls' lovable Uncle Joe Carson (Edgar Buchanan) served as Shady Rest's slow-moving manager and fire chief of Hooterville. Also on hand were handsome Steve Elliott (Mike Minor), a pilot who crashed outside Hooterville and became Betty Jo's beau and eventual husband; Charley Pratt and Floyd Smoot (Smiley Burnette and Rufe Davis), the engineers of the antiquated steam train Cannonball; and Higgins (Benji), Uncle Joe's faithful dog.

When *Green Acres*, likewise set in Hooterville, premiered in 1965, its characters, such as general-store owner Sam Drucker (Frank Cady), farmer Newt Kiley (Kay Kuter), and handyman Eb Dawson (Tom Lester), often showed up on *Petticoat Junction*. In 1968, June Lockhart joined the cast as country doctor Janet Craig, after Benaderet passed away from cancer.

FYI: ▸ Sharon Tate, murder victim of Charles Manson, was originally cast in the role of Billie Jo, but because she had posed in *Playboy* (an act considered quite scandalous in 1963) she was taken off before an episode could be filmed.

PETUNIA PIG
Pigtailed, black-haired swine girlfriend of Looney Tunes character Porky Pig who made her debut in the 1937 cartoon short "Porky's Romance."

PEZ
"If I could have only one food for the rest of my life? That's easy. Pez. Cherry-flavored Pez. There's no doubt about it." This line from the 1986 movie *Stand by Me*, director Rob Reiner's homage to Baby Boomer childhood, could be a communal response from millions who have snacked on the popular candy since the 1950s. Pez was initially developed by Austrian inventor Edward Hass as a breath mint for smokers in 1927. Hass conceived its name by shortening the German word for peppermint, *pfeffermintz*, to Pez. In 1948, the Pez automatic dispenser was invented. It originally resembled a plain cigarette lighter, with the brick-shaped candy loaded in stacks just like staples in a stapler and ejected one at a time from a flip top. In 1952, the Pez Candy Company came to the United States and targeted the kids market by putting a character head on the plastic dispenser that unloaded pastel-colored, fruit-flavored Pez from the neck. These colorful, jazzed-up dispensers featured Disney characters, superheroes, and other personalities of cartoons and folklore. Today, in America alone, one billion Pez tablets are ejected from the dispensers yearly.

FYI: ▸ Disney's Mickey Mouse was the first to top a Pez dispenser. Other Pez favorites have included Bugs Bunny, Bullwinkle, Popeye, Snoopy, Superman, Uncle Sam, Santa Claus, and even Bart Simpson.

PHANTASM
"If this one doesn't scare you, you're already dead!" Screwy horror fantasy about two Oregon brothers, thirteen-year-old Mike Pearson (Michael Baldwin) and older Jody (Bill Thornbury), who heedlessly investigate the weird goings-on at the Morningside Cemetery funeral parlor. What they discover inside the white, marbled halls is a sinister mortician, The Tall Man, a.k.a. Jebediah Morningside (Angus Scrimm), who sends newly deceased victims into another dimension, where they are shrunk into black-robed zombie dwarves and put into slavery. Watch out for the flying silver ball with protruding hooks that thuds into foreheads and drills out brains. Produced, written, and directed on a shoestring budget by newcomer Don Coscarelli in 1979, *Phantasm* has become a classic, spawning a cult of fans worldwide. Oh, and it was followed by the obligatory sequels. "Booyyyy!"

PHANTOM OF THE OPERA
A music-loving madman (Erik) who hides his disfigured face underneath a mask and haunts a Paris opera house. Although featured in movies since the silent era (Lon Chaney's 1925 version is still the best), the scary Phantom's plight was romanticized in Andrew Lloyd Webber's Tony-winning, long-running Broadway musical (1988) starring Michael Crawford and featuring the tune "Music of the Night."

PHILIP DRUMMOND
On *Diff'rent Strokes*, Conrad Bain starred as the wealthy white widower and president of a huge conglomerate, Trans Allied Inc., who adopted the two black sons of his deceased maid—Arnold and Willis Jackson. Married feisty Maggie McKinney (actress Dixie Carter) in 1984.

PHOEBE FIGALILLY
Juliet Mills's beloved governess, who traveled all the way from England to Los Angeles to take care of the three children of Professor Howard Everett on the sitcom *Nanny and the Professor.* Phoebe was gifted with magical powers, which were never quite explained, and she obviously had ESP and could talk to the animals, just like Dr. Dolittle. Her work uniform included a blue cape and matching nanny's cap.

PHOENIX, RIVER
"I don't see any point or any good in drugs that are as disruptive as cocaine." Talented Hollywood star whose career of portraying troubled youths left a major impact on the big screen before drugs abruptly ended his life at age twenty-three. Born on August 23, 1970, in a log cabin in rural Oregon, Phoenix was the eldest son of God-worshiping hippie parents who gave their five offspring weird names—River Jude (after the river of life in Hermann Hesse's novel *Siddhartha* and after The Beatle's "Hey Jude"), Leaf Joaquim, Rainbow Joan of Arc, Liberty Mariposa, Summer Joy—and raised them on a religious commune (the Children of God) in South America.

At age sixteen, the pensive actor garnered critical approval with his performance of Chris Chambers, a tough boy from the wrong side of the tracks, in the film adaptation of Stephen King's *Stand by Me* (1986). His heartrending role as Danny Pope, the son of radical fugitives, in *Running on Empty* earned him an Academy Award nomination as Best Supporting Actor in 1988. Other key performances were in *The Mosquito Coast* (1986), as Charlie, Harrison Ford's son; *Little Nikita* (1988), as Jeff Grant, the Air Force cadet son of Soviet spies; *Indiana Jones and the Last Crusade* (1989), as young Indy; and *My Own Private Idaho* (1991), as Jeff, a narcoleptic gay hustler, opposite close pal Keanu Reeves. When not acting, he played guitar and sang with his own rock band, Aleka's Attic.

However, it could be said that the blond Phoenix, an ardent animal rights activist, environmentalist, and vegetarian, gave his best performance by convincing his Hollywood co-workers and Gen-X fan base that he was clean-living, by not partaking in drug use. The world was stunned on Halloween night 1993 when he died on the sidewalks outside Johnny Depp's L.A. club, the Viper Room, from a lethal mixture of cold medicine, Valium, marijuana, cocaine, and heroin. Like James Dean, Marilyn Monroe, and other youthful ill-fated stars who blazed before him, Phoenix burned out too soon, leaving us with the somber awareness that there would have been so much more to come. Damn drugs.

FYI: ▸ "For River." Michael Stipe, lead singer of R.E.M., dedicated their 1994 album *Monster* to friend River Phoenix.

PHYLLIS LINDSTROM
Bitchy and high-strung landlord who owns the apartment building in Minneapolis where Mary Richards rents. This busybody is the mother of angst-ridden teenager Bess Lindstrom and wife of dull dermatologist Lars Lindstrom. Played by Emmy-winning Cloris Leachman on *The Mary Tyler Moore Show* (1970–75) and spin-off *Phyllis* (1975–77).

"PHYSICAL"
"Let me hear your body talk. . . ." The biggest-selling single of the 1980s! Recorded by Olivia Newton-John in 1981, "Physical" was number one for an astonishing ten weeks, tying Debby Boone's "You Light Up My Life" (1977) as the second longest-holding chart-topper in the history of pop music (behind Elvis Presley's "Don't Be Cruel"). The first and most identifiable aerobic theme, "Physical" was "the" anthem for those who worked their bodies during the early 1980s. Some dirty-minded souls felt the lyrics were highly suggestive, full of sexual innuendo, so they had it banned from American radio stations. The best thing about the song was its playful music video. It featured an aerobicizing Olivia—sporting a short bi-level haircut and essential headband and leg warmers gym wear—displaying an athletic, sexy side to her personality as she tried to inspire some fat men in the weight room to get in shape. In the end, the guys are transformed into beefy, half-naked hunks who walk off hand-in-hand with one another, leaving poor Livvy all by herself. It won the Best Video Award at the twenty-fifth annual Grammy ceremonies in 1982 and helped kick off the aerobics craze of the 1980s.

FYI: ▸ Other aerobic anthems of the era were "Let's Work" (1981) by Prince, "Work That Body" (1982) and "Muscles" (1982) by Diana Ross, and "Maniac" (1983) by Michael Sembello.

PICTIONARY

"The Game of Quick Draw." Pictionary was created by a twenty-four-year-old waiter from Seattle named Rob Angel and first distributed by Milton Bradley in 1987. Similar to charades, the fun board game had players drawing something that resembled a picture while their teammates guessed what word or phrase was being drawn. Its high popularity inspired the 1987 TV game show *Win, Lose, or Draw*, hosted by Vicki Lawrence.

PIGLET

Naive little pig dressed in a pink-striped sweater who lives in a beech tree and is the best friend of "silly old bear" Winnie the Pooh. Piglet is the only animal in Hundred Acre Woods to ever see a real Heffalump.

PIG PEN

> "Pig Pen is the only person who can get dirty walking in a snowstorm."
> —CHARLIE BROWN

The "messiest boy in the world" is a perpetually dirty kid who roams around in a cloud of dust and sprinkles dirt on everything he comes in contact with. Pig Pen made his debut in the *Peanuts* comic strip on July 13, 1954.

"PIGS IN SPACE"

A spoof of both *Star Trek* and *Star Wars*, starring brave Captain Link Heartthrob and amorous Miss Piggy on the starship Swinetrek, seen on *The Muppet Show* (1976–81) as a regular segment.

PIKACHU

The fuzzy yellow critter with the rosy red cheeks is the best known of Japan's Pokemon creatures.

PILLBOX HAT

Created by designer Halston for ultrachic Jackie Kennedy, this style of feminine headwear—resembling a box for carrying pills (round brim and flat top)—first became fashionable in 1961 after Jackie was photographed wearing one at husband John F. Kennedy's presidential inauguration ceremony. Its popularity came to an abrupt halt on November 22, 1963, when the First Lady, wearing a pink pillbox hat, cradled the President's bloody head in her lap after he was struck down by an assassin's bullets while riding in a motorcade in Dallas, Texas. Bob Dylan sang an ode to the hat with "Leopard-Skin Pillbox Hat" (1966).

PILLSBURY DOUGHBOY (POPPIN' FRESH)

"Nothing says loving like something in the oven!" According to a recent *Advertising Age* poll, Poppin' Fresh is the favorite ad character of all time. Since 1966, the plump little fellow made out of white dough and dressed in a chef's hat and kerchief has been entertaining kids and moms alike as the spokesperson for Pillsbury ready-to-bake products. A long-running series of TV spots features the Doughboy popping out of a just-opened Pillsbury container and bashfully blushing, then giggling—tee-hee-hee—after someone playfully pokes a finger in his doughy belly. His popularity led to an onslaught of collectible items—ceramic banks, cookie jars, refrigerator magnets, salt and pepper shakers, and telephones. During the 1970s, vinyl dolls of Poppin' Fresh and his entire family were sold, including wife Poppy Fresh, son Popper, daughter Poppie, baby Bun Bun, grandparents Grandpopper and Grandmopper, Uncle Rollie, cat Biscuit, and dog Flapjack.

FYI: ▸ The Pillsbury Doughboy was created by animator Hal Marsh, the man responsible for giving us other such advertising icons as Mr. Clean, the Frito Bandito, the Hamm's Beer Bear, and the Raid Roaches.

PINE VALLEY

Fictional suburban community somewhere in Pennsylvania (yet not far from New York City), where all the dastardly doings on the ABC-TV daytime soap opera *All My Children* take place. Most famous denizen: the one and only Erica Kane—model, actress, cosmetics executive, and bitch of all bitches.

PINHEAD

"I am pain!" Featured in Clive Barker's *Hellraiser* film series, this acupunctured-head leader of a group of pain-loving demons called the Cenobites is summoned to earth from hell by a mysterious puzzle box. His mission: to find human sinners worthy of a place in hell. Totally scary.

PINK LADIES

Pink-jacketed, gum-smacking, tough-girl gang from Rydell High, led by the scandalous Betty Rizzo and featured in the musical *Grease*.

PINK LADY

Mie Nemoto and Kei Masuda, otherwise known as Pink Lady, were Japan's hottest disco act of the 1970s. Young and beautiful, the spandex-pantsed, tube-topped twosome had a moderately successful record, "Kiss in the Dark," which barely cracked the American Top Forty in the summer of 1979. In 1980, some genius at NBC thought the pair should have their own TV variety show, despite their not being able to speak English and their squeaky "little-girl" singing voices. Produced by Sid and Marty Krofft and titled *Pink Lady and Jeff*, the program's ongoing gimmick was that the girls spoke hardly any English and had to learn about American customs from an unknown comedian, Jeff Altman, who served as their interpreter. Between unfunny comedy sketches, all Pink Lady seemed to do was giggle continually, change into a gazillion skimpy outfits, and sing totally unintelligible versions of American pop hits. Television at its lowest form, and it was canceled after a mere six episodes.

PINK PANTHER

Suave, slinky, and silent, the animated, pink feline who walked upright on two legs was first seen in the opening title sequence of the 1964 spy spoof *The Pink Panther*, starring Peter Sellers as bumbling French Inspector Clouseau. Abetted by Henry Mancini's catchy theme ("Da dum, Da dum, Da dum Da dum Da dum, Da dum, Da dum . . ."), the film's popularity led to a series of *Pink Panther* theatrical cartoon shorts, created by legendary Warner Brothers animator Friz Freleng, which ran throughout the 1960s. In 1968, the Pink Panther came to TV, headlining his own Saturday-morning show. It aired on NBC for nine straight years, becoming one of the network's longest-running cartoon series. Also featured on the program were two other animated segments: "The Ant and the Aardvark," featuring the ongoing strife between a resourceful red ant and an inept blue aardvark, and "Inspector Clouseau," showcasing the misadventures of the Paris police inspector.

How many of you remember the Pink Panther Flakes cereal introduced in the mid-1970s that turned milk an odd shade of pink? Or a joke that played off the *Pink Panther* theme? Q: What did the aardvark say when the ant crossed his path? A: Dead ant, dead ant, dead ant dead ant dead ant, dead ant, dead ant!

FYI: ▸ The *Pink Panther* movie title referred to the panther-like image captured in a diamond when light hit the jewel at the right angle.

PINKY TUSCADERO

Fonzie's old girlfriend (played by Roz Kelly), a fiery-haired motorcycle queen and leader of the pink-jacketed Pinkettes who had Milwaukee's "King of Cool" wrapped around her finger. Younger sister was Leather Tuscadero (Suzi Quatro), a rock star who fronted the Suedes. Pinky and Leather were popular guest stars on *Happy Days* throughout the sitcom's 1976–77 season.

PINTO

The legendary "lemon" of the 1970s! Manufactured by the Ford Motor Company from 1970 to 1976, the friendly-appearing subcompact car came equipped with some serious flaws. It was underpowered—as in having no get-up-and-go, unlike a real-life pinto pony—and cursed with engine and transmission problems. The 1976 model's automatic transmission was infamous for habitually slipping from park to reverse—which was not a good thing because the car also had a tendency to explode when struck from behind. A defect in the gas-tank ventilation system caused the Pinto to ignite on impact, so even the most minimal fender-bender could turn it into an exploding ball of fire. Once a common sight on the roads, it's rare to see a Pinto these days. (Did all of them explode into oblivion?)

PIPPI LONGSTOCKING

"Don't you worry about me. I'll always come out on top." The heroine of a Swedish book series, created by Astrid Lindgren in 1950, who has become one of the most beloved and enduring characters of children's literature. Mischievous, free-spirited, and remarkably strong, Pippi Longstocking was a nine-year-old tomboy, with freckles and carrot-colored, gravity-defying pigtails, whose last name came from the mismatched thigh-high stockings she wore. She lived by herself at Villa Villekulla, a rickety old house on the edge of a little town in Sweden (Pippi's mother was in heaven and her father was a sea captain), with a little monkey, Mr. Nilsson, and a horse, General. Best friends Annika and Tommy, two average kids who lived next door, accompanied Pippi on many incredible escapades.

Extreme fame came for Pippi throughout the 1970s, fueled by a series of Swedish films starring Inger Nilsson as the spunky redhead: *Pippi Longstocking, Pippi in the South Seas, Pippi Goes on Board,* and *Pippi on the Run.* These motion pictures were all filmed in 1969 but never released in the States until the mid-1970s. They're notable for being simplistic, technically flawed, poorly dubbed, and almost unbearable to watch.

PIRANHA

"People eat fish. Fish don't eat people." Frightening movie about a school of toothy little fish developed to be more ferocious in a laboratory experiment for the military. When they are accidentally unleashed in a Texas resort river, Paul Grogran (Bradford Dillman) and Maggie McKeown (Heather Menzies) race against time to warn summer vacationers about the flesh-eating menace swimming their way. Unfortunately for a few swimmers (and one dog), the warning comes too late. Released in 1978, this Roger Corman–produced *Jaws* takeoff was directed by Joe Dante and followed by a sequel, *Piranha II: The Spawning* (1981).

PIRATES OF THE CARIBBEAN

"Dead men tell no tales." Elaborate Disney theme-park attraction employing 123 lifelike audio-animatronic figures that has guests traveling by boat to view scenes of a pirate lair, ghost ships, and a seaport village being pillaged by buccaneers. Located in Disneyland's New Orleans Square and Walt Disney World's Adventureland, POTC is a favorite ride of many visitors. Its theme song is titled "Yo Ho (A Pirate's Life for Me)." Inspired a highly successful big-screen adaptation, *Pirates of the Caribbean: The Curse of the Black Pearl* (2003), starring Johnny Depp as scalawag pirate Jack Sparrow.

FYI: ▸ Pirates of the Caribbean was the last Disneyland attraction the great Walt Disney personally worked on. He passed away four months before it opened on March 18, 1967.

PITT, BRAD

"Being a sex symbol all the time hampers my work." If Pitt isn't the current generation's greatest movie actor, he's definitely its primo male sex symbol; his golden locks and chiseled biceps conjure up memories of a young Robert Redford. Born December 18, 1963, in Oklahoma and raised in Springfield, Missouri, Pitt attended the University of Missouri, where he studied journalism before heading for California in search of fame. A short stint on the daytime soap *Another World* garnered him minor attention, but it was a bit part as a sexy hitchhiker exposing his bare derriere in *Thelma and Louise* (1991) that made viewers worldwide take notice. Quirky, rebellious types are the film roles he's best at performing. Stand-outs include Early Grayce in *Kalifornia* (1993), Floyd in *True Romance* (1993), Louis in *Interview with the Vampire* (1994), Tristan Ludlow in *Legends of the Fall* (1994), Detective David Mills in *Se7en* (1995), Jeffrey Goines in *Twelve Monkeys* (1995), Tyler Durden in *Fight Club* (1999), Mickey O'Neil in *Snatch* (2000), and Rusty Ryan in *Ocean's Eleven* (2001). After long-term romances with actresses Juliette Lewis and Gwyneth Paltrow (remember Brad's and Gwyneth's matching blond shag cuts?), he settled into marriage in 2000 with *Friends* star Jennifer Aniston (and settled out of it in 2005). His clique of high-profile Hollywood friends, dubbed the "Frat Pack," includes George Clooney, Matt Damon, and Julia Roberts.

FYI: ▸ To support himself in prestardom days, Brad Pitt dressed in a chicken suit for El Pollo Loco restaurants.

PIXIE AND DIXIE

A pair of carefree mice, seen as a separate cartoon segment on *The Huckleberry Hound Show,* who constantly pestered a cordial tomcat named Mr. Jinks. ("I love those meeces to pieces!")

PIXIE CUT

Intensely short and waifish, this boyish hairstyle worn by women was named so because it resembled the tresses found on merrymaking elves and other sprite types. First originating overseas, it's believed that four European-flavored actresses—Audrey Hepburn, Leslie Caron, Jean Seberg, and Gina Lollobrigida—introduced this trendy cut to American women in the late 1950s. The pixie's peak years were in the late 1960s and early 1970s, when it was seen on impish celebs like British model Twiggy, comedienne Sandy Duncan, gamine actress Mia Farrow, energetic showgirl Liza Minnelli, "Downtown" singer Petula Clark, Australian songbird Helen Reddy, and kooky Goldie Hawn. Many of the undernourished and gloomy Big Eyes children painted by San Francisco artist Margaret Keane sport this hairdo. It was revived in the 1990s after Canadian supermodel Linda Evangelista, movie actress Demi Moore (for her role in *Ghost*), Wilson Phillips's vocalist Chynna Phillips, and *Dallas* starlet Kimberly Foster had shorn their long locks into this style. The male equivalent is known as the Caesar.

FYI: ▸ Mia Farrow's pixie was a $5,000 cut from Vidal Sassoon. In the horror film *Rosemary's Baby* (1968), her character, Rosemary Woodhouse, returns from the hair salon and inquires of her shocked husband, Guy, "Do you like? It's a Sassoon."

PIXY STIX

A powdered-sugar candy that's packaged in waxy, colored-striped straws. (The stripes match the color and flavor of the Stix: red for cherry, yellow for lemon, green for lime, orange for orange, and so on.) Kids do some dorky things with Pixy Stix. Some slurp all the powder out of the straw at once, and end up with a hacking cough from the dust settling in their throats, while others try snorting it up their nose and wind up with a painful burning sensation in the nose cavity. And by the way, if you want to make a Kool-Aid-type drink from the Pixy Stix powder, it doesn't work. I tried.

PIZZA HUT

Pizza Hut is the world's largest pizza restaurant chain, both in sales and in number of stores. Founded by two brothers, Frank and Dan Carney, college students in Wichita, Kansas, in 1958. The restaurant's trademark is the red roof, and its best-known pizzas are Thin 'n Crispy, Thick 'n Chewy, Super Supreme, Meat Lovers, Stuffed Crust, Pan Pizza, and Personal Pan Pizza. Major competitors over the years have included Chuck E. Cheese, Domino's, Godfather's, Little Caesars, Papa John's, Pizza Inn, Pizza Shoppe, Shakey's, and ShowBiz.

P.J.

"Hey, wow! P.J.'s here!" Move over, Midge. This "far-out" and "with it" gal is Barbie's new best friend. She debuted in 1969 as a talking doll (New 'n Groovy Talking P.J.) dressed in a flower-power micro-mini with hot pants and wearing platinum-blonde hair in twin ponytails wrapped with love beads. Talking P.J. spoke the latest slang, such as "Wow! You're the grooviest!" Other things the fun-loving lass adored were mod hip bubble glasses and zingy knee-high go-go boots of every color. A fashion-doll favorite, P.J. once gave the ever-popular Barbie a run for the money.

FYI: ▸ If you are wondering what the initials P.J. stand for, wonder no more: They stand for nothing!

PLANET OF THE APES

"Take your stinking paws off me, you damn dirty ape!" Director Franklin J. Schaffner's thrilling cinematic sci-fi adventure based on Pierre Boulle's 1963 novel *Monkey Planet*. In the 1968 film, a team of American astronauts led by heroic Colonel George Taylor (Charlton Heston) crash-lands their spaceship (the Icarus) on an unknown planet in the future (A.D. 3978) where evolution has taken a bizarre twist: Human beings are mute primitives, and apes are their intelligent masters. In no time at all, Taylor and crew are captured by an army of horseback-riding simians ruled over by orangutan Dr. Zaius (Maurice Evans) and are caged as animals to be experimented on.

Discovering that Taylor is different because he has higher-than-average intelligence (for a human) and he can talk, a sympathetic chimpanzee scientist couple, Cornelius (Roddy McDowall) and Dr. Zira (Kim Hunter), help him and a beautiful female savage, Nova (Linda Harrison), escape to the Forbidden Zone. The twist at the finale—depicting a half-buried Statue of Liberty—shocked moviegoers because it revealed that the strange world Taylor had landed on is actually earth, where mankind's inclination toward war had destroyed the world, leaving the apes to take over. John Chambers received an Oscar for the exceptional makeup effects; he encased actors in full-body fur and monkey makeup, transforming them into living apes.

The movie was followed by four sequels: *Beneath the Planet of the Apes* (1970), *Escape from the Planet of the Apes* (1971), *Conquest of the Planet of the Apes* (1972), and *Battle for the Planet of the Apes* (1973). It also inspired a 1974 prime-time series, a Saturday-morning cartoon, and a multitude of toy tie-ins, including action figures by Mego, games, model kits, Halloween masks, bubblegum cards, and a lunch box. In the summer of 2001, director Tim Burton's remake of *Planet of the Apes* was released; it starred Mark Wahlberg and had computer-animated special effects.

PLASTIGOOP

Colorful, sludgy liquid plastic that came in squeeze bottles and was used in Mattel's highly popular Thingmaker sets (including Creepy Crawlers, Fright Factory, Creeple People) during the 1960s.

PLATFORM SHOES

It's Friday night, 1977. The disco music is pulsating ("Toot, Toot . . . Heeeey . . . Beep, Beep . . ."), the glittery disco ball is whirling, and the dazzling light show shooting across the nightclub is reminiscent of a laser scene from *Star Wars*. In the middle of all this are sweet young things of every gender, strutting (or wobbling, depending on your perspective) out on the crowded dance floor in a pair of clunky, sky-scraping shoes known as platforms.

Flashy and gaudy, platforms are the footwear associated with the 1970s. On average, a pair had one-to-three-inch soles and heels made out of wood, rubber, or plastic. Before the end of their heyday, they would tower as high as five inches to a toe-deforming, ankle-breaking, orthopedic nightmare of twelve inches. Though not new to the fashion scene—spicey "Brazilian Bombshell" Carmen Miranda, of the extravagant costumes and fruity headgear, wore platforms that had a twelve-inch heel (plus a secret compartment for stashing cocaine while filming her movie musicals in the 1940s)—they were innovative during the 1970s as a balance for the sky-high miniskirt and hot-pants styles that were the rage. Exaggerated versions could be found on glitter rockers Elton John, David Bowie, and KISS and on funkadelic soulsters like George Clinton's Parliament, K.C.'s Sunshine Band, and Rick James, as well as on the female groupies who had the pleasure of being associated with them.

FYI: ▸ In the state of Oklahoma, platforms with heels five inches or taller were illegal to wear when driving a car.

PLAYBOY

"Entertainment for Men." Founded in 1953 by Hugh Hefner, this archetypal girlie magazine, with heavy emphasis on female nudity and ribald humor, is heralded as the leader of the 1960s and 1970s sexual revolution. *Playboy*'s trademark is the stapled-in nude centerfold known as the "Playmate of the Month." Its mascot: a rabbit head that is always cleverly used or hidden somewhere on the magazine cover. Many guys would jokingly declare that they bought the magazine for "reading the interesting articles." *Playboy* paved the way for other girlie magazines, such as *Penthouse* and *Hustler*.

FYI: ▸ *Playboy* magazine's first "Playmate of the Month" was none other than sex goddess Marilyn Monroe (December 1953). Famous Playmates to follow Miss Monroe's belly staple were Jayne Mansfield (February 1955), Claudia Jennings (November 1969), Barbi Benton (March 1970), Dorothy Stratten (August 1979), Shannon Tweed (November 1981), Pamela Anderson (February 1990), Anna Nicole Smith (May 1992), and Jenny McCarthy (October 1993).

PLAYBOY BUNNIES

Swanky Playboy Clubs, for key-holding members only (male of course), employed Bunnies: well-built, gorgeous waitresses in skimpy satin uniforms complete with rabbit ears on their heads and fluffy white tails on their rears. In 1963, feminist Gloria Steinem went undercover as an actual Playboy Bunny to write an exposé of the sexist treatment of the women employed at these clubs. Her story was made into a TV movie, *A Bunny's Tale* (1985), starring Kirstie Alley.

PLAY-DOH

In 1955, Cincinnati inventor Joseph McVicker developed the much-loved modeling compound after his sister-in-law, a nursery school teacher, complained she needed a modeling material that was easy for her young students to manipulate and that wouldn't dry after sitting out for a while. Manufactured by Rainbow Crafts and packaged in tightly sealed little cans, McVicker's Play-Doh was cleaner, softer, and more pliable than regular modeling clay. Parents approved because it wasn't messy and could be used over and over. Kids liked Play-Doh because they could make all kinds of neat creations and it smelled good enough to eat. (Many were tempted to eat the nontoxic stuff, only to be discouraged by the yucky flavor.)

Play-Doh originally came in an off-white color, but in 1956 the color line expanded when blue, red, and yellow were added. In the early 1980s, Play-Doh's palette got another increase with the addition of green, orange, pink, and purple. The distinctive Play-Doh smell (sort of salty and vanilla-ish) is the one toy scent that can make adults recall the days of childhood (runner-ups include Crayola Crayons and Liddle Kiddle Kolognes). Play-Doh's advertising mascot, the blond boy (Play-Doh Pete) wearing a beret and an artist smock on the label, is a drawing of a young French lad who was among the first to test the product before it hit the stores.

FYI: ▸ September 16 is National Play-Doh Day.

PLAY-DOH FUN FACTORY

Introduced in 1960, this play set was actually a toy extruder shaped like a miniature plastic factory, into which you placed a lump of pliable Play-Doh and then pressed a pump handle to squeeze out a shape from one of twelve interchangeable dies. Youngsters had hours of fun churning out blocks, bricks, logs, beads, and various other clay items at assembly-line speed. It later inspired the Fuzzy Pumper Barber and Beauty Shop set, the Fuzzy Pumper Monster set, the Dr. Drill 'n Fill set, the Bakery and Chef's oven set, the Pizza Party and Sandwich set, and the McDonaldland Happy Meal Playshop set.

***PLAYGIRL* MAGAZINE**

Premiering in 1973, this feminine take on Hugh Hefner's *Playboy* and Bob Guccione's *Penthouse* was inspired by the then-current women's lib movement and by movie actor Burt Reynolds's nude centerfold in *Cosmopolitan* magazine (April 1972). Playgirl was the first magazine for women to feature naked male photo spreads, including a foldout centerfold (their version of *Playboy*'s Playmate of the Year and *Penthouse*'s Pet of the Year was called Man of the Year). There were also celebrity interviews, cartoons, a reader's fantasy forum titled "Erotic Encounters," and "how to" sex advice—for example, "How to make your muff irresistible" and "How to give him awesome oral sex."

The early *Playgirl* centerfolds, labeled the "ideal man for every woman," were rugged outdoorsy hunks or suave seductive Europeans or macho stars, including Jim Brown, Fred Williamson, Gary Conway, Peter Lupus, Fabian, George Maharis, Lyle Waggoner, and Sam J. Jones. The nude pictorials at first were shy, with a strategically placed hand or inanimate object (fern, boulder, wine bottle, housecat) covering a man's penis. A year or two later, the magazine got braver and started showing men in all their glory. As the 1980s got under way, the object of *Playgirl*'s centerfolds became the clean-cut Chippendales type: shaven body, six-pack abs, and perfectly coifed hair.

In the early 1990s, believing that their female readers were too sophisticated for nudity, *Playgirl* stopped showing the penis in pictorials, including the famed centerfold. But sales dropped drastically and the monthly periodical went back to "showing it all." A 1995 documentary, *Man of the Year*, by Dirk Shafer, *Playgirl*'s 1992 Centerfold of the Year, revealed the lie behind the myth: A homosexual with a boyfriend, he had been faking being the world's most sexually desirable man for women. *Playgirl*'s success launched a massive wave of gay-oriented publications showcasing naked men: *Advocate Men*, *Blueboy*, *Colt*, *Freshmen*, *Honcho*, *Inches*, *Jock*, *Playguy*, and *Torso*.

"PLAYGROUND IN MY MIND"

Back in the early 1970s, the radio airwaves seemed saturated with sappy, oversentimental pop tunes, such as Ray Stevens's "Everything Is Beautiful" (1970),

Bobby Goldboro's "Watching Scotty Grow" (1971), Sammy Davis's "The Candy Man" (1972), Wayne Newton's "Daddy, Don't You Walk so Fast" (1972), and Donna Fargo's "Funny Face" (1972). However, the one that outsapped them all was this sickeningly-sweet number recorded by a black Tom Jones soundalike named Clint Holmes. In the song, Holmes wistfully recalls the carefree joy of childhood ("My name is Michael / I've got a nickel / I've got a nickel, shiny and new / I'm gonna buy me all kinds of candy / That's what I'm gonna do") in order to lift his spirits when "the whole world gets him down." It sold a million copies and went to the number-two spot for two weeks on the *Billboard* Top Forty in 1973.

PLAYMOBIL

These colorful, elaborate themed play sets for youngsters (medieval kingdoms, ocean worlds, city neighborhoods, and so on) are notable for being the number-one rival of the Fisher-Price Little People sets. Created by Hans Beck, a cabinetmaker in Germany, Playmobil sets have been manufactured and sold worldwide since debuting in 1971 and now come in more than 275 different varieties.

PLEASE DON'T EAT THE DAISIES

A prime-time sitcom (1965–67) about a happy family living in a big, rundown house in the New York suburbs. Set in the community of Ridgemont, it starred Patricia Crowley as Joan Nash, a nontraditional housewife and mother of four sons. Joan was nontraditional in that she didn't cook, disliked housework, slept until midafternoon, had a career (a freelance writer), and couldn't care less about what the nosy neighbors thought (a giant step for a woman back in the prefeminist 1960s). Also featured were Mark Miller as her English professor husband Jim Nash, Kim Tyler as older son Kyle, Brian Nash as middle son Joe, Jeff and Jason Fithian as twins Trevor and Tracey, Ellen Corby as housemaid Martha, and Lord Nelson as Ladadog, the family's large sheepdog. The NBC-TV series was based on Doris Day's 1960 film of the same title, itself based on Jean Kerr's 1957 best-selling book.

PLUTO

Seen in Walt Disney cartoons since debuting in 1930's "The Chain Gang," this lovable orange-colored dog with the playful nature belongs to Mickey Mouse. In Pluto's own cartoon shorts, annoying chipmunks Chip 'n' Dale and little kitten Figaro often bedevil him.

POGO

Quintessential 1980s dance in which you spastically bounced up and down as if riding a pogo stick to songs by The Go-Go's ("We Got the Beat") and other New Wave artists.

POGO STICKS

Boing! Boing! Boing! Fun only for those who could balance and hop at the same time. Those who couldn't, just fell down. Invented by George B. Hansburg in 1919.

POGS

This mid-1990s fad had kids feverishly collecting and trading small, milkcap-like discs (Pogs) that came with all sorts of designs.

POINT

Unusual but charming animated TV special about the adventures of Oblio (voiced by Mike Lookinland of *The Brady Bunch*), a young boy who is banished from the Land of Point because his head is rounded, not pointed like everyone else's. Accompanied by dog Arrow, Oblio journeys to the Point-less Forest, where he encounters strange beings, like a three-headed man, an old Rockman, and a tree known as Leafman who teaches him that prejudice and conformity are pretty silly stuff. Dustin Hoffman narrates this 1971 children's fable, and Harry Nilsson provided the songs, including the Top Forty hit "Me and My Arrow."

POKEMON

"Gotta catch 'em all!" Magical creatures—an assortment of colorful animals and monsters who like to battle—that have been the center of an enormous trading-card fad since the late 1990s. You can also catch 'em on a slew of cartoons, video games, and movies. Pokemon stands for Pocket Monsters.

POKEY

Gumby the Green Clayboy's best pal and sidekick was this spunky black-maned orange pony. Cautious and full of worry, Pokey was often the voice of reason on the *Gumby* TV adventures of the 1950s and 1960s. He also joined Gumby as a bendable rubber toy in the mid-1960s.

POLICE

Sexy, bottle-blond, and showcasing a postpunk reggae pop sound, the British trio was the first New Wave superstar band of the 1980s. Formed in 1977, the group consisted of vocalist Gordon Sumner (Sting), guitarist Andy Summers, and drummer Stewart Copeland. They first arrested the ears of Americans in 1979 with "Roxanne," a song inspired by a Paris prostitute. Other hits included "Message in the Bottle" (1979), "De Do Do Do, De Da Da Da" (1980), "Don't Stand So Close to Me" (1981), "Every Little Thing She Does Is Magic" (1981), "Every Breath You Take" (1983), and "King of Pain" (1983). "Every Breath You Take" topped the American Top Forty for an incredible eight weeks, and its million-selling parent album, *Synchronicity*, crested at number one for an even more incredible seventeen weeks. (It would've been the top-seller of 1983, but that was the year of Michael Jackson's *Thriller.*) Like so many superstar bands, personal disagreements developed among the members, and the band became inactive around 1986.

POLICE WOMAN

Angie Dickinson starred as Sergeant Suzanne "Pepper" Anderson, a sexy blonde divorcée, who worked as an undercover cop for the Los Angeles Police Department. Busting street scum never seemed sexier as Pepper's assignments called for her to pose in many disguises, ranging anywhere from a hooker to a gangster's moll. Her partners on the vice-squad team were Joe Styles (Ed Bernard) and Pete Royster (Charles Dierkop), and all three reported directly to their boss, Lieutenant Bill Crowley (Earl Holliman). Airing on NBC from 1974 to 1978, the TV series was inspired by an episode of the crime anthology *Police Story* titled "The Gamble," also starring Dickinson.

POLLY POCKET

Expansive line of tiny dolls (about one inch high) featuring blonde Polly Pocket. Each came with a plastic compact-like play set that flipped open to reveal colorful, highly detailed houses, shops, zoos, carnivals, playgrounds, pools, and otherworldly fairylands. Bluebird Toys of England introduced Polly and her Lilliputian accessories to the United States in 1989. Today she is manufactured by toy giant Mattel.

POLTERGEIST

Produced by Steven Spielberg, directed by Tobe Hooper, and loaded with spine-tingling special effects, *Poltergeist* is one of the scariest ghost stories ever filmed. It concerns an average California family, the Freelings, set upon by furious poltergeists (German for "noisy ghosts") that turn their suburban home into a house of horrors and mysteriously abduct their youngest daughter via the TV set. It appears that the Freelings' fancy housing development was built on a sacred Indian burial ground and the spirits are angry—and, as all horror fans know, an angry ghost is not a friendly ghost.

The 1982 frightfest starred Craig T. Nelson as concerned father Steve Freeling, JoBeth Williams as brave mother Diane Freeling, Dominique Dunne as overwhelmed eighteen-year-old daughter Dana Freeling, Oliver Robbins as worrisome eight-year-old son Robbie Freeling, and Heather O'Rourke as kidnapped five-year-old Carol Anne Freeling. Also featured are Beatrice Straight as Dr. Lesh, a paranormal psychologist, and Zelda Rubinstein as Tangina, a diminutive psychic. Unforgettable moments are Diane Freeling's chilling dip in the family swimming pool full of rotten corpses, son Robbie's nightmarish bedtime attack by a malevolent clown doll during a lightning storm, and Dr. Lesh's assistant, Ryan (Richard Lawson), ripping his own face off in a bathroom mirror. This cinematic roller coaster of humor-aided terror was followed by two sequels, *Poltergeist II: The Other Side* (1986) and *Poltergeist III* (1988).

FYI: ▸ Along with *Poltergeist*, a list of the greatest ghost stories in movie history would have to include *The Uninvited* (1944), *The House on Haunted Hill* (1959), *Carnival of Souls* (1962), *The Haunting* (1963), *The Amityville Horror* (1979), *The Changeling* (1979), *The Shining* (1980), *The Lady in White* (1988), *Ghost* (1990), *The Sixth Sense* (1999), and *The Others* (2001).

POLTERGEIST CURSE

The horror movie was rumored to have a curse, particularly after the unexpected deaths of two of its young stars, Dominique Dunne and Heather O'Rourke. On Halloween of 1982, the twenty-two-year-old daughter of writer Dominick Dunne and sister of actor Griffin Dunne, was strangled by her estranged boyfriend during a quarrel outside her West Hollywood home. In February 1988, twelve-year-old Heather died suddenly from complications due to a congenital intestinal obstruction.

POLYESTER

"Smelling is believing." Not the cheesy 1970s fabric, but the 1981 cult film by shock director John Waters. After filming tasteless, often bizarre stuff like *Pink Flamingos* (1972), *Female Trouble* (1974), and *Desperate Living* (1977), this was the first of Waters's more mainstream work, which later included *Hairspray* (1988), *Cry-Baby* (1990), *Serial Mom* (1994), and *Pecker* (1998). An outrageous satire on middle-class life, *Polyester* stars obese transvestite Divine as Francine Fishpaw, a forlorn Baltimore housewife whose nightmarish family is driving her to alcoholism.

Francine's awful husband, Elmer (David Samson), a porno-theater proprietor, is sleeping with his secretary, Sandra Sullivan (Mink Stole), a cornrowed floozy, and the neighbors are on the front lawn protesting his being a smut king. Feathered-haired, beer-guzzling teen daughter Lu-Lu (Mary Garlington) go-go dances for boys during school lunch ("For a quarter, I will, I will, I will") and gets knocked up by hoodlum boyfriend Bo-Bo Belsinger (Stiv Bators). Glue-snorting teen son Dexter (Ken King) is the infamous Baltimore Foot Stomper. It's enough to drive a "good Christian" wife and mother to drink. And it does. But all is not lost, thanks to the goodwill of best pal Cuddles Kovinsky (Edith Massey), an aging, dentally challenged debutante; dreamboat Todd Tomorrow (Tab Hunter), a dashing drive-in theater owner; and a can of air freshener.

Polyester featured a wacky gimmick called Odorama. Audience members received a scratch-and-sniff card containing specific scents, ranging from pleasant to putrid, that corresponded to key scenes. When scent-sensitive Francine smelled something, a number appeared on the screen, allowing moviegoers (screaming with delightful disgust) to scratch and then sniff the same smell. The ten scents on the Odorama card were as follows: a rose, a fart, airplane glue, pizza, gasoline, a skunk, natural gas, a new car, a stinky tennis shoe, and air freshener.

POLYESTER LEISURE SUITS

This polyester-woven uniform of the 1970s lounge lizard featured flashy big lapels and wide-flare bells. He would wear a colorful polyester shirt underneath, with half the upper buttons undone to reveal an abundance of chest hair and gold medallion chainage. Throw in platform shoes, blow-dried-to-perfection hair, and the aroma of Aqua Velva—and it's stud city, man! The khaki-toned safari suit was its alternative.

POLYNESIA

The name of the beautiful blue parrot with the yellow chest (a South American macaw) that was the companion of Doctor Dolittle in the 1967 film version of the children's stories.

POM POM GIRLS

Gimme an S! Gimme an E! Gimme an X! What's it spell? "Sex!" Drive-in sleeper about a team of cheerleaders whose only focus was having sex, drinking beer, having more sex, smoking pot, having sex again, taking part in riotous hijinks—oh, and did I mention sex? Laurie, Sally, Judy, Sue Ann, and Roxanne—vivacious members of Rosedale High's pom-pom squad—are intent on raising more than school spirit. They help their football team prepare for the Big Game by making love to various players (including young Robert Carradine), partying, and stealing a fire truck to hose down the opposition, Hardin High. Released by Crown International Pictures in 1976, *The Pom Pom Girls* should be credited as the forerunner of poorly acted, low-budget teen comedies centering on the sophomoric capers of promiscuous, empty-headed chicks and their naked boobies. Seen mostly as drive-in fodder, the most memorable of these titles include *Revenge of the Cheerleaders* (1976), *Gas Pump Girls* (1978), *H.O.T.S.* (1979), *Gimme an "F"* (1984), *Hollywood Hot Tubs* (1984), *Malibu Bikini Shop* (1985), *Stewardess School* (1987), *Assault of the Killer Bimbos* (1988), and *The Bikini Carwash Company* (1990)

PONCHO

Spanish-style, blanket-like cloak with a center slit for the head, popular with both gals and guys in the early 1970s. (The guys who wore these thought they were cool, like Clint Eastwood.) The cool girls had brightly colored ponchos made out of yarn with ornamental yarn pom-poms that dangled at the bottom.

PONDEROSA

A 600,000-acre ranch located on the outskirts of Virginia City, Nevada, owned by Ben Cartwright and sons on the TV western *Bonanza* and named for the ponderosa pines growing there.

PONDEROSA RESTAURANTS

Steakhouse chain inspired by the popularity of *Bonanza* and known for inexpensive, charbroiled steaks and all-you-can-eat salad bars. Sister restaurant is the similar-concept Bonanza.

PONG

It seems archaic compared to today's action-packed, computer-generated Nintendo and Sony play stations, but Atari's Pong, the "father of all electronic games," was the first to feature a video screen and will always be cited as the one that started it all. Pong was first introduced to arcade parlors, bars, and restaurants, before being marketed in 1975 as a home game to be hooked up to TV screens (Tele-Game Pong). Simulating a game of ping-pong, it featured an electronic net that split the TV screen down the center, and an electronic "blip" that served as the ball. A tabletop knob allowed players to move their electronic paddles, and volley the ball back and forth. The longer you played, the faster the volleys would get, making the game more exciting and challenging.

Pong captivated youths of the 1970s, who spent hours glued to TV sets, eyes moving side to side, thumbs and index fingers numb from manipulating the knobs, until weary parents made them turn off the addictive game. By the early 1980s, it would be cast aside as kids flocked to local arcades to play more-sophisticated video games, such as Asteroids, Space Invaders, Galaga, Tempest, Centipedes, Pac-Man, Donkey Kong, and Frogger. Pong inventors Nolan Bushnell and Shigeru Miyamoto would later create Nintendo's Super Mario Brothers.

PONY

Cute 1960s dance: prance like a pony—step, ball, change, step, ball, change, and so on. Introduced by Chubby Checker in 1961 with his "Pony Time" single.

POODLE SKIRTS

These full circular skirts decorated with felt patches of well-coiffed French poodles were the fashion rage for teen gals, called bobby-soxers, in the late 1950s. Poodle skirts looked real nifty when paired with two-tone saddle shoes and a crisp white shirt or soft angora sweater and a tightly cinched neck scarf. Poodle dogs themselves were also the rage. A best-selling canine of the era (rivaling the collie and the Chihuahua), associated with women of the rich and pampered variety (for example, Mrs. Drysdale of *The Beverly Hillbillies*), the froufrou beast appeared commonly as stuffed animals, figurines, and on wall prints.

POP CULTURE EVENTS 101

Welcome, class! Now take a seat. Sit straight and listen up. I'm here to give you the 101 greatest events of pop culture history, beginning with President Kennedy's assassination in 1963 and ending with the Millennium New Year's Eve of 1999.

1963

- President John F. Kennedy is assassinated by Lee Harvey Oswald while riding in a motorcade in Dallas (November 22).

1964

- The Beatles invasion of America begins as screaming fans welcome them at New York's Kennedy Airport (February 7).

1965

- Muhammad Ali wins the first of many world heavyweight boxing titles (February 25).
- The first American combat troops land in South Vietnam (March 8).
- Some 25,000 civil-rights marchers converge on Montgomery, Alabama (March 26).
- "Where were you when the lights went out?" New York is hit by the biggest power outage in history, and nine months later the city has a huge population increase (November 9).

1966
- John Lennon touches off international protest after declaring he and fellow Beatles are "more popular than Jesus Christ" (March 3).
- U.S. deaths exceed Vietnamese for the first time since American soldiers arrived in Vietnam (April).
- Television sci-fi series *Star Trek* takes off into outer space (September 9).

1967
- Football's very first Super Bowl is played as the NFL's Green Bay Packers defeat the AFL's Kansas City Chiefs, 35–10 (January 15).

1968
- Civil-rights leader the Reverend Dr. Martin Luther King Jr. is assassinated in Memphis by James Earl Ray (April 5).
- Presidential contender Senator Bobby Kennedy is assassinated in Los Angeles by Sirhan Sirhan (June 8).
- Bloody clashing between antiwar protesters and police officers marks the Democratic National Convention in Chicago as the most violent political convention in history (August).
- Richard M. Nixon is narrowly elected President of the United States (November 5).

1969
- The Gay Rights movement officially starts when homosexuals, unfairly harassed by police officers for many years, violently fight back outside the Stonewall Inn, a gay hangout in New York's Greenwich Village (June 27).
- After leaving a party, Massachusetts senator Ted Kennedy drives a car off a Chappaquiddick bridge and flees the scene, leaving female passenger Mary Jo Kopechne to drown (July 18).
- Apollo 11's Neil Armstrong becomes the first man to set foot on the moon (July 20).
- Followers of cult leader Charles Manson commit bloody Helter Skelter on movie sex symbol Sharon Tate and four others in the hills above Hollywood (August 9).
- "Three days of peace and music." More than 400,000 Baby Boomer hippies gather in Woodstock, New York, for a weekend of peace, music, and love (August 17).
- Hundreds of thousands evacuate when Hurricane Camille ravages the Gulf Coast, killing 300 (August 17).
- "Here's a story. . . ." TV's favorite family, *The Brady Bunch*, debuts (September 26).
- Sesame Street and its lovable Muppets debut on PBS (November 10).

1970
- Four students are shot dead on the campus of Kent State University in Ohio after National Guardsmen open fire during an antiwar protest (April 4).
- The first Earth Day, a celebration of the earth's ecology, is observed (April 22).
- Legendary rock guitarist Jimi Hendrix dies of a drug overdose at age twenty-seven (September 18).
- Legendary rock vocalist Janis Joplin dies of a drug overdose at age twenty-seven (October 4).

1971
- Controversial rock star Jim Morrison of the Doors dies of a drug overdose at age twenty-seven (July 3).
- The vote is granted to eighteen-year-old Americans (July 25).
- Walt Disney World opens in Orlando, Florida (October 1).

1972
- Hirsute movie actor Burt Reynolds poses in the buff for a centerfold in the women's lib magazine *Cosmopolitan* (April).

1973
- At 1,700 feet aloft, completion of Chicago's Sears Tower makes it the tallest building in the world, beating the twin towers of New York's World Trade Center (May 3).

1974
- Nineteen-year-old newspaper heiress Patricia Hearst is kidnapped in Berkeley, California, by the Symbionese Liberation Army (SLA) and brainwashed into becoming "Citizen Tania," a bank-robbing terrorist (February 4).
- Richard Nixon becomes the first President of the United States ever to resign, because of his involvement in the Watergate scandal (August 8).

- Daredevil stuntman Evel Knievel makes a highly publicized but unsuccessful one-mile jump over Idaho's Snake River in his rocket-powered motorcycle (September 8).

1975
- The last remaining U.S. citizens are airlifted out of Saigon as the South Vietnam capital falls to Vietnamese Communist forces, leading to the end of the Vietnam War (April 29).
- Microsoft (short for microcomputer software) is founded by Bill Gates (November 29).

1976
- America celebrates its Bicentennial (July 4).
- Former Georgia governor Jimmy Carter is elected U.S. President (November 2).

1977
- The dance party is on as the legendary Manhattan discotheque Studio 54 opens its doors (April 16).
- The awe-inspiring, F/X-laden *Star Wars*—the most influential sci-fi flick in the history of cinema—is released (May 25).
- "The King is dead." More than 80,000 mourn the death of singer Elvis Presley at his Graceland mansion in Memphis, Tennessee (August 17).
- The sensational dancing of John Travolta in *Saturday Night Fever,* and the accompanying Bee Gees soundtrack, sets off an international epidemic of disco fever (December 16).

1978
- Louise Brown, the world's first test-tube baby, is born in Manchester, England (July 26).
- The Reverend Jim Jones and 908 of his followers of the People's Temple, a religious cult, commit mass suicide through cyanide-laced Kool-Aid in Jonestown, Guyana (November 28).

1979
- Three Mile Island near Harrisburg, Pennsylvania, becomes the site of the worst nuclear accident in U.S. history (March 31).
- Followers of the Ayatollah Khomeini seize the U.S. Embassy in Tehran, Iran, and hold sixty-six Americans hostage for 444 days (November 26).

1980
- The underdog U.S. hockey team wins the gold medal after beating the favored Finnish and Russian teams at the Winter Olympics (February 22).
- Mount Saint Helens, a long-dormant volcano, erupts in southeastern Washington State (May 19).
- The era of Reagonomics and *Star Wars* begins when conservative Republican Ronald Reagan defeats liberal Democrat Jimmy Carter as America's fortieth President (November 4).
- Who shot J.R.? (November 21).
- John Lennon is shot dead outside his Manhattan apartment by crazed fan Mark David Chapman (December 8).

1981
- Would-be assassin John Hinckley Jr. shoots and wounds President Ronald Reagan outside the Washington Hilton Hotel (March 30).
- Japan's hungry Pac-Man arrives in American arcades and revolutionizes the video-game industry (June).
- Britain's Prince Charles and Lady Diana Spencer marry (July 29).
- MTV debuts, and the way we look at music will never be the same (August 1).
- The first reports of homosexual men dying of a mysterious immune-damaging plague begin to surface (December).

1982
- Like totally, the teenage gals from Southern California's San Fernando Valley are, like, the focus of a bitchin' novelty song, "Valley Girl" (August).
- Princess Grace of Monaco is killed when her car hurtles 120 feet off a mountain road (September 14).
- Michael Jackson's landmark *Thriller* is released, becoming the number-one album of all time (December).

1983
- Pop singer Karen Carpenter dies of anorexia at the age of thirty-two (February 4).
- Vinyl beware. . . . The CD (compact disc) is launched by Philips and Sony (March 2).
- First Lady Nancy Reagan appears on an episode

of TV's *Diff'rent Strokes* to promote her "Just say no" antidrug campaign (March 19).

1984

- American and French research scientists discover the micro-organisms that cause AIDS (Acquired Immune Deficiency Syndrome), a terrible disease that attacks the immune system and leaves victims unable to resist infections (April 23).
- Vanessa Williams, the first black to be crowned Miss America, is forced from her throne after prepageant nudes appear in *Penthouse* magazine (July 23).
- Scientists give the first warnings of global warming, also known as the "greenhouse effect" (October).

1985

- Screen idol Rock Hudson dies of AIDS (October 2).

1986

- Seventy-four seconds after liftoff from Cape Canaveral, the space shuttle Challenger explodes into a ball of fire, killing all seven crew members, including schoolteacher Christa McAuliffe (January 31).

1987

- The Reverend Jim Bakker and teary-eyed wife Tammy Faye fall from grace following his sexual affair with Jessica Hahn and charges of embezzling money from their TV ministry, The PTL (Praise the Lord) Club (July 3).
- Eighteen-month-old Baby Jessica (McClure) falls down an abandoned well shaft in Midland, Texas, and—as an on-edge nation watches—is rescued two and a half days later (October 16).
- Worldwide stock markets crash on "Black Monday," ending the era of yuppies (October 19).

1988

- "I have sinned." Self-righteous tele-evangelist Jimmy Swaggart is nabbed red-handed with a New Orleans prostitute (February 21).
- Brat-Packer Rob Lowe gets caught with his pants down after a videotaped sexual rendezvous with two others, including a minor, in a hotel room becomes a bootlegged favorite (July).
- Terrorists bomb Pan Am Flight 103—en route to New York City from London—over Lockerbie, Scotland, killing all 259 aboard, plus eleven people on the ground (December 21).

1989

- Spoiled rich kids Erik and Lyle Menendez murder their parents in Beverly Hills for insurance money (August 20).
- During live TV coverage of the World Series between the San Francisco Giants and Oakland A's, the San Francisco area is shaken by a devastating earthquake (October 17).
- The Berlin Wall falls (November 10).

1991

- The title of Douglas Coupland's book, *Generation X*, is adopted as the name for the generation born in the 1960s and 1970s (January).
- "The mother of all battles." Gen-Xers get their first taste of combat (the Persian Gulf War, a.k.a. Operation Desert Storm) when the United States and its allies attack Iraq to liberate Kuwait (January 16).
- A jury in Indianapolis finds boxing thug Mike Tyson guilty of raping Desirée Washington, a Miss Black America contestant (February 10).

1992

- "People, can't we all get along?" For several days, race riots ravage Los Angeles, particularly the neighborhoods of South Central, after four white police officers are handed a verdict of not guilty for the severe beating of black Rodney King in a videotaped incident (April 29).
- Amy Fisher, the sixteen-year-old "Long Island Lolita," shoots Mary Jo Buttafuoco, the wife of her much older lover, Joey (May 19).
- With 150-mile-an-hour winds, Hurricane Andrew slams into the southern Florida coast (barely missing downtown Miami), killing thirteen, rendering 250,000 homeless, and causing $20 billion in damages (August 24).
- Bill Clinton becomes the first Baby Boomer elected President of the United States (November 3).

1993

- Foreshadowing future events, New York's World Trade Center is rocked after bombs planted by Islamic terrorists explode in the underground parking garage (February 26).
- The "Great Flood of 1993" leaves thirty-three dead and 70,000 homeless and causes $12 billion in property damage along the Mississippi River and its tributaries in the Midwest (April–July).
- L.A. party girl Heidi Fleiss is busted by cops for being a madam for high-class call girls catering to the rich and famous of Hollywood (June 9).

1994

- Early-morning peace in Los Angeles comes to an abrupt halt when a major earthquake (Northridge Quake), measuring somewhere between 6.6 and 6.8 on the Richter scale, shatters the vicinity (January 17).
- White-trash figure skater Tonya Harding hires an assailant to club the knee of Olympic rival Nancy "Whymeeee!" Kerrigan (January 6).
- "Run, O.J., Run!" In an eerie low-speed chase, O.J. Simpson flees from police in his white Ford Bronco—watched live on TV by ninety-five million people—and later surrenders to be charged with the brutal murders of ex-wife Nicole Brown Simpson and her friend Ronald Goldman (June 12).
- Drug-addicted Kurt Cobain, lead singer of the grunge rock band Nirvana, dies of a self-inflicted gunshot at age twenty-seven (August 4).
- The twentysomething favorite *Friends*, a sitcom centering on six young New Yorkers, debuts to high ratings (September 22).

1995

- After telling officers a lie that a black carjacker had kidnapped her two sons, South Carolina mother Susan Smith confesses to drowning the boys by driving them into a lake (January 16).
- A powerful truck bomb rips apart the Alfred P. Murrah Federal Building in Oklahoma City, killing 168 people, including young children in a day-care center (April 19).

1996

- Six-year-old beauty queen JonBenet Ramsey is found murdered in the basement of her affluent parents' home in Boulder, Colorado (December 25).

1997

- Italian fashion designer Gianni Versace is gunned down outside his South Beach residence by gay serial killer Andrew Cunanan in Miami (July 15).
- People worldwide mourn Princess Diana after she, and boyfriend Dodi Fayed, dies in a car crash in a Paris tunnel while trying to flee pursuing paparazzi (August 31).

1998

- "I never had sex with that woman." President Bill Clinton admits to having sexual encounters (oral sex) with White House intern Monica Lewinsky (September 21).

1999

- At Columbine High School in Littleton, Colorado, two students go on a shooting rampage, killing fourteen students, one teacher, and themselves (April 20).
- John F. Kennedy Jr.; his wife, Carolyn; and her sister Lauren Bessette are killed when the small plane he is piloting crashes into the Atlantic Ocean (July 17).
- Instead of three days of peace and love, Woodstock '99 features three days of mud wars, fires, and rape (July 27).
- The Millennium Y2K doomsayers were wrong. The world didn't end at midnight on December 31, 1999 (December 31).

POPEYE

"I yam what I yam." Well, blow me down! The spinach-chomping, pipe-smoking sailorman with the oversized forearms was originally introduced as a comic-book character by Elzie Segar in 1929, before becoming the star of more than 450 animated shorts for the Fleischer Studios. (Popeye has appeared in more theatrical and TV cartoons than any other character.) As all kids know, spinach gave Popeye his massive strength to fell bully opponents, like Bluto or Brutus, for trying to move on gangly sweetheart Olive Oyl. Regulars featured with crafty-faced Popeye included hamburger-mooching Wimpy, adopted infant Swee'pea, crusty papa

Poopdeck Pappy, witch Sea Hag, and a fantastic African creature known as Eugene the Jeep. Popeye inspired many food-finicky types to eat their spinach, a leafy green vegetable considered yucky by most youths. A big-screen musical directed by Robert Altman was filmed in 1980, starring comic Robin Williams as Popeye, Shelley Duvall as Olive Oyl, and Paul Smith as Bluto. "I'm strong to the finich, 'cause I eats my spinich!"

POP-O-MATIC

The "automatic cube shaker" that comes with the games Trouble, Headache, and Frustration lets you roll the playing dice by pushing on a clear dome in the center of the game board. (A hidden spring underneath pops it back up, scrambling the dice.)

POPPLES

A collection of colorful fuzzy and magical creatures who were able to produce just about any object out from pouches on their backs when in a scrape. They also could flip into their pouches to become balls of fuzz for bouncing and hiding. The name Popples came from the popping sound they made when they sprang back to normal out of a ball. Only two children, Bonnie and Billy (in whose attic they lived), knew of their existence. Featured in a TV cartoon (1986–87) based on a series of toys created by American Greeting Cards.

POP ROCKS

Pop Rocks were the hottest-selling candy fad in pop culture history, with more than 500 million packages sold, from 1975 to 1980. Originally manufactured by cereal maker General Mills, the colorful, fruit-flavored, sugar-sweet little pieces of carbonated nuggets fizzed and popped when mixed with saliva in your mouth. Many schools—including my senior high—banned Pop Rocks because the popping noise annoyed teachers, who also felt that students were being distracted from learning.

The crackling noise could be annoying, and some users found the exploding Pop Rocks painful to the palate—but a false rumor caused General Mills to halt production of the candy in 1980: Little Mikey (Michael Gilchrist), the "He likes it!" tot who had starred in Life cereal commercials in the early 1970s, had swallowed one to three packages of Pop Rocks, then washed it all down with a can of Coca-Cola (or Dr. Pepper, depending on who tells the story). The high concentration of carbonation from both the candy and the soda combined caused Mikey's stomach to explode, and he died. (In reality, Gilchrist is alive and well, working today as a radio ad executive in New York.) In 1985, Carbonated Candy Ventures of Buffalo reintroduced Pop Rocks, now calling them an "action candy" that "provides entertainment for the entire mouth."

POP-TARTS

Loved by those who can never get enough sugar, these frosted toaster pastries introduced by Kellogg's in 1964 are distinguished by their flat rectangular shape and cream- or fruit-filled centers and come packed in twos in a foil package. You pop Pop-Tarts in the toaster to heat them (a word of warning: let them cool down a bit before you bite into them, because the just-heated filling is a mouth-scorcher) or eat them cold—my favorite way. Over the years, some of the delicious flavors of Pop-Tarts have included Blueberry, Cherry, Strawberry, Grape, Raspberry, Apple Cinnamon, Brown Sugar, Chocolate Fudge, Vanilla Creme, S'mores, and Peanut Butter and Jelly. Milton the Toaster was once the Pop-Tarts animated advertising icon, and its toaster food rivals were Danish-Go-Rounds and Eggos.

PORIZKOVA, PAULINA

Known simply as Paulina, a supermodel from Poland who gave men of average looks hope when she dated and later married the odd-looking tall and lanky Ric Ocasek, frontman of The Cars, in 1989 (David Letterman called him the "luckiest man alive"). She had been previously featured in two of The Cars' award-winning music videos, "You Might Think" and "Drive." Throughout the 1980s, the blue-eyed brunette—a *Sports Illustrated* swimsuit favorite—was the spokes-model for the prestigious Estée Lauder cosmetics line. Paulina turned to acting in the films *Anna* (1987) and *Her Alibi* (1989).

PORKY PIG

This shy, simpleminded, speech-impaired swine was the first Looney Tunes superstar. After making his debut in 1935's "I Haven't Got a Hat," he went on to star in more than 100 cartoon shorts, frequently appearing with sweetheart Petunia Pig and nemeses Daffy Duck, Bugs Bunny, and Sylvester the Cat. His stutter, voiced by Mel Blanc, is famous for ending Warner Brothers cartoon shorts with the sign-off "Th-th-th—that's all folks!" From 1964 to 1967, *The Porky Pig Show* aired on Saturday-morning TV.

FYI: ▸ Animator Friz Freleng named Porky Pig after a childhood playmate he recalled as being "very fat."

PORKY'S

"You'll be glad you came!" A raunchy, low-budget sex comedy—full of dumb humor and naked women—that appealed to the average horny teenage boy of the 1980s. Set in South Florida during the 1950s, it centered on a group of testosterone-driven youths attending school at Angel Beach High who try to lose their virginity at a redneck cathouse called Porky's. It's a funny, now-legendary shower scene that the movie is best remembered for: The guys are peeping through a hole in the locker room at naked girls until an encounter with bulldog-esque gym mistress Miss Balbricker. (You have to pity the unfortunate lad who decides to stick his penis through the hole. Ouch!) The cast of mostly unknowns included Mark Herrier as Billy, Wyatt Knight as Tommy, Roger Wilson as Mickey, Dan Monahan as Pee Wee, Scott Colomby as Brian Schwartz, Kaki Hunter as Wendy Williams, Kim Cattrall as Miss Honeywell, Alex Karras as the Sheriff, Susan Clark as Cherry Forever, and Nancy Parsons as Miss Balbricker. Directed by Bob Clark, *Porky's* was the surprise box-office hit of 1982, spawning two sequels: *Porky's 2: The Next Day* (1983) and *Porky's Revenge* (1985). It procreated a teen-sex genre brimming with countless B-movie rip-offs, including *The Last American Virgin* (1982), *Losin' It* (1983), *My Tutor* (1983), *Private School* (1983), *Screwballs* (1983), *Spring Break* (1983), *Hardbodies* (1984), and *Hot Dog . . . The Movie* (1984).

PORT CHARLES

Fictional hometown of the long-running soap opera *General Hospital*, said to be located near Buffalo, New York.

PORTER RICKS

The chief ranger at the Coral Key Park, a marine refuge in Florida, responsible for keeping the wildlife and scuba divers in the area safe. Nicknamed "Po," he is a humane and strong widower who lives in a small beach cottage with two young sons, Sandy and Bud, and who befriends a courageous dolphin called Flipper. Handsome Brian Kelly starred as Porter Ricks in the kid-friendly *Flipper* show of the 1960s.

POSEIDON ADVENTURE

"Hell, upside down!" It's New Year's Eve, and the crew and passengers of the luxury ocean liner S.S. *Poseidon*, en route from New York to Athens, are reveling in the festivities of champagne and "Auld Lang Syne" totally unaware of what's in store for them. An undersea earthquake spawning a monstrous ninety-foot tidal wave has occurred, and the *Poseidon* is headed in its path. Exactly at midnight, the gigantic wave slams into the *Poseidon* and overturns her. Stunned partyers in the Grand Salon Ballroom are left tilting and sliding toward the ceiling, while others dangle from upside-down bolted tables and eventually fall to their death. Left capsized and on the verge of sinking, a handful of survivors struggles to make the perilous adventure to the bottom—now the top—of the ship in order to escape the steadily rising water. Who will survive?

Based on Paul Gallico's 1969 suspense novel, the granddaddy of all 1970s disaster films was directed by Ronald Neame in 1972. Its cast included Gene Hackman as the determined Reverend Frank Scott, Ernest Borgnine as tough cop Mike Rogo, Stella Stevens as Rogo's ex-prostitute wife, Linda, Jack Albertson as middle-aged Manny Rosen, Oscar-nominated Shelley Winters as Manny's mountainous, life-saving wife, Belle, Red Buttons as lonely bachelor James Martin, Carol Lynley as freaked-out pop singer Nonnie Parry, Pamela Sue Martin as pretty seventeen-year-old Susan Shelby, Eric Shea as Susan's inquisitive ten-year-old brother, Robin, Roddy McDowall as steward Acres, and Leslie Nielsen as the ship's doomed captain.

The Poseidon Adventure's Oscar-winning special effects, all-star cast, and whopping $100 million box-office gross inspired a new genre of filmmaking: the big-cast disaster extravaganza (for example, *The Towering Inferno* and *Earthquake*). The theme, "The Morning After," won an Academy Award for Best Song and became a number-one Top Forty hit for Maureen McGovern (sang by Lynley in the film). A lifeless sequel was released in 1979, *Beyond the Poseidon Adventure*, starring Michael Caine, Sally Field, and Telly Savalas.

POTSIE WEBBER
First name: Warren. Richie Cunningham's cute but slightly nerdy best friend, played by Anson Williams on the TV sitcom *Happy Days*.

POTTSYLVANIA
Fictional dictatorship on the *Bullwinkle* cartoon show, located somewhere in Eastern Europe during the cold war, where everyone is a spy. Most famous citizens: the dastardly Boris Badenov and Natasha Fatale, whose mission is to destroy Rocky and Bullwinkle.

POUND PUPPIES
Introduced in 1985 by the Tonka Corporation, these were "Lovable puppies that need a home!" Like the Cabbage Patch Kids, these adorable, adoptable stuffed pups were looking for children to provide them with a good home and lots of love. Their first-year success inspired a kitty version known as Pound Purries, and together they became the biggest-selling toy line of 1986.

POWERPUFF GIRLS
What are little girls made of? Sugar, spice, and everything nice—or so thought Professor Utonium when he used these ingredients in his laboratory to make the perfect little girl. However, his lab assistant, a mad monkey genius named Mojo Jojo, put a dash of Chemical X into the mix, leaving the Professor with not one but three perfect little girls gifted with mighty crime-fighting powers. Called the Powerpuff Girls, the superhero trio—sweetie-pie blonde Bubbles (sugar), hot-headed brunette Buttercup (spice), and take-charge redhead Blossom (everything nice)—reside with the Professor in a suburban home on the outskirts of Townsville. They attend kindergarten at Pokey Oaks School, supervised by sunny teacher Miss Keane, where they like to color (Bubbles's fave pastime), play superpowered games of hopscotch in the schoolyard, and have puppy-love crushes on boys (except for Elmer, a glue-eating classmate). Saving Townsville (and the rest of the world) before bedtime, they battle such would-be conquering villains as the Gang Green Gang, redneck Fuzzy Lumpkins, "Him" (the devil), and the Professor's ex-assistant Mojo Jojo. The animated *Powerpuff Girls* TV show was developed by Craig McCracken, who originally called them "Whoopass Girls," for the Cartoon Network in 1997.

PRAIRIE DAWN
The sweet, levelheaded Muppet with the blonde pigtail braids was featured as a supporting player on *Sesame Street* throughout the 1970s.

PRECIOUS MOMENTS
These Christian-oriented, pastel-colored figurines of teardrop-eyed children accompanied by inspirational sayings on their base were created by midwesterner Sam Butcher in the 1970s. Those who collect Hummel figurines from Germany tend to also collect these.

PRECIOUS PUPP
The prankish cartoon hound with a snickering laugh, who fools his owner, Granny Sweet, a motorcycle-riding old biddy, into believing he's a "precious pup," appeared on a regular supporting cartoon segment on *The Atom Ant Show*.

PRELL
Had memorable TV ads in the late 1960s of a pearl being dropped in its bottle to prove how rich and thick the iridescent green shampoo was as it sunk to the bottom. In the 1980s, spokes-model Christie Brinkley claimed to use Prell (perhaps, but most likely not on her hair). Truth be known, Prell is great for stripping out unwanted hair color.

PREPPIES
Bored with bell-bottoms, polyester, and disco glitz, middle-class American youths took a conservative swing in the early 1980s and adopted the appearance and characteristics of preppies, a term used to describe the privileged upper class who attend exclusive prep schools scattered throughout the northeastern United States. A stereotypical preppy

was a collegiate Wasp type (think sorority or fraternity) who habitually dressed in a pastel-colored polo shirt (Lacoste Izod or Ralph Lauren Polo) with collar turned up, sweater draped over shoulders, khaki pants, or a khaki skirt belted with a thin canvas belt, and moccasin-like Sperry Top-Siders sans socks. Or they sported a blazer over an argyle vest over an oxford-cloth button-down shirt, a pair of corduroy slacks, Bass penny loafers with pennies inserted in the slits, and Ray-Ban sunglasses. Other fashion faves were Bermuda shirts, boxer shorts, cable knits, cashmere, Duck shoes, hair bands, madras plaid, and monograms.

Preppies had nicknames like Biff, Skip, Chip, Muffy, and Buffy and shopped at such clothiers as Brooks Brothers, J. Crew, Lands' End, and L. L. Bean. Smelled like Ralph Lauren's Polo (guys) or Lauren (girls). Attended prestigious Ivy League colleges like Brown, Harvard, Princeton, Vassar, and Yale. Took part in field hockey, golf, lacrosse, rowing, rugby, and tennis. Socialized at exclusive country clubs, where they drank "G and Ts" (gin and tonics). Vacationed at Martha's Vineyard (yachting), Vail (skiing), and Bermuda (swimming). Drove Jeeps and Alfa Romeos. Owned Labrador retrievers. Voted Republican, as in Ronald Reagan and George H. W. Bush. And spoke in snobbish-sounding, drawn-out acce-e-e-ented vowels, known as Locust Valley Lockjaw.

Preppy prototypes seen on prime-time TV: Michael J. Fox's Alex Keaton of *Family Ties*, Lisa Whelchel's Blair Warner of *The Facts of Life*, and both Julia Duffy's Stephanie Vanderkellen and Peter Scolari's Michael Harris of *Newhart*. Inevitably, preppies evolved into the materialistic, power-suited yuppies of the later 1980s.

FYI: ▸ Tacky, tacky. A big preppy no-no was to sport a Lacoste Alligator simultaneously with a Ralph Lauren Polo Pony. And never, ever be caught dead wearing the LeTigre Tiger.

PREPPY HANDBOOK

"Look, Muffy, a book for us." *The Official Preppy Handbook* was a 1980 best-seller in which author Lisa Birnbach, tongue planted firmly in cheek, guided readers on how to look, speak, and act like an Ivy League prepster. It inspired a handful of parodies, such as *The Joy of Stuffed Preppies, The Official I Hate Preppies Handbook*, and *101 Uses for a Dead Preppy*.

PRETENDERS

Strumming a mean guitar, singing in a brash style, and wearing a jet-black, spiky, bi-level hairdo, Chrissie Hynde (born September 7, 1951, in Akron, Ohio) fronted this landmark group, whose popularity led to the emergence of early-1980s rock acts headed by female vocalists (for instance, Motels' Martha Davis, Quarterflash's Rindy Ross, Blackhearts' Joan Jett, and Scandal's Patty Smyth). After attending school at Ohio's Kent State University, Hynde moved to London, where in 1978 she assembled a band consisting of Brits: guitarist James Honeyman-Scott, bassist Peter Farndon, and drummer Martin Chambers. Inspired by The Platters' 1955 tune "The Great Pretender," the quartet named themselves The Pretenders. Hit songs included the moody "Brass in Pocket (I'm Special)" (1980) and the festive "2000 Miles" (1983), along with "Back on the Chain Gang" (1983), "Middle of the Road" (1984), "Thin Line Between Love and Hate" (1984), and "Don't Get Me Wrong" (1986). In 1985, Hynde dueted with reggae octet UB40 in a remake of Sonny and Cher's "I Got You Babe."

PRETTY IN PINK

Written by John Hughes and directed by Howard Deutch, this 1986 film tells the timeless story of the poor kid from the wrong side of the tracks who falls for a rich kid from the right side of the tracks. This one stars Brat Pack princess Molly Ringwald as Andie Walsh, a virtuous teenager living in a working-class home with her unemployed dad (Harry Dean Stanton). Andie wears second-hand, thrift-store duds, works part time at a record shop (Trax) run by zany Iona (Annie Potts), hangs out with nerdy New Wave pal Duckie Dale (Jon Cryer), and has a crush on popular, well-to-do kid Blaine McDonnagh (Andrew McCarthy). She attends Meadowbrook High, a suburban school ruled by an affluent clique known as "the richies," led by Blaine's hissably evil buddy Steff McKee (James Spader), who enjoys tormenting the lower-class students. In one heart-tugging scene, Andie gets taunted by the rich bitches in history class, who inquire sneeringly: "Where'd you get your clothes? Five-and-dime store? Attractive."

When adorable Blaine asks Andie out on a date, the twosome encounter social pressure from both sets of peers, who succeed in keeping them apart—that is, until the night of the senior prom, when Andie, dressed "pretty in pink" in a converted vintage prom dress, and Blaine, realizing what a fool he's been to let Steff dictate how he should feel, reunite and kiss while OMD's "If You Leave" plays in the background. Ahhhh, love conquers all. The top-selling soundtrack featured not only "If You Leave" but also an assortment of New Wave nuggets, like Echo and the Bunnymen's "Bring on the Dancing Horses," New Order's "Shell-Shock," and the 1981 title cut by The Psychedelic Furs.

PRETTY WOMAN

This modern spin on the Cinderella fairy tale has lovable streetwalker Vivian Ward (Oscar-nodded Julia Roberts) hired to escort a rich corporate raider for a week in Los Angeles. Not really digging the hooking thing (she's just a runaway who fell on tough times), Vivian has fantasies that come true rooming with handsome Edward Lewis (Richard Gere) at the exclusive Beverly Wilshire Hotel. She accompanies him to fancy soirees, fine restaurants, and Rodeo Drive shopping in Beverly Hills (where the stuck-up salesclerks try to burst her bubble). Alas, the week is over—Vivian and Edward's business arrangement is finished. She has real feelings for Edward, and he has feelings for her too, but, sadly, a Wall Street millionaire and a Hollywood hooker can never be together. Wipe your tears—it's a movie, which means the ending is joyful. Before Edward leaves for home, he whisks Vivian off the streets to live happily ever after. Directed by Garry Marshall, the 1990 mega-hit made twenty-three-year-old Georgia native Julia Roberts an overnight star. Distinguished by a vivacious smile and spiral-curled hair, Roberts is among Hollywood's highest-paid actresses, reportedly getting $20 million per film.

PRICE IS RIGHT

"Come on down!" Exciting price-guessing game show that features four contestants from the studio audience bidding on merchandise, with the successful bidder proceeding on to various games. It's been hosted by the amiable Bob Barker, assisted by a bevy of beautiful showcase models, since 1972. Barker is also known for hosting another game show, *Truth or Consequences* (1956–77), and the Miss U.S.A. Pageant. (An avid animal lover, he quit the pageant because they gave real furs as one of the prizes.)

PRINCE

Back in the 1980s, before changing his name to that unpronounceable symbol, the "Artist Formerly Known as Prince" was the most innovative, influential, and controversial artist of the modern music world. His keyboard-dominated, funky-erotic "Minneapolis Sound" ruled over dance floors across the nation while monopolizing the soul and pop charts as well. The self-taught multimusician and songwriter with a flair for sexually explicit lyrics was born Prince Rogers Nelson on June 7, 1958, in Minneapolis, Minnesota. His raw "I Wanna Be Your Lover" (1979) led a string of dance hits, including "Controversy" (1981), "Little Red Corvette" (1983), and the ultimate Millennium New Year's Eve party song, "1999" (1983).

In 1984, Prince wrote and starred in the blockbuster semi-autobiographical movie *Purple Rain*. Its soundtrack sold a million albums on the first day of release, topped the charts for twenty-four weeks, and spawned two number-one songs: "When Doves Cry" and "Let's Go Crazy." Other chart-smashing Prince songs, "Raspberry Beret" (1985), "Pop Life" (1985), "Kiss" (1986), and a duet with Sheena Easton, "U Got the Look" (1987). Over time, he has written and produced many tunes for other singers, like Easton's naughty "Sugar Walls" (1985), The Bangles' wistful "Manic Monday" (1986), and Sinead O'Connor's heartfelt "Nothing Compares 2 U" (1990), and played a major role in discovering and nurturing such acts as Morris Day, Vanity, Appollonia, Sheila E., and Wendy and Lisa (his backup singers).

During the mid-1980s, Prince's flamboyant fashion style, reminiscent of romantic eighteenth-century France—satin duster-jackets, tight-fitting pants, ruffled shirts, high-heeled boots (he's short), and lace clothing (fingerless gloves, bibs, shirt cuffs)—was a trendy look for both men and women.

PRINCESS CHARMA

Residing in *Harvey* comics' Enchanted Forest, this lovely blonde fairy could charm the devil out of Hot Stuff, the Little Devil.

PRINCESS DI CUT
Throughout fair-haired Diana's life as a celebrated princess, her wash-and-wear cuts were cloned by women on both sides of the Atlantic, particularly hairdresser Kevin Shanley's feathered and layered page boy, which she wore around the time she wed Charles in 1981, and the stylish, ultramodern, chin-level bob she sported at the time of her death in 1997.

PRINCESS JASMINE
In Disney's 1992 *Aladdin* movie, this exotic beauty is the spunky daughter of the royal Sultan of Agrabah. Bored with palace life, she sneaks out incognito to the busy marketplace, where she meets her true love—a handsome street thief named Aladdin. Jasmine has a benevolent and protective pet tiger named Rajah.

PRINCESS LEIA ORGANA
The Rebel Alliance's beautiful and strong-willed leader—daughter of Viceroy Bail Organa of the planet Alderaan—in George Lucas's *Star Wars* saga (played by Carrie Fisher, daughter of actress Debbie Reynolds and singer Eddie Fisher). Princess Leia's trademark was wearing her brunette hair in braided buns on both sides of her head.

PRINCESS TOADSTOOL
In Nintendo's *Super Mario* video game, the blonde, pink-robed princess is the kindhearted heir of Mushroom Kingdom who is kidnapped by the evil King "Bowser" Koopa and—if lucky—rescued by hardworking Brooklyn plumber Super Mario (or his brother Luigi). First name: Peach.

PRINCIPAL ED ROONEY
Suspicious principal (played by Jeffrey Jones) of Glenbrook North High School in suburban Chicago, who despises Ferris Bueller (Matthew Broderick) and spends the whole day (in *Ferris Bueller's Day Off*) trying to nab the quick-witted teenager in the act of playing hooky. Rooney's secretary is Grace, a fluttery busybody.

PRINGLES
"I've got the fever for the flavor of a Pringle!" "Newfangled" potato chips—made from a mixture of potato flour and water (not from actual potatoes)—that are cloned into the perfect saddle-shape and packaged in a crushproof, airtight, space-saving cylinder. A product of the 1970s, the Pringles container and its convenient pop-top symbolized the decade's fascination with familiar items that have a new and unusual shape, such as the donut-shaped telephone, the sky-high platform shoe, and the bulbous Pacer car. "It's out of the bag!"

PRINZE, FREDDIE
Born on June 2, 1954, in Harlem, the self-proclaimed "Hungarican" (half Hungarian, half Puerto Rican) was the comic whiz-kid of the 1970s whose sudden overnight fame led to an early demise at the age of twenty-two. Following graduation from New York's High School of the Performing Arts in 1973, Prinze started doing stand-up comic routines at improvisational clubs around Manhattan, which eventually earned him an appearance on Johnny Carson's *Tonight Show*. In 1974, at the age of nineteen, he won the role of Chico "Eet's not my job" Rodriquez, opposite veteran character actor Jack Albertson, on the NBC-TV sitcom *Chico and the Man*. An immediate smash, it quickly hurled the good-looking and naturally charming comedian into superstardom.

Hollywood's hot young thing, Prinze headlined standing-room-only clubs in Las Vegas and appeared on highly rated TV specials. Sadly, he also fell into Hollywood's notorious lifestyle of big money and drugs. On January 29, 1977, tormented by the pressure of fame and anguished over wife Kathy Cochrane's taking their baby son and filing for divorce because of his drug addiction (allegedly he ingested as many as 100 quaaludes a day and had a $2,000-a-week cocaine habit), a despondent Prinze committed suicide. ("I cannot go on any longer," read his suicide note.) In 1979, this tragic rise to fame was made into a biographical TV movie, *Can You Hear the Laughter? The Story of Freddie Prinze*, starring Ira Angustain.

FYI: ▸ Freddie Prinze's legacy lives on in the form of his handsome and very grown-up son, Freddie Prinze Jr., who has become one of Hollywood's hottest young actors, starring in the big-screen films *I Know What You Did Last Summer* (1997) and *She's All That* (1999).

PROFESSOR HINKLE
"Think nasty, think nasty!" Known as the "Worst Magician in the World," this cad's discarded magic hat brought snowman Frosty to life "one magic Christmas Eve" in the Rankin/Bass animated TV special *Frosty the Snowman* (1969). Wanting his hat back, Hinkle ruthlessly pursues Frosty all the way to the North Pole, until a stern lecture from Santa Claus makes him change his nasty ways.

PROFESSOR JOHN ROBINSON
Handsome leading man Guy Williams (formerly of Disney's *Zorro*) played the stalwart astrophysicist and leader of the Robinson family aboard the wayward spaceship Jupiter 2. He desperately spends his time on TV's *Lost in Space* trying to find a way to get his wife, Maureen, and three kids home to planet earth.

PROFESSOR LUDWIG VON DRAKE
Donald Duck's eccentric elderly uncle, from the European side of the family, became a cartoon star after many TV appearances on *Walt Disney's Wonderful World of Color*. Beginning with 1961's "The Hunting Instinct," the self-styled expert (on practically everything) with a German accent gave humorous lectures on various topics introducing a Disney cartoon short that coincided with the topic.

FYI: ▸ Ludwig Von Drake is the grandson of Mother Goose.

PROFESSOR ROY HINKLEY
An absentminded science teacher who took a three-hour cruise in Hawaii and found himself as one of seven castaways on *Gilligan's Island*. Amazingly, the Professor used his great wisdom to create all kinds of screwball contraptions on the deserted isle, but he could never quite figure out how to fix the hole in the side of the S.S. *Minnow*.

PROTEUS
Featured in the sci-fi film *Fantastic Voyage*, a hi-tech, submarine-like vessel that is shrunk to microscopic size, along with a crew of doctors, and injected into the body of a wounded scientist rescued from behind the Iron Curtain. In the Saturday-morning cartoon series, the miniaturized ship was called the *Voyager*.

PRUDENCE EVERETT
On *Nanny and the Professor*, Kim Richards—future star of Disney films (*Escape to Witch Mountain*) and TV sitcoms (*Hello, Larry*)—stars as cute five-year-old Prudence, a musical genius who plays only one piano piece and has nightmares about an imaginary beast she calls the Wiblet.

PSSSSSST SHAMPOO
You didn't need to wet your hair for this instant shampoo, made for those busy souls on the go. Just spray it on dry hair, brush it through, and the powder in the product would soak up the oil and dirt.

PSYCHED YOU OUT
Bothersome practical joke in which some doofus points at your chest (as if you had something dribbled on it) and asks, "What's that?" When you look down to see what he's pointing at, he flicks you in the nose with his finger while saying, "Psyched you out! Made you look!"

PTERRI
A pterodactyl who was Pee-Wee Herman's lime-green, lispy-talking pet on his *Playhouse* TV show in the 1980s.

PUDDIN' POPS
The TV commercials for this Jell-O brand product had pitchman Bill Cosby dressed as an ice-cream man, saying: "Jell-O Puddin' Pops, frozen pudding on a stick." Flavors included Chocolate, Vanilla, and Banana.

PUDDLEBY-ON-THE-MARSH
This charming coastal location in England is the hometown of Doctor Dolittle, the veterinarian hero of a children's book series by Hugh Lofting.

PUERTO VALLARTA
Exciting beach resort located on Mexico's Pacific coast, made famous in the 1970s as the destination of TV's *Love Boat*. Once a sleepy fishing village surrounded by breathtaking mountains and jungles, Puerto Vallarta was put on the map only a decade earlier (1963) when Hollywood screen goddess Elizabeth Taylor arrived for a rendezvous with lover Richard Burton, who was there filming John Huston's *Night of the Iguana*.

"PUFF THE MAGIC DRAGON"
The 1962 children's song performed by folk trio Peter, Paul, and Mary (Peter Yarrow, Paul Stookey, and Mary Travers) that some people believe is about drugs and others believe is simply about the innocence of childhood lost. Its lyrics had little Jackie Paper (his last name refers to rolling papers) visiting Puff the Magic Dragon (Puff is slang for smoking pot), who lives in the land of Honalee by the Sea (the Hawaiian village of Hanalei is known in the drug world for its particularly potent marijuana plants). Together they would frolic in the autumn mist (marijuana smoke) and venture out on a boat to encounter pirates (drug-tripping). Sadly, one gray night Jackie grew up and came no more (was it because he'd gone to rehab?). Denying the drug references, "Puff" co-writer Peter Yarrow commented: "What kind of a mean-spirited SOB would write a children's song with a covert drug message?"

PUGSLEY ADDAMS
Gomez and Morticia's pudgy eldest child with the morbid outlook on life was seen in *The Addams Family* TV show, cartoons, and movies. Mother Morticia once sent Pugsley to see a shrink after witnessing him helping an old woman across the street. Played by juvenile actor Ken Weatherwax, nephew of Lassie's trainer, Rudd Weatherwax.

FYI: ▸ In Hanna-Barbera's *Addams Family* cartoon series (1973–75), child actress Jodie Foster provides the voice of Pugsley.

PUKKA-SHELL NECKLACES
Surf-oriented, choker-style jewelry made of small white shells strung on a leather cord and worn by "with it" guys of the 1970s. Let's give teen idol David Cassidy a nod for making pukka-shell necklaces a fashion hit (males rarely if ever wore necklaces, particularly chokers, until seeing Cassidy sporting them on TV's *Partridge Family).*

PULL MY FINGER
Geez, you knew when your dad or brother asked you to pull a finger (usually the index finger) it could mean only one thing: He's gonna let out one big, stinky fart. But you only fell for this once. After that, wise to the fact that a blast of rank air (ew!) was going to invade your senses, you'd just say no and bolt away

PULL-STRING TALKING DOLLS
The phenomenal success in 1960 of Mattel Toys' Chatty Cathy—who talked after you pulled a ring attached to a string on her back, causing a tiny record player hidden inside her body to play—paved the way for hundreds of other talkers, often based on popular cartoon and TV characters. The most memorable of these childhood playmates, produced from 1960 throughout the 1980s, included Casper (1961), Matty Mattel and Sister Belle (1961), Beany and Cecil (1962), Bugs Bunny (1962), Bozo (1964), Herman Munster (1964), Drowsy (1965), Mr. Ed (1965), Woody Woodpecker (1965), Captain Kangaroo (1967), G.I. Joe (1967), Mrs. Beasley (1967), Barbie (1968), Doctor Dolittle (1968), The Cat in the Hat (1970), Flip Wilson / Geraldine (1970), Mother Goose (1970), Mork from Ork (1979), Big Bird (1985), and Pee-Wee Herman (1987).

PUNK AND NEW WAVE HAIR
Popular with those on the cutting edge in the late 1970s and throughout the 1980s (and still found on today's punk-wannabes), these unusual hairdos came in diverse styles and shapes, including Mohawks, asymmetricals, spikes, shaves, wedges, and tails. They had names like the Statue of Liberty (hair pointed in every direction), the Kingfisher (like the bird, two massive fins growing on each side and meeting in the middle), and the Goth (spidery-looking locks, just like Robert Smith's The Cure). Garish and top-heavy, these coiffures were styled using the strongest of gels and household glues. They were tinted unnatural hues, such as blue, fuchsia, pink, green, and jet black, or simply bleached Billy Idol white. Music acts sported the most interesting hair of the era, particularly The Sex Pistols (the founding fathers of punk hair) and the Human League, Culture Club, Thompson Twins, Eurythmics, A Flock of Seagulls, 'Til Tuesday, Sigue Sigue Sputnik, Kajagoogoo, Siouxsie Sioux, and Cyndi Lauper.

PUNK MUSIC
Influential genre of rock characterized by short songs, antisocial lyrics, speedy tempos, and noisy

guitars. Some music historians argue that it started in 1976 with Malcolm McClaren's Sex Pistols at Liverpool's Cavern Club in the United Kingdom, while others argue for The Ramones at New York's CBGBs in the United States. Other familiar punk bands of the era were Blondie, The Buzzcocks, The Clash, Billy Idol's Generation X, Siouxsie and the Banshees, Patti Smith, and Talking Heads. The archetypal punk look consists of torn jeans, studded jackets, combat boots, multiple body piercings, and of course spiked hair (see preceding entry). Violent slam-dancing, in which participants slammed their bodies into one another, is the style of dance associated with punk music.

PUNKY BREWSTER

"That's Punky power!" Spunky seven-year-old tomboy played by Soleil Moon Frye on prime-time TV (1984–86), who, along with pet puppy Brandon, was abandoned by her parents in Chicago and adopted by a crusty tenement manager named Henry Warnimont. Punky's pals included Eddie Malvin, Cherie Johnson, and stuck-up Margaux Kramer. Real name: Penelope.

PUPPET BAND

A jazz music combo of beatnik puppet animals, seen on *Pee-Wee's Playhouse*, that consisted of Dirty Dog, Cool Cat, and Chicky Baby.

PURPLE PIEMAN

"Ratt a tat ta ta tat tah!" Peculiar Purple Pieman of Porcupine Peak is the wicked cartoon villain of Strawberry Shortcake Land. He hangs with bad guys Sour Grapes, Dregs the Snake, and Cackles the Crow.

PUSH-BUTTON PUPPETS

By pushing a button underneath the base of these plastic puppets—which were based on such cartoon icons as Atom Ant, Fred Flintstone, and Yogi Bear—you could make them spastically contort their upper bodies, arms, and heads.

PUSHMI-PULLYU

Wonderful furry white llama with two heads—one on each end, facing in opposite directions. This exotic creature, known as the "Rarest Animal in the World," appeared in the 1967 film *Doctor Dolittle*.

PUSSY GALORE

The sexy lesbian villainess with the double-entendre name is the best known of all the Bond girls. Played by Honor Blackman in the 1964 James Bond thriller *Goldfinger*, Pussy is the no-nonsense leader of a female crime syndicate who partners with fiendish Auric Goldfinger to rob Fort Knox of all its gold. Also the name of a trashy punk band from Washington, D.C., fronted by Jon Spencer, in the early 1980s.

PUTTIN' ON THE HITS

Lame mid-1980s TV game show that featured contestants lip-synching to rock records and then being judged on their performance. It was hosted by curly-haired blond Allen Fawcett, formerly of the daytime soap *The Edge of Night* (he played young Kelly McGrath from 1980 to 1982).

Q-BERT

Introduced by Gottlieb in 1982, this video-game star is a foul-mouthed ("@!#?@!"), snorkel-nosed little ball of orange fur who jumps on squares of a 3-D pyramid while avoiding bouncing pitfalls.

QUANT, MARY

Hip fashion designer from "Swingin' London" who is acclaimed for inventing the miniskirt in the mid-1960s.

QUEEN

In the 1992 movie comedy *Wayne's World*, there's a memorable scene where Wayne and Garth, cruising in their AMC Pacer, begin jamming and bobbing their heads furiously to Queen's 1976 rock operetta "Bohemian Rhapsody." This scene perfectly captured both the inanity of teen male bonding and the strange influence this flamboyant British band—fronted by hairy-chested, bad-toothed Freddie Mercury (born September 9, 1946)—had on young metal heads. As global superstars, Queen were famed for elaborate stage performances mixing glam-rock and opera and showcasing Mercury's falsetto vocals. The other band members consisted of guitarist Brian May, bassist John Deacon, and drummer Roger Taylor. Hit songs included "Killer Queen" (1975), "Somebody to Love" (1976), "We Are the Champions / We Will Rock You" (1977), "Crazy Little Thing Called Love" (1980), "Another One Bites the Dust" (1980), and a duet with fellow Brit David Bowie, "Under Pressure" (1981). On November 24, 1991, the rock 'n' roll world mourned the death of Mercury after he lost his battle with AIDS.

QUENTIN COLLINS

Handsome David Selby starred as the family werewolf and all-around bad guy on the TV sensation *Dark Shadows* from 1968 to 1971. Loved by viewers, this nasty fellow inspired the celestial piano instrumental "Quentin's Theme" by The Charles Randolph Grean Sounde in 1969.

QUICK CURL BARBIE

"Magic hair! Curl it instantly! Easily!" The big hit of the doll world in 1973 was this Barbie whose special locks could go from straight to curly with a twist of a plastic curling wand. There was no setting, no wetting, and no waiting! The secret? Quick Curl Barbie had tiny wire fibers rooted into the strands of her hair, giving it extra styleability. The only flaw was that after much curling and straightening the wires could break, leaving Barbie with a frizzy finger-in-an-electrical-outlet hairdo. Along with Barbie, the Quick Curl series included a new friend—redhead Quick Curl Kelley, plus African-American Quick Curl Cara, cousin Quick Curl Francie, little sister Quick Curl Skipper, and a Quick Curl Miss America.

QUICK DRAW McGRAW

"Hold on thar!" A drawling, white-mustang sheriff of the Old West whose pistol-shooting law-and-order skills were more legendary than factual. His deputy was little Baba Looey, a sombrero-wearing Mexican burro who frequently cautioned the bumbling Quick Draw about the cartoon dangers ahead. The duo's pals included Snuffles, a biscuit-loving dog, and Sagebrush Sal, Quick Draw's filly sweetheart. Created by Hanna-Barbera and voiced by versatile Daws Butler (Huckleberry Hound and Yogi Bear), Quick Draw McGraw starred in his own self-titled Saturday-morning show from 1959 to 1966.

QUISP AND QUAKE CEREALS

It all began around 1963, when Quaker Oats hired animator Jay Ward (of Rocky and Bullwinkle) to help advertise a new sugar-crusted cereal called Cap'n Crunch. Children loved the TV commercials, featuring the cartoon adventures of a ship captain, and made the cereal a huge success. In 1965, Quaker Oats rehired Ward to create two characters for competing cereals, Quisp and Quake.

"Vitamin-powered sugary cereal Quisp for Quazy energy" was the slogan for Quisp, "the biggest-selling cereal from Saturn to Alpha Centauri" (and one of the best-loved cereals for a generation of earth's children). Quisp's advertising mascot was a cross-eyed pink spaceman dressed in a green jumpsuit with a "Q" on the belt buckle and a spinning propeller on top of his head. Quake had "deep-down sweetness, and vitamins to give you the power of an earthquake." Its mascot was a big-jawed miner with bulging biceps enthusiastically claiming to come from the center of the earth, who wore a cavern helmet and lumberjack boots and sported a "Q" on his powerful chest.

Appearing in each other's commercials, the two characters constantly quarreled over which similar-tasting corn-based cereal tasted best ("For Quazy energy, Quisp is best!" or "Quake is best!"). It led to an actual nationwide popularity contest in 1971 in which kids voted for their favorite. Quake lost, and was discontinued by 1975, while popular Quisp and his saucer-shaped cereal has remained in and out of production ever since. Quaker Oats also manufactured another character to duke it out with Quisp, Simon the Quangaroo, whose cereal was orange-flavored.

r

RABBIT
"Oh dear, mercy me." Fretful, fussy, know-it-all yellow hare who occasionally invites the Winnie the Pooh gang over for a cup of tea and a bite to eat at his house. One afternoon, chubby Pooh Bear ate so much honey that when he tried to leave he found himself tightly wedged in Rabbit's hole. ("Why did I ever invite that bear to lunch?")

RACE BANNON
Handsome and virile, the bodyguard and jack-of-all-trades pilot assisted famous scientist Dr. Benton Quest and his young son Jonny Quest on fantastic global expeditions on their Saturday-morning cartoon adventures. First name: Roger.

FYI: ▸ An oft-repeated rumor is that Race Bannon and Dr. Quest were gay lovers.

RACER X
"You must not enter the race!" The mysterious masked racer would appear driving the revved-up Shooting Star just as Speed Racer faced a perilous moment and would turn the race around in Speed's favor. No one, not even Speed Racer, knew who this protective loner was (except for the TV cartoon's home viewers, of course). He was Speed's long-lost older brother, Rex Racer, who vanished at the age of eighteen to work undercover as a top secret agent for Interpol.

FYI: ▸ A rumor about a jinx that followed Racer X to every competition abounded: Whenever he was in a race, there was bound to be a terrible crash.

RACHEL HAIRCUT
Once in vogue in the 1970s, the shag haircut had a revival in the 1990s with the modified version worn by and named after Rachel, Jennifer Aniston's character on the Gen-X friendly prime-time comedy *Friends*. Emulated by much of the female population, the sexy cut, notable for its long bangs and choppy layers accented with highlight streaks, was created by L.A. stylist Chris McMillan. It got dubbed "America's first hairdo" by *Rolling Stone* magazine.

RADIO FLYERS
First introduced by craftsman Anton Pasin in 1933, the little red wagons with the words "Radio Flyer" stenciled on the side are a classic of the Baby Boom childhood.

RAGGEDY ANN

Hailed as "America's Folk Doll," the wholesome ragamuffin—whose unique features include red yarn hair, black shoe-button eyes, triangular nose, red-and-white-striped legs, pinafore, bloomers, and a silk-screened "I Love You" heart—has been a favorite of generations of children. But this soft, cheery doll that has given us so much love had somber beginnings. Around 1915, political cartoonist Johnny Gruelle's young daughter Marcella was stricken with tuberculosis. To entertain his dying child, the doting father found an old handmade rag doll in the attic. He christened her Raggedy Ann—a combination of title characters from the James Whitcomb Riley poems "The Raggedy Man" and "Little Orphan Annie"—and made up stories about her. After Marcella's death in 1917, Gruelle wanted to ensure that in some way his daughter's memory would live on, so he had his stories published with each book, accompanied by a Raggedy Ann doll. Several months after the Raggedy Ann books were released, the doll was mass-manufactured by the Volland Company, making it—along with brother Raggedy Andy, introduced in 1920, the first and longest-running licensed character in toy history.

FYI: ▸ Arcola, Illinois (the birthplace of Johnny Gruelle), is the host of the Raggedy Ann and Andy Festival, held annually on the weekend before Memorial Day.

RAH-RAH SKIRTS

These Valley Girl–era miniskirts, featuring ruffles or pleats (à la cheerleaders) and made out of polyester or sweatsuit-like fabric, were often paired with leg warmers or ankle-high pixie boots. In 2004, this style of skirt made a fashion comeback, along with off-the-shoulder sweatshirts, worn by the daughters of women who originally wore it back in the 1980s.

RAIDERS OF THE LOST ARK

Steven Spielberg took our breath away with the mega-blockbuster that made mega-bucks at the box office (as 1981's high grosser, it has earned more than $115,600,000) and spawned two just-as-breathtaking mega-sequels, *Indiana Jones and the Temple of Doom* (1984) and *Indiana Jones and the Last Crusade*. Directed by Spielberg and written by George Lucas (*Star Wars*), this special-effects extravaganza—a dizzying thrill ride of a film, reminiscent of the 1930s and 1940s Saturday matinee serials—stars Harrison Ford as college professor Dr. Henry Jones, a.k.a. Indiana Jones, an adventurous archaeologist.

The time is 1936, and Jones sets out on a globe-trotting journey to save the Lost Ark of the Covenant—a mythical biblical artifact containing the Ten Commandments and a powerful supernatural force—from the hands of dastardly Nazis. Along the way, he encounters bloodcurdling dangers, hidden spears, a giant renegade boulder, burning airplanes, runaway trucks, a short-lived duel with a swordsman, and (gasp!) a pit of snakes (he can't stand the squirmy creatures). "Indy" is aided by the spunky Marion Ravenwood (Karen Allen), his beautiful, hard-drinking ex-girlfriend, who operates a bar high in the mountains of Tibet, and the gentlemanly Marcus Brody (Denholm Elliott), his British colleague. *Raiders of the Lost Ark* earned eight Oscar nominations, including Best Picture and Best Director.

RAINBOW BRITE

Another nauseatingly cute toy-cum-cartoon character from the 1980s who, like many of her comrades (Strawberry Shortcake and Care Bears, for instance), originated as a greeting card (for Hallmark, in 1983). This one gallantly travels the world via rainbows spreading happiness, riding on Starlite, a faithful white horse , with a rainbow-colored mane and tail, and clashing against gloomy bad guy Murky Dismal. Residing at the magical Color Castle in Rainbow Land (where all the colors of the earth are created), she lives with furry white Twink, her personal sprite, and an entourage of eight pals, all representing different hues of the rainbow, called the Color Kids: environmentally friendly Patty O'Brien, overambitious Red Butler, French joker La La Orange, bookworm Shy Violet, giggly Tickled Pink, lovable Canary Yellow, sweet Indigo, and athletic Buddy Blue.

RALPH FURLEY

Don Knotts's jittery, karate-chopping landlord-manager, who ran the *Three's Company* apartment building on the popular ABC-TV sitcom after Stanley and Helen Roper sold it to his brother, Bart.

RALPHIE PARKER

Bespectacled young boy in a small midwestern city whose obsession with getting a Red Ryder Carbine Action, 200 Shot, Range Model Air Rifle as a Christmas present in the 1983 holiday film *A Christmas Story* leads to opposition from his parents, his teacher, and even good ol' Santa Claus himself.

RALPH LAUREN POLO

These colorful yet conservative polo shirts with the little polo player on the upper-left chest rivaled Izod as the "got-to-have-it" clothing item of the early-1980s preppy era. Also the name of the designer's green-hued, odoriferous cologne for men (his women's fragrance was called Lauren).

RALPH MALPH

Redheaded actor Donny Most starred as Jefferson High's annoying class clown, the son of a dentist, who palled around with Richie Cunningham and Potsie Webber on *Happy Days*. Ralph's practical jokes and sight-gags usually weren't funny to anyone except himself.

RAMBO

Sylvester Stallone embodies a lean, mean fighting machine as the sullen, moderately deranged Vietnam War vet John Rambo who became an icon of American patriotism in the 1980s. The oft-grunting, bicep-flexing former Green Beret, highly skilled at survival and attack, is sent by Uncle Sam on one-man commando missions to rescue American MIAs still imprisoned in Southeast Asia. Loved by testosterone-driven guys, Rambo can be seen in a trilogy of action-packed films, starting with *First Blood* in 1982 and followed by *Rambo: First Blood II* (1985) and *Rambo III* (1988).

RAMONES

"Hey ho, let's go!" The Yankee contemporaries of England's Sex Pistols were the influential forerunners of just about every American alternative music act of the 1980s and 1990s. Formed in 1974 in New York, these self-proclaimed "juvenile delinquents," clad in torn denim jeans and leather jackets, shared the adopted surname of Ramone (but they weren't related). There was lead singer Joey Ramone (Jeffrey Hyman), guitarist Johnny Ramone (John Cummings), bassist Dee Dee Ramone (Douglas Colvin), and drummer Tommy Ramone (Thomas Erdelyi). The Ramones were distinguished by an edgy, fast-paced, three-cord music formula with "1-2-3-4" intros to every song. Although never charting on the American Top Forty, their best-known tunes included "Blitzkrieg Bop" (1976), "Sheena Is a Punk Rocker" (1977), "I Wanna Be Sedated" (1979), and a cover of The Ronettes' "Baby I Love You" (1980). In 1979, the quartet starred in the Roger Corman cult flick *Rock 'n' Roll High School*, co-starring P. J. Soles and Vince Van Patten. "Gabba Gabba Hey!"

RANGER JOHN SMITH

Earnest and honest guardian of Jellystone National Park (voiced by Don Messick) who is continually out to stop the misbehaving Yogi Bear from continuing his picnic-basket-nabbing ways on the animated *Yogi Bear Show*.

RANKIN/BASS

Producer Arthur Rankin Jr. and director Jules Bass are the pioneers of three-dimensional, stop-motion animation known as "Animagic," a laborious technique in which you posed a puppet figure, shot a few frames, moved the figure just a little, shot a few frames, and so on and on. The prolific pair are responsible for producing the enchanting holiday TV specials featuring jerky little puppet characters voiced by film-star celebrities. (How many of you grew up thinking Burl Ives was a talking snowman?) Their Animagic TV career began in 1964 when the legendary *Rudolph the Red-Nosed Reindeer*, which became the most popular Rankin/Bass production and the longest-running special in the history of television, made its prime-time debut. Other Rankin/Bass Animagic fantasies include *The Ballad of Smokey the Bear* (1966), *The Little Drummer Boy* (1968), *Here Comes Peter Cottontail* (1971), *Santa Claus Is Comin' to Town* (1970), *The Year Without a Santa Claus* (1974), *The Easter Bunny Is Comin' to Town* (1977), *Nestor, the Long-Eared Christmas Donkey* (1977), *Rudolph and Frosty's Christmas in July* (1979), and *Jack Frost* (1979). Rankin/Bass was also responsible for two Animagic big-screen features, *The Daydreamer* (1966) and *Mad Monster Party* (1967), and the Yuletide cartoon favorite *Frosty the Snowman* (1969).

RAP

A type of music characterized by rapid, lyrical talking backed by sounds sampled from other songs. Can be traced back to America's inner-city streets before hitting the mainstream in the 1980s. The different types of rap music include East Coast, West Coast, gangsta, new school, hip-hop, and alternative rap.

"RAPPER'S DELIGHT"

The 1980 record by The Sugarhill Gang, a rapping trio from Harlem, is credited with introducing rap music to the Top Forty *Billboard* pop chart.

"RAPTURE"

The inventive Blondie tune, about a man from Mars who went around eating cars, is distinguished for being the first rap song to top the American pop charts in 1981. Its accompanying music video is noteworthy as well—it was the first rap clip to air on MTV. It featured Debbie Harry rapping while walking wobbly among artsy-fartsy Soho-types.

RAT FINK

Capitalizing on the nation's love affair with funny cars and movie monsters, Revell, the leading model manufacturer, got together with cartoonist Ed "Big Daddy" Roth in 1963 and created a line of kits featuring offbeat cars driven by the ugliest creatures you ever laid eyes on. Big Daddy's most famous monster was an oversized rodent named Rat Fink, an "anti-Mickey Mouse" with bloodshot bug-eyes, wide-open mouth, dagger teeth, and a long drooling tongue. This huge rat was seen driving far-out dragsters and twisted hot rods. There were thirteen variations of the character, including Angel Fink, Brother Rat Fink, Robbin' Hood Fink, Surfink, Super Fink, Scuz Fink, Boss Fink, Drag Nut, and Mr. Gasser. The popularity of Rat Fink led to one of the biggest fads of the 1960s: the funny monster craze, which spawned knockoffs Weird-Ohs and Nutty Mads.

RAT PACK

Popular in the early 1960s with our parents' generation, a way-too-hip clique of martini-sipping actors and swingin' singers whose members included Frank Sinatra, Dean Martin, Sammy Davis Jr., Peter Lawford, Joey Bishop, and Bing Crosby. Marilyn Monroe, Shirley MacLaine, and Judy Garland were considered female members of this high-profile gang. To see them in celluloid action, check out these three films: *Ocean's Eleven* (1960), *Sergeants 3* (1962), and *Robin and the 7 Hoods* (1964).

RAT PACK (BEACH MOVIES)

Name of the pesty, leather-jacketed motorcycle club led by the detestable Eric Von Zipper, who constantly harassed Frankie, Dee Dee, and the rest of the beach gang during their surfing shindigs. Von Zipper called his male members "rats" and the females "mice."

RAT PATROL

"Leapin' jeeps!" Riding on the heels of TV's highly popular *Combat!* (1962–67), this wartime action-adventure series focused on a four-man team of commandos, armed with machine-gun mounted jeeps, who traveled the desert sands of North Africa fighting General Rommel's Afrika Korps during World War II. The Rat Patrol consisted of three Americans—Sergeant Sam Troy (Christopher George), Private Mark Hitchcock (Lawrence Casey), and Private Tully Pettigrew (Justin Tarr)—and one Englishman, Sergeant Jack Moffitt (Gary Raymond). Premiering in 1966, this was the only new show of the season to premiere in Nielsen's Top Ten; it ran until 1968.

RAT TAIL

A late-1980s fashion fad in which people would let a thin bunch of hair at the neckline grow out long enough to resemble the tail of a rodent. The rat-tail wearer was always adamant about "never" cutting it off (it was their claim to fame) and would be style savvy by braiding or cornrowing it. For others, it was hard to resist the temptation to sneak up behind a rat-tailed person and snip it off.

RAVES

Large, all-night underground youth parties of the 1990s enhanced by throbbing techno and acid-house music and the mind-altering designer drug ecstasy. An out-of-control rave is known as a "rager."

RAY-BAN SUNGLASSES

The Wayfarer pair that movie hunk Tom Cruise sported in 1983's *Risky Business* ignited a renewed popularity for Ray-Ban sunglasses, which had been around since the 1950s.

READING IS FUNDAMENTAL (RIF)

Yes, Reading Is Fundamental and these are 100 childhood books published in the twentieth century loved best by Baby Boomers and Gen-Xers. Following each title is the year it debuted and the name of the author(s).

- *All Creatures Great and Small* (1972) by James Herriot
- *Amelia Bedelia* (1963) by Peggy Parish
- *Annie on My Mind* (1982) by Nancy Garden
- *Are You My Mother?* (1960) by P. D. Eastman
- *Are You There God? It's Me, Margaret* (1970) by Judy Blume
- *Babar* (1933) by Jean de Brunhoff
- *Bambi* (1926) by Felix Salten
- *A Bear Called Paddington* (1960) by Michael Bond
- *The Berenstain Bears* (1967) by Stan and Jan Berenstain
- *Best Word Book Ever* (1963) by Richard Scarry
- *Big Red* (1945) by Jim Kjelgaard
- *The Black Cauldron* (1965) by Lloyd Alexander
- *The Black Stallion* (1941) by Walter Farley
- *Bless the Beasts and the Children* (1970) by Gordon Swarthout
- *Blubber* (1974) by Judy Blume
- *The Bobbsey Twins* (1904) by Laura Lee Hope
- *Born Free* (1960) by Joy Adamson
- *The Borrowers* (1953) by Mary Norton
- *Caddie Woodlawn* (1935) by Carol Ryrie Brink
- *The Call of the Wild* (1903) by Jack London
- *The Cat Ate My Gymsuit* (1974) by Paula Danziger
- *The Cat in the Hat* (1956) by Dr. Seuss
- *Charlie and the Chocolate Factory* (1963) by Roald Dahl
- *Charlie and the Great Glass Elevator* (1972) by Roald Dahl
- *Charlotte's Web* (1952) by E. B. White
- *Chitty Chitty Bang Bang* (1964) by Ian Fleming
- *The Chronicles of Narnia* (1950) by C. S. Lewis
- *Clifford, the Big Red Dog* (1966) by Norman Bridwell
- *The Cricket in Times Square* (1960) by George Selden
- *Curious George* (1942) by H. A. and Margret Rey
- *The Diary of Anne Frank* (1947) by Anne Frank
- *Doctor Dolittle* (1920) by Hugh Lofting
- *Eloise* (1955) by Kay Thompson
- *Encyclopedia Brown* (1963) by Donald J. Sobol
- *Forever* (1975) by Judy Blume
- *Fox in Socks* (1966) by Dr. Seuss
- *Freaky Friday* (1972) by Mary Rodgers
- *From the Mixed-Up Files of Mrs. Basil E. Frankweiler* (1967) by E. L. Konigsburg
- *Gentle Ben* (1965) by Walt Morey
- *Go Ask Alice* (1971) by Anonymous
- *Green Eggs and Ham* (1960) by Dr. Seuss
- *Happiness Is a Warm Puppy* (1962) by Charles Schulz
- *The Hardy Boys* (1927) by Franklin W. Dixon
- *Harold and the Purple Crayon* (1955) by Crockett Johnson
- *Harriet the Spy* (1964) by Louise Fitzhugh
- *The Hobbit* (1937) by J. R. R. Tolkien
- *Hop on Pop* (1963) by Dr. Seuss
- *Horton Hears a Who!* (1954) by Dr. Seuss
- *How the Grinch Stole Christmas* (1957) by Dr. Seuss
- *The Incredible Journey* (1961) by Sheila Burnford
- *Island of the Blue Dolphins* (1960) by Scott O'Dell
- *James and the Giant Peach* (1961) by Roald Dahl
- *Lassie Come Home* (1940) by Eric Knight
- *The Little Engine That Could* (1930) by Watty Piper
- *Little House in the Big Woods* (1932) by Laura Ingalls Wilder
- *The Little Prince* (1943) by Antoine de Saint-Exupéry
- *The Littlest Angel* (1946) by Charles Tazewell
- *The Lord of the Rings* (1954) by J. R. R. Tolkien
- *Madeline* (1939) by Ludwig Bemelman
- *Mary Poppins* (1934) by P. L. Travers

- *Mike Mulligan and His Steam Shovel* (1939) by Virginia Lee Burton
- *Misty of Chincoteague* (1947) by Marguerite Henry
- *Mrs. Piggle-Wiggle* (1957) by Betty MacDonald
- *My Friend Flicka* (1941) by Mary O'Hara
- *Nancy Drew* (1930) by Carolyn Keene
- *National Velvet* (1935) by Enid Bagnold
- *Old Yeller* (1957) by Fred Gipson
- *One Fish, Two Fish, Red Fish, Blue Fish* (1960) by Dr. Seuss
- *The Outsiders* (1967) by S. E. (Susan Eloise) Hinton
- *Pat the Bunny* (1940) by Dorothy Kunhardt
- *Peter Pan* (1904) by James M. Barrie
- *Peter Rabbit* (1902) by Beatrix Potter
- *The Phantom Tollbooth* (1961) by Norman Juster
- *Pippi Longstocking* (1950) by Astrid Lindgren
- *The Poky Little Puppy* (1942) by Janet Sebring Lowrey
- *Pollyanna* (1913) by Eleanor H. Porter
- *Ramona the Pest* (1952) by Beverly Cleary
- *Rudolph the Red-Nosed Reindeer* (1939) by Robert L. May
- *The Saggy Baggy Elephant* (1947) by Kathryn and Byron Jackson
- *Scuffy the Tugboat* (1946) by Gertrude Crampton
- *The Secret Garden* (1912) by Frances Hodgson Burnett
- *Sounder* (1969) by William H. Armstrong
- *Stuart Little* (1945) by E. B. White
- *Superfudge* (1980) by Judy Blume
- *The Sweet Smell of Christmas* (1970) by Patricia Scarry
- *Tales of a Fourth Grade Nothing* (1972) by Judy Blume
- *Tarzan of the Apes* (1914) by Edgar Rice Burroughs
- *The Tawny Scrawny Lion* (1952) by Kathryn Jackson
- *There's a Wocket in My Pocket* (1974) by Dr. Seuss
- *The Trumpet of the Swan* (1970) by E. B. White
- *The Twenty-One Balloons* (1947) by William Pene du Bois
- *The Velveteen Rabbit* (1926) by Margery Williams
- *Watership Down* (1972) by Richard Adams
- *Where the Red Fern Grows* (1961) by Wilson Rawls
- *Where the Sidewalk Ends* (1974) by Shel Silverstein
- *Where the Wild Things Are* (1963) by Maurice Sendak
- *The Wind in the Willows* (1908) by Kenneth Grahame
- *Winnie the Pooh* (1926) by A. A. Milne
- *The Wonderful Wizard of Oz* (1900) by L. Frank Baum
- *The Yearling* (1938) by Marjorie Kinnan Rawlings

READING IS FUNDAMENTAL (RIF) II

Reading Is Fundamental for adults too. Here are 100 can't-put-it-down reads for maturer readers, from the late 1950s through to the end of the 1990s.

- *Airport* (1968) by Arthur Hailey
- *All I Really Need to Know I Learned in Kindergarten* (1989) by Robert Fulghum
- *All the President's Men* (1974) by Carl Bernstein and Bob Woodward
- *The Amityville Horror* (1977) by Jay Anson
- *And the Band Played On* (1987) by Randy Shilts
- *The Andromeda Strain* (1969) by Michael Crichton
- *The Beauty Myth* (1991) by Naomi Wolf
- *The Bell Jar* (1962) by Sylvia Plath
- *The Bermuda Triangle* (1974) by Charles Berlitz
- *The Betsy* (1971) by Harold Robbins
- *The Bonfire of the Vanities* (1987) by Tom Wolfe
- *The Book of Lists* (1977) by David Wallechinsky, Irving Wallace, and Amy Wallace
- *Breakfast at Tiffany's* (1958) by Truman Capote
- *The Bridges of Madison County* (1993) by Robert James Waller
- *Bright Lights, Big City* (1984) by Jay McInerney
- *Bury My Heart at Wounded Knee* (1971) by Dee Brown
- *Carrie* (1974) by Stephen King
- *Cat* (1975) by B. Kliban
- *Catch-22* (1961) by Joseph Heller
- *Chariots of the Gods* (1968) by Erich Von Daniken
- *Coffee, Tea, or Me?* (1967) by Trudy Baker and Rachel Jones
- *The Color Purple* (1982) by Alice Walker
- *Coma* (1977) by Robin Cook

- *The Complete Book of Running* (1978) by James Fixx
- *Cosmos* (1980) by Carl Sagan
- *Dancing in the Light* (1985) by Shirley MacLaine
- *The Day of the Jackal* (1971) by Frederick Forsyth
- *The Dead Zone* (1979) by Stephen King
- *Deliverance* (1969) by James Dickey
- *Dune* (1965) by Frank Herbert
- *Elvis and Me* (1985) by Priscilla Presley
- *Everything You Always Wanted to Know About Sex But Were Afraid to Ask* (1970) by David Reuben
- *The Executioner's Song* (1979) by Norman Mailer
- *The Exorcist* (1971) by William Peter Blatty
- *Faeries* (1978) by Brian Froud
- *Fear of Flying* (1973) by Erica Jong
- *The Firm* (1991) by John Grisham
- *Flowers in the Attic* (1979) by V. C. Andrews
- *Generation X* (1991) by Douglas Coupland
- *Gnomes* (1978) by Wil Huygen and Rien Poortvliet
- *The Godfather* (1969) by Mario Puzo
- *The Grass Is Always Greener over the Septic Tank* (1977) by Erma Bombeck
- *The Happy Hooker* (1972) by Xaviera Hollander
- *Hawaii* (1959) by James Michener
- *Helter Skelter* (1974) by Vincent Bugliosi
- *The Hitchhiker's Guide to the Galaxy* (1979) by Douglas Adams
- *Hollywood Wives* (1983) by Jackie Collins
- *Hotel* (1965) by Arthur Hailey
- *The Hunt for Red October* (1984) by Tom Clancy
- *I Know Why the Caged Bird Sings* (1969) by Maya Angelou
- *I'm O.K., You're O.K.* (1971) by Thomas Harris
- *In Cold Blood* (1965) by Truman Capote
- *Interview with a Vampire* (1976) by Anne Rice
- *Jackie Oh!* (1978) by Kitty Kelley
- *Jane Fonda's Workout Book* (1982) by Jane Fonda
- *Jaws* (1974) by Peter Benchley
- *Jonathan Livingston Seagull* (1972) by Richard Bach
- *The Joy of Sex* (1973) by Alex Comfort
- *Kids Say the Darndest Things* (1957) by Art Linkletter
- *Lake Wobegon Days* (1985) by Garrison Keillor
- *Less Than Zero* (1985) by Brett Easton Ellis
- *The Life and Times of Heidi Abromowitz* (1984) by Joan Rivers
- *Looking for Mr. Goodbar* (1975) by Judith Rossner
- *The Love Machine* (1969) by Jacqueline Susann
- *Love Story* (1970) by Erich Segal
- *Marilyn* (1973) by Norman Mailer
- *Men Are from Mars, Women Are from Venus* (1993) by John Gray
- *Mommie Dearest* (1978) by Christina Crawford
- *Naked Lunch* (1959) by William S. Burroughs
- *Nancy Reagan: The Unauthorized Biography* (1991) by Kitty Kelley
- *The Official Preppy Handbook* (1980) by Lisa Birnbach
- *On the Road* (1957) by Jack Kerouac
- *Once Is Not Enough* (1973) by Jacqueline Susann
- *The Other Side of Midnight* (1973) by Sidney Sheldon
- *Pet Sematary* (1983) by Stephen King
- *The Poseidon Adventure* (1969) by Paul Gallico
- *The Prince of Tides* (1986) by Pat Conroy
- *Rabbit Run* (1960) by John Updike
- *Ragtime* (1975) by E. L. Doctorow
- *Rich Man, Poor Man* (1970) by Irwin Shaw
- *Roots* (1976) by Alex Haley
- *Rosemary's Baby* (1967) by Ira Levin
- *Salem's Lot* (1976) by Stephen King
- *Scruples* (1978) by Judith Krantz
- *Secrets* (1985) by Danielle Steele
- *Sex* (1992) by Madonna
- *The Shining* (1976) by Stephen King
- *Shogun* (1975) by James Clavell
- *Slaughterhouse Five* (1969) by Kurt Vonnegut Jr.
- *Slaves of New York* (1989) by Tama Janowitz
- *Sophie's Choice* (1979) by William Styron
- *Space* (1982) by James A. Michener
- *The Stand* (1978) by Stephen King
- *Sun Signs* (1969) by Linda Goodman
- *Sybil* (1973) by Flora R. Schreiber
- *The Thorn Birds* (1977) by Colleen McCullough
- *Up the Down Staircase* (1965) by Bel Kaufman
- *Valley of the Dolls* (1966) by Jacqueline Susann
- *The Winds of War* (1971) by Herman Wouk
- *The World According to Garp* (1980) by John Irving

READY-TO-FLY PLANES
Inexpensive planes made out of thin balsa wood that you assembled in seconds. When thrown, they would glide effortlessly in the air (just like a paper airplane), at least until crash-landing in a tree or on a rooftop.

REALITY BITES
Released in 1994, this is noteworthy for being the first film deliberately geared to Generation X about Generation X. It centers on a group of twentysomethings facing the reality of life after recently graduating from college in Houston, Texas. There's Lelaina Pierce (Winona Ryder), college valedictorian and aspiring filmmaker, looking for work and love by camcording her pals in a documentary on postcollege life titled "Reality Bites." Lelaina's three best buds are Troy Dyer (Ethan Hawke), perpetually unemployed slacker full of pseudo-philosophical musings; Vickie Miner (Janeane Garofalo), sarcastic Gap manager and slut (sixty men and counting) who's worried about the results of an AIDS test; and Sammy Gray (Steve Zahn), a homosexual yearning to come out of the closet. Earnest yuppie Michael Grates (Ben Stiller), a TV executive for an MTV-like station, enters the group and offers cynical Lelaina a shot at becoming a successful film journalist—and at being in love. Stiller, the son of comedians Jerry Stiller and Anne Meara, also made his directorial debut with this movie. With the exception of the brilliant Garofalo, whose dry wit always steals the show, *Reality Bites* bites. It's not very good, because it plays into the stereotype of Gen-X's being a generation of overeducated, overprivileged, smugly hip, contemptuous, unloved whiners who go around blurting out oh-so-ironic pop culture-based quips.

REAL WORLD
MTV's "soap-umentary" series about a group of multicultural young adults living in cool pads in cool places like New York, L.A., Chicago, South Beach, Seattle, New Orleans, San Diego, Honolulu, London, and Paris while being filmed by eighteen-hour-a-day camera crews. Originally premiering in 1992, *The Real World* is the forerunner of today's reality shows, including *Big Brother*, *Survivor*, *The Bachelor*, and MTV's own *Road Rules*.

REBOUND
Introduced in 1971, Ideal's action game, a hybrid of bowling and shuffleboard, relied on precision aiming skills, such as bank shots, angle shots, and trick shots. The game's object was to slide a puck up the alley (like bowling), rebound it off the rubberband cushion, and watch it zip down to land in the score area (like shuffleboard). With the right touch, you could tally up a high score or knock your opponent's puck in the pit area to keep him from scoring, but if you used too much force you could land in the pit area. The first player to reach "500" was the champ.

RED BARON
"Curse you, Red Baron!" Flying astride the Sopwith Camel doghouse, Charlie Brown's daredevil dog Snoopy engaged this infamous German fighter pilot (Baron von Richthofen) in fierce aerobatic battles over war-ravaged France. The Red Baron's airplane of choice was a Fokker Triplane. Inspired the Royal Guardsmen's Top Ten song "Snoopy vs. The Red Baron" (1966) and the holiday album *Snoopy's Christmas*, and featured the Peter Pan Singers and Orchestra. (The illustration on the cover showed Santa Claus in the Sopwith Camel throwing candy canes at the Red Baron.)

REDDY, HELEN
In the 1970s, the Australian songbird, born October 25, 1942, in Melbourne, made a name for herself by singing a trio of feminist-oriented tunes about dysfunctional women. These million-sellers included "Delta Dawn" (1973), about Brownsville's crazy forty-one-year-old "Baby" who wore a faded rose from days gone by; "Leave Me Alone (Ruby Red Dress)" (1973), about a brokenhearted, antisocial soul who talked to herself as she wandered around town; and "Angie Baby" (1974), about a weird young gal who lived in a world of make-believe (her bedroom), where she enslaved male visitors via her radio. Other American Top Forty hits for Reddy included "I Don't Know How to Love Him" (1971) from the rock opera *Jesus Christ Superstar*, "I Am Woman" (1973), "You and Me Against the World" (1974), and "Ain't No Way to Treat a Lady" (1975). The short-haired brunette singer experienced a minor film career playing a guitar-strumming nun

in the disastrous *Airport 1975* (1974) and starring opposite a fire-breathing cartoon dragon in Disney's *Pete's Dragon* (1977). From 1975 to 1977, she hosted *The Midnight Special*, TV's late-night rock concert series.

REESE, MASON

Redheaded munchkin whose fifteen minutes of fame were for Underwood Deviled Ham commercials of the early 1970s in which he acclaimed the processed meat product as "a borgasmord in a can."

REESE'S PEANUT BUTTER CUPS

"There's no wrong way to eat a Reese's." This delectable chocolate and peanut butter confection from Hershey's was known also for its TV commercials aired throughout the 1970s. These featured two people, one with a jar of peanut butter, the other with a chocolate bar, who accidentally collide and exclaim: "You got your chocolate in my peanut butter!" "You got your peanut butter in my chocolate!" The chocolate cups with the peanut butter center were named after H. B. (Harry Burnett) Reese, an employee of Milton S. Hershey, who invented them in the 1920s. Variations on the candy included Reese's Crunchy (with nuts), Reese's Crunchy Cookie Cups, ReeseSticks, and Reese's Pieces.

REESE'S PIECES

Debuting in 1978, Hershey's M&M-esque confection has peanut butter in the center of candy-coated orange, yellow, and brown shells. These were a favorite of space alien E.T.

REEVES, KEANU

Many of the moviegoing public question this leading man's acting abilities. Although perfectly cast in offbeat films like *River's Edge* (1986), *Bill and Ted's Excellent Adventure* (1989), and *My Own Private Idaho* (1991), or in action flicks, such as *Point Break* (1991), *Speed* (1994), and *The Matrix* (1999), his surfer-esque vocal delivery doesn't quite cut it in more serious fare—*Bram Stoker's Dracula* (1992), *A Walk in the Clouds* (1995), and *The Devil's Advocate* (1997). Reeves's smoldering dark looks come from his Chinese, Hawaiian, and English heritage (he was born in Beirut, Lebanon, on September 2, 1964). On off-time from acting, he plays bass guitar in a rock band called Dogstar.

FYI: ▸ Keanu Reeves's first name means "cool breeze over the mountains" in Hawaiian.

REGAL BEAGLE

When not hanging out at the fern-laden apartment or Jack's Bistro (Jack Tripper's French cuisine restaurant), prime time's *Three's Company* gang can be found at this swingin' neighborhood pub in Santa Monica, California.

REGAN MACNEIL

"Mother, make it stop!" Wholesome twelve-year-old girl who gets possessed by the devil and turns into a revolting, foul-mouthed, crucifix-masturbating creature in *The Exorcist*. Her mother is a famous movie star. Played by Oscar-nominated Linda Blair in the 1973 horror film.

REGGIE MANTLE

Handsome and extremely vain, the dark-haired wiseguy from the *Archies* comics constantly competes against Archie Andrews in just about everything. A talented athlete, Reggie has won trophies for football, baseball, basketball, track, and tennis, but he once lost a tiddlywinks tournament to Archie. Reggie thinks he's God's gift to women and has a thing for slinky Veronica Lodge (or is it for her daddy's money?), but she usually has a thing for Archie. He also has a thing for down-to-earth intellect Midge Klump, who is the sweetheart of hulking football jock Moose Mason. This incenses Moose, and Reggie customarily ends up on the receiving end of Moose's beatings.

REGGIE VAN DOUGH

Richie Rich's jealous and snobbish prankster cousin. (Why are all Reggies in comic books scoundrels?)

R.E.M.

Singer Michael Stipe, bassist Mike Mills, guitarist Peter Buck, and drummer Bill Berry formed R.E.M. in 1980 as students at the University of Georgia in Athens. Led by Stipe (born January 4, 1960), whose high, keening vocals became the rock band's trademark sound, the foursome dropped out of school to pursue a full-time recording career. As one of the first alternative music acts, they developed a vast following among college audiences in the 1980s with hauntingly edgy songs containing socially conscious lyrics: "Radio Free Europe," "The One I Love," "It's the End of the World as We Know It (And I Feel Fine)," and "Stand." By the mid-1990s, R.E.M. would rule the world as the biggest band (at least for a short time), earning a few Grammys and a few MTV Music Awards, and a few Top Forty hits: "Losing My Religion," "Shiny Happy People," "Man on the Moon," "Everybody Hurts, and "What's the Frequency, Kenneth?"

FYI: ▸ R.E.M.'s initials stand for Rapid Eye Movement, a physiological term for the sleep-cycle stage in which dreaming occurs.

REMOTE CONTROL

Airing from 1987 to 1990, MTV's pop-culture-oriented game show starred a trio of twentysomething contestants holding remote controls and munching on bowls of popcorn and answering questions about TV and music while strapped into La-Z-Boy recliners. Hosted by Ken Ober and his deadpan sidekick Colin Quinn.

REMOTE-CONTROL CARS

Favorite toys for boys were these battery-operated stunt vehicles with antennas and motors, which you maneuvered with handheld control pads.

REN AND STIMPY

"Happy! Happy! Joy! Joy!" Premiering on the Nickelodeon cable channel in 1991, animator John Kricfalusi's cartoon show, starring Ren Höek (a scrawny, hairless Chihuahua with big, bloodshot eyes and an overcaffeinated disposition) and Stimpson J. "Stimpy" Cat (a slobbering, slow-witted, obese feline) provided a gross-out alternative to traditional cartoons. The show's twisted tales had Ren and Stimpy wallowing in every bodily function imaginable: farts, boogers, vomit, spit, shit—you name it, they produced it. The twosome were an instant hit with college-age viewers (ages eighteen to twenty-four) and are credited with influencing other "bad taste" cartoons, like *2 Stupid Dogs, Cow and Chicken, Rocko's Modern Life, Beavis and Butt-Head,* and *South Park.*

REN McCORMACK

Headstrong teenager who just wants to get loose—footloose—put on his dancing shoes in a Bible Belt town in the Midwest that has banned all forms of dancing ("the devil's rhythm"). Portrayed by Kevin Bacon in the 1984 *Footloose* film.

RESCUE RACER

The emergency vehicle (sort of a cross between an ambulance and a police paddy-wagon) was driven by two miniature Keystone Cops named Cling and Clang on TV's *H. R. Pufnstuf.*

RESCUERS

"To Morningside Orphanage, New York. I am in terrible, terrible trouble. Hurry. Help!"

—PENNY

This 1977 feature-length cartoon from the Disney Studios is a sweet gem about two heroic mice, reticent Bernard and chic Miss Bianca (voiced by Bob Newhart and Eva Gabor), who are members of the Mouse Rescue Aid Society. Their motto: "We never fail to do what's right." Their mission: to rescue a kidnapped little orphan girl named Penny from the evil Madame Medusa and her sinister accomplice, Mr. Snoop, and a pair of alligator bodyguards, Brutus and Nero. Madame Medusa is after the fabulous Devil's Eye diamond (stuffed in Penny's teddy bear) and holds the girl prisoner in a swamp called Devil's Bayou. On their mission, Bernard and Bianca are assisted by albatross Orville, elderly cat Rufus, and dragonfly Evinrude. *The Rescuers* was based on stories by novelist Margery Sharp. A 1990 sequel followed, *The Rescuers Down Under,* in which the sleuthing mice travel to Australia to save a boy and a golden eagle from deadly poachers.

REUBEN KINCAID

"Mr. Kincaid" was the smarmy, fast-talking manager of *The Partridge Family,* who detested kids—especially smart-ass Danny Partridge—and sorta had a thing for mom Shirley Partridge. Portrayed by former *Laugh-In* comedian Dave Madden from 1970 to 1974.

REVENGE OF THE NERDS

Directed by Jeff Kanew, this raunchy but totally likeable low-budget comedy gave dweebs their day. Filmed in 1984, freshmen geeks Lewis Skolnick

(Robert Carradine) and Gilbert Lowell (Anthony Edwards) arrive at Adams College only to find themselves tormented by the jocks of the Alpha Beta fraternity. In desperation, they unite with other nerds to form their own campus fraternity, Lambda Lambda Lambda, and along with a sorority of sister misfits, Omega Mu, fight back against the hot-shot antagonists. Co-starring nerds included aptly named Booger (Curtis Armstrong), Poindexter (Timothy Busfield), Wormser (Andrew Cassese), Takashi (Brian Tochi), and Lamar (Larry B. Scott), the aerobicizing black homosexual. This surprise box-office hit was followed by three sequels: 1987's *Revenge of the Nerds II: Nerds in Paradise* (the geeks travel to Fort Lauderdale for an all-frat conference), 1992's *Revenge of the Nerds III: The Next Generation* (a TV movie), and 1994's *Revenge of the Nerds IV: Nerds in Love* (another TV movie).

REY, H. A., AND MARGRET REY

> "Curious George does things that children wish they could do."
> —MARGRET REY

Husband-and-wife team from Germany who wrote and illustrated the enchanting *Curious George* picture books. Since 1941, more than twenty million copies in twelve different languages have been sold worldwide. H. A.'s first name is Hans.

REYNOLDS, BURT

"The only way to handle a reputation for being a sex symbol is to have fun with it. Sex symbols don't last long." Without a doubt, Hollywood's foremost male sex symbol of the 1970s was this handsome, virile actor. Fueled by a completely nude centerfold in the April 1972 issue of *Cosmopolitan* magazine (he was the first celebrity male to pose for a centerfold, and, disappointingly, his penis was covered by his hand), the mustached, fuzzy-chested, dark-haired Reynolds epitomized the sexy macho-male type that so ruled the decade. Born February 11, 1936, in Georgia and raised in Florida, Reynolds was a football star at Florida State University, before an auto accident sidelined his sports career. Turning to acting, from 1959 until 1972 he starred in a string of western and detective TV programs, *Riverboat* (1959–60), *Gunsmoke* (1962–65), *Hawk* (1966), *Dan August* (1970–71), and a string of western and detective movies, *100 Rifles* (1969), *Sam Whiskey* (1969), *Shark!* (1969), *Fuzz* (1972), *Shamus* (1973), before hitting the big time as a doomed white-water rafter in John Boorman's terrifying *Deliverance* (1972).

Charming and with an easygoing, self-mocking nature, Reynolds was a movie superstar, known best for playing car-chasing, skirt-chasing good ol' boys in action comedies, such as *White Lightning* (1973), *The Longest Yard* (1974), *W.W. and the Dixie Dancekings* (1975), *Semi-Tough* (1977), *Smokey and the Bandit* (1977), *Hooper* (1978), and *The Cannonball Run* (1981). Other notable hits included *The End* (1978), *Starting Over* (1979), *Sharky's Machine* (1981), *Best Friends* (1982), and *The Best Little Whorehouse in Texas* (1982). After experiencing an embarrassing career decline throughout most of the 1980s and 1990s, he brilliantly transformed into a character actor in supporting roles, like Congressman David Dilbeck in *Striptease* (1996) and porno king Jack Horner in *Boogie Nights* (1997), which earned him an Oscar nomination. He is also known for well-publicized romances, including that with first wife Judy Carne (*Laugh-In*'s "Sock It to Me" girl), girlfriends Dinah Shore, Sally Field, and Chris Evert, and second wife Loni Anderson (that marriage ended in a messy "he said, she said" divorce).

FYI: ▸ Burt Reynolds was the number-one box-office draw for five consecutive years, 1978 to 1982.

"RHINESTONE COWBOY"

After a fourteen-year chart career, boyish-looking country singer Glen Campbell gained his first number one on the American pop charts with this tale of a country boy trying to make it in New York City. Written by Larry Weiss, it sold more than two million copies in 1975, became *Billboard*'s country single of the year, and earned Song of the Year honors from both the Academy of Country Music and the Country Music Association. It inspired the Sylvester Stallone / Dolly Parton big-screen dud *Rhinestone* in 1984.

RHODA MORGENSTERN

Mary Richard's worrywart best friend and upstairs neighbor who was a transplanted New Yorker from the Bronx working as a window dresser at Hempel's Department Store in Minneapolis. Sister is the whiny, overweight Brenda Morgenstern, mother is the meddlesome, guilt-giving Ida Morgenstern. Valerie Harper played this well-loved kook on *The Mary Tyler Moore Show* from 1970 to 1974, before having her own spin-off *Rhoda* series, from 1974 to 1978.

RICARDO

Cute, muscular, and energetic Latin-American soccer player who regularly visited TV's *Pee-Wee's Playhouse* to give the wacky host and home viewers tips on eating healthily and exercising. Vic Trevino played Ricardo.

RICARDO TUBBS

Sophisticated former New York street cop played by Philip Michael Thomas on *Miami Vice*, who moved to warmer climates (Miami, Florida) in the 1980s to work as an undercover detective. His loyal partner was the more rough-edged Sonny Crockett.

RICE-A-RONI

Introduced by the DeDomenico family in 1958, this boxed rice was advertised by a San Francisco cable car and a famous slogan: "The San Francisco Treat!"

RICHIE CUNNINGHAM

"I found my thrill on Blueberry Hill. . . ." On the sitcom *Happy Days*, freckle-faced redhead Ron Howard starred as the straitlaced nice-guy teen from Milwaukee who attended Jefferson High School (where he lettered in basketball) and once entered a Howdy Doody look-alike contest. Best buddies: Potsie Webber, Ralph Malph, and Fonzie.

RICHIE RICH

Since 1956, the "Poor Little Rich Boy" has been the inspiration of every child's million-dollar fantasy. Also called the "Richest Kid in the World," the bow-tied, yellow-haired eight-year-old resides with his parents, Richard and Regina, in the superlavish Rich mansion, a spectacular estate equipped with a swimming pool shaped like a dollar sign. Richie has a weekly allowance of $100,000 (wow!), plus all the luxuries money can buy, including his own yacht, jet plane, and helicopter. Never a spoiled brat, the young master enjoys spending his wealth on good causes and various globe-trotting adventures. Aiding him in his comic-book tales are middle-class girlfriend Gloria Glad, lower-class pal Freckles Friendly and little brother Pee Wee, Dalmatian Dollar, resourceful butler Cadbury, superpowered robotic maid Irona, wacky inventor Professor Keenbean, bratty cousin Reggie Van Dough, spoiled rich girl Mayda Munny, and young comedian Jackie Jokers.

Richie Rich debuted as a supporting character in *Harvey* comics' *Little Dot* number 6 (1956) before headlining his own self-titled comic book a year later (November 1957). By the late 1970s, he was *Harvey*'s leading star and had a dozen different comic books, with titles like *Richie Rich Billions, Richie Rich Diamonds, Richie Rich Dollars and Cents, Richie Rich Jackpots, Richie Rich Riches,* and *Richie Rich and Casper.* From 1980 to 1986, the comic star could be seen in a Saturday-morning cartoon TV series, *The Richie Rich Show.* A big-screen adaptation starring Macaulay Culkin in the title role played at theaters in 1994.

RICKIE TICKIE STICKIES

Flower Power! These groovy, brightly colored, daisy-shaped decals (yes, they actually had a name) are everlasting icons of the late 1960s and early 1970s, along with the peace sign and the smiley face. Rickie Tickie Stickies were created in 1967 by Don Kracke, a Los Angeles inventor, whose inspiration came from all the vehicles actually painted with flowers driven by hippies on Southern California's roadways. These stickers were easy to apply, stayed on forever (no amount of elbow grease could remove them), and were great for adding sunshiny cheer to boring, everyday objects. In their heyday, no object was safe. From kitchen appliances to bathroom fixtures, notebooks to school lockers, garage doors to automobiles—especially dune buggies and VW Beetles—everything was bedecked with these happy daisies. By mid-1968, the adhesive mod flowers sold at a rate of more than one million a week!

RICK MARSHALL

Handsome forest ranger who takes his children, Will and Holly, on a river-rafting expedition in the Grand Canyon, where they find themselves tumbling over a waterfall and transported to Saturday morning's

Land of the Lost. He disappears from this lost land three years later and is mysteriously replaced by brother Jack Marshall.

RICOCHET RABBIT
The persevering hare was a sheriff of the Old West who moved so quick it appeared as if he was bouncing off every surface in his vicinity ("ping, ping, ping"). On the other hand, his deputy assistant, Droop-a-Long Coyote, moved painfully slow. The law-abiding twosome were featured as a cartoon segment on Hanna-Barbera's *Magilla Gorilla Show* from 1964 to 1967.

RIDDLER
Maniacal villain from *Batman* who spoke in riddles and wore a green bodysuit with question marks all over it. Played by comedian Frank Gorshin on the 1960s TV series and by Jim Carrey in the 1995 *Batman Forever* movie.

RIFF RAFF
Bald hunchbacked henchman of Dr. Frank N. Furter who carried on an incestuous affair with his sister Magenta in the cult musical *The Rocky Horror Picture Show*. New Zealander Richard O'Brien created *Rocky Horror* and portrayed freaky Riff Raff in the 1975 film version.

RIFF RANDLE
Bouncy and pigtailed, the teen cutie loves The Ramones (especially Joey) so much that she invites the punk band to her high school. A student leader and cheerleader, she leads fellow students in a takeover of the school, resulting in its demolition. Played by P. J. Soles in the 1979 teen flick *Rock 'n' Roll High School*.

RIN TIN TIN
"Yo ho, Rinty!" Heroic German shepherd star whose adventures—based on a orphan puppy found in a trench by an American soldier during World War I—were featured in nineteen films for Warner Brothers, in a radio show sponsored by Ken-L Ration, and in a prime-time TV series (*The Adventures of Rin Tin Tin*), in which he joined young Corporal Rusty (Lee Aaker) and troopers of the 101st Cavalry in the Old West around the 1880s.

RINGWALD, MOLLY
The young actress with the pouty, full lips and soulful doe eyes was the personification of the suburban teen girl of the 1980s, dubbed the "model modern teen" by *Time* magazine. Born February 18, 1968, the California native garnered attention in the mid-1980s by association with director John Hughes, who transformed her not only into a movie star but also into a role model for adolescent girls. Ringwald's memorable film roles were about moody, misunderstood teens, such as angst-ridden Samantha Baker in *Sixteen Candles* (1984), spoiled Claire Standish in *The Breakfast Club* (1985), and lower-class Andie Walsh in *Pretty in Pink* (1986). Droves of "Molly Wannabes" copied the redhead's wavy hair and vintage clothing style by perming their tresses and dying them red and flocking to second-hand stores. These days, as a mature actress, the onetime princess of the Brat Pack appears to have lost her niche in Hollywood and is struggling to find it.

FYI: ▸ In 1979, Molly Ringwald appeared as Molly Parker on TV's *The Facts of Life*. She was fired after the sitcom down-sized to only four girls—Blair, Tootie, Jo, and Natalie—the following year.

RIPPY, RODNEY ALLEN
"Take life a little easier." Diminutive African-American lad famed for a series of TV commercials for Jack in the Box restaurants airing in the mid-1970s, in which he tried to take a bite out of a big, big burger. Led the way for two other overtly precocious black sprites: Gary Coleman and Emmanuel Lewis.

"RISE"
Instrumental song by trumpeter-bandleader Herb Alpert infamous for being played in the background when Luke Spencer raped future wife Laura Vining in his deserted Campus Disco club on the October 5, 1979, airing of *General Hospital*. The throbbing, disco-laced single had topped the American Top Forty for two weeks the previous summer (August 1979).

RISKY BUSINESS
The film that put Tom Cruise on the road to superstardom was both a critical and a popular hit, grossing more than $65 million in the United States

alone. Cruise plays Joel Goodsen, an overachieving and repressed Chicago teenager who is studying for his college entrance exams while his parents are away on vacation. Like all healthy young men, he can't take his mind off sex, and he eventually meets up with a kittenish, frosted-blonde hooker named Lana (Rebecca De Mornay). The laughs begin when Lana and Joel turn his parents' swank suburban home into a one-night brothel to repay money owed to Guido the Killer Pimp (Joe Pantoliano). Cruise's star-making scene is when he does a humorous yet sexy air-guitar dance in his Jockey briefs to Bob Seger's "Old Time Rock 'n' Roll." The sight of the young hunk's muscular legs alone was well worth the ticket price. Directed by Paul Brickman, this 1983 comedy was 'way above its contemporaries in the teen-sex genre (for instance, *Porky's*). It's stylish, funny, smart, cynical, and the closest thing to *The Graduate* (1967) that Generation X has.

RIVERDALE
Hometown setting of *Archie* comic books—located somewhere, anywhere, in Middle America (and near a beach)—where Archie Andrews and the gang live. Neighboring Midvale is where Josie and the Pussycats are from.

RIVERDALE HIGH
Alma mater of the Archies, ruled over by harried Principal Mr. Wetherbee. Other school employees included teachers Miss Grundy and Miss Haggly, science teacher Professor Flutesnoot, gym teacher Coach Kleats, cafeteria cook Miss Beazly, and Swedish janitor Mr. Svenson ("Yumpin' Yimminy!"). Riverdale's school colors are blue and gold. Central High School is its main rival.

RIVERS, JOAN
"Can we talk?" Big-mouth blonde comedienne and advocate of plastic surgery, born on June 8, 1933, in Brooklyn, known for late-night talk-show standup routines in which she ruthlessly dishes the dirt on celebs, particularly Elizabeth Taylor and Queen Elizabeth. Since 1995, the fashionable Rivers and no-talent daughter Melissa have stood alongside the red carpet before awards shows (Oscars, Emmys, Grammys), critiquing what the stars are wearing for the E! Entertainment network.

ROACH CLIP WITH FEATHERS
For stoner chicks of the 1980s, this contraption had two purposes. It was a dandy feathered accessory to be worn in the hair, and/or it could be used to hold a burning roach. (For the marijuana illiterate out there, a roach is not a bug but a joint smoked down until you can't hold it in your fingers without burning.)

ROAD RUNNER AND WILE E. COYOTE
Poor Road Runner *(acceleratii incredibilus)*. The speedy bird is eternally chased across the desert landscapes of the American Southwest by pesty Wile E. Coyote *(carnivorous vulgaris)*. The ravenous Coyote would like to make a meal out of the fowl, and he enlists an endless supply of Rube Goldberg-ish gadgets to help nab him (ordered from the world-famous Acme company, of course), such as Rocket-Powered Roller Skates, Do-It Yourself Tornadoes, Sling-Shot Anvils, and Axle Grease (guaranteed slippery). Invariably these nutty contraptions backfire, leaving the scheming Coyote with one whopping headache and the Road Runner free to "Beep! Beep!" for the next cartoon adventure. The desert twosome were created by animator Chuck Jones in 1949 for the animated Warner Brothers short "Fast and Furry-ous." In 1966, the Road Runner was given his own Saturday-morning TV program before sharing top billing with Bugs Bunny on *The Bugs Bunny / Road Runner Hour* in 1968.

ROBBIE DOUGLAS
At age fourteen, former *Mickey Mouse Club* Mouseketeer Don Grady starred as the cute, dimple-cheeked middle son of Steve Douglas on the TV sitcom *My Three Sons*. As the show progressed, Robbie grew up to marry his college sweetheart, Katie Miller, and to father triplet sons—Steve Jr., Charley (after his beloved Uncle Charley), and Robbie II.

ROBIN
Nicknamed the Boy Wonder, the enthusiastic orphan fond of starting exclamations with "Holy" ("Holy mackerel, Batman!") is millionaire Bruce Wayne's young ward (alias Dick Grayson) and crime-fighter Batman's sidekick. Robin would later moonlight as leader of a team of teenage superheroes called the Teen Titans in the early twenty-first century.

ROBIN'S-EGG-BLUE FROSTED EYE SHADOW

The ultimate 1970s eyelid color—named after the flat blue color of a robin's egg—a version of which every major cosmetic company featured (Revlon's China Blue Frost, for example).

ROBOT

The Robot was a mimelike dance, popularized by The Jackson 5 and their Top Ten hit "Dancing Machine" (1974), involving robotic-like stiff, start-and-stop jerks (a.k.a. "popping"). The dance evolved into the Electric Boogie in the 1980s, which was the Robot combined with hand waves and the gravity-defying Moonwalk made famous by Michael Jackson.

FYI: ▸ You haven't seen anything until you've seen forty white-gloved babes doing a synchronized Robot, followed by astonishing high-kicks, like the trophy-winning Indianettes drill team of Garfield High School (in suburban Woodbridge, Virginia) did to Heatwave's "Groove Line" back in 1978.

ROBOT B-9

"Danger! Danger! Will Robinson!" Trustworthy and logically inclined, this mechanical being (just call him "Robot") with the bubble head and accordion arms guided the Robinson family on their explorations in outer space. Had a friendship with young electronics whiz Will Robinson—whom he usually saved—and a "love-hate" relationship with sinister Dr. Smith, an agent for an enemy foreign government who once tried to use the Robot to destroy the Robinsons. In the 1960s sci-fi TV series *Lost in Space*, Bob May maneuvered the Robot, and Dick Tufeld provided its voice (Tufeld was also the show's announcer).

FYI: ▸ Other famous pop culture robots include Rosie (*Jetsons*), Conky 2000 (*Pee-Wee's Playhouse*), R2-D2 and C3PO (*Star Wars*), Robby (*Forbidden Planet*), Hymie (*Get Smart*), Yul Brynner's Gunslinger (*Westworld*), and the sexy but deadly Fembots (*Austin Powers*).

ROCK

Late 1970s disco dance often alternated with the Freak ("Rock . . . Freak!"). Dancers rocked side to side—with wrist action—to the beat of the disco rhythm. Best songs to do the Rock: "Disco Nights (Rock-Freak)" (1979) by GQ and "Rock with You" (1979) by Michael Jackson.

ROCK 'EM SOCK 'EM ROBOTS

"You knocked his block off!" We rocked 'em, we socked 'em. We knocked their blocks off. Popular with boys, this was the ultimate action game of the era, not to mention the coolest as well. It featured two robot gladiators—beautiful Blue Bomber from Saultarus II and rollicking Red Rocker, pride of Umgluk—duking it out in a yellow boxing ring for the title of "Heavyweight Champion of the Universe." Two players, serving as managers, operated each robot by hand controls outside the ring. The plastic robots could move forward, backward, and sideways while throwing punches with each arm. The contenders kept fighting and slugging away until a Sunday punch squarely to the jaw made the loser's head pop up. Rock 'Em Sock 'Em was introduced by Marx Toys in 1966.

ROCK FLOWERS

"Spin my record! Watch me spin!" Presented by Mattel in 1970, Rock Flowers were a "swingin', singin'" trio of rock-star fashion dolls. Dressed in psychedelic outfits replete with bell-bottoms, maxiskirts, and go-go boots, the band of six-inch-high bendable dolls, all named after flowers, consisted of brunette Lilac, blonde Heather, and African-American Rosemary. The following year, two new members were introduced: raven-haired Iris and token male Doug (What! No floral name?). The gimmick was that each doll came with a plastic 45 rpm single featuring her own hit on one side and a song ("Sweet Times") by all the Rock Flowers on the other. By using a plastic holder, you could position the doll on the middle top of the record—and as the disc played, the Rock Flower would twirl, seeming to dance and sing to the tune.

ROCKING HORSES

Ride 'em cowboy! These bouncy, spring-based replicas of frisky palominos and pinto ponies were a staple of childhood playtime.

ROCK 'N' ROLL HIGH SCHOOL

A high-energy, low-budget cult flick, from the Roger Corman Factory and directed by Allan Arkush, about the ongoing conflict between adult authority and youth rebellion. At Vince Lombardi High School in Southern California, stern Miss Evelyn Togar (played by Mary Woronov), a rock-'n'-roll-hating principal, suppresses the student body, led by spirited cheerleader Riff Randell (P. J. Soles), by banning the popular music. Riff is the number-one fan of The Ramones (America's numero-uno punk band) and rebelliously succeeds in bringing them to Vince Lombardi High, setting off a revolution against the stodgy administration. In the end, the kids take over the school, rename it Rock 'n' Roll High, and then blow it up (every youngster's fantasy).

Supporting players of *Rock 'n' Roll High School* include teen idol Vince Van Patten as Tom Roberts, the straitlaced quarterback who has a crush on Riff; Dey Young as Kate Rambeau, Riff's straitlaced best friend who has a crush on Tom; Clint Howard as Eaglebauer, the school's fix-it guy with an office in the boy's bathroom who is capable of delivering hall passes, absentee excuses, A+ reports, and setting up fellow students with their hot crushes; Loren Lester and Daniel Davies as Fritz Hansel and Fritz Gretel, a pair of dorky hall monitors; Lynn Farrell as slutty Angel Dust, a Ramones groupie; and Paul Bartel as Mr. McGree, the classical-music instructor who has an appreciation for rock music. *Rock 'n' Roll High School*'s soundtrack includes virtually all the best of The Ramones, such as "I Wanna Be Sedated," "Sheena Is a Punk Rocker," "Teenage Lobotomy," "Blitzkrieg Bop," and the title anthem, remixed by legendary Wall-of-Sound producer Phil Spector.

ROCK, PAPER, SCISSORS

"Go!" Two-player hand game used to determined teams or to see who would have to do something, or simply to relieve boredom. To play, each participant would make a fist with one hand and hold the other hand, palm face-up. Simultaneously, they thump their fist three times in the upright palm. On the third thump, they randomly form one of three items: a rock (a fist), a sheet of paper (hand flat down), or a pair of scissors (two fingers extended apart). The winner of the round is determined by what item each person chose to form—a rock crushes scissors, paper covers rock, and scissors cut paper.

ROCKY

"Yo, Adrian!" Released in 1976, the cinematic story of an underdog boxer who gets his million-to-one shot for fame and respect in a championship battle for the world heavyweight title. Italian Stallion newcomer Sylvester Stallone starred as Rocky Balboa, the loutish two-bit palooka from South Philly who "only wants to go the distance." Supporting Rocky was his painfully shy girlfriend (and, later, wife) Adrian (Talia Shire), his manager and Adrian's brother Paulie (Burt Young), and his feisty elderly trainer Mickey (Burgess Meredith). Carl Weathers played Apollo Creed, the cocky world heavyweight champ.

As the feel-good movie of the 1970s, this rags-to-riches story mirrored Stallone's own fight for Hollywood success. It went on to win him the coveted Oscar for Best Picture, and an Oscar for John G. Avildsen as Best Director. Spawned four sequels: *Rocky II* (1979), in which Rocky is rematched with Apollo Creed; *Rocky III* (1982), in which Rocky fights obnoxious Clubber Lang (Mr. T); *Rocky IV* (1985), where Rocky confronts superhuman Russian Ivan Drago (Dolph Lundgren); and *Rocky V* (1990), where Rocky brawls with young protégé Tommy Morrison. Bill Conti's rousing theme, "Gonna Fly Now," remindful of Rocky's now-famous run through the streets of Philadelphia, became a chart-topping single in May 1977.

ROCKY AND HIS FRIENDS

This fun-filled, pun-filled satirical TV cartoon starred dauntless Rocky, a flying squirrel, and dim-witted Bullwinkle, a moose, who hailed from Frostbite Falls, Minnesota. Their adventures centered on the patriotic twosome's battling a cold-war baddie, Mr. Big, and his dastardly yet ineffective Pottsylvanian henchpeople: Boris Badenov and Natasha Fatale. Created by animator Jay Ward and narrated by William "Cannon" Conrad, the half-program first aired from 1959 to 1961 before being renamed *The Bullwinkle Show* from 1961 to 1973. Supporting segments included "Fractured Fairy Tales," "Peabody's Improbable History," "Adventures of Dudley Do-Right," and "Aesop and Son." Popular with kids and adults alike, Rocky and Bullwinkle have developed an almost legendary cult following over the years, spawning hundreds of merchandise spin-offs, such as games, toys, dolls, coloring books, and a now-sought-after lunch box.

ROCKY HORROR
Dr. Frank N. Furter's "creature of the night," a blond, tanned hunk with an extremely well-built muscular body clad only in scanty gold briefs. Created in a laboratory to be the "ultimate sexual man," Rocky awakens to fear the transvestite scientist and reject his sexual advances. Played by Peter Hinwood, whose flawless face (and body) put him at the top of the male modeling industry before filming *The Rocky Horror Picture Show* (1975).

ROCKY HORROR PICTURE SHOW
"Give yourself over to absolute pleasure!" The ultimate queen of the midnight movie started out as a box-office dud in 1975 but eventually developed an unprecedented cult following, due to audience participation. Every Friday and Saturday at midnight, filmgoers equipped with props—toast, rice, squirt guns, newspapers, and cigarette lighters—and often dressed as one of the film's campy characters would line up outside theaters nationwide, waiting in anticipation of the event to come. (The typical *Rocky* fan was a young thespian type; first-time viewers were known as "virgins.") During the screening, the audience threw all manners out the window as they talked aloud to the onscreen characters, changed the dialogue around, danced the "Time Warp," and used the props for a night of outrageous behavior.

Based on Richard O'Brien's British musical stage play and directed by Jim Sharman, the hilarious and sexy horror spoof told the story of nerdy Brad and virginal Janet (played by Barry Bostwick and Susan Sarandon), a straitlaced, newly engaged couple from Denton, Ohio, whose car breaks down at night during the middle of a rainstorm. They take refuge at a nearby castle owned by vampy transvestite Dr. Frank N. Furter (Tim Curry), who happens to be a mad scientist from outer space—Planet Transsexual in the galaxy Transylvania, to be exact! Frank N. Furter, along with a group of bizarre cohorts, has been working on a laboratory creation—the blond, muscled hunk named Rocky (Peter Hinwood)—the ultimate sexual man. Before daylight breaks, Brad and Janet get initiated to "absolute pleasure" and the darker side of life.

Co-starring in the legendary cast is Richard O'Brien as humpbacked Riff Raff, a handyman; Patricia Quinn as Riff Raff's incestuous sister Magenta, a domestic; Nell Campbell as Betty Boop-ish tap dancer Columbia, a groupie; Meat Loaf as Columbia's deceased boyfriend, Eddie, a hoodlum; Jonathan Adams as wheelchair-confined Dr. Everett Von Scott, a rival scientist; and Charles Gray as the film's "no-neck" narrator. The fun musical numbers include "Sweet Transvestite," "Dammit Janet," "Science Fiction / Double Feature," "The Time Warp," "I Can Make You a Man," and "Touch-a, Touch-a, Touch Me."

In December 1999, the Amazing World of Cult Movies, an Internet film group, named *The Rocky Horror Picture Show* the Cult Movie of the Century. "Don't dream it—be it!"

FYI: ▸ *Rocky Horror*'s recognized logo, the red lips, belonged to actress Patricia "Magenta" Quinn.

ROCKY J. SQUIRREL
"And now, here's something you'll really like!" This plucky, pint-sized flying squirrel teamed up with best pal Bullwinkle Moose to save Frostbite Falls (and the rest of the world, for that matter) from the evil Mr. Big and his cronies, Natasha and Boris. "Hokey smokes!"

RODAN
A giant mutant pterodactyl whose colossal wingspan (250 feet) creates destructive shockwaves on poor Tokyo after ill-considered atomic bomb tests awaken the monster from a deep slumber in its underground cavern nest. Rodan is featured in the sci-fi film *Rodan the Flying Monster* (1956), directed by Inoshiro Honda, the creator of another creature of mayhem—Godzilla.

ROE, TOMMY
American recording artist from the 1960s, known best for a string of youthful bubblegum hits: "Sweet Pea" (1966), "Hooray for Hazel" (1966), "Heather Honey" (1969), "Jam Up Jelly Tight" (1969), and the classic chart-topper "Dizzy" (1969). First number-one hit occurred in 1962 with "Sheila."

ROGER HEALEY
Major Tony Nelson's babe-loving bachelor buddy who is the only other person wise to Jeannie the wish-

granting genie. He secretly wants a genie like Jeannie. Played by Bill Daily on TV's *I Dream of Jeannie.*

ROGER RABBIT (DANCE)

Energetic late-1980s dance inspired by the movie *Who Framed Roger Rabbit?* You kept both arms bent at the elbow, making a fist, and as you pumped your arms back and forth you step-ball-changed with your right foot two times, then repeated with your left foot.

ROGER RAMJET

This "daredevil, flying fool, and all-around good guy," voiced by TV personality Gary Owens (*Laugh-In*), was the patriotic star of a satirical Saturday-morning TV cartoon first airing in 1965. A scientist by day, our superhero led an American Eagle Squadron of kids—Yank, Doodle, Dan, and Dee—and swallowed proton energy capsules, which gave him "the power of twenty atom bombs for a period of twenty seconds." He used the amazing power to battle Noodle Romanov of N.A.S.T.Y. (the National Association of Spies, Traitors, and Yahoos). The lovely Lotta Love was Roger's oft-concerned girlfriend.

ROLLER BOOGIE

"It's love on wheels!" A mostly awful teen pic made quickly to cash in on the mercifully brief roller-disco craze. It starred Linda Blair as Terry Barkley, a rebellious rich girl from Beverly Hills who goes slumming at a roller-skating rink in Venice Beach. She finds romance with the rink's disco king, Bobby James (real-life skating champ Jim Bray), an ambitious yet poor local. Together Terry and Bobby prevent a crooked businessman (Mark Goddard, from TV's *Lost in Space*) from closing the rink so that they can compete in the climactic disco-skating contest. Directed by Mark L. Lester, the 1979 low-budgeter also featured Kimberly Beck and Jimmy Van Patten as skating pals Lana and Hoppy.

ROLLER DISCO

It's believed that people under the age of twenty started the roller-boogie fad of the late 1970s, an inevitable union between disco-dancing and roller-skating. Weekend nights at the local roller rink was the place to be for teens who were unable to get into discotheques that served liquor because they were under the drinking age. So, off to the rink they went! There they simply strapped on a pair of wheels and shuffled and boogied all night around the skating arena to such songs as Heatwave's "Boogie Nights" and Peaches and Herb's "Shake Your Groove Thing."

From D.C. to N.Y. to L.A., the skating craze streaked across the United States, fueled by celebs like Cher, Olivia Newton-John, Robin Williams, Erik Estrada, Brooke Shields, and John Kennedy Jr., who were at the rinks as roller-disco devotees. Hollywood reflected roller disco with three movies: *Roller Boogie* (1979), starring Linda Blair; *Skatetown U.S.A.* (1979), starring Scott Baio; and *Xanadu* (1980), starring Olivia Newton-John. Fashion-teen Barbie even joined the eight-wheel fad when Mattel released Roller Skating Barbie in 1980 ("She's queen of the roller scene!"). An essential roller-disco outfit for women consisted of rainbow-striped knee-high tube socks, shiny Dolphin shorts (with little slits up the sides), a rainbow-striped tube top, and a satiny jacket (to wear as a cover-up inside chilly roller rinks).

FYI: ▸ The Roxy in New York City was the hotspot for disco-skating in the 1970s.

ROMPER ROOM

Similar to *Bozo the Clown*, this was a children's educational program, locally produced by individual TV stations who used their own hosts. Created in 1953 by Bert Claster and wife Nancy, *Romper Room* originated on WBAL-TV in Baltimore, and a decade later more than 115 stations nationwide were airing the series—called the "world's largest classroom" by *Time* magazine. The *Romper Room* set looked like an elementary school classroom. It was filled with in-studio kids (generally six five-year-olds), and the teacher was a pleasant hostess who used the courtesy title of Miss followed by her first name (Miss Sally, Miss Gloria, Miss Molly, Miss Nancy . . .).

The program featured music, songs, stories, games, and other related entertainment geared toward the preschool set. Children were taught the basics of safety and manners with Mr. Do Bee and Mr. Don't Bee ("Do Bees look both ways before crossing the street, Don't Bees never look both ways before crossing the street"). Most memorable was the Magic Mirror roll call at the show's end, when the teacher gazed through an empty mirror frame to "see" all the kids watching the show from home ("I see Pam, I see Matt, I see Tina, I see Darren . . .").

RONALD McDONALD

"The McFriendliest Fellow in Town!" Highly adored by wee ones, this redheaded advertising clown from magical McDonaldland has happily slaved for the McDonald's fast-food chain since 1963. Famed weatherman Willard Scott played the first Ronald McDonald (initially named Donald McDonald), in televised commercials that aired in the Washington, D.C., area. McDonald's replaced the portly Scott in favor of somebody thinner, actor King Moody, when they went nationwide with the character. (Moody starred as Ronald throughout the 1970s and 1980s.)

FYI: ▸ Recent surveys show that Ronald McDonald is so popular that more than 96 percent of school-aged children in the U.S. can identify him (he rates second only to Santa Claus).

RONSTADT, LINDA

Born July 15, 1946, in Tucson, Arizona, the dark-haired, shy-eyed singer of Mexican and German descent was one of the best-loved and sexiest female rockers of the 1970s. She began her career in 1964, at age eighteen, as lead vocalist for the Stone Poneys, accompanying Bobby Kimmel and Ken Edwards. In 1967, the folksy threesome had a Top Twenty single with "Different Drum," featuring Ronstadt's soulful country-rock voice. The following year, she ventured out as a solo singer, giving superb live performances.

Superstar success arrived in the mid-1970s with a string of million-selling LPs: *Heart Like a Wheel* (1974), *Prisoner in Disguise* (1975), *Hasten Down the Wind* (1976), *Simple Dreams* (1977), and *Living in the U.S.A.* (1978). Hit singles (many covers of other artists' songs) included "Long Long Time" (1970), "You're No Good" (1975), "When Will I Be Loved" (1975), "Heat Wave" (1975), "Tracks of My Tears" (1976), "Blue Bayou" (1977), "It's So Easy" (1977), "Ooh Baby Baby" (1978), "How Do I Make You" (1980), and "Hurt So Bad" (1980).

In the 1980s, Ronstadt branched away from her rock roots by taking several surprising detours, displaying her musical diversity. She was an operetta actress, starring opposite Rex Smith in the Tony-winning Broadway musical *Pirates of Penzance* by Gilbert and Sullivan (made into a movie in 1983); a chanteuse, backed by legendary orchestra conductor Nelson Riddle, crooning pop standards of the 1950s on the albums *What's New* (1983), *Lush Life* (1984), and *Sentimental Reasons* (1986); a country singer in a Grammy-winning trio, along with Dolly Parton and Emmylou Harris in 1987; and a Mexican folksinger, performing songs from her childhood in Spanish on the 1988 album *Canciones de Mi Padre* (*My Father's Songs*). Other Ronstadt highlights: making the cover of *Rolling Stone* (December 1976); coming in second on Mr. Blackwell's list of Ten Worst Dressed Women of 1978 (Farrah Fawcett-Majors was number one); and dating Jerry Brown, the Democratic governor of California.

FYI: ▸ Linda Ronstadt's regular tour band in the early 1970s—guitarist Glenn Frey, guitarist Bernie Leadon, bassist Randy Meisner, and drummer Don Henley—later became The Eagles.

ROOM 222

Set at fictional Walt Whitman High, an integrated high school in Los Angeles, this award-winning drama series aired on ABC-TV from 1969 to 1974. It focused on the relationship between the teachers and students by examining various problems associated with youths of the era, such as drug abuse, dropping out, and racial intolerance. Lloyd Haynes starred as idealist Pete Dixon, the black history teacher, whose homeroom was Room 222. Other faculty members included Seymour Kaufman (Michael Constantine), the sardonic principal; Liz McIntyre (Denise Nicholas), the guidance counselor and Pete's girlfriend; and Alice Johnson (Karen Valentine), the high-spirited English teacher. Regular students were Helen Loomis (Judy Strangis), Richie Lane (Howard Rice), Al Cowley (Pendrant Netherly), Jason Allen (Heshimu), Pam (Ta-Tanisha), Bernie (David Jolliffe), and Larry (Eric Laneuville). Strangis later starred as ElectraWoman's young sidekick, DynaGirl, on *The Krofft Supershow.*

FYI: ▸ *Room 222* was based on and filmed at Los Angeles High School, which housed a 3,000-plus student body.

ROPERS
Married middle-aged landlords and owners of the apartment building in which prime time's *Three's Company* gang (Jack, Chrissy, and Janet) resided. Husband Stanley Roper was cantankerous, sexually impotent, and suspicious of the renters—particularly "gay" Jack—living above him. On the other hand, wife Helen, although frustratedly horny and frocked in sight-blinding, psychedelic-floral dresses, was friendlier and couldn't care less about what occurred among the apartment tenants.

ROSANNE ROSANNADANNA
"It just goes to show you, it's always something." Weekend Update's fuzzy-haired consumer-affairs reporter who inevitably rambles on about some issue of personal hygiene, such as belly-button lint, warts, or things that get stuck in teeth, and therefore earns the disdain of uptight anchorwoman Jane Curtin. Played delightfully by the late Gilda Radner, Rosanne Rosannadanna is one of the most beloved characters ever created for *Saturday Night Live*.

ROSEANNE

> "This is why some animals eat their young."
> —ROSEANNE CONNER (ROSEANNE BARR)

Sardonic comedienne Roseanne Barr's groundbreaking sitcom about a lower-class family of five struggling to make ends meet in the blue-collar town of Lanford, Illinois. It centered on Roseanne Conner (Barr), the hefty queen of the house and working mother of three who was always ready to deliver a teasing, wiseass remark to those she loved—followed by a loving smile and a laugh. Equally hefty Dan Conner (John Goodman), Roseanne's high school sweetheart husband, was constantly job-hopping (his dream was to own a Harley-Davidson motorcycle shop). Their offspring consisted of oldest Becky (Lecy Goranson), the boy-crazy ditz; middle-child Darlene (Sara Gilbert), the dour tomboy; and youngest D.J. (Michael Fishman), the slightly peculiar son. Goofball Jackie Harris (Laurie Metcalf), Roseanne's supportive sister and best friend, was trying to find her way through careers and a love life. Premiering on ABC-TV in 1988, *Roseanne*, showcasing charismatic characters and sharper-than-average writing, was the biggest hit of the late 1980s and aired for nearly a decade.

ROSEMARY
Ditsy but sweet nasal-voiced switchboard operator who worked alongside custodian Penry Pooch at the police station in the Saturday-morning cartoon *Hong Kong Phooey*.

ROSEMARY WOODHOUSE
Manhattan housewife who is impregnated by Satan after her husband sells the soul of their unborn son to better his acting career. Played by the gamine Mia Farrow in director Roman Polanski's terrifying *Rosemary's Baby* (1968).

ROSE PETAL PLACE
The 1984 Kenner doll line showcasing a flower that was turned into a young girl, Rose Petal, and her friends—Daffodil, Iris, Orchid, Lily Fair, and Sunny Sunflower—who resided in a teapot in a magic garden. Each flower fairy came scented to match her floral personality.

ROSIE THE ROBOT
The Jetsons' robot maid, who delivered wisecracks in a Brooklyn accent, on the Saturday-morning cartoon program. Although Rosie was outdated, the Jetsons loved her and would never think of trading her in for a newer model from the U-Rent-a-Robot Maid Service.

ROSIE THE WAITRESS
Server in a small diner who constantly demonstrated, to the astonishment of her dining customers, what a "better picker-upper" Bounty paper towels were. Played by wisecracking Nancy Walker of *Rhoda* fame on a long-running series of TV commercials.

ROSS, DIANA
Born on March 26, 1944, the petite lead singer of The Supremes—the biggest girl group of all time—started her solo career in 1970 with the single "Ain't No Mountain High Enough." It was the first of many Top Ten hits, including "Touch Me in the Morning" (1973), "Theme from *Mahogany*" (1975), "Love Hangover" (1976), "Upside Down" (1980), "I'm Coming Out" (1980), "It's My Turn" (1980), and a

duet with Lionel Richie, "Endless Love" (1981). Ross's performance as Billie Holiday in the 1972 biopic *Lady Sings the Blues* earned her an Oscar nomination for Best Actress. Other notable film roles included fashion-model Mahogany in 1975's *Mahogany* (Ross designed her own clothing) and Dorothy in 1978's all-black musical *The Wiz*, based on the Broadway hit starring Stephanie Mills. Called the "Female Entertainer of the Century" by *Billboard* magazine, the big-haired "Diva of Pop" has remained at the top of her profession for four decades.

R2-D2

Spunky, squatty, barrel-shaped, three-legged droid that communicates by a series of electronic beeps and whistles. In 1977's *Star Wars*, Artoo delivered the important holographic message to Luke Skywalker from the captive Princess Leia. Usually teamed with fastidious protocol droid C-3PO.

RUBBER BRACELETS

Black, round, and stretchy, these were actually typewriter drive-belts made famous as an arm bangle by Madonna in the mid-1980s. New Wave club kids would wear tons of these around each wrist. The thin plastic bracelets, found in a variety of colors, were sold by Claire's Boutiques at your nearest shopping mall and were known as Jelly or Gummy bracelets.

RUBIK'S CUBE

"Over three billion combinations . . . just one solution." Along with Pac-Man and the Izod alligator, the Rubik's Cube is an enduring icon of the 1980s. It was invented in 1974 by Hungarian architecture professor Erno Rubik, who used it as a mental exercise for students at the Academy for the Applied Arts in Budapest. In 1980, Ideal Toys bought the rights to manufacture Rubik's Cube, and by the following year more than ten million had been sold worldwide.

The Rubik's Cube is a baffling 3-D geometric puzzle consisting of six sides of smaller cubes, each showing nine colored squares in rows of three. The object of playing is to obtain solid colors on each side of the Cube by twisting and turning the rows in any direction. Except for a few Cubist elites (a sixteen-year-old British boy solved it in twenty-eight seconds), it's difficult to solve and even harder to put down. It can take most people days, weeks, or even months of twiddling and thumbing, and many others never do solve the riddle of the Cube. In 1983, the complex puzzle was featured in a Saturday-morning TV cartoon, *Rubik, the Amazing Cube* (voiced by Ron "Arnold Horshack" Palillo), considered by many to be the worst of the decade!

RUB-ONS

Described as "the most exciting craft for children since coloring," Rub-Ons were an assortment of picture transfers that you rubbed onto illustrated backgrounds. Originally manufactured by Hasbro Toys in the 1960s, these kits featured some of the era's most beloved icons: Bozo, Superman, Popeye, G.I. Joe, Mary Poppins, Mickey Mouse, Casper, Flipper, and Herman Munster.

RUDOLPH THE RED-NOSED REINDEER

"Rudolph, with your nose so bright, won't you guide my sleigh tonight?"

—SANTA CLAUS

Burl Ives gives voice to Sam the Snowman, narrator of the endearing Christmas TV special about the brave little buck with the shiny red nose. Rudolph, the fawn of Santa's lead reindeer, Donner, is shunned by all the other reindeer and banned from playing with them because of his glowing snout (which gives a slight high-pitched cheep each time it glows). He teams up with fellow misfit Hermey, a reluctant toy-making elf who yearns to be a dentist, and the twosome run away from Christmastown, a.k.a. North Pole, leaving behind Rudolph's sweet doe-friend, Clarice. During their journey in the Arctic wilderness, the outcasts encounter the furious Abominable Snow Monster, fearless prospector Yukon Cornelius, and the Island of Misfit Toys.

Upon returning home to Christmastown, Rudolph learns that his parents and Clarice have set off to look for him. He finds them captive in Abominable's cave and ready to become dinner for the Snow Monster. With the aid of Yukon and Hermey (the elf removes all the giant beast's teeth), Rudolph courageously rescues them. On Christmas Eve, a fierce blizzard ravages the land and threatens to cancel the holiday. Realizing that Rudolph's bright-red nose would make a terrific beacon, Santa asks him for help in guiding his sleigh through the dark, snowy night. Rudolph agrees and goes down in history for saving the Christmas holiday.

Rudolph the Red-Nosed Reindeer was filmed using Animagic, stop-motion animated puppets created by Arthur Rankin Jr. and Jules Bass. Since first airing December 6, 1964, it has become the longest-running and highest-rated TV special of all time. It is based on the 1939 poem by Robert L. May, who penned it for employer Montgomery Ward, and on the million-selling Johnny Marks tune made famous by Gene Autry in 1949. Marks also wrote all the other songs for the musical fantasy, including "A Holly Jolly Christmas," "Jingle Jingle Jingle," "We Are Santa's Elves," "There's Always Tomorrow," "We're a Couple of Misfits," "Silver and Gold," and "The Most Wonderful Time of the Year." The program's popularity fostered three sequels: *Rudolph's Shiny New Year* (1976), *Rudolph and Frosty* (1979), and the computer-animated *Rudolph the Red-Nosed Reindeer and the Island of Misfit Toys* (2001).

RUFF

The shaggy-haired, not-so-intelligent dog was owned by the Mitchell family in Hank Ketcham's *Dennis the Menace* comic tales. He tagged along with menace Dennis on mischief-making adventures.

RUFFLED BLOUSES

Like—omigawd—these frilly tops were a totally hot fashion item, worn with miniskirts by Valley Girls in the early 1980s!

RUGRATS

Slang term for little kids, and the title of an incredibly popular cartoon about a group of diaper-clad toddlers, premiering on the Nickelodeon cable channel in 1991. The TV show's stories revolved around the floor-hugging antics of good-natured one-year-old Tommy Pickles and his crew of babies: one-tooth, four-eyed worrywart Chuckie Finster, double-trouble infant twins Phil and Lil Deville, bullying older cousin Angelica Pickles, and pet dog Spike. Susie Carmichael, a sweet African-American tot, and Dil Pickles, Tommy's new baby brother, were added to the series later. The precocious kids appeared in a variety of holiday TV specials, including *Rugrats Hollyween* (1993), *Rugrats Santa Experience* (1996), and *Rugrats Chanukah* (1997) and in two full-length feature films, *Rugrats Movie* (1998) and *Rugrats in Paris* (2000).

FYI: ▸ Actress-singer E. G. Daily, famed for playing Loryn in the 1983 cult teen flick *Valley Girl*, provided the voice of Tommy Pickles.

RUNAROUND

A Saturday-morning TV game show for children hosted by ventriloquist Paul Winchell and airing from 1972 to 1973. It showcased nine youngsters who, when a question was asked, ran (the "runaround") to certain colored squares on a stage resembling a life-sized board game, which contained the correct answers. After a series of eliminations (those who picked the wrong answers were sent to a penalty box), the last player on stage was the winner and would go on to the big final round.

FYI: ▸ Paul Winchell is best known for his act with dummies Jerry Mahoney and Knucklehead Smiff and as the voice of many Hanna-Barbera cartoon characters: Fleegle of *The Banana Splits* (1968–70), Dick Dastardly of *Dastardly and Muttley* (1969–71), canine Goober of *Goober and the Ghost Chasers* (1973–75), and the evil Gargamel of *The Smurfs* (1981–90).

RUNAWAYS

Formed in Los Angeles in 1975, the near-legendary group is considered to be the first all-female teenage rock act and the fore-sisters of such alternative girl acts as Babes in Toyland, The Bangles, The Breeders, Fuzzbox, The Go-Go's, Hole, L7, Veruca Salt, and The Donnas. Nicknamed the "Female Ramones," The Runaways consisted of five sixteen-year-old girls: bleached-blonde lead vocalist Cherie Currie, guitarists Lita Ford and Joan Jett, bassist Jackie Fox, and drummer Sandy West. Although music superstars in Japan, they were only moderately successful in America, noted for three LPs: *The Runaways* (1976), *Queens of Noise* (1977), and *Live in Japan* (1977) and a riotous single, "Cherry Bomb" (1976).

In 1977, black-haired Jett moved to lead singer after Currie left to form a music duo with identical twin sister Marie. In April 1979, The Runaways disbanded to try their luck as soloists, with varying degrees of success. Ford landed a modest heavy-metal smash in 1988 with "Kiss Me Deadly," while Jett had better luck. She formed Joan Jett and The Blackhearts and scored a string of hits, including a number-one song for seven weeks, "I Love Rock 'n' Roll" (1982). Cherie Currie co-starred with Jodie Foster and Scott Baio in the 1980 teen flick *Foxes* (she played the doomed Annie).

RUN, JOE, RUN

This live-action Saturday-morning series, airing on NBC-TV from 1974 to 1976, told the sad tale of an army K-9 German shepherd on the lam after being wrongly accused of attacking his master. As he runs from his pursuers each week, Joe (played by a dog named Heinrich of Midvale) manages to aid those in need.

"RUN, JOEY, RUN"

A depressing ditty about a young woman named Julie who is shot by her enraged father while trying to protect her boyfriend, Joey. It's not quite clear why he is so angry, but I think it's because Julie might be pregnant—because of lyrics like "Daddy, please don't! It wasn't his fault. He means so much to me. Daddy, please don't! We're going to get married. Just you wait and see." "Run, Joey, Run" was a Top Ten hit for pop singer David Geddes in the summer of 1975. It was a throwback to the "death pop" hits of the early 1960s, such as Mark Dinning's "Teen Angel" (1960), Ray Peterson's "Tell Laura I Love Her," and The Shangri-Las' "Leader of the Pack" (1964).

RUSSELL, KURT

Before he played macho action-heroes in blockbuster movies (*Escape to New York, The Thing, Backdraft,* and *Stargate*) and became Goldie Hawn's longtime companion, this cute, dimpled blond actor was the leading juvenile star of the Disney Studios back in the late 1960s and early 1970s. Born March 17, 1951, Russell made his film debut opposite Elvis Presley in 1963's *It Happened at the World's Fair* (he played the little boy who kicked Elvis in the shin). A string of popular but silly Disney comedies made him a teen favorite with a wholesome boy-next-door image: *Follow Me, Boys* (1966), *The Horse in the Gray Flannel Suit* (1968), *The Computer Wore Tennis Shoes* (1969), *The Barefoot Executive* (1971), *Now You See Him, Now You Don't* (1972), *Charley and the Angel* (1973), *Superdad* (1973), and *The Strongest Man in the World* (1975). His stunning portrayal of Elvis Presley in the 1979 TV biopic *Elvis* earned him an Emmy nod and helped tarnish the clean-cut stereotype.

RYDELL HIGH

The Southern California school where most of the action in the musical *Grease* takes place. Alma mater of Danny Zuko, Sandy Olsson, the T-Birds, Pink Ladies, Patty Simcox, Tom Chisum, and Eugene Felsnick. Nickname: Rydell Rangers.

RYDER, WINONA

Born on October 29, 1971, in Winona, Minnesota, and raised in a commune in Northern California, the elfin beauty with dark hair and woeful eyes was the top teen-film actress of the late-1980s and early-1990s grunge era. Ryder's claim to fame is movie roles, in which she played peculiar, passionate youths, such as Lydia in *Beetle Juice* (1988), Veronica in *Heathers* (1989), Kim in *Edward Scissorhands* (1990), Charlotte in *Mermaids* (1990), Dinky in *Welcome Home, Roxy Carmichael* (1990), Mina in *Bram Stoker's Dracula* (1992), Jo in *Little Women* (1994), Lelaina in *Reality Bites* (1994), Annalee in *Alien: Resurrection* (1997), and Susanna in *Girl, Interrupted* (1999). In 1993, she earned an Oscar nomination as Best Supporting Actress for director Martin Scorsese's *Age of Innocence* (1993). Sweethearts over the years have included Christian Slater, Matt Damon, Spin Doctors' David Pirner, and Johnny Depp (her former fiancé, he once wore a tattoo that read "Winona Forever"). In December 2001, Ryder experienced the embarrassment of getting arrested for shoplifting $4,760 worth of clothing items at Saks Fifth Avenue in Beverly Hills and for carrying pharmaceutical drugs without a prescription. She was convicted and sentenced to three years of probation, community service, and drug counseling. A popular T-shirt worn by supporters during her 2002 trial proclaimed "Free Winona."

FYI: ▸ Winona Ryder's godfather is Timothy Leary, the famed counterculture philosopher and LSD connoisseur.

SABRINA DUNCAN

This resourceful and intellectual brunette beauty was the leader of Charlie's trouble-tracking Angels who always kept her cool no matter how dicey the situation. She was also the Angel who wore high turtlenecks and other less-sexy attire, while the other sleuthing foxes (Jill, Kelly, and Kris) let it all hang out. "Bri" was played by Kate Jackson, formerly of *Dark Shadows* and *The Rookies*.

SABRINA, THE TEENAGE WITCH

Blonde and winsome, the young enchantress was first introduced with The Archies on their Saturday-morning TV cartoon in 1969. Sabrina Spellman appears to be your typical sixteen-year-old who enjoys cheerleading, dating Harvey Kinkle, and hanging out at the Chocklit Shoppe with Archie Andrews and the gang. But there's one thing that sets Sabrina apart from other teenage girls: She possesses witchy powers (unknowing to her Riverdale friends). With a tweak of her ear and the rhyme of a spell, she entangles herself, and often boyfriend Harvey, in magical misadventures. Sabrina lives with her two wacky sorceress aunts, Hilda and Zelda; a warlock cousin, Ambrose; and a pet black feline named Salem.

In 1970, at the height of her popularity, she was given her own spin-off cartoon called *Sabrina and the Groovie Goolies*. (The Goolies were a group of musical monsters who resided in Horrible Hall.) The following year, Sabrina starred in her very own self-titled TV cartoon and headlined a comic-book series for *Archie* comics. It wasn't until 1977 that Sabrina and The Archies were reunited for TV on the series *The New Archie/Sabrina Hour*. In the fall of 1996, a new generation of children discovered Sabrina when she reappeared in a live-action sitcom starring Melissa Joan Hart as the Teenage Witch.

SADDLE SHOES

Created by Spalding Sports in 1906, these clunky shoes with the trademark colored "saddle" (black and white) were extremely cool in the 1950s among teen girls, who wore them with bobby socks and poodle skirts. Later, they became the footwear associated with rah-rah cheerleaders.

"SAFETY DANCE"

Not a dance, but a chart-smashing 1983 song by Men Without Hats, accompanied by a memorable video rotated on MTV featuring a medieval-dressed lot prancing through the British countryside.

SAILOR MOON

The mid-1990s action cartoon is based on a Japanese TV hit called *Pretty Soldier Sailor Moon* (1992–93). It centers on a high school girl named Serena and her four friends, Amy, Lita, Mina, and Raye, who are given awesome powers from two mystifying felines, Luna and Artemis, and are transformed into fighters called Sailor Scouts: Sailor Moon (Serena), Sailor Mercury (Amy), Sailor Jupiter (Lita), Sailor Venus (Mina), and Sailor Mars (Raye). Their mission is to battle the evil Queen Beryl, ruler of the Negaverse, whose goal is to destroy planet earth.

SALEM

Every good witch has to have her trademark cat—Gillian Holroyd's Pyewacket and Alexandra Cabot's Sebastian (the Pussycats' nemesis isn't really a witch, she only rhymes with it)—so this mischievous black feline does the deed for teenage sorceress Sabrina Spellman.

FYI: ▸ According to the *Sabrina, the Teenage Witch* TV series of the 1990s, Salem was really a warlock, Salem Saberhagen, stripped of his powers and turned into a cat by a witch council as punishment for not performing misdeeds.

SALLY

Stitched-together rag doll created by wheelchair-bound mad scientist Dr. Finkelstein. She's always escaping from his laboratory home. Thoughtful and somewhat sad, Sally loves Jack Skellington, the Pumpkin King of Halloweentown, and rescues him from bad guy Oogie Boogie Man. Comedienne Catherine O'Hara, formerly of SCTV, provided the voice of Sally in Tim Burton's *Nightmare Before Christmas* (1993).

SALLY BROWN

Charlie Brown's sassy little sister from the *Peanuts* cartoons who has a schoolgirl crush on Linus Van Pelt, her Sweet Babboo, and supports him in his search for the Great Pumpkin of Halloween.

SAMANTHA BAKER

Teenage character played by Molly Ringwald in the film *Sixteen Candles* (1984). Lovelorn, cynical, and unsure of herself, Samantha epitomized the typical 1980s suburban girl, particularly girls with average popularity in school and who at home were the middle child, often stuck in the shadow of a prettier older sister. Samantha's heart pounded for hunk Jake Ryan, but not for Ted the Geek, who got on her nerves.

SAMANTHA STEPHENS

"Oh, my stars!" Levelheaded, pretty blonde sorceress (played by Elizabeth Montgomery on *Bewitched*) married to a mere mortal and living in suburbia as a housewife, who promises hubby Darrin she'll never use witchcraft but goes against his wishes to clean up the pandemonium, with a twitch of the nose, created by her spell-casting family. It should be noted that Sam (for short) makes a mean martini.

FYI: ▸ Samantha Stephens's birthday is "April 15, Ages Ago."

SAM DRUCKER

Hooterville's general-store owner (played by Frank Cady) who did double-duty on the classic TV sitcoms *Green Acres* and *Petticoat Junction*. Drucker also served as the Hooterville postmaster, mayor, and publisher of the local newspaper, the *Hooterville World Guardian*.

SAM-I-AM

"Do you like green eggs and ham?" Very pushy, very persuasive, this red-capped Dr. Seuss storybook character really, really liked green eggs and ham.

SAMMY JO CARRINGTON

Krystle Carrington's trampy, social-climbing, white-trash niece who married her husband Blake's gay son, Steven, on *Dynasty*. Played by Heather Locklear, at the time a twenty-year-old blonde (born September 25, 1961) with a Farrah Fawcett hairdo, who simultaneously starred in another prime-time series, *T. J. Hooker*, as police officer Stacy Sheridan.

SAM THE BUTCHER

> "I've been digging Sam so long that by the time he proposes, I'll be six feet under."
>
> —ALICE NELSON (ANN B. DAVIS)

Housemaid Alice's meat-chopping boyfriend on TV's *Brady Bunch* was "six feet tall and two hundred pounds of unbudgeable bachelor." Sam's last name: Franklin.

SAM THE SNOWMAN
"What's the matter? Haven't you ever seen a talking snowman before?" Voiced by folksinger Burl Ives, the congenial snowman is the storyteller in the Rankin/Bass yuletide TV classic *Rudolph the Red-Nosed Reindeer* (1964). On the special, Sam sings "Holly Jolly Christmas" and "Silver and Gold."

SAMURAI
John Belushi's best-known character on NBC's *Saturday Night Live* was a ponytailed, saber-bearing Asian warrior whose sketches were set in urban American surroundings, like a psychiatrist's office, a divorce court, a drycleaner, a discotheque, and a bakery.

SANDY OLSSON
"How's it hangin', stud?" This pretty, blonde cheerleader, who's as virginal as Sandra Dee, transferred to California's Rydell High from Sydney, Australia, and fell in love with hoodlum Danny Zuko, the leather-jacketed leader of the T-Bird gang. Pop recording sensation Olivia Newton-John made her American film debut playing sweet Sandy in the 1978 musical *Grease*. She took the role after Marie Osmond turned it down. Brooke Shields played Sandy in the 1980s *Grease* revival on Broadway.

SAN PUEBLO
Southern California hometown of TV's *Partridge Family*, who lived there in a modest two-story house at 689 Sycamore Road (a location you couldn't miss, on account of the colorful Mondrian-painted bus parked out front).

SANTA CLAUS

"Dear Editor,
I am eight years old. Some of my little friends say there is no Santa Claus. Papa says if you see it in *The Sun*, it's so. Please tell me the truth, is there a Santa Claus?"
—VIRGINIA O'HANLON

Yes, Virginia, there is a Santa Claus. He's a plump old fellow with a white beard, rosy cheeks, and a jolly "Ho-ho-ho." Dressed in a red suit and black boots, he comes down chimneys every Christmas Eve to deliver gifts to the world's "nice" boys and girls (the "naughty" receive only a lump of coal). Santa Claus lives in the freezy North Pole with spouse Mrs. Claus and a team of happy elves who spend their time in a workshop making toys for the December 25 deadline.

On Christmas Eve, Santa, lugging a bottomless bag of toys, rides in a sled flown by eight magical reindeer—Dasher, Dancer, Prancer, Vixen, Comet, Cupid, Donner, and Blitzen. (Some years, Rudolph the Red-Nosed Reindeer leads the way, when visibility is poor due to inclement weather.) Santa travels quickly from house to house at great speed, placing presents under the Christmas tree and in stockings hung by the fireplace (with care). He even finds time to consume all the cookies kids put out for him. (Thoughtful children will also leave a few carrots for the reindeer. It's their favorite!) A rite of childhood is visiting Santa at the local department store to sit on his lap and spill your guts out about how good you've been all year, before listing the many toys you want him to bring. But a significant day in childhood is the day you realize your know-it-all friend was right, that Santa Claus is only a myth and that mom and dad are, and have always been, the real Santa.

The modern-day Santa Claus is based on Saint Nicholas, a fourth-century Dutch bishop known throughout the world for his kind giving of gifts of gold to those less fortunate. Around the world, Santa is known as Father Christmas (England), Père Noel (France), Babbo Natale (Italy), Old Man Christmas (Chile), Christmas Man (Germany), Christmas Brownie (Norway), and Grandfather Frost (Russia). In pop culture, his tale is told best in Clement C. Moore's story *The Night Before Christmas* (a.k.a. *A Visit from Saint Nicholas*), as well as in the movie *Miracle on 34th Street* and in the animated TV special *Santa Claus Is Comin' to Town*.

SANTA CLAUS IS COMIN' TO TOWN
In 1970, the Animagic puppets of Rankin/Bass enchanted children once again with this holiday musical special. Narrated by mailman S. D. Kluger (voice of Fred Astaire), it told the mythical story of Santa Claus, a.k.a. Kris Kringle, and answered the

mysterious questions surrounding the jolly old fellow: Why does he live in the North Pole? How did he learn to "Ho-ho-ho"? Where did he get reindeer that fly? Why does he deliver presents only on Christmas Eve? And so on.

The tale begins when a baby with the birth name of Claus is abandoned in the forest. The forest animals rescue the baby and bring him to Rainbow River Valley, where he is adopted by kindly Tanta Kringle, grand matriarch of toy-making elves Dingle, Wingle, Tingle, Zingo, and Bingo Kringle. Christened Kris Kringle, the cheerful lad grows up to learn the art of making toys. When he becomes a young man, Kris sets off across the perilous Mountain of the Whispering Wind to deliver toys to the children of a doleful village called Sombertown, where tyrannical ruler Burgermeister Meisterburger has forbidden toys. Along the way he meets a host of captivating characters, including amiable penguin Topper, terrible Winter Warlock, and pretty schoolteacher Miss Jessica, who later becomes his wife.

The delightful TV special was based on the classic title song, written by J. Fred Coots and Haven Gillespie. Other tunes featured were "Put One Foot in Front of the Other" and "The First Toymaker to the King."

SANTA'S LITTLE HELPER

Santa's Little Helper is the Simpson family's pet greyhound. Abandoned by his previous owner for losing too many races at the Springfield Downs dog race track, the orange-colored canine was brought home one Christmas Eve by Homer Simpson as the family's Christmas present. Santa's Little Helper likes burying things in the backyard, begging for food, chewing on furniture, and being doted on by his master, Bart.

SARAH T.: PORTRAIT OF A TEENAGE ALCOHOLIC

This 1975 TV movie was one of many depicting the teenage Generation X as a dysfunctional lot. It starred Linda Blair (in another of her inevitable teenager-in-distress roles) as fifteen-year-old Sarah Travis. Her parents are separating, she's moving to a new town, and glee-club auditions are tomorrow—so what's a girl to do but drink, drink, drink! Sarah is secretly an alcoholic who boozes it up to escape from everyday problems and a lack of love at home. Larry Hagman co-starred as Sarah's estranged traveling artist dad, Jerry Travis.

SARA LEE

Frozen desserts (pies, iced cakes, pound cakes, cheesecakes, Danishes, and so on) that are advertised with the slogan "Nobody doesn't like Sara Lee!" The company was founded in 1932 by Charles Lubin.

SASSOON, VIDAL

London hairdresser, probably the most famous beautician in pop culture history, who created the short, asymmetrical Sassoon cut during the mod era of the 1960s. His popularity launched a product line of shampoos and styling aids. ("If you don't look good, we don't look good.")

SATIN JACKETS

Supershiny, supersilky sports jackets like the kind you would have seen on Leif Garrett or Kristy McNichol in the late 1970s. Chic during the disco era, these accented the designer-jean look or matching satin shorts with tube socks. Extra cool, if you had your name in cursive on the front and a groovy decal on the back.

"SATURDAY NIGHT"

"I hate to blow the mystique, but at the time we really liked bubblegum music, and we really liked the Bay City Rollers. Their song 'Saturday Night' had a great chant in it, so we wanted a song with a chant in it: 'Hey! Ho! Let's Go!' or 'Blitzkrieg Bop' was our 'Saturday Night.'"

—JOEY OF THE RAMONES

Scotland's Bay City Rollers scored international success with this 1975 mega-smash that landed at number one on the American Top Forty. A Rollers' concert was a sight to behold, as thousands of squealing plaid-attired teenyboppers, fanatically waving tartan scarves, chanted at the top of their lungs "S-a-t-u-r-d-a-y Night!" The "do it all, have a ball" song was written by Phil Coulter and Bill Martin.

SATURDAY NIGHT FEVER

"Catch it!" The definitive disco movie is a time capsule of what it was like to be young and dancing in the 1970s. Its pulse-pounding soundtrack, electrifying choreography, and late-1970s street slang captured the spirit of the prevailing disco dance movement. It also fueled the fancy of young people who turned disco into a national pastime. In urban areas across America, local discotheques were packed to capacity with disco-crazed patrons who imitated the film's clothing (three-piece polyester suits, platform heels, and gold medallions for guys; gold lamé gowns, strappy stilettos, and fashion scarves for gals) and competed in disco dance competitions or John Travolta look-alike contests.

Based on a story in *New York* magazine, "Tribal Rites of the New Saturday Night" by Nik Cohn, the 1977 film starred John Travolta as Tony Manero, a cocky Brooklyn teen with a dead-end life whose escape is boogying at the neighborhood discotheque (2001 Odyssey Disco), where he is king of the dance floor. Tony falls for Stephanie (Karen Lynn Gorney), a yuppie from Manhattan, who partners with him for the big dance contest that could lead to a way out of his working-class environment. Costars include Donna Pescow as disco slut Annette and Tony's spurned girlfriend; Martin Shakar as Frank, Tony's seminarian brother; and Barry Miller, Paul Pape, and Joseph Cali as Bobby C., Double J., and Joey, Tony's buddies.

Saturday Night Fever catapulted Travolta—who at the time was TV's current teen idol, starring as Vinnie Barbarino on *Welcome Back, Kotter*—into movie stardom and earned him an Oscar nomination for Best Actor. Directed by John Badham, the disco extravaganza featured an exciting Bee Gees music score, along with dazzling dance scenes choreographed by Lester Wilson (one of the best is the synchronized number to "Night Fever"). Its double-album soundtrack became the top-selling movie LP of all time. It was followed by a lackluster sequel in 1983, *Staying Alive*, directed by Sylvester Stallone and again starring a very buff Travolta as Tony Manero, now a Broadway dancer.

SATURDAY NIGHT FEVER (LP)

The pulsating, disco-fueled Grammy winner (Album of the Year) to Travolta's legendary flick sold more than thirty million copies, becoming the first in history to go triple platinum, topped the charts for twenty-four weeks, and remains to this day the best-selling soundtrack ever. It housed three number-one hits for the Bee Gees: "How Deep Is Your Love," "Stayin' Alive," and "Night Fever." Also includes Yvonne Elliman's chart-topper "If I Can't Have You," as well as "Boogie Shoes" by K.C. and the Sunshine Band, "Disco Inferno" by The Trammps, "A Fifth of Beethoven" by Walter Murphy, and "More Than a Woman" by Tavares.

SATURDAY NIGHT LIVE BEES

"Live from New York, it's *Saturday Night*!" The first of the long-running late-night show's recurring skit characters. Had all the original Not Ready for Prime-Time Players—Dan Aykroyd, John Belushi, Chevy Chase, Jane Curtin, Garrett Morris, Laraine Newman, and Gilda Radner—at one time or another donning silly black-and-yellow-striped bee outfits with bobbing antennae. "Buzzzzzz!"

SATURDAY NIGHT LIVE NERDS

"Todd, that's so funny I forgot to laugh." Airing throughout the late 1970s, the recurring skit centered on the geeky escapades of Lisa "Four Eyes" Loopner (Gilda Radner) and Todd "Pizza Face" DiLaMuca (Bill Murray). Lisa was fond of Todd, Todd liked to torment Lisa with "noogies," and Lisa's equally geeky mother, Mrs. Enid Loopner (Jane Curtin), perpetually dressed in a housecoat, enjoyed serving egg salad and jugs of Tang to these nerdy high schoolers.

SAUCER SLEDS

Wintertime fun was had by all with these disc-shaped plastic or steel sleds that gave you hardly any control when gliding and sliding down a snow-covered slope. (In other words, a tree trunk or another sledder was often what stopped you.)

SAVED BY THE BELL

Known for having a huge base of dedicated fans, this teen-oriented fare began its run on the Disney cable channel as *Good Morning Miss Bliss*, starring Hayley Mills as teacher Carrie Bliss, before changing its name, dropping Miss Mills, and moving to NBC as a Saturday-morning series from 1989 to 1993. It detailed the high school hijinks of a clique of popular teenagers attending Bayside High in Palisades, California. The lead character was preppy blond Zack Morris (Mark-Paul Gosselaar), a girl-crazy prankster who would stop the show's action to address the camera directly. Zack's best pals at Bayside included brunette babe Kelly Kapowski (Tiffani-Amber Thiessen), the head cheerleader; Latin hunk Alfred Clifford "A.C." Slater (Mario López), the wrestling captain; curly-haired Jessie Spano (Elizabeth Berkley), the class president and valedictorian; African-American Lisa Turtle (Lark Voorhies), the gossipy fashion queen; and fuzzy-headed Samuel "Screech" Powers (Dustin Diamond), the luckless geek. Principal Richard Belding (Dennis Haskins) fluctuated between being the group's friend and foe.

Like most other teen shows, *Saved by the Bell*'s weekly episodes dealt with growing up and facing life-issues. It was followed by a sequel, *Saved by the Bell: The College Years*, which had Zack and company enrolled at California University.

SCARRY, RICHARD

Born June 5, 1919, in Boston, the prolific writer and illustrator of the "Best Ever" picture books, which have sold more than 100 million copies worldwide and have been translated into thirty languages. Aimed at ages two to ten, Scarry's work is distinguished by colorful, detailed illustrations of people-like animals, such as Pickles Pig, Lowly Worm, Huckle Cat, Bananas Gorilla, and Hilda Hippo, doing everyday jobs and activities in the municipality of Busytown. His first commercial breakthrough occurred in 1963 with the publication of *Richard Scarry's Best Word Book Ever*. It was followed by *Richard Scarry's Busy, Busy World* (1965), *Richard Scarry's What Animals Do* (1968), *Richard Scarry's What Do People Do All Day?* (1968), *Richard Scarry's Great Big Schoolhouse* (1969), *Richard Scarry's Best Mother Goose Ever* (1970), *Richard Scarry's Funniest Storybook Ever* (1972), *Richard Scarry's Best Rainy Day Book Ever* (1973), and *Richard Scarry's Cars and Trucks and Things That Go* (1974). His wife, Patricia Murphy Scarry, authored the best-selling scratch-and-sniff book *Sweet Smell of Christmas* (1970).

SCHIFFER, CLAUDIA

Born on August 25, 1970, in Rheinberg, Germany, the Bardot-esque supermodel (the light-haired rival of Cindy Crawford) gained international popularity with a smoldering-hot ad campaign for Guess Jeans in 1989. High-profile jobs with Chanel, Revlon, and Victoria's Secret, as well as 400 magazine covers, made Schiffer one of the top models of the 1990s. She was engaged to magician David Copperfield from 1994 to 1999.

FYI: ▸ Claudia Schiffer always considered herself too tall and too thin, but that didn't stop a Metropolitan Modeling Agency representative from approaching her in a Düsseldorf discotheque at age seventeen. Six months later, the statuesque five-foot-eleven beauty with tousled long blonde hair and sky-blue eyes made her first appearance on the cover of *Elle* magazine.

SCHLEPROCK

On *The Pebbles and Bamm-Bamm Show* cartoon (airing Saturday mornings from 1971 to 1976), this fellow with the sullen demeanor and hat worn low was a bad-luck sign capable of jinxing anyone who crossed his path. Schleprock always had a persistent thundercloud overhead—complete with lightning bolts—and his catchphrase was the depressing mutter, "Wowsy-wowsy-woo-woo."

SCHMOO

Bell-shaped white blob, originally a recurring character from Al Capp's *Li'l Abner* comic strip and later seen on *The Flintstones* cartoon, that morphed into all kinds of shapes and sizes.

SCHOLASTIC BOOKS

For those who loved reading, these were among the high points of their elementary school years. Once a month or so, students would be given Scholastic Books catalogs that listed a wide variety of paperbacks. They would take it home, contemplate what stories to buy, check them off on an order form, and turn their order in by the end of the week, accompanied by cash or a check written by parents. After eagerly waiting more than a month (which seemed like forever), it was exciting to arrive at class and see the gigantic brown cardboard box with the tiny red Scholastic logo in the bottom corner sitting on the teacher's desk. The books—all new and shiny—would be handed out, and little bookworms couldn't wait to rush home to begin reading a new storybook adventure! Those who didn't love reading could order silly animal posters featuring cute kittens, puppies, and chimps, or youth-oriented magazines full of no-brainer stories and glossy photos, such as *Dynamite* (for younger kids) or *Bananas* (for older kids).

SCHOOLHOUSE ROCK

"As your body grows bigger, your mind must flower / It's great to learn, 'cause knowledge is power!" Short educational capsules sandwiched between regular Saturday-morning cartoons on ABC-TV that taught the fundamentals of math, grammar, history, and science using a jazzy tune. *Schoolhouse Rock*'s story is "elementary, my dear." It originated from the brilliant mind of David B. McCall, president of the McCaffrey & McCall advertising agency, after realizing that his son Davey was having trouble memorizing multiplication math but had no problem remembering the words to rock songs that played on the radio. McCall thought Davey might have an easier time of learning if he had a catchy song to go with his math timetables. So he united with McCaffrey & McCall's creative directors, George Newell and Tom Yohe, plus jazz musician-composer Bob Dorough, and invented more than forty episodes of three-minute animated musicals known as *Schoolhouse Rock*.

For a generation of kids camped out in pajamas in front of the TV set each Saturday morning from 1972 to 1985, *Schoolhouse Rock* taught that a zero was a hero, how a bill became a law, the function of a conjunction, and the Preamble to the U.S. Constitution. Its *Multiplication Rock* (1972) taught the mechanics of the multiplication tables (for instance, "Three Is a Magic Number" and "My Hero Zero"). *Grammar Rock* (1973) educated kids on the proper use of the various parts of speech ("Conjunction Junction" and "Lolly, Lolly, Lolly, Get Your Adverbs Here"). *America Rock* (1974) gave various history lessons to celebrate the upcoming Bicentennial (including "The Preamble" and "I'm Just a Bill"). And *Science Rock* (1979) introduced subjects dealing with outer space and energy (for example, "Interplanet Janet" and "The Energy Blues").

As for the show's impact on this TV generation, well, there are many grammar experts, history buffs, math whizzes, and rocket scientists of adult age who are indebted to *Schoolhouse Rock* for the infectious songs they hum while driving in the fast lane or waiting in long lines at the bank. "Darn! That's the end!"

SCHOOLHOUSE ROCKY

The orange-haired superhero mascot of *Schoolhouse Rock* who is featured in the opening segment of each of the educational cartoons. Rocky has the letters S and R displayed on the front of his superhero uniform.

SCHOONER BAY

Coastal New England setting—haunted by ghosts of old sea captains—where the TV sitcom *The Ghost and Mrs. Muir* takes place.

SCHRODER, RICKY

Born April 13, 1970, in New York, the adorable tow-headed child star of the early 1980s could be seen in the films *The Champ* (1979), *The Last Flight of Noah's Ark* (1980), and *The Earthling* (1980). From 1982 to 1987, he played spoiled rich-kid Ricky Stratton on the TV sitcom *Silver Spoons*. Upon shortening his first name to the mature "Rick," Schroder successfully made the transition from juvenile actor to leading man with the TV miniseries *Lonesome Dove* and the prime-time cop-drama *NYPD Blue*.

FYI: ▸ Ricky Schroder named his first son, Holden, after actor William Holden, with whom he co-starred in *The Earthling*.

SCHROEDER

This blond-haired lad from the *Peanuts* cartoons was a Beethoven aficionado and a musical prodigy who played virtuoso pieces on his toy piano while ignoring the amorous advances of lovesick Lucy Van Pelt. Favorite holiday: Beethoven's birthday on December 17.

SCHULZ, CHARLES

"Charles Schulz said that he guessed that in the final analysis Charlie Brown was him the way he was, and Snoopy was him the way he wished he could be."

—LEE MENDELSON,
PRODUCER OF THE *CHARLIE BROWN* TV SPECIALS

Born in Minneapolis, Minnesota, on November 26, 1922, Schulz was the inventor of *Peanuts*, starring Charlie Brown and Snoopy, one of the most successful comic strips ever created. He won an Emmy Award for *A Charlie Brown Christmas* in 1966.

SCHWINN STING-RAY BIKES

The top-selling brand of the hi-rise style of bikes, accessorized with banana seats and sissy bars, was in high demand by kids during the 1960s and 1970s. You were the envy of the neighborhood cul-de-sac if your Sting-Ray was "Cherry Red."

SCOOBY-DOO

"Hey, Scooby!" The cowardly, scratchy-voiced Great Dane, who shook and shivered at any sign of danger and had a ravenous appetite for Scooby Snacks, is one of the most endearing cartoon icons of all time. The furry brown pooch made his debut in 1969 on the *Scooby-Doo, Where Are You?* Saturday-morning comedy-mystery TV show. He starred as the traveling companion of four groovy teenage detectives: hunky Freddy Jones, foxy Daphne Blake, brainy Velma Dinkley, and bumbling Shaggy Rogers. The gang traveled around the country in the Mystery Machine, a psychedelic-painted van, to solve supernatural whodunits involving ghosts, ghouls, witches, and mummies that inevitably turned out to be flesh-and-blood con artists out to scam money or seek revenge.

Created by Hanna-Barbera, *Scooby-Doo* holds the record for longest-running consecutively produced cartoon show (eighteen years). It has appeared in various forms with different titles—*The New Scooby-Doo Movies, The Scooby-Doo/Dynomutt Hour, Scooby's All-Star Laff-a-Lympics, Scooby and Scrappy-Doo*—and inspired a number of copycat programs: *Funky Phantom, Clue Club, Jabberjaw, Speed Buggy*, and *Goober and the Ghost Chasers*. Why the continuing popularity of the canine sleuth? This quote from Don Messick, the voice of Scooby, may hold the answer: "I've loved Scooby from inception, and so has everyone else. I think it's because he embraces a lot of human foibles. He's not the perfect dog. In fact, you might say he's a coward. Yet with everything he does, he seems to land on his four feet. He comes out of every situation unscathed. I think the audience—kids and more mature people as well—can identify with Scooby's character and a lot of his imperfections." "Ruh-Roh . . . Rooby Rooby Rooooo!"

FYI: ▸ The name Scooby-Doo was inspired by "Dooby dooby doo," a phrase heard in the 1966 Frank Sinatra song "Strangers in the Night."

SCRAPPY-DOO

"Puppy Power!" Who ever decided that Scooby-Doo needed a sidekick? Wasn't Shaggy good enough? The introduction in 1979 of Scooby's overzealous little puppy nephew with the irritating voice was the worst thing ever to happen in Saturday-morning cartoon history. Overall, it ranks right up there with the day annoying cousin Oliver moved in with *The Brady Bunch*.

SCREAM

"Don't answer the phone. Don't open the door. Don't try to escape. And whatever you do, don't scream." The surprise box-office smash of 1996 became the highest-grossing horror movie ever and revived the teen-slasher genre of the 1990s. Set in the small California town of Woodsboro, *Scream* opens with one of the most frightening scenes in the recent history of horror films: Lovely seventeen-year-old Casey Becker (played by Drew Barrymore), home alone, receives bone-chilling prank phone calls involving trivia questions from a mysterious caller, who then kills her football-player boyfriend after she misses an answer, attacks her in the house, and finally guts her in the backyard.

The film's heroine is teenager Sidney Prescott (Neve Campbell, from TV's *Party of Five*), a friend of Casey's who is still fragile from the loss of her mother a year ago to a brutal slaying. The last thing Sidney needs right now is for her group of high school chums to be murdered by a raving lunatic—particularly one who wields a huge knife, wears a black cloak and startling ghoul mask (based on Munch's "Scream" painting), and terrorizes his victims via cordless phone, taking his cues from horror movies. An offbeat group of then mostly unknowns made up the rest of the cast: Courteney Cox as tabloid-news reporter Gale Weathers, David Arquette as Deputy Dewey Riley, Skeet Ulrich as Sidney's boyfriend, Billy Loomis, Liev Schreiber as framed-killer Cotton Weary, Rose McGowan as Sidney's best friend, Tatum Riley, Matthew Lillard as party-boy Stu Macher, and Jamie Kennedy as film-geek Randy Meeks, an expert on slasher-movie rules (for example, "Never have sex . . ."). Look for uncredited cameos by Henry Winkler as principal of Woodsboro High School, Linda Blair as a reporter, and director Wes Craven as Fred the janitor.

Scary thrills aside, what makes *Scream* stand out from the rest is screenwriter Kevin Williamson, who tweaked the old slasher formula by using clever plot twists and joking references to other horror films. It inspired two sequels plus a tidal wave of imitations: *I Know What You Did Last Summer* (1997), *Disturbing Behavior* (1998), *Halloween H2O* (1998), *Urban Legend* (1998), *Final Destination* (2000), *Valentine* (2001), a spoof, *Scary Movie* (2000), and its two sequels, *Scary Movie 2* (2001) and *Scary Movie 3* (2003).

FYI: ▸ Courteney Cox (of *Friends* fame) and David Arquette (of the Rosanna and Patricia Arquette family fame) met and fell in love while filming *Scream.* They married in 1999 and are the proud parents of a daughter, Coco, born in 2004.

SCROOGE MCDUCK

The crotchety millionaire uncle of Donald Duck (yes, even more crotchety than our dear Donald) experienced popularity as a Disney comic-book favorite before starring in his first animated feature, *Scrooge McDuck and Money*, in 1967. In the 1980s, the "world's richest tightwad" appropriately played Ebenezer Scrooge, Charles Dickens's misanthropic miser, in the movie *Mickey's Christmas Carol* (1983) and starred in the cartoon series *DuckTales* (1987) on the Disney Channel, which had him adventuring around the world with his three devilish grandnephews, Huey, Dewey, and Louie. Scrooge's sister, Matilda McDuck, married wacked scientist Ludwig Von Drake.

SCRUMDIDILYUMPTIOUS BAR

"Did you say Scrumdidilyumptious Bar? What is it?" It's an extralarge, extrascrumptious chocolate bar created by Willy Wonka and featured in the 1971 film *Willy Wonka and the Chocolate Factory*, starring Gene Wilder, and manufactured for real during the 1970s.

S. D. KLUGER

Looking and sounding a lot like movie hoofer Fred Astaire, the friendly North Pole postman who rode a snowmobile mail car was narrator of the TV yuletide special *Santa Claus Is Comin' to Town* (1970). His initials stood for "Special Delivery."

SEADOG

The animated pooch served as Cap'n Crunch's first mate aboard the sea-travelin' S.S. *Guppy* in the Cap'n Crunch cereal commercials.

SEA MONKEYS

"The world's first instant pet!" Do you remember thumbing through the back of comic books and coming across the colorfully illustrated advertisements featuring smiling, human-like, mermaid-esque playmates with heads shaped like tiaras and cute tails, called Sea Monkeys? The ads were enticing. What kid wouldn't want his or her own amazing Sea Monkey family that came to life instantly just by adding water? So kids mailed their dollar allowance to the manufacturer, Honey Toy Industries (later renamed Transcience), and in a few weeks received a kit containing a packet of Sea Monkeys in "suspended animation," a little plastic aquarium, water purifier, growth food, and *The Official Sea Monkey Handbook.*

In reality, the Sea Monkeys were a big disappointment. They looked nothing like the creatures in the ads. Actually a type of brine shrimp, a.k.a. plankton, from the seas of northern Canada, Sea Monkeys were dull in color and about the size of a pinhead (after feeding, they could grow to about half an inch). And all they seemed to want to do was swim around aimlessly in their plastic-encased sea. Nevertheless, they sold big, and a variety of accessory kits were offered, including the Sea Monkey Speedway, which pitted Sea Monkey against Sea Monkey in an aquatic race to the finish line, and the Incredible Sea Bubble, a mini aquarium attached to a golden chain that you could wear around your neck!

Sea Monkeys were the brainchild of magician Harold von Braunhut (the man who invented x-ray specs), who began manufacturing them in 1960. "It's fun to raise pet Sea Monkeys!"

SEARS CHRISTMAS WISH BOOK

My childhood experience of wishing over the Sears Wish Book probably echoes yours. In the weeks before Christmas, mom and dad would want us kids to go through its huge toy section and circle the items we wished "Santa" would bring. Decisions, decisions, decisions. How would we ever choose among the thousands of toys perfectly displayed on the catalog's colorful pages? We would spend hours staring at everything we dreamed of having. Rival department stores J. C. Penney and Montgomery Ward also had their own versions of the Sears Wish Book.

"SEASONS IN THE SUN"

"We had joy, we had fun, we had seasons in the Sun. . . ." One of the great story songs of our era (1970s) that left many a prepubescent a bundle of tears and many cynics reaching to turn the radio dial. Penned by Jacques Brel and Rod McKuen and weepingly sung by Terry Jacks, the tearjerker was an ode to a father from his son, "the black sheep of the family." The son was dying (we never knew what of, possibly "too much wine and too much song") and trying to make amends with his family. "Seasons in the Sun" went to the top of the charts for three weeks in 1974. Terry Jacks originally recorded with wife Susan as members of The Poppy Family, a pop group from Canada that had a hit with "Which Way You Goin', Billy?" in 1970.

SEATTLE

What San Francisco was to the hippie movement of the 1960s, what New York was to the disco movement of the 1970s, and what Los Angeles was to the New Wave movement of the 1980s, this rainy northwestern city in Washington was to the alternative-music movement of the 1990s. Hometown of angst-ridden, flannel-clad grunge bands like Kurt Cobain's Nirvana, Courtney Love's Hole, and Eddie Vedder's Pearl Jam. Also the home of Boeing (until recently), Microsoft, and Starbucks Coffee.

SEAVIEW

Futuristic glass-nosed atomic submarine that journeys through the ocean depths, where it discovers giant octopuses, lobstermen, alien spaceships, Nazi labs, lost civilizations, and other fantastic underwater objects. The *Seaview* is featured in the 1961 *Voyage to the Bottom of the Sea* movie and TV spin-off of the same name (1964–68), both produced by Irwin Allen.

SEAWORLD

First opened in 1964 in San Diego, California, the aquatic theme park SeaWorld is home to Shamu, the world-famous killer whale, and a stadium of splashy, back-flipping dolphins.

SEBASTIAN (*JOSIE AND THE PUSSYCATS*)

Alexandra Cabot's devilish cat, who was similar to her in both looks (skunk-striped black hair) and personality (bitch) in the *Josie and the Pussycats* cartoon and comics. In the comic books, Alexandra could cast spells by stroking Sebastian's back. (The feline was the reincarnation of Alexandra's deceased uncle, who was prosecuted 300 years earlier for being a witch.)

SEBASTIAN (*LITTLE MERMAID*)

Full name: Horatio Felonious Ignacious Crustaceous Sebastian. The singing crab with a Jamaican accent was one of Princess Ariel's comrades in Disney's 1989 animated classic *The Little Mermaid*. In the movie, he sings the calypso-reggae "Under the Sea" and "Kiss the Girl."

SECRET AGENT MAN

British TV import starring Patrick McGoohan as John Drake, a secret security agent whose schtick was he didn't carry a weapon and he steered clear of violent confrontations. The show is remembered best for its theme song, "Secret Agent Man," recorded by Johnny Rivers in 1966.

SECRET AGENTS

Populating movie and TV screens throughout the 1960s, secret agents were modern-day superheroes, a product of the cold war between America and Russia. As diplomatic tensions heated up between the two nations, there was a growing fascination with espionage, which in turn sired an interest in Ian Fleming's novels featuring James Bond, Agent 007. Creating the archetype for all superspies, Bond was a strong, suave, smooth, sophisticated, stylish, swingin', martini-swilling bachelor capable of bedding a succession of gorgeous gals—the kind you find only in the pages of Hugh Hefner's *Playboy*. Equipped with a fast car and fancy gadgetry, the globe-trotting agent never lost his cool as he thwarted sinister archvillains in their quest to take over the world. He was every man's fantasy of who they wanted to be, and every woman's fantasy of what they wanted their man to be. In 1962, a big-screen adaptation of Fleming's *Dr. No*, starring sexy newcomer Sean Connery as James Bond, broke box-office records and spawned countless sequels (including *Goldfinger* and *From Russia with Love*) and imitators (Matt Helm, Derek Flint, and more). In 1966 alone, there were twenty-three films and ten regular TV shows featuring secret agents.

SECRET DEODORANT

Best-selling female-friendly antiperspirant, produced by Procter & Gamble, that's "strong enough for a man but made for a woman."

SECRET SQUIRREL

Inspired by the popularity of James Bond, Hanna-Barbera's Secret Squirrel, a.k.a. Agent 000, was a cartoon superspy who headlined his own Saturday-morning show in 1965. Dressed in traditional spy garb of a trench coat (laden with amazing crime-fighting gadgetry) and a purple fedora with eyeholes cut in the brim, the buck-toothed agent worked for the International Sneaky Service. Agency boss Double Q handed Secret Squirrel and fez-wearing sidekick Morocco Mole assignments to thwart such villains as the Masked Granny, Robin and the Merry Muggs, and Yellow Pinkie (a nod to *Goldfinger*). From 1967 to 1969, Secret Squirrel joined forces with tiny superhero Atom Ant on *The Atom Ant / Secret Squirrel Show*.

SEE 'N SAY

"The cow says moooooo!" This fun learning tool is Mattel's biggest-selling preschool toy ever. First introduced in 1965, the See 'n Say is a round, plastic talking toy imprinted with a circle of illustrations keyed to prerecorded phrases. To activate a phrase, you rotate the pointer toward the picture you want to hear, then pull a ring attached to a string (known as the Chatty Ring). These toys help preschoolers develop listening and speaking skills, learn the fundamentals of spelling and counting, and become acquainted with sound-word-object associations.

The many different versions of See 'n Say over the years included "The Farmer Says," featuring the sounds farm animals make; "The Bee Says," featuring alphabet sayings from A to Z; "Mother Goose Says," featuring familiar rhymes, such as Humpty Dumpty and Little Miss Muffet; "The Clock Says," featuring the times of the day; "Mr. Music Says," featuring the sounds of various music instruments; "Snoopy Says," featuring *Peanuts* phrases; "Doctor Dolittle Says," featuring the film's animals, like Pushmi-Pullyu and Polynesia Parrot; and a "Dr. Seuss' Zoo Says," featuring a dozen kooky characters talking and singing about themselves.

SEGALL, RICKY

Adorable moppet with long, black shaggy hair who joined *The Partridge Family* cast in 1973 as little Ricky Stevens, a singing four-year-old who lived next door.

SEGO

At only 225 calories a can, this 1970s diet drink was the predecessor of today's Slim-Fast. Flavors included Banana, Chocolate, Orange, and Vanilla.

SESAME STREET

"Sunny day / Sweepin' the clouds away / On my way to where the air is sweet / Can you tell me how to get, how to get to *Sesame Street*. . . ." Since 1969, generations of children have been able to tell you how to get to this legendary thoroughfare populated by live actors and Jim Henson's cute and cuddly Muppets. Developed by Joan Ganz Cooney, executive director of the Children's Television Network (CTW), and airing on the Public Broadcasting Station (PBS), *Sesame Street* revolutionized children's TV by setting a new standard for teaching the A-B-Cs and 1-2-3's: employing quick-paced commercial-like skits, songs, puppetry, and cartoons. Each episode was "sponsored" by a letter and a number ("And now a word from the letter 'A'" or "Brought to you by the number three").

Originally, the show targeted the educationally deprived minority kids living in America's inner cities. That's why its studio set is a ghetto street lined with brownstone townhouses and filled with a multiethnic cast. However, youngsters from all areas of America—rich, poor, suburban, rural—quickly caught on to the program that made learning so much fun. The human performers familiar to the first generation of *Sesame Street* viewers included Gordon (Matt Robinson), Susan (Loretta Long), Bob (Bob McGrath), Maria (Sonia Manzano), Luis

(Emilio Delgado), David (Northern J. Calloway), and candy-shop owner Mr. Hooper (Will Lee). But, as we all know, the real stars are the Muppets—most notably, roommates Bert and Ernie, cookie-ravishing Cookie Monster, irritable Oscar the Grouch, playful Grover, counting Count von Count, and lovable, huggable Big Bird. Today, *Sesame Street* is viewed around the world in almost 100 countries! "One of these things is not like the other. . . ."

7-ELEVEN

"Oh, thank heaven, for 7-Eleven!" The sight of a 7-Eleven, or the mere mention of the name, brings back memories of being a kid and walking to the nearest convenience store with a dollar allowance and an armload of empty soda bottles to be returned for a few cents apiece. Once there, you'd head straight for the candy aisle to pick out a long stick of Big Buddy Bubblegum or a Tootsie Roll Pop or a Reese's Peanut Butter Cup or a handful of penny candy. Then off to the comic-book display to buy the latest *Spider-Man* comic or *Mad* magazine. Your final destination was the Slurpee machine, where the dilemma was choosing between cola flavor or cherry flavor. You couldn't decide on either, so you combined both to make a "Suicide."

During your teen years, 7-Elevens were often the place to chill with the gang after school. When you weren't hanging out in front of the store being a public nuisance, you were inside playing pinball or the latest video game. Twentysomething memories are of stumbling into a brightly illuminated 7-Eleven in the wee morning hours after a dose of partying. To take care of the munchies, you could buy a frozen microwaveable burrito, a bag of Doritos, a Hostess snack cake, a huge thirty-two-ounce Big Gulp, and a pack of Marlboros for a smoke afterward. Today, as busy adults, it's easy to understand why it's called a convenience store when you're in dire need of a loaf of bread, a can of cat food, or a roll of toilet paper and don't feel like hassling with the crowd at the grocery mart (and you can fill up your gas tank too). Originated by the Southland Company of Dallas in 1946, the 7-Eleven moniker refers to the store's first morning-to-night hours, 7 A.M. to 11 P.M. 7-Eleven pioneered the convenience-store concept during its first years of operation as an ice company, when its retail outlets began selling milk, bread, and eggs as a convenience to customers. In 1963, stores began the twenty-four-hour-a-day operation. Today, it's the country's largest convenience-store chain (more than 5,000 stores nationwide), inspiring countless imitators: Quik Trip, Circle K, Stop 'n Go, U Totem, Cumberland Farm, High's, Handy Dandy, AM/PM, and Zarda, to name just a few.

Critics and comics alike cite 7-Eleven as an example of American capitalism gone amuck. There seems to be one on every corner; they have put many mom-and-pop general stores out of business; they employ rude foreigners who can barely speak English; and they take advantage of consumers by charging sky-high prices. (After the L.A. Northridge earthquake, stores in the San Fernando Valley charged up to six dollars for a bottle of water.)

7-UP

This clear, lemony-lime cola is a popular alternative to caffeinated dark sodas like Coke or Pepsi. Invented by Charles Leiper Grigg from Missouri in 1929, it was originally called "Bib-Label Lithiated Lemon-Lime Soda" and marketed as a cure for upset stomach and hangover. In the 1970s, Wacky Packages spoofed it as "7-Urp," and deep-voiced Jamaican Geoffrey Holder hawked it as the "Un-Cola." 7-Up's major rival is Sprite.

FYI: ▸ Lithium was the main ingredient in 7-Up's original recipe!

SEYMOUR S. SASSAFRASS

Voiced by Danny Kaye, the narrator of the Rankin/Bass Easter special *Here Comes Peter Cottontail* (1971) who helps Peter Cottontail become Chief Easter Bunny with his miraculous time-tripping Yestermorrow Mobile.

SGT. PEPPER'S LONELY HEARTS CLUB BAND

What were they thinking when they filmed this big-screen fiasco based on The Beatles' 1967 concept album? Awful, is what I was thinking. Many people believe it single-handedly terminated the recording careers of the Bee Gees, Peter Frampton, Paul Nicholas, Earth, Wind, and Fire, Alice Cooper, and actress Sandy Farina (did she even have one?). The only good thing to come out of the 1978 atrocity was Aerosmith's performance of "Come Together" and comedian Steve Martin's off-the-wall version of "Maxwell's Silver Hammer."

FYI: ▸ Duck and cover. Other big-screen rock 'n' roll bombs of the era were the Village People's *Can't Stop the Music* (1980), Neil Diamond's *The Jazz Singer* (1980), Olivia Newton-John's *Xanadu* (1980), Michelle Pfeiffer's *Grease 2* (1982), John Travolta's *Staying Alive* (1983), and Rick Springfield's *Hard to Hold* (1984).

SHADY REST HOTEL

Somewhat peaceful bed-and-breakfast establishment owned and operated by widow Kate Bradley in the 1960s TV sitcom *Petticoat Junction.* Located down the tracks outside rural Hooterville at Petticoat Junction, a train stop named after Kate's three knockout daughters—Betty Jo, Billie Jo, and Bobbie Jo—who wore petticoats under their dresses.

SHAFT

Influential 1971 action-packed film directed by Gordon Parks that is credited for kicking off the blaxploitation genre. It stars Richard Roundtree as John Shaft, the superstar private dick, and one bad mother ("Shut ya mouth"), who takes on the Mafia in Harlem. Shaft's specialty: sex and violence. Isaac Hayes's funky theme song, with the uptown instrumental groove and cool byplay, topped the pop charts and earned the singer-composer an Academy Award for Best Song—making him the first African-American to win in that category. Followed by sequels *Shaft's Big Score* (1972) and *Shaft in Africa* (1973). Remade in 2000 by director John Singleton and starring Samuel L. Jackson as John Shaft.

SHAG CARPETS

Throughout the 1960s and 1970s, this type of carpeting—constructed of exceptionally long cut-pile (one to three inches deep) made of twisted, shaggy strands of synthetic fibers, like nylon or polyester—was a common sight in most suburban homes. From room to room, these fluffy rugs could be found in spectacular shades of hot pink, sunshine yellow, baby blue, and snowy white (all popular during the pop-op 1960s) or in gold, olive green, rusty brown, and sea blue (fashionable during the earthy 1970s). A status symbol with an aura of luxury, shag carpets were something our mothers took extra pride in; they would comb them to perfection with a special shag rake after they got that trampled-on, lived-in look. The downside was that all the dirt, dust, hair, crumbs, Lite Brite pieces, Lego blocks, and other unidentifiable objects would get lost forever in the fuzzy pile. (The strongest Hoover vacuum cleaner couldn't suck the gunk out of the thick, lengthy strands.)

FYI: ▸ Elvis Presley, shag carpets' best friend, had them installed throughout Graceland in Memphis, including the Jungle Room (the mansion's rumpus room), in which the floor, walls, and ceilings were covered with furry olive green carpeting.

SHAGGY DOG

Disney's first live-action comedy was an appealing fantasy starring Tommy Kirk as Wilby Daniels, a misfit teenage boy who turns into a shaggy sheepdog via the spell of a magic ring. Co-stars included Fred MacMurray as Wilby's dog-allergic father Wilson Daniels, Annette Funicello as Wilby's high school girlfriend Allison D'Allessio, and Jordan Blake Warkol as Wilby's younger brother Moochie. Directed by Charles Barton, the 1959 movie was followed by two sequels, *The Shaggy D.A.* (1976) and *Return of the Shaggy Dog* (1987). It set the formula for future Disney comedies: youngsters, animals, and strange circumstances.

SHAGGY ROGERS

"Zoinks!" Actual first name: Norville. Scooby-Doo's bumbling, squeaky-voiced beatnik buddy, with bushy hair and soul-patch on the chin, who shared the same cowardice and gluttonous appetite as the cartoon canine in Hanna-Barbera's popular Saturday-morning series. "Yikes! Scoooob! Let's get outta-heeeeeere!"

SHAG HAIRCUT

Shag—a sex act, a style of carpet, and, most important to us pop culture aficionados, a haircut. Invented by hairstylist Paul McGregor, the unisex shag cut was fashionable during the first half of the 1970s. Like its name, it's a very shaggy style with lots of choppy layers and fringy ends, usually cut about shoulder length. In the 1971 movie *Klute*, Jane Fonda's call girl Bree Daniel sported the perfect shag hairdo, and in the 1975 film *Shampoo*, Warren Beatty's promiscuous hairdresser George Roundy gave Goldie Hawn great sex and great shag. Groovy TV moms Carol Brady (Flo Henderson) of *The Brady Bunch* and Shirley Partridge (Shirl Jones) of *The Partridge Family* both had shags their kids could be proud of. It was the hairdo of choice for male teen heartthrobs of the 1970s as well, seen on David Cassidy, Bobby Sherman, Jack Wild, Tony DeFranco, and all five members of the Bay City Rollers. In the 1990s, the shag had a revival, influenced by two actress with modified versions, Jennifer Aniston's slicey "Rachel" cut and Meg Ryan's cutesy chopped-up bob.

SHAKE 'N BAKE
Famous brand of breaded coating for cut chicken pieces, in which you shake pieces of chicken and then bake them. It has one of pop culture's best advertising catchphrases: "It's Shake 'n Bake, and I helped!" (Remember to say it in the sassy voice of a little Southern girl.)

SHAKER MAKER
"It's fun. It's silly. It's fantastic!" Produced by Ideal Toys in the 1970s, these craft sets let kids create different ceramic-esque figures based on licensed characters like Batman and Mickey Mouse. You combined a powder (the Magic Mix) and water in the special Shaker Maker mold, then shook and shook and shook. Then you waited a short time for the figure to dry, removed it from the Shaker Maker mold, and carefully painted it with a brush. The final work of art could then be given as a gift, to be admired by mom, then set on a shelf or tabletop.

"SHAKE YOUR BOOTY"
What you did with your butt at discotheques in the 1970s—oh, and the title of a 1976 K.C. and the Sunshine Band song.

SHAKEY'S PIZZA
Now-expired kid-friendly restaurant chain featuring pizza crust reminiscent of cardboard, a jazzy ragtime band, and a kitchen with a huge glass picture window (so you could watch the cooks show off by tossing the dough in the air like pros). The first Shakey's restaurant was opened by founders Sherwood "Skakey" Johnson and Ed Plummer in Sacramento, California, in 1954.

SHA NA NA
"Grease for peace!" The 1970s vocal group dressed up as greaser hoodlums (ducktail haircuts and leather jackets) while performing oldies but goodies from the 1950s and early 1960s. Unofficially led by Jon "Bowzer" Bauman, they got their name from the background chant heard on the Silhouettes' 1957 recording of "Get a Job." Hollywood credits include hosting a self-titled musical-variety TV show (1977–81) and starring in the movie *Grease* (1978) as Johnny Casino and the Gamblers, the band that performs at the National Bandstand Dance-Off at Rydell High.

SHANGRI-LAS
"Betty, is that Jimmy's ring you're wearing?" Formed in 1963, the "bad girl" group of the 1960s consisted of two sets of teenage sisters (Betty and Mary Weiss, and twins Marge and Mary Anne Ganser) from Andrew Jackson High School in Queens, New York. What set the Shangri-Las apart from other girl groups of the era was their raw, impassioned vocals—accented by a New York twang—heard on melodramatic pop recordings about teen love and heartache, such as "Leader of the Pack," "Remember (Walkin' in the Sand)," "Give Him a Great Big Kiss," and "I Can Never Go Home Anymore." Their cool, slightly delinquent appearance, with vulgarian makeup, big hair, and cycle-chick outfits with leather boots, also made them stand out. The Shangri-Las split up in 1969.

SHARK-TOOTH NECKLACE
Usually worn by guys, this fashion accessory had a single tooth dangling from a leather cord that was tied around the neck as a necklace. As part of the California pukka-shell necklace craze of the mid-1970s, it became even more popular with the success of the film *Jaws*.

SHAZAM!
"O Elder, leave me strong and wise, appear before my seeking eyes!" Live-action Saturday-morning show based on the 1940s comic superhero Captain Marvel, starring Michael Gray as Billy Batson, a

teenager on a never-ending mission to fight injustice. Billy was endowed with mighty powers of six immortal elders—Solomon, Hercules, Atlas, Zeus, Achilles, and Mercury. When trouble brewed, he yelled "Shazam!" (an acronym derived from the first initial of each ancient figure) and in a lightning flash was transformed into brawny alter-ego Captain Marvel, "the World's Mightiest Mortal," with the gift of amazing strength. Billy traveled around the country in a specially equipped van. When he needed advice, he summoned an elderly master, aptly named Mentor, whose face materialized in a blue light to offer words of wisdom. Premiering in 1974, the wholesome show focused on social cooperation, tolerance, honesty, and good citizenship and never used violence. It united with feminine superhero Isis to form the highly rated *Shazam/Isis Hour* in 1975.

FYI: ▸ For the 1940s comic books, movie actor Fred MacMurray reportedly served as the model for Captain Marvel's face.

SHELDON THE SEA GENIE

Bumbling magical genie who lived in a seashell and couldn't "whammy" a spell correctly. Played by flamboyant Rip Taylor on Saturday morning's *Sigmund and the Sea Monsters.*

SHEP

Witless ape-man George thought this friendly pet elephant called Shep was a large puppy dog ("great big gray, peanut-loving bow-wow") on his *George of the Jungle* cartoon program.

SHE-RA

Just as the previous generation picked Wonder Woman or Isis as superheroine role models, young girls of the 1980s chose this "Princess of Power" as theirs. Spinning off on her own Saturday-morning cartoon in 1985, He-Man's vigorous sister was the alter ego of Princess Adora from the land of Etheria. By acclaiming, "For the honor of Grayskull! I am She-Ra!" she metamorphosed into the courageous heroine, holding her Sword of Protection to guard Etheria's mystical Crystal Castle against baddie Hordak from the Horde World. Loyal friends included Lighthope, Madame Razz, owl-like Kowl, and little fairy Loo-Kee. She-Ra's devoted horse, Spirit, could also change into a magically altered version of itself called Swiftwind.

SHERIFF ELROY P. LOBO

Trucker B.J. McCay's larcenous nemesis from Orly County, Georgia, who along with imbecilic brother-in-law Deputy Perkins went on to have his own misadventures on prime-time TV's *The Misadventures of Sheriff Lobo*, starring Claude Akins, from 1979 to 1981.

SHERMAN, BOBBY

Once referred to as the "King of the Bubblegum Set," Bobby Sherman caused the hearts of young girls to flutter and throb as the first legitimate teen idol of the 1970s. Born on July 22, 1943, in Santa Monica, California, Sherman had a laid-back style, a pleasant disposition, and boy-next-door good looks: dreamy blue eyes, shaggy sandy-brown hair, and a sparkling smile. His first break came as a singer on the rock 'n' roll TV show *Shindig* from 1964 to 1966. In 1968, he landed the role that made him a star: Jeremy Bolt (the world's cutest lumberjack), on the comedy-adventure prime-time series *Here Come the Brides*. Spurred on by the success of the show, Sherman's music career exploded in 1969 with four consecutive gold singles: "Little Women" (1969), "La La La (If I Had You)" (1969), "Easy Come, Easy Go" (1970), and his best-known, "Julie, Do Ya Love Me" (1970).

At the peak of his reign, teenyboppers couldn't get enough of Sherman. The heartthrob virtually dominated the outside and inside of such teen mags as *Tiger Beat* and *16*. His adorable mug could be found on pinup posters, jewelry, lunch boxes, and even the backs of cereal boxes on a cardboard 45 rpm record that could be cut out and played. Alas, teen idolship is fleeting, and by 1971 Sherman found himself replaced as teendom's favorite dreamboat by both David Cassidy and Donny Osmond, the new pinup Kings of the Bubblegum Set.

SHERMAN OAKS GALLERIA

> "So for now, the Galleria is as empty as an airhead, except in the memories buried in the minds of the Valley Girls."
>
> —COMEDIENNE JULIA SWEENEY, 1999

Opening in 1980, the gleaming shopping complex, located at the intersection of Ventura and Sepulveda

Boulevards in Southern California's San Fernando Valley, is the architectural icon to a teenage generation. It was there—999,000 square feet of escalator-strewn retail space—the Valley Girl roamed with her friends, squealing "Omigod!" and spending daddy's money on trendy threads. In 1982, Moon Unit Zappa's record "Valley Girl" and the youth flick *Fast Times at Ridgemont High* immortalized the Galleria as the most famous mall in the world. It was closed and subsequently torn down in the late 1990s, after failing to keep up with changing times and falling victim to the devastating Northridge earthquake of 1994.

SHERMER HIGH SCHOOL

Fictional high school located in suburban Chicago in the 1985 film *The Breakfast Club*, where you would find a group of delinquent students sentenced to an all-day Saturday detention period in the school library, overseen by Richard Vernon, the strict dean of students.

SHIELDS, BROOKE

Born May 31, 1965, in New York City, the beautiful actress started her career at the wee age of eleven months as an Ivory Snow baby. Shortly after, she was signed by the prestigious Ford Agency as their very first child model. Aided by mature photo shoots with famed fashion photographer Francesco Scavullo, along with ad work for Colgate toothpaste and Breck shampoo, Shields became America's first and only juvenile supermodel. In 1978, film director Louis Malle cast her in his scandalous *Pretty Baby*. Her performance as Violet, a prepubescent New Orleans prostitute, had antipornography groups in an uproar because of some scenes showing the twelve-year-old in various states of undress and having sex with an adult lover. The hoopla made her one of Hollywood's youngest sex symbols and an international celebrity—known simply as "Brooke."

Pushed by overambitious stage mother Teri Shields, Brooke was a hard worker whose movies included tepid comedies—*Tilt* (1979), *Wanda Nevada* (1979), and *Just You and Me, Kid* (1979)—and teen-sex dramas, *The Blue Lagoon* (1980) and *Endless Love* (1981). By the beginning of the 1980s, she had developed into a tall (five-foot-eleven), lithe, and leggy older teenager sporting long and lustrous chestnut-colored hair, thick sculpted eyebrows (her trademark), pouty lips, and a smart but rather bland personality. Deemed the official "Face of the 1980s" by *Time* magazine, Brooke was everywhere: on the cover of hundreds of fashion and gossip magazines, as a TV commercial spokes-model for Calvin Klein jeans, as a fashion doll for LJN Toys, and as a multimillion-dollar corporation, Brooke Shields & Company.

In 1983, she took four years off from the busy Hollywood lifestyle to attend and graduate from Princeton University (majoring in French literature). The "World's Most Famous" coed added "author" to her resumé in 1985 with *On Your Own*, a self-help book aimed at young women just starting off for college. Romantically, she has been linked with Scott Baio, John Travolta, Prince Albert of Monaco, John Kennedy Jr., Dean Cain, George Michael, Michael Bolton, Michael Jackson, and Ted McGinley (the *Love Boat* hunk escorted Brooke to her high school prom). Yet, it a was wild-haired, rebellious tennis player who won her heart, and, following a long courtship, Brooke became Mrs. Andre Agassi in 1997. Two years later, Brooke surprised the public by ending the union, citing "incompatible tastes and temperament."

Over the years, the debate over Brooke Shields has been whether she is an actor or just a very gorgeous celeb. After a string of big-screen stinkers—*Sahara* (1983), *Brenda Starr* (1989), and *Speed Zone!* (1989)—the now fortysomething actress has proved that she has comedic talent, with the prime-time sitcom *Suddenly Susan* (1996–2000).

FYI: ▸ Legend has it that Teri Shields was pushing infant Brooke down Manhattan's Fifty-second Street when they came upon screen-great Greta Garbo, who stopped to admire the child.

SHIELDS AND YARNELL

In the 1970s, America went through a brief mime craze that peaked when this husband-and-wife act was given its own prime-time variety TV series (the first and only mime program in the history of television). Sporting matching Prince Valiant haircuts and toothy smiles, the young duo of Robert Shields and Lorene Yarnell began as street mimes in San Francisco. Upon winning a Ted Mack amateur contest, they guest-starred on TV's *Mac Davis Show* and

The Sonny and Cher Show, which led to their own summer series on CBS in 1977. *The Shields and Yarnell Show* did surprisingly well in the ratings, so CBS reinstated it the next season to compete opposite the top-rated *Laverne and Shirley*. Getting their asses whipped by the girls from Milwaukee, the silent twosome faded into obscurity, but not before starting trends in fashion (satin knickers, rainbow-striped suspenders, and toe socks) and in dance (the Robot, for all ya dancing machines).

FYI: ▸ Shields and Yarnell were married in an actual mime ceremony held at San Francisco's Union Square!

SHIMMY

Now associated with strippers, the 1960s dance consisted of rapidly shaking the chest or butt—or both! Introduced in 1960s with the songs "(I Do The) Shimmy Shimmy" by Bobby Freeman and "Shimmy, Shimmy, Ko-Ko-Bop" by Little Anthony.

SHIRLEY FEENEY

Brunette half of TV's *Laverne and Shirley* (played by Cindy Williams), a pert goody-goody whose naiveté usually lands her and best pal Laverne in some awkward situation. Likes poodle skirts, Boo Boo Kitty (her lucky stuffed black cat), and macho boyfriend Carmine Ragusa.

SHIRLEY PARTRIDGE

"She's the quintessential mother.
She's just extremely maternal, and loving,
nurturing, forgiving."
—DAVID CASSIDY

In 1970, you couldn't help but think: "Move over, Carol Brady, there's a new mom on the prime-time block—and with a groovy blonde shag hairdo as well!" This ultracool mother of the Partridge Family, played by award-winning actress Shirley Jones, was caring, wise, and beautiful, and shared vocals with teenage son Keith (played by Jones's real-life stepson David Cassidy, son of Jack Cassidy) on their hit pop recordings.

SHIRT TALES

Airing from 1982 to 1985, a Hanna-Barbera Saturday-morning cartoon series inspired by a popular line of greeting cards that depicted a group of cuddly animals: raccoon Rick, panda Pammy, mole Digger, monkey Bogey, tiger Tyg, and kangaroo Kit. The do-good critters' trademarks were shirts marked with words that randomly proclaim their feelings or thoughts, such as "Wild 'n' Crazy," "Hug Me," and "Let's Go." They lived in Oak Tree, a city park, attended by friendly superintendent Mr. Dinkle.

SHORTALLS

A cross between overalls and shorts sported originally by toddlers as a durable playsuit on the playground before grown-up versions made the fashion rounds in the 1980s.

SHORT N' SASSY

Manufactured by Clairol, the essential shampoo for those sporting the short and sassy Dorothy Hamill wedge in the 1970s; once advertised by the figure-skating champ herself.

SHOTGUN

What the place of honor in the front seat of a car nearest the passenger door is called. In most cases, before entering the vehicle someone would claim that seat by shouting "Shotgun!" and all the other passengers would have to settle for the lowly backseat.

SHOTZ BREWERY

Milwaukee-based beer manufacturer, from the *Laverne and Shirley* TV show, where Laverne DeFazio and Shirley Feeney work together on an assembly line in the bottle-cap division, and annoying Lenny and Squiggy are employed as delivery-truck drivers.

SHOW 'N TELL

The closest thing kids had to a VCR back in the early 1970s was General Electric's Show 'n Tell phonoviewer, a little TV set that had a phonograph player on top. It played full-color film strips that changed automatically ("Show") while an accompanying record told the story and performed songs ("Tell"). The different story sets included many Disney characters, like Winnie the Pooh, 101 Dalmatians, Mary Poppins, Three Little Pigs, Bambi, Pinocchio, Cinderella, Snow White, and It's a Small World. Show 'n Tell's competitors included the View-Master and Kenner's Give-a-Show.

SHRIMPTON, JEAN

"The changing face of the fashion model."
—*VOGUE* MAGAZINE, 1967

British mannequin Jean Shrimpton, with her trademark long, straight hair and bangs, baby blue eyes, a cleft underlip, and long-limbed stick figure, was truly the first great supermodel. Before Twiggy, she was the world's top cover girl during the swinging 1960s. In fact, she was to the 1960s what Cheryl Tiegs was to the 1970s, Christie Brinkley was to the 1980s, and Cindy Crawford was to the 1990s. Shrimpton is also renowned for a romantic relationship with fashion photographer David Bailey. (David Hemmings's character in the film *Blow-Up* is loosely based on Bailey.) Her nickname: "The Shrimp."

FYI: ▸ In 1989, *Model* magazine ranked Jean Shrimpton as the number-one model of the past twenty years.

SHRINKY DINKS

"Shrinks like magic!" Introduced by Colorforms in 1973, a craft toy in which clear, plastic-like cutouts of different characters were colored and then baked in the oven for a few minutes to shrink them down to a smaller, harder version. Originally the sets included generic themes, like clowns, dogs, cats, and dolls. By the 1980s, famous childhood favorites were added to the Shrinky Dinks line, such as Star Wars, E.T., Barbie, Holly Hobbie, Strawberry Shortcake, He-Man, and Pac-Man.

SIGMUND AND THE SEA MONSTERS

Another wacky live-action TV program from the strange and beautiful world of Sid and Marty Krofft, airing on Saturday mornings from 1973 to 1975. It starred redhead Johnny Whitaker (formerly Jody on *Family Affair*) and blond Scott Kolden as Southern California brothers Johnny and Scott Stuart. One afternoon, while surfing at Cypress Beach, the brothers bumped into a multiple-tentacled, green sea monster with a blob of seaweed for hair and one pointed tooth, named Sigmund Ooz. The friendly little creature, who had been mistreated by his rotten family—Big Daddy, Sweet Mama, brothers Blurp and Slurp, Great Uncle Siggy, and pet lobster Prince—ran away from their sea cave at Dead Man's Point.

Zany adventures followed as Johnny and Scott hid lovable Sigmund in their backyard clubhouse and helped him elude the monstrous clan, who wanted him back so they could continue bossing him around. The show co-starred famous Hollywood short person Billy Barty as costumed Sigmund, Mary Wickes as the Stuart family's suspicious housekeeper, Zelda, Margaret "Wicked Witch of the West" Hamilton as nosy neighbor Miss Eddels, Rip Taylor as Sheldon the Sea Genie, and Pamelyn Ferdin as neighborhood friend Peggy, whose dog Fluffy was the apple of Sigmund's eye. The theme tune, "Friends," sung by Whitaker, was written by Danny Janssen and Bobby Hart, the guys responsible for numerous bubblegum hits of the 1960s, including many for The Monkees and Bobby Sherman.

FYI: ▸ One day at the beach in La Jolla, California, Sid Krofft saw some seaweed floating up from a cave. He thought the seaweed appeared to be alive and thus was inspired to create *Sigmund and the Sea Monsters.*

SILLY PUTTY

The pinkish-peach glob of glorious goop was invented in 1944 by James Wright at General Electric's New Haven laboratory as an inexpensive silicone-based rubber substitute during World War II. It failed as a replacement for rubber, but the G.E. scientists had fun molding and bouncing the blob-like substance around the lab (they dubbed it "Gooey Gupp"). In 1949, entrepreneur Peter Hodgson, realizing the fun goo would make a great toy, bought the rights to it. He called it Silly Putty, packaged it in egg-shaped plastic containers, and advertised it as "real solid liquid." Hailed as "the biggest novelty fad in years," the versatile Silly Putty was rolled, stretched, molded, bounced, and snapped by Americans of all ages, who also used it to lift images off the pages of newspapers and comic books. Following Hodgson's death in 1976, Binney & Smith, the manufacturers of Crayola Crayons, acquired the rights to Silly Putty. As of today, more than 200 million eggs of Silly Putty have been sold.

FYI: ▸ Apollo 8 astronauts used Silly Putty to fasten down weightless tools during their space flight.

SILLY SAND
A colorful, sandlike mixture that you dripped from a squeeze bottle to create castles, forts, igloos, creatures, and other works of art. This craft toy, produced in the late 1960s and early 1970s, was basically a hybrid of Magic Rocks and Wham-O's Magic Sand.

SILLY STRAW
A clear-plastic drinking straw full of wacky curves, twists, and loop-the-loops that made sipping boring milk and other beverages a delightful pastime. Introduced in the early 1970s by Wham-O.

SILLY STRING
Many of us have been victims of a stringy Silly String attack—when, minding our own business, all of a sudden we're blasted and covered with gooey, neon-colored string squirted out of an aerosol can. It's fun to have Silly String strung (more like webbed) all over, just as it's fun to squirt it all over someone else. Introduced in 1969, Silly String is cool and wet when initially ejected, but it quickly solidifies into a plastic-like substance. It livens up parties, sporting events, school hallways, graduation, and even weddings—but at all costs, avoid the bride in her sacred white gown unless you want a very, very enraged woman after you for blood.

SILVER
"Hi-ho, Silver! Away-y-y!" On the extremely popular *Lone Ranger* TV series of the 1950s, Silver is the trusty white steed with lightning speed belonging to the masked hero, the Lone Ranger. He is named after the Lone Ranger's unique calling card, a silver bullet.

SILVER SPOONS
"The Rickster!" Half-hour sitcom starring Ricky Schroder as twelve-year-old Ricky Stratton, the sagacious son of divorced parents, who left military school to live with his immature but well-meaning tycoon father, Edward Stratton III, a toy-inventing genius played by Joel Higgins. Stratton's vast mansion was filled floor to ceiling with every game and toy imaginable, plus he had a nearly life-sized railroad in which you could ride a train through the rooms. Co-starring were Erin Gray as Kate Summers, Edward's secretary, who later became his wife; and Jason Bateman and Alfonso Ribeiro as Derek Taylor and Alfonso Spears, Ricky's friends. The TV series aired from 1982 to 1987 on NBC.

SILVER SURFER
The Sentinel of the Spaceways! Introduced in 1966, *Marvel* comics' silver-colored superhero (real name: Norrin Radd) from a faraway planet called Zenn-La, who soars through the galaxy on a shiny surfboard.

SIMBA
The determined lion son of King Mufasa of the African Pride Land who is tricked out of his place as heir to the throne by his evil Uncle Scar, but later regains it with the aid of lioness girlfriend Nala, warthog Pumbaa, and meerkat Timon, in *The Lion King* movie.

SIMMONS, RICHARD
Ostentatious and overenergetic fitness guru whose trademark curly locks remind one of a Brillo pad. A friend of the fat, he inspires them to shed pounds with his mail-order weight-loss program called "Deal-a-Meal" and his exercise-dance videos, such as the best-selling "Sweating to the Oldies." From 1979 to 1981, Simmons appeared as himself on the soap smash *General Hospital.* (He instructed a weight-loss and exercise class at the Campus Disco in Port Charles.)

FYI: ▸ The vanity plates on Richard Simmons's sports car once read YRUFATT. (Get it?)

SIMON (CHIPMUNKS)
Blue-sweatered, bespectacled bookworm who was regularly dragged into comical mischief by his brothers Alvin and Theodore in The Chipmunks cartoon series.

SIMON (GAME)
A memory-testing, spherical electronic game with four lighted, colored panels (blue, green, red, and yellow), introduced by Milton Bradley in 1978. The battery-operated game's rules are similar to Simon Says (hence the name). When you turn it on, Simon beeps, flashes one of the colored panels, and in return you push that panel. Then it repeats that color,

adds a new color, and you then push both panels. It continues repeating and adding new colors with each sequence becoming longer, faster, and more difficult. When your memory can't hold out any longer and you push a wrong panel, Simon lets out a rather insulting electronic "Razzzzz," and the game is over. Its obnoxiously loud beeps get on the nerves of parents so much that the batteries go missing or the game is crushed or mysteriously disappears.

SIMONE

Belonging to TV's Partridge Family, this fluffy dog (half sheepdog) once chased a stinky skunk inside their tour bus, resulting in tomato baths for the whole group.

SIMPSON, O.J.

Once upon a time, before becoming involved in the biggest murder trial of the twentieth century, O.J. Simpson had the adoration and respect of millions of fans. Born Orenthal James Simpson on July 9, 1947, in San Francisco, the football running back led the University of Southern California to two Rose Bowls in the late 1960s and was the recipient of the Heisman Trophy in 1968. In 1969, he signed with the Buffalo Bills, with whom he played until he joined the San Francisco Forty-Niners for two seasons in 1978. Nicknamed "The Juice" (because his initials also stand for "orange juice"), Simpson was one of the AFC's leading rushers, setting a record in 1973 for most yards gained in a single season. The same year, the NFL voted him Most Valuable Player.

Held in high esteem long after the end of his remarkable football career, Simpson had everything: handsome looks, wealth, respect from his peers, public admiration, product endorsements (most notable were the Hertz Rent-a-Car TV spots), an active role as a sports commentator, a steady film career (*The Towering Inferno, Capricorn One,* and *The Naked Gun*), and a blonde trophy-wife, Nicole Brown Simpson, who gave him two beautiful children. His life changed on June 14, 1994, the night the brutally slain bodies of Nicole and friend Ron Goldman were found outside her fashionable Brentwood condominium. After an eerie low-speed chase on the freeways of Southern California, watched live on TV by ninety-five million people, Simpson was arrested and charged with the murders. We all know the outcome of the trial (a "not guilty" verdict), and God knows enough has been said about it, so I won't go any further except to say, guilty or not, it's tragic to witness the fall of the man once considered our greatest football hero.

SIMPSONS

Cartoonist Matt (*Life in Hell*) Groening's outlandish spin on the American middle-class family is the longest-running prime-time animated series of all time. Set in the seemingly idyllic hamlet of Springfield, Middle America, the location of a nuclear power plant, a toxic waste dump, and a prison, the show focuses on the Simpsons, a rather crude and obnoxious family made up of characters with bizarre hairdos, yellow skin, four fingers, and severe overbites. There's Homer Simpson, the lazy, slobbish doofus of a dad; Marge Simpson, the blue-haired diplomatic wife and mother; Bart, the troublemaking, underachieving ten-year-old son; Lisa, the underappreciated, overachieving eight-year-old daughter; and Maggie, the pacifier-sucking baby. Extended family members include Bart's pet greyhound Santa's Little Helper, Lisa's deceased cat Snowball I, current cat Snowball II, senile Grampa (Abe Simpson), and Marge's chain-smoking sisters Patty and Selma (whom Homer loathes).

The Simpsons were originally featured in thirty-second segments on FOX's *Tracey Ullman Show* (1987–89), before headlining their own weekly series beginning in January 1990. It is cited as the first prime-time cartoon hit since the prehistoric days of *The Flintstones* in the 1960s and has paved the way for edgier adult fare, like *Beavis and Butt-Head, The Critic, Futurama, King of the Hill, Ren and Stimpy,* and *South Park.*

SINATRA, NANCY

> "My first pop idol was Nancy Sinatra—Nancy with go-go boots, miniskirt, and fake eyelashes. She was cool."
>
> —MADONNA

A second-generation pop sensation whose smash records in the mid-1960s included the chart-topping "These Boots Are Made for Walkin'" (1966), "How Does That Grab You, Darlin'?" (1966), "Sugar Town" (1966), "You Only Live Twice" (1967), and

"Somethin' Stupid" (1967), a duet with papa, Frank Sinatra. Born on June 8, 1940, in New Jersey, Nancy had an image of being one tough cookie. She wore calf-hugging vinyl boots, tight miniskirts, black leather jackets, a long mane of frosted blonde hair, and vulgarian-style makeup, consisting of false eyelashes, heavy eyeliner, and pale frosted lipstick. Sassy and sexy, Nancy represented the "now" generation as she performed go-go hits on the TV dance shows *Hullabaloo* and *Shindig*. On the big screen, she was seen sharing a Harley chopper with supercool Peter Fonda (1966's *The Wild Angels*) and frugging with hip-swiveling Elvis Presley (1968's *Speedway*).

Little girls of the 1960s watched Sinatra in curious amazement. Unlike their pert Laura Petrie–type moms and perky Gidget-type teen sisters, Sinatra was hard and liberated. She talked as if she had been around the block a few times, and even had the courage to wear go-go boots with a bikini (wow!). She was later acclaimed as a role model for such strong and independent singers as Pat Benatar and Madonna.

FYI: ▸ Nancy's 1967 album *Sugar* caused so much commotion—because of its cover featuring Miss Sinatra in a fetching pink bikini—that it was banned in Boston.

SINCLAIR DINOSAUR

The bright-green advertising icon found at Sinclair gas stations nationwide was always a sight for the travel-weary eyes of children. He actually has a name: "Dino."

SINGING NUN

Vespa-riding, guitar-strumming, habit-wearing Sister Luc-Gabrielle, a.k.a. Jeanine Deckers, a.k.a. Soeur Sourire (Sister Smile), from the Fichermont, Belguim, convent, became the wildest pop star around with her worldwide hit "Dominique" in 1963. It topped the U.S. charts for four weeks. Her story was made into a film, *The Singing Nun* (1966), starring Debbie Reynolds. The Singing Nun committed suicide with her female lover in 1985.

FYI: ▸ Throughout the 1960s, American pop culture seemed to be obsessed with nuns. Just check out these big-screen movies featuring habit-clad women: *The Nun's Story* (1959), *The Sound of Music* (1965), *The Trouble with Angels* (1966) and its sequel, *Where Angels Go, Trouble Follows* (1968), *Change of Habit* (1969), and *Two Mules for Sister Sara* (1970). And then there's prime-time TV's *The Flying Nun* (1967–70).

SIR NILSSON

The little pet monkey belonged to pigtailed, mischief-making Pippi Longstocking, from Astrid Lindgren's classic storybooks.

SISSY BARS

Very high (around forty-two inches) chrome backrest equipped with a back pad, found on hi-rise bicycles in early 1970s. Obviously named because it kept scaredy-cat kids from falling off the back of the bike while doing wheelies and other stunts (if the sissies even bothered), unlike the shorter backrests.

SISTER SLEDGE

Four singing sisters from North Philadelphia—Debbie, Joni, Kim, and Kathy Sledge—who had a bunch of Top Forty disco hits, including "He's the Greatest Dancer" (1979), "We Are Family" (1979), and a remake of the Mary Wells classic "My Guy" (1980).

SIT 'N SPIN

Little kids would sit on this lazy Susan type of riding toy and use the steering wheel at its center to spin themselves silly. Kenner Toys first produced the Sit 'n Spin in 1973.

SIX MILLION DOLLAR MAN

A fantasy-adventure TV series, airing on ABC from 1974 to 1978, based on Martin Caidin's 1972 sci-fi novel *Cyborg*. It starred Lee Majors as Colonel Steve Austin, an astronaut grievously injured after crashing an M3F5 test jet in a Southwestern desert. "A man barely alive," Austin was rebuilt, using six million dollars' worth of nuclear-powered bionic parts, by a secret government agency called the Office of Scientific Information (OSI). Half-man, half-robot, Austin had superhuman strength and was capable of running at speeds up to sixty miles an hour, jumping over buildings, and crashing through cement walls. Oscar Goldman (Richard Anderson), the head of OSI, sent Austin on special assignments to stop evildoers from destroying the world. *The Six Million Dollar Man* is notable for launching a wave of mid-1970s superhero shows, such as *Wonder Woman* (1976–79), *Man from Atlantis* (1977), *The Incredible Hulk* (1978–82), *The Amazing Spider-Man* (1978–79), and the just-as-popular spin-off *The Bionic Woman* (1976–78), starring Lindsay Wagner as Jaime Sommers, Steve Austin's supercharged true love.

SIXTEEN CANDLES

"It's the time of your life that may last a lifetime." In the 1984 teen comedy, Molly Ringwald stars as Samantha Baker, your average angst-ridden high school sophomore going through a severe case of the puberty blues. It's Samantha's Sweet Sixteen, and she's a teen with problems. Her family has totally forgotten her birthday because they're preoccupied with the impending wedding of Ginny (Blanche Baker), her self-centered older sister. Sam has to endure the immature taunts of smart-alecky younger brother Mike (Justin Henry). Her grandparents have invaded her bedroom, not to mention her breasts. Long Duk Dong (Gedde Watanabe), a wacky Chinese foreign-exchange student who thinks he's a regular party animal, is staying at her house. Nerdy freshman hornball Ted the Geek, a.k.a. Farmer Ted (Anthony Michael Hall), is putting the moves on her. And Samantha's crush, Jake Ryan (Michael Schoeffling), who happens to be the senior-class heartthrob dating Caroline (Haviland Morris), the blonde prom queen, doesn't know she's alive. But wait! Things just might turn out fine, as dreamboat Jake begins to show signs of interest in Samantha.

As director John Hughes's debut, the heartwarming *Sixteen Candles* is considered his best; it also launched the Brat Pack careers of Ringwald and Hall. It has developed a cult following among Gen-Xers who were in high school in the 1980s because of its low-brow humor and clever one-liners, such as Samantha's "I can't believe my grandmother actually felt me up," "I loathe the bus," and "I can't believe I gave my panties to a geek."

FYI: ▸ Look for the Cusack siblings in cameos—John as a fellow nerd friend of Ted's, and Joan as the geeky girl wearing the orthodontic headgear.

SIZZLERS

"Race the fastest Hot Wheels of them all!" Ultrafast Hot Wheels got even faster when Mattel Toys introduced the Sizzlers line in 1970. These three-inch cars sizzled around the orange Hot Wheels track at the extraordinary speed of 1,200 (scale) miles an hour for more than a roaring nonstop five minutes. What gave Sizzlers their incredible energy was the Juice Machine, a gas-pump-shaped battery pack into which you plugged its hose to the car. When the top of the Juice Machine was pushed down, a battery charge went through the hose to the power cells of the Sizzler car, allowing it to zoom totally around the track. When drained of power, the car could be recharged again for hot racing. The many different types of Sizzler vehicles included Back Fire, Hot Head, Indy Eagle, Live Wire, Revvin' Heaven, Spoil Sport, and Fata Police Car.

SKATEBOARDING

> "They're not going to stop kids from skateboarding. Skateboarders have an attitude. It's a freedom thing."
>
> —KEVIN THATCHER, EDITOR OF *THRASHER* MAGAZINE

When two surfers from Dana Point, California, nailed roller-skate wheels to a plank of wood and then discovered that they could hang-ten down a sidewalk in 1958, who would have guessed that the ingenious creation would lead to a recreational sport that has become a way of life for millions of kids? Skateboarding experienced three waves in popularity. The first was from 1964 to 1967, when skateboards were manufactured as simple, flat pieces of wood, resembling mini-surfboards mounted on metal skate wheels. Although primitive in design and movement compared with today's boards, they caught on with youngsters nationwide and become the biggest sport fad of the decade. It inspired a 1964 pop-music hit by Jan and Dean, "Sidewalk Surfin'," complete with wheels-on-pavement sound effects.

Unfortunately, by the end of the 1960s the sport was discouraged by parents because of a rise in the number of broken bones and other injuries, as well as complaints by unwary pedestrians who were bombarded by skateboarders on busy sidewalks. "No Skateboarding" signs were posted in parking lots and on city walkways, so the police would often confiscate skateboards and cite them as dangerous and a public nuisance.

Skateboarding's second wave, known as the "golden age," occurred from 1973 to 1979, following the revolutionary development of the urethane wheel. Skateboards now had a kickback and were made out of fiberglass decorated with wild graphics, and the urethane wheels provided excellent traction, faster speed, and tighter maneuverability. Teen boys (the average age of a skateboarding enthusiast is fourteen) turned the sport into an amazing art form by performing various tricks with such names as ollies, kickflips, wheelies, handplants, slappies, shove-its, fingerflips, and indy airs. Celebrities like Farrah Fawcett, Kristy McNichol, Scott Baio, and Leif Garrett took to skateboarding on TV shows and in the movies. This skate era saw the rise of specially designed skateboard parks where riders could strut their stuff in areas equipped with concrete ramps, bowls, and banked tracks. Once again, it was accidents that caused the second waning of the skateboard craze, after high insurance rates forced most of the 200 parks nationwide to close in 1979. (At its peak, more than 27,000 skateboard injuries were reported per year.)

The third wave, from 1983 to the present, saw skateboarding not so much as a fad but more as a separate subculture, a lifestyle adopted by young punk-rebel types who had a distinctive way of talking, dressing, and listening to speed-metal rock groups, such as Suicidal Tendencies, Offspring, and Cypress Hill. *Thrasher* magazine, the "bible of skate style," was launched in 1979 ("thrasher" is slang for a skateboarder). Currently, skateboarding is the sixth largest participant sport in America and considered an "extreme" sport, along with surfing, skydiving, and snowboarding. Pro skaters travel the world making mega-bucks off endorsement deals.

SKEDIDDLE KIDDLES

"I walk! Watch me move along!" Introduced in 1968, this line of Liddle Kiddle dolls actually walked with the help of a Skediddler mechanism inserted in their backs. The different Skediddle Kiddles included Sheila Skediddle, Shirley Skediddle, Suki Skediddle, Swingy Skediddle, Rah-Rah Skediddle (a cheerleader), and Cherry Blossom (an Oriental).

SKELETOR

One of Saturday-morning cartoons' most ominous villains ever was He-Man's hooded, skull-faced nemesis from Snake Mountain. Skeletor's evil horde included Beastman, Trapjaw, Triclops, Mer-Man, and female witch Evil-Lyn.

SKINNY TIES

Absurdly thin neckwear often made out of cool leather (men) or flashy lamé (women) that made a huge fashion statement for nightclub-hopping New Wavers in the early 1980s.

SKIPPER

In 1964, Barbie became a big sister when Mattel introduced Skipper, a nine-inch-tall preteen sibling with an undeveloped body and straight blonde hair. Skipper was your typical elementary school girl who loved ice cream, roller-skating, and playing with best-buddy Skooter, a pigtailed tomboy who had a wacky grin on her face. Because Skipper was too young to have a boyfriend, her "special friend" was redheaded Ricky, "the cutest freckle-faced kid in town." Skipper's appeal is attributed to two things: She was closer in age to the little girls who played with Barbie dolls, reminding them of themselves, and she represented the idea of growing up to be just as wonderful as the glamorous Barbie.

SKIPPER JONAS GRUMBY

Congenial captain of the marooned S.S. *Minnow* who refers to his bumbling first mate Gilligan as "my little buddy." Played by Alan Hale Jr. on the TV sitcom *Gilligan's Island* (1964–67).

SKIPPY HANDLEMAN

A hopelessly dense nerd, Erwin "Skippy" Handleman was the next-door neighbor of the Keatons of Columbus, Ohio, and eldest son Alex's closest friend. He had an enormous crush on scatter-brained Mallory Keaton. Marc Price played Skippy on the NBC-TV sitcom *Family Ties* from 1982 to 1989.

SKITTLE BOWL

Introduced in 1969 by Aurora (the company known primarily for model kits) and advertised by *Get Smart*'s Don Adams, this was the next best thing to having a bowling alley in your living room. Based on a classic game from the United Kingdom, Skittle Bowl was similar to bowling, complete with the same scoring and rules, but it had a twist: The miniature wooden pins were set on a plastic game board, and the ball was attached to a pole by an adjustable metal chain. As players took turns swinging the ball, the right swing could score spares and strikes. Its popularity led to a whole series of Skittle games characterized by the swinging ball, including Skittle Golf, Skittle Baseball, Skittle Horseshoes, Skittle Tic-Tac-Toe, Skittle Poker, Skittle Bingo, and Skittle Pool. The TV commercial for Skittle Pool featured comedienne Lucille Ball walking into a pool hall with a swimsuit and asking, "Where's the pool?"

SKORTS

Shorts that looked like a skirt—or was it a skirt that looked like shorts? Either way, it seemed that gals got to wear the best of both worlds.

SKY DANCERS

Introduced by Galoob in 1994, these princess ballerina dolls propelled high into the sky after a cord from a handheld launching pad was pulled. Although lovely to look at, Sky Dancers could be dangerous. In 2000, they were recalled and soon discontinued because they would fly quickly in unpredictable directions, hitting and injuring—black eyes and broken teeth—those in near proximity.

SKYPAD

Swanky, ultramodern (in a retro sort of way) apartment complex located in Orbit City and built on towering hydraulic lifts that were raised and lowered to avoid inclement weather conditions. Home of George Jetson and family.

SLACKER

An unmotivated adult with no direction—unique to Generation X—who doesn't work and still lives at home with the parental unit. All talk (they have big ideas) and no action (they're lazy), the slacker types are glorified in director Richard Linklater's semi-documentary film, *Slacker* (1991).

SLAM BOOKS

"Write small to save space!" Do you remember these? They were question-and-answer books that you had your friends and classmates fill out. To do a Slam Book, you needed a notebook, preferably a spiral. Then you wrote a topical question at the top of every page. These ranged from the innocent (such as "What's your favorite food?") to the topical ("Who do you love more, Shaun Cassidy or Leif Garrett?") to the personal ("Do you like sex and fooling around?"). After writing the questions, you carried the Slam Book to school or around the neighborhood and made everyone fill it out. Those who answered the questions had a personal number, and their answer was represented by that number. A list of the names and their numbers were kept somewhere in the book, usually after the title page, so you could peek to see who answered what. The answers revealed much about a person's personality and were a great way to find out what your secret crush was thinking and if you were compatible with him or her.

SLAM DANCING

Punk-rock dancing from the late 1970s in which participants (usually young men) violently slammed their bodies up against each other; evolved into moshing during the grunge–alternative music era of the 1990s.

SLANG

Bodacious. Bogus. Diss. Gnarly. Groovy. Rad. Skank. Spaz. Stoked. Can you believe we actually used these words in everyday conversation, and that many are still used today? Here's a lexicon, with pseudo-definitions, with more than 200 common slang terms and phrases used by young people from the 1960s through the 1990s.

- "Ain't"—Contraction of "am not" or "are not," loathed by those with high regard for the English language; commonly spoken by lower-class Americans.
- "Airhead"—Empty-headed, self-absorbed person, usually of the female gender.
- "As if"—Sarcastic expression of doubt; catchphrase of Cher Horowitz from the movie *Clueless*.
- "Awesome"—Really cool; oft-associated with surfers and skaters.
- "Babe"—A sweet-looking person of either sex.

- "Bad"—Originating among inner-city black youths of the 1970s, means its opposite: good.
- "Ballistic"—To go wildly insane or lose control of emotions, or both.
- "Barf me out"—What a Valley Girl would say after being told something offensive.
- "Beach bunny"—A beautiful girl (usually blonde) at the beach (the same girl at a mountain ski resort would be referred as a "ski bunny").
- "Beer goggles"—Having blurry vision from being drunk, which makes everyone in the bar, including the appearance-challenged, look attractive.
- "Bimbo"—A ditzy, self-centered girl with big hair and slutty clothing.
- "Bitchin'"—Southern California slang—originating among surfers before Val-Gals overused it—meaning something cool.
- "Bite me"—An insult response; also, there is "Bite the big one" and "Eat me."
- "Blow chunks"—The act of vomiting caused from drinking too much booze.
- "Blow your mind"—Getting very high on drugs, particularly mind-altering ones like acid and ecstasy.
- "Bodacious"—Valley Boy types first spoke this to describe a well-shaped girl, before using it as a term for describing anything cool.
- "Bogart"—To hog something, generally in reference to hoarding a marijuana joint.
- "Bogus"—Double-meaning here: awfully fake or totally cool.
- "Boogie down"—A phrase commonly used during the disco era, meaning to dance.
- "Booty"—Butt, as in "Shake your booty."
- "Booty call"—To show up at someone's house for the sole purpose of having sex.
- "Boss"—Something or someone extremely awesome.
- "Boy toy"—Term invented by Madonna for a girl who plays around with boys. (The pop star wore a "boy toy" belt on her 1984 *Like a Virgin* album cover.) Later used to describe a cute, well-built guy.
- "Brain fart"—To lose your train of thought or be unable to recall a simple memory in mid-sentence.
- "Bread"—Money; cash.
- "Brewski"—Frat-speak for beer.
- "Brickhouse"—A well-built woman; from 1977 Commodores dance song of the s name ("She's a brick . . . house").
- "Bro'"—What a dude would call his friend.
- "Buff"—A well-muscled body found on gyn bunnies of both genders.
- "Bummer"—A major let down.
- "Burn-out"—Describing someone who has d so many drugs they can't function in norma everyday life. (The past participle, "burned-out," is used to describe someone who is tire of doing the same thing over and over.)
- "Bust a move"—Early 1990s hip-hop term for dancing.
- "Butt floss"—A thong bikini.
- "Butt ugly"—Uglier than ugly; sometimes shortened to "bugly."
- "Buzz"—To cop a light high from booze or pot. A "buzz kill" is when the high is brought down by some kind of bad news.
- "Cheesy"—Characterizing a person or event that is in poor taste.
- "Cherry"—Something totally pristine, usually in reference to an automobile.
- "Chick"—Hippie-speak for those of the female gender. (Most women today consider this slang term offensive, if not sexist.)
- "Chick flick"—Gal-oriented movie often starring the likes of Meg Ryan or Sandra Bullock and not featuring graphic violence, unnecessary female nudity, high-speed chases, and things being blown up.
- "Chillin'"—Hanging out and relaxing; made popular by black Americans in the rap era of the 1980s.
- "Chill pill"—To tell someone to calm down, say: "Take a chill pill."
- "City"—Suffix used as a way to put great emphasis on something (for example, drag-city, surf-city); similar to the suffix "-ville" (dulls-ville, squares-ville, and so on).
- "Cool"—Classic slang meaning laid back, not a problem, really good: "It's cool!"
- "Cop-out"—Not coming through on a promise.
- "Couch potato"—Someone who plops their ass on a sofa in front of the TV all the time.
- "Cowabunga"—Surfer lingo for "Wow!"

- "Crack up"—Something hilarious.
- "Crap"—Cleaner alternative to the naughty "shit": "That car is a piece of crap."
- "Da bomb"—Describes something or someone favorably: "Carmen's da bomb!"
- "Dang it!"—Polite way to say "damn it" after hurting yourself or receiving some bad news.
- "Deep shit"—When someone is in big trouble.
- "Def"—Rap lingo for anything cool.
- "Dickhead"—An unpleasant person of the male sex.
- "Dig it"—Classic 1970s expression for acknowledging something good.
- "Dipstick"—A stupid person.
- "Diss"—To insult or disrespect someone; often used by African-American women: "Girl, I know you ain't dissin' me!"
- "Do lunch"—Overused yuppie phrase meaning to get together for power lunches (mixing lunch with business).
- "Dog"—Once slang for a homely person, now slang for a male who sleeps around.
- "Dud"—A boring event or person.
- "Dude"—Surf slang for a guy friend, often used in a salutation.
- "Duh"—An expression commonly used as a sarcastic reply after someone stupidly says something you already knew ("No, duh!"); when the comment was really, really stupid, a long drawn-out "Du-u-h-h-h!" was uttered.
- "Dynomite!"—A 1970s expression meaning "wonderful," linked to Jimmie "J.J." Walker of TV's *Good Times*.
- "Easy does it"—The 1970s phrase meaning to take it nice and slow.
- "Eat shit and die"—An extreme way of telling someone to drop dead.
- "Excellent"—Classic 1980s term for something very good.
- "Eye candy"—Sights that are pleasing to the eyes: "Brad Pitt is eye candy."
- "Fab"—Short for "fabulous," originating during the mod 1960s: "The Beatles are the Fab Four."
- "Fake bake"—A glowing suntan acquired from tanning salon.
- "Far-out"—Classic term associated with hippies of the 1960s used to described something really great: "It's far-out!"
- "Fer shur"—Variation of "for sure"; Val-Gal agreement, often overenunciated: "Ferrr shurrr, I'd love to go to the Galleria with you!"
- "Fink"—The act of tattling, or someone who tattles.
- "Five finger discount"—Shoplifting.
- "Flaky"—Having an unreliable or unpredictable personality.
- "Flip out"—Lose control of your emotions.
- "Fly"—Early-1990s term for someone cool or good-looking.
- "Foxy"—A 1970s term for someone totally attractive, male or female.
- "Freak out"—In the 1960s, this phrase meant having a bad acid trip; in the 1970s it meant having a really good disco trip.
- "Fresh"—Hip-hop for something cool and new.
- "Funky"—Once used to characterize something smelly or quaintly unsophisticated, it was adopted by African-Americans in the 1970s to describe anything good, as in "Play that funky music, white boy."
- "Fuzz"—Term for police used by hippies and other antiestablishment types during the late 1960s and early 1970s.
- "Gag me with a spoon"—Val-Gal response uttered after seeing or hearing something really distasteful.
- "Get on down"—To party and dance.
- "Gnarly"—Exclamation used by Valley Boys of the 1980s to describe something especially cool; for Valley Girls, it meant something especially uncool.
- "Go for it!"—Classic yuppie catchphrase of the 1980s often found on a bumper sticker on yuppie mobiles, such as BMWs, Saabs, and Audis.
- "Gonzo"—Surf-speak for outrageous.
- "Goober"—An idiot: "Don't be such a goober."
- "Gravy"—Word meaning cool or sweet.
- "Grody"—Something really, really, really gross.
- "Groovy"—First used by London mods and San Francisco hippies, before becoming an overused expression of mainstream Americans, this is the definitive slang term of the late 1960s and early 1970s, used as a simple description for anything extraordinarily nice.
- "Hang loose"—Surf lingo for hanging out and waiting patiently without getting uptight.

- "Hang ten"—Surf lingo meaning to hang ten toes over the front of your surfboard.
- "Happenin'"—A 1960s slang term for an event or where the action takes place: "It's my happenin', and welcome to it!"
- "Haul ass"—To leave someplace really fast.
- "Head rush"—A big thrill that makes one dizzy in the head: "Hearing Jimmy Page's awesome guitar solo gave Misty a head rush."
- "Heavy"—Term used to describe highly serious subject matter; a downer: "I don't mean to get heavy on you but. . . ."
- "Heinous"—Anything bad and ugly, such as a heinous zit on your face.
- "Hellacious" There are two meanings for this slang word: difficult ("The algebra final was hellacious") or fine: "That babe's got a hellacious bod."
- "Hip"—From "hipster," referring to someone or something extremely fashionable and up-to-date.
- "Homey"—What a rapper calls his closest friend; also, homey.
- "Hoochie"—A slut.
- "Horn-dog"—A horny dude.
- "Hot"—Something so feverishly good it's burning up; also employed to add heated emphasis (hot love, hot number, hot stuff . . .).
- Hottie—Cute gal or guy.
- "Hot-doggin'"—Surfer and skater slang for showing off.
- "How's it hangin'?"—Simply, "Hello."
- "Hump Day"—Nickname for middle-of-the-week Wednesday.
- "I am so sure"—Sarcastic disbelief uttered by Valley Girls: "I am sooooo sure. Like, *he'd* go out with *you*."
- "Jacked"—Extremely messed up; used particularly in reference to being drunk or stoned on drugs.
- "Jive"—African-American slang from the 1970s meaning to bullshit someone; often used in conjunction with the term "turkey," as in "jive turkey," which meant a phony, uncool person.
- "Jonesin'"—To really crave something; drug-addict term for badly in need of a fix.
- "Keen"—Someone or something sharp-looking or cool; often coupled with "peachy," as in "peachy keen."
- "Kick ass"—Two meanings for this one: (1) to beat someone up or (2) something really fine.
- "Kick back"—To relax.
- "Killer"—A term to describe something great: "Dude, I've got some killer weed to toke."
- "Kooky"—Crazy in an amusing sort of Gidget way.
- "Kudos"—Slang from the early 1960s meaning good-bye.
- "Laid back"—To be mellow, relaxed, and not in a hurry.
- "Lame"—Not so great.
- "Later"—Good-bye; see you soon, as in "Later, dudes!"
- "Let's boogie"—This 1970s phrase had no connection with disco-dancing; instead, it meant to leave in a hurry.
- "Let's roll"—A 1990s term meaning "to leave," immortalized as the last words uttered by the heroic Todd Beamer when he and other passengers fought the hijackers on the doomed United Airlines Flight 93 (September 11, 2001).
- "Like"—Teen girls of the 1980s garnished their sentences with this verbal tic, frequently used after every third or fourth word: "She, like, wanted to go to, like, this party last night, and it was, like, such a dud, like, there were hardly any, like, cute guys there, like, y'know?"
- "Macho"—Derived from the Spanish "machismo," a term fashionable in the disco era to describe overtly masculine men.
- "Major"—Slang commonly used by young people to put great emphasis on something: "He's a major dodo" or "The party was a major bummer."
- "Mall rats"—Annoying adolescents who invade suburban shopping malls in packs, without adult supervision, after school hours and on weekends.
- "Man"—Not referring to a male person, but an expression used as a sentence starter or ending: "Man, check out those hot wheels over there" or "Cool, man."
- "Mellow out"—To relax, take it easy.
- "Mrs. Robinson"—From Anne Bancroft's character in *The Graduate*, a much-older woman (like your mom's age) who sleeps with much-younger men.

- "Narc"—To tattle, squeal, snitch, rat; or, the person who does these things.
- "Neat-o"—Expression used to describe something you really like.
- "No shit, Sherlock"—Expression stating the obvious—as in already knowing it.
- "Not!"—Contradicting term used at the end of a statement as a way of expressing disapproval: "I like your new poodle-perm hairdo—not!"
- "Oh my gawd"—Usually spoken by a girl to express disbelief. Users often paused between each word: "Oh (pause) my (pause) gawd. Did you see the fat ass on that girl!" (See also "Omigod.")
- "Omigod"—"Oh my gawd" squealed quickly and excitably as if one word, usually by a girl expressing disbelief. "Omigod! That cute boy just looked at me!" (See "Oh my gawd.")
- "Outtasight"—To be outtasight is to be the grooviest one can get!
- "Pad"—Hipster slang for living space, usually an apartment where one crashes.
- "Pantywaist"—A mama's boy or wimpy geek.
- "Party-hardy"—From the 1970s, a term for heavy partying or kicking ass.
- "Phat"—In the 1990s, someone cool, hip, and in style. (If you get called "phat" don't be insulted unless you really are fat.)
- "Pig"—Derogatory term for a police officer, commonly used by radical anti-establishment types in the early 1970s.
- "Pissed-off"—Angry; often shortened to "P.O.'d."
- "Pizza face"—A put-down directed to somebody whose facial complexion is marked by a lot of pimples and blackheads.
- "Player"—A man who screws around and convinces each woman she's "the one."
- "Playing hooky"—Skipping school.
- "Poseur"—A fake person who is trying to fit in with a cooler social group, also known as "a wannabe."
- "Psyched"—Two meanings: (1) to fool someone, as in "psyched you out" and (2) to describe excitement, as in "I'm psyched about going to Padre Island for Spring Break."
- "Rad"—Short for radical, skater slang used to describe something extremely cool.
- "Rag"—To bitch at someone; derived from "being on the rag," as in when a woman has her period she is on the rag (tampon) and overly sensitive and bitchy.
- "Right on!"—Classic Black Power term signifying agreement; those who used it would often hold a fist up.
- "Righteous"— Describes someone or something really fine or beautiful, from the 1980s.
- "Rock on"—Rocker lingo for good-bye in the 1970s.
- "Rocks"—Something that's very good: "The new KISS record rocks!"
- "Schmooze"—Yuppie term from the 1980s meaning to kiss ass (not literally) for something you want.
- "Scumbag"—A used condom, or an undesirable person.
- "Shag"—Short for shagging, a British word for doing the dirty deed, a.k.a. fornicating, making love, getting it on, screwing, boinking, boffing, and so on.
- "Shake it, don't break it"—What you said to a girl who had an awesome wiggle in her walk; also, there's "Can I have some fries with that shake?"
- "Shindig"—Surf slang for a 1960s party.
- "Shit-faced"—Drunk.
- "Shitting bricks"—Being stupendously nervous.
- "Skag"—Put-down directed to an ugly girl.
- "Skank"—Nasty put-down directed to a trashy and slutty girl. (The worst was to be called a "skanky skag" or a "skaggy skank.")
- "Smash"—Short for "smashing," a term describing an event or something that went over well: "The party was a smash!"
- "Space cadet"—An absentminded person.
- "Spaz"—Short for "spastic," someone who is annoyingly overexcited and overemotional.
- "Spiffy"—Okay, in a good way.
- "Square"—An uncool person, such as Lawrence Welk or your parents.
- "Stacked"—A chick who is well endowed (having big breasts).
- "Stoked"—Slang for ecstatic: "The team is in the lead and the fans are stoked."
- "Stud"—A virile guy.
- "Stud-muffin"—A cute virile guy.

- "Sucks"—Used to indicate something is bad: "Disco sucks."
- "Super-"—Prefix commonly used in modern pop culture to describe something or someone so great and powerful that they surpass all others (supercool, superhero, supermarket, supermodel, supersonic, superstar . . .).
- "Swingin'"—Lingo from the 1960s, describing things that are fun and groovy.
- "Take it easy"— Be mellow, from the 1970s.
- "Talk to the hand"—When someone is exchanging insults with you and you don't want to listen anymore, you hold up your hand as if to block their words, cock your head, and utter in a swarmy tone, "Talk to the hand." Commonly used in the 1990s by both tough-talking black women and nelly gay men.
- "Tie one on"—To get drunk.
- "To the max"—Val-Gals used this phrase to put heavy emphasis on something: "I like to shop to the max!"
- "Toss cookies"—The act of vomiting.
- "Totally"—Expression used either to signify agreement or to put great emphasis on something: "Like, totally, that was cool!"
- "Tripendicular"—Southern California term used to describe something totally amazing.
- "Trippin'"—Two meanings: (1) To be high on drugs, as in a drug trip, and (2) to be amazed by incredible news.
- "Tubular"—Early-1980s slang for something great.
- "Turkey"—Someone who is stupid or silly.
- "Up yours"—A slang insult along the lines of "Up your ass!"
- "Veg-out"—Term meaning to take it easy, be mellow, chill out, or just plain relax.
- "Wastoid"—An uninspired person who spends every day high on drugs.
- "Wanking"—Masturbating. Other slang terms for this solo sex act are beating off, jacking off, jerking off, pulling the pud, spanking the monkey, and waxing the dolphin.
- "Wasted"—To be really drunk, really high, or both.
- "Way"—Slang prefix used to indicate the extra importance of something (for example, "Way-good," "Way-hot," "Way-dumb"); also an affirmative response to the statement "No way." "Way."
- "Way-out"—A variant of far-out: "Like, that's way-out, man!"
- "Weenie"—A wimp.
- "Whacked"—Used to describe someone out of his or her mind.
- "Whatever"—Sarcastic 1990s "I couldn't care less" reply.
- "Whassup?"—Guy talk for "What's up?" Popularized by Budweiser commercials in the 1990s; a short variation is "S'up?"
- "Wicked"—Something so good it's bad, or something so bad it's good.
- "Wigged-out"—As stressed out and upset as a person can get before having a mental breakdown.
- "Woody"—An erect penis.
- "Word up"—Lingo for the whole truth, from the 1980s.
- "Wow!"—Classic exclamation used after hearing or seeing something extraordinary.
- "Wussie"—Slang for a wimpy person, commonly of the male sex. (This is a more acceptable put-down than the hard-on-the-ears "pussy.")
- "Yadda, yadda, yadda"—Made famous by the 1990s sitcom *Seinfeld,* this phrase was used to make a long story short, while skipping over the boring details: "We went to lunch, yadda, yadda, yadda, then she accused me of kissing the boss' ass, yadda, yadda, yadda, so I punched her." A variation of "yadda, yadda, yadda" is "blah, blah, blah."
- "Y'know"—From "you know," poor English that is commonly overused in the everyday conversation of many young Americans: "It's like, y'know, way tubular how Bobby, y'know, looks at me, y'know."
- "Yo!"—Inquiring "hello" used by rappers in the 1980s.
- "You go, girl!"—From one woman to another, an exclamation showing emotional support.
- "Your mama"—Derogatory response used after someone says something insulting to you; most likely came from the classic put-down "Your mama wears combat boots."
- "Yucky"—Something disgusting.

SLASHER FILMS

To the dismay of adults, slasher films were all the rage among teenagers during the late 1970s and 1980s. Extremely gory, violent, and poorly filmed, they caused most grown-ups to worry about youthful morals and I.Q.s. Nevertheless, these movies were the rage for a simple reason: Kids love to be scared, and the films provide a safe and controlled fright, the same way a thrilling roller-coaster ride at the amusement park would—when it was all over, you could take a deep breath, uncover your eyes, and be unharmed.

The prototypical slasher film generally had no plot and lots of nudity and was a low-budget splatterfest highlighting imaginative ways to kill off teens. They commonly contained the same generic "dead teenager" formula: An isolated group of young people, at a summer camp or spooky house or high school after hours, who are terrorized and killed off one by one by some maniacal-psychotic-ghostly-being with superhuman powers in an act of deep-seated revenge. This evil beast obviously had an inclination for skinny-dippers and the promiscuously inclined, because they seemed to be the first to be slashed. At the end, there would likely be a sole survivor, usually the virginal female, who showed remarkable courage plus strength and "killed" off the villain (or at least until the next sequel).

FYI: ▸ According to Wes Craven's *Scream,* a 1996 horror spoof, there are four cardinal rules for surviving a slasher film: (1) Never drink alcohol. (2) Never smoke. (3) Never have sex. (4) Never say, "I'll be right back."

SLATER, KELLY

Born February 11, 1972, the greatest surfer of his generation, a six-time world champion who learned to hang ten not in California or Hawaii but on the waves off the coast of home state Florida (he's from Cocoa Beach). The eye-catching brunet is nicknamed "the Michael Jordan of surfing," and he played Jimmy Slade on the TV series *Baywatch* (1992–93).

FYI: ▸ Before *People* magazine chose Kelly Slater as one of the Fifty Most Beautiful People in the world (1991), he was voted Cutest Boy in high school.

SLEESTACKS

"Sssssssssssss!" Scary, scary, scary! These malicious reptilian humanoids dwelled in the dark caves of TV's *Land of the Lost*. They made dreadful hissing sounds, had green skin and eyes like a bug, were seven feet tall, and were so highly intelligent that they posed more of a threat to the Marshalls than any dinosaur, including Grumpy the T-Rex. Sadly, the Sleestacks would feast on the kindhearted Pakuni tribe.

FYI: ▸ Sid and Marty Krofft, creators of *Land of the Lost*, hired many of their Sleestak actors from high school basketball teams, including future Detroit Piston Bill Laimbeer.

SLICKER

"I'll be soft. I'll be wild. I'll be whatever I want. I'll be Slicker!" The 1960s mod lip color by Yardley came in frosted shades, like Fainting Pink and Helpless Pink. Brit Jean Shrimpton was the spokes-model for Slicker.

SLIME

"I've been Slimed!" Slime was the gooey and goopy, cold and clammy, snotlike, booger-colored substance packaged in plastic miniature garbage cans. Introduced in 1978, Slime grossed out many people (particularly grown-ups) because it was perfect for faking a messy sneeze. Kids would secretly put Slime in the palm of their hand, pretend to sneeze covering their nose with the hand, and then produce a gross-out handful of fake snot! The downside was that Slime could be next-to-impossible to remove from fabrics, especially shag carpeting. In the late 1980s, a new generation of children discovered it after tuning into the Nickelodeon TV network, where not only kids but also adults were frequently getting Slimed on the head.

SLINKY

The springy coil of flat steel that makes a "Slinkety" sound when played with is acclaimed as a classic toy of the twentieth century. Slinky originated in 1943, when Richard James, a twenty-six-year-old naval engineer, was inspecting a ship in Philadelphia's Cramp Shipyard and accidentally knocked a torsion spring off a table. As the spring hit the ground, it didn't just stay put, but instead bounced across the floor, coil by coil, end over end. James took the spring home to show his wife, Betty, and the couple decided to turn it into a toy.

For more than two years, they tested various types of steel, thicknesses, and dimensions before finding the exact formula for the perfect spring toy. Betty combed the dictionary in search of the right name, and she found "Slinky." In 1945, Richard and Betty persuaded Gimbel's department store in Philadelphia to let them set up an in-store demonstration. They put up a sloping board as a display and allowed a Slinky to slink its way down. Shoppers were amazed, and ninety minutes later they sold the entire stock of 400 Slinkies at a dollar apiece.

In the 1950s, Slinky reached fad-buying proportions, largely because of the interest of young Baby Boomers (in 1953 alone, 7,000 of the walking spring toys were sold each day). The most famous Slinky trick is walking it down stairs. Besides the classic steel Slinky, there have been many variations, including Slinky Jr., a miniature version; plastic Slinky, colored in neon shades (pink is a favorite); Slinky Crazy Eyes, eyeglass frames with eyeballs attached to steel coils, causing them to bug out; Slinky Pull Toys, embraced by younger kids, consisting of a dog, a kitten, a worm, a bunny, a seal, and a train (you dragged them along and their tails would fall behind, then suddenly pull up); and a Slink 'Em board game. These days, Slinky sells at a rate of more than two million a year.

FYI: ▸ According to *The Whole Pop Catalog*, "All the Slinkies ever made could slink end to end down a stairway from the moon."

"SLINKY SONG"

Since 1962, this happy tune has been used in Slinky's TV spots, making it the longest-running jingle in advertising history. It goes: "It's Slinky, it's Slinky / For fun it's a wonderful toy / It's Slinky, it's Slinky / It's fun for a girl or a boy."

SLIP 'N SLIDE

"Easy fun, just run and slide a mile!" Introduced by Wham-O in 1961, this is a twenty-five-foot-long, forty-inch-wide, yellow plastic strip that got its name from what kids did on it after it was unrolled in the yard and attached to a garden hose. Swimsuit-clad youngsters took a running start and leaped feet-first or dived head-first onto the water-oozing contraption, slipping all the way down the wet runway (a special lubricating compound made it slick). The Slip 'n Slide was unpopular with parents because it killed the grass underneath, leaving the yard looking like an airport runway. Another fitting name for the water toy would be "Slip 'n Scrape" because of all the grass burns, scratches, belly-busters, bruises, and sprained limbs caused by playing on it!

SLOGANS

These are some of the best-known slogans, epigrams, and catchphrases from the late 1960s through the 1980s. They were commonly found on bumper stickers, buttons, posters, T-shirts, statuettes, and plaques.

"Keep on truckin'"
"Keep on keepin' on"
"Sock it to me"
"What's your sign?"
"You've come a long way, Baby"
"Here comes da judge"
"The devil made me do it"
"What you see is what you get"
"Black is beautiful"
"Black power"
"Right on"
"Dy-no-mite"
"I love you this much"
"Hang in there, baby"
"Butterflies are free"
"To know me is to love me"
"God is dead"
"Jesus is coming"
"Jesus is coming—look busy"
"Honk if you love Jesus"
"Honk if you are Jesus"
"Jesus saves"
"Save the whales"
"Save water—shower with a friend"
"Save a tree—eat a beaver"
"Real people wear fake furs"
"Think peace"
"Make love, not war"
"Make babies, not bombs"

"One nuclear bomb can ruin your whole day"
"Ban the bomb"
"War is not healthy for children and other living things"
"Suppose they gave a war and nobody came"
"Give peace a chance"
"Draft beer, not boys"
"POW/MIA: You are not forgotten"
"Don't trust anyone over thirty"
"When guns are outlawed, only outlaws will have guns"
"America—Love it or leave it"
"American and proud of it"
"Keep America beautiful"
"Give a hoot—Don't pollute"
"WIN" (for "Whip Inflation Now")
"Eat beans—America needs gas"
"Question authority"
"I'm okay, You're so-so"
"Today is the first day of the rest of your life"
"Have a nice day"
"I'm with stupid ☞"
"Sit on it"
"Sit on a happy face"
"Up your nose with a rubber hose"
"Kiss my grits"
"Bag your face"
"Nanu, Nanu"
"I can't believe I ate the whole thing"
"Beam me up, Scotty—There's no intelligent life here"
"I ♥ New York"
"Virginia is for lovers"
"Love means never having to say you're sorry"
"TGIF" (for "Thank God it's Friday")
"Let's boogie"
"Disco sucks"
"Shit happens"
"Take it easy"
"Easy does it"
"Hang ten"
"Life's a beach"
"Life's a bitch, and then you die"
"I'm a bitch, and you are too"
"Take this job and shove it"
"Love thy neighbor, but don't get caught"
"Go naked"
"Cure virginity"
"I'm a virgin (this is a very old t-shirt)"
"If this van is rockin', don't bother knockin'"
"Smile if you're horny"
"If it feels good . . . do it"
"Sex, drugs, and rock 'n' roll"
"A friend with weed is a friend indeed"
"Live fast, die young"
"Born to be wild"
"Party hardy"
"Tune in, turn on, drop out"
"A mind is a terrible thing to waste"
"Try it you'll like it"
"Don't take drugs, give them to me"
"If it's too loud, you're too old"
"Cancer cures smoking"
"Love is a many-gendered thing"
"Have you hugged your kid today?"
"Choose life"
"Just say no"
"Just do it"
"Go for it"
"To the max"
"Born to shop"
"A woman's place is in the mall"
"Girls just want to have funds"
"The one who dies with the most toys wins"
"Greed is good"
"Save an alligator, shoot a preppy"
"Die yuppie scum"
"Who shot J.R.?"
"May The Force be with you"
"I brake for unicorns"
"Baby on board"
"Baby in trunk"
"Nobody on board"
"Where's the beef?"
"Read my lips"
"Go ahead—make my day"
"Don't have a cow"
"Homework causes brain damage"
"Free Tibet"
"Mean people suck"
"Hate is not a family value"
"Visualize world peace"
"Visualize whirled peas"
"Don't worry, be happy"

SLOT CAR RACING SETS

These miniature sets featured souped-up race cars powered by electric current insets in curved tracks. The cars' fast speed was controlled by separate hand controls for each driver. They were the subject of a nationwide fad, which began in 1962 and peaked in the late 1960s.

SLOW DANCE SONGS

Do you remember your first slow dance? If you were like most teens of the era, it probably was in junior high during the year the opposite sex stopped having cooties and became interesting (eighth grade?). At school dances, a slow song often played after a set of fast ones. The timing was convenient, because it gave sweaty fast-dancers a chance to rest their dancing feet and allowed budding couples to see how intimate they could get with each other on the dance floor (until an adult monitor broke up the heavy petting). The typical guy didn't really like to slow-dance, but if he wanted to show a girl how much he liked her he had to. For girls, it was a status thing. It meant she was desirable to a boy and not a wallflower like some of the other girls.

Here are the twenty-five quintessential slow-dance songs from around the early 1970s to the mid-1980s.

- "Always and Forever" (1978) by Heatwave
- "Baby, I'm-a Want You" (1971) by Bread
- "Beth" (1976) by KISS
- "The Closer I Get to You" (1978) by Roberta Flack and Donny Hathaway
- "Color My World" (1971) by Chicago
- "Crazy for You" (1985) by Madonna
- "Dream Weaver" (1976) by Gary Wright
- "Emotion" (1978) by Samantha Sang
- "Endless Love" (1981) by Diana Ross and Lionel Richie
- "Free Bird" (1975) by Lynyrd Skynyrd
- "How Can You Mend a Broken Heart" (1971) by The Bee Gees
- "I'm Not in Love" (1975) by 10cc
- "Lead Me On" (1979) by Maxine Nightingale
- "Please Don't Go" (1980) by K.C. and the Sunshine Band
- "Precious and Few" (1972) by Climax
- "Reunited" (1978) by Peaches and Herb
- "Sad Eyes" (1979) by Robert John
- "Slow Dancing (Swayin' to the Music)" by Johnny Rivers
- "Sometimes When We Touch" (1978) by Dan Hill
- "Stairway to Heaven" (1971) by Led Zeppelin
- "Three Times a Lady" (1978) by Commodores
- "Tonight's the Night" (1976) by Rod Stewart
- "True" (1983) by Spandau Ballet
- "Truly" (1982) by Lionel Richie
- "Wonderful Tonight" (1978) by Eric Clapton

SLURPEE

Premiering in 1965, the brightly colored, sweet-tasting slushy drink is 7-Eleven's signature product, named from the sound it made when slurped through a straw. A combination of water, carbon dioxide, and flavored syrup, Slurpees are frozen just enough to come out of a self-serve machine, into a cup, and up a straw. If you drink them too fast, you'll get a momentary yet agonizing brain freeze. A wide variety of exotic flavors are available today—Banana Split, Blue Raspberry, Bubblegum, Pina Colada, Tangerine—but in the old days there were only two choices: Coca-Cola and Cherry, which kids often mixed together to create a concoction known as a "suicide." Well-known Slurpee-like beverages sold at other convenient stores are the Icee and the Slush Puppie.

FYI: ▸ Brrrrrrrr! According to a 7-Eleven press release, 5.3 billion Slurpees have been sold since they first appeared.

SMALLVILLE

After fleeing the exploding planet of Krypton, the space pod carrying the baby who was Superman lands in this fictional farming community located somewhere in rural Kansas. He would grow up on a farm in Smallville under the alias Clark Kent, before heading off to the big city of Metropolis to work as a reporter and superhero.

SMASH-UP DERBY

"All the thrills of a real smash-up derby!" Contributing to the headaches of mothers everywhere, in 1971 Kenner Toys created the SSP Smash-Up Derby to capitalize on the popularity of their best-selling SSP (Super-Sonic Power) Racers. This was a wild new kind of action, with cars designed to roar off ramps, jump, and come apart after a mid-air collision—just like a real demolition derby. After each thrilling smash-up, you simply snapped the pieces (doors, hoods, trunk lids, and wheels) back together and started all over again. The two demolition cars featured were a 1957 Chevy wagon and a 1957 Ford sedan.

SMEDLEY THE ELEPHANT

This animated elephant character from the Cap'n Crunch TV commercials couldn't get enough of Peanut Butter Crunch cereal and had a tendency to smash things because he didn't know his own weight. His skin was the color of peanut butter (yellowish brown).

"SMELLS LIKE TEEN SPIRIT"

Named after a cheap teen deodorant, Nirvana's grunge anthem is regarded by critics as an alternative-rock classic for Generation X. Its music video—hotly rotated on MTV in 1991—starred Kurt Cobain and company performing in a school gym and joined by a hellish cheerleading squad personifying heroin chic while shaking pom-poms.

SMILEY FACE

The best-known smile since Mona Lisa's is the gleaming grin set inside a noseless yellow circle with a pair of black eyes, also referred to as a happy face. Representing happiness and good cheer, the smiley face was the most famous symbol to come out of the 1970s. N. G. Slater, a New York button manufacturer, is credited for making the world break out in yellow-smile fever after mass-producing the sweeping grin on pin-backed buttons and a variety of other items in 1969. By 1971, more than twenty million smiley buttons were sold.

The cheerful smiley face beamed from everywhere and was on just about everything: T-shirts, lapel buttons, purses, lighters, lamps, cookie jars, mugs, stationery, balloons, bath mats, toilet seats, and huge municipal water tanks. Teachers used the happy face to reward good work (bad work got an unhappy face), waitresses put it on restaurant checks, young girls dotted their "i's" with it, and graffiti artists filled up any blank circular shape with eyes and a curved smile line. In 1972, presidential candidate George McGovern used the smiley face as a campaign logo (he lost to the more somber Richard Nixon). Lisa Marie Presley wore a fourteen-karat-gold happy-face ring with diamonds for eyes, given to her by daddy Elvis.

The smiley face often appears accompanied by the chipper salutation "Have a nice day," which became the decade's most mindless and insincere farewell. Cynics preferred the smiley-face version with a bleeding bullet-hole between the eyes. In the late 1980s, the enchanting face made a comeback among X-tripping club kids who felt that its dopey grin captured the feeling of rolling on the mind-altering drug.

SMITH, REX

Born on September 19, 1955, in Jacksonville, Florida, Smith was a minor teen heartthrob—in the shaggy-tressed-blond tradition of Leif Garrett and Shaun Cassidy—who became the object of affection for juvenile girls in 1979 as star of the tele-flick *Sooner or Later.* Smith scored a Top Ten hit in June 1979 with "You Take My Breath Away" from the *Sooner or Later* soundtrack. In 1981, he dueted with New Wave rocker Rachel Sweet on a redo of "Everlasting Love." He later appeared with Linda Ronstadt in both the stage version and the big-screen version of *The Pirates of Penzance* and as co-host with Marilyn McCoo on TV's *Solid Gold.*

SMOKEY THE BEAR

The gentle-hearted brown bear wearing a ranger hat and denim jeans and toting a spade has been the animated advertising icon for the U.S. Forest Service since 1944. He was created to encourage fire safety, commonly using the refrain "Remember, only you can prevent forest fires." In 1950, rangers found a four-pound bear cub orphaned by a New Mexico forest fire. Nursed back to health, he was called Smokey and sent to the National Zoo in Washington, D.C., where he became the living symbol of the beloved spokes-bear. From 1969 to 1971, *The Smokey Bear Show,* a half-hour cartoon series, aired on Saturday mornings. Smokey's balloon form has floated in the Macy's Thanksgiving Day Parade since 1968.

FYI: ▸ "Smokey the Bear" is CB radio jargon for a

state policeman, because the officers' hats are much like forest rangers' hats.

"SMOKIN' IN THE BOYS' ROOM"

According to this 1974 rock anthem, the best remedy for teachers on your case and for classes that are a drag is sneaking a smoke in the boys' bathroom. But remember, dudes: "Smokin' ain't allowed in school!" The best-selling song by Brownsville Station was the ultimate expression of 1970s teen rebellion. It appealed to the bad kids in school who were referred to as freaks, hoods, stoners, druggies, heads, antisocials, hippies—whatever they were called in your region of the country. These kids had long, unruly hair and commonly wore a uniform of bell-bottom jeans, rock concert T-shirts (Black Sabbath, Led Zeppelin, Lynyrd Skynyrd, KISS, AC/DC), and jewelry made out of drug paraphernalia. They often came to school stoned, had a strong antipathy for authority figures (parents, teachers, principals, and policemen), despised goody-goody cheerleaders and jocks, and dropped out of high school before junior year. "Smokin' in the Boys' Room" was later covered by metal-heads Motley Crue in 1985.

SMURFETTE

The sole female of Saturday morning's *Smurfs* show started out as a femme fatale created by naughty magician Gargamel as a way to fool the other Smurfs. Reaction to criticism that the cartoon's depiction of the flirtatious blonde Smurfette was sexist led to Papa Smurf's transforming her into a sweetie by way of magic.

SMURFS

"La la la la la la, sing a happy song / La la la la la la, Smurf the whole day long. . . ." A race of squeaky-voiced blue gnomes with white stocking caps who stand just three apples high and live in mushroom dwellings in a tiny village located in the middle of an enchanted forest. These wee creatures consist of ninety-eight males with monikers reflecting their personalities, like Happy Smurf, Grouchy Smurf, Lazy Smurf, Clumsy Smurf, Brainy Smurf, Vanity Smurf, Jokey Smurf, and so on. Wise Papa Smurf, the 543-year-old leader, and vivacious Smurfette, the solitary female, round out the Smurf population to an even one hundred. Benign and cheerful, the Smurfs have an all-for-one and one-for-all attitude and use the word "smurf" in every possible way (for example, "It's such a smurfy day!"). Evil wizard Gargamel, along with his Smurf-hungry feline Azriel, try in vain to capture the pint-sized pixies.

Belgian illustrator Pierre "Peyo" Culliford created the Smurfs for a children's book in 1957. They were originally known as Schtroumphs, loosely translated as "whatchamacallits," before becoming the easier-to-say "Smurfs." Although popular in Europe throughout the 1960s and 1970s, it wasn't until 1978 that various Smurf toys became licensed in America. In 1981, Fred Silverman, then president of NBC-TV, cleverly noticed his young daughter playing with a Smurf doll and commissioned Hanna-Barbera Productions to devise a cartoon series. Nauseatingly precious with simple story lines, *The Smurfs* had kid appeal written all over it and was the smash of the 1981–82 Saturday-morning TV season. It experienced phenomenal ratings, boosted last-place NBC to first place, and earned an Emmy for Outstanding Children's Entertainment Series. The Smurfs remained a fixture of Saturday-morning programming all through the 1980s, ending its run in 1990.

Although wildly adored by preschoolers, the Smurfs drove anyone over kindergarten age—who considered them insipid, sexist, loathsome, and a blue-colored eye sore—completely bonkers. There was no escaping the overkill, as the coyingly cute imps spawned a galaxy of toys and other tie-ins, such as two-inch-tall figurines, transistor radios, lunch boxes, bed sheets, clothing, pedal cars (Smurfmobiles), and a breakfast cereal called Smurfberry Crunch (suspiciously like one of Cap'n Crunch's Crunchberries). In 1982 alone, they generated some $600 million in retail sales. The Smurfs inspired a swarm of adorable fantasy urchins that likewise were marketed as toys (their cartoon shows on TV seemed like one big half-hour commercial), including Astroniks, Care Bears, The Get Along Gang, The Littles, The Monchichis, My Little Pony, Rainbow Brite, Shirt Tales, The Snorks, Strawberry Shortcake, The Trollkins, and The Wuzzles.

SNAGGLEPUSS

From 1958 to 1963, Hanna-Barbera's furry pink mountain lion was featured as a separate segment of Yogi Bear's Saturday-morning cartoon show. A cowardly stage actor, Snagglepuss was always in a state of comical calamity, especially when pursued by the aggressive Lion Hunter. He's distinguished by lispy exclamations (voiced by Daws Butler) of "Heavens to Murgatroyd!" and "Exit stage left. Better yet, exit stage right!"

SNAP! CRACKLE! AND POP!
Rice Krispies' well-known elf trio are notable for two firsts: They were the first (and longest-running) characters to represent a Kellogg's product, and the first animated characters to ever appear in a cereal commercial (a 1937 theatrical spot titled "Breakfast Pals"). Good-natured Snap, topped by a baker's cap; know-it-all Crackle, wearing a red-striped stocking cap; and funny-guy Pop, sporting a military hat, made their debut in 1933 on the Rice Krispies cereal box. Originally drawn by Vernon Grant, these colorful sprites personified the clicking sound that a bowl of Rice Krispies made when milk was added ("snap, crackle, pop"). Since the 1950s, innovative TV ads have featured the threesome singing and dancing their way into the hearts of young viewers everywhere. Other notable advertising icons for Kellogg's cereals include Tony the Tiger (Frosted Flakes), Toucan Sam (Froot Loops), Dig 'Em Frog (Sugar Smacks), Cornelius the Rooster (Kellogg's Corn Flakes), Sunny the Sun (Raisin Bran), and the Cocoa Krispies Monkey.

SNIDELY WHIPLASH
"Heh heh!" The fiendish, green-skinned, mustached foe of Canadian Mountie Dudley Do-Right had a sadistic thing for putting sweet Nell Fenwick in various life-threatening situations. Voiced by character actor Hans Conried on the *Dudley Do-Right* cartoon show.

SNOOPY
This original "Joe Cool" was a philosophical, floppy-eared beagle owned by Charlie Brown who lived in a well-furnished doghouse and had fantasy adventures about being a courageous World War I flying ace out to gun down German archenemy, the Red Baron. His best friend is a little yellow bird named Woodstock. Worldwide, Charles Schulz's Snoopy is one of the most recognized cartoon idols, rivaling Disney's Mickey Mouse and Warner Brothers' Bugs Bunny.

SNOOPY COME HOME
In this 1972 theatrical release, independent Snoopy hits the road with bird-buddy Woodstock on a journey to visit previous owner Lila, who is sick in the hospital. Meanwhile, owner Charlie Brown and pals search frantically for the runaway beagle. Planning on permanently staying with Lila, Snoopy learns there is no place like home when he encounters many unwelcoming "No Dogs Allowed" signs. Directed by Bill Melendez, the animated musical followed *A Boy Named Charlie Brown* (1969) as the second entry to star Charles Schulz's popular Peanuts characters. It is marked by the playful songs of songwriting brothers Richard and Robert Sherman (Disney's *Mary Poppins*), such as "Snoopy Come Home," "Lila's Tune," "Best of Buddies," "Fun on the Beach," and the stick-in-your-head motif "No Dogs Allowed." Later entries in the series include 1977's *Race for Your Life, Charlie Brown* and 1980's *Bon Voyage, Charlie Brown (And Don't Come Back!).*

SNORKS
Smurf-esque snorkel-topped creatures who lived in the underwater world of Snorkland. Created by Belgian animator Freddy Monnickendam for a highly viewed Hanna-Barbera cartoon series airing from 1984 to 1986.

SNORKY
On Hanna-Barbera's *Banana Splits Adventure Hour,* this wistful little elephant with pink-polka-dotted ears and long hair couldn't talk, so he simply honked. "Honk! Honk!"

SNOWBALL I AND II
Two black cats (not white, as their name would imply) that belong to Lisa Simpson of *The Simpsons* cartoon show. Lisa's beloved Snowball (I) mysteriously died one day, so parents Homer and Marge tried to fool the distraught girl by replacing it with an identical-looking Snowball (II). The feline-switching scam didn't go over well, but Lisa eventually accepted Snowball II, who was more scrappy than Snowball I, as her new pet.

SNUFFLEUPAGUS
The benign dinosaur-like creature was Big Bird's imaginary pal on the children's TV series *Sesame*

Street. Snuffy's first name is Aloysius, and he has a sister called Alice Snuffleupagus.

SOAP OPERAS

"Like sands through the hourglass, so are the days of our lives. . . ." Episodic melodramas with massive fan bases—generally female—that air on all three of the major TV networks (ABC, CBS, and NBC) during weekday afternoons. Awash with outlandish plot lines, soaps focus on the personal dilemmas (love, heartbreak, villainy, scandal, and sex) of the beautiful people living in small-town America (Genoa City, Llanview, Pine Valley, Port Charles, Salem, and Somerset). These shows are commonly popular with bored housewives and college coeds looking for a sense of adventure and romance in their mundane lives. A list of daytime's most memorable serials would have to include *All My Children, Another World, As the World Turns, The Bold and the Beautiful, Days of Our Lives, The Doctors, The Edge of Night, General Hospital, Guiding Light, Love of Live, Loving, One Life to Live, Ryan's Hope, Santa Barbara, Search for Tomorrow,* and *The Young and the Restless.*

FYI: ▸ Soap operas are so called because the early ones were sponsored by soap manufacturers, such as Procter & Gamble.

SOFT DRINKS

A&W Root Beer. Big Red. Bubble Up. C&C Cola. Canada Dry. Coca-Cola. Dad's Root Beer. Diet Coke. Diet Pepsi. Diet-Rite Cola. Double Cola. Dr. Pepper. Fanta. Fresca. Frostie Root Beer. Grape Crush. Hire's Root Beer. Jolt Cola. Mellow Yello. Mountain Dew. Mr. Pibb. Nehi. Orange Crush. Pepsi-Cola. Pop Shoppe. Quench. RC Cola. 7-Up. Shasta. Slice. Sprite. Squirt. Sunkist Orange. Tab. Wink. Yoo-Hoo. Those are the names of popular carbonated soft drinks—also known as colas or soda pop, depending on what part of the country you're from.

It's odd that, during the first quarter of the twentieth century, most soft drinks were used as medicinal tonics before evolving into today's refreshing fountain and bottled beverages. They tell a lot about the tastes and personalities of Americans over the years. You knew Jason was a feisty fellow for drinking Pepsi; that Holly was a calorie counter for drinking Tab; that Steve was an outgoing guy for drinking Mountain Dew; and that Christian was a chocolate lover for drinking Yoo-Hoo. In the world of soft drinks, you could be a pepper (Dr. Pepper), do the dew (Mountain Dew), taste the Un-Cola (7-Up), teach the world to sing (Coca-Cola), and be part of a new generation (Pepsi-Cola).

FYI: ▸ Americans consume an average of 486 cans of soda per person every year.

SOLID GOLD

"Solid Gold / Filling up my life with music / Solid Gold / Putting rhythm in my soul . . ." This variety show was once known as "TV's flashiest hour of music and dance." Its mainstays were a countdown of the nation's Top Ten records; lip-synch performances by current recording stars; and a coed dance troupe called the Solid Gold Dancers. Airing in syndication for eight years (1980–88), *Solid Gold* was hosted by a string of pop-music personalities: pre-Psychic Network's Dionne Warwick (1980–81, 1985–86), teen heartthrob Andy Gibb (1981–82), 5th Dimension's Marilyn McCoo (1981–84, 1986–88), rock idol Rex Smith (1982–83), and disc jockey Rick Dees (1984–85). Regulars on the program included ventriloquist Wayland Flowers and his foul-mouthed puppet Madame, comedian Marty Cohen, comedian Jeff Altman (of Pink Lady fame), and MTV V.J. Nina Blackwood. Robert W. Morgan served as the show's "announcer."

SOLID GOLD DANCERS

Forget about the Rockettes or the Fly Girls, this was the best-known dance troupe of the 1980s. Consisting of eight or so members of both sexes, these overtly sexy hoofers wore flashy spandex outfits while performing high-energy interpretations of the hottest hits of the week, even slow ones like Air Supply's "All Out of Love" and Kenny Rogers's "Lady." The original members, from 1980 to 1982, included Deborah, Kahea, Pam, Alex, Darcel (the principal dancer with the trademark long cornrows), Helene, Paula, and Tony.

SONIC

The 1950s-style burger chain based in Oklahoma where drive-up customers order via intercom from a menu board located at every parking spot and where carhops (sometimes on roller skates) deliver such food as cheese coneys, tater tots, and cherry limeades. In the 1990s, Sonic's ad campaigns used 1950s teen idol Frankie Avalon as its national spokesperson.

SONIC THE HEDGEHOG

Introduced in 1991, the spiky-haired, blue-hued hedgehog was Sega's best-selling answer to Nintendo's popular video game Mario Brothers. And like his competitor, speedy Sonic starred in a Saturday-morning animated adventure from 1993 to 1995 (voiced by Jaleel White of prime time's *Family Matters*). Tails was his red-fox sidekick.

SONNY AND CHER

Salvatore Phillip Bono and Cherilyn Sarkisian LaPierre, otherwise known as Sonny and Cher, personified the freewheeling style of the Flower Power era with their kooky hippie fashions (sandals, furry vests, bell-bottoms, and love beads), long hair, and laid-back demeanor. The music duo first met in 1963 in Los Angeles as session performers for legendary music-producer Phil Spector. Sonny, eleven years her senior, became teenager Cher's mentor, and together they formed Caesar and Cleo, an unsuccessful folk-music act. A union of marriage followed in 1964.

Using their own names, Sonny and Cher, the outwardly mismatched couple (Sonny was diminutive, Cher was lanky) released "I Got You Babe" in 1965. A chart-topper, the single sold millions of records and made the two hep-cats overnight stars. A string of best-sellers followed, including "The Beat Goes On" (1967), "All I Ever Need Is You" (1971), "A Cowboy's Work Is Never Done" (1972), and an adaptation of a Budweiser beer jingle, "When You Say Love" (1972).

Following a stint on a prime-time music-variety show, *The Sonny and Cher Comedy Hour*, the couple divorced and embarked on separate careers. Cher emerged as a multitalented pop icon whose occupational titles included rock star, TV star, Broadway star, movie star, fitness instructor, home and clothing designer, and infomercial spokesperson. Sonny reinvented himself as a successful politician. In 1988, the citizens of Palm Springs elected him mayor, and in 1994 he became a Republican congressman for the state of California. (The same week that Sonny was elected mayor, Cher won her Best Actress Oscar for *Moonstruck*.)

On January 6, 1998, Sonny died instantaneously after striking a pine tree while skiing on a Nevada ski slope. As a touching tribute to a resilient and hardworking man, federal flags flew at half-mast around the nation, and a teary-eyed Cher read the eulogy at his funeral service.

SONNY AND CHER COMEDY HOUR

From 1971 to 1974, puppyish Sonny and the outlandishly dressed Cher headlined this successful musical variety show on CBS-TV. It featured the groovy husband-and-wife duo singing, dancing, and doing a comedy repertoire built around ribbing each other (Sonny's short stature was often the butt of Cher's jokes). Regular highlights included the "Vamp" skit, with Cher portraying notorious famous women like Cleopatra and Miss Sadie Thompson; the "Dirty Linen" skit, with frumpy-housewife Laverne (Cher) gossiping at the neighborhood laundromat; the "Sonny's Pizza" skit, with Sonny as the dense proprietor of a pizzeria; and the semi-regular appearances of the couple's towheaded, future-lesbian daughter, Chastity, who, despite being a cute toddler, had no stage presence. Sonny and Cher opened the show with their anthem "The Beat Goes On" and closed it with "I Got You Babe." The Bonos ended the highly rated series in the spring of 1974, when it was announced they were getting a divorce.

SONNY CROCKETT

Rough around the edges, this Miami undercover vice detective (played by Don Johnson on TV's *Miami Vice*) drove a Ferrari and lived on a boat called *Saint Vitus' Dance* with a pet alligator named Elvis. Known for wearing pastel-hued suit jackets and for his two-day facial stubble.

SONNY THE CUCKOO BIRD

"I go cuckoo for Cocoa Puffs!" Since 1962, the orange-crested, yellow-beaked excitable fowl had been going cuckoo for Cocoa Puffs—General Mills' chocolaty-tasting corn-puff cereal.

SOONER OR LATER

The 1979 made-for-TV romance—a first-crush classic—was popular with teen females of the late 1970s. It starred mop-top Rex Smith as seventeen-year-old rock idol Michael Skye, the object of worship for a thirteen-year-old fan, Jessie Walters (played by Denise Miller). To attract his attention, Jessie passes herself off as a much-older, more worldly sixteen-year-old. After hooking up with Michael, she invariably must decide whether to go all the way or fess up to the sham. The soundtrack, featuring Smith's vocals, did well on the charts and housed his swooning love song "You Take My Breath Away." Miller is best remembered for playing youngsters on prime-time sitcoms, such as Jilly Papalardo on *Fish* (1977–78), Tina Manucci on *Makin' It* (1979), and niece Billie on *Archie Bunker's Place* (1981–83).

SOOPER GOOPER

Mattel's electric oven for the Incredible Edibles play set was actually a hot plate in the shape of a wacky, buck-toothed, big-eyed, orange-wigged head.

SOPHIE

Trained circus seal in England, a friend of Doctor Dolittle's, who is worried sick about her husband back at the North Pole. After helping Sophie escape from the circus by disguising her in women's clothing and throwing her into the Bristol Channel, the good doctor finds himself arrested for murder because the authorities think he threw a helpless old lady off the cliff.

SOPWITH CAMEL

During his aviation fantasies, this became the name of Snoopy's doghouse, which he flew as a World War I flying ace—outfitted in traditional gear (helmet, goggles, and scarf)—while fighting the Red Baron in the skies over war-torn France.

SOUL TRAIN

"S-o-o-o-u-u-u-l Train!" The African-American alternative to Dick Clark's *American Bandstand* brings back memories of viewing Saturday-afternoon TV and seeing black urban teens shaking their groove thangs to the latest dances—the Bump, the Robot, the Hustle, the Rock, the Freak, and the Electric Boogie—and realizing how totally un-hip white suburban kids were. Many critics cite *Soul Train* as the TV show that did the most to bring black culture into American households. First broadcast out of Philadelphia in 1971, *Soul Train* was created and hosted by deep-voiced Don Cornelius, who had the hippest if not the largest Afro on TV. Cornelius's weekly extravaganza featured about seventy African-American youths dancing to soul music and watching guest recording artists lip-synch to their latest hits. Two favorite segments were the Soul Train Line, a funky update of the 1950s dance the Stroll, in which the kids lined up—girls on one side, guys on the other—while couples took turns gyrating down the center trying to out-dance one another; and the Soul Train Scramble, in which a couple tried to unscramble the title of a song that was playing, within forty-five seconds. The rousing theme song, "TSOP (The Sound of Philadelphia)," performed by the session group MFSB with vocals by the Three Degrees, topped the Top Forty for two weeks in 1974. The Johnson Products Company, maker of Afro-Sheen, was the sponsor of *Soul Train*. "Peace, love, and soul."

FYI: ▸ Singer Jody Watley ("Looking for a New Love") was once a dance regular on *Soul Train*.

SOUNDER

A heart-wrenching family drama about a black sharecropper family in rural Louisiana during the Great Depression. It centers around a proud father, Nathan Lee Morgan (Paul Winfield), who is unjustly sentenced to a year in a prison work camp for stealing a ham to feed his hungry family. His strong-willed wife, Rebecca Morgan (Cicely Tyson), endures various crises to keep her three children, dog Sounder, and the family farm together. Engaging Kevin Hooks stars as David Lee Morgan, the eldest son on the verge of manhood, who discovers education as a way out of poverty. Nominated for four Academy Awards, including Best Picture, Best Actor (Winfield), and Best Actress (Tyson), the 1972 movie was adapted from William Armstrong's book, winner of the 1970 Newberry Award for Children's Literature.

SOUND OF MUSIC

"The happiest sound in all the world!" One of the most beloved musicals in cinema history, based on the true account of the singing Von Trapp family, who fled Austria to escape Nazi oppression during World War II. Wholesome Julie Andrews, fresh from her Oscar-winning performance as Mary Poppins, plays spunky Maria, a postulant nun too busy daydreaming and singing about how the "hills are alive with the sound of music" to fit in at her Austrian convent. Maria is sent away by concerned Mother Abbess (Peggy Wood) to become governess for the seven young offspring of stern Captain Von Trapp (Christopher Plummer), a handsome widower and retired naval officer, in Salzburg.

With soprano rectitude abounding, Maria befriends the Captain's repressed children, enlightening them on the joys of everyday life. (How could a kid resist a nanny who sings the reassuring "My Favorite Things" during a frightening thunderstorm?) Eventually, she softens the heart of the irascible Captain, and they fall in love and marry. While all this goodness is occurring, evil is lurking around the corner as the Nazis of Germany invade Austria. Maria transforms the family into a singing troupe, and as such they elude the Germans and flee to the safe haven of Switzerland. The Von Trapp children were played by Charmain Carr (Liesl), Nicholas Hammond (Friedrich), Heather Menzies (Louisa), Duane Chase (Kurt), Angela Cartwright (Brigitta), Debbie Turner (Marta), and Kym Karath (Gretl).

The Sound of Music first appeared as a 1959 Broadway musical, starring Mary Martin as Maria. The 1965 movie is noted for its spectacular photography (filmed on location in Salzburg and the Austrian Alps) and for its array of unforgettable songs by Richard Rodgers and Oscar Hammerstein. These include the round "Do-Re-Mi" and the beautiful "Edelweiss," as well as "(How Do You Solve a Problem Like) Maria," "Climb Every Mountain," "Sixteen Going on Seventeen," "Have Confidence in Me," "The Lonely Goatherd," "So Long, Farewell," "My Favorite Things," and the title tune. It won the Academy Award for Best Picture and Best Director (Robert Wise).

FYI: ▸ So long, farewell, Rhett and Scarlett. *The Sound of Music* climbed every mountain to become the highest-grossing film ever, knocking 1939's *Gone with the Wind* off the top.

SOUR GRAPES BUNCH

A gang of white-booted, go-go dancing, juvenile girls, all called Charlie, who regularly joined The Banana Splits in song and dance on their Saturday-morning adventure hour.

SOUTH BEACH

This two-mile oceanfront strip (Ocean Drive) in Miami Beach, Florida, became the heart and soul of the fashion world in the 1990s when the late designer Gianni Versace and his supermodel entourage called it home. Casually trendy, SoBe (as referred to by the locals) is characterized by palm-tree-lined streets, art deco structures painted in eye-popping pastels, sidewalk cafés and designer stores, world-famous nightclubs, and a population of beautiful people who make just about everyone else feel inadequate. Local eateries offer up exotic multiethnic cuisines, such as "New World," "Nuevo Latino," and "Eurasian," so it's no wonder that South Beach is the home of the low-fat, low-carb South Beach Diet.

SOUTHFORK

Sprawling fictional ranch on the outskirts of Dallas (set twenty miles north of downtown in Parker, Texas) where the prosperous and powerful Ewing clan reside in the 1980s prime-time soap *Dallas*.

SOUTH PARK

"The following program contains coarse language, and, due to its content, it should not be viewed by anyone. . . ." Rude, crude, and very funny TV series, done in a distinctive paper-cutout animation, that stirs up much controversy for its politically incorrect humor poking fun at social taboos, religion, and celebrities. Set in the Colorado town of South Park, which is beset by bizarre occurrences, it follows the misadventures of four potty-mouth elementary school boys. There's Stan Marsh, the normal one; Kyle Broslofski, the smart one; Eric Cartman, the fat one; and Kenny McCormick, the unlucky one (in almost every episode Kenny gets killed in some grisly, unexpected way). Only in South Park can you get your ass probed by alien invaders or own a gay dog with the voice of George Clooney or have Hollywood diva Barbra Streisand turn into Mecha-Streisand, a Godzilla-like monster out to destroy the world, or witness Jesus and Satan fighting a pay-per-view battle for spiritual domination.

Other South Park characters include amorous school chef Jerome "Chef" McElroy, homosexual teacher Mr. Herbert Garrison and his aggressive hand puppet named Mr. Hat, Stan's girlfriend Wendy Testaburger, Wendy's best friend Bebe, Stan's bully older sister Shelly, Kyle's adopted little brother Ike, wheelchair retard Timmy, overcaffeinated Tweek, stuttering Butters, famished Ethiopian Starvin' Marvin, Kyle's cousin Kyle, and jolly Mr. Hankey—the Christmas Poo. Created in 1997, *South Park* is based on a short film created by Trey Parker and Matt Stone called "The Spirit of Christmas." A big-screen musical, *South Park: Bigger, Longer, and Uncut*, played in theaters in 1999.

SPACE CHARIOT

The Robinson family's twelve-wheeled (six on each side), mostly glass-encased vehicle, reminiscent of today's SUV, is best known for the 1965 *Lost in Space* episode ("There Were Giants in the Earth") involving the attack by a carnivorous one-eyed giant known as the Cyclops.

SPACE FOOD STICKS

"The energy snack developed by Pillsbury under a government contract, in support of the U.S. Aerospace Program." This fondly remembered 1970s snack food was supposedly eaten by Apollo astronauts when they traveled on space missions. (Did they wash it down with Tang?) The cylinder-shaped sticks (like a Tootsie Roll in thickness but longer and not as taffy-like) came in tasty chocolate and peanut butter flavors and were packaged in futuristic-looking silver wrappers. They allegedly gave you an energy burst, so I like to think of them as the predecessor of today's power bars.

SPACE GHOST

"Great galaxies!" Endowed with the powers of speed and invisibility, Hanna-Barbera's interplanetary crime-fighter ruled as the Protector of the Universe. The yellow-caped, black-hooded Space Ghost, whose magic Invisi-Belt rendered him invisible, rocketed through the cosmos in the Phantom Cruiser to battle villainous members of the Council of Doom, such as the Black Widow, Creature King, Heat Thing, Iceman, Metallis, Sorcerer, Moltar, and Zorak. Aiding him were two teenage sidekicks, Jan and Jayce, and their pet space monkey, Blip. Space Ghost's stiff deep voice was provided by Gary Owens, better known as the announcer for *Rowan and Martin's Laugh-In*.

Those of us old enough to remember this cartoon's original run, from 1966 to 1968, will recall that it was accompanied by a separate Dino Boy segment. Space Ghost is distinguished for being the first superhero to originate on Saturday-morning TV. His popularity launched numerous fantasy-adventure crime-fighting cartoons, including *Frankenstein Jr. and the Impossibles* (1966–68), *Birdman and the Galaxy Trio* (1967–69), *Samson and Goliath* (1967), *The Herculoids* (1967–69), *Moby Dick and the Mighty Mightor* (1967–69), and *Shazzan!* (1967–69).

FYI: ▸ Move over, Dave and Jay! The superhero gave up chasing galactic bad guys in 1997 when he became the animated host of a hilarious talk show interviewing real-life celebrities for the Cartoon Network titled *Space Ghost Coast to Coast*. Longtime adversaries molten Moltar and praying mantis Zorak joined Space Ghost as sidekicks (just like Ed McMahon and Doc Severinson).

SPAGHETTIOS

"Uh, oh! SpaghettiOs!" Introduced in 1965, Franco-American's fun macaroni shaped like little O's was an instant meal for the "latchkey" generation. While liberated mom was busy working and unable to cook dinner, her children could fix it themselves simply by opening a can of SpaghettiOs, heating it in a pan, and then eating it with a spoon. For variety, there were SpaghettiOs that had meatballs or sliced hot dogs mixed in. Rival was Chef Boyardee's Beefaroni. The wonderful "Wizard of O's" advertised SpaghettiOs from 1978 to 1993.

SPAM

"Cold or hot, Spam hits the spot!" The legendary processed-meat product, crammed in a can and named from a shortened version of "spiced ham," was introduced by the Hormel Company in 1937. Scorned by gourmets and nongourmets alike, Spam originated as a surplus food for G.I.'s during

World War II (it needs no refrigeration), and then sold more than five billion cans to household consumers as a breakfast and luncheon meat. Besides the traditional flavor, Spam of modern times can be found in several flavors, including smoked, low-salt, laden with chunks of pasteurized processed American cheese, and, for those of you counting calories, Spam Lite. Spam-lovers worldwide take part in in Spamorama cooking contests to show off the versatility of the "miracle meat."

FYI: ▸ Following World War II, Hawaiians developed a love affair with Spam, which to this day has them consuming an average of four cans per person per year.

SPANDEX PANTS

Glistening, skintight, camel-toe-revealing or penis-outlining slacks donned by disco queens and male rock stars alike. Foxy mamas commonly wore halter tops and Candies slides with 'em.

SPEARS, BRITNEY

Provocative teenage singer who, along with fellow pop princess Christina Aguilera, had a whopping influence on adolescent females in the late 1990s. Unfortunately that influence wasn't too keen. There's nothing more unsettling than seeing an army of preteen Lolitas imitating Britney and Christina by looking and acting like tarts. They copied the blonde divas' dress codes with belly-baring midriffs and low-riding hip-huggers (so low you can see the pelvic bone). They went around twirping seductive lyrics like Britney's "Hit me baby one more time" and Christina's "I wanna get dirrty (oh, oh)" and performed freaky dance moves consisting of nasty crotch-grinding and booty-shaking. It didn't help matters that seventeen-year-old Spears was sending out mixed messages of being a good Christian girl from Louisiana amid rumors of breast implants and lost virginity while in a heated romance with 'N Sync's Justin Timberlake. It makes one yearn for the days of Madonna.

SPEED BUGGY

"Rodger-Dodger, Putt-Putt!" Airing from 1973 to 1978, a Saturday-morning cartoon from Hanna-Barbera, loosely inspired by Disney's *Love Bug,* about a lovable dune buggy with magical powers. Nicknamed "Speedy," the orange-colored automobile could talk (the front grille was his sputtering mouth), see (his headlights were eyes), fly, and even cruise under water. The show was reminiscent of Hanna-Barbera's own *Scooby-Doo* as Speed Buggy, who had Scooby-Doo mannerisms, carried a trio of wacky teenagers on various TV adventures. There was Tinker, the Shaggy-esque mechanic and driver; Mark, the Freddy-esque handsome brain; and Debbie, Mark's Daphne-esque pretty girlfriend. A 1973 Milton Bradley board game based on this program had players racing dune buggies in an exciting cross-country race set in Baja California, Mexico. "Speedy thinking, Speedy!"

SPEED RACER

"Go, Speed Racer, go!" One of the best-loved and best-remembered cartoons of our times. The highly energetic show followed the adventures of heroic Speed Racer, an eighteen-year-old race driver who drove the powerful Mach V, the world's coolest car. Dark-haired and handsome, Speed encountered excitement and danger at every turn while competing on grueling international race courses and being pursued by an array of colorful racing villains. He was accompanied by a loyal pit crew consisting of cute girlfriend Trixie, inquisitive little brother Spridal, mischievous pet chimp Chim Chim, hotheaded mechanic father Pops, caring mother Moms, best buddy and assistant Sparky, and the mysterious Racer X. Premiering on American syndicated TV in 1967, the Japanimation program was based on a comic book from Japan, *Mach Go Go* ("Go" is the Japanese word for "5"). *Speed Racer* is noted for having the most memorable cartoon theme song ever: "Here he comes / Here comes Speed Racer / He's a demon on wheels / He's a demon and he's gonna be chasin' after someone. . . ."

FYI: ▸ Real-life speed racer Michael Andretti credits *Speed Racer* as an inspirational favorite.

SPEEDY ALKA-SELTZER

Created to reflect Alka-Seltzer's promotional theme, "Speedy Relief," the ever-cheerful little redhead was one of the first TV advertising icons. He appeared in more than 200 commercials over a ten-year span, from 1954 to 1964.

SPEEDY GONZALEZ
"Ar-riba! Ar-riba!" Mischievous, sombrero-wearing cartoon rodent boasted as "the fastest mouse in all of Mexico" (he had a running speed of 100 miles an hour). Made his debut in the cartoon short "Cat-Tails for Two" (1953).

SPELLING, TORI
Born May 16, 1973, in Los Angeles, Victoria Spelling is TV mogul Aaron Spelling's big-eyed, cleavage-altered stringbean daughter who starred as the virginal Donna Martin on the hit series *Beverly Hills 90210*. (Contrary to rumors, she claims that producer daddy didn't have any part in her getting cast as a main character of his financially backed show.) In the 1990s, Tori frequently got parodied as a shallow, spoiled Beverly Hills princess (the kind of girl you love to hate) by Melanie Hutsell on *Saturday Night Live*. After starring in trashy TV movies, like *Co-ed Call Girl* (1996), she has been trying to revamp her image by taking quirky roles in indie movies, including two Sundance Festival hits: *The House of Yes* (1997) and *Trick* (1999). Tori has also been coloring her once-bleached-blonde hair back to its true dark color. Smart moves, Tori.

SPENCER'S
For anyone under the age of twenty-one, this retail store—found primarily at shopping malls across the nation—was the best gift shop of them all! The reason: all the cool junk found at this one-stop, youth-oriented emporium. No other place in the mall had such a wide array of funny greeting cards and gag gifts, "Over the hill" items, naughty sex toys—vibrators, edible undies, penis-shaped lollipops, handcuffs—decaled T-shirts, pinup posters of current celebrity hunks and hunkettes, trippy black-light paraphernalia, lava lamps, hippie jewelry, faddish toys, and so much other bric-a-brac you never knew existed.

SPICE GIRLS
"Girl Power!" The all-girl British pop band, once acclaimed as the "fastest-selling new act since The Beatles," was characterized by its tasty bubblegum songs, colorful clothing, and a cheeky in-your-face attitude. Constructed by producer Simon Fuller in 1993, the six babes used stage monikers to describe their individual personalities: cool Posh Spice (Victoria Adams), loud Scary Spice (Melanie Brown), cute Baby Spice (Emma Bunton), energetic Sporty Spice (Melanie Chisholm), and fun Ginger Spice (Geri Halliwell). After hitting number one for seven weeks in 1996 with their debut single "Wannabe," the Spice Girls ruled the music charts for a couple of years more and sold out concert halls worldwide. Popularity waned in 1998 when redhead Ginger Spice left, but not before the Girls starred in a lukewarm movie titled *Spice World*. Victoria Adams is the wife of hottie English footballer David Beckham.

FYI: ▸ Ginger Spice's very short dress in the design of England's Union Jack flag was a fashion craze in the late 1990s.

SPIDER-MAN
Representing a new breed of superheroes, Spidey was created by writer Stan Lee and artist Steve Ditko for *Marvel* comics in 1962. Mild-mannered Peter Parker was your typical high school science geek until the day he was bitten by a radioactive lab spider, transforming him into the "Amazing Spider-Man." Acquiring superhero strength, along with unusual spider-like skills, such as wall-climbing, web-throwing, and a danger-warning "spider-sense," Parker moonlighted as a crime-fighter costumed in a red-and-blue bodysuit. In the dark corners and on the rooftops of New York City, Spider-Man nabbed thieves like flies and battled evil-doers, like the Scorpion, Sorcerer, Dr. Octopus, and the Green Goblin. When not fighting injustice, he lived with doting Aunt May and between classes worked as a photographer for the *Daily Bugle* newspaper, where he assisted pretty reporter Betty Brandt and avoided antagonistic editor J. Jonah Jameson.

From 1967 to 1970, Spider-Man starred on a Saturday-morning cartoon series, renowned for having the most groovy theme song around: "Spider-Man, Spider-Man / Friendly neighborhood Spider-Man / Spins a web, any size, catches thieves just like flies / Look out, here comes the Spider-Man!"

FYI: ▸ The 2002 live-action, big-screen adaptation of *Spider-Man,* starring Tobey Maguire as Peter Parker, made history by having the highest opening-weekend gross ever ($114 million). It was followed by an even more successful sequel in 2004.

SPIKE

Snoopy's brother, who moved to the desert (Needles, California) after graduating from the Daisy Hill Puppy Farm. Hangs out with a cactus named "Joe" and a few friendly tumbleweeds.

SPINDRIFT

While zooming from Los Angeles to London, this commercial orange rocket ship with three crew members and four passengers is drawn into a spacely time warp and crash-lands on a strange planet occupied by giant-sized people on the sci-fi TV series *Land of the Giants*.

SPIRAL PERMS

The bigger the better was the motto when it came to women's hair in the late 1980s and early 1990s, so this unique way of perm wrapping left wearers with outrageous spiralcurled big hair. It left many wearers with outrageous frizzy, damaged big hair as well. Fortunately, fluffy permed manes went the straight way when Jennifer Aniston's supersleek Rachel cut became all the rage in the mid-1990s.

SPIROGRAPH

"No limit to the different designs you can make!" Created by an Englishman named Denys Fisher, this was America's best-selling toy of 1968, the same year it was introduced by Kenner. By using an assortment of gears, discs, and color pens, kids could draw millions of geometrically perfect designs, like ovals, squares, trapezoids, circles, clovers, and so on. A Spirograph set consisted of two large rings, eighteen small plastic wheels, and two racks—all with tiny gearlike teeth on the outer rim. Each wheel had holes in which color pens (red, blue, green, and black) could be placed. The wheels were put in contact with the rings, interlocking the teeth, and then turned by the pen to create a never-ending array of quasi-psychedelic patterns. In the early 1970s, a Super Spirograph, a Magnetic Spirograph, and a Motorized Spirograph were introduced.

FYI: ▸ In 1968, Spirograph was awarded the Educational Toy of the Year award in Britain, the Artistic Toy Oscar in France, and the Design Idea of the Month award by *Design News* in the United States.

SPITZ, MARK

Dark-haired, mustached swimming champion from California who won an unprecedented seven gold medals at the 1972 Summer Olympics. A subsequent poster featuring the attractive twenty-two-year-old swimmer adorned with his prized gold and a pair of skimpy Speedos was a pinup sensation.

SPLASH

Enormously popular big-screen fantasy about a lonely New York City bachelor, Allen Bauer (Tom Hanks), who is saved from drowning off the coast of Cape Cod by a lovely blonde mermaid (Daryl Hannah). Sprouting legs when her tail dries, the mermaid called Madison later arrives in New York in search of Allen, and they fall in love. Complications (and laughs) set in as Madison adapts to human city-life and attempts are made by a bungling scientist, Walter Kornbluth (Eugene Levy), to catch and study her. Co-star John Candy is hilarious as Allen's lecherous brother, Freddie Bauer. Directed by Ron Howard, the 1984 Disney comedy turned both Hanks and Hannah into movie stars.

SPLITTIN' IMAGE

The two-sided miniature racing car, one of the best-known of all Hot Wheels, was introduced during the premier year (1968) of the popular Mattel toy line.

SPONGEBOB SQUAREPANTS

"Oh, barnacles!" Nonsensical yet earnest, this cartoon character is a square yellow sea sponge who resides in Bikini Bottom, a ocean-floor village located beneath Bikini Atoll, a tropical isle in the Pacific. SpongeBob lives in a two-story pineapple house with pet snail Gary and works as a fry cook at the Krusty Krab, owned by money-hungry Mr. Krabs. His underwater comrades include grumpy next-door neighbor Squidward Tentacles (a clarinet-playing squid), simpleminded best buddy Patrick Star (a chubby starfish), and thrill-seeking Sandy Cheeks (a Texas squirrel wearing an air helmet). An embarrassing misfortune of SpongeBob's is that his pants frequently fall down to expose his tighty-whitey briefs underneath. Stephen Hillenburg created him in the late 1990s for Nickelodeon TV.

SPOOKY

Created by *Harvey* comics, this "Tuff Little Ghost" first joined cousin Casper as a supporting regular in the friendly specter's comic books and cartoon shorts in 1958. Unlike Casper, Spooky was a mischievous prankster in search of some unsuspecting soul to pull a practical joke on and shout a scary "Boo!" A freckle-faced spook, he spoke in a Brooklyn accent ("Ha! The poifect victim!" "It woiked!" and "Ow! That hoit!"), wore a black "doiby," and was fond of a sweet orange-haired "goil" ghost named "Poil" (Pearl). In 1961, he branched off from supporting status with his own comic-book series, titled *Spooky Spooktown*.

SPOT

Eddie Munster's pet dragon, who stays under the Munsters' staircase in their creepy home. On the sitcom, Eddie likes to play with Spot in the backyard, but sometimes the fire-breathing beast runs away and chases cars (which he often catches).

SPRIDAL

Speed Racer's little brother was a ridiculously cute, candy-crazed kid who truly idolized his bigger sibling and always got underfoot during an important auto race. He hung around with a troublemaking pet monkey named Chim Chim on the *Speed Racer* cartoon.

SPRINGFIELD, DUSTY

Born Mary O'Brien on April 16, 1939, in London, the mascaraed, beehived blonde known for "blue-eyed soul" was England's top female pop star of the 1960s. So soulful were Dusty's vocals that some people, such as Motown singer Martha Reeves, were at first under the impression that she was black. Cliff Richard commented that she had the "blackest" voice he had ever heard, while Aretha Franklin refused to record "Son of a Preacher Man" (1968) after being impressed with Dusty's husky-voiced rendition. Her stream of American Top Forty hits included "I Only Want to Be with You" (1964), "Wishin' and Hopin'" (1964), "You Don't Have to Say You Love Me" (1966), "The Look of Love" (1967), and "The Windmills of Your Mind" (1969). Semi-retired in the 1970s and early 1980s, Dusty marked a comeback in 1988 when she joined forces with the Pet Shop Boys on "What Have I Done to Deserve This" and recorded "Nothing Has Been Proved," for the *Scandal* movie soundtrack. She died of cancer in 1999.

SPRINGFIELD, RICK

Born on August 23, 1949, in Sydney, the cute, dark-haired rocker initially experienced success as a member of Zoot, Australia's reigning teen idol band of the early 1970s. In 1972, Springfield left Zoot when he signed with Capitol Records in London, which unsuccessfully tried to make him another David Cassidy across the Atlantic in America. After moving to the States in 1972, Springfield had problems with immigration work permits and management contracts, forcing him out of performance. He eventually settled in Los Angeles and enrolled in acting school.

In 1981, Springfield was cast as dreamy Dr. Noah Drake on daytime's highly rated soap opera *General Hospital*. The same year, he released the album *Working Class Dog*, which landed in the Top Ten and spawned a number-one single, "Jessie's Girl." The music and the TV show cemented Springfield's popularity in America and made him the dominant teen heartthrob of the early 1980s. Other recording hits included "I've Done Everything for You" (1981), "Don't Talk to Strangers" (1982), "Affair of the Heart" (1983), and "Love Somebody" (1984), from his big-screen movie *Hard to Hold*.

FYI: ▸ Often mistaken for Bruce Springsteen, Rick Springfield penned a 1985 autobiographical song about the experience, titled "Bruce."

SPRINGSTEEN, BRUCE

In the late 1970s and early 1980s, New Jersey–born Springsteen (on September 23, 1949), a.k.a. the "Boss," embodied the Baby Boomer's search for the American Dream, particularly the blue-collar male segment of the generation, with the critically applauded LPs *Born to Run* (1975) and *The River* (1980). Younger Boomers (Tweeners) and Gen-Xers may recall Springsteen as a headbanded, beefed-up rocker on MTV in the mid-1980s, shaking his butt in a tight pair of faded 501's on stage while "Dancing in the Dark" with an unknown Courteney Cox, or emoting sexually as a love-struck auto mechanic in "I'm on Fire." Hit singles by Springsteen and his E Street Band included "Born to Run" (1975), "Hungry Heart" (1980), and seven from the renowned best-selling album *Born in the U.S.A.* (1984): "Dancing in the Dark," "Cover Me," "I'm on Fire," "Glory Days," "I'm Goin' Down," "My Hometown," and the booming title track. In 1993, he won an Oscar for the heartfelt "Streets of Philadelphia," the theme song from the AIDS drama *Philadelphia* starring Tom Hanks and Antonio Banderas.

SPROCKETS

"Now is the time on Sprockets when we dance. . . ." Regular skit on *Saturday Night Live* featuring Mike Myers as black-clothed Dieter, the angstful host of a TV talk show, *Sprockets*, for mod West Germans of the late 1980s.

SPUDS MACKENZIE

"The Original Party Animal" was a black-eyed bull terrier sporting a Hawaiian shirt that starred in a series of commercials for Bud Light Beer in the 1980s. The studly canine surrounded himself with a group of bikini-clad, two-legged gals known as the Spudettes.

FYI: ▸ Dudes, I hate to burst your bubble, but our pal Spuds was actually no stud. A female terrier named Honey Tree Evil Eye played him.

SPY VS. SPY

Regular comic-strip segment found in *Mad* magazine, featuring two pointy-faced spies—one dressed in all black, the other in all white—who try to assassinate each other with an elaborate scheme of sorts, only to have it backfire.

SQUARE PEGS

"I'd like it if they liked us, but I don't think they like us. . . ." Wonderful offbeat prime-time series that spoofed high school social cliques of the early 1980s. It starred Sarah Jessica Parker and Amy Linker as Patty Greene and Lauren Hutchinson, best friends and "square pegs" who were freshmen at Weemawee High in suburban Los Angeles. Patty was the tall, gawky one with glasses, Lauren was the short, stout one with braces on her teeth. Both girls were somewhat geeky and yearned desperately to belong to the school's popular crowd, led by preppy cheerleader Muffy Tepperman (Jami Gertz), wealthy Val-Gal Jennifer DeNuccio (Tracy Nelson), self-centered hunk Vinnie Pasetta (Jon Caliri), and bigoted black LaDonna Fredericks (Claudette Wells). Comrades of Patty and Lauren were New Wave rocker John "Johnny Slash" Ulasewicz (Merritt Butrick) and aspiring comedian Marshall Blechtman (John Femia). Mr. Dingleman (Basil Hoffman) served as Weemawee's principal.

Airing on CBS from 1982 to 1983, *Square Pegs* is noted for being the big sister of high school sitcoms targeting social cliques, like *Head of the Class* (1986–91), *The Wonder Years* (1988–93), *Saved by the Bell* (1989–93), *Ferris Bueller* (1990–91), *Parker Lewis Can't Lose* (1990–93), *Clueless* (1996–99), *Freaks and Geeks* (1999–2000), and *Popular* (1999–2001). Its theme song was written and sung by The Waitresses.

FYI: ▸ Sarah Jessica Parker (born March 25, 1965) would later go on to play the quirky SanDeE* in Steve Martin's *L.A. Story* (1991), become the wife of Matthew "Ferris Bueller" Broderick, and star as Carrie Bradshaw in the award-winning *Sex and the City* on HBO.

SQUIDDLY DIDDLY

Hanna-Barbera's star-struck octopus, who resided at Bubbleland, an aquatic park run by annoyed Chief Winchley. He headlined his own cartoon segment on Saturday morning's *Secret Squirrel Show* from 1965 to 1967.

S.S. *GUPPY*

The seafaring ship guided by cereal-loving captain Cap'n Crunch; seen on animated TV commercials created by Jay (*Rocky and Bullwinkle*) Ward.

S.S. *MINNOW*

This is the sightseeing charter boat, captained by the Skipper, that wrecked ashore an uncharted South Pacific island, marooning its crew and passengers in the TV sitcom *Gilligan's Island*.

SSP RACERS
"World's fastest big racers! No motor. No batteries. No push. No track." First introduced in 1969, Kenner's SSP (for Super-Sonic Power) Racers were the biggest-selling boys' toy of the early 1970s. These racing cars were cool. They could travel up to 800 scale miles an hour, race more than eighty feet, and make a powerful sound as they revved up to 20,000 rpm. What made the SSP Racers run was simple. They were activated by the ratcheted Power T-Stick inserted into the Gyro-Wheel (a flywheel) located in the middle of the car's base. After yanking the stick out, it caused the wheel to spin, giving the SSP its mighty speed. The exciting SSP line showcased an assortment of fantastic-looking vehicles with names like Black Widow, Bonneville Bike, Can-Am Racer, Jet Star, Mod Mercer, Siamese Slingshot, Sidewinder, Super Stocker, Tee-riffic, and Two Much.

STACEY Q.
"I-I-I-I need you, I-I-I-I need you. . . ." The synthesized sweetie of the mid-1980s, nicknamed the "Queen of Retro Dance," was born Stacey Swain on November 30, 1958, in Los Angeles. Her sexy, quirky vocals were heard on two Top Forty dance hits in 1986: "Two of Hearts" and "We Connect." What really set this pretty singer apart from all others were her awesome dancing and her totally hot fashion sense, emulated by young female dance artists like Jody Watley, Expose, Debbie Gibson, Tiffany, and Paula Abdul. (Allegedly, Madonna stood in the wings, captivated by Paula's dance moves at an AIDS benefit in 1986.) Stacey Q's trademark look was long blonde hair worn ratted, sometimes crimped, with matching hair extensions applied here and there. She dressed her five-foot-two slender frame in voluminous crinoline skirts, belly-button-revealing half-tops, leggings, high-heeled ankle boots, and an immense array of bangles, necklaces, and hoop earrings. She appeared twice on the hit TV series *The Facts of Life*, as Cinnamon, a singer who bested Tootie in an audition for a Broadway rock musical. Today, she is a Buddhist and a student of Tibetan culture who incorporates the mystical religion into her music.

FYI: ▸ Q, the high-tech weapons wizard in the James Bond novels, inspired the "Q" in Stacey Q's name.

"STAIRWAY TO HEAVEN"
The 1971 masterpiece was a cut off the *Led Zeppelin IV* album (a.k.a *The Four Symbols* album). Despite never being released as a single, it is the British rock band's most recognized tune, which to this day still populates "all-time" song polls and radio airwaves. It was also "the" song to slow dance to at school dances in the 1970s.

STAN MARSH
Considered the leader of the *South Park* group, Stan is just your average mixed-up third-grade kid who has a gay dog named Sparky and vomits when his love crush, Wendy Testeburger, speaks to him. Shelly Marsh, his older sister with headgear for teeth, beats the crap out of him on a regular basis.

STARBUCKS
Where else but Starbucks could one order a grande decaf vanilla latte, nonfat milk, with extra foam? With a store seemingly on every block in America, the yuppiefied coffeehouse franchise from Seattle (founded in 1971) became the McDonald's of the 1990s. Starbucks made specialized coffees (espresso, cappuccino, latte, mocha) as common as the coffeepot-style coffee of yesteryear.

STARLITE
The white stallion with rainbow-colored mane and tail was the devoted mount of rainbow-traveling cartoon sprite Rainbow Brite.

STARSKY AND HUTCH
The TV series that brings back memories of screeching tires, screaming sirens, and surly manliness. Airing from 1975 to 1979, the crime drama featured a pair of young and handsome plainclothes detectives named Dave Starsky (Paul Michael Glaser, the brunet) and Ken "Hutch" Hutchinson (David Soul, the blond). The duo tackled cases involving thieves, hookers, drug dealers, and other lowlife scum while racing around the streets of Los Angeles in Starsky's souped-up Ford Torino. Other regulars included Captain Harold Dobey (Bernie Hamilton), their hot-tempered boss; and Huggy Bear (Antonio Fargas), their showy pimp informant. *Starsky and Hutch* was one of many youth-friendly cop shows occupying prime time in the 1970s. Extremely popular, it was

also very violent, and by the 1977–78 season the ABC-TV network ordered its producers to tone it down. In 2004, it was remade as a big-screen comedy starring Ben Stiller as Starsky and Owen Wilson as Hutch.

"STARSKY" SWEATERS

Cardigans with black-and-white geometrical designs made trendy in the mid-1970s thanks to Paul Michael Glaser, who wore them as trademark clothing on the police detective series *Starsky and Hutch.*

STAR TREK

"Space, the final frontier. . . ." Klingons, Romulans, Tribbles, Vulcan V-fingered salutes, phaser guns, transporters, tricorders, warp engines, velveteen-polyester shirts—all this can mean only one thing: *Star Trek*, the most famous sci-fi TV series in prime-time history. Created by Gene Roddenberry, the show followed the space voyages of a multicultural, multispecies crew aboard the U.S.S. Enterprise, a large science-military exploration starship commissioned by the United Federation of Planets in the twenty-third century for a five-year mission "to seek out new life and new civilizations" and "boldly go where no man has gone before." The large cast included William Shatner as the ship's commander, Captain James T. Kirk, Leonard Nimoy as half-Vulcan, half-human first officer Mr. Spock, DeForest Kelley as Enterprise physician Dr. Leonard McCoy, Nichelle Nichols as communications officer Lieutenant Uhura, James Doohan as chief engineer Montgomery Scott, George Takei as helms officer Mr. Sulu, Walter Koenig as navigator Pavel Chekov, and Majel Barrett as head nurse Christine Chapel.

Although hugely successful today, during its original run on NBC (1966 to 1969) *Star Trek* suffered from chronic low ratings (it never ranked higher than fifty-second in the year-end Nielsen ratings). It now claims one of the largest fan bases of any TV show ever, known as "Trekkies," who have turned it into a billion-dollar-a-year franchise. *Star Trek*'s legacy includes eight theatrical movies; a Saturday-morning cartoon (airing from 1973 to 1975); three spin-off TV series, *Star Trek: The Next Generation*, *Voyager*, and *Deep Space Nine*, and a Tribble-load of action figures and other toys. The familiar theme music was composed by Alexander Courage.

STAR WARS

"A long time ago, in a galaxy far, far away" began the saga of *Star Wars*, the most successful and influential sci-fi film of the twentieth century. Created and directed by George Lucas, the action-packed 1977 epic showcased dazzling high-tech special effects—thundering spaceships, exploding planets, and dueling light sabers—along with a rousing John Williams music score and a grand old-fashioned story line of good versus evil.

Plucky farm youth Luke Skywalker (Mark Hamill), from the desert planet Tatooine, aspires to be a revered Jedi Knight and joins freedom-fighting rebels, led by spirited Princess Leia (Carrie Fisher), in an intergalactic revolt against the evil, universe-dominating Galactic Empire. The Empire's greatest weapon is the menacing Death Star, a huge spacecraft with the awesome capability of blowing up entire worlds, commanded by sinister despot Grand Moff Tarkin (Peter Cushing). Tarkin's terrifying henchman is Darth Vader (David Prowse, voiced by James Earl Jones), a black-masked, black-robed, heavy-breathing onetime "good" Jedi Knight who had crossed over to the Dark Side to become the military leader of the white-garbed Imperial Stormtroopers. Along the way, Luke and Princess Leia are aided by noble Ben "Obi-Wan" Kenobi (Sir Alec Guinness), a mystical Jedi Knight; roguish Han Solo, the swashbuckling space pilot of the Millennium Falcon; and a trio of nonhumans: fussy C-3PO (Anthony Daniels), a golden android; sassy R2-D2 (Kenny Baker), a bleeping and whistling robot; and hairy Chewbacca (Peter Mayhew), Solo'sWookie co-pilot.

With moviegoers lining up around the block for months, *Star Wars* became the box-office champ of the year. It received seven Academy Awards for various technical achievements, including Best Sound, Best Original Score, Best Visual Effects, and Best Costume Design. A disco version of Williams's prolific score, mixed with the "Cantina" number, "Star Wars Theme / Cantina Band," by Meco, topped the pop charts for a couple of weeks in August 1977. Two sequels completed the *Star Wars* trilogy: 1980's *Empire Strikes Back*, introducing suave Lando Calrissian (Billy Dee Williams) and wise Jedi master Yoda; and 1983's *Return of the Jedi*, introducing the furry Ewoks and vile crime lord Jabba the Hutt. In 1999, a highly anticipated prequel, *Star*

Wars Episode 1: Phantom Menace, took fans back to a time when Darth Vader was an innocent slave boy named Anakin Skywalker.

As the highest-grossing film series ever, these movies launched a complete industry of merchandising tie-ins, such as novels, comic books, trading cards, posters, T-shirts, lunch boxes, bed sheets, wallpaper, alarm clocks, and, most notable, a line of action figures by Kenner.

STAR WARS ACTION FIGURES

Let the action-figure revolution begin! For Christmas 1977, Kenner Toys released the first of their *Star Wars* action-figure line with a preorder package set consisting of four characters: Luke Skywalker, Princess Leia, Chewbacca, and R2-D2. At about three inches high, these plastic, poseable figures were instant sellouts, prompting Kenner to introduce others from the blockbuster movie. In no time, Han Solo, Obi-Wan Kenobi, C-3PO, Darth Vader, Stormtroopers, and Jawas joined the action-figure party. But that wasn't enough. Kids needed to act out their interplanetary *Star Wars* fantasies, so Kenner followed up with spacecraft—Luke's Land Speeder, Han's Millennium Falcon, R2-D2's A-Wing Fighter—and play sets: Tattoine's Creature Cantina, Darth Vader's Death Star, Droid Factory. With the release of the *Star Wars* sequels in 1980 and 1983 came more action figures and play sets, with a phenomenal 300 million sold between the years of 1977 and 1984. Kenner's success prompted practically every movie and TV show slanted toward action-adventure to release a line of action figures.

FYI: ▸ Did you hold on to your *Star Wars* figures? A Luke Skywalker, with telescoping saber, can net you more than $3,000 (mint-in-box condition, of course).

STAY ALIVE

"I'm the sole survivor!" Billed as the "Ultimate Survival Game," this was introduced by Milton Bradley in 1971. The object of the action game was for players to strategically pull levers to open and close holes on an elevated plastic board, allowing opponents' marbles to drop down and out of the game. The last player with marbles left was the winner (or "sole survivor") of Stay Alive.

ST. ELMO'S FIRE

This *Big Chill* for the twentysomething generation was sarcastically labeled "The Little Chill" by film critics. The 1985 movie starred a now-legendary Brat Pack ensemble cast as a group of self-indulgent friends sorting out their lives and love affairs during their first postgraduate year from Georgetown University in Washington, D.C. Directed and written by Joel Schumacher, the cast included Emilio Estevez as Kirby Keger, a law student obsessed with a thirtysomething doctor (Andie MacDowell); Rob Lowe as Billy Hicks, a reckless pretty-boy musician; Andrew McCarthy as Kevin Dolenz, a struggling writer mistaken for being gay; Demi Moore as Jules, a cocaine abuser sleeping with her boss; Judd Nelson as Alec Newbary, a promiscuous up-and-coming yuppie; Ally Sheedy as Leslie Hunter, who's torn between Kevin and Alec; and Mare Winningham as Wendy Beamish, a wealthy social worker yearning for Billy. John Parr's overplayed title theme topped the charts. St. Elmo's Fire, the Georgetown bar the Brats spend their youth reveling in, was named after a seafaring fable about a fire in the sky.

FYI: ▸ In order to play coke addict Jules in *St. Elmo's Fire*, party-girl Demi Moore had to sign a contract stipulating that she would stop using alcohol and drugs, an agreement that caused her to turn her life around.

STEPFORD WIVES

"Something strange is happening in the town of Stepford." Male chauvinists who feel threatened by the women's lib movement will delight in the chilling 1975 horror film directed by Bryan Forbes and based on Ira Levin's 1972 novel. Set in the tranquil small burb of Stepford, Connecticut, three newly transplanted housewives, Joanna Eberhart (Katharine Ross), Bobbie Markowe (Paula Prentiss), and Charmaine Wimperis (Tina Louise)—all free spirits and pseudo-feminists—are perplexed by the weird state of the other women in the community.

Placidly smiling and perpetually blissful, the Stepford wives seem perfect in every way. They love to do housework. They drone on and on about cleaning products as if spokes-models in a TV commercial. They happily exchange recipes ("I've just been so busy with baking. I know I shouldn't say this, but I just love my brownies"). They keep every strand of hair in place. They wear pretty picture-hats and long gowns while pushing shopping carts to the bland rhythm of Muzak at the supermarket. And they never argue with their husbands, being devoted to satisfying them in every way ("Whatever you want, darling").

What's causing them to be faultless models of domesticity? It seems the Stepford hubbies have replaced their real wives with robot replicas designed to be mindlessly compliant and forever beautiful. Will our trio of heroines be next? A don't-miss favorite scene is when Stepford android Carol (Nanette Newman), wife of the movie's adversary, Dale Coba (Patrick O'Neal), goes on the blink at a cocktail party, telling every guest, "I'll just die if I don't get that recipe. I'll just die if I don't get that recipe. I'll just die if I don't get that recipe. . . ."

Look for Mary Stuart Masterson making her film debut at age seven, playing the daughter of real-life dad Peter Masterson and Katharine Ross. Three inferior TV movie sequels followed: *Revenge of the Stepford Wives* (1980), *The Stepford Children* (1987), and *The Stepford Husbands* (1996). Director Frank Oz refilmed it as a black comedy in 2004, starring Oscar-winning Nicole Kidman, comedienne Bette Midler, and country singer Faith Hill as Stepford Wives.

FYI: ▸ "Stepford" has become part of the American lexicon, used as an adjective for robotic mindlessness and usually describing the younger, obedient trophy-wives of middle-aged corporate types. These women live in affluent suburbs, don't have work careers, volunteer at the Junior League, vote Republican, and emulate Martha Stewart.

STEVE AUSTIN

After a plane crash leaves this athletic and handsome astronaut severely injured, he is rebuilt with $6 million worth of superhuman bionic parts. The new and improved *Six Million Dollar Man* has powerful bionic legs that allow him to run at speeds up to sixty miles an hour or jump buildings in a single bound; a mighty bionic right arm that can crash through a concrete wall or throw an object far, far away; and a bionic left eye equipped with a built-in grid screen for amazing penetrating vision. The OSI, a government agency headed by Oscar Goldman, assigned Austin top-secret tasks, pitting him against mad scientists, evil fembots, diabolical aliens, and even Bigfoot!

STEVE DOUGLAS

On TV's *My Three Sons*, film star Fred MacMurray starred as the patient, even-keeled widower and father of three sons—Mike, Robbie, and Chip (actually four sons and one daughter, if you count adopted Ernie and stepdaughter Dodie)—who worked as an aerodynamics engineer in a medium-sized city in the Midwest.

STEVE McGARRETT

On the smash police series *Hawaii Five-O*, craggy-faced, helmet-haired Jack Lord played the hard-driving head honcho of the Hawaii State Police's Five-O, an elite detective unit.

STEVEN CARRINGTON

Al Corley, and later Jack Coleman, starred as the mild-mannered, sexually confused (straight or gay?) black-sheep son of Blake and Alexis Carrington on *Dynasty*. He's renowned for being one of the first recurring gay characters on a prime-time series.

STEVE URKEL

"Did I do th-a-a-a-a-t?!" Urkel's large, thick glasses, high-waisted trousers with suspenders, high-pitched voice, snorting laugh, and annoying demeanor made him the nerdiest of all nerds and the stand-out star of the TV sitcom *Family Matters* (1989–98). Played by Jaleel White on the show, the teen geek has a whopping crush on school classmate and next-door neighbor Laura Winslow and virtually stalks her.

STEWART, ROD

In 1979, the rocker sang the tongue-in-cheek question "Da Ya Think I'm Sexy?" and fans everywhere answered yes by making the disco-laden song number one for four weeks. Born on January 10, 1945, in London, Stewart is known for a raspy singing voice and his glitzy image: frosted-blond cockatoo shag, leopard-printed spandex pants, and a penchant for hooking up with blonde models who seem to get younger as he gets older (Britt Ekland, Alana Hamilton, Kelly Emberg, and Rachel Hunter). Stewart's early music career was spent as a folksinger-harmonica player before joining The Jeff Beck Group in 1967 and, later, Faces in 1969. While with Faces, he started a solo career with the release of the 1971 album *Every Picture Tells a Story*, which carried his first hit single, "Maggie May." In 1976, Stewart's ballad "Tonight's the Night" topped the charts for an amazing eight weeks. It found itself banned across the nation because of the controversial subject matter: the seduction of a sixteen-year-old virgin. Other hits included "You Wear It Well" (1972), "The Killing of Georgie" (1977), a two-part saga about the murder of a gay friend, "You're in My Heart" (1977), "Hot Legs" (1977), "Passion" (1980), "Young Turks" (1981), "Infatuation" (1984), "Some Guys Have All the Luck" (1984), "Forever Young" (1988), and "Downtown Train" (1989).

FYI: ▸ Since the late 1970s, Rod Stewart has been the subject of an urban legend that has him rushed to a hospital emergency room to have three gallons of semen pumped out of his stomach as a result of preconcert antics.

STING

Real name: Gordon Sumner (born October 2, 1951). The bleached-blond lead vocalist of New Wave mega-band The Police got his nickname, "Sting," because he wore a black-and-yellow-striped rugby jersey—just like a bee. Being the most popular of The Police because of his unusual personality and sexy good looks, he appeared in the films *Dune* (1984), as space-aged villain Feyd-Rautha; *The Bride* (1985), as Baron Frankenstein; and *Plenty* (1985), opposite Meryl Streep, as working-class Mick. When the band broke up, it was not surprising that Sting started a solo recording career with such jazz-sprinkled hits as "If You Love Somebody Set Them Free" (1985), "Fortress Around Your Heart" (1985), and "We'll Be Together" (1987). Of recent years, he has used his celebrity to raise consciousness and cash worldwide for environmental issues, most notable being Amnesty and the Brazilian Rainforest.

FYI: ▸ According to *People* magazine, Sting claims that by practicing meditation he can make love for more than five hours at a time.

STIRRUP PANTS

Feminine pants made out of body-hugging, stretchy material, characterized by a band of fabric worn under the foot to help keep the pant leg pulled down. First popular in the 1950s as a garment for ski bunnies, stirrup pants made a comeback in the 1980s paired with oversized sweaters and flats.

STORY SONGS

Reminiscent of tearjerker "death pop" songs from earlier years (including "Leader of the Pack" and "Tell Laura I Love Her"), these tragic tales were particularly popular with impressionable adolescent music buyers of the 1970s who didn't mind being woeful and—according to record sales—wanted more of the same. The ill-fated dilemmas told in these melancholy, rather cheesy ballads included:

Love affairs gone astray

- "Ode to Billy Joe" (1967) by Bobbie Gentry
- "Which Way You Goin' Billy?" (1970) by The Poppy Family
- "Brandy (You're a Fine Girl)" (1972) by Looking Glass
- "Side Show" (1974) by Blue Magic
- "Please Mr. Please" (1975) by Olivia Newton-John
- "Torn Between Two Lovers" (1977) by Mary MacGregor
- "Escape (The Piña Colada Song)" (1979) by Rupert Holmes
- "Same Old Lang Syne" (1981) by Dan Fogelberg

Regrettable life-altering decisions

- "Billy, Don't Be a Hero" (1974) by Bo Donaldson and The Heywoods
- "Please Come to Boston" (1974) by Dave Loggins
- "Rhinestone Cowboy" (1975) by Glen Campbell
- "The Wreck of the Edmund Fitzgerald" (1976) by Gordon Lightfoot
- "I've Never Been to Me" (1982) by Charlene

Beloved pets lost forever

- "Ben" (1972) by Michael Jackson
- "Wildfire" (1975) by Michael Murphey
- "Shannon" (1976) by Henry Gross

Families stricken with dysfunction
- "D-I-V-O-R-C-E" (1968) by Tammy Wynette
- "Fancy" (1970) by Bobbie Gentry
- "Gypsies, Tramps, and Thieves" (1971) by Cher
- "Daddy, Don't You Walk So Fast" (1972) by Wayne Newton
- "Delta Dawn" (1973) by Helen Reddy
- "Angie Baby" (1974) by Helen Reddy
- "Cat's in the Cradle" (1974) by Harry Chapin

Victims of social injustice
- "Love Child" (1968) by Diana Ross and The Supremes
- "In the Ghetto" (1969) by Elvis Presley
- "One Tin Solder" (1971) by Coven
- "Half-Breed" (1968) by Cher

Loved ones dying from illness
- "Honey" (1968) by Bobby Goldsboro
- "Patches" (1970) by Clarence Carter
- "Seasons in the Sun" (1974) by Terry Jacks
- "Rocky" (1975) by Austin Roberts

Fatal shootings
- "The Night the Lights Went Out in Georgia (1973) by Vicki Lawrence
- "Dark Lady" (1974) by Cher
- "I Shot the Sheriff" (1974) by Eric Clapton
- "The Night Chicago Died" (1974) by Paper Lace
- "Run Joey Run" (1975) by David Geddes
- "Copacabana (At the Copa)" (1978) by Barry Manilow

STRANGE CHANGE TIME MACHINE

Odd 1960s toy set. Inside the Strange Change Time Machine, a domed expansion chamber, you placed a square plastic capsule that heat would transform into a prehistoric creature. After its visit on modern earth has expired, you simply place the monster in a compression chamber, crushing it back into a reusable square shape. Introduced in 1967, this "Lost World" was part of Mattel's Thingmaker line, which included Creepy Crawlers, Fright Factory, and Incredible Edibles.

STRATTEN, DOROTHY

On August 14, 1980, twenty-year-old Dorothy Stratten, *Playboy* Playmate and film starlet, was found shot to death after being raped in her Hollywood home. Her grisly murder by estranged husband Paul Snider, who consequently committed suicide, ranks as one of the saddest tragedies in Hollywood history.

Born on February 28, 1960, good-hearted Stratten was a beautiful teenager from the middle-class suburbs of Vancouver when she was discovered by Snider, a small-time hustler and photographer, while working at a Dairy Queen in the late 1970s. As her much-older boyfriend, Snider persuaded the blonde, buxom Stratten to let him photograph her in the nude and then sent the pictures to *Playboy* magazine. Impressed with what they saw, *Playboy* made the Canadian stunner its August 1979 centerfold, and soon afterward Hugh Hefner selected her as the celebrated Playmate of the Year. The same year, Stratten married Snider in a small Las Vegas wedding.

Evoking memories of a young Marilyn Monroe, Hollywood beckoned, and the budding actress made two movies: *Galaxina* (1980), a low-budget sci-fi (she played a sexy robot), and *They All Laughed* (1981), a romantic comedy. All the attention bestowed on Stratten drove the domineering Snider insanely jealous and possessive, fearing he was losing his wife—and hence his meal ticket. The erratic behavior led Stratten to separate from him and find comfort in the arms of Peter Bogdanovich, director of *They All Laughed*. This sent Snider over the edge and caused him to viciously stalk her and finally kill her. In 1981, Jamie Lee Curtis portrayed her in a TV movie, *Death of a Centerfold: The Dorothy Stratten Story*, and in 1983, Mariel Hemingway played her in a theatrical release, *Star 80*, directed by Bob Fosse. A grief-stricken Bogdanovich wrote the 1984 best-selling book *The Killing of the Unicorn*, which chronicled the life and death of Stratten.

STRAWBERRY SHORTCAKE

Ugh. Probably the second most annoying toy-cartoon character of the 1980s after The Smurfs. Manufactured by Kenner Toys, the doll version of the freckled and bonneted Strawberry Shortcake and her Strawberry Land friends—Apple Dumplin', Blueberry Muffin, Huckleberry Pie, Lemon Meringue, Lime Chiffon, Orange Blossom, Peach Blush, Plum Puddin', Raspberry Tart, Crepe Suzette, Angel Cake, and Butter Cookie—came scented like their fruit or dessert names. Peculiar Purple Pieman from Porcupine Peak—and his cohorts, henchwoman Sour Grapes and Cackles the Crow—were their nemeses. Based on the best-selling line of American Greeting Cards from the late 1970s, the Strawberry dolls and accessories are now becoming sought-after collectibles with adult Gen-Xers.

STRAY CATS

The wild rock trio, formed in New York's Long Island, consisted of former school buddies: lead singer Brian Setzer, string bassist Lee Rocker (real name: Leon Drucker), and drummer Slim Jim Phantom (real name: Jim McDonnell). Heavily tattooed and with towering pompadour hairstyles, the Stray Cats had a taste for hard-edged 1950s-style rockabilly music reminiscent of artists like Eddie Cochran, Gene Vincent, and Johnny Burnette. Hits included "Rock This Town" (1982), "Stray Cat Strut" (1983), and "(She's) Sexy + 17" (1983). After disbanding in 1984, Phantom married actress Britt Ekland, and Setzer went on to front a sixteen-piece big-band orchestra, The Brian Setzer Orchestra, credited with bringing back the swing dance movement in the 1990s.

STREAKING

To streak is to race openly through a public place wearing nothing but your birthday suit (if you were modest, you could wear a ski mask). Nowhere in America was safe from this nude run-for-fun in the mid-1970s. Young people were streaking on college campuses, through crowded cafeterias, unsuspecting dormitories, libraries, and school commencements. Streakers disrupted city traffic as they darted out of cars at stoplights and at busy intersections. Housewives were shocked silly by dashing derrieres and wiggling genitalia inside suburban grocery stores and laundromats. A "Streaker of the House" interrupted Hawaii's state legislative assembly. Singer Ray Stevens capitalized on the pastime with the novelty tune "The Streak" (1974), which streaked straight to the number-one spot ("Don't look, Ethel!").

FYI: ▸ The fad's most famous streak occurred when Robert Opel mooned the world during the 1974 Oscar telecast while David Niven was at the podium, prompting the actor's famous quip about the streaker's "shortcomings."

STRETCH ARMSTRONG

"S-T-R-E-T-C-H him . . . He returns to normal size!" Introduced by Kenner Toys in 1976, a rubbery action doll with blond superhero looks whose arms and legs could be stretched and twisted four times their natural span. His limbs were supposed to return to their original shape, but after prolonged and overextended stretching they never did. Stretch's insides consisted of a mysterious purplish, jelly-like substance. In 1977, the green-skinned nemesis, Stretch Monster, was introduced.

STRIDEX PADS

Anyone who was once a teenager will recall these round cotton pads, presoaked in pimple lotion in a jar, which you used to wipe your face to remove acne-causing facial grime.

STRIPED RUGBY SHIRTS

In the mid-1970s, the kids on *Zoom* sported these long-sleeve knit shirts with horizontal stripes, and so did we.

STROLL

Popular 1950s line dance had boys on one side, girls on the other, with each couple taking turns dancing down the center. Reinvented in the 1970s on TV's *Soul Train* as young black couples showed off their most funky boogie moves.

STUART LITTLE

First published in 1945, E. B. White's beloved children's book about a little mouse born to a family of humans, the Littles. It focuses on the adventures of Stuart as he grows up around the house, explores New York City, and leaves home to follow Margalo, a sweet wren who has flown north. In 1999, the story was made into a live-action film featuring Michael J. Fox as the voice of Stuart Little.

STUDIO 54

"Steve [Rubell] changed forever what people think of as nightlife in New York."
—DESIGNER CALVIN KLEIN

Epicenter of the late-1970s disco dance movement, located on West Fifty-fourth Street in Manhattan, where the beautiful party people—rich and famous (including regulars Bianca Jagger, Halston, Liza Minnelli, and Andy Warhol) or not—mingled, boozed, snorted coke, took part in in bawdy sex acts, and most important—danced, danced, danced. Noted for having beefy doormen who decided which of the patrons waiting eagerly in a line outside could enter through the doors. (It helped to be a high-profile celeb, extremely gorgeous, or outlandishly costumed.) The nightclub's reign ended when the extravagant proprietor, Steve Rubell, was busted by the IRS for tax evasion.

STUFFED ANIMALS

Cuddly faves were those won by your dad or a sweetie at a carnival. But the best were the life-sized ones you could crawl all over and fall asleep on. Well-known stuffed-animal manufacturers are Applause, Dankin, Gund, and Ty.

STUMBO THE GIANT

The giant from Giantland whose well-meaning intentions toward diminutive Tinytown, his new place of residence, usually backfire. Has been a supporting comic segment in *Harvey* comics' *Hot Stuff* series since 1957.

SUB-MARINER

The exotic-looking underwater superhero from Atlantis with the black hair and pointed Spock ears was *Marvel* comics' answer to *DC* comics' Aquaman. "Subbie," alias Prince Namor, made his debut in 1939.

SUDDEN TAN

Coppertone's fake tanning product, which came as a bronzing foam or a bronzing lotion, gave consumers an "instant California look" by temporarily dyeing skin on contact. According to Sudden Tan ads of the late 1970s, the self-tanning product was supposed to make you "a more colorful personality." Unfortunately, the tan you achieved looked unnatural—and didn't do anything for your personality. Blotchy where it wasn't spread evenly, it gave your skin the same color (orange) as someone afflicted with some tropical unknown skin disease.

SUE ANN NIVENS

Aggressive, man-starved TV hostess on WJM-TV's *Happy Homemaker Show* who dishes out household cleaning tips and cooking advice to her viewing audience. Actress Betty White brilliantly played the manipulative Sue Ann on *The Mary Tyler Moore Show*, copping two Best Supporting Actress Emmy Awards in 1975 and 1976. In a turnabout performance, she would later star as sweet but dippy Rose Nylund on *The Golden Girls*, this time scoring a 1986 Emmy for Best Actress in a Comedy Series.

SUE ELLEN EWING

On the prime-time soap *Dallas*, Linda Gray starred as hard-hearted J.R. Ewing's beautiful but troubled alcoholic wife and mother of his son John Ross III.

SUE SNELL

One of Carrie White's classmates at Bates High School who participated in "the shower incident." Remorseful, she convinces her football hero boyfriend, Tommy Ross, to take Carrie to the senior prom. Bad move, Sue! Played by clear-eyed, curly-haired Amy Irving in the 1976 film version of Stephen King's novel *Carrie*.

SUGAR BEAR

Wearing a trademark blue turtleneck sweater, hipster Sugar Bear premiered in 1963 as the animated spokes-bear for Super Sugar Crisp, a honey-flavored puffed-wheat cereal. With a smooth banter sounding a lot like Bing Crosby, Sugar Bear would croon "Can't get enough of that Super Sugar Crisp" while searching for the cereal in his commercials. Crazy adversary Granny Goodwitch tried to keep Sugar Bear away from the sugar stuff he loved so much.

The cereal, today known as Golden Crisp, was the one offering The Archies record cutouts on the back of the box in 1969. These cardboard discs featured swingin' tunes from their Saturday-morning cartoon, like "Jingle Jangle" and "Bang Shang-a-Lang." In 1974, Sugar Bear copied The Archies by forming his own groovy band, The Sugar Bears, with drummer Shoobee Bear, guitarist Doobee Bear, and girl tambourine-player Honey Bear. Similar to the teens from Riverdale, the singing bear quartet offered actual records performed by anonymous studio musicians that could be cut out from the back of the Super Sugar Crisp box.

SUGAR KANE
In *Beach Blanket Bingo* (1965), this gorgeous blonde singer (played by Linda "Big Valley" Evans) parachutes into the Malibu surf and is rescued by Frankie Avalon and his surfing buddies, who are unaware that it's actually a publicity stunt to promote her latest record. Also, the name of Marilyn Monroe's luscious ukulele player in *Some Like It Hot*.

"SUGAR, SUGAR"
The Archies scored a number-one smash in 1969 with this sugary-sweet, candy-coated song about a guy (Archie?) wanting his "Sugar, Sugar" (Betty?), "Honey, Honey" (Veronica?), "Candy Girl" (Betty? Veronica?). Based on the cartoon gang, The Archies on vinyl were actually an anonymous studio group created by producer Don Kirshner, consisting of lead singer Ron Dante, along with Toni Wine, Andy Kim, and Tony Passalacqua. On the Saturday-morning cartoon, The Archies featured Archie Andrews on guitar and lead vocals, Reggie Mantle on bass guitar, Jughead Jones on drums, Veronica Lodge on keyboards, Betty Cooper doing her thing on the tambourine, and Hot Dog as the band's mascot. Written by Jeff Barry and Andy Kim, "Sugar, Sugar" represented the best of the bubblegum music genre.

SUICIDE BARS
Handlebars found on the hi-rise bicycles of the late 1960s and early 1970s that were characterized by an extended forward U-shape with the handle grips pulled down at the top.

SULU
First name: Hikaru. Loyal and hardworking Japanese helm officer of the starship Enterprise, portrayed by George Takei in the *Star Trek* sci-fi series.

SUMMER, DONNA
Hailed as the "Queen of Disco," Summer was the most successful recording artist to emerge from the 1970s disco era. Before her reign ended, she had accumulated more than twenty-four gold and platinum records and four Grammy awards. Born in Boston on New Year's Eve of 1948, Summer started her career singing gospel music, then traveled to Europe, where she performed musical stage productions of *Hair* and *Godspell*. While in Germany, she recorded the oft-banned "Love to Love You Baby" (1975), a sixteen-minute orgasmic extravaganza, which made the Top Ten in America, selling more than a million copies.

Summer's recording career has been spectacular, gifted with many Top Forty disco hits (all classics), including "I Feel Love" (1977), "MacArthur Park" (1978), "Heaven Knows" (1979), "Hot Stuff" (1979), "Bad Girls" (1979), "Dim All the Lights" (1979), "On the Radio" (1980), "The Wanderer" (1980), "She Works Hard for the Money" (1983), and the showy duet with Babs Streisand, "No More Tears (Enough Is Enough)" (1979). In 1978, Summer starred in the disco-oriented movie *Thank God It's Friday*, in which she warbled the Oscar-winning song "Last Dance." In the 1980s, she rejected her disco-diva lifestyle after becoming a "born-again" Christian.

"SUMMER NIGHTS"
"Tell me more, tell me more. . . ." Witty ditty sung as a duet by John Travolta and Olivia Newton-John in the movie musical *Grease* (1978). A Top Ten recording hit, it featured the two sweethearts telling school chums their own version of a summer beach date: hers, a sweet romance ("We went strolling, drank lemonade"); his, a horny encounter ("We made out under the dock"). It has become one of today's most overdone karaoke numbers.

SUNDRESS
Colorful warm-weather dress made of soft cotton and marked by ribbon-style straps and a smocked bodice. We'll have to give pretty pop singer Olivia Newton-John credit for making this the trendy dress of the mid-1970s.

"SUNGLASSES AT NIGHT"
This song contributed to one of the dumbest clothing fads of the 1980s (and, believe me, there were many)—wearing sunglasses at night! It was common to see young people wearing sleek sunglasses (Ray-Bans, just like Tom Cruise, if you were cool) while posing in dark nightclubs or walking around happenin' urban hot spots during the evening hours. Thinking they looked way awesome, these foolish folks only came off appearing to be trying too hard. Unfortunately, they missed out on a lot of

fun because they couldn't see anything. "Sunglasses at Night" was a Top Ten hit for Canadian-born Corey Hart in 1984.

SUN-IN

"Sun-In and sunlight, and you'll be glowing tonight." Sun-In is an instant hair lightener used to achieve natural-looking summer highlights. Heat activated (basically hydrogen peroxide), users often apply the product while tanning in the hot sun, and if there isn't any sunshine, a heated hair dryer at home does the trick. Sun-In comes in a handy spray pump, making it easy to use for a quick spritz (many people used it as frequently as hair spray). The problem with Sun-In is that it often, if not always, colors your hair an unsightly brassy orange (especially brunettes) and gives it a dried-out, strawlike feel, and anyone who used it never admitted that ("It's natural, the sun did it"). Beware: If combined with Coppertone's self-tanning Sudden Tan or QT (for Quick Tan) for skin, users could end up looking like an orange version of a Willy Wonka Oompa Lompa. "Here comes the sun."

SUN 'N FUN BUGGY

Malibu Barbie and her suntanned friends drove this cute daisy-decaled dune buggy on the sandy shores of the California beaches.

SUNSHINE

A three-hankie tearjerker based on the true life story of Kate Hayden, a twenty-year-old wife and mother dying of bone cancer who tape-recorded a journal of her last days alive. Played by Cristina Raines in this 1973 TV movie, Kate was a free-spirited idealist residing in a cabin in the woods with struggling musician husband Sam (Cliff De Young) and a young daughter from a previous marriage, Jill (Robin Bush). The tele-film's success led to a short-lived *Sunshine* TV series on NBC in 1975, starring De Young and Elizabeth Cheshire as Jill, and a 1977 sequel, *Sunshine Christmas*. John Denver scored a number-one hit with the movie's theme "Sunshine on My Shoulders" in 1974 (it was Kate's favorite song).

SUNSHINE FAMILY

"Doing things together and with you!" These were the nature-loving, granola-eating, posthippie doll family of the 1970s. Introduced by Mattel in 1973, the earthy trio consisted of cute brunet father Steve, pretty, blonde mother Stephie, and adorable baby daughter Sweets. The Sunshine Family's clothing reflected the latest in 1970s fashions: prairie dresses and earth sandals for mom, turtlenecks and bells for dad, and overall jumpers for Sweets. The family resided in a four-room house decorated in earth-tone colors: burnt orange, avocado green, mustard yellow, and rusty brown. Other play accessories included The Sunshine Family Watch 'em Grow Greenhouse, complete with real growing bean seeds; The Sunshine Family Surrey Cycle, built for three; The Sunshine Family Van, with Piggyback Shack for an outing at the country fair; The Sunshine Family Craft Store; and The Sunshine Family Farm. In 1977, the threesome became a foursome when a baby boy was introduced (Sweets was now a toddler). Gray-haired Grandpa and Grandma Sunshine were added in 1976.

SUPER BALL

"The ball with the incredible super-high bounce!" Wham-O, producers of the Hula-Hoop and the Frisbee, introduced this high-bouncing ball in 1965. Invented by chemist Norman Stingley, it's a hard rubber (Zectron) black ball with amazing elasticity and strength. According to Wham-O, the Super Ball allegedly had 50,000 pounds of compressed energy with 92 percent resiliency. It could bounce on for about a minute when dropped from a short height; when released from shoulder level, it leaped nearly all the way back; and when thrown down hard, it could soar over a building. By 1966, the Super Ball craze was at its peak, selling more than three million balls a year. One disadvantage of the mighty ball: It wasn't easy to catch, and its vigor meant you had to duck or be struck—leaving many kids with black eyes and painful body welts.

SUPER CHARGER

Introduced in 1969, this Hot Wheels accessory was a pit-stop/tune-up shop that attached over the orange-colored track and was capable of giving a racing car an amazing power boost as it zoomed through.

SUPER CHICKEN

This supporting segment on *George of the Jungle* told the animated tale of Henry Cabot Henhouse II, an aristocratic fowl who transforms into crime-fighting Super Chicken, a caped and masked superhero, after swigging his famed Super Sauce.

SUPER ELASTIC BUBBLE PLASTIC

Manufactured by Wham-O, this had not only the best name of any toy item of the early 1970s but also the coolest "got-to-have-it" TV ads, featuring kids blowing gigantic, psychedelic-hued bubbles that hovered gloriously in the sky. After squeezing a small amount of the plastic-like goo out of a tube, you rolled it into a ball, placed it at the end of a little straw, and blew up these lightweight, bigger-than-big bubbles. I remember not being able to make it work—my fingers just ended up sticky— and giving up in frustration. (It did work, though, because my brother could always make a pretty cool bubble, which inevitably shriveled up into a hard wad a few days later.) Super Elastic Bubble Plastic's odor was unique, sort of like model-airplane glue. I wonder how many kids unintentionally got stoned out of their minds, and how many freakers purposely tried to get high from its smell.

SUPERFRIENDS

A long-running Hanna-Barbera cartoon show depicting the adventures of the Justice League of America, whose members included various superheroes based on the *DC* comic series of the same name: Superman, Aquaman, Wonder Woman, Green Lantern, Flash, and Batman and Robin. Assisting them in crime fighting were young superhero hopefuls Marvin and Wendy, and pooch Wonder Dog, forming the Junior Justice League. In the fall of 1977, *SuperFriends* dropped Marvin, Wendy, and Wonder Dog and added the Wonder Twins, Zan and Jayna, along with sidekick monkey Gleek. The Twins were more developed in maturity and in strength than Marvin and Wendy and could morph into a powerful form or shape by touching each other's rings and shouting, "Wonder Twin powers, activate!" The wicked Legion of Doom was the JLA's archvillain. The program aired on Saturday mornings from 1973 to 1986 with various titles: *SuperFriends*, *The All-New SuperFriends Hour*, *Challenge of the SuperFriends*, and *The World's Greatest SuperFriends*.

FYI: ▸ *The Mary Tyler Moore Show*'s Ted Knight was the narrator of *SuperFriends*.

SUPERFLY

Handsome Ron O'Neal stars as Priest, the ultracool, ultrastudly Harlem cocaine dealer out to score one more big deal before calling it quits. This 1972 film was blaxploitation at its best. Followed by two lesser sequels, *Superfly T.N.T.* (1973) and *The Return of Superfly* (1990). Curtis Mayfield, formerly of The Impressions, earned a gold disc for the Superfly theme song, "Freddie's Dead."

SUPERGIRL

Superman's younger cousin, Kara Zor-El, who likewise came to earth from the exploding planet of Krypton. Raised at the Midvale Orphanage in Illinois, the buxom blonde crime-fighter wearing a blue-and-red bodysuit with red cape adopted the alter ego of Linda Lee. She made her debut in *DC's Action Comics* in May 1959.

SUPER JOCK

Action game introduced by Schaper in 1975 that had young athletes thumping the top of the head of an eleven-inch-high plastic jock, which allowed him to kick a football into a field goal, shoot a puck past the goalie, launch a basketball into a hoop, and smack a baseball for a home run.

SUPERMAN

"Look! Up in the sky! It's a bird! It's a plane! It's . . . Superman!" This champion of truth, justice, and the American way is faster than a speeding bullet, more powerful than a locomotive, and able to leap tall buildings in a single bound. He can bend steel with his bare hands, freeze objects with his breath, push whole planets together, see with x-ray vision—and he has super hearing.

Created by two seventeen-year-olds from Ohio, Jerry Siegel and Joe Shuster, Superman made his debut in *DC* comics' *Action Comics* number 1 in 1938. Scientist Jor-El and mother Lara sent their baby son, Kal-El, to earth on a rocket ship from the exploding planet of Krypton. The alien orphan is adopted and raised by an elderly farm couple, Jonathan and Martha Kent, who name him Clark, in the rural community of Smallville, Kansas.

As an adult, the Man of Steel (his superpowers come from earth's yellow sun) moves to the big city of Metropolis, where he disguises himself as a mild-mannered reporter at the *Daily Planet* newspaper. There he works with diligent newshound Lois Lane, cub photographer Jimmy Olsen, and grouchy editor Perry White. When trouble is around, Clark Kent secretly dashes into a nearby phone booth and emerges as the vigorous crime-fighting Superman, flying around in a skintight bodysuit with a large "S" on the chest, boots, and a red cape. His arch-nemesis is the evil Lex Luthor, who diminishes Superman's power with Kryptonite, green rock fragments from his long-dead home.

Over the years, Superman's comic-book legacy has been superpowerful. He has inspired numerous champions of virtue that have secret identities, including Batman, Spider-Man, and Wonder Woman, and spawned other Kryptonian superheroes, such as Supergirl, Superboy, Superhorse, and a Superdog named Krypto. He has appeared in three successful TV series: *The Adventures of Superman* (1952–57), starring George Reeves (who proved not so invincible after dying of an apparent suicide in 1959), *Lois and Clark: The New Adventures of Superman* (1993–97), starring Dean Cain; and *Smallville* (2001–), starring Tom Welling; two Saturday-morning cartoons: *The New Adventures of Superman* (1966–70) and *SuperFriends* (1973–86); four state-of-the-art blockbuster films, starring Christopher Reeve; and hundreds of merchandise items, like toys, lunch boxes, clothing, and bed sheets. "This is a job for Superman!"

SUPERMODELS

"Don't hate me because I'm beautiful."
—KELLY LEBROCK, BEAUTIFUL SUPERMODEL

Not your ordinary, run-of-the-mill fashion models, but modern-day goddesses, blessed with good genes and even better luck whose million-dollar faces commanded million-dollar salaries. These supermodels graced the covers of such magazines as *Vogue, Harper's Bazaar, Elle, Glamour,* and *Cosmopolitan,* which featured them on the inside pages wearing high fashion from New York, London, Paris, and Milan. Their tall, thin, storklike frames sashayed down catwalks adorned with clothing designed by such greats as Valentino, Chanel, Yves Saint Laurent, Perry Ellis, Calvin Klein, Ralph Lauren, and Versace. As spokes-models, their print and TV ads stirred up endless fantasies and persuaded consumers to purchase products they didn't necessarily need yet felt that by owning them they could be in the same league as a supermodel. Many of these supermodels were so famous they didn't even need last names: Linda, Naomi, Christy, Cindy, Claudia, Cheryl, and Twiggy. In 1994, statuesque drag queen RuPaul sang a tribute to these cover girls with the song "Supermodel (You Better Work)."

FYI: ▸ Supermodels have a fondness for rockers and often marry them. Check out these cover girl / rock star combos: Patti Boyd and George Harrison, Jerry Hall and Mick Jagger, Patti Hansen and Keith Richards, Christie Brinkley and Billy Joel, Paulina Porizkova and Ric Ocasek, Rachel Hunter and Rod Stewart, Elaine Irwin and John Cougar Mellencamp, and Iman and David Bowie.

SUPER MARIO

Mario, along with brother Luigi, a plumber from Brooklyn, finds himself flushed through a Warp Zone to the exciting Mushroom Kingdom, where he searches for and rescues (hopefully) the kidnapped Princess Peach Toadstool from the menacing dragon-esque King Bowser Koopa and his minions. First appearing as a support for Nintendo's Donkey Kong in 1981, Super Mario was bestowed with his own wildly popular multiple-world arcade game in 1983. Ever since, he has gone on to be the Japanese-based company's biggest star, appearing in more than a dozen home video games (including Super Mario Land, Super Mario World, and Yoshi's Island) for Game Boy, Super Nintendo, and Nintendo 64, as well as starring in a Saturday-morning cartoon (1989) and a feature film (1993).

FYI: ▸ In a 1991 poll, it was found that more children could recognize a picture of Super Mario than Mickey Mouse!

SUPER RALLY CASE

Classic plastic carrying case, shaped like a racing wheel with a red stripe, that stored up to twenty-four of Mattel's Hot Wheels cars.

SUPER SOAKERS
"Wetter is Better!" Forget those old, leaky plastic water pistols that squirt water like a baby boy peeing freely. These marvels of modern toy weaponry are ideal for rather painful backyard ambush attacks on pesky siblings. Brightly colored Super Soakers are large, high-powered water guns (more like rifles) meant to hold a lot of water so you don't have to refill as often (the water supply could last up to an hour). They are capable of propelling water up to great distances: At fifty feet or more you can stand across the street and soak your neighborhood foe like the wet rat he really is. A lot of guys enjoy spraying water on an assembly of young women at recreational parks. (Do wet T-shirts on ample breasts come to mind?)

"SUPERSTAR"
Undeniably, this is the epitome of Karen Carpenter's emotionally haunting singing style and rich contralto voice. In the years following her untimely death, it has become the song frequently identified with her. Written by Leon Russell and Bonnie Bramlett, "Superstar" is a melancholy ballad about a young groupie's sorrow over the lost love of a rock star who once passed through her life. Every downhearted soul who ever loved an elusive music idol related strongly when Karen wailed the opening lines, "Long ago, and oh, so far away / I fell in love with you, before the second show." In September 1971, "Superstar" became The Carpenters' fifth Top Ten single, selling a million records in a mere eight weeks.

SUPERSTAR BARBIE
"She's got SuperStar sparkle!" Barbie's dazzling SuperStar era began in 1977 when Mattel gave the fashion doll a makeover, based loosely on the appearance of golden girl Farrah Fawcett-Majors and consisting of a wide, dimpled smile, fluffy sunstreaked blonde hair, and permanently bent arms (this look remained well into the 1990s). Barbie was now one of the "beautiful people," a glamorous SuperStar living in the SuperStar land of sunshine, palm trees, and earthquakes (Southern California). She drove the SuperVette, a hot-pink Corvette convertible, to happenin' Hollywood parties and movie premieres, escorted by blond SuperStar Ken ("Barbie Doll's boyfriend with the movie-star look!"), whose body was more muscular than ever and who resembled Robert Redford. SuperStar Barbie's chic clothing (slinky, glittery gowns, frilly boas, and strappy shoes) symbolized the glamorous disco scene. A giant eighteen-inch version of the doll, called SuperSize Barbie, was also available.

SUPERSTAR: THE KAREN CARPENTER STORY
Director Todd Hayne's notorious 1990 film in which Barbie dolls are used to dramatize the crystalline-voiced pop singer's tragic death. It was withdrawn from theaters because of its illegal use of The Carpenters' music and of Mattel's Barbie, so the only way to view it is via bootlegged videotape copies.

SUPREMES
Florence Ballard. Diana Ross. Mary Wilson. Three attractive girls from Detroit's poverty-stricken Brewster Projects who became the most popular girl group of all time and the most successful American recording act of the 1960s. As teenagers, the girls were introduced to Berry Gordy, president of Motown Records, who carefully groomed and trained them as an R&B vocal trio called The Primettes, later changed to The Supremes. In 1964, The Supremes, featuring nightclub-esque dance moves and Diana Ross's incomparable voice, hit it big with the infectious song "Where Did Our Love Go." It went to the top of the pop charts, leading the way for ten more number-ones: "Baby Love" (1964), "Come See About Me" (1964), "Stop! In the Name of Love" (1965), "Back in My Arms Again" (1965), "I Hear a Symphony" (1965), "You Can't Hurry Love" (1966), "You Keep Me Hangin' On" (1966), "Love Is Here and Now You're Gone" (1967), "The Happening" (1967), and "Love Child" (1968).

By the end of the 1960s, a darkness fell over the sparkle after Gordy, showing obvious favoritism, made the overtly ambitious Ross frontwoman of the group and renamed them Diana Ross and The Supremes. This enraged the other girls, especially Ballard (said to be the true talent behind The Supremes), who in 1967 was dismissed from the group for drinking and being unreliable by not showing up for concerts. She was replaced by Cindy Birdsong, and, in 1969, Jean Terrell took over for Ross, who had left to start a solo career with

"Ain't No Mountain High Enough." Brokenhearted, Ballard died on welfare in the Brewster Projects in 1976. The phenomenal story of The Supremes inspired a movie, *Sparkle* (1976), and a Broadway show, *Dreamgirls.*

FYI: ▸ "Where Did Our Love Go" (1964) earned The Supremes a place in the record books by being the first U.S. number one by an all-female act, and the last until The Bangles' "Eternal Flame" (1989).

SURFING

> "If everybody had an ocean
> across the U.S.A., then everybody'd
> be surfin' like Californi-ay. . . . "
>
> —THE BEACH BOYS

Cowabunga! Awesome American pastime, associated with Southern California, that's extremely popular with young people (mostly male) who live near a beach with large, rolling breakers. The sport involves riding an incoming ocean wave to shore ("hot-dogging") by standing on a lightweight, polyurethane-foam surfboard without getting toppled off (a.k.a. "wiping out"). Fueled by the music of The Beach Boys and the movie *Endless Summer* (1966), surfing became a national fad in the 1960s. Today, it has evolved into a million-dollar enterprise with a pro circuit that has dozens of international competitions.

For nonsurfing hodads, here are ten boss surfing movies, including *Endless Summer* and its 1994 sequel, worth checking out:

Beach Blanket Bingo (1965)
Big Wednesday (1978)
Blue Crush (2002)
Endless Summer (1966)
Endless Summer II (1994)
Gidget (1959)
North Shore (1987)
Point Break (1991)
Red Surf (1990)
Ride the Wild Surf (1964)

FYI: ▸ Although associated with modern Californians, surfing is actually an ancient Hawaiian custom, first reported by British explorer Captain James Cook in 1771.

SURVIVAL OF DANA

Once again a TV movie exploited the dysfunctional lifestyle of the 1970s teenager. In this one, blue-eyed blonde Melissa Sue Anderson plays Dana Lee, a pretty high school girl from Fargo, North Dakota, who moves to Los Angeles and—to the dismay of her mother (Marion Ross of *Happy Days*)—falls in with the wrong crowd. The 1979 drama made a lame effort to explain why young people raised with values in an affluent society turn to mindless violence and senseless destruction (maybe they're just bored).

SURVIVOR

> "I've got the million-dollar check
> written in my name."
>
> —*SURVIVOR* WINNER RICHARD HATCH ON DAY 1

"Outwit. Outplay. Outlast." Hosted by handsome Jeff Probst, CBS-TV's groundbreaking reality game series has sixteen people, placed in a remote location on the other side of the world, playing to survive harsh terrain, extreme weather conditions, unrelenting hunger, and each other. The contestants consist of eight men and eight women from all walks of American life, many with conflicting personalities (for example, a gay corporate trainer, a retired Navy Seal, a mousy homemaker, a brash truck driver, a yuppie neurologist, and a twentysomething student).

On Day 1 of *Survivor*, the castaways arrive at a deserted location (an island, desert, or jungle), with little more than the clothes on their backs, where they are split into two opposing teams (tribes). Receiving a sack of rice and hardly anything else, each tribe immediately starts building camp shelters while rounding up whatever natural food source they can find, such as fish, snails, and edible vegetation. Right away, alliances begin and personalities clash—for example, some are know-it-alls or bossy or ignorant or simply lazy, and so on. (A hidden camera crew captures every moment.)

On each episode (which spans three days on actual location), the tribes compete against one another in a Reward Challenge, with the winners receiving such much-needed items as blankets, cooking utensils, luxury food items, grooming aids, or getaway day trips. At episode's end, the tribes compete in the Immunity Challenge, in which physical endurance, mental awareness, and an iron stomach are all that are required to win showdowns involving strenuous races, mazes, puzzles, and live-beetle-larva-eating. The team losing the Immunity Challenge is sent to the dreaded Tribal Council, where they have to strategically vote a member off the show (symbolized by Probst extinguishing the contestant's personal torch). This plays out every week until the numbers are reduced to ten contestants. At this point the tribes merge into one. Alliances are broken and strategies change as each contestant scrambles to play for himself, winning individual Reward Challenges and, more important than ever, the Immunity Challenge, in which the winner receives the coveted Immunity Idol (meaning he can't be voted out at the next Tribal Council).

By Day 39, the ten have been narrowed down to two, and the cast-out players now become a jury of peers. The jury—many angry about being stabbed in the back by those they once thought of as allies—plays a key role at the show's Tribal Council finale. After quizzing and berating the final pair ("If you were lying there, dying of thirst, I would not give you a drink of water . . . "), they get to vote. However, it's a different kind of vote. They aren't voting someone off, they're voting for the player who deserves the title of "Survivor," the person who played the game best, whether by honesty and hard work or by lies and manipulation. The winner receives one million dollars.

Since airing its very first episode from the tropical island of Pulau Tiga (Borneo) in the South China Sea, *Survivor* has survived consistently high ratings and huge fanfare. It paved the way for other reality-based programs starring nonactors competing in elimination challenges, like *The Amazing Race*, *Big Brother*, *The Mole*, *Fear Factor*, and *The Apprentice*.

FYI: ▸ *Survivor* is based on the Swedish game show *Operation Robinson*.

SUZY HOMEMAKER

Introduced by Topper Toys in 1966, a miniature line of actual working household appliances that were highly desired by little housewives-to-be. Styled in modern colors (lots of turquoise and chrome) and marked by the symbol of a ponytailed girl profile (Suzy Homemaker?), these battery-operated and electrical gadgets included a Budget Blender, Deluxe Grill, Dishwasher-Sink, Hair Dryer, High Speed Mixer, Ice Cream Maker, Ice Delight Maker, Jet Spray Iron, Juicer, Popcorn Popper, Refrigerator, Super Oven, Soda Fountain, Taffy Puller, and Washing Machine. There was also a Suzy Homemaker doll to help you with all those laborious chores. Went out of vogue in the early 1970s, when homemaking came to be looked down on by women's libbers.

SWANSON TV DINNERS

"The next best thing to your good cooking." Introduced in 1954 by Swanson Frozen Foods of Omaha, Nebraska, these complete meals—served in partitioned aluminum trays—changed the way Americans ate dinner. In the past, a busy mother spent all day slaving over a hot stove trying to whip up a well-balanced meal for her brood. But in these modern times, she could easily take the frozen TV dinners out of a freezer, slip them out of their cardboard boxes, and put them in the oven.

After cooking for forty-five minutes, the hot meal, complete with meat and vegetables, was served to the family, usually on fold-up TV trays in the living room so everyone could eat while viewing favorite TV shows. Afterward, there were no dirty dishes to clean because you simply threw away the aluminum trays. The great thing for mom was the extra free time she now had for herself. She could go to bridge club with the other mothers, do a little evening shopping, or just sit around with dad and the kids and catch up on the day's events.

Some interesting tidbits about Swanson TV dinners:

- The first frozen dinner consisted of turkey and stuffing, mashed potatoes and gravy, and peas served in a three-compartment aluminum tray; later, roast beef, Salisbury steak (the quintessential frozen meat), meatloaf, chopped sirloin, ham with raisin sauce, fried chicken, fish and chips, and Mexican meals would be available.
- In the 1960s, a fourth compartment was added for dessert—brownies, apple or cherry cobbler, or chocolate pudding—making the TV dinner a complete meal. During this convenience-crazed

decade, the frozen dinner flourished, and millions were sold each year.

- In 1973, the Hungry Man dinners, offering jumbo portions, were introduced for those with big, big appetites.
- By the beginning of the 1980s, TV dinners had become associated with lowbrow, trailer-park living.
- The year 1982 saw the introduction of Le Menu, a "designer dinner" line created to appeal to upscale yuppies.
- The aluminum trays were discontinued in 1987 in favor of the plastic microwaveable ones, making this great convenience food even more convenient.

FYI: ▸ Another classic food by Swanson is the frozen potpie, introduced in 1951.

SWATCH WATCHES

First manufactured in 1983, these low-priced timepieces with hundreds of fun, colorful designs have become the top-selling watches in the world. Swatch fanatics would wear two or three at one time.

SWEATHOGS

> "A sweathog is somebody who perspires a lot and acts like a pig."
> —JOHN TRAVOLTA

A rambunctious gang of underachieving delinquents who attend James Buchanan High in Brooklyn in the 1970s sitcom *Welcome Back, Kotter.* Kept away from the rest of the student body in a remedial classroom and instructed by Mr. Gabriel Kotter (himself once a Sweathog at Buchanan), its core members included dumb dreamboat Vinnie Barbarino, excusable Juan Epstein, cool Freddie "Boom Boom" Washington, and geeky Arnold Horshack.

SWEDISH BIKINI TEAM

A bevy of beautiful, blonde, big-boobed, bikinied bimbos (try saying that when you're drunk) who bring relief to males dying of thirst and boredom in the form of Old Milwaukee Beer on a series of popular TV commercials airing in the early 1990s.

SWEENEY SISTERS

The big-haired singing siblings, Liz (Nora Dunn) and Candy (Jan Hooks), played the motel-lounge circuit and did a scat-laden act consisting only of medleys, beginning with "Everything's Coming Up Roses" and ending with their trademark tune, "The Trolley Song." (I wonder if they ever double-billed with Nick the Lounge Singer.) This was a favorite recurring sketch on NBC's *Saturday Night Live* during the late 1980s.

SWEE'PEA

"Glop!" Popeye's adopted infant who arrived one day in a box left outside his door. This infant from the *Popeye* cartoons was baptized in a pot of spinach.

SWEET POLLY PUREBRED

"Oh where, oh where has my Underdog gone? Oh where, oh where can he be?" When the blonde canine investigative TV reporter became a damsel in distress, superhero boyfriend Underdog would come and save the day. Norma McMillan voiced Sweet Polly in the *Underdog* cartoon show of the 1960s.

SWEET VALLEY HIGH

Teenage book series written by the ever-prolific Francine Pascal about a set of identical twins named Elizabeth and Jessica Wakefield. Set in the fictitious Southern California town of Sweet Valley, the sixteen-year-old blondes are popular, smart, and beautiful. However, that's where the similarity stops. Though would-be journalist Elizabeth is friendly and sincere, cheerleader Jessica is snobbish and scheming. The twins' soap-opera-like adventures center on school, family, friends, boys, vacations, and the occasional kidnapping or two.

Only one week after the first *Sweet Valley High* paperback, "Double Love," was published in 1984, it rocketed to the number-one spot in *Publisher's Weekly*. Since then, more than 140 *Sweet Valley High* books have been written, selling more than 100 million copies. Its popularity led to a sequel series (*Sweet Valley University*), two prequel series (*Sweet Valley Kids* and *Sweet Valley Twins*), and a TV show starring real-life twins Brittany and Cynthia Daniels as Jessica and Elizabeth. Also inspired competitors, notably Christopher Pike's *Cheerleaders* and Ann M. Martin's *Baby-Sitters Club*.

SWIM

"Beach Blanket Bingo!" Favorite 1960s dance, especially among the surfing crowd, in which you did the Twist with your lower body while doing a variety of swimming and diving motions with hands and arms. "Hold your nose and jump in!"

SWINGY

"Because girls would love a friend to dance with, Mattel makes Swingy." This eighteen-inch-tall battery-operated doll, introduced in 1969, was gifted with the ability to be a swingin' go-go dancer. Turn Swingy on, and the blonde with the flip hairdo and mod minidress would swing her arms, shake her body back and forth, turn her head, and take swingin' steps as if dancing. She came with her very own groovy pop record too. Swingy is one of many well-remembered action dolls of the era.

SWISS FAMILY ROBINSON

Adapted from the classic children's story by Johann Wyss, a delightful Disney film about a nineteenth-century Swiss family en route to New Guinea who are shipwrecked on an uncharted tropical isle. Remaining optimistic, the Robinsons build an idyllic life, living in a huge tree house while successfully fighting off a band of raiding pirates. The cast includes John Mills (Hayley's pop) as inventive Father, Dorothy McGuire as loving Mother, James MacArthur as oldest son Fritz, Tommy Kirk as scholarly son Ernst, Kevin Corcoran as youngest son Francis, and Janet Munro as the sea captain's granddaughter Roberta. Directed by Ken Annakin, the 1960 adventure was filmed on the lush Caribbean island of Tobago. A favorite scene is the wild animal race in which the whole family participates, riding ostriches, zebras, and elephants. (Nobody questions why these native African creatures are living on an island in the Tropics.)

FYI: ▸ Am I the only child of the 1960s out there who finds it sad that the Swiss Family Robinson Tree House located in Adventureland at Disneyland, in which guests could climb and explore, has now been converted into Tarzan's Tree House?

SWISS MISS

"Yo-de-lay-hee-hoo!" Dressed in a blue jumper with white apron and wearing blonde pigtails, the yodeling dairy maid from the Swiss Alps has been the sweet spokesperson for Swiss Miss Hot Chocolate since 1960.

SYLVERS

Formed in the wake of successful musical family acts of the 1970s, such as The Jackson 5 and The Osmonds, the group from Memphis consisted of ten siblings: Olympia, Leon, Charmaine, James, Edmund, Ricky, Angie, Pat, Jonathan, and youngest member Foster, the lead vocalist and lead heartthrob. Hits included the exhilarating chart-topper "Boogie Fever" (1976), along with "Hot Line" (1976) and "High School Dance" (1977). The Sylvers are noteworthy for sporting the most enormous Afros of the era.

SYLVESTER SNEEKLY

A scheming lawyer—secretly the cloaked and masked Hooded Claw—who was out to destroy his trusting client Penelope Pitstop, a beautiful race car driver, because he was next in line to inherit her vast fortune. Fiendish Sneekly's incompetent accomplices were the Bully Brothers. Uncredited, comedian Paul Lynde performed the voice of Sylvester Sneekly on *The Perils of Penelope Pitstop* cartoon show.

SYLVESTER THE PUSSYCAT AND TWEETY PIE

Cartoon's most famous cat-and-bird twosome. The always-famished black feline made his debut, sans Tweety, in "Life with Feathers" in 1945, exasperatedly spluttering the phrase "Sufferin' succotash!" The big-eyed, baby-talking yellow canary first appeared in the Warner Bros. short "A Tale of Two Kitties" in 1942, in which he jabbered the phrase "I tawt I taw a puddytat!" Their fateful union occurred in 1947's "Tweety Pie." The pair's on-going tussle involved Sylvester trying his darnedest to devour the bird and Tweety cleverly dodging the "bad old puddytat." They were both owned by gentle Granny (gentle, yes, unless you're trying to hurt her sweet Tweety bird).

FYI: ▸ Tweety Pie originally had pink feathers, but after censors barked that he looked naked, he became a yellow canary.

qrstu

TABITHA STEPHENS
On January 13, 1966, the question on everybody's mind was "Will she be a witch or a mortal?" when Samantha and Darrin Stephens gave birth to their first child on the hit sitcom *Bewitched*. Played by fraternal twins Erin and Diane Murphy (Erin eventually played her full time), Tabitha inherited not only her mother's blonde hair but also her magical powers (unlike mom, she had to use her finger to wiggle her nose). The Stephenses later had a son named Adam (born October 16, 1969) who was brunet and mortal, like dad. From 1977 to 1978, Lisa Hartman played the little sprite as a grown-up on a spin-off series titled simply *Tabitha.*

FYI: ▸ Jodie Foster and Helen Hunt were both up for the role of Tabitha Stephens.

TABU
Not the cheap-smelling perfume by Dana, but an ancient tiki idol discovered by Bobby Brady on his family's vacation to Hawaii. Thought to be symbol of "good luck" at first, Tabu is later believed to bestow "bad luck" after the Bradys are plagued by a series of mishaps (for instance, Greg almost drowns while surfing, and a tarantula crawls on Peter). To rid themselves of the curse, the Brady boys return the idol to an ancient Hawaiian burial cave. Seen in a three-part episode of *The Brady Bunch* in 1972 ("Hawaii Bound," "Pass the Tabu," and "The Tiki Caves").

TACO BELL
Make a run for the border (or at least a bathroom) with America's most famous Mexican fast-food chain, first established by Glen Bell in Downey, California, in 1962. The mission-style restaurants' 1990s advertising icon was the Taco Bell Chihuahua (actually a female, named Gidget) who used the catchphrase "Yo quiero Taco Bell" ("I want Taco Bell"). Also known as Taco Hell and Taco Smell.

"TAKE ON ME"
A 1985 chart-topping, synthesizer-driven song by a-ha, a pop trio from Norway famous for having one of the best-loved videos of MTV's first decade. Directed by Steve Barron, the groundbreaking clip mixed live-action with animation as a young woman entered the pages of an action comic book and found true love with its animated hero—a-ha's deliciously cute lead singer, Morten Harket. It won a then-record six awards at the 1986 MTV Video Music Awards: Best New Artist, Best Direction, Best

Concept, Best Special Effects, Most Experimental, and Viewer's Choice.

TALES FROM THE CRYPT

"Greeting fright fans. . . ." Premiering on HBO in 1989, this TV anthology series featured bone-chilling tales with star-studded casts based on Al Feldstein's gloriously gruesome EC horror comic books of the 1950s. Hosting the show was the Crypt Keeper, a creepy skeleton puppet whose tongue was placed firmly in cheek (voiced by comedian John Kassir). Some of the stars seen in *Tales'* six-season run included Demi Moore, Brad Pitt, Martin Sheen, Whoopi Goldberg, Dan Aykroyd, Bobcat Goldthwait, Mariel Hemingway, Kyle MacLachlan, Teri Garr, and Christopher Reeve.

TALLAHATCHIE BRIDGE

Billy Joe McAllister's fatal suicide jump into the muddy Tallahatchie River off this bridge, located up at Choctow Ridge in rural Mississippi, was made famous in the 1967 Bobbie Gentry song "Ode to Billy Joe."

TAMAGOTCHI

Released by Bandai of Japan, these tiny virtual pets from the planet Tamagotchi needed to be constantly fed and loved. If neglected, they would fall ill and die. All the rage in 1997, children would carry them around in egg-shaped cases everywhere they went. Many adults questioned whether these high-maintenance cyber pets taught youngsters responsibility or simply stressed them out. Gigapet was Tamagotchi's rival.

TAMMY

"The doll you love to dress!" Fashion doll with a girl-next-door wholesomeness whose popularity came closest to rivaling the more worldly Barbie doll in the 1960s. Loosely based on the movie starring Debbie Reynolds, Tammy was introduced in 1962 by the Ideal Toy Company. Compared with Barbie, she had a younger look, a more youthful figure, and a far less sophisticated wardrobe. Tammy lived like an everyday middle-class teenager. She wasn't a jet-setting stewardess or a high-fashion model or an award-winning actress. Her passions were gabbing with best friend Misty on the phone, attending record hops with beau Bud (who looked a lot like dreamy George Maharis of TV's *Route 66*), and shopping for clothes. Members of Tammy's family included Dad, Mom, spunky little sister Pepper, and brothers Ted and Pete. Dodi, Patti, and Salty were a few of Pepper's pals.

TANG

A favorite from childhood was this "orangy-tasting powder drink" introduced by General Foods in 1959. Called "yesterday's drink of tomorrow" by authors Jane and Michael Stern in their *Encyclopedia of Pop Culture,* Tang symbolized the modern jet-age for the busy soul on the go. It was convenient to make (just mix a spoonful of Tang's orange crystals in a glass of water), nutritious (full of vitamins A and C), and aromatic (like oranges, but with a flavor all its own), and its airtight jar gave it a long shelf life. In the late 1960s, Tang went from modern jet-age to futuristic space-age when it was adopted as part of NASA's nutritionally balanced food supply. As "the astronauts' favorite breakfast beverage," it traveled aboard space capsules Gemini IV and Gemini V in 1965 and zoomed to the moon with the Apollo crew in 1969.

All over America, youngsters eagerly imitated their galaxy-traveling heroes by drinking Tang for breakfast (usually accompanied by two other futuristic items: Eggos and Pop-Tarts). It seems that kids always left at least one inch of Tang on the bottom of the glass, to avoid drinking the orange sludge that settled there. Some people used Tang as an ingredient for creative food and drink ideas, such as Tangy Coffeecakes, Tangy Cookies, Tangy Cakes (the powder was added to the mix and the frosting), Tangy Screwdrivers (Tang mixed with vodka), and Tangy Ice (a yummy frozen treat consisting of crushed ice and Tang).

FYI: ▸ Tang was the favorite beverage of *Saturday Night Live*'s nerdy Loopner ladies, Lisa and her mom, who drank it by the pitcher.

TANK TOPS

First fashionable in the early 1970s, these unisex tops, featuring a scooped neck and no sleeves, were named after the style of shirt men wore for swimming at the beginning of the twentieth century. Not to be confused with the male-oriented hard-rocking muscle tee popular in the 1980s.

TARZAN

One of the greatest action characters of all time was storyteller Edgar Rice Burrough's vine-hopping, loinclothed bellowing jungle hero, a young English lord who had been orphaned in the wilds of Africa as a baby and raised by apes. Most of us first became acquainted with the Ape Man by viewing old black-and-white *Tarzan* movies that aired on TV almost every weekend afternoon. These cinematic adventures had Tarzan grappling with a giant croc or a ferocious lion, all the while swinging through treetops via hanging vines to defend his habitat against villainous white hunters or to rescue sweetheart Jane from evil witch doctors. When unable to use his brawny strength, Tarzan's acute senses allowed him to communicate with and control wild animals to his advantage.

Many actors have stepped into the famous loincloth, but the definitive Lord of the Jungle would be Olympic-swimming champ Johnny Weissmuller, who originated the trademark Tarzan yell, "Aaaaaah-eeee-Aaaaaah!" and made a dozen films between 1932 and 1948. Along with the many big-screen ventures (more than forty films since 1918), there have been a prime-time TV series (1966–68) starring Ron Ely as Tarzan; a Saturday-morning cartoon (1976–81) showcasing the Jungle King as a superhero in the ranks of Batman, Hercules, Isis, Sinbad, and The Lone Ranger; and a Walt Disney animated feature (1999).

FYI: ▸ After Lord and Lady Greystoke died following an ill-fated African expedition, their infant son, John Clayton, was named Tarzan, meaning "white skin" in Ape, by his adopted simian mother, Kala.

***TARZAN* (TV SERIES)**

From 1966 to 1968, the Ape Man could be seen on a hit NBC-TV adventure starring Ron Ely in the title role (he was the fourteenth actor to play him). Ely's Tarzan, who returns to the jungle forest after becoming fed up with civilization, was well educated and had a refined vocabulary from his years of formal schooling (no more "Ungawa!"). Loyal chimpanzee Cheetah and small orphan Jai (Manuel Padilla Jr.) are there to assist him in combating poachers and other African bad guys.

TASMANIAN DEVIL

Nicknamed Taz, this slobbering, snarling, and buzz-sawing whirl of a beast from Down Under has become one of the most popular Looney Tunes characters of recent years. Taz had his very own Saturday cartoon TV show, *Taz-Mania* (1991–93), in which he worked as a hotel bellhop, along with dad Hugh, mom Jean, and sister Molly.

TATE, SHARON

"My whole life has been decided by fate. I think something more powerful than we are decides our fate for us. I know one thing—I've never planned anything that ever happened to me."

—SHARON TATE, IN HER LAST INTERVIEW, JULY 26, 1969

Hauntingly gorgeous (the *Saturday Evening Post* heralded her as "the most beautiful girl in the world"), characterized by honey-blonde hair, large brown eyes, high cheekbones, a dazzling smile, and majestic curvage (36C-22-35), sweet-natured Sharon Tate seemed to have it all. An up-and-coming movie career and comparisons to sexy contemporaries Ann-Margret and Raquel Welch, marriage to acclaimed director Roman Polanski, friendship with filmdom's elite (including Steve McQueen and Warren Beatty), and the upcoming birth of her first child. It all changed on August 9, 1969, the ill-fated night she met up with the drug-ravaged disciples of Charlie Manson and became the victim of Hollywood's most gruesome murder, dubbed the "Helter Skelter Killings."

Tate started young—way young, like at the age of six months—when she was crowned Miss Tiny Tot of Dallas. A popular cheerleader in high school, she was both homecoming queen and prom queen and held two local beauty titles, Miss Richland and Miss Autorama. Her Hollywood break came in 1963, when she donned a brunette wig to play the shapely Janet Trego, one of Milton Drysdale's bank secretaries, on fourteen episodes of *The Beverly Hillbillies*. It didn't take long for movies to come knocking.

Her most famous role would be that of Jennifer North, the slinky sex symbol turned porn actress who later commits suicide, in Jacqueline Susann's *Valley of the Dolls* (1967). She was also good as

Sarah Shagal, the Jewish innkeeper's daughter who is kidnapped by bloodsuckers in Polanski's atmospheric horror comedy *The Fearless Vampire Killers* (1967); as Malibu, the swingin', surfin' beach bunny and obvious prototype of Mattel's Malibu Barbie, in the Southern California satire *Don't Make Waves* (1967); and as Freya Carlson, Matt Helm's koo-koo karate-chopping sidekick, in the spy spoof *The Wrecking Crew* (1969).

Tate's gruesome murder at age twenty-six extinguished a Hollywood rising star. (Eight months pregnant, she was stabbed sixteen times, with a futile attempt made to cut out the unborn baby, and her blood was used to write "Pig" on the front door.) Seen purely in decorative roles, she died a starlet whose career teetered on the edge of a major breakthrough. Sadly, she is remembered today chiefly in association with Manson and not for her movies.

FYI: ▸ Headstrong and determined, mother Doris Tate led a successful crusade—in memory of Sharon and her unborn grandson, Paul Richard Polanski—for legislation that would permit victims' families to speak out during sentencing and parole hearings, known as the "Victim's Bill of Rights."

TATOOINE
Luke Skywalker's homeworld is this desert planet where much of the *Star Wars* story takes place. There you can find the Cantina, a sleazy spaceport bar—located in the city of Mos Eisley—filled with a host of alien riffraff swilling drinks.

TATTOO
"Yezz, boss." Mr. Roarke's heavily accented dwarf manservant (played by Herve Villechaize) from the dream vacation spot Fantasy Island. When planes bringing guests appeared on the horizon, Tattoo would climb the tropical island's bell tower and yelled "Dee plane! Dee plane!"

TATTOOS
Ancient Polynesian body art achieved by etching indelible pigments into one's skin. At one time, tattoos were seen only on servicemen, biker gangs, jailbirds, and other low-class types. However, in the 1990s they became a trendy yet permanent fashion statement for young men and women from all walks of life. It's ill-advised to get your lover's name etched on your skin unless you want to go through the embarrassment of having it removed (for example, Johnny Depp's "Winona Forever" and Angelina Jolie's "Billy Bob Thornton"), which I hear can be quite painful.

FYI: ▸ The word "tattoo" is derived from "tatau," the Polynesian word for "scarification."

T-BIRDS
Short for Thunderbirds, the greaser hoodlum gang featured in the musical *Grease*, whose members included Danny, Kenickie, Sonny, Putzie, and Doody. Rival gang was the Scorpions, led by crater-faced Leo, from the other side of town.

TEA SETS
Miniature plastic teapots, cups, plates, knives, forks, and spoons that allowed little hostesses to host tea parties for guests consisting of dolls and teddy bears.

TED BAXTER
"Good night and good news." This bumbling, pompous white-haired newscaster worked for the Six O'Clock News on WJM-TV in Minneapolis. Played by Ted Knight on the TV sitcom *The Mary Tyler Moore Show* (1970–77).

TEDDY BEARS
The first lovable stuffed toy bear was created in 1903 by Morris and Rose Michtom, founders of the Ideal Toy Company, and named for President Teddy Roosevelt. Roosevelt had refused to shoot a bear cub on a hunting expedition the previous year.

TEDDY RUXPIN
As the toy phenomenon of 1985, this storytelling and singing teddy bear moved his mouth to the words of a cassette tape that you placed in a player installed in his back. The friendly bear's best friend was Grubby, a multiple-limbed octopede who could actually converse with Teddy when you attached a special cord to each. Ken Forsse, an engineer who helped develop the talking creatures seen at the Disneyland attractions, invented these interactive toys manufactured by Worlds of Wonder.

TEENAGE MUTANT NINJA TURTLES
"Heroes in a half shell . . . Turtle Power!" A quartet of feisty, pizza-loving, sewer-dwelling, crime-fighting green turtles who mastered the fine art of ninja and were named after Italian Renaissance artists: Leonardo (the leader), Donatello (the genius), Michelangelo (the party dude), and Raphael (the prankster). Created first as a comic book by Kevin Eastman and Peter Laird, the Turtles' cartoon adventures began in 1987 as a syndicated show, before becoming a Saturday-morning favorite on CBS-TV from 1990 to 1997. In 1990, the first of three *Teenage Mutant Ninja Turtles* action-packed, live-action films was released.

TEEN IDOL MAGAZINES
When it came to info on teen heartthrobs, magazines such as *Flip*, *16*, *Teen Beat*, and *Tiger Beat* were the handbooks. They were full of all kinds of frivolous stuff that only a teenybopper girl (or boy) would care about. You could find out Leif Garrett's 100 sizzling secrets or Bobby Sherman's loves and hates or Shaun Cassidy's superstar statistics or the Bay City Rollers' zodiac signs or Michael Jackson's address or how to pass the John Travolta kissing test or how to turn David Cassidy on (by the girls who have) or—God forbid—whom Donny Osmond was dating. For readers full of angst about family life, dating, popularity, or personal appearance, popular teen actresses offered monthly advice in such columns as Susan Dey's "Girl to Girl," Maureen McCormick's "Dear Maureen," Eve Plumb's "Beauty Tips," LaToya Jackson's "Tell It to Toya," and Marie Osmond's "Secret Sister Marie." There were all these supercool contests and giveaways, where you could win a lunch date or a trip to Disneyland with your dream hunk, or autographed items ranging from photos to records to stuffed animals. Best of all, these mags were full of awesome pinups, which ended up adorning the bedroom walls of many adolescents.

The following is a list of the top twenty-five teen idols, chosen by the amount of coverage they were given in a selection of *Flip*, *16*, *Teen Beat*, and *Tiger Beat* magazines from the late 1960s to the mid-1980s. Which of these "fave raves" were tacked on your walls and taped inside your school locker?

Scott Baio
Bay City Rollers
Brady Bunch
David Cassidy / Partridge Family
Shaun Cassidy
Tony DeFranco / DeFranco Family
Matt Dillon
Duran Duran
Peter Frampton
Leif Garrett
Andy Gibb / Bee Gees
Hudson Brothers
Michael Jackson / Jackson 5
Elton John
Davy Jones/Monkees
KISS
Randolph Mantooth
Jimmy and Kristy McNichol
Donny Osmond / Osmonds
Bobby Sherman
Rick Springfield
John Travolta
Vince Van Patten
Andy and David Williams
Henry Winkler

Honorable teen idol mentions: Willie Aames, Desi Arnaz Jr., Robby Benson, Clark Brandon, Alice Cooper, Cowsills, Tom Cruise, Bo Donaldson / Heywoods, Jeff East, Erik Estrada, Wesley Eure, Greg Evigan, Paul Michael Glaser, Michael Gray, Corey Hart, Rob Lowe, Ralph Macchio, Philip McKeon, Menudo, Michael Ontkean, Freddie Prinze, John Schneider, Rex Smith, David Soul, Parker Stevenson, Sylvers, Richard Thomas, Jan-Michael Vincent, Jack Wagner, Wham!, Johnny Whitaker, and Jack Wild.

TEEN SPIRIT
The youth-oriented antiperspirant's pop culture fate was sealed in 1991 when used as part of the title in the grunge anthem "Smells Like Teen Spirit" by Kurt Cobain's Nirvana. Produced by Mennen and marketed to females, Teen Spirit came in fun fragrances like Berry Blossom, Caribbean Cool, Orchard Blossom, and Shower Fresh.

TELEPHONE-BOOTH PACKING
Our crazy parents! The amount of people you could squash into a standard-sized phone booth was the goofy fad of 1959 (the record: thirty-two, set at

Modesto Junior College in California). Inspired VW Beetle-packing in the 1960s.

TEMPLE, SHIRLEY
Considered Hollywood's number-one child star of all time, Shirley Temple gave me and countless other children a lesson in movie immortality. As a youngster, I was captivated by the magical charms of Miss Temple: the curly mop, dimpled cheeks, twinkly eyes, chirpy singing voice, cutesy dancing, and optimistic innocence. When watching her old black-and-white movies (including *Bright Eyes, Curly Top, The Littlest Rebel, Captain January, Stowaway,* and *Heidi*), I couldn't comprehend that they were filmed in the 1930s. I thought Shirley was a kid just like me, a child of the 1960s, not an adult older than most parents. Eventually that did sink in. Captured forever on celluloid, her timeless appeal led to Shirley Temple matinees on TV and Ideal Toys' best-selling Shirley Temple dolls aimed at Baby Boomer girls. Long live Shirley!

10
In the late 1970s and early 1980s, it became common practice to rate someone's personal appearance on a numerical scale of 1 through 10. A 10 was a super-good-looking person—a hot buff hunk (like Jon-Erik Hexum or John Schneider) or foxy brickhouse babe (like Heather Locklear or Heather Thomas). A rating around 5 meant a person was average-looking but somewhat cute (like Erin Moran, Ron Howard, and the whole cast of *The Waltons*). A lowly score of 1 was reserved for the unlucky souls who'd been shortchanged in the looks department (like Phyllis Diller or Marty Feldman). The lowest of low was a 0 rating, which often had nothing to do with appearance but was bestowed on the girl who stole your boyfriend or the pesky nerd who sat behind you in Spanish class. This superficial trend was made popular by the 1979 comedy movie *10* , directed by Blake Edwards and starring Dudley Moore, Julie Andrews, and Bo Derek (the "10" in the title).

TEN-O-SIX
The brown-colored Bonne Bell astringent with the distinctive smell, marketed to zit-faced youngsters.

TERMINATOR
"I'll be back." Apparently indestructible cyborg sent to present-day earth (1984) from the future earth (2029) to assassinate Sarah Connor, the woman who will conceive the child destined to lead humankind to victory in a bitter war with a race of machines. Played by Arnold Schwarzenegger in three sci-fi films: *The Terminator* (1984), *Terminator 2: Judgment Day* (1991), and *Terminator 3: Rise of the Machines* (2003).

TERROR ON THE BEACH
In this 1973 TV movie, a suburban family, led by dad Neil Glynn (Dennis Weaver), has their beach vacation turn into a nightmare when a gang of delinquents driving dune buggies terrorizes them. Susan Dey co-starred as teenage daughter Dee Dee Glynn.

TERRYTOONS
Cartoon production company formed by Paul Terry in the 1940s that has gifted pop culture with such gems as Mighty Mouse, Heckle and Jeckle, Deputy Dawg, Hector Heathcote, Tom Terrific, Sidney the Elephant, Hashimoto-San, and the Mighty Heroes.

TETRIS
The colorful 1980s arcade game with Russian graphics is a puzzle in which players quickly position various block shapes as they drop down on top of each other. As you play, Tetris gets faster and faster, so if you aren't quick enough the blocks will back up and game's over.

TEXAS CHAINSAW MASSACRE
"Who will survive, and what will be left of them?" Directed by Tobe Hooper, this 1974 low-budget gorefest, laden with never-ending suspense and a sweat-inducing pace, has been acclaimed as an influential and groundbreaking movie of modern-day horror. Set in rural Texas, the terrifying yarn begins with the sunny afternoon drive of five carefree teens—Sally (Marilyn Burns), boyfriend Jerry (Allen Danziger), brother Franklin (Paul A. Partain), and friends Pam (Teri McMinn) and Kirk (William Vail). After visiting the grave of Sally's grandfather, which has been ritualistically desecrated, the youths pick up a weird hitchhiker (Edwin Neal), who turns out

to be a psychopath, subsequently cutting himself and slashing wheelchair-confined Franklin with a knife. So they kick the wacko out of their van and proceed to the old family farm to take a dip in an isolated swimming hole.

Things turn more nightmarish upon encountering a deranged clan of slaughterhouse workers, the Sawyers: three inbred brothers (including the sinister hitchhiker) and their bloodsucking, corpselike grandfather. This ghastly bunch eat and sell human flesh (as smoked meat at a roadside stand) and have a particular knack for decorating their desolate home with grisly items made out of body parts. One by one, the hapless teens fall victim to squealing, mask-wearing Leatherface (Gunnar Hansen), who menaces them with a sledgehammer (Kirk), a meat hook (Pam), and of course the notorious chainsaw (Franklin, Jerry, and Sally). Loosely inspired by the exploits of real-life cannibal-killer Edward "The Wisconsin Ghoul" Gein, *TCM* loosely inspired three sequels and a not-so-bad remake in 2003.

FYI: ▸ The narrator at the beginning of the film is a young John Larroquette.

THAT DARN CAT

Amusing Walt Disney romp about a kidnapped woman, Margaret Miller (Grayson Hall), who hides a clue to her whereabouts on the collar of a Siamese named D.C. (for Darn Cat) owned by sixteen-year-old Patti Randall (Hayley Mills). After discovering the clue, the enthusiastic teen calls in Zeke Kelso (Dean Jones), a feline-allergic FBI agent, and together, with the help of D.C., they track down the bank-robbing kidnappers and rescue Mrs. Miller. Based on the book *Undercover Cat*, by Gordon and Mildred Golden, the 1965 comedy film was directed by Robert Stevenson. It co-starred Dorothy Provine as pretty Ingrid Randall, Patti's older sister, and Roddy McDowall as nosy Gregory Benson, the next-door neighbor. As Disney's biggest child star of the 1960s, this was Mills's last theatrical film with the Studio. Hipster Bobby Darin sang the catchy title song.

THAT GIRL

Airing from 1966 to 1971, this beloved ABC-TV series was one of the first to feature a career-oriented, forward-thinking, single woman as the lead character. In the past, a gal left home either to get married or to go to college and then get married, and even after marriage she rarely got the chance to pursue her college major because husband and children came first. *That Girl* provided a new role model for women, that it's just grand to be independent and seek a career. It set a trend in prime-time sitcoms and became the precursor of such shows as *Julia*, *The Doris Day Show*, *The Mary Tyler Moore Show*, *Rhoda*, *Murphy Brown*, *Caroline in the City*, and *Suddenly Susan*.

That Girl starred Marlo Thomas, daughter of Danny, as wholesome, big-eyed Ann Marie, an aspiring actress-model trying to make it on her own in New York City. Adorable and fashionably dressed, Ann was the kind of woman young gals dreamed of being, and the type young guys wanted to go steady with. The program's opening credits captured how charmingly high-spirited she was—whirling around Fifth Avenue, spinning and hugging herself, shaking her brunette flip hairdo, flying a kite, and winking at a look-alike mannequin in a department store window. She lived by herself in a small apartment in the Upper West Side (627 East Fifty-Fourth, to be exact).

Always on the verge of a big break, Ann spent most of her time acting in TV advertisements and bit parts in plays, or taking on a variety of odd jobs, such as office worker, department store clerk, and cocktail waitress. Handsome Ted Bessell co-starred as Ann's long-suffering boyfriend, Donald Hollinger. Also featured were Lew Parker and Rosemary DeCamp as doting parents Lew and Helen Marie, owners of a French restaurant in Ann's suburban hometown of Brewster, New York. After years of anticipation, Ann and Donald finally became engaged in 1970, but they never married because the show was canceled before the wedding could take place.

FYI: ▸ The reason a kite is featured in the opening credit sequence is that it's the symbol of Marlo Thomas's college sorority, Kappa Alpha Theta, at USC. (Ann Marie's kite had the *That Girl* caricature imprinted on it.)

THAT '70s SHOW

"Be groovy. Be very groovy." FOX-TV's nostalgic look back at the 1970s was more popular with those born after the decade than those who actually lived it. Set sometime in the late 1970s, the series centered on seventeen-year-old Eric Foreman (Topher Grace), son of Red and Kitty (Kurtwood Smith and Debra Jo Rupp), who lived in the suburbs of fictional Point Place, Wisconsin. A typical high school junior, Eric was constantly getting involved in some lame sitcom plot lampooning the 1970s (streaking, disco-dancing, pot-smoking, and the like) with a gang of bell-bottomed, feathered-haired pals: foxy next-door-neighbor Donna Pinciotti (Laura Prepon), dumb hunk Michael Kelso (Ashton Kutcher), spoiled Jackie Burkhardt (Mila Kunis), conspiracy theorist Steve Hyde (Danny Masterson), and Fez (Wilmer Valderrama) a foreign-exchange student from an unknown country. The gang spent most of their time in hanging out in Eric's basement. Laurie Foreman was Eric's older sister with the blonde Farrah Fawcett hairdo who attended the University of Wisconsin before flunking out. Like many teen-popular sitcoms before it, *That '70s Show* was a launching pad for one breakout star, and Ashton Kutcher was it.

THAT'S INCREDIBLE!
"Kids, don't try this at home." Reality-based TV show featuring everyday citizens doing incredible stunts, like jumping out of a plane handcuffed and straitjacketed, catching a bullet with your teeth, and eating a ten-speed bike (spokes and all). Airing on ABC from 1980 to 1984, the variety program was hosted by the trio of John Davidson, Cathy Lee Crosby, and ex-football player Fran Tarkenton. In the search for high ratings, the show allegedly staged and rigged several stunts, while others were too dangerous. For example, a man who ran through a tunnel of flames was badly burned, and a motorcyclist broke his hip and legs after a jump went awry. In 1980, *Time* magazine awarded it a Dubious Achievement Award for "Most Sadistic Show." The notoriety (and high ratings) inspired a host of imitators, centering around everyday folks—*Real People*, *Those Amazing Animals*, *TV's Bloopers and Practical Jokes*, and *America's Funniest Home Videos* among them.

THELMA EVANS
Florida Evans's "baby girl" on *Good Times* is significant for being one of the only black female teenagers featured as a regular character on a TV show in the 1970s. Played by BernNadette Stanis, the intelligent (she made straight A's), pretty (great figure and beautiful smile) sixteen-year-old who wore an Afro puff and big hoop earrings, had no qualms about trading insults with know-it-all big brother J.J.

THEODORE
In the *Alvin and the Chipmunks* cartoon show, this giggling, gullible chubster dressed in a green floor-length sweater was Alvin's sidekick when it came to mischief-making.

"THESE BOOTS ARE MADE FOR WALKIN'"
As the go-go craze swept the nation in 1966, vinyl-booted, miniskirted Nancy Sinatra kicked her way to the top of the pop charts with this sassy, bass-laden anthem. More than just a tribute to footwear, the song was a prefeminist warning to a cheating and lying boyfriend that if he didn't straighten up, "these boots are going to walk all over you." At first, when Sinatra went into the studio to record "Boots" she sang it sweetly and prettily, which wasn't what the producers wanted to hear. They told her to perform it "for the truck drivers," and the finished product, featuring a tough, flat, and rather dolorous voice, became Sinatra's trademark sound.

THING
Fierce alien being that mutates into frightening shapes while running amok through an isolated Arctic outpost. It starred in the 1951 sci-fi-horror film *The Thing from Another World* and its 1982 remake *The Thing*.

THING (*ADDAMS FAMILY*)
This pale, disembodied hand pops out of a black box for various errands on TV's *Addams Family*. The hand actually belonged to actor Ted Cassidy, who moonlighted as butler Lurch on the hit sitcom.

THING (FANTASTIC FOUR)
After being exposed to cosmic radiation, robust Ben Grimm, a friend of Dr. Reed Richards and his wife, Sue, was changed into an extraordinarily powerful rocklike creature with the strength of a thousand horses. A member of *Marvel* comics' Fantastic Four

(along with the Richards), his might and appearance made him the superhero equal to The Incredible Hulk.

THINGMAKER SETS
Electric heating units used to bake prestamped metal molds filled with a liquid plastic called Plasti-goop to create all sorts of shapes and creatures. Although these casting sets by Mattel (for instance, Creepy Crawlers and Fright Factory) were some of the best-selling toys of the 1960s, not all kids were allowed to have one, because parents thought the ovens might cause burns.

THOMAS MAGNUM
Mustached, hairy-chested, strapping (six-foot-four), hunky Tom Selleck made this private investigator from Hawaii the hottest TV detective (*Magnum, P.I.*) of the early 1980s. Magnum resided on Oahu's North Shore, and his typical wardrobe choice was a casual Hawaiian shirt, shorts or jeans, scuffed sneakers, and a baseball cap from the Detroit Tigers (his favorite team).

THOMAS O'MALLEY
The red-coated tomcat, with a devil-may-care attitude and a heart as big as his ego, that rescued and fell in love with the aristocratic Duchess in Walt Disney's animated *The Aristocats* (1970). Full name: Abraham de Lacy Giuseppe Casey Thomas O'Malley.

THOMPSON TWINS
Not really twins, but a British pop trio who rode high on the New Wave invasion of the 1980s. Consisting of handsome lead singer-keyboardist Tom Bailey, girl saxophonist Alannah Currie, and black bongo-player Joe Leeway, the band was noted for glossy electronic dance hits. These included "In the Name of Love" (1982), "Lies" (1983), "Hold Me Now" (1984), "Doctor, Doctor" (1984), and "Lay Your Hands on Me" (1985). Like most acts of the era, the threesome was distinguished by a bizarre fashion sense: Bailey's colored spiky locks, Currie's oddly shaved platinum hair topped with a Foreign Legion cap, and Leeway's shaved eyebrows. In 1986, the Thompson Twins became twins (kind of) when Leeway quit the group.

FYI: ▸ The Thompson Twins were named after a pair of identical detectives in German cartoonist Herge's adventure comic strip, *Tin Tin.*

THONG SANDALS
Trendy in the late 1970s and early 1980s, this warm-weather footwear, marked by rainbow-layered rubber soles and blue faux-velvet toe straps, was first worn by Hang Ten surfers with pukka-shell necklaces, before catching on with the masses.

THOR
In the early 1960s, *Marvel* comics experienced an extraordinary rise to prominence thanks to the creation of several new superheroes: The Fantastic Four, The Incredible Hulk, The Amazing Spider-Man, and The Mighty Thor, created by Stan Lee and drawn by Jack Kirby. Loosely based on ancient Norse mythology, Thor originated as a supporting strip in *Journey into Mystery,* number 83 (August 1962). Emaciated and weak, Dr. Donald Blake could turn into the legendary God of Thunder by whacking his magic cane on the ground. In a flash, the cane converted into a powerful hammer and Blake transformed into the muscular superhero with long blond locks and a winged Viking cap. In March 1966, the Dr. Blake alter ego was dropped when Thor headlined his own comic-book series.

Thor lived in Asgard, where he commingled with other Nordic gods, such as Oldin, the god of gods and ruler of Asgard; Heimdall, the protector of the Rainbow Bridge; and Lady Sif, Thor's beloved. He constantly fought a troupe of Norse evildoers, including Loki, the god of mischief, who happened to be his half-brother. These battles took place not only on Asgard but also on earth, in heaven, in hell, and in every netherworld between.

THREE DOG NIGHT
America's most commercially successful rock group of the early 1970s, formed in Los Angeles in 1968 by Danny Hutton, who envisioned an act centering on three lead vocalists: Cory Wells, Chuck Negron, and himself. The band's forte was funky cover versions of material by then-unknown composers, including Harry Nilsson's "One" (1969), *Hair*'s "Easy to Be Hard" (1969), Laura Nyro's "Eli's Coming" (1969), Randy Newman's "Mama Told Me (Not to

Come)" (1970), Hoyt Axton's "Joy to the World" (1971) and "Never Been to Spain" (1972), Greyhound's "Black and White" (1972), Dave Loggin's "Pieces of April" (1972), and Leo Sayer's "The Show Must Go On" (1973). Three Dog Night disbanded in the 1977 because of personal problems among its members.

FYI: ▸ The band's name derives from an old Australian saying: In the outback, the colder the night, the more dingo dogs you sleep next to to stay warm, with the coldest night being a "three dog night."

THREE'S COMPANY

"Come on knock on our door / We've been waiting for you / Where the kisses are hers and hers and his / *Three's Company* too. . . ." The ABC-TV sex-com (1977–84) was the leader of the jiggly tits-and-ass prime-time shows popular during the sexual revolution of the late 1970s. Loosely based on the British series *Man About the House*, its racy subject matter, fraught with sexy double-entendres and out-of-context misunderstandings, made it an enormous success (a Top Ten show for six out of seven seasons) and a perpetual target of critics and religious groups.

Set in sunny Santa Monica, California, the *Three's Company* story revolved around two beautiful women in need of a roommate for their apartment (No. 201) who settled for a young man they find passed out drunk in their bathtub after a farewell bash for the last roomie. To be able to stay, he pretends to be homosexual so that the landlord, suspicious of swingin' behavior, will allow him to share the pad with the girls. The gender-mixed roommates were Jack Tripper (John Ritter, son of cowboy-star Tex), a fun-loving, bumbling chef; Janet Wood (Joyce DeWitt), a sensible, smart brunette florist; and Chrissy Snow (Suzanne Somers), a ding-dong, sexy, blonde secretary. Other characters on the hit show included cranky landlord Stanley Roper (Norman Fell), his horny wife, Helen (Audra Lindley), and Jack's swinger buddy Larry Dallas (Richard Kline).

In 1979, the Ropers spun off onto a self-titled series and were replaced by fidgety Ralph Furley (Don Knotts), the new landlord, who managed the building for his brother. Also joining the cast was sexually voracious Lana Shields (Ann Wedgeworth), an older upstairs neighbor who is hot for Jack. Typical of all overnight TV sensations, Suzanne Somers left *Three's Company* in the summer of 1980 after a contract dispute (she demanded a salary increase from $30,000 to $150,000 per episode). To fill the empty-head void, ex-L.A. Rams cheerleader Jenilee Harrison as Chrissy's cousin Cindy Snow (1980–82), and Priscilla Barnes as nurse Terri Alden (1981–84), were hired.

THRILLER (ALBUM)

The most celebrated and successful LP of all time was a recording tour de force for song-and-dance superstar Michael Jackson and producer Quincy Jones. Released in late 1982, it sold forty million-plus copies worldwide, becoming the best-selling album in history (one million records alone were sold in Los Angeles). *Thriller* spent a record thirty-seven weeks at the top of the American charts, hitting number one in every western country worldwide. An unprecedented seven Top Ten singles were released, including the title track, featuring a ghostly rap from fright-master Vincent Price, and "Billie Jean," "Beat It," "Wanna Be Startin' Somethin'," "Human Nature," "P.Y.T. (Pretty Young Thing)," and a duet with Paul McCartney, "The Girl Is Mine." In 1983, Jackson and his masterpiece received a record twelve Grammy nominations, winning eight (another record), including Album of the Year. Presenter Mickey Rooney jokingly referred to that year's broadcast as "The Michael Jackson Show."

"THRILLER" (MUSIC VIDEO)

On December 2, 1983, a fourteen-minute, mini-epic video of Michael Jackson's title, cut from his phenomenal *Thriller* album, made its world premiere on MTV. Directed by John Landis and costing somewhere in the million-dollar range, it is considered by critics to be the greatest music video ever filmed (and the first intentionally horror-oriented one). Jackson stars as a leather-jacketed heartthrob who turns into a scary werewolf when the moon is full. He terrorizes his sugar-sweet girlfriend (Ola Ray) and merrily dances with a horde of decaying zombies (elaborately choreographed by the Gloved One himself). Not to offend elders of the Jehovah Witnesses (Jackson's religion of choice), he added this disclaimer at the beginning of the landmark video: "Due to my strong personal convictions, I wish to stress that this film in no way endorses a belief in the occult."

"THRILLER" JACKET

The famous candy-apple-red jacket, covered with zippers-deluxe and worn by Michael Jackson in the "Thriller" video, launched a gazillion imitations and became the hottest outerwear fad of the mid-1980s.

THUNDARR THE BARBARIAN

Star Wars–like sci-fi series, airing Saturday mornings from 1980 to 1982, starring ex-slave Thundarr, a blond Adonis-type who uses the Sun Sword to fight for justice on planet earth 2,000 years into the future. Helping him is beautiful Ariel, daughter of a wizard, and friendly Ookla the Mok, a mutant ape.

THUNDERBIRDS

"5 . . . 4 . . . 3 . . . 2 . . . 1 . . . Thunderbirds Are Go!" One of Britain's most enduring childhood sci-fi shows, originally airing on TV from 1965 to 1966, was another marionette adventure created by Gerry (*Fireball XL-5*) Anderson. Set in the year 2026, this told the exploits of American billionaire Jeff Tracy and his five sons, who operated a high-tech interplanetary lifeguard agency called International Rescue using elaborate Thunderbird crafts. Concealed in hangars at a top-secret base on an unmapped island in the Pacific, each Thunderbird, numbered one to five, was piloted by one of Tracy's heroic sons: Scott: Thunderbird 1 (an atomic-powered craft that can soar with speeds of more than 15,000 mph); Virgil: Thunderbird 2 (a heavy-duty freight transporter): Alan: Thunderbird 3 (a rocket ship for space rescues); Gordon: Thunderbird 4 (a submarine for undersea rescues); and John: Thunderbird 5 (an elaborate space monitor capable of receiving messages of distress from anywhere in the world). I.R.'s security was handled by the blonde Lady Penelope Creighton-Ward, a cool-as-ice special agent from London who had a pink Rolls-Royce driven by chauffeur Parker. Many of Anderson's character puppets were based on the famous faces of the era (for instance, Scott Tracy was based on Sean Connery). A genuine cult item, *Thunderbirds* has inspired spin-offs, feature films, and even a rock band.

THUNDERCATS

"Thunder . . . Thunder . . . THUNDER . . . THUNDER-CATS . . . HOOOOOO!" Typical 1980s action-figure toy line turned cartoon series (including He-Man and the Masters of the Universe). This one was about a team of good guys who are hybrids of cats and humans: Lion-O (the sword-wielding leader), Tygra, Panthro, Cheetara, Jaga, and Pumrya. Set in futuristic Third Earth, our muscular feline heroes came from the doomed planet Thundera to take on the evil Mutants, led by the hideous Mumm-Ra. LJN manufactured the action figures (1985–87), and Rankin/Bass produced the Saturday-morning cartoon (1985–86).

THURSTON HOWELL III

A millionaire with a snooty accent who, along with beloved wife Lovey and a trunkful of money and liquor, is shipwrecked on a deserted Pacific isle called *Gilligan's Island*. Portrayed by Jim "Mr. Magoo" Backus.

TIC TAC

"Put a Tic Tac in your mouth and get a bang out of life!" Itty-bitty breath mints packaged in cool plastic containers small enough to fit in your pocket for easy use in case of halitosis emergencies.

TIE-DYE

Hippies in the late 1960s and early 1970s made these at home by tying white cotton fabrics into a wad with rubber bands and putting them into a tub of colorful dye (Rit dye). The dye would only penetrate the loose fabric and create a swirling psychedelic pattern. Tie-dyeing made a considerable comeback in the 1980s with young people who yearned for the carefree days of the San Francisco hippie movement.

TIEGS, CHERYL

The highest-paid model of the 1970s had the appearance of the outdoorsy California blonde, a look so desired during that "Me" decade. Actually, Tiegs wasn't a native Californian; she was a midwesterner born in Minnesota on September 25, 1947. She began her career as a teenager in the mid-1960s modeling for youth-oriented fashion magazines, such as *Seventeen* and *Teen*. National recognition came in the 1970s when she was hired as the dimpled-smile, lean-framed spokes-model for Cover Girl cosmetics and Virginia Slims cigarettes ("You've come a long way, baby"). In 1978, Tiegs hit supermodel status after gracing the much-coveted cover of the *Sports Illustrated* annual swimsuit issue. The same year, a poster of her wearing an itsy-bitsy teenie-weenie lavender bikini sold a million copies, rivaling Farrah Fawcett's legendary red-swimsuit pinup. As the 1980s began, Tiegs padded her portfolio with multi-million-dollar TV and modeling contracts, including her own line of clothing for Sears department stores.

TIFFANY

Auburn-haired teen singing sensation with the tall bangs, born Tiffany Darwish on October 2, 1971, in California, who performed her pop hits at shopping malls across America. Those hits included two number-ones: "I Think We're Alone Now" (1987) and "Could've Been" (1987). The typical Tiffany fan was a young mall-rat type of white-trash nature who didn't like her rival, Debbie Gibson, because she was such a stuck-up goody-goody.

FYI: ▸ In 1990, Tiffany voiced the role of Judy Jetson for the animated *Jetsons* movie.

TIFFANY TAYLOR

"She's a blonde! She's a brunette! Nineteen inches of what you want her to be." A beautiful fashion doll, introduced by Ideal in 1974, whose uniqueness was that by rotating the crown of her head she could be either a fun-loving blonde or a luscious brunette. (If only hair-coloring could be so easy!) Tiffany came with many sophisticated teenage cover-girl fashion choices to go with her hair-color options. In 1976, Ideal shrunk her down to Barbie size (eleven and a half inches), changed her name to Tuesday Taylor, and gave her a black girlfriend named Taylor Jones. Suntan Tuesday Taylor came to toy stores in 1977. She was the first doll that could actually tan when exposed to the sun, because of a photochronic substance in her plastic body. She had a handsome blond boyfriend, Suntan Eric, and a cute little sister, Suntan Dodi (those dolls did not have the changing hair feature).

TIGER

In the first episode of *The Brady Bunch* (titled "The Honeymoon"), this adorable shaggy dog, belonging to the boys, caused havoc during Mike and Carol's wedding ceremony when he got loose and chased after cat Fluffy, owned by the girls. He was played by two different Tigers after the first ran off the set and got iced by a car.

FYI: ▸ In 1976, the second Tiger won a Patsy Award (Performing Animal Top Star of the Year) for his work as Blood in the film *A Boy and His Dog,* starring Don Johnson.

TIGGER

"The most wonderful thing about Tiggers is that I'm the only one!" The overly enthusiastic "bouncy, flouncy, pouncy" tiger made his debut in Disney's *Winnie the Pooh and the Blustery Day* (1968). What is Tigger's favorite pastime? Bouncing, of course! "Boing! Boing! Boing!"

TIME BOMB

"Tic . . . tic . . . tic. . . ." An extra-exciting action game, introduced in 1964 by Milton Bradley, that had players tossing back and forth a round, black plastic time bomb with a windup fuse serving as its timer. The person stuck holding the bomb, which "exploded" in an unnerving loud bang when time was up, lost the game. For those of you old enough to remember, Remco Toys marketed a similar game in the 1960s called Hot Potato.

"TIME WARP"

Thrilling song-and-dance number performed by Magenta and fellow party guests at the "Annual Transylvania Convention" in *The Rocky Horror Picture Show* (1975). During midnight screenings of the cult movie, audience members would get up out of their seats and do the Time Warp in the aisles or on stage. How to do it? Just followed these six easy steps:

1. It's just a jump to the left (with hands up)
2. A step to the right (very wide step)
3. With your hands on your hips
4. Then the pelvic thrust (repeat five times—it nearly drives you insane)
5. Hip swivel
6. "Let's do the Time Warp again!"

TIMON AND PUMBAA

Timon's a wisecracking meerkat, Pumbaa's a flatulent warthog, and together they teach Simba, Africa's future Lion King, the carefree life of "hakuna matata." Wildly popular in *The Lion King* movie, the twosome were given their own TV series on the Disney Channel, simply titled *Timon and Pumbaa*, from 1995 to 1998.

TINKER BELL

Little fairy from the Walt Disney animated *Peter Pan* movie who sprinkles magical pixie dust with a wave of her wand while darting through the sky. Since the early 1960s, she has moonlighted as the introductory image of Disney TV programs and flies above Sleeping Beauty's castle, heralding the nightly fireworks display at Disneyland. Persistent rumors have the blonde and curvy Tink modeled after Marilyn Monroe, but in reality it was actress Margaret Kerry who posed for the pouty sprite.

TINKERTOYS

Packaged in the familiar tubular cardboard box with metal lid, a Tinkertoy set consists of brightly colored wooden rods, connecting spools, moving parts, and wheels. Kids can stick the rods into the rounded spools with holes around the sides and top to create all kinds of cool contraptions, such as ferris wheels, windmills, skyscrapers, and towers. Tinkertoy was invented by a tinkerer from Evanston, Illinois, named Charles Pajeau. Its inspiration came after Pajeau witnessed his own children playing with pencils and empty spools of thread. Since premiering at a New York toy fair in 1914, millions of Tinkertoy sets have been sold each year, making it one of the great construction toys of all time. (Others include Erector Sets, Lincoln Logs, and Legos.)

TINKY WINKY

Three reasons that the Reverend Jerry Falwell outed TV's beloved Teletubbie for being a secret gay role-model for preschoolers:

1. He totes a purse but has a male voice.
2. His purple tint is the color of gay pride.
3. His antenna is shaped like a triangle, the symbol of gay pride.

They are also the three reasons that the reverend proved himself to be a complete idiot.

TINY TEARS

"My eyes close as I'm rocked. I drink. I wet. I cry real tears." This popular seller of the 1950s and 1960s, manufactured by American Character, was one of the first baby dolls who drank from a bottle, cried real tears, and wet her diapers. Tiny Tears also had unique "rock-a-bye eyes," which gradually closed as she was rocked to sleep. Throughout the 1960s, the doll's name was expanded to include Baby Tiny Tears, Lifesize Tiny Tears, Teeny Tiny Tears, and Teeny Weenie Tiny Tears.

TIP-IT

"The wackiest balancing game ever!" Created by toy designer Marvin Glass and introduced by Ideal Toys in 1965, this was a wacky and suspenseful balancing game designed to test your skill and dexterity. It featured an acrobat, Mr. Tip-It, perched upside-down on a rod attached to a tripod balancing on a plastic base. Players took turns removing plastic chips from the tripod, causing Mr. Tip-It to weave back and forth. The player who caused him to topple off his perch was the loser of the game. In the 1990s, Tip-It was rereleased as an appeal to the Baby Boomer parent who had gleefully played it as a kid and would purchase it for their own children. (It's still just as fun to play.)

TIPPEE TOES

Battery-operated sixteen-inch-high doll, introduced by Mattel in 1967, whose moving legs allowed her to toddle across the floor, ride her tricycle and horse, or use a baby walker called the "Walkabout." As Tippee rides, her head sways merrily back and forth as if she's having the best time of her life.

TITANIC

Claimed as unsinkable, the grandest ocean liner of all time met its doom on her maiden voyage, from England to New York, after striking an iceberg on April 14, 1912. Eighty-five years later, director James Cameron gave voice to the 1,513 passengers lost during the Titanic's sinking, whose untold stories remain a mystery at two and a half miles below the surface of the choppy North Atlantic. Cameron's voice was this glorious yet simple love story between a rich girl, Rose (actress Kate Winslet), and a poor boy, Jack (actor Leonardo DiCaprio), set against the spectacular backdrop of the ship's icy demise. As the most expensive movie ever made ($285 million), the three-hour-long *Titanic* drew adoration from critics and fans alike. It earned eleven Oscars, including Best Picture, Best Director, and Best Song ("My Heart Will Go On"), and became the biggest box-office film in history, grossing more than $1 billion worldwide. "I'm the king of the world!"

TOBY TYLER
A twelve-year-old orphan who runs away from his aunt and uncle to join a circus, where he finds tremendous success as a boy equestrian with the aid of Mr. Stubbs, a mischievous chimpanzee. Played by Kevin "Moochie" Corcoran in the 1960 *Toby Tyler* Disney film.

TOE SOCKS
Gloves for the feet! The rainbow-striped ones with the multicolored toes were the coolest back in the 1970s. They looked fantastic with open-toed shoes, such as clogs and platform sandals.

TOGA PARTIES
These wild and raunchy get-togethers were inspired by the 1978 John Belushi film *National Lampoon's Animal House* (1978), a comedy about Faber College's Delta House Fraternity, where underachieving members throw bashes wearing bed sheets and laurel wreaths in Roman fashion. Throughout the late 1970s and early 1980s, the rowdy chant of "Toga! Toga! Toga!" could be heard in college towns across America as toga-clad party animals partied away in fraternities, sororities, dorm rooms, and off-campus apartments. They wore sheets draped around their bodies in every imaginable (and unimaginable) way, while wearing nothing but birthday suits underneath. (Okay, there were the modest few who kept their undergarments on.) For some unfortunate souls, toga parties led to the embarrassing "I wish I were dead" moment upon realizing their sheets had come undone and were giving everybody in sight a glimpse of unmentionables. But for exhibitionists, the fun of wearing a toga was knowing that somebody might just tear it off.

FYI: ▸ At the University of Wisconsin in 1978, thousands of reveling undergrads tried to get their toga party into the *Guinness Book of World Records* by creating and consuming the world's largest mixed cocktail: a vat of various BYOB (Bring Your Own Booze).

TOM AND JERRY
Ever-feuding cat and mouse duo created by William Hanna and Joseph Barbera for the cartoon short "Puss Gets the Boot" in 1940. Tom, a mischievous housecat, and Jerry, a plucky mouse, silently appeared together in more than 114 theatrical cartoons for the MGM Studios, winning their creators seven Academy Awards. Considered the flagship of the legendary Hanna-Barbera team, in 1965 they landed their own Saturday-morning series, with all-new cartoons, which aired for eight years. Their friends included baby mouse Tuffy, bulldog Spike, and basset hound Droopy. Jerry's career highlight came when he did an irresistible dance with sailor-man Gene Kelly in the 1945 big-screen musical *Anchors Aweigh*.

FYI: ▸ Tom and Jerry was the original stage name of Simon and Garfunkel ("Mrs. Robinson" and "The Sounds of Silence").

TOM CORBETT
Dark-haired Bill Bixby played the handsome widower on the ABC-TV sitcom *The Courtship of Eddie's Father* (1969–72) who juggles both a career as a magazine publisher and single fatherhood. His young son, Eddie, constantly gets Tom entangled with women, thanks to his juvenile matchmaking efforts.

"TOM JONES" SHIRTS
In style during the late 1960s and early 1970s, mod button-up shirts for men, distinguished by flouncy, ultrafull sleeves and a large collar. I could never figure out whether they were made fashionable by Albert Finney's Tom Jones or by pop music's Tom Jones, or both. Also known as pirate shirts.

TOMMY
Directed by Ken Russell in 1975, this film adaptation of The Who's 1969 rock opera—conceived and written by Pete Townshend—stars mop-haired lead singer Roger Daltrey as the "deaf, dumb, and blind

kid" who shuns the rest of the world after the death of his father. Also starring were Ann-Margret as Tommy's frustrated mother, Nora Walker, Oliver Reed as cruel stepfather Frank Hobbs, Elton John as the glittery Pinball Wizard, Eric Clapton as the guitar-playing preacher of the Church of Marilyn Monroe, Tina Turner as the rousing Acid Queen, and drummer Keith Moon as perverted Holiday Camp counselor Uncle Ernie. Bizarre movie highlight is when the screen of a TV set vomits black beans all over a sexually wallowing Ann-Margret, a scene so powerful it helped earn her a Best Actress Golden Globe and a Best Actress Oscar nomination.

TOMMY BRADFORD
Middle son of *Eight Is Enough*'s Bradford family, an attractive, curly-headed youth (played by teen idol Willie Aames) who was often misunderstood and prone to mischief-making, especially following the death of his beloved mother, Joan.

FYI: ▸ A former drug abuser, actor Willie Aames is currently "born again" and performing on church stages around the nation as a Christian superhero called Bible Man.

TOMMY FLANAGAN
"Yeah, that's the ticket!" Fast-talking member of Pathological Liars Anonymous, made famous by Jon Lovitz, who claimed to be the husband of actress Morgan Fairchild, a friend of Ferdinand Marcos, the manager of The Rolling Stones, and the producer of NBC's *Saturday Night Live.*

TOMMY ROSS
Blond, curly-haired football jock—the most handsome and popular boy at Bates High School—who escorts telekinetic misfit Carrie White to the senior prom. Due to rigged votes, Tommy and Carrie are announced as prom king and queen, and we all know what tragic event follows (thanks to a bucket of pig's blood). Tommy was portrayed by William Katt in the 1976 horror film *Carrie.* Katt is the son of actress Barbara Hale (secretary Della Street on TV's *Perry Mason*).

TOM SLICK
The All-American auto racer who always played by the rules was a supporting segment on the *George of the Jungle* cartoon show (1967–70). Aiding Tom during his race car competitions were girlfriend Marigold and grandma Gertie.

TONI HOME PERM
"Which twin has the Toni?" The home permanent for those too cheap to go to a salon (or too embarrassed to be seen with smelly, tight perm rods atop their head) was advertised on TV by various look-alike twin models with curly hair.

TONKA TRUCKS
In the Native American language of the Dakota Sioux, the word "tonka" means "great," and for generations of American boys the name Tonka translates to "great toy." Originating in Lake Minnetonka, Minnesota, in 1946, Tonka trucks were created by the trio of Lynn Baker, Avery Crounse, and Alvin Tesch, owners of a metal-stamping business. Made out of steel and plastic, these realistic-looking toys are so durable and long-lasting that parents actually allow kids to play with them outside in the dirt and mud. Throughout the years, the wide variety of Tonka vehicles have included fire trucks, dump trucks, bulldozers, graders, cement mixers, steam shovels, cranes, wreckers, moving vans, farm tractors, pickup trucks, a dune buggy, and even a Winnebago camper. Tonka's all-time best-sellers were the yellow Mighty Dump Truck (introduced in 1964) and the cherry-red Fire Engine (introduced in 1956). Buddy L is its main rival.

TONTO
The Lone Ranger's loyal Indian companion whose pet name for the legendary western hero was "Kemo Sabe" (faithful friend) and whose devoted mount was named Scout. Real-life American Indian Jay Silverheels played Tonto in the *Lone Ranger* TV western.

TONY BARETTA
"You can take that to the bank." Italian-American undercover cop who works the inner city by blending in using a variety of disguises or dressed in white T-shirt, blue jeans, and trademark cap. He lives at the run-down King Edward Hotel with best pal Fred, an expressive cockatoo. Played by Robert

Blake on the hit TV detective series *Baretta* from 1975 to 1978.

TONY MANERO
"Don't hit my hair. I work hard on my hair, and you hit it." John Travolta's cocky Brooklyn youth whose only meaning in a dead-end life is dancing at the local discotheque, where he is king of the disco floor. A nineteen-year-old, Tony works as a minimum-wage clerk in a paint store, lives at home with his nagging parents, and dreams of one day crossing the river to a better life in Manhattan. From the opening scene in *Saturday Night Fever* (1977), as Travolta struts through the streets with "Stayin' Alive" by the Bee Gees pulsating on the soundtrack, it is clear that he was made for the role of Tony Manero and that only he could make blow-dried hair and polyester suits look so cool!

TONY NELSON
Larry Hagman's good-looking, dark-haired NASA astronaut from the *I Dream of Jeannie* TV show, a resolute bachelor who reluctantly becomes the master of Jeannie, a gorgeous blonde genie who lives in a bottle. Major Nelson and Jeannie would eventually fall in love, marry, and live happily ever after in a swank house at 1020 Palm Drive in Cocoa Beach, Florida (although she generally stayed in a genie bottle).

TONY THE TIGER
"They're Gr-r-r-reat!" roared Tony the Tiger, the most popular cereal spokes-animal of all time. Created by Martin Provensen, a children's book illustrator, the robust jungle cat with the red neck-scarf has graced the front of Kellogg's Frosted Flakes cereal boxes since 1952. Tony's young son, Tony Jr., joined him in a series of TV commercials about the importance of eating Frosted Flakes for breakfast and later became the advertising character for Kellogg's Frosted Rice cereal. Rounding out the Tiger family is a wife, known only as Mrs. Tony, and a daughter, Antoinette. Thurl Ravenscroft provided the voice for Tony the Tiger.

TOOKI TOOKI BIRD
The squawking African fowl who served as a telephone for George and Ursula on the *George of the Jungle* cartoon program.

TOONTOWN

"We 'toons may act idiotic,
but we're not stupid."
—ROGER RABBIT

Fictional community on "the wrong side of the tracks" in the Disney movie *Who Framed Roger Rabbit?* (1988), where all cartoon characters reside. Called "'toons," these animated residents are considered second-class citizens by flesh-and-blood people. Go to Disneyland in Anaheim, California, if you care to visit.

TOOT-A-LOOP RADIO
"It's an S, it's an O, it's a crazy radio!" Manufactured in the 1970s, Panasonic's brightly colored plastic transistor radio with a hole in the middle could be twisted into various fun shapes.

TOOTIE RAMSEY
Since age eleven, the naive, gossipy, braces-adorned black girl—the youngest of her tight-knit group of friends—has attended the Eastland School for Young Women in upstate New York. Played by Kim Fields on *The Facts of Life* TV sitcom.

FYI: ▸ Tootie facts: Her real name is Dorothy; her best friend is wiseacre Natalie Green; her cat's name is Jeffrey; and she was the first African-American to play Romeo's Juliet at Eastland.

TOOTSIE CARS
These low-priced, die-cast tiny toy vehicles were generally found at five-and-dime stores during the Baby Boomer childhood era.

TOOTSIE ROLL POPS
Do you remember the amusing animated TV commercial for the lollipop with the Tootsie Roll center? Airing in the early 1970s, it had a little boy asking a wise owl, "How many licks does it take to get to the Tootsie Roll center of a Tootsie Pop?" and the owl demonstrating: "A one, a two, a three . . . (crunch) . . . three!" Tootsie Roll Pops have been around since 1931.

FYI: ▸ Debuting in 1896, candy inventor Leo Hirshfield named the beloved Tootsie Roll after his daughter's nickname, "Tootsie."

TOOT SWEETS

"The eatable, tweetable treats!" Candy whistles invented by Caractacus Potts in *Chitty Chitty Bang Bang* that attract the attention of every dog (including his own pet sheepdog, Edison) within earshot.

TOP CAT

Hanna-Barbera cartoon show about a streetwise, sharp-tongued furry yellow feline who was the enterprising leader of a gang of con-artist alley cats, including right-hand cat Benny the Ball, dim-witted Brain, overanxious Choo-Choo, "catsanova" Fancy-Fancy, and hep-cat Spook. Living in well-equipped trash cans in Manhattan, Top Cat (T.C. to pals) and cronies were constantly cooking up some get-rich caper while avoiding suspicious Officer Dibble, the cop on the beat. Officer Dibble didn't appreciate the cats, making personal calls from a police telephone pole and drinking milk from bottles left at the doors of local residents. *Top Cat* was first introduced as a prime-time series in 1961; it aired for one season, before landing on Saturday-morning TV from 1962 to 1969, where it found a loyal audience who remember it fondly today.

TOP GUN

"A Top Gun instructor told me that there are only four occupations worthy of a man: actor, rock star, jet fighter pilot, or President of the United States."

—TOM CRUISE, ACTOR

The number-one movie of 1986, with a gross of more than $150 million, confirmed Tom Cruise's superstar status and put leather bomber-jackets in the fashion forefront. Directed by Tony Scott, it's a slick, calculated actioner about student pilots at the elite Top Gun Naval Flying School. Set to a pounding rock score, *Top Gun* offers up high-tech aerial dogfighting mixed with a planeload of masculine beefcake. Cruise plays Pete Mitchell, a hotshot young lieutenant nicknamed "Maverick" who aspires to be the Navy's number-one pilot. Co-stars include Kelly McGillis as Charlotte "Charlie" Blackwood, the astrophysicist teacher and Maverick's love interest; Anthony Edwards as Nick "Goose" Bradshaw, the radar intercept officer and Maverick's best buddy; Tom Skerrit as Mike "Viper" Metcalf, the commanding officer; Val Kilmer as Tom "Iceman" Kazanski, Maverick's nemesis; and Meg Ryan as Carole, Goose's wife. On the soundtrack you can find Kenny Loggin's "Danger Zone" and Berlin's "You Take My Breath Away," the year's Oscar-winner for Best Song.

TOPPER

Cute lost penguin searching for the South Pole who joins Santa-to-be, Kris Kringle, on his first journey to deliver toys to the children of Sombertown; seen in the animated TV special *Santa Claus Is Comin' to Town* (1970).

TOP-SIDERS

Originating as a classic sailing shoe, a.k.a. deck shoe, Sperry's Top-Siders were the must-have footwear during the preppy craze of the early 1980s. A Top-Sider is a moccasin-like shoe made out of teak-brown leather that had a suede cord outlining the top and a matching suede cord as a shoelace. Prepsters preferred to wear them without socks (totally cool) and with khakis and Izods. Notable copycats included Sebago's Docksiders and Dexter's Deck Shoes.

TORS, IVAN

Hollywood producer best remembered for producing family-friendly action-adventure TV shows, usually revolving around animals: *Sea Hunt* (1958–61), *Flipper* (1964–68), *Daktari* (1966–69), *Cowboy in Africa* (1967–68), and *Gentle Ben* (1967–69). Tors help established Africa U.S.A., a wild-animal park in Southern California where *Cowboy in Africa* and *Daktari* were filmed.

"TO SIR, WITH LOVE"

Uplifting title-track to the 1967 movie of the same name, starring Sidney Poitier as Mark Thackeray, an American teacher assigned to a rough high school in a London's slummy East End who inspires a classroom of undisciplined teens ("taking them from crayons to perfume"). At the film's end, pop singer Lulu as student Barbara Pegg performs the heartfelt ballad as a respectful tribute to Poitier's influence. In the United States, Lulu's song topped the charts for an amazing five weeks!

FYI: ▸ A singing star in Britain, Lulu was once married to a Bee Gee (Maurice Gibb), from 1969 to 1973.

TOSS ACROSS

"Go . . . go . . . go . . . for three in a row!" A fun family game introduced by Ideal Toys in 1969. Toss Across was an updated take on tic-tac-toe in which players took turns throwing little bean bags at a large game board made up of plastic rotating squares with the symbols of X or O on them. You could toss to score for yourself or to block your opponent. The first to turn up X or O three in a row won the game.

TOUCAN SAM

The blue jungle bird with the big multicolored beak has been entertaining kids in his Kellogg's Froot Loops commercials since 1964. These animated ads for the donut-shaped, fruity-colored (lemon-yellow, strawberry-red, lime-green, and orange) oat cereal had Sam following his nose, because "it always knows the flavor of fruit wherever it goes."

FYI: ▸ Froot Loops in pig Latin is "Oot-fray Oops-lay."

TOUGHSKINS

In the 1970s, many kids were forced by their cruel parents to wear these jeans sold only at Sears department stores. Plain-looking and with a yellow X stitched on each rear pocket, Toughskins represented total dorkdom—no kid in their right mind would have picked them out. Why, you ask? Well, the denim fabric was rather stiff and came in ugly shades like clay brown, moss green, rhubarb red, thunderstorm blue, and military gray. But parents liked them (they didn't have to wear 'em) because they were economical (as in inexpensive, and they looked it too) and durable (they weren't called Toughskins for nothin'), and because it was easy to find the right size (they came in only three size-types: slim, regular, and the humiliating husky). At the school playground, it was hard not to pity the overweight child who had to stick his or her fat derriere in a husky pair, especially when the "in crowd" wasn't even wearing Toughskins (they had on status jeans, such as Levi's, Brittania, or Bugle Boy).

TOWERING INFERNO

"One tiny spark becomes a night of blazing suspense!" In this 1974 disaster epic, catastrophe strikes San Francisco's Glass Tower, the world's tallest skyscraper (135 stories), on the night of its grand-opening gala. Due to cost-cutting by a greedy developer, shoddy electrical wiring causes a fire to break out in a storage room on the 85th floor. As massive flames spread up the colossal structure, the swanky partygoers on the top floor are trapped, not knowing whether they will be rescued or perish. Down below, a team of daring firemen led by heroic fire chief Michael O'Hallorhan (Steve McQueen) and the building's stunned but also heroic architect, Doug Roberts (Paul Newman), are fighting their way up through the burning tower to save the trapped party, including Roberts's sweetheart, Susan Franklin (Faye Dunaway), on the 135th floor.

Directed by John Guillermin and Irwin Allen (the man who gave us 1972's *Poseidon Adventure*), the multi-million-dollar extravaganza is praised by many as the best if not the biggest disaster movie ever (one critic called it the "Cadillac of Disaster Films"). It showcases spectacular special effects and a terrific all-star supporting cast, including William Holden as greedy developer Jim Duncan, Richard Chamberlain as Roger Simmons, Susan Blakely as Patty Simmons, Fred Astaire as Harlee Claiborne, Jennifer Jones as Lisolette Mueller, Robert Vaughn as Senator Gary Parker, Robert Wagner as Don Bigelow, Susan Flannery as Lorrie, O.J. Simpson as Harry Jernigan, and Mike Lookinland as Phillip Allbright. Two novels inspired the Oscar-nominated picture, *The Tower* by Richard Martin Stern and *The Glass Inferno* by Thomas N. Scortia.

TOXIC AVENGER

A 1985 film created by New Jersey–based Troma Studios, a company infamous for such low-budget cult faves as *Class of Nuke 'em High* (1986), *Troma's War* (1988), and *Chopper Chicks in Zombietown* (1989). It starred Mitchell Cohen as Melvin Junko, a ninety-pound weakling who is bullied by the buff jocks at the local Tromaville health club. After one particular bullying incident, geeky Melvin falls into a tub of toxic waste and is transformed into a hideously deformed mutant with superhuman strength known as the Toxic Avenger. He immediately seeks revenge on his jock antagonists, on criminals, and on the evil industries that pollute New Jersey's landscapes. "Toxie" also falls in love with Claire, a "beautiful, blind buxom bimbo" whom he saved from a robbery at a fast-food joint. It inspired three sequels and a 1991 syndicated cartoon series, *The Toxic Crusaders*.

TOY PISTOLS AND RIFLES

"Bang! Bang! You're dead!" What would a boyhood romp of cowboys versus Indians, cops versus robbers, or Americans versus Nazis be without these? Topper's Johnny Eagle line was the best of the Baby Boom era.

TOY STORY

In 1995, the Walt Disney Company united with the Pixar Animation Studios and gave us the first-ever feature-length film animated entirely by computer. Simply delightful, *Toy Story* is about the secret world of toys that come to life when people are not around. Woody, a pull-string cowboy (voiced by Oscar-winning Tom Hanks), is six-year-old Andy Davis's top toy. Then one day, Andy acquires flashy space-ranger Buzz Lightyear, a high-tech action figure (voiced by comedian Tim Allen), as a birthday present that takes the place as "top toy." Threatened and jealous, Woody schemes to get rid of Buzz (who doesn't realize he is a toy), but the plan backfires and the two rivals find themselves lost outside Andy's toy room.

Working together as friends, Woody and Buzz journey back to Andy while avoiding the clutches of Sid Phillips, a toy-torturing boy who lives next door. Co-starring in the film are many classic toys of our childhood brought to vivid life, such as an Etch-a-Sketch, Barrel of Monkeys, green plastic army men, Slinky Dog, and Mr. Potato Head (voiced by the puckish Don Rickles). A winner at the box office (grossing $354 million worldwide), *Toy Story* earned three Academy Award nominations, including Best Song ("You've Got a Friend in Me"), and inspired Disney and Pixar to produce a line of computer-animated tales: *A Bug's Life* (1998), *Toy Story 2* (1999), *Monsters Inc.* (2001), and *Finding Nemo* (2003). Its superior sequel, *Toy Story 2*, has the toys encountering a greedy toy collector out to nab Woody.

T.P. (TOILET-PAPERING)

Juvenile prank of throwing rolls of toilet paper across the foliage in someone's front yard at night to the surprise—or anger—of its occupants the next morning. The mischief-making act was done to someone you really liked (for example, cheerleaders toilet-papering the team before the big game) or to someone you really disliked (the bitch in class, for instance).

TRACY PARTRIDGE

The youngest member of the Partridges, TV's groovy music family, was a dour five-year-old girl with strawberry-blonde locks whose versatility in playing the tambourine, the triangle, the cowbell, and wood blocks more than made up for her lack of rhythm. Played by Suzanne Crough (born March 6, 1963) on *The Partridge Family* from 1970 to 1974.

TRACY TURNBLAD

A spunky teen queen who, despite her hefty size and even heftier bouffant hairdo, mashed-potatoes her way to the top spot on a 1962 Baltimore dance program, *The Corny Collins Show*, and teaches the local citizens a thing or two about civil rights. (Tracy spoke out for African-American youths, who were banned from appearing on the show.) Adored by working-class parents Edna and Wilbur Turnblad, the dancing chubbette is best friends with Penny Pingleton (who's constantly "permanently, positively punished" by her mother) but enemies with rich witch Amber Von Tussle and her snooty parents, Franklin and Velma. Tracy was played by Ricki Lake in director John Waters's teenage satire, *Hairspray* (1988).

TRAMP

The furry sheepdog (actually a mixed briard) owned by Steve Douglas and family on the *My Three Sons* TV sitcom. Good-natured Speed, and later replacement Spud, who played Tramp during the series' thirteen-year run, won three Patsy Awards.

TRANS AM

> "A hard-muscled lightning-reflexed commando of a car, the likes of which doesn't exist anywhere in the world."
>
> —*CAR AND DRIVER* MAGAZINE

The coolest of the cool (and the cockiest of the cocky) drove this spirited muscle car, part of Pontiac's Firebird line and created in 1967 to compete with Ford's phenomenal Mustang. The Trans Am was a showy road warrior, a sexy modern machine, a car with machismo written all over. It had distinctive qualities, such as twin scoops on the hood, front air dams, rear-end ducktail spoiler, Rally II tires, and a speedometer that clocked an amazing 160 miles an hour. Most Trans Ams were marked with a huge, flaming trademark Firebird painted on the hood. In 1977, the automobile became extremely popular because of the movie *Smokey and the Bandit*, which had the hero, Burt Reynolds's Bandit, driving a high-flying Trans Am.

FYI: ▸ Pontiac Firebird's rival, the Chevrolet Camaro, had its own version of the Trans Am called the Z/28.

TRANSFORMERS
"More than meets the eye!" Premiering in 1984, the enormously successful Hasbro toy line and cartoon series starred the Autobots, heroic robots able to transform into various vehicles or weapons and battle the Decepticons, evil robots out to control the universe. They inspired two other cars-that-turn-into-robots: GoBots and Voltron.

TRANQUILITY FOREST
Mystical woodland home of The Bugaloos, a musical group whose members are half-human and half-insect, seen on Saturday-morning TV in the 1970s.

TRAVOLTA, JOHN
"I don't think I'm very cool as a person. I'm just better than anyone else at acting cool." Born in New Jersey on February 18, 1954, Travolta's Hollywood break came in 1975, at age twenty-one, when he was cast as one of the Sweathogs on TV's *Welcome Back, Kotter.* His portrayal of the dim-witted but charmingly cool Vinnie Barbarino, combined with handsome looks—sparkling blue eyes, dimpled chin, shaggy dark hair, and a hunky, long-limbed build—made him the show's breakout star and a hot idol for the *Tiger Beat* crowd. Capitalizing on this heartthrob appeal in 1976, he starred in a touching TV movie, *The Boy in the Plastic Bubble*, as immune-deficient Tod Lubitch, and in a big-screen horror flick, *Carrie*, as bruiser villain Billy Nolan; he also recorded a Top Ten bubblegum song called "Let Her In."

In 1977, Travolta hit pay dirt when cast as cool dance king Tony Manero in the legendary disco film *Saturday Night Fever.* Earning him a Best Actor Oscar nomination, the role established him as an international star and an icon of the disco era whose blow-dried hair and white-lapel suit with open shirt became the archetype for male dancers everywhere (Travolta was dubbed "The King of Disco"). Other notable movie performances include cool greaser Danny Zuko, opposite Olivia Newton-John's wholesome Sandy, in the retro 1950s musical *Grease* (1978), and two-stepping, mechanical bull–riding cool country-stud Bud Davis in *Urban Cowboy* (1980). After experiencing a lengthy career slump throughout most of the 1980s and early 1990s, Travolta was rediscovered by moviegoers in director Quentin Tarentino's *Pulp Fiction* (1994), playing cool hit man Vincent Vega. He married actress Kelly Preston (*SpaceCamp*) in 1991.

FYI: ▸ John Travolta has been a member of the Church of Scientology for more than twenty years. In 2000, he starred in the stinker of the Millennium year, *Battlefield Earth*, a critic-panned film based on the book by Scientology founder L. Ron Hubbard.

TREKKIES
Star Trek claims one of the biggest cult followings of any show ever. Known as Trekkies, these rabidly devoted fans are nerdy techno types who fiercely worship and breathe any and all things *Star Trek* and flock to annual *Star Trek* conventions held around the world. They have turned the 1960s TV show—which aired on prime time for only three years, with low ratings—into pop culture's most successful sci-fi franchise and a multi-billion-dollar industry.

TRESSY
Long before those other hair-growing dolls (Ideal's Crissy and Velvet) made the toy scene in the late 1960s, there was Tressy. Introduced by American Character in 1963, this eleven-and-a-half-inch fashion doll's hair grew to different lengths by pushing a button on her stomach, which made it longer, or turning a key inserted in her back, to make it shorter. A fashion booklet packaged with her gave instructions on how to construct a variety of high-fashion coiffures, like the Beach Beauty Bob, the Royal Pouf, and the Beehive Bubble. Created to rival Mattel's

fashion-queen Barbie, Tressy likewise came with a variety of clothes, carrying cases, and other accessories, such as the essential penthouse apartment and beauty salon. Tressy had a younger, nine-inch-tall sister, Cricket, and a best friend, Mary Make-Up.

TRIBBLES

These alien space critters—featured on a legendary *Star Trek* episode titled "The Trouble with Tribbles" (originally airing on December 29, 1967)—were lovably annoying, purring little balls of fur that reproduced faster than you could say "Beam me up, Scotty!" Brought on the starship Enterprise by Lieutenant Uhura, Tribbles happened to be born pregnant and to love to eat, and the more they ate—the more they multiplied!

FYI: ▸ Archenemies of the evil Klingons, Tribbles squeaked whenever one was in proximity.

TRILOGY OF TERROR

Directed by Dan Curtis, creator of daytime's *Dark Shadows*, a 1975 TV movie starring cockeyed Karen Black as four anguished females in a trio of bizarre horror stories. These episodes included "Millicent and Therese," the opening tale, in which Black plays both an amorous seductress and the tormented spinster sister she taunts; "Julie," the second story, about a withdrawn, sexually repressed schoolteacher who is blackmailed by one of her students; and "Amelia" (a.k.a. "Prey"), the final segment, concerning a mother-dominated woman who is viciously stalked in her modern high-rise apartment by a spear-toting, devilish African doll come to life. It is this third episode—with frenetic pacing, low-angle shots, and a terrifying final scene—that lingers in our memories and that was acclaimed by critics as the best TV horror tale ever filmed.

TRIVIAL PURSUIT

People who read books like this are probably good at playing games like this. Created by two fellows from Canada, Scott Abbott and Chris Haney, and introduced by Parker Brothers in 1981, the game let players show off their trivia know-how (or lack of it) by asking and answering endless questions (6,000 were featured in the first edition, known as Genus) from six different categories separated by colors: Geography (blue), Entertainment (pink), History (yellow), Art and Literature (brown), Science and Nature (green), and Sports and Leisure (orange). As the best-selling game of the 1980s (in 1984, the peak of trivia mania, nineteen million sets were sold), Trivial Pursuit spawned a variety of special editions, including Silver Screen, TV, RPM, All-Star Sports, Baby Boomer, Disney, Star Wars, Biblical, and a Young Players edition. It's credited with relaunching the adult board-game industry, inspiring numerous trivia-word games, such as Pictionary, Charades, Balderdash, Boggle, Scattergories, and Taboo.

TRIXIE

Although at times she worries about her thrill-seeking, car-racing boyfriend Speed Racer, this spunky, pretty cartoon brunette, with the seductive wink in her wide eyes, will forever be devoted to him.

TRIX RABBIT

"I'm a rabbit, and rabbits are supposed to like carrots. But I hate carrots. I like Trix." White hare who joneses for Trix cereal and has to be reminded all the time, "Silly rabbit. Trix are for kids!" General Mills started marketing Trix fruit-flavored corn puffs in 1955. In 1960, the kooky rabbit was introduced as its Trix-loving spokes-hare and star of animated TV spots that never allowed him to eat the popular cereal. This denial went on for a decade and a half, until 1976, when kids were asked to vote in a much-ballyhooed election—"Yes! Let the rabbit eat Trix" or "No! Trix are for kids"—by submitting box-top ballots. In a landslide victory, 99 percent voted "Yes!" allowing the rabbit his own bowl of "raspberry red, lemon yellow, and orange orange."

TROLL DOLLS

In the late 1950s, a poor Danish woodcutter named Thomas Dam carved a Troll Doll out of wood as a birthday present for his daughter. The doll was based on the mythical forest elves of Scandinavian folklore who were as old as time and visible to no one, except children and kindhearted grown-ups. It was believed if caught, these little gnomes would bring their captors a lifetime of good luck. The young daughter's gift caught the attention of a local toy-store owner, who encouraged Dam to create more of them to sell.

Known as Dammit Dolls and made out of plastic instead of wood, the homely but cute imps were quickly embraced throughout Europe. When they were introduced to the United States in the early 1960s, Dam's dolls were an immediate smash, inspiring American toy companies to produce their own lines (Uneeda's Wishnik and Scandia House Enterprises' Trolls) and becoming the second-best-selling doll of the decade, topped only by Barbie.

Troll dolls were comically ugly and goofy in appearance. Ranging from three inches to roughly twelve inches in height, they had naked pudgy bodies with stubby-fingered hands and oversized heads with big, glassy eyes, flared nostrils, toothless grins, jug ears, and wild bushy hair colored in groovy psychedelic hues, such as bright green, fluorescent orange, hot pink, and sky blue. In the early years (1963 and 1964), Trolls were largely faddish among high school and college girls, who carried them in their pockets and purses for their promise of good fortune (by stroking the hair). It didn't take long for small tots to catch on to the crazy fad. Kids collected them by the dozens, including Animal Trolls and Superhero Trolls, and played with them in vinyl Troll Houses and a Troll Village by Marx Toys, complete with cave, rocks, and trees. Trolls enjoyed a massive revival in the 1980s when a new generation of youngsters discovered them.

FYI: ▸ In 1963, believing that the little pixies gave their owners good luck, daredevil pilot Betty Miller duplicated Amelia Earhart's 1935 solo flight of 7,400 miles with only a Troll Doll as copilot.

TROUBLE

Released by Kohner in 1965, this is the game that introduced the famous Pop-o-Matic placed at the center of the playing board, which rolled the dice when its clear plastic dome was pushed down. A variant of Parcheesi and advertised as a "frustrating chase game," Trouble's object was to move your game piece quickly around the plastic board while trying to land on your opponents' pieces to send them back to the start—that's how you gave them "trouble."

TRUE GRIT

The enormously successful movie earned legendary John Wayne his first and only Oscar and is considered by many to be the last of the great western epics. Wayne played Reuben J. "Rooster" Cogburn, a crusty, hard-drinking, over-the-hill U.S. Marshal with a patch over one eye and a trusty horse named Beau. Believing that Rooster is a man of "true grit," Mattie Ross (Kim Darby), a spunky fourteen-year-old tomboy, hires him to help her find the killer of her father. Together with straight-as-an-arrow Texas Ranger La Boeuf (singer Glen Campbell), they set off into dangerous Indian territory to track and capture murderer Tom Chaney (Jeff Corey) and accomplices Lucky and Moon (Robert Duvall and Dennis Hopper). Directed by Henry Hathaway, the rousing 1969 film was based on the best-selling novel by Charles Portis. Wayne reprised his role in 1975's *Rooster Cogburn*, co-starring Katharine Hepburn.

FYI: ▸ Did you know 1969 was a banner year for movie westerns? Joining *True Grit* on the big screen were *Butch Cassidy and the Sundance Kid*, *Charro*, *MacKenna's Gold*, *100 Rifles*, *Sam Whiskey*, *Support Your Local Sheriff*, and *The Wild Bunch*. And, if you're askin' where's *Midnight Cowboy*, it doesn't count—it's not about a cowpoke at twilight, but a modern-day Texan who becomes a male hustler in New York City.

TRULY SCRUMPTIOUS

"Truly Scrumptious, you're truly, truly scrumptious / Scrumptious as a cherry peach parfait . . ." Pretty, blonde lady friend of *Chitty Chitty Bang Bang's* inventor, Caractacus Potts, and his young twins, Jemima and Jeremy. Her father is Lord Scrumptious, owner of a large British candy factory (Scrumptious Candy Company). Mattel's Truly Scrumptious Barbie dolls, manufactured in 1969, are some of the most sought-after among collectors, with a price tag up to $600 mint-in-the-box.

T-SHIRTS

> "My grandparents went to Las Vegas and all I got was this lousy T-shirt."
> —POPULAR T-SHIRT STATEMENT

The power of expressing one's personal feelings on a T-shirt can be incredible. Just by going to a T-shirt parlor, you can let people know where you went on vacation, which presidential candidate you are voting for, what kind of beer you like, and if you think life stinks. You can display your beliefs with radical statements like "Disco sucks," "I'm with stupid," "Bowlers make better lovers," "Jesus saves," "Keep on truckin'," or "Dy-no-mite!" You can tell the world what kind of person you are with descriptives like "Hot Stuff, "Foxy Lady," "Evil Woman," "Born Loser, "Party Animal," or "I'm a 10!" You can be a walking billboard, advertising big names like "Adidas" or "Budweiser" and slogans like "Just do it!" or "Coke—It's the real thing!" (the drink not the drug). You can show everyone who your teen idol is or what your favorite shows are by wearing transfers of Shaun Cassidy, The Fonz, Baretta, Wonder Woman, Jaws, or Star Wars (with the back of the shirt reading, "May The Force be with you"). And you can be the coolest of the cool by wearing a concert T-shirt the day after witnessing a live performance by Aerosmith, Foreigner, Van Halen, Journey, Styx, Rush, KISS, or AC/DC.

TUBE SOCKS

White calf-high socks marked by athletic stripes circling the upper calf. Youths commonly wore them with sneakers and shorts back in the 1970s. For me, they stir up unwanted memories of junior high school and being a gawky adolescent in second period P.E. class.

TUBE TOPS

These tops with elasticized round bands were ideal for small-titted babes at the disco or roller rink, but they could be dangerously revealing if a large-breasted woman wearing one hopped around too much. (That actually happened to a bouncing woman who was overelated as a contestant on Bob Barker's TV game show *The Price Is Right*.)

TUBSY

"Gee . . . Tubsy splashes all by herself!" Gleeful baby doll with the cute two-tooth smile, introduced by Ideal Toys in 1967, that actually splashes with her arms when placed in a tub of tummy-high water.

"TUBULAR BELLS"

Incredibly chilling multi-instrumental theme for the 1973 frightfest *The Exorcist*. It earned composer Mike Oldfield a Top Ten single in the early winter of 1974.

TUCKER, TANYA

Country-and-western music has always been dominated by adult singers who perform songs containing mature subject matter relating to sex, adultery, divorce, drinking, abuse, and so on. In 1972, the country world was shocked to discover that the distinctively husky, lusty voice behind the latest hit-maker belonged not to a grown woman but to a thirteen-year-old girl named Tanya Tucker.

Born October 10, 1958, in Seminole, Texas, the pretty, blonde teen rarely sang about topics relating to youthful innocence, like teddy bears, butterflies, and funny faces. She preferred story songs with provocative lyrics: "What's Your Mama's Name?" (1973), "Blood Red and Goin' Down" (1973), "Would You Lay with Me (In a Field of Stone)" (1974), "Lizzie and the Rainman" (1975), and "San Antonio Stroll" (1975). Although it most likely had a religious connotation, "Would You Lay with Me" was particularly controversial and banned from radio stations (some listeners interpreted it as a song about fornication). These hits earned Tucker, who by age sixteen was one of the industry's biggest stars, a reputation as a country-western Lolita.

In 1979, Tucker moved from Nashville to L.A., where she changed her image by promoting herself as a rock 'n' roll vixen—dressed in sexy threads (spandex pants, tube tops, and stiletto heels)—for the album *TNT*. But that move backfired. Her country fans weren't supportive of the new Tanya Tucker, so her hot career fizzled. In the early 1980s, she hit even harder times. First, there was the very publicized stormy relationship with much-older boyfriend Glen Campbell, followed by a succession of short-lived love affairs with such beaus as pop singer Andy Gibb, actor Don Johnson, and boxer George Cooney. Then financial trouble emerged, accompanied by a bout with alcohol and drug addiction, and a three-year absence from recording. Tough as a cookie, Tucker persevered and, throughout the 1990s, remained a prominent country hit-maker (named the Country Music Association's Female Vocalist of the Year in 1991), with such songs as "If Your Heart Ain't Busy Tonight" and "Two Sparrows in a Hurricane" (both in 1992).

TUTTI AND TODD

Barbie's Dream House became crowded when Mattel introduced her five-year-old twin siblings in 1966. Previously, the fashion queen had shared it only with younger sister Skipper. Then MOD'ern teen cousin Francie and her chum Casey, a foreign-exchange student from London, moved in. So now she had to make more room for the cute-as-a-button brother and sister. Accompanied by a variety of play sets and matching outfits, the look-alike Tutti and Todd provided Barbie with a lot of babysitting responsibilities. (Maybe she could pawn them off on wallflower pal Midge in order to spend extra cuddle time with sweetheart Ken.) In 1967, a playmate named Chris was added, and in 1968, *Family Affair*'s Buffy Davis and Mrs. Beasley became friends of the young twins.

TV MOVIES

The made-for-TV movies of the 1970s and 1980s portrayed teenagers as a dysfunctional bunch. Did the adult programmers at the three networks (ABC, CBS, and NBC) really think this way of us youths, or was it an example of art imitating real life? The many social ills showcased included:

- **Drug abuse:** *Maybe I'll Come Home in the Spring* (1970); *The People Next Door* (1970); *Go Ask Alice* (1973); *The Death of Richie* (1977); *Stoned* (1980); *Angel Dusted* (1981); and *Not My Daughter* (1985).
- **Alcoholism:** *Sarah T.: Portrait of a Teenage Alcoholic* (1975) and *The Boy Who Drank Too Much* (1980).
- **Prostitution:** *Dawn: Portrait of a Teenage Runaway* (1976); *Alexander: The Other Side of Dawn* (1977); *Little Ladies of the Night* (1977); *Off the Minnesota Strip* (1980); and *Girls of the White Orchid* (1983).
- **Delinquency:** *Outrage* (1973); *Terror on the Beach* (1973); *All the Kind Strangers* (1974); *Born Innocent* (1974); *A Cage Without a Key* (1975); *Nightmare in Badham County* (1976); *The Survival of Dana* (1979); *In the Custody of Strangers* (1982); and *Baby Sister* (1983).
- **Teen pregnancy:** *Mr. and Mrs. Bo Jo Jones* (1971); *The Girls of Huntington House* (1973); *I Want to Keep My Baby!* (1976); and *Daddy* (1987).
- **Devil-worship:** *The Devil's Daughter* (1973); *Satan's School for Girls* (1973); *The Spell* (1977); *The Initiation of Sarah* (1978); *A Stranger in Our House* (1978); *Midnight Offerings* (1981); and *The Midnight Hour* (1985).
- **Religious fanaticism:** *Can Ellen Be Saved?* (1974) and *Blinded by the Light* (1980).
- **Mental illness:** *Lisa, Bright and Dark* (1973); *Bad Ronald* (1974); and *A Last Cry for Help* (1979).
- **Suicide:** *Silence of the Heart* (1984) and *Surviving* (1985).
- **Anorexia nervosa:** *The Best Little Girl in the World* (1981).
- **Hitchhiking:** *Diary of a Teenage Hitchhiker* (1979).
- **Child pornography:** *Fallen Angel* (1981).

TV WESTERNS

Howdy, pardners! As the 1960s began, there were no fewer than thirty westerns airing on prime-time TV. The following are twenty-five favorite shoot-em-uppers from the once-popular genre.

The Adventures of Rin Tin Tin (1954–59)
Alias Smith and Jones (1971–73)
The Big Valley (1965–69)
Bonanza (1959–73)
Branded (1965–66)
Bronco (1958–62)
Cheyenne (1955–63)
The Cisco Kid (1950–56)
Daniel Boone (1964–70)
Gunsmoke (1955–75)
Have Gun Will Travel (1957–63)
The Lawman (1958–62)
The Life and Times of Wyatt Earp (1955–61)
The Lone Ranger (1949–57)
Maverick (1957–62)
Rawhide (1959–66)
The Rebel (1959–62)
The Rifleman (1958–63)
Sugarfoot (1957–61)
Tales of Wells Fargo (1957–62)
The Virginian (1962–71)
Wagon Train (1957–65)
Wanted: Dead or Alive (1958–61)
Wild, Wild West (1965–70)
Zorro (1957–59)

TWEENERS

"Flower power, the Vietnam era, the drug age—I don't identify with that. But we're not Generation X either. We float at the end of the Baby Boomer generation."

—LAURIE FRINGS, AGE THIRTY-THREE, IN *USA TODAY*, 1996

The twenty million or so Americans born in the first five years of the 1960s, associated with the Baby Boom demographically, and linked to Generation X socially. Truth be known, these people haven't felt like a part of either generation—post-Boomer, pre-Xer—just stuck in between, hence the name. According to a *USA Today* cover story written by Andrea Stone, tweeners started grade school in the 1960s, became teenagers in the 1970s, and graduated from school in the 1980s. They often resent being lumped statistically with Baby Boomers. Why? The older Boomers, born in the 1940s and 1950s, have incessantly basked in the media spotlight with their idealism, social issues, and pastimes, while the younger ones simply went ignored.

Think about this. How can you be an archetypal Baby Boomer if you don't remember Howdy Doody or Davy Crockett coonskin caps? If you don't remember John F. Kennedy's assassination because you were an infant or not born yet. If you can't recall when The Beatles invaded America. If you didn't march for civil rights, burn your bra, protest Vietnam, or attend Woodstock. If you didn't drop acid or practice free love. If you're younger than the actors who played Jan Brady and Danny Partridge. If you weren't old enough to Hustle inside Studio 54. And if your lowly McJob didn't allow you enough income to be a BMW-driving yuppie. As for Generation X, consider them lucky to have inherited the Tweeners' cynicism.

21 JUMP STREET

An updated version of *The Mod Squad*, this hip TV crime drama airing from 1987 to 1992 was created by the new FOX network to attract a younger audience. The series focused on a special unit of cops whose youthful looks allowed them to pass as high school or college students and go undercover in local schools to fight crime. The building they were based out of was an abandoned church at 21 Jump Street in Los Angeles. The cast included Johnny Depp as Tommy Hanson, Holly Robinson as Judy Hoffs, Dustin Nguyen as H.T. (for Harry Truman) Ioki, and Peter DeLuise as Doug Penhall. In 1988, brooding Richard Grieco joined the cast as streetwise new member Dennis Booker.

FYI: ▸ *21 Jump Street* holds the distinction of being the first FOX series ever to beat an ABC, CBS, or NBC series in its time slot (August 23, 1987).

TWIGGY

"Is it a girl? Is it a boy? No, it's Twiggy!"

—*LOOK* MAGAZINE, 1967

She was an original, a superstar, a 1960s phenomenon, and at seventeen years of age the first model to achieve genuine international celebrity. Born Leslie Hornby on September 19, 1949, in London, Twiggy, with her trademark elfin cap of pale-blonde hair and heavily lashed eyes, was the most unlikely of candidates to become a supermodel. Skinny as a twig (hence the name) at five feet six inches tall, ninety pounds, and measuring a mere 31-23-31, Twiggy had long, bony legs, no bust, pale skin, and large doe-eyes. She was a working-class lass with a strong Cockney twang (it's been said that she sounded like a demented parrot), a limited vocabulary, a lack of sophistication, and a happy-go-lucky nature. In fact, she looked like a little lost waif who had somehow ended up in a fashion shoot.

Twiggy's knobby knees and frightened deer-in-the-headlights look enchanted the world, and in 1966 the teen model was dubbed the "Face of the Year" by London's *Daily Express*. Along with Mary Quant's miniskirt and the Fab Four from Liverpool, she became a swingin' symbol of London's pop scene. Teen girls on both sides of the Atlantic copied her short, boyish pixie and starved themselves silly trying to mimic her emaciated appearance. They purchased a kaleidoscope of mod clothing and hosiery from the Twiggy fashion collection and stocking line. Mannequins were created from an actual cast of Twiggy's body, to display these groovy fashions at department stores and clothing boutiques. Yardley cosmetics sold "Twiggy Lashes" so gals could make their eyes look just like the Twig's. (Fashion note: Three sets of false lashes on top, and drawn-on lashes on the bottom, is the way to acquire this wide-eyed look.)

For little girls, Mattel in 1967 introduced the Twiggy doll, sporting a multicolored minidress and bright-yellow go-go boots, to hang out with Barbie and Francie. You could dress her for a make-believe photo shoot in an array of colorful fashions with names like Twiggy-Do's, Twiggy Turnouts, and Twiggy Gear, and you could play the Twiggy board game ("A game that makes every girl like Twiggy, the Queen of Mod") and carry a vinyl Twiggy lunch box to school.

At the height of her popularity, and "a skillion dollars" wealthy from being the world's top cover girl, Twiggy dropped out of modeling in 1970. Her reason? "You can't be a clothes-hanger for your entire life." Twiggy remained in the spotlight as an accomplished actress and singer, whose credits include the 1971 Ken Russell film, *The Boyfriend*, and the 1983 Broadway musical *My One and Only*, opposite Tommy Tune. In the mid-1990s, the Twiggy waif look was revived by a horde of ultraskinny models, led by fellow Brit Kate Moss.

TWINKIE

Once called the "Cream Puff of the Proletariat," the golden sponge delight with the creamy filling and oblong shape is considered to be the most famous snack cake of all time. Over the years, the Twinkie has left its remarkable mark on pop culture. In the 1950s, Howdy Doody and fellow citizens of Doodyville claimed it was their favorite food. Songwriter Larry Groce sang favorably about the Twinkie in his 1976 Top Ten hit, "Junk Food Junkie." TV's Archie Bunker referred to it as "Wasp soul food" and demanded the snack cake in his lunch box every day. President Jimmy Carter had a Twinkie vending machine installed in the White House. And in the 1979 murder trial known for "the Twinkie defense," Dan White successfully claimed that he had killed San Francisco Mayor George Moscone and Supervisor Harvey Milk only because his diet of Twinkies and other sugary items had made him insane.

Manufactured by Hostess, the Twinkie was created in 1930 by James Dewar, a Chicago baker, who came up with the name after spotting a sign advertising "Twinkle Toe Shoes." Twinkie the Kid, a Twinkie-shaped cowboy, has been the cake's lasso-swinging advertising mascot since 1971. An estimated one billion Twinkies are sold every year!

FYI: ▸ More Twinkies are devoured in the Midwest than in any other region of the United States.

TWIST

"C'mon baby, let's do the Twist. . . ." The mega-classic dance belonging to our parents' generation, introduced by nineteen-year-old Chubby Checker in 1960 with the number-one song "The Twist," involved hips and legs twisting as if stamping out a cigarette. Other great Twistin' tunes: "Let's Twist Again" (1961) by Chubby Checker, "Peppermint Twist" (1962) by Joey Dee and The Starliters, "Twist and Shout" (1962) by The Isley Brothers (The Beatles did a fab remake in 1964), and "Twistin' the Night Away" (1962) by Sam Cooke.

TWISTER (GAME)

"The game that ties you up in knots!" On May 3, 1966, host Johnny Carson and Hungarian actress Eva Gabor demonstrated a brand-new game, called Twister, on TV's *Tonight Show*. Delighted to witness the puckish Carson and the lovely Gabor twisted and knotted in hilarious and somewhat provocative positions, home viewers swiftly purchased Twister by the millions, making it the best-selling game of the year.

Designed by Chuck Foley for Milton Bradley, the game appealed to children and adults alike. Actually, before becoming an enduring favorite of tots, Twister seemed to be marketed toward older folks; even the original box cover featured an illustration of grown-ups playing the popular party game. Imagine, if you will, that it's the mid-1960s and our parents have been fueled by one too many martinis and Winstons at a cocktail soiree—fathers in ties and dinner jackets, mothers in pearls and capri pants, all in stockin' feet, and all are stretched and entwined into a mass resembling human pretzels on a big vinyl game sheet emblazoned with dots of different colors (blue, green, red, yellow). A nonplayer, the "Referee," spins the giant spinner, which tells the participants the next hand or foot to be placed on which colored dot. Uncontrollable gaiety fills the rumpus room after "right hand yellow" is shouted and each player scrambles for a yellow circle. Then "left foot red," and everyone shuffles to a red dot, all the while trying not to fall down—because the person who outlasts his opponents will be the champion of Twister.

Unlike all other boxed board games to that point, Twister was the first to let players become physically involved in the play. Milton Bradley's sales department—unsure about the game's potential—thought their bosses had gone completely wacko to even consider manufacturing it. Nonetheless, it turned out to be one of the company's all-time biggest sellers, and it launched a slew of goofball body-action games, such as Tight Squeeze (1967), Bump Ball (1968), Funny Bones (1968), Grab a Loop (1968), Hip Flip (1968), Limbo Legs (1969), and Swivel (1972).

TWISTER (MOVIE)

Big-screen blockbuster about a team of caravaning weather meteorologists led by an estranged couple, Bill and Jo Harding (Bill Paxton and Helen Hunt), who chase an intense storm system of tornadoes bursting across Oklahoma. Directed by Jan de Bont (*Speed*), this 1996 movie is one fun ride, but the plot, dialogue, and acting definitely take second place to the magnificent twister special effects.

TWIST 'N TURN BARBIE

"Barbie has a new look!" The Queen of Fashion Dolls received her first total transformation and entered the MODern era when Mattel Toys introduced the innovative Twist 'n Turn Barbie in 1967. Incited by a large population of teenage Baby Boomers and the mighty influence they had on popular culture, America was in the middle of a youth movement. The old Barbie doll with her heavy eyeliner, arched eyebrows, bubble-cut hairstyle, and unbendable legs seemed rather rigid and matronly. So Mattel gave her a hip new younger look to reflect the times.

Barbie now appeared more innocent, more open-eyed, and more poseable than ever before. She had big, blue eyes with real rooted lashes, bee-stung lips, and softer makeup. Her hair was styled long and straight with bangs and came in four different colors: Summer Sand, Chocolate Bon-Bon, Go-Go Co-Co, and Sun Kissed. Best of all, Barbie had "lifelike" bendable legs and a waist that swiveled back and forth, allowing her to do all the new dances, like the Frug or Jerk.

"But what do I do with my old Barbie?" asked a thrilled pre–*Brady Bunch* Maureen McCormick on the TV advertisement. According to Mattel, the answer was "just as easy as one (take your old doll to the nearest toy store), two (along with $1.50), and three (and trade her for the new Twist 'n Turn Barbie)." More than one million Barbies were returned, and the old dolls were donated to various children's charities. This trade-in program caused the original Barbie dolls to become scarce. (Known as Barbie Ponytail #1 and Barbie Ponytail #2, those dolls are now worth from $5,000 to $10,000 mint-in-box.)

The Twist 'n Turn Barbie turned the children of the late 1960s and early 1970s on to the groovy world of mod. Her clothing and vinyl carrying cases featured cartoon-colored psychedelic patterns, daisy flowers, giant paisley prints, polka dots, and outtasight optical art. The far-out fashions had mod names like Smasheroo, Zokko, Fancy Dancy, Groovin' Gauchos, Swirly-Cue, Fab City, and Flower Wower and came accessorized with go-go boots, micro-miniskirts, fringed vests, bell-bottoms, fishnet tights, faux furs, swingy earrings, and love beads. Fresh, exciting friends were added to Barbie's world, like smashin' British model Stacey, swingin' blonde P.J., and cool African-American Christie. But the Twist 'n Turn era, from 1967 to 1972, seems to have been Barbie's last glorious years of stylish hairdos and fashionable clothing. In the mid-1970s, she adopted the stereotypical brainless blonde look—dressed in the cheap, simple-looking, froufrou outfits commonly seen today.

2001 ODYSSEY DISCO

Discotheque in Brooklyn where feverish Tony Manero and crew strutted their disco moves on Saturday nights in the 1970s. The nightclub's name is a reference to Stanley Kubrick's trippy sci-fi classic *2001: A Space Odyssey* (1968).

TY-D-BOL MAN

The miniaturized fellow who floated on a boat inside a toilet tank hawking the glories of Ty-D-Bol Toilet Bowl Cleaner. (And you thought your job was bad?)

rstuv

UBBI-DUBBI

The educationally fun children's program *Zoom* featured a weird language called Ubbi-Dubbi, in which you put "ub" before every pronounced vowel in a word. For example, turning "Hi, friends!" into "Hub-i, Frub-iends!" It was perfect for talking behind someone's back in lunch lines (hopefully they were *Zoom*-illiterate) and for discussing secret things parents didn't need to know about.

ULTRAMAN

Before a badly dubbed English version premiered on American syndicated TV in 1967, the bug-eyed metallic giant superhero was already a popular favorite in his home country of Japan. Set on twenty-first-century earth, the live-action series centered around Ultraman's alter ego, Hayata, a bold agent of Japan's Scientific Investigative Agency (SIA), who metamorphosed into the flying colossal titan by swallowing a pill (Beta Capsule) given to him by an alien from planet Nebula M-78 in the fortieth galaxy. Assisting Hayata at SIA are Commander Muramatsu, Arashi, Ide, and Akiko Fuji, his girlfriend, whose curious little brother, Hoshino, repeatedly stumbles across some odd creature bent on causing world destruction.

When a rampaging monster is on the prowl, Ultraman, the "Protector of the World," uses his strong steel hands in a wicked karate chop, shoots powerful Specium beams, or wrestles the monstrosity to defeat. On his chest is a warning light that activates when his energy level is depleting. The incredible array of rubber-suited invaders includes Antlar, a creature that blasts magnetic rays from its horn; Dodongo, a mountain-dwelling dragon; Gabora, a uranium-craving beast; Hydro, a half-bird, half-dinosaur; Neronga, an electricity-craving monster; Ragon, a prehistoric sea demon; Phantom Mountain's snow monster; and Geronimon, a supermonster that's a resurrection of all Ultraman's previous opponents. Ultraman was created by Eiji Tsuburaya, who also created Godzilla, "King of Monsters."

UNCLE ARTHUR

Samantha Stephen's zany and rather outrageous warlock relative (comedian Paul Lynde), who played practical jokes and caused nothing but trouble on prime time's *Bewitched.*

UNCLE CHARLEY

The retired seaman—a grouch on the outside, a softy on the inside—moved in with Steve Douglas and sons to clean and cook after his brother, Bub O'Casey, the original housekeeper, moved home to Ireland. Played by William Demarest on *My Three Sons* from 1965 to 1972.

UNCLE FESTER
Gomez Addams's bald-headed, bulging-eyed weirdo brother who dresses like a monk and can pop a lightbulb in his mouth and light it. Uncle Fester was portrayed by former child star Jackie Coogan on *The Addams Family* TV series and by *Taxi*'s Christopher Lloyd in the 1990s *Addams Family* films.

UNCLE JOE CARSON
Kate Bradley's "moving kind of slow" brother who assumed the position of manager of the Shady Rest Hotel and moonlighted as the Hooterville fire chief. His beloved dog was a little mutt named Higgins. Portrayed from 1963 to 1970 by Edgar Buchanan on the sitcom *Petticoat Junction.*

UNDERDOG
"There's no need to fear, Underdog is here!" Residing in Washington, D.C., lovable, meek Shoeshine Boy was the alter ego of the rhyme-spewing canine superhero. Underdog's magic cape and energy pills gave this courageous fighter for truth and justice the power to overcome despicable foes like scientist Simon Bar Sinister and gangster Riff Raff while rescuing TV reporter Sweet Polly Purebred, his true love. Airing from 1964 to 1973, the durable cartoon featured the voice of frequent *Hollywood Squares* guest Wally Cox as Underdog. In 1965, the superpowered pooch achieved further fame when he became a huge balloon perennial in the Macy's Thanksgiving Day Parade. "Not plane, nor bird nor even frog, it's just little ole me, Underdog!"

UNDEROOS
"Underwear that's fun to wear!" Tighty-whiteys for both little boys and girls, featuring superheroes—like Batman, Spider-Man, Superman, and Wonder Woman—on the crotch. For most tots these were the next step up from diapers and training pants.

UNKNOWN COMIC
A regular on *The Gong Show* TV series who wore a paper sack over his head while telling corny jokes. Performed his act during the program's interludes. His real name: Murray Langston.

UNO
Launched in 1972, the fast-paced card game involves four suits of cards, plus special cards for skipping players, reversing the direction of play, and making players draw cards. The object of the game is to get rid of all your cards, being sure to shout "Uno!" when you get down to your last one.

"UPTOWN GIRL"
In the promo video clip for Billy Joel's 1983 harmony-laced single, a Downtown auto mechanic (played by Joel) finds love with a leggy Uptown girl (Joel's blonde supermodel girlfriend—and future wife—Christie Brinkley).

"UP, UP, AND AWAY"
Unabashedly cute and breezy tune by the 5th Dimension about hot-air ballooning. Released in 1967, it was the group's first Top Ten hit and swept the 1968 Grammy telecast, winning seven awards, including Record of the Year, Song of the Year, and Best Performance by a Vocal Group.

URBAN COWBOY
In the early 1980s, all America appeared to be caught up in the Urban Cowboy craze. Country music was always popular in the South and the Midwest, but now urban cities like L.A., Chicago, and New York were embracing it. It was everywhere! Music acts like Kenny Rogers, Dolly Parton, Willie Nelson, Eddie Rabbitt, and Alabama dominated the pop charts. Cowboy hats, boots, denim, fringe, and bolo ties captured the fashion world. On TV, we watched country-themed shows such as *Dallas*, *The Dukes of Hazzard*, and *B.J. and the Bear*. And *Urban Cowboy* heated up the big screen.

The 1980 film, starring John Travolta and Debra Winger as Bud and Sissy Davis, did for country music what *Saturday Night Fever* (1977) did for disco. It had a familiar tale of boy-meets-girl, boy-loses girl, boy-meets-girl-again—spiced with a down-home Texas flavor, sassy honky-tonk music, electrifying two-stepping, and Winger's sexy ride on the mechanical bull. After viewing *Urban Cowboy,* movie audiences left the theater and flocked to country-western clubs, where they line-danced, two-stepped, guzzled long-necks, and rode the bull. Yee-haa!

URBAN LEGENDS

Modern myths—you know, those too-good-to-be-true accounts that you hear about a friend of a friend's sister's neighbor. Often overheard in the workplace or at parties, these supposedly true tales about microwaved pups and lovers-lane slashers are amazing. But as they unfold, it's hard not to suspect that they're just too good, too outrageous, to have really occurred, or maybe you've heard a different yet similar version before. For the gullible, here are fifteen classic stories that never happened, told for true:

- **AIDS Mary.** A man traveling in New Orleans picks up a woman at a bar and takes her back to his hotel for a one-night stand. The next morning, he wakes up to find her gone, but she had left him a message written on the bathroom mirror in bright-red lipstick: "Welcome to the world of AIDS."
- **Alligators in the Sewers.** Unwanted pet baby gators are flushed down the toilet. They survive, grow to maturity, and roam New York City's vast sewer system.
- **The Babysitter.** A teenage babysitter is getting phone calls from a deadly lunatic. She notifies the police, who trace the calls and discover they are coming from an upstairs phone extension in her suburban home.
- **The Back-Seat Killer.** A woman traveling alone at night stops for gas. The gas station attendant fills the tank and takes her credit card. He comes back to her, says there is something wrong with her card and would she please step out of the car. Reluctantly, she steps out of the car, and he escorts her into the station, locks the door, and says, "There's a guy hidden in the back seat with an axe."
- **The Body in the Bed.** A couple rent a motel room that has a horrendous stench. After enduring a night in the stinky room, they find out what is causing the smell—a corpse is hidden in the bed's box springs.
- **The Boyfriend's Death.** Two sweethearts are necking in a car under a tree in an isolated lovers's lane on the outskirts of town. They hear a strange noise coming from outside, so he tells her to lie low in the locked car while he goes to investigate. He never comes back, and throughout the night the scared girl hears a scrape, scrape, scrape sound on the roof of the car. The next morning she is rescued by the cops, who tell her not to look back. However, she looks back to discover the source of the scraping—her dead boyfriend is hanging from the tree with his feet scraping against the roof of the car.
- **The Doggie Dinner.** In a third-world country, a pampered woman on vacation arrives in a restaurant for dinner carrying her little froufrou dog. Because of language difficulties, she has trouble communicating to the waiter, so she gestures to him to give her pooch a meal. He takes the animal away to the kitchen. Later he returns to serve her beloved pet, now cooked, on a platter, as her dinner entree.
- **The Drug-Tripping Babysitter.** A hippie teen does a hit of LSD while babysitting. She becomes totally freaked out, mistakes the infant for a turkey, and roasts him.
- **The Hook.** Young couple parked on a moonlit lovers' lane in the country overhear a radio broadcast about a crazed killer with a hook for a hand who has escaped from the local insane asylum and was last seen in their area. Spooked, the girl panics and pleads to go home; disappointed, the boy eventually agrees, and in her driveway the pair discover a bloody hook attached to the car door handle.
- **The Microwaved Pet.** An elderly lady gives her dirty kitty a bath and makes the bad decision to dry her in the microwave. Seconds later, the feline explodes.
- **The Missing Kidney.** In some big city, a traveling businessman picks up a seductive woman at a bar. She takes him back to her hotel room for a night of sex. Soon after being served a cocktail, he becomes disoriented and blacks out. As the drugs wear off, he awakens alone in a tub of ice with a surgical closure on his back. Someone had stolen his kidney to sell on the black market.
- **The Shaking Cactus.** A woman brings a cactus home from a trip to the desert. It begins to quiver and shake, so she telephones a cactus expert. He tells her to put the phone down and flee her house right away. The reason? The innards of the cactus are filled with a nest of deadly tarantulas and it's getting ready to explode. Kablam!

- **The Spider in the Hairdo.** There once was a high school gal who had a large, overly hairsprayed and teased bouffant hairdo that she never took down or combed or shampooed. One day a spider climbs into it. A few weeks later, while sitting in history class, the teen's head begins to bleed and she drops dead. A nest of baby spiders had eaten into her brain.
- **The Surprise Birthday Party.** It's a significant birthday for an aging executive. Feeling old, depressed, maybe unattractive, he gleefully responds to his young and gorgeous secretary's invite for lunch. After a couple of martinis, he takes her up on a suggestion that they not go back to the office but go instead to her apartment for another drink. She excuses herself to slip into something more comfortable in the bedroom. Thinking he's gonna get a little afternoon nookie, he strips naked. Minutes later, the bedroom door opens and—"Happy Birthday!"—out pops his secretary, his wife, his kids, other relatives, and the entire office staff.
- **The Toothbrushes.** A family vacationing in a foreign country returned to their hotel room to find it completely ransacked. A thief had taken everything except their toothbrushes and—luckily—their expensive camera. When they return home, they get their vacation pictures developed. To their surprise and utter disgust, they find a succession of photos showing each family member's toothbrush, bristles and all, sticking out of the thief's hairy ass.

URSULA (*GEORGE OF THE JUNGLE*)

Endowed with hourglass curves and luscious red hair, George's sweetheart is definitely one gorgeous cartoon female. She's highly unappreciated by the dim-witted George, who values his yo-yo and autographed pix of Sonny Tufts more and refers to her as "the soft fella who never shaves!"

URSULA (*LITTLE MERMAID*)

Part octopus, part human, this purple-skinned sea witch—who's ugly and overweight—grants the Little Mermaid her wish to have human legs, as a scheme to overtake her father's underwater kingdom. Ursula hangs with two hench-eels, Flotsam and Jetsam, and takes her place—rightly so—as another in Disney's marvelous lineage of wicked villains.

U.S.S. ENTERPRISE

Large, distinctive twenty-third-century starship that carries a diverse crew of courageous scientists and military leaders on a trek to explore deep outer space in the *Star Trek* movie and TV series.

U2

Simply stated, the Irish rockers, formed in Dublin in 1976, were the biggest rock band on the planet during the last two decades of the twentieth century. U2 consists of vocalist Paul "Bono" Hewson, guitarist Dave "The Edge" Evans, bassist Adam Clayton, and drummer Larry Mullern. The best of their alternative-tinged hits include "New Year's Day" (1983), "Sunday Bloody Sunday" (1983), "Pride (In the Name of Love)" (1984), "With or Without You" (1987), "Where the Streets Have No Name" (1987), "Desire" (1988), "Who's Gonna Ride Your Wild Horses" (1992), and "Discotheque" (1997). In 1988, they released *U2: Rattle and Hum*, a documentary film of their North American concert tour.

V

VAC-U-FORM

Electric-oven-like contraption by Mattel Toys used for molding colorful plastic (called Plastigoop) into toys, jewelry, buttons, and various other shapes. Inspiration for Mattel's enormously successful Creepy Crawlers and Incredible Edibles.

VALERIE BROWN

Smart, sensible African-American who played the tambourine for the all-girl rock band Josie and the Pussycats. (Josie might be the leader, but Valerie's the brains behind the group.) However, she's most noteworthy for being the first minority heroine featured in a Saturday-morning cartoon.

VALLEY GIRL

"She's cool. He's hot. She's from the Valley. He's not." Loosely inspired by Moon Unit Zappa's novelty record, and cleverly directed by Martha Coolidge, *Valley Girl* was a teenage love story—sort of a "Romeo and Juliet"—set in modern Los Angeles. The 1983 film follows sweet Julie (played by Deborah Foreman), a popular Val-Gal from the San Fernando Valley, and surly Randy (played by newcomer Nicolas Cage), a punk rocker from across the hills in Hollywood, who meet one night at a party and start to date (Oh my gawd!). The other Vals are of course mortified about one of their own dating a guy from "Hollyweird" (I'm soooo sure!). Julie ultimately caves in to peer pressure and dumps the "tripendicular" Randy, so her old boyfriend, Tommy, a cocky and brainless jock, can take her to the prom (gag me with a spoon!). Randy shows up at the Valley High prom to fight for Julie's hand, and love wins the night (like, totally!). Co-stars were blonde vixen Elizabeth Daily as slutty Loryn, Heidi Holicker as shallow Stacey, Michelle Meyrink as lovestruck Suzi, Michael Bowen as jerky Tommy, Cameron Dye as Randy's cheesy pal Fred, and Fredric Forrest and Colleen Camp as Julie's ex-hippie parents.

A great gem of the 1980s, the movie's awesome soundtrack boasts an incredible collection of New Wave songs, like Modern English's "I Melt with You," The Plimsouls' "A Million Miles Away," Psychedelic Furs' "Love My Way," and Josie Cotton's "Johnny, Are You Queer?" From the fashions (skinny ties, leather miniskirts, decorated headbands, and leg warmers) to the Val-speak ("grody," "fer shur," "bitchin'," and "rad") to the music (Devo, Culture Club, Men at Work, and Sparks), *Valley Girl* is a time capsule of what it was like to be a teen in the early years (1980–84) of the Reagan era.

VALLEY GIRLS

"Okay, fine, fer shur, fer shur, I'm a Valley Girl, and there ain't no cure. . . ." Valley Girls were empty-headed, self-absorbed, shopping-obsessed, spoiled young women who lived in California's San Fernando Valley, the sprawling suburban region north of Los Angeles. A Val-Gal's biggest characterization was the funny way she talked: enthusiastic squeals and overenunciated words, derived from stoner-surfer jargon and babbled at rapid speed (for example, "Like, ferrr shurrr" or "Ohmigod!"). During the summer of 1982, the girls from the Valley became the focus of the nation, following rock satirist Frank Zappa's novelty song "Valley Girl," in which his teen daughter, Moon Unit, spoke a monologue brimming with Valley slang, such as the disdainful "Bag your face" and "Gag me with a spoon." Known as Val-speak, this lingo spread like a plague across America. Wherever there was a suburb, there was a mall, and in those malls teen girls, adopting the Val-Gal's way of life, could be found with their quaint expressions: "To the max," "Bitchin'," "Tubular," "Gnarly," "Awesome," "Excellent," and "I'm soooo sure!"

The look of the stereotypical Valley Girl consisted of trendy fashions: a miniskirt (leather was way-cool); a striped, polka-dotted, or ruffled blouse; white pumps with anklet socks; headbands and leg warmers; costume jewelry; and gooey lip-gloss. She preferred to wear her long hair blow-dried, center-parted, and feathered, or, if she was mondo outrageous, in the daringly short Pat Benatar hairdo. Along with shopping for clothes, the Vals liked (in no particular order) manicures, fast food (especially Mexican), Pac-Man, unicorns, Brooke Shields, MTV, New Wave rock, The Go-Go's, gossip, parties, bubble gum, and rockin' dudes with buff bods (guys from the Valley were called Valley Dudes). Their favorite place, besides Taco Bell and the Sherman Oaks Galleria, was the beach. They tended to flock north on the PCH to Zuma, because the surfing locals at Malibu, Santa Monica, and Venice hated them for crowding their beaches (nonsurfers were called "hodads").

A complete culture was spawned from the Valley Girls. There were two movies, the classic *Valley Girl* (1983), starring Nicolas Cage and Deborah Foreman, and the not-so-classic *The Vals* (1982), starring nobody famous; a prime-time TV series, *Square Pegs* (1982–83), starring Tracy Nelson as Val-Gal Jennifer; and two books, *The Totally Awesome Val Guide* (1982), by Jodie Ann Posserello and Sue Black, and *The Valley Girls Guide to Life* (1982), by Mimi Pond.

VALLEY OF THE DOLLS (BOOK)

"You've got to climb Mount Everest to reach the Valley of the Dolls" began Jacqueline Susann's notoriously trashy, record-breaking, best-selling novel about the drug-filled, love-starved, sex-satiated world of show business. As kids, we only had to look under our parents' mattress to reach the *Valley of the Dolls*, because that's where they hid this once-shocking book full of steamy good-stuff like sex, booze, drugs, deceit, and revenge. It told the saga of three beautiful girls—singer Neely O'Hara, model Anne Welles, and sex symbol Jennifer North—who become best friends when they are young and struggling in New York City. They climb to the top of the entertainment industry, only to find there's no place left to go but down—into the Valley of the Dolls ("dolls" was 1960s slang for pep pills and sleeping pills). *Valley of the Dolls* sold more than twenty-two million copies in its debut year of 1966, becoming America's all-time best-seller. Remarkably, it was novelist Susann's first book. She later penned *The Love Machine* (1969) and *Once Is Not Enough* (1973), two more tales about the sleazy lifestyles of the rich and famous, before succumbing to cancer in 1975.

VALLEY OF THE DOLLS (MOVIE)

> "They drummed you right out of Hollywood,
> so you came crawling back to Broadway.
> Well, Broadway doesn't go for booze and dope!"
>
> —HELEN LAWSON (SUSAN HAYWARD)

In 1967, Jacqueline Susann's mega-selling novel about three women who claw their way to Hollywood stardom and end up hellishly hooked on pills was made into a major motion picture. Directed by Mark Robson, it starred Patty Duke as self-destructive star Neely O'Hara, Barbara Parkins as Gillian Girl model Anne Welles, Sharon Tate as ill-fated sexpot Jennifer North, and Susan Hayward as Broadway bitch Helen Lawson. Also featured were Paul Burke as high-powered entertainment attorney Lyon

Burke, Tony Scotti as ill-fated lounge singer Tony Polar, Martin Milner as emasculated manager Mel Anderson, and Lee Grant as Tony's lesbian sister Miriam Polar.

Despite being a critical bomb (author Susann herself called it "a piece of shit"), *Valley of the Dolls* grossed more than $80 million at the box office. As one of Hollywood's "so bad it's good" movies, it has developed a mammoth cult following, particularly among gay men who adore its camp. There's corny dialogue galore, brimming with grandiose lines like "I am not nutty! I'm just hooked on dolls!" and "Ted Casablanca is not a fag, and I'm the dame who can prove it!" Then there's the unintentionally funny acting—especially Duke's over-the-top performance. (Her catfight scene, where she rips Hayward's wig off and gleefully flushes it down the toilet, is a classic.) There's the now-dated 1960s pop-art appearance, sprinkled with kicky montages, split screens, freeze-frame sequences, and kitschy set designs, including the most enormous kaleidoscopic mobile you've ever seen. And finally, the actresses' groovy mod fashions are spectacular, and so are the hairdos, allegedly costing the film $13,000 on wigs alone (we're talking towering fall wiglets upon fall wiglets upon fall wiglets here).

The haunting theme, sung by Parkins in the film, was a Top Ten hit for Dionne Warwick in 1968. Followed by an even more racy "nonsequel," *Beyond the Valley of the Dolls* (1970), about an all-girl rock group, The Carrie Nations (Cynthia Myers, Marcia McBroom, and Dolly Read), written by film critic Roger Ebert and directed by Russ Meyer.

VAN

The low-budget sex comedy that experienced surprise box-office success in 1977 was about a shy teenager, Bobby (Stuart Geetz), who uses his flashy new custom van to pick up and seduce sweet California chicks. Also known as *Chevy Van*.

VANILLA ICE

White rapper with the strange flat-top haircut (head-lines shaved into the sides, and a bleach-streaked, off-center bang puff), born Robert Van Winkle on October 31, 1968, in Miami, who experienced a sudden rise to fame in 1990 with a crossover rap hit, "Ice Ice Baby." Experienced an equally sudden fall from fame because many in the rap industry viewed him as a fake who tried to pass himself off as a "street kid" (he claimed to have been stabbed a few times during various gang fights), despite a suburban Dallas upbringing. It didn't help that there was a Vanilla Ice fashion doll and a Vanilla Ice board game, or that he had starred in two big-screen turkeys, *Cool as Ice* (1991), as a motor-cross rebel, and *Teenage Mutant Ninja Turtles II* (1991). After suffering bouts of depression and drug addiction through most of the 1990s, he is still trying to recover the music fame he once had.

VAN PATTEN, VINCE

Dick Van Patten's clean-cut cutie-pie son, born October 17, 1957, who was a teen idol for a while in the mid-1970s and known best for two short-lived TV series—*Apple's Way* (1974–75) and *Three for the Road* (1975)—and the big-screen cult favorite *Rock 'n' Roll High School* (1979). In a November 1976 episode of *The Six Million Dollar Man* titled "Bionic Boy," he played sixteen-year-old athlete Andy Sheffield, whose paralyzed legs were replaced by bionics. Van Patten was once romantically linked with TV sex symbol Farrah Fawcett-Majors by the tabloids. (Just close friends, the California-blonde toothsome twosome were often photographed playing tennis together.) Van Patten brothers Jimmy, Nels, and Timothy acted too; you might remember them in the low-budget films 1979's *California Dreaming* (Jimmy), 1980's *Lunch Wagon* (Jimmy and Nels), and 1982's *Class of 1984* (Timothy).

FYI: ▸ Vince Van Patten became a professional tennis player who was ranked number forty-one in 1981.

VANS SNEAKERS

These were all the rage during the early 1980s, especially after Sean Penn's surfing rebel, Jeff Spicoli, was seen sporting a pair of checkered slip-ons in the teen pic *Fast Times at Ridgemont High* (1982). Vans were the coolest of all shoes, totally hot among the action-oriented youth subcultures, such as surfers, skaters, breakdancers, and New Wavers. They came in a variety of styles: hi-tops, low-tops, and the famed slip-ons that had no shoelaces. The checkered or Hawaiian-print ones were gnarly. (Many kids would take a pair of less-expensive white Vans and draw their own checker-board pattern with a Magic Marker.)

VELMA DINKLEY

"My glasses! I can't see without them!" Bespectacled, brainy, brave brunette—dressed in knee-highs, miniskirt, and lumpy orange-hued turtleneck—who did most of the mystery-cracking on the *Scooby-Doo* cartoons. Often cited as the first fantasy chick for juvenile lesbians. "Jinkies!"

VELVET

"Hair that grows. Hair that goes . . . to here . . . to there . . . to anywhere!" The adorable hair-growing little cousin (around fifteen inches tall) of the beautiful Crissy doll was introduced by Ideal Toys in 1970. Velvet had shiny platinum-blonde hair and big violet-colored eyes. Her best girlfriends included dark-haired Mia, auburn-haired Cricket, champagne-blonde Dina, and African-American Tara.

VELVET JONES

"Be somebody. Be a ho." Eddie Murphy's hustling TV pimp—er—pitchman for the Velvet Jones School of Technology and author of *I Wanna Be a Ho* was seen on *Saturday Night Live* during the early 1980s.

VENTURES

Highly influential guitar-based rock band from Seattle whose rousing instrumentals, including 1960's "Walk-Don't Run" and "Perfidia," paved the way for the surf sound of the 1960s. Best known hit: "Hawaii Five-O" (1969), the theme from the police TV series starring Jack Lord. Contemporaries of The Ventures included The Surfaris ("Wipe Out"), The Chantays ("Pipeline"), Dick Dale and The Del-Tones ("Miserlou"), The Lively Ones ("Surf Rider"), The Mar-Kets ("Surfer's Stomp"), The Sandals ("Endless Summer"), and The Shadows ("Apache").

FYI: ▸ In Japan, The Ventures' popularity rivals that of The Beatles.

VERMICIOUS KNIDS

Fierce and predatory, these supermorphing extra-terrestrials are featured in author Roald Dahl's *Charlie and the Great Glass Elevator*, his 1972 sequel to the classic story *Charlie and the Chocolate Factory*. Held up at the Space Hotel, Vermicious Knids are show-off carnivores (Oompa Loompas are their snack of choice) that spell out the warning "Scram!" with their twisty bodies when space-venturing Willy Wonka and the Bucket Family, including young Charlie Bucket, arrive there in the Great Glass Elevator.

VERONICA LODGE

Daughter of millionaire Hiriam Lodge, she's Riverdale's teen socialite, a vivacious and spoiled cartoon brunette who shares a friendly rivalry with blonde girl-next-door Betty Cooper—particularly when it comes to redhead Archie Andrews. Forever fashion-conscious, Veronica needs a large space to store all her designer threads, so it comes as no surprise that her closet is the size of a bedroom. (She boasts it even has its own zip code!)

VERTIBIRDS

Various action play sets consisting of a remote-controlled helicopter that could lift off, land, hover, circle, and swoop down to perform rescue missions with a flight hook. Manufactured by Mattel from 1971 through the early 1980s, VertiBirds are remembered fondly by men who had them as children.

VERUCA SALT

Spoiled, selfish, pampered, impatient, and obnoxious are words that best describe the rich brat, one of the lucky ticket-holders from *Willy Wonka and the Chocolate Factory.* Dressed in a red-velvet dress and white mink coat, Veruca has her wealthy daddy wrapped around her greedy fingers (and viewers too, who love to hate her). But Veruca's foot-stamping demands for a Golden Goose, via a singing temper tantrum ("I want it now!"), lead to rejection as a "bad egg," and she tumbles down a garbage chute. An all-girl alternative rock band fronted by Nina Gordon named itself after Veruca Salt in the 1990s.

FYI: ▸ British child actress Julie Dawn Cole (born October 26, 1957), who starred as Veruca Salt in the 1971 *Willy Wonka* film, actually hated chocolate!

VH-1

The sister channel of MTV was launched in 1985 to appeal to the more mellow musical tastes of the older (thirtysomething and beyond) audience. More recently, VH-1 has been airing such fun, retro-oriented TV programs as *I Love the 70s* (and *80s* and *90s*), *Before They Were Rock Stars*, and *Where Are They Now?*

VICTORIA WINTERS

Young woman (played by Alexandra Moltke on daytime TV's *Dark Shadows*) who comes to the brooding manor of Collinwood located in Collinsport, a coastal town in Maine, to act as governess to young David Collins. She soon discovers the odd behavior of various Collins family members, including vampirism and witchcraft.

VIDEO GAMES

The video-game revolution began in 1978, when Bally's Space Invaders took arcade parlors to a galactic new level. Before its introduction, kids were perfectly satisfied playing an action-packed round of pinball, skee-ball, foosball, Air Hockey, or Whac-a-Mole. But now those games seemed primitive and somewhat boring compared with the fast-paced, high-tech Space Invaders—a quarter-operated game housed in a stand-up video cabinet—which featured computer microchips, making it more complicated and challenging. Those who scored the most points could show off to others by leaving their name or initials on a high-score chart that automatically kept track (until someone unplugged the game). Soon more electronic games followed: Asteroids (1979), Berzerk (1980), Burgertime (1980), Centipede (1980), Defender (1980), Dig-Dug (1982), Donkey Kong (1981), Dragon's Lair (1983), Frogger (1981), Galaxian (1979), Missile Command (1980), Q-Bert (1982), Tempest (1980), Tron (1982), Zaxxon (1982), and the enormously popular (and addictive) Pac-Man (1980) and sequel Ms. Pac-Man (1981).

There was no escaping the distinctive sound of beeps, boings, and buzzes as video games became a multi-billion-dollar industry and new arcade parlors popped up like zits on a teenager all across America. Eventually they found a place in American households as game cartridges for Atari 2000, Commodore VIC-20, and Mattel's Intellivision home video systems. These early homevideo games led the way to the biggest phenomenon in electronic playtime: Nintendo and its competitor, Sega.

Introduced in 1986, Nintendo and Sega entertainment systems came with a box that hooked up to the TV set and were controlled by a joystick, a power pad, or a power glove. They offered a variety of game cartridges to own and play, such as Super Mario Brothers, Sonic the Hedgehog, The Legend of Zelda, Mortal Kombat, Streetfighter, Resident Evil, and Donkey Kong Country. Their graphics were significantly sharper, colors were brighter, and the sound was clearer, compared with the earlier arcade games. They also gave impassioned video fanatics blistered fingers (especially the thumbs), inflamed tendons, joint pain, tennis elbow, and weary eyes from playing hour after hour.

"VIDEO KILLED THE RADIO STAR"

The so-so Buggles' tune was made history-making famous by its video, the very first ever to air on MTV (August 1, 1981).

FYI: ▸ Did you know that Pat Benatar's "You Better Run" was the second video to be broadcast on MTV?

VIEW-MASTER

Invented by William Gruber, View-Master offers its beholder a 3-D look at the world. It allows you to travel the far corners of the world, visit scenic wonders, join in the adventures of beloved cartoon and TV characters, and relive exciting historic events of the past. A typical View-Master set consists of a handheld viewer resembling space-age binoculars, made from black- or gray-colored Bakelite, and a packet of three reels accompanied by a story booklet. The reels are inserted through a slit at the top of the viewer. Each reel contains seven full-color, three-dimensional scenes that seem to spring to life when held toward a light source, such as a lamp or a window. A fingertip lever on the side allows the reel to advance to the next picture.

The View-Master was first introduced at the 1939 New York World's Fair. Throughout the 1940s and 1950s, it sold as a photographic souvenir of various national parks and other scenic spots. In the late 1950s, it became a favorite toy of the young when it began featuring popular TV, movie, cartoon, and fairy-tale characters, as well as reels on nature, travel, and famous events. Over the years, many different companies have owned View-Master, including Sawyers, GAF, Ideal Toys, Tyco Toys, and presently Fisher-Price. In 1971, GAF introduced the Talking View-Master, which had a small record attached to each reel.

VILLAGE OF THE DAMNED

"Beware the eyes that paralyze!" In the sci-fi thriller, the small English village of Midwich experiences a mysterious sleep-induced blackout, resulting in the pregnancy of every female with childbearing capability. Nine months later, the women give birth—all at the same time—to twelve weird, nonemotional offspring, referred to by the townspeople as "the devil's children." Maturing quickly, these strange moppets all look the same, with bright blonde hair and piercing ray-gun eyes, and act the same, with superior intelligence, telekinetic powers, and cold-hearted, murderous dispositions. It seems that they also have a terrifying secret: They are the front line of an alien invasion of earth!

Directed by Wolf Rilla, this 1960 film starred George Sanders as Gordon Zellaby, a scientist who tries to stop the children's evil plans for world domination, and Barbara Shelley as Anthea Zellaby, his wife, who gives birth to one of the spooky tots. Based on *The Midwich Cuckoo*, a 1957 novel by John Wyndham, the movie was followed by a 1964 sequel, *Children of the Damned*. It is interesting that the two *Damned* features were released as the first members of Generation X were being born. They are notable for bringing in the demonic "evil kid" genre, which includes such classics as *Rosemary's Baby* (1968), *The Exorcist* (1973), *It's Alive!* (1974), *The Omen* (1976), *Carrie* (1976), *Halloween* (1978), *The Brood* (1979), *Firestarter* (1984), and *Children of the Corn* (1984).

VILLAGE PEOPLE

A campy, all-male disco act, formed by French composer-producer Jacques Morali and named after New York City's Greenwich Village, that made us believe it was fun to stay at the Y.M.C.A. in the late 1970s. The sextet of singers had a gimmick: They wore costumes representing macho stereotypes: a Cowboy (Randy Jones), a Construction Worker (David Hodo), an Indian (Felipe Rose), a Policeman (Alex Briley), a G.I. (Victor Willis, the lead vocalist), and a Biker (Glenn Hughes). These boys from the Village were loved by mainstream America, who at the time didn't have a clue that they were a gay-oriented bunch singing homosexual anthems: "San Francisco" (1978), "Macho Man" (1978), "Y.M.C.A." (1978), "In the Navy" (1979), and "Go West" (1979). In 1980, they starred with Valerie Perrine, Steve Guttenberg, and Bruce Jenner (of 1976 Summer Olympics fame) in the appalling disco movie *Can't Stop the Music*.

FYI: ▸ The Village People's million-seller "In the Navy" nearly became a recruitment song until its gay message was pointed out to Navy officials.

VILLA VILLEKULLA

Rickety old house on the outskirts of a small village in Sweden where storybook heroine Pippi Longstocking resides, sans parental guidance, with horse General and monkey Sir Nilsson.

VINCE LOMBARDI HIGH SCHOOL

Also known as *Rock 'n' Roll High School*, this fictional Southern California educational institution was blown up in 1979 after its student body revolted against the stuffy, rock-music-hating administration.

VINNIE BARBARINO

"What? Where? When?" John Travolta's dense but oh-so-cute and cool leader of the rowdy Sweathog gang on TV's *Welcome Back, Kotter*. "I'm so confused."

VIOLET

Lucy Van Pelt's snooty friend from the *Peanuts* cartoons who wore her brunette hair in a bun on top of her head and hosted parties to which Charlie Brown was never invited.

VIOLET BEAUREGARDE

"What is this? A freak out!" The daughter of a used-car salesman was a fervent gum-chewer (she chewed on the same piece for three months solid) and winner of the second Golden Ticket from Willy Wonka. Against Wonka's wishes, brassy Violet ate a three-course meal gum and got transformed into a huge blueberry. "Violet, you're turning violet, Violet."

FYI: ▸ Eleven-year-old actress Denise Nickerson, who played the gum-smacker in *Willy Wonka and* *the Chocolate Factory* (1971), could also be seen on TV as Amy Jennings in the daytime serial *Dark Shadows* and as a regular on *The Electric Company*.

VOGUEING

"Strike a pose." This style of dance originated with drag queens in New York City who would stand in the middle of a nightclub and strike the poses favored by high-fashion models in the pages of *Vogue* magazine. Pop goddess Madonna popularized the dance with her 1990 song "Vogue."

"VOICES CARRY"

"Hush, hush, keep it down now . . ." 'Til Tuesday's rat-tailed lead singer Aimée Mann starred in the video clip for their 1985 song as a frustrated girlfriend who finally tells her no-good guy off while in the audience at the opera.

VOLKSWAGEN BEETLE

The cute pint-sized, bug-shaped automobile brings back groovy recollections of happy faces, daisies, and sunshiny days. The VW Beetle (or Bug) was designed and first manufactured in Nazi Germany in 1938 (its name is a derivative of the German words *volks*, for "people," and *wagen*, for "car") and introduced in America in 1949. In the mid-1960s, helped by a clever ad campaign ("Ugly is only skin deep" and "Drivers wanted"), the inexpensive Beetle (at around $1,595)—with its rear-mounted engine and a top speed of only sixty miles an hour—became a happy-go-lucky "anti-status" symbol that mirrored the times. You would spot them on college campuses driven by young, intellectual hippie types, or as breezy convertibles on American beaches surrounded by the fun-in-the-sun crowd. Beetles came in cheery shades like yellow, lime, orange, baby blue, and pink, and owners sometimes decorated them with colorful flower decals, making them cuter than they already were. So loved was the VW Beetle that Walt Disney featured it as the kooky "Herbie" in the 1969 film *The Love Bug*. In 1997, a redesigned, just-as-cute Beetle was introduced.

FYI: ▸ A fad among teenagers in the 1960s was cramming as many people as possible into the little Volkswagen Bug.

VOYAGE TO THE BOTTOM OF THE SEA

Created and produced by Irwin Allen, this was one of TV's all-time favorite sci-fi series. Airing from 1964 to 1968, it followed the futuristic (set in 1983!) exploits of the *Seaview*, an atomic-powered research submarine whose crew traveled the seven seas encountering an assortment of monsters, aliens, and human villains. Featured players included Richard Basehart as Admiral Harriman Nelson, David Hedison as Captain Lee Crane, Bob Dowdell as Lieutenant Commander Chip Morton, and Henry Kulky as CPO Curley Jones. Based on the 1961 film of the same name.

VROOM BROOM

On *H. R. Pufnstuf*, this was the official name of the gaudy, rocket-powered broom flown by the evil Witchiepoo. Came equipped with an umbrella-shaded seat for Witchiepoo and a bathtub sidecar for her silly sidekick, Orson the Vulture.

VULGARIA

All youngsters should avoid this faraway land (somewhere in Eastern Europe, I think) found in *Chitty Chitty Bang Bang*, because its amoral child-hating rulers, Baron and Baroness Bomburst, have passed a law that children ("Ugh! Nasty, creepy, crawly things!") are forbidden and will be imprisoned in their castle.

W

WACKY PACKAGES

Created by comic-book artist Jay Lynch for Topps, these self-adhesive trading cards bitingly parodied common supermarket products and their slogans. We're talking nostalgia city here—memories of being a young boy and venturing into the local convenience store to purchase a pack or two of these *Mad* magazine-influenced stickers (they were usually located near the cash register). From 1973 to 1976, sixteen different series were produced, showcasing thirty different cards per set, and I feverishly collected each one. They were plastered all over every surface in my childhood domain. Notebook binders, math books, lunch boxes, school lockers, bicycles, Tonka trucks, bedroom furniture, and hallway doors—all were bedecked with the crazy, colorful Wacky Packs stickers.

For your enjoyment, here are thirty examples of the consumer brands spoofed by Wacky Packages. Can you guess their real names?

Awful Bits Cereal
Band-Ache
Bar-Kist Tuna
Bloodweiser Beer
Blisterine
Blunder Bread
Cover Ghoul Makeup
Fang Breakfast Drink
Fearasil Complexion Cream
Fibby's Juice
Footsieroll
Freetoes
Hex Lax
Hopeless Snow Balls
Kentucky Fried Fingers
Killy Putty
Kook-Aid
Lifeservers
Log Cave-In Syrup
Minute Lice
Play-Dumb Moldy Clay
Raw Goo Uncooked Spaghetti Sauce
Rice A Phoni
Shot Wheels
Slopicana 100% Peels Orangutan Juice
Stinkertoy
Sugar Daffy
3 Mosquitoes
Weakies Cereal
Wormy Packages

WACKY RACES

Saturday-morning cartoon about a madcap transcontinental automobile race featuring a menagerie of far-out characters driving bizarre vehicles while competing for the title of "World's Wackiest Racer." The eleven contestants included the prehistoric Slag Brothers, Rock and Gravel, in the Boulder Mobile (car number 1); the Gruesome Twosome, Big and Little, in the dragon-driven Creepy Coupe (car number 2); inventor-professor Pat Pending in the Ring-a-Ding Convert-a-Car (car number 3); flying-ace Red Max in the Crimson Haybaler (car number 4); dainty Southern Belle Penelope Pitstop in the Compact Pussycat (car number 5); military men—General, Sarge, and Private

Pinkley—in the tanklike Army Surplus Special (car number 6); gangster Clyde and his Ant Hill Mob in the Bulletproof Bomb (car number 7); hillbillies Luke and Blubber Bear in the Arkansas Chugga-Bug (car number 8); dashing hero Peter Perfect in the Turbo Terrific (car number 9); lumberjack Rufus Ruffcut and bucktoothed beaver sidekick Sawtooth in the Buzz Wagon (car number 10); and the dirty, despicable, diabolical, devious Dick Dastardly and snickering canine accomplice Muttley in the Mean Machine (car number 00). In every episode, Dastardly set out to sabotage the other drivers but failed in his attempts, only to reap a nasty snicker from Muttley.

Airing from 1968 to 1970, the Hanna-Barbera show was based loosely on the smash 1965 movie *The Great Race*, starring Tony Curtis, Jack Lemmon, and Natalie Wood. In the fall of 1969, two of the teams got their own spin-off shows, *Dastardly and Muttley in Their Flying Machines* and *The Perils of Penelope Pitstop*, while still competing in the *Wacky Races*.

WACKY WALL WALKERS

This short-lived 1980s fad consisted of sticky spider-like rubber creatures that slithered down walls and other vertical surfaces after being flung up against them.

WAFFLE STOMPERS

These lace-up ankle boots are characterized by waffle-like treads and associated with outdoorsy, sportsmen types.

WAITRESSES

Another one of the New Wave girl groups from the early 1980s inspired by the success of The Go-Go's. This sextet based in Akron, Ohio, never scored a Top Forty hit, but their notable songs, teeming with witty lyrics and lead singer Patty Donahue's sassy, laconic vocals, included "I Know What Boys Like" (1982), "It's My Car" (1982), "Square Pegs" (1982), the hip theme to the same-titled TV sitcom, and "Christmas Wrapping" (1982), a wonderful Yuletide number destined to be a classic. Donahue died from lung cancer on December 9, 1996, at the age of forty.

"WAKE ME UP BEFORE YOU GO-GO"

The upbeat video for this upbeat song starred the sensational Wham! boys, George Michael and Andrew Ridgeley, go-going on stage while wearing black short-shorts and T-shirts with the logo "Choose Life" in big black letters. Wham!'s single sold more than a million records and topped the American pop charts for three weeks in the fall of 1984.

WALKABOUT

A superb 1971 film, beautifully photographed by the master of visual imagery, director Nicolas Roeg (*Don't Look Back* and *The Man Who Fell to Earth*). It starred Jenny Agutter as a teenage schoolgirl stranded in the Australian Outback with her younger brother (Lucien John) after their father goes insane and kills himself. The children wander aimlessly through the desert wasteland with little hope of rescue until they run into a young aborigine (David Gulpilil) who is on his "journey to manhood," a ritualistic tribal trek known as a "walkabout." As he leads them back to the safety of civilization, sexual tension arises: The uptight, nonconformist white teen, dressed in a very short school uniform, finds herself physically attracted to the black Australian native, dressed in a loincloth. Often compared to fellow British teen stars Hayley Mills and Pamela Franklin, wide-eyed Agutter had other noteworthy movies, including *The Railway Children* (1970), *The Snow Goose* (1971), *Logan's Run* (1976), *Equus* (1977), and *An American Werewolf in London* (1981).

WALKER, JIMMIE

Long-legged, toothpick-shaped, platform-shoed star of the TV sitcom *Good Times* (he played J.J. Evans). The show made the self-titled "Ebony Prince" instantly popular as a young comic, and his supercool expression of "Dyn-O-Mite!" became a national catchphrase.

WALKING TALL

In this 1973 movie, directed by Phil Karlson, Joe Don Baker starred as Buford Pusser, the legendary sheriff from Tennessee who takes on local mobsters to avenge the death of his wife with nothing but determination and a baseball bat. Based on real-life events, the ultraviolent tale was a huge theatrical success spawning two sequels, *Walking Tall: Part 2* (1975) and *Walking Tall: The Final Chapter* (1977), plus a short-lived TV series in 1981, all featuring Bo Svenson as Sheriff Pusser. It goes hand in hand (or should I say fist in fist) with the *Billy Jack* and *Death*

Wish sagas. In 2004, *Walking Tall* was remade with a story line that barely resembled the original's, starring wrestling superstar The Rock and Johnny Knoxville (from MTV's *Jackass*).

WALLABEES

Clark, the creators of the much-popular desert boots, introduced this casual footwear named after an Australian marsupial. Popular as well, this tan suede shoe had a unique gummy-eraser-like sole that seemed to melt or crumble with long-term wear.

WALLY CLEAVER

"Gee, Wally." Beaver Cleaver's older brother (played by Tony Dow on *Leave It to Beaver*) was a good-looking, popular All-American teen who attended Mayfield High, where he excelled in sports and academics. Beaver never could understand why Wally fussed so much with personal hygiene and clothes just to impress the girls. Yuck! Buddies were hooligan Eddie Haskell and the aptly named Lumpy Rutherford.

WALLY GATOR

"Oh, fuddle dee doo!" A "swinging alligator from the swamp" who mimics the voice style of movie comic Ed Wynn and strives to be free from the confines of the city zoo. Created by Hanna-Barbera in 1962, Wally's cartoon segments were usually featured alongside Touche Turtle and Lippy the Lion and Hardy Har Har.

WALLY WORLD

Fictional Disneyland-esque amusement park in Southern California to which the ill-fortuned Griswold family of Chicago, headed by bungling dad Clark, trek in the *National Lampoon's Vacation* movie (1983). Marty Moose is Wally World's mascot.

WALTONS

A long-running CBS-TV series (1972–81) about a financially poor but emotionally rich family, based on the childhood experiences of creator Earl Hammer Jr. and the 1971 Christmas special *The Homecoming*. Set during the Great Depression of the 1930s, the prime-time drama concentrated on the trials, tribulations, and love of John and Olivia Walton and their seven offspring, who lived in a farmhouse on Walton's Mountain, a tiny Jefferson County hamlet in the Blue Ridge Mountains of rural Virginia. These stories were told through the eyes of oldest son John-Boy, a reflective dreamer and aspiring writer much revered by his younger siblings. It starred Ralph Waite as salt-of-the-earth father John Walton; Michael Learned as no-nonsense but caring mother Olivia; Richard Thomas as earnest John-Boy; Jon Walmsley as sensitive musician Jason; Judy Norton-Taylor as rebellious eldest daughter Mary Ellen; Eric Scott as dependable Ben; Mary Beth McDonough as quiet Erin; David W. Harper as carefree Jim-Bob; and Kami Cotler as pigtailed youngest Elizabeth. Co-starring were Ellen Corby and Will Geer as Esther and Zeb Walton, John's feisty mother and mischievous father (Esther's "old coot").

Featuring no sex or violence, the warm and unpretentious *Waltons* was the first successful family-oriented prime-time drama of the 1970s, and inspired an assortment of similar shows: *Apple's Way* (1974–75), *Little House on the Prairie* (1974–83), *Swiss Family Robinson* (1975–76), *Family* (1976–80), *Mulligan's Stew* (1977), *The Fitzpatricks* (1977–78), *Eight Is Enough* (1977–81), and *Shirley* (1979–80).

FYI: ▸ Earl Hammer's first effort at dramatizing his boyhood memories ended up as a 1963 movie, *Spencer's Mountain*, starring Henry Fonda, Maureen O'Hara, Donald Crisp, Veronica Cartwright, and James MacArthur as Clay-Boy.

WARD, JAY

The Baby Boom cartoon genius best known for creating animated TV icons, such as Rocky and Bullwinkle, Crusader Rabbit, George of the Jungle, Cap'n Crunch, and Quisp and Quake.

WARRIORS

"Warriors, come out and play. . . ." A dazzling big-screen thriller about a tough street gang, the Warriors, who are framed for the assassination of a big-time gang messiah during a rally of 200 gangs in the Bronx. The Warriors flee to the safety of home turf, Coney Island, while crossing through enemy territory belonging to vicious rival gangs—the Gramercy Riffs, the Rogues, the Baseball Furies, and the all-girl Lizzies—who are out for revenge. The cast includes Michael Beck as leader Swan, James Remar as Ajax, Thomas Waites as Fox, Dorsey Wright as Cleon,

Brian Tyler as Snow, David Harris as Cochise, Tom McKitterick as Cowboy, Marcelino Sánchez as Rembrandt, Terry Michos as Vermin, and *Too Close for Comfort*'s Deborah Van Valkenburgh as Mercy. Directed by Walter Hill, the 1979 movie is marked by a nonstop pace, well-choreographed fight sequences, and a surrealistic portrayal of New York City.

FYI: ▸ When initially released, *The Warriors* was widely criticized for inciting gang warfare because of a few violent acts that broke out in theaters.

WATERSHIP DOWN

The best-selling novel written by Richard Adams in 1974, based on stories he told to his daughters, in which all the central characters were rabbits. Led by Hazel, a heroic colony of bunnies flee their doomed warren and search for a new home, a hill called Watership Down. The hares encounter many perils along the way, including owls, foxes, dogs, and, worst of all, humans. In 1978, the allegorical saga was made into a film that many critics considered to be the best non-Disney animated feature ever made.

WATER WIGGLE

"It's cool-splashing fun!" Always on target with what makes kids happy, Wham-O turned the garden hose into a fun summer toy with the introduction of this wacky creation in the late 1960s. The Water Wiggle was a goofy clownlike head attached to the end of the garden hose, which when the water was turned on became a water-spraying snake that wiggled wildly at youngsters, who excitedly darted around it. Wham-O also created another outdoor water favorite, the Slip 'n Slide.

WATUSI

Shimmy-esque dance that involved swaying hips from side to side with a jump; introduced in 1964 with the song "The Wah Wahtusi" by The Orlons.

WAYLAND FLOWERS AND MADAME

Puppeteer and his sidekick puppet, a saucy-mouthed old screen queen from yesteryear who still thought of herself as a glamorous star. The comedy duo were semi-regulars on TV's *Gong Show*, *Hollywood Squares*, and *Solid Gold* throughout the late 1970s and early 1980s. Wayland Flowers died of AIDS in 1988.

WAYNE'S WORLD

"Party on!" Airing from his parents' basement, long-haired freaker Wayne Campbell (Mike Myers), with spacey sidekick Garth Algar (Dana Carvey), was the tongue-in-cheek host of this totally excellent show seen on Cable 10, a public-access channel in suburban Aurora, Illinois. Slackers extraordinaire, these teenage dudes cruised the neighborhood streets in the Murfmobile (an AMC Pacer), listened to heavy-metal music, like Queen's "Bohemian Rhapsody," and found blonde babe Heather Locklear most worthy of a "Schwing!" Seen as a regular *Saturday Night Live* skit during the late 1980s, it inspired two big-screen films, *Wayne's World* (1992) and *Wayne's World 2* (1993), and several "stupid buddy" imitators, including *Dumb and Dumber* (1994), *Tommy Boy* (1995), and more recently, *Dude, Where's My Car?* (2000).

FYI: ▸ Wayne and Garth's motto is "Babum, partium, tuneum," translated as "Babes, parties, tunes."

"WE ARE FAMILY"

The 1979 disco smash by Sister Sledge is notable for being adopted as an anthem for gays and lesbians who have become a "family" based on unity, freedom, and pride.

"WE ARE THE WORLD"

A 1985 benefit song performed by a slew of American rock stars under the title U.S.A. for Africa (United Support of Artists), formed to help raise money for and consciousness of the millions dying in Ethiopia from a drought-induced famine. Initiated by Harry Belafonte, it was inspired by Bob Gedlof's "Do They Know It's Christmas?" (1984), which featured a collection of U.K. artists under the name Band Aid (including George Michael, Boy George, Bono, Annie Lennox, Sting, Phil Collins, David Bowie, and Paul McCartney). Belafonte contacted Lionel Richie and Michael Jackson, who wrote the anthem, and producer Quincy Jones, who recruited the music superstars. To try to get as many big names as possible, Jones held the recording session on January 28, 1985, immediately following the televised American Music Awards. Among the forty-five singers featured were Kim Carnes, Ray Charles, Bob Dylan, Hall and Oates, James Ingram, Al Jarreau, Michael Jackson, Billy Joel, Cyndi Lauper, Huey Lewis, Kenny Loggins,

Bette Midler, Willie Nelson, Steve Perry, The Pointer Sisters, Lionel Richie, Kenny Rogers, Diana Ross, Paul Simon, Bruce Springsteen, Tina Turner, Dionne Warwick, and Stevie Wonder. (If you listen closely, you can tell who sings what lyrics.) "We Are the World" became the biggest-selling single ever; topped the charts for four weeks; won four Grammy Awards, including Record and Song of the Year; and raised more than $60 million for the African famine relief.

WEDGE HAIRCUT

A haircut created especially for figure-skater Dorothy Hamill and her gold-winning performance at the 1976 Winter Olympics in Innsbruck. It became the favorite of sassy cheerleaders and other jock gals during the late 1970s. The wedge was short, pert, and displayed a considerable amount of movement, particularly when spinning around on a skating rink, chasing balls on the tennis court, doing the Hustle at discos, or just plain giggling. The coiffure was so popular that it even had its own shampoo, called Short n' Sassy, advertised by Miss Hamill herself!

WEDGIE

To pull another person's underwear upward in a jerking motion until it wedges in the butt crack. A wedgie is given from behind to keep the victim defenseless.

WEDNESDAY TUESDAY ADDAMS

The Addams Family's cute (in a macabre sort of way) but somber pigtailed daughter whose favorite pastime is decapitating her dolls with a miniature toy guillotine (her favorite is a headless doll named Marie Antoinette) and playing with pet spider Homer. Portrayed by Lisa Loring (TV) and Christina Ricci (film).

WEEBLES

"Weebles wobble—but they don't fall down!" That's the best advertising catchphrase of any toy of its era. Introduced by Hasbro for Romper Room in 1969, they are noted for friendly little egg-shaped Weeble people whose plastic bodies were weighted at the bottom, allowing them to sway back and forth but never fall over. The Weebles came with play sets—such as the Tree House, Haunted House, Treasure Island, Wild West Ranch, Circus, Car and Camper, Sesame Street, and Mickey Mouse Club—and competed strongly with the Fisher-Price Little People in popularity and sales. Years later, when someone got staggering drunk at parties, we would say: "He's a Weeble. He wobbles, but he won't fall down" or "I'm so bombed I'm wobbling like a Weeble."

WEENIE THE GENIE

Amiable but incompetent genie, housed in a magic ring and possessed by wicked Hoo Doo the Magician on the Saturday-morning kiddie program *Lidsville* (1971–73). She (or he?) becomes the sidekick of stranded youngster Mark after he steals the ring that leads to both of them being pursued by Hoo Doo, who wants the red-faced Weenie back.

WEE PALS

> "I decided that just by exposing readers to the sight of Negroes and whites playing together in harmony, rather than pointing up aggravations, a useful, if subliminal, purpose would be served, and ultimately would have as great effect for good as all the freedom marchers in Mississippi."
>
> —CARTOONIST MORRIE TURNER

African-American cartoonist Morrie Turner created this national syndicated comic strip in 1965. Inspired by Charles Schulz's *Peanuts*, it was the first truly integrated strip, inhabited by schoolchildren from different cultural and ethnic backgrounds. There was Oliver, the overweight, bespectacled white boy who was leader of the gang and Arch Foe of Intolerance; Nipper, the little black lad named after comedian Nipsey Russell, who wore a Confederate soldier cap; Sybil, the no-nonsense black girl fond of fortune-telling; George, the Confucius-quoting Chinese-American; Connie, the blonde feminist; Jerry, the intellectual Jew; Rocky, a full-blooded American Indian; Diz, the African-American kid who wore a Dashiki shirt, beret, sunglasses, and cool attitude; Randy, the black boy with leadership skills; Wellington, the Latin-American whose pet parrot was called Polly; and Ralph, the prejudiced bully. The multicultural gang members belonged to the Rainbow Club, a worldwide organization that dealt with environmental issues and racial prejudice. From 1972 to 1974, *Wee Pals* could be seen as a Saturday-morning cartoon series titled *Kid Power*.

"WE GOT THE BEAT"

"Go-go music really makes us dance. . . ." The signature tune of The Go-Go's, the most successful all-female band of the 1980s, written by guitarist Charlotte Caffey. Housed on the 1981 multiplatinum album *Beauty and the Beat*, it peaked at the number-two spot on the American Top Forty for three weeks in 1982.

WEIRD-OHS

These goony-looking model kids were created by artist Bill Campbell for the Hawk Model Company to capitalize on the success of competitor Revell's Rat Fink funny monster-car series in 1963. Influenced by the fun-loving California lifestyle, the whacked-out Weird-Ohs featured wild, oddball hot-rods driven by strange characters with names like Daddy the Way-Out Suburbanite, Davy the Way-Out Cyclist, Hot Dogger Hangin' Ten, Beach Bunny, Hidad Silly Surfer, Drag Hag, Freddy Flame-Out, Huey's Hot Rod, Leaky Boat Louie, Sling Rave Corvette, Endsville Eddie, Wild Woodie, and Woodie on a Surfari.

WEIRD SCIENCE

Director John Hughes's 1985 film comedy centers around two horny high school geeks—Gary (Anthony Michael Hall) and Wyatt (Ilan Mitchell-Smith)—who cop an idea from Frankenstein and use their home computer to create the perfect babe: Lisa (in the form of supermodel Kelly LeBrock). Thinking hanging out with a gorgeous "10" will make them popular at Farber High, the plan backfires for the geeks as Lisa wreaks zany havoc in their lives. Oingo Boingo performed the theme song.

WELCH, RAQUEL

"I pity any actor who gets second billing to Raquel Welch. He's really getting third billing to her breasts."

—EDWARD G. ROBINSON

Enormously famous during the Vietnam War era of the late 1960s and early 1970s, Welch was the first love goddess—post-Marilyn, pre-Farrah—for the Baby Boom generation. Gorgeous beyond belief, she had an Amazonian physique with alpine breasts, striking long legs, rounded hips and thighs, a fantastic face with high cheekbones, sensual brown eyes, dazzling white teeth, a well-defined jaw, and long, full chestnut-colored hair. (I remember seeing TV footage of her dancing wildly in a crocheted minidress and white knee-high go-go boots on Bob Hope's 1967 USO Christmas tour in Vietnam—and boy, did the troops go wild!)

She was born Raquel Tejada (Welch was the surname of her first husband, Jim) on September 5, 1940, of Bolivian (father) and English (mother) descent in Chicago. As a youngster, she moved with her family to La Jolla, California, where her stunning looks led to perennial beauty-contest titles (Miss La Jolla, Miss San Diego, Miss Photogenic Teen, Miss Contour, and Maid of California) and to modeling. Welch's second marriage, to Patrick Curtis, a shrewd press agent, was a life turning-point. The twosome set out to promote her by aggressively exploiting her spectacular physique (five-foot-six, 118 pounds, and a voluptuous 39-22-33). The heavy publicity campaign, fueled by countless pinups, paid off with Welch becoming an international celebrity and one of Hollywood's top money-earners (in one year she landed on a record eighty magazine covers).

Often referred to as a "star" instead of an "actress," Welch's acting ability is questionable. Most of her films were low-budget action flicks or comedy romps. Memorable roles were Cora Peterson, a miniaturized medic wearing a skintight rubber diver's suit, in *Fantastic Voyage* (1966); Loana, a prehistoric cavegirl clad in a strategically placed fur bikini, in *One Million Years B.C.* (1966); Lilian Lust, the sinful "Babe with the Bust," in *Bedazzled* (1967); Michele, a swingin' dancer at the Pussy Cat A-Go-Go Club, in *Flareup* (1969); and K.C. Carr, a gum-chewing, tough-talking roller-derby queen, in *Kansas City Bomber* (1972). Other movies include *The Biggest Bundle of Them All* (1968), *100 Rifles* (1969)—renowned for an interracial sex scene with Jim Brown—*Myra Breckingridge* (1970), *Fuzz* (1972), *The Three Musketeers* (1974), and *Mother, Jugs, and Speed* (1976).

The ravishing bombshell's career stalled in the late 1970s, most likely because of her arrogant interviews and repeated complaints about being a sex symbol ("To be a sex symbol is not to be a legitimate member of society"). In the early 1980s, Welch proved respectable when she succeeded Lauren Bacall on Broadway in the musical *Woman of the Year* and published a best-selling fitness book,

Raquel: The Raquel Welch Total Beauty and Fitness Program, with an accompanying videotape.

FYI: ▸ In 1971, Herb Kelleher's Texas-based Southwest Airlines put out a full-page ad to Raquel Welch ("Dear Raquel Welch . . . ") to recruit her (or any young woman who resembled her) to become a stewardess with the then-fledgling airline. The original SWA flight-attendant uniform consisted of sexy hot pants and knee-high boots, unlike today's casual polo shirt and shorts combo.

WELCH'S JELLY GLASSES

In the late 1960s, Welch's began imprinting beloved cartoon characters, like The Flintstones, Looney Tunes, Tom and Jerry, Scooby-Doo, and The Archies, on miniature glass jars containing their sugary-sweet jelly. When the jar was empty, you had yourself a free drinking glass. The ones featuring The Archies were the most popular; manufactured from 1971 to 1973, those twelve glasses had the Riverdale teens in various scenarios (including Betty and Veronica modeling mod fashions for a show, Jughead winning a pie-eating contest, and cheerleader Sabrina the Teenage Witch using her magic to assist Archie in a football play). On the bottom of each glass was a different Archies member's face.

WELCOME BACK, KOTTER

> "Kotter is not a show, it is my life.
> Kotter is the make-believe teacher
> I wanted to have in Brooklyn."
> —GABE KAPLAN

Airing on ABC-TV from 1975 to 1979, a sitcom based on comedian Gabriel Kaplan's real-life high school experiences as a remedial student. On the show, he plays Gabe Kotter, a wisecracking and compassionate teacher who returns to his Brooklyn alma mater, James Buchanan High, to teach a class of delinquent underachievers known as "Sweathogs." As the misfits of the school system, the Sweathogs are tough but funny street kids who can't make it in regular classes. At the core of this rowdy gang is Vinnie Barbarino (John Travolta), the good-looking, somewhat dense leader; Juan Epstein (Robert Hegyes), a Puerto Rican Jew who never does his homework; Freddie "Boom Boom" Washington (Lawrence Hilton-Jacobs), the smooth-talking black basketball star; and Arnold Horshack (Ron Palillo), the class goofball with the patented hand-raise and "Oooh, Oooh, Oooh!" shout. Other regulars include Gabe's patient wife, Julie Kotter (Marcia Strassman), cranky vice-principal Michael Woodman (John Sylvester White), class slut Rosalie "Hotzy" Totzy (Debralee Scott), goody-goody honor student Judy Borden (Helaine Lembeck), Freddie's girlfriend Verna Jean Williams (Vernee Watson-Johnson), and the Sweathogs' archrival Carvelli (Charles Fleischer).

Heartthrob John Travolta became the breakout star, skyrocketing to superstardom via popular music ("Let Her In") and motion pictures (*Saturday Night Fever* and *Grease*). In 1978, when Travolta's contract allowed him to appear less frequently, two new Sweathogs were added to Mr. Kotter's classroom: Angie Globagoski (Melonie Haller), the first female Sweathog, and Beau De Labarre (Stephen Shortridge), a slick Southern boy with many school expulsions to his credit. Catchphrases like "Up your nose with a rubber hose!" "Off my case, toilet face!" and "Very impressive, Mr. Kotter!" entered the vocabulary of teenagers of the era. The theme song, "Welcome Back," by John Sebastian (formerly of The Lovin' Spoonfuls), was a number-one hit in 1976.

WELLA BALSAM

Before Charlie recruited her as an Angel, Farrah Fawcett was the spokes-model for this shampoo. In the early 1980s, the Dallas Cowboys Cheerleading squad from Texas was its spokes-group. It's famed for the TV commercials about telling two friends, who then tell two other friends, and so on and so on and so on. . . .

WENDY'S

Fast-food burger-and-shake chain named after founder Dave Thomas's Pippi Longstocking-esque daughter. Gave pop culture one of its most popular advertising catchphrases of the 1980s: "Where's the beef?" The first Wendy's opened in Columbus, Ohio, in 1969.

WENDY THE GOOD LITTLE WITCH

This cute little sorceress with the sweet disposition was Casper's best friend. Created by *Harvey* Publications in 1958, she first appeared with the friendly ghost in his cartoons and comics, before spinning off on her own bewitching comic-book series in 1960. Wearing a red-hooded jumpsuit and holding a magic wand, the yellow-haired enchantress flew a broom through the skies of the Enchanted Forest to protect the woodland animals (her soft spot) from harm. Wendy lived with a trio of wart-infested, green-faced witch aunts—Auntie Thelma, Auntie Velma, and Auntie Zelma—who pestered her for not being wicked and ugly like them.

WESSON OIL

This bottled cooking oil had cheesy mid-1970s TV commercials starring spokesperson Florence "Carol Brady" Henderson, who danced around a kitchen while singing something about fried chicken having a certain "Wessonality!"

WEST DALE HIGH

Brady Bunch alma mater in Southern California where Greg was once student-body president, Marcia was a cheerleader, Peter was editor of the newspaper's "Whole Truth" column (as "Scoop" Brady), and Jan was a pom-pom squad bomb-out (but in all fairness, she was named the high school's "Most Popular Girl in the Class"). Before advancing to fictional West Dale, the Brady kids attended Fillmore Junior High.

WET T-SHIRT CONTESTS

Competitions held at singles-friendly nightclubs and during spring breaks, where a whole lot of boozing goes on among young adults. The typical contest had bimbos with boobs of all sizes and shapes wearing white undershirts, minus bra underneath, lined up on a stage. One by one, the event's host-emcee would douse the chest of each contestant with water from a pitcher or a garden hose. As the cheering crowd of horny fellows egged them on, the gals—often three sheets to the wind—would gleefully shake their goods, nipples erect in all their wet glory. The winner of this disreputable honor was commonly judged by audience applause. It pointed the way for other frolicking games involving not only women but men as well, such as Wet Boxer, Best Butt, Best Legs, Best Six Pack, Best Tan Line, and Best Thong contests.

WET WILLIE

A very juvenile trick played when someone licks a finger and puts it in your ear.

"WE WILL ROCK YOU"

Originally released as the B-side of the 1977 single "We Are the Champions," Queen's power ballad has become an anthem for virtually every sports team with a marching band and cheerleading squad. Other rock songs bestowed with the same fate are Gary Glitter's "Rock and Roll, Part 2" (1972), Wild Cherry's "Play That Funky Music" (1976), and Queen's "Another One Bites the Dust" (1980).

WHAM!

Born of Greek descent, George Michael (born Georgios Panayiotou on June 25, 1963) met Andrew Ridgeley (born January 26, 1963) while attending the Bushey Meads Comprehensive School in the London suburbs. In 1979, the twosome formed a ska-friendly band called The Executives, and by 1981, with Michael as chief vocalist-songwriter and Ridgeley as guitarist, they had changed their name to Wham! Wham!-mania gripped Europe and, thanks to MTV, the States, as the teenybopper twosome exploded onto the music scene in the mid-1980s. Their fun bebop songs and male-model good looks—consisting of two-toned moussed hair and a cutesy clothing style (short-shorts with white T-shirts inscribed with giddy messages like "Choose Life" in bold black lettering)—had girls and gay guys screaming for more (straight guys hated Wham!). Hits included "Bad Boys" (1983), "Young Guns (Go for It)" (1983), "Club Tropicana" (1983), "Wake Me Up Before You Go-Go" (1984), "Careless Whisper" (1984), "Everything She Wants" (1985), "Freedom" (1985), and "I'm Your Man" (1985).

By 1986, they had become Britain's most successful pop duo of the decade. But, Michael had grown musically independent, and it was no surprise when the two members announced they were separating. As a successful solo artist, Michael was a one-man hit machine with a string of million-selling singles, including "I Want Your Sex" (1987), "Faith" (1988), "Father Figure" (1988), "Kissing a Fool" (1988), "Monkey" (1988), and "Freedom '90" (1990). Sporting a trendy Caesar haircut, Michael is now divorced from his earlier work and takes himself seriously as an artist while dodging cops in public restrooms. As for Ridgeley, after an unsuccessful solo career he became a California surfer working for environmental issues with an organization called Surfers Against Sewage.

WHAM-O

San Francisco-based toy company, formed in 1948 by Arthur "Spud" Melin and Richard Knerr, notable for manufacturing a myriad of faddish yet innovative play items: Frisbee, Hula-Hoop, Hacky Sack, Super Ball, Air Blaster, Silly Straw, Slip 'n Slide, Water Wiggle, and Super Elastic Bubble Plastic. The company got its distinctive name from its first product, a slingshot that made a "Wham-O" sound when its missile hit a target.

WHAT'S HAPPENING!

Loosely based on the 1975 comedy movie *Cooley High*, this TV sitcom centered on the shenanigans of three black teenagers in urban Los Angeles. Airing on ABC from 1976 to 1978, it starred Ernest Thomas as Roger "Raj" Thomas, the studious idealist whose ambition is to write; Haywood Nelson Jr. as Dwayne Clemons, the not-so-bright tagalong; and Fred Berry as Freddie "Rerun" Stubbs, the roly-poly jokester and far-out dancin' machine. Also featured were Mabel King as Mrs. Thomas, Roger's no-nonsense divorced mama; Danielle Spencer as Dee Thomas, Roger's sassy and tattling little sister; and Shirley Hemphill as Shirley Wilson, the surly, rotund waitress at the boys' favorite hangout, Rob's, a diner near their high school. In 1985, most of the original cast was reunited for a syndicated revival titled *What's Happening Now!* which aired until 1988.

WHAT'S UP DOC?

"Once upon a time, there was a plaid overnight case. . . ." No, this isn't the title of a Bugs Bunny cartoon short, it's director Peter Bogdanovich's 1972 screwball farce, starring Barbra Streisand as Judy Maxwell and Ryan O'Neal as Howard Bannister. Filmed in San Francisco, the madcap action begins when Howard, a shy, absentminded musicologist from Iowa, is led astray by the attentions of daffy, free-spirited Judy, who continually forces herself into his life. Things heat up after four identical flight bags, containing (1) top-secret information, (2) a wealth of jewels, (3) Howard's prehistoric musical rocks, and (4) Judy's clothes, become mixed up. It all ends with Howard and Judy being pursued in a VW Beetle by government spies and jewel thieves through the hilly, twisty streets of San Francisco (considered one of Hollywood's best car-chase scenes). Madeline Kahn makes a delightful screen-stealing debut as Howard's whiny, uptight fiancée, Eunice Burns. In 1979, Streisand and O'Neal reteamed for the boxing comedy *The Main Event.*

"WHAT'S YOUR SIGN?"

Aries. Taurus. Gemini. Cancer. Leo. Virgo. Libra. Scorpio. Sagittarius. Capricorn. Aquarius. Pisces. What sign are you? Before it became notorious for being one of the cheesiest pickup lines ever, this was the question on everybody's mind during the astrology (a.k.a. zodiac or horoscope) craze of the 1970s. In 1969, The 5th Dimension scored the biggest-selling single of the year with "Aquarius / Let the Sunshine In," from the Broadway rock musical *Hair*, which charted for seventy-two weeks—six of those at number one. The song and its lyrics ("When the moon is in the seventh house / And Jupiter aligns with Mars / Then peace will guide the planets / And love will steer the stars") epitomized people's fascination with the zodiac and its mystical New Age connections (for instance, crystals, reincarnation, psychics, and ESP).

Astrology-mania was everywhere! In newspapers you could read the daily horoscope column to find out if you would have a good day or a bad day ("Love is in the air today for all you romantic Pisces out there"). Televised beauty pageants announced each contestant's statistics accompanied by her sign ("This lovely blue-eyed brunette from Oklahoma is a Cancer"). Linda Goodman's *Sun Signs* and *Love Signs* topped the best-selling book lists. Astrology memorabilia in the form of wall plaques, black light posters, and T-shirts crowded the shelves at stores like Spencer's Gifts in shopping malls nationwide. Diana Ross and her Supremes had a Top Forty hit with "No Matter What Sign You Are" (1969), as did guitarist Dennis Coffey with the instrumental "Scorpio" (1971). On the morbid side, an uncaught serial killer, dubbed the Zodiac, viciously stalked the San Francisco area throughout the 1970s (after each of his killings, he taunted the police with letters ending with an astrological symbol). And yes, "What's your sign?" was taken very seriously as lonesome singles searched for their perfect soul mate at single bars everywhere ("I'm a Virgo, baby!").

WHEATIES

General Mills breakfast cereal advertised by the jock superstar of the moment, on the front of its box. Gold Medal Wheat Flakes was the original name of Wheaties when it was first introduced in 1924.

FYI: ▸ To celebrate its seventy-fifth anniversary, Wheaties had the American public select their ten favorite sports champions featured on the box. The winners: John Elway, Lou Gehrig, 1980 U.S. Men's Hockey Team, Michael Jordan, Walter Payton, Mary Lou Retton, Cal Ripken Jr., Jackie Robinson, Babe Ruth, and Tiger Woods.

WHEELIE AND THE CHOPPER BUNCH

"Charge!" This lively cartoon series from Hanna-Barbera about a brave car battling a gang of motorcycles aired on Saturday mornings for only one season (1974–75). Set in the world of automobiles, Wheelie, a champion stunt-racing VW Bug, constantly had to defend himself and sweet convertible girlfriend, Rota Ree, from spike-helmeted bully Chopper and his dubious Bunch—nervous Scrambles, snickering Revs, and stupid Hi-Riser.

WHEE-LO

A two-pronged piece of wire curved like a "J" that had a red plastic wheel with a powerful magnetized axle spinning up, down, and all around its edge without ever falling off. The first Whee-lo toys were produced by Maggie Magnetic Inc. in the early 1950s.

WHEEL OF FORTUNE

"I would like to buy a vowel." Since 1975, this popular TV game show has had contestants spinning a large wheel for money and guessing the letters in a mystery phrase or word. First hosted by Chuck Woolery and later by Pat Sajak. Attractive blonde Vanna White has assisted Sajak as the show's letter-turner since 1983.

WHEN A STRANGER CALLS

"Have you checked the children lately?" Chilling horror movie based on the urban legend about a teenage babysitter being tormented by threatening phone calls from a psychopath. The scared teen notifies the police, who then do a trace on the calls. They later phone her back to warn—yikes—that the fearful calls are coming from inside the house! Directed by Fred Walton, the 1979 thriller starred Carol Kane as babysitter Jill Johnson, and Charles Durning as police investigator John Clifford. A made-for-TV sequel, *When a Stranger Calls Back*, followed four years later.

"WHEN DOVES CRY"

Sexy Prince tune, from his semi-autobiographical film *Purple Rain* (1984), critically regarded as "the most influential record of the 1980s." It sold more than a million copies and topped the pop charts for five weeks and the R&B charts for eight. Its promo video clip had Prince emoting erotically in a bathtub.

WHERE HAVE ALL THE PEOPLE GONE?

Anyone who saw this as a child when it first aired in 1974 would definitely agree it's one frightening and unforgettable TV movie. A strange series of solar flares decimates the inhabitants of the planet earth. Human beings are turned into white powder with only traces of clothing left behind. A father, Steven Anders (Peter Graves), and his two teen children, David and Deborah (George O'Hanlon Jr. and future Oscar-nominee Kathleen Quinlan), on a camping expedition in California, are a few who survived the sun's deadly radiation. They head back to Los Angeles to discover the fate of the mother, Barbara (Jay W. MacIntosh), and to start anew on a depopulated earth.

"WHERE'S THE BEEF?"

The catchphrase of the 1980s. Introduced on a famed TV commercial for the Wendy's hamburger chain, featuring a trio of old ladies at a fast-food restaurant counter. When they get their hamburgers with the oversized buns and undersized patties, the crotchety Clara Peller barks, "Where's the beef?" A pop culture phenomenon was born when Democratic presidential candidate Walter Mondale asked that question of rival Gary Hart during the 1984 debates.

WHERE'S WALDO?

Series of best-selling picture-puzzle books, created by British artist Martin Handford in 1987, that had readers trying to find the gangly bespectacled Waldo—with the red-and-white-striped sweater and ski cap—hidden among a heavily detailed crowd scene in a variety of globe-trotting illustrations. Usually accompanying Waldo on his adventures were girlfriend Wilma and pet dog Woof.

WHERE THE WILD THINGS ARE

"How much does it cost to get to where the wild things are? If it is not expensive, my sister and I want to spend the summer there. Please answer soon."

—LETTER FROM A SEVEN-YEAR-OLD BOY TO MAURICE SENDAK

"And now," cried Max, "let the rumpus start!" First published in 1963, author-illustrator Maurice Sendak's groundbreaking tale about Max, a small boy wearing a wolf suit, who argues with his mother and is sent to bed without any supper. Max copes with this displeasure by sailing off to the island of the Wild Things, a place ruled by big, frightening monsters. In this dream world, Max is crowned king by the Wild Things—Aaron, Bernard, Moishe, Tzippy, and Goat Boy—and can be as terrible as he pleases. He soon misses his family and returns home.

Considered a modern classic, the popular story won Sendak the 1964 Caldecott Medal for Children's Picture Book. Some school libraries banned the book after a few critics found it too scary for young tots and believed it could cause psychological harm. In 1970, Sendak was the first American illustrator to be awarded the prestigious Hans Christian Andersen Award, for his entire body of work, which also included *The Nutshell Library* (1963) and *In the Night Kitchen* (1970).

FYI: ▸ The monsters in *Where the Wild Things Are* were inspired by Brooklyn relatives whom Maurice Sendak despised as a child.

WHICH WITCH?

A fun, tricky, three-dimensional game by Milton Bradley that allowed players to travel through four rooms (Broom Room, Witchin' Kitchen, Spell Cell, and Bat's Ballroom) of a haunted house owned by three witches, Wanda the Wicked, Goulish Gerty, and Glenda the Good. As players moved through the rooms, they had to avoid tripping a snare, which in return released a whammy ball that would knock their playing piece off the board and turn them into a mouse. The first to reach the Charmed Circle, set in the middle of the house at the top of stairs, was the winner. Released in 1970, the game was created by Marvin Glass, the genius behind Mouse Trap and Rock 'Em Sock 'Em Robots.

WHINERS

Doug and Wendy Whiner (Joe Piscopo and Robin Duke) were a suburban New Jersey couple, seen on *Saturday Night Live* in the early 1980s, who complained about everything in incredibly loud, whiny voices.

"WHIP IT"

Ultrahyper Devo song, their only Top Forty hit, accompanied by a memorable music video of the boys from Akron dressed in red caps and black suits cracking whips and trying to snap a cigarette out of the mouth of an Asian woman.

WHIPPLE-SCRUMPTIOUS FUDGEMALLOW DELIGHT

The name of the Willy Wonka chocolate bar in which young Charlie Bucket finds the fifth (and last) Golden Ticket in *Charlie and the Chocolate Factory.*

WHITAKER, JOHNNY

Born on December 13, 1959, in Van Nuys, California, the curly-haired, freckle-faced redhead was best known for playing Jody Davis on TV's popular *Family Affair* from 1966 to 1971. Brian Keith, Whitaker's Uncle Bill on the sitcom, personally hired him as one of the adorable twins (the other was look-alike Anissa Jones as Buffy) after becoming fond of the youngster while on the set of the 1966 film *The Russians Are Coming, the Russians Are Coming*. And, we all know no one could say "Uncle Beiill" as disgustingly cutely as raspy-voiced Whitaker could. In 1969, his angelic looks got him cast in the title role of the Christmas TV special *The Littlest Angel.*

After *Family Affair*'s prime-time expiration, Whitaker went on to further success as Disney's leading juvenile actor of the early 1970s with the movies *The Biscuit Eater* (1972), *Napoleon and Samantha* (1972), *Snowball Express* (1972), *Mystery in Dracula's Castle* (1973), and *Tom Sawyer* (1973). Before the end of his acting career, he starred in another hit TV series, playing teenager Johnny Stuart opposite a sea monster on Sid and Marty Krofft's *Sigmund and the Sea Monster*, airing Saturday mornings from 1973 to 1975. Today, Whitaker is a recovered drug addict and devout Mormon who attended Brigham Young University in Utah and once did missionary work overseas. He works at his sister's Los Angeles talent agency, where the late Dana Plato was a client, and hosts a radio show, *The Dr. Zod and Johnny Show*, with his psychiatrist Dr. Ron Zodkevitch.

FYI: ▸ While filming *Family Affair*, six-year-old Johnny Whitaker had a whopping crush on TV sibling Anissa Jones. She, being a sophisticated eight-year-old, did not return the crush.

WHITE, E. B.

American author whose children's books, *Stuart Little* (1945), *Charlotte's Web* (1952), and *The Trumpet of the Swan* (1970), have become classics. Initials stand for Elwyn Brooks.

WHITE CASTLE

"Buy 'em by the sack." People either really like or really hate these small, square, ultra-inexpensive fast-food burgers. Founded by Edgar "Billy" Ingram in Wichita, Kansas, in 1921.

FYI: ▸ White Castle burgers are known as Belly-Bombers, Beef Cookies, Gut-Busters, Sliders, and Whiteys.

WHITE SHADOW

Airing on CBS from 1978 to 1981, a TV drama starring blonde-haired Ken Howard as Ken Reeves, a basketball star with the Chicago Bulls who, after an injury sidelines his pro career, accepts a job as coach at Carver High School, an inner-city school in Los Angeles. Featured players included Ed Bernard as principal Jim Willis, Joan Pringle as vice-principal Sybil Buchanan, and a cast of talented youngsters who made up the racially mixed basketball team: Kevin Hooks as Morris Thorpe, Erik Kilpatrick as Curtis Jackson, Ira Angustain as Ricardo Gomez, Thomas Carter as James Hayward, Nathan Cook as Milton Reese, Ken Michelman as Abner Goldstein, Byron Stewart as Warren Coolidge, and Timothy Van Patten as Mario "Salami" Petrino.

Howard co-created the series based on his own experiences playing high school basketball in New York City. It dealt with the personal conflicts surrounding the students, their encounters with crime and drugs, and the struggles of living in a tough area. In a memorable episode, innocent bystander Curtis Jackson was shot to death during a liquor store robbery. Reflecting real life, *The White Shadow* had the students moving on; in the spring of 1980, several players graduated from Carver and were succeeded by new ones in the fall.

"WHITE WEDDING"

Sneering peroxide-blonde Billy Idol's 1983 punk rock tribute to Holy Matrimony was his second hit in America, following "Hot in the City" (1982).

WHITMAN FRAME-TRAY PUZZLES

If preschoolers looked close enough, they could spot puzzle pieces shaped like hearts, stars, bells, planes, autos, bunnies, ducks, and so on. The Whitman Publishing Company also specialized in paper-doll and coloring books.

WHO FRAMED ROGER RABBIT

From Walt Disney Productions and Steven Spielberg's Amblin Entertainment comes the top-grossing film of 1988, an innovative, technically brilliant and vastly entertaining *film noir* spoof that wonderfully blends live action and animation. Set in 1947 Hollywood, Bob Hoskins stars as Eddie Valiant, a down-and-out cartoon-hating private detective investigating the murder of gag tycoon Marvin Acme. By his side is slaphappy cartoon star Roger Rabbit (voice of Charles Fleischer), the prime suspect, whose motivation for the killing was jealousy. His sultry wife, Jessica Rabbit (voice of Kathleen Turner), played "pat-a-cake" with the victim. Along the way, they uncover a plot to wipe out all the 'toons residing in Toontown. Directed by Robert Zemeckis, *Roger Rabbit* won Oscars for Special Visual Effects and a special Oscar for animation. Extra fun is trying to spot the many cartoon characters from the Disney, Warner Brothers, and Fleischer studios who make cameo appearances, like Mickey Mouse, Donald Duck, Bugs Bunny, Daffy Duck, and Betty Boop.

WHOPPER

"It takes two hands to handle a Whopper!" Now, get your mind out of the gutter, this is Burger King's gigantic mayo-laden hamburger, first introduced in 1957 and the closest competitor to McDonald's Big Mac. The Junior Whopper is for those with smaller appetites.

"WHO SHOT J.R.?"

During the summer of 1980, the prime-time mega-soap *Dallas* had the whole world asking that question. The cliffhanging season finale ended with nasty J.R. Ewing being shot in the chest while working late in his office, leaving viewers pondering over which character actually pulled the trigger. (J.R. was so despised that anyone could've done it.) The answer to the burning question was such a well-kept secret that the show's cast and crew didn't even know it, and five alternative endings were filmed, using wife Sue Ellen, rival Cliff Barnes, mother Miss Ellie, father Jock Ewing, and sister-in-law Kristin Shepard. On November 21, 1980, nearly 80 percent of TV viewers tuned in to find out that Sue Ellen's trampy younger sister Kristin shot J.R. She did it because she was pregnant with J.R.'s baby and he was blackmailing her: Leave Dallas or everyone would know her dirty little secret of being a prostitute. The telecast was the most widely watched program in the history of TV (it would later be beat by the final showing of *M*A*S*H* in 1983).

WHOVILLE

Minuscule community, home of the plucky Whos, located in the Land of Seuss just south of snowy Mount Crumpit. Once was rescued by the gentle-hearted elephant Horton and had Christmas stolen by the mean-spirited Grinch. Distinguished citizens: wise Dr. Whoovy, the leader of Whoville, and sweet little Cindy Lou Who, who actually encountered the mean old Grinch on Christmas Eve.

WIDETTES

Junk-food-consuming family on *Saturday Night Live* with wide, wide, wide, wide (I mean really wiiiiide) asses: mom Betty (Jane Curtin), dad Bob (Dan Aykroyd), and son Jeff (John Belushi).

WIENERMOBILE

The unique hot-dog-shaped vehicle tours around the country to promote Oscar Mayer wieners. First built in 1936, the eye-catching Wienermobile has been redesigned six times. The current version includes a "bun" roof, relish-colored seats, a ketchup-hued walkway, and a stereo system that broadcasts the famed Oscar Mayer wiener jingle.

WIENIE ROLLS

Also known as wienie curls. Late-1970s and early-1980s slang for bad feathered hair, occurring because a girl didn't brush out curling-iron rolls to form those well-known layers of feathery waves (à la Farrah) or because she just had wimpy, limp hair that couldn't hold a feather.

WILBUR

"Terrific" little farm pig who is saved from the butcher's block by a word-weaving spider named Charlotte in E. B. White's classic children's book *Charlotte's Web*.

WILBUR POST

Alan Young's good-natured city architect, who discovers a horse isn't a horse when he moves to a quiet home in the countryside. The property came with a barn housing a fabulously talking horse in the 1960s *Mr. Ed* TV series.

WILD, JACK

Talented juvenile actor and teen dreamboat from England—with shaggy dark hair, an impish grin, and a cockney accent—who first gained attention and a Best Supporting Actor Oscar nod at age fifteen playing the Artful Dodger in the 1968 movie musical *Oliver!* Probably best remembered for his role of Jimmy, the shipwrecked lad, on *H. R. Pufnstuf*, airing Saturday mornings from 1969 to 1971.

WILD KINGDOM

Mutual of Omaha's long-running nature documentary program (1968–88), hosted by famed naturalist and zoologist Marlin Perkins, which gave TV audiences exciting close-up views of wildlife in natural habitats in different parts of the world, particularly the plains of Africa and the jungles of South America. Less exciting were the Mutual of Omaha commercials in which Perkins served as spokesman.

WILD THORNBERRYS

Fun late-1990s Nickelodeon cartoon series about a family of naturalists involved in various wildlife adventures while traveling to exotic locales (including the Serengeti, the Amazon, and the North Pole) in a rigged-out RV. The program's star is inquisitive twelve-year-old Eliza Thornberry, geeky with pigtails, glasses, and a mouthful of braces, who has the uncanny ability—thanks to a magical shaman—to communicate with animals in their native tongue. Eliza's parents are dashing Nigel and wary Marianne, acclaimed host and producer of the documentary TV program, *Nigel Thornberry's Animal World.* Whiny sibling Debbie Thornberry is the typical American sixteen-year-old, more interested in her appearance and in boy singers than the wilds of nature. Donnie is the wild boy from the jungles of Borneo, adopted by the Thornberrys, and Darwin, Eliza's best friend, is the family's tagalong chimp. Tim Curry of *Rocky Horror* fame provides Nigel Thornberry's British voice.

WILD, WILD WEST

Innovative western fantasy, airing from 1965 to 1969, starring Robert Conrad as supercool James T. West, and Ross Martin as master-of-disguise Artemus Gordon, government intelligence agents sent to the American frontier by President Grant to battle crazed adversaries. What set the show apart from the onslaught of westerns cluttering the era's TV screens was the use of Bond-like weaponry and gizmos to nab criminal masterminds. Highly memorable are the cliffhanger scenes—involving seemingly escape-proof traps—that turn animated before commercial breaks.

WILLARD STILES

"Tear him up!" An oddball misfit who communicates with rats—led by Ben—and trains them as his agents of revenge. Played by Bruce Davison in the 1971 horror film *Willard.*

WILLIAMS, ROBIN

Hairy, hyperactive improv comic whose hilarious portrayal of extra-terrestrial Mork from Ork on the hit TV sitcom *Mork and Mindy* (1978–82) made him the hot new celebrity of the late 1970s. Following the series run, Williams went on to become a movie star, appearing in such box-office bonanzas as *Popeye* (1980), *The World According to Garp* (1982), *Good Morning, Vietnam* (1987), *Dead Poets Society* (1989), *Awakenings* (1990), *The Fisher King* (1991), *Hook* (1991), *Mrs. Doubtfire* (1993), *Jumanji* (1995), *The Birdcage* (1996), *Good Will Hunting* (1997), which earned him an Oscar for Best Supporting Actor, and *Patch Adams* (1998).

WILLIAMS, VANESSA

"I am not a lesbian and I am not a slut, and somehow I am going to make people believe me." In 1983, she became the first black woman to win the Miss America title—and the first to give it up for violating the pageant's moral code. Born in New York on March 18, 1963, Williams was a novice contestant when she won the Miss New York crown in 1982. From there she went on to Atlantic City to participate in the Miss America Pageant, and, following her show-stopping rendition of "Happy Days Are Here Again," went on to make history.

Green-eyed and light-skinned, the twenty-year-old Williams was a popular winner, but a regrettable scandal developed. Sometime before she began competing in beauty contests, she had posed nude for sexually explicit photographs, including those of a lesbian bondage nature. *Penthouse* magazine purchased this notorious photo collection, and owner Bob Guccione announced he would publish them before her reign was over. The conservative Miss America board promptly requested that she submit her resignation. On July 24, 1984, a distraught Williams informed journalists at a mobbed press conference—telecast live—that she was relinquishing her crown.

In the years following the scandal, Williams showed strength and perseverance. Proving that talent wins out in the end, she has since gone on to achieve success in movies (*Eraser*), TV (*Bye Bye Birdie*), stage (*Kiss of the Spider Woman*), and music. In 1992, her romantic single "Save the Best for Last" topped the American Top Forty for five weeks. Other hits included "The Right Stuff" (1988), "Dreamin'" (1989), "Running Back to You" (1991), and "Colors of the Wind" (1995), from Disney's *Pocahontas.* It is interesting that, now that Vanessa Williams is a big star, the Miss America Pageant namedrops and claims her as one of their own, after years of excluding her in shame and embarrassment.

WILLIS JACKSON

Juvenile actor Todd Bridges, who previously starred as Loomis in Abe Vigoda's *Fish*, played Arnold Jackson's more reserved twelve-year-old brother on *Dif-f'rent Strokes*.

WILL MARSHALL

The cute teenage son on the *Land of the Lost* was played by blue-eyed, curly- and dark-haired teen idol Wesley Eure. Eure co-starred for eight years as Michael Horton on the soap opera *Days of Our Lives* (1973–81).

WILLONA WOODS

Sexy, single, and swingin', she was the next-door neighbor and best confidante of Florida Evans on the prime-time sitcom *Good Times*. Became a mother when she adopted little Penny Gordon, a victim of child abuse.

WILL ROBINSON

Adventurous ten-year-old boy-genius on the TV sci-fi classic *Lost in Space*, portrayed by Billy Mumy. More enthusiastic than his family about being marooned in space, Will liked to spend his time exploring the strange planets they landed on, accompanied by trusty Robot, treasonous Dr. Smith, and—when she's not being a pesky know-it-all—middle sister Penny.

WILLY WONKA AND THE CHOCOLATE FACTORY

"Little surprises around every corner, but nothing dangerous. Don't be alarmed."
—WILLY WONKA (GENE WILDER)

"It's scrumdidilyumptious! It's everybody's non-polluttionary, anti-institutionally, pro-confectionery factory of fun!" The film that caught a generation's fancy (it's my personal all-time favorite) is acclaimed by many as the best kids' cinematic feature ever made. Directed by Mel Stuart and filmed in beautiful Bavaria, the 1971 musical-fantasy was adapted from Roald Dahl's classic *Charlie and the Chocolate Factory* (1964). It starred Gene Wilder as candy mogul Willy Wonka, the eccentric yet mysterious owner of the world's greatest chocolate factory. Wonka holds a contest in which the winners of five Golden Tickets—concealed in chocolate bars—are awarded a tour of his candy empire and a lifetime supply of sweets.

One by one, the coveted tickets are discovered by decidedly disgusting children: gluttonous Augustus Gloop (Michael Bollner), gum-smacker Violet Beauregarde (Denise Nickerson), spoiled brat Veruca Salt (Julie Dawn Cole), and TV-addicted Mike Teevee (Paris Themmen). The mold is broken when honest but poor Charlie Bucket (Peter Ostrum) discovers the last Golden Ticket. The winners, along with Charlie's feisty Grandpa Joe (Jack Albertson), are led on a thrilling journey through the secret gates of Wonka's factory. Once inside, they discover a fantasy world of edible plants, chocolate rivers, lickable wallpaper, fizzy lifting drinks, golden-egg-laying geese, a psychedelic boat ride, a foam-spewing Wonkamobile, miniaturizing Wonkavision, a glass elevator, and orange-skinned dwarf employees known as Oompa Loompas.

Unbeknownst to the youngsters, Wonka has set up pitfalls along the way to test their honesty and integrity, because his real motive for the tour is to find a "good" child to be the heir to the chocolate factory. Before the end of the deliciously twisted tale, we see fatso Augustus get sucked up a chocolate river pipe, rude Violet blow up into a gigantic blueberry, bad egg Veruca fall down the Golden Goose garbage chute, and hellion Mike hop into Wonkavision and hop out a few inches tall. This leaves pure-hearted Charlie as Wonka's lucky protégé. The Oscar-nominated music score includes tuneful songs, written by Anthony Newley and Leslie Bricusse, such as "The Candy Man," "(I've Got a) Golden Ticket," "Pure Imagination," "I Want It Now," and four different versions of "Oompa Loompa (Doompa-Dee-Doo)."

Unlike most kid-friendly movies, *Willy Wonka* didn't offer the usual merchandise tie-ins (coloring books, board games, lunch boxes, and so on); the only exception seems to be a toy Willy Wonka Chocolate Factory that came as a send-away from Quaker Oats cereal. It allowed tots to make candy bars with "W" molds and wrap them up in Wonka wrappers, complete with Golden Tickets. There was also a Willy Wonka candy line in stores, which included Everlasting Gobstoppers, Oompas, Scrunch Bars, and Scrumdidilyumptious Bars. "And Charlie, don't forget what happened to the man that suddenly got everything he ever wanted. He lived happily ever after. . . ."

WILMA FLINTSTONE

The pretty redhead is Fred Flintstone's even-tempered, long-suffering, dutiful wife. The model of

Stone Age housekeeping, she often spends her time cleaning up the trouble her hubby makes on *The Flintstones* cartoon. Maiden name: Wilma Slaghoopal.

WIMPY

"I'll gladly pay you Tuesday for a hamburger today." The best friend of seadog Popeye was a rotund, lazy coward with a *great* love for hamburgers. Also used as a slang word for a weak person.

WINGS

Not Paul McCartney's post-Beatles' rock band, but the name of bangs cut parted in the middle and styled so that the hair feathered outward and away, reminiscent of bird wings. Fashionable around 1975, this style was the halfway point between the Marcia Brady center-parted straight hair of the 1970s and the Farrah Fawcett feathered hair of the late 1970s. The celebrity who comes to mind for wearing wings would be Olivia Newton-John, during her country-rock music phase (pre-*Grease*).

WINNIE THE POOH

Children's author A. A. Milne (1882–1956) created the tubby, butterscotch-hued bear dressed in trademark red shirt and endowed with a huge appetite for "hunny" in 1926. The kindhearted bear "of little brain" resided at Pooh Corner in the enchanted Hundred Acre Woods. He shared his woodland adventures with an array of friends, including timid tiny Piglet, intellectual Owl, fussbudget Rabbit, mama Kanga and baby Roo, gloomy old donkey Eeyore, hyperactive Tigger, and little boy Christopher Robin. (The tales were based on the real-life Christopher Robin's stuffed animals.)

In 1966, Walt Disney gave new life to the cherished storybook characters with a thirty-minute animated feature, *Winnie the Pooh and the Honey Tree*, narrated by Sebastian "Mr. French" Cabot and featuring the charming voice of Sterling Holloway as Pooh. It was followed by *Winnie the Pooh and the Blustery Day* (1968) and *Winnie the Pooh and Tigger Too* (1974). In 1977, all three films were combined as a feature-length theatrical release titled *The Many Adventures of Winnie the Pooh*. Popular with audiences of all ages, Pooh has since joined the ranks of Mickey Mouse, Donald Duck, and Goofy as a regular of the Disney lineup.

WINSOME WITCH

Good-hearted sorceress, called Winnie for short, with the motto "Have Broom, Will Travel." She starred in a supporting cartoon segment of *The Secret Squirrel Show* in the mid 1960s.

WINTER WARLOCK

"You are trespassing on the land of the Winter Warlock." Raging, powerful hermit who resides in an icy lair on the Mountain of the Whispering Winds. When Kris Kringle presents him with a Christmas gift (a choo-choo train), ol' Winter Warlock transforms into a big sweetheart. He was voiced by Keenan Wynn in the 1970 TV special *Santa Claus Is Comin' to Town*.

WISHNIK

"Rub my hair for good luck." Uneeda Doll Company's version of the so-ugly-I've-got-to-have-one Trolls. First manufactured in 1964, these faddish dolls were characterized by naked bodies, glassy eyes, and flowing, neon-colored hair. Other noteworthy dolls of the era produced by Uneeda included Pee-Wees, Petal People, and Dollikin.

WISK

The TV ads for this laundry detergent claimed annoyingly that if you didn't use their product you would get the embarrassing "Ring around the collar."

WITCHIEPOO

"Alarm! Alarm! Witchiepoo is coming, Witchiepoo is coming!" Sinister but kooky green-skinned hag who menaces the citizens of Living Island, particularly a young teen named Jimmy, because she wants his magical golden flute. Witchiepoo shares her spooky-faced castle with a trio of dimwit sidekicks—Orson the Vulture, Seymour the Spider, and Stupid Bat—and soars through the skies on her rocket-powered Vroom Broom. Played overtly campy by character actress Billie Hayes on *H. R. Pufnstuf* from 1969 to 1971, she is considered by many to be one of the best villains of kid-oriented Saturday-morning TV. Her wicked Krofft contemporaries included Martha Raye's Benita Bizarre (*The Bugaloos*) and Charles Nelson Reilly's Hoo Doo (*Lidsville*).

WIZ-WHEEL
A round, low-slung riding toy where you sat in the middle and used your arms to crank two large plastic wheels, causing it to move forward, backward, and spin dizzily like a top.

WIZ-Z-ZER
The "World's Wildest Whirler" was this plastic, two-toned-colored top introduced by Matchbox in 1969 and named after the noisy "wizzzing" sound it made. The dizzyingly fast spinner ("over 10,000 rpm!") was unique because it didn't need to be pulled by a string (it had a friction-activated rubber tip), could boomerang around a room, and could get right back up if it toppled over. Each Wiz-z-zer came packaged with a "Pocket Trick Book" that illustrated all kinds of neat-o tricks, such as finger balancing, pencil-point teetering, string spinning, stair skipping, tightrope walking, and duking it out with one another (like a homemade version of Ideal's Battling Tops).

WJM-TV
Fictional Minneapolis TV station on Channel 12 (seen in the 1970s sitcom *The Mary Tyler Moore Show*) whose poorly rated Six O'Clock News program employs producer Lou Grant, associate producer Mary Richards, anchorman Ted Baxter, news writer Murray Slaughter, and TV hostess Sue Ann Nivens. The station's call letters are from the initials of owner Wild Jack Monroe.

WOLFGANG
Arte Johnson's cigarette-smoking, myopic German soldier on TV's *Laugh-In* who lurked behind a potted palm, muttering "Verrrry interesting."

WOLFIE THE WOLFMAN
Cool, sandal-wearing werewolf, one of Saturday morning's *Groovie Goolies*, who skateboarded, surfed, and drove the custom-built, fur-covered Wolf Wagon. Wolfie's pet was a flying piranha fish named Fido.

WOLF MAN
From the 1942 *Wolf Man* movie, a human named Larry Talbot (actor Lon Chaney) who changes into a bloodthirsty werewolf every time there is a full moon. Only a silver bullet can kill the Wolf Man. Great werewolf films from twentieth-century cinema include *An American Werewolf in London* (1981), *The Company of Wolves* (1984), *The Curse of the Werewolf* (1961), *The Howling* (1981), *I Was a Teenage Werewolf* (1957), *Silver Bullet* (1985), *The Wolf Man* (1941), *Wolfen* (1981), and the teen comedy *Teen Wolf* (1985) starring Michael J. Fox.

WONDER BREAD
Packaged in the familiar color-dotted wrapper, the "King of White Bread" is popular with kids because of its sweet taste and spongy texture (it's fun to roll into balls). Moms like Wonder Bread because it comes presliced and enriched with vitamins ("Helps build strong bodies twelve ways"). It has been America's best-selling bread since first being introduced by the Taggart Baking Company in 1920. Today, Wonder Bread is owned by Continental Bakeries, which also produces Hostess snack cakes.

WONDERBUG
The kid-oriented TV drama appeared on Saturday mornings, from 1976 to 1978, as one of the installments on *The Krofft Supershow*. It told the crime-busting tale of a dune buggy that went from a junky, falling-apart car called Schlepp to an awe-inspiring four-wheeler via the squeeze of a magic horn. Heralded as Wonderbug, with headlights resembling eyes, and the front grille a smiling mouth, old Schlepp now had the power to talk and fly and help three teenagers—leader Barry (David Levy), rhyme-talking C.C. (John Anthony Bailey), and sensible Susan (Carol Anne Seflinger)—capture wrongdoers.

WONDER TWINS
Zan and Jayna—the young Asian-esque siblings clad in purple tights—who assist the Justice League of America's crime-fighting superheroes on Saturday-morning TV. By sticking out their fists, touching each other's power rings, and declaring, "Wonder Twin powers, activate!" they would morph into *SuperFriends* themselves. Jayna, took the shape of some kind of animal, while Zan assumed the form of water. Their sidekick was a lovable but bumbling blue monkey called Gleek.

WONDER WOMAN
"You're a wonder, Wonder Woman!" Wonder Woman, pop culture's first superheroine, acclaimed

as the "fabulous forerunner of the feminist movement," debuted in *All Star Comics* number 8 in December 1941, before headlining her own comic-book series the following summer. A beautiful brunette, Wonder Woman originates from the all-female Paradise Island, where she is known as Diana, daughter of Hippolyte, Queen of the Amazons. Gifted by the gods, the princess Diana has the loveliness of Aphrodite, the wisdom of Athena, the speed of Mercury, and the strength of Hercules.

After rescuing a pilot whose plane has crashed, Major Steve Trevor, she becomes smitten and follows him to World War II–era Washington, D.C., in guise as bespectacled secretary Diana Prince. It's there that she helps the Americans fight dastardly Nazis and other bad guys. When trouble erupts, she whirls herself into Wonder Woman, dressed in snazzy red-white-and-blue hot pants, matching breastplate and cape, knee-high boots, and golden headband. Wonder Woman uses her mighty power—aided by a golden lasso, bullet-deflecting bracelets, and an invisible plane—to avenge injustice and right a wrong.

Wonder Woman made her first prime-time appearance in a 1974 TV movie starring Cathy Lee Crosby. From 1976 to 1979, a highly viewed TV series aired, starring glamorous and statuesque (at five-foot-ten) Lynda Carter, a former Miss World, in the title role. From 1973 to 1986, Wonder Woman joined Superman, Batman, Robin, and Aquaman as a member of the Justice League of America (JLA) on a Saturday-morning cartoon titled *SuperFriends*. Superheroines following in her mighty footsteps include Batgirl, Supergirl, Ms. Marvel, Spider-Woman, Invisible Girl, ElectraWoman and DynaGirl, and Wonder Girl (Wonder Woman's kid sister).

FYI: ▸ Dr. William Moulton Marston, a Harvard-educated psychologist who created Wonder Woman, also invented the lie detector machine.

WONDER YEARS

A sweet coming-of-age series that took a nostalgic look back at suburban life circa 1968, through the eyes of young Kevin Arnold (played by angelic-faced Fred Savage). Each episode was narrated by Daniel Stern, as the voice of the adult Kevin, who reminisced about the day-to-day ordeals common to adolescents growing up in the late 1960s. During the program's prime-time run on ABC (1988–93), Kevin matured from a twelve-year-old attending John F. Kennedy Junior High to a teenager graduating from McKinley High. He lived in a comfortable middle-class home with weary father Jack (Dan Lauria), nurturing mother Norma (Alley Mills), hippie older sister Karen (Olivia d'Abo), and bullying older brother Wayne (Jason Hervey). Best friends were Gwendolyn "Winnie" Cooper (Danica McKellar), a pretty neighbor whom he had a crush on, and Paul Pfeiffer (Josh Saviano), a nerdy confidante.

FYI: ▸ According to Wonder Bread, the Wonder Years are ages one to twelve.

WONKAMOBILE

This odd-looking, sound-sputtering, foam-spewing vehicle is found in Willy Wonka's Chocolate Factory.

WONKATANIA

"Is it raining? Is it snowing? Is a hurricane a-blowing?" The boat from *Willy Wonka and the Chocolate Factory* that took candymaker Wonka and his Golden Ticket winners on a psychedelic ride through a scary tunnel.

WOODSEY OWL

"Give a hoot, don't pollute!" exclaimed this animated owl wearing a green Robin Hood suit, in a TV ad campaign for the U.S. Forest Service to remind kids to help fight pollution. Smokey Bear, who helps prevents forest fires, introduced Woodsey as one of his pals in 1974. Remember, kiddies: "Never be a dirty bird in the city, or in the woods. Help keep America looking good."

WOODSTOCK (COMIC CHARACTER)

You know you're not a Baby Boomer when the name Woodstock is mentioned and the first thing that comes to mind is not acid-tripping hippies gyrating in the rainy mud at a music festival, but the image of Snoopy's little yellow bird-buddy. Charles Schulz created the Peanuts' Woodstock in 1970 as a loyal chum for Charlie Brown's headstrong beagle. So constant was this fledgling's devotion to Snoopy that he even ran (or fluttered) away from home with him in the 1972 animated film *Snoopy Come Home*.

WOODSTOCK (MUSIC FESTIVAL)

You know you're a Baby Boomer when the name Woodstock is mentioned and the first thing that comes to mind is acid-tripping hippies gyrating in the rainy mud at a music festival. The most famous event in the cultural history of the post–World War II generation occurred on farmland near Woodstock, New York, in the summer of 1969. Estimated at 400,000, the crowd of young people—half-naked, grubby, and on drugs—experienced three days (August 15, 16, and 17) in torrential rain and thick mud peacefully groovin' to now-legendary rock performances by Jimi Hendrix, Janis Joplin, Jefferson Airplane, Crosby, Stills, Nash, and Young, The Who, The Band, Arlo Guthrie, Joe Cocker, Joan Baez, Canned Heat, Santana, and Sly and the Family Stone. This groovy happenin' is endlessly evoked in the minds of aging Boomers—dubbed the "Woodstock Nation"—as "the best of times."

WOODY

"Reach for the sky." The pull-string talking cowboy was little Andy's number-one toy but now shares the honor with action-figure Buzz Lightyear. According to the Disney/Pixar *Toy Story* movies, Woody (voiced with warm sincerity by screen actor Tom Hanks) was once the star of a 1950s marionette kid TV program titled *Woody's Roundup*, co-starring spunky cowgirl Jessie, crusty prospector Stinky Pete, and his trusty horse Bullseye. His love interest is Bo Peep, a porcelain doll with a flock of sheep, belonging to Andy's baby sister Molly.

WOODY STATION WAGONS

Manufactured by the Ford Motor Company throughout the 1940s and 1950s, these roomy station wagons, characterized by wood-sided panels, were commonly used by surfers in the 1960s to transport their surfboards to the ocean.

WOODY WOODPECKER

"Guess who? . . . Hahahahaha . . . Hahahahaha . . . Hagugugugugughu!" Created by animator Walter Lantz, the fun-loving, ultrahyper woodpecker with the staccato laugh made his debut as Andy Panda's foil in the 1940 cartoon "Knock Knock." Hammering into the hearts of children everywhere, the redheaded bird appeared in more than 200 cartoon shorts and headlined a long-running TV series, *The Woody Woodpecker Show*, from 1957 to 1972. In 1948, his musical theme, "The Woody Woodpecker Song," recorded by Kay Kyser's swing band, topped the charts for six weeks and garnered an Academy Award nomination. Along with Woody Woodpecker and Andy Panda, Lantz's other characters include penguin Chilly Willy, Oswald the Rabbit, Wally Walrus, Space Mouse, Gabby Gator, and Knothead and Splinter—Woody's nephew and niece. Lantz's wife, Grace, supplied the distinctive voice of Woody Woodpecker.

FYI: ▸ They say Woody Woodpecker was inspired by Walter Lantz on his honeymoon with Grace after a continuously pecking woodpecker bore a hole through their cottage roof.

WOOLY WILLY

By using the Magic Wand, you could draw whiskers, hair, and eyebrows on this "magnetic personality," a classic novelty toy of the Baby Boom era. Also known as Dapper Dan.

WORLD OF LOVE

"Love is today's American teenager. . . . The Love scene is your scene. Wherever you're going, Love is already there." Introduced by Hasbro Toys in 1971, the seven-inch-tall World of Love fashion dolls were a reflection of the free-spirited, peace-loving hippie era. The doll line included blonde Love, the leader, and her friends: brunette Peace, redhead Flower, Afro-haired Soul, shag-cut Harmony, and token male Adam. Love's color-coordinated fashions featured the hippest of mod clothing—quilted pants, jumpers, miniskirts, midis, gauchos, knickers, ponchos, and fringy suede vests. Accessories included Love's Favorite Places, a round case that opened to become a far-out discotheque, a groovy record shop, and an outtasight clothing boutique. There was also a Love's Beauty Salon and Wig Set, a portable beauty parlor complete with wiglets and hair accessories to create many exciting coiffures. Wow!

WORLD'S GREATEST ATHLETE

The 1973 Disney comedy starred young Jan-Michael Vincent and his cute blonde surfer looks as Nanu, a naive and superathletic African jungle boy. The Tarzan-like youth is discovered by Sam Archer (John

Amos), the luckless coach of Merrivale College, and his assistant Milo (Tim Conway), while on safari in Africa. They bring him, along with pet tiger Harri, back to America to be a star athlete. As expected, Nanu wins the trophies, plus the heart of a pretty campus coed named Jane (model Dayle Haddon), yet he yearns to go back to his African home. Directed by Robert Scheerer, this was one of Disney Studios' better live-action films of the 1970s. It's filled with hilarious slapstick action, especially the scene where Conway gets shrunk to a height of three inches by the vengeful witch doctor Gazenga (Roscoe Lee Brown).

WORLD TRADE CENTER

Soaring twin skyscrapers built between 1968 and 1973 that came to symbolize the concrete landscape of New York's lower Manhattan in the late twentieth century. Before Chicago's Sears Tower was erected in 1984, they were the tallest buildings in the world (110 stories), housing a work force of more than 40,000 people, the population of a small city. In the 1976 remake of *King Kong*, the Towers were featured prominently as the lovesick ape's fatal climb. On the infamous morning of September 11, 2001, mad followers of Al Qaeda, a radical Islamic organization led by Osama bin Laden, hijacked two passenger airliners and plowed them into the top floors of each building (American Airlines Flight 11 into the South Tower, United Airlines Flight 175 into the North Tower). Structurally weakened by the impact of the crash and by the intense heat of burning jet fuel, the Towers collapsed within minutes of each other, killing thousands of office workers and hundreds of firefighters and rescue workers below. This horrific event—along with the simultaneous airborne assault on the Pentagon (using American Airlines Flight 77) and the crash in Pennsylvania of the hijacked United Airlines Flight 93, allegedly headed for an unknown target in Washington, D.C. (the Capitol Building? White House?)—would become the deadliest attack on American soil and the worst terrorist act in history.

WOSSAMOTTA U.

What's the matter? You didn't know this is the university at Frostbite Falls, Minnesota, that Rocky J. Squirrel and Bullwinkle Moose attended in Jay Ward's *Bullwinkle* cartoon series?

WRAPAROUND SKIRTS

So popular in the 1970s, these sexy dresses wrapped around from one side to the other and were tied together at the waist. Many women fell victim on a windy day to the wraparound skirt coming unfastened and giving people nearby a peek of more skin than they would prefer.

WRAPPLES

Making caramel apples got a lot easier in 1977 when Kraft Foods introduced its crafty sweet Wrapples. Wrapples came with sheets of caramel that you wrapped over fresh apples (hence the name) then stuck a popsicle stick through the top. After being placed on a cookie sheet and baking in the oven for a few minutes to melt the caramel around the apples, you'd have instant caramel apples for a delicious autumn treat.

WUZZLES

Odd group of creatures from the magical Island of Wuz that were two animals in one. This hybrid menagerie included Bumblelion (part bee, part lion), Eleroo (part elephant, part kangaroo), Hoppotamus (part rabbit, part hippo), Moosel (part moose, part seal), Rhinokey (part rhino, part monkey), Butterbear (part butterfly, part bear), and Girafbra (part giraffe, part zebra). The cartoon series aired on the Disney Channel from 1985 to 1987.

X

XANADU

"A fantasy! A musical! A place where dreams come true!" The 1980 movie starred Australian rocker Olivia Newton-John as Kira, a beautiful roller-skating muse on a wall mural who comes to life and inspires a struggling young artist, Sonny Malone (Michael Beck), and a lonely rich man, Danny McGuire (Gene Kelly), who had also been inspired by her forty years earlier. Kira convinces the two mortals to open a roller-boogie nightclub called Xanadu ("The place where nobody dared to go"). This glitzy discothon mixes 1940s big-band swing music with 1970s glam rock, 1980s giddy-up country, and some punk-ish New Wave thrown in—and in the big production number we get to see Newton-John perform it all. (Whew!)

A poor remake of the 1947 Rita Hayworth production *Down to Earth*, *Xanadu* is another one of those "so bad it's good" movies. It's infamous for being a big-budget flop, rivaling other musicals of its era—*Sgt. Pepper's Lonely Hearts Club Band* (1978), *Can't Stop the Music* (1980), *Grease 2* (1982), and *Staying Alive* (1983)—as the worst ever made. Its redeeming features are Newton-John, who's very lovely to look at, and the great soundtrack, housing the songs "Magic," "Suddenly," "All Over the World," "I'm Alive," and the title track sung by Olivia and the Electric Light Orchestra.

FYI: ▸ Olivia Newton-John met her much-younger husband Matt Lattanzi during the film's production. He was cast to play Gene Kelly as a young man and allegedly Livvy picked him up hitchhiking on the PCH in Malibu following a day of filming. The couple married in 1985 and divorced ten years later.

XENA

Raven-haired Warrior Princess who was the lead character in a sword-and-sorcery fantasy adventure airing on syndicated TV from 1995 to 2001. Originally an evil character on *Hercules: The Legendary Journeys*, Xena (played by Lucy Lawless, muscular and tall at five-foot-eleven) vowed to change her wicked habits when she got her own spin-off series. She roamed the mystical countryside of New Zealand, joined by female companion Gabrielle (Renée O'Connor), a stereotypical blonde ditz, on crusades against the forces of evil. The sword-wielding, leather-clad heroine employed acrobatic flips with karate chops, an eardrum-shattering war cry, and a paralyzing two-finger neck pinch known as the "Xena Touch," and could hurl a chakram (a razor-sharp disc) great distances. Regular foes included handsome Ares (Kevin Smith), the god of war; scheming Autolycus (Bruce Campbell), a bandit prince; and troublemaking Callisto (Hudson Leick), a villainess from Hades.

X-FILES

"The truth is out there"—the truth being that UFOs and other paranormal activities really do exist on earth, according to this cult hit created and produced by Chris Carter for FOX-TV. Airing from 1993 to 2002, the series centered around two FBI agents, levelheaded skeptic Dana Scully (Gillian Anderson) and more-believing Fox Mulder (David Duchovny), who investigated unusual cases ("X-Files") involving mysterious phenomena like extra-terrestrial encounters, telekinetic beings, supernatural monsters, genetically altered or mutant whatevers, and so on. Throughout Scully and Mulder's investigations, a top-secret government agency known as "The Project" worked to obstruct their efforts. I love the eerie instrumental theme by Mark Snow (the best whistling in a theme song since *The Andy Griffith Show*), later tweaked by DJ Dado into a pulsating, techno-thumping dance hit in 1996.

X-MEN

"The Strangest Superheroes of All!" Introduced in 1963, one of the largest-selling comic-book lines in history from Marvel, centering on a team of mutant crime-fighters run by telepathic Professor Charles Xavier and consisting of Slim Summers (Cyclops), Bobby Drake (Iceman), Hank McCoy (Beast), Warren Worthington the Third (Angel), and Jean Grey (Marvel Girl). Later add-ons included Wolverine, Storm, Gambit, Morph, Rogue, and Jubilee. Two big-screen adaptations of the comic were released in 2000 and 2003, starring Patrick Stewart as Professor Xavier, Hugh Jackman as Wolverine, and Halle Berry as Storm.

"XYZ"

"eXamine Your Zipper." That's what you'd say to the clueless person who has been walking about with his pants unzipped. Some will follow XYZ with PDQ (for "examine your zipper, pretty darn quick").

wxyz

YAKKY DOODLE
A self-consciously cute yellow cartoon duckling who has a tendency to yak on and on about the most trivial nonsense. Yakky's best pal was an overprotective bulldog named Chopper who kept the playful "little fella" from becoming duck soup for hungry con artist Fibber Fox. Created by Hanna-Barbera in 1960 as a supporting segment on *The Yogi Bear Show*.

YANKEE DOODLE PIGEON
"Charge!" Unflappable courier pigeon carrying secret messages for America during World War I, who always avoids the evil clutches of Dick Dastardly and hench-dog Muttley, on the Saturday-morning cartoon *Dastardly and Muttley in Their Flying Machines* (1969–71). "Stop that pigeon, now!"

YANKOVIC, "WEIRD AL"
Nerdy-looking novelty singer from California who specializes in song parodies. The better known of these include "Ricky" (Toni Basil's "Mickey"), "Eat It" (Michael Jackson's "Beat It"), "I Lost on Jeopardy" (Greg Kihn Band's "Jeopardy"), "Like a Surgeon" (Madonna's "Like a Virgin"), and "Smells Like Nirvana" (Nirvana's "Smells Like Teen Spirit").

YEAR WITHOUT A SANTA CLAUS
The extraordinary TV special about "the Christmas that almost wasn't" is remembered by many children of the 1970s as the one starring the Heat Miser and the Snow Miser. Filmed using the Rankin/Bass Animagic puppets, the 1974 classic told about the time, before you were born, when a dispirited Santa Claus declared, "Nobody cares about Christmas anymore," and canceled his gift-giving journey. Eager to help her husband, Mrs. Claus (or just "Mrs. C") sends two elves, Jingle Bells and Jangle Bells, along with young reindeer Vixen, down to the town of Southland U.S.A. to find out where the Christmas Spirit had disappeared.

It appears that Southland's lack of cheer stems from not having any seasonal snow (it hasn't snowed there in a hundred years). Jingle and Jangle trek off to visit the fiery-haired Heat Miser, who rules over warm climates (including Southland),

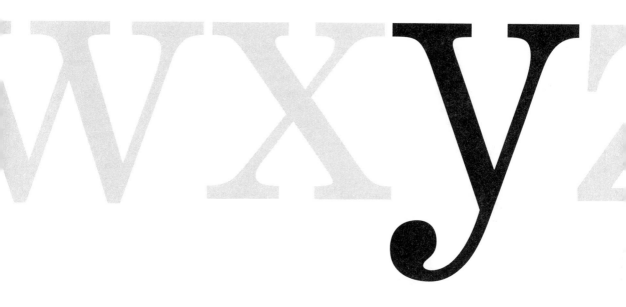

and his brother, the icy-haired Snow Miser, who rules over colder climates. Mrs. C steps in and tries to convince the bickering brothers to let it snow just once in Southland. The wacky siblings can't stop arguing, so it's off to visit their mother, Mother Nature, who sets those nasty boys straight.

Meanwhile, Santa sets off for Southland on reindeer Dasher to find little Vixen, who's taken ill from all the warm weather. Santa meets a doubting lad named Iggy Thistlewhite, who doesn't believe in him. Upon convincing Iggy he is real, and receiving gifts and letters from the rest of the world's children, particularly one girl's poignant "Blue Christmas" note, Santa becomes jolly again. It snows in Southland, and Christmas is back. Adapted from Phyllis McGinley's book, *The Year Without a Santa Claus* is narrated by Shirley Booth (better known as TV's Hazel) as the persistent Mrs. Claus and features the voice of Mickey Rooney as Santa Claus.

YELLOW RIBBONS

Inspired by Tony Orlando and Dawn's hit 1973 tune, "Tie a Yellow Ribbon 'Round the Ole Oak Tree," yellow ribbons tied around front-lawn trees became symbols of hope for families with loved ones off fighting in wars, held hostage by terrorists, or incarcerated in prison.

YELLOW SUBMARINE

Wiggy-animated fantasy that has The Beatles summoned to join Captain Fred in his Yellow Submarine to save the magical world of Pepperland, located beneath the sea, from the music-hating Blue Meanies. Along the way, they encounter Sergeant Pepper, Strawberry Fields, Nowhere Land, and the Sea of Holes. Released in 1968, the film is acclaimed for its stunning psychedelic pop art and wonderful soundtrack showcasing mid-career Beatles songs: "Lucy in the Sky with Diamonds," "Eleanor Rigby," "All You Need Is Love," "When I'm Sixty Four," and the title tune.

"Y.M.C.A."

In 1978, the Young Men's Christian Association (Y.M.C.A.) gained unwanted notoriety when the flamboyant disco group the Village People sang about it on this smash single. You see, the organization—known for athletic, social, and educational programs and men down on their luck—didn't want the publicity because of the song's homosexual undertones. (The Y.M.C.A. threatened to boycott Dick Clark's *American Bandstand* when the Village People appeared on the program.) Like all the disco act's records, the song was a gay creed containing campy tongue-in-cheek lyrics like "It's fun to stay at the Y.M.C.A. / They got everything for a man to enjoy / You can hang out with all the boys!" A massive hit, "Y.M.C.A." sold more than two million copies (150,000 a day at its retail peak) and stayed on the Top Forty charts for five months, three weeks at the number-one spot. Still popular today, the tune is a disco standard played regularly at dance clubs for a new generation of dancers, who use their arms and hands to spell out the letters "Y.M.C.A." just like they did during its original heyday.

YODA

"A Jedi uses The Force for knowledge. Never for attack." In the *Star Wars* film dynasty, Yoda is the 900-year-old, green-tinted, troll-like, wise master of The Force and teacher of the Jedi. He can be found in hiding in the swamps on planet Dagobah.

YOGI BEAR

One of the most famous cartoon characters to come out of Hanna-Barbera studios. Yogi Bear first appeared in 1959 on *The Huckleberry Hound Show*, and two years later he was starring in his own self-titled series. A cheery and earnest fellow with an incomparable singsong voice (provided by Daws Butler), Yogi was "smarter than the av-er-age bear" and wore a green pork-pie hat plus matching necktie. He lived in Jellystone Park with diminutive cub pal Boo Boo and Southern sweetheart Cindy Bear. His cartoons centered around avoiding Ranger Smith while concocting schemes for stealing "pic-a-nic" baskets full of goodies from the park's vacationers.

Throughout the 1960s, Yogi's enormous popularity extended into merchandising, and he also turned up in holiday parades, TV commercials, and comic books. In 1964, he got to be a movie star in Hanna-Barbera's first feature-length cartoon, *Hey There, It's Yogi Bear*. He later teamed up with an array of Hanna-Barbera characters (including Huckleberry Hound, Quick Draw McGraw, Snagglepuss, Wally Gator, Top Cat, Magilla Gorilla, and Scooby-Doo) in various Saturday-morning shows: *Yogi's Gang* (1973–75), *Scoo-*

by's All-Star Laff-a-Lympics (1977–80), *Yogi's Space Race* (1978–79), and *Yogi's Treasure Hunt* (1985).

YOSEMITE SAM

"I'm the roughest, toughest, meanest hombre ever to terrorize the West!" Pint-sized, hot-tempered, gun-slinging cowpoke with a big, droopy moustache, first featured in 1948's "Hare Trigger" cartoon opposite Bugs Bunny.

"(YOU GOTTA) FIGHT FOR YOUR RIGHT (TO PARTY)!"

The promo video for this Beastie Boys' brat-rant had the boisterous white rappers from New York City crashing a nerd's party. The song's influential parent LP, *License to Ill*, made pop history in 1987 for being the first rap album to top the American charts.

"YOU LIGHT UP MY LIFE"

In 1977, Debby Boone scored the hit of the decade with the inspirational song (yes, she sang it to God) from the movie of the same name. Written by Joseph Brooks (who also produced, directed, and scripted the movie, starring Didi Conn and Joe Silver), the single sold more than two million copies and became the top-selling record of the 1970s. It also was number one for ten weeks on the American Top Forty and won the Oscar for Best Song. Born September 22, 1956, to Pat and Shirley Boone, Debby went on to have a lucrative career in gospel music.

FYI: ▸ On TV's *The Simpsons*, Marge and Homer's "song" was "You Light Up My Life."

"YOU'RE THE ONE THAT I WANT"

In the 1978 blockbuster *Grease*, this was the electrifying duet sung by Olivia Newton-John and John Travolta after her sweet-as-pie character, Sandy Olsson, got made over into a leather-jacketed sex kitten for the film's finale. As the first single released off the soundtrack, it sold more than two million copies and landed at number one on the Top Forty charts.

YOURS, MINE, AND OURS

"The bride had eight boys and girls. The groom had ten boys and girls. . . . Their wedding night set new attendance records!" The motion-picture precursor to TV's *Brady Bunch* was the first to show two separate households coming together to form a "conglomerate" family. It stars Lucille Ball as navy nurse Helen North, a widowed mother of eight (Colleen, Nicky, Janette, Tommy, Jean, Phillip, Gerald, and Teresa), who married a naval officer, Frank Beardsley (Henry Fonda), a widower with ten children (Nancy, Howard, Mike, Rosemary, Rusty, Greg, Louise, Veronica, Germaine, and Jean). This union creates a family of twenty (plus one on the way) and a household filled with chaotic and amusing situations. Directed by Melville Shavelson, the 1968 comedy was based on the true story of the Beardsley family of northern California featured in Helen's book *Who Gets the Drumstick?* Notable actors cast as the youngsters included Grant Goodeve (*Eight Is Enough*), Morgan Brittany—billed as Suzanne Cupito (*Dallas*)—Eric Shea (*The Poseidon Adventure*), and a four-year-old Tracy Nelson (*The Father Dowling Mysteries*).

YO-YO

The name "yo-yo" is Filipino for "spring," which is fitting for a toy that springs back when you throw it: Yo-yo-ing frequently becomes a national craze, then dies out, then springs back. In the 1920s, a Filipino immigrant, Pedro Flores, began manufacturing a small number of his native toy in Los Angeles. It caught the eye of a local businessman named Donald Duncan, the marketing wizard responsible for inventing the Eskimo Pie, originating the Good Humor ice-cream truck, and developing the premium incentive ("Kids! Send in two box tops and receive a . . ."). Buying the rights from Flores, he added the slip-string, a sliding loop around the axle instead of a knot, and the Duncan Yo-Yo yo-yoed into national glory.

Over the years, the yo-yo's popularity has gone up and down. Its highest peak occurred during the 1960s and early 1970s, when sixteen million a year were sold. The modern yo-yos are showy models made out of brightly-colored plastic instead of the old-fashioned wood. Yo-yo-coordinated kids could do flashy tricks, such as "Rock the Cradle," "Walk the Dog," "Skin the Cat," "Around the World, and "Double Delight." These skills could make them a world champion at the Yo-Yo Olympics, sponsored by Duncan.

FYI: ▸ In 1999, cable TV's Arts and Entertainment network picked the yo-yo as the number-one toy of the twentieth century.

YO-YOS
A brand of 1970s platform shoes with a distinctive look: holes in the middle of the soles.

YUCCA-DEW
This extinct 1970s hair shampoo supposedly included dew from the southwestern yucca plant. Referred to as "yucka-ew" by those who didn't care for it.

YUKON CORNELIUS
"The Greatest Prospector in the North!" Courageous Canadian, searching for silver and gold on a dog sled at the North Pole, who aids Rudolph the Red-Nosed Reindeer and Hermey the Misfit Elf against the Abominable Snow Monster in the well-loved Rankin/Bass Christmas special.

YUMMY MUMMY
A late entry in the General Mills spooky monster lineup (1988–90), the funky-looking mummy's breakfast cereal was described as "fruit-flavor cereal with vanilla-flavor marshmallows."

"YUMMY YUMMY YUMMY"
This is considered by many to be the ultimate bubblegum rock song. No other from the sweeter-than-sweet music genre even came close to matching its sugarcoated juvenile lyrics, like "Yummy yummy yummy, I've got love in my tummy" or "Kinda like sugar, kinda like spices, kinda like, like what you do." (Well, maybe The Archies' "Sugar, Sugar" gives it some competition.) The Top Ten ditty from 1968 was written by Joey Levine and Arthur Resnick and recorded by Ohio Express, a group from Mansfield, Ohio.

FYI: ▸ When *Rolling Stone* magazine asked R.E.M.'s Michael Stipe whether 1960s icons like The Beatles or The Rolling Stones meant anything to him when he was growing up, he replied: "The Beatles and Stones didn't mean a thing to me. The Monkees and Banana Splits meant more—and whoever did 'Yummy, Yummy, Yummy.'"

YUPPIES
Oft-loathed young urban professionals from President Reagan's "greed is good" era (1980–88) who ostentatiously purchased expensive, trendy, designer-brand belongings and voted Republican. Their car of choice: the high-priced BMW, a.k.a. Beemer. Fortunately, "Yuptopia" ended with the stock market crash of October 19, 1987.

Z

ZAPPED!

Released in 1982, a silly *Carrie* spoof where *Tiger Beat* hunk Scott Baio plays Barney Springboro, a telekinetic nerd who uses his powers to undress hot cheerleader Jane Mitchell (Heather Thomas). Also starred Willie Aames, another *Tiger Beat* hunk, as Peyton Nichols, his best bud, and Felice Schachter as Bernadette, his best gal. Displaying chemistry of some sort, Baio and Aames would co-star again in 1984 in the long-running syndicated sitcom *Charles in Charge.*

ZAVARONI, LENA

Now, here's an obscure one from the past—a talented child singer, born November 4, 1963, from Rothesay, on the remote Scottish Isle of Bute, whose belting of "Ma! He's Making Eyes at Me" in 1973 made her a winner of *Opportunity Knocks*, a British TV talent show. Her singing voice drew comparison to the young Judy Garland, and she went on to star in several U.K. TV series (for example, *Lena Zavaroni and Her Music*). She toured the world, including America, where she sang for President Gerald Ford at the White House in 1975, and she worked with such entertainment greats as Frank Sinatra and Liza Minnelli. Zavaroni died in 1999 from complications due to a long-term anorexia nervosa disorder.

ZERO

The loyal ghost dog of Jack Skellington resides in a cemetery grave, and if you look closely while viewing *The Nightmare Before Christmas* movie, you'll see that his nose is actually a tiny jack-o'-lantern.

ZIGGY

A short, bald, big-nosed, wide-eyed fellow, created by cartoonist Tom Wilson, whose life-pondering wonderment helped people laugh at the ironies in life. In 1971, Ziggy—along with pet dog Fuzz, pet cat Sid, pet goldfish Goldie, pet parrot Josh, and pet duck Wack—made his comic-strip debut in only fourteen daily newspapers, and today he appears in more than 600 periodicals around the world. He can also be seen in countless best-selling paperbacks and animated TV specials (including the Emmy-winning *Ziggy's Gift* in 1982), as well as in a line of popular greeting cards.

ZIGGY STARDUST

For a couple of years in the early 1970s, chameleon-like rocker David Bowie adopted a glam-rock persona as a preening and pouting androgynous space diva from Mars. He's featured on the 1972 futuristic conceptual album *The Rise and Fall of Ziggy Stardust and the Spiders from Mars.*

ZINGERS

These little Twinkie-like creme-filled cakes are the signature of the Dolly Madison snack cake line. They come in three flavors: Iced Devil's Food, Iced Vanilla, and Raspberry.

ZIPPER-RING SHIRTS

Pullover style of shirt, generally short-sleeved, with a zippered collar instead of buttons and made out of a ribbed material with multicolored stripes, like the kind Peter Brady would have worn on *The Brady Bunch.*

ZOMBIES

It should be noted that after years of portrayal in the movies as mindless voodoo-controlled corpses from Haiti, the zombies in director George Romero's *Night of the Living Dead* (1968) were not the nicest dead people to find decomposing on your front lawn because of their insatiable appetite for warm human flesh. Zombies shuffle, they lumber, and sometimes they just sway slowly back and forth to the rhythm of nothing, so you might be able to fight them off one-on-one (if you happen to find one lurking around, a blow directly to the brain can kill it). However, their strength came in sheer numbers: As a group they would encircle human victims to trap, rip to threads, and devour. What makes zombies truly frightening is that in living death they don't care if you were once their parent, child, sibling, spouse, or friend. All they care about is eating you. Cannibalistic zombies are also featured in two *Living Dead* sequels: *Dawn of the Dead* (1978) and *Day of the Dead* (1985), a *Night of the Living Dead* remake (1990), a *Dawn of the Dead* remake (2004), plus countless imitations, including *Zombie* (1980), *Night of the Comet* (1984), *Return of the Living Dead* (1985), *Night of the Creeps* (1986), *Zombie High* (1987), *C.H.U.D. 2* (1989), *Dead Alive* (1993), *Cemetery Man* (1995), *Resident Evil* (2002), and *28 Days Later* (2002).

ZOOM

"C'mon and Zoom a Zoom a Zoom a Zoom!" Airing on PBS in the late afternoon from 1972 to 1979, this daily half-hour TV program could get kids zooming home quicker than you could say "Ubbi-Dubbi." Telecast from WGBH in Boston, it was created to capture the whimsy and humor of children in the six-to-twelve age-bracket. Serving as hosts were a group of seven talented kids—known by first name only—who wore identical striped rugby shirts and whose membership changed twice a year. Bernadette was the most popular because she could do a real keen twisty-twirl thing with her arms. Children from all over America were envious of the Zoomers and wanted to audition for the show, but there was one catch: You had to live in the Boston area. Rats!

The Emmy-winning series zoomed to the top of the PBS charts, becoming its second most-popular show, behind *Masterpiece Theatre*. It showcased a potpourri of skits, songs, dances, games, stunts, jokes, filmed sketches (suggested by the legions of fans), and letter-reading. At its peak, a staggering 20,000 letters a week were received ("That's Zoom, Box Three-Five-Oh, Boston, Mass, Oh-Two-One-Three-Four"). The letters were filled with drawings, poems, puzzles, and ideas for the program to consider (most of the show's ideas came from viewers). Twenty years later, in 1999, PBS bought back a new *Zoom*, which followed the old series' format and starred a new batch of youngsters.

bibliography

The following are the many sources that helped in my extensive research and are recommended reading and viewing. As a fan of the authors listed, I applaud their pop culture expertise and thank them for inspiring me to write *From ABBA to Zoom*.

BOOKS

Asakawa, Gil, and Leland Rucker. *The Toy Book*. New York: Alfred A. Knopf, 1991.

Augustyniak, J. Michael. *Thirty Years of Mattel Fashion Dolls*. Paducah, Ky.: Collector Books, 1998.

Bernstein, Jonathan. *Pretty in Pink: The Golden Age of Teenage Movies*. New York: St. Martin's Griffin, 1997.

Betrock, Alan. *Girl Groups: The Story of a Sound*. New York: Delilah Books, 1982.

Blackwell, Earl. *Earl Blackwell's Entertainment Celebrity Register*. Detroit: Visible Ink, 1991.

Boy, Billy. *Barbie: Her Life and Times*. New York: Crown Publishing, 1987.

Brooks, Tim. *The Complete Directory to Prime Time TV Stars*. New York: Ballantine Books, 1987.

Brooks, Tim, and Earl Marsh. *The Complete Directory to Prime Time Network and Cable TV Shows*. Eighth edition. New York: Ballantine Books, 2003.

Bruegman, Bill. *Cartoon Friends of the Baby Boom Era: A Pictorial Price Guide*. Akron, Ohio: Cap'n Penny Productions, 1993.

Bruegman, Bill. *Toys of the Sixties: A Pictorial Guide*. Akron, Ohio: Toy Scouts, 1996.

Brunvard, Jan Harold. *Too Good to Be True: The Colossal Book of Urban Legends*. New York: W. W. Norton and Company, 1999.

Bugliosi, Vincent, with Curt Gentry. *Helter Skelter: The True Story of the Manson Murders*. New York: W. W. Norton and Company, 1974.

Burke, Timothy and Kevin. *Saturday Morning Fever*. New York: St. Martin's Griffin, 1999.

Cader, Michael, and Edie Baskin. *Saturday Night Live: The First Twenty Years*. New York: Houghton Mifflin, 1994.

Cain, Dana. *Saturday Morning TV Collectibles*. Iola, Wis.: Krause Publications, 2000.

Cameron-Wilson, James. *Young Hollywood*. Lanham, Md.: Madison Books, 1994.

Clark, Dick, with Fred Bronson. *Dick Clark's American Bandstand*. New York: Collins Publishers, 1997.

Cooper, Kim, and David Smay. *Bubblegum Music Is the Naked Truth*. Los Angeles: Feral House, 2000.

Courtney-Thompson, Fiona, and Kate Phelps. *The 20th Century Year by Year*. New York: Barnes & Noble Books, 1998.

Cox, Stephen. *The Beverly Hillbillies*. Chicago: Contemporary Books, 1988.

Cox, Stephen. *Dreaming of Jeannie*. New York: St. Martin's Griffin, 2000.

Cox, Stephen. *The Hooterville Handbook: A Viewer's Guide to Green Acres*. New York: St. Martin's Press, 1993.

Crenshaw, Marshall. *Hollywood Rock*. New York: HarperPerennial, 1994.

Daly, Steven, and Nathaniel Wice. *Alt. Culture: An A-to-Z Guide to the '90s—Underground, Online, and Over-the-Counter*. New York: HarperPerennial, 1995.

Dotz, William, and Jim Morton. *What a Character! 20th-Century American Advertising Icons*. San Francisco: Chronicle Books, 1996.

Du Noyer, Paul. *Encyclopedia of Albums*. London: Dempsey Parr, 1998.

Du Noyer, Paul. *Encyclopedia of Singles*. London: Dempsey Parr, 1998.

Eagen, Daniel. *HBO's Guide to Movies on Video-Cassette and Cable TV*. New York: HarperPerennial, 1991.

Ebert, Roger. *Roger Ebert's Video Companion 1997.* Kansas City: Andrews McMeel, 1996.

Edelstein, Andrew J., and Frank Lovece. *The Brady Bunch Book.* New York: Warner Books, 1990.

Entertainment Weekly Guide to the Greatest Movies Ever Made. New York: Warner Books, 1996.

Entertainment Weekly: The 100 Greatest TV Shows of All Times. New York: Time, 1998.

Epstein, Dan. *20th Century Pop Culture.* London: Carlton Books Limited, 1999.

Fennick, Janine. *The Collectible Barbie Doll: An Illustrated Guide to Her Dreamy World.* Philadelphia: Courage Books, 1999.

Fox-Sheinwold, Patricia. *Too Young to Die.* New York: Emson, 1997.

Frey, Tom. *Toy Bop! Kid Classics of the 50's & 60's.* Murrysville, Penn.: Fuzzy Dice, 1994.

Gaslin, Glenn, and Rick Porter. *The Complete, Cross-Referenced Guide to* the *Baby Buster Generation's Collective Unconscious.* New York: Boulevard Books, 1998.

Gifford, Denis. *The International Book of Comics.* New York: Crescent Books, 1984.

Goldschmidt, Rick. *The Enchanted World of Rankin/Bass.* Issaquah, Wash.: Tiger Mountain Press, 1997.

Gordon, Seth. *The Encyclopedia of Fictional People.* New York: Boulevard Books, 1996.

Green, Joey. *The Partridge Family Album.* New York: HarperPerennial, 1994.

Guttmacher, Peter. *Legendary Horror Films.* New York: Metro Books, 1995.

Hake, Ted. *Hake's Price Guide to Character Toy Premiums.* Timonium, Md.: Gemstone Publishing, 1996.

Hake, Ted. *Hake's Price Guide to Character Toys.* Third edition. Timonium, Md: Gemstone Publishing, 2000.

Handler, Ruth, with Jacqueline Shannon. *Dream Doll: The Ruth Handler Story.* Stamford, Conn: Longmeadow Press, 1994.

Harvey, Diana Karanikas and Jackson. *Dead Before Their Time.* New York: Metro Books, 1996.

Hoffman, David. *Kid Stuff.* San Francisco: Chronicle Books, 1996.

Hollis, Richard, and Brian Sibley. *The Disney Studio Story.* New York: Crown Publishers, 1988.

Holston, Kim. *Starlet.* Jefferson, N.C.: McFarland and Company, 1988.

Horn, Maurice. *100 Years of American Newspaper Comics.* New York: Gramercy Books, 1996.

Hyatt, Wesley. *The Encyclopedia of Daytime Television.* New York: Billboard Books, 1997.

Izen, Judith. *Collector's Guide to Ideal Dolls.* Paducah, Ky.: Collector Books, 1994.

Javna, John and Gordon. *60s!* New York: St. Martin's Griffin, 1988.

Johnson, Richard A. *American Fads.* New York: Beech Tree Books, 1985.

Karney, Robyn. *The Movie Stars Story.* New York: Crescent Books, 1984.

Knopper, Steve. *MusicHound Lounge: The Essential Album Guide to Martini Music and Easy Listening.* Detroit: Invisible Ink Press, 1998.

Korbeck, Sharon. *Toys & Prices: 1999.* Sixth edition. Iola, Wis.: Krause Publications, 1998.

Lamphier, Mary Jane. *Zany Characters of the Ad World.* Paducah, Ky.: Collector Books, 1995.

Langford, Paris. *Liddle Kiddles: Identifcation and Value Guide.* Paducah, Ky.: Collector Books, 1996.

Lenburg, Jeff. *The Encyclopedia of Animated Cartoons.* Second edition. New York: Checkmark Books, 1999.

Lewis, Jon E., and Penny Stempl. *Cult TV: The Comedies.* San Francisco: Bay Books, 1998.

Lipson, Eden Ross. *The New York Times Parent's Guide to the Best Books for Children.* New York: Three Rivers Press, 2000.

Maltin, Leonard. *Leonard Maltin's 2002 Movie and Video Guide.* New York: Signet, 2001.

Maltin, Leonard. *Leonard Maltin's Movie Encyclopedia.* New York: Dutton, 1994.

Mandeville, A. Glenn. *5th Doll Fashion Anthology and Price Guide*. Grantsville, Md.: Hobby House Press, 1996.

Mandeville, A. Glenn. *Sensational '60s: Doll Album and Price Guide*. Grantsville, Md.: Hobby House Press, 1996.

Marill, Alvin H. *Movies Made for Television: The Telefeature and the Mini-Series, 1964-86*. New York: New York Zoetrope, 1987.

Martin, Mick, and Marsha Porter. *Video and DVD Guide 2002*. New York: Ballantine Books, 2002.

Martindale, David. *Pufsntuf and Other Stuff*. Los Angeles: Renaissance Books, 1998.

Matthews, Scott, Jay Kerness, Tamara Nikuradse, Jay Steele, and Greg White. *Stuck in the Seventies: 113 Things from the 1970s That Screwed Up* the *Twentysomething Generation*. Chicago: Bonus Books, 1991.

McCall, Michael. *The Best of 50s TV*. New York: Mallard Press, 1992.

McCall, Michael. *The Best of 60s TV*. New York: Mallard Press, 1992.

McNeil, Alex. *Total Television*. Third edition. New York: Penguin Books, 1991.

Moore, Darrell. *Consumer Guide—The Best, Worst, and Most Unusual: Horror Films*. Skokie, Ill.: Publications International, 1983.

Moran, Elizabeth. *Bradymania!* Holbrook, Mass.: Bob Adams, 1992.

Nelson, Craig. *Bad TV*. New York: Delta, 1995.

Pallot, James. *The Movie Guide*. New York: Perigee, 1995.

Panati, Charles. *Panati's Parade of Fads, Follies, and Manias*. New York: HarperPerennial, 1991.

Peary, Danny. *Cult Movie Stars*. New York: Simon & Schuster/Fireside, 1991.

People Magazine Almanac 2004. New York: Time, 2003.

Pilato, Herbie J. *The Bewitched Book*. New York: Delta, 1992.

Polizzi, Rick. *Baby Boomer Games*. Paducah, Ky.: Collector Books, 1995.

Reader's Digest America A to Z. New York: *Reader's Digest* Association, Inc., 1997.

Rees, Dafydd, and Luke Crampton. *Encyclopedia of Rock Stars*. New York: DK Publishers, 1996.

Reisfeld, Randi, and Danny Fields. *16 Magazine: Who's Your Fave Rave?* New York: Boulevard Books, 1997.

Retrohell: Life in the '70s and '80s, from Afros to Zotz, by the editors of *Ben Is Dead* magazine. Boston: Little, Brown and Company, 1997.

Rettenmuno, Matthew. *Totally Awesome 80s*. New York: St. Martin's Griffin, 1996.

Rich, Mark. *100 Greatest Baby Boomer Toys*. Iola, Wis.: Krause Publications, 2000.

Rich, Mark. *Toys A to Z*. Iola, Wis.: Krause Publications, 2001.

Rivlin, Holly, and Michael Cavanaugh. *The Barnes & Noble Guide to Children's Books*. New York: Barnes & Noble Books, 1999.

Sabulis, Cindy. *Collector's Guide to Dolls of the 1960s and 1970s*. Paducah, Ky.: Collector Books, 2000.

Sackett, Susan. *The Hollywood Reporter of Box Office Hits*. New York: Billboard Books, 1996.

Scheuer, Steven H. *Movies on TV and Videocassette*. New York: Bantam Books, 1992.

Schneider, Steve. *That's All Folks! The Art of Warner Bros. Animation*. New York: Barnes & Noble Books, 1988.

Searles, Baird. *Films of Science Fiction and Fantasy*. New York: AFI Press, 1988.

Sennett, Ted. *The Art of Hanna-Barbera*. New York: Viking Studio Books, 1989.

Smith, Dave. *The Updated Official Encyclopedia Disney A to Z*. New York: Hyperion, 1998.

Smith, Ronald L. *Sweethearts of '60s TV*. New York: St. Martin's Griffin, 1989.

Sommer, Robin Langley. *"I Had One of Those" Toys of Our Generation*. Greenwich, Conn.: Crescent Books, 1992.

Spitznagel, Eric. *The Junk Food Companion*. New York: Plume, 1999.

Stanley, John. *Creature Features: The Science Fiction, Fantasy, and Horror Movie Guide*. New York: Berkley Boulevard, 2000.

Stern, Jane and Michael. *The Encyclopedia of Bad Taste*. New York: HarperCollins, 1990.

Stern, Jane and Michael. *Jane and Michael Stern's Encyclopedia of Pop Culture*. New York: HarperCollins, 1992.

Stern, Jane and Michael. *Sixties People*. New York: Alfred A. Knopf, 1990.

Sternfield, Jonathan. *The Look of Horror: Scary Moments from Scary Movies*. Philadelphia: Courage Books, 1990.

Strodder, Chris. *Swingin' Chicks of the '60s*. San Rafael, Calif.: Cedco, 2000.

Sullivan, Steve. *Glamour Girls*. New York: St. Martin's Griffin, 1999.

Thomson, Liz. *New Women in Rock*. New York: Delilah/Putnam, 1982.

Tobler, John. *Who's Who in Rock and Roll*. New York: Crescent Books, 1991.

Tuleja, Tad. *The New York Public Library Book of Popular Americana*. New York: Stonesong Press, 1994.

VideoHound's Complete Guide to Cult Flicks and Trash Pics. Detroit: Visible Ink Press, 1996.

VideoHund's Family Video Guide. Detroit: Visible Ink Press, 1995.

VideoHound's Golden Movie Retriever 2002. Detroit: Visible Ink Press, 2001.

VideoHound's Horror Show. Detroit: Visible Ink Press, 1998.

VideoHound's Sci-Fi Experience. Detroit: Visible Ink Press, 1997.

Wesson, Vann. *Generation X Field Guide and Lexicon*. San Diego: Orion Media, 1997.

Whitburn, Joel. *The Billboard Book of Top 40 Albums*. Third edition. New York: Billboard Books, 1995.

Whitburn, Joel. *The Billboard Book of Top 40 Country Hits*. New York: Billboard Books, 1996.

Whitburn, Joel. *The Billboard Book of Top 40 Hits*. Seventh edition. New York: Billboard Books, 2000.

The Whole Pop Catalog. Revised edition. New York: Avon Books, 1991.

Woolery, George W. *Animated TV Specials*. London: Scarecrow Press, Inc., 1989.

Yohe, Tom, and George Newall. *The Official Guide to Schoolhouse Rock*. New York: Hyperion, 1996.

Zillner, Dian. *Collectible Television Memorabilia*. Atglen, Penn.: Schiffer, 1996.

PERIODICALS

J.C. Penney Christmas Catalogs, 1973–87.

Montgomery Ward Christmas Catalogs, 1964–84.

Sears Wish Book [Christmas catalogs], 1967–72.

WEB SITES

BBC, I Love the 1960s (the 1970s, the 1980s, the 1990s): www.bbc.co.uk/cult/ilove/

Big Red Toy Box: www.bigredtoybox.com

Crazy Fads: www.crazyfads.com

In the 70s: www.inthe70s.com

In the 80s: www.inthe80s.com

In the 90s: www.inthe90s.com

The Interactive 80s Network: www.i80s.com

The Internet Movie Database: www.imdb.com

Topher's Breakfast Cereal Guide: www.lavasurfer.com

TV Tome: www.tvtome.com

Wikipedia, the Free Enyclopedia: www.wikipedia.org

Yesterdayland, Your Childhood Is Here: www.yesterdayland.com